BRIEF CONTENTS

CONTENTS

Key Terms, Chapter Summary, and Selected Print and Media Resources appear at the end of each chapter.

PREFACE

As always, the new 2009–2010 edition of *American Government and Politics Today* includes significant revisions and reflects our commitment to producing the most up-to-date text possible. In the past year, the nation witnessed one of the most spirited contests for the presidential nomination in the past 40 years, culminating with a general election contest that spurred public interest in the political process and increased voter turnout. Both political parties found flaws and successes in their nomination systems, and we are sure to see changes before 2012. Voters made clear choices for control of the Congress and for the presidency. Now, the interest turns to seeing how President Barack Obama and his administration address such issues as Social Security reform, the extension of health-care benefits, and the economy. The foreign policy challenges facing the new president include ending the American engagement in Iraq, dealing with instability and threats from other nations in the Middle East, and building more positive relationships with allies in all parts of the globe.

The changes we have made to this edition are not limited to bringing the text up to date, however. We have also made major revisions based on the latest research. The entire textbook is more focused on showing students how participation in the system can result in changes in the political system. Each chapter now opens with a *Making a Difference* feature that highlights political change brought about by citizens, groups, or organizations. Finally, pedagogy in the profession has evolved over time, and this edition represents our latest and best approach to introducing American government and politics to today's students.

2008 ELECTION RESULTS INCLUDED AND ANALYZED

Our experience has been that students respond to up-to-date information about political events. Consequently, we have included results of the November 2008 elections. We also analyze how these results will affect our political processes at the national, state, and local levels. While we have updated all of the text to be consistent with these results, in particular we have added throughout the text numerous special subsections dedicated to the elections.

THE INTERACTIVE FOCUS OF THIS TEXT

Whether the topic is voter participation, terrorism, or the problems that face the president, we constantly strive to involve the student reader in the analysis. We make sure that the reader comes to understand that politics is not an abstract process but a very human enterprise. We emphasize how different outcomes can affect students' civil rights and liberties, employment opportunities, and economic welfare.

Throughout the text, we encourage the reader to think critically. The features titled *Beyond Our Borders* encourage students to think globally. We further encourage interaction with the political system by ending each chapter with features titled *You Can Make a Difference*, which show students not only what they can do to become politically involved, but also *why* they should care enough to do so. Online exercises that conclude each chapter show students how to access and analyze political information.

SPECIAL PEDAGOGY AND FEATURES

The 2009–2010 edition of *American Government and Politics Today* contains many pedagogical aids and high-interest features to assist both students and instructors. The following list summarizes the special elements that can be found in each chapter:

- **Questions to Consider**—New chapter-opening "Questions to Consider" lay out for students the most important questions explored in the chapter, allowing them to target their reading, and prompting them to think critically.

- **Making a Difference**—These chapter-opening features, from contributor Rebecca Deen of the University of Texas at Arlington, highlight how a group or individual has made a difference in navigating our political system. These engaging and relevant openers succinctly incorporate a literature review of key scholarship on the topic and offer a balance of positive and negative, modern and historical examples. Examples include "Friends of the Court and Civil Liberties," about *amicus curiae* briefs in Chapter 4; "Using the Courts as a Strategy in the Fight for Civil Rights" in Chapter 5; and "Let's Put It to a Vote," concerning ballot efforts and the debate between representative and direct democracy in Chapter 9. A complete listing of these features can be found in this Preface under "For Users of the Previous Edition."

- **Beyond Our Borders**—Appearing in nearly every chapter, this feature discusses a topic such as globalization, the war on terrorism, immigration, or comparative government that is relevant to the chapter. Half of the chapters in the new edition feature new or heavily revised *Beyond Our Borders* features: "What Makes a Constitution?" (new, Chapter 2); "Flexible Federalism" (new, Chapter 3); "World Opinion of the United States" (revised, Chapter 6); "Why Do Other Nations Have Higher [Voter] Turnout?" (new, Chapter 9); "Do We Need a President *and* a King?" (new, Chapter 13); "Privatizing the Military Abroad" (revised, Chapter 14); "The Legal System Based on *Sharia*" (revised, Chapter 15); "The Canadian Health-Care System" (revised, Chapter 16); and "China: A Superpower Under the Spotlight" (updated, Chapter 18).

- **Margin Definitions**—For all important terms. All terms and definitions are compiled in a complete glossary at the end of the book as well.

- **Did You Know?**—Margin features presenting various facts and figures that add interest to the learning process.

- **You Can Make a Difference**—These chapter-ending features give the students some specific reasons why they should care about the topics covered in the chapter and provide ways in which they can become actively involved in American politics. Completely new or significantly revised and updated, these features now include coverage of the proposed Every Vote Counts legislation (Chapter 1); discussion of individual state and Department of Homeland Security grants (Chapter 3); dealing with discrimination in the workplace (Chapter 5); being a critical consumer of opinion polls (Chapter 6); critically consuming news, especially that from new media (Chapter 11); watching the White House (Chapter 13); and planning for the future (Chapter 17).

- **Key Terms**—A chapter-ending list, with page numbers, of all terms in the chapter that were boldfaced and defined in the margins.

- **Chapter Summary**—A point-by-point summary of the chapter text.

- **Selected Print and Media Resources**—An annotated list of suggested scholarly readings, as well as popular books and films relevant to chapter topics.

- **E-mocracy**—A feature that discusses politics and the Internet and suggests Web sites and Internet activities related to the chapter's topics.

APPENDICES

Because we know that this book serves as a reference, we have included important documents for the student of American government to have close at hand. A fully annotated copy of the U.S. Constitution appears at the end of Chapter 2, as an appendix to that chapter. In addition, we have included the following appendices:

The Declaration of Independence

Federalist Papers **Nos. 10 and 51**

Useful material is also located immediately inside the front and back covers of this text. Inside the front cover, you will find a cutaway view of the Capitol Building, describing the different chambers and what goes on inside. Inside the back cover you will find a list of the presidents of the United States.

A COMPREHENSIVE SUPPLEMENTS PACKAGE

We are proud to be the authors of a text that has the most comprehensive, accessible, and fully integrated supplements package on the market. Together, the text and the supplements listed as follows constitute a total learning and teaching package for you and your students. For further information on any of these supplements, contact your Wadsworth Cengage Higher Education sales representative.

SUPPLEMENTS FOR INSTRUCTORS

PowerLecture DVD with JoinIn
(ISBN-10: 0495568759 | ISBN-13: 9780495568759)

This one-stop lecture and class preparation tool makes it easy for you to assemble, edit, publish, and present custom lectures for your course. The interactive **PowerPoint® lectures** bring together text-specific outlines; audio and video clips from historic to current events (including clips from our 2008 ABC video collection); NEW animated learning modules illustrating key concepts; tables, statistical charts, and graphs; and photos from the book as well as outside sources. In addition, you can add your own materials, culminating in a powerful, personalized, media-enhanced presentation.

A **test bank** in Microsoft Word® and ExamView® computerized testing offer a large array of well-crafted multiple-choice and essay questions, along with their answers and page references.

An **Instructor's Manual** includes learning objectives, chapter outlines, discussion questions, suggestions for stimulating class activities and projects, tips on integrating media into your class (including step-by-step instructions on how to create your own podcasts), suggested readings and Web resources, and a section specially designed to help teaching assistants and adjunct instructors.

JoinIn™ offers book-specific "clicker" questions that test and track student comprehension of key concepts. Political Polling questions simulate voting, engage students, foster dialogue on group behaviors and values, and add personal relevance; the results can be compared to national data, leading to lively discussions. Visual Literacy questions are tied to images from the book and add useful pedagogical tools and high-interest feedback during your lecture. Save the data from students' responses all semester—track their progress and show them how political science works by incorporating this exciting new tool into your classroom. It is available for college and university adopters only.

The **Resource Integration Guide** outlines the rich collection of resources available to instructors and students within the chapter-by-chapter framework of the book, suggesting how and when each supplement can be used to optimize learning.

A new **AP Instructor's Guide** includes resources for instructors who teach Advanced Placement American Government, including chapter overviews, details on how the text aligns with AP themes, chapter outlines and lecture guides, discussion questions, and suggested activities.

FOR STUDENTS: THE MOST ONLINE RESOURCES

We continue to make sure that our text leads the industry in its integration with the Web. For this edition, you will find the following Web-based resources:

Resource Center with InfoTrac College Edition® Instant Access Code
(ISBN-10: 0495569488 | ISBN-13: 9780495569480)

Resource Center with InfoTrac College Edition Instant Access Code, Alternate Edition
(ISBN-10: 0495569518 ISBN-13: 9780495569510)
The Resource Center for *American Government and Politics Today* offers a variety of rich online learning resources designed to enhance the student experience. These resources include podcasts from author Steffen Schmidt, quizzes, all-new simulations, animated learning modules, Internet activities, an Associated Press newslink, videos, and links to Election 2008 information and analysis. All resources are correlated with key chapter learning concepts, and users can browse or search for content in a variety of ways. The *American Government and Politics Today* Resource Center is updated throughout the semester. We provide separate options for the delivery of an e-book.

Companion Web site for *American Government and Politics Today*
At the **companion Web site**, students will find free and open access to Learning Objectives, Quizzes, Chapter Glossaries, Flash Cards, and Crossword Puzzles. Adopting instructors will receive password-protected access to an electronic version of the Instructor's Manual, a new **AP Instructor's Guide**, and Microsoft PowerPoint® lecture presentations.

WebTutor™ on WebCT or Blackboard:
WebTutor on WebCT IAC
(ISBN-10: 0495568910 | ISBN-13: 9780495568919)

WebTutor on Blackboard IAC
(ISBN-10: 0495568872 | ISBN-13: 9780495568872)
Rich with content for your American government course, this Web-based teaching and learning tool includes course management, study/mastery, and communication tools. Use WebTutor™ to provide virtual office hours, post your syllabus, and track student progress with WebTutor's quizzing material. For students, WebTutor™ offers real-time access to interactive online tutorials and simulations, practice quizzes, and Web links—all correlated to *American Government and Politics Today*.

Study Guide
(ISBN-10: 0495568767 | ISBN-13: 9780495568766)
The Study Guide includes a Chapter Summary, Key Terms, and a Practice Exam for every chapter of the book.

Political Theatre DVD 2.0
(ISBN-10: 0495793604 | ISBN-13: 9780495793601)
This three-DVD set, perfect for classroom use, contains video and audio clips drawn from key political events from the past 75 years: presidential speeches, campaign ads, debates, news reports, national convention coverage, demonstrations, speeches by civil rights leaders, and more.

ABC News Videos for American Government 2010 DVD
(ISBN-10: 0495573094 | ISBN-13: 9780495573098)
This collection of three- to six-minute video clips on relevant political issues serves as a great lecture or discussion launcher. It has been updated to include coverage of

the Democratic and Republican National Conventions. These clips are available on the DVD and include Primary 2008: Three States Dominate; Mitt Romney: The Role of Religion in the Race for the Presidency; The Ailing Economy Rescue Plan; Joe Biden on CIA Interrogation Techniques and Iran Report; and many more.

Election 2008: An American Government Supplement
(ISBN-10: 0495567485 | ISBN-13: 9780495567486)
The use of real examples in this election booklet, which addresses the 2008 presidential, Congressional, and gubernatorial races, makes the concepts covered come alive for students.

The Handbook of Selected Court Cases
(ISBN-10: 0495127744 | ISBN-13: 9780495127741)
This handbook includes more than 30 Supreme Court cases.

The Handbook of Selected Legislation and Other Documents
(ISBN-10: 0495127825 | ISBN-13: 9780495127826)
This handbook features excerpts from laws passed by the U.S. Congress that have had a significant impact on American politics.

FOR USERS OF THE PREVIOUS EDITION

As usual, we thank you for your past support of our work. We have made numerous changes to this text for the 2009–2010 edition, many of which we list as follows. We have rewritten much of the text, added numerous new features, and updated the book to reflect the results of the 2008 elections.

NEW *Making a Difference* **features intelligently kick off each chapter:**

When Passions Mobilize (Chapter 1)

How to Form a More Perfect Union? (Chapter 2)

Learning from Each Other (Chapter 3)

Friends of the Court and Civil Liberties (Chapter 4)

Using the Courts as a Strategy in the Fight for Civil Rights (Chapter 5)

Opinion Gaps and Advocacy (Chapter 6)

Lobby U (Chapter 7)

Shifting Party Coalitions (Chapter 8)

Let's Put It to a Vote (Chapter 9)

The Emergence of 527 Groups (Chapter 10)

Have YouTube and Jon Stewart Changed How Politicians Campaign? (Chapter 11)

Keeping Tabs on Congress (Chapter 12)

"For the Record" versus "That's Privileged Information" (Chapter 13)

Holding Government Accountable (Chapter 14)

Political Struggles Fought in the Court (Chapter 15)

Defining Problems and Finding Solutions in Education (Chapter 16)

Managing Your Money (Chapter 17)

Think Tanks (Chapter 18)

Who Should Run the City, Professionals or Politicians? (Chapter 19)

New design: An entirely new, contemporary, and dynamic interior design and more streamlined content allow for better focus on the core material and fewer distractions. Dozens of new photographs with captions have been added to encourage critical thinking and draw in students. The "What If . . ." features that opened the chapters in the previous edition have been shortened and moved inside the chapter. New "What If . . ." sections in the new edition include the following:

- What If the Constitution Had Banned Slavery Outright? (Chapter 2)
- What If Public Opinion Polls Were Regulated by the Government? (Chapter 6)
- What If the Public Graded Federal Bureaucracies? (Chapter 14)
- What If the United States Brought Back the Draft? (Chapter 18)

Two boxed feature strands from the previous edition have been moved into the Instructor's Manual: "Politics and . . ." boxes, which tie current topics and issues to politics; and "Which Side Are You On?" features, which challenge the reader to find a connection between controversial issues facing the nation and the reader's personal positions on these issues.

New political science scholarship: New citations in every chapter highlighting cutting-edge research and the latest scholarship are included. The literature review that is part of the new chapter-opening *Making a Difference* features also contributes to this end. Figures and tables have been updated with the most recent data available, some added at press time.

SIGNIFICANT CHANGES WITHIN CHAPTERS

Each chapter contains new features—such as an entirely new *Making a Difference* feature that begins each chapter, updated data in figures and tables in every chapter, updated citations throughout, and whenever feasible, the most current information available on the problems facing the nation.

In addition, significant chapter-by-chapter changes have been made as follows:

Chapter 1 (The Democratic Republic)—A revamped Chapter 1 now more effectively sets the tone for the text by emphasizing the importance of an active citizenry, civic responsibility, and how individuals—including students—drive change. It includes expanded and reorganized coverage of political ideologies and up-to-the-minute content on the following election-related topics: online voting, the demographic breakdown of voters, and a discussion of how Hispanic Americans voted in 2008.

Chapter 2 (The Constitution)—Includes expanded, updated, and better organized coverage of the events and issues of the Constitutional Convention and the creation of the federal republic, and a closer look at the lack of women and minority delegates.

Chapter 3 (Federalism)—Includes expanded, updated, and better organized coverage of the concept of privileges and immunities, federalism generally and also as it relates to Hurricane Katrina, the concept of "necessary and proper," interstate commerce, and the full faith and credit clause.

Chapter 4 (Civil Liberties)—Includes expanded, updated, and better organized coverage of the debates about school prayer and teaching of intelligent design; modifications to the clear and present danger rule; and privacy rights and 2008 changes to the PATRIOT Act, such as the eavesdropping bill.

Chapter 5 (Civil Rights)—Includes an updated section, "Challenging Gender Discrimination in the Courts and Legislatures." Up-to-the-minute content was added on the following election-related topics: the race for the nominations, the historic candidates, and the increased role of women in Congress and the judiciary following the 2008 elections.

Chapter 6 (Public Opinion and Political Socialization)—A new chapter introduction uses the topic of the war in Iraq to discuss public opinion and the approval rating of the president. The chapter includes updated content about how demographic influences impact political preferences and voting behavior. Up-to-the-minute content was added on the accuracy of the 2008 polls and perception of candidates.

Chapter 7 (Interest Groups)—The data and text within the chapter have been updated to reflect new scholarship on interest groups and lobbying activities. A section discussing the lobbying reforms of 2007 has been added, as well as updated information on Common Cause and new content on MoveOn.org.

Chapter 8 (Political Parties)—This chapter includes a recap of the Democrats retaking both houses of Congress in 2006; election updates to the sections "Partisan Trends in the 2008 Elections" and "The 2008 Elections: Economics and National Security"; and new content on party polarization and "safe seats."

Chapter 9 (Voting and Elections)—The topic of campaigning has been pulled out into its own chapter (Chapter 10), and a more streamlined Chapter 9 now offers new content in the section "Factors Influencing Who Votes"; a new *Beyond Our Borders* feature, "Why Do Other Nations Have Higher Turnout?"; a new section, "The Importance of the Voting Machine," which explores the Florida punchcard controversy; coverage of the 2002 Help America Vote Act; and discussions of proposals for reform of the electoral college.

Chapter 10 (Campaigning for Office)—A new Chapter 10 fills the need for increased coverage of this timely topic on the heels of the 2008 presidential election and in a time when voter turnout, especially in primary elections, is on the rise. (Previously, the topic of campaigning had been discussed along with voting and elections.) The chapter offers expanded coverage of the following topics: women as candidates for office; EMILY's list; campaign finance reform and 2008 campaign finance; campaign staffing; and spending limits. This new chapter also features a recap of both sides of the 2008 primary contest; engaging 2008 convention coverage; coverage of the seating controversies at 2008 Democratic Convention; and coverage and analysis of the 2008 election outcomes. The data in the figures reflect recent election results.

Chapter 11 (The Media and Cyberpolitics)—Includes a new section on investigative reporting; a new section on racial bias in the media; and new content on how candidates use new media like e-mail, Web sites like YouTube, and blogs in campaigning.

Chapter 12 (The Congress)—Includes new sections, "Checks on the Congress" and "Logrolling, Earmarks, and 'Pork.'" The section on Congressional oversight has been revised to reflect the Democrats' recent investigations and other oversight activities. The chapter includes revised coverage of the Rules Committee; updates to the section "The Committee Structure"; and a new discussion about how the popularity of the president impacted the 2002 and 2006 midterm elections. Coverage of Congressional representation for the District of Columbia is now incorporated into the chapter.

Chapter 13 (The President)—Includes new coverage of the power to pardon; wartime powers and the use of military force; the expansion of presidential power over time; the State of the Union message; strategies for passing legislation; presidential approval ratings; and emergency powers.

Chapter 14 (The Bureaucracy)—Includes a new section on "Challenges to the Bureaucracy" that covers government reorganizing efforts to deal with terrorism and natural disasters; coverage of the controversy over the EPA and coal-burning power plants; and a discussion of the 2006 United States Supreme Court decision placing restrictions on lawsuits brought by public workers, which has been included in the whistleblowing section.

Chapter 15 (The Courts)—Coverage of judicial review now appears earlier in the chapter; updated coverage of the Rehnquist court has been added, as well as updated coverage of John Roberts; and a new figure is included, "Dual Structure of the American Court System."

Chapter 16 (Domestic Policy)—Includes updated information on prescription drug coverage; and coverage of environmental policy is followed by a new section on energy policy. Also included is updated immigration policy coverage and a new section on school shootings. Two new figures, "Oil Consumption by the Top Fifteen Oil Producers, 2007," and "U.S. Crude Oil and Retail Gasoline Prices from 1976 to 2007," have been added.

Chapter 17 (Economic Policy)—Includes new content on the Fed and interest rates; content on the privatization of Social Security now appears in-text; new content on import restrictions in the automobile industry has been added, as well as updates on the World Trade Organization and a new figure, "Medicare, Medicaid, and Social Security Spending as a Percentage of GDP, 2005–2050."

Chapter 18 (Foreign Policy and National Security)—Includes a new discussion of President Jimmy Carter's efforts in the Israel–Egypt peace accords and the UN working with Hezbollah and Israel to reach a peace settlement; a new section has been added, "The Emerging World Order," as well as updates on the Iraq War and up-to-date coverage of the nuclear ambitions of Iran and North Korea.

Chapter 19 (State and Local Politics)—Includes new coverage of state policies dealing with immigration; new in-text coverage of salary differences among state legislators; and a new section, "Ethics and Campaign Finance Reform in the States." New coverage of states' financial recovery from the Medicaid crisis has been added in "The Struggle to Balance State Budgets," and a new section, "States as Policy Pioneers," closes the chapter.

ACKNOWLEDGMENTS

Since we started this project several years ago, a sizable cadre of individuals has helped us in various phases of the undertaking. The following academic reviewers offered numerous constructive criticisms, comments, and suggestions during the preparation of all previous editions:

Danny M. Adkison, Oklahoma State University, Stillwater

Ahrar Ahmad, Black Hills State University, Spearfish, South Dakota

Sharon Z. Alter, William Rainey Harper College, Palatine, Illinois

Hugh M. Arnold, Clayton College and State University, Morrow, Georgia

William Arp III, Louisiana State University, Baton Rouge

Kevin Bailey, North Harris Community College, Houston, Texas

Evelyn Ballard, Houston Community College, Texas

Orlando N. Bama, McLennan Community College, Waco, Texas

Dr. Charles T. Barber University of Southern Indiana, Evansville

Clyde W. Barrow, Texas A&M University, College Station

Shari Garber Bax, Central Missouri State University, Warrensburg

David S. Bell, Eastern Washington University, Cheney

David C. Benford, Jr., Tarrant County Junior College, Fort Worth, Texas

John A. Braithwaite, Coastline Community College, Fountain Valley, California

Lynn R. Brink, North Lake College, Irving, Texas

Barbara L. Brown, Southern Illinois University at Carbondale

Richard G. Buckner, Santa Fe Community College, New Mexico

Kenyon D. Bunch, Fort Lewis College, Durango, Colorado

Ralph Bunch, Portland State University, Oregon

Carol Cassell, University of Alabama, Tuscaloosa

Dewey Clayton, University of Louisville, Kentucky

Frank T. Colon, Lehigh University, Bethlehem, Pennsylvania

Frank J. Coppa, Union County College, Cranford, New Jersey

Irasema Coronado, University of Texas at El Paso

James B. Cottrill, Santa Clara University, California

Robert E. Craig, University of New Hampshire, Durham

Doris Daniels, Nassau Community College, Garden City, New York

Carolyn Grafton Davis, North Harris County College, Houston, Texas

Paul B. Davis, Truckee Meadows Community College, Reno, Nevada

Richard D. Davis, Brigham Young University, Salt Lake City, Utah

Ron Deaton, Prince George's Community College, Largo, Maryland

Marshall L. DeRosa, Louisiana State University, Baton Rouge

Michael Dinneen, Tulsa Junior College, Oklahoma

Gavan Duffy, University of Texas at Austin

Don Thomas Dugi, Transylvania University, Lexington, Kentucky

George C. Edwards III, Texas A&M University, College Station

Gregory Edwards, Amarillo College, Texas

Mark C. Ellickson, Southwestern Missouri State University, Springfield

Larry Elowitz, Georgia College, Milledgeville

John W. Epperson, Simpson College, Indianola, Indiana

Victoria A. Farrar-Myers, University of Texas at Arlington

Daniel W. Fleitas, University of North Carolina at Charlotte

Elizabeth N. Flores, Del Mar College, Corpus Christi, Texas

Joel L. Franke, Blinn College, Brenham, Texas

Barry D. Friedman, North Georgia College, Dahlonega

Robert S. Getz, SUNY–Brockport, New York

Kristina Gilbert, Riverside Community College, Riverside, California

William A. Giles, Mississippi State University, Starkville, Mississippi

Donald Gregory, Stephen F. Austin State University, Nacogdoches, Texas

Forest Grieves, University of Montana, Missoula

Dale Grimnitz, Normandale Community College, Bloomington, Minnesota

Stefan D. Haag, Austin Community College, Texas

Justin Halpern, Northeastern State University, Muskogee, Oklahoma

Willie Hamilton, Mount San Jacinto College, San Jacinto, California

Jean Wahl Harris, University of Scranton, Pennsylvania

David N. Hartman, Rancho Santiago College, Santa Ana, California

Robert M. Herman, Moorpark College, Moorpark, California

Richard J. Herzog, Stephen F. Austin State University, Nacogdoches, Texas

Paul Holder, McLennan Community College, Waco, Texas

Michael Hoover, Seminole Community College, Sanford, Florida

J. C. Horton, San Antonio College, Texas

Robert Jackson, Washington State University, Pullman

Willoughby Jarrell, Kennesaw State University, Kennesaw, Georgia

Loch K. Johnson, University of Georgia, Athens, Georgia

Donald L. Jordan, United States Air Force Academy, Colorado Springs, Colorado

John D. Kay, Santa Barbara City College, California

Charles W. Kegley, University of South Carolina, Columbia

Bruce L. Kessler, Shippensburg University, Shippensburg, Pennsylvania

Robert King, Georgia Perimeter College, Clarkston, Georgia

Jason F. Kirksey, Oklahoma State University, Stillwater

Nancy B. Kral, Tomball College, Tomball, Texas

Dale Krane, Mississippi State University, Starkville, Mississippi

Samuel Krislov, University of Minnesota, Minneapolis, Minnesota

William W. Lamkin, Glendale Community College, Glendale, California

Harry D. Lawrence, Southwest Texas Junior College, Uvalde, Texas

Ray Leal, Southwest Texas State University, San Marcos

Sue Lee, Center for Telecommunications, Dallas County Community College District, Texas

Alan Lehmann, Blinn College, Brenham, Texas

Carl Lieberman, University of Akron, Ohio

Orma Linford, Kansas State University, Manhattan

James J. Lopach, University of Montana, Missoula, Montana

Eileen Lynch, Brookhaven College, Dallas, Texas

James D. McElyea, Tulsa Junior College, Oklahoma

Thomas J. McGaghie, Kellogg Community College, Battle Creek, Michigan

William P. McLauchlan, Purdue University, West Lafayette, Indiana

William W. Maddox, University of Florida, Gainesville, Florida

S. J. Makielski, Jr., Loyola University, New Orleans, Louisiana

Jarol B. Manheim, George Washington University, District of Columbia

J. David Martin, Midwestern State University, Wichita Falls, Texas

Bruce B. Mason, Arizona State University, Tempe

Thomas Louis Masterson, Butte College, Oroville, California

Steve J. Mazurana, University of Northern Colorado, Greeley

Stanley Melnick, Valencia Community College, Orlando, Florida

Robert Mittrick, Luzerne County Community College, Nanticoke, Pennsylvania

Helen Molanphy, Richland College, Dallas, Texas

James Morrow, Tulsa Community College, Oklahoma

Keith Nicholls, University of South Alabama, Mobile, Alabama

Stephen Osofsky, Nassau Community College, Garden City, New York

John P. Pelissero, Loyola University of Chicago, Illinois

Neil A. Pinney, Western Michigan University, Kalamazoo

George E. Pippin, Jones County Community College, Ellisville, Mississippi

Walter V. Powell, Slippery Rock University, Slippery Rock, Pennsylvania

Michael A. Preda, Midwestern State University, Wichita Falls, Texas

Jeffrey L. Prewitt, Brewton-Parker College, Mt. Vernon, Georgia

Mark E. Priewe, University of Texas at San Antonio

Charles Prysby, University of North Carolina at Greensboro

Donald R. Ranish, Antelope Valley College, Lancaster, California

John D. Rausch, Fairmont State University, Fairmont, West Virginia

Renford Reese, California State Polytechnic University, Pomona

Curt Reichel, University of Wisconsin, Madison, Wisconsin

Russell D. Renka, Southeast Missouri State University, Cape Girardeau

Donna Rhea, Houston Community College—Northwest, Texas

Paul Rozycki, Charles Stewart Mott Community College, Flint, Michigan

Bhim Sandhu, West Chester University, West Chester, Pennsylvania

Gregory Schaller, Villanova University, Villanova, Pennsylvania; and St. Joseph's University, Philadelphia, Pennsylvania

Pauline Schloesser, Texas Southern University, Houston

Eleanor A. Schwab, South Dakota State University, Brookings

Charles R. Shedlak, Ivy Tech State College, South Bend, Indiana

Len Shipman, Mount San Antonio College, Walnut, California

Scott Shrewsbury, Minnesota State University, Mankato

Alton J. Slane, Muhlenberg College, Allentown, Pennsylvania

Joseph L. Smith, Grand Valley State University, Allendale, Michigan

Michael W. Sonnlietner, Portland Community College, Oregon

Gilbert K. St. Clair, University of New Mexico

Robert E. Sterken, Jr., University of Texas, Tyler

Carol Stix, Pace University, Pleasantville, New York

Gerald S. Strom, University of Illinois at Chicago

Regina Swopes, Northeastern Illinois University, Chicago

John R. Todd, North Texas State University, Denton, Texas

Ron Velton, Grayson County College, Denison, Texas

Albert C. Waite, Central Texas College, Killeen, Texas

Benjamin Walter, Vanderbilt University, Nashville, Tennessee

B. Oliver Walter, University of Wyoming, Laramie

Mark J. Wattier, Murray State University, Murray, Kentucky

Paul Weizer, Fitchburg State College, Fitchburg, Massachusetts

Thomas L. Wells, Old Dominion University, Norfolk, Virginia

Jean B. White, Weber State College, Ogden, Utah

Lance Widman, El Camino College, Torrance, California

Allan Wiese, Minnesota State University, Mankato

J. David Woodard, Clemson University, Columbia, South Carolina

Robert D. Wrinkle, Pan American University, Edinburg, Texas

The 2009–2010 edition of this text is the result of our working closely with reviewers, who each offered us penetrating criticisms, comments, and suggestions. Although we have not been able to take account of all requests, each of the reviewers listed will see many of his or her suggestions taken to heart:

Martin J. Adamian
California State University, Los Angeles

Dr. Joshua G. Behr
Old Dominion University, Norfolk, Virginia

Dr. Curtis Berry
Shippensburg University, Shippensburg, Pennsylvania

Jodi Empol
Montgomery County Community College, Pennsylvania

Matthew Hansel
McHenry County College, Crystal Lake, Illinois

Alice Jackson
Morgan State University, Baltimore, Maryland

Susan J. Martin
Indiana University of Pennsylvania

Sandra O'Brien
Florida Gulf Coast University, Fort Myers, Florida

Maxine Swaikowsky
Hubbard High School

Joseph Swarner
Garfield High School, Seattle, Washington

Richard Vollmer
Oklahoma City Community College, Oklahoma

Stella Webster
Wayne County Community College—Downtown, Detroit, Michigan

In preparing this edition of *American Government and Politics Today*, we were the beneficiaries of the expert guidance of a skilled and dedicated team of publishers and editors. We would like, first of all, to thank Sean Wakely, Executive Vice President, Cengage Arts & Sciences, for the support he has shown for this project. We have benefited greatly from the supervision and encouragement given by Carolyn Merrill, executive editor; Clark Baxter, publisher; and P. J. Boardman, editor-in-chief.

We are very grateful to Professor Rebecca Deen of the University of Texas at Arlington for her thoughtful suggestions and for her substantial contributions to this edition. Jennifer Jacobson and Ohlinger Publishing Services, our developmental editors, also deserve our thanks for their many aspects of project development. We are also indebted to editorial assistant Nathan Gamache for his contributions to this project.

We are grateful to Josh Allen, our content production manager, Jennifer Bonnar, project manager at Lachina Publishing Services, and Linda Helcher, for a remarkable design and for making it possible to get the text out on time. In addition, our gratitude goes to all of those who worked on the various supplements offered with this text, especially Katherine Hayes and Caitlin Holroyd, who coordinates the Web site. We would also like to thank Amy Whitaker, marketing manager, for her tremendous efforts in marketing the text.

Any errors remain our own. We welcome comments from instructors and students alike. Suggestions that we have received in the past have helped us to improve this text and to adapt it to the changing needs of instructors and students.

STEFFEN SCHMIDT • MACK SHELLEY • BARBARA BARDES

ABOUT THE AUTHORS

STEFFEN W. SCHMIDT

Steffen W. Schmidt is a professor of political science at Iowa State University. He grew up in Colombia, South America, and studied in Colombia, Switzerland, and France. He obtained his Ph.D. from Columbia University, New York, in public law and government.

Schmidt has published six books and more than 150 journal articles. He is also the recipient of numerous prestigious teaching prizes, including the Amoco Award for Lifetime Career Achievement in Teaching and the Teacher of the Year award. He is a pioneer in the use of Web-based and real-time video courses and is a member of the American Political Science Association's section on computers and multimedia. He is on the editorial board of the *Political Science Educator* and is the technology and teaching editor of the *Journal of Political Science Education*.

Schmidt has a political talk show on WOI Radio, where he is known as Dr. Politics, streaming live once a week at **www.woi.org**. The show has been broadcast live from various U.S. and international venues. He is a frequent political commentator for *CNN en Español* and the British Broadcasting Corporation.

Schmidt likes to snow ski, ride hunter jumper horses, race sailboats, and scuba dive.

MACK C. SHELLEY II

Mack C. Shelley II is professor of political science, professor of statistics, and director of the Research Institute for Studies in Education at Iowa State University. After receiving his bachelor's degree from American University in Washington, D.C., he completed graduate studies at the University of Wisconsin at Madison, where he received a master's degree in economics and a Ph.D. in political science. He taught for two years at Mississippi State University before arriving at Iowa State in 1979.

Shelley has published numerous articles, books, and monographs on public policy. From 1993 to 2002, he served as elected coeditor of the *Policy Studies Journal*. His published books include *The Permanent Majority: The Conservative Coalition in the United States Congress; Biotechnology and the Research Enterprise* (with William F. Woodman and Brian J. Reichel); *American Public Policy: The Contemporary Agenda* (with Steven G. Koven and Bert E. Swanson); and *Redefining Family Policy: Implications for the 21st Century* (with Joyce M. Mercier and Steven Garasky). Other recent work has focused on electronic government and the "digital divide," learning communities, how to improve student life (especially in residence halls), and public health.

His leisure time activities include traveling, working with students, and playing with the family dog and three cats.

BARBARA A. BARDES

Barbara A. Bardes is a professor of political science and director of graduate studies in that department at the University of Cincinnati. She received her bachelor of arts degree and master of arts degree from Kent State University. After completing her Ph.D. at the University of Cincinnati, she held faculty positions at Mississippi State University and Loyola University in Chicago. She returned to the University of Cincinnati as Dean of the Raymond Walters College. She has also worked as a political consultant and directed polling for a research center.

Bardes has written articles on public opinion and foreign policy, and on women and politics. She has authored *Thinking about Public Policy; Declarations of Independence: Women and Political Power in Nineteenth-Century American Fiction*; and *Public Opinion: Measuring the American Mind* (with Robert W. Oldendick). Her current research interests include public opinion on terrorism and homeland security and media effects in elections.

Bardes's home is located in a very small hamlet in Kentucky called Rabbit Hash, famous for its 150-year-old general store. Her hobbies include traveling, gardening, needlework, and antique collecting.

American Government & Politics Today

CHAPTER

(1)

Immigration rights supporters rally
at the Capitol to urge Congressional
action on visas for skilled workers.
(Mandel Ngan/AFP/Getty Images)

THE DEMOCRATIC REPUBLIC

QUESTIONS TO CONSIDER

What is the fundamental reason for having a democracy?

Why is it so important for citizens to participate in a democratic system?

What are the cultural values and ideological views that support the American democracy?

CHAPTER CONTENTS

Making a DIFFERENCE

WHEN PASSIONS MOBILIZE

"We the People. . ." has profound meaning in the 21st century. A quick Internet search reveals literally millions of Web sites with the title "citizens against. . ." and just as many more with "citizens for. . ." in their title. People organize into groups in order to influence the system and affect changes in public policy. Individual citizens can make a difference.

Many groups mobilize to monitor government power. Citizen groups rally for good government, against taxes, against government waste, for responsible ethics, and against government encroachment. Some groups address specific policy problems: the environment, handgun violence, urban gas well drilling. Some tackle specific local issues: citizens against lawsuit abuse in Houston or those against liquefied natural gas storage in Oregon. The focus can be quite narrow: groups against car alarms, noise, ugly street spam, and litter, or those for midwifery or dog parks.

Some of the most energized groups are those that are concerned with activities seen as social vices: pornography, gambling, or liquor sales. In fact, some groups explicitly share information with others faced with similar issues. At **www.noliquor.us/liquor/noliquor1.html**, one can learn about previous "dry" efforts to prohibit alcohol sales in specific counties or cities. People can download documents, templates for campaign literature, and suggestions for campaign strategy to prepare for alcohol referenda.

Many of these issues affect young people directly. You might be familiar with the vigorous debate about the appropriate minimum age (for voting, drinking, driving) and maximum age (driving, employment) for certain privileges. College campuses are natural spots for healthy disagreement over all sorts of issues, and learning how to mobilize to affect change is a valuable life skill.

What is your passion? What are the issues about which you care most deeply? Chances are good that other similarly motivated individuals would welcome your help!

FRIENDS, FAMILY, JOBS, and school fill our lives. Why should it be important for anyone to be active in politics? Why should ordinary Americans take an interest in political issues or campaigns? The reason is that the citizens of the United States are more powerful than the president, Supreme Court justices, or any member of Congress. Democracies, especially this democracy, derive their powers from the citizens. Believe it or not, citizens can affect a local issue such as the level of taxes in their own town or national issues such as politics. As in the previous examples, individuals who participate in the system can create change. The flip side of this truth is that if the people of a democracy fail to pay attention and fail to participate, decisions that impact their lives will be made for them, either for good or for ill. And, like other skills we have, if we don't use the power to influence government, we may lose our inclination to do so.

What are the ways in which we can participate? Voting first comes to mind. Voting draws public attention, particularly as news coverage of campaigns fills the airwaves. Although voting is extremely important, it is only one of the ways that citizens can exercise their political influence. Americans can also join a political organization or interest group, stage

DID YOU KNOW?

That the Greek philosopher Aristotle favored enlightened despotism over democracy, which to him meant mob rule?

a protest, or donate funds to a political campaign or cause. Countless ways to become involved exist. Informed participation begins with knowledge, however, and this text aims to provide you with a strong foundation in American government and politics. We hope that this book helps introduce you to a lifetime of political awareness and activity.

POLITICS AND GOVERNMENT

What is politics? **Politics** can be understood as the process of resolving conflicts and deciding, as political scientist Harold Lasswell put it, "who gets what, when, and how."[1] More specifically, politics is the struggle over power or influence within organizations or informal groups that can grant or withhold benefits or privileges.

We can identify many such groups and organizations. In families, all members may meet together to decide on values, priorities, and actions. Wherever a community makes decisions through formal or informal rules, politics exists. For example, when a church decides to construct a new building or hire a new minister, the decision may be made politically. Politics is particularly intense when decisions are made that hit close to home, such as decisions about local schools: Where will the school be built? How will it be paid for? Will the curriculum include controversial subjects such as human sexuality? Parents, teachers, and board members will all "politic" on these issues. Of all of the organizations that are controlled by political activity, however, the most important is the government.

What is the government? Certainly, it is an **institution**—that is, an ongoing organization with a life separate from the lives of the individuals who are part of it at any given moment in time. The **government** can be defined as an institution in which decisions are made that resolve conflicts or allocate benefits and privileges. The government is also the *preeminent* institution within society. It is unique because it has the ultimate authority for making decisions and establishing political values.

Politics
The struggle over power or influence within organizations or informal groups that can grant or withhold benefits or privileges.

Institution
An ongoing organization that performs certain functions for society.

Government
The institution in which decisions are made that resolve conflicts or allocate benefits and privileges. It is unique because it has the ultimate authority within society.

WHY IS GOVERNMENT NECESSARY?

Perhaps the best way to assess the need for government is to examine circumstances in which government, as we normally understand it, does not exist. What happens when multiple groups compete with each other for power within a society? There are places around the world where such circumstances exist. A current example is the African nation of Somalia. Since 1991, Somalia has not had a central government. The nation has disintegrated into a collection of tribal areas, each of which has some autonomy. Neighboring nations supported the creation of the Transitional National Government in 2004, but it only controls one town near the capital. The capital, Mogadishu, is currently controlled by a coalition of clerics and other leaders. When Somali warlords compete for the control of a particular locality, the result is war, widespread devastation, and famine. In general, multiple armed forces compete by fighting, and the absence of a unified government is equivalent to civil war.

SECURITY

As the example of Somalia shows, one of the original purposes of government is the maintenance of security, or **order**. By keeping the peace, the government protects the

Order
A state of peace and security. Maintaining order by protecting members of society from violence and criminal activity is the oldest purpose of government.

[1]Harold Lasswell, *Politics: Who Gets What, When, and How* (New York: McGraw-Hill, 1936).

people from violence at the hands of private or foreign armies. It dispenses justice and protects the people against the violence of criminals. If order is not present, it is not possible to provide any of the other benefits that people expect from government.

Consider the situation in Iraq. In March and April 2003, U.S. and British coalition forces invaded that nation, which was governed by the dictator Saddam Hussein. The relatively small number of coalition troops had little trouble in defeating their military opponents, but they experienced serious difficulties in establishing order within Iraq when the war was over.

Once it became clear that Saddam Hussein was no longer in control of the country, widespread looting broke out. Ordinary citizens entered government buildings and made off with the furniture. Looters stole crucial supplies from hospitals, making it difficult to treat Iraqis injured during the war. Thieves stripped the copper from electrical power lines, which made it impossible to quickly restore electrical power. In 2005, it became clear that numerous groups within Iraqi society were engaged in the struggle for power. Some groups focused on attacks on the coalition forces, while others engaged in terrorist activities against other Iraqi religious or ethnic sects.

By 2007, when the Bush administration initiated a troop surge, it was clear that the Iraq situation had deteriorated badly, and no clear agreement among Iraqis about the future of their society had emerged. The new Bush strategy created local teams, including U.S. troops with aid officials and Iraqi local leaders, to rebuild towns and local institutions. It was understood that a degree of security and order would have to be restored before it would be possible to begin the reconstruction of Iraqi society. Order is a political value that we will return to later in this chapter.

BUDDHIST MONKS PROTEST the suppression of liberty by the ruling military elite in Myanmar. Does international attention to the regime help or hurt the movement for more freedom there? (AFP/Getty Images)

LIBERTY

Order cannot be the only important political value. There are many examples of countries where order exists but other threats to individuals loom large. In Myanmar, formerly called Burma, the military rulers have kept order by restricting the rights of opposition leaders, suppressing all protests including those led by Buddhist monks in 2007, and cutting off access to the Internet. Protection from the violence of domestic criminals or foreign armies is not enough. Citizens also need protection from abuses of power by the government if they are to experience any form of liberty.

Liberty—the greatest freedom of the individual consistent with the freedom of other individuals—is a second major political value, along with order. Liberty is a value that may be promoted by government, but it can also be invoked *against* government. We will further discuss this value later in this chapter.

Liberty
The greatest freedom of individuals that is consistent with the freedom of other individuals in the society.

AUTHORITY AND LEGITIMACY

Every government must have **authority**—that is, the right and power to enforce its decisions. Ultimately, the government's authority rests on its control of the armed forces and the police. Virtually no one in the United States, however, bases his or her day-to-day activities on fear of the government's enforcement powers. Most people, most of the time, obey the law because this is what they have always done, and they have been taught to believe that this is the right way to behave. Also, if they did not obey the law, they would face the disapproval of friends and family. Consider an example: Do you obey traffic laws and drive on the right side of the road because you are fearful of arrest or because you understand that these rules provide order, prevent accidents, and give you the freedom to travel where you wish to go?

Authority
The right and power of a government or other entity to enforce its decisions and compel obedience.

Under most circumstances, the government's authority has broad popular support. People accept the government's right to establish rules and laws. When authority is broadly accepted, we say that it has **legitimacy**. Authority without legitimacy is a recipe for trouble. Iraq can serve as an example. Although many Iraqis were happy to see the end of Saddam Hussein's regime, they were displeased that their nation was occupied by foreign troops. Many Iraqis, especially in districts inhabited by Sunni Arabs (the former politically dominant group in Iraq), did not accept the legitimacy of the U.S.-led Coalition Provisional Authority (CPA).

Legitimacy
Popular acceptance of the right and power of a government or other entity to exercise authority.

ON APRIL 13, 2007, the Iraqi parliament meets even though its cafeteria was attacked by a suicide bomber the day before. Progress toward a stable Iraqi government has been uneven due to such events. (Ceerwan Aziz, Pool/AP Photos)

Terrorists and other groups hostile to the CPA planned and carried out violent attacks on coalition forces and other groups, knowing the people would not call on government for help. A perceived precondition of making progress toward a fully peaceful country was that the CPA yield its authority to a government chosen by the Iraqis—a government with substantial legitimacy, rather than one imposed by outside forces. After several interim steps, the Iraqi people elected the new Council of Representatives in 2005, and all ministers in the new constitutional government were in place by May 2006.

WHY CHOOSE DEMOCRACY?

Today, more than 200 nations exist in the world. All have some form of government that possesses authority and some degree of legitimacy. The crucial question for every nation is who controls the government? The answer could be a group, one person, perhaps the monarch or a dictator, or no one.

Totalitarian Regime
A form of government that controls all aspects of the political and social life of a nation.

At one extreme is a society governed by a **totalitarian regime**. In such a political system, a small group of leaders or a single individual—a dictator—makes all political decisions for the society. An example of such a regime is the Soviet Union in the 1930s, 1940s, and 1950s. The leaders of the Communist Party controlled every facet of the society, including the church, schools, commerce, and government. The power of the ruler is total (thus, the term *totalitarianism*).

Authoritarianism
A type of regime in which only the government is fully controlled by the ruler. Social and economic institutions exist that are not under the government's control.

A second type of system is authoritarian government. **Authoritarianism** differs from totalitarianism in that only the government is fully controlled by the ruler. Social and economic institutions exist that are not under the government's control.

Aristocracy
Rule by the "best"; in reality, rule by an upper class.

Many of our terms for describing the distribution of political power are derived from the ancient Greeks, who were the first Western people to study politics systematically. One form of rule by the few was known as **aristocracy**, literally meaning "rule by the best." In practice, this meant rule by leading members of wealthy families who were, in theory, the best educated and dedicated to the good of the state. The ancient Greeks had another term for rule by the few, **oligarchy**, which means rule by a small group for corrupt and self-serving purposes.

Oligarchy
Rule by the few in their own interests.

Democracy
A system of government in which political authority is vested in the people. Derived from the Greek words *demos* ("the people") and *kratos* ("authority").

The Greek term for rule by the people was **democracy**, which means that the authority of the government is granted to it from the people as a whole. Within the limits of their culture, some of the Greek city-states operated as democracies. Today, in much of the world, the people will not grant legitimacy to a government unless it is based on democracy.

Anarchy
The absence of any form of government or political authority.

If totalitarianism is control of all aspects of society by the government, **anarchy** is the complete opposite. It means that there is no government at all. Each individual or family in a society decides for themselves how they will behave, and there is no institution with the authority to keep order in any way.

DIRECT DEMOCRACY AS A MODEL

Direct Democracy
A system of government in which political decisions are made by the people directly, rather than by their elected representatives; probably attained most easily in small political communities.

The system of government in the ancient Greek city-state of Athens is usually considered the purest model of **direct democracy**, because the citizens of that community debated and voted directly on all laws, even those put forward by the ruling council of the city. The most important feature of Athenian democracy was that the **legislature** was composed of all of the citizens. Women, foreigners, and slaves, however, were excluded because they were not citizens. This form of government required a high level of participation from every citizen; that participation was seen as benefiting the individual and the city-state. The Athenians believed that although a high level of participation might lead to instability in government, citizens, if informed about the issues, could be trusted to make wise decisions.

Legislature
A governmental body primarily responsible for the making of laws.

Direct Democracy Today. Direct democracy has also been practiced in Switzerland and in the United States, in New England town meetings. At New England town meetings, which can include all of the voters who live in the town, important decisions—such as levying taxes, hiring city officials, and deciding local ordinances—are made by majority vote. Some states provide a modern adaptation of direct democracy for their citizens; representative democracy is supplemented by the **initiative** or the **referendum**—processes by which the people may vote directly on laws or constitutional amendments. The **recall** process, which is available in many states, allows the people to vote to remove an official from state office.

Teledemocracy. Today, because of the Internet, Americans have more access to political information than ever before. Voters can now go online to examine the record of any candidate for any office. Constituents can badger their congressional representatives and state legislators by sending them e-mail. Individuals can easily and relatively inexpensively form political interest groups using the Internet. They can even contribute to a particular politician's campaign through the Internet. Therefore, to some extent, we are gradually progressing toward a type of teledemocracy in which citizens and their political representatives communicate with each other easily and frequently online.

Although Colorado offered its citizens the opportunity of voting online in 2000, the Pentagon cancelled a plan for troops overseas to vote online in 2004 due to Internet security concerns. In 2008, the Democratic Party used online primary voting for Democrats residing overseas. On February 5, 2008, registered Democrats could go to specified cities overseas and vote online to select the candidate who would win the 11 convention delegates who would represent them. Barack Obama won the vote handily.[2]

THE DANGERS OF DIRECT DEMOCRACY

Although they were aware of the Athenian model, the framers of the U.S. Constitution had grave concerns about the stability of such a society. The Founding Fathers were well-educated men who had read the new political philosophers of the 17th and

Initiative
A procedure by which voters can propose a law or a constitutional amendment.

Referendum
An electoral device whereby legislative or constitutional measures are referred by the legislature to the voters for approval or disapproval.

Recall
A procedure allowing the people to vote to dismiss an elected official from state office before his or her term has expired.

THIS TOWN MEETING in Vermont allows every citizen of the town to vote directly and in person for elected officials, for proposed policies, and, in some cases, for the town budget. To be effective, such a form of direct democracy requires that the citizens stay informed about local politics, attend town meetings, and devote time to discussion and decision making. Why might citizens be willing to spend the time necessary to attend town meetings? (AP Photo/Toby Talbot)

---

[2]Since then, other jurisdictions have offered online voting.

THIS CAMPAIGN WORKER in Chicago is helping a recent immigrant register to vote. If this person ends up voting in the next election, is he participating in a direct or a representative democracy? (AP Photo/Nam Y. Huh)

Consent of the People
The idea that governments and laws derive their legitimacy from the consent of the governed.

18th centuries. The arguments for government based on the **consent of the people** were put forward by philosopher John Locke, who held that all individuals have certain inalienable rights and that governments are created by the people in a "social contract."[3] During America's colonial period, the idea of government based on the consent of the people gained increasing popularity. Such a government was the main aspiration of the American Revolution, the French Revolution in 1789, and many subsequent revolutions. At the time of the American Revolution, however, the masses were still considered to be too uneducated to govern themselves, too prone to the influence of demagogues (political leaders who manipulate popular prejudices), and too likely to subordinate minority rights to the tyranny of the majority.

James Madison defended the new scheme of government set forth in the U.S. Constitution, while warning of the problems inherent in a "pure democracy":

A common passion or interest will, in almost every case, be felt by a majority of the whole . . . and there is nothing to check the inducements to sacrifice the weaker party or an obnoxious individual. Hence it is that such democracies have ever been spectacles of turbulence and contention, and have ever been found incompatible with personal security or the rights of property; and have in general been as short in their lives as they have been violent in their deaths.[4]

Like other politicians of his time, Madison feared that pure, or direct, democracy would deteriorate into mob rule. What would keep the majority of the people, if given direct decision-making power, from abusing the rights of minority groups?

A DEMOCRATIC REPUBLIC

Republic
A form of government in which sovereignty rests with the people, as opposed to a king or monarch.

Popular Sovereignty
The concept that ultimate political authority is based on the will of the people.

Democratic Republic
A republic in which representatives elected by the people make and enforce laws and policies.

The framers of the U.S. Constitution chose to craft a **republic**, meaning a government in which sovereign power rests with the people, rather than with a king or monarch. A republic is based on **popular sovereignty**. To Americans of the 1700s, the idea of a republic also meant a government based on common beliefs and virtues that would be fostered within small communities. The rulers were to be amateurs—good citizens who would take turns representing their fellow citizens.

The U.S. Constitution created a form of republican government that we now call a **democratic republic**. The people hold the ultimate power over the government through the election process, but all policy decisions are made by elected officials. For the founders, even this distance between the people and the government was not sufficient. The Constitution made sure that the Senate and the president would be selected by political elites rather than by the people, although later changes to the Constitution allowed the voters to elect members of the Senate directly.

[3]John Locke, *Two Treatises on Government*, 1680.
[4]James Madison, in Alexander Hamilton, James Madison, and John Jay, *The Federalist Papers*, No. 10 (New York: Mentor Books, 1964), p. 81. See Appendix B of this textbook.

Despite these limits, the new American system was unique in the amount of power it granted to ordinary citizens. Over the course of the following two centuries, democratic values became increasingly popular, at first in the West and then throughout the rest of the world. The spread of democratic principles gave rise to another name for our system of government—**representative democracy**. The term *representative democracy* has almost the same meaning as *democratic republic*, with one exception. In a republic, not only are the people sovereign, but there is no king. What if a nation develops into a democracy, but preserves the monarchy as a largely ceremonial institution? This is exactly what happened in Britain. Not surprisingly, the British found the term *democratic republic* to be unacceptable, and they described their system as a representative democracy instead.

Principles of Democratic Government. All representative democracies rest on the rule of the people as expressed through the election of government officials. In the 1790s in the United States, only free white males were able to vote, and in some states they had to be property owners as well. Women did not receive the right to vote in national elections in the United States until 1920, and the right to vote was not secured in all states by African Americans until the 1960s. Today, **universal suffrage** is the rule.

Because everyone's vote counts equally, the only way to make fair decisions is by some form of **majority** will. But to ensure that **majority rule** does not become oppressive, modern democracies also provide guarantees of minority rights. If political minorities were not protected, the majority might violate the fundamental rights of members of certain groups, especially groups that are unpopular or that differ from the majority population, such as racial minorities.

To guarantee the continued existence of a representative democracy, there must be free, competitive elections. Thus, the opposition always has the opportunity to win elective office. For such elections to be totally open, freedom of the press and speech must be preserved so that opposition candidates may present their criticisms of the government.

Constitutional Democracy. Yet another key feature of Western representative democracy is that it is based on the principle of **limited government**. Not only is the government dependent on popular sovereignty, but the powers of the government are also clearly limited, either through a written document or through widely shared beliefs. The U.S. Constitution sets down the fundamental structure of the government and the limits to its activities. Such limits are intended to prevent political decisions based on the whims or ambitions of individuals in government rather than on constitutional principles.

Representative Democracy
A form of government in which representatives elected by the people make and enforce laws and policies; may retain the monarchy in a ceremonial role.

DID YOU KNOW?

That the phrase "In God We Trust" was made the national motto on July 30, 1956, but had appeared on U.S. coins as early as 1864?

Universal Suffrage
The right of all adults to vote for their representatives.

Majority
More than 50 percent.

Majority Rule
A basic principle of democracy asserting that the greatest number of citizens in any political unit should select officials and determine policies.

Limited Government
The principle that the powers of government should be limited, usually by institutional checks.

WHO REALLY RULES IN AMERICA?

Americans feel free to organize, to call and e-mail their representatives, to vote candidates in and out of office. We always describe our political system as a democracy or democratic republic. However, do the people of the United States actually hold power today? Political scientists have developed several theories about American democracy, including *majoritarian* theory, *elite* theory, and theories of *pluralism*. Advocates of these theories use them to describe American democracy either as it actually is or as they believe it should be.

MAJORITARIANISM

Many people believe that in a democracy, the government ought to do what the majority of the people want. This simple proposition is the heart of majoritarian theory. As

a theory of what democracy should be like, **majoritarianism** is popular among both political scientists and ordinary citizens. In the presidential election of 2000, the idea that George W. Bush should become president although he did not win the majority of the popular vote led to many debates over our electoral system. He did, however, win the majority of votes in the electoral college; that is, electoral votes assigned to each state, as specified by the U.S. Constitution. The workings of the electoral college are explained in more detail in Chapter 9.

Rooted in majoritarian theory are the contemporary debates in many states over which type of voting machine would be completely accurate and tamperproof. Many scholars, however, consider majoritarianism to be a surprisingly poor description of how U.S. democracy actually works. In particular, they point to the low level of turnout for elections. Polling data have shown that many Americans are neither particularly interested in politics nor well informed. Few are able to name the persons running for Congress in their districts, and even fewer can discuss the candidates' positions. As discussed following, a requirement that all citizens vote might bring the United States closer to a true majoritarian democracy.

ELITISM

If ordinary citizens are not really making policy decisions with their votes, then who is? One answer suggests that elites really govern the United States. American government, in other words, is a sham democracy. **Elite theory** is usually used simply to describe the American system. Few people today believe it is a good idea for the country to be run by a privileged minority. In the past, however, many people believed that it was appropriate for the country to be run by an elite. Consider the words of Alexander Hamilton, one of the framers of the Constitution:

> All communities divide themselves into the few and the many. The first are the rich and the wellborn, the other the mass of the people.... The people are turbulent and changing; they seldom judge or determine right. Give therefore to the first class a distinct, permanent share in the government. They will check the unsteadiness of the second, and as they cannot receive any advantage by a change, they therefore will ever maintain good government.[5]

Some versions of elite theory posit a small, cohesive, elite class that makes almost all of the important decisions for the nation,[6] whereas others suggest that voters choose among competing elites. New members of the elite are recruited through the educational system so that the brightest children of the masses allegedly have the opportunity to join the elite stratum. One view suggests that the members of the elite are primarily interested in

SUPREME COURT JUSTICE Louis Brandeis, who served 1916–1939, said, "The greatest menace to freedom is an inert people." (Topham/Image Works)

[5]Alexander Hamilton, "Speech in the Constitutional Convention on a Plan of Government," in *Writings*, ed. Joanne B. Freeman (New York: Library of America, 2001).
[6]Michael Parenti, *Democracy for the Few*, 7th ed. (Belmont, CA: Wadsworth Publishing, 2002).

WHAT IF...

CITIZENS WERE REQUIRED TO VOTE?

If all eligible Americans were required to vote, elected representatives would reflect the views of a majority of the entire voting-age population. Passive consent of the nonvoters aside, today's politicians frequently ascend to their positions with the support of only a relatively small minority of citizens.

Consider the election of George W. Bush in 2004. In that election, Bush garnered roughly 51 percent of the total popular vote. When voter turnout is considered, however, Bush was elected by only 27.6 percent of the voting-age population. Given that 72.4 percent of age-eligible voters did *not* cast a ballot for him in 2004, Bush's post-election claim to have earned "a mandate from the people" seemed overstated. How would the political system be changed if all citizens voted?

EFFECTS ON POLICY DECISIONS

If citizens were required to vote, elected officials would have to consider all of their constituents when making policy decisions. Today, the groups who are less likely to vote include the younger voters, the less-educated citizens, and those who are economically disadvantaged. If all citizens were required to vote, policies to assist the poor and less-skilled Americans might be implemented. On the other hand, older citizens tend to turn out in higher numbers today, keeping politicians anxious about any changes to the Social Security program.

POSSIBLE OBJECTIONS

Optimism over mandatory voting must be tempered by some of the unintended consequences that might result.

First of all, requiring every citizen to vote would undoubtedly increase the number of uninformed voters. A common complaint in our existing system is that voters do not adequately follow politics or know individual candidates' stances on important issues. Uninformed voters might be more likely to be swayed by the charisma of candidates or impractical promises made by politicians. And, in the United States, voting is seen as a voluntary activity; those who are unhappy with the entire system are entitled to stay home and not vote. Imposing a fine or other punishment for not voting seems to run counter to our view of citizenship as voluntary.

FOR CRITICAL ANALYSIS

1. Do you agree with the concept that every American should be required to cast a ballot? Why or why not?
2. If citizens were required to vote, should they also be required to be well informed on the candidates and the issues? Explain your answer.
3. What are possible implications of such a change to the electoral system? Would this accomplish the reform's goals or create unintended consequences?

controlling the political system to protect their own wealth and the capitalist system that produces it.[7] Studies of elite opinion, however, have suggested that elites are more tolerant of diversity, more willing to defend individual liberties, and more supportive of democratic values than are members of the mass public.

PLURALISM

A different school of thought holds that our form of democracy is based on group interests. As early as 1831, the French traveler and commentator Alexis de Tocqueville noted the American penchant for joining groups: "As soon as the inhabitants of the United States have taken up an opinion or a

DID YOU KNOW?

That more than 500,000 officials are elected in the United States, which is more than all the bank tellers in the country?

[7]G. William Domhoff, *Who Rules America*, 4th ed. (New York: McGraw-Hill Higher Education, 2002).

feeling which they wish to promote in the world, they look out for mutual assistance; and as soon as they have found one another out, they combine. From that moment they are no longer isolated men, but a power seen from afar, . . ."[8]

Pluralist theory proposes that even if the average citizen cannot keep up with political issues or cast a deciding vote in any election, the individual's interests will be protected by groups that represent her or him. Theorists who subscribe to **pluralism** see politics as a struggle among groups to gain benefits for their members. Given the structures of the American political system, group conflicts tend to be settled by compromise and accommodation. Because there are a multitude of interests, no one group can dominate the political process. Furthermore, because most individuals have more than one interest, conflict among groups need not divide the nation into hostile camps.

Many political scientists believe that pluralism works very well as a descriptive theory. As a way to defend the practice of democracy in the United States, however, pluralism has problems. Poor citizens are rarely represented by interest groups. At the same time, rich citizens are often overrepresented, in part because they understand their own interests. As political scientist E. E. Schattschneider observed, "The flaw in the pluralist heaven is that the heavenly chorus sings with a strong upper-class accent."[9] There are also serious doubts as to whether group decision making always reflects the best interests of the nation.

Critics see a danger that groups may become so powerful that all policies become compromises crafted to satisfy the interests of the largest groups. The interests of the public as a whole, then, are not considered. Critics of pluralism have suggested that a democratic system can be virtually paralyzed by the struggle among interest groups. We will discuss interest groups at greater length in Chapter 7.

Some scholars argue that none of these three theories—majoritarianism, elite theory, or pluralism—fully describes the workings of American democracy. These experts say that each theory captures a part of the true reality, but that we need all three theories to gain a full understanding of American politics.

FUNDAMENTAL VALUES

The writers of the American Constitution believed that the structures they had created would provide for both democracy and a stable political system. They also believed that the nation could be sustained by its **political culture**—the set of ideas, values, and ways of thinking about government and politics that are shared by all citizens.

There is considerable consensus among American citizens about certain concepts basic to the U.S. political system. Given that the vast majority of Americans are descendants of immigrants with diverse cultural and political backgrounds, how can we account for this consensus? Primarily, it is the result of **political socialization**—the process by which beliefs and values are transmitted to new immigrants and to our children. The nation depends on families, schools, houses of worship, and the media to transmit the precepts of our national culture.

The most fundamental concepts of the American political culture are those of the **dominant culture**. Those beliefs are rooted in Western European civilization and the ideas of the Enlightenment, including the ideas of popular sovereignty, and the right to life, liberty, and property as expressed in the Declaration of Independence. That

Pluralism
A theory that views politics as a conflict among interest groups. Political decision making is characterized by bargaining and compromise.

Political Culture
The collection of beliefs and attitudes toward government and the political process held by a community or nation.

Political Socialization
The process through which individuals learn a set of political attitudes and form opinions about social issues. Families and the educational system are two of the most important forces in the political socialization process.

Dominant Culture
The values, customs, and language established by the group or groups that traditionally have controlled politics and government in a society.

---

[8]Alexis de Tocqueville, *Democracy in America*, Volume II, Section 2, Chapter V, "Of the uses which the Americans make of Public Associations." (Available in many editions, and as full text in several Web locations.)
[9]E. E. Schattschneider, *The Semi-Sovereign People* (Hinsdale, IL: The Dryden Press, 1975; originally published in 1960).

EACH YEAR THOUSANDS of immigrants are sworn in as new U.S. citizens. The U.S. Constitution, in Article I, Section 8, declares that Congress shall have the power to "establish a uniform Rule of Naturalization." Naturalization is the process by which individuals become U.S. citizens. Are the values that immigrants bring with them from their homelands likely to influence the values of their new country? (Joseph Sohm/Visions of America/Corbis)

said, it is important to note that while Americans express broad support for these ideas and values, there are many conflicts over which values are most important to various groups within the society.

INDIVIDUAL FREEDOM

In the United States, our civil liberties include religious freedom—both the right to practice whatever religion one chooses and freedom from any state-imposed religion. Our civil liberties also include freedom of speech—the right to express our opinions freely on all matters, including government actions. Freedom of speech is perhaps one of our most prized liberties, because a democracy could not endure without it. These and many other basic guarantees of liberty are found in the Bill of Rights, the first 10 amendments to the Constitution.

Liberty, however, is not the only value widely held by Americans. A substantial portion of the American electorate, those qualified to vote, believes that certain kinds of liberty threaten the traditional social order. The right to privacy is a particularly controversial liberty. The United States Supreme Court has held that the right to privacy can be derived from other rights that are explicitly stated in the Bill of Rights. The Supreme Court has also held that under the right to privacy, the government cannot ban either abortion[10] or private homosexual behavior by consenting adults.[11] Some Americans believe that such rights threaten the sanctity of the family and the general cultural commitment to moral behavior. Of course, other Americans disagree with this point of view.

Security is another issue. When Americans perceive serious external or internal threats, they have supported government actions to limit individual liberties in the name of national security. Such limits were imposed during the Civil War, World War II, and during the McCarthy era of the Cold War. Following the terrorist attacks on the World Trade Center and the Pentagon on September 11, 2001, Congress passed legislation designed to provide greater security at the expense of some civil liberties. In particular, the USA PATRIOT Act (which stands for Uniting and Strengthening

---

[10]*Roe v. Wade*, 410 U.S. 113 (1973).
[11]*Lawrence v. Texas*, 539 U.S. 558 (2003).

America by Providing Appropriate Tools Required to Intercept and Obstruct Terrorism) gave law enforcement and intelligence-gathering agencies greater latitude to search out and investigate suspected terrorists. Many Americans objected to the PATRIOT Act, pointing out that it compromised numerous civil liberties, such as protection from unreasonable searches and seizures. When the news broke in December 2005 that the National Security Agency (NSA) had been engaging in warrantless secret surveillance, many wondered if civil liberties had been eroded too far in the name of national security.

EQUALITY

The Declaration of Independence states, "All men are created equal." The proper meaning of equality, however, has been disputed by Americans since the Revolution.[12] Much of American history—and world history—is the story of how the value of **equality** has been extended and elaborated.

First, the right to vote was granted to all adult white males regardless of whether they owned property. The Civil War resulted in the end of slavery and established that, in principle at least, all citizens were equal before the law. The civil rights movement of the 1950s and 1960s sought to make that promise of equality a reality for African Americans. Other movements have sought equality for other racial and ethnic groups, for women, for persons with disabilities, and for gay men and lesbians. We discuss these movements in Chapter 5.

To promote equality, it is often necessary to place limits on the desire by some to treat people unequally. In this sense, equality and liberty are conflicting values. Today, the denial of equal treatment to members of a particular race has very few defenders. Yet as recently as 60 years ago, such denial was a cultural norm.

Economic Equality. Equal treatment regardless of race, religion, gender, and other characteristics is a popular value today. Equal opportunity for individuals to develop their talents and skills is another value with substantial support. Equality of economic status, however, is a controversial value.

For much of history, few people even contemplated the idea that the government could do something about the division of society between rich and poor. Most people assumed that such an effort was either impossible or undesirable. This assumption began to lose its force in the 1800s. As a result of the growing wealth of the Western world and a visible increase in the ability of government to take on large projects, some people began to advocate the value of universal equality, or *egalitarianism*. Some radicals dreamed of a revolutionary transformation of society that would establish an egalitarian system—that is, a system in which wealth and power would be redistributed on a more equal basis.

Many others rejected this vision but still came to endorse the values of eliminating poverty and at least reducing the degree of economic inequality in society. Antipoverty advocates believed then and believe now that such a program could alleviate much suffering. In addition, they believed that reducing economic inequality would promote fairness and enhance the moral tone of society generally.

A HIGH POINT OF the civil rights movement of the 1950s and 1960s was the March on Washington on August 8, 1963, led by Martin Luther King, Jr. Nearly 250,000 people participated in the event. The following year, Congress passed the Civil Rights Act of 1964, one of the most important civil rights acts in the nation's history. Why does the mandate of equal treatment for all groups of Americans sometimes come into conflict with the concept of liberty? (Library of Congress, Prints & Photographs Division, U.S. News & World Report Magazine Collection [LC-U9- 10363-5])

Equality
As a political value, the idea that all people are of equal worth.

----

[12]Gary B. Nash, *The Unknown American Revolution: The Unruly Birth of Democracy and the Struggle to Create America* (New York: Viking, 2005); and Alfred F. Young, ed., *Beyond the American Revolution: Explorations in the History of American Radicalism* (DeKalb, IL: Northern Illinois University Press, 1993).

ORDER

As noted earlier in this chapter, individuals and communities create governments to provide for stability and order in their lives. John Locke justified the creation of governments as a way to protect every individual's property rights and to organize a system of impartial justice. In the United States, laws passed by local, state, and national governments create order and stability in every aspect of life ranging from traffic laws to business laws to a national defense system. Citizens expect these laws to create a society in which individuals can pursue opportunities and live their lives in peace and prosperity. However, the goal of maintaining order and security can run counter to the values of liberty and equality.

SECURITY

The attacks on the United States on September 11, 2001, forced Americans to consider the tension between order and liberty once again. One of the goals of any national government is to provide security for its citizens against all enemies, domestic or foreign. The terrorist attacks of September 11 convinced the President to seek dramatic changes to the federal laws regarding evidence gathering, including wiretapping and other surveillance techniques used to catch criminals, so that it would be possible to find and prosecute terrorists more easily. Congress quickly passed the PATRIOT Act.

Within months of approving the legislation, more liberal members of Congress, civil liberties watchdogs, and individuals began to question the new powers given to the federal government. Did the PATRIOT Act go too far in allowing surveillance of law-abiding Americans? Shouldn't libraries be free from such surveillance? What would happen if the government overstepped its boundaries with no real judicial scrutiny? All of these questions point to the inherent tension between individual liberty and the tools used to provide security to the nation. The PATRIOT Act has been revised to some extent, but most of the basic provisions remain in effect. You can learn more about the act and its impact on your life by reading the "E-mocracy" section at the end of the chapter.

SECRETARY OF HOMELAND SECURITY Michael Chertoff testifies before a Senate Judiciary Committee oversight hearing on the Department of Homeland Security in Washington on April 2, 2008. How successful has the new department been in keeping the nation secure? (Kevin Dietsch/UPI/ Landov Media)

PROPERTY

Property
Anything that is or may be subject to ownership. As conceived by the political philosopher John Locke, the right to property is a natural right superior to human law (laws made by government).

Capitalism
An economic system characterized by the private ownership of wealth-creating assets, free markets, and freedom of contract.

The value of reducing economic inequality is in conflict with the right to **property**. This is because reducing economic inequality typically involves the transfer of property (usually in the form of money) from some people to others. For many people, liberty and property are closely entwined. A capitalist system is based on private property rights. Under **capitalism**, property consists not only of personal possessions but also of wealth-creating assets, such as farms and factories. The investor-owned corporation is in many ways the preeminent capitalist institution. The funds invested by the owners of a corporation are known as *capital*—hence, the very name of the system. Capitalism is also typically characterized by considerable freedom to make binding contracts and by relatively unconstrained markets for goods, services, and investments.

Property—especially wealth-creating property—can be seen as giving its owner political power and the liberty to do whatever he or she wants. At the same time, the ownership of property immediately creates inequality in society. The desire to own property, however, is so widespread among all classes of Americans that egalitarian movements have had a difficult time securing a wide following here.

A conflict between property rights and commercial development came before the United States Supreme Court in the 2005 case of *Kelo v. City of New London*.[13] The case arose when the city of New London, Connecticut, attempted to seize property from numerous homeowners through the power of **eminent domain**, which allows government to take private land for *public use* in return for *just compensation*. Some homeowners resisted because they did not want to move, regardless of the compensation being offered by the city. They also objected because the city planned to turn the land over to private developers, who wished to build an office park and expensive condominiums. The homeowners claimed that such a transfer did not constitute a public use. The Supreme Court disagreed, stating that the economic stimulation and increased tax revenues that the city would gain by the transfer of ownership fulfilled the public use requirement for eminent domain takings. The Court's decision caused an immediate uproar across the nation. The widespread disapproval compelled many state and local governments to pass laws against the kind of takings at issue in the *Kelo* case.

Eminent Domain
A power set forth in the Fifth Amendment to the U.S. Constitution that allows government to take private property for public use under the condition that just compensation is offered to the landowner.

THIS HOUSE IN Weare, New Hampshire, belongs to United States Supreme Court Justice David Souter. The man in front, Logan Darrow Clements, led a signature drive for a ballot initiative that would have asked the town of Weare to seize Souter's land for the purpose of building a hotel. Clements and others were annoyed at the Supreme Court's 2005 decision to allow the city of New London, Connecticut, to seize private land in order to allow private developers to build an office park and expensive apartments. How does this issue relate to the concept of eminent domain? (AP Photo/Jim Cole)

[13]545 U.S. 469 (2005).

POLITICAL IDEOLOGIES

A political **ideology** is a closely linked set of beliefs about politics. Political ideologies offer their adherents well-organized theories that propose goals for the society and the means by which those goals can be achieved. At the core of every political ideology is a set of guiding values. The two ideologies most commonly referred to in discussions of American politics are *liberalism* and *conservatism*. In the scheme of ideologies embraced across the globe, these two, especially as practiced in the United States, are in the middle of the ideological spectrum, as noted in Table 1–1.

THE TRADITIONAL POLITICAL SPECTRUM

A traditional method of comparing political ideologies is to array them on a continuum from left to right, based primarily on how much power the government should exercise to promote economic equality as well as the ultimate goals of government activity. Table 1–1 shows how ideologies can be arrayed in a traditional political spectrum. In addition to liberalism and conservatism, the table includes the ideologies of socialism and libertarianism.

Socialism falls on the left side of the spectrum. Socialists play a minor role in the American political arena, although socialist parties and movements are very important in other countries around the world. In the past, socialists typically advocated replacing investor ownership of major businesses with either government ownership or ownership by employee cooperatives. Socialists believed that such steps would break the power of the very rich and lead to an egalitarian society. In more recent times, socialists in Western Europe have advocated more limited programs that redistribute income.

On the right side of the spectrum is **libertarianism**, a philosophy of skepticism toward most government activities. Libertarians strongly support property rights and typically oppose regulation of the economy and redistribution of income. Libertarians support *laissez-faire* capitalism. (*Laissez-faire* is French for "let it be.") Libertarians also tend to oppose government attempts to regulate personal behavior and promote moral values.

IN THE MIDDLE: LIBERALISM AND CONSERVATISM

The set of beliefs called **conservatism** includes a limited role for the government in helping individuals. These values usually include a strong sense of patriotism. Conservatives believe that the private sector probably can outperform the government in almost any activity. Believing that the individual is primarily responsible for his or her own well-being, conservatives typically oppose government programs to redistribute income or change the status of individuals. Conservatism may also include support for what they refer to as traditional values regarding individual behavior and the importance of the family.

The set of beliefs called **liberalism** includes advocacy of government action to improve the welfare of individuals, support for civil rights, and tolerance for social change. American liberals believe that government should take positive action to reduce poverty, to redistribute income from wealthier classes to poorer ones, and to regulate the economy. Those who espouse liberalism may also be more supportive of the rights of women and gays and diverse lifestyles. Liberals are often seen as an influential force within the

"You'll be happy to know, Father, he's not a Liberal, Moderate or Conservative. Jason's a nothing."

Ideology
A comprehensive set of beliefs about the nature of people and about the role of an institution or government.

Socialism
A political ideology based on strong support for economic and social equality. Socialists traditionally envisioned a society in which major businesses were taken over by the government or by employee cooperatives.

Libertarianism
A political ideology based on skepticism or opposition toward almost all government activities.

Conservatism
A set of beliefs that includes a limited role for the national government in helping individuals, support for traditional values and lifestyles, and a cautious response to change.

Liberalism
A set of beliefs that includes the advocacy of positive government action to improve the welfare of individuals, support for civil rights, and tolerance for political and social change.

PRESIDENT GERALD FORD, served 1974–1976. President Ford is quoted as saying, "A government big enough to give you everything you want is a government big enough to take from you everything you have." (Dick Halstead/Time Life Pictures/Getty Images)

Democratic Party, and conservatives are often regarded as the most influential force in the Republican Party.

THE DIFFICULTY OF DEFINING LIBERALISM AND CONSERVATISM

While political candidates and commentators are quick to label candidates and voters as "liberals" and "conservatives," the meanings of these words have evolved over time. Moreover, each term may represent a quite different set of ideas to the person or group that uses it.

Liberalism. The word *liberal* has an odd history. It comes from the same root as *liberty*, and originally it simply meant "free." In that broad sense, the United States as a whole is a liberal country, and all popular American ideologies are variants of liberalism. In a more restricted definition, a *liberal* was a person who believed in limited government and who opposed religion in politics. A hundred years ago, liberalism referred to a philosophy that in some ways resembled modern-day libertarianism. For that reason, many libertarians today refer to themselves as *classical liberals*.

How did the meaning of the word *liberal* change? In the 1800s, the Democratic Party was seen as the more liberal of the two parties. The Democrats of that time stood for limited government and opposition to moralism in politics. Democrats opposed Republican projects such as building roads, freeing the slaves, and prohibiting the sale of alcoholic beverages. Beginning with Democratic president Woodrow Wilson (served 1913–1921), however, the party's economic policies began to change. President Franklin Delano Roosevelt won a landslide election in 1932, by pledging to take steps to end the Great Depression. Roosevelt and the Democratic Congress quickly passed several measures that increased federal government intervention in the economy and improved conditions for Americans. By the end of Roosevelt's presidency in 1945, the Democratic Party had established itself as standing for positive government action to help the economy. Although Roosevelt stood for new policies, he kept the old language—as Democrats had long done, he called himself a liberal. We will discuss the history of the two parties in greater detail in Chapter 8.

Outside the United States and Canada, the meaning of the word *liberal* never changed. For this reason, you might hear a left-of-center European denounce U.S. President Ronald Reagan (served 1981–1989) or British Prime Minister Margaret Thatcher

TABLE 1–1 The Traditional Political Spectrum

	SOCIALISM	LIBERALISM	CONSERVATISM	LIBERTARIANISM
How much power should the government have over the economy?	Active government control of major economic sectors	Positive government action in the economy	Positive government action to support capitalism	Almost no regulation of the economy
What should the government promote?	Economic equality, community	Economic security, equal opportunity, social liberty	Economic liberty, morality, social order	Total economic and social liberty

(served 1979–1990) for their "liberalism." What is meant is that these two leaders were enthusiastic advocates of *laissez-faire* capitalism.

Conservatism. The term *conservatism* suffers from similar identity problems. In the United States and Western Europe, conservatives tended to believe in maintaining traditions and opposing change. Conservatives were more likely to support the continuation of the monarchy, for example. At the end of World War II, Senator Robert A. Taft of Ohio was known as "Mr. Conservative," and he steadfastly opposed the Democratic Party's platform of an active government. However, he was not a spokesperson for conservative or traditional personal values.

Today, conservatism is often considered to have two quite different dimensions. Some self-identified conservatives are "economic conservatives" who believe in less government, support for capitalism and private property, and allowing individuals to pursue their own route to achievement with little government interference. Recent presidential campaigns have seen great efforts to motivate those individuals who might be called "social conservatives" to support Republican candidates. Social conservatives are much less interested in economic issues than in supporting traditional social values, including opposition to abortion, support for the death penalty or the right to own firearms, and opposition to gay marriage. Given these two different dimensions of conservatism, it is not surprising that conservatives are not always united in their political preferences.

Libertarianism. Although libertarians make up a much smaller proportion of the population in the United States than do conservatives or liberals, this ideology shares the more extreme positions of both groups. If the only question is how much power the government should have over the economy, this is where they belong. Libertarians, however, advocate the most complete possible freedom in social matters. They oppose government action to promote traditional moral values, although such action is often favored by other groups on the political right. Libertarians' strong support for civil liberties seems to align them more closely with modern liberals than with conservatives.

THE GLOBAL RANGE OF IDEOLOGIES

Several other ideologies have adherents today. Two of these, **communism** and **fascism**, have few followers in the United States. Their impact on Europe and Asia, however, determined the course of 20th-century history.

The first communists were a radical faction that broke away from the socialist movement. Traditionally, socialists had always considered themselves to be democrats. The communists, however, believed that they could abolish capitalism and institute socialism through a severe partisan dictatorship. The Soviet Union, founded by Russian Communists after World War I (1914–1918), succeeded in establishing government control of farms, factories, and businesses of all kinds and in replacing the market system with central planning. Under Joseph Stalin (served 1924–1953), the Soviet Union also developed into a brutal totalitarian regime.

Today, a hybrid of communism and limited capitalism is practiced by the People's Republic of China. In Cuba, Raul Castro, appointed by his brother, Fidel Castro, is the new leader of a communist nation that is repressive but has considerable support from its citizens. The leader of Venezuela, President Hugo Chavez, is a self-described socialist who has quickly moved to extend the state's reach of the economy.

The most famous example of fascism was Nazi Germany (1933–1945). As with communism, the success of fascism depended on a large body of disciplined followers and a populist appeal. Fascism, however, championed elitism rather than egalitarianism. It was strongly influenced by Charles Darwin's concept of "the survival of the fittest."

DID YOU KNOW?

That about 14 percent of all legal immigrants to the United States plan to live in the Los Angeles/Long Beach, California, area?

Communism
A revolutionary variant of socialism that favors a partisan (and often totalitarian) dictatorship, government control of all enterprises, and the replacement of free markets by central planning.

Fascism
A 20th-century ideology—often totalitarian—that exalts the national collective united behind an absolute ruler. Fascism rejects liberal individualism, values action over rational deliberation, and glorifies war.

It valued action over rational deliberation and explicitly rejected liberal individualism; it exalted the national collective, united behind an absolute ruler. Fascism appealed to patriotism or nationalism, but it shaped these common sentiments into virulent racism.

RADICAL ISLAM

The terrorists who attacked the World Trade Center and the Pentagon on September 11, 2001, were ideologically motivated. These terrorists were members of the al Qaeda[14] network led by Osama bin Laden. The ideology embraced by al Qaeda and several other terrorist and political movements is based on a radical and fundamentalist interpretation of Islam, an interpretation sometimes called *Islamism* or *Radical Islam*. This view rejects all Western democratic and cultural values, including equal rights for women, and calls for the establishment of a worldwide Islamic political order (the *caliphate*). The goal of this ideology is to bring all Muslim peoples back to a form of government ruled by religious leaders according to the strict interpretation of the Koran.

Given the complexity of ideological beliefs within the United States as well as the vitality of other ideologies that are directly opposed to democracy, it is clear that American representative democracy will face political challenges in the future. In addition, our form of government will need to be durable enough to deal with many future challenges.

THE AL QAEDA TERRORIST GROUP frequently uses the Internet to broadcast messages from their leader, Osama bin Laden. In the spring of 2008, al Qaeda released a video with a new audio recording from bin Laden about the 60th anniversary of the state of Israel. While such Internet postings are captured by a U.S. government contractor, there is no way to verify that the speech was made by bin Laden. (IntelCenter/AP Photo)

THE CHALLENGE OF CHANGE

In the next 50 years, the United States will face internal and external challenges. Not only will the face of America change as its citizens age, become more diverse, and generate new needs for laws and policies, but it will also have to contend with a lessening of its economic dominance in the world. Other nations, including China and India, have much larger populations than the United States and are assuming their respective roles in the world. The United States and its citizens will need to meet the challenges of a global economy and the impact of global environmental change. All of these challenges—demographic change, globalization, and environmental change—will impact how the American political system functions in the future.

That Russia is expected to lose 30 million people by 2050 and will have a population of only 118 million, compared to the predicted 420 million for the United States?

DEMOGRAPHIC CHANGE IN A DEMOCRATIC REPUBLIC

The population of the United States is changing in fundamental ways that will impact the political and social system of the nation. Long a nation of growth, the United States has become a middle-aged nation with a low birthrate and an increasing number of older citizens who want services from the government. Both the aging of the population and its changing ethnic composition will have significant political consequences.

---

[14]*Al Qaeda*, sometimes transliterated as *al Qaida* or *al-Qa'idah*, is Arabic for "the base."

BEYOND OUR B RDERS

IMMIGRATION: CHALLENGING CULTURES IN EUROPE

One of the hottest issues on the American political scene in recent years is the debate over what to do about undocumented immigrants who have come to the United States for employment. Currently, it is estimated that approximately 12 million individuals reside in the United States without legal status. Some conservatives believe that the best solution is deporting them all to their respective native countries. Others, including President George W. Bush and moderate leaders of both parties, have argued that the United States should recognize its need for workers and implement some system by which individuals can come to this country to work and someday possibly earn a right to citizenship.

Other nations, especially in Europe, have long admitted immigrants as unskilled and semiskilled workers to fuel their economies. Today, the immigrant population of Germany is about 12 percent while that of Austria is 15 percent. Luxembourg has a 37 percent immigrant population and Switzerland about 23 percent. For many decades, Great Britain has allowed individuals who were subjects in the British Commonwealth to enter the country, while France extended legal residency to many French citizens from the former colonies in North Africa.*

These European nations and many others on the European continent have faced many serious problems as their immigrant populations have reached 10 percent or more. Youths rioted in France in the last few years over the lack of employment opportunities for nonwhite French residents, while the Netherlands has seen outbreaks of violence by Muslim residents against other Dutch citizens. In Great Britain, especially after the bombings of the London subway, concern was raised over the motivations for homegrown terrorists in a nation that sees itself as offering opportunities to all its residents. Many of these states are engaged in serious internal discussion about how to socialize new residents to the culture of their new home and how to ensure that immigrants can find economic opportunities for themselves and their children. Some have even turned to examine the ways in which Americans used their school systems in the early 20th century to integrate immigrant children into the dominant culture.

FOR CRITICAL ANALYSIS

1. To what extent do you think that immigrant families should give up their customs to become part of their host country?
2. Should countries make specific efforts to socialize the children of immigrants into the language and customs of their new home?
3. How do nations ensure that immigrants accept the cultural and political values of their new home?

*United Nations statistics, 2005.

Like other economically advanced countries, the United States has in recent decades experienced falling birthrates and an increase in the number of older citizens (see Figure 1-1). The "aging of America" is a weaker phenomenon than in many other wealthy countries, however. Today, the median age of the population is 35.5 in the United States and 38.2 in Europe. By 2050, the median age in the United States is expected to rise slightly to 36.2. In Europe, it is expected to reach 52.7. As is already the case in many European nations, older citizens demand that their need for pensions and health care dominate the political agenda. Young people in the United States, already apathetic about politics, may become even more alienated as they witness the tilting of policies and benefits toward the aging.

FIGURE 1–1
The Aging of America

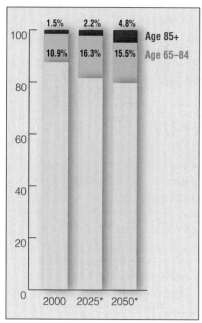

*Data for 2025 and 2050 are projections.
Source: U.S. Bureau of the Census.

Hispanic
Someone who can claim a heritage from a Spanish-speaking country (other than Spain). The term is used only in the United States or other countries that receive immigrants—Spanish-speaking persons living in Spanish-speaking countries do not normally apply the term to themselves.

ETHNIC CHANGE

As a result of differences in fertility rates and immigration, the ethnic character of the United States is also changing. Non-Hispanic white Americans have a fertility rate of just over 1.8 per two people; African Americans have a fertility rate of 2.1; and Hispanic Americans have a current fertility rate of almost 3.0. (The fertility rate in Mexico is only 2.5.) Figure 1–2 shows the projected changes in the U.S. ethnic distribution in future years.

A large share of all new immigrants is Hispanic, which also increases the Hispanic proportion of the U.S. population. A **Hispanic** is someone who can claim a heritage from a Spanish-speaking country (other than Spain). Table 1–2 shows the top 10 countries of origin for foreign-born populations in the United States projected to 2010. Immigration, of course, includes both legal and illegal immigration. Dealing with illegal immigration has spread far beyond the border states to become a major political issue in U.S. political campaigns. The existence of more than 12 million illegal immigrants within our borders presents a huge political and logistical problem. Even if all of these individuals could be identified, how could any policy—whether deportation or a path to citizenship—be implemented effectively?

Hispanics may come from any of about 20 primarily Spanish-speaking countries,[15] and they differ among themselves in many ways. Hispanic Americans, as a result, are a highly diverse population. The three largest Hispanic groups are Mexican Americans at 58.5 percent of all Hispanics; Puerto Ricans (all of whom are U.S. citizens) at 9.6 percent of the total; and Cuban Americans at 3.5 percent.

The diversity among Hispanic Americans results in differing political behavior. The majority of Hispanic Americans vote Democratic. In 2004, they backed Democratic presidential candidate John Kerry over Republican George W. Bush by 53 to 44 percent. Cuban Americans, however, are usually Republican. Most Cuban Americans left Cuba because of Fidel Castro's communist regime, and their strong anticommunism beliefs translate into conservative politics. In 2008, Barack Obama captured the major-

FIGURE 1–2 Distribution of the U.S. Population by Race and Hispanic Origin, 1980–2075

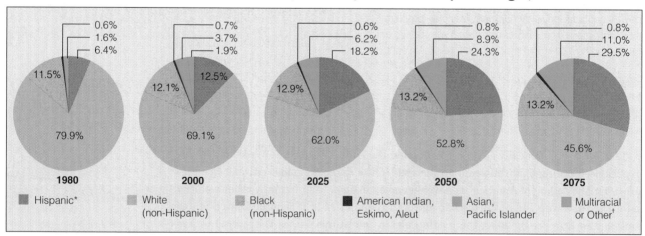

Data for 2025, 2050, and 2075 are projections.
*Persons of Hispanic origin can be of any race.
†The "multiracial or other" category in 2000 is not an official census category but represents all non-Hispanics who chose either "some other race" or two or more races in the 2000 census.
Source: U.S. Bureau of the Census.

[15]According to the census definition, "Hispanic" includes the relatively small number of Americans whose ancestors came directly from Spain. Few of these people are likely to check the "Hispanic" box on a census form, however.

TABLE 1–2 Top Ten Countries of Origin for Foreign-Born Populations in the United States

COUNTRY	2000	2004	2010*	PERCENT
Mexico	7,841,000	8,544,600	8,600,000	23.7
China	1,391,000	1,594,600	1,900,000	4.7
Philippines	1,222,000	1,413,200	1,700,000	4.2
India	1,007,000	1,244,200	2,600,000	4.0
Ireland	863,000	997,800	1,200,000	3.0
Cuba	952,000	1,011,200	1,100,000	2.7
El Salvador	765,000	899,000	1,100,000	2.7
Canada	678,000	774,800	920,000	2.3
Dominican Republic	692,000	791,600	941,000	2.3
Korea	701,000	772,600	880,000	2.2
TOTAL POPULATION—TOP TEN COUNTRIES				
	16,112,000	18,043,600	20,941,000	51.8
TOTAL FOREIGN-BORN—POPULATION				
	31,100,000	34,860,000	40,500,000	100

*Projected.
Sources: U.S. Bureau of the Census; U.S. Bureau of Citizenship and Immigration Services.

DID YOU KNOW?

That people of Hispanic origin are estimated to make up almost one-quarter of the U.S. population by 2025?

ity of Hispanic votes across the nation. In Florida, Hispanic voters favored him by a margin of 57 percent to 42 percent, an increase of 14 percent over the prior presidential race. Strong voter turnout, combined with an increase in the number of Hispanic voters in the Southwestern states, resulted in Obama victories in Colorado and New Mexico. The Hispanic share of the electorate increased from 8 percent to 17 percent in Colorado, and Obama received 73 percent of their votes. In New Mexico, where Hispanics comprise 41 percent of the vote, Obama carried 69 percent of the Latino vote. Commentators suggested that the strong opposition of conservative talk radio to any form of immigration reform alienated many Hispanic voters from the Republican Party.

The United States is continuing to become a more ethnically diverse nation in every way. Nothing could be more telling than the election of Bobby Jindal, an American of Indian descent, as the governor of Louisiana in 2007. A former Republican Congressman, Jindal did not represent any major ethnic group in that state but ran on a platform of effective government and ending corruption. The campaign of Jindal—and even more significantly of Barack Obama for President of the United States—may signal the end of white dominance in political leadership at state and national levels. A multiethnic, multiracial society, however, poses some real challenges in keeping the various groups from exacerbating racial differences to obtain benefits for their respective groups. If the United States could achieve a higher level of economic equality for all Americans, group differences could be minimized.

GLOBALIZATION

DID YOU KNOW?

That in 2006, Washington became the first state to have both a female governor and two female U.S. Senators at the same time?

The globalization of the world economy has occurred with relatively little notice by Americans. The power of the American economy and its expansion into other parts of the world spurred similar actions by the European, South American, and Asian nations. Huge international corporations produce and

THE ELECTION OF BOBBY JINDAL, an Indian American, as governor of Louisiana in 2007 is an indication of how diverse the nation has become. Jindal, a Republican, was formerly a Congressman. (Tim Mueller/AP Photos)

market products throughout the world. American soft drinks are produced and sold in China, while Americans buy clothing manufactured in China or the former states of the Soviet Union. Jobs are outsourced from the United States to India, the Philippines, or Vietnam, while other nations outsource jobs to the United States. Companies such as General Electric employ design teams that collaborate in the design and production of jet engines, with employees working around the clock, across all time zones.

Globalization brings a multitude of challenges to the United States and all other nations, beginning with the fact that no single government can regulate global corporations. Globalization changes employment patterns, reducing jobs in one nation and increasing employment in another. Products produced in low-wage nations are cheaper to buy in the United States, but the result is little control over quality and safety for consumers. Economic recession may, however, affect the entire globe if one nation has an economic decline. Clearly, nations must come together to meet the issues of globalization, but collaborative efforts may weaken the power of the United States or any sovereign nation.

ENVIRONMENTAL CHANGE

The challenges posed by environmental change are political, technological, and global. The great majority of scientists agree that global warming is taking place. Many scien-

tists and global organizations are focusing their efforts on measures to reduce humankind's contribution to global warming through carbon emissions and other actions. The United States, under the Bush administration, balked at joining in the imposition of the measures on all nations until developing nations such as China and India were included. Signing any kind of treaty on this matter is a serious issue for the United States because, as we will see in Chapter 2, treaties override U.S. law according to our Constitution. American citizens would have their own lives determined by these treaties whether they approve these policies or not.

While many scientists are working on the technologies to slow global warming, others believe that it is more important to concentrate on mitigating the impact of global warming, whatever the cause. The United States, like many other nations, has a concentration of population on the seacoasts: how should policies change in the face of rising seas and more hurricanes and coastal damage? Global warming is predicted to have more immediate and dire consequences on nations in Africa, where droughts will cause starvation to millions. Should the United States play a much greater role in ameliorating these disasters and others caused by global warming in the near future, or should our policy priorities focus on technologies to change our lifestyles years from now?

Other challenges on a global scale include biological dangers such as bird flu and other sources of pollution. For each of these environmental threats, the challenge facing American democracy is to make these issues a priority, even above domestic issues. Given the normal tendency for politics to focus on those issues most important to each of us personally, it will be very difficult to move global environmental issues to the top of the American agenda.

You can make a difference

SEEING DEMOCRACY IN ACTION

One way to begin to understand the American political system is to observe a legislative body in action. There are thousands of elected legislatures in the United States at all levels of government. You might choose to visit a city council, a school board, a township board of trustees, a state legislature, or the U.S. Congress.

WHY SHOULD YOU CARE?

State and local legislative bodies can have a direct impact on your life. For example, local councils or commissions typically oversee the police, and the behavior of the police is a matter of interest even if you live on-campus. If you live off-campus, local authorities are responsible for an even greater number of issues that affect you directly. Are there items that the Sanitation Department refuses to pick up? You might be able to change its policies by lobbying your councilperson.

Even if no local issues concern you, benefits can still be gained from observing a local legislative session. You may discover that local government works rather differently than you expected. You might learn, for example, that the representatives of your political party do not serve your interests as well as you thought—or that the other party is much more sensible than you had presumed.

WHAT CAN YOU DO?

To find out when and where local legislative bodies meet, look up the number of the city hall or county building in the telephone directory, and call the clerk of the council. In many communities, city council meetings and county board meetings can be seen on public-access TV channels. Many cities and almost all state governments have Web sites.

Before attending a business session of the legislature, try to find out how the members are elected. Are the members chosen by the at-large method of election, so that each member represents the whole community, or are they chosen by specific geographic districts or wards? Is there a chairperson or official leader who controls the meetings? What are the responsibilities of this legislature?

When you visit the legislature, keep in mind the theory of representative democracy. The legislators or council members are elected to represent their constituents (those who live in their geographic area). Observe how often the members refer to their constituents or to the special needs of their community or electoral district. Listen for sources of conflict within a community. If there is a debate, for example, over a zoning proposal that involves the issue of land use, try to figure out why some members oppose the proposal.

If you want to follow up on your visit, try to get a brief interview with one of the members of the council or board. In general, legislators are very willing to talk to students, particularly students who are also voters. Ask the member how he or she sees the job of representative. How can the wishes of constituents be identified? How does the representative balance the needs of the ward or district with the good of the entire community? You can write to many legislators via e-mail. You might ask how much e-mail they receive and who actually answers it.

KEY TERMS

anarchy 8
aristocracy 8
authoritarianism 8
authority 7
capitalism 18
communism 21
consent of the people 10
conservatism 19
democracy 8
democratic republic 10
direct democracy 8
dominant culture 14
elite theory 12
eminent domain 18
equality 16

fascism 21
government 5
Hispanic 24
ideology 19
initiative 9
institution 5
legislature 8
legitimacy 7
liberalism 19
libertarianism 19
liberty 7
limited government 11
majoritarianism 12
majority 11
majority rule 11

oligarchy 8
order 5
pluralism 14
political culture 14
political socialization 14
politics 5
popular sovereignty 10
property 18
recall 9
referendum 9
representative democracy 11
republic 10
socialism 19
totalitarian regime 8
universal suffrage 11

CHAPTER SUMMARY

1. Politics is the process by which people decide which members of society get certain benefits or privileges and which members do not. It is the struggle over power or influence within institutions and organizations that can grant benefits or privileges. Government is the institution within which decisions are made that resolve conflicts or allocate benefits and privileges. It is unique because it has the ultimate authority within society.

2. Fundamental political values are order, which includes security against violence, and liberty, the greatest freedom of the individual consistent with the freedom of other individuals. Liberty can be both promoted by government and invoked against government. To be effective, government authority must be backed by legitimacy.

3. In a direct democracy, such as ancient Athens, the people make the important political decisions. The United States is a representative democracy, where the people elect representatives to make the decisions.

4. Theories of American democracy include majoritarianism, in which the government does what the majority wants; elite theory, in which the real power lies with one or more elites; and pluralist theory, in which organized interest groups contest for power.

5. Fundamental American values include liberty, order, equality, and property. Not all of these values are fully compatible. The value of order often competes with civil liberties, and economic equality competes with property rights.

6. Popular political ideologies can be arrayed from left (liberal) to right (conservative). We can also analyze economic liberalism and conservatism separately from cultural liberalism and conservatism. However, other ideologies on the left (communism) and the right (fascism) also exist in the world.

7. Many challenges face the United States in the future. Among these challenges are demographic changes in the nation, the impact of globalization, and the threats of environmental change.

SELECTED PRINT AND MEDIA RESOURCES

SUGGESTED READINGS

Harrison, Lawrence E., and Samuel P. Huntington, eds. *Culture Matters: How Values Shape Human Progress.* New York: Basic Books, 2001. Each of the essays included in this book gives insight into an important question: How and why do some cultures do a better job of creating freedom, prosperity, and justice than others?

Lasswell, Harold. *Politics: Who Gets What, When and How.* New York: McGraw-Hill, 1936. This classic work defines the nature of politics.

Levy, Bernard-Henri. *American Vertigo: Traveling America in the Footsteps of Tocqueville.* New York: Random House, 2006. The author, a French journalist and philosopher, seeks to explore the question of what it means to be an American today. Just as Alexis de Tocqueville did in the 1820s, Levy provides a foreigner's description of American culture and life.

Ngai, Mae M. *Impossible Subjects: Illegal Aliens and the Making of Modern America.* Princeton, NJ: Princeton University Press, 2005. This study explains why and how illegal immigration became the central problem in U.S. immigration policy. Ngai delves into the complex subjects of citizenship, race, and state authority.

Tocqueville, Alexis de. *Democracy in America.* Edited by Phillips Bradley. New York: Vintage Books, 1945. Life in the United States is described by a French writer who traveled through the nation in the 1820s.

MEDIA RESOURCES

All Things Considered—A daily broadcast of National Public Radio (NPR) that provides extensive coverage of political, economic, and social news stories.

The Conservatives—A TV program that shows the rise of the conservative movement in America from the 1940s, from the presidential candidacy of Barry Goldwater to the presidency of Ronald Reagan. In addition to Goldwater and Reagan, leaders interviewed include William F. Buckley, Jr., Norman Podhoretz, and Milton Friedman.

Liberalism vs. Conservatism—A 2001 film from Teacher's Video that focuses on two contrasting views of the role of government in society.

Mr. Smith Goes to Washington—A classic movie, produced in 1939, starring Jimmy Stewart as the honest citizen who goes to Congress trying to represent his fellow citizens. The movie dramatizes the clash between representing principles and representing corrupt interests.

The Values Issue and American Politics: Values Matter Most—Ben Wattenberg travels around the country in this 1995 TV program speaking to a broad range of ordinary Americans. He examines what he calls the "values issue"—the issues of crime, welfare, race, discipline, drugs, and prayer in the schools. Wattenberg believes that candidates who can best address these issues will win elections.

e-mocracy

CONNECTING TO AMERICAN GOVERNMENT AND POLITICS

The Web has become a virtual library, a telephone directory, a contact source, and a vehicle to improve your understanding of American government and politics today. To help you become familiar with Web resources, we conclude each chapter in this book with an *E-mocracy* feature. The *Logging On* section in each of these features includes Internet addresses, or uniform resource locators (URLs), that will take you to Web sites focusing on topics or issues discussed in the chapter. Realize that Web sites come and go continually, so some of the Web sites that we include in the *Logging On* section may not exist by the time you read this book. Each *E-mocracy* feature also includes an InfoTrac® College Edition Internet activity. These activities are designed to lead you to Web sites that you can explore to learn more about an important political issue.

A word of caution about Internet use: Many students surf the Web for political resources. When doing so, you need to remember to approach these sources with care. For one thing, you should be very careful when giving out information about yourself. You also need to use good judgment, because the reliability or intent of any given Web site is often unknown. Some sites are more concerned with accuracy than others, and some sites are updated to include current information, whereas others are not.

LOGGING ON

- We have a powerful and interesting Web site for this textbook, which you can access through the Wadsworth American Government Resource Center. Go to: **www.politicalscience.wadsworth.com/amgov**
- You may also want to visit the home page of Dr. Politics—offered by Steffen Schmidt, one of the authors of this book—for some interesting ideas and activities relating to American government and politics. Go to: **www.public.iastate.edu/~sws/**

- Information about the rules and requirements for immigration and citizenship can be found at the Web site of the U.S. Citizenship and Immigration Services: **www.uscis.gov/graphics/index.htm**
- For a basic "front door" to almost all U.S. government Web sites, click onto the very useful site maintained by the University of Michigan: **www.lib.umich.edu/govdocs/govweb.html**
- For access to federal government offices and agencies, go to the U.S. government's official Web site at: **www.usa.gov**
- To learn about the activities of one of the nation's oldest liberal political organizations, go to the Web site of the Americans for Democratic Action (ADA) at the following URL: **www.adaction.org**
- For more information about conservative positions, go to the Web site of the American Conservative Union: **www.conservative.org**
- You can find a wealth of information about the changing face of America at the Web site of the Bureau of the Census: **www.census.gov**
- To learn more about the National Security Agency, including its history, visit: **www.nsa.gov**

ONLINE REVIEW

At **www.cengage.com/politicalscience/schmidt/agandpt14e**, you will find a Tutorial Quiz for this chapter providing questions on the chapter contents, including the features. The questions are organized to match the major sections of the chapter. You'll have access to other helpful study tools, including the book's glossary and flashcards, crossword puzzles, and Web links, as well as "Which Side Are You On?" and "Politics and . . ." features written by the authors of the book.

CHAPTER

(2)

A family looks at the U.S. Constitution
at the National Archives in Washington,
D.C. (Alex Wong/Getty Images)

THE CONSTITUTION

QUESTIONS TO CONSIDER

Why does the Constitution divide the powers of government among the three branches?

Why is it so difficult to amend the Constitution?

Should the Constitution be changed to better address the needs of the nation in the 21st century?

CHAPTER CONTENTS

Making a DIFFERENCE

HOW TO FORM A MORE PERFECT UNION?

We the People of the United States, in Order to form a more perfect Union, establish Justice, insure domestic Tranquility, provide for the common defence, promote the general Welfare, and secure the Blessings of Liberty to ourselves and our Posterity, do ordain and establish this Constitution for the United States of America.

Did you ever wonder what the framers of the Constitution meant by "a more perfect union"? Or why establishing justice and insuring domestic tranquility would be at the top of their list? As you will learn in this chapter, the framers were reacting to problems with the early form of government for the new country: the Articles of Confederation.

During the Revolution, the Continental Congress created a confederate form of government.

As you will learn in this chapter and Chapter 3, a confederation is a loose alliance among members—in this case, a "league of friendship among states." Because of their frustrations with King George's tyranny, the framers created a national government with very little power. Adopted in 1781, the Articles of Confederation governed the emerging nation until our existing Constitution replaced it in 1787. The Articles held competing and disparate interests together for more than a decade.

Any time political rules are changed, there are winners and losers. Some wish to maintain the *status quo* and others want change. Whether to amend or replace the Articles of Confederation was a dispute between those who enjoyed power under the Articles and those who found their weaknesses too dangerous and unprofitable. Let's look at a couple of examples of ways the Articles weren't working.

In a confederal system that gave all autonomy to the member states, the Congress had very little power. It could

EVERY SCHOOLCHILD IN AMERICA has at one time or another been exposed to the famous words that appear in the *Making a Difference* box that are taken from the Preamble to the U.S. Constitution. The document itself is remarkable. The U.S. Constitution, compared with others in the 50 states and in the world, is relatively short. Because amending it is difficult, it also has relatively few amendments. The Constitution has remained largely intact for more than 200 years. To a great extent, this is because the principles set forth in the Constitution met the needs of the diverse and independent states of the confederacy (as noted above) and, over time, have also met the needs of a changing nation.

How and why the U.S. Constitution was created is a story that has been told and retold. It is worth repeating, because knowing the historical and political context in which this country's governmental machinery was formed is essential to understanding American government and politics today. The Constitution did not result just from creative thinking. Many of its provisions were grounded in the political philosophy of the time. The delegates to the Constitutional Convention in 1787 brought with them two important sets of influences: their political culture and their political experience. In the years between the first settlements in the New World and the writing of the Constitution, Americans had developed a political philosophy about how people should be governed and had tried out several forms of government. These experiences gave the founders the tools with which they constructed the Constitution. Milestones in the nation's early political history are shown in Table 2–1 later in this chapter.

DID YOU KNOW?

That the first English claim to territory in North America was made by John Cabot, on behalf of King Henry VII, on June 24, 1497?

not regulate commerce or foreign trade nor levy taxes, and it had to depend on the state to begin to pay down the war debt. To deal with the difficulty of deficits without power to tax, Congress simply printed more money. This led to inflation, a lack of trust in the printed currency, and reliance on gold and silver. The national government commanded such little respect that ratifying the Treaty of Paris, which ended the Revolutionary War in 1783, was a problem because a sufficient number of Congressional delegates were not present![a]

Members of Congress, as well as those whose economic interests were hurt by the economic instability, were frustrated. In addition to the aforementioned problems, the national government could not effectively regulate trade (all 13 states could negotiate separate trading arrangements with each other and with foreign governments). For people like seaport merchants, large plantation owners, and commercial farmers who depended on trade, this was a trying and unstable situation.[b]

On the other hand, some people did approve of the Articles. Smaller farmers and those who lived inland depended less on trade and were more likely to believe the state governments were sufficient to solve their problems. In fact, they generally preferred a less active government that would keep taxes low and provide debt relief. Also, many state legislative districts were apportioned to benefit westward-expanding portions of their states. With the success of the Articles in creating the Northwest Territory, there was a contingent in state governments that was suspicious of national encroachment on their power.

So, why would states give up the enormous power they enjoyed under the Articles of Confederation? Initially, they did not. As early as 1786, calls were made to reform the Articles, and it was through crises like the rebellion led by Daniel Shays in Massachusetts (about which you will learn more in this chapter) that those favoring a stronger national government were able to organize to form a Constitutional Convention. Meeting in 1787, they deliberated for months in secret to draft a document that was acceptable to the participants. The new Constitution was ratified in July 1788 through intense efforts to persuade state leaders (including promises of positions in the new government), a promise of greater protection of civil liberties, and lobbying efforts modern politicians would recognize.[c]

[a] www.loc.gov/rr/program/bib/ourdocs/articles.html, accessed September 22, 2008.

[b] Robert A. McGuire, "Review of Keith L. Dougherty," *Collective Action under the Articles of Confederation*, EH.Net Economic History Services, April 11, 2002, http://eh.net/bookreviews/library/0469.

[c] Lee Epstein and Thomas G. Walker, *Constitutional Law for a Changing America*, 5th ed., 2 vols. (Washington, DC: CQ Press, 2004).

THE COLONIAL BACKGROUND

In 1607, the English government sent a group of farmers to establish a trading post, Jamestown, in what is now Virginia. The Virginia Company of London was the first to establish a permanent English colony in the Americas. The king of England gave the backers of this colony a charter granting them "full power and authority" to make laws "for the good and welfare" of the settlement. The colonists at Jamestown instituted a **representative assembly**, setting a precedent in government that was to be observed in later colonial adventures.

Representative Assembly
A legislature composed of individuals who represent the population.

Jamestown was not an immediate success. Of the 105 men who landed, 67 died within the first year. But 800 new arrivals in 1609 added to their numbers. By the spring of the next year, frontier hazards had cut their numbers to 60. Of the 6,000 people who left England for Virginia between 1607 and 1623, 4,800 perished. This period is sometimes referred to as the "starving time for Virginia." Climatological researchers suggest that this "starving time" may have been brought about by a severe drought in the Jamestown area, which lasted from 1607 to 1612.

SEPARATISTS, THE *MAYFLOWER*, AND THE COMPACT

The first New England colony was established in 1620. A group of mostly extreme Separatists, who wished to break with the Church of England, came over on the ship *Mayflower* to the New World, landing at Plymouth (Massachusetts). Before going onshore, the adult males—women were not considered to have any political status—drew up the

THE SIGNING OF THE compact aboard the *Mayflower*. In 1620, the Mayflower Compact was signed by almost all of the men aboard the *Mayflower* just before they disembarked at Plymouth, Massachusetts. It stated, "We . . . covenant and combine ourselves togeather into a civil body politick . . . ; and by vertue hearof to enacte, constitute, and frame such just and equal laws . . . as shall be thought [necessary] for the generall good of the Colonie." (The Granger Collection)

Mayflower Compact, which was signed by 41 of the 44 men aboard the ship on November 21, 1620. The reason for the compact was obvious. This group was outside the jurisdiction of the Virginia Company of London, which had chartered its settlement in Virginia, not Massachusetts. The Separatist leaders feared that some of the *Mayflower* passengers might conclude that they were no longer under any obligations of civil obedience. Therefore, some form of public authority was imperative. As William Bradford (one of the Separatist leaders) recalled in his accounts, there were "discontented and mutinous speeches that some of the strangers amongst them had let fall from them in the ship; That when they came a shore they would use their owne libertie; for none had power to command them."[1]

The compact was not a constitution. It was a political statement in which the signers agreed to create and submit to the authority of a government, pending the receipt of a royal charter. The Mayflower Compact's historical and political significance is twofold: it depended on the consent of the affected individuals, and it served as a prototype for similar compacts in American history. According to Samuel Eliot Morison, the compact proved the determination of the English immigrants to live under the rule of law, based on the *consent of the people*.[2]

MORE COLONIES, MORE GOVERNMENT

Another outpost in New England was set up by the Massachusetts Bay Colony in 1630. Then followed Rhode Island, Connecticut, New Hampshire, and others. By 1732, the last of the 13 colonies, Georgia, was established. During the colonial period, Americans developed a concept of limited government, which followed from the establishment of the first colonies under Crown charters. Theoretically, London governed the colonies. In practice, owing partly to the colonies' distance from London, the colonists exercised a large measure of self-government. The colonists were able to make their own laws, as

[1]John Camp, *Out of the Wilderness: The Emergence of an American Identity in Colonial New England* (Middleton, CT: Wesleyan University Press, 1990).
[2]See Morison's "The Mayflower Compact," in Daniel J. Boorstin, ed., *An American Primer* (Chicago: University of Chicago Press, 1966), p. 18.

in the Fundamental Orders of Connecticut in 1639. The Massachusetts Body of Liberties in 1641 supported the protection of individual rights and was made a part of colonial law. In 1682, the Pennsylvania Frame of Government was passed. Along with the Pennsylvania Charter of Privileges of 1701, it foreshadowed our modern Constitution and Bill of Rights. All of this legislation enabled the colonists to acquire crucial political experience. After independence was declared in 1776, the states quickly set up their own new constitutions.

TABLE 2–1 Milestones in Early U.S. Political History

YEAR	EVENT
1607	Jamestown established; Virginia Company lands settlers.
1620	Mayflower Compact signed.
1630	Massachusetts Bay Colony set up.
1639	Fundamental Orders of Connecticut adopted.
1641	Massachusetts Body of Liberties adopted.
1682	Pennsylvania Frame of Government passed.
1701	Pennsylvania Charter of Privileges written.
1732	Last of the 13 colonies (Georgia) established.
1756	French and Indian War declared.
1765	Stamp Act; Stamp Act Congress meets.
1774	First Continental Congress.
1775	Second Continental Congress; Revolutionary War begins.
1776	Declaration of Independence signed.
1777	Articles of Confederation drafted.
1781	Last state (Maryland) signs Articles of Confederation.
1783	"Critical period" in U.S. history begins; weak national government until 1789.
1786	Shays' Rebellion.
1787	Constitutional Convention.
1788	Ratification of Constitution.
1791	Ratification of Bill of Rights.

BRITISH RESTRICTIONS AND COLONIAL GRIEVANCES

The conflict between Britain and the American colonies, which ultimately led to the Revolutionary War, began in the 1760s when the British government decided to raise revenues by imposing taxes on the American colonies. Policy advisers to Britain's young King George III, who ascended the throne in 1760, decided that it was only logical to require the American colonists to help pay the costs of Britain's defending them during the French and Indian War (1756–1763). The colonists, who had grown accustomed to a large degree of self-government and independence from the British Crown, viewed the matter differently.

In 1764, the British Parliament passed the Sugar Act. Many colonists were unwilling to pay the tax imposed by the Act. Further regulatory legislation was to come. In 1765, Parliament passed the Stamp Act, providing for internal taxation—or, as the colonists' Stamp Act Congress, assembled in 1765, called it, "taxation without representation." The colonists boycotted the purchase of English commodities in return. The success of the boycott (the Stamp Act was repealed a year later) generated a feeling of unity within the colonies.

The British, however, continued to try to raise revenues in the colonies. When Parliament passed duties on glass, lead, paint, and other items in 1767, the colonists again

KING GEORGE III (1738–1820) was king of Great Britain and Ireland from 1760 until his death on January 29, 1820. Under George III, the British Parliament attempted to tax the American colonies. Ultimately, the colonies, exasperated at repeated attempts at taxation, proclaimed their independence on July 4, 1776. (*King George III*, studio of Allan Ramsay, oil on canvas [1761–1762], 58 in. x 42 in., purchased 1866. On display in Room 14 at the National Portrait Gallery, London.)

boycotted British goods. The colonists' fury over taxation climaxed in the Boston Tea Party: colonists dressed as Mohawk Indians dumped close to 350 chests of British tea into Boston Harbor as a gesture of tax protest. In retaliation, Parliament passed the Coercive Acts (the "Intolerable Acts") in 1774, which closed Boston Harbor and placed the government of Massachusetts under direct British control. The colonists were outraged—and they responded.

THE COLONIAL RESPONSE: THE CONTINENTAL CONGRESSES

New York, Pennsylvania, and Rhode Island proposed the convening of a colonial congress. The Massachusetts House of Representatives requested that all colonies hold conventions to select delegates to be sent to Philadelphia for such a congress.

THE FIRST CONTINENTAL CONGRESS

The First Continental Congress was held at Carpenter's Hall on September 5, 1774. It was a gathering of delegates from 12 of the 13 colonies (delegates from Georgia did not attend until 1775). At that meeting, there was little talk of independence. The Congress passed a resolution requesting that the colonies send a petition to King George III expressing their grievances. Resolutions were also passed requiring that the colonies raise their own troops and boycott British trade. The British government condemned the Congress's actions, treating them as open acts of rebellion.

The delegates to the First Continental Congress declared that in every county and city, a committee was to be formed whose mission was to spy on the conduct of friends and neighbors and to report to the press any violators of the trade ban. The formation of these committees was an act of cooperation among the colonies, which represented a step toward the creation of a national government.

THE SECOND CONTINENTAL CONGRESS

By the time the Second Continental Congress met in May 1775 (this time all of the colonies were represented), fighting had already broken out between the British and the colonists. One of the main actions of the Second Congress was to establish an army. It did this by declaring the militia that had gathered around Boston an army and naming George Washington as commander in chief. The participants in that Congress still attempted to reach a peaceful settlement with the British Parliament. One declaration of the Congress stated explicitly that "we have not raised armies with ambitious designs of separating from Great Britain, and establishing independent states." But by the beginning of 1776, military encounters had become increasingly frequent.

Public debate was acrimonious. Then Thomas Paine's *Common Sense* appeared in Philadelphia bookstores. The pamphlet was a colonial best seller. (To do relatively as well today, a book would have to sell between nine and 11 million copies in its first year of publication.) Many agreed that Paine did make common sense when he argued that

a government of our own is our natural right: and when a man seriously reflects on the precariousness [instability, unpredictability] of human affairs, he will become convinced, that it is infinitely wiser and safer, to form a constitution of our own in a cool and deliberate manner, while we have it in our power, than to trust such an interesting event to time and chance.[3]

Students of Paine's pamphlet point out that his arguments were not new—they were common in tavern debates throughout the land. Rather, it was the near poetry of his words—which were at the same time as plain as the alphabet—that struck his readers.

DECLARING INDEPENDENCE

On April 6, 1776, the Second Continental Congress voted for free trade at all American ports with all countries except Britain. This act could be interpreted as an implicit declaration of independence. The next month, the Congress suggested that each of the colonies establish state governments unconnected to Britain. Finally, in July, the colonists declared their independence from Britain.

THE RESOLUTION OF INDEPENDENCE

On July 2, the Resolution of Independence was adopted by the Second Continental Congress:

> RESOLVED, That these United Colonies are, and of right ought to be free and independent States, that they are absolved from allegiance to the British Crown, and that all political connection between them and the state of Great Britain is, and ought to be, totally dissolved.

The actual Resolution of Independence was not legally significant. On the one hand, it was not judicially enforceable, for it established no legal rights or duties. On the other hand, the colonies were already, in their own judgment, self-governing and independent of Britain. Rather, the Resolution of Independence and the subsequent Declaration of Independence were necessary to establish the legitimacy of the new nation in the eyes of foreign governments, as well as in the eyes of the colonists. What the new nation needed most were supplies for its armies and a commitment of foreign military aid. Unless it appeared to the world as a political entity separate and independent from Britain, no foreign government would enter into a contract with its leaders.

"You know, the idea of taxation with representation doesn't appeal to me very much either." (Cartoon by J. B. Handelsman; published in *The New Yorker*, June 27, 1970, © cartoonbank .com. All rights reserved.)

JULY 4, 1776—THE DECLARATION OF INDEPENDENCE

By June 1776, Thomas Jefferson already was writing drafts of the Declaration of Independence in the second-floor parlor of a bricklayer's house in Philadelphia. On adoption of the Resolution of Independence, Jefferson argued that a declaration clearly putting forth the causes that compelled the colonies to separate from Britain was necessary. The Second Congress assigned the task to him, and he completed his work on the declaration, which enumerated the colonists' major grievances against Britain. Some of his work was amended to gain unanimous acceptance (for example, his condemnation of the slave trade was eliminated to satisfy Georgia and North Carolina), but the bulk of it was passed intact on July 4, 1776. On July 19, the modified draft became "the

[3]*The Political Writings of Thomas Paine*, Vol. 1 (Boston: J. P. Mendum Investigator Office, 1870), p. 46.

unanimous declaration of the thirteen United States of America." On August 2, it was signed by the members of the Second Continental Congress.

Universal Truths. The Declaration of Independence has become one of the world's most famous and significant documents. The words opening the second paragraph of the Declaration are known most widely:

> We hold these Truths to be self-evident, that all Men are created equal, that they are endowed by their Creator with certain unalienable Rights, that among these are Life, Liberty, and the Pursuit of Happiness—That to secure these Rights, Governments are instituted among Men, deriving their just Powers from the Consent of the Governed, that whenever any Form of Government becomes destructive of these Ends, it is the Right of the People to alter or abolish it, and to institute new Government.

Natural Rights and a Social Contract. The assumption that people have **natural rights** ("unalienable Rights"), including the rights to "Life, Liberty, and the Pursuit of Happiness," was a revolutionary concept at that time. Its use by Jefferson reveals the influence of the English philosopher John Locke (1632–1704), whose writings were familiar to educated American colonists, including Jefferson.[4] In his *Two Treatises on Government*, published in 1690, Locke had argued that all people possess certain natural rights, including the rights to life, liberty, and property, and that the primary purpose of government was to protect these rights. Furthermore, government was established by the people through a **social contract**—an agreement among the people to form a government and abide by its rules. As you read earlier, such contracts, or compacts, were not new to Americans. The Mayflower Compact was the first of several documents that established governments or governing rules based on the consent of the governed. In citing the "pursuit of happiness" instead of "property" as a right, Jefferson clearly meant to go beyond Locke's thinking.

Natural Rights
Rights held to be inherent in natural law, not dependent on governments. John Locke stated that natural law, being superior to human law, specifies certain rights of "life, liberty, and property." These rights, altered to become "life, liberty, and the pursuit of happiness," are asserted in the Declaration of Independence.

Social Contract
A voluntary agreement among individuals to secure their rights and welfare by creating a government and abiding by its rules.

MEMBERS OF THE SECOND Continental Congress adopted the Declaration of Independence on July 4, 1776. Minor changes were made in the document in the following two weeks. On July 19, the modified draft became the "unanimous declaration of the thirteen United States of America." On August 2, the members of the Second Continental Congress signed it. The first official printed version carried only the signatures of the Congress's president, John Hancock, and its secretary, Charles Thompson. (Library of Congress Prints & Photographs Division, Washington, D.C. [LC-H8-CT-C01-0621])

[4]Not all scholars believe that Jefferson was truly influenced by Locke. For example, Jay Fliegelman states that "Jefferson's fascination with Homer, Ossian, Patrick Henry, and the violin is of greater significance than his indebtedness to Locke," in Jay Fliegelman, *Declaring Independence: Jefferson, Natural Language, and the Culture of Performance* (Palo Alto, CA: Stanford University Press, 1993).

After setting forth these basic principles of government, the Declaration of Independence goes on to justify the colonists' revolt against Britain. Much of the remainder of the document is a list of what "He" (King George III) had done to deprive the colonists of their rights. (See Appendix A at the end of this book for the complete text of the Declaration of Independence.)

Once it had fulfilled its purpose of legitimating the American Revolution, the Declaration of Independence was all but forgotten for many years. According to scholar Pauline Maier, the Declaration did not become enshrined as what she calls "American Scripture" until the 1800s.[5]

THE RISE OF REPUBLICANISM

Although the colonists had formally declared independence from Britain, the fight to gain actual independence continued for five more years—until the British general Charles Cornwallis surrendered at Yorktown in 1781. In 1783, after Britain formally recognized the independent status of the United States in the Treaty of Paris, Washington disbanded the army. During these years of military struggles, the states faced the additional challenge of creating a system of self-government for an independent United States.

Some colonists had demanded that independence be preceded by the formation of a strong central government. But others, who called themselves Republicans, were against a strong central government. They opposed monarchy, executive authority, and virtually any form of restraint on the power of local groups.

From 1776 to 1780, all of the states adopted written constitutions. Eleven of the constitutions were completely new. Two of them—those of Connecticut and Rhode Island—were old royal charters with minor modifications. Republican sentiment led to increased power for the legislatures. In Pennsylvania and Georgia, **unicameral** (one-body) **legislatures** were unchecked by executive or judicial authority. Basically, the Republicans attempted to maintain the politics of 1776. In almost all states, the legislature was predominant.

Unicameral Legislature
A legislature with only one legislative chamber, as opposed to a bicameral (two-chamber) legislature, such as the U.S. Congress. Today, Nebraska is the only state in the Union with a unicameral legislature.

THE ARTICLES OF CONFEDERATION: THE FIRST FORM OF GOVERNMENT

The fear of a powerful central government led to the passage of the Articles of Confederation, which created a weak central government. The term **confederation** is important; it means a voluntary association of *independent* **states**, in which the member states agree to only limited restraints on their freedom of action. As a result, confederations seldom have an effective executive authority.

In June 1776, the Second Continental Congress began the process of drafting what would become the Articles of Confederation. The final form of the Articles was achieved by November 15, 1777. It was not until March 1, 1781, however, that the last state, Maryland, agreed to ratify what was called the Articles of Confederation and Perpetual Union. Well before the final ratification of the Articles, however, many of them were implemented: the Continental Congress and the 13 states conducted American military, economic, and political affairs according to the standards and the form specified by the Articles.[6]

Confederation
A political system in which states or regional governments retain ultimate authority except for those powers they expressly delegate to a central government. A voluntary association of independent states, in which the member states agree to limited restraints on their freedom of action.

State
A group of people occupying a specific area and organized under one government; may be either a nation or a subunit of a nation.

---

[5]See Pauline Maier, *American Scripture: Making the Declaration of Independence* (New York: Knopf, 1997).
[6]Robert W. Hoffert, *A Politics of Tensions: The Articles of Confederation and American Political Ideas* (Niwot, CO: University Press of Colorado, 1992).

FIGURE 2–1 The Confederal Government Structure under the Articles of Confederation

Congress
Congress had one house. Each state had two to seven members, but only one vote. The exercise of most powers required approval of at least nine states. Amendments to the Articles required the consent of all the states.

Committee of the States
A committee of representatives from all the states was empowered to act in the name of Congress between sessions.

Officers
Congress appointed officers to do some of the executive work.

The States

Under the Articles, the 13 original colonies, now states, established on March 1, 1781, a government of the states—the Congress of the Confederation. The Congress was a unicameral assembly of so-called ambassadors from each state, with each state possessing a single vote. Each year, the Congress would choose one of its members as its president (that is, presiding officer), but the Articles did not provide for a president of the United States.

The Congress was authorized in Article X to appoint an executive committee of the states "to execute in the recess of Congress, such of the powers of Congress as the United States, in Congress assembled, by the consent of nine [of the 13] states, shall from time to time think expedient to vest with them." The Congress was also allowed to appoint other committees and civil officers necessary for managing the general affairs of the United States. In addition, the Congress could regulate foreign affairs and establish coinage and weights and measures, but it lacked an independent source of revenue and the necessary executive machinery to enforce its decisions throughout the land. Article II of the Articles of Confederation guaranteed that each state would retain its sovereignty. Figure 2–1 illustrates the structure of the government under the Articles of Confederation; Table 2–2 summarizes the powers—and the lack of powers—of Congress under the Articles of Confederation.

ACCOMPLISHMENTS UNDER THE ARTICLES

The new government had some accomplishments during its eight years of existence under the Articles of Confederation. Certain states' claims to western lands were settled. Maryland had objected to the claims of the Carolinas, Connecticut, Georgia, Massachusetts, New York, and Virginia. It was only after these states consented to give up their land claims to the United States as a

TABLE 2–2 Powers of the Congress of the Confederation

CONGRESS HAD POWER TO	CONGRESS LACKED POWER TO
• Declare war and make peace.	• Provide for effective treaty-making power and control foreign relations; it could not compel states to respect treaties.
• Enter into treaties and alliances.	• Compel states to meet military quotas; it could not draft soldiers.
• Establish and control armed forces.	• Regulate interstate and foreign commerce; it left each state free to set up its own tariff system.
• Requisition men and revenues from states.	• Collect taxes directly from the people; it had to rely on states to collect and forward taxes.
• Regulate coinage.	• Compel states to pay their share of government costs.
• Borrow funds and issue bills of credit.	• Provide and maintain a sound monetary system or issue paper money; this was left up to the states, and monies in circulation differed tremendously in value.
• Fix uniform standards of weight and measurement.	
• Create admiralty courts.	
• Create a postal system.	
• Regulate Indian affairs.	
• Guarantee citizens of each state the rights and privileges of citizens in the several states when in another state.	
• Adjudicate disputes between states on state petition.	

whole that Maryland signed the Articles of Confederation. Another accomplishment under the Articles was the passage of the Northwest Ordinance of 1787, which established a basic pattern of government for new territories north of the Ohio River. All in all, the Articles represented the first real pooling of resources by the American states.

WEAKNESSES OF THE ARTICLES

Despite these accomplishments, the Articles of Confederation had many defects. Although Congress had the legal right to declare war and to conduct foreign policy, it did not have the right to demand revenues from the states. It could only ask for them. Additionally, the actions of Congress required the consent of nine states. Any amendments to the Articles required the unanimous consent of the Congress and confirmation by every state legislature. Furthermore, the Articles did not create a national system of courts.

Basically, the functioning of the government under the Articles depended on the goodwill of the states. Article III of the Articles simply established a "league of friendship" among the states—no national government was intended.

Probably the most fundamental weakness of the Articles, and the most basic cause of their eventual replacement by the Constitution, was the lack of power to raise funds for the militia. The Articles contained no language giving Congress coercive power to raise revenues (by levying taxes) to provide adequate support for the military forces controlled by Congress. When states refused to send revenues to support the government (not one state met the financial requests made by Congress under the Articles), Congress resorted to selling off western lands to speculators or issuing bonds that sold for less than their face value. Due to a lack of resources, the Continental Congress was forced to disband the army, even in the face of serious Spanish and British military threats.

SHAYS' REBELLION AND THE NEED FOR REVISION OF THE ARTICLES

Because of the weaknesses of the Articles of Confederation, the central government could do little to maintain peace and order in the new nation. The states bickered among themselves and increasingly taxed each other's goods. At times they prevented trade altogether. By 1784, the country faced a serious economic depression. Banks were calling in old loans and refusing to give new ones. People who could not pay their debts were often thrown into prison.

By 1786, in Concord, Massachusetts, the scene of one of the first battles of the Revolution, there were three times as many people in prison for debt as there were for all other crimes combined. In Worcester County, Massachusetts, the ratio was even higher—20 to one. Most of the prisoners were small farmers who could not pay their debts because of the disorganized state of the economy.

In August 1786, mobs of musket-bearing farmers led by former Revolutionary War captain Daniel Shays seized county courthouses and disrupted the trials of debtors in Springfield, Massachusetts. Shays and his men then launched an attack on the federal arsenal at Springfield, but they were repulsed. Shays' Rebellion demonstrated that the central government could not protect the citizenry from armed rebellion or provide

That the Articles of Confederation specified that Canada could be admitted to the Confederation if it ever wished to join?

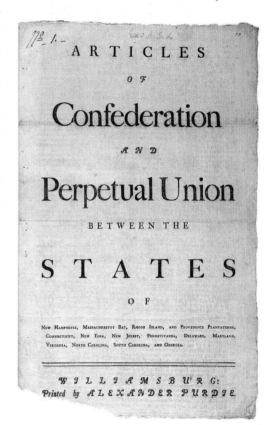

THE TITLE PAGE from an early printing of the Articles of Confederation. (Library of Congress Prints & Photographs Division, Washington, D.C.)

adequately for the public welfare. The rebellion spurred the nation's political leaders to action. As John Jay wrote to Thomas Jefferson,

> Changes are Necessary, but what they ought to be, what they will be, and how and when to be produced, are arduous Questions. I feel for the Cause of Liberty . . . . If it should not take Root in this Soil[,] Little Pains will be taken to cultivate it in any other.[7]

DRAFTING THE CONSTITUTION

DID YOU KNOW?

That the 1776 constitution of New Jersey granted the vote to "all free inhabitants," including women, but the large number of women who turned out to vote resulted in male protests and a new law limiting the right to vote to "free white male citizens"?

Concerned about the economic turmoil in the young nation, five states, under the leadership of the Virginia legislature, called for a meeting to be held at Annapolis, Maryland, on September 11, 1786—ostensibly to discuss commercial problems only. It was evident to those in attendance (including Alexander Hamilton and James Madison) that the national government had serious weaknesses that had to be addressed if it were to survive. Among the important problems to be solved were the relationship between the states and the central government, the powers of the national legislature, the need for executive leadership, and the establishment of policies for economic stability.

Those attending the meeting prepared a petition to the Continental Congress for a general convention to meet in Philadelphia in May 1787 "to consider the exigencies of the union." Congress approved the convention in February 1787. When those who favored a weak central government realized that the Philadelphia meeting would in fact take place, they endorsed the convention. They made sure, however, that the convention would be summoned "for the sole and express purpose of revising the Articles of Confederation." Those in favor of a stronger national government had different ideas.

The designated date for the opening of the convention at Philadelphia, now known as the Constitutional Convention, was May 14, 1787. Because few of the delegates had actually arrived in Philadelphia by that time, however, the convention was not formally opened in the East Room of the Pennsylvania State House until May 25.[8] Fifty-five of the 74 delegates chosen for the convention actually attended. (Of those 55, only about 40 played active roles at the convention.) Rhode Island was the only state that refused to send delegates.

WHO WERE THE DELEGATES?

Who were the 55 delegates to the Constitutional Convention? They certainly did not represent a cross section of American society in the 1700s. Indeed, most were members of the upper class. Consider the following facts:

1. Thirty-three were members of the legal profession.
2. Three were physicians.
3. Almost 50 percent were college graduates.
4. Seven were former chief executives of their respective states.
5. Six were owners of large plantations.
6. Eight were important businesspersons.

---

[7]Excerpt from a letter from John Jay to Thomas Jefferson written in October 1786, as reproduced in Winthrop D. Jordan et al., *The United States*, combined ed., 6th ed. (Englewood Cliffs, NJ: Prentice Hall, 1987), p. 135.
[8]The State House was later named Independence Hall. This was the same room in which the Declaration of Independence had been signed 11 years earlier.

They were also relatively young by today's standards: James Madison was 36, Alexander Hamilton was only 32, and Jonathan Dayton of New Jersey was 26. The venerable Benjamin Franklin, however, was 81 and had to be carried in on a portable chair borne by four prisoners from a local jail. Not counting Franklin, the average age was just over 42. What almost all of them shared, however, was prior experience in political office or military service. Most of them were elected members of their own states' legislatures. George Washington, the esteemed commander of the Revolutionary War troops, was named to chair the meeting. There were, however, no women or minorities among this group. Women could not vote anywhere in the confederacy and, while free African Americans played an important part in some Northern states, they were certainly not likely to be political leaders.[9]

THE WORKING ENVIRONMENT

The conditions under which the delegates worked for 115 days were far from ideal and were made even worse by the necessity of maintaining total secrecy. The framers of the Constitution believed that if public debate took place on particular positions, delegates would have a more difficult time compromising or backing down to reach agreement. Consequently, the windows were usually shut in the East Room of the State House. Summer quickly arrived, and the air became heavy, humid, and hot by noon of each day. Also, when the windows were open, flies swarmed into the room. The delegates did, however, have a nearby tavern and inn to which they retired each evening. The Indian Queen became the informal headquarters of the delegates.

FACTIONS AMONG THE DELEGATES

We know much about the proceedings at the convention because James Madison kept a daily, detailed personal journal. A majority of the delegates were strong nationalists—they wanted a central government with real power, unlike the central government under the Articles of Confederation. George Washington and Benjamin Franklin preferred limited national authority based on a separation of powers. They were apparently willing to accept any type of national government, however, as long as the other delegates approved it. A few advocates of a strong central government, led by Gouverneur Morris of Pennsylvania and John Rutledge of South Carolina, distrusted the ability of the common people to engage in self-government.

Among the nationalists, several went so far as to support monarchy. This group included Alexander Hamilton, who was chiefly responsible for the Annapolis Convention's call for the Constitutional Convention. In a long speech on June 18, he presented his views: "I have no scruple in declaring . . . that the British government is the best in the world and that I doubt much whether anything short of it will do in America."

Another important group of nationalists were of a more democratic stripe. Led by James Madison of Virginia and James Wilson of Pennsylvania, these democratic nationalists wanted a central government founded on popular support.

Still another faction consisted of nationalists who were less democratic in nature and who would support a central government only if it was founded on very narrowly defined republican principles. This group was made up of a relatively small number of delegates, including Edmund Randolph and George Mason of Virginia, Elbridge Gerry of Massachusetts, and Luther Martin and John Francis Mercer of Maryland.

[9]For a detailed look at the delegates and their lively debates, see Carol Berkin, *A Brilliant Solution: Inventing the American Constitution* (New York: Harcourt, 2002).

ELBRIDGE GERRY (1744–1814), from Massachusetts, was a patriot during the Revolution. He was a signatory of the Declaration of Independence and later became governor of Massachusetts (1810–1812). He became James Madison's new vice president when Madison was re-elected in December 1812. (Library of Congress Prints & Photographs Division, Washington, D.C.)

Bicameral Legislature
A legislature made up of two parts, called chambers. The U.S. Congress, composed of the House of Representatives and the Senate, is a bicameral legislature.

Supremacy Doctrine
A doctrine that asserts the priority of national law over state laws. This principle is rooted in Article VI of the Constitution, which provides that the Constitution, the laws passed by the national government under its constitutional powers, and all treaties constitute the supreme law of the land.

Many of the other delegates from Connecticut, Delaware, Maryland, New Hampshire, and New Jersey were concerned about only one thing—claims to western lands. As long as those lands became the common property of all of the states, they were willing to support a central government.

Finally, there was a group of delegates who were totally against a national authority. Two of the three delegates from New York quit the convention when they saw the nationalist direction of its proceedings.

POLITICKING AND COMPROMISES

The debates at the convention started on the first day. James Madison had spent months reviewing European political theory. When his Virginia delegation arrived ahead of most of the others, it got to work immediately. By the time George Washington opened the convention, Governor Edmund Randolph of Virginia was prepared to present 15 resolutions. In retrospect, this was a masterful stroke on the part of the Virginia delegation. It set the agenda for the remainder of the convention—even though, in principle, the delegates had been sent to Philadelphia for the sole purpose of amending the Articles of Confederation. They had not been sent to write a new constitution.

The Virginia Plan. Randolph's 15 resolutions proposed an entirely new national government under a constitution. It was, however, a plan that favored the large states, including Virginia. Basically, it called for the following:

1. A **bicameral** (two-chamber) **legislature**, with the lower chamber chosen by the people and the smaller upper chamber chosen by the lower chamber from nominees selected by state legislatures. The number of representatives would be proportional to a state's population, thus greatly favoring the states with larger populations, including slaves, of course. The legislature could void any state laws.
2. The creation of an unspecified national executive, elected by the legislature.
3. The creation of a national judiciary, appointed by the legislature.

It did not take long for the smaller states to realize they would fare poorly under the Virginia plan, which would enable Virginia, Massachusetts, and Pennsylvania to form a majority in the national legislature. The debate on the plan dragged on for many weeks. It was time for the small states to come up with their own plan.

The New Jersey Plan. On June 15, lawyer William Paterson of New Jersey offered an alternative plan. After all, argued Paterson, under the Articles of Confederation, all states had equality; therefore, the convention had no power to change this arrangement. He proposed the following:

1. The fundamental principle of the Articles of Confederation—one state, one vote—would be retained.
2. Congress would be able to regulate trade and impose taxes.
3. All acts of Congress would be the supreme law of the land.
4. Several people would be elected by Congress to form an executive office.
5. The executive office would appoint a Supreme Court.

Basically, the New Jersey plan was simply an amendment of the Articles of Confederation. Its only notable feature was its reference to the **supremacy doctrine**, which was later included in the Constitution.

The "Great Compromise." The delegates were at an impasse. Most wanted a strong national government and were unwilling even to consider the New Jersey plan, but when the Virginia plan was brought up again, the small states threatened to leave. The issues involved in the debate included how states and their residents would be represented. Small states feared that the Virginia plan with its powerful national government would pass laws that would disadvantage smaller states. The larger states, aware that they would be the economic force in the new nation, absolutely opposed a government in which smaller states had the balance of power. Roger Sherman of Connecticut proposed a solution that gave power to both the small states and the larger states. On July 16, the **Great Compromise** was put forward for debate:

1. A bicameral legislature in which the lower chamber, the House of Representatives, would be apportioned according to the number of free inhabitants in each state, plus three-fifths of the slaves.
2. An upper chamber, the Senate, which would have two members from each state elected by the state legislatures.

This plan, also called the Connecticut Compromise because of the role of the Connecticut delegates in the proposal, broke the deadlock. It did exact a political price, however, because it permitted each state to have equal representation in the Senate. Having two senators represent each state in effect diluted the voting power of citizens living in more heavily populated states and gave the smaller states disproportionate political powers. But the Connecticut Compromise resolved the large-state/small-state controversy. In addition, the Senate acted as part of a checks-and-balances system against the House, which many feared would be dominated by, and responsive to, the masses. However, another important piece to the debate needed a resolution: How were slaves to be counted in determining the number of members of Congress allotted to a state?

The Three-Fifths Compromise. Part of the Connecticut Compromise dealt with this problem. Slavery was still legal in many Northern states, but it was concentrated in the South. Many delegates were opposed to slavery and wanted it banned entirely in the United States. Charles Pinckney of South Carolina led strong Southern opposition to a ban on slavery. Furthermore, the South wanted slaves to be counted along with free persons in determining representation in Congress. Delegates from the Northern states

Great Compromise
The compromise between the New Jersey and Virginia plans that created one chamber of the Congress based on population and one chamber representing each state equally; also called the Connecticut Compromise.

That during the four centuries of slave trading, an estimated 10 million to 11 million Africans were transported to North and South America—and that only 6 percent of these slaves were imported into the United States?

GEORGE WASHINGTON presided over the Constitutional Convention of 1787. Although the convention was supposed to start on May 14, 1787, few of the delegates had actually arrived in Philadelphia by that date. The convention formally opened in the East Room of the Pennsylvania State House (later named Independence Hall) on May 25. Only Rhode Island did not send any delegates. (Corbis)

objected. Sherman's three-fifths proposal was a compromise between Northerners who did not want the slaves counted at all and Southerners who wanted them counted in the same way as free whites. Actually, Sherman's Connecticut plan spoke of three-fifths of "all other persons" (and that is the language of the Constitution itself). It is not hard to figure out, though, who those other persons were.

The three-fifths compromise illustrates the power of the Southern states at the convention.[10] The three-fifths rule meant that the House of Representatives and the electoral college would be apportioned in part on the basis of *property*—specifically, property in slaves. Modern commentators have referred to the three-fifths rule as valuing African Americans only three-fifths as much as whites. Actually, the additional Southern representatives elected because of the three-fifths rule did not represent the slaves at all. Rather, these extra representatives were a gift to the slave owners—the additional representatives enhanced the power of the South in Congress.

The three-fifths compromise did not completely settle the slavery issue. There was also the question of the slave trade. Eventually, the delegates agreed that Congress could not ban the importation of slaves until after 1808. The compromise meant that the matter of slavery was never addressed directly. The South won 20 years of unrestricted slave trade and a requirement that escaped slaves in free states be returned to their owners in slave states. Could the authors of the Constitution have done more to address the issue of slavery?

[10]See Garry Wills, *"Negro President": Jefferson and the Slave Power* (New York: Houghton Mifflin, 2003).

WHAT IF...

THE CONSTITUTION HAD BANNED SLAVERY OUTRIGHT?

One of the most hotly debated issues at the Constitutional Convention concerned slavery. As noted previously, the three-fifths compromise was the result of that debate. There was also another compromise: the importation of slaves would not be banned until after 1808. The debate over slavery—or, more specifically, over how the founders dealt with it—continues to this day. Some contend that those delegates who opposed slavery should have made greater efforts to ban it completely.*

DID THE FOUNDERS HAVE NO OTHER CHOICE?

Some historians argue that the founders had no choice. The South was an important part of the economy, and the Southern states had more than 600,000 slaves. Major leaders from Virginia, such as George Washington, had serious doubts about slavery. It appears, however, that the delegates from North Carolina, South Carolina, and Georgia and, perhaps, Virginia itself would never have agreed to the Constitution if slavery had been threatened—meaning that these states would not have joined the new nation. The founders believed, as James Madison said, "Great as the evil is, a dismemberment of the Union would be worse. . . . If those states should disunite from the other states, . . . they might solicit and obtain aid from foreign powers."** Benjamin Franklin, then president of the Pennsylvania Society for the Abolition of Slavery, also feared that without a slavery compromise, delegates from the South would abandon the convention.

CRITICS ARGUE THAT ETHICS SHOULD HAVE PREVAILED

Critics of the founders' actions nonetheless believe that any compromise on slavery implicitly acknowledged the validity of the institution. According to these critics, the delegates who opposed slavery had a moral obligation to make greater efforts to ban it. At the time, many of the writers felt that slavery would eventually end. They did not foresee the expansion of the nation to the Mississippi River and beyond and the fierce struggle in the 19th century to expand slavery to the new territories. It was, of course, the importance of slaves to the economy of the Southern states as well as the moral opposition to slavery that brought the nation to civil war.

FOR CRITICAL ANALYSIS

1. Do you think that antislavery delegates to the convention could have obtained a better result if they had taken a stronger stand?
2. If Georgia and the Carolinas had stayed out of the Union, what would subsequent American history have been like?
3. Would the eventual freedom of the slaves have been advanced—or delayed?

*See Paul Finkelman's criticism of the founders' actions on the slavery issue in *Slavery and the Founders: Race and Liberty in the Age of Jefferson*, 2nd ed. (Armonk, NY: M. E. Sharpe, 2001).
**Speech before the Virginia ratifying convention on June 17, 1788, as cited in Bruno Leone, ed., *The Creation of the Constitution* (San Diego, CA: Greenhaven Press, 1995), p. 159.

Other Issues. The South also worried that the Northern majority in Congress would pass legislation that was unfavorable to its economic interests. Because the South depended on agricultural exports, it feared the imposition of export taxes. In return for acceding to the Northern demand that Congress be able to regulate commerce among the states and with other nations, the South obtained a promise that export taxes would not be imposed. As a result, the United States is among the few countries that do not tax their exports.

There were other disagreements. The delegates could not decide whether to establish only a Supreme Court or to create lower courts as well. They deferred the issue by mandating a Supreme Court and allowing Congress to establish lower courts. They also disagreed over whether the president or the Senate would choose the Supreme Court justices. A compromise was reached with the agreement that the president would nominate the justices and the Senate would confirm the nominations. These compromises, as well as others, resulted from the recognition that if one group of states refused to ratify the Constitution, it was doomed.

WORKING TOWARD FINAL AGREEMENT

The Connecticut Compromise was reached by mid-July. The makeup of the executive branch and the judiciary, however, was left unsettled. The remaining work of the convention was turned over to a five-man Committee of Detail, which presented a rough draft of the Constitution on August 6. It made the executive and judicial branches subordinate to the legislative branch.

The Madisonian Model—Separation of Powers. The major issue of **separation of powers** had not yet been resolved. The delegates were concerned with structuring the government to prevent the imposition of tyranny—either by the majority or by a minority. Madison proposed a governmental scheme—sometimes called the **Madisonian model**—to achieve this: the executive, legislative, and judicial powers of government were to be separated so that no one branch had enough power to dominate the others, nor could any one person hold office in two different branches of the government at the same time. The separation of powers was by function, as well as by personnel, with Congress passing laws, the president enforcing and administering laws, and the courts interpreting laws in individual circumstances.

Each of the three branches of government would be independent of the others, but they would have to share power to govern. According to Madison, in *Federalist Paper No. 51* (see Appendix B), "the great security against a gradual concentration of the several powers in the same department consists in giving to those who administer each department the necessary constitutional means and personal motives to resist encroachments of the others."

The Madisonian Model—Checks and Balances. The "constitutional means" Madison referred to is a system of **checks and balances** through which each branch of the government can check the actions of the others. For example, Congress can enact laws, but the president has veto power over congressional acts. The Supreme Court has the power to declare acts of Congress and of the executive unconstitutional, but the president appoints the justices of the Supreme Court, with the advice and consent of the Senate. (The Supreme Court's power to declare acts unconstitutional was not mentioned in the Constitution, although arguably the framers assumed that the Court would have this power—see the discussion of judicial review later in this chapter.) Figure 2–2 outlines these checks and balances.

Madison's ideas of separation of powers and checks and balances were not new. The influential French political thinker Baron de Montesquieu (1689–1755) had explored these concepts in his book *The Spirit of the Laws*, published in 1748. Montesquieu not only discussed the "three sorts of powers" (executive, legislative, and judicial) that were necessarily exercised by any government but also gave examples of how, in some nations, certain checks on these powers had arisen and had been effective in preventing tyranny.

Separation of Powers
The principle of dividing governmental powers among different branches of government.

Madisonian Model
A structure of government proposed by James Madison in which the powers of the government are separated into three branches: executive, legislative, and judicial.

Checks and Balances
A major principle of the American system of government whereby each branch of the government can check the actions of the others.

That Alexander Hamilton wanted the American president to hold office for life and to have absolute veto power over the legislature?

In the years since the Constitution was ratified, the checks and balances built into it have evolved into a sometimes complex give-and-take among the branches of government. Generally, for nearly every check that one branch has over another, the branch that has been checked has found a way of getting around it. For example, suppose that the president checks Congress by vetoing a bill. Congress can override the presidential veto by a two-thirds vote. Additionally, Congress holds the "power of the purse." If it disagrees with a program endorsed by the executive branch, it can simply refuse to appropriate the funds necessary to operate that program. Similarly, the president can impose a countercheck on Congress if the Senate refuses to confirm a presidential appointment, such as a judicial appointment. The president can simply wait until Congress is in recess and then make what is called a "recess appointment," which does not require the Senate's approval. Recess appointments last until the end of the next session of the Congress.

The Executive. Some delegates favored a plural executive made up of representatives from the various regions. This was abandoned in favor of a single chief executive. Some argued that Congress should choose the executive. To make the presidency completely independent of the proposed Congress, however, an electoral college was adopted. To be sure, the electoral college created a cumbersome presidential election process (see Chapter 9). The process even made it possible for a candidate who came in second in the popular vote to become president by being the top vote-getter in the electoral college, which happened in 2000 and in three prior contests. The electoral college insulated the president, however, from direct popular control. The seven-year single term that some of the delegates had proposed was replaced by a four-year term and the possibility of re-election.

A Federal Republic. The Constitution creates a **federal system** of government that divides the sovereign powers of the nation between the states and the national government. This structure allows for states to make their own laws about many of the issues of direct concern for their citizens while granting the national government far more power over the states and their citizens than under the Articles of Confederacy. As you will read in Chapter 3, the Constitution expressly granted certain powers to the national government.

For example, the national government was given the power to regulate commerce among the states. The Constitution also declared that the president is the nation's chief executive and the commander in chief of the armed forces. Additionally, the Constitution made it clear that laws made by the national government take priority over conflicting state laws. At the same time, the Constitution provided for extensive states' rights, including the right to control commerce within state borders and to exercise those governing powers that were not delegated to the national government.

JAMES MADISON (1751–1836) earned the title "master builder of the Constitution" because of his persuasive logic during the Constitutional Convention. His contributions to the *Federalist Papers* showed him to be a brilliant political thinker and writer. (Library of Congress Prints & Photographs Division, Washington, D.C. [LC-USZ62-13004])

Federal System
A system of government in which power is divided between a central government and regional, or subdivisional, governments. Each level must have some domain in which its policies are dominant and some genuine political or constitutional guarantee of its authority.

THE FINAL DOCUMENT

On September 17, 1787, the Constitution was approved by 39 delegates. Of the 55 who had attended originally, only 42 remained. Three delegates refused to sign the Constitution. Others disapproved of at least parts of it but signed anyway to begin the ratification debate.

The Constitution that was to be ratified established the following fundamental principles:

1. Popular sovereignty, or control by the people.
2. A republican government in which the people choose representatives to make decisions for them.
3. Limited government with written laws, in contrast to the powerful British government against which the colonists had rebelled.
4. Separation of powers, with checks and balances among branches to prevent any one branch from gaining too much power.
5. A federal system that allows for states' rights, because the states feared too much centralized control.

THE DIFFICULT ROAD TO RATIFICATION

Ratification
Formal approval.

The founders knew that **ratification** of the Constitution was far from certain. Because it was almost guaranteed that many state legislatures would not ratify it, the delegates agreed that each state should hold a special convention. Elected delegates to these conventions would discuss and vote on the Constitution. Further departing from the Articles of Confederation, the delegates agreed that as soon as nine states (rather than all 13) approved the Constitution, it would take effect, and Congress could begin to organize the new government.

The federal system created by the founders was a novel form of government at that time—no other country in the world had such a system. It was invented by the founders as a compromise solution to the controversy over whether the states or the central

FIGURE 2–2 Checks and Balances

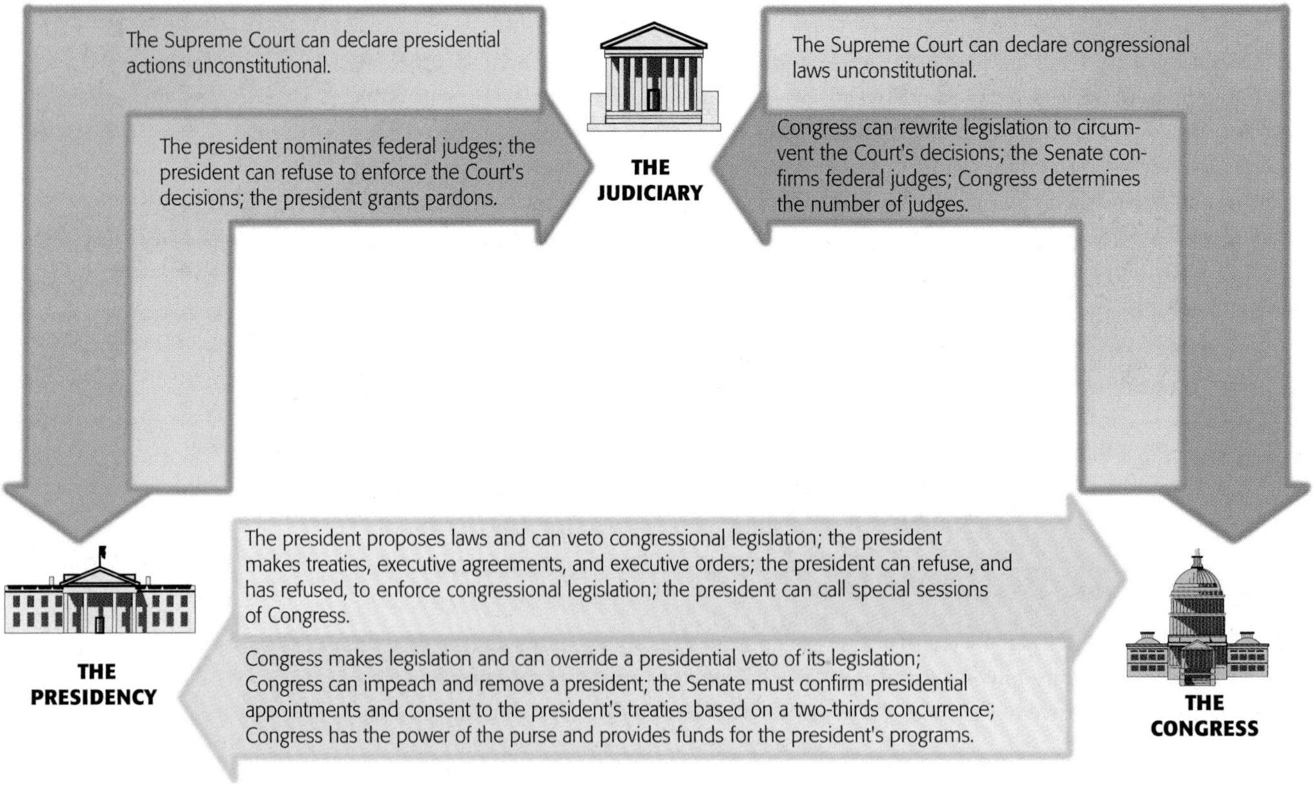

The Supreme Court can declare presidential actions unconstitutional.

The president nominates federal judges; the president can refuse to enforce the Court's decisions; the president grants pardons.

THE JUDICIARY

The Supreme Court can declare congressional laws unconstitutional.

Congress can rewrite legislation to circumvent the Court's decisions; the Senate confirms federal judges; Congress determines the number of judges.

The president proposes laws and can veto congressional legislation; the president makes treaties, executive agreements, and executive orders; the president can refuse, and has refused, to enforce congressional legislation; the president can call special sessions of Congress.

Congress makes legislation and can override a presidential veto of its legislation; Congress can impeach and remove a president; the Senate must confirm presidential appointments and consent to the president's treaties based on a two-thirds concurrence; Congress has the power of the purse and provides funds for the president's programs.

THE PRESIDENCY

THE CONGRESS

government should have ultimate sovereignty. As you will read in Chapter 3, the debate over where the line should be drawn between states' rights and the powers of the national government has characterized American politics ever since. The founders did not go into detail about where this line should be drawn, thus leaving it up to scholars and court judges to divine the founders' intentions.

THE FEDERALISTS PUSH FOR RATIFICATION

The two opposing forces in the battle over ratification were the Federalists and the Anti-Federalists. The **Federalists**—those in favor of a strong central government and the new Constitution—had an advantage over their opponents, called the **Anti-Federalists**, who wanted to prevent the Constitution as drafted from being ratified. In the first place, the Federalists had assumed a positive name, leaving their opposition the negative label of *Anti*-Federalist.[11] More important, the Federalists had attended the Constitutional Convention and knew of all the deliberations that had taken place. Their opponents had no such knowledge, because those deliberations had not been open to the public. Thus, the Anti-Federalists were at a disadvantage in terms of information about the document. The Federalists also had time, power, and money on their side. Communications were slow. Those who had access to the best communications were Federalists—mostly wealthy bankers, lawyers, plantation owners, and merchants living in urban areas, where communications were better. The Federalist campaign was organized relatively quickly and effectively to elect Federalists as delegates to the state ratifying conventions.

The Anti-Federalists, however, had at least one strong point in their favor: they stood for the status quo. In general, the greater burden is always placed on those advocating change.

The *Federalist Papers*. In New York, opponents of the Constitution were quick to attack it. Alexander Hamilton answered their attacks in newspaper columns over the signature "Caesar." When the Caesar letters had little effect, Hamilton switched to the pseudonym Publius and secured two collaborators—John Jay and James Madison. In a very short time, those three political figures wrote a series of 85 essays in defense of the Constitution and of a republican form of government.

These widely read essays, called the *Federalist Papers*, appeared in New York newspapers from October 1787 to August 1788 and were reprinted in the newspapers of other states. Although we do not know for certain who wrote every one, it is apparent that Hamilton was responsible for about two-thirds of the essays. These included the most important ones interpreting the Constitution, explaining the various powers of the three branches, and presenting a theory of *judicial review*—to be discussed later in this chapter. Madison's *Federalist Paper* No. 10 (see Appendix B), however, is considered a classic in political theory; it deals with the nature of groups—or factions, as he called them. Despite the rapidity with which the *Federalist Papers* were written, they

THE ORIGINAL COPY OF THE Constitution is stored in a special case at the National Archives. The case is lowered into a safe underground every evening. (Michael Ventura/ Alamy Limited)

Federalist
The name given to one who was in favor of the adoption of the U.S. Constitution and the creation of a federal union with a strong central government.

Anti-Federalist
An individual who opposed the ratification of the new Constitution in 1787. The Anti-Federalists were opposed to a strong central government.

---

[11]There is some irony here. At the Constitutional Convention, those opposed to a strong central government pushed for a federal system because such a system would allow the states to retain some of their sovereign rights (see Chapter 3). The label *Anti-Federalists* thus contradicted their essential views.

are considered by many to be perhaps the best example of political theorizing ever produced in the United States.[12]

The Anti-Federalist Response. The Anti-Federalists used such pseudonyms as Montezuma and Philadelphiensis in their replies. Many of their attacks on the Constitution were also brilliant. The Anti-Federalists claimed that the Constitution was written by aristocrats and would lead to aristocratic tyranny. More important, the Anti-Federalists believed that the Constitution would create an overbearing and overburdening central government hostile to personal liberty. (The Constitution said nothing about freedom of the press, freedom of religion, or any other individual liberty.) They wanted to include a list of guaranteed liberties, or a bill of rights. Finally, the Anti-Federalists decried the weakened power of the states.

The Anti-Federalists cannot be dismissed as unpatriotic extremists. They included such patriots as Patrick Henry and Samuel Adams. They were arguing what had been the most prevalent contemporary opinion. This view derived from the French political philosopher Montesquieu, who, as mentioned earlier, was an influential political theorist at that time. Montesquieu believed that liberty was safe only in relatively small societies governed by direct democracy or by a large legislature with small districts. The Madisonian view favoring a large republic, particularly expressed in *Federalist Papers* No. 10 and No. 51 (see Appendix B), was actually the more *un*popular view at the time. Madison was probably convincing because citizens were already persuaded that a strong national government was necessary to combat foreign enemies and to prevent domestic insurrections. Still, some researchers believe it was mainly the bitter experiences with the Articles of Confederation, rather than Madison's arguments, that persuaded the state conventions to ratify the Constitution.[13]

THE MARCH TO THE FINISH

The struggle for ratification continued. Strong majorities were procured in Delaware, Pennsylvania, New Jersey, Georgia, and Connecticut. After a bitter struggle in Massachusetts, that state ratified the Constitution by a narrow margin on February 6, 1788. By the spring, Maryland and South Carolina had ratified by sizable majorities. Then on June 21 of that year, New Hampshire became the ninth state to ratify the Constitution. Although the Constitution was formally in effect, this meant little without Virginia and New York—the latter did not ratify for another month (see Table 2–3).

DID THE MAJORITY OF AMERICANS SUPPORT THE CONSTITUTION?

In 1913, historian Charles Beard published *An Economic Interpretation of the Constitution of the United States*.[14] This book launched a debate that has continued ever since—the debate over whether the Constitution was supported by a majority of Americans.

Beard's Thesis. Beard's central thesis was that the Constitution had been produced primarily by wealthy property owners who desired a stronger government able to protect their

[12]Some scholars believe that the *Federalist Papers* played only a minor role in securing ratification of the Constitution. Even if this is true, they still have lasting value as an authoritative explanation of the Constitution.
[13]Of particular interest is the view of the Anti-Federalist position contained in Herbert J. Storing, *What the Anti-Federalists Were For* (Chicago: University of Chicago Press, 1981). Storing also edited seven volumes of the Anti-Federalist writings, *The Complete Anti-Federalist* (Chicago: University of Chicago Press, 1981). See also Josephine F. Pacheco, *Antifederalism: The Legacy of George Mason* (Fairfax, VA: George Mason University Press, 1992).
[14]Charles A. Beard, *An Economic Interpretation of the Constitution of the United States* (New York: MacMillan, 1913; New York: Free Press, 1986).

TABLE 2–3 Ratification of the Constitution

STATE	DATE	VOTE FOR–AGAINST
Delaware	Dec. 7, 1787	30–0
Pennsylvania	Dec. 12, 1787	43–23
New Jersey	Dec. 18, 1787	38–0
Georgia	Jan. 2, 1788	26–0
Connecticut	Jan. 9, 1788	128–40
Massachusetts	Feb. 6, 1788	187–168
Maryland	Apr. 28, 1788	63–11
South Carolina	May 23, 1788	149–73
New Hampshire	June 21, 1788	57–46
Virginia	June 25, 1788	89–79
New York	July 26, 1788	30–27
North Carolina	Nov. 21, 1789*	194–77
Rhode Island	May 29, 1790	34–32

*Ratification was originally defeated on August 4, 1788, by a vote of 84–184.

property rights. Beard also claimed that the Constitution had been imposed by undemocratic methods to prevent democratic majorities from exercising real power. He pointed out that there was never any popular vote on whether to hold a constitutional convention in the first place.

Furthermore, even if such a vote had been taken, state laws generally restricted voting rights to property-owning white males, meaning that most people in the country (white males without property, women, Native Americans, and slaves) were not eligible to vote. Finally, Beard pointed out that even the word *democracy* was distasteful to the founders. The term was often used by conservatives to smear their opponents.

That not all the states had ratified the Constitution by April 30, 1789, when George Washington became President of the United States of America?

State Ratifying Conventions. As for the various state ratifying conventions, the delegates had been selected by only 150,000 of the approximately 4 million citizens. That does not seem very democratic—at least not by today's standards. Some historians have suggested that if a Gallup poll could have been taken at that time, the Anti-Federalists would probably have outnumbered the Federalists.[15]

Certainly, some of the delegates to state ratifying conventions from poor, agrarian areas feared that an elite group of Federalists would run the country just as oppressively as the British had governed the colonies. Amos Singletary, a delegate to the Massachusetts ratifying convention, contended that those who urged the adoption of the Constitution "expect to get all the power and all the money into their own hands, and then they will swallow up all us little folks . . . just as the whale swallowed Jonah."[16] Others who were similarly situated, though, felt differently. Jonathan Smith, who was also a delegate to the Massachusetts ratifying convention, regarded a strong national government as a "cure for disorder"—referring to the disorder caused by the rebellion of Daniel Shays and his followers.[17]

Support Was Probably Widespread. Much has also been made of the various machinations used by the Federalists to ensure the Constitution's ratification (and they did resort to

[15]Jim Powell, "James Madison—Checks and Balances to Limit Government Power," *The Freeman*, March 1996, p. 178.
[16]As quoted in Bruno Leone, ed., *The Creation of the Constitution* (San Diego, CA: Greenhaven Press, 1995), p. 215.
[17]*Ibid.*, p. 217.

BEYOND OUR B🌐RDERS

WHAT MAKES A CONSTITUTION?

When Americans think of the Constitution, most visualize an old handwritten document that is protected in our National Archives. They may also reflect on the basic principles of the Constitution—checks and balances, separation of powers, the Bill of Rights—that structure how the national government carries out its work. However, just because a nation has a constitution does not mean that it is a short document like ours or that the constitution actually reflects the way the government operates.

WRITTEN OR UNWRITTEN

The United States Constitution is a written document that contains many lessons from that of Great Britain. However, Great Britain does not adhere to its constitution; few would argue this point. In fact, the British do not have a written constitution. They consider multiple historic documents, conventions, royal declarations, and other agreements to be their founding documents. And, the House of Commons can pass further legislation that would change the "constitution" of their nation. Canada's constitution is also a "set of documents" including the original Constitution Act of the 19th century creating the country and their much more recent (1982) bill of rights. Australia's constitution was approved by referendum in the Australian states between 1898 and 1900. However, in contrast to the constitution written by Americans after becoming an independent nation, the Australian constitution was submitted to the British Parliament for approval after it was approved by the Australian people.

WRITTEN OR DICTATED

In the case where one nation or group of allies defeats another nation in a war, the victorious nation may decide to take a hand in the future organization of the defeated country. After World War II, General Douglas McArthur, the commander of the Pacific forces, occupied Japan and gave strong direction to the writing of the new Japanese Constitution. That document, which is still in force and has never been amended, makes it clear that the Japanese imperial family has no political power at all. The Basic Law of Germany was also written after the allied victory in World War II and contains provisions that are intended to prohibit the rise of a political movement like that of Adolf Hitler.

After the United States defeated the forces of Saddam Hussein in Iraq in 2003, the process to rebuild the nation began. Although many different types of insurgencies have arisen and extended that conflict for the United States, it was decided to have the Iraqi people adopt a new constitution. After several interim governments (backed by the United States), a new Iraqi constitution was approved by referendum in 2005. Various other political issues, such as sharing oil revenues and the relative autonomy of provinces, are still in discussion.

CONSTITUTION OR WINDOW-DRESSING

During the Cold War between the United States and the Soviet Union, the Soviet republics held elections and called themselves democratic nations. They all had written constitutions that they strictly adhered to. However, the elections were not contested, and no opposition candidates or political parties emerged. Newspapers and other media were strictly controlled, as was any access to external information. Today, all of the former Soviet republics have new constitutions and are democracies with the same freedoms as other nations in Western Europe or the United States. In 2008, Russia, following its popularly approved constitution of 1993, held a free election and chose a new president who was the protégé of former President Vladimir Putin. Opposition leaders claim that they are harassed and that investigative journalists have been murdered.

Similarly, the People's Republic of North Korea has a fairly new constitution (1998) and claims to be democratic. However, the military and the Premier, Kim Jong II, direct all aspects of life there, including limiting the frequencies available on radios and televisions to those approved by the government. So, it seems that just having a written document outlining the structures of government and freedoms of the people may not be enough to guarantee any form of democratic government, at least in the sense that we know it.

FOR CRITICAL ANALYSIS

1. Do you think the United States could have survived without a written constitution?

2. How important is it for the people of a nation to have approved their constitution?
3. How can you tell if a nation is following the letter and the spirit of its constitution?

If you would like to read the constitution of any country in the world, go to http://confinder.richmond.edu.

a variety of devious tactics, including purchasing at least one printing press to prevent the publication of Anti-Federalist sentiments). Yet the perception that a strong central government was necessary to keep order and protect the public welfare appears to have been fairly pervasive among all classes—rich and poor alike.

Further, although the need for strong government was a major argument in favor of adopting the Constitution, even the Federalists sought to craft a limited government. Compared with constitutions adopted by other nations in later years, the U.S. Constitution, through its checks and balances, favors limited government over "energetic" government to a marked degree.

THE BILL OF RIGHTS

The U.S. Constitution would not have been ratified in several important states if the Federalists had not assured the states that amendments to the Constitution would be passed to protect individual liberties against incursions by the national government. Certainly, the idea of including certain rights in the Constitution had been discussed in the convention. There were those who believed that including these rights was simply unnecessary, whereas others suggested that carefully articulating certain rights might encourage the new national government to abuse any that were not specifically defined. Some rights, including prohibiting *ex post facto lawmaking*, were included in the document. *Ex post facto lawmaking* is passing laws that make one liable for an act that has already taken place. Also prohibited were *bills of attainder*, through which a legislature could pass judgment on someone without legal process. However, many of the recommendations of the state ratifying conventions included specific rights that were considered later by James Madison as he labored to draft what became the Bill of Rights.

A "BILL OF LIMITS"

Although called the Bill of Rights, essentially the first 10 amendments to the Constitution were a "bill of limits," because the amendments limited the powers of the national government over the rights and liberties of individuals.

Ironically, a year earlier Madison had told Jefferson, "I have never thought the omission [of the Bill of Rights] a material defect" of the Constitution. But Jefferson's enthusiasm for a bill of rights apparently influenced Madison, as did his desire to gain popular support for his election to Congress. Madison promised in his campaign letter to voters that, once elected, he would force

That 52 percent of Americans do not know what the Bill of Rights is?

Congress to "prepare and recommend to the states for ratification, the most satisfactory provisions for all essential rights."

Madison had to cull through more than 200 state recommendations.[18] It was no small task, and in retrospect he chose remarkably well. One of the rights appropriate for constitutional protection that he left out was equal protection under the laws—but that was not commonly regarded as a basic right at that time. Not until 1868 did the states ratify an amendment guaranteeing that no state shall deny equal protection to any person. (The Supreme Court has since applied this guarantee to certain actions of the federal government as well.)

The final number of amendments that Madison and a specially appointed committee came up with was 17. Congress tightened the language somewhat and eliminated five of the amendments. Of the remaining 12, two—dealing with the apportionment of representatives and the compensation of the members of Congress—were not ratified immediately by the states. Eventually, Supreme Court decisions led to reform of the apportionment process. The amendment on the compensation of members of Congress was ratified 203 years later—in 1992!

NO EXPLICIT LIMITS ON STATE GOVERNMENT POWERS

On December 15, 1791, the national Bill of Rights was adopted when Virginia agreed to ratify the 10 amendments. On ratification, the Bill of Rights became part of the U.S. Constitution. The basic structure of American government had already been established. Now the fundamental rights and liberties of individuals were protected, at least in theory, at the national level. The proposed amendment that Madison characterized as "the most valuable amendment in the whole lot"—which would have prohibited the states from infringing on the freedoms of conscience, press, and jury trial—had been eliminated by the Senate. Thus, the Bill of Rights as adopted did not limit state power, and individual citizens had to rely on the guarantees contained in a particular state constitution or state bill of rights. The country had to wait until the violence of the Civil War before significant limitations on state power in the form of the Fourteenth Amendment became part of the national Constitution.

ALTERING THE CONSTITUTION: THE FORMAL AMENDMENT PROCESS

The U.S. Constitution consists of 7,000 words. It is shorter than any state constitution except that of Vermont, which has 6,880 words. One of the reasons the federal Constitution is short is that the founders intended it to be only a framework for the new government, to be interpreted by succeeding generations. One of the reasons it has remained short is that the formal amending procedure does not allow for changes to be made easily. Article V of the Constitution outlines the ways in which amendments may be proposed and ratified (see Figure 2–3).

Two formal methods of proposing an amendment to the Constitution are available: (1) a two-thirds vote in each chamber of Congress or (2) a national convention that is called by Congress at the request of two-thirds of the state legislatures (the second method has never been used).

Ratification can occur by one of two methods: (1) by a positive vote in three-fourths of the legislatures of the various states or (2) by special conventions called in the states and a positive vote in three-fourths of them. The second method has been used only

[18]For details on these recommendations, including their sources, see Leonard W. Levy, *Origins of the Bill of Rights* (New Haven, CT: Yale University Press, 1999).

FIGURE 2–3 The Formal Constitutional Amending Procedure

There are two ways of proposing amendments to the U.S. Constitution and two ways of ratifying proposed amendments. Among the four possibilities, the usual route has been proposal by Congress and ratification by state legislatures.

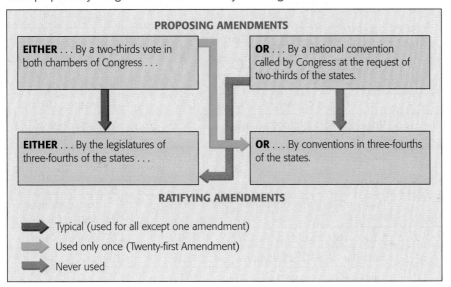

PROPOSING AMENDMENTS

EITHER . . . By a two-thirds vote in both chambers of Congress . . .

OR . . . By a national convention called by Congress at the request of two-thirds of the states.

EITHER . . . By the legislatures of three-fourths of the states . . .

OR . . . By conventions in three-fourths of the states.

RATIFYING AMENDMENTS

Typical (used for all except one amendment)

Used only once (Twenty-first Amendment)

Never used

once, to repeal Prohibition (the ban on the production and sale of alcoholic beverages). That situation was exceptional because it involved an amendment (the Twenty-first) to repeal an amendment (the Eighteenth, which had created Prohibition). State conventions were necessary for repeal of the Eighteenth Amendment, because the "pro-dry" legislatures in the most conservative states would never have passed the repeal. (Note that Congress determines the method of ratification to be used by all states for each proposed constitutional amendment.)

MANY AMENDMENTS PROPOSED, FEW ACCEPTED

Congress has considered more than 11,000 amendments to the Constitution. Many proposed amendments have been advanced to address highly specific problems. An argument against such narrow amendments has been that amendments ought to embody broad principles, in the way that the existing Constitution does. For that reason, many people have opposed such narrow amendments as one to protect the American flag.

Only 33 amendments have been submitted to the states after having been approved by the required two-thirds vote in each chamber of Congress, and only 27 have been ratified—see Table 2–4. (The full, annotated text of the U.S. Constitution, including its amendments, is presented in a special appendix at the end of this chapter.) It should be clear that the amendment process is much more difficult than a graphic depiction such as Figure 2–3 can indicate. Because of competing social and economic interests, the requirement that two-thirds of both the House and Senate approve the amendments is difficult to achieve. Thirty-four senators, representing only 17 sparsely populated states, could block any amendment. For example, the Republican-controlled House approved the Balanced Budget Amendment within the first 100 days of the 104th Congress in 1995, but it was defeated in the Senate by one vote.

After approval by Congress, the process becomes even more arduous. Three-fourths of the state legislatures must approve the amendment. Only those amendments that have wide popular support across parties and in all regions of the country are likely to be approved.

TABLE 2–4 Amendments to the Constitution

AMENDMENT	SUBJECT	YEAR ADOPTED	TIME REQUIRED FOR RATIFICATION
1st–10th	The Bill of Rights	1791	2 years, 2 months, 20 days
11th	Immunity of states from certain suits	1795	11 months, 3 days
12th	Changes in electoral college procedure	1804	6 months, 3 days
13th	Prohibition of slavery	1865	10 months, 3 days
14th	Citizenship, due process, and equal protection	1868	2 years, 26 days
15th	No denial of vote because of race, color, or previous condition of servitude	1870	11 months, 8 days
16th	Power of Congress to tax income	1913	3 years, 6 months, 22 days
17th	Direct election of U.S. senators	1913	10 months, 26 days
18th	National (liquor) prohibition	1919	1 year, 29 days
19th	Women's right to vote	1920	1 year, 2 months, 14 days
20th	Change of dates for congressional and presidential terms	1933	10 months, 21 days
21st	Repeal of the Eighteenth Amendment	1933	9 months, 15 days
22nd	Limit on presidential tenure	1951	3 years, 11 months, 3 days
23rd	District of Columbia electoral vote	1961	9 months, 13 days
24th	Prohibition of tax payment as a qualification to vote in federal elections	1964	1 year, 4 months, 9 days
25th	Procedures for determining presidential disability and presidential succession and for filling a vice-presidential vacancy	1967	1 year, 7 months, 4 days
26th	Prohibition of setting minimum voting age above 18 in any election	1971	3 months, 7 days
27th	Prohibition of Congress's voting itself a raise that takes effect before the next election	1992	203 years

Why was the amendment process made so difficult? The framers feared that a simple amendment process could lead to a tyranny of the majority, which could pass amendments to oppress disfavored individuals and groups. The cumbersome amendment process does not seem to stem the number of amendments that are proposed each year in Congress, however, particularly in recent years.

LIMITS ON RATIFICATION

A reading of Article V of the Constitution reveals that the framers of the Constitution specified no time limit on the ratification process. The Supreme Court has held that Congress can specify a time for ratification as long as it is "reasonable." Since 1919, most proposed amendments have included a requirement that ratification be obtained within seven years. This was the case with the proposed Equal Rights Amendment, which sought to guarantee equal rights for women. When three-fourths of the states had not ratified in the allotted seven years, however, Congress extended the limit by an additional three years and three months. That extension expired on June 30, 1982, and the amendment still had not been ratified. Another proposed amendment, which would have guaranteed congressional representation to the District of Columbia, fell far short of the 38 state ratifications needed before its August 22, 1985, deadline.

On May 7, 1992, Michigan became the 38th state to ratify the Twenty-seventh Amendment (on congressional compensation)—one of the two "lost" amendments of the 12 that originally were sent to the states in 1789. Because most of the amendments proposed in recent years have been given a time limit of only seven years by Congress, it was questionable for a time whether the amendment would take effect even if the necessary number of states ratified it. Is 203 years too long a lapse of time between the proposal and the final ratification of an amendment? It apparently was not, because the amendment was certified as legitimate by archivist Don Wilson of the National Archives on May 18, 1992.

THE NATIONAL CONVENTION PROVISION

The Constitution provides that a national convention requested by the legislatures of two-thirds of the states can propose a constitutional amendment. Congress has received approximately 400 convention applications since the Constitution was ratified; every state has applied at least once. Fewer than 20 applications were submitted during the Constitution's first hundred years, but more than 150 have been filed in the last two decades. No national convention has been held since 1787, and many national political and judicial leaders are uneasy about the prospect of convening a body that conceivably could do as the Constitutional Convention did—create a new form of government. The

SENATOR RUSSELL FEINGOLD, D.-Wis., speaks at a news conference to oppose the proposed Flag Protection Amendment. Senator Feingold, Senator Edward Kennedy, D.-Mass., and Veterans Defending the Bill of Rights, a national grassroots coalition, held the news conference on Flag Day, June 14, 2006. (Shauneil Scott/Landov Media)

state legislative bodies that originate national convention applications, however, do not appear to be uncomfortable with such a constitutional modification process; more than 230 state constitutional conventions have been held.

INFORMAL METHODS OF CONSTITUTIONAL CHANGE

Formal amendments are one way of changing our Constitution, and, as is obvious from their small number, they have been resorted to infrequently. If we discount the first 10 amendments (the Bill of Rights), which were adopted soon after the ratification of the Constitution, there have been only 17 formal alterations of the Constitution in the more than 200 years of its existence.

But looking at the sparse number of formal constitutional amendments gives us an incomplete view of constitutional change. The brevity and ambiguity of the original document have permitted great alterations in the Constitution by way of varying interpretations over time. As the United States grew, both in population and territory, new social and political realities emerged. Congress, presidents, and the courts found it necessary to interpret the Constitution's provisions in light of these new realities. The Constitution has proved to be a remarkably flexible document, adapting itself repeatedly to new events and concerns.

CONGRESSIONAL LEGISLATION

The Constitution gives Congress broad powers to carry out its duties as the nation's legislative body. For example, Article I, Section 8, of the Constitution gives Congress the power to regulate foreign and interstate commerce. Although there is no clear definition of foreign commerce or interstate commerce in the Constitution, Congress has cited the *commerce clause* as the basis for passing thousands of laws that have defined the meaning of foreign and interstate commerce.

Similarly, Article III, Section 1, states that the national judiciary shall consist of one supreme court and "such inferior courts, as Congress may from time to time ordain and establish." Through a series of acts, Congress has used this broad provision to establish the federal court system of today, which includes the Supreme Court, the Courts of Appeal, and District Courts. This provision allows Congress to create a court such as the Foreign Intelligence Surveillance Act (FISA) court to review requests for wiretapping suspected terrorists.

In addition, Congress has frequently delegated to federal agencies the legislative power to write regulations. These regulations become law unless challenged in the court system. Nowhere does the Constitution outline this delegation of legislative authority.

PRESIDENTIAL ACTIONS

Even though the Constitution does not expressly authorize the president to propose bills or even budgets to Congress,[19] presidents since the time of Woodrow Wilson (who served as president from 1913 to 1921) have proposed hundreds of bills to Congress each year. Presidents have also relied on their Article II authority as commander in chief of the nation's armed forces to send American troops abroad into combat, although the Constitution provides that Congress has the power to declare war.

---

[19]Note, though, that the Constitution, in Article II, Section 3, does state that the president "shall from time to time . . . recommend to [Congress's] consideration such measures as he shall judge necessary and expedient." Some scholars interpret this phrase to mean that the president has the constitutional authority to propose bills and budgets to Congress for consideration.

The president's powers in wartime have waxed and waned through the course of American history. President Abraham Lincoln instituted a draft and suspended several civil liberties during the Civil War. During World War II, President Franklin Roosevelt approved the internment of thousands of Japanese American citizens. President George W. Bush significantly expanded presidential power in the wake of the terrorist attacks of 2001, especially in regard to the handling of individuals who could be defined as "enemy combatants." The creation of the detention facility at Guantánamo Bay, Cuba, made it possible for those prisoners to be held and interrogated by the military under the full control of the executive branch.

Presidents have also conducted foreign affairs by the use of executive agreements, which are legally binding documents made between the president and a foreign head of state. The Constitution does not mention such agreements.

That the states have still not ratified an amendment (introduced by Congress in 1810) barring U.S. citizens from accepting titles of nobility from foreign governments?

JUDICIAL REVIEW

Another way of changing the Constitution—or of making it more flexible—is through the power of judicial review. Judicial review refers to the power of U.S. courts to examine the constitutionality of actions undertaken by the legislative and executive branches of government. A state court, for example, may rule that a statute enacted by the state legislature is unconstitutional. Federal courts (and ultimately, the United States Supreme Court) may rule unconstitutional not only acts of Congress and decisions of the national executive branch but also state statutes, state executive actions, and even provisions of state constitutions.

Not a Novel Concept. The Constitution does not specifically mention the power of judicial review. Those in attendance at the Constitutional Convention, however, probably expected that the courts would have some authority to review the legality of acts by the executive and legislative branches, because, under the common law tradition inherited from England, courts exercised this authority. Alexander Hamilton, in *Federalist Paper* No. 78, explicitly outlined the concept of judicial review. Whether the power of judicial review can be justified constitutionally is a question that has been subject to some debate, particularly in recent years. For now, suffice it to say that in 1803, the Supreme Court claimed this power for itself in *Marbury v. Madison*,[20] in which the Court ruled that a particular provision of an act of Congress was unconstitutional.

Allows Court to Adapt the Constitution. Through the process of judicial review, the Supreme Court adapts the Constitution to modern situations. Electronic technology, for example, did not exist when the Constitution was ratified. Nonetheless, the Supreme Court has used the Fourth Amendment guarantees against unreasonable searches and seizures to place limits on the use of wiretapping and other electronic eavesdropping methods by government officials. The Court has needed to decide whether antiterrorism laws passed by Congress or state legislatures, or executive orders declared by the president, violate the Fourth Amendment or other constitutional provisions. Additionally, the Supreme Court has changed its interpretation of the Constitution in accordance with changing values. It ruled in 1896 that "separate-but-equal" public facilities for African Americans were constitutional; but by 1954, the times had changed, and the Supreme Court reversed that decision.[21] Woodrow Wilson summarized the Supreme Court's work when he described it as "a constitutional convention in continuous session." Basically, the law is what the Supreme Court says it is at any given time. In saying what the law is, the Supreme Court sometimes consults the laws of other countries, as this chapter's *Beyond Our Borders* feature describes.

[20]5 U.S. 137 (1803). See Chapter 15 for a further discussion of the *Marbury v. Madison* case.
[21]*Brown v. Board of Education of Topeka*, 347 U.S. 483 (1954).

INTERPRETATION, CUSTOM, AND USAGE

The Constitution has also been changed through interpretation by both Congress and the president. Originally, the president had a staff consisting of personal secretaries and a few others. Today, because Congress delegates specific tasks to the president and the chief executive assumes political leadership, the executive office staff alone has increased to several thousand persons. The executive branch provides legislative leadership far beyond the expectations of the founders.

Changes in the ways of doing political business have also altered the Constitution. The Constitution does not mention political parties, yet these informal, "extraconstitutional" organizations make the nominations for offices, run the campaigns, organize the members of Congress, and in fact change the election system from time to time. The emergence and evolution of the party system, for example, has changed the way the president is elected. The entire nominating process with its use of primary elections and caucuses to choose delegates to the party's nominating convention is the creation of the two major political parties. The president is then selected by the electors who are, in fact, chosen by the parties and are pledged to a party's candidate.

A recent book by Bruce Ackerman argues that the rise of political parties and growth of the executive represent the failure of the founding fathers to understand how the government would develop over time. He proposes that the only reason that the system has maintained its checks is the development of the Supreme Court into the guarantor of our rights and liberties.[22] Perhaps most striking, the Constitution has been adapted from serving the needs of a small, rural republic to providing a framework of government for an industrial giant with vast geographic, natural, and human resources.

[22]Bruce Ackerman, *The Failure of the Founding Fathers: Jefferson, Marshall, and the Rise of Presidential Democracy* (Cambridge: The Belknap Press, 2005).

You can make a difference

HOW CAN YOU AFFECT THE U.S. CONSTITUTION?

The U.S. Constitution is an enduring document that has survived more than 200 years of turbulent history. It is also a changing document, however. Twenty-seven amendments have been added to the original Constitution. How can you, as an individual, actively influence constitutional amendments?

WHY SHOULD YOU CARE?

The laws of the nation have a direct impact on your life, and none more so than the Constitution—the supreme law of the land. The most important issues in society are often settled by the Constitution. For example, for the first 75 years of the Republic, the Constitution implicitly protected the institution of slavery. If the Constitution had never been changed through the amendment process, slavery might still be legal today.

Since the passage of the Fourteenth Amendment in 1868, the Constitution has defined who is a citizen and who is entitled to the protections the Constitution provides. Constitutional provisions define our liberties. The First Amendment protects our freedom of speech more thoroughly than do the laws of many other nations. Few other countries have constitutional provisions governing the right to own firearms (the Second Amendment). All of these are among the most fundamental issues we face.

WHAT CAN YOU DO?

One way that you can affect the Constitution is by protecting your existing rights and liberties under it. In the wake of the September 11 attacks, several new laws have been enacted that many believe go too far in curbing our constitutional rights. If you agree and want to join with others who are concerned about this issue, a good starting point is the Web site of the American Civil Liberties Union (ACLU) at **www.aclu.org**.

Do you feel that your vote makes a difference? Many voters are beginning to feel disenfranchised by the political process in presidential elections through the effects of the electoral college. A 2007 poll found that 72 per-

cent of Americans favored replacing the electoral college with a direct election.* The Every Vote Counts Amendment proposes to abolish the electoral college and would provide for the direct popular election of the president. If you would like to further investigate Every Vote Counts, go to **www.washingtonwatch.com**, a forum for monitoring proposed legislation in Washington, D.C. Visit the Take Action box, where you can comment on the amendment, alert your friends and colleagues about the issue, and write your representative in Congress.

At the time of this writing, national coalitions of interest groups are supporting or opposing several proposed amendments. Constitutional amendments are difficult to pass, needing supermajorities in the House and Senate, as well as three-fourths of the state legislatures. The National Popular Vote Bill seeks to reform the electoral college through individual state legislatures, who may change state laws regarding the distribution of electoral votes. With the National Popular Vote bill, all state electoral votes would be awarded to the presidential candidate winning the popular vote in all 50 states and the District of Columbia. Check out National Popular Vote, Inc., a nonprofit group, at **www.nationalpopularvote.com**, for more information regarding this bill. Their Web site offers numerous ways to become informed and take action. You can even check the bill's progress in your own state.

*The Washington Post-Kaiser Family Foundation-Harvard University Survey of Political Independents, Public Opinion and Media Research Program, *Kaiser Family Foundation*, July 1, 2007, p. 14; www.kff.org/kaiserpolls/7665.cfm.

KEY TERMS

Anti-Federalist 53
bicameral legislature 46
checks and balances 50
confederation 41
federal system 51
Federalist 53

Great Compromise 47
Madisonian model 50
natural rights 40
ratification 52
representative assembly 35
separation of powers 50

social contract 40
state 41
supremacy doctrine 46
unicameral legislature 41

CHAPTER SUMMARY

1. The first permanent English colonies were established at Jamestown in 1607 and Plymouth in 1620. The Mayflower Compact created the first formal government for the British colonists. By the mid-1700s, other British colonies had been established along the Atlantic seaboard from Georgia to Maine.

2. In 1763, the British tried to impose a series of taxes and legislative acts on their increasingly independent-minded colonies. The colonists responded with boycotts of British products and protests. Representatives of the colonies formed the First Continental Congress in 1774. The delegates sent a petition to the British king expressing their grievances. The Second Continental Congress established an army in 1775 to defend the colonists against attacks by British soldiers.

3. On July 4, 1776, the Second Continental Congress approved the Declaration of Independence. Perhaps the most revolutionary aspects of the Declaration were its assumptions that people have natural rights to life, liberty, and the pursuit of happiness; that governments derive their power from the consent of the governed; and that people have a right to overthrow oppressive governments. During the Revolutionary War, the colonies adopted written constitutions that severely curtailed the power of executives, thus giving their legislatures predominant powers. By the end of the Revolutionary War, the states had signed the Articles of Confederation, creating a weak central government with few powers. The Articles proved to be unworkable because the national government had no way to ensure compliance by the states with such measures as securing tax revenues.

4. General dissatisfaction with the Articles of Confederation prompted the call for a convention at Philadelphia in 1787. Although the delegates ostensibly convened to amend the Articles, the discussions soon focused on creating a constitution for a new form of government. The Virginia plan and the New Jersey plan did not garner widespread support. A compromise offered by Connecticut helped to break the large-state/small-state disputes dividing the delegates. The final version of the Constitution provided for the separation of powers, checks and balances, and a federal form of government.

5. Fears of a strong central government prompted the addition of the Bill of Rights to the Constitution. The Bill of Rights secured for Americans a wide variety of freedoms, including the freedoms of religion, speech, and assembly. It was initially applied only to the federal government, but amendments to the Constitution following the Civil War made it clear that the Bill of Rights would apply to the states as well.

6. An amendment to the Constitution may be proposed either by a two-thirds vote in each house of Congress or by a national convention called by Congress at the request of two-thirds of the state legislatures. Ratification can occur either by a positive vote in three-fourths of the legislatures of the various states or by special conventions called in the states for the specific purpose of ratifying the proposed amendment and a positive vote in three-fourths of these state conventions. Informal methods of constitutional change include congressional legislation, presidential actions, judicial review, and changing interpretations of the Constitution.

SELECTED PRINT AND MEDIA RESOURCES

SUGGESTED READINGS

Ackerman, Bruce. *The Failure of the Founding Fathers: Jefferson, Marshall, and the Rise of Presidential Democracy.* Cambridge: Belknap Press, 2005. In this book, the author sees the contested election of 1800 as exposing the failure of the new Constitution to account for the rise of presidential power and the appearance of *political parties.*

Bailyn, Bernard. *To Begin the World Anew: The Genius and Ambiguities of the American Founders.* New York: Knopf, 2003. In a series of essays, a two-time Pulitzer Prize-winning historian discusses the themes of order and liberty in the *Federalist Papers* and the advantages of the founders' provincialism.

Breyer, Stephen G. *Active Liberty: Interpreting Our Democratic Constitution.* New York: Knopf, 2005. Supreme Court justice Stephen Breyer offers his thoughts on the Constitution as a living document. He argues that the genius of the Constitution rests in the adaptability of its great principles to cope with current problems.

Dahl, Robert A. *How Democratic Is the American Constitution?* New Haven, CT: Yale University Press, 2002. This book compares the U.S. Constitution with the constitutions of other democratic countries in the world.

Gibson, Alan. *Understanding the Founding: The Crucial Questions.* Lawrence: The University Press of Kansas, 2007. The author looks at several oft-debated questions concerning the motivation and political views of the Founding Fathers.

Hamilton, Alexander, et al. *The Federalist: The Famous Papers on the Principles of American Government.* Benjamin F. Wright, ed. New York: Friedman/Fairfax Publishing, 2002. This is an updated version of the papers written by Alexander Hamilton, James Madison, and John Jay, and published in the *New York Packet,* in support of the ratification of the Constitution.

Philbrick, Nathaniel. *Mayflower: A Story of Courage, Community and War.* New York: Penguin, 2007. The author investigates many of the myths surrounding the first colony in New England and sheds light on some little-known history.

MEDIA RESOURCES

In the Beginning—A 1987 Bill Moyers TV program that features discussions with three prominent historians about the roots of the Constitution and its impact on our society.

John Locke—A 1994 video exploring the character and principal views of John Locke.

Thomas Jefferson—A 1996 documentary by acclaimed director Ken Burns. The film covers Jefferson's entire life, including his writing of the Declaration of Independence, his presidency, and his later years in Virginia. Historians and writers interviewed include Daniel Boorstin, Garry Wills, Gore Vidal, and John Hope Franklin.

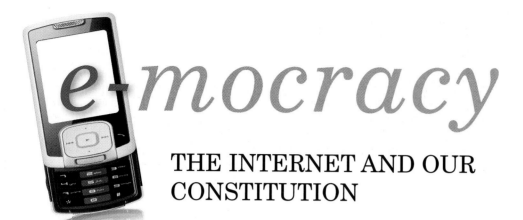

e-mocracy

THE INTERNET AND OUR CONSTITUTION

Today, you can find online many important documents from the founding period, including descriptions of events leading up to the American Revolution, the Articles of Confederation, notes on the Constitutional Convention, the Federalists' writings, and the Anti-Federalists' responses.

You are able to access the Internet and explore a variety of opinions on every topic imaginable because you enjoy the freedoms—including freedom of speech—guaranteed by our Constitution. Even today, more than 200 years after the U.S. Bill of Rights was ratified, citizens in some countries do not enjoy the right to free speech. Nor can they surf the Web freely, as U.S. citizens do.

For example, the Chinese government employs several methods to control Internet use. One method is to use filtering software to block electronic pathways to objectionable sites, including the sites of Western news organizations. Another technique is to prohibit Internet users from sending or discussing information that has not been publicly released by the government. Still another practice is to monitor the online activities of Internet users. None of these methods is foolproof, however, and some observers claim that the Internet, by exposing citizens in politically oppressive nations to a variety of views on politics and culture, will eventually transform those nations.

We should note that such restrictions can also exist in the United States. For example, there have been persistent efforts by Congress and many courts to limit access to Web sites deemed pornographic. Free-speech advocates have attacked these restrictions as unconstitutional, as you will read in Chapter 4.

LOGGING ON

- For U.S. founding documents, including the Declaration of Independence, scanned originals of the U.S. Constitution, and the *Federalist Papers*, go to Emory University School of Law's Web site at:
  www.law.emory.edu/erd/docs/federalist
- If you would like to read James Madison's notes on the Constitutional Convention debates, taken from his daily journal, they are online at:
  http://www.yale.edu/lawweb/avalon/
- The University of Oklahoma Law Center has several U.S. historical documents online, including many of those discussed in this chapter. Go to:
  www.law.ou.edu/hist
- The National Constitution Center provides information on the Constitution—including its history, current debates over constitutional provisions, and news articles—at the following site:
  www.constitutioncenter.org
- To look at state constitutions, go to:
  www.findlaw.com/casecode/state.html

ONLINE REVIEW

At **www.cengage.com/politicalscience/schmidt/agandpt14e**, you will find a Tutorial Quiz for this chapter providing questions on the chapter contents, including the features. The questions are organized to match the major sections of the chapter. You'll have access to other helpful study tools, including the book's glossary and flashcards, crossword puzzles, and Web links, as well as "Which Side Are You On?" and "Politics and . . ." features written by the authors of the book.

APPENDIX TO CHAPTER 2

the Constitution

OF THE UNITED STATES*

THE PREAMBLE

We the People of the United States, in Order to form a more perfect Union, establish Justice, insure domestic Tranquility, provide for the common defence, promote the general Welfare, and secure the Blessings of Liberty to ourselves and our Posterity, do ordain and establish this Constitution for the United States of America.

The Preamble declares that "We the People" are the authority for the Constitution (unlike the Articles of Confederation, which derived their authority from the states). The Preamble also sets out the purposes of the Constitution.

ARTICLE I. *(Legislative Branch)*

The first part of the Constitution, Article I, deals with the organization and powers of the lawmaking branch of the national government, the Congress.

Section 1. *Legislative Powers*

All legislative Powers herein granted shall be vested in a Congress of the United States, which shall consist of a Senate and House of Representatives.

Section 2. *House of Representatives*

Clause 1: Composition and Election of Members. The House of Representatives shall be composed of Members chosen every second Year by the People of the several States, and the Electors in each State shall have the Qualifications requisite for Electors of the most numerous Branch of the State Legislature.

Each state has the power to decide who may vote for members of Congress. Within each state, those who may vote for state legislators may also vote for members of the House of Representatives (and, under the Seventeenth Amendment, for U.S. senators). When the Constitution was written, nearly all states limited voting rights to white male property owners or taxpayers at least 21 years old.

Subsequent amendments granted voting power to African American men, all women, and everyone at least 18 years old.

Clause 2: Qualifications. No Person shall be a Representative who shall not have attained to the Age of twenty five Years, and been seven Years a Citizen of the United States, and who shall not, when elected, be an Inhabitant of that State in which he shall be chosen.

Each member of the House must be at least 25 years old, a citizen of the United States for at least seven years, and a resident of the state in which she or he is elected.

Clause 3: Apportionment of Representatives and Direct Taxes. Representatives [and direct Taxes][1] shall be apportioned among the several States which may be included within this Union, according to their respective Numbers [which shall be determined by adding to the whole Number of free Persons, including those bound to Service for a Term of Years, and excluding Indians not taxed, three fifths of all other Persons].[2] The actual Enumeration shall be made within three Years after the first Meeting of the Congress of the United States, and within every subsequent Term of ten Years, in such Manner as they shall by Law direct. The Number of Representatives shall not exceed one for every thirty Thousand, but each State shall have at Least one Representative; and until such enumeration shall be made, the State of New Hampshire shall be entitled to chuse three, Massachusetts eight, Rhode Island and Providence Plantations one, Connecticut five, New York six, New Jersey four, Pennsylvania eight, Delaware one, Maryland six, Virginia ten, North Carolina five, South Carolina five, and Georgia three.

A state's representation in the House is based on the size of its population. Population is counted in each decade's census, after which Congress reapportions House seats. Since early in the 20th century, the number of seats has been limited to 435.

---

*The spelling, capitalization, and punctuation of the original have been retained here. Brackets indicate passages that have been altered by amendments to the Constitution. We have added article titles (in parentheses), section titles, and clause designations. We have also inserted annotations in blue italic type.
[1]Modified by the Sixteenth Amendment.
[2]Modified by the Fourteenth Amendment.

Clause 4: Vacancies. When vacancies happen in the Representation from any State, the Executive Authority thereof shall issue Writs of Election to fill such Vacancies.

The "Executive Authority" is the state's governor. When a vacancy occurs in the House, the governor calls a special election to fill it.

Clause 5: Officers and Impeachment. The House of Representatives shall chuse their Speaker and other Officers; and shall have the sole Power of Impeachment.

The power to impeach is the power to accuse. In this case, it is the power to accuse members of the executive or judicial branch of wrongdoing or abuse of power. Once a bill of impeachment is issued, the Senate holds the trial.

Section 3. *The Senate*

Clause 1: Term and Number of Members. The Senate of the United States shall be composed of two Senators from each State [chosen by the Legislature thereof],[3] for six Years; and each Senator shall have one Vote.

Every state has two senators, each of whom serves for six years and has one vote in the upper chamber. Since the Seventeenth Amendment in 1913, all senators have been elected directly by voters of the state during the regular election.

Clause 2: Classification of Senators. Immediately after they shall be assembled in Consequence of the first Election, they shall be divided as equally as may be into three Classes. The Seats of the Senators of the first Class shall be vacated at the Expiration of the second Year, of the second Class at the Expiration of the fourth Year, and of the third Class at the Expiration of the sixth Year, so that one third may be chosen every second Year; [and if Vacancies happen by Resignation, or otherwise, during the Recess of the Legislature of any State, the Executive thereof may make temporary Appointments until the next Meeting of the Legislature, which shall then fill such Vacancies].[4]

One-third of the Senate's seats are open to election every two years (in contrast, all members of the House are elected simultaneously).

Clause 3: Qualifications. No Person shall be a Senator who shall not have attained to the Age of thirty Years, and been nine Years a Citizen of the United States, and who shall not, when elected, be an Inhabitant of that State for which he shall be chosen.

Every senator must be at least 30 years old, a citizen of the United States for a minimum of nine years, and a resident of the state in which he or she is elected.

Clause 4: The Role of the Vice President. The Vice President of the United States shall be President of the Senate, but shall have no Vote, unless they be equally divided.

The vice president presides over meetings of the Senate but cannot vote unless there is a tie. The Constitution gives no other official duties to the vice president.

Clause 5: Other Officers. The Senate shall chuse their other Officers, and also a President pro tempore, in the Absence of the Vice President, or when he shall exercise the Office of President of the United States.

The Senate votes for one of its members to preside when the vice president is absent. This person is usually called the president pro tempore because of the temporary nature of the position.

Clause 6: Impeachment Trials. The Senate shall have the sole Power to try all Impeachments. When sitting for that Purpose, they shall be on Oath or Affirmation. When the President of the United States is tried, the Chief Justice shall preside: And no Person shall be convicted without the Concurrence of two thirds of the Members present.

The Senate conducts trials of officials that the House impeaches. The Senate sits as a jury, with the vice president presiding if the president is not on trial.

Clause 7: Penalties for Conviction. Judgment in Cases of Impeachment shall not extend further than to removal from Office, and disqualification to hold and enjoy any Office of honor, Trust, or Profit under the United States: but the Party convicted shall nevertheless be liable and subject to Indictment, Trial, Judgment, and Punishment, according to Law.

On conviction of impeachment charges, the Senate can only force an official to leave office and prevent him or her from holding another office in the federal government. The individual, however, can still be tried in a regular court.

Section 4. *Congressional Elections: Times, Manner, and Places*

Clause 1: Elections. The Times, Places and Manner of holding Elections for Senators and Representatives, shall be prescribed in each State by the Legislature thereof; but the Congress may at any time by Law make or alter such Regulations, except as to the Places of chusing Senators.

Congress set the Tuesday after the first Monday in November in even-numbered years as the date for congressional elections. In states with more than one seat in the House, Congress requires that representatives be elected from districts within each state. Under the Seventeenth Amendment, senators are elected at the same places as other officials.

[3]Repealed by the Seventeenth Amendment.
[4]Modified by the Seventeenth Amendment.

Clause 2: Sessions of Congress. [The Congress shall assemble at least once in every Year, and such Meeting shall be on the first Monday in December, unless they shall by Law appoint a different Day.][5]

Congress has to meet every year at least once. The regular session now begins at noon on January 3 of each year, subsequent to the Twentieth Amendment, unless Congress passes a law to fix a different date. Congress stays in session until its members vote to adjourn. Additionally, the president may call a special session.

Section 5. *Powers and Duties of the Houses*

Clause 1: Admitting Members and Quorum. Each House shall be the Judge of the Elections, Returns, and Qualifications of its own Members, and a Majority of each shall constitute a Quorum to do Business; but a smaller Number may adjourn from day to day, and may be authorized to compel the Attendance of absent Members, in such Manner, and under such Penalties as each House may provide.

Each chamber may exclude or refuse to seat a member-elect.

The quorum rule requires that 218 members of the House and 51 members of the Senate be present to conduct business. This rule normally is not enforced in the handling of routine matters.

Clause 2: Rules and Discipline of Members. Each House may determine the Rules of its Proceedings, punish its Members for disorderly Behaviour, and, with the Concurrence of two thirds, expel a Member.

The House and the Senate may adopt their own rules to guide their proceedings. Each may also discipline its members for conduct that is deemed unacceptable. No member may be expelled without a two-thirds majority vote in favor of expulsion.

Clause 3: Keeping a Record. Each House shall keep a Journal of its Proceedings, and from time to time publish the same, excepting such Parts as may in their Judgment require Secrecy; and the Yeas and Nays of the Members of either House on any question shall, at the Desire of one fifth of those Present, be entered on the Journal.

The journals of the two chambers are published at the end of each session of Congress.

Clause 4: Adjournment. Neither House, during the Session of Congress, shall, without the Consent of the other, adjourn for more than three days, nor to any other Place than that in which the two Houses shall be sitting.

Congress has the power to determine when and where to meet, provided, however, that both chambers meet in the same city. Neither chamber may recess for more than three days without the consent of the other.

Section 6. *Rights of Members*

Clause 1: Compensation and Privileges. The Senators and Representatives shall receive a Compensation for their services, to be ascertained by Law, and paid out of the Treasury of the United States. They shall in all Cases, except Treason, Felony and Breach of the Peace, be privileged from Arrest during their Attendance at the Session of their respective Houses, and in going to and returning from the same; and for any Speech or Debate in either House, they shall not be questioned in any other Place.

Congressional salaries are to be paid by the U.S. Treasury rather than by the members' respective states. The original salaries were $6 per day; in 1857 they were $3,000 per year. Both representatives and senators were paid $165,200 in 2006.

Treason is defined in Article III, Section 3. A felony is any serious crime. A breach of the peace is any indictable offense less than treason or a felony. Members cannot be arrested for things they say during speeches and debates in Congress. This immunity applies to the Capitol Building itself and not to their private lives.

Clause 2: Restrictions. No Senator or Representative shall, during the Time for which he was elected, be appointed to any civil Office under the Authority of the United States, which shall have been created, or the Emoluments whereof shall have been encreased during such time; and no Person holding any Office under the United States, shall be a Member of either House during his Continuance in Office.

During the term for which a member was elected, he or she cannot concurrently accept another federal government position.

Section 7. *Legislative Powers: Bills and Resolutions*

Clause 1: Revenue Bills. All Bills for raising Revenue shall originate in the House of Representatives; but the Senate may propose or concur with Amendments as on other Bills.

All tax and appropriation bills for raising money have to originate in the House of Representatives. The Senate, though, often amends such bills and may even substitute an entirely different bill.

---

[5]Changed by the Twentieth Amendment.

Clause 2: The Presidential Veto. Every Bill which shall have passed the House of Representatives and the Senate, shall, before it becomes a Law, be presented to the President of the United States; If he approve he shall sign it, but if not he shall return it, with his Objections to the House in which it shall have originated, who shall enter the Objections at large on their Journal, and proceed to reconsider it. If after such Reconsideration two thirds of that House shall agree to pass the Bill, it shall be sent together with the Objections, to the other House, by which it shall likewise be reconsidered, and if approved by two thirds of that House, it shall become a Law. But in all such Cases the Votes of both Houses shall be determined by Yeas and Nays, and the Names of the Persons voting for and against the Bill shall be entered on the Journal of each House respectively. If any Bill shall not be returned by the President within 10 Days (Sundays excepted) after it shall have been presented to him, the Same shall be a Law, in like Manner as if he had signed it, unless the Congress by their Adjournment prevent its Return in which Case it shall not be a Law.

When Congress sends the president a bill, he or she can sign it (in which case it becomes law) or send it back to the chamber in which it originated. If it is sent back, a two-thirds majority of each chamber must pass it again for it to become law. If the president neither signs it nor sends it back within 10 days, it becomes law anyway, unless Congress adjourns in the meantime.

Clause 3: Actions on Other Matters. Every Order, Resolution, or Vote to which the Concurrence of the Senate and House of Representatives may be necessary (except on a question of Adjournment) shall be presented to the President of the United States; and before the Same shall take Effect, shall be approved by him, or being disapproved by him, shall be repassed by two thirds of the Senate and House of Representatives, according to the Rules and Limitations prescribed in the Case of a Bill.

The president must have the opportunity to either sign or veto everything that Congress passes, except votes to adjourn and resolutions not having the force of law.

Section 8. *The Powers of Congress*

Clause 1: Taxing. The Congress shall have Power to lay and collect Taxes, Duties, Imposts and Excises, to pay the Debts and provide for the common Defence and general Welfare of the United States; but all Duties, Imposts and Excises shall be uniform throughout the United States;

Duties are taxes on imports and exports. Impost is a generic term for tax. Excises are taxes on the manufacture, sale, or use of goods.

Clause 2: Borrowing. To borrow Money on the credit of the United States;

Congress has the power to borrow money, which is normally carried out through the sale of U.S. treasury bonds on which interest is paid. Note that the Constitution places no limit on the amount of government borrowing.

Clause 3: Regulation of Commerce. To regulate Commerce with foreign Nations, and among the several States, and with the Indian Tribes;

This is the commerce clause, which gives to Congress the power to regulate interstate and foreign trade. Much of the activity of Congress is based on this clause.

Clause 4: Naturalization and Bankruptcy. To establish an uniform Rule of Naturalization, and uniform Laws on the subject of Bankruptcies throughout the United States;

Only Congress may determine how aliens can become citizens of the United States. Congress may make laws with respect to bankruptcy.

Clause 5: Money and Standards. To coin Money, regulate the Value thereof, and of foreign Coin, and fix the Standard of Weights and Measures;

Congress mints coins and prints and circulates paper money. Congress can establish uniform measures of time, distance, weight, and so on. In 1838, Congress adopted the English system of weights and measurements as our national standard.

Clause 6: Punishing Counterfeiters. To provide for the Punishment of counterfeiting the Securities and current Coin of the United States;

Congress has the power to punish those who copy American money and pass it off as real. Currently, the fine is up to $5,000 and/or imprisonment for up to 15 years.

Clause 7: Roads and Post Offices. To establish Post Offices and post Roads;

Post roads include all routes over which mail is carried—highways, railways, waterways, and airways.

Clause 8: Patents and Copyrights. To promote the Progress of Science and useful Arts, by securing for limited Times to Authors and Inventors the exclusive Right to their respective Writings and Discoveries;

Authors' and composers' works are protected by copyrights established by copyright law, which currently is the Copyright Act of 1976, as amended. Copyrights are valid for the life of the author or composer plus 70 years. Inventors' works are protected by patents, which vary in length of protection from 14 to 20 years. A patent gives a person the exclusive right to control the manufacture or sale of her or his invention.

Clause 9: Lower Courts. To constitute Tribunals inferior to the supreme Court;

Congress has the authority to set up all federal courts, except the Supreme Court, and to decide what cases those courts will hear.

Clause 10: Punishment for Piracy. To define and punish Piracies and Felonies committed on the high Seas, and Offences against the Law of Nations;

Congress has the authority to prohibit the commission of certain acts outside U.S. territory and to punish certain violations of international law.

Clause 11: Declaration of War. To declare War, grant Letters of Marque and Reprisal, and make Rules concerning Captures on Land and Water;

Only Congress can declare war, although the president, as commander in chief, can make war without Congress's formal declaration. Letters of marque and reprisal authorized private parties to capture and destroy enemy ships in wartime. Since the middle of the 19th century, international law has prohibited letters of marque and reprisal, and the United States has honored the ban.

Clause 12: The Army. To raise and support Armies, but no Appropriation of Money to that Use shall be for a longer Term than two Years;

Congress has the power to create an army; the money used to pay for it must be appropriated for no more than two-year intervals. This latter restriction gives ultimate control of the army to civilians.

Clause 13: Creation of a Navy. To provide and maintain a Navy;

This clause allows for the maintenance of a navy. In 1947, Congress created the U.S. Air Force.

Clause 14: Regulation of the Armed Forces. To make Rules for the Government and Regulation of the land and naval Forces;

Congress sets the rules for the military mainly by way of the Uniform Code of Military Justice, which was enacted in 1950 by Congress.

Clause 15: The Militia. To provide for calling forth the Militia to execute the Laws of the Union, suppress Insurrections and repel Invasions;

The militia is known today as the National Guard. Both Congress and the president have the authority to call the National Guard into federal service.

Clause 16: How the Militia Is Organized. To provide for organizing, arming, and disciplining the Militia, and for governing such Part of them as may be employed in the Service of the United States, reserving to the States respectively, the Appointment of the Officers, and the Authority of training the Militia according to the discipline prescribed by Congress;

This clause gives Congress the power to "federalize" state militia (National Guard). When called into such service, the National Guard is subject to the same rules that Congress has set forth for the regular armed services.

Clause 17: Creation of the District of Columbia. To exercise exclusive Legislation in all Cases whatsoever, over such District (not exceeding ten Miles square) as may, by Cession of particular States, and the Acceptance of Congress, become the Seat of the Government of the United States, and to exercise like Authority over all Places purchased by the Consent of the Legislature of the State in which the Same shall be, for the Erection of Forts, Magazines, Arsenals, dock-Yards, and other needful Buildings;—And

Congress established the District of Columbia as the national capital in 1791. Virginia and Maryland had granted land for the District, but Virginia's grant was returned because it was believed it would not be needed. Today, the District covers 69 square miles.

Clause 18: The Elastic Clause. To make all Laws which shall be necessary and proper for carrying into Execution the foregoing Powers, and all other Powers vested by this Constitution in the Government of the United States, or in any Department or Officer thereof.

This clause—the necessary and proper clause, or the elastic clause—grants no specific powers, and thus it can be stretched to fit different circumstances. It has allowed Congress to adapt the government to changing needs and times.

Section 9. *The Powers Denied to Congress*

Clause 1: Question of Slavery. The Migration or Importation of such Persons as any of the States now existing shall think proper to admit, shall not be prohibited by the Congress prior to the Year one thousand eight hundred and eight, but a Tax or duty may be imposed on such Importation, not exceeding ten dollars for each Person.

"Persons" referred to slaves. Congress outlawed the slave trade in 1808.

Clause 2: Habeas Corpus. The privilege of the Writ of Habeas Corpus shall not be suspended, unless when in Cases of Rebellion or Invasion the public Safety may require it.

A writ of habeas corpus is a court order directing a sheriff or other public officer who is detaining another person to "produce the body" of the detainee so the court can assess the legality of the detention.

Clause 3: Special Bills. No Bill of Attainder or ex post facto Law shall be passed.

A bill of attainder is a law that inflicts punishment without a trial. An ex post facto law is a law that inflicts punishment for an act that was not illegal when it was committed.

Clause 4: Direct Taxes. [No Capitation, or other direct, Tax shall be laid, unless in Proportion to the Census or Enumeration herein before directed to be taken.][6]

A capitation is a tax on a person. A direct tax is a tax paid directly to the government, such as a property tax. This clause was intended to prevent Congress from levying a tax on slaves per person and thereby taxing slavery out of existence.

Clause 5: Export Taxes. No Tax or Duty shall be laid on Articles exported from any State.

Congress may not tax any goods sold from one state to another or from one state to a foreign country. (Congress does have the power to tax goods that are bought from other countries, however.)

Clause 6: Interstate Commerce. No Preference shall be given by any Regulation of Commerce or Revenue to the Ports of one State over those of another: nor shall Vessels bound to, or from, one State, be obliged to enter, clear, or pay Duties in another.

Congress may not treat different ports within the United States differently in terms of taxing and commerce powers. Congress may not give one state's port a legal advantage over the ports of another state.

Clause 7: Treasury Withdrawals. No Money shall be drawn from the Treasury, but in Consequence of Appropriations made by Law; and a regular Statement and Account of the Receipts and Expenditures of all public Money shall be published from time to time.

Federal funds can be spent only as Congress authorizes. This is a significant check on the president's power.

Clause 8: Titles of Nobility. No Title of Nobility shall be granted by the United States: And no Person holding any Office of Profit or Trust under them, shall, without the Consent of the Congress, accept of any present, Emolument, Office, or Title, of any kind whatever, from any King, Prince, or foreign State.

No person in the United States may hold a title of nobility, such as duke or duchess. This clause also discourages bribery of American officials by foreign governments.

Section 10. *Those Powers Denied to the States*

Clause 1: Treaties and Coinage. No State shall enter into any Treaty, Alliance, or Confederation; grant Letters of Marque and Reprisal; coin Money; emit Bills of Credit; make any Thing but gold and silver Coin a Tender in Payment of Debts; pass any Bill of Attainder, ex post facto Law, or Law impairing the Obligation of Contracts, or grant any Title of Nobility.

Prohibiting state laws "impairing the Obligation of Contracts" was intended to protect creditors. (Shays' Rebellion—an attempt to prevent courts from giving effect to creditors' legal actions against debtors—occurred only one year before the Constitution was written.)

Clause 2: Duties and Imposts. No State shall, without the Consent of the Congress, lay any Imposts or Duties on Imports or Exports, except what may be absolutely necessary for executing its inspection Laws; and the net Produce of all Duties and Imposts, laid by any State on Imports or Exports, shall be for the Use of the Treasury of the United States; and all such Laws shall be subject to the Revision and Controul of the Congress.

Only Congress can tax imports. Further, the states cannot tax exports.

Clause 3: War. No State shall, without the Consent of Congress, lay any Duty of Tonnage, keep Troops, or Ships of War in time of Peace, enter into any Agreement or Compact with another State, or with a foreign Power or engage in War, unless actually invaded, or in such imminent Danger as will not admit of delay.

A duty of tonnage is a tax on ships according to their cargo capacity. No states may tax ships according to their cargo unless Congress agrees. Additionally, this clause forbids any state to keep troops or warships during peacetime or to make a compact with another state or foreign nation unless Congress so agrees. A state, in contrast, can maintain a militia, but its use has to be limited to disorders that occur within the state—unless, of course, the militia is called into federal service.

ARTICLE II. *(Executive Branch)*

Section 1. *The Nature and Scope of Presidential Power*

Clause 1: Four-Year Term. The executive Power shall be vested in a President of the United States of America. He shall hold his Office during the Term of four Years, and, together with the Vice President, chosen for the same Term, be elected, as follows.

The president has the power to carry out laws made by Congress, called the executive power. He or she serves in office for a four-year term after election. The Twenty-second Amendment limits the number of times a person may be elected president.

Clause 2: Choosing Electors from Each State. Each State shall appoint, in such Manner as the Legislature thereof may direct, a Number of Electors, equal to the whole Number of Senators and Representatives to which the State may be entitled in the Congress; but no Senator or Representative, or Person holding an Office of Trust or Profit under the United States, shall be appointed an Elector.

---

[6]Modified by the Sixteenth Amendment.

The "Electors" are known more commonly as the "electoral college." The president is elected by electors—that is, representatives chosen by the people—rather than by the people directly.

Clause 3: The Former System of Elections. [The Electors shall meet in their respective States, and vote by Ballot for two Persons, of whom one at least shall not be an Inhabitant of the same State with themselves. And they shall make a List of all the Persons voted for, and of the Number of Votes for each; which List they shall sign and certify, and transmit sealed to the Seat of the Government of the United States, directed to the President of the Senate. The President of the Senate shall, in the Presence of the Senate and House of Representatives, open all the Certificates, and the Votes shall then be counted. The Person having the greatest Number of Votes shall be the President, if such Number be a Majority of the whole Number of Electors appointed; and if there be more than one who have such Majority, and have an equal Number of Votes, then the House of Representatives shall immediately chuse by Ballot one of them for President; and if no Person have a Majority, then from the five highest on the List the said House shall in like Manner chuse the President. But in chusing the President, the Votes shall be taken by States, the Representation from each State having one Vote; A quorum for this Purpose shall consist of a Member or Members from two thirds of the States, and a Majority of all the States shall be necessary to a Choice. In every Case, after the Choice of the President, the Person having the greater Number of Votes of the Electors shall be the Vice President. But if there should remain two or more who have equal Votes, the Senate shall chuse from them by Ballot the Vice President.][7]

The original method of selecting the president and vice president was replaced by the Twelfth Amendment. Apparently, the framers did not anticipate the rise of political parties and the development of primaries and conventions.

Clause 4: The Time of Elections. The Congress may determine the Time of chusing the Electors, and the Day on which they shall give their Votes; which Day shall be the same throughout the United States.

Congress set the Tuesday after the first Monday in November every fourth year as the date for choosing electors. The electors cast their votes on the Monday after the second Wednesday in December of that year.

Clause 5: Qualifications for President. No person except a natural born Citizen, or a Citizen of the United States, at the time of the Adoption of this Constitution, shall be eligible to the Office of President; neither shall any Person be eligible to that Office who shall not have attained to the Age of thirty five Years, and been fourteen Years a Resident within the United States.

The president must be a natural-born citizen, be at least 35 years of age when taking office, and have been a resident within the United States for at least 14 years.

Clause 6: Succession of the Vice President. [In Case of the Removal of the President from Office, or of his Death, Resignation or Inability to discharge the Powers and Duties of the said Office, the same shall devolve on the Vice President, and the Congress may by Law provide for the Case of Removal, Death, Resignation or Inability, both of the President and Vice President, declaring what Officer shall then act as President, and such Officer shall act accordingly, until the Disability be removed, or a President shall be elected.][8]

This section provided for the method by which the vice president was to succeed to the presidency, but its wording is ambiguous. It was replaced by the Twenty-fifth Amendment.

Clause 7: The President's Salary. The President shall, at stated Times, receive for his Services, a Compensation, which shall neither be encreased nor diminished during the Period for which he shall have been elected, and he shall not receive within that Period any other Emolument from the United States, or any of them.

The president maintains the same salary during each four-year term. Moreover, she or he may not receive additional cash payments from the government. Originally set at $25,000 per year, the salary is currently $400,000 a year plus a $50,000 non-taxable expense account.

Clause 8: The Oath of Office. Before he enter on the Execution of his Office, he shall take the following Oath or Affirmation: "I do solemnly swear (or affirm) that I will faithfully execute the Office of President of the United States, and will to the best of my Ability, preserve, protect and defend the Constitution of the United States."

The president is "sworn in" prior to beginning the duties of the office. The taking of the oath of office occurs on January 20, following the November election. The ceremony is called the inauguration. The oath of office is administered by the chief justice of the United States Supreme Court.

Section 2. *Powers of the President*

Clause 1: Commander in Chief. The President shall be Commander in Chief of the Army and Navy of the United States, and of the Militia of the several States, when called into the actual Service of the United States; he may require the Opinion, in writing, of the principal Officer in each of the executive Departments, upon any Subject relating to

[7]Changed by the Twelfth Amendment.
[8]Modified by the Twenty-fifth Amendment.

the Duties of their respective Offices, and he shall have Power to grant Reprieves and Pardons for Offences against the United States, except in Cases of Impeachment.

The armed forces are placed under civilian control because the president is a civilian but still commander in chief of the military. The president may ask for the help of the head of each of the executive departments (thereby creating the Cabinet). The Cabinet members are chosen by the president with the consent of the Senate, but they can be removed without Senate approval.

The president's clemency powers extend only to federal cases. In those cases, he or she may grant a full or conditional pardon, or reduce a prison term or fine.

Clause 2: Treaties and Appointment. He shall have Power, by and with the Advice and Consent of the Senate, to make Treaties, provided two thirds of the Senators present concur; and he shall nominate, and by and with the Advice and Consent of the Senate, shall appoint Ambassadors, other public Ministers and Consuls, Judges of the supreme Court, and all other Officers of the United States, whose Appointments are not herein otherwise provided for, and which shall be established by Law; but the Congress may by Law vest the Appointment of such inferior Officers, as they think proper, in the President alone, in the Courts of Law, or in the Heads of Departments.

Many of the major powers of the president are identified in this clause, including the power to make treaties with foreign governments (with the approval of the Senate by a two-thirds vote) and the power to appoint ambassadors, Supreme Court justices, and other government officials. Most such appointments require Senate approval.

Clause 3: Vacancies. The President shall have Power to fill up all Vacancies that may happen during the Recess of the Senate, by granting Commissions which shall expire at the end of their next Session.

The president has the power to appoint temporary officials to fill vacant federal offices without Senate approval if the Congress is not in session. Such appointments expire automatically at the end of Congress's next term.

Section 3. *Duties of the President*

He shall from time to time give to the Congress Information of the State of the Union, and recommend to their Consideration such Measures as he shall judge necessary and expedient; he may, on extraordinary Occasions, convene both Houses, or either of them, and in Case of Disagreement between them, with Respect to the Time of Adjournment, he may adjourn them to such Time as he shall think proper; he shall receive Ambassadors and other public Ministers; he shall take Care that the Laws be faithfully executed, and shall Commission all the Officers of the United States.

Annually, the president reports on the state of the union to Congress, recommends legislative measures, and proposes a federal budget. The State of the Union speech is a statement not only to Congress but also to the American people. After it is given, the president proposes a federal budget and presents an economic report. At any time, the president may send special messages to Congress while it is in session. The president has the power to call special sessions, to adjourn Congress when its two chambers do not agree on when to adjourn, to receive diplomatic representatives of other governments, and to ensure the proper execution of all federal laws. The president further has the ability to empower federal officers to hold their positions and to perform their duties.

Section 4. *Impeachment*

The President, Vice President and all civil Officers of the United States, shall be removed from Office on Impeachment for, and Conviction of, Treason, Bribery, or other high Crimes and Misdemeanors.

Treason denotes giving aid to the nation's enemies. The phrase high crimes and misdemeanors is usually considered to mean serious abuses of political power. In either case, the president or vice president may be accused by the House (called an impeachment) and then removed from office if convicted by the Senate. (Note that impeachment does not mean removal but rather refers to an accusation of treason or high crimes and misdemeanors.)

ARTICLE III. *(Judicial Branch)*

Section 1. *Judicial Powers, Courts, and Judges*

The judicial Power of the United States, shall be vested in one supreme Court, and in such inferior Courts as the Congress may from time to time ordain and establish. The Judges, both of the supreme and inferior Courts, shall hold their Offices during good Behaviour, and shall, at stated Times, receive for their Services a Compensation, which shall not be diminished during their Continuance in Office.

The Supreme Court is vested with judicial power, as are the lower federal courts that Congress creates. Federal judges serve in their offices for life unless they are impeached and convicted by Congress. The payment of federal judges may not be reduced during their time in office.

Section 2. *Jurisdiction*

Clause 1: Cases under Federal Jurisdiction. The judicial Power shall extend to all Cases, in Law and Equity, arising under this Constitution, the Laws of the United States, and Treaties made, or which shall be made, under their Authority;—to all Cases affecting Ambassadors, other public Ministers and Consuls;—to all Cases of admiralty and maritime Jurisdiction;—to Controversies to which the United States shall be a Party;—to Controversies between two or more States; [—between a State and Citizens of another State;—]⁹ between Citizens of different States;—between Citizens of the same State claiming Lands under Grants of different States, [and between a State, or the Citizens thereof, and foreign States, Citizens or Subjects.]¹⁰

The federal courts take on cases that concern the meaning of the U.S. Constitution, all federal laws, and treaties. They also can take on cases involving citizens of different states and citizens of foreign nations.

Clause 2: Cases for the Supreme Court. In all Cases affecting Ambassadors, other public Ministers and Consuls, and those in which a State shall be a Party, the supreme Court shall have original Jurisdiction. In all the other Cases before mentioned, the supreme Court shall have appellate Jurisdiction, both as to Law and Fact, with such Exceptions, and under such Regulations as the Congress shall make.

In a limited number of situations, the Supreme Court acts as a trial court and has original jurisdiction. These cases involve a representative from another country or involve a state. In all other situations, the cases must first be tried in the lower courts and then can be appealed to the Supreme Court. Congress may, however, make exceptions. Today, the Supreme Court acts as a trial court of first instance on rare occasions.

Clause 3: The Conduct of Trials. The Trial of all Crimes, except in Cases of Impeachment, shall be by Jury; and such Trial shall be held in the State where the said Crimes shall have been committed; but when not committed within any State, the Trial shall be at such Place or Places as the Congress may by Law have directed.

Any person accused of a federal crime is granted the right to a trial by jury in a federal court in that state in which the crime was committed. Trials of impeachment are an exception.

Section 3. *Treason*

Clause 1: The Definition of Treason. Treason against the United States, shall consist only in levying War against them, or, in adhering to their Enemies, giving them Aid and Comfort. No Person shall be convicted of Treason unless on the Testimony of two Witnesses to the same overt Act, or on Confession in open Court.

Treason is the making of war against the United States or giving aid to its enemies.

Clause 2: Punishment. The Congress shall have Power to declare the Punishment of Treason, but no Attainder of Treason shall work Corruption of Blood, or Forfeiture except during the Life of the Person attainted.

Congress has provided that the punishment for treason ranges from a minimum of five years in prison and/or a $10,000 fine to a maximum of death. "No Attainder of Treason shall work Corruption of Blood" prohibits punishment of the traitor's heirs.

ARTICLE IV. *(Relations among the States)*

Section 1. *Full Faith and Credit*

Full Faith and Credit shall be given in each State to the public Acts, Records, and judicial Proceedings of every other State. And the Congress may by general Laws prescribe the Manner in which such Acts, Records and Proceedings shall be proved, and the Effect thereof.

All states are required to respect one another's laws, records, and lawful decisions. There are exceptions, however. A state does not have to enforce another state's criminal code. Nor does it have to recognize another state's grant of a divorce if the person obtaining the divorce did not establish legal residence in the state in which it was given.

Section 2. *Treatment of Citizens*

Clause 1: Privileges and Immunities. The Citizens of each State shall be entitled to all Privileges and Immunities of Citizens in the several States.

A citizen of a state has the same rights and privileges as the citizens of another state in which he or she happens to be.

Clause 2: Extradition. A Person charged in any State with Treason, Felony, or other Crime, who shall flee from Justice, and be found in another State, shall on Demand of the executive Authority of the State from which he fled, be delivered up, to be removed to the State having Jurisdiction of the Crime.

Any person accused of a crime who flees to another state must be returned to the state in which the crime occurred.

Clause 3: Fugitive Slaves. [No Person held to Service or Labour in one State, under the Laws thereof, escaping into another, shall, in Consequence of any Law or Regulation therein, be discharged from such Service or Labour, but shall be delivered up on Claim of the Party to whom such Service or Labour may be due.]¹¹

This clause was struck down by the Thirteenth Amendment, which abolished slavery in 1865.

Section 3. *Admission of States*

Clause 1: The Process. New States may be admitted by the Congress into this Union; but no new State shall be

⁹Modified by the Eleventh Amendment.
¹⁰Modified by the Eleventh Amendment.
¹¹Repealed by the Thirteenth Amendment.

formed or erected within the Jurisdiction of any other State; nor any State be formed by the Junction of two or more States, or Parts of States, without the Consent of the Legislatures of the States concerned as well as of the Congress.

Only Congress has the power to admit new states to the union. No state may be created by taking territory from an existing state unless the state's legislature so consents.

Clause 2: Public Land. The Congress shall have Power to dispose of and make all needful Rules and Regulations respecting the Territory or other Property belonging to the United States; and nothing in this Constitution shall be so construed as to Prejudice any Claims of the United States, or of any particular State.

The federal government has the exclusive right to administer federal government public lands.

Section 4. *Republican Form of Government*

The United States shall guarantee to every State in this Union a Republican Form of Government, and shall protect each of them against Invasion; and on Application of the Legislature, or of the Executive (when the Legislature cannot be convened) against domestic Violence.

Each state is promised a republican form of government— that is, one in which the people elect their representatives. The federal government is bound to protect states against any attack by foreigners or during times of trouble within a state.

ARTICLE V. *(Methods of Amendment)*

The Congress, whenever two thirds of both Houses shall deem it necessary, shall propose Amendments to this Constitution, or on the Application of the Legislatures of two thirds of the several States, shall call a Convention for proposing Amendments, which, in either Case, shall be valid to all Intents and Purposes, as Part of this Constitution, when ratified by the Legislatures of three fourths of the several States, or by Conventions in three fourths thereof, as the one or the other Mode of Ratification may be proposed by the Congress; Provided that no Amendment which may be made prior to the Year One thousand eight hundred and eight shall in any Manner affect the first and fourth Clauses in the Ninth Section of the First Article; and that no State, without its Consent, shall be deprived of its equal Suffrage in the Senate.

Amendments may be proposed in either of two ways: a two-thirds vote of each chamber (Congress) or at the request of two-thirds of the states. Ratification of amendments may be carried out in two ways: by the legislatures of three-fourths of the states or by the voters in three-fourths of the states. No state may be denied equal representation in the Senate.

ARTICLE VI. *(National Supremacy)*

Clause 1: Existing Obligations. All Debts contracted and Engagements entered into, before the Adoption of this Constitution shall be as valid against the United States under this Constitution, as under the Confederation.

During the Revolutionary War and the years of the Confederation, Congress borrowed large sums. This clause pledged that the new federal government would assume those financial obligations.

Clause 2: Supreme Law of the Land. This Constitution, and the Laws of the United States which shall be made in Pursuance thereof; and all Treaties made, or which shall be made, under the Authority of the United States, shall be the supreme Law of the Land; and the Judges in every State shall be bound thereby, any Thing in the Constitution or Laws of any State to the Contrary notwithstanding.

This is typically called the supremacy clause; it declares that federal law takes precedence over all forms of state law. No government at the local or state level may make or enforce any law that conflicts with any provision of the Constitution, acts of Congress, treaties, or other rules and regulations issued by the president and his or her subordinates in the executive branch of the federal government.

Clause 3: Oath of Office. The Senators and Representatives before mentioned, and the Members of the several State Legislatures, and all executive and judicial Officers, both of the United States and of the several States, shall be bound by Oath or Affirmation, to support this Constitution; but no religious Test shall ever be required as a Qualification to any Office or public Trust under the United States.

Every federal and state official must take an oath of office promising to support the U.S. Constitution. Religion may not be used as a qualification to serve in any federal office.

ARTICLE VII. *(Ratification)*

The Ratification of the Conventions of nine States shall be sufficient for the Establishment of this Constitution between the States so ratifying the Same.

Nine states were required to ratify the Constitution. Delaware was the first and New Hampshire the ninth.

Done in Convention by the Unanimous Consent of the States present the Seventeenth Day of September in the Year of our Lord one thousand seven hundred and Eighty seven and of the Independence of the United States of America the Twelfth. In witness whereof we have hereunto subscribed our Names,

Go. WASHINGTON
*Presid't.
and deputy from Virginia*

Attest William Jackson Secretary

Delaware	{ Geo. Read Gunning Bedford jun John Dickinson Richard Bassett Jaco. Broom	New Hampshire	{ John Langdon Nicholas Gilman	
Maryland	{ James McHenry Dan of St. Thos. Jenifer Danl. Carroll	Massachusetts	{ Nathaniel Gorham Rufus King	
Virginia	{ John Blair James Madison Jr.	Connecticut	{ Wm. Saml. Johnson Roger Sherman	
North Carolina	{ Wm. Blount Richd. Dobbs Spaight Hu. Williamson	New York	{ Alexander Hamilton	
South Carolina	{ J. Rutledge Charles Cotesworth Pinckney Charles Pinckney Pierce Butler	New Jersey	{ Wh. Livingston David Brearley Wm. Paterson Jona. Dayton	
Georgia	{ William Few Abr. Baldwin	Pennsylvania	{ B. Franklin Thomas Mifflin Robt. Morris Geo. Clymer Thos. FitzSimons Jared Ingersoll James Wilson Gouv. Morris	

AMENDMENTS TO THE CONSTITUTION OF THE UNITED STATES (The Bill of Rights)[12]

Articles in addition to, and amendment of, the Constitution of the United States of America, proposed by Congress and ratified by the Legislatures of the several states, pursuant to the Fifth Article of the original Constitution.

AMENDMENT I. *(Religion, Speech, Assembly, and Petition)*

Congress shall make no law respecting an establishment of religion, or prohibiting the free exercise thereof; or abridging the freedom of speech, or of the press; or the right of the people peaceably to assemble, and to petition the Government for a redress of grievances.

Congress may not create an official church or enact laws limiting the freedom of religion, speech, the press, assembly, and petition. These guarantees, like the others in the Bill of Rights (the first 10 amendments), are not absolute—each may be exercised only with regard to the rights of other persons.

AMENDMENT II. *(Militia and the Right to Bear Arms)*

A well regulated Militia, being necessary to the security of a free State, the right of the people to keep and bear Arms, shall not be infringed.

To protect itself, each state has the right to maintain a volunteer armed force. States and the federal government regulate the possession and use of firearms by individuals.

AMENDMENT III. *(The Quartering of Soldiers)*

No Soldier shall, in time of peace be quartered in any house, without the consent of the Owner, nor in time of war, but in a manner to be prescribed by law.

Before the Revolutionary War, it had been common British practice to quarter soldiers in colonists' homes. Military troops do not have the power to take over private houses during peacetime.

AMENDMENT IV. *(Searches and Seizures)*

The right of the people to be secure in their persons, houses, papers, and effects, against unreasonable searches and seizures, shall not be violated, and no Warrants shall issue, but upon probable cause, supported by Oath or affirmation, and particularly describing the place to be searched, and the persons or things to be seized.

Here the word warrant means "justification" and refers to a document issued by a magistrate or judge indicating the name, address, and possible offense committed. Anyone asking for the warrant, such as a police officer, must be able to convince the magistrate or judge that an offense probably has been committed.

AMENDMENT V. *(Grand Juries, Self-Incrimination, Double Jeopardy, Due Process, and Eminent Domain)*

No person shall be held to answer for a capital, or otherwise infamous crime, unless on a presentment or indictment of a Grand Jury, except in cases arising in the land or naval forces, or in the Militia, when in actual service in time of War or public danger; nor shall any person be subject for the same offence to be twice put in jeopardy of life or limb; nor shall be compelled in any criminal case to be a witness against himself, nor be deprived of life, liberty, or property, without due process of law; nor shall private property be taken for public use, without just compensation.

There are two types of juries. A grand jury considers physical evidence and the testimony of witnesses and decides whether there is sufficient reason to bring a case to trial. A petit jury hears the case at trial and decides it. "For the same offence to be twice put in jeopardy of life or limb" means to be tried twice for the same crime. A person may not be tried for the same crime twice or forced to give evidence against herself or himself. No person's right to life, liberty, or property may be taken away except by lawful means, called the due process of law. Private property taken for use in public purposes must be paid for by the government.

AMENDMENT VI. *(Criminal Court Procedures)*

In all criminal prosecutions, the accused shall enjoy the right to a speedy and public trial, by an impartial jury of the State and district wherein the crime shall have been committed, which district shall have been previously ascertained by law, and to be informed of the nature and cause of the accusation; to be confronted with the witnesses against him; to have compulsory process for obtaining witnesses in his favor, and to have the Assistance of Counsel for his defence.

Any person accused of a crime has the right to a fair and public trial by a jury in the state in which the crime took place. The charges against that person must be indicated. Any accused person has the right to a lawyer to defend him or her and to question those who testify against him or her, as well as the right to call people to speak in his or her favor at trial.

---

[12]On September 25, 1789, Congress transmitted to the state legislatures 12 proposed amendments, two of which, having to do with congressional representation and congressional pay, were not adopted. The remaining 10 amendments became the Bill of Rights. In 1992, the amendment concerning congressional pay was adopted as the Twenty-seventh Amendment.

AMENDMENT VII. *(Trial by Jury in Civil Cases)*

In Suits at common law, where the value in controversy shall exceed twenty dollars, the right of trial by jury shall be preserved, and no fact tried by jury, shall be otherwise re-examined in any Court of the United States, than according to the rules of the common law.

A jury trial may be requested by either party in a dispute in any case involving more than $20. If both parties agree to a trial by a judge without a jury, the right to a jury trial may be put aside.

AMENDMENT VIII. *(Bail, Cruel and Unusual Punishment)*

Excessive bail shall not be required, nor excessive fines imposed, nor cruel and unusual punishments inflicted.

Bail is that amount of money that a person accused of a crime may be required to deposit with the court as a guaranty that she or he will appear in court when requested. The amount of bail required or the fine imposed as punishment for a crime must be reasonable compared with the seriousness of the crime involved. Any punishment judged to be too harsh or too severe for a crime shall be prohibited.

AMENDMENT IX. *(The Rights Retained by the People)*

The enumeration in the Constitution, of certain rights, shall not be construed to deny or disparage others retained by the people.

Many civil rights that are not explicitly enumerated in the Constitution are still held by the people.

AMENDMENT X. *(Reserved Powers of the States)*

The powers not delegated to the United States by the Constitution, nor prohibited by it to the States, are reserved to the States respectively, or to the people.

Those powers not delegated by the Constitution to the federal government or expressly denied to the states belong to the states and to the people. This amendment in essence allows the states to pass laws under their "police powers."

AMENDMENT XI. *(Ratified on February 7, 1795—Suits against States)*

The Judicial power of the United States shall not be construed to extend to any suit in law or equity, commenced or prosecuted against one of the United States by Citizens of another State, or by Citizens or Subjects of any Foreign State.

This amendment has been interpreted to mean that a state cannot be sued in federal court by one of its own citizens, by a citizen of another state, or by a foreign country.

AMENDMENT XII. *(Ratified on June 15, 1804— Election of the President)*

The Electors shall meet in their respective states, and vote by ballot for President and Vice-President, one of whom, at least, shall not be an inhabitant of the same State with themselves; they shall name in their ballots the person voted for as President, and in distinct ballots the person voted for as Vice-President, and they shall make distinct lists of all persons voted for as President, and of all persons voted for as Vice-President, and of the number of votes for each, which lists they shall sign and certify, and transmit sealed to the seat of the government of the United States, directed to the President of the Senate;—The President of the Senate shall, in the presence of the Senate and House of Representatives, open all the certificates and the votes shall then be counted;—The person having the greatest number of votes for President, shall be the President, if such number be a majority of the whole number of Electors appointed; and if no person have such majority, then from the persons having the highest numbers not exceeding three on the list of those voted for as President, the House of Representatives shall choose immediately, by ballot, the President. But in choosing the President, the votes shall be taken by States, the representation from each State having one vote; a quorum for this purpose shall consist of a member or members from two-thirds of the States, and a majority of all States shall be necessary to a choice. [And if the House of Representatives shall not choose a President whenever the right of choice shall devolve upon them, before the fourth day of March next following, then the Vice-President shall act as President, as in the case of the death or other constitutional disability of the President.][13]— The person having the greatest number of votes as Vice-President, shall be the Vice-President, if such number be a majority of the whole number of Electors appointed, and if no person have a majority, then from the two highest numbers on the list, the Senate shall choose the Vice-President; a quorum for the purpose shall consist of two-thirds of the whole number of Senators, and a majority of the whole number shall be necessary to a choice. But no person constitutionally ineligible to the office of President shall be eligible to that of Vice-President of the United States.

The original procedure set out for the election of president and vice president in Article II, Section 1, resulted in a tie in 1800 between Thomas Jefferson and Aaron Burr. It was not until the next year that the House of Representatives chose Jefferson to be president. This amendment changed the procedure by providing for separate ballots for president and vice president.

---

[13]Changed by the Twentieth Amendment.

AMENDMENT XIII. *(Ratified on December 6, 1865— Prohibition of Slavery)*

Section 1.

Neither slavery nor involuntary servitude, except as a punishment for crime whereof the party shall have been duly convicted, shall exist within the United States, or any place subject to their jurisdiction.

Some slaves had been freed during the Civil War. This amendment freed the others and abolished slavery.

Section 2.

Congress shall have power to enforce this article by appropriate legislation.

AMENDMENT XIV. *(Ratified on July 9, 1868—Citizenship, Due Process, and Equal Protection of the Laws)*

Section 1.

All persons born or naturalized in the United States, and subject to the jurisdiction thereof, are citizens of the United States and of the State wherein they reside. No State shall make or enforce any law which shall abridge the privileges or immunities of citizens of the United States; nor shall any State deprive any person of life, liberty, or property, without due process of law; nor deny to any person within its jurisdiction the equal protection of the laws.

Under this provision, states cannot make or enforce laws that take away rights given to all citizens by the federal government. States cannot act unfairly or arbitrarily toward, or discriminate against, any person.

Section 2.

Representatives shall be apportioned among the several States according to their respective numbers, counting the whole number of persons in each State, excluding Indians not taxed. But when the right to vote at any election for the choice of electors for President and Vice President of the United States, Representatives in Congress, the Executive and Judicial officers of a State, or the members of the Legislature thereof, is denied to any of the male inhabitants of such State, being [twenty-one][14] years of age, and citizens of the United States, or in any way abridged, except for participation in rebellion, or other crime, the basis of representation therein shall be reduced in the proportion which the number of such male citizens shall bear to the whole number of male citizens twenty-one years of age in such State.

Section 3.

No person shall be a Senator or Representative in Congress, or elector of President and Vice President, or hold any office, civil or military, under the United States, or under any State, who having previously taken an oath, as a member of Congress, or as an officer of the United States, or as a member of any State legislature, or as an executive or judicial officer of any State, to support the Constitution of the United States, shall have engaged in insurrection or rebellion against the same, or given aid or comfort to the enemies thereof. But Congress may by a vote of two-thirds of each House, remove such disability.

This provision forbade former state or federal government officials who had acted in support of the Confederacy during the Civil War to hold office again. It limited the president's power to pardon those persons. Congress removed this "disability" in 1898.

Section 4.

The validity of the public debt of the United States, authorized by law, including debts incurred for payment of pensions and bounties for services in suppressing insurrection or rebellion, shall not be questioned. But neither the United States nor any State shall assume or pay any debt or obligation incurred in aid of insurrection or rebellion against the United States, or any claim for the loss or emancipation of any slave, but all such debts, obligations and claims shall be held illegal and void.

Section 5.

The Congress shall have power to enforce, by appropriate legislation, the provisions of this article.

AMENDMENT XV. *(Ratified on February 3, 1870— The Right to Vote)*

Section 1.

The right of citizens of the United States to vote shall not be denied or abridged by the United States or by any State on account of race, color, or previous condition of servitude.

No citizen can be refused the right to vote simply because of race or color or because that person was once a slave.

Section 2.

The Congress shall have power to enforce this article by appropriate legislation.

AMENDMENT XVI. *(Ratified on February 3, 1913— Income Taxes)*

The Congress shall have power to lay and collect taxes on incomes, from whatever source derived, without apportionment among the several States, and without regard to any census or enumeration.

This amendment allows Congress to tax income without sharing the revenue so obtained with the states according to their population.

[14]Changed by the Twenty-sixth Amendment.

AMENDMENT XVII. *(Ratified on April 8, 1913—The Popular Election of Senators)*

Section 1.

The Senate of the United States shall be composed of two Senators from each State, elected by the people thereof, for six years; and each Senator shall have one vote. The electors in each State shall have the qualifications requisite for electors of the most numerous branch of the State legislatures.

Section 2.

When vacancies happen in the representation of any State in the Senate, the executive authority of such State shall issue writs of election to fill such vacancies: *Provided,* That the legislature of any State may empower the executive thereof to make temporary appointments until the people fill the vacancies by election as the legislature may direct.

Section 3.

This amendment shall not be so construed as to affect the election or term of any Senator chosen before it becomes valid as part of the Constitution.

This amendment modified portions of Article I, Section 3, that related to election of senators. Senators are now elected by the voters in each state directly. When a vacancy occurs, either the state may fill the vacancy by a special election, or the governor of the state involved may appoint someone to fill the seat until the next election.

AMENDMENT XVIII. *(Ratified on January 16, 1919—Prohibition)*

Section 1.

After one year from the ratification of this article the manufacture, sale, or transportation of intoxicating liquors within, the importation thereof into, or the exportation thereof from the United States and all territory subject to the jurisdiction thereof for beverage purposes is hereby prohibited.

Section 2.

The Congress and the several States shall have concurrent power to enforce this article by appropriate legislation.

Section 3.

This article shall be inoperative unless it shall have been ratified as an amendment to the Constitution by the legislatures of the several States, as provided in the Constitution, within seven years from the date of the submission hereof to the States by the Congress.[15]

This amendment made it illegal to manufacture, sell, and transport alcoholic beverages in the United States. It was repealed by the Twenty-first Amendment.

AMENDMENT XIX. *(Ratified on August 18, 1920—Women's Right to Vote)*

Section 1.

The right of citizens of the United States to vote shall not be denied or abridged by the United States or by any State on account of sex.

Section 2.

Congress shall have power to enforce this article by appropriate legislation.

Women were given the right to vote by this amendment, and Congress was given the power to enforce this right.

AMENDMENT XX. *(Ratified on January 23, 1933—The Lame Duck Amendment)*

Section 1.

The terms of the President and Vice President shall end at noon on the 20th day of January, and the terms of Senators and Representatives at noon on the 3d day of January, of the years in which such terms would have ended if this article had not been ratified; and the terms of their successors shall then begin.

This amendment modified Article I, Section 4, Clause 2, and other provisions relating to the president in the Twelfth Amendment. The taking of the oath of office was moved from March 4 to January 20.

Section 2.

The Congress shall assemble at least once in every year, and such meeting shall begin at noon on the 3rd day of January, unless they shall by law appoint a different day.

Congress changed the beginning of its term to January 3. The reason the Twentieth Amendment is called the Lame Duck Amendment is that it shortens the time between when a member of Congress is defeated for re-election and when he or she leaves office.

Section 3.

If, at the time fixed for the beginning of the term of the President, the President elect shall have died, the Vice President elect shall become President. If a President shall not have been chosen before the time fixed for the beginning of his term, or if the President elect shall have failed to qualify, then the Vice President elect shall act as President until a President shall have qualified; and the Congress may by law provide for the case wherein neither a President elect nor a Vice President elect shall have qualified, declaring who shall then act as President, or the manner in which one who is to act shall be selected, and such person shall act accordingly until a President or Vice President shall have qualified.

This part of the amendment deals with problem areas left ambiguous by Article II and the Twelfth Amendment. If

---

[15]The Eighteenth Amendment was repealed by the Twenty-first Amendment.

the president dies before January 20 or fails to qualify for office, the presidency is to be filled as described in this section.

Section 4.

The Congress may by law provide for the case of the death of any of the persons from whom the House of Representatives may choose a President whenever the rights of choice shall have devolved upon them, and for the case of the death of any of the persons from whom the Senate may choose a Vice President whenever the right of choice shall have devolved upon them.

Congress has never created legislation pursuant to this section.

Section 5.

Sections 1 and 2 shall take effect on the 15th day of October following the ratification of this article.

Section 6.

This article shall be inoperative unless it shall have been ratified as an amendment to the Constitution by the legislatures of three-fourths of the several States within seven years from the date of its submission.

AMENDMENT XXI. *(Ratified on December 5, 1933—The Repeal of Prohibition)*

Section 1.

The eighteenth article of amendment to the Constitution of the United States is hereby repealed.

Section 2.

The transportation or importation into any State, Territory, or possession of the United States for delivery or use therein of intoxicating liquors, in violation of the laws thereof, is hereby prohibited.

Section 3.

This article shall be inoperative unless it shall have been ratified as an amendment to the Constitution by conventions in the several States, as provided in the Constitution, within seven years from the date of the submission hereof to the States by the Congress.

The amendment repealed the Eighteenth Amendment but did not make alcoholic beverages legal everywhere. Rather, they remained illegal in any state that so designated them. Many such "dry" states existed for a number of years after 1933. Today, there are still "dry" counties within the United States, in which the sale of alcoholic beverages is illegal.

AMENDMENT XXII. *(Ratified on February 27, 1951—Limitation of Presidential Terms)*

Section 1.

No person shall be elected to the office of the President more than twice, and no person who has held the office of President, or acted as President, for more than two years of a term to which some other person was elected President shall be elected to the office of President more than once. But this Article shall not apply to any person holding the office of President when this Article was proposed by the Congress, and shall not prevent any person who may be holding the office of President, or acting as President, during the term within which this Article becomes operative from holding the office of President or acting as President during the remainder of such term.

Section 2.

This article shall be inoperative unless it shall have been ratified as an amendment to the Constitution by the legislatures of three-fourths of the several States within seven years from the date of its submission to the States by the Congress.

No president may serve more than two elected terms. If, however, a president has succeeded to the office after the halfway point of a term in which another president was originally elected, then that president may serve for more than eight years, but not to exceed 10 years.

AMENDMENT XXIII. *(Ratified on March 29, 1961—Presidential Electors for the District of Columbia)*

Section 1.

The District constituting the seat of Government of the United States shall appoint in such manner as the Congress may direct:

A number of electors of President and Vice President equal to the whole number of Senators and Representatives in Congress to which the District would be entitled if it were a State, but in no event more than the least populous State; they shall be in addition to those appointed by the States, but they shall be considered, for the purposes of the election of President and Vice President, to be electors appointed by a State; and they shall meet in the District and perform such duties as provided by the twelfth article of amendment.

Section 2.

The Congress shall have power to enforce this article by appropriate legislation.

Citizens living in the District of Columbia have the right to vote in elections for president and vice president. The District of Columbia has three presidential electors, whereas before this amendment it had none.

AMENDMENT XXIV. *(Ratified on January 23, 1964—The Anti-Poll Tax Amendment)*

Section 1.

The right of citizens of the United States to vote in any primary or other election for President or Vice President, for electors for President or Vice President, or for Senator or Representative in Congress, shall not be denied or abridged by the United States, or any State by reason of failure to pay any poll tax or other tax.

Section 2.

The Congress shall have power to enforce this article by appropriate legislation.

No government shall require a person to pay a poll tax to vote in any federal election.

AMENDMENT XXV. *(Ratified on February 10, 1967—Presidential Disability and Vice Presidential Vacancies)*

Section 1.

In case of the removal of the President from office or of his death or resignation, the Vice President shall become President.

Whenever a president dies or resigns from office, the vice president becomes president.

Section 2.

Whenever there is a vacancy in the office of the Vice President, the President shall nominate a Vice President who shall take office upon confirmation by a majority vote of both Houses of Congress.

Whenever the office of the vice presidency becomes vacant, the president may appoint someone to fill this office, provided Congress consents.

Section 3.

Whenever the President transmits to the President pro tempore of the Senate and the Speaker of the House of Representatives his written declaration that he is unable to discharge the powers and duties of his office, and until he transmits to them a written declaration to the contrary, such powers and duties shall be discharged by the Vice President as Acting President.

Whenever the president believes she or he is unable to carry out the duties of the office, she or he shall so indicate to Congress in writing. The vice president then acts as president until the president declares that she or he is again able to carry out the duties of the office.

Section 4.

Whenever the Vice President and a majority of either the principal officers of the executive departments or of such other body as Congress may by law provide, transmit to the President pro tempore of the Senate and the Speaker of the House of Representatives their written declaration that the President is unable to discharge the powers and duties of his office, the Vice President shall immediately assume the powers and duties of the office as Acting President.

Thereafter, when the President transmits to the President pro tempore of the Senate and the Speaker of the House of Representatives his written declaration that no inability exists, he shall resume the powers and duties of his office unless the Vice President and a majority of either the principal officers of the executive department or of such other body as Congress may by law provide, transmit within four days to the President pro tempore of the Senate and the Speaker of the House of Representatives their written declaration that the President is unable to discharge the powers and duties of his office. Thereupon Congress shall decide the issue, assembling within forty-eight hours for that purpose if not in session. If the Congress, within twenty-one days after receipt of the latter written declaration, or, if Congress is not in session, within twenty-one days after Congress is required to assemble, determines by two-thirds vote of both Houses that the President is unable to discharge the powers and duties of his office, the Vice President shall continue to discharge the same as Acting President; otherwise, the President shall resume the powers and duties of his office.

Whenever the vice president and a majority of the members of the cabinet believe that the president cannot carry out her or his duties, they shall so indicate in writing to Congress. The vice president shall then act as president. When the president believes that she or he is able to carry out her or his duties again, she or he shall so indicate to the Congress. However, if the vice president and a majority of the cabinet do not agree, Congress must decide by a two-thirds vote within three weeks who shall act as president.

AMENDMENT XXVI. *(Ratified on July 1, 1971—The 18-Year-Old Vote)*

Section 1.

The right of citizens of the United States, who are eighteen years of age or older, to vote shall not be denied or abridged by the United States or by any State on account of age.

No one over 18 years of age can be denied the right to vote in federal or state elections by virtue of age.

Section 2.

The Congress shall have power to enforce this article by appropriate legislation.

AMENDMENT XXVII. *(Ratified on May 7, 1992—Congressional Pay)*

No law, varying the compensation for the services of the Senators and Representatives, shall take effect, until an election of representatives shall have intervened.

This amendment allows the voters to have some control over increases in salaries for congressional members. Originally submitted to the states for ratification in 1789, it was not ratified until 203 years later, in 1992.

President George W. Bush addresses
the National Governors Association
in the State Dining Room of the White
House. Why do governors want to meet
with the president? (Denis Brack/Pool/
epa/CORBIS)

FEDERALISM

Why did the founders think it important to divide power between the national government and the states?

Is a federal system flexible enough to address the problems of the 21st century?

How can a federal system protect local decision making and subcultures?

CHAPTER CONTENTS

Making a DIFFERENCE

LEARNING FROM EACH OTHER

Have you ever moved to a new city or town? It's a challenge to locate the goods and services you need. How do you activate your utilities or enroll yourself or your children in school? If you attend school out of state, you may wonder if you are eligible to vote and, if you are, how do you register? Or, if you wish to vote by absentee ballot in your hometown, how do you get one? Federalism is responsible for many of the differences in the answers to these questions and countless others that exist across cities and states.

The nature of power held by national, state, and local governments has changed over time. State governments, rather than the federal government, increasingly have been asked to solve the problems of their citizens' education, health care, clean air, and safe streets, to name a few. How do states accomplish these tasks? Do they decide independently, or can they work cooperatively to learn from each other how best to solve policy problems?

One way states can cope with these challenges is through associations and organizations designed to share policy ideas and provide members with support. For example, the State Legislative Leaders Foundation hosts educational programs for key state legislators (e.g., Speakers of the House, committee chairs, majority leaders) so that leaders can learn from experts and each other. Other examples are mayors' groups (The United States Confer-

THE UNITED STATES IS, as the name implies, a union of states. Unlike many other nations, the national government does not have all of the authority in the system; rights and powers are reserved to the states by the Tenth Amendment. But the situation is even more complicated than having just state governments and the national government: there are almost 89,000 separate governmental units in this nation, as you can see in Table 3–1.

Visitors from France or Spain are often awestruck by the complexity of our system of government. Consider that a criminal action can be defined by state law, national law, or both. Thus, a criminal suspect can be prosecuted in the state court system or in the federal court system (or both). Think about such a simple matter as getting a driver's license. Each state has separate requirements for the driving test, the written test, the number of years between renewals, and the cost for the license. In 2005, Congress passed the REAL ID Act requiring states to include a specified set of information on the license so that it can be used as an identity card for travel, but the Act was opposed by several states that insisted on maintaining their own requirements. If the licenses issued by those states do not meet the new requirements by 2011, the IDs will not be accepted at airports for travel.

Relations between central governments and local units are structured in various ways. *Federalism* is one of these ways. Understanding **federalism** and how it differs from other forms of government is important in understanding the American political system. Many political issues today are shaped by the policies of the different states, as noted in the *Making a Difference* box. The impact of policies on the individual would be substantially different if we did not have a federal form of government in which governmental authority is divided between the central government and various subunits.

Federalism
A system of government in which power is divided by a written constitution between a central government and regional or subdivisional governments. Each level must have some domain in which its policies are dominant and some genuine constitutional guarantee of its authority.

ence of Mayors; the National Conference of Democratic Mayors; the Republican Mayors and Local Officials), governors' associations (National Governors Association), and groups for state government officials (Council of State Governments).[a] These organizations provide networking opportunities for state and local officials to learn from each other.[b]

This sharing of experiences has led to *policy innovation and diffusion*.[c] *Policy entrepreneurs* find new solutions to problems. States and localities adopt these policies, adapt them to their needs, and share information and ideas.[d] This diffusion of public policy occurs in areas as diverse as health care, disability accessibility, education, and resource management, just to name a few.

[a]http://usmayors.org, www.ncdm.org, www.nga.org, www.csg.org

[b]For example, see Jill Clark and Thomas H. Little, "National Organizations as Sources of Information for State Legislative Leaders," *State and Local Government Review*, Volume 34 (1), Winter 2002, pp. 38–45; and T. Heikkila and A. Gerlak, "The Formation of Large-scale Collaborative Resource Management Institutions: Clarifying the Roles of Stakeholders, Science, and Institutions," *Policy Studies Journal*, Volume 33 (4), pp. 583–612.

[c]For example, see John W. Kingdon, *Agenda, Alternative, and Public Policies* (Boston: Little, Brown, and Co., 1984); M. Mintrom, "Policy Entrepreneurs and the Diffusion of Innovation," *American Journal of Political Science*, Volume 41 (3), p. 738; and M. Mintrom and S. Vergari, "Policy Networks and Innovation Diffusion: The Case of State Education Reforms," *Journal of Politics*, Volume 60 (1), February 1998, p. 126.

[d]F. Meyer and R. Baker, "An Overview of State Policy Problems," *Policy Studies Review*, Volume 11 (1), Spring 1992, pp. 75–90.

TABLE 3–1 Governmental Units in the United States

With almost 89,000 separate governmental units in the United States today, it is no wonder that intergovernmental relations in the U.S. are so complicated. Actually, the number of school districts has decreased over time, but the number of special districts created for single purposes, such as flood control, has increased from only about 8,000 during World War II to more than 36,000 today.

Federal government	1
State governments	50
Local governments	88,525
Counties	3,034
Municipalities (mainly cities or towns)	19,429
Townships (less extensive powers)	16,504
Special districts (water, sewer, and so on)	36,052
School districts	13,506
TOTAL	88,576

Source: U.S. Census Bureau.

THREE SYSTEMS OF GOVERNMENT

There are more than 200 independent nations in the world today. Each of these nations has its own system of government. Generally, though, we can describe how nations structure relations between central governments and local units in terms of three models: (1) the unitary system, (2) the confederal system, and (3) the federal system. The most popular, both historically and today, is the unitary system.

A UNITARY SYSTEM

Unitary System
A centralized governmental system in which local or subdivisional governments exercise only those powers given to them by the central government.

A **unitary system** of government is the easiest to define. Unitary systems allow ultimate governmental authority to rest in the hands of the national, or central, government. Consider a typical unitary system—France. There are regions, departments, and municipalities (communes) in France. The regions, departments, and communes have elected and appointed officials. So far, the French system appears to be very similar to the U.S. system, but the similarity is only superficial. Under the unitary French system, the decisions of the lower levels of government can be overruled by the national government. The national government can also cut off the funding of many local government activities. Moreover, in a unitary system such as that in France, all questions of education, police, the use of land, and welfare are handled by the national government. Britain, Egypt, Ghana, Israel, Japan, the Philippines, and Sweden—in fact, the majority of countries today—have unitary systems of government.[1]

A CONFEDERAL SYSTEM

Confederal System
A system consisting of a league of independent states, each having essentially sovereign powers. The central government created by such a league has only limited powers over the states.

You were introduced to the elements of a **confederal system** of government in Chapter 2, when we examined the Articles of Confederation. A *confederation* is the opposite of a unitary governing system. It is a league of independent states in which a central government or administration handles only those matters of common concern expressly

THIS MASSACHUSETTS RESIDENT is demonstrating in favor of legally sanctioned same-sex marriages. Under the U.S. federal system of government, the states can regulate certain aspects of the lives of their residents, such as marriage. Is there a way to ban the legality of same-sex marriages in *all* states? (Darren McCollester/ Getty Images)

---

[1]Recent legislation has altered somewhat the unitary character of the French political system. In Britain, the unitary nature of the government has been modified by the creation of the Scottish Parliament.

delegated to it by the member states. The central government has no ability to make laws directly applicable to member states unless the members explicitly support such laws. The United States under the Articles of Confederation was a confederal system.

Few, if any, confederations of this kind exist. One possible exception is the European Union, a league of countries that is developing unifying institutions, such as a common currency. Nations have also formed organizations with one another for limited purposes, such as military or peacekeeping cooperation. Examples are the North Atlantic Treaty Organization (NATO) and the United Nations. These organizations, however, are not true confederations.

A FEDERAL SYSTEM

The federal system lies between the unitary and confederal forms of government. As mentioned in Chapter 2, in a *federal system*, authority is divided, usually by a written constitution, between a central government and regional, or subdivisional, governments (often called *constituent governments*). The central government and the constituent governments both act directly on the people through laws and through the actions of elected and appointed governmental officials. Within each government's sphere of authority, each is supreme, in theory. Thus, a federal system differs sharply from a unitary one, in which the central government is supreme and the constituent governments derive their authority from it. Australia, Brazil, Canada, Germany, India, and Mexico are other examples of nations with federal systems. (See Figure 3–1 for a comparison of the three systems.)

WHY FEDERALISM?

Why did the United States develop in a federal direction? We look here at that question, as well as at some of the arguments for and against a federal form of government. Remember that the delegates at the Constitutional Convention were often divided over how much power the national government would have over their respective states.

A PRACTICAL CONSTITUTIONAL SOLUTION

As you saw in Chapter 2, the historical basis of our federal system was laid down in Philadelphia at the Constitutional Convention, where advocates of a strong national government opposed states' rights advocates. This dichotomy continued through to the ratifying conventions in the several states. The resulting federal system was a compromise.[2] The supporters of the new Constitution were political pragmatists—they realized that without a federal arrangement, the new Constitution would not be ratified. The appeal of federalism was that it retained state traditions and local power while establishing a strong national government capable of handling common problems.

Even if the colonial leaders had agreed on the desirability of a unitary system, size and regional isolation would have made such a system difficult operationally. At the time of the Constitutional Convention, the 13 colonies taken together were much larger geographically than England or France. Slow travel and communication, combined with geographic spread, contributed to the isolation of many regions within the colonies. It could take several weeks for all of the colonies to be informed about a particular political decision.

DID YOU KNOW?

That in Florida, Michigan, Mississippi, North Carolina, North Dakota, Virginia, and West Virginia, male-female unmarried cohabitation is against the law and punishable by a short jail term, a fine of up to $500, or both?

DID YOU KNOW?

That under Article I, Section 10, of the Constitution, no state is allowed to enter into any treaty, alliance, or confederation?

---

[2]For a contemporary interpretation of this compromise and how the division of power between the national government and the states has changed, see Edward A. Purcell, *Originalism, Federalism and the American Constitutional Enterprise: A Historical Inquiry* (New Haven, CT: Yale University Press, 2007).

FIGURE 3–1 The Flow of Power in Three Systems of Government

In a unitary system, power flows from the central government to the local and state governments. In a confederal system, power flows in the opposite direction—from the state governments to the central government. In a federal system, the flow of power, in principle, goes both ways.

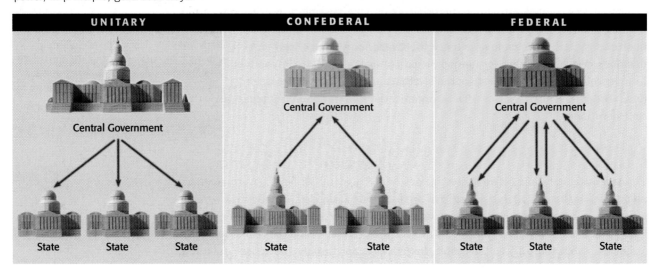

That state governments in the United States typically are unitary governments—that is, most local governments are mere creatures of the states?

Given the size of the United States, even in the 18th century, a federal form of government allows many functions to be delegated by the central government to the states or provinces. The lower levels of government that accept these responsibilities thereby can become the focus of political dissatisfaction rather than the national authorities. Second, even with modern transportation and communications systems, the large area or population of some nations makes it impractical to locate all political authority in one place. Finally, federalism brings government closer to the people. It allows more direct access to, and influence on, government agencies and policies, rather than leaving the population restive and dissatisfied with a remote, faceless, all-powerful central authority.

Benefits for the United States. In the United States, federalism historically has yielded many benefits. State governments long have been a training ground for future national leaders. Many presidents made their political mark as state governors. The states have been testing grounds for new government initiatives. As United States Supreme Court Justice Louis Brandeis once observed:

> It is one of the happy incidents of the federal system that a single courageous state may, if its citizens choose, serve as a laboratory and try novel social and economic experiments without risk to the rest of the country.[3]

Examples of programs pioneered at the state level include unemployment compensation, which began in Wisconsin, and air-pollution control, which was initiated in California. Statewide health-care plans have been pioneered in Hawaii and Massachusetts. Today, states are experimenting with policies ranging from education reforms to environmental policies to homeland security defense strategies. Since the passage of the 1996 welfare reform legislation—which gave more control over welfare programs to state governments—states also have been experimenting with different methods of delivering welfare assistance.

[3]*New State Ice Co. v. Liebmann*, 285 U.S. 262 (1932).

Allowance for Many Political Subcultures. The American way of life always has been characterized by many political subcultures, which divide along the lines of race and ethnic origin, region, wealth, education, and, more recently, degree of religious fundamentalism and sexual preference. At the time of the writing of the Constitution, the diversity of the 13 "states" was seen as an obstacle to the survival of the nation. How could the large, rural, slaveholding states ever coexist with states where slavery was illegal? What would prevent a coalition of the larger states from imposing unfair laws on smaller states and minority groups? In *Federalist Paper* No. 51 (see Appendix B), Madison argued that adopting a federal system would protect the people from the absolute power of the national government and the will of an unjust majority. He put it this way:

> In the compound republic of America, the power surrendered by the people is first divided between two distinct governments, and then the portion allotted to each subdivide among distinct and separate departments. Hence a double security arises to the rights of the people. The different governments will control each other, at the same time that each will be controlled by itself.

Had the United States developed into a unitary system, various political subcultures certainly would have been less able to influence government behavior than they have been, and continue to be, in our federal system.

Political scientist Daniel Elazar has claimed that one of federalism's greatest virtues is that it encourages the development of distinct political subcultures. These political subcultures reflect differing needs and desires for government, which vary from region to region. Federalism, he argues, allows for "a unique combination of governmental strength, political flexibility, and individual liberty."[4] The existence of political subcultures allows a wider variety of factions to influence government. As a result, political subcultures have proved instrumental in driving reform even at the national level.

ARGUMENTS AGAINST FEDERALISM

Not everyone thinks federalism is such a good idea. Some see it as a way for powerful state and local interests to block progress and impede national plans. Smaller political units are more likely to be dominated by a single political group, and the dominant groups in some cities and states have resisted implementing equal rights for minority groups. (This was essentially the argument that James Madison put forth in *Federalist Paper* No. 10, which you can read in Appendix B of this text.) Some argue, however, that the dominant factions in other states have been more progressive than the national government in many areas, such as the environment.

Critics of federalism also argue that too many Americans suffer as a result of the inequalities across the states. Individual states differ markedly in educational spending and achievement, crime and crime prevention, and even the safety of their buildings. Not surprisingly, these critics argue for increased federal legislation and oversight. This might involve creating national educational standards, national building code standards, national expenditure minimums for crime control, and so on.

Others see dangers in the expansion of national powers at the expense of the states. President Ronald Reagan (served 1981–1989) said, "The Founding Fathers saw the federalist system as constructed something like a masonry wall. The States are the bricks,

[4]Daniel Elazar, *American Federalism: A View from the States,* 2nd ed. (New York: Crowell, 1972).

the national government is the mortar. . . . Unfortunately, over the years, many people have increasingly come to believe that Washington is the whole wall."[5]

THE CONSTITUTIONAL BASIS FOR AMERICAN FEDERALISM

The term *federal system* cannot be found in the U.S. Constitution. Nor is it possible to find a systematic division of governmental authority between the national and state governments in that document. Rather, the Constitution sets out different types of powers. These powers can be classified as (1) the powers of the national government, (2) the powers of the states, and (3) prohibited powers. The Constitution also makes it clear that if a state or local law conflicts with a national law, the national law will prevail.

POWERS OF THE NATIONAL GOVERNMENT

The powers delegated to the national government include both expressed and implied powers, as well as the special category of inherent powers. Most of the powers expressly delegated to the national government are found in Article I, Section 8, of the Constitution. These enumerated powers include coining money, setting standards for weights and measures, making uniform naturalization laws, admitting new states, establishing post offices, and declaring war. Another important enumerated power is the power to regulate commerce among the states—a topic we deal with later in this chapter.

----

[5]Text of the address by the president to the National Conference of State Legislatures, Atlanta, Georgia (Washington, DC: The White House, Office of the Press Secretary, July 30, 1981), as quoted in Edward Millican, *One United People: The Federalist Papers and the National Idea* (Lexington: The University Press of Kentucky, 1990).

The Necessary and Proper Clause. The implied powers of the national government are also based on Article I, Section 8, which states that Congress shall have the power

> [t]o make all Laws which shall be necessary and proper for carrying into Execution the foregoing Powers, and all other Powers vested by this Constitution in the Government of the United States, or in any Department or Officer thereof.

This clause is sometimes called the **elastic clause**, or the **necessary and proper clause**, because it provides flexibility to the U.S. constitutional system. It gives Congress all of those powers that can be reasonably inferred but that are not expressly stated in the brief wording of the Constitution. The clause was first used in the Supreme Court decision of *McCulloch v. Maryland*[6] (discussed later in this chapter) to develop the concept of implied powers. Through this concept, the national government has succeeded in strengthening the scope of its authority to meet the numerous problems that the framers of the Constitution did not, and could not, anticipate.

Inherent Powers. A special category of national powers that is not implied by the necessary and proper clause consists of what have been labeled as the inherent powers of the national government. These powers derive from the fact that the United States is a sovereign power among nations, and so its national government must be the only government that deals with other nations. Under international law, it is assumed that all nation-states, regardless of their size or power, have an *inherent* right to ensure their own survival. To do this, each nation must have the ability to act in its own interest among and with the community of nations—by, for instance, making treaties, waging war, seeking trade, and acquiring territory. In 2006, many Americans were outraged to learn that the federal government had considered allowing a Middle East-based company to take over the contracts for operating several American ports. Such an action would have been an exercise of the federal government's inherent powers. To learn more about this issue, see this chapter's *Beyond Our Borders* feature.

Note that no specific clause in the Constitution says anything about the acquisition of additional land. Nonetheless, through the federal government's inherent powers, we made the Louisiana Purchase in 1803 and then went on to acquire Florida, Texas, Oregon, Alaska, Hawaii, and other lands. The United States grew from a mere 13 states to 50 states, plus several "territories."

The national government has these inherent powers whether or not they have been enumerated in the Constitution. Some constitutional scholars categorize inherent powers as a third type of power, completely distinct from the delegated powers (both expressed and implied) of the national government.

POWERS OF THE STATE GOVERNMENTS

The Tenth Amendment states that the powers not delegated to the United States by the Constitution, nor prohibited by it to the states, are reserved to the states, or to the people. These are the reserved powers that the national government cannot deny to the states. Because these powers are not expressly listed—and because they are not limited to powers that are expressly listed—there is sometimes a question as to whether a certain power is delegated to the national government or reserved to the states. State powers have been held to include each state's right to regulate commerce within its borders and to provide for a state militia. States also have the reserved power to make laws on all matters not prohibited to the states by the U.S. Constitution or state constitutions

Elastic Clause, or Necessary and Proper Clause
The clause in Article I, Section 8, that grants Congress the power to do whatever is necessary to execute its specifically delegated powers.

---

[6]4 Wheaton 316 (1819).

and not expressly, or by implication, delegated to the national government. Furthermore, the states have **police power**—the authority to legislate for the protection of the health, morals, safety, and welfare of the people. Their police power enables states to pass laws governing such activities as crimes, marriage, contracts, education, intrastate transportation, and land use.

The ambiguity of the Tenth Amendment has allowed the reserved powers of the states to be defined differently at different times in our history. When there is widespread support for increased regulation by the national government, the Tenth Amendment tends to recede into the background. When the tide turns the other way (in favor of states' rights), the Tenth Amendment is resurrected to justify arguments supporting increased states' rights.

> **Police Power**
> The authority to legislate for the protection of the health, morals, safety, and welfare of the people. In the United States, most police power is reserved to the states.

CONCURRENT POWERS

> **Concurrent Powers**
> Powers held jointly by the national and state governments.

In certain areas, the states share **concurrent powers** with the national government. Most concurrent powers are not specifically listed in the Constitution; they are only implied. An example of a concurrent power is the power to tax. The types of taxation are divided between the levels of government. For example, states may not levy a tariff (a set of taxes on imported goods); only the national government may do this. Neither government may tax the facilities of the other. If the state governments did not have the power to tax, they would not be able to function other than on a ceremonial basis.

Other concurrent powers include the power to borrow funds, to establish courts, and to charter banks and corporations. To a limited extent, the national government exercises police power, and to the extent that it does, police power is also a concurrent power. Concurrent powers exercised by the states are normally limited to the geographic area of each state and to those functions *not* granted by the Constitution exclusively to the national government (such as the coinage of money and the negotiation of treaties).

PROHIBITED POWERS

The Constitution prohibits or denies several powers to the national government. For example, the national government expressly has been denied the power to impose taxes on goods sold to other countries (exports). Moreover, any power not granted expressly or implicitly to the federal government by the Constitution is prohibited to it. For example, the national government cannot create a national divorce law system. The states are also denied certain powers. For example, no state is allowed to enter into a treaty on its own with another country.

THE SUPREMACY CLAUSE

> **Supremacy Clause**
> The constitutional provision that makes the Constitution and federal laws superior to all conflicting state and local laws.

The supremacy of the national constitution over subnational laws and actions is established in the **supremacy clause** of the Constitution. The supremacy clause (Article VI, Clause 2) states the following:

> This Constitution, and the Laws of the United States which shall be made in Pursuance thereof; and all Treaties made . . . under the Authority of the United States, shall be the supreme Law of the Land; and the Judges in every State shall be bound thereby, any Thing in the Constitution or Laws of any State to the Contrary notwithstanding.

In other words, states cannot use their reserved or concurrent powers to thwart national policies. All national and state officers, including judges, must be bound by oath to support the Constitution. Hence, any legitimate exercise of national governmental power

BEYOND OUR B RDERS

FLEXIBLE FEDERALISM

The United States Constitution pretty clearly lays out the division of powers and authority between the states and the national government, as well as creating a complex election scheme to further guarantee representation for the states. As we will see, the decisions of the Supreme Court over the centuries have reinterpreted this division numerous times.

Several other large, diverse countries have also adopted the federal system of government. Have they been able to construct a clear division of powers between the national government and states that has lasted? Or is federalism as a system flexible enough for nations to change their internal arrangements in response to need?

The government of Canada is a federal system with a national government and multiple provinces and territories. At its founding in 1867, the Canadian federal system differed from that of the United States in at least two major ways: (1) it was created by the United Kingdom, and the new nation owed allegiance to the British monarch; and (2) from the very beginning, provinces were divided by culture and language, with one of the largest provinces being French-speaking Quebec.

The division of powers in the Canadian system is also different from that of the United States. In general, the government has operated on the principle that all Canadians, regardless of where they live, should be taxed about equally and receive equal government benefits. The national government had power over defense, trade, transportation, and so on, whereas the provinces had control over education, civil rights, hospitals, and all natural resources within their boundaries. In the 20th century, the Canadian national government has acquired much more power over social services, the national health system, and other direct services to the people.

In contrast to the American states, provinces have won increased economic independence from the central government through their control over natural resources and the money they earn from taxing their use. Today, with the price of oil skyrocketing, the province of Alberta has become the world capital of oil sand production, and the province has earned a windfall in revenue from its natural resources.*

Another large federal system is that of India, formed after the end of British rule in 1948. India adopted federalism to deal with its huge number of ethnic minorities and local cultures and languages. At the beginning, while powers were constitutionally divided between the capital of New Delhi and the states, the drive for economic development led to national control of some industries directly and considerable control over state decisions and economic initiatives. In the 1990s, India began to reform its economic system to encourage more development. One of the principles of that reform was to end much of the national control of the economy and allow states to develop their own laws and incentives for development. Today, the balance of power has shifted toward the states.**

FOR CRITICAL ANALYSIS

1. Do you think there would be a time when power would shift from the national government to the states in the United States?
2. What conditions might make that possible?

*Canadian Embassy, "A Strong Partnership," accessed at www .canadianembassy.org/government/federalism-en.asp.
**Aseema Sinha, "The Changing Political Economy of Federalism in India; A Historical Institutional Approach," *India Review* 3, January 2004, p. 25–63.

supersedes any conflicting state action.[7] Of course, deciding whether a conflict actually exists is a judicial matter, as you will see when we discuss the case of *McCulloch v. Maryland*.

National government legislation in a concurrent area is said to *preempt* (take precedence over) conflicting state or local laws or regulations in that area. One of the ways in which the national government has extended its powers, particularly during the 20th century, is through the preemption of state and local laws by national legislation. In the first decade of the 20th century, fewer than 20 national laws preempted laws and regulations issued by state and local governments. By the beginning of the 21st century, the number had risen to nearly 120.

Some political scientists believe that national supremacy is critical for the longevity and smooth functioning of a federal system. Nonetheless, the application of this principle has been a continuous source of conflict. As you will see, the most extreme example of this conflict was the Civil War.

VERTICAL CHECKS AND BALANCES

Recall from Chapter 2 that one of the concerns of the founders was to prevent the national government from becoming too powerful. For that reason, they divided the government into three branches—legislative, executive, and judicial. They also created a system of checks and balances that allowed each branch to check the actions of the others. The federal form of government created by the founders also involves checks and balances. These are sometimes called *vertical checks and balances* because they involve relationships between the states and the national government. They can be contrasted with *horizontal checks and balances*, in which the branches of government that are on the same level—either state or national—can check one other.

....

[7]An example of this is President Dwight Eisenhower's disciplining of Arkansas Governor Orval Faubus in 1957 by federalizing the National Guard to enforce the court-ordered desegregation of Little Rock High School.

For example, the reserved powers of the states act as a check on the national government. Additionally, the states' interests are represented in the national legislature (Congress), and the citizens of the various states determine who will head the executive branch (the presidency). The founders also made it impossible for the central government to change the Constitution without the states' consent, as you read in Chapter 2. Finally, national programs and policies are administered by the states. This gives the states considerable control over the ultimate shape of those programs and policies.

The national government, in turn, can check state policies by exercising its constitutional powers under the clauses just discussed, as well as under the commerce clause (to be examined later). Furthermore, the national government can influence state policies indirectly through federal grants, as you will learn later in this chapter.

INTERSTATE RELATIONS

So far we have examined only the relationship between central and state governmental units. The states, however, have constant commercial, social, and other dealings among themselves. The national Constitution imposes certain "rules of the road" on interstate relations. These rules have prevented any one state from setting itself apart from the other states. The three most important clauses governing interstate relations in the Constitution, all derived from the Articles of Confederation, require each state to do the following:

1. Give full faith and credit to every other state's public acts, records, and judicial proceedings (Article IV, Section 1).
2. Extend to every other state's citizens the privileges and immunities of its own citizens (Article IV, Section 2).
3. Agree to return persons who are fleeing from justice in another state back to their home state when requested to do so (Article IV, Section 2).

The Full Faith and Credit Clause. This provision of the Constitution protects the rights of citizens as they move from state to state. It provides that "full faith *and credit* shall be given in each State to the public Acts, Records and judicial Proceedings of every other State." This clause applies only to civil matters. It ensures that rights established under deeds, wills, contracts, and the like will be honored by any other states. It also ensures that any judicial decision with respect to such property rights will be honored as well as enforced, in all states. The **full faith and credit clause** has contributed to the unity of American citizens, particularly as we have become a more mobile society.

> **Full Faith and Credit Clause**
> This section of the Constitution requires states to recognize one another's laws and court decisions. It ensures that rights established under deeds, wills, contracts, and other civil matters in one state will be honored by other states.

Privileges and Immunities. Privileges and immunities are defined as special rights and exemptions provided by law. Under Article IV, "The Citizens of each State shall be entitled to all Privileges and Immunities of Citizens in the several States." This clause indicates that states are obligated to extend to citizens of other states protection of the laws, the right to work, access to courts, and other privileges they grant their own citizens. It means that if you are a student from Iowa attending college in Ohio, you have the same rights as Ohioans to protest a traffic ticket, to buy a car, to hold a job, and to travel freely throughout the state.

> **Privileges and Immunities**
> Special rights and exceptions provided by law. States may not discriminate against one another's citizens.

Interstate Extradition. The Constitution clearly addressed the issue of how states should cooperate in catching criminals. Article IV, Section 2, states that "[a] person charged in any State with Treason, Felony, or another Crime who shall flee from Justice and be found in another State, shall on Demand of the executive Authority of the State from which he fled, be delivered up, to be removed to the State having jurisdiction of the Crime." While the language is clear, a federal judge will not order such an action. It is the moral duty of the governor to **extradite** the accused. From time to time, the governor of a state

> **Extradite**
> To surrender an accused or convicted criminal to the authorities of the state from which he or she has fled; to return a fugitive criminal to the jurisdiction of the accusing state.

WHAT IF...

ONE STATE'S SAME-SEX MARRIAGES HAD TO BE RECOGNIZED NATIONWIDE?

The full faith and credit clause of the Constitution certainly requires states to recognize that a couple married in California is also married when they move to Nebraska. But what if one state recognizes same-sex marriages? Does that mean that all other states must recognize such marriages and give each partner the benefits accorded to partners in opposite-sex marriages?

FEDERAL LAW INTERVENES

In 1996, Congress attempted to prevent such a result through the Defense of Marriage Act, which allows state governments to ignore same-sex marriages performed in other states. But what would happen if the United States Supreme Court ruled that the Defense of Marriage Act is unconstitutional? If this happened, then all of the state laws that refuse to recognize same-sex marriages performed in another state would be unconstitutional as well, because the U.S. Constitution is the supreme law of the land.

What about federal benefits? The national government has traditionally left marriage to the states. In the past, the Internal Revenue Service, the Social Security Administration, and other federal agencies recognized marriages when, and only when, the states recognized them. With the Defense of Marriage Act, the national government established its own definition of marriage for the first time. Under the Act, no matter what the states do, federal agencies cannot recognize same-sex marriages. If the Defense of Marriage Act were declared unconstitutional, however, the federal government might again have to accept all state-defined marriages, and a same-sex marriage in a state that allowed such unions would entitle the couple to federal benefits, including spousal benefits under Social Security.

WHAT MUST HAPPEN TO CHANGE THE LAW

Two things must happen for nationwide recognition of same-sex marriages. One is that the Defense of Marriage Act be ruled unconstitutional. It is open to question whether the Supreme Court would actually issue such a ruling. The other requirement, however—legalization of same-sex marriage by one or more states—is in place already. In November 2003, the Massachusetts Supreme Judicial Court ruled that same-sex couples have a right to civil marriage under the Massachusetts state constitution. In 2008, the California Supreme Court overturned a law banning same-sex marriages, and ceremonies to wed couples began in June of that year. However, a referendum to amend California's constitution to outlaw same-sex marriages was on the ballot in November 2008. Voters approved the proposition to ban same sex marriage by a vote of 52 percent to 48 percent.

Civil unions are legally recognized partnerships that provide some or all of the state benefits provided to married couples. By 2008, civil unions were recognized in Vermont, Connecticut, New Jersey (for persons older than 62), and New Hampshire. Several states have established "domestic partnerships" that include some of the legal benefits of marriage.

FOR CRITICAL ANALYSIS

1. If marriage is a contract between two individuals, should it be recognized in the same way as other contracts under the full faith and credit clause?
2. Why do you think that a state might adopt different marriage laws from those in other states? Can you think of an example?
3. Would a national recognition of civil unions reduce the controversies over same-sex marriages?

may refuse to do so, either because he or she does not believe in capital punishment, which might be ordered upon conviction, or because the accused has lived a law-abiding life for many years outside the state in which the crime was committed.

Following these constitutional mandates is not always easy for the states. For example, one question that has arisen in recent years is whether states will be constitutionally obligated to recognize same-sex marriages performed in other states, as you read in the *What If . . .* feature.

Additionally, states may enter into agreements called **interstate compacts**, if consented to by Congress. In reality, congressional consent is necessary only if such a compact increases the power of the contracting states relative to other states (or to the national government). Typical examples of interstate compacts are the establishment of the Port Authority of New York and New Jersey by an interstate compact between those two states in 1921 and the regulation of the production of crude oil and natural gas by the Interstate Oil and Gas Compact of 1935. Recently, the federal government has attempted to mediate the dispute between Georgia and Tennessee over a prior agreement about how much water can be sent from a Tennessee lake to meet Georgia's needs.

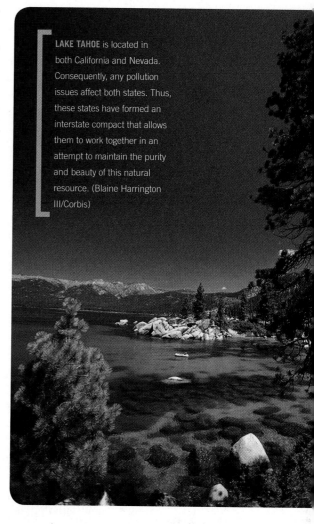

LAKE TAHOE is located in both California and Nevada. Consequently, any pollution issues affect both states. Thus, these states have formed an interstate compact that allows them to work together in an attempt to maintain the purity and beauty of this natural resource. (Blaine Harrington III/Corbis)

DEFINING CONSTITUTIONAL POWERS—THE EARLY YEARS

Recall from Chapter 2 that constitutional language, to be effective and to endure, must have some degree of ambiguity. Certainly, the powers delegated to the national government and the powers reserved to the states contain elements of ambiguity, thus leaving the door open for different interpretations of federalism. Disputes over the boundaries of national versus state powers have characterized this nation from the beginning. In the early 1800s, the most significant disputes arose over differing interpretations of the implied powers of the national government under the necessary and proper clause and over the respective powers of the national government and the states to regulate commerce.

Although political bodies at all levels of government play important roles in the process of settling such disputes, ultimately the Supreme Court casts the final vote. As might be expected, the character of the referee will have an impact on the ultimate outcome of any dispute. From 1801 to 1835, the Supreme Court was headed by Chief Justice John Marshall, a Federalist who advocated a strong central government. We look here at two cases decided by the Marshall Court: *McCulloch v. Maryland*[8] and *Gibbons v. Ogden*.[9] Both cases are considered milestones in defining the boundaries between federal and state power.

Interstate Compact
An agreement between two or more states. Agreements on minor matters are made without congressional consent, but any compact that tends to increase the power of the contracting states relative to other states or relative to the national government generally requires the consent of Congress. Such compacts serve as a means by which states can solve regional problems.

McCULLOCH V. MARYLAND (1819)

Nowhere in the U.S. Constitution does it grant the Congress the power to create a national bank, although it does have the express power to regulate currency. Twice in the history of the nation has the Congress chartered banks—the First and Second Banks of the United States—and provided part of their initial capital; thus, they were national banks. The government of Maryland, which intended to regulate its own banks and did not want a national bank competing with its own institutions, imposed a tax on the Second Bank's Baltimore branch in an attempt to put that branch out of business. The branch's cashier, James William McCulloch, refused to pay the Maryland

[8]4 Wheaton 316 (1819).
[9]9 Wheaton 1 (1824).

tax. When Maryland took McCulloch to its state court, the state of Maryland won. The national government appealed the case to the Supreme Court.

The Constitutional Questions. The questions before the Supreme Court were of monumental proportions. The very heart of national power under the Constitution as well as the relationship between the national government and the states, was at issue. Congress has the authority to make all laws that are "necessary and proper" for the execution of Congress's expressed powers. Strict constitution constructionists looked at the word necessary and contended that the national government had only those powers *indispensable* to the exercise of its designated powers. To them, chartering a bank and contributing capital to it were not necessary, for example, to coin money and regulate its value.

Loose constructionists disagreed. They believed that the word *necessary* could not be looked at in its strictest sense. As Alexander Hamilton once said, "It is essential to the being of the national government that so erroneous a conception of the meaning of the word *necessary* be exploded." The important issue was, if the national bank was constitutional, could the state tax it?

Marshall's Decision. Three days after hearing the case, Chief Justice John Marshall announced the court's decision. (Given his Federalist allegiance, it is likely he made his decision before he heard the case.) It is true, Marshall said, that Congress's power to establish a national bank was not expressed in the Constitution. He went on to say, however, that if establishing such a national bank aided the government in the exercise of its designate powers, that the authority to set up such a bank could be implied. To Marshall, the necessary and proper clause embraced "all means which are appropriate: to carry out the 'legitimate ends' of the Constitution." Only when such actions are forbidden by the letter and spirit of the Constitution are they thereby unconstitutional. There was nothing in the Constitution, according to Marshall, "which excludes incidental or implied powers; and which requires that everything granted shall be expressly and minutely described." It would be impossible to spell out every action that Congress might legitimately take—the Constitution "would be enormously long and could scarcely be embraced by the human mind."

JOHN MARSHALL (1755–1835) was the fourth chief justice of the Supreme Court. When Marshall took over, the Court had little power and almost no influence over the other two branches of government. Some scholars have declared that Marshall is the true architect of the American constitutional system, because he single-handedly gave new power to the Constitution. What consequences might have followed if Marshall had taken a more restrictive view of the national government's powers? (Library of Congress Prints & Photographs Division)

In perhaps the single most famous sentence every uttered by a Supreme Court justice, Marshall said, "[W]e must never forget it is a constitution we are expounding." In other words, the Constitution is a living instrument that has to be interpreted to meet the practical needs of government. Having established this doctrine of implied powers, Marshall then answered the other important question before the Court and established the doctrine of national supremacy. Marshall stated that no state could use its taxing power to tax an arm of the national government. If it could, "the declaration that the

Constitution . . . shall be the supreme law of the land, is an empty and unmeaning declamation."

Marshall's decision enabled the national government to grow and to meet problems that the Constitution's framers were unable to foresee. Today, practically every expressed power of the national government has been expanded in one way or another by use of the necessary and proper clause.

GIBBONS V. OGDEN (1824)

One of the most important parts of the Constitution included in Article I, Section 8, is the so-called **commerce clause**, in which Congress is given the power "[t]o regulate Commerce with foreign Nations, and among the several States, and with the Indian Tribes." What exactly does "to regulate commerce" mean? What does "commerce" entail? The issue here is essentially the same as that raised by *McCulloch v. Maryland*: how strict an interpretation should be given to a constitutional phrase? As might be expected given his Federalist loyalties, Marshall used a liberal approach in interpreting the commerce clause in *Gibbons v. Ogden*.

The Background of the Case. Robert Fulton and Robert Livingston secured a monopoly on steam navigation on New York waters from the New York legislature in 1803. They licensed Aaron Ogden to operate steam-powered ferryboats between New York and New Jersey. Thomas Gibbons, who had obtained a license from the U.S. government to operate boats in interstate waters, decided to compete with Ogden, but he did so without New York's permission. Ogden sued Gibbons. The New York state courts prohibited Gibbons from operating in New York waters. Gibbons appealed to the Supreme Court.

There were actually several issues before the Court in this case. The first issue was how the term *commerce* should be defined. New York's highest court had defined the term narrowly to mean only the shipment of goods, or the interchange of commodities, *not* navigation or the transport of people. The second issue was whether the national government's power to regulate interstate commerce extended to commerce within a state (*intra*state commerce) or was limited strictly to commerce among the states (*inter*state commerce). The third issue was whether the power to regulate interstate commerce was a concurrent power (as the New York court had concluded), meaning a power that could be exercised by both the state or national governments, or an exclusive national power. Clearly, if such powers were concurrent, there would be many instances of laws that conflicted with each other.

Marshall's Ruling. Marshall defined *commerce* as all commercial intercourse—all business dealings—including navigation and the transport of people. Marshall used this opportunity not only to expand the definition of commerce but also to validate and increase the power of the national legislature to regulate commerce. Declared Marshall, "What is this power? It is the power . . . to prescribe the rule by which commerce is to be governed. This power, like all others vested in Congress, is complete in itself." Marshall also held that the commerce power of the national government could be exercised in state jurisdictions, even though it cannot reach *solely* intrastate commerce. Finally, Marshall emphasized that the power to regulate interstate commerce was an *exclusive* national power. Marshall held that because Gibbons was duly authorized by the national government to navigate in interstate waters, he could not be prohibited from doing so by a state court.

Marshall's expansive interpretation of the commerce clause in *Gibbons v. Ogden* allowed the national government to exercise increasing authority over all areas of economic affairs throughout the land. Congress did not immediately exploit this broad grant of power. In the 1930s and subsequent

Commerce Clause
The section of the Constitution in which Congress is given the power to regulate trade among the states and with foreign countries.

That the Liberty Bell cracked when it was rung at the funeral of John Marshall in 1835?

decades, however, the commerce clause became the primary constitutional basis for national government regulation—as you will read later in this chapter.

STATES' RIGHTS AND THE RESORT TO CIVIL WAR

The controversy over slavery that led to the Civil War took the form of a dispute over national government supremacy versus the rights of the separate states. Essentially, the Civil War brought to an ultimate and violent climax the ideological debate that had been outlined by the Federalist and Anti-Federalist parties even before the Constitution was ratified.

THE SHIFT BACK TO STATES' RIGHTS

As we have seen, while John Marshall was chief justice of the Supreme Court, he did much to increase the power of the national government and to reduce that of the states. During the Jacksonian era (1829–1837), however, a shift back to states' rights began. The question of the regulation of commerce became one of the major issues in federal-state relations. When Congress passed a tariff in 1828, the state of South Carolina unsuccessfully attempted to nullify the tariff (render it void), claiming that in cases of conflict between a state and the national government, the state should have the ultimate authority over its citizens.

Over the next three decades, the North and South became even more sharply divided—over tariffs that mostly benefited Northern industries and over the slavery

PRESIDENT LINCOLN meets with some of his generals and other troops on October 3, 1862. While many believe that the Civil War was fought over the issue of slavery, others point out that it was really a battle over the supremacy of the national government. In any event, once the North won the war, what happened to the size and power of our national government? (Bettmann/Corbis)

issue. On December 20, 1860, South Carolina formally repealed its ratification of the Constitution and withdrew from the Union. On February 4, 1861, representatives from six Southern states met at Montgomery, Alabama, to form a new government called the Confederate States of America.

WAR AND THE GROWTH OF THE NATIONAL GOVERNMENT

The ultimate defeat of the South in 1865 permanently ended any idea that a state could successfully claim the right to secede, or withdraw, from the Union. Ironically, the Civil War—brought about in large part because of the South's desire for increased states' rights—resulted in the opposite: an increase in the political power of the national government.

The War Effort. Thousands of new employees were hired to run the Union war effort and to deal with the social and economic problems that had to be handled in the aftermath of war. A billion-dollar ($1.3 billion, which is over $11.9 billion in today's dollars) national government budget was passed for the first time in 1865 to cover the increased government expenditures. The first (temporary) income tax was imposed on citizens to help pay for the war. This tax and the increased national government spending were precursors to the expanded future role of the national government in the American federal system. Civil liberties were curtailed in the Union and in the Confederacy in the name of the wartime emergency. The distribution of pensions and widows' benefits also boosted the national government's social role. Many scholars contend that the North's victory set the nation on the path to a modern industrial economy and society.

The Civil War Amendments. The expansion of the national government's authority during the Civil War was reflected in the passage of the Civil War Amendments to the Constitution. Before the war, legislation with regard to slavery was some of the most controversial ever to come before the Congress. In fact, in the 1830s, Congress prohibited the submission of antislavery petitions being brought before it. When new states were admitted into the Union, the primary decision was whether slavery would be allowed.

DID YOU KNOW?

That only after the Civil War did people commonly refer to the United States as "it" instead of "they"?

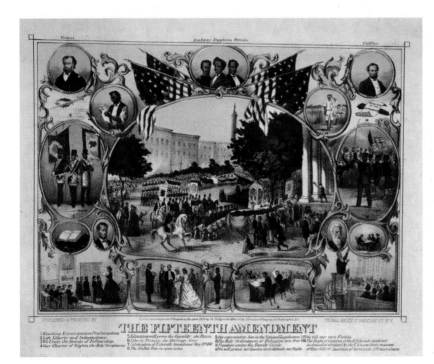

THE CENTRAL IMAGE of this print by Thomas Kelly, published in 1870, depicts a parade celebrating the ratification of the Fifteenth Amendment. The surrounding portraits and vignettes illustrate African American life and the rights granted by the Amendment. The key to the illustrations in the lower margin reads as follows: 1. Reading Emancipation Proclamation. 2. Life, Liberty, and Independence. 3. We Unite the Bonds of Fellowship. 4. Our Charter of Rights the Holy Scriptures. 5. Education will prove the Equality the Races [sic]. 6. Liberty Protects the Mariage [sic] Alter [sic]. 7. Celebration of Fifteenth Amendment May 19th, 1870. 8. The Ballot Box is open to us. 9. Our representative Sits in the National Legislature. 10. The Holy Ordinances of Religion are free. 11. Freedom unites the Family Circle. 12. We will protect our Country as it defends our Rights. 13. We till our own Fields. 14. The Right of Citizens of the U.S. to vote shall not be denied or abridged by the U.S. or any State on account of Race Color or Condition of Servitude 15th Amendment. (Library of Congress Prints & Photographs Division, Washington, D.C. [LC-USZ62-36272])

Immediately after the Civil War, at a time when former officers of the Confederacy were barred from voting, the three Civil War Amendments were passed. The Thirteenth Amendment, ratified in 1865, did more than interfere with slavery—it abolished the institution altogether. By abolishing slavery, the amendment also in effect abolished the rule by which three-fifths of the slaves were counted when apportioning seats in the House of Representatives (see Chapter 2). African Americans were now counted in full.

The Fourteenth Amendment (1868) defined who was a citizen of each state. It sought to guarantee equal rights under state law, stating that

[no] State [shall] deprive any person of life, liberty, or property, without due process of law; nor deny to any person within its jurisdiction the equal protection of the laws.

For a brief time after the ratification of these amendments, the rights of African Americans in the South were protected by the local officials appointed by the Union forces. Within two decades, the Fourteenth Amendment lost much of its power as states reinstituted separate conditions for the former slaves. Decades later, the courts interpreted these words to mean that the national Bill of Rights applied to state governments, a development that we will examine in Chapter 4. The Fourteenth Amendment also confirmed the abolition of the three-fifths rule. Finally, the Fifteenth Amendment (1870) gave African Americans the right to vote in all elections, including state elections, although a century would pass before that right was enforced.

THE CONTINUING DISPUTE OVER THE DIVISION OF POWER

Although the outcome of the Civil War firmly established the supremacy of the national government and put to rest the idea that a state could secede from the Union, the war by no means ended the debate over the division of powers between the national government and the states. The debate over the division of powers in our federal system can be viewed as progressing through at least two general stages since the Civil War: dual federalism and cooperative federalism.

DUAL FEDERALISM AND THE RETREAT OF NATIONAL AUTHORITY

Dual Federalism
A system in which the states and the national government each remain supreme within their own spheres. The doctrine looks on nation and state as co-equal sovereign powers. Neither the state government nor the national government should interfere in the other's sphere.

During the decades following the Civil War, the prevailing model was what political scientists have called **dual federalism**—a doctrine that emphasizes a distinction between federal and state spheres of government authority. Various images have been used to describe different configurations of federalism over time. Dual federalism is commonly depicted as a layer cake, because the state governments and the national government are viewed as separate entities, like separate layers in a cake. The national government is the top layer of the cake; the state government is the bottom layer. Nevertheless, the two layers are physically separate. They do not mix. For the most part, advocates of dual federalism believed that the state and national governments should not exercise authority in the same areas.

A Return to Normal Conditions. The doctrine of dual federalism represented a revival of states' rights following the expansion of national authority during the Civil War. Dual federalism, after all, was a fairly accurate model of the prewar consensus on state-national relations. For many people, it therefore represented a return to normal. The national income tax, used to fund the war effort and the reconstruction of the South, was ended in 1872. The most significant step to reverse the wartime expansion of national power took place in 1877, when President Rutherford B. Hayes withdrew the last federal troops from the South. This meant that the national government was no longer in a position to regulate state actions that affected African Americans. While the black population was now free, it was again subject to the authority of Southern whites.

The Role of the Supreme Court. The Civil War crisis drastically reduced the influence of the United States Supreme Court. In the prewar *Dred Scott* decision,[10] the Court had attempted to abolish the power of the national government to restrict slavery in the territories. In so doing, the Court placed itself on the losing side of the impending conflict. After the war, Congress took the unprecedented step of exempting the entire process of Southern reconstruction from judicial review. The Court had little choice but to acquiesce.

In time, the Supreme Court reestablished itself as the legitimate constitutional umpire. Its decisions tended to support dual federalism, defend states' rights, and limit the powers of the national government. In 1895, for example, the Court ruled that a national income tax was unconstitutional.[11] In subsequent years, the Court gradually backed away from this decision and eventually might have overturned it. In 1913, however, the Sixteenth Amendment explicitly authorized a national income tax.

For the Court, dual federalism meant that the national government could intervene in state activities through grants and subsidies, but for the most part, it was barred from regulating matters that the Court considered to be purely local. The Court generally limited the exercise of police power to the states. For example, in 1918, the Court ruled that a 1916 national law banning child labor was unconstitutional because it

THIS PHOTOGRAPH shows teenagers and young boys leaving a coal mine near Fairmont, West Virginia. In the 1800s, even very young children worked in coal mines. Today, national child-labor laws prohibit employers from hiring young workers for dangerous occupations. Why do you think the parents of these youths and children allowed them to work at such dangerous jobs? If no child-labor laws existed today, would a large percentage of children still be working in dangerous occupations? Why or why not? (Lewis Wickes Hine, Library of Congress Prints & Photographs Division, Washington, D.C. [LC-DIG-nclc-01082])

---

[10]*Dred Scott v. Sanford*, 19 Howard 393 (1857).
[11]*Pollock v. Farmers' Loan & Trust Co.*, 157 U.S. 429 (1895); *Pollock v. Farmers' Loan & Trust Co.*, 158 U.S. 601 (1895).

attempted to regulate a local problem.[12] In effect, the Court placed severe limits on the ability of Congress to legislate under the commerce clause of the Constitution.

THE NEW DEAL AND COOPERATIVE FEDERALISM

The doctrine of dual federalism receded into the background in the 1930s as the nation attempted to deal with the Great Depression. Franklin D. Roosevelt was inaugurated on March 4, 1933, as the 32nd president of the United States. In the previous year, nearly 1,500 banks had failed (and 4,000 more would fail in 1933). Thirty-two thousand businesses had closed down, and almost one-fourth of the labor force was unemployed. The public expected the national government to do something about the disastrous state of the economy. But for the first three years of the Great Depression (1930–1932), the national government did very little.

The "New Deal." President Herbert Hoover (served 1929–1933) clung to the doctrine of dual federalism and insisted that unemployment and poverty were local issues. The states, not the national government, had the sole responsibility for combating the effects of unemployment and providing relief to the poor. Roosevelt, however, did not feel bound by this doctrine, and his new Democratic administration energetically intervened in the economy. Roosevelt's "New Deal" included large-scale emergency antipoverty programs. In addition, the New Deal introduced major new laws regulating economic activity, such as the National Industrial Recovery Act of 1933, which established the National Recovery Administration (NRA). The NRA, initially the centerpiece of the New Deal, provided codes for every industry to restrict competition and regulate labor relations.

PRESIDENT FRANKLIN DELANO ROOSEVELT (served 1933–1945). Roosevelt's national approach to addressing the effects of the Great Depression was overwhelmingly popular, although many of his specific initiatives were controversial. How did the Great Depression change the political beliefs of many ordinary Americans? (Bettmann/Corbis)

The End of Dual Federalism. Roosevelt's expansion of national authority was challenged by the Supreme Court, which continued to adhere to the doctrine of dual federalism. In 1935, the Court ruled that the NRA program was unconstitutional.[13] The NRA had turned out to be largely unworkable and was unpopular. The Court, however, rejected the program on the ground that it regulated intrastate, not interstate, commerce. This position appeared to rule out any alternative recovery plans that might be better designed. Subsequently, the Court struck down the Agricultural Adjustment Act, the Bituminous Coal Act, a railroad retirement plan, legislation to protect farm mortgages, and a municipal bankruptcy act.

In 1937, Roosevelt proposed legislation that would allow him to add up to six new justices to the Supreme Court. Presumably, the new justices would be more friendly to the exercise of national power than were the existing members. Roosevelt's move was widely seen as an assault on the Constitution. Congressional Democrats refused to support the measure, and it failed. Nevertheless, the "court-packing scheme" had its intended effect. Although the membership of the Court did not change, after 1937 the

---

[12]*Hammer v. Dagenhart*, 247 U.S. 251 (1918). This decision was overruled in *United States v. Darby*, 312 U.S. 100 (1940).
[13]*Schechter Poultry Corp. v. United States*, 295 U.S. 495 (1935).

Court ceased its attempts to limit the national government's powers under the commerce clause. For the next half-century, the commerce clause would provide Congress with an unlimited justification for regulating the economic life of the country.

Cooperative Federalism. Some political scientists have described the era since 1937 as characterized by **cooperative federalism**, in which the states and the national government cooperate in solving complex common problems. Roosevelt's New Deal programs, for example, often involved joint action between the national government and the states. The pattern of national-state relationships during these years created a new metaphor for federalism—that of a marble cake. Unlike a layer cake, in a marble cake the two types of cake are intermingled, and any bite contains cake of both flavors.

As an example of how national and state governments work together under the cooperative federalism model, consider Aid to Families with Dependent Children (AFDC), a welfare program that was established during the New Deal. (In 1996, AFDC was replaced by Temporary Assistance to Needy Families—TANF.) Under the AFDC program, the national government provided most of the funding, but state governments established benefit levels and eligibility requirements for recipients. Local welfare offices were staffed by state, not national, employees. In return for national funding, the states had to conform to a series of regulations on how the program was to be carried out. These regulations tended to become more elaborate over time.

The 1960s and 1970s were a time of even greater expansion of the national government's role in domestic policy. The evolving pattern of national-state-local government relationships during the 1960s and 1970s yielded yet another metaphor—**picket-fence federalism**, a concept devised by political scientist Terry Sanford. The horizontal boards in the fence represent the different levels of government (national, state, and local), while the vertical pickets represent the various programs and policies in which each level of government is involved. Officials at each level of government work together to promote and develop the policy represented by each picket.

METHODS OF IMPLEMENTING COOPERATIVE FEDERALISM

Even before the Constitution was adopted, the national government gave grants to the states in the form of land to finance education. The national government also provided land grants for canals, railroads, and roads. In the 20th century, federal grants increased significantly, especially during Roosevelt's administration during the Great Depression and again during the 1960s, when the dollar amount of grants quadrupled. These funds were used for improvements in education, pollution control, recreation, and highways. With this increase in grants, however, came a bewildering number of restrictions and regulations.

Categorical Grants. By 1985, **categorical grants** amounted to more than $100 billion per year. They were spread out across 400 separate programs, but the largest five accounted for more than 50 percent of the revenues spent. These five programs involved Medicaid (health care for the poor), highway construction, unemployment benefits, housing assistance, and welfare programs to assist mothers with dependent children and people with disabilities. For fiscal year 2006, the national government gave an estimated $225 billion to the states through federal grants. The shift toward a greater role for the central government in the United States can be seen clearly in Figure 3–2, which shows the increase in central government spending as a percentage of total government spending.

Before the 1960s, most categorical grants by the national government were *formula grants*. These grants take their name from the method used to allocate funds. They fund state programs using a formula based on such variables as the state's needs, population, or willingness to come up with matching funds. Beginning in the 1960s, the national government began increasingly to offer *program grants*. This funding requires

Cooperative Federalism
The theory that the states and the national government should cooperate in solving problems.

Picket-Fence Federalism
A model of federalism in which specific programs and policies (depicted as vertical pickets in a picket fence) involve all levels of government—national, state, and local (depicted by the horizontal boards in a picket fence).

Categorical Grants
Federal grants to states or local governments that are for specific programs or projects.

states to apply for grants for specific programs. The applications are evaluated by the national government, and the applications may compete with one another. Program grants give the national government a much greater degree of control over state activities than formula grants.

Why have federal grants to the states increased so much? One reason is that Congress has decided to offload some programs to the states and provide a major part of the funding for them. Also, Congress continues to use grants to persuade states and cities to operate programs devised by the federal government. Finally, states often are happy to apply for grants because they are relatively "free," requiring only that the state match a small portion of each grant. States can still face criticism for accepting the grants, because their matching funds may be diverted from other state projects.

Feeling the Pressure—The Strings Attached to Federal Grants. No dollars sent to the states are completely free of strings, however; all funds come with requirements that must be met by the states. Often, through the use of grants, the national government has been able to exercise substantial control over matters that traditionally have been under the purview of state governments. When the federal government gives federal funds for highway improvements, for example, it may condition the funds on the state's cooperation with a federal policy. This is exactly what the federal government did in the 1980s and 1990s to force the states to raise their minimum drinking age to 21.

Such carrot-and-stick tactics have been used as a form of coercion in recent years as well. In 2002, for example, President George W. Bush signed the No Child Left Behind (NCLB) Act into law. Under NCLB, Bush promised billions of dollars to the states to bolster their education budgets. The funds would only be delivered, however, if states agreed to hold schools accountable to new federal achievement benchmarks on standardized tests designed by the federal government. Education traditionally had been under state control, and the conditions for receiving NCLB funds effectively stripped the states of some autonomy in creating standards for public schools.

Block Grants
Federal programs that provide funds to state and local governments for general functional areas, such as criminal justice or mental-health programs.

Block Grants. Block grants lessen the restrictions on federal grants given to state and local governments by grouping several categorical grants under one broad heading. Governors and mayors generally prefer block grants because such grants give the states more flexibility in how the money is spent.

FIGURE 3–2 The Shift Toward Central Government Spending

Before the Great Depression, local governments accounted for 60 percent of all government spending, with the federal government accounting for only 17 percent. By 2007, federal government spending was almost two-thirds of the total.

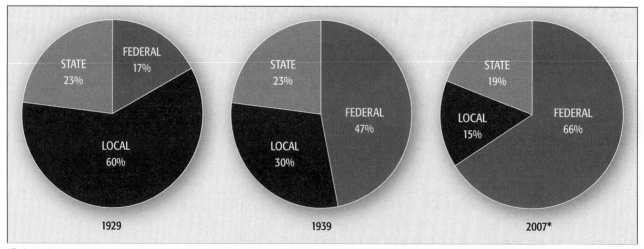

*Estimated.
Sources: U.S. Department of Commerce, Bureau of the Census, and Bureau of Economic Analysis; Congressional Budget Office.

One major set of block grants provides aid to state welfare programs. The Personal Responsibility and Work Opportunity Reconciliation Act of 1996 ended the AFDC program. The TANF program that replaced AFDC provided a welfare block grant to each state. Each grant has an annual cap. According to some, this is one of the most successful block grant programs. Although state governments prefer block grants, Congress generally favors categorical grants, because the expenditures can be targeted according to congressional priorities.

Federal Mandates. For years, the federal government has passed legislation requiring that states improve environmental conditions and the civil rights of certain groups. Since the 1970s, the national government has enacted literally hundreds of **federal mandates** requiring the states to take some action in areas ranging from the way voters are registered, to ocean-dumping restrictions, to the education of persons with disabilities. The Unfunded Mandates Reform Act of 1995 requires the Congressional Budget Office to identify mandates that cost state and local governments more than $50 million to implement. Nonetheless, the federal government routinely continues to pass mandates for state and local governments that cost more than that to implement.

For example, the estimated total cost of complying with federal mandates concerning water purity, over just a four-year period, is in the vicinity of $29 billion. In all, the estimated cost of federal mandates to the states in the early 2000s was more than $70 billion annually. One way in which the national government has moderated the burden of federal mandates is by granting *waivers*, which allow individual states to try out innovative approaches to carrying out the mandates. For example, Oregon received a waiver to experiment with a new method of rationing health-care services under the federally mandated Medicaid program.

Federal Mandate
A requirement in federal legislation that forces states and municipalities to comply with certain rules.

Speech bubbles in cartoon: "WAIT A MINUTE... WHEN DID OUR CLASS SIZE REACH 3,704,552?" "THIS WAS THE ONLY SCHOOL THAT WASN'T FAILING, SO THEY TRANSFERRED ALL OF US HERE."

UNDER THE NO CHILD LEFT BEHIND ACT, a school that is rated "in need of improvement" over a period of five years must be "restructured." Presumably, this could mean closing the school, as suggested by the cartoonist. The No Child Left Behind Act imposes certain federal mandates on the states in return for funding by the national government. In what way might this act represent a shift away from the federal system? (© Tom Toles. Reprinted with permission of Universal Press Syndicate. All rights reserved.)

PRESIDENT LYNDON B.
JOHNSON'S Great Society and
War on Poverty were among
programs that asserted the
most national authority since
the New Deal. The top photo
shows Johnson shaking the
hand of one of the residents
of Appalachia during his
Poverty Tour on May 7, 1964.
The photo on the bottom
shows Johnson signing the
Poverty Bill (also known as the
Economic Opportunity Act)
on August 20, 1964, while
press and supporters of the bill
look on. (Cecil Stoughton/LBJ
Library Collection, National
Archives)

THE POLITICS OF FEDERALISM

As we have observed, the allocation of powers between the national and state governments continues to be a major issue. In 2005, the devastation caused by Hurricane Katrina in Louisiana unleashed a heated debate about federalism, as Americans disagreed on which level of government should be held accountable for inadequate preparations and the failures in providing aid afterward. As you know, some 1,300 people died as a result of the storm, while property damage totaled tens of billions of dollars. Many Americans felt that the federal government's response to Katrina was woefully inadequate. Much of their criticism centered on the failures of the Federal Emergency Management Agency (FEMA) in the aftermath of Katrina.

FEMA, the government agency responsible for coordinating disaster preparedness and relief efforts, was disorganized and slow to respond in the days following the storm. On their arrival in the Gulf Coast, FEMA officials often acted counterproductively—on some occasions denying the delivery of storm aid that their agency had not authorized. Many critics of the federal government's handling of Katrina pointed out that FEMA's director, Michael Brown, had no disaster management experience: He was a political appointee, earning the job through his campaign efforts to help the president.

Other Americans claimed that state and local politicians, including Louisiana Governor Kathleen Blanco and New Orleans Mayor Ray Nagin, were not adequately prepared for the storm. Local officials knew the region and its residents best, yet they failed to make proper provisions for evacuating vulnerable residents.

The real reason for the disaster was the failure of the levees that protect New Orleans from Mississippi River floods. The levees were constructed by the Army Corps of Engineers (a federal agency) and maintained by the Corps; however, those employees took orders from both federal officials and state and local politicians, including the multiple local levee boards that could and did divert funds to other purposes.[14] It was widely known that the levees needed replacement, but Congress had declined to fund the design for many years. The aftermath of Hurricane Katrina was a classic case of failure due, perhaps, to the design of our federal system of government.

WHAT HAS NATIONAL AUTHORITY ACCOMPLISHED?

Why have conservatives favored the states and liberals favored the national government? One answer is that throughout American history, the expansion of national authority typically has been an engine of social change. Far more than the states, the national government has been willing to alter the status quo. The expansion of national authority during the Civil War freed the slaves—a major social revolution. During the New Deal, the expansion of national authority meant unprecedented levels of government intervention in the economy. In both the Civil War and New Deal eras, support for states' rights was a method of opposing these changes and supporting the status quo.

Some scholars believe that this equation was also a subtext in the Supreme Court's defense of states' rights between the Civil War and 1937. These scholars argue that the

[14]Douglas Brinkley, *The Great Deluge: Hurricane Katrina, New Orleans and the Mississippi Gulf Coast* (New York: HarperCollins, 2006).

Supreme Court, in those years, came increasingly under the influence of *laissez-faire* economics—a belief that any government intervention in the economy was improper. When the Court struck down national legislation against child labor, for example, it was not acting only in defense of the states; an underlying motivation was the Court's belief that laws banning child labor were wrong no matter which level of government implemented them.

Civil Rights and the War on Poverty. A final example of the use of national power to change society was the presidency of Lyndon B. Johnson (1963–1969). Johnson oversaw the greatest expansion of national authority since the New Deal. Under Johnson, a series of civil rights acts forced the states to grant African Americans equal treatment under the law. Crucially, these acts included the abolition of all measures designed to prevent African Americans from voting. Johnson's Great Society and War on Poverty programs resulted in major increases in spending by the national government. As before, states' rights were invoked to support the status quo—states' rights meant no action on civil rights and no increase in antipoverty spending.

Why Should the States Favor the Status Quo? When state governments have authority in a particular field, there may be great variations from state to state in how the issues are handled. Inevitably, some states will be more conservative than others. Therefore, bringing national authority to bear on a particular issue may impose national standards on states that, for whatever reason, have not adopted such standards. One example is the voting rights legislation passed under President Johnson. By the 1960s, there was a national consensus that all citizens, regardless of race, should have the right to vote. A majority of the white electorate in former Confederate states, however, did not share this view. National legislation was necessary to impose the national consensus on the recalcitrant states.

Another factor that may make the states more receptive to limited government, especially on economic issues, is competition among the states. It is widely believed that major corporations are more likely to establish new operations in states with a "favorable business climate." Such a climate may mean low taxes and therefore relatively more limited social services. If states compete with one another to offer the best business climate, the competition may force down taxes all around. Competition of this type also may dissuade states from implementing environmental regulations that restrict certain business activities. Those who deplore the effect of such competition often refer to it as a "race to the bottom." National legislation, in contrast, is not constrained by interstate competition.

A final factor that may encourage the states to favor the status quo is the relative power of local economic interests. A large corporation in a small state, for example, may have a substantial amount of political influence. Such a corporation, which has experienced success within the existing economic framework, may be opposed to any changes to that framework. These local economic interests may have less influence at the national level. This observation echoes James Madison's point in *Federalist Paper No. 10* (see Appendix B of this text). Madison argued that a large federal republic would be less subject to the danger of factions than a small state.

FEDERALISM BECOMES A PARTISAN ISSUE

In the years after 1968, the **devolution** of power from the national government to the states became a major ideological theme for the Republican Party. Republicans believed that the increased size and scope of the federal government—which began with the New Deal programs of Franklin Roosevelt and continued unabated through Lyndon Johnson's Great Society programs—was a threat to individual liberty and to the power

Devolution
The transfer of powers from a national or central government to a state or local government.

of the states. As the Republicans became more conservative in their views of the extent of national government power, Democrats have become more liberal and supportive of that power.

The "New Federalism." The architects of Lyndon Johnson's War on Poverty were reluctant to let state governments have a role in the new programs. This reluctance was a response to the resistance of many southern states to African American civil rights. The Johnson administration did not trust the states to administer antipoverty programs in an impartial and efficient manner.

Republican president Richard Nixon (served 1969–1974), who succeeded Johnson in office, saw political opportunity in the Democrats' suspicion of state governments. Nixon advocated what he called a "New Federalism" that would devolve authority from the national government to the states. In part, the New Federalism involved the conversion of categorical grants into block grants, thereby giving state governments greater flexibility in spending. A second part of Nixon's New Federalism was revenue sharing. Under the revenue-sharing plan, the national government provided direct, unconditional financial support to state and local governments.

Nixon was able to obtain only a limited number of block grants from Congress. The block grants he did obtain, plus revenue sharing, substantially increased financial support to state governments. Republican President Ronald Reagan was also a strong advocate of federalism, but some of his policies withdrew certain financial support from the states. Reagan was more successful than Nixon in obtaining block grants, but Reagan's block grants, unlike Nixon's, were less generous to the states than the categorical grants they replaced. Under Reagan, revenue sharing was eliminated.

Federalism in the 21st Century. Today, federalism (in the sense of limited national authority) continues to be an important element in conservative ideology. At this point, however, it is not clear whether competing theories of federalism truly divide the Republicans

PRESIDENT BILL CLINTON prepares to sign the Welfare Reform Act of 1996, overhauling America's welfare system, replacing Aid to Families with Dependent Children (AFDC), a categorical program, with Temporary Assistance to Needy Families (TANF), a block grant program that transfers control from the federal government to state governments. How is this explained, given the traditional divide the Democrats have from the Republicans in setting the theoretical limits of national authority? (AP Photo/J. Scott Applewhite)

A New Beginning

Welfare to Work

from the Democrats in practice. Consider that under Democratic president Bill Clinton (served 1993–2001), Congress replaced AFDC, a categorical welfare program, with the TANF block grants. This change was part of the Welfare Reform Act of 1996, which was perhaps the most significant domestic policy initiative of Clinton's administration. In contrast, a major domestic initiative of Republican president George W. Bush was increased federal funding and control of education—long a preserve of state and local governments.

Also, in some circumstances, liberals today may benefit from states' rights. One example is the issue of same-sex marriages, which we examined in the *What If . . .* feature. A minority of the states are much more receptive than the rest of the nation to same-sex marriages or to civil unions for gay or lesbian partners. Liberals who favor such marriages or civil unions therefore have an incentive to oppose national legislation or an amendment to the national Constitution on this topic.

FEDERALISM AND THE SUPREME COURT TODAY

The United States Supreme Court, which normally has the final say on constitutional issues, necessarily plays a significant role in determining the line between federal and state powers. Consider the decisions rendered by Chief Justice John Marshall in the cases discussed earlier in this chapter. Since the 1930s, Marshall's broad interpretation of the commerce clause has made it possible for the national government to justify its regulation of virtually any activity, even when an activity would appear to be purely local in character.

Since the 1990s, however, the Supreme Court has been reining in somewhat the national government's powers under the commerce clause. The Court also has given increased emphasis to state powers under the Tenth and Eleventh Amendments to the Constitution. At the same time, other recent rulings have sent contradictory messages with regard to states' rights and the federal government's power.

REINING IN THE COMMERCE POWER

In a widely publicized 1995 case, *United States v. Lopez*,[15] the Supreme Court held that Congress had exceeded its constitutional authority under the commerce clause when it passed the Gun-Free School Zones Act in 1990. The Court stated that the Act, which banned the possession of guns within 1,000 feet of any school, was unconstitutional because it attempted to regulate an area that had "nothing to do with commerce, or any sort of economic enterprise." This marked the first time in 60 years that the Supreme Court had placed a limit on the national government's authority under the commerce clause.

In 2000, in *United States v. Morrison*,[16] the Court held that Congress had overreached its authority under the commerce clause when it passed the Violence against Women Act in 1994. The Court invalidated a key section of the Act that provided a federal remedy for gender-motivated violence, such as rape. The Court noted that in enacting this law, Congress had extensively documented that violence against women had an adverse "aggregate" effect on interstate commerce: it deterred potential victims from traveling, from engaging in employment, and from transacting business in interstate commerce. It

[15]514 U.S. 549 (1995).
[16]529 U.S. 598 (2000).

also diminished national productivity and increased medical and other costs. Nonetheless, the Court held that evidence of an aggregate effect on commerce was not enough to justify national regulation of noneconomic, violent criminal conduct.

STATE SOVEREIGNTY AND THE ELEVENTH AMENDMENT

In recent years, the Supreme Court has issued a series of decisions that bolstered the authority of state governments under the Eleventh Amendment to the Constitution. As interpreted by the Court, that amendment in most circumstances precludes lawsuits against state governments for violations of rights established by federal laws unless the states consent to be sued. For example, in a 1999 case, *Alden v. Maine*,[17] the Court held that Maine state employees could not sue the state for violating the overtime pay requirements of a federal act. According to the Court, state immunity from such lawsuits "is a fundamental aspect of the sovereignty which [the states] enjoyed before the ratification of the Constitution, and which they retain today."

In 2000, in *Kimel v. Florida Board of Regents*,[18] the Court held that the Eleventh Amendment precluded employees of a state university from suing the state to enforce a federal statute prohibiting age-based discrimination. In 2003, however, in *Nevada v. Hibbs*,[19] the Court ruled that state employers must abide by the federal Family and Medical Leave Act (FMLA). The reasoning was that the FMLA seeks to outlaw gender bias, and government actions that may discriminate on the basis of gender must receive a "heightened review status" compared with actions that may discriminate on the basis of age or disability. Also, in 2004, the Court ruled that the Eleventh Amendment could not shield states from suits by individuals with disabilities who had been denied access to courtrooms located on the upper floors of buildings.[20]

TENTH AMENDMENT ISSUES

The Tenth Amendment states: "The powers not delegated to the United States by the Constitution, nor prohibited by it to the States, are reserved to the States respectively, or to the people." In 1992, the Court held that requirements imposed on the state of New York under a federal act regulating low-level radioactive waste were inconsistent with the Tenth Amendment and thus unconstitutional. According to the Court, the act's "take title" provision, which required states to accept ownership of waste or regulate waste following Congress's instructions, exceeded the enumerated powers of Congress. Although Congress can regulate the handling of such waste, "it may not conscript state governments as its agents" in an attempt to enforce a program of federal regulation.[21]

In 1997, the Court revisited this Tenth Amendment issue. In *Printz v. United States*,[22] the Court struck down the provisions of the federal Brady Handgun Violence Prevention Act of 1993 that required state employees to check the backgrounds of prospective handgun purchasers. Said the Court:

> [T]he federal government may neither issue directives requiring the States to address particular problems, nor command the States' officers, or those of their political subdivisions, to administer or enforce a federal regulatory program.

[17]527 U.S. 706 (1999).
[18]528 U.S. 62 (2000).
[19]538 U.S. 721 (2003).
[20]*Tennessee v. Lane*, 541 U.S. 509 (2004).
[21]*New York v. United States*, 505 U.S. 144 (1992).
[22]521 U.S. 898 (1997).

IN 2005, THESE PEOPLE waited at the steps of the United States Supreme Court building because they wished to be the first to find out about the Court's decision in the government's appeal against Oregon's "Death with Dignity" law. The Court decided against the federal government and in favor of Oregon. Why would the federal government go to court in an attempt to prevent legally assisted suicide in one state? (AP Photo/Charles Dharapak)

OTHER FEDERALISM CASES

In recent years, the Supreme Court has sent mixed messages in federalism cases. At times the Court has favored states' rights, whereas on other occasions it has backed the federal government's position.

There has been a general drift toward favoring the states in cases involving federalism issues. Despite this trend, the Supreme Court argued in 2005 that the federal government's power to seize and destroy illegal drugs trumped California's law legalizing the use of marijuana for medical treatment.[23] Yet, less than a year later, the Court favored states' rights in another case rife with federalism issues, *Gonzales v. Oregon*.[24] After a lengthy legal battle, the Court upheld Oregon's controversial "Death with Dignity" law, which allows patients with terminal illnesses to choose to end their lives early and thus alleviate suffering.

As you read in Chapter 1, the decision handed down in *Kelo v. City of New London*[25] created an uproar among property rights advocates. Many state and local governments proposed legislation that would bar the taking of private land unaffected by blight if it would be transferred to a private developer. Steps taken by the states to combat *Kelo* gained so much political traction that the U.S. Congress is considering legislation that would forbid such takings nationwide. If such a law is passed, it will eventually be tested in the courts.

[23]*Gonzales v. Raich*, 545 U.S. 1 (2005).
[24]126 S.Ct. 904 (2006).
[25]545 U.S. 469 (2005).

You can make a *difference*

YOUR STATE AND DEPARTMENT OF HOMELAND SECURITY GRANTS

Since September 11, 2001, nearly $20 billion in federal grants have been awarded to state and local municipalities for establishing our national response to terrorism preparedness. The National Strategy for Homeland Security and the Homeland Security Act of 2002 attempted to mobilize our nation against terrorist attacks. This new federal organization, the Department of Homeland Security (DHS), unified 22 governmental agencies in 2003 and now employs 180,000 people. Do you ever wonder how your tax dollars are being spent? How much of this money does your state or city receive?

WHY SHOULD YOU CARE?

The Constitution and the Tenth Amendment, in particular, are supposed to define and limit the power of the national government and define the relationship between the national government and individual state governments. Federalism establishes that power be shared between the national and state governments. Since 9/11, however, it may appear that the federal government dominates the national conversation with regard to homeland security. The federal government determines risk factors for terrorism and decides how much money each state and, in some cases, cities receive. State and local officials then administer the grants awarded.

But, how is that money being spent? Critics say that questionable projects are being funded and argue that homeland security money should be off limits for "pork-barrel" spending. In 2005, Kentucky secured a $36,000 grant to protect bingo halls from terrorist infiltration. Five days before Christmas in 2004, the government announced a $153 million

homeland security grant to provide food and shelter for the homeless. In 2006, $15.7 million in homeland security funds went for enforcement of child-labor laws. Often, Congress earmarks spending; in other cases, the DHS decides how to allocate state and local grants.

WHAT CAN YOU DO?

You can find out how much money your state and local government has received from DHS, but you may have little chance of knowing how that money was spent. Some states have laws or policies that preclude public disclosure of certain details on homeland security purchases; officials say that the information could be useful to terrorists. Some states, such as New York, will disclose general categories of purchases, such as personal protection gear, but will not give specifics. Other states are still developing disclosure policies on homeland security purchases, with requests for spending details decided on a case-by-case basis. Alabama forbids disclosure of homeland security spending specifics. Colorado passed a secrecy law in 2003 that, some critics say, was misinterpreted to mean anything related to homeland security is not public information; in 2005, lawmakers discovered that the state did not have a homeland security plan, yet spent $130 million.

To research your state's 2007 DHS grant awards and total funding history, go to **www.dhs.gov/xgovt/grants**. This page displays state grant award information for all 50 states and territories. You can click on your state for your homeland security contact and fiscal year 2007 allocation totals. A comparative state grant document is available to download. Check to see how your city and state compare with the rest of the nation in grant money.

1. The state grant document gives details about grant program breakdowns. The Urban Areas Security Initiative (UASI) gives specific grants to the 45 highest-risk urban areas. Is your city designated a high-risk urban area?
2. The State Homeland Security Program (SHSP) is the core assistance program for all 50 states to implement their antiterror readiness programs. How do your fund levels compare with other states?

3. The Law Enforcement Terrorism Prevention Program (LETPP) provides resources to your state's public safety communities. How does your state rank?
4. The Metropolitan Medical Response System (MMRS) supports local efforts to respond to mass casualty incidents such as epidemic disease outbreaks, natural disasters, and hazardous materials. About 124 cities were eligible for funding. Is your city included?
5. The Citizens Corps Program (CCP) brings community and government leaders together to coordinate community involvement in emergency preparedness. How much did your state receive?

REFERENCES

http://bensguide.gpo.gov/9-12/government/federalism.html
www.dhs.gov/xabout/strategicplan/index.shtm
www.dhs.gov/xgovt/grants
Fred Lucas, "Homeland Security Funding 'Pork' Under Fire," CNSNews.com, accessed February 23, 2007.
Eileen Sullivan, "Billions in States' Homeland Purchases Kept in the Dark," *Congressional Quarterly*, accessed June 22, 2005, at www.cq.com.

KEY TERMS

block grants 110
categorical grants 109
commerce clause 103
concurrent powers 96
confederal system 90
cooperative federalism 109
devolution 113
dual federalism 106

elastic clause, or necessary and proper clause 95
extradite 99
federalism 88
federal mandate 111
Full Faith and Credit Clause 99

interstate compact 101
picket-fence federalism 109
police power 96
privileges and immunities 99
supremacy clause 96
unitary system 90

CHAPTER SUMMARY

1. There are three basic models for ordering relations between central governments and local units: (1) a unitary system (in which ultimate power is held by the national government), (2) a confederal system (in which ultimate power is retained by the states), and (3) a federal system (in which governmental powers are divided between the national government and the states). A major reason for the creation of a federal system in the United States is that it reflected a compromise between the views of the Federalists (who wanted a strong national government) and those of the Anti-Federalists (who wanted the states to retain their sovereignty).

2. The Constitution expressly delegated certain powers to the national government in Article I, Section 8. In addition to these expressed powers, the national government has implied and inherent powers. Implied powers are those that are reasonably necessary to carry out the powers expressly delegated to the national government. Inherent powers are those held by the national government by virtue of its being a sovereign state with the right to preserve itself.

3. The Tenth Amendment to the Constitution states that powers not delegated to the United States by the Constitution, nor prohibited by it to the states, are reserved to the states, or to the people. In certain areas, the Constitution provides for concurrent powers, such as the power to tax, which are powers that are held jointly by the national and state governments. The Constitution also denies certain powers to both the national government and the states.

4. The supremacy clause of the Constitution states that the Constitution, congressional laws, and national treaties are the supreme law of the land. States cannot use their reserved or concurrent powers to override national policies. Vertical checks and balances allow the states to influence the national government and vice versa.

5. The three most important clauses in the Constitution on interstate relations require that each state (1) give full faith and credit to every other state's public acts, records, and judicial proceedings; (2) extend to every other state's citizens the privileges and immunities of its own citizens; and (3) agree to return persons who are fleeing from justice back to their home state when requested to do so.

6. Two landmark Supreme Court cases expanded the constitutional powers of the national government. Chief Justice John Marshall's expansive interpretation of the necessary and proper clause of the Constitution in *McCulloch v. Maryland* (1819) permitted the "necessary and proper" clause to be used to enhance the power of the national government. Additionally, his decision made it clear that no state could tax a national institution. Marshall's broad interpretation of the commerce clause in *Gibbons v. Ogden* (1824) further extended the constitutional regulatory powers of the national government.

7. The controversy over slavery that led to the Civil War took the form of a fight over national government supremacy versus the rights of the separate states. Ultimately, the South's

desire for increased states' rights and the subsequent Civil War resulted in an increase in the political power of the national government.

8. Since the Civil War, federalism has evolved through at least two general phases: dual federalism and cooperative federalism. In dual federalism, each of the states and the federal government remain supreme within their own spheres. The era since the Great Depression has sometimes been labeled one of cooperative federalism, in which states and the national government cooperate in solving complex common problems.

9. Categorical grants from the federal government to state governments help finance many projects, such as Medicaid, highway construction, unemployment benefits, and welfare programs. By attaching special conditions to the receipt of federal grants, the national government can effect policy changes in areas typically governed by the states. Block grants, which group several categorical grants together, usually have fewer strings attached, thus giving state and local governments more flexibility in using funds. Federal mandates—laws requiring states to implement certain policies, such as policies to protect the environment—have generated controversy because of their cost.

10. Traditionally, conservatives have favored states' rights, and liberals have favored national authority. In part, this is because the national government has historically been an engine of change, while state governments have been more content with the status quo. States have also been reluctant to increase social spending because of a fear that the resulting taxes could interfere with a "favorable business climate" and discourage new business enterprises.

11. Resistance to African American civil rights by the Southern states prejudiced many people against states' rights in the 1960s. Renamed "federalism," the states' rights cause received Republican support in the 1970s and 1980s. Republican presidents Richard Nixon and Ronald Reagan sought to return power to the states through block grants and other programs. Under Republican President George W. Bush, however, the national government has gained power relative to that of the states.

12. The United States Supreme Court plays a significant role in determining the line between state and federal powers. Since the 1990s, the Court has been reining in somewhat the national government's powers under the commerce clause and has given increased emphasis to state powers under the Tenth and Eleventh Amendments to the Constitution.

SELECTED PRINT AND MEDIA RESOURCES

SUGGESTED READINGS

Gerston, Larry A. *American Federalism: A Concise Introduction.* New York: M. E. Sharpe, 2007. The author introduces the reader to the philosophical and historical foundations of the federal system. He examines cases of conflict throughout our history.

Hamilton, Alexander, et al. *The Federalist: The Famous Papers on the Principles of American Government.* Benjamin F. Wright, ed. New York: Friedman/Fairfax Publishing, 2002. These essays remain an authoritative exposition of the founders' views on federalism.

Karmis, Dimitrios, and Wayne Norman, eds. *Theories of Federalism: A Reader.* New York: Palgrave MacMillan, 2005. This reader brings together the most significant writings on Federalism from the late 18nth century to the present.

Manna, Paul. *School's In: Federalism and the National Education Agenda.* Washington, DC: Georgetown University Press, 2006. The author examines the changing relationship between the federal government and the states with regard to our public education system.

Nagel, Robert F. *The Implosion of American Federalism.* New York: Oxford University Press, 2002. The author contends that despite the states' rights trend of recent

years, which has been given force by the Supreme Court in several of its decisions, the nation faces the danger of increasingly centralized power.

MEDIA RESOURCES

Can the States Do It Better?—A 1996 film in which various experts discuss how much power the national government should have. The film uses documentary footage and other resources to illustrate this debate.

City of Hope—A 1991 movie by John Sayles. The film is a story of life, work, race, and politics in a modern New Jersey city. An African American alderman is one of the several major characters.

The Civil War—The PBS documentary series that made director Ken Burns famous. *The Civil War*, first shown in 1990, marked a revolution in documentary technique. Photographs, letters, eyewitness memoirs, and music are used to bring the war to life. The DVD version was released in 2002.

McCulloch v. Maryland and ***Gibbons v. Ogden***—These programs are part of the series *Equal Justice under Law: Landmark Cases in Supreme Court History*. They provide more details on cases that defined our federal system.

e-mocracy

YOUR FEDERAL, STATE, AND LOCAL GOVERNMENTS ARE AVAILABLE AT A CLICK OF YOUR MOUSE

Although online voting remains rare, your access to federal, state, and local government offices has improved dramatically since the Internet entered just about everybody's life. The number of government services available online is growing rapidly. Some researchers now talk about *e-government*. Instead of waiting in line to renew car registrations, residents of Scottsdale, Arizona, can renew online. In Colorado, heating and air-conditioning contractors can obtain permits from a Web site run by NetClerk, Inc. In many jurisdictions, all parking tickets can be handled with a credit card and a computer connected to the Internet.

At most colleges, it is now possible to apply online for financial aid. The federal government allows online applications for Social Security benefits and strongly encourages taxpayers to file their income tax returns electronically. Many citizens have found that e-government programs such as these make interactions with the government much simpler. It is no longer necessary to wait in line or to put up with the "bureaucratic shuffle."

LOGGING ON

Federalism is an important aspect of our democracy. To learn more about the establishment of our federal form of government and about current issues relating to federalism, visit the Web sites listed in the remainder of this section.

- To learn the founders' views on federalism, you can access the *Federalist Papers* at:
  www.law.emory.edu/erd/docs/federalist
- The following site has links to U.S. state constitutions, the *Federalist Papers*, and international federations, such as the European Union:
  www.constitution.org/cs_feder.htm
- The Council of State Governments is a good source for information on state responses to federalism issues. Go to:
  www.csg.org

- Another good source of information on issues facing state governments and federal-state relations is the National Governors Association's Web site at:
  www.nga.org
- If you would like to see the complete listing of the federal grants that may be distributed to states and local governments, look at the Catalog of Federal Domestic Assistance at:
  www.cfda.gov
- The Brookings Institution's policy analyses and recommendations on a variety of issues, including federalism, can be accessed at:
  www.brookings.edu
- For a libertarian approach to issues relating to federalism, go to the Cato Institute's Web page at:
  www.cato.org

ONLINE REVIEW

At **www.cengage.com/politicalscience/schmidt/agandpt14e**, you will find a Tutorial Quiz for this chapter providing questions on the chapter contents, including the features. The questions are organized to match the major sections of the chapter. You'll have access to other helpful study tools, including the book's glossary and flashcards, crossword puzzles, and Web links, as well as "Which Side Are You On?" and "Politics and . . ." features written by the authors of the book.

CHAPTER (4)

A college student holds a peace sign as he speaks to a group about race relations and racist symbols at Denison College in Ohio. (Columbus Dispatch/David Foster/AP Photos)

CIVIL LIBERTIES

QUESTIONS TO CONSIDER

Why is freedom of expression so fundamental to democracy?

What should be the relationship between religion and the political system?

What should be the balance between the rights of the accused and the rights of society to be protected from criminals?

CHAPTER CONTENTS

Making a DIFFERENCE

FRIENDS OF THE COURT AND CIVIL LIBERTIES

Freedom of Speech. Freedom of Religion. The Right to Bear Arms. Protection against Self-Incrimination. These basic civil liberties ensure that individuals are protected against overreaching government power. This truth, while fundamental to the American ethos, oversimplifies the relationship between society and government. There are often deep-seated disagreements over the appropriate balance between the rights of an individual or a group of individuals with the needs of society. These disagreements are often settled by the Supreme Court. Groups representing these individuals' interests have honed strategies for winning these conflicts; **amicus curiae briefs** are one such strategy.

As you will learn in Chapter 15, in cases before the Supreme Court, sometimes groups who are not named in the case but who have an interested stake in the outcome will file *amicus curiae* or "friend of the Court" briefs. Briefs are essays, laying out a position for a preferred outcome, framing the debate in a way that is advantageous to the brief's author, and suggesting appropriate legal grounding to support the position argued. "Friend of the Court" suggests neutrality, but most often these briefs support one party over the other. Research suggests that savvy attorneys will even solicit *amicus* briefs in order to bolster the arguments they are presenting. This is especially effective at the *certiorari* stage, or the point at which a litigant asks the Court to hear the case.[a]

Friends of the Court are often groups who have organized around particular interests, and the legal arguments they make are often premised on issues of civil liberties. For example, the research just described also found that groups like the American Civil Liberties Union (ACLU,

---

Amicus Curiae **Brief**
A legal document filed by an organization that is not a party to a lawsuit to provide additional information and attempt to influence the outcome of the case.

Civil Liberties
Those personal freedoms that are protected for all individuals. Civil liberties typically involve restraining the government's actions against individuals.

"THE LAND OF THE FREE." When asked what makes the United States distinctive, Americans commonly say that it is a free country. Americans have long believed that limits on the power of government are an essential part of what makes this country free. The first ten amendments to the U.S. Constitution—the Bill of Rights—place such limits on the national government. Of these amendments, none is more famous than the First Amendment, which guarantees freedom of religion, speech, the press, and other rights.

Most other democratic nations have laws to protect these and other **civil liberties**, but none of the laws is quite like the First Amendment, which states, "Congress shall make no law . . . abridging the freedom of speech, or of the press." Think about the issue of "hate speech." What if someone makes statements that stir up hatred toward a particular race or other group of people? In Germany, where memories of Nazi anti-Semitism remain alive, such speech is unquestionably illegal. In the United States, such speech may well be constitutionally protected, depending on the circumstances under which it occurred. Organizations like the American Civil Liberties Union mentioned in the *Making a Difference* box have often filed *amicus curiae* in support of people using such speech.

In this chapter, we describe the civil liberties provided by the Bill of Rights and some of the controversies that surround them. We look at the First Amendment liberties, including religion, speech, press, and assembly, and then discuss the right to privacy and the rights of the accused.

www.aclu.org) is highly sought to be an *amicus*. The ACLU's stated mission is to preserve all of the rights and protections found in the Bill of Rights, the post-Civil War amendments (Thirteenth, Fourteenth, and Fifteenth), and the Nineteenth Amendment that provided for women's suffrage. In fact, in a famous case, *Mapp v. Ohio* (1961),[b] the ACLU was instrumental in influencing the Court's decision making when it ruled that the exclusionary rule, barring admission of illegally obtained evidence in court, must extend to state laws. While political scientists debate whether the ACLU's *amicus* role is the exception or the norm, interest groups of all ideological viewpoints actively pursue an *amici* strategy.[c]

In fact, some of the most important, landmark Supreme Court cases have engendered record-setting numbers of *amici*. In *Webster v. Reproductive Health Services* (1989),[d] 78 *amici* briefs were filed on behalf of more than 400 individuals and organizations. This case was one in a long string of cases that began with *Roe v. Wade* (1973),[e] which provided a constitutionally protected right for a woman to terminate her pregnancy within the first trimester of gestation. As a result of *Roe*, many state legislatures whose majorities were conservative and who disapproved of the Court's decision in *Roe* passed laws designed to make it more difficult for a woman to obtain a first-trimester abortion. The proliferation of *amici* in *Webster* from groups as diverse as the American Medical Association, Americans United for the Separation of Church and State, Lutherans for Life, and the National Organization for Women, illustrates the way in which civil liberties groups use friend of the Court briefs to battle for their preferred outcomes.[f]

[a]Kevin T. McGuire, "Amici Curiae and Strategies for Gaining Access to the Supreme Court," *Political Research Quarterly*, 47, 1994, p. 821–837.

[b]367 U.S. 643

[c]Donald Songer, Ashlyn Kuersten, and Erin Kaheny, "Why the Haves Don't Always Come out Ahead: Repeat Players Meet Amici Curiae for the Disadvantaged," *Political Research Quarterly*, 53, 2000, p. 537–556.

[d]492 U.S. 490

[e]410 U.S. 113

[f]To read the text of these and other *amicus curiae* briefs, see http://curiae.law.yale.edu.

THE BILL OF RIGHTS

As you read through this chapter, bear in mind that the Bill of Rights, like the rest of the Constitution, is relatively brief. The framers set forth broad guidelines, leaving it up to the courts to interpret these constitutional mandates and apply them to specific situations. Thus, judicial interpretations shape the true nature of the civil liberties and rights that we possess. Because judicial interpretations change over time, so do our rights. As you will read in the following pages, there have been many conflicts over the meaning of such simple phrases as *freedom of religion* and *freedom of the press*. To understand what freedoms we actually have, we need to examine how the courts—and particularly the United States Supreme Court—have resolved some of those conflicts. One important conflict was over the issue of whether the Bill of Rights in the federal Constitution limited the powers of state governments as well as those of the national government.

DID YOU KNOW?

That one of the proposed initial constitutional amendments—"No State shall infringe the equal rights of conscience, nor the freedom of speech, nor of the press, nor of the right of trial by jury in criminal cases"—was never sent to the states for approval because the states' rights advocates in the First Congress defeated this proposal?

EXTENDING THE BILL OF RIGHTS TO STATE GOVERNMENTS

Many citizens do not realize that, as originally intended, the Bill of Rights limited only the powers of the national government. At the time the Bill of Rights was ratified, there was little concern over the potential of state governments to curb civil liberties. For

THESE EMPLOYEES of the National Security Agency (NSA) are working at the Threat Operations Center in Fort Meade, Maryland. This "super-secret" intelligence operation is heavily guarded. The NSA has admitted that it has engaged in domestic surveillance. Why were the actions of this agency seen as a threat to our First Amendment freedoms? (AP Photo/Evan Vucci)

one thing, state governments were closer to home and easier to control. For another, most state constitutions already had bills of rights. Rather, the fear was of the potential tyranny of the national government. The Bill of Rights begins with the words, "Congress shall make no law . . ." It says nothing about *states* making laws that might abridge citizens' civil liberties.

In 1833, in *Barron v. Baltimore*,[1] the United States Supreme Court held that the Bill of Rights did not apply to state laws. The issue in the case was whether a property owner could sue the city of Baltimore for recovery of his losses under the Fifth Amendment to the Constitution. Chief Justice Marshall spoke for a united court, declaring that the Supreme Court could not hear the case because the amendments were meant only to limit the national government.

We mentioned that most states had bills of rights. These bills of rights were similar to the national one, but there were some differences. Furthermore, each state's judicial system interpreted the rights differently. Citizens in different states, therefore, effectively had different sets of civil rights. Remember that the Thirteenth, Fourteenth, and Fifteenth Amendments were passed after the Civil War to guarantee equal rights to the former slaves and free black Americans, regardless of the states in which they lived. It was not until after the Fourteenth Amendment was ratified in 1868 that civil liberties guaranteed by the national Constitution began to be applied to the states. Section 1 of that amendment provides, in part, as follows:

No State shall . . . deprive any person of life, liberty, or property, without due process of law.

[1]7 Peters 243 (1833).

INCORPORATION OF THE FOURTEENTH AMENDMENT

There was no question that the Fourteenth Amendment applied to state governments. For decades, however, the courts were reluctant to define the liberties spelled out in the national Bill of Rights as constituting "due process of law," which was protected under the Fourteenth Amendment. Not until 1925, in *Gitlow v. New York*,[2] did the United States Supreme Court hold that the Fourteenth Amendment protected the freedom of speech guaranteed by the First Amendment to the Constitution.

Only gradually, and never completely, did the Supreme Court accept the **incorporation theory**—the view that most of the protections of the Bill of Rights are incorporated into the Fourteenth Amendment's protection against state government actions. Table 4–1 shows the rights that the Court has incorporated into the Fourteenth Amendment and the case in which it first applied each protection. As you can see in that table, in the 15 years following the *Gitlow* decision, the Supreme Court incorporated into the Fourteenth Amendment the other basic freedoms (of the press, assembly, the right to petition, and religion) guaranteed by the First Amendment. These and the later Supreme Court decisions listed in Table 4–1 have bound the 50 states to accept for their citizens most of the rights and freedoms that are set forth in the U.S. Bill of Rights. We now look at some of those rights and freedoms, beginning with the freedom of religion.

DID YOU KNOW?

That in a recent survey, nearly one-fourth of the respondents could not name any First Amendment rights?

Incorporation Theory
The view that most of the protections of the Bill of Rights apply to state governments through the Fourteenth Amendment's due process clause.

FREEDOM OF RELIGION

In the United States, freedom of religion consists of two main principles as they are presented in the First Amendment. The **establishment clause** prohibits the establishment of a church that is officially supported by the national government, thus guaranteeing a division between church and state. The *free exercise clause* constrains the national government from prohibiting individuals from practicing the religion of their choice. These two precepts can inherently be in tension with one another, however. For example, would prohibiting a group of students from holding prayer meetings in a public school classroom infringe on the students' right to free exercise of religion? Or would allowing the meetings amount to unconstitutional government support for religion? You will read about several difficult freedom of religion issues in the following discussion.

Establishment Clause
The part of the First Amendment prohibiting the establishment of a church officially supported by the national government. It is applied to questions of state and local government aid to religious organizations and schools, the legality of allowing or requiring school prayers, and the teaching of evolution versus intelligent design.

THE SEPARATION OF CHURCH AND STATE— THE ESTABLISHMENT CLAUSE

The First Amendment to the Constitution states, in part, that "Congress shall make no law respecting an establishment of religion." In the words of Thomas Jefferson, the establishment clause was designed to create a "wall of separation of Church and State."[3]

Perhaps Jefferson was thinking about the religious intolerance that characterized the first colonies. Many of the American colonies were founded by groups that were pursuing religious freedom for their own particular denomination. Nonetheless, the early colonists were quite intolerant of religious beliefs that did not conform to those held by the majority of citizens within their own communities. Jefferson undoubtedly was also aware that established churches (denominations) existed within nine of the original 13 colonies.

---

[2]268 U.S. 652 (1925).
[3]"Jefferson's Letter to the Danbury Baptists, The Final Letter, as Sent," January 1, 1802, The Library of Congress, Washington, D.C.

TABLE 4–1 Incorporating the Bill of Rights into the Fourteenth Amendment

YEAR	ISSUE	AMENDMENT INVOLVED	COURT CASE
1925	Freedom of speech	I	*Gitlow v. New York*, 268 U.S. 652
1931	Freedom of the press	I	*Near v. Minnesota*, 283 U.S. 697
1932	Right to a lawyer in capital punishment cases	VI	*Powell v. Alabama*, 287 U.S. 45
1937	Freedom of assembly and right to petition	I	*De Jonge v. Oregon*, 299 U.S. 353
1940	Freedom of religion	I	*Cantwell v. Connecticut*, 310 U.S. 296
1947	Separation of church and state	I	*Everson v. Board of Education*, 330 U.S. 1
1948	Right to a public trial	VI	*In re Oliver*, 333 U.S. 257
1949	No unreasonable searches and seizures	IV	*Wolf v. Colorado*, 338 U.S. 25
1961	Exclusionary rule	IV	*Mapp v. Ohio*, 367 U.S. 643
1962	No cruel and unusual punishment	VIII	*Robinson v. California*, 370 U.S. 660
1963	Right to a lawyer in all criminal felony cases	VI	*Gideon v. Wainwright*, 372 U.S. 335
1964	No compulsory self-incrimination	V	*Malloy v. Hogan*, 378 U.S. 1
1965	Right to privacy	I, III, IV, V, IX	*Griswold v. Connecticut*, 381 U.S. 479
1966	Right to an impartial jury	VI	*Parker v. Gladden*, 385 U.S. 363
1967	Right to a speedy trial	VI	*Klopfer v. North Carolina*, 386 U.S. 213
1969	No double jeopardy	V	*Benton v. Maryland*, 395 U.S. 784

As interpreted by the United States Supreme Court, the establishment clause in the First Amendment means at least the following:

Neither a state nor the federal government can set up a church. Neither can pass laws which aid one religion, aid all religions, or prefer one religion over another. Neither can force nor influence a person to go to or to remain away from church against his will or force him to profess a belief or disbelief in any religion. No person can be punished for entertaining or professing religious beliefs or disbeliefs, for church attendance or nonattendance. No tax in any amount, large or small, can be levied to support any religious activities or institutions, whatever they may be called, or whatever form they may adopt to teach or practice religion. Neither a state nor the federal government can, openly or secretly, participate in the affairs of any religious organizations or groups and vice versa.[4]

[4]*Everson v. Board of Education*, 330 U.S. 1 (1947).

The establishment clause is applied to all conflicts about such matters as the legality of state and local government aid to religious organizations and schools, allowing or requiring school prayers, the teaching of evolution versus intelligent design, the posting of the Ten Commandments in schools or public places, and discrimination against religious groups in publicly operated institutions. The establishment clause's mandate that government can neither promote nor discriminate against religious beliefs raises particularly complex questions at times.

Aid to Church-Related Schools. Throughout the United States, all property owners except religious, educational, fraternal, literary, scientific, and similar nonprofit institutions must pay property taxes. A large part of the proceeds of such taxes goes to support public schools. But not all children attend public schools. Fully 12 percent of school-aged children attend private schools, of which 85 percent have religious affiliations. Many cases have reached the United States Supreme Court; the Court has tried to draw a fine line between permissible public aid to students in church-related schools and impermissible public aid to religion. These issues have arisen most often at the elementary and secondary levels.

In 1971, in *Lemon v. Kurtzman*,[5] the Court ruled that direct state aid could not be used to subsidize religious instruction. The Court in the *Lemon* case gave its most general statement on the constitutionality of government aid to religious schools, stating that the aid had to be secular (nonreligious) in aim, that it could not have the primary effect of advancing or inhibiting religion, and that the government must avoid "an excessive government entanglement with religion." The three phrases above became known as the "three-part *Lemon* test" which has been applied in most of the cases under the establishment clause since 1971. The interpretation of the test, however, has varied over the years.

DID YOU KNOW?

That on the eve of the American Revolution, fewer than 20 percent of American adults adhered to a church in any significant way, compared with the 60 percent that do so today?

[5]403 U.S. 602 (1971).

In several cases, the Supreme Court has held that state programs helping church-related schools are unconstitutional. The Court also has denied state reimbursements to religious schools for field trips and for developing achievement tests. In a series of other cases, however, the Supreme Court has allowed states to use tax funds for lunches, textbooks, diagnostic services for speech and hearing problems, standardized tests, computers, and transportation for students attending church-operated elementary and secondary schools. In some cases, the Court argued that state aid was intended to directly assist the individual child, and in other cases, such as bus transportation, the Court acknowledged the state's goals for public safety.

A Change in the Court's Position. Generally, today's Supreme Court has shown a greater willingness to allow the use of public funds for programs in religious schools than was true at times in the past. Consider that in 1985, in *Aguilar v. Felton*,[6] the Supreme Court ruled that state programs providing special educational services for disadvantaged students attending religious schools violated the establishment clause. In 1997, however, when the Supreme Court revisited this decision, the Court reversed its position. In *Agostini v. Felton*,[7] the Court held that *Aguilar* was "no longer good law." What had happened between 1985 and 1997 to cause the Court to change its mind? Justice Sandra Day O'Connor answered this question in the *Agostini* opinion: What had changed since *Aguilar*, she stated, was "our understanding" of the establishment clause. Between 1985 and 1997, the Court's makeup had changed significantly. In fact, six of the nine justices who participated in the 1997 decision were appointed after the 1985 *Aguilar* decision.

School Vouchers. Questions about the use of public funds for church-related schools are likely to continue as state legislators search for new ways to improve the educational system in this country. An issue that has come to the forefront in recent years is school vouchers. In a voucher system, educational vouchers (state-issued credits) can be used to "purchase" education at any school, public or private.

School districts in Florida, Ohio, and Wisconsin have all been experimenting with voucher systems. In 2000, the courts reviewed a case involving Ohio's voucher program. Under that program, some $10 million in public funds is spent annually to send 4,300 Cleveland students to 51 private schools, all but five of which are Catholic schools. The case presented a straightforward constitutional question: Is it a violation of the principle of separation of church and state for public tax money to be used to pay for religious education?

In 2002, the Supreme Court held that the Cleveland voucher program was constitutional.[8] The Court concluded, by a five-to-four vote, that Cleveland's use of taxpayer-paid school vouchers to send children to private schools was constitutional, even though more than 95 percent of the students use the vouchers to attend Catholic or other religious schools. The Court's majority reasoned that the program did not unconstitutionally entangle church and state, because families theoretically could use the vouchers for their children to attend religious schools, secular private academies, suburban public schools, or charter schools, even though few public schools had agreed to accept vouchers. The Court's decision raised a further question that will need to be decided—whether religious and private schools that accept government vouchers must comply with disability and civil rights laws, as public schools are required to do.

Despite the United States Supreme Court's decision upholding the Cleveland voucher program, in 2006 the Florida Supreme Court declared Florida's voucher program

---

[6]473 U.S. 402 (1985).
[7]521 U.S. 203 (1997).
[8]*Zelman v. Simmons-Harris*, 536 U.S. 639 (2002).

unconstitutional. The Florida court held that the Florida state constitution bars public funding from being diverted to private schools that are not subject to the uniformity requirements of the state's public school system. The decision could have national implications if other states mount similar challenges to voucher programs. It remains to be seen whether the United States Supreme Court will review the Florida ruling.

The Issue of School Prayer—*Engel v. Vitale.* Do the states have the right to promote religion in general, without making any attempt to establish a particular religion? That is the question raised by school prayer and was the precise issue in 1962 in *Engel v. Vitale*,[9] the so-called Regents' Prayer case in New York. The State Board of Regents of New York had suggested that a prayer be spoken aloud in the public schools at the beginning of each day. The recommended prayer was as follows:

> Almighty God, we acknowledge our dependence upon Thee, And we beg Thy blessings upon us, our parents, our teachers, and our Country.

Such a prayer was implemented in many New York public schools. The parents of several students challenged the action of the regents, maintaining that it violated the establishment clause of the First Amendment. At trial, the parents lost. The Supreme Court, however, ruled that the regents' action was unconstitutional because "the constitutional prohibition against laws respecting an establishment of a religion must mean at least that in this country it is no part of the business of government to compose official prayers for any group of the American people to recite as part of a religious program carried on by any government." The Court's conclusion was based in part on the "historical fact that governmentally established religions and religious persecutions go hand in hand." In *Abington School District v. Schempp*,[10] the Supreme Court outlawed officially sponsored daily readings of the Bible and recitation of the Lord's Prayer in public schools.

The Debate over School Prayer Continues. Although the Supreme Court has ruled repeatedly against officially sponsored prayer and Bible-reading sessions in public schools, other means for bringing some form of religious expression into public education have been attempted. In 1983, the Tennessee legislature passed a bill requiring public school classes to begin each day with a minute of silence. Alabama had a similar law. In 1985, in *Wallace v. Jaffree*,[11] the Supreme Court struck down as unconstitutional the Alabama law authorizing one minute of silence for prayer or meditation in all public schools. Applying the three-part *Lemon* test, the Court concluded that the law violated the establishment clause because it was "an endorsement of religion lacking any clearly secular purpose."

THIS RALLY IN FAVOR OF a school voucher program was held on the grounds of the state capitol in Salt Lake City, Utah, during the spring of 2007. What groups might oppose school vouchers? Why? (AP Photo/Douglas C. Pizac)

[9]370 U.S. 421 (1962).
[10]374 U.S. 203 (1963).
[11]472 U.S. 38 (1985).

Since then, the lower courts have interpreted the Supreme Court's decision to mean that states can require a moment of silence in the schools as long as they make it clear that the purpose of the law is secular, not religious.

Prayer outside the Classroom. The courts have also dealt with cases involving prayer in public schools outside the classroom, particularly prayer during graduation ceremonies. In 1992, in *Lee v. Weisman*,[12] the United States Supreme Court held that it was unconstitutional for a school to invite a rabbi to deliver a nonsectarian prayer at graduation. The Court said nothing about *students* organizing and leading prayers at graduation ceremonies and other school events, however, and these issues continue to come before the courts. A particularly contentious question in the last few years has been the constitutionality of student-initiated prayers before sporting events, such as football games. In 2000, the Supreme Court held that while school prayer at graduation did not violate the establishment clause, students could not use a school's public-address system to lead prayers at sporting events.[13]

Despite the Court's ruling, students at several schools in Texas continue to pray over public-address systems at sporting events. In other areas, the Court's ruling is skirted by avoiding the use of the public-address system. For example, in a school in North Carolina, a pregame prayer was broadcast over a local radio station and heard by fans who took radios to the game for that purpose.

The Ten Commandments. A related church–state issue is whether the Ten Commandments may be displayed in public schools—or on any public property. In recent years, several states have considered legislation that would allow or even require schools to post the Ten Commandments in school buildings. Supporters of the "Hang Ten" movement claim that schoolchildren are not being taught the fundamental religious and family values that frame the American way of life. They argue further that the Ten Commandments are more than just religious documents. The Commandments are also secular in nature because they constitute a part of the official and permanent history of American government.

Opponents of such laws claim that they are an unconstitutional government entanglement with the religious life of citizens. Still, various Ten Commandments installations have been found to be constitutional. For example, the Supreme Court ruled in 2005 that a granite monument on the grounds of the Texas state capitol that contained the commandments was constitutional because the monument as a whole was secular in nature.[14] In another 2005 ruling, however, the Court ordered that displays of the Ten Commandments in front of two Kentucky county courthouses had to be removed because they were overtly religious.[15]

DID YOU KNOW?

That about two-thirds of 18- to 25-year-old Americans believe that humans and other living things evolved over time, whereas about one-third believe that all living things have existed in their present form since creation?

MARIAN WARD, RIGHT, who caused a controversy in 1999 with a pregame prayer, listens to her lawyer Kelly Coghlan, left, talk about their disappointment with a 6-3 Supreme Court decision barring students from leading stadium crowds in prayer. Why shouldn't a person be able to lead her friends in prayer in a public place? (Michael Stravato/AP Photos)

---

[12]505 U.S. 577 (1992).
[13]*Santa Fe Independent School District v. Doe*, 530 U.S. 290 (2000).
[14]*Van Orden v. Perry*, 125 S.Ct. 2854 (2005).
[15]*McCreary County v. American Civil Liberties Union*, 125 S.Ct. 2722 (2005).

WORKERS REMOVE a monument of the Ten Commandments from the rotunda area of the Alabama Judicial Building where Superior Court Justice Roy Moore had refused to take it down on August 27, 2003, in Montgomery, Alabama. Judge Moore was suspended by the state judicial review board for refusing to comply with the federal court order to remove the monument. (REUTERS/Tami Chappell/Landov Media)

The Ten Commandments controversy took an odd twist in 2003 when, in the middle of the night, former Alabama chief justice Roy Moore installed a two-and-a-half-ton granite monument featuring the Commandments in the rotunda of the state courthouse. When Moore refused to obey a federal judge's order to remove the monument, the Alabama Court of the Judiciary was forced to expel him from the judicial bench. The monument was wheeled away to a storage room.

Forbidding the Teaching of Evolution. For many decades, certain religious groups, particularly in Southern states, have opposed the teaching of evolution in the schools. To these groups, evolutionary theory directly counters their religious belief that human beings did not evolve but were created fully formed, as described in the biblical story of creation. State and local attempts to forbid the teaching of evolution, however, have not passed constitutional muster in the eyes of the United States Supreme Court. For example, in 1968, the Supreme Court held in *Epperson v. Arkansas*[16] that an Arkansas law prohibiting the teaching of evolution violated the establishment clause because it imposed religious beliefs on students. The Louisiana legislature passed a law requiring the teaching of the biblical story of the creation alongside the teaching of evolution. In 1987, in *Edwards v. Aguillard*,[17] the Supreme Court declared that this law was unconstitutional, in part because it had as its primary purpose the promotion of a particular religious belief.

Nonetheless, state and local groups around the country, particularly in the so-called Bible Belt, continue their efforts against the teaching of evolution. The Cobb County school system in Georgia attempted to include a disclaimer in its biology textbooks that proclaims, "Evolution is a theory, not a fact, regarding the origin of living things."

KEN HAM, president of Answers in Creation, previews the group's new Creation Museum. The museum, which presents the creationist view of the beginning of life, includes exhibits of children playing with dinosaurs. Far more visitors have come to the museum since its opening in 2007 than had been expected. (REUTERS/John Sommers II/Landov Media)

---

[16]393 U.S. 97 (1968).
[17]482 U.S. 578 (1987).

A federal judge later ruled that the disclaimer stickers must be removed. Other school districts have considered teaching "intelligent design" as an alternative explanation of the origin of life. Proponents of intelligent design contend that evolutionary theory has gaps that can be explained only by the existence of an intelligent creative force (God). They believe that teaching intelligent design in the schools is simply teaching another kind of scientific theory, so it would not breach the separation of church and state.

Critics of intelligent design have pointed out that many of its proponents have a religious agenda. Conservative evangelical Christians have often been the driving force behind efforts to teach intelligent design alongside evolution. The same religious groups also once backed creationism, a discredited theory that attempted to provide scientific evidence for the Bible's creation narrative. Furthermore, say the critics, intelligent design is not even a theory in the scientific sense of the word, as its claims cannot be disproved by examining real-world data. Therefore, intelligent design is a belief system. They insist that such religious agendas have no place in the public school system, where a firm separation between church and state must be respected.

Religious Speech. Another controversy in the area of church-state relations concerns religious speech in public schools or universities. For example, in *Rosenberger v. University of Virginia*,[18] the issue was whether the University of Virginia violated the establishment clause when it refused to fund a Christian group's newsletter but granted funds to more than 100 other student organizations. The Supreme Court ruled that the university's policy unconstitutionally discriminated against religious speech. The Court pointed out that the funds came from student fees, not general taxes, and was used for the "neutral" payment of bills for student groups.

Later, the Supreme Court reviewed a case involving a similar claim of discrimination against a religious group, the Good News Club. The club offers religious instruction to young schoolchildren. The club sued the school board of a public school in Milford, New York, when the board refused to allow the club to meet on school property after the school day ended. The club argued that the school board's refusal to allow the club to meet on school property, when other groups—such as the Girl Scouts and the 4-H Club—were permitted to do so, amounted to discrimination on the basis of religion. Ultimately, the Supreme Court agreed, ruling in *Good News Club v. Milford Central School*[19] that the Milford school board's decision violated the establishment clause.

THE FREE EXERCISE CLAUSE

Free Exercise Clause
The provision of the First Amendment guaranteeing the free exercise of religion.

The First Amendment constrains Congress from prohibiting the free exercise of religion. Does this **free exercise clause** mean that no type of religious practice can be prohibited or restricted by government? Certainly, a person can hold any religious belief that he or she wants, or a person can have no religious beliefs. When, however, religious *practices* work against public policy and the public welfare, the government can act. For example, regardless of a child's or parent's religious beliefs, the government can require certain types of vaccinations. The sale and use of marijuana for religious purposes has been held illegal, because a religion cannot make legal what would otherwise be illegal. Additionally, public school students can be required to study from textbooks chosen by school authorities.

The extent to which government can regulate religious practices has always been a subject of controversy. For example, in 1990 in *Oregon v. Smith*,[20] the United States Supreme Court ruled that the state of Oregon could deny unemployment benefits to two

---

[18]515 U.S. 819 (1995).
[19]533 U.S. 98 (2001).
[20]494 U.S. 872 (1990).

drug counselors who had been fired for using peyote, an illegal drug, in their religious services. The counselors had argued that using peyote was part of the practice of a Native American religion. Many criticized the decision as going too far in the direction of regulating religious practices.

The Religious Freedom Restoration Act. In 1993, Congress responded to the public's criticism by passing the Religious Freedom Restoration Act (RFRA). One of the specific purposes of the Act was to overturn the Supreme Court's decision in *Oregon v. Smith*. The Act required national, state, and local governments to "accommodate religious conduct" unless the government could show that there was a *compelling* reason not to do so. Moreover, if the government did regulate a religious practice, it had to use the least restrictive means possible.

Some people believed that the RFRA went too far in the other direction—it accommodated practices that were contrary to the public policies of state governments. Proponents of states' rights complained that the Act intruded into an area traditionally governed by state laws, not by the national government. In 1997, in *City of Boerne v. Flores*,[21] the Supreme Court agreed and held that Congress had exceeded its constitutional authority when it passed the RFRA. According to the Court, the Act's "sweeping coverage ensures its intrusion at every level of government, displacing laws and prohibiting official actions of almost every description and regardless of subject matter."

Free Exercise in the Public Schools. The courts have repeatedly held that U.S. governments at all levels must remain neutral on issues of religion. In the *Good News Club* decision discussed previously, the Supreme Court ruled that "state power is no more to be used to handicap religions than it is to favor them." Nevertheless, by overturning the RFRA, the Court cleared the way for public schools to set regulations that, while ostensibly neutral, effectively limited religious expression by students. An example is a

A MUSLIM GIRL in France arrives at school with her head covered in a traditional scarf. The French government has prohibited the wearing of such religious symbols in the schools. Could a state in the U.S. prohibit wearing a cross or another religious symbol in public schools? (Olivier Morin/AFP/Getty Images)

[21]521 U.S. 507 (1997).

rule banning hats, which has been instituted by many schools as a way of discouraging the display of gang insignia. This rule has also been interpreted as barring yarmulkes, the small caps worn by strictly observant Jewish boys and men.

The national government found a new way to ensure that public schools do not excessively restrict religion. To receive funds under the No Child Left Behind Act of 2002, schools must certify in writing that they do not ban prayer or other expressions of religion as long as they are made in a constitutionally appropriate manner.

FREEDOM OF EXPRESSION

Perhaps the most frequently invoked freedom that Americans have is the right to free speech and a free press without government interference. Each of us has the right to have our say, and all of us have the right to hear what others say. For the most part, Americans can criticize public officials and their actions without fear of reprisal by any branch of government.

NO PRIOR RESTRAINT

Prior Restraint
Restraining an action before the activity has actually occurred. When expression is involved, this means censorship.

Restraining an activity before that activity has actually occurred is called **prior restraint**. When expression is involved, prior restraint means censorship, as opposed to subsequent punishment. Prior restraint of expression would require, for example, that a permit be obtained before a speech could be made, a newspaper published, or a movie or TV show exhibited. Most, if not all, Supreme Court justices have been very critical of any governmental action that imposes prior restraint on expression. The Court clearly displayed this attitude in *Nebraska Press Association v. Stuart*,[22] a case decided in 1976:

> A prior restraint on expression comes to this Court with a "heavy presumption" against its constitutionality. . . . The government thus carries a heavy burden of showing justification for the enforcement of such a restraint.

One of the most famous cases concerning prior restraint was *New York Times v. United States*[23] in 1971, the so-called Pentagon Papers case. The *Times* and the *Washington Post* were about to publish the Pentagon Papers, an elaborate secret history of the U.S. government's involvement in the Vietnam War (1964–1975). The secret documents had been obtained illegally by a disillusioned former Pentagon official. The government wanted a court order to bar publication of the documents, arguing that national security was threatened and that the documents had been stolen. The newspapers argued that the public had a right to know the information contained in the papers and that the press had the right to inform the public. The Supreme Court ruled six to three in favor of the newspapers' right to publish the information. This case affirmed the no-prior-restraint doctrine.

THE PROTECTION OF SYMBOLIC SPEECH

Symbolic Speech
Nonverbal expression of beliefs, which is given substantial protection by the courts.

Not all expression is in words or in writing. Articles of clothing, gestures, movements, and other forms of expressive conduct are considered **symbolic speech**. Such speech is given substantial protection today by our courts. For example, in a landmark decision

---

[22]427 U.S. 539 (1976). See also *Near v. Minnesota*, 283 U.S. 697 (1931).
[23]403 U.S. 713 (1971).

DEMONSTRATORS burn U.S. flags in front of the World Bank headquarters in 2002, protesting the international meetings there. Why is it legal to burn the flag in protest? (Hiroko Masuike/ AFP/Getty Images)

issued in 1969, *Tinker v. Des Moines School District*,[24] the United States Supreme Court held that the wearing of black armbands by students in protest against the Vietnam War was a form of speech protected by the First Amendment. The case arose after a school administrator in Des Moines, Iowa, issued a regulation prohibiting students in the Des Moines School District from wearing the armbands. The Supreme Court reasoned that the school district was unable to show that the wearing of the armbands had disrupted normal school activities. Furthermore, the school district's policy was discriminatory, as it banned only certain forms of symbolic speech (the black armbands) and not others (such as lapel crosses and fraternity rings).

In 1989, in *Texas v. Johnson*,[25] the Supreme Court ruled that state laws that prohibited the burning of the American flag as part of a peaceful protest also violated the freedom of expression protected by the First Amendment. Congress responded by passing the Flag Protection Act of 1989, which was ruled unconstitutional by the Supreme Court in June 1990.[26] Congress and President George H. W. Bush immediately pledged to work for a constitutional amendment to "protect our flag"—an effort that has yet to be successful.

In 2003, however, the Supreme Court held that a Virginia statute prohibiting the burning of a cross with "an intent to intimidate" did not violate the First Amendment. The Court concluded that a burning cross is an instrument of racial terror so threatening that it overshadows free speech concerns.[27]

------

[24]393 U.S. 503 (1969).
[25]488 U.S. 884 (1989).
[26]*United States v. Eichman*, 496 U.S. 310 (1990).
[27]*Virginia v. Black*, 538 U.S. 343 (2003).

THE PROTECTION OF COMMERCIAL SPEECH

Commercial speech usually is defined as advertising statements. Can advertisers use their First Amendment rights to prevent restrictions on the content of commercial advertising? Until the 1970s, the Supreme Court held that such speech was not protected at all by the First Amendment. By the mid-1970s, however, more commercial speech had been brought under First Amendment protection. According to Justice Harry A. Blackmun, "Advertising, however tasteless and excessive it sometimes may seem, is nonetheless dissemination of information as to who is producing and selling what product for what reason and at what price."[28] Nevertheless, the Supreme Court will consider a restriction on commercial speech valid as long as it (1) seeks to implement a substantial government interest, (2) directly advances that interest, and (3) goes no further than necessary to accomplish its objective. In particular, a business engaging in commercial speech can be subject to liability for factual inaccuracies in ways that do not apply to noncommercial speech.

PERMITTED RESTRICTIONS ON EXPRESSION

At various times, restrictions on expression have been permitted. As we have seen after the terrorist attacks of September 11, 2001, periods of perceived foreign threats to the government sometimes lead to more repression of speech that is thought to be dangerous to the nation. It is interesting to note that the Supreme Court changes its view of what might be dangerous speech depending on the times.

Clear and Present Danger. When a person's remarks create a clear and present danger to the peace or public order, they can be curtailed constitutionally. Justice Oliver Wendell

IN 2002, A STUDENT who held this banner outside his school in Alaska was suspended for supporting drug use with his "speech." The Supreme Court upheld the principal's decision in the 2007 case *Morse v. Frederick*,[29] saying that public schools are able to regulate what students say about promoting illegal drug use. Do you think banning such speech is a violation of students' free speech rights? Should colleges be able to implement such a ban as well? (Clay Good/Zuma Press)

[28]*Virginia State Board of Pharmacy v. Virginia Citizens Consumer Council, Inc.*, 425 U.S. 748 (1976).
[29]*Morse v. Frederick*, 550 U.S. ___ (2007).

Holmes used this reasoning in 1919 when examining the case of a socialist who had been convicted for violating the Espionage Act by distributing a leaflet that opposed the military draft. Holmes stated:

> The question in every case is whether the words are used in such circumstances and are of such a nature as to create a *clear and present danger* that they will bring about the substantive evils that Congress has a right to prevent. It is a question of proximity and degree.[30] [Emphasis added.]

According to the **clear and present danger test**, then, expression may be restricted if evidence exists that such expression would cause a condition, actual or imminent, that Congress has the power to prevent. Commenting on this test, Justice Louis D. Brandeis in 1920 said, "Correctly applied, it will reserve the right of free speech . . . from suppression by tyrannists, well-meaning majorities, and from abuse by irresponsible, fanatical minorities."[31]

Clear and Present Danger Test
The test proposed by Justice Oliver Wendell Holmes for determining when government may restrict free speech. Restrictions are permissible, he argued, only when speech creates a *clear and present danger* to the public order.

Modifications to the Clear and Present Danger Rule. Since the clear and present danger rule was first enunciated, the United States Supreme Court has modified it. In 1925, during a period when many Americans feared the increasing power of communist and other left-wing parties in Europe, the Supreme Court heard the case *Gitlow v. New York*.[32] In its opinion, the Court introduced the *bad-tendency rule*. According to this rule, speech or other First Amendment freedoms may be curtailed if there is a possibility that such expression might lead to some "evil." In the *Gitlow* case, a member of a left-wing group was convicted of violating New York State's criminal anarchy statute when he published and distributed a pamphlet urging the violent overthrow of the U.S. government. In its majority opinion, the Supreme Court held that although the First Amendment afforded protection against state incursions on freedom of expression, Gitlow could be punished legally in this particular instance because his expression would tend to bring about evils that the state had a right to prevent.

The Supreme Court again modified the clear and present danger test in a 1951 case, *Dennis v. United States*.[33] During the early years of the Cold War, Americans were anxious about the activities of communists and the Soviet Union within the United States. Congress passed several laws that essentially outlawed the Communist Party of the United States and made its activities illegal. Twelve members of the American Communist Party were convicted of violating a statute that made it a crime to conspire to teach, advocate, or organize the violent overthrow of any government in the United States. The Supreme Court affirmed the convictions, significantly modifying the clear and present danger test in the process. The Court applied a *grave and probable danger rule*. Under this rule, "the gravity of the 'evil' discounted by its improbability justifies such invasion of free speech as is necessary to avoid the danger." This rule gave much less protection to free speech than did the clear and present danger test.

Six years after the *Dennis* case, the Supreme Court heard another case in which members of the Communist Party in California were accused of teaching and advocating the overthrow of the government of the United States. The ruling of the court in this case greatly reduced the scope of the law passed by Congress. In *Yates v. United States*,[34] the court held that there was a difference between "advocacy and teaching of forcible overthrow as an abstract principle" and actually proposing concrete action. The

[30]*Schenck v. United States*, 249 U.S. 47 (1919).
[31]*Schaefer v. United States*, 251 U.S. 466 (1920).
[32]268 U.S. 652 (1925).
[33]341 U.S. 494 (1951).
[34]354 U.S. 298 (1957).

Court overturned the convictions of the party leaders because they were essentially engaging in speech rather than action. This was the beginning of a series of cases that eventually found the original Congressional legislation to be unconstitutional for violating the First and Fourth Amendments.

Some claim that the United States did not achieve true freedom of political speech until 1969. In that year, in *Brandenburg v. Ohio*,[35] the Supreme Court overturned the conviction of a Ku Klux Klan leader for violating a state statute. The statute prohibited anyone from advocating "the duty, necessity, or propriety of sabotage, violence, or unlawful methods of terrorism as a means of accomplishing industrial or political reform." The Court held that the guarantee of free speech does not permit a state "to forbid or proscribe advocacy of the use of force or of law violation except where such advocacy is directed to inciting or producing imminent lawless actions and is likely to incite or produce such action." The incitement test enunciated by the Court in this case is a difficult one for prosecutors to meet. As a result, the Court's decision significantly broadened the protection given to advocacy speech.

UNPROTECTED SPEECH: OBSCENITY

Many state and federal statutes make it a crime to disseminate obscene materials. Generally, the courts have not been willing to extend constitutional protections of free speech to what they consider to be obscene materials. But what is obscenity? Justice Potter Stewart once stated, in *Jacobellis v. Ohio*,[36] a 1964 case, that even though he could not define *obscenity*, "I know it when I see it." The problem is that even if it were agreed on, the definition of *obscenity* changes with the times. Victorians deeply disapproved of the "loose" morals of the Elizabethan Age. The works of Mark Twain and Edgar Rice Burroughs at times have been considered obscene (after all, Tarzan and Jane were not legally wedded).

Definitional Problems. The Supreme Court has grappled from time to time with the difficulty of specifying an operationally effective definition of *obscenity*. In 1973, in *Miller v. California*,[37] Chief Justice Warren Burger created a formal list of requirements that must be met for material to be considered legally obscene. Material is obscene if (1) the average person finds that it violates contemporary community standards; (2) the work taken as a whole appeals to a prurient interest in sex; (3) the work shows patently offensive sexual conduct; and (4) the work lacks serious redeeming literary, artistic, political, or scientific merit. The problem is that one person's prurient interest is another person's medical interest or artistic pleasure. The Court went on to state that the definition of *prurient interest* would be determined by the community's standards. The Court avoided presenting a definition of *obscenity,* leaving this determination to local and state authorities. Consequently, the *Miller* case has been applied in a widely inconsistent manner.

Protecting Children. The Supreme Court has upheld state laws making it illegal to sell materials showing sexual performances by minors. In 1990, in *Osborne v. Ohio*,[38] the Court ruled that states can outlaw the possession of child pornography in the home. The Court reasoned that the ban on private possession is justified because owning the material perpetuates commercial demand for it and for the exploitation of the children involved. At the federal level, the Child Protection Act of 1984 made it a crime to receive knowingly through the mails sexually explicit depictions of children.

....

[35]395 U.S. 444 (1969).
[36]378 U.S. 184 (1964).
[37]413 U.S. 5 (1973).
[38]495 U.S. 103 (1990).

CHILDREN USE COMPUTERS at a Boston public library. Under the Children's Internet Protection Act (CIPA), public schools and libraries must install filtering software on their computers to prevent children from viewing pornographic material. What problems might the CIPA pose for adult library patrons? (AP Photo/Chitose Suzuki)

Pornography on the Internet. A significant problem facing Americans and lawmakers today is how to control obscenity and child pornography disseminated via the Internet. In 1996, Congress first attempted to protect minors from pornographic materials on the Internet by passing the Communications Decency Act (CDA). The Act made it a crime to make available to minors online any "obscene or indecent" message that "depicts or describes, in terms patently offensive as measured by contemporary community standards, sexual or excretory activities or organs." The Act was immediately challenged in court as an unconstitutional infringement on free speech. The Supreme Court held that the Act imposed unconstitutional restraints on free speech and was therefore invalid.[39] In the eyes of the Court, the terms *indecent* and *patently offensive* covered large amounts of nonpornographic material with serious educational or other value.

Later attempts by Congress to curb pornography on the Internet also encountered stumbling blocks. For example, the Child Online Protection Act (COPA) of 1998 banned the distribution of material "harmful to minors" without an age-verification system to separate adult and minor users. In 2002, the Supreme Court upheld a lower court injunction suspending the COPA, and in 2004, the Court again upheld the suspension of the law on the ground that it was probably unconstitutional.[40] In 2000, Congress enacted the Children's Internet Protection Act (CIPA), which requires public schools and libraries to install filtering software to prevent children from viewing Web sites with "adult" content.

Should "Virtual" Pornography Be Deemed a Crime? In 2001, the Supreme Court agreed to review a case challenging the constitutionality of another federal act attempting to protect minors in the online environment—the Child Pornography Prevention Act (CPPA) of 1996. This Act made it illegal to distribute or possess computer-generated images that appear to depict minors engaging in lewd and lascivious behavior. At issue was whether digital child pornography should be considered a crime even though it uses only digitally rendered images and no actual children are involved.

[39]*Reno v. American Civil Liberties Union*, 521 U.S. 844 (1997).
[40]*Ashcroft v. American Civil Liberties Union*, 542 U.S. 656 (2004).

The Supreme Court, noting that virtual child pornography is not the same as child pornography, held that the CPPA's ban on virtual child pornography restrained a substantial amount of lawful speech.[41] The Court stated, "The statute proscribes the visual depiction of an idea—that of teenagers engaging in sexual activity—that is a fact of modern society and has been a theme in art and literature throughout the ages." The Court concluded that the act was overbroad and thus unconstitutional.

UNPROTECTED SPEECH: SLANDER

Defamation of Character
Wrongfully hurting a person's good reputation. The law imposes a general duty on all persons to refrain from making false, defamatory statements about others.

Can you say anything you want about someone else? Not really. Individuals are protected from **defamation of character**, which is defined as wrongfully hurting a person's good reputation. The law imposes a general duty on all persons to refrain from making false, defamatory statements about others. Breaching this duty orally is the wrongdoing called *slander*. Breaching it in writing is the wrongdoing called *libel*, which we discuss later. The government does not bring charges of slander or libel. Rather, the defamed person may bring a civil suit for damages.

Slander
The public uttering of a false statement that harms the good reputation of another. The statement must be made to, or within the hearing of, persons other than the defamed party.

Legally, **slander** is the public uttering of a false statement that harms the good reputation of another. Slanderous public uttering means that the defamatory statements are made to, or within the hearing of, persons other than the defamed party. If one person calls another dishonest, manipulative, and incompetent to his or her face when no one else is around, that does not constitute slander. The message is not communicated to a third party. If, however, a third party accidentally overhears defamatory statements, the courts have generally held that this constitutes a public uttering and therefore slander, which is prohibited.

CAMPUS SPEECH

In recent years, students have been facing free-speech challenges on campuses. One issue has to do with whether a student should have to subsidize, through student activity fees, organizations that promote causes that the student finds objectionable.

Student Activity Fees. In 2000, this question came before the United States Supreme Court in a case brought by several University of Wisconsin students. The students argued that their mandatory student activity fees—which helped to fund liberal causes with which they disagreed, including gay rights—violated their First Amendment rights of free speech, free association, and free exercise of religion. They contended that they should have the right to choose whether to fund organizations that promoted political and ideological views that were offensive to their personal beliefs. To the surprise of many, the Supreme Court rejected the students' claim and ruled in favor of the university. The Court stated that "the university may determine that its mission is well served if students have the means to engage in dynamic discussions of philosophical, religious, scientific, social, and political subjects in their extracurricular life. If the university reaches this conclusion, it is entitled to impose a mandatory fee to sustain an open dialogue to these ends."[42]

Campus Speech and Behavior Codes. Another free speech issue is the legitimacy of campus speech and behavior codes. Some state universities have established codes that challenge the boundaries of the protection of free speech provided by the First Amendment. These codes are designed to prohibit so-called hate speech—abusive speech attacking persons on the basis of their ethnicity, race, or other criteria. For example, a University

---

[41]*Ashcroft v. Free Speech Coalition*, 535 U.S. 234 (2002).
[42]*Board of Regents of the University of Wisconsin System v. Southworth*, 529 U.S. 217 (2000).

of Michigan code banned "any behavior, verbal or physical, that stigmatizes or victimizes an individual on the basis of race, ethnicity, religion, sex, sexual orientation, creed, national origin, ancestry, age, marital status, handicap" or Vietnam-veteran status. A federal court found that the code violated students' First Amendment rights.[43]

Although the courts generally have held, as in the University of Michigan case, that campus speech codes are unconstitutional restrictions on the right to free speech, such codes continue to exist. Whether hostile speech should be banned on high school campuses has also become an issue. In view of school shootings and other violent behavior in the schools, school officials have become concerned about speech that consists of veiled threats or that could lead to violence. Some schools have even prohibited students from wearing clothing, such as T-shirts bearing verbal messages (such as sexist or racist comments) or symbolic messages (such as the Confederate flag), that might generate "ill will or hatred."

Defenders of campus speech codes argue that they are necessary not only to prevent violence but also to promote equality among different cultural, ethnic, and racial groups on campus and greater sensitivity to the needs and feelings of others. In recent years, law schools even attempted to bar military recruiters from their campuses. The law schools argued that the military's policy toward homosexuals was discriminatory and violated their own antidiscrimination policies.

In response, Congress passed the Solomon Amendment, which required all colleges and universities receiving federal funds to open their campuses to military recruiters. Unless the recruiters were granted the same access as any other company or prospective employer, federal funding would be forfeited.

In 2003, law schools and numerous concerned faculty members formed the Forum for Academic and Institutional Rights (FAIR) and filed a suit in federal court. The law schools claimed that the Solomon Amendment violated their rights to free speech and freedom of association. The United States Supreme Court disagreed. In March 2006, the Court handed down a unanimous eight-to-zero decision holding the Solomon Amendment constitutional.[44] Chief Justice John Roberts noted in his opinion that the Amendment does not infringe in any way on an institution's freedom of speech. Roberts also held that Congress could even directly force schools to allow recruiting through the "raise and support Armies" clause of the Constitution.

HATE SPEECH ON THE INTERNET

Extreme hate speech appears on the Internet, including racist materials and denials of the Holocaust (the murder of millions of Jews by the Nazis during World War II). Can the federal government restrict this type of speech? Should it? Content restrictions can be difficult to enforce. Even if Congress succeeded in passing a law prohibiting particular speech on the Internet, an army of "Internet watchers" would be needed to enforce it. Also, what if other countries attempt to impose their laws that restrict speech on U.S. Web sites? This is not a theoretical issue. In 2000, a French court found Yahoo! in violation of French laws banning the display of Nazi memorabilia. In 2001, however, a U.S. district court held that this ruling could not be enforced against Yahoo! in the United States.[45]

---

[43]*Doe v. University of Michigan*, 721 F.Supp. 852 (1989).
[44]*Rumsfeld v. Forum for Academic and Institutional Rights, Inc.*, 547 U.S. 47.
[45]*Yahoo!, Inc. v. La Ligue Contre le Racisme et l'Antisemitisme*, 169 F.Supp. 2d 1181 (N.D. Cal. 2001).

FREEDOM OF THE PRESS

Freedom of the press can be regarded as a special instance of freedom of speech. Of course, at the time of the framing of the Constitution, the press meant only newspapers, magazines, and books. As technology has modified the ways in which we disseminate information, the laws touching on freedom of the press have been modified. What can and cannot be printed still occupies an important place in constitutional law, however. (To see how freedom of the press is viewed elsewhere in the world, see this chapter's *Beyond Our Borders* feature.)

DEFAMATION IN WRITING

Libel
A written defamation of a person's character, reputation, business, or property rights.

Libel is defamation in writing (or in pictures, signs, films, or any other communication that has the potentially harmful qualities of written or printed words). As with slander, libel occurs only if the defamatory statements are observed by a third party. If one person writes a private letter to another person wrongfully accusing him or her of embezzling funds, that does not constitute libel. It is interesting that the courts have generally held that dictating a letter to a secretary constitutes communication of the letter's contents to a third party, and therefore, if defamation has occurred, the wrongdoer can be sued.

Actual Malice
Either knowledge of a defamatory statement's falsity or a reckless disregard for the truth.

A 1964 case, *New York Times Co. v. Sullivan*,[46] explored an important question regarding libelous statements made about public officials. The Supreme Court held that only when a statement against a public official was made with **actual malice**—that is, with either knowledge of its falsity or a reckless disregard of the truth—could damages be obtained.

Public Figure
A public official, movie star, or other person known to the public because of his or her position or activities.

The standard set by the Court in the *New York Times* case has since been applied to **public figures** generally. Public figures include not only public officials but also public employees who exercise substantial governmental power and any persons who are generally in the limelight. Statements made about public figures, especially when they are

POLICE COMMISSIONER L. B. Sullivan (second from right) celebrates his $500,000 libel suit victory in the case *New York Times Co. v. Sullivan.* From left are attorneys J. Roland Nachman, Jr., who directed the plaintiff's suit, Calvin Whitesell, Sullivan, and Sam Rice Baker. (Bettmann/CORBIS)

[46]376 U.S. 254 (1964).

made through a public medium, usually are related to matters of general public interest; they are made about people who substantially affect all of us. Furthermore, public figures generally have some access to a public medium for answering disparaging falsehoods about themselves, whereas private individuals do not. For these reasons, public figures have a greater burden of proof (they must prove that the statements were made with actual malice) in defamation cases than do private individuals.

A FREE PRESS VERSUS A FAIR TRIAL: GAG ORDERS

Another major issue relating to freedom of the press concerns media coverage of criminal trials. The Sixth Amendment to the Constitution guarantees the right of criminal suspects to a fair trial. In other words, the accused have rights. The First Amendment guarantees freedom of the press. What if the two rights appear to be in conflict? Which one prevails?

Jurors certainly may be influenced by reading news stories about the trial in which they are participating. In the 1970s, judges increasingly issued **gag orders**, which restricted the publication of news about a trial in progress or even a pretrial hearing. In a landmark 1976 case, *Nebraska Press Association v. Stuart*,[47] the Supreme Court unanimously ruled that a Nebraska judge's gag order had violated the First Amendment's guarantee of freedom of the press. Chief Justice Warren Burger indicated that even pervasive adverse pretrial publicity did not necessarily lead to an unfair trial, and that prior restraints on publication were not justified. Some justices even went so far as to suggest that gag orders are never justified.

Despite the *Nebraska Press Association* ruling, the Court has upheld certain types of gag orders. In *Gannett Co. v. De Pasquale*[48] in 1979, for example, the highest court held that if a judge found a reasonable probability that news publicity would harm a defendant's right to a fair trial, the court could impose a gag rule: "Members of the public have no constitutional right under the Sixth and Fourteenth Amendments to attend criminal trials."

Gag Order
An order issued by a judge restricting the publication of news about a trial or a pretrial hearing to protect the accused's right to a fair trial.

RADIO "SHOCK JOCK" Howard Stern offended the sensibilities of the Federal Communications Commission (FCC). That regulatory body fined Stern's radio station owner hundreds of thousands of dollars for Stern's purportedly obscene outbursts on radio in 1992 and again in 2004. The extent to which the FCC can regulate speech over the air involves the First Amendment. But the current FCC regulation does not apply to pay-for-service satellite radio, pay-for-service cable TV, or satellite TV. To take advantage of this, in December of 2005, Stern took his show to satellite radio, thus, for now, evading FCC regulation. Why is it that what is permissible and acceptable on radio and TV today probably would have been considered obscene three decades ago? (Getty Images)

[47] 427 U.S. 539 (1976).
[48] 443 U.S. 368 (1979).

BEYOND OUR B RDERS

AN UPROAR OVER CARTOONS

An international imbroglio erupted when a Danish newspaper printed cartoon images that were deemed offensive by many Muslims. The cartoons, many of which depicted the Prophet Muhammad unfavorably and linked the Islamic faith to international terrorism, enraged Muslims all over the globe. When newspapers in some other European countries reprinted the offensive cartoons, riots broke out, European embassies were attacked, and already tense relations between Muslims and Westerners degraded. The dispute over the cartoons opened an international debate about freedom of expression.

THE FREEDOM TO OFFEND?

Without question, the caricatures of Muhammad were offensive. In the Islamic faith, creating any kind of image of the Prophet or Allah (God) is strictly forbidden. Thus, the offensive nature of the cartoons merely added further insult to an already taboo portrayal. Moreover, many Muslims living in Europe perceived the cartoons as yet another example of racial and religious discrimination.

In contrast, many Westerners saw the publication of the cartoons as a freedom of expression issue. Nonetheless, most Westerners viewed the cartoons as offensive and unnecessarily inflammatory. The European newspaper editors argued that they had every right to publish the images, even as they apologized for offending the Muslim community. The editors felt that freedom of expression should not be restrained, regardless of the reaction it may cause. French and German newspapers insisted that democratic freedoms include the "right to blasphemy."

REVEALING DEEPER TENSIONS AND DIFFERENCES

The cartoon dispute also revealed a deeper cultural rift between many Muslims and Westerners. Significant numbers of Muslims living in Europe and North America have been revolted by what they consider to be overly "liberal" attitudes toward personal freedom, individualism, sex, family structure, and religion. For their part, many Westerners have been critical of what they perceive as Muslims' religious fundamentalism and immigrant Muslims' unwillingness to assimilate culturally and politically to their new surroundings.

Most Westerners were shocked at the reaction spurred by the cartoons. The violent attacks on European and American embassies in the Middle East and other Muslim areas were perhaps the most bewildering. In Gaza, for example, gunmen appeared at the offices of the European Union, firing automatic weapons and threatening further violence unless the offending nations apologized for the cartoons.

U.S. MEDIA AND THE CARTOONS

Most U.S. media sources decided not to reprint the offending cartoons. Some outlets, such as NBC News, chose to offer links to the images via their Web sites. Nonetheless, the cartoons were a hot topic on television news channels and in newspaper editorial sections across the country. Some defended the cartoons as free speech, whereas others focused on the need to be more respectful of sensitive religious and cultural topics. Columnist Kathleen Parker summed up the difficulty of reconciling Western notions of free expression with the fundamentalist reactions of some Muslims: "Until Muslim nations and peoples get the idea that free expression means freedom to offend as well as the necessary correlative—to be offended—we have a problem."*

FOR CRITICAL ANALYSIS

Some commentators spoke of the need to find a balance between freedom of expression and respect for religious beliefs.

1. Do you believe that such a balance can be found?
2. Is it desirable to restrict freedom of expression in some instances? Explain.

*Kathleen Parker, *Washington Post*, February 2, 2006.

The *Nebraska* and *Gannett* cases, however, involved pretrial hearings. Could a judge impose a gag order on an entire trial, including pretrial hearings? In 1980, in *Richmond Newspapers, Inc. v. Virginia*,[49] the Court ruled that actual trials must be open to the public except under unusual circumstances.

FILMS, RADIO, AND TV

As we have noted, only in a few cases has the Supreme Court upheld prior restraint of published materials. The Court's reluctance to accept prior restraint is less evident with respect to motion pictures. In the first half of the 20th century, films were routinely submitted to local censorship boards. In 1968, the Supreme Court ruled that a film can be banned only under a law that provides for a prompt hearing at which the film is shown to be obscene. Today, few local censorship boards exist. Instead, the film industry regulates itself primarily through the industry's rating system.

Radio and television broadcasting has the least First Amendment protection. Broadcasting initially received less protection than the printed media because, at that time, the number of airwave frequencies was limited. In 1934, the national government established the Federal Communications Commission (FCC) to regulate electromagnetic wave frequencies. No one has a right to use the airwaves without a license granted by the FCC. The FCC grants licenses for limited periods and imposes a variety of regulations on broadcasting. Based on a case decided by the Supreme Court in 1978,[50] the FCC can impose sanctions on radio or TV stations that broadcast "filthy words," even if the words are not legally obscene. During the George W. Bush administration, the FCC acted more frequently to sanction radio and television broadcasters for the use of words, phrases, and pictures that might be considered in the category of "filthy words."

THE RIGHT TO ASSEMBLE AND TO PETITION THE GOVERNMENT

The First Amendment prohibits Congress from making any law that abridges "the right of the people peaceably to assemble, and to petition the Government for a redress of grievances." Inherent in such a right is the ability of private citizens to communicate their ideas on public issues to government officials, as well as to other individuals. The Supreme Court has often put this freedom on a par with freedom of speech and freedom of the press. Nonetheless, it has allowed municipalities to require permits for parades, sound trucks, and demonstrations so that public officials can control traffic or prevent demonstrations from turning into riots.

The freedom to demonstrate became a major issue in 1977 when the American Nazi Party sought to march through Skokie, Illinois, a largely Jewish suburb where many Holocaust survivors resided. The American Civil Liberties Union defended the Nazis' right to march (despite its opposition to the Nazi philosophy). The Supreme Court let stand a lower court's ruling that the city of Skokie had violated the Nazis' First Amendment guarantees by denying them a permit to march.[51]

---

[49]448 U.S. 555 (1980).
[50]*FCC v. Pacifica Foundation*, 438 U.S. 726 (1978). The phrase "filthy words" refers to a monologue by comedian George Carlin, which became the subject of the court case.
[51]*Smith v. Collin*, 439 U.S. 916 (1978).

ONLINE ASSEMBLY

A question for Americans today is whether individuals should have the right to "assemble" online to advocate violence against certain groups (such as physicians who perform abortions) or advocate values that are opposed to our democracy (such as terrorism). While some online advocacy groups promote interests consistent with American political values, other groups aim to destroy those values. Whether First Amendment freedoms should be sacrificed (by the government's monitoring of Internet communications, for example) in the interests of national security is a question that will no doubt be debated for some time to come.

MORE LIBERTIES UNDER SCRUTINY: MATTERS OF PRIVACY

No explicit reference is made anywhere in the Constitution to a person's right to privacy. Until the second half of the 1990s, the courts did not take a very positive approach toward the right to privacy. For example, during Prohibition, suspected bootleggers' telephones were tapped routinely, and the information obtained was used as a legal basis for prosecution. In *Olmstead v. United States*[52] in 1928, the Supreme Court upheld such an invasion of privacy. Justice Louis Brandeis, a champion of personal freedoms, strongly dissented from the majority decision in this case. He argued that the framers of the Constitution gave every citizen the right to be left alone. He called such a right "the most comprehensive of rights and the right most valued by civilized men."

....

[52]277 U.S. 438 (1928). This decision was overruled later in *Katz v. United States*, 389 U.S. 347 (1967).

WHAT IF...

THE GOVERNMENT MONITORED ALL E-MAIL?

Shortly after the terrorist attacks of September 11, 2001, the U.S. government passed the USA PATRIOT Act (which stands for Uniting and Strengthening America by Providing Appropriate Tools Required to Intercept and Obstruct Terrorism). Designed to help law enforcement and intelligence-gathering agencies combat terrorism threats, the PATRIOT Act expanded the possible ways that government agencies can obtain information about individuals, including, in some cases, reading a suspect's e-mail.

If the government filtered all e-mail, Americans would experience the kind of invasion of privacy that is commonplace in nations such as China. Software that can track Internet activity, such as spyware and keystroke-capturing programs, has existed for quite some time. The use of such programs is typically associated with criminal activities such as identity theft and cyberstalking. The government could easily employ variations of these types of software to monitor individuals' e-mail and Internet activity.

There is already precedent for using electronic monitoring programs in the United States. Numerous U.S. corporations have implemented electronic surveillance to monitor their employees' e-mail and Web use. In several instances, the information gleaned from such practices has resulted in employees being terminated or having criminal charges brought against them.

Such electronic monitoring would also represent a serious threat to freedom of speech. Americans would be less likely to express themselves candidly or research topics that might cast suspicion on them. Web logs (blogs), especially those with political content, would undoubtedly suffer. The Internet has become an important marketplace of ideas and information, and any threat to freedom of expression would likely curtail its growth, scope, and diversity of content.

Consider the level of surveillance imposed by the Chinese government. In China, the government employs more than 30,000 individuals to monitor Internet traffic of all forms. E-mail and blogs are censored and scrutinized. Many words, including *freedom*, are blocked out by software and government employees. In addition, most Internet users are forced to log in and register through a government program so that their activities can be tracked and subjected to surveillance. Privacy on the Internet is almost completely nonexistent. Interestingly, much of the software used in China was developed by U.S. and other Western companies.

FOR CRITICAL ANALYSIS

1. Would you use the Internet any differently if you thought that the government might be monitoring your e-mail and Internet activity?
2. Your college or university owns the rights over all e-mail activity you engage in through the school's e-mail server. To what extent do you think the university monitors use of the Internet?
3. Should hate speech, bomb-making instructions, or government documents be censored on the Internet?

In the 1960s, the highest court began to modify the majority view. In 1965, in *Griswold v. Connecticut*,[53] the Supreme Court overturned a Connecticut law that effectively prohibited the use of contraceptives, holding that the law violated the right to privacy. Justice William O. Douglas formulated a unique way of reading this right into the Bill of Rights. He claimed that the First, Third, Fourth, Fifth, and Ninth Amendments created "penumbras [shadows], formed by emanations [things sent out from] those guarantees that help give them life and substance," and he went on to describe zones of privacy that are guaranteed by these rights. When we read the Ninth Amendment, we

[53]381 U.S. 479 (1965).

can see the foundation for his reasoning: "The enumeration in the Constitution, of certain rights, shall not be construed to deny or disparage [belittle] others retained by the people." In other words, just because the Constitution, including its amendments, does not specifically talk about the right to privacy does not mean that this right is denied to the people.

Some of today's most controversial issues relate to privacy rights. One issue involves the erosion of privacy rights in an information age, as computers make it easier to compile and distribute personal information. Other issues concern abortion and the "right to die." Since the terrorist attacks of September 11, 2001, Americans have faced another crucial question regarding privacy rights: To what extent should Americans sacrifice privacy rights in the interests of national security?

PRIVACY RIGHTS IN AN INFORMATION AGE

An important privacy issue, created in part by new technology, is the amassing of information on individuals by government agencies and private businesses, such as marketing firms, grocery stores, and casinos, to name just a few. Personal information on the average American citizen also is filed away in dozens of agencies—such as the Social Security Administration and the Internal Revenue Service. Because of the threat of indiscriminate use of private information by unauthorized individuals, Congress passed the Privacy Act in 1974. This was the first law regulating the use of federal government information about private individuals. Under the Privacy Act, every citizen has the right to obtain copies of personal records collected by federal agencies and to correct inaccuracies in such records.

The ease with which personal information can be obtained by using the Internet for marketing and other purposes has led to unique privacy issues. Some fear that privacy rights in personal information may soon be a thing of the past. However, for today's young adults, the concept of privacy seems to have evolved into a concept that individuals define for themselves. Portraits on public Web sites such as MySpace or other networking sites are created by the user and can protect personal data or make certain facts *very public*. The person who submits the information gets to decide. Whether privacy rights can survive in an information age is a question that Americans and their leaders continue to confront.

A STUDENT at the University of Missouri browses Facebook while in class. The popular online social networking site is sometimes used by school administrators and prospective employers to check out student behavior. (L. G. Patterson/ AP Photo)

IN 2006, ON THE 33rd anniversary of *Roe v. Wade*, opposing sides on the abortion issue argued with each other in front of the United States Supreme Court building in Washington, D.C. What was the major argument against laws prohibiting abortion that the Court used in the *Roe* case? (AP Photo/Pablo Martinez Monsivais)

PRIVACY RIGHTS AND ABORTION

Historically, abortion was not a criminal offense before the "quickening" of the fetus (the first movement of the fetus in the uterus, usually between the 16th and 18th weeks of pregnancy). During the last half of the 19th century, however, state laws became more severe. By 1973, performing an abortion at any time during pregnancy was a criminal offense in a majority of the states.

Roe v. Wade. In 1973, in Roe v. Wade,[54] the United States Supreme Court accepted the argument that the laws against abortion violated "Jane Roe's" right to privacy under the Constitution. The Court held that during the first trimester (three months) of pregnancy, abortion was an issue solely between a woman and her physician. The state could not limit abortions except to require that they be performed by licensed physicians. During the second trimester, to protect the health of the mother, the state was allowed to specify the conditions under which an abortion could be performed. During the final trimester, the state could regulate or even outlaw abortions, except when necessary to preserve the life or health of the mother.

After *Roe*, the Supreme Court issued decisions in several cases defining and redefining the boundaries of state regulation of abortion. During the 1980s, the Court twice struck down laws that required a woman who wished to have an abortion to undergo counseling designed to discourage abortions. In the late 1980s and early 1990s, however, the Court took a more conservative approach. For example, in *Webster v. Reproductive Health Services*[55] in 1989, the Court upheld a Missouri statute that, among other things, banned the use of public hospitals or other taxpayer-supported facilities for performing abortions. And, in *Planned Parenthood v. Casey*[56] in 1992, the Court upheld a Pennsylvania law that required preabortion counseling, a waiting period of 24 hours, and, for girls under the age of 18, parental or judicial permission. The *Casey* decision was remarkable for several reasons. The final decision was a five-to-four vote with Sandra Day O'Connor writing the opinion. While the opinion explicitly upheld

---

[54]410 U.S. 113 (1973). Jane Roe was not the real name of the woman in this case. It is a common legal pseudonym used to protect a person's privacy.
[55]492 U.S. 490 (1989).
[56]505 U.S. 833 (1992).

Roe, it changed the grounds on which the states can regulate abortion. The court found that states could not place an "undue burden" on a woman who sought an abortion. In this case, the court found that spousal notification was such a burden. Because many other conditions were upheld, abortions continue to be more difficult to obtain in some states than others.

The Controversy Continues. Abortion continues to be a divisive issue. Right-to-life forces continue to push for laws banning abortion, to endorse political candidates who support their views, and to organize protests. Because of several episodes of violence attending protests at abortion clinics, in 1994 Congress passed the Freedom of Access to Clinic Entrances Act. The Act prohibits protesters from blocking entrances to such clinics. The Supreme Court ruled in 1993 that such protesters can be prosecuted under laws governing racketeering, and in 1998 a federal court in Illinois convicted right-to-life protesters under these laws. In 1997, the Supreme Court upheld the constitutionality of prohibiting protesters from entering a 15-foot "buffer zone" around abortion clinics and from giving unwanted counseling to those entering the clinics.[57] In 2006, however, the Supreme Court unanimously reversed its earlier decision that antiabortion protesters could be prosecuted under laws governing racketeering.[58]

In a 2000 decision, the Court upheld a Colorado law requiring demonstrators to stay at least eight feet away from people entering and leaving clinics unless people consent to be approached. The Court concluded that the law's restrictions on speech-related conduct did not violate the free speech rights of abortion protesters.[59]

In the same year, the Supreme Court again addressed the abortion issue directly when it reviewed a Nebraska law banning "partial-birth" abortions. Similar laws had been passed by at least 27 states. A partial-birth abortion, which physicians call intact dilation and extraction, is a procedure that can be used during the second trimester of pregnancy. Abortion rights advocates claim that in limited circumstances the procedure is the safest way to perform an abortion, and that the government should never outlaw specific medical procedures. Opponents argue that the procedure has no medical merit and that it ends the life of a fetus that might be able to live outside the womb. The Supreme Court invalidated the Nebraska law on the grounds that, as written, the law could be used to ban other abortion procedures, and it contained no provisions for protecting the health of the pregnant woman.[60] In 2003, legislation similar to the Nebraska statute was passed by the U.S. Congress and signed into law by President George W. Bush. It was immediately challenged in court. In 2007, the Supreme Court heard several challenges to the partial-birth abortion law and upheld the constitutionality of that legislation, saying that the law was specific enough that it did not "impose an undue burden" on women seeking an abortion.[61]

In a move that will likely set off another long legal battle, in 2006 the South Dakota legislature passed a law that banned almost all forms of abortion in the state. The bill's supporters hope that it will eventually force the United States Supreme Court to reconsider *Roe v. Wade*. Opponents of the bill have already filed suit.

PRIVACY RIGHTS AND THE "RIGHT TO DIE"

A 1976 case involving Karen Ann Quinlan was one of the first publicized right-to-die cases.[62] The parents of Quinlan, a young woman who had been in a coma for nearly a year and who had been kept alive during that time by a respirator, wanted her

---

[57]*Schenck v. ProChoice Network*, 519 U.S. 357 (1997).
[58]*Scheidler v. National Organization for Women*, 126 S.Ct. 1264 (2006).
[59]*Hill v. Colorado*, 530 U.S. 703 (2000).
[60]*Stenberg v. Carhart*, 530 U.S. 914 (2000).
[61]*Gonzales v. Carhart*, 550 U.S. ___ (2007) and *Gonzales v. Planned Parenthood*, 550 U.S.___ (2007).
[62]*In re Quinlan*, 70 N.J. 10 (1976).

respirator removed. In 1976, the New Jersey Supreme Court ruled that the right to privacy includes the right of a patient to refuse treatment and that patients who are unable to speak can exercise that right through a family member or guardian. In 1990, the Supreme Court took up the issue. In *Cruzan v. Director, Missouri Department of Health*,[63] the Court stated that a patient's life-sustaining treatment can be withdrawn at the request of a family member only if there is "clear and convincing evidence" that the patient did not want such treatment.

What If There Is No Living Will? Since the 1976 *Quinlan* decision, most states have enacted laws permitting people to designate their wishes concerning life-sustaining procedures in "living wills" or durable health care powers of attorney. These laws and the Supreme Court's *Cruzan* decision have resolved the right-to-die controversy for situations in which the patient has drafted a living will. Disputes are still possible if there is no living will. An example is the case of Terri Schiavo. The husband of the Florida woman, who had been in a persistent vegetative state for more than a decade, sought to have her feeding tube removed on the basis of oral statements that she would not want her life prolonged in such circumstances. Schiavo's parents fought this move in court but lost on the ground that a spouse, not a parent, is the appropriate legal guardian for a married person. Although the Florida legislature passed a law allowing Governor Jeb Bush to overrule the courts, the state Supreme Court held that the law violated the state constitution.[64]

The case escalated into a national drama in March 2005 when the U.S. Congress intervened and passed a law allowing Schiavo's case to be heard in the federal court system. The federal courts, however, essentially agreed with the Florida state courts' findings and refused to order the reconnection of the feeding tube, which had been disconnected a few days earlier. After twice appealing to the United States Supreme Court without success, the parents gave up hope, and Schiavo died shortly thereafter.

Physician-Assisted Suicide. In the 1990s, another issue surfaced: Do privacy rights include the right of terminally ill people to end their lives through physician-assisted suicide? Until 1996, the courts consistently upheld state laws that prohibited this practice, either through specific statutes or under their general homicide statutes. In 1996, after

IN 2006, the United States Supreme Court upheld Oregon's position on its physician-assisted suicide law. In this photo, Scott Rice, whose wife used Oregon's law to end her life, shows an artist's sketch of the Court's proceedings. Why would the federal government challenge Oregon's Death with Dignity Act? (AP Photo/Don Ryan)

[63]497 U.S. 261 (1990).
[64]*Bush v. Schiavo*, 885 So.2d 321 (Fla. 2004).

two federal appellate courts ruled that state laws banning assisted suicide (in Washington and New York) were unconstitutional, the issue reached the United States Supreme Court. In 1997, in *Washington v. Glucksberg*,[65] the Court stated, clearly and categorically, that the liberty interest protected by the Constitution does not include a right to commit suicide, with or without assistance. In effect, the Supreme Court left the decision in the hands of the states. Since then, assisted suicide has been allowed in only one state—Oregon. In 2006, the Supreme Court upheld Oregon's physician-assisted suicide law against a challenge from the Bush administration.[66]

PRIVACY RIGHTS VERSUS SECURITY ISSUES

As former Supreme Court Justice Thurgood Marshall once said, "Grave threats to liberty often come in times of urgency, when constitutional rights seem too extravagant to endure." Not surprisingly, antiterrorist legislation since the attacks on September 11, 2001, has eroded certain basic rights, in particular the Fourth Amendment protections against unreasonable searches and seizures. Several tools previously used against certain types of criminal suspects (e.g., "roving wiretaps" and National Security Letters) have been authorized for use against a broader array of terror suspects. Many civil liberties organizations argue that abuses of the Fourth Amendment are ongoing.

While it has been possible for a law enforcement agency to gain court permission to wiretap a telephone virtually since telephones were invented, a roving wiretap allows the agency to tap all forms of communication used by the named person, including cell phones and e-mail, and it applies across legal jurisdictions. Previously, roving wiretaps could only be requested for persons suspected of one of a small number of serious crimes. Now if persons are suspected of planning a terrorist attack, they can be monitored no matter what form of electronic communication they use. Such roving wiretaps appear to contravene the Supreme Court's interpretation of the Fourth Amendment, which requires a judicial warrant to describe the *place* to be searched, not just the person, although the Court has not banned them to date. One of the goals of the framers was to avoid *general* searches. Further, once a judge approves an application for a roving wiretap, when, how, and where the monitoring occurs will be left to the discretion of law enforcement agents. Supporters of these new procedures say that they allow agents to monitor individuals as they move about the nation. Previously, a warrant issued in one federal district might not be valid in another.

Moreover, President George W. Bush approved a plan by the National Security Agency to eavesdrop on telephone calls between individuals overseas and those in the United States if one party was a terrorist suspect. This plan was carried out without warrants because the administration claimed that speed was more important. Critics called for immediate termination of such eavesdropping. The Congress has continued to reform legislation on this issue.

The USA PATRIOT Act. Much of the government's failure to anticipate the attacks of September 11, 2001, has been attributed to a lack of cooperation among government agencies. At that time, barriers prevented information sharing between the law enforcement and intelligence arms of the government. A major objective of the USA PATRIOT Act was to lift those barriers. Lawmakers claimed that the PATRIOT Act would improve lines of communication between agencies such as the Federal Bureau of Investigation (FBI) and the Central Intelligence Agency (CIA), thereby allowing the government to better anticipate terrorist plots. With improved communication, various agencies could more effectively coordinate their efforts in combating terrorism.

In addition, the PATRIOT Act eased restrictions on the government's ability to investigate and arrest suspected terrorists. Because of the secretive nature of terrorist groups,

---

[65]521 U.S. 702 (1997).
[66]*Gonzales v. Oregon*, 126 S.Ct. 904 (2006).

supporters of the PATRIOT Act argue that the government must have greater latitude in pursuing leads on potential terrorist activity. After receiving approval of the Foreign Intelligence Surveillance Court (known as FISA), the Act authorizes law enforcement officials to secretly search a suspected terrorist's home. It also allows the government to monitor a suspect's Internet activities, phone conversations, financial records, and book purchases. Although a number of these search and surveillance tactics have long been a part of criminal investigations, the PATRIOT Act expanded their scope to include individuals as suspects even if they are not agents of a foreign government.

Civil Liberties Concerns. Proponents of the PATRIOT Act insist that ordinary, law-abiding citizens have nothing to fear from the government's increased search and surveillance powers. Groups such as the ACLU have objected to the PATRIOT Act, however, arguing that it poses a grave threat to constitutionally guaranteed rights and liberties. Under the PATRIOT Act, FBI agents are required to certify the need for search warrants to the FISA Court. Rarely are such requests rejected.

In the last few years, the FBI began using another tool that it has had for several years, the National Security Letter (NSL), to avoid the procedures required by the FISA Court. The NSL allows the FBI to get records of telephone calls, subscriber information, and other kinds of transactions, although it does not give the FBI access to the content of the calls. However, as Congress tightened the requirements for warrants under the PATRIOT Act, the FBI evidently began to use the NSLs as a shortcut. While the use of NSLs has been legal for more than 20 years, recent massive use of this technique has led Congress to consider further restrictions on the FBI and its investigations in order to preserve the rights of U.S. citizens.

Opponents of the PATRIOT Act fear that these expanded powers of investigation might be used to silence government critics or to threaten members of interest groups who oppose government polices today or in the future. Congress debated all of these issues in 2005 and then renewed most of the provisions of the Act in 2006. One of the most controversial aspects of the PATRIOT Act permits the government to eavesdrop on telephone calls with a warrant from the FISA court. In 2005, it became known that the Bush administration was eavesdropping on U.S. telephone calls without a warrant if the caller was from outside the U.S. After almost three years of controversy, Congress passed the FISA Amendments Act in June 2008, which regulates such calls and gives immunity from prosecution to telecommunications companies.

THE ACLU HAS consistently opposed the PATRIOT Act as an unconstitutional violation of a citizen's right to privacy. These information sheets were passed out to both the Republican and Democratic delegates at the national conventions in 2004. What argument does the federal government use to support the PATRIOT Act? (Courtesy of aclu.org)

THE GREAT BALANCING ACT: THE RIGHTS OF THE ACCUSED VERSUS THE RIGHTS OF SOCIETY

The United States has one of the highest murder rates in the industrialized world. It is not surprising, therefore, that many citizens have extremely strong opinions about the rights of those accused of violent crimes. When an accused person, especially one who has confessed to some criminal act, is set free because of an apparent legal technicality, many people believe that the rights of the accused are being given more weight than the rights of society and of potential or actual victims. Why, then, give criminal suspects rights? The answer is partly to avoid convicting innocent people, but mostly because all criminal suspects have the right to due process of law and fair treatment.

The courts and the police must constantly engage in a balancing act of competing rights. At the basis of all discussions about the appropriate balance is the U.S. Bill of Rights. The Fourth, Fifth, Sixth, and Eighth Amendments deal specifically with the rights of criminal defendants. (You will learn about some of your rights under the Fourth Amendment in the *You Can Make a Difference* feature at the end of this chapter.)

RIGHTS OF THE ACCUSED

The basic rights of criminal defendants are outlined in Table 4-2. When appropriate, the specific constitutional provision or amendment on which a right is based is also given.

TABLE 4–2 Basic Rights of Criminal Defendants

LIMITS ON THE CONDUCT OF POLICE OFFICERS AND PROSECUTORS
No unreasonable or unwarranted searches and seizures (Amend. IV)
No arrest except on probable cause (Amend. IV)
No coerced confessions or illegal interrogation (Amend. V)
No entrapment
On questioning, a suspect must be informed of her or his rights
DEFENDANT'S PRETRIAL RIGHTS
Writ of *habeas corpus* (Article I, Section 9)
Prompt **arraignment** (Amend. VI)
Legal counsel (Amend. VI)
Reasonable bail (Amend. VIII)
To be informed of charges (Amend. VI)
To remain silent (Amend. V)
TRIAL RIGHTS
Speedy and public trial before a jury (Amend. VI)
Impartial jury selected from a cross section of the community (Amend. VI)
Trial atmosphere free of prejudice, fear, and outside interference
No compulsory self-incrimination (Amend. V)
Adequate counsel (Amend. VI)
No cruel and unusual punishment (Amend. VIII)
Appeal of convictions
No double jeopardy (Amend. V)

Writ of *habeas corpus*
Habeas corpus means, literally, "you have the body." A writ of *habeas corpus* is an order that requires jailers to bring a prisoner before a court or judge and explain why the person is being held.

Arraignment
The first act in a criminal proceeding, in which the defendant is brought before a court to hear the charges against him or her and enter a plea of guilty or not guilty.

EXTENDING THE RIGHTS OF THE ACCUSED

During the 1960s, the Supreme Court, under Chief Justice Earl Warren, significantly expanded the rights of accused persons. In *Gideon v. Wainwright*,[67] a case decided in 1963, the Court held that if a person is accused of a felony and cannot afford an attorney, an attorney must be made available to the accused person at the government's expense. This case was particularly interesting because Gideon, who was arrested for stealing a small amount of money from a vending machine, was not considered a dangerous man, nor was his intellect in any way impaired. As related by Anthony Lewis,[68] Gideon pursued his own appeal to the Supreme Court because he believed that every accused person who might face prison should be represented. Although the Sixth Amendment to the Constitution provides for the right to counsel, the Supreme Court had established a precedent 21 years earlier in *Betts v. Brady*,[69] when it held that only criminal defendants in capital (death penalty) cases automatically had a right to legal counsel.

Miranda v. Arizona. In 1966, the Court issued its decision in *Miranda v. Arizona*.[70] The case involved Ernesto Miranda, who was arrested and charged with the kidnapping and rape of a young woman. After two hours of questioning, Miranda confessed and was later convicted. Miranda's lawyer appealed his conviction, arguing that the police had never informed Miranda that he had a right to remain silent and a right to be represented by counsel. The Court, in ruling in Miranda's favor, enunciated the *Miranda* rights that are now familiar to virtually all Americans:

> Prior to any questioning, the person must be warned that he has a right to remain silent, that any statement he does make may be used against him, and that he has a right to the presence of an attorney, either retained or appointed.

Two years after the Supreme Court's *Miranda* decision, Congress passed the Omnibus Crime Control and Safe Streets Act of 1968. Section 3501 of the act reinstated a rule that had been in effect for 180 years before *Miranda*—that statements by defendants

AN OFFICER IN TRAINING reads *Miranda* rights to a handcuffed suspect at the Edward M. Davis LAPD Training Facility in Los Angeles during a training situation involving arresting a violent criminal. Why is using the correct procedure so important in securing an arrest? (Kim Kulish/CORBIS)

[67]372 U.S. 335 (1963).
[68]Anthony Lewis, *Gideon's Trumpet* (New York: Vintage, 1964).
[69]316 U.S. 455 (1942).
[70]384 U.S. 436 (1966).

can be used against them if the statements were made voluntarily. The Justice Department immediately disavowed Section 3501 as unconstitutional and has continued to hold this position. As a result, Section 3501, although it was never repealed, has never been enforced. In 2000, in a surprise move, a federal appellate court held that the all-but-forgotten provision was enforceable, but the Supreme Court held that the *Miranda* warnings were constitutionally based and could not be overruled by a legislative act.[71]

Exceptions to the *Miranda* Rule. As part of a continuing attempt to balance the rights of accused persons against the rights of society, the Supreme Court has made several exceptions to the *Miranda* rule. In 1984, for example, the Court recognized a "public-safety" exception to the rule. The need to protect the public warranted the admissibility of statements made by the defendant (in this case, indicating where he had placed a gun) as evidence in a trial, even though the defendant had not been informed of his *Miranda* rights.

In 1985, the Court further held that a confession need not be excluded even though the police failed to inform a suspect in custody that his attorney had tried to reach him by telephone. In an important 1991 decision, the Court stated that a suspect's conviction will not be automatically overturned if the suspect was coerced into making a confession. If the other evidence admitted at trial is strong enough to justify the conviction without the confession, then the fact that the confession was obtained illegally in effect can be ignored. In yet another case, in 1994, the Supreme Court ruled that suspects must unequivocally and assertively state their right to counsel in order to stop police questioning. Saying "Maybe I should talk to a lawyer" during an interrogation after being taken into custody is not enough. The Court held that police officers are not required to decipher the suspect's intentions in such situations.

Video Recording of Interrogations. In view of the numerous exceptions, there are no guarantees that the *Miranda* rule will survive indefinitely. Increasingly, though, law enforcement personnel are using digital cameras to record interrogations. According to some scholars, the recording of *all* custodial interrogations would satisfy the Fifth Amendment's prohibition against coercion and in the process render the *Miranda* warnings unnecessary. Others argue, however, that recorded interrogations can be misleading.

DID YOU KNOW?

That in 18th-century England, pocket picking and similar crimes were punishable by the death penalty?

THE EXCLUSIONARY RULE

Exclusionary Rule
A policy forbidding the admission at trial of illegally seized evidence.

At least since 1914, judicial policy has prohibited the admission of illegally seized evidence at trials in federal courts. This is the so-called **exclusionary rule**. Improperly obtained evidence, no matter how telling, cannot be used by prosecutors. This includes evidence obtained by police in violation of a suspect's *Miranda* rights or of the Fourth Amendment. The Fourth Amendment protects against unreasonable searches and seizures and provides that a judge may issue a search warrant to a police officer only on *probable cause* (a demonstration of facts that permit a reasonable belief that a crime has been committed). The question that must be determined by the courts is what constitutes an unreasonable search and seizure.

The reasoning behind the exclusionary rule is that it forces police officers to gather evidence properly, in which case their due diligence will be rewarded by a conviction. Nevertheless, the exclusionary rule has always had critics who argue that it permits guilty persons to be freed because of innocent errors.

This rule was first extended to state court proceedings in a 1961 United States Supreme Court decision, *Mapp v. Ohio*.[72] In this case, the Court overturned the convic-

---

[71]*Dickerson v. United States*, 530 U.S. 428 (2000).
[72]367 U.S. 643 (1961).

tion of Dollree Mapp for the possession of obscene materials. Police found pornographic books in her apartment after searching it without a search warrant and despite her refusal to let them in.

Over the last several decades, the Supreme Court has diminished the scope of the exclusionary rule by creating some exceptions to its applicability. For example, in 1984, the Court held that illegally obtained evidence could be admitted at trial if law enforcement personnel could prove that they would have obtained the evidence legally anyway. In another case decided in the same year, the Court held that a police officer who used a technically incorrect search warrant form to obtain evidence had acted in good faith and therefore the evidence was admissible at trial. The Court thus created the "good faith" exception to the exclusionary rule.

THE DEATH PENALTY

Capital punishment remains one of the most debated aspects of our criminal justice system. Those in favor of the death penalty maintain that it serves as a deterrent to serious crime and satisfies society's need for justice and fair play. Those opposed to the death penalty do not believe it has any deterrent value and hold that it constitutes a barbaric act in an otherwise civilized society.

CRUEL AND UNUSUAL PUNISHMENT?

The Eighth Amendment prohibits cruel and unusual punishment. Throughout history, "cruel and unusual" referred to punishments that were more serious than the crimes— the phrase referred to torture and to executions that prolonged the agony of dying. The Supreme Court never interpreted "cruel and unusual" to prohibit all forms of capital punishment in all circumstances. Indeed, several states had imposed the death penalty for a variety of crimes and allowed juries to decide when the condemned could be sentenced to death. However, many believed that the imposition of the death penalty was random and arbitrary, and in 1972 the Supreme Court agreed in *Furman v. Georgia*.[73]

GEORGE WHITE, PICTURED in the foreground, spent seven years in an Alabama prison after he was convicted of murdering his wife. The state ultimately admitted that he had been falsely accused of the crime and released him from prison. Here, he speaks out against the death penalty. What are some of the arguments for and against capital punishment? (Independent Record/George Lane/AP Photo)

[73]408 U.S. 238 (1972).

The Supreme Court's 1972 decision stated that the death penalty, as then applied, violated the Eighth and Fourteenth Amendments. The Court ruled that capital punishment is not necessarily cruel and unusual if the criminal has killed or attempted to kill someone. In its opinion, the Court invited the states to enact more precise laws so that the death penalty would be applied more consistently. By 1976, 25 states had adopted a two-stage, or *bifurcated*, procedure for capital cases. In the first stage, a jury determines the guilt or innocence of the defendant for a crime that has been determined by statute to be punishable by death. If the defendant is found guilty, the jury reconvenes in the second stage and considers all relevant evidence to decide whether the death sentence is, in fact, warranted.

In *Gregg v. Georgia*,[74] the Supreme Court ruled in favor of Georgia's bifurcated process, holding that the state's legislative guidelines had removed the ability of a jury to "wantonly and freakishly impose the death penalty." The Court upheld similar procedures in Texas and Florida, establishing a procedure for all states to follow that would assure them protection from lawsuits based on Eighth Amendment grounds. On January 17, 1977, Gary Mark Gilmore became the first American to be executed (by Utah) under the new laws.

FIGURE 4–1 The States and the Death Penalty: Executions Since 1976 and the Death Row Population

Today, as shown in this figure, 36 states and the federal government and military have laws permitting capital punishment. Since 1976, there have been 1,119 executions in the U.S., with 42 in 2007 and 20 in 2008 at the time this book went to press.

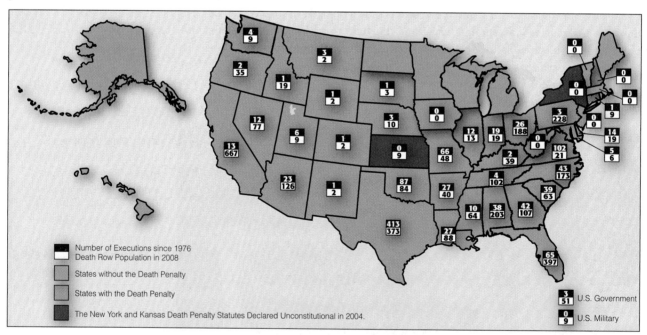

Sources: U.S. Department of Justice, Bureau of Justice Statistics, "Capital Punishment, 2006," www.ojp.usdoj.gov/bjs; Death Penalty Information Center, "Death Row Inmates of State and Size of Death Row by Year," January/February 2008; and "Facts About the Death Penalty," September 15, 2008, www.deathpenaltyinfo.org.

[74]428 U.S. 153 (1976).

THE DEATH PENALTY TODAY

Today, 38 states (see Figure 4–1) and the federal government have capital punishment laws based on the guidelines established by the *Gregg* case. State governments are responsible for almost all executions in this country. The executions of Timothy McVeigh and Juan Raul Garza in 2001 marked the first death sentences carried out by the federal government since 1963. At this time, about 3,700 prisoners are on death row across the nation.

The number of executions per year reached a high in 1998 at 98, and then began to fall. Some believe that the declining number of executions reflects the waning support among Americans for the imposition of the death penalty. In 1994, polls indicated that 80 percent of Americans supported the death penalty. Recent polls, however, suggest that this number has dropped to between 50 and 60 percent, depending on the poll, possibly because of public doubt about the justice of the system. Recently, DNA testing has shown that some innocent people may have been convicted unjustly of murder. Since 1973, more than 100 prisoners have been freed from death row after new evidence suggested that they were wrongfully convicted.

The number of executions may decline even further due to the Supreme Court's 2002 ruling in *Ring v. Arizona.*[75] The Court held that only juries, not judges, could impose the death penalty, thus invalidating the laws of five states that allowed judges to make this decision. The ruling meant that the death sentences of 168 death row inmates would have to be reconsidered by the relevant courts. The sentences of many of these inmates have been commuted to life in prison.

TIME LIMITS FOR DEATH ROW APPEALS

In 1996, Congress passed the Anti-Terrorism and Effective Death Penalty Act. The law limits access to the federal courts for all defendants convicted in state courts. It also imposes a severe time limit on death row appeals. The law requires federal judges to hear these appeals and issue their opinions within a specified time period. Many are concerned that the shortened appeals process increases the possibility that innocent persons may be put to death before evidence that might free them can be discovered. On average, it takes about seven years to exonerate someone on death row; however, the time between conviction and execution has been shortened from an average of 10 to 12 years to an average of six to eight years.

[75]536 U.S. 548 (2002).

You can make a difference

YOUR CIVIL LIBERTIES: SEARCHES AND SEIZURES

Our civil liberties include numerous provisions, many of them listed in the Bill of Rights, that protect persons who are suspected of criminal activity. Among these are limits on how the police—as agents of the government—can conduct searches and seizures.

WHY SHOULD YOU CARE?

You may be the most law-abiding person in the world, but that will not guarantee that you will never be stopped, arrested, or searched by the police. Sooner or later, most citizens will have some kind of interaction with the police. People who do not understand their rights or how to behave toward law enforcement officers can find themselves in serious trouble. The words of advice in this feature actually provide you with key survival skills for life in the modern world.

WHAT CAN YOU DO?

How should you behave if you are stopped by police officers? Your civil liberties protect you from having to provide information other than your name and address. Normally, even if you have not been placed under arrest, the officers have the right to frisk you for weapons, and you must let them proceed. The officers cannot, however, check your person or your clothing further if, in their judgment, no weaponlike object is produced.

The officers may search you only if they have a search warrant or probable cause to believe that a search will likely produce incriminating evidence. What if the officers do not have probable cause or a warrant? Physically resisting their attempt to search you can lead to disastrous results. It is best simply to refuse orally to give permission for the search, preferably in the presence of a witness. Being polite is better than acting out of anger and making the officers irritable. It is usually advisable to limit what you say to the officers. If you are arrested, it is best to keep quiet until you can speak with a lawyer.

If you are in your car and are stopped by the police, the same fundamental rules apply. Always be ready to show your driver's license and car registration. You may be asked to get out of the car. The officers may use a flashlight to peer inside the car if it is too dark to see otherwise. None of this constitutes a search. A true search requires either a warrant or probable cause. No officer has the legal right to search your car simply to find out if you may have committed a crime. Police officers can conduct searches that are incident to lawful arrests, however.

If you are in your home and a police officer with a search warrant appears, you can ask to examine the warrant before granting entry. A warrant that is correctly made out will state the place or persons to be searched, the object sought, and the date of the warrant (which should be no more than 10 days old), and it will bear the signature of a judge or magistrate. If the warrant is in order, you need not make any statement. If you believe the warrant to be invalid, or if no warrant is produced, you should make it clear orally that you have not consented to the search, preferably in the presence of a witness. If the search later is proved to be unlawful, normally any evidence obtained cannot be used in court.

Officers who attempt to enter your home without a search warrant can do so only if they are pursuing a suspected felon into the house. Rarely is it advisable to give permission for a warrantless search. You, as the resident, must be the one to give permission if any evidence obtained is to be considered legal. The landlord, manager, or head of a college dormitory cannot give legal permission. A roommate, however, can give permission for a search of his or her room, which may allow the police to search areas where you have belongings.

If you are a guest in a place that is being legally searched, you may be legally searched as well. But unless you have been placed under arrest, you cannot be compelled to go to the police station or get into a squad car.

If you would like to find out more about your rights and obligations under the laws of searches and seizures, you might wish to contact the following organization:

American Civil Liberties Union
125 Broad St., 18th Floor
New York, NY 10004
212-549-2500
www.aclu.org

KEY TERMS

CHAPTER SUMMARY

1. Originally, the Bill of Rights limited only the power of the national government, not that of the states. Gradually and selectively, however, the Supreme Court accepted the incorporation theory, under which no state can violate most provisions of the Bill of Rights.

2. The First Amendment protects against government interference with freedom of religion by requiring a separation of church and state (under the establishment clause) and by guaranteeing the free exercise of religion. Controversial issues that arise under the establishment clause include aid to church-related schools, school prayer, the teaching of evolution versus intelligent design, school vouchers, the posting of the Ten Commandments in public places, and discrimination against religious speech. The government can interfere with the free exercise of religion only when religious practices work against public policy or the public welfare.

3. The First Amendment protects against government interference with freedom of speech, which includes symbolic speech (expressive conduct). The Supreme Court has been especially critical of government actions that impose prior restraint on expression. Commercial speech (advertising) by businesses has received limited First Amendment protection. Restrictions on expression are permitted when the expression creates a clear and present danger to the peace or public order. Speech that has not received First Amendment protection includes expression that is judged to be obscene or slanderous.

4. The First Amendment protects against government interference with the freedom of the press, which can be regarded as a special instance of freedom of speech. Speech by the press that does not receive protection includes libelous statements. Publication of news about a criminal trial may be restricted by a gag order in some circumstances.

5. The First Amendment protects the right to assemble peaceably and to petition the government. Permits may be required for parades, sound trucks, and dem-

onstrations to maintain the public order, and a permit may be denied to protect the public safety.

6. Under the Ninth Amendment, rights not specifically mentioned in the Constitution are not necessarily denied to the people. Among these unspecified rights protected by the courts is a right to privacy, which has been inferred from the First, Third, Fourth, Fifth, and Ninth Amendments. A major privacy issue today is how best to protect privacy rights in cyberspace. Whether an individual's privacy rights include a right to an abortion or a "right to die" continues to provoke controversy. Another major challenge concerns the extent to which Americans must forfeit privacy rights to control terrorism.

7. The Constitution includes protections for the rights of persons accused of crimes. Under the Fourth Amendment, no one may be subject to an unreasonable search or seizure or be arrested except on probable cause. Under the Fifth Amendment, an accused person has the right to remain silent. Under the Sixth Amendment, an accused person must be informed of the reason for his or her arrest. The accused also has the right to adequate counsel, even if he or she cannot afford an attorney, and the right to a prompt arraignment and a speedy and public trial before an impartial jury selected from a cross section of the community.

8. In *Miranda v. Arizona* (1966), the Supreme Court held that criminal suspects, before interrogation by law enforcement personnel, must be informed of certain constitutional rights, including the right to remain silent and the right to be represented by counsel.

9. The exclusionary rule forbids the admission in court of illegally seized evidence. There is a "good faith exception" to the exclusionary rule: illegally seized evidence need not be thrown out due to, for example, a technical defect in a search warrant. Under the Eighth Amendment, cruel and unusual punishment is prohibited. Whether the death penalty is cruel and unusual punishment continues to be debated.

SELECTED PRINT AND MEDIA RESOURCES

SUGGESTED READINGS

Ackerman, Bruce. *Before the Next Attack: Preserving Civil Liberties in an Age of Terrorism.* New Haven, CT: Yale University Press, 2006. The author advocates creating an "emergency constitution" with specific time limits that would give the government enhanced national security powers in times of crisis. He argues that such a solution would better protect civil liberties during normal circumstances.

Behe, Michael. *Darwin's Black Box: The Biochemical Challenge to Evolution.* New York: Simon and Schuster, 2006. Considered a seminal work in the intelligent design movement, Behe's book has been updated to include further evidence for his claims that evolution does not fully explain the origins of life.

Epps, Garrett. *To an Unknown God: Religious Freedom on Trial.* New York: St. Martin's Press, 2001. The author chronicles the journey through the courts of *Oregon v. Smith* (discussed earlier in this chapter), a case concerning religious practices decided by the Supreme Court in 1990. The author regards this case as one of the Supreme Court's most momentous decisions on religious freedom in the last 50 years.

Lewis, Anthony. *Gideon's Trumpet.* New York: Vintage, 1964. This classic work discusses the background and facts of *Gideon v. Wainwright,* the 1963 Supreme Court case in which the Court held that the state must make an attorney available for any person accused of a felony who cannot afford a lawyer.

MEDIA RESOURCES

*The Abortion War: Thirty Years after **Roe v. Wade***—An ABC News program released in 2003 that examines the abortion issue.

The Chamber—A movie, based on John Grisham's novel by the same name, about a young lawyer who defends a man (his grandfather) who has been sentenced to death and faces imminent execution.

Execution at Midnight—A video presenting the arguments and evidence on both sides of the controversial death penalty issue.

Gideon's Trumpet—An excellent 1980 movie about the *Gideon v. Wainwright* case. Henry Fonda plays the role of the convicted petty thief Clarence Earl Gideon.

May It Please the Court: The First Amendment—A set of audiocassette recordings and written transcripts of the oral arguments made before the Supreme Court in 16 key First Amendment cases. Participants in the recording include nationally known attorneys and several Supreme Court justices.

The People vs. Larry Flynt—An R-rated 1996 film that clearly articulates the conflict between freedom of the press and how a community defines pornography.

Skokie: Rights or Wrong?—A documentary by Sheila Chamovitz. The film documents the legal and moral crisis created when American Nazis attempted to demonstrate in Skokie, Illinois, a predominantly Jewish suburb that was home to many concentration camp survivors.

UNDERSTANDING YOUR CIVIL LIBERTIES

Today, the online world offers opportunities for Americans to easily access information concerning the nature of their civil liberties, how they originated, and how they may be threatened by various government actions. Several of the Web sites in the *Logging On* section of Chapter 2 present documents that set forth and explain the civil liberties guaranteed by the Constitution. In the *Logging On* section that follows, we list other Web sites you can visit to gain insights into the nature of these liberties.

LOGGING ON

- The American Civil Liberties Union (ACLU), the nation's leading civil liberties organization, provides an extensive array of information and links concerning civil rights issues at:
  www.aclu.org
- The Liberty Counsel describes itself as "a nonprofit religious civil liberties education and legal defense organization established to preserve religious freedom." The URL for its Web site is:
  www.lc.org
- The Center for Democracy and Technology is a nonprofit institute that monitors threats to the freedom of the Internet and provides a wealth of information about issues involve the Bill of Rights. It also focuses on how developments in communications technology are affecting the constitutional liberties of Americans. Their Web site can be found at:
  www.cdt.org
- Summaries and the full text of Supreme Court decisions concerning constitutional law, plus a virtual tour of the Supreme Court, are available at:
  www.oyez.org

- If you want to read historic Supreme Court decisions, you can search for them at:
  http://supct.law.cornell.edu/supct/search/index.html
- The American Library Association's Web site provides information on free-speech issues, especially issues of free speech on the Internet. Go to:
  www.ala.org
- You can find current information on Internet privacy issues at the Electronic Privacy Information Center's Web site. Go to:
  www.epic.org/privacy
- For the history of flag protection and the First Amendment, as well as the status of the proposed flag amendment in Congress, go to:
  www.freedomforum.org/packages/first/Flag/timeline .htm

ONLINE REVIEW

At **www.cengage.com/politicalscience/schmidt/agandpt14e**, you will find a Tutorial Quiz for this chapter providing questions on the chapter contents, including the features. The questions are organized to match the major sections of the chapter. You'll have access to other helpful study tools, including the book's glossary and flashcards, crossword puzzles, and Web links, as well as "Which Side Are You On?" and "Politics and . . ." features written by the authors of the book.

(5)

Barack Obama speaks with a diverse group of students and their teacher at Wayne County Community College, 2008. (Paul Sancya/AP/Wide World Photos)

CIVIL RIGHTS

QUESTIONS TO CONSIDER

Why does discrimination against groups exist in the United States?

How can the government best ensure equal rights for all?

Why is the Supreme Court so important in determining civil rights?

CHAPTER CONTENTS

Making a DIFFERENCE

USING THE COURTS AS A STRATEGY IN THE FIGHT FOR CIVIL RIGHTS

Many groups have struggled for civil rights, such as the Constitutional right to vote, full participation in the democratic process, access to education, and fair and equal treatment under the law. Although each group's experiences are to a degree unique, they share certain approaches. One strategy that could become a template for other groups was that of the National Association for the Advancement of Colored People (NAACP) in challenging *Plessy v. Ferguson* (1896),[a] a Supreme Court case that established the doctrine of *separate but equal*, which argued that segregation was constitutionally acceptable as long as the facilities were equal.

Because facilities (accommodations, transportation, education) for African Ameri-

cans and other groups were rarely if ever equal, the NAACP and a group of black attorneys focused on enforcement of the equality mandate as a mechanism to attack the larger structure of laws and norms known as *Jim Crow*. They believed that because it would have been prohibitively expensive for states and localities to provide truly equal facilities, desegregation would be a more attractive option. In 1935, the NAACP began to target institutions of higher education—law schools or postgraduate programs—to insist on qualified teachers, public money for transportation costs, equity in buildings and equipment, and equality in per capita state funds spent on each student.

Several cases were argued successfully using this strategy. Law schools in Maryland, Missouri, Oklahoma, and Texas were forced to change their policies regarding admittance or matriculation of law school students. There are many poignant examples of the injustices that remained.[b] One of the most intriguing is the 1938 case of

DESPITE THE WORDS set forth in the Declaration of Independence that "all Men are created equal," the concept of equal treatment under the law was a distant dream in those years. In fact, the majority of the population had few rights. As you learned in Chapter 2, the framers of the Constitution permitted slavery to continue. Slaves thus were excluded from the political process. Women also were excluded for the most part, as were Native Americans, African Americans who were not slaves, and even white men who did not own property. In reality, it has taken this nation more than 200 years to approach even a semblance of equality among all Americans. As you learned from the *Making A Difference* feature, a concerted effort and strategic legal campaign made possible major gains in civil rights for African Americans. In this chapter, you will learn about that campaign and those waged by other groups to gain an equal footing in American society.

Equality is at the heart of the concept of civil rights. Generally, the term **civil rights** refers to the rights of all Americans to equal treatment under the law, as provided for by the Fourteenth Amendment to the Constitution. Although the terms *civil rights* and *civil liberties* are sometimes used interchangeably, scholars make a distinction between the two. As you learned in Chapter 4, civil liberties are basically limitations on government; they specify what the government *cannot* do. Civil rights, in contrast, specify what the government *must* do—to ensure equal protection and freedom from discrimination.

Civil Rights
Generally, all rights rooted in the Fourteenth Amendment's guarantee of equal protection under the law.

DID YOU KNOW?

That at the time of the American Revolution, African Americans made up nearly 25 percent of the American population of about 3 million?

Lloyd Gaines, who brought suit to be admitted to the law school at the University of Missouri. The Court decided in Gaines's favor, ruling that the University of Missouri must provide equal facilities.[c] Mr. Gaines, however, disappeared, and the university did not have to adapt its policies.[d] As you will learn in the chapter on the judiciary, individuals who bring suit in these landmark cases often are not the immediate beneficiaries of their actions. Rather, their legal victories are critical in the establishment of precedent—a series of legal decisions that form the basis for future Supreme Court decisions.

The NAACP's Legal Defense and Education Fund, in conjunction with Howard University's Law School,[e] are owed much of the credit for these legal successes that paved the way for *Brown v. Board of Education* (1954).[f] As you will learn in this chapter, the Court's unanimous ruling in this case reversed more than fifty years of legal segregation in education. The facts surrounding the case are fascinating. First argued in 1952, the votes were almost evenly split to uphold or strike down *separate but equal*; Chief Justice Fred Vinson held the swing vote. In 1953, the Chief died, and President Dwight Eisenhower appointed Earl Warren to replace him. *Brown* was reargued, and Warren wrote a unanimous decision to strike down *separate but equal*, arguing that "separate" is inherently unequal. Warren's political skills are often credited with this impressive achievement.

This legal strategy was only one of many African Americans found successful in their struggle for civil rights, and

there would be many difficult days ahead. The success of civil rights groups in *Brown* was a flashpoint, sparking an enormous wave of backlash among segregationists. They defied the Court, closed public schools rather than integrate them, and vowed to maintain inequality in other areas like voting. Violence and sometimes death for civil rights activists often resulted. Despite that this was only a beginning, the legal strategies utilized by the NAACP's Legal Defense Fund were instrumental in marking a change in the law. Today, contemporary civil rights groups model their tactics on those of almost a century before.

[a]163 U.S. 537 (1896).
[b]See www.brownvboard.info for a good description of this history, especially the cses of Ms. Ada Sipuel (332 U.S. 631) and Mr. Herman Sweatt (339 U.S. 629 (1950)).
[c]305 U.S. 337 (1938).
[d]In 2006, the State Supreme Court of Missouri and the Missouri State Bar Association posthumously awarded Gaines a license to practice law and his law degree; www.jbhe.com/latest/index091406_p.html.
[e]The Legal Defense and Education Fund was founded in 1940 (www.naacpldf.org). Howard University, founded in 1867 for the education of former slaves and their descendents, remains today a premier institution of higher education and a leader among Historical Black Colleges and Universities (HBCUs); www.howard.edu.
[f]347 U.S. 483 (1954).

Essentially, the history of civil rights in America is the story of the struggle of various groups to be free from discriminatory treatment. In this chapter, we first look at two movements that had significant consequences for the history of civil rights in America: the civil rights movement of the 1950s and 1960s and the women's movement, which began in the mid-1800s and continues today. Each of these movements resulted in legislation that secured important basic rights for all Americans—the right to vote and the right to equal protection under the laws. We then explore a question with serious implications for today's voters and policymakers: What should the government's responsibility be when equal protection under the law is not enough to ensure truly equal opportunities for Americans?

AFRICAN AMERICANS AND THE CONSEQUENCES OF SLAVERY IN THE UNITED STATES

Before 1863, the Constitution protected slavery and made equality impossible in the sense in which we use the word today. African American leader Frederick Douglass pointed out that "Liberty and Slavery—opposite as Heaven and Hell—are both in the Constitution." As Abraham Lincoln stated sarcastically, "All men are created equal, except Negroes."

THIS IS A PORTRAIT of Dred Scott (1795–1858), an American slave who was born in Virginia and who later moved with his owner to Illinois, where slavery was illegal. He was the nominal plaintiff in a test case that sought to obtain his freedom on the ground that he lived in the free state of Illinois. Although the Supreme Court ruled against him, he was soon emancipated and became a hotel porter in St. Louis. (Missouri Historical Society)

The constitutionality of slavery was confirmed just a few years before the outbreak of the Civil War in the famous *Dred Scott v. Sanford*[1] case of 1857. The Supreme Court held that slaves were not citizens of the United States, nor were they entitled to the rights and privileges of citizenship. The Court also ruled that the Missouri Compromise, which banned slavery in the territories north of 36°30' latitude (the southern border of Missouri), was unconstitutional. The *Dred Scott* decision had grave consequences. Most observers contend that the ruling contributed to making the Civil War inevitable.

ENDING SERVITUDE

With the emancipation of the slaves by President Lincoln's Emancipation Proclamation in 1863 and the passage of the Thirteenth, Fourteenth, and Fifteenth Amendments during the Reconstruction period following the Civil War, constitutional inequality was ended.

The Thirteenth Amendment (1865) states that neither slavery nor involuntary servitude shall exist within the United States. The Fourteenth Amendment (1868) tells us that *all* persons born or naturalized in the United States are citizens of the United States. It states, furthermore, that "[n]o State shall make or enforce any law which shall abridge the privileges or immunities of citizens of the United States; nor shall any State deprive any person of life, liberty, or property, without due process of law; nor deny to any person within its jurisdiction the equal protection of the laws." Note the use of the terms *citizen* and *person* in this amendment. Citizens have political rights, such as the right to vote and run for political office. Citizens also have certain privileges or immunities (see Chapter 4). All *persons*, however, including noncitizen immigrants, have a right to due process of law and equal protection under the law.

The Fifteenth Amendment (1870) reads as follows: "The right of citizens of the United States to vote shall not be denied or abridged by the United States or by any State on account of race, color, or previous condition of servitude." Pressure was brought to bear on Congress to include in the Fourteenth and Fifteenth Amendments a prohibition against discrimination based on sex, but with little success.

THE CIVIL RIGHTS ACTS OF 1865 TO 1875

At the end of the Civil War, President Lincoln's Republican Party controlled the national government and most state governments, and the so-called radical Republicans, with their strong antislavery stance, controlled the party. From 1865 to 1875, the Republican majority succeeded in passing a series of civil rights acts that were aimed at enforcing the Thirteenth, Fourteenth, and Fifteenth Amendments. Even Republicans who were not very sympathetic to the antislavery position saw these amendments as a way to undercut Democratic Party domination of the South by enfranchising the ex-slaves.

The first Civil Rights Act in the Reconstruction period was passed in 1866 over the veto of President Andrew Johnson. That act extended citizenship to anyone born in the United States and gave African Americans full equality before the law. It gave the president authority to enforce the law with military force. It was considered to be unconstitutional, but the passage of the Fourteenth Amendment two years later ended that concern.

Among the six other civil rights acts passed after the Civil War, one of the most important was the Enforcement Act of 1879, which set out specific criminal sanctions

DID YOU KNOW?

That the holiday Juneteenth, or Freedom Day, celebrates the day in 1865 that slaves in Galveston, Texas, found out they were free three years after Lincoln signed the Emancipation Proclamation?

---

[1]19 Howard 393 (1857).

FEMALE MEMBERS of the Ku Klux Klan march in Atlanta, Georgia, in 1936. The parade was a Memorial Day remembrance of Confederate soldiers. Why was such a parade permitted in a major American city? (AP/Wide World Photos)

for interfering with the right to vote as protected by the Fifteenth Amendment and by the Civil Rights Act of 1866. Equally important was the Civil Rights Act of 1872, known as the Anti-Ku Klux Klan Act. This Act made it a federal crime for anyone to use law or custom to deprive an individual of his or her rights, privileges, and immunities secured by the Constitution or by any federal law.

The last of these early civil rights acts, known as the Second Civil Rights Act, was passed in 1875. It declared that everyone is entitled to full and equal enjoyment of public accommodations, theaters, and other places of amusement, and it imposed penalties for violators. What is most important about all of the Civil Rights Acts was the belief that Congressional power applied to official or government action or to private action. If a state government did not secure rights, then the federal government could do so. Thus, Congress could legislate directly against individuals who were violating the constitutional rights of others. As we will see, these acts were quickly rendered ineffective by law and by custom. However, they became important in the civil rights struggles of the 1960s, 100 years after their passage.

ABRAHAM LINCOLN reads the Emancipation Proclamation on July 22, 1862. The Emancipation Proclamation did not abolish slavery (that was done by the Thirteenth Amendment in 1865), but it ensured that slavery would be abolished if and when the North won the Civil War. After the Battle of Antietam on September 17, 1862, Lincoln publicly announced the Emancipation Proclamation and declared that all slaves residing in states that were still in rebellion against the United States on January 1, 1863, would be freed once those states came under the military control of the Union Army. (Library of Congress, Prints & Photographs Division, Washington, D.C. [LC-USZ62-2070])

THE INEFFECTIVENESS OF THE CIVIL RIGHTS LAWS

The Reconstruction statutes, or civil rights acts, ultimately did little to secure equality for African Americans. Both the *Civil Rights Cases* and the case of *Plessy v. Ferguson* (discussed in this section) effectively nullified these acts. Additionally, Southern and border states created legal barriers that prevented African Americans from exercising their right to vote.

The Civil Rights Cases. The Supreme Court invalidated the 1875 Civil Rights Act when it held, in the *Civil Rights Cases*[2] of 1883, that the enforcement clause of the Fourteenth Amendment (which states that "[n]o State shall make or enforce any law which shall abridge the privileges or immunities of citizens") was limited to correcting actions by states in their *official* acts; thus, the discriminatory acts of private citizens were not illegal. ("Individual invasion of individual rights is not the subject matter of the Amendment.") The 1883 Supreme Court decision met with widespread approval throughout most of the United States.

Twenty years after the Civil War, the white majority was all too willing to forget about the three Civil War Amendments and the civil rights legislation of the 1860s and 1870s. The other civil rights laws that the Court did not specifically invalidate became dead letters in the statute books, although they were never repealed by Congress. At the same time, many former proslavery secessionists had regained political power in the Southern states.

Plessy v. Ferguson: **Separate but Equal.** A key decision during this period concerned Homer Plessy, a Louisiana resident who was one-eighth African American. In 1892, he boarded a train in New Orleans. The conductor made him leave the car, which was restricted to whites, and directed him to a car for nonwhites. At that time, Louisiana had a statute providing for separate railway cars for whites and African Americans.

....

[2]109 U.S. 3 (1883).

Plessy went to court, claiming that such a statute was contrary to the Fourteenth Amendment's equal protection clause. In 1896, the United States Supreme Court rejected Plessy's contention. The Court concluded that the Fourteenth Amendment "could not have been intended to abolish distinctions based upon color, or to enforce social . . . equality." The Court stated that segregation alone did not violate the Constitution: "Laws permitting, and even requiring, their separation in places where they are liable to be brought into contact do not necessarily imply the inferiority of either race to the other."[3] So was born the **separate-but-equal doctrine**.

Plessy v. Ferguson became the judicial cornerstone of racial discrimination throughout the United States. Even though Plessy upheld segregated facilities in railway cars only, it was assumed that the Supreme Court was upholding segregation everywhere as long as the separate facilities were equal. The result was a system of racial segregation, particularly in the South—supported by laws collectively known as Jim Crow laws—that required separate drinking fountains; separate seats in theaters, restaurants, and hotels; separate public toilets; and separate waiting rooms for the two races. "Separate" was indeed the rule, but "equal" was never enforced, nor was it a reality.

Voting Barriers. The brief enfranchisement of African Americans ended after 1877, when the federal troops that occupied the South during the Reconstruction era were withdrawn. Southern politicians regained control of state governments and, using everything except race as a formal criterion, passed laws that effectively deprived African Americans of the right to vote. By using the ruse that political parties were private bodies, the Democratic Party was allowed to keep black voters from its primaries. The **white primary** was upheld by the Supreme Court until 1944 when, in *Smith v. Allwright*,[4] the Court ruled it a violation of the Fifteenth Amendment.

Another barrier to African American voting was the **grandfather clause**, which restricted voting to those who could prove that their grandfathers had voted before 1867. **Poll taxes** required the payment of a fee to vote; thus, poor African Americans—as well as poor whites—who could not afford to pay the tax were excluded from voting. Not until the Twenty-fourth Amendment to the Constitution was ratified in 1964 was the poll tax eliminated as a precondition to voting. **Literacy tests** were also used to deny the vote to African Americans. Such tests asked potential voters to read, recite, or interpret complicated texts, such as a section of the state constitution, to the satisfaction of local registrars—who were, of course, never satisfied with the responses of African Americans.

Black Codes. Southern states, counties, and towns passed numerous ordinances and laws to maintain a segregated society and to control the movements and activities of African American residents. In Florida, for example, no "negro, mulatto, or person of color" was permitted to own or carry a weapon, including a knife, without a license. This law did not apply to white residents. Other laws set curfews for African Americans, set limits on the businesses they could own or run and on their rights to assembly, and required the newly freed men and women to find employment quickly or be subject to penalties. The penalty sometimes meant that the men would be forced into labor at very low wages at large farms or factories against their will.

Extralegal Methods of Enforcing White Supremacy. The second-class status of African Americans was also a matter of social custom, especially in the South. In their interactions

Separate-but-Equal Doctrine
The doctrine holding that separate-but-equal facilities do not violate the equal protection clause.

DID YOU KNOW?

That the original Constitution failed to describe the status of *citizen* or how this status could be acquired?

White Primary
A state primary election that restricts voting to whites only; outlawed by the Supreme Court in 1944.

Grandfather Clause
A device used by Southern states to disenfranchise African Americans. It restricted voting to those whose grandfathers had voted before 1867.

Poll Tax
A special tax that must be paid as a qualification for voting. The Twenty-fourth Amendment to the Constitution outlawed the poll tax in national elections, and in 1966, the Supreme Court declared it unconstitutional in all elections.

Literacy Test
A test administered as a precondition for voting, often used to prevent African Americans from exercising their right to vote.

---

[3]*Plessy v. Ferguson*, 163 U.S. 537 (1896).
[4]321 U.S. 649 (1944).

DID YOU KNOW?

That by September 1961, more than 3,600 students had been arrested for participating in civil rights demonstrations, and that 141 students and 58 faculty members had been expelled by colleges and universities for their part in civil rights protests?

with Southern whites, African Americans were expected to observe an informal but detailed code of behavior that confirmed their inferiority. The most serious violation of the informal code was "familiarity" toward a white woman by an African American man or boy. The code was backed up by the common practice of *lynching*—mob action to murder an accused individual, usually by hanging and sometimes accompanied by torture. Lynching was a common response to an accusation of "familiarity." Of course, lynching was illegal, but Southern authorities rarely prosecuted these cases, and white juries would not convict.

African Americans outside the South were subject to a second kind of violence—race riots. In the early 20th century, race riots were typically initiated by whites. Frequently, the riots were caused by competition for employment. For example, there were several serious riots during World War II (1939–1945), when labor shortages forced Northern employers to hire more black workers.

THE END OF THE SEPARATE-BUT-EQUAL DOCTRINE

As described in *Making a Difference*, the successful attack on the separate-but-equal doctrine began with a series of lawsuits in the 1930s that sought to admit African Americans to state professional schools. By 1950, the Supreme Court had ruled that African Americans who were admitted to a state university could not be assigned to separate sections of classrooms, libraries, and cafeterias.

In 1951, Oliver Brown decided that his eight-year-old daughter, Linda Carol Brown, should not have to go to an all-nonwhite elementary school 21 blocks from her home, when there was a white school only seven blocks away. The National Association for the Advancement of Colored People (NAACP), formed in 1909, decided to support Oliver Brown. The outcome would have a monumental impact on American society.

Brown v. Board of Education of Topeka. The 1954 unanimous decision of the United States Supreme Court in *Brown v. Board of Education of Topeka*[5] established that segrega-

---

[5]347 U.S. 483 (1954).

tion of races in the public schools violates the equal protection clause of the Fourteenth Amendment. Concluding that separate schools are inherently unequal, Chief Justice Earl Warren stated that "to separate [African Americans] from others of similar age and qualifications solely because of their race generates a feeling of inferiority as to their status in the community that may affect their hearts and minds in a way unlikely every to be undone." Chief Justice Warren said that separation implied inferiority, whereas the majority opinion in *Plessy v. Ferguson* had said the opposite.

"With All Deliberate Speed." The following year, in *Brown v. Board of Education*[6] (sometimes called the second *Brown* decision), the Court declared that the lower courts needed to ensure that African Americans would be admitted to schools on a nondiscriminatory basis "with all deliberate speed." The district courts were to consider devices in their desegregation orders that might include "the school transportation system, personnel, [and] revision of school districts and attendance areas into compact units to achieve a system of determining admission to the public schools on a nonracial basis."

THESE THREE LAWYERS successfully argued in favor of desegregation of the schools in the famous *Brown v. Board of Education of Topeka* case. On the left is George E. C. Hayes; on the right is James Nabrit, Jr.; and in the center is Thurgood Marshall, who later became the first African American Supreme Court justice. The *Brown* decision overruled which previous Supreme Court case? (Bettmann/Corbis)

REACTIONS TO SCHOOL INTEGRATION

The white South did not let the Supreme Court ruling go unchallenged. Governor Orval Faubus of Arkansas used the state's National Guard to block the integration of Central High School in Little Rock in September 1957. The federal court demanded that the troops be withdrawn. Finally, President Dwight Eisenhower had to federalize the Arkansas National Guard and send in the Army's 101st Airborne Division to quell the violence. Central High became integrated.

The universities in the South, however, remained segregated. When James Meredith, an African American student, attempted to enroll at the University of Mississippi in Oxford in 1962, violence flared there, as it had in Little Rock. The white riot at Oxford was so intense that President John Kennedy was forced to send in 30,000 U.S. combat troops, a larger force than the one then stationed in Korea. There were 375 military and civilian injuries, many from gunfire, and two bystanders were killed. Ultimately, peace was restored, and Meredith began attending classes.[7]

AN INTEGRATIONIST ATTEMPT AT A CURE: BUSING

In most parts of the United States, residential concentrations by race have made it difficult to achieve racial balance in schools. Although it is true that many school boards in

[6]349 U.S. 294 (1955).
[7]William Doyle, *An American Insurrection: James Meredith and the Battle of Oxford, Mississippi, 1962* (New York: Anchor, 2003).

ANGRY WHITES shout epithets at one of eight African American students who were admitted to the previously segregated Little Rock Central High School in September 1957. Successful integration of that school required the federalization of the Arkansas National Guard with the help of the Army's 101st Airborne Division. (Bettmann/Corbis)

De Facto Segregation
Racial segregation that occurs because of past social and economic conditions and residential racial patterns.

De Jure Segregation
Racial segregation that occurs because of laws or administrative decisions by public agencies.

Busing
In the context of civil rights, the transportation of public school students from areas where they live to schools in other areas to eliminate school segregation based on residential patterns.

Northern districts created segregated schools by drawing school district lines arbitrarily, the residential concentration of African Americans and other minorities in well-defined geographic locations has contributed to the difficulty of achieving racial balance. This concentration results in ***de facto* segregation**, as distinct from ***de jure* segregation**, which results from laws or administrative decisions.

Court-Ordered Busing. The obvious solution to both *de facto* and *de jure* segregation seemed to be transporting some African American schoolchildren to white schools and some white schoolchildren to African American schools. Increasingly, the courts ordered school districts to engage in such **busing** across neighborhoods. Busing led to violence in some Northern cities, such as in south Boston, where African American students were bused into blue-collar Irish Catholic neighborhoods. Indeed, busing was unpopular with many groups. In the mid-1970s, almost 50 percent of African Americans interviewed were opposed to busing, and approximately three-fourths of the whites interviewed held the same opinion. Nonetheless, throughout the next decade, the Supreme Court fairly consistently upheld busing plans in the cases it decided.

The End of Integration? During the 1980s and the early 1990s, the Supreme Court tended to back away from its earlier commitment to busing and other methods of desegregation. By the late 1990s and early 2000s, the federal courts were increasingly unwilling to uphold race-conscious policies designed to further school integration and diversity—outcomes that are not mandated by the Constitution. For example, in 2001, a federal appellate court held that the Charlotte-Mecklenburg school district in North Carolina had achieved the goal of integration,[8] meaning that race-based admission quotas could no longer be imposed constitutionally.

The Resurgence of Minority Schools. Today, schools around the country are becoming segregated again, in large part because of *de facto* segregation. The rapid decline in the relative proportion of whites who live in large cities and high minority birthrates have increased the minority presence in those urban areas. Today, one out of every three African American and Hispanic students goes to a school with more than 90 percent minority enrollment. In the largest U.S. cities, 15 out of 16 African American and Hispanic students go to schools with almost no non-Hispanic whites.

Generally, Americans are now taking another look at what desegregation means. The attempt to integrate the schools, particularly through busing, has largely failed to improve educational resources and achievement for African American children. The goal of racially balanced schools envisioned in the 1954 *Brown v. Board of Education of Topeka* decision is giving way to the goal of better education for children, even if that means educating them in schools in which students are of the same race or in which race is not considered. In 2007, the Supreme Court handed down a decision that would dramatically change the way school districts across the country assigned students to schools. In cases brought by white parents in Seattle and Louisville, the court, by a narrow five-to-four majority, found that using race to determine which schools students

---

[8]*Belk v. Charlotte-Mecklenburg Board of Education*, 269 F.3d 305 (4th Cir. 2001).

could attend was a violation of the Fourteenth Amendment. White children could not be denied admission to magnet schools or other schools designed to have racially balanced populations on account of their race.[9]

THE CIVIL RIGHTS MOVEMENT

The *Brown* decision applied only to public schools. Not much else in the structure of existing segregation was affected. In December 1955, a 43-year-old African American woman, Rosa Parks, boarded a public bus in Montgomery, Alabama. When the bus became crowded and several white people stepped aboard, Parks was asked to move to the rear of the bus (the "colored" section). She refused, was arrested, and was fined $10, but that was not the end of the matter. For an entire year, African Americans boycotted the Montgomery bus line. The protest was headed by a 27-year-old Baptist minister, Dr. Martin Luther King, Jr. During the protest period, he went to jail, and his house was bombed. In the face of overwhelming odds, King won. In 1956, a federal district court issued an injunction prohibiting the segregation of buses in Montgomery. The era of civil rights protests had begun.

KING'S PHILOSOPHY OF NONVIOLENCE

The following year, in 1957, King formed the Southern Christian Leadership Conference (SCLC). King advocated nonviolent **civil disobedience** as a means to achieve racial justice. King's philosophy of civil disobedience was influenced, in part, by the life and teachings of Mahatma Gandhi (1869–1948). Gandhi had led resistance to the British colonial system in India from 1919 to 1947. He used tactics such as demonstrations and marches, as well as nonviolent, public disobedience to unjust laws. King's followers successfully used these methods to gain wider public acceptance of their cause.

Civil Disobedience
A nonviolent, public refusal to obey allegedly unjust laws.

MORE THAN 30,000 visitors filed past the casket of Rosa Parks in the U.S. Capitol Rotunda on Monday, October 31, 2005. Parks became the first African American woman to lay in honor in the Rotunda. Born in Alabama, Rosa Parks was active in the Montgomery Voters' League and the NAACP League Council. After the successful boycott of the Montgomery bus system, which was sparked by her actions, she was fired from her job and subsequently moved to Detroit. Can actions by an ordinary person change history? Why or why not?
(AP Photo/Susan Walsh)

[9]*Parents Involved v. Seattle School District No. 1,* 550 U.S (2007) and *Meredith v. Jefferson County Board of Education,* 550 U.S. (2007).

Nonviolent Demonstrations. For the next decade, African Americans and sympathetic whites engaged in sit-ins, freedom rides, and freedom marches. Organizations including the NAACP, the Congress of Racial Equality (CORE), and the Student Nonviolent Coordinating Committee (SNCC) organized and supported these actions. In the beginning, such demonstrations were often met with violence, and the contrasting image of nonviolent African Americans and violent, hostile whites created strong public support for the civil rights movement. In 1960, when African Americans in Greensboro, North Carolina, were refused service at a Woolworth's lunch counter, they organized a sit-in that was aided day after day by sympathetic whites and other African Americans. Enraged customers threw ketchup on the protesters. Some spat in their faces. The sit-in movement continued to grow, however. Within six months of the first sit-in at the Greensboro Woolworth's, hundreds of lunch counters throughout the South were serving African Americans.

The sit-in technique also was successfully used to integrate interstate buses and their terminals, as well as railroads engaged in interstate transportation. Although buses and railroads engaged in interstate transportation were prohibited by law from segregating African Americans from whites, they stopped doing so only after the sit-in protests.

Marches and Demonstrations. One of the most famous of the violence-plagued protests occurred in Birmingham, Alabama, in 1963, when Police Commissioner Eugene "Bull" Connor unleashed police dogs and used electric cattle prods against the protesters. People throughout the country viewed the event on television with indignation and horror. King was thrown in jail. The media coverage of the Birmingham protest and the violent response by the city government played a key role in the process of ending Jim Crow laws in the United States. The ultimate result was the most important civil rights act in the nation's history, the Civil Rights Act of 1964 (to be discussed shortly).

In August 1963, African American leaders A. Philip Randolph and Bayard Rustin organized a massive March on Washington for Jobs and Freedom. Before nearly a quarter-million white and African American spectators and millions watching on television, King told the world his dream: "I have a dream that my four little children will one day live in a nation where they will not be judged by the color of their skin but by the content of their character."

ANOTHER APPROACH—BLACK POWER

Not all African Americans agreed with King's philosophy of nonviolence or with the idea that King's strong Christian background should represent the core spirituality of African Americans. Black Muslims and other African American separatists advocated a more militant stance and argued that desegregation should not result in cultural assimilation. During the 1950s and 1960s, when King was spearheading nonviolent protests and demonstrations to achieve civil rights for African Americans, black power leaders insisted that African Americans should "fight back" instead of turning the other cheek. Some would argue that without the fear generated by black militants, a "moderate" such as King would not have garnered such widespread support from white America.

Malcolm Little (who became Malcolm X when he joined the Black Muslims in 1952) and other leaders in the black power movement believed that African Americans fell into two groups: the "Uncle Toms," who peaceably accommodated the white establish-

MALCOLM X, right, shown here in March 1964, along with Martin Luther King, Jr., opposed the philosophy of nonviolence espoused by Dr. King, and he urged African Americans to "fight back" against white supremacy. Some people have argued that such a militant approach is almost always counterproductive. Others believe that a militant alternative may have made King's peaceful appeal more attractive. Is either of these arguments persuasive? Why or why not? (Library of Congress, Prints & Photographs Division, Washington, D.C. [LC-USZ6-1847])

ment, and the "New Negroes," who took pride in their color and culture and who preferred and demanded racial separation as well as power. Malcolm X was assassinated in 1965, but he became an important reference point for a new generation of African Americans and a symbol of African American identity.

THE CLIMAX OF THE CIVIL RIGHTS MOVEMENT

Police-dog attacks, cattle prods, high-pressure water hoses, beatings, bombings, the March on Washington, and black militancy—all of these events and developments led to an environment in which Congress felt compelled to act on behalf of African Americans. The second era of civil rights acts, sometimes referred to as the second Reconstruction period, was under way.

MODERN CIVIL RIGHTS LEGISLATION

As the civil rights movement mounted in intensity, equality before the law came to be "an idea whose time has come," in the words of then Republican Senate Minority Leader Everett Dirksen. The legislation passed during the Eisenhower administration was relatively symbolic. The Civil Rights Act of 1957 established the Civil Rights Commission and a new Civil Rights Division within the Department of Justice. The Civil Rights Act of 1960 was passed to protect voting rights. Whenever a pattern or practice of discrimination was documented, the Justice Department, on behalf of the voter, could bring suit, even against a state. However, this Act, which had little enforcement power, was relatively ineffective.

The 1960 presidential election was one of the most exciting in our nation's history, pitting Vice President Richard Nixon against Senator John F. Kennedy. Kennedy sought the support of African American leaders, promising to introduce tougher civil rights legislation. When Martin Luther King was imprisoned in Georgia after participating in a sit-in in Atlanta, candidate Kennedy called Mrs. King to express his support, and his brother, Robert, made telephone calls to expedite King's release on bond. However, President Kennedy's civil rights legislation was stalled in the Senate in 1963, and his assassination ended the effort in his name. When Lyndon B. Johnson became president in 1963, he committed himself to passing civil rights bills, and the 1964 Act was the result.

The Civil Rights Act of 1964. The Civil Rights Act of 1964, the most far-reaching bill on civil rights in modern times, forbade discrimination on the basis of race, color, religion, gender, and national origin. The major provisions of the act were as follows:

1. It outlawed arbitrary discrimination in voter registration.
2. It barred discrimination in public accommodations, such as hotels and restaurants, whose operations affect interstate commerce.
3. It authorized the federal government to sue to desegregate public schools and facilities.
4. It expanded the power of the Civil Rights Commission and extended its life.
5. It provided for the withholding of federal funds from programs administered in a discriminatory manner.
6. It established the right to equality of opportunity in employment.

Title VII of the Civil Rights Act of 1964 is the cornerstone of employment-discrimination law. It prohibits discrimination in employment based on race, color, religion, gender, or national origin. Under Title VII, executive orders were issued that banned employment discrimination by firms that received any federal funding. The 1964 Civil Rights Act created a five-member commission, the Equal Employment Opportunity Commission (EEOC), to administer Title VII.

The EEOC can issue interpretive guidelines and regulations, but these do not have the force of law. Rather, they give notice of the commission's enforcement policy. The EEOC also has investigatory powers. It has broad authority to require the production of documentary evidence, to hold hearings, and to **subpoena** and examine witnesses under oath.

Subpoena
A legal writ requiring a person's appearance in court to give testimony.

The equal employment provisions of the 1964 act have been strengthened several times since its first passage. In 1965, President Johnson signed an Executive Order (11246) that prohibited any discrimination in employment by any employer who received federal funds, contracts, or subcontracts. It also required all such employers to establish *affirmative action plans*, which will be discussed later in this chapter. A revision of that order extended the requirement for an affirmative action plan to public institutions and medical and health facilities with more than 50 employees. In 1972, the Equal Employment Opportunity Act extended the provisions prohibiting discrimination in employment to the employees of state and local governments and most other not-for-profit institutions.

The Voting Rights Act of 1965. As late as 1960, only 29.1 percent of African Americans of voting age were registered in the Southern states, in stark contrast to 61.1 percent of whites. The Voting Rights Act of 1965 addressed this issue. The Act had two major provisions. The first one outlawed discriminatory voter-registration tests. The second authorized federal registration of voters and federally administered voting procedures in any political subdivision or state that discriminated electorally against a particular

PRESIDENT LYNDON B. JOHNSON
is shown signing the Civil Rights
Act of 1968. What are some of the
provisions of that far-reaching law?
(Bettmann/Corbis)

group. In part, the Act provided that certain political subdivisions could not change their voting procedures and election laws without federal approval. The Act targeted counties, mostly in the South, in which less than 50 percent of the eligible population was registered to vote. Federal voter registrars were sent to these areas to register African Americans who had been kept from voting by local registrars. Within one week after the act was passed, 45 federal examiners were sent to the South. A massive voter-registration drive covered the country.

Urban Riots. Even as the civil rights movement was experiencing its greatest victories, a series of riots swept through African American inner-city neighborhoods. These urban riots were different in character from the race riots described earlier in this chapter. The riots in the first half of the 20th century were street battles between whites and blacks. The urban riots of the late 1960s and early 1970s, however, were not directed against individual whites—in some instances, whites actually participated in small numbers. The riots were primarily civil insurrections, although these disorders were accompanied by large-scale looting of stores. Inhabitants of the affected neighborhoods attributed the riots to racial discrimination.[10] The riots dissipated much of the goodwill toward the civil rights movement that had been built up earlier in the decade among

---

[10]Angus Campbell and Howard Schuman, *ICPSR 3500: Racial Attitudes in Fifteen American Cities, 1968* (Ann Arbor, MI: Inter-University Consortium for Political and Social Research, 1997). Campbell and Schuman's survey documents both white participation and the attitudes of the inhabitants of affected neighborhoods. This survey is available online at www.grinnell.edu/academic/data/sociology/minorityresearch/raceatt1968.

Northern whites. Together with widespread student demonstrations against the Vietnam War (1964–1975), the riots pushed many Americans toward conservatism.

The Civil Rights Act of 1968 and Other Housing Reform Legislation. Martin Luther King, Jr., was assassinated on April 4, 1968. Despite King's message of peace, his death was followed by the most widespread rioting to date. Nine days after King's death, President Johnson signed the Civil Rights Act of 1968, which forbade discrimination in most housing and provided penalties for those attempting to interfere with individual civil rights (giving protection to civil rights workers, among others). Subsequent legislation added enforcement provisions to the federal government's rules against discriminatory mortgage-lending practices. Today, all lenders must report to the federal government the race, gender, and income of all mortgage-loan seekers, along with the final decision on their loan applications.

CONSEQUENCES OF CIVIL RIGHTS LEGISLATION

As a result of the Voting Rights Act of 1965 and its amendments, and the large-scale voter-registration drives in the South, the number of African Americans registered to vote climbed dramatically. By 1980, 55.8 percent of African Americans of voting age in the South were registered. In recent elections, the percentage of voting-age African Americans who have registered to vote has been just slightly less than the percentage of voting-age whites who have done so. Some of the provisions in the Voting Rights Act of 1965 were due to "sunset" (expire) in 2007. In July 2006, President George W. Bush signed a 25-year extension of these provisions, following heated congressional debate.

FOLLOWING THE ASSASSINATION of Martin Luther King in April, 1968, riots erupted across the nation. Federal troops were sent to protect all government buildings and memorials in Washington, D.C., from the rioters and fires. (Bettmann/CORBIS)

Political Participation by African Americans. Today, there are more than 8,500 African American elected officials in the United States. The movement of African American citizens into high elected office has been sure, if exceedingly slow. Notably, recent polling data show that most Americans do not consider race a significant factor in choosing a president. In 1958, when the Gallup poll first asked whether respondents would be willing to vote for an African American as president, only 38 percent of the public said yes. By 2007, this number had reached 94 percent. After a hard fought and closely contested race with New York Senator Hillary Clinton, in June 2008, Barack Obama had become the presumptive Democratic nominee for president. At this time, 88 percent of white respondents said that Obama's race would make no difference to them in deciding on whom to vote for for president.[11] In recent years, several African Americans emerged who were widely considered to be of presidential caliber. They include Colin Powell, former chair of the Joint Chiefs of Staff and later secretary of state under President George W. Bush, and Bush's secretary of state, Condoleezza Rice, who had been championed by some Republicans as a possible successor to Bush.

Although his opponent, Senator John McCain, managed to even the race shortly after the Republican convention, Senator Obama built a lead through the fall emphasizing the economy. In a decisive victory, he was elected the first African American president on November 4, 2008. Obama's campaign theme, "Change You Can Believe In," was proven true with his election to the highest office in the land. In his acceptance speech on election night, the president-elect stressed the need for all Americans to come together regardless of race or ethnic background to solve the problems facing the nation.

Political Participation by Other Minorities. As mentioned earlier, the civil rights movement focused primarily on the rights of African Americans. Yet, the legislation resulting from the movement has ultimately benefited all minority groups. The Civil Rights Act of 1964, for example, prohibits discrimination against any person because of race, color, or national origin. Subsequent amendments to the Voting Rights Act of 1965 extended its protections to other minorities, including Hispanic Americans, Asian Americans, Native Americans, and Native Alaskans. To further protect the voting rights of minorities, the law now provides that states must make bilingual ballots available in counties where 5 percent or more of the population speaks a language other than English.

That after the assassination of Martin Luther King, Jr., riots took place in more than 100 cities, 75,000 troops and members of the National Guard were mobilized, 27,000 African Americans were jailed, and 39 African Americans were killed?

The political participation of other minority groups in the United States has also been increasing. Hispanics are gaining political power in several states. Even though political participation by minorities has increased dramatically since the 1960s, the number of political offices held by members of minority groups remains disproportionately low compared with their numbers in the overall population. This will likely change in the future due to the continued influx of immigrants, particularly from Mexico. Collectively, Hispanics, African Americans, Native Americans, and Asian Americans are now a majority of the populations in California, Hawaii, and New Mexico. It is estimated that by 2015, minority populations will collectively outnumber whites in Texas as well. The impact of immigration will be discussed in more detail later in this chapter.

Lingering Social and Economic Disparities. According to Joyce Ladner of the Brookings Institution, one of the difficulties with the race-based civil rights agenda of the 1950s and 1960s is that it did not envision remedies for cross-racial problems. How, for example, should the nation address problems, such as poverty and urban violence, that affect underclasses in all racial groups? In 1967, when Martin Luther King, Jr., proposed a Poor People's Campaign, he recognized that a civil rights coalition based entirely on race would not be sufficient to address the problem of poverty among whites as well

---

[11] The Gallup Poll, June 8, 2008.

IN THE SPAN OF YEARS since a 1958 poll when only 38 percent of Americans said they would be willing to vote for an African American candidate for president, public opinion shifted to a point in 2008 when 92 percent said they would do so. The change in American opinions may have been influenced by the rise to prominence of such gifted political leaders as former Secretary of State Colin Powell (right), Bush administration Secretary of State Condoleezza Rice (center), and the 44th President of the United States, Barack Obama (left). To what extent do you think that race has really diminished as a factor for American voters? (Photos courtesy of Barack Obama and the U.S. Department of State)

as blacks. During his 1984 and 1988 presidential campaigns, African American leader Jesse Jackson also acknowledged the inadequacy of a race-based model of civil rights when he attempted to form a "Rainbow Coalition" of minorities, women, and other underrepresented groups, including the poor.[12]

Some, including many liberals, contend that government intervention is necessary to eliminate the social and economic disparities that persist within the American population (see Figure 5–1 on the opposite page). Others, including many conservatives, believe that the most effective means of addressing these issues is through coalitions of government groups, private businesses, community-based groups, and individuals. Some civil rights activists currently are pursuing the latter strategy.

Finally, even today, race consciousness continues to divide African Americans and white Americans. Whether we are talking about college attendance, media stereotyping, racial profiling, or academic achievement, the black experience is different from the white one. As a result, African Americans view the nation and many specific issues differently than their white counterparts do.[13] In survey after survey, when blacks are asked whether they have achieved racial equality, few believe that they have. In contrast, whites are five times more likely than blacks to believe that racial equality has been achieved.[14] Despite the civil rights movement and civil rights legislation, African Americans continue to feel a sense of injustice in matters of race, and this feeling is often not apparent to, or appreciated by, the majority of white America.

WOMEN'S STRUGGLE FOR EQUAL RIGHTS

Like African Americans and other minorities, women also have had to struggle for equality. During the first phase of this struggle, the primary goal of women was to obtain the right to vote. As early as 1776, Abigail Adams petitioned her husband to "not forget the ladies" of the new republic. Some women had hoped that the founders would provide such a right in the Constitution. The Constitution did not include a provision guaranteeing women the right to vote, but neither did it deny to women—or to any others—this right. Rather, the founders left it up to the states to decide such issues, and,

[12]Joyce A. Ladner, "A New Civil Rights Agenda," *The Brookings Review*, Vol. 18, No. 2, Spring 2000, pp. 26–28.
[13]Lawerence D. Bobo et al., "Through the Eyes of Black America," *Public Perspective*, May/June 2001, p. 13.
[14]*Ibid.*, p. 15, Figure 2.

as mentioned earlier, by and large, the states limited the franchise to adult white males who owned property.

EARLY WOMEN'S POLITICAL MOVEMENTS

The first political cause in which women became actively engaged was the movement to abolish slavery. Yet even male abolitionists felt that women should not take an active role on the subject in public. When the World Antislavery Convention was held in London in 1840, women delegates were barred from active participation. Partly in response to this rebuff, two American delegates, Lucretia Mott and Elizabeth Cady Stanton, returned from that meeting with plans to work for women's rights in the United States.

In 1848, Mott and Stanton organized the first women's rights convention in Seneca Falls, New York. The 300 people who attended approved a Declaration of Sentiments: "We hold these truths to be self-evident: that all men and *women* are created equal." In the following 12 years, groups that supported women's rights held seven conventions in different cities in the Midwest and East. With the outbreak of the Civil War, however, advocates of women's rights were urged to put their support behind the war effort, and most agreed.

FIGURE 5–1 Median Household Income by Race, 1975–2006.

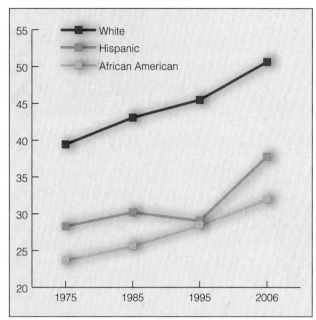

Source: U.S. Bureau of the Census Income, Poverty, and Health Insurance Coverage in the United States, 2007.

WOMEN'S SUFFRAGE ASSOCIATIONS

Susan B. Anthony and Elizabeth Cady Stanton formed the National Woman Suffrage Association in 1869. In their view, women's **suffrage** was a means to achieve major improvements in the economic and social situation of women in the United States. In other words, the vote was to be used to seek broader goals. Nowadays, we commonly see the women's rights movement as a liberal cause, but many of the broader goals of the suffrage advocates would not be regarded as liberal today. An example was the prohibition of alcoholic beverages, which received widespread support among women in general and women's rights activists in particular. It should be noted that many women considered prohibition to be a method of combating domestic violence.

Unlike Anthony and Stanton, Lucy Stone, a key founder of the rival American Woman Suffrage Association, believed that the vote was the only major issue. Members of the American Woman Suffrage Association traveled to each state; addressed state legislatures;

Suffrage
The right to vote; the franchise.

ELIZABETH CADY STANTON (1815–1902), left, was a social reformer and a women's suffrage leader. At her wedding to Henry B. Stanton in 1840, she insisted on dropping the word *obey* from the marriage vows. She wrote *The History of Women's Suffrage,* which was published in 1886. Susan B. Anthony (1820–1906), right, a leader of the women's suffrage movement, was also active in the antialcohol and antislavery movements. In 1869, with Elizabeth Cady Stanton, she founded the National Woman Suffrage Association. In 1888, she organized the International Council of Women and, in 1904, the International Women's Suffrage Alliance, in Berlin. (Library of Congress, Prints & Photographs Division, Washington, D.C. [LC-USZ61-791])

TABLE 5–1 Years, by Country, in which Women Gained the Right to Vote

1893: New Zealand	**1919**: Germany	**1945**: Italy	**1953**: Mexico
1902: Australia	**1920**: United States	**1945**: Japan	**1956**: Egypt
1913: Norway	**1930**: South Africa	**1947**: Argentina	**1963**: Kenya
1918: Britain	**1932**: Brazil	**1950**: India	**1971**: Switzerland
1918: Canada	**1944**: France	**1952**: Greece	**1984**: Yemen

Source: Center for the American Woman and Politics.

That in 1916, four years before the Nineteenth Amendment gave women the right to vote, Jeannette Rankin became the first woman to be elected to the U.S. House of Representatives?

and wrote, published, and argued their convictions. They achieved only limited success. In 1880, the two organizations joined forces. The resulting National American Woman Suffrage Association had only one goal—the enfranchisement of women—but it made little progress.

The Congressional Union, founded in the early 1900s by Alice Paul, rejected the state-by-state approach. Instead, the Union adopted a national strategy of obtaining an amendment to the U.S. Constitution. The Union also employed militant tactics. It sponsored large-scale marches and civil disobedience—which resulted in hunger strikes, arrests, and jailings. Finally, in 1920, the Nineteenth Amendment was passed: "The right of citizens of the United States to vote shall not be denied or abridged by the United States or by any State on account of sex." (Today, the word *gender* is typically used instead of sex.)

Although it may seem that the United States was slow to give women the vote, it was really not too far behind the rest of the world (see Table 5–1). For more on women's rights around the world, see this chapter's *Beyond Our Borders* feature.

THE MODERN WOMEN'S MOVEMENT

Feminism
The movement that supports political, economic, and social equality for women.

Historian Nancy Cott contends that the word *feminism* first began to be used around 1910.[15] At that time, **feminism** meant, as it does today, political, social, and economic equality for women—a radical notion that gained little support among members of the suffrage movement.

After gaining the right to vote in 1920, women engaged in little independent political activity until the 1960s. The civil rights movement of that decade resulted in a growing awareness of rights for all groups, including women. Increased participation in the workforce gave many women greater self-confidence. Additionally, the publication of Betty Friedan's *The Feminine Mystique* in 1963 focused national attention on the unequal status of women in American life.

In 1966, Friedan and others who were dissatisfied with existing women's organizations, and especially with the failure of the Equal Employment Opportunity Commission to address discrimination against women, formed the National Organization for Women (NOW). Many observers consider the founding of NOW to be the beginning of the modern women's movement—the feminist movement. NOW immediately adopted a blanket resolution designed "to bring women into full participation in the mainstream of American society *now*, exercising all the privileges and responsibilities thereof in truly equal partnership with men."

[15] Nancy F. Cott, *The Grounding of Modern Feminism* (New Haven: Yale University Press, 1987).

BEYOND OUR BRDERS

THE STRUGGLE FOR WOMEN'S RIGHTS AROUND THE WORLD

Although in the last several decades women's rights have emerged as a global issue, progress has been slow. The struggle for women's rights in countries where cultural or legal practices perpetuate the inequality of women is especially difficult.

THE PROBLEM OF VIOLENCE

Most people consider the right to be free from violence as one of the most basic human rights. Women's rights advocates point out that this right is threatened in societies that do not accept the premise that men and women are equal. Some parts of India, for example, implicitly tolerate the practice of dowry killing. (A *dowry* is a sum of money given to a husband by the bride's family.) In a number of cases, husbands, dissatisfied with the size of dowries, have killed their wives in order to remarry for a "better deal"—a crime that is rarely prosecuted.

THE SITUATION IN AFGHANISTAN

In 2001, a startling documentary, "Behind the Veil," was aired repeatedly on CNN. A courageous female reporter had

IRAQI GIRLS wait for the start of class at the Eastern Secondary School in Baghdad. The role of women in the new Iraq remains uncertain. What negative consequences could result if discriminatory laws forced Iraqi women—among the region's most educated—to retreat to their homes? (AP Photo/Alexander Zemlianichenko)

secretly filmed Afghan women being beaten in the streets, killed in public for trivial offenses, and generally subjugated in extreme ways. For the first time ever, women's rights became a major issue in our foreign policy. Americans learned that Afghan girls were barred from schools, and by law women were not allowed to work. Women who had lost their husbands during Afghanistan's civil wars were forced into begging and prostitution. Women had no access to medical care. Any woman found with an unrelated man could be executed by stoning, and many were.

NATION BUILDING AND WOMEN'S RIGHTS

After the collapse of the Taliban regime, the United States and its allies were able to influence the status of Afghan women. The draft constitution of Afghanistan, adopted in January 2004, gave women equality before the law and 20 percent of the seats in the National Assembly. Much of the country remained outside the control of the national government, however. Women continued to face daunting abuse, including arson attacks on girls' schools, forced marriages, and imposition of the all-covering burka garment.

Women in Iraq have enjoyed greater equality than in most Arab nations. In line with the secular ideology of the Baath Party, Saddam Hussein's government tended to treat men and women alike. A problem for the U.S.-led Coalition Provisional Authority (CPA) that governed Iraq until June 2004 was ensuring that women did not lose ground under the new regime. Some members of the Iraqi Governing Council, for example, advocated traditional Islamic laws that would have deprived women of equal rights. Women's organizations campaigned against these provisions, and they were vetoed by the CPA. The interim Iraqi constitution, adopted in March 2004, allotted 25 percent of the seats in the parliament to women.

FOR CRITICAL ANALYSIS

Is it fair or appropriate for one country to judge the cultural practices of another? Why or why not?

Feminism gained additional impetus from young women who entered politics to support the civil rights movement or to oppose the Vietnam War. Many of them found that despite the egalitarian principles of these movements, women remained in second-class positions. These young women sought their own movement. In the late 1960s, "women's liberation" organizations began to spring up on college campuses. Women also began organizing independent "consciousness-raising groups," in which they discussed how gender issues affected their lives. The new women's movement experienced explosive growth, and by 1970 it had emerged as a major social force.

Who are the feminists today? It is difficult to measure the support for feminism at present because the word means different things to different people. When the dictionary definition of *feminist*—"someone who supports political, economic, and social equality for women"—was read to respondents in a survey, 67 percent labeled themselves as feminists.[16] In the absence of such prompting, however, the term *feminist* (like the term *liberal*) implies radicalism to many people, who therefore shy away from it.

The Equal Rights Amendment. The initial focus of the modern women's movement was not on expanding the political rights of women. Rather, leaders of NOW and other liberal women's rights advocates sought to eradicate gender inequality through a constitutional amendment. The proposed Equal Rights Amendment (ERA), which was first introduced in Congress in 1923 by leaders of the National Women's Party (a successor to the Congressional Union), states: "Equality of rights under the law shall not be denied or abridged by the United States or by any state on account of sex." For years the amendment was not even given a hearing in Congress, but finally it was approved by both chambers and sent to the state legislatures for ratification in 1972.

As was noted in Chapter 2, any constitutional amendment must be ratified by the legislatures (or conventions) in three-fourths of the states before it can become law. Since the early 1900s, most proposed amendments have required that ratification occur within seven years of Congress's adoption of the amendment. The necessary 38 states failed to ratify the ERA within the seven-year period specified by Congress, even though it was supported by numerous national party platforms, six presidents, and both chambers of Congress. To date, efforts to reintroduce the amendment have not succeeded.

During the national debate over the ratification of the ERA, a women's countermovement emerged. Many women perceived the goals pursued by NOW and other liberal women's organizations as a threat to their way of life. At the head of the countermovement was Republican Phyllis Schlafly and her conservative organization, Eagle Forum. Eagle Forum's "Stop ERA" campaign found significant support among fundamentalist religious groups and various other conservative organizations. The campaign was effective in blocking the ratification of the ERA, although almost all states have passed such amendments to their own constitutions.

Additional Women's Issues. While NOW concentrated on the ERA, a large number of other women's groups, many of them entirely local, addressed a spectrum of added issues. One of these was the issue of *domestic violence*—that is, assaults within the family. Typically, this meant husbands or boyfriends assaulting their wives or girlfriends. During the 1970s, feminists across the country began opening *battered women's shelters* to house victims of abuse.

That in 1922, at age 87, Rebecca Latimer Felton was the first and oldest woman to serve in the U.S. Senate—although she was appointed as a token gesture and was allowed to serve only one day?

---

[16]Nancy E. McGlen and Karen O'Connor, *Women, Politics, and American Society*, 4th ed. (Upper Saddle River, NJ: Prentice Hall, 2004).

Abortion soon emerged as a key concern. Virtually the entire organized women's movement united behind the "freedom-of-choice" position, at the cost of alienating potential women's rights supporters who favored the "right-to-life" position instead. Because abortion was a national issue, the campaign was led by national organizations such as NARAL Pro-Choice America, formerly the National Abortion and Reproductive Rights Action League. As noted in the discussion in Chapter 4, the right to an abortion has been tightly regulated in many states and partial-birth abortions banned by federal law. Each of these legislative actions has met opposition from the groups that seek to preserve a woman's right to choose an abortion.

Another issue—pornography—tended to divide the women's movement rather than unite it. While a majority of feminists found pornography demeaning to women, many were also strong supporters of free speech. Others, notably activists Andrea Dworkin and Catharine Mackinnon, believed that pornography was so central to the subjugation of women that First Amendment protections should not apply.

Challenging Gender Discrimination in the Courts and Legislatures. When the ERA failed to be ratified, women's rights organizations began a campaign to win more limited national and state laws that would guarantee the equality of women. This more limited campaign met with much success. In 1978, the Civil Rights Act of 1964 was amended by the Pregnancy Discrimination Act, which prohibits discrimination in employment against pregnant women. In addition, Title IX of the Education Amendments was passed in 1972. This legislation has greatly impacted college and university athletic programs as they try to equalize the numbers of men and women playing varsity sports.

DID YOU KNOW?

That a Gallup poll taken in early 2000 found that 15 percent of the women polled described themselves as homemakers, but not one man described himself as such?

THE UNIVERSITY OF SOUTHERN California's women's soccer team celebrates their championship in 2007. Would USC even have a women's soccer team if Title IX had not existed? (Matt Slocum/AP Photos)

Gender Discrimination
Any practice, policy, or procedure that denies equality of treatment to an individual or to a group because of gender.

Women's rights organizations also challenged discriminatory statutes and policies in the federal courts, contending that **gender discrimination** violated the Fourteenth Amendment's equal protection clause. Since the 1970s, the Supreme Court has tended to scrutinize gender classifications closely and has invalidated a number of such statutes and policies. For example, in 1977, the Court held that police and firefighting units cannot establish arbitrary rules, such as height and weight requirements, that tend to keep women from joining those occupations.[17] In 1983, the Court ruled that life insurance companies cannot charge different rates for women and men.[18]

A question that the Court has not ruled on is whether women should be allowed to participate in military combat. Generally, the Supreme Court has left this decision up to Congress and the Department of Defense. Recently, women have been allowed to serve as combat pilots and on naval warships. To date, however, they have not been allowed to join infantry direct-combat units, although they are now permitted to serve in combat-support units. During the Persian Gulf War, women served in forward support units and flew in combat. The Iraq War has seen a rapid increase in the number of women who serve in a combat zone, particularly in the National Guard units who have been called up to serve in that theater. In 1996, the Supreme Court held that the state-financed Virginia Military Institute's policy of accepting only males violated the equal protection clause.[19]

Expanding Women's Political Opportunities. Following the failure of the ERA, in addition to fighting discrimination in the courts, the women's movement began to work for increased representation in government. Several women's political organizations that are active today concentrate their efforts on getting women elected to political offices. These organizations include the National Women's Political Caucus, the Coalition for Women's Appointments, the Feminist Majority Foundation, and the National Education for Women's Leadership (the NEW Leadership).

SHOWN HERE is Sergeant Leigh Ann Hester of the 617th Military Police Company. She received a Silver Star, making her the first female soldier serving in Operation Iraqi Freedom to receive such an award. As team leader and vehicle commander, Hester helped thwart an insurgent attack against a coalition convoy. What reasoning was previously used for preventing female soldiers from being put into combat situations in military engagements? (Spc. Jeremy D. Crisp/AP Photo)

---

[17]*Dothard v. Rawlinson*, 433 U.S. 321 (1977).
[18]*Arizona v. Norris*, 463 U.S. 1073 (1983).
[19]*United States v. Virginia*, 518 U.S. 515 (1996).

WOMEN IN POLITICS TODAY

The efforts of women's rights advocates have helped increase the number of women holding political offices at all levels of government.

Women in Congress. Although a men's club atmosphere still prevails in Congress, the number of women holding congressional seats has increased significantly in recent years. Elections during the 1990s brought more women to Congress than either the Senate or the House had seen before. In 2001, for the first time, a woman was elected to a top leadership post in Congress and, in 2007, Nancy Pelosi of California became the first female Speaker of the House, the most powerful member of the majority party and second in the line of succession to the presidency.

Women in Congress After the 2008 Elections. The success of Democratic candidates for the House in 2008 gave a boost to the popularity and power of Speaker Pelosi. The election also brought a record number of women to Congress, although the number of women candidates did not increase that year. In the House of Representatives, 74 women took their seats. Of that number, 64 are incumbents who won re-election, while 10 new congresswomen (eight Democrats and two Republicans) joined the House of Representatives. In the Senate, a record number of 17 women took seats. In 2008, two of the winners were challengers who defeated incumbent senators. Jeanne Shaheen, the former Democratic governor of New Hampshire, defeated the incumbent senator there, while Democrat Kay Hagan of North Carolina defeated Republican Elizabeth Dole, a two-term incumbent.

Women in the Executive and Judicial Branches. Although no woman has yet been nominated for president by a major political party, in 1984 a woman, Geraldine Ferraro, became the Democratic nominee for vice president. Another woman, Elizabeth Dole, made a serious run for the Republican presidential nomination in the 2000 campaigns. Of course, in 2008, Hillary Rodham Clinton, senator from New York, became one of two contenders for the presidential nomination of the Democratic Party, but ultimately lost to Barack Obama. In a surprise move, Senator John McCain chose the Alaskan governor, Sarah Palin, for his running mate. While Governor Palin drew criticism for her inexperience in foreign policy and occasional verbal gaffes, she found strong support among working-class mothers and families with special needs children.

ALL OF THE FOURTEEN women senators from the 109th Congress are shown here. What obstacles have women faced in their attempts to reach the highest political ranks in America? (AP Photo)

Increasing numbers of women are also being appointed to Cabinet posts. President Bill Clinton (served 1993–2001) appointed four women to his Cabinet, more than any previous president. Madeleine Albright was appointed to the important post of secretary of state. President George W. Bush also appointed several women to Cabinet positions, including Condoleezza Rice as his secretary of state in 2005, and a number of other women to various federal offices.

Increasing numbers of women are sitting on federal judicial benches as well. President Ronald Reagan (served 1981–1989) was credited with a historic first when he appointed Sandra Day O'Connor to the Supreme Court in 1981. President Clinton appointed a second woman, Ruth Bader Ginsburg, to the Court. O'Connor retired from the Court in 2006. President Bush initially nominated another woman, Harriet Miers, to take her place on the bench. Miers, however, later withdrew her nomination.

Continuing Disproportionate Leadership. For all their achievements in the political arena, the number of women holding political offices remains disproportionately low compared with their participation as voters. In recent elections, the turnout of female voters nationally has been slightly higher than that of male voters.

GENDER-BASED DISCRIMINATION IN THE WORKPLACE

Traditional cultural beliefs concerning the proper role of women in society continue to be evident not only in the political arena but also in the workplace. Since the 1960s, however, women have gained substantial protection against discrimination through laws mandating equal employment opportunities and equal pay.

TITLE VII OF THE CIVIL RIGHTS ACT OF 1964

Title VII of the Civil Rights Act of 1964 prohibits gender discrimination in employment and has been used to strike down employment policies that discriminate against employees on the basis of gender. Even so-called protective policies have been held to violate Title VII if they have a discriminatory effect. In 1991, for example, the Supreme Court held that a fetal protection policy established by Johnson Controls, Inc., the country's largest producer of automobile batteries, violated Title VII. The policy required all women of childbearing age working in jobs that entailed periodic exposure to lead or other hazardous materials to prove that they were infertile or to transfer to other positions. Women who agreed to transfer often had to accept cuts in pay and reduced job responsibilities. The Court concluded that women who are "as capable of doing their jobs as their male counterparts may not be forced to choose between having a child and having a job."[20]

In 1978, Congress amended Title VII to expand the definition of gender discrimination to include discrimination based on pregnancy. Women affected by pregnancy, childbirth, or related medical conditions must be treated—for all employment-related purposes, including the receipt of benefits under employee benefit programs—the same as other persons not so affected but similar in ability to work.

SEXUAL HARASSMENT

Sexual Harassment
Unwanted physical or verbal conduct or abuse of a sexual nature that interferes with a recipient's job performance, creates a hostile work environment, or carries with it an implicit or explicit threat of adverse employment consequences.

The Supreme Court has also held that Title VII's prohibition of gender-based discrimination extends to **sexual harassment** in the workplace. Sexual harassment occurs when job opportunities, promotions, salary increases, and the like are given in return

[20]*United Automobile Workers v. Johnson Controls, Inc.*, 499 U.S. 187 (1991).

for sexual favors. A special form of sexual harassment, called hostile-environment harassment, occurs when an employee is subjected to sexual conduct or comments that interfere with the employee's job performance or are so pervasive or severe as to create an intimidating, hostile, or offensive environment.

In two 1998 cases, the Supreme Court clarified the responsibilities of employers in preventing sexual harassment. In *Faragher v. City of Boca Raton*, the question was the following: Should an employer be held liable for a supervisor's sexual harassment of an employee even though the employer was unaware of the harassment? The Court ruled that the employer in this case was liable but stated that the employer might have avoided such liability if it had taken reasonable care to prevent harassing behavior, which the employer had not done.

In the second case, *Burlington Industries v. Ellerth*, the Court similarly held that an employer was liable for sexual harassment caused by a supervisor's actions even though the employee had suffered no tangible job consequences as a result of those actions. Again, the Court emphasized that a key factor in holding the employer liable was whether the employer had exercised reasonable care to prevent and promptly correct any sexually harassing behavior.[21]

In another 1998 case, *Oncale v. Sundowner Offshore Services, Inc.*,[22] the Supreme Court addressed a further issue: Should Title VII protection be extended to cover situations in which individuals are harassed by members of the same gender? The Court answered this question in the affirmative.

WAGE DISCRIMINATION

By 2010, women will constitute a majority of U.S. workers. Although Title VII and other legislation since the 1960s have mandated equal employment opportunities for men and women, women continue to earn less, on average, than men do.

The Equal Pay Act of 1963. The issue of wage discrimination was first addressed during World War II (1939–1945), when the War Labor Board issued an "equal pay for women" policy. In implementing the policy, the board often evaluated jobs for their comparability and required equal pay for comparable jobs. The board's authority ended with the war. Although it was supported by the next three presidential administrations, the Equal Pay Act was not enacted until 1963 as an amendment to the Fair Labor Standards Act of 1938.

Basically, the Equal Pay Act requires employers to provide equal pay for substantially equal work. In other words, males cannot legally be paid more than females who perform essentially the same job. The Equal Pay Act did not address the fact that certain types of jobs traditionally held by women pay lower wages than the jobs usually held by men. For example, more women than men are salesclerks and nurses, whereas more men than women are construction workers and truck drivers. Even if all clerks performing substantially similar jobs for a company earned the same salaries, they typically would still be earning less than the company's truck drivers.

When Congress passed the Equal Pay Act in 1963, a woman, on average, made 59 cents for every dollar earned by a man. Figures recently released by the U.S. Department of Labor suggest that women now earn 77.8 cents for every dollar that men earn. In some areas, the wage gap is widening. According to the results of a General Accounting Office survey reported in 2002, female managers in 10 industries made less money relative to male managers in 2000 than they did in 1995. In the entertainment industry,

---

[21]524 U.S. 725 (1998), and 524 U.S. 742 (1998).
[22]523 U.S. 75 (1998).

for example, in 2000 female managers earned 62 cents for every dollar earned by male managers—down from 83 cents in 1995.[23]

The Glass Ceiling. Although greater numbers of women are holding jobs in professions or business enterprises that were once dominated by men, few women hold top positions in their firms. Less than 12 percent of the Fortune 500 companies in the United States—the nation's leading corporations—have a woman as one of their five highest-paid executives. In all, according to Census Bureau statistics, men still hold 93 percent of the top corporate management positions in this country. Because the barriers faced by women in the corporate world are subtle and not easily pinpointed, they have been referred to as the "glass ceiling."

Over the last decade, women have been breaking through the glass ceiling in far greater numbers than before. Alternatively, some corporations have offered a "mommy track" to high-achieving women. The mommy track allows a woman more time to pursue a family life but usually rules out promotion to top jobs. The mommy track therefore tends to reinforce the glass ceiling.

IMMIGRATION, HISPANICS, AND CIVIL RIGHTS

Time and again, this nation has been challenged and changed—and culturally enriched—by immigrant groups. All of these immigrants have faced the challenges involved in living in a new and different political and cultural environment. Most of them have had to overcome language barriers, and many have had to deal with discrimination in one form or another because of their color, their inability to speak English fluently, or their customs. The civil rights legislation passed during and since the 1960s has done much to counter the effects of prejudice against immigrant groups by ensuring that they obtain equal rights under the law.

One of the questions facing Americans and their political leaders today concerns the effect of immigration on American politics and government. This is especially true with regard to the Hispanic American community. With the influx of individuals from Latin American countries growing exponentially, issues related to immigration and Hispanic Americans will continue to gain greater attention in years to come.

THE CONTINUED INFLUX OF IMMIGRANTS

Today, immigration rates are the highest they have been since their peak in the early 20th century. Every year, about 1 million people immigrate to this country, and those who were born on foreign soil now constitute more than 10 percent of the U.S. population—twice the percentage of 30 years ago.

Since 1977, more than 80 percent of immigrants have come from Latin America or Asia. Hispanics are now overtaking African Americans as the nation's largest minority. If current immigration rates continue, minority groups collectively will constitute the "majority" of Americans by the year 2050. If Hispanics, African Americans, and perhaps Asians were to form coalitions, they could increase their political strength dramatically and would have the numerical strength to make significant changes. According to Ben Wattenberg of the American Enterprise Institute, in the future the "old guard" white majority will no longer dominate American politics.[24]

---

[23]The results of this survey are online at www.gao.gov/audit.htm. To view a copy of the results, enter "GAO-02-156" in the search box. In 2004, the name of this agency was changed to the "Government Accountability Office."
[24]Ben J. Wattenberg, *Fewer: How the New Demography of Depopulation Will Shape our Future* (Chicago: Ivan R. Dee Publisher, 2004).

ILLEGAL IMMIGRATION

In the past few years, the issue of illegal immigration has become both a hot political issue and a serious policy problem. It is estimated that there may be as many as 12 million undocumented aliens residing and working in the United States. How could any government find and deport or identify that many individuals? The immigrants typically come to the United States to work, and their labor tends to be in high demand. The most recent housing boom across the nation, for example, was partially fueled by the steady stream of illegal immigrants seeking construction jobs.

One civil rights question that has often surfaced is whether the government should provide services to those who enter the country illegally. At one point, a bill that would criminalize assisting illegal immigrants circulated in the House of Representatives. This bill and similar measures at the state level have come in response to residents of Southwestern states that have complained about the need to shore up border control. These citizens perceive illegal immigrants as a burden on government-provided social services and the health-care industry. Some schools have become crowded with the children of illegal immigrants. Often, these children require greater attention because of their inability to speak English. Moreover, hospitals and health-care providers in many communities have been overwhelmed because a significant proportion of illegal immigrants do not have any type of health insurance.

Citizenship. Illegal immigrants are not without advocates, however. Members of Congress from both parties have proposed legislation that would either immediately or gradually extend citizenship to illegal immigrants now residing in the United States. Although not all Americans agree that citizenship should be extended to illegal immigrants, the

IN A MAY 1, 2007, demonstration, immigrants fill the streets of Los Angeles to protest the possible passing of a bill that would criminalize illegal immigrants. Congress did not pass such a bill, but it did pass a law approving the construction of a border fence to deter illegal immigration. (David McNew/Getty Images)

WHAT IF...

ILLEGAL IMMIGRANTS WERE GRANTED CITIZENSHIP?

Granting citizenship to every illegal immigrant now residing in the United States would have significant repercussions. The illegal immigrants' sheer numbers would command attention from both political parties. The already important "Hispanic vote" would take on even greater significance.

A massive grant of citizenship would make employment and income tax practices (or lack thereof) associated with illegal immigrants more transparent. Finally, by granting citizenship to those who had entered the country illegally, the United States would likely face a tide of new immigrants.

INCREASED POLITICAL CLOUT FOR THE HISPANIC COMMUNITY

In recent years, Hispanics have begun to reverse their reputation for being politically inactive or disinterested. Voter participation within the Hispanic community has increased. Hispanics have become more politically active and outspoken. Indeed, such developments are reflected in the growing number of individuals of Hispanic descent holding public office as mayors of major cities, governors, and members of Congress.

The fact that granting citizenship to illegal immigrants is even a topic of discussion represents a significant turn of events for Hispanic Americans. Factions within both major parties have proposed different measures that would lead to citizenship for illegals. Political interest groups have formed to champion immigrant rights. Some broader-based groups have advocated on behalf of both legal and illegal immigrants of Hispanic origin.

EMPLOYMENT AND TAXES

Most illegal immigrants come to the United States to work. Many illegal immigrants send part of their earnings in America back to relatives in their home countries. The wages sent home to family members by individuals working in the United States (both legally and illegally) are the second-largest source of foreign income in Mexico.

The Internal Revenue Service has had difficulty collecting taxes on the wages that illegal immigrants earn, however. Some employers who knowingly hire illegal immigrants simply pay those workers "under the table" to avoid a paper trail. Often, the arrangement is a cash transaction, which is difficult to track. If all illegal immigrants were granted citizenship, most employers would no longer be able to engage in such tax-evasion schemes.

Employers sometimes take advantage of illegal immigrants by refusing to pay them for work or changing the terms of work agreements. Other employers use illegal immigrants as employees because they often accept lower wages than American citizens would. Some employers break the law by hiring illegal immigrants to get around paying state or federal minimum wages. If citizenship were granted to illegal immigrants, employers would have to reconsider their practices. Moreover, as wages were properly reported, tax revenues would increase. Employers, however, might eliminate some jobs if they were forced to pay higher wages.

U.S. IMMIGRATION POLICY

Obviously, illegal immigrants violate U.S. immigration laws. Anyone seeking to enter the United States legally faces a lengthy application process and annual quota limitations that depend on national origin. Enforcement of immigration law has always been difficult. Record numbers of illegal immigrants continue to enter the United States despite increased efforts to control the borders.

Granting citizenship to all illegal immigrants now residing in the United States could be considered unfair to all those who are waiting for legal entry. It would be difficult for the United States to justify keeping its borders closed if citizenship were granted to those already within its borders illegally.

FOR CRITICAL ANALYSIS

1. Some politicians have advocated a gradual process for granting citizenship to illegal immigrants. Do you think that a gradual process would be more appropriate than an automatic grant of citizenship? Or do you oppose any proposal—gradual or immediate—to offer citizenship to illegal immigrants? Explain your position

2. Do you think immigration would significantly increase if the United States unveiled some type of policy to grant citizenship to illegal immigrants? Why or why not?

greater Hispanic community in the United States has taken up the cause. Numerous protests and marches calling for citizenship occurred in 2006, with more than 1 million individuals participating in demonstrations on May 1, 2006, alone. To be sure, the citizenship question will be an important political topic for the foreseeable future.

Border Crime. Crime is another concern related to illegal immigration and border control. Smugglers who help illegal immigrants cross the border are quite common in border towns. Although some smugglers simply collect a fee, others take advantage of the situation. Many individuals attempting to enter the United States illegally are swindled or physically harmed by criminals. Many Mexican women trying to enter the United States have been raped and sexually abused by smugglers. Some of these women have said that such abuse is the price of a better life on the American side of the border. Drugs have also been a significant problem along the U.S.–Mexican border. In 2005, federal agents discovered an extensive underground tunnel that was being used as a pipeline for a lucrative drug-trafficking scheme. The governors of Arizona and New Mexico had to declare a state of emergency in 2005 because of border-control problems.

BILINGUAL EDUCATION

The continuous influx of immigrants into this country presents another ongoing challenge—how to overcome language barriers. About half of the states have responded to this challenge by passing English-only laws, making English the official language of those states. Language issues have been particularly difficult for the schools. Throughout our history, educators have been faced with the question of how best to educate children who do not speak English or do not speak it very well.

During the 1950s, increased immigration from Mexico and Latin American countries caused many educators to be concerned about the language problems facing these immigrants. Spanish had effectively become America's second language, yet local school districts in some parts of the Southwest prohibited children from speaking Spanish, even on school playgrounds. In the 1960s, bilingual education programs began to be implemented as a solution to the language problems facing immigrants.

Accommodating Diversity with Bilingual Education. Bilingual education programs teach children in their native language while also teaching them English. To some extent, today's bilingual education programs are the result of the government policies favoring multiculturalism that grew out of the civil rights movement. Multiculturalism involves the belief that the government should accommodate the needs of different cultural groups and should protect and encourage ethnic and cultural differences.

Children attending classes taught in English were frequently encouraged by their teachers as well as their parents to speak English as much as possible, both at school and at home. Children who did so felt distanced from their grandparents and family members who spoke no English and, as a result, felt cut off from their ethnic backgrounds. Bilingual education was premised on the hope that, over time, Hispanic children would become truly bilingual without having to sacrifice their close family relationships and cultural heritage.

Congress authorized bilingual education programs in 1968 when it passed the Bilingual Education Act, which was intended primarily to help Hispanic children learn English. In a 1974 case, *Lau v. Nichols*,[25] the Supreme Court bolstered the claim that children have a right to bilingual education. In that case, the Court ordered a California school district to provide special programs for Chinese students with language difficulties

---

[25]414 U.S. 563 (1974).

if a substantial number of these children attended school in the district. Today, most bilingual education programs are for Hispanic American children, particularly in areas of the country such as California and Texas, where there are large numbers of Hispanic residents.

Controversy over Bilingual Education. The bilingual programs established in the 1960s and subsequently have increasingly come under attack. In 1998, California residents passed a ballot initiative that called for the end of bilingual education programs in that state. The law allowed schools to implement English-immersion programs instead. In these programs, students are given intensive instruction in English for a limited period of time and then placed in regular classrooms.

The law was immediately challenged in court on the ground that it unconstitutionally discriminated against non-English-speaking groups. A federal district court, however, concluded that the new law did not violate the equal protection clause and allowed the law to stand, thus ending bilingual education efforts in California.

AFFIRMATIVE ACTION

As noted earlier in this chapter, the Civil Rights Act of 1964 prohibited discrimination against any person on the basis of race, color, national origin, religion, or gender. The Act also established the right to equal opportunity in employment. A basic problem remained, however: minority groups and women, because of past discrimination, often lacked the education and skills to compete effectively in the marketplace. In 1965, the federal government attempted to remedy this problem by implementing the concept of affirmative action. **Affirmative action** policies attempt to "level the playing field" by giving special preferences in educational admissions and employment decisions to groups that have been discriminated against in the past.

In 1965, President Lyndon B. Johnson ordered that affirmative action policies be undertaken to remedy the effects of past discrimination. All government agencies, including those of state and local governments, were required to implement such policies. Additionally, affirmative action requirements were imposed on companies that sell goods or services to the federal government and on institutions that receive federal funds. Affirmative action policies were also required whenever an employer had been ordered to develop such a plan by a court or by the Equal Employment Opportunity Commission because of evidence of past discrimination. Finally, labor unions that had been found to discriminate against women or minorities in the past were required to establish and follow affirmative action plans.

Affirmative action programs have been controversial because they allegedly result in discrimination against majority groups, such as white males (or discrimination against other minority groups that may not be given preferential treatment under a particular affirmative action program). At issue in the current debate over affirmative action programs is whether such programs, because of their discriminatory nature, violate the equal protection clause of the Fourteenth Amendment to the Constitution.

THE *BAKKE* CASE

The first Supreme Court case addressing the constitutionality of affirmative action plans examined a program implemented by the University of California at Davis. Allan Bakke, a white student who had been turned down for medical school at the Davis campus, discovered that his academic record was better than those of some of the minority applicants who had been admitted to the program. He sued the University of Cali-

Affirmative Action
A policy in educational admissions or job hiring that gives special attention or compensatory treatment to traditionally disadvantaged groups in an effort to overcome present effects of past discrimination.

fornia regents, alleging **reverse discrimination**. The UC-Davis Medical School had held 16 places out of 100 for educationally "disadvantaged students" each year, and the administrators at that campus admitted to using race as a criterion for admission for these particular minority slots. At trial in 1974, Bakke said that his exclusion from medical school violated his rights under the Fourteenth Amendment's provision for equal protection of the laws. The trial court agreed. On appeal, the California Supreme Court agreed also. Finally, the regents of the university appealed to the United States Supreme Court.

In 1978, the Supreme Court handed down its decision in *Regents of the University of California v. Bakke*.[26] The Court did not rule against affirmative action programs. Rather, it held that Bakke must be admitted to the UC-Davis Medical School because its admissions policy had used race as the sole criterion for the 16 "minority" positions. Justice Lewis Powell, speaking for the Court, indicated that while race can be considered "as a factor" among others in admissions (and presumably hiring) decisions, race cannot be the sole factor. So affirmative action programs, but not specific quota systems, were upheld as constitutional.

FURTHER LIMITS ON AFFIRMATIVE ACTION

Several cases decided during the 1980s and 1990s placed further limits on affirmative action programs. In a landmark decision in 1995, *Adarand Constructors, Inc. v. Peña*,[27] the Supreme Court held that any federal, state, or local affirmative action program that uses racial or ethnic classifications as the basis for making decisions is subject to "strict scrutiny" by the courts. Under a strict-scrutiny analysis, to be constitutional, a discriminatory law or action must be narrowly tailored to meet a *compelling* government interest. In effect, the Court's opinion in *Adarand* means that an affirmative action program cannot use quotas or preferences for unqualified persons, and once the program has succeeded in achieving that compelling government interest, the program must be changed or dropped.

In 1996, a federal appellate court went even further. In *Hopwood v. State of Texas*,[28] two white law school applicants sued the University of Texas School of Law in Austin, alleging that they had been denied admission because of the school's affirmative action program. The program allowed admissions officials to take race and other factors into consideration. The federal appellate court held that the program violated the equal protection clause because it discriminated in favor of minority applicants. Significantly, the court directly challenged the *Bakke* decision by stating that the use of race even as a means of achieving diversity on college campuses "undercuts the Fourteenth Amendment."

In 2003, however, in two cases involving the University of Michigan, the Supreme Court indicated that limited affirmative action programs continue to be acceptable and that diversity is a legitimate goal. The Court struck down the affirmative action plan used for undergraduate admissions at the university, which automatically awarded a substantial number of points to applicants based on minority status.[29] At the same time, it approved the admissions plan used by the law school, which took race into consideration as part of a complete examination of each applicant's background.[30]

> **Reverse Discrimination**
> The charge that an affirmative action program discriminates against those who do not have minority status.

---

[26]438 U.S. 265 (1978).
[27]515 U.S. 200 (1995).
[28]84 F.3d 720 (5th Cir. 1996).
[29]*Gratz v. Bollinger*, 539 U.S. 244 (2003).
[30]*Grutter v. Bollinger*, 539 U.S. 306 (2003).

STATE BALLOT INITIATIVES

A ballot initiative passed by California voters in 1996 amended that state's constitution to end all state-sponsored affirmative action programs. The law was challenged immediately in court by civil rights groups and others. These groups claimed that the law violated the Fourteenth Amendment by denying racial minorities and women the equal protection of the laws. In 1997, however, a federal appellate court upheld the constitutionality of the amendment. Thus, affirmative action is now illegal in California in all state-sponsored institutions, including state agencies and educational institutions. In 1998, Washington voters also approved a law banning affirmative action in that state.

SPECIAL PROTECTION FOR OLDER AMERICANS

Americans are getting older. In colonial times, about half the population was under the age of 16. In 2000, fewer than one in four Americans was under the age of 16. Today, about 38 million Americans (nearly 13 percent of the population) are aged 65 or older. By the year 2025, this figure is projected to reach about 70 million. By 2050, the portion of the population over age 65 will have almost doubled from the current figure.

Older citizens face a variety of difficulties unique to their group. One problem that seems to endure, despite government legislation designed to prevent it, is age discrimination in employment.

AGE DISCRIMINATION IN EMPLOYMENT

Age discrimination is potentially the most widespread form of discrimination, because anyone—regardless of race, color, national origin, or gender—could be a victim at some point in life. The unstated policies of some companies not to hire or to demote or dismiss people they feel are "too old" have made it difficult for some older workers to succeed in their jobs or continue with their careers. Additionally, older workers have fallen victim at times to cost-cutting efforts by employers. To reduce operational costs, companies may replace older, higher-salaried workers with younger, lower-salaried workers.

THE AGE DISCRIMINATION IN EMPLOYMENT ACT OF 1967

In an attempt to protect older employees from such discriminatory practices, Congress passed the Age Discrimination in Employment Act (ADEA) in 1967. The Act, which applies to employers, employment agencies, and labor organizations and covers individuals over the age of 40, prohibits discrimination against individuals on the basis of age unless age is shown to be a bona fide occupational qualification reasonably necessary to the normal operation of the particular business.

To succeed in a suit for age discrimination, an employee must prove that the employer's action, such as a decision to fire the employee, was motivated, at least in part, by age bias. Even if an older worker is replaced by a younger worker falling under the protection of the ADEA—that is, by a younger worker who is also over the age of 40—the older worker is entitled to bring a suit under the ADEA.[31] As discussed in Chapter 3 in the context of federalism, in 2000 the Supreme Court limited the applicability of the ADEA in its decision in *Kimel v. Florida Board of Regents*.[32] The Court held that the

[31] *O'Connor v. Consolidated Coin Caterers Corp.*, 517 U.S. 308 (1996).
[32] 528 U.S. 62 (2000).

sovereign immunity granted to the states by the Eleventh Amendment to the Constitution precluded suits against a state by private parties alleging violations of the ADEA. Victims of age discrimination can bring actions under state statutes, however, and most states have laws protecting their citizens from age discrimination.

The ADEA, as initially passed, did not address one of the major problems facing older workers—**mandatory retirement** rules, which require employees to retire when they reach a certain age. Mandatory retirement rules often mean that competent, well-trained employees who want to continue working are unable to do so. In 1978, in an amendment to the ADEA, Congress prohibited mandatory retirement rules for most employees under the age of 70. In 1986, Congress outlawed mandatory retirement rules entirely for all but a few selected occupations, such as firefighting.

Mandatory Retirement
Forced retirement when a person reaches a certain age.

SECURING RIGHTS FOR PERSONS WITH DISABILITIES

Like older Americans, persons with disabilities did not fall under the protective umbrella of the Civil Rights Act of 1964. In 1973, however, Congress passed the Rehabilitation Act, which prohibited discrimination against persons with disabilities in programs receiving federal aid. A 1978 amendment to the Act established the Architectural and Transportation Barriers Compliance Board. Regulations for ramps, elevators, and the like in all federal buildings were implemented. Congress passed the Education for All Handicapped Children Act in 1975. It guarantees that all children with disabilities will receive an "appropriate" education. The most significant federal legislation to protect the rights of persons with disabilities, however, is the Americans with Disabilities Act (ADA), which Congress passed in 1990.

THE AMERICANS WITH DISABILITIES ACT OF 1990

The ADA requires that all public buildings and public services be accessible to persons with disabilities. The Act also mandates that employers must reasonably accommodate the needs of workers or potential workers with disabilities. Physical access means ramps; handrails; wheelchair-accessible restrooms, counters, drinking fountains, telephones, and doorways; and easily accessible mass transit. In addition, other steps must be taken to comply with the Act. Car rental companies must provide cars with hand controls for disabled drivers. Telephone companies are required to have operators to pass on messages from speech-impaired persons who use telephones with keyboards.

The ADA requires employers to "reasonably accommodate" the needs of persons with disabilities unless to do so would cause the employer to suffer an "undue hardship." The ADA defines persons with disabilities as persons who have physical or mental impairments that "substantially limit" their everyday activities. Health conditions that have been considered disabilities under federal law include blindness, alcoholism, heart disease, cancer, muscular dystrophy, cerebral palsy, paraplegia, diabetes, acquired immune deficiency syndrome (AIDS), and infection with the human immunodeficiency virus (HIV) that causes AIDS.

The ADA does not require that *unqualified* applicants with disabilities be hired or retained. If a job applicant or an employee with a disability, with reasonable

A MAN AND A WOMAN communicating in sign language at work. Sign language is not a method of representing English, but is an entirely unique language system. Despite the fact that it is not English, could sign language be exempted from the effects of English-only laws that have been adopted in some jurisdictions? Why or why not? (Michael Newman/PhotoEdit)

accommodation, can perform essential job functions, however, then the employer must make the accommodation. Required accommodations may include installing ramps for a wheelchair, establishing more flexible working hours, creating or modifying job assignments, and creating or improving training materials and procedures.

LIMITING THE SCOPE AND APPLICABILITY OF THE ADA

Beginning in 1999, the Supreme Court has issued a series of decisions that effectively limit the scope of the ADA. In 1999, for example, the Court held in *Sutton v. United Airlines, Inc.*[33] that a condition (in this case, severe nearsightedness) that can be corrected with medication or a corrective device (in this case, eyeglasses) is not considered a disability under the ADA. In other words, the determination of whether a person is substantially limited in a major life activity is based on how the person functions when taking medication or using corrective devices, not on how the person functions without these measures. Since then, the courts have held that plaintiffs with bipolar disorder, epilepsy, diabetes, and other conditions do not fall under the ADA's protections if the conditions can be corrected with medication or corrective devices—even though the plaintiffs contended that they were discriminated against because of their conditions.

In a 2002 decision, the Court held that carpal tunnel syndrome did not constitute a disability under the ADA. The Court stated that although an employee with carpal tunnel syndrome could not perform the manual tasks associated with her job, the injury did not constitute a disability under the ADA because it did not "substantially limit" the major life activity of performing manual tasks.[34]

The Supreme Court has also limited the applicability of the ADA by holding that lawsuits under the ADA cannot be brought against state government employers.[35] In a 2001 case, the Court concluded—as it did with the ADEA, as mentioned earlier—that states, as sovereigns, are immune from lawsuits brought against them by private parties under the federal ADA.

THE RIGHTS AND STATUS OF GAYS AND LESBIANS

On June 27, 1969, patrons of the Stonewall Inn, a New York City bar popular with gays and lesbians, responded to a police raid by throwing beer cans and bottles because they were angry at what they felt was unrelenting police harassment. In the ensuing riot, which lasted two nights, hundreds of gays and lesbians fought with police. Before Stonewall, the stigma attached to homosexuality and the resulting fear of exposure had tended to keep most gays and lesbians quiescent. In the months immediately after Stonewall, however, "gay power" graffiti began to appear in New York City. The Gay Liberation Front and the Gay Activist Alliance were formed, and similar groups sprang up in other parts of the country. Thus, Stonewall has been called "the shot heard round the homosexual world."

....

[33]527 U.S. 471 (1999).
[34]*Toyota Manufacturing, Kentucky, Inc. v. Williams*, 534 U.S. 184 (2002).
[35]*Board of Trustees of the University of Alabama v. Garrett*, 531 U.S. 356 (2001).

GROWTH IN THE GAY AND LESBIAN RIGHTS MOVEMENT

The Stonewall incident marked the beginning of the movement for gay and lesbian rights. Since then, gays and lesbians have formed thousands of organizations to exert pressure on legislatures, the media, schools, churches, and other organizations to recognize their right to equal treatment.

To a great extent, lesbian and gay groups have succeeded in changing public opinion—and state and local laws—relating to their status and rights. Nevertheless, they continue to struggle against age-old biases against homosexuality, often rooted in deeply held religious beliefs, and the rights of gays and lesbians remain an extremely divisive issue in American society. These attitudes were clearly illustrated in a widely publicized case involving the Boy Scouts of America. The case arose after a Boy Scout troop in New Jersey refused to allow gay activist James Dale to be a Scout leader. In 2000, the case came before the Supreme Court, which held that, as a private organization, the Boy Scouts had the right to determine the requirements for becoming a Scout leader.[36]

That in October 1999, Scouts Canada, the Canadian equivalent of the Boy Scouts of America, officially approved North America's first gay Scout troop?

STATE AND LOCAL LAWS TARGETING GAYS AND LESBIANS

Before the Stonewall incident, 49 states had sodomy laws that made various kinds of sexual acts, including homosexual acts, illegal (Illinois, which had repealed its sodomy law in 1962, was the only exception). During the 1970s and 1980s, more than half of these laws were either repealed or struck down by the courts.

The trend toward repealing state antigay laws was suspended in 1986 with the Supreme Court's decision in *Bowers v. Hardwick.*[37] In that case, the Court upheld, by a five-to-four vote, a Georgia law that made homosexual conduct between two adults

---

[36]*Boy Scouts of America v. Dale*, 530 U.S. 640 (2000).
[37]478 U.S. 186 (1986).

a crime. In 2003, the Court reversed its earlier position on sodomy with its decision in *Lawrence v. Texas*.[38] In this case, the Court held that laws against sodomy violate the due process clause of the Fourteenth Amendment. The Court stated: "The liberty protected by the Constitution allows homosexual persons the right to choose to enter upon relationships in the confines of their homes and their own private lives and still retain their dignity as free persons." The result of *Lawrence v. Texas* was to invalidate all remaining sodomy laws throughout the country.

Today, 12 states[39] and more than 230 cities and counties have special laws protecting lesbians and gays against discrimination in employment, housing, public accommodations, and credit. At one point, Colorado adopted a constitutional amendment to invalidate all state and local laws protecting homosexuals from discrimination. Ultimately, however, the Supreme Court, in *Romer v. Evans*,[40] invalidated the amendment, ruling that it violated the equal protection clause of the U.S. Constitution because it denied to homosexuals in Colorado—but to no other Colorado residents—"the right to seek specific protection of the law." Several laws at the national level have also been changed over the past two decades. Among other things, the government has lifted a ban on hiring gays and lesbians and voided a 1952 law prohibiting gays and lesbians from immigrating to the United States.

DID YOU KNOW?

That Albert Einstein was among 6,000 persons in Germany in 1903 who signed a petition to repeal a portion of the German penal code that made homosexuality illegal?

THE GAY COMMUNITY AND POLITICS

Politicians at the national level have not overlooked the potential significance of homosexual issues in American politics. While conservative politicians generally have been critical of efforts to secure gay and lesbian rights, liberals, by and large, have been speaking out for gay rights in the last 25 years. In 1980, the Democratic platform included a gay plank for the first time.

President Bill Clinton long embraced much of the gay rights agenda and became the first sitting president to address a gay rights organization. In 1997, in a speech intentionally reminiscent of Harry Truman's 1947 speech to an African American civil rights group, Clinton pledged his support for equal rights for gay and lesbian Americans at a fundraiser sponsored by the Human Rights Campaign Fund. In 2000, George W. Bush became the first Republican presidential candidate to meet with a large group of openly gay leaders to discuss their issues. Although Bush asserted that he would continue to oppose gay marriage and adoption, he also said that being openly gay would not disqualify a person from serving in a prominent position in his administration.

To date, 11 openly gay men and lesbians have been elected to the House of Representatives, but none has succeeded yet in gaining a seat in the Senate. Gay rights groups continue to work for increased political representation in Congress, however.

GAYS AND LESBIANS IN THE MILITARY

The U.S. Department of Defense traditionally has viewed homosexuality as incompatible with military service. Supporters of gay and lesbian rights have attacked this policy in recent years, and in 1993, the policy was modified. In that year, President

[38]539 U.S. 558 (2003).
[39]California, Connecticut, Hawaii, Maryland, Massachusetts, Minnesota, Nevada, New Hampshire, New Jersey, Rhode Island, Vermont, and Wisconsin. Maine also had a law protecting gay and lesbian rights until February 1998, when the law was repealed in a referendum.
[40]517 U.S. 620 (1996).

Clinton announced that a new policy, generally characterized as "don't ask, don't tell," would be in effect. Enlistees would not be asked about their sexual orientation, and gays and lesbians would be allowed to serve in the military so long as they did not declare that they were gay or lesbian or commit homosexual acts. Military officials endorsed the new policy, after opposing it initially, but supporters of gay rights were not enthusiastic. Clinton had promised during his presidential campaign to repeal outright the long-standing ban.

Several gays and lesbians who have been discharged from military service have protested their discharges by bringing suit against the Defense Department. Often at issue in these cases are the constitutional rights to free speech, privacy, and the equal protection of the laws. A widely publicized 1998 case involved the Navy's dismissal of a naval officer, Timothy McVeigh,[41] on the ground that he had entered "gay" on a profile page for his account with America Online (AOL). Naval officers claimed that this amounted to a public declaration of McVeigh's gay status and thus justified his discharge. McVeigh argued that it was not a public declaration. Furthermore, contended McVeigh, the Navy had violated a 1986 federal privacy law governing electronic communications by obtaining information from AOL without a warrant or a court order. In 1998, a federal court judge agreed and ordered the Navy to reinstate McVeigh.[42]

SAME-SEX MARRIAGES

Perhaps one of the most sensitive political issues with respect to the rights of gay and lesbian couples is whether they should be allowed to marry, just as heterosexual couples are.

Defense of Marriage Act. The controversy over this issue was fueled in 1993, when the Hawaii Supreme Court ruled that denying marriage licenses to gay couples might

CITIZENS CALLING for a ballot measure to prohibit legal recognition of same-sex marriages demonstrate their cause near the Minnesota Senate chamber on March 27, 2006, in St. Paul, Minnesota. Two groups at the forefront of the fight against gay marriage have filed as political committees and not lobby groups, allowing them to avoid more stringent reporting of expenditures on salaries, advertising and public relations campaigns, and other political spending. (AP Photo/Jim Mone, File)

---

[41]This is not the Timothy McVeigh who was convicted for the 1995 bombing of the Alfred P. Murrah Federal Building in Oklahoma City.
[42]*McVeigh v. Cohen*, 983 F.Supp. 215 (D.C. 1998).

violate the equal protection clause of the Hawaii constitution.[43] In the wake of this event, other states began to worry about whether they might have to treat gay men or lesbians who were legally married in another state as married couples in their state as well. Opponents of gay rights pushed for state laws banning same-sex marriages, and the majority of states enacted such laws or adopted constitutional amendments. At the federal level, Congress passed the Defense of Marriage Act of 1996, which bans federal recognition of lesbian and gay couples and allows state governments to ignore same-sex marriages performed in other states.

The controversy over gay marriages was fueled again by developments in the state of Vermont. In 1999, the Vermont Supreme Court ruled that gay couples are entitled to the same benefits of marriage as opposite-sex couples.[44] Subsequently, in April 2000, the Vermont legislature passed a law permitting gay and lesbian couples to form "civil unions." The law entitled partners forming civil unions to receive some 300 state benefits available to married couples, including the rights to inherit a partner's property and to decide on medical treatment for an incapacitated partner. It did not, however, entitle those partners to receive any benefits allowed to married couples under federal law, such as spousal Social Security benefits. In 2005, Connecticut became the second state to adopt civil unions. Some felt that the Vermont and Connecticut legislatures did not go far enough—they should have allowed full legal marriage rights to same-sex couples.

State Recognition of Gay Marriages. Massachusetts was the first state to recognize gay marriage. In November 2003, the Massachusetts Supreme Judicial Court ruled that same-sex couples have a right to civil marriage under the Massachusetts state constitution.[45] The court also ruled that civil unions would not suffice. In 2005, the Massachusetts legislature voted down a proposed ballot initiative that would have amended the state constitution to explicitly state that marriage could only be between one man and one woman (but would have extended civil union status to same-sex couples). Although the highest courts in several states have upheld bans on gay marriage, in 2008 the Supreme Court of California held that the state was required to recognize gay marriages. Citizens immediately prepared petitions to put a constitutional amendment on the ballot in November of 2008 to outlaw such marriages. The campaign for and against Proposition 6, which would ban gay marriages in California, cost at least $74 million and was funded by contributions from almost every state. It was predicted that the outcome would impact gay rights everywhere. Proposition 6 was approved by a margin of 4 percent. The effect the proposition will have on the 18,000 marriages that took place after the Supreme Court decision will eventually be determined in the California state courts.

Same-sex marriage is currently accepted nationwide in Belgium, Canada, the Netherlands, Norway, South Africa, and Spain.

CHILD CUSTODY AND ADOPTION

Gays and lesbians have also faced difficulties in obtaining child-custody and adoption rights. Courts around the country, when deciding which of two parents should have custody, have wrestled with how much weight, if any, should be given to a parent's sexual orientation. For some time, the courts were split fairly evenly on this issue. In about half the states, courts held that a parent's sexual orientation should not be a significant factor in determining child custody. Courts in other states, however, tended to give more weight to sexual orientation. In one case, a court even went so far as to award custody

---

[43]*Baehr v. Lewin*, 852 P.2d 44 (Hawaii 1993).
[44]*Baker v. Vermont*, 744 A.2d 864 (Vt. 1999).
[45]*Goodridge v. Department of Public Health*, 798 N.E.2d 941 (Mass. 2003).

to a father because the child's mother was a lesbian, even though the father had served eight years in prison for killing his first wife. Today, however, courts in the majority of states no longer deny custody or visitation rights to persons solely on the basis of their sexual orientation.

The last decade has also seen a sharp climb in the number of gays and lesbians who are adopting children. To date, 22 states have allowed lesbians and gay men to adopt children through state-operated or private adoption agencies.

That only one state, Florida, has a law explicitly banning gay adoptions?

THE RIGHTS AND STATUS OF JUVENILES

Approximately 76 million Americans—almost 30 percent of the total population—are under 21 years of age. The definition of children ranges from persons under age 16 to persons under age 21. However defined, children in the United States have fewer rights and protections than any other major group in society.

The reason for this lack of rights is the common presumption of society and its law-makers that children basically are protected by their parents. This is not to say that children are the exclusive property of the parents. Rather, an overwhelming case in favor of not allowing parents to control the actions of their children must be presented before children can be given authorization to act without parental consent (or before the state can be given authorization to act on children's behalf without regard to their parents' wishes).

Supreme Court decisions affecting children's rights began a process of slow evolution with *Brown v. Board of Education of Topeka*, the landmark civil rights case of 1954 discussed earlier in this chapter. In *Brown*, the Court granted children the status of rights-bearing persons. In 1967, in *In re Gault*,[46] the Court expressly held that children have a constitutional right to be represented by counsel at the government's expense in a criminal action. Five years later, the Court acknowledged that "children are 'persons' within the meaning of the Bill of Rights. We have held so over and over again."[47] In 1976, the Court recognized a girl's right to have an abortion without consulting her parents.[48] (More recently, however, the Court has allowed state laws to dictate whether the child must obtain consent.)

VOTING RIGHTS AND THE YOUNG

The Twenty-sixth Amendment to the Constitution, ratified on July 1, 1971, reads as follows:

> The right of citizens of the United States, who are eighteen years of age or older, to vote shall not be denied or abridged by the United States or by any State on account of age.

Before this amendment was ratified, the age at which citizens could vote was 21 in most states. Why did the Twenty-sixth Amendment specify age 18? Why not 17 or 16? And why did it take until 1971 to allow those between the ages of 18 and 21 to vote? One of the arguments used for granting the right to 18-year-olds was that, because they could be drafted to fight in the country's wars, they had a stake in public policy. At the time, the example of the Vietnam War (1964–1975) was paramount.

[46]387 U.S. 1 (1967).
[47]*Wisconsin v. Yoder*, 406 U.S. 205 (1972).
[48]*Planned Parenthood of Central Missouri v. Danforth*, 428 U.S. 52 (1976).

Have 18- to 20-year-olds used their right to vote? Yes and no. In 1972, immediately after the passage of the Twenty-sixth Amendment, 58 percent of 18- to 20-year-olds were registered to vote, and 48.4 percent reported that they had voted. But by the 2004 presidential elections, of the 11.5 million U.S. residents in the 18-to-20 age bracket, 50.7 percent were registered, and 41 percent reported that they had voted. Subsequent elections have shown similar results. In contrast, voter turnout among Americans aged 65 or older is very high, usually between 60 and 70 percent.

THE RIGHTS OF CHILDREN IN CIVIL AND CRIMINAL PROCEEDINGS

Children today have limited rights in civil and criminal proceedings in our judicial system. Different procedural rules and judicial safeguards apply under civil and criminal laws. **Civil law** relates in part to contracts among private individuals or companies. **Criminal law** relates to crimes against society that are defined by society acting through its legislatures.

Civil Rights of Juveniles. The civil rights of children are defined exclusively by state law with respect to private contract negotiations, rights, and remedies. The legal definition of **majority** varies from 18 to 21 years of age, depending on the state. As a rule, an individual who is legally a minor cannot be held responsible for contracts that he or she forms with others. In most states, only contracts entered into for so-called **necessaries** (things necessary for subsistence, as determined by the courts) can be enforced against minors. Also, when minors engage in negligent behavior, their parents are typically liable. If, for example, a minor destroys a neighbor's fence, the neighbor may bring suit against the child's parent but not against the child.

Civil law also encompasses the area of child custody. Child-custody rulings traditionally have given little weight to the wishes of the child. Courts have maintained the right to act on behalf of the child's "best interests" but have sometimes been constrained from doing so by the "greater" rights possessed by adults. For instance, a widely publicized Michigan Supreme Court ruling awarded legal custody of a two-and-a-half-year-old Michigan resident to an Iowa couple, the child's biological parents. A Michigan couple, who had cared for the child since shortly after her birth and who had petitioned to adopt the child, lost out in the custody battle. The court said that the law had allowed it to consider only the parents' rights and not the child's best interests.

Children's rights and their ability to articulate their rights for themselves in custody matters were strengthened, however, by several well-publicized rulings involving older children. In one case, for example, an 11-year-old Florida boy filed suit in his own name, assisted by his own privately retained legal counsel, to terminate his relationship with his biological parents and to have the court affirm his right to be adopted by foster parents. The court granted his request, although it did not agree procedurally with the method by which the boy initiated the suit.[49] The news media characterized the case as the first instance in which a minor child had "divorced" himself from his parents.

Criminal Rights of Juveniles. One of the main requirements for an act to be criminal is intent. The law has given children certain defenses against criminal prosecution because of their presumed inability to have criminal intent. Under the common law, children up to seven years of age were considered

Civil Law
The law regulating conduct between private persons over noncriminal matters. Under civil law, the government provides the forum for the settlement of disputes between private parties in such matters as contracts, domestic relations, and business interactions.

Criminal Law
The law that defines crimes and provides punishment for violations. In criminal cases, the government is the prosecutor because crimes are violations of the public order.

Majority
Full age; the age at which a person is entitled by law to the right to manage her or his own affairs and to the full enjoyment of civil rights.

Necessaries
In contract law, necessaries include whatever is reasonably necessary for suitable subsistence as measured by age, state, condition in life, and so on.

DID YOU KNOW?

That the United Nations Convention on the Rights of the Child calls for the provision of effective legal assistance for children so that their interests can be "heard directly"?

---

[49]*Kingsley v. Kingsley*, 623 So.2d 780 (Fla.App. 1993).

incapable of committing a crime because they did not have the moral sense to understand that they were doing wrong. Children between the ages of seven and 14 were also presumed to be incapable of committing a crime, but this presumption could be challenged by showing that the child understood the wrongful nature of the act. Today, states vary in their approaches. Most states retain the common law approach, although age limits vary from state to state. Other states have simply set a minimum age for criminal responsibility.

All states have juvenile court systems that handle children below the age of criminal responsibility who commit delinquent acts. The aim of juvenile courts is allegedly to reform rather than to punish. In states that retain the common law approach, children who are above the minimum age but are still juveniles can be turned over to the criminal courts if the juvenile court determines that they should be treated as adults. Children sent to juvenile court still do not have the right to trial by jury or to post bail. Also, in most states, parents can commit their minor children to state mental institutions without allowing the child a hearing.

Although minors do not usually have the full rights of adults in criminal proceedings, they have certain advantages. In felony, manslaughter, murder, armed robbery, and assault cases, juveniles were not traditionally tried as adults. They were often sentenced to probation or "reform" school for a relatively short term, regardless of the seriousness of their crimes. Today, however, most states allow juveniles to be tried as adults (often at the discretion of the judge) for certain crimes, such as murder. When they are tried as adults, they are given due process of law and tried for the crime, rather than being given the paternalistic treatment reserved for the juvenile delinquent. Juveniles who are tried as adults may also face adult penalties. These used to include the death penalty. In 2005, however, the Supreme Court ruled that executing persons who were under the age of 18 when they committed their crimes would constitute cruel and unusual punishment. The Court opined that 16- and 17-year-olds do not have a fully

DID YOU KNOW?

That the first juvenile court in the United States opened in Chicago on July 3, 1899?

developed sense of right and wrong, nor do they necessarily understand the full gravity of their misdeeds.[50]

Approaches to Dealing with Crime by Juveniles. What to do about crime committed by juveniles is a pressing problem for today's political leaders. One approach to the problem is to treat juveniles as adults, which more judges seem to be doing. There appears to be widespread public support for this approach, as well as for lowering the age at which juveniles should receive adult treatment in criminal proceedings. Polling data show that two-thirds of U.S. adults think that juveniles under the age of 13 who commit murder should be tried as adults.

Another method is to hold parents responsible for the crimes of their minor children (a minority of the states do so under so-called parental-responsibility laws). These are contradictory approaches, to be sure. Yet they reflect the divided opinion in our society concerning the rights of children versus the rights of parents.

In the wake of crimes committed in the schools, many districts have implemented what are called zero-tolerance policies. These policies have become controversial in recent years because, according to some, they are enforced without regard to the particular circumstances surrounding an incident. Should they be modified or revoked?

That the number of juveniles sent to adult prisons for violent offenses in the United States has tripled since 1985?

[50]*Roper v. Simmons,* 543 U.S. 551 (2005).

You can make a difference

DEALING WITH DISCRIMINATION

You may think you know what "discrimination" means while applying for or working at a job. But do you really understand how it applies to your work life? To "discriminate" means to treat differently or less favorably, and can happen while you are at school or at work. Discrimination can come from friends, teachers, coaches, co-workers, managers, and business owners, and be based on race, color, gender, religion, age, sexual preference, or disability. There may be tests while applying for a job that could have a discriminatory effect on being hired. Agencies at the state and federal government examine the fairness and validity of criteria used in screening job applicants and, as a result, there are ways of addressing the problem of discrimination.

WHY SHOULD YOU CARE?

Some people may think that discrimination is only a problem for members of racial or ethnic minorities. Actually, almost everyone can be affected. Consider that in some instances, white men have actually experienced "reverse discrimination"—and have obtained redress for it. Also, discrimination against women is common, and women constitute half the population. Even if you are male, you probably have female friends whose well-being is of interest to you. Therefore, the knowledge of how to proceed when you suspect discrimination is another useful tool to have when living in the modern world.

WHAT CAN YOU DO?

If you believe that you have been discriminated against by a potential employer, consider the following steps:

1. Evaluate your own capabilities, and determine if you are truly qualified for the position.
2. Analyze the reasons why you were turned down. Would others agree with you that you have been the object of discrimination, or would they uphold the employer's claim?
3. If you still believe that you have been treated unfairly, you have recourse to several agencies and services.

You should first speak to the personnel director of the company and explain politely that you believe you have not been evaluated adequately. If asked, explain your concerns clearly. If necessary, go into explicit detail, and indicate that you may have been discriminated against.

If you feel further action is warranted, there are many states and localities that have antidiscrimination laws and agencies responsible for enforcing these laws. They are referred to as Fair Employment Practices Agencies (FEPAs). They can be found on your state's official government Web site and include your state attorney general; state commissions on civil rights, equal rights, equal opportunity, and antidiscrimination; and departments of labor and industry. You can access all local and state government agencies through **www.usa.gov**, the U.S. government's official Web portal to all federal, state, and local government resources and services.

Finally, the U.S. Equal Employment Opportunity Commission (EEOC) enforces federal laws concerning job discrimination and harassment, processing about 80,000 complaints a year, and partners with 90 state and local agencies that investigate an additional 50,000 complaints. You can contact the EEOC anytime you feel you are being treated unfairly on the job because of race, religion, sex (including pregnancy), national origin, disability, or age. This federal agency is an extensive resource and will answer questions about job discrimination even if you do not want to file a formal complaint.

The EEOC's main office is located in Washington, D.C., but there are 51 field offices around the country. You should contact the field office closest to you. The EEOC should be contacted promptly if you have an unresolved complaint. A charge must be filed within 180 days from the date of the alleged violation; the deadline is extended to 300 days if the charge is also covered by a state or local antidiscrimination law. To find the field office closest to you, please contact:

The U.S. Equal Employment Opportunity Commission
1801 L St. NW
Washington, D.C.
20507

KEY TERMS

affirmative action 198	**feminism** 186	**reverse discrimination** 199
busing 176	**gender discrimination** 190	**separate-but-equal**
civil disobedience 177	**grandfather clause** 173	**doctrine** 173
civil law 208	**literacy test** 173	**sexual harassment** 192
civil rights 168	**majority** 208	**subpoena** 180
criminal law 208	**mandatory retirement** 201	**suffrage** 185
de facto **segregation** 176	**necessaries** 208	**white primary** 173
de jure **segregation** 176	**poll tax** 173	

CHAPTER SUMMARY

1. The civil rights movement started with the struggle by African Americans for equality. Before the Civil War, most African Americans were slaves, and slavery was protected by the Constitution and the Supreme Court. Constitutional amendments after the Civil War legally ended slavery, and African Americans gained citizenship, the right to vote, and other rights through legislation. This legal protection was largely a dead letter by the 1880s, however, and politically and socially African American inequality continued.

2. Legal segregation was declared unconstitutional by the Supreme Court in *Brown v. Board of Education of Topeka* (1954), in which the Court stated that separation implied inferiority. In *Brown v. Board of Education* (1955), the Supreme Court ordered federal courts to ensure that public schools were desegregated "with all deliberate speed." Also in 1955, the modern civil rights movement began with a boycott of segregated public transportation in Montgomery, Alabama. Of particular impact was the Civil Rights Act of 1964. The Act bans discrimination on the basis of race, color, religion, gender, or national origin in employment and public accommodations. The Act created the Equal Employment Opportunity Commission to administer the legislation's provisions.

3. The Voting Rights Act of 1965 outlawed discriminatory voter-registration tests and authorized federal registration of persons and federally administered procedures in any state or political subdivision evidencing electoral discrimination or low registration rates. The Voting Rights Act and other protective legislation passed during and since the 1960s apply not only to African Americans but to other ethnic groups as well. Minorities have been increasingly represented in national and state politics, although they have yet to gain representation proportionate to their numbers in the U.S. population. Lingering social and economic disparities have led to a new civil rights agenda—one focusing less on racial differences and more on economic differences.

4. In the early history of the United States, women were considered citizens, but by and large they had no political rights. After the first women's rights convention in 1848, the women's movement gained momentum. Not until 1920, when the Nineteenth Amendment was ratified, did women finally obtain the right to vote. The modern women's movement began in the 1960s in the wake of the civil rights and anti-Vietnam War movements. The National Organization for Women (NOW) was formed in 1966 to bring about complete equality for women in all walks of life. Efforts to secure the ratification of the Equal Rights Amendment failed, but the women's movement has been successful in obtaining new laws, changes in social customs, and increased political representation of women.

5. Although women have found it difficult to gain positions of political leadership, their numbers in Congress and in other government bodies increased significantly in the 1990s and early 2000s. Women continue to struggle against gender discrimination in employment. Federal government efforts to eliminate gender discrimination in the workplace include Title VII of the Civil Rights Act of 1964, which prohibits, among other things, gender-based discrimination, including sexual harassment on the job. Wage dis-

crimination also continues to be a problem for women, as does the "glass ceiling" that prevents them from rising to the top of business or professional firms.

6. America has always been a land of immigrants and will continue to be so. Today, more than 1 million immigrants enter the United States each year, and more than 10 percent of the U.S. population consists of foreign-born persons. In particular, the Hispanic American community in the United States has experienced explosive growth. In recent years, illegal immigration has surfaced as a significant national issue. Indeed, one of the pressing concerns facing today's politicians is whether U.S. immigration policy should be reformed.

7. Affirmative action programs have been controversial because they can lead to reverse discrimination against majority groups or even other minority groups. Supreme Court decisions have limited affirmative action programs, and voters in California and Washington passed initiatives banning state-sponsored affirmative action in those states. Two Supreme Court decisions in cases brought against the University of Michigan have confirmed the principle that limited affirmative action programs are constitutional.

8. Problems associated with aging and retirement are becoming increasingly important as the number of older persons in the United States increases. The Age Discrimination in Employment Act of 1967 prohibited job-related discrimination against individuals who are over 40 years old on the basis of age, unless age is shown to be a bona fide occupational qualification reasonably necessary to the normal operation of the business. Amendments to the Act prohibit mandatory retirement except in a few selected professions.

9. The Rehabilitation Act of 1973 prohibited discrimination against persons with disabilities in programs receiving federal aid. Regulations implementing the Act provide for ramps, elevators, and the like in federal buildings. The Education for All Handicapped Children Act (1975) provides that children with dis-

abilities should receive an "appropriate" education. The Americans with Disabilities Act of 1990 prohibits job discrimination against persons with physical and mental disabilities, requiring that positive steps be taken to comply with the Act. The Act also requires expanded access to public facilities, including transportation, and to services offered by such private concerns as car rental and telephone companies.

10. Gay and lesbian rights groups, which first began to form in 1969, now number in the thousands. These groups work to promote laws protecting gays and lesbians from discrimination and to repeal antigay laws. After 1969, sodomy laws that criminalized specific sexual practices were repealed or struck down by the courts in all but 18 states, and in 2003 a Supreme Court decision effectively invalidated all remaining sodomy laws nationwide. Twelve states and more than 230 cities and counties now have laws prohibiting discrimination based on sexual orientation. Gays and lesbians are no longer barred from federal employment or from immigrating to this country. Since 1980, liberal Democrats at the national level have supported gay and lesbian rights and sought electoral support from these groups. The military's "don't ask, don't tell" policy has fueled extensive controversy, as have same-sex marriages and child-custody issues.

11. Although children form a large group of Americans, they have the fewest rights and protections, in part because it is commonly presumed that parents protect their children. The Twenty-sixth Amendment grants the right to vote to those aged 18 or older. In most states, only contracts entered into for necessaries can be enforced against minors. When minors engage in negligent acts, their parents may be held liable. Minors have some defense against criminal prosecution because of their presumed inability to have criminal intent below certain ages. For those under the age of criminal responsibility, there are state juvenile courts. When minors are tried as adults, they are entitled to the procedural protections afforded to adults and are sometimes subject to adult penalties.

SELECTED PRINT AND MEDIA RESOURCES

SUGGESTED READINGS

Anderson, Terry H. *The Pursuit of Fairness: A History of Affirmative Action.* New York: Oxford University Press, 2004. Anderson offers an even-handed history of affirmative action. His account extends from the administrations of Franklin D. Roosevelt and Harry Truman in the 1940s to the 2003 University of Michigan cases that have established the current constitutional parameters of affirmative action policies.

Friedan, Betty. *The Feminine Mystique.* New York: W. W. Norton & Co., 2001. Friedan's 1963 work is the feminist classic that helped launch the modern women's movement in the United States. This edition contains an up-to-date introduction by columnist Anna Quindlen.

Moats, David. *Civil Wars: A Battle for Gay Marriage.* New York: Harcourt, 2004. Moats, a Pulitzer Prize-winning Vermont journalist, chronicles the battle over same-sex marriage in Vermont. The result was a law legalizing civil unions.

Ngai, Mae M. *Impossible Subjects: Illegal Aliens and the Making of Modern America.* Princeton, NJ: Princeton University Press, 2005. The author explains why and how illegal immigration became the central problem in U.S. immigration policy.

Roberts, Gene, and Hank Kilbanoff. *The Race Beat: The Press, Civil Rights Struggle, and the Awakening of a Nation.* New York: Knopf, 2006. The authors recount the story of how the press finally recognized the civil rights struggle in the 1950s and 1960s. This book describes the awakening of the public to America's race problems.

Woodward, C. Vann. *The Strange Career of Jim Crow.* New York: Oxford University Press, 1957. This is the classic study of how segregation was created in the Southern states.

MEDIA RESOURCES

Beyond the Glass Ceiling—A CNN-produced program showing the difficulties women face in trying to rise to the top in corporate America.

G.I. Jane—A 1997 film about a woman who is out to prove that she can survive Navy SEAL training that is so rigorous that many (60 percent) of the men do not make it.

I Have a Dream—A film on Martin Luther King, Jr., focusing on the 1963 March on Washington and King's "I Have a Dream" speech, which some consider to be one of the greatest speeches of all time.

Malcolm X—A 1992 film, directed by Spike Lee and starring Denzel Washington, that depicts the life of the controversial "black power" leader Malcolm X. Malcolm X, who was assassinated on February 21, 1965, clearly had a different vision from that of Martin Luther King, Jr., regarding how to achieve civil rights, respect, and equality for black Americans.

Separate but Equal—A video focusing on Thurgood Marshall, the African American lawyer (and later Supreme Court justice) who took the struggle for equal rights to the Supreme Court, and on the rise and demise of segregation in America.

Shot by a Kid—A film documenting the relationship among children, guns, and violence in four major U.S. cities.

CIVIL RIGHTS INFORMATION ONLINE

Today, thanks to the Internet, information on civil rights issues is literally at your fingertips. By simply accessing the American Civil Liberties Union's (ACLU) Web site (the URL for this organization is given later, in the *Logging On* section), you can learn about the major civil rights issues facing Americans today. A host of other Web sites offer data on the extent to which groups discussed in this chapter are protected under state and federal laws. You can also find numerous advocacy sites that indicate what you can do to help promote the rights of a certain group.

LOGGING ON

- For information on, and arguments in support of, affirmative action and the rights of the groups discussed in this chapter, a good source is the American Civil Liberties Union's Web site. Go to:
  www.aclu.org
- The National Organization for Women (NOW) offers online information and updates on the status of women's rights, including affirmative action cases involving women. Go to:
  www.now.org
- An excellent source of information on issues facing African Americans is the Web site of the National Association for the Advancement of Colored People at:
  www.naacp.org

- You can find information on the Americans with Disabilities Act (ADA) of 1990, including the Act's text, at:
  www.jan.wvu.edu/links/adalinks.htm
- You can access the Web site of the Human Rights Campaign Fund, the nation's largest gay and lesbian political organization, at:
  www.hrc.org
- If you are interested in children's rights and welfare, a good starting place is the Web site of the Child Welfare Institute. Go to:
  www.gocwi.org

ONLINE REVIEW

At **www.cengage.com/politicalscience/schmidt/agandpt14e**, you will find a Tutorial Quiz for this chapter providing questions on the chapter contents, including the features. The questions are organized to match the major sections of the chapter. You'll have access to other helpful study tools, including the book's glossary and flashcards, crossword puzzles, and Web links, as well as "Which Side Are You On?" and "Politics and . . ." features written by the authors of the book.

A voter completes a *Los Angeles Times* exit poll after voting in the 2006 California primary. (Bob Daemmrich/The Image Works)

PUBLIC OPINION AND POLITICAL SOCIALIZATION

QUESTIONS TO CONSIDER

How does public opinion impact government actions?

How do individuals come to hold political opinions?

Should government officials always follow public opinion?

CHAPTER CONTENTS

Making a DIFFERENCE

OPINION GAPS AND ADVOCACY

Have you ever noticed that when your friends are discussing something, the same group of people seems to be on one side of the debate more often than not? It could be that in discussing the latest movies, the fine arts majors tend to agree. Or perhaps, in conversations about politics, Democrats and Republicans find themselves on opposite sides of the fence.

Opinion split along group lines (e.g., gender, partisanship, socioeconomic status, race, or ethnicity) is called an opinion gap. Public opinion research yields many interesting gaps. One of the most widely covered is the gender gap, which occurs when women as a group have similar opinions or behaviors as compared to those of

men. For example, since the 1980 presidential election, women have tended to vote for the Democratic candidate for president at rates higher than men. Sometimes these differences can be significant; in the 2004 presidential election, 51 percent of women said they supported Senator John Kerry, and only 48 percent said they voted to re-elect President Bush. Contrast this with men, 55 percent of whom said they voted to re-elect the President, and only 41 percent said they voted for Senator Kerry.[a]

Another example of an opinion gap is among racial or ethnic groups. African Americans historically have been more likely to identify as Democrats. In 2007, 78 percent of those African Americans polled identified themselves as Democrats or leaning toward the Democratic Party. That percentage was only 50 percent for whites surveyed.[b] The same survey explored attitudes about racial discrimination, and a clear gap among the races emerged. While

IN A DEMOCRACY, the people express their opinions in many different ways. First and foremost, they express their views in political campaigns and vote for the individuals who will represent their views in government. Between elections, individuals express their opinions in many ways, ranging from writing to the editor to calling their Senator's office to responding to a blog. Public opinion is also expressed and conveyed to public officials through public opinion polls, which are reported almost daily in the media. As noted in the *Making a Difference* feature, there are often striking differences in opinion between groups that have an impact on political debates and the decision-making process.

In 2003, when President George W. Bush asked the Congress to authorize the use of force against Iraq, public approval for the war was 72 percent. At that time, more than 80 percent of Americans either believed or considered it possible that Saddam Hussein was building an arsenal of biological and other extremely dangerous weapons. By 2005, support for the use of troops in Iraq had declined to 39 percent and, by mid-2007, had fallen to 36 percent. Senator Barack Obama made withdrawal of American troops from Iraq a priority of his campaign and claimed that if he had been in the Senate at that time, he would not have supported the authorization of the use of force. Senator Hillary Clinton, who had voted for the resolution, no longer supported the Iraqi campaign and claimed that she had been misled at the time of the debate. The approval rating of President Bush, inevitably connected with the unpopular war, fell to 30 percent or less. However, as of 2007, the gap between Republicans and Democrats was surprisingly large, with Republicans expressing 67 percent approval of the president as compared to only 7 percent of Democrats.

67 percent of African Americans reported experiencing discriminatory practices in searching for a job, only 20 percent of whites and 36 percent of Hispanics perceived that anti-black discrimination in employment exists.

Yet another way to understand opinion gaps is to examine differences between average people and "opinion leaders" like elected officials, clergy, educators, and journalists. In a 2005 report on attitudes toward immigration policy, 51 percent of the public reported that reducing illegal immigration should be a top priority. Contrast this with roughly one-third of military leaders and religious leaders.[c] A 2006 report similarly found that 58 percent of the public believed that reducing illegal immigration should be among the top foreign policy goals.[d]

These opinion gaps can mobilize groups to form in advocacy for awareness and social change. For example, in addition to the many reports on gender equity produced by the American Association of University Women, this advocacy group also publishes a "woman-to-woman" voter turnout manual. This effort is designed to increase voter turnout among women and to aid women candidates in reaching women voters.[e]

Groups concerned with the racial gap described previously have organized to address existing inequities and to facilitate communication on these delicate issues. For example, the Open Society Institute, funded by the Soros Foundation Network, has sponsored a project examining youth criminal offenders and the criminal justice sys-

tem. As part of this initiative, they have conducted public opinion polling to determine attitudes about minority offenders and so-called get-tough initiatives. One of the project's aims is to address the differential treatment of minority youth by the criminal justice system found by their studies, and they hope to use public opinion as a tool to accomplish their aims.[f]

[a]www.cawp.rutgers.edu/Facts/Elections/GGPresVote.pdf

[b]"Blacks See Growing Values Gap Between Poor and Middle Class: Optimism about Black Progress Declines," November 13, 2007 report from the Pew Research Center: Social and Demographic Trends, http://pewsocialtrends.org/assets/pdf/Race.pdf, accessed March 20, 2008.

[c]http://people-press.org/reports/pdf/263.pdf

[d]www.thechicagocouncil.org/dynamic_page.php?id=56

[e]www.aauw.org/advocacy/issue_advocacy/voter_ed/Woman-to-WomanVoterTurnout.cfm

[f]www.soros.org/initiatives/usprograms/focus/justice/articles_publications/publications/public_opinion_youth_20011001?skin=printable (accessed September 16, 2008)

In the past, public opinion also has had a dramatic impact on presidents. In 1968, President Lyndon B. Johnson decided not to run for re-election because of the intense and negative public reaction to the war in Vietnam. In 1974, President Richard Nixon resigned in the wake of a scandal when it was obvious that public opinion no longer supported him. The extent to which public opinion affects policy making is not always so clear, however. For example, suppose that public opinion strongly supports a certain policy. If political leaders adopt that position, is it because they are responding to public opinion or to their own views on the issue? In addition, to some extent, political leaders can shape public opinion. For these and other reasons, scholars must deal with many uncertainties when analyzing the impact of public opinion on policy making.

DEFINING PUBLIC OPINION

There is no single public opinion, because there are many different publics. In a nation of almost 300 million people, there may be innumerable gradations of opinion on an issue. What we do is describe the distribution of opinions among the members of the public about a particular question. Thus, we define **public opinion** as the aggregate of individual attitudes or beliefs shared by some portion of the adult population.

Typically, public opinion is distributed among several different positions, and the distribution of opinion can tell us how divided the public is on an issue and whether compromise is possible. When a large proportion of the American public appears to express

Public Opinion
The aggregate of individual attitudes or beliefs shared by some portion of the adult population.

Consensus
General agreement among the citizenry on an issue.

Divisive Opinion
Public opinion that is polarized between two quite different positions.

Nonopinion
The lack of an opinion on an issue or policy among the majority.

the same view on an issue, we say that a **consensus** exists, at least at the moment the poll was taken. Figure 6–1 shows a pattern of opinion that might be called consensual. Issues on which the public holds widely differing attitudes result in **divisive opinion** (see Figure 6–2). Sometimes, a poll shows a distribution of opinion indicating that most Americans either have no information about the issue or are not interested enough in the issue to formulate a position. This is sometimes referred to as **nonopinion** (see Figure 6–3). Politicians may believe that the public's lack of knowledge about an issue gives them more room to maneuver, or they may be wary of taking any action for fear that opinion will crystallize after a crisis.

An interesting question arises as to when private opinion becomes public opinion. Everyone probably has a private opinion about the competence of the president, as well as private opinions about more personal concerns, such as the state of a neighbor's lawn. We say that private opinion becomes public opinion when the opinion is publicly expressed and concerns public issues. When someone's private opinion becomes so strong that the individual is willing to go to the polls to vote for or against a candidate or an issue—or is willing to participate in a demonstration, discuss the issue at work, speak out on television or radio, or participate in the political process in any one of a dozen other ways—then the opinion becomes public opinion.

HOW PUBLIC OPINION IS FORMED: POLITICAL SOCIALIZATION

Political Socialization
The process by which people acquire political beliefs and attitudes.

Most Americans are willing to express opinions on political issues when asked. How do people acquire these opinions and attitudes? Typically, views that are expressed as political opinions are acquired through the process of **political socialization**. By this

FIGURE 6–1
Consensus Opinion

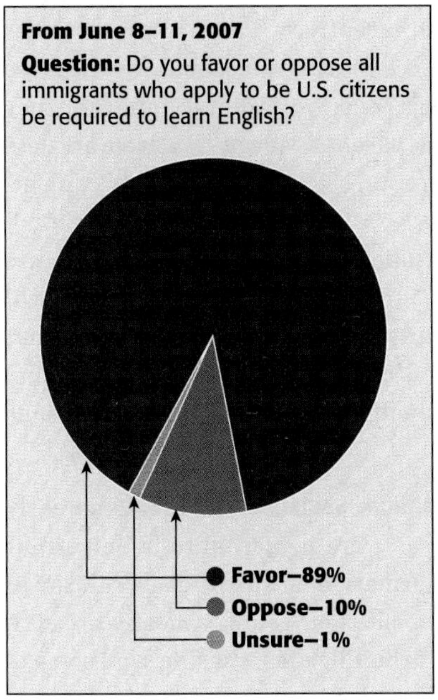

From June 8–11, 2007

Question: Do you favor or oppose all immigrants who apply to be U.S. citizens be required to learn English?

● Favor–89%
● Oppose–10%
● Unsure–1%

Source: NBC News/Wall Street Journal Poll

FIGURE 6–2
Divisive Opinion

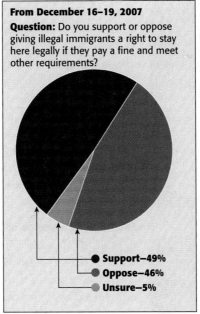

From December 16–19, 2007

Question: Do you support or oppose giving illegal immigrants a right to stay here legally if they pay a fine and meet other requirements?

● Support–49%
● Oppose–46%
● Unsure–5%

Source: ABCNews/Facebook Poll

FIGURE 6–3
Nonopinion

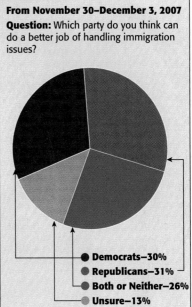

From November 30–December 3, 2007

Question: Which party do you think can do a better job of handling immigration issues?

● Democrats–30%
● Republicans–31%
● Both or Neither–26%
● Unsure–13%

Source: Los Angeles Times/Bloomberg Poll

we mean that people acquire their political attitudes, often including their party identification, through relationships with their families, friends, and co-workers.

MODELS OF POLITICAL SOCIALIZATION

The most important early sources of political socialization are found in the family and the schools. Children learn their parents' views on politics and on political leaders through observation and approval-seeking. When parents are strong supporters of a political party, children are very likely to identify with that same party. If the parents are alienated from the political system or totally disinterested in politics, children will tend to hold the same attitudes. It is clear that children who are very young, say about five or six, will express political views even when they are not mature enough to comprehend very much about the political institutions. This is the result of socialization.

In the last few decades, more sources of information about politics have become available to all Americans and especially to young people. Although their basic outlook on the political system may be formed by early family influences, young people are now exposed to many other sources of information about issues and values. It is not unusual for young adults to express support for the same party as their parents but to hold very different views on issues. The exposure of younger Americans to many sources of ideas may also support their more liberal views on such issues as tolerance for gay rights and environmentalism.

THE FAMILY AND THE SOCIAL ENVIRONMENT

Not only do our parents' political attitudes and actions affect our opinions, but the family also links us to other factors that affect opinion, such as race, social class, edu-

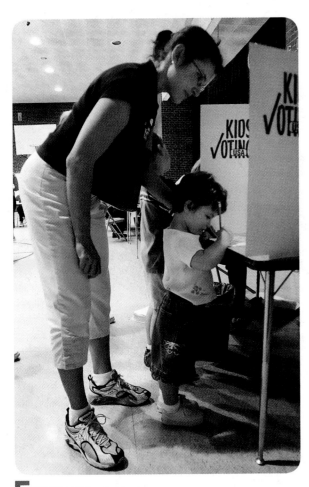

THE KIDS VOTE project involves teachers, parents, and children in encouraging children to vote on an unofficial ballot in the presidential election. Do you think this project will increase the children's desire to vote when they are adults? (Charlotte Observer, John D. Simmons/AP/Wide World Photos)

Peer Group
A group consisting of members sharing common social characteristics. These groups play an important part in the socialization process, helping to shape attitudes and beliefs.

cational environment, and religious beliefs. How do parents transmit their political attitudes to their offspring?

Studies suggest that the influence of parents is due to two factors: communication and receptivity. Parents communicate their feelings and preferences to children constantly. Because children have such a strong need for parental approval, they are very receptive to their parents' views. Children are less likely to influence their parents, because parents expect deference from their children.[1]

Nevertheless, other studies show that if children are exposed to political ideas at school and in the media, they will share these ideas with their parents, giving the parents what some scholars call a second chance at political socialization. Children can also expose their parents to new media, such as the Internet.[2]

Education as a Source of Political Socialization. From the early days of the Republic, schools were perceived to be important transmitters of political information and attitudes. Children in the primary grades learn about their country mostly in patriotic ways. They learn about the Pilgrims, the flag, and some of the nation's presidents. They also learn to celebrate national holidays. Later, in the middle grades, children learn more historical facts and come to understand the structure of government and the functions of the president, judges, and Congress. By high school, students have a more complex understanding of the political system, may identify with a political party, and may take positions on issues. Additionally, students in grade school and high school may gain some experience in political participation: first, through student elections and activities, and second, through their introduction to registration and voting while still in school.

Generally, education is closely linked to political participation. The more education a person receives, the more likely it is that person will be interested in politics, be confident in his or her ability to understand political issues, and be an active participant in the political process. Public opinion polls, however, suggest that even well-educated younger Americans are not strongly interested in politics.[3]

Peers and Peer Group Influence. Once a child enters school, the child's friends become an important influence on behavior and attitudes. For children and for adults, friendships and associations in **peer groups** affect political attitudes. We must, however, separate the effects of peer group pressure on opinions and attitudes in general from the effects of peer group pressure on political opinions. For the most part, associations among peers are nonpolitical. Political attitudes are more likely to be shaped by peer groups when the peer groups are involved directly in political activities.

[1]Barbara A. Bardes and Robert W. Oldendick, *Public Opinion: Measuring the American Mind*, 3rd ed. (Belmont, CA: Wadsworth Publishing, 2006), p. 73.
[2]For a pioneering study in this area, see Michael McDevitt and Steven H. Chaffee, "Second Chance Political Socialization: 'Trickle-up' Effects of Children on Parents," in Thomas J. Johnson et al., eds., *Engaging the Public: How Government and the Media Can Reinvigorate American Democracy* (Lanham, MD: Rowman & Littlefield, 1998), pp. 57–66.
[3]Jane Eisner, *Taking Back the Vote: Getting American Youth Involved in Our Democracy* (Boston: Beacon Press, 2004).

Individuals who join interest groups based on ethnic identity may find, for example, a common political bond through working for the group's civil liberties and rights. African American activist groups may consist of individuals who join together to support government programs that will aid the African American population. Members of a labor union may be strongly influenced to support certain pro-labor candidates.

Opinion Leaders' Influence. We are all influenced by those with whom we are closely associated or whom we hold in high regard—friends at school, family members and other relatives, and teachers. In a sense, these people are **opinion leaders**, but on an *informal* level; that is, their influence on our political views is not necessarily intentional or deliberate. We are also influenced by *formal* opinion leaders, such as presidents, lobbyists, congresspersons, news commentators, and religious leaders, who have as part of their jobs the task of swaying people's views. Their interest lies in defining the political agenda in such a way that discussions about policy options will take place on their terms.

Opinion Leader
One who is able to influence the opinions of others because of position, expertise, or personality.

THE IMPACT OF THE MEDIA

Clearly, the **media**—newspapers, television, radio, and Internet sources—strongly influence public opinion. This is because the media inform the public about the issues and events of our times and thus have an **agenda setting** effect. In other words, to borrow from Bernard Cohen's classic statement about the media and public opinion, the media may not be successful in telling people what to think, but they are "stunningly successful in telling their audience what to think about."[4]

DID YOU KNOW?

That CNN reaches more than 1.5 billion people in 212 countries?

Today, many contend that the media's influence on public opinion has grown to equal that of the family. For example, in her analysis of the role played by the media in American politics,[5] media scholar Doris A. Graber points out that high school students, when asked where they obtain the information on which they base their attitudes, mention the mass media far more than they mention their families, friends, and teachers. This trend, combined with the increasing popularity of such information sources as cable satires such as *The Daily Show,* talk radio, blogs, social networking sites, and the Internet, may significantly alter the nature of the media's influence on public debate in the future. The media's influence will be discussed in more detail in Chapter 11.

Media
Channels of mass communication.

Agenda Setting
Determining which public-policy questions will be debated or considered.

THE INFLUENCE OF POLITICAL EVENTS

Generally, older Americans tend to be somewhat more conservative than younger Americans, particularly on social issues and, to some extent, on economic issues. This effect is known as the **lifestyle effect**. It probably occurs because older adults are concerned about their own economic situations and are likely to retain the social values that they learned at a younger age. Young people, especially today, are more liberal than their grandparents on social issues such as the rights of gays and lesbians and racial and gender equality. Nevertheless, a more important factor than a person's age is the impact of important political events that shape the political attitudes of an entire generation. When events produce such a long-lasting result, we refer to it as a **generational effect** (also called the *cohort effect*).

Voters who grew up in the 1930s during the Great Depression were likely to form lifelong attachments to the Democratic Party, the party of Franklin D. Roosevelt. In

Lifestyle Effect
The phenomenon of certain attitudes occurring at certain chronological ages.

Generational Effect
A long-lasting effect of the events of a particular time on the political opinions of those who came of political age at that time.

---

[4]*The Press and Foreign Policy* (Princeton, NJ: Princeton University Press, 1963), p. 81.
[5]See Doris A. Graber, *Mass Media and American Politics*, 7th ed. (Chicago: University of Chicago Press, 2005).

Watergate Break-In
The 1972 illegal entry into the Democratic National Committee offices by participants in President Richard Nixon's re-election campaign.

the 1960s and 1970s, the war in Vietnam and the **Watergate break-in** and the subsequent presidential cover-up fostered widespread cynicism toward government. There is evidence that the years of economic prosperity under President Ronald Reagan during the 1980s led many young people to identify with the Republican Party. It is less clear whether more recent presidents—including Democrat Bill Clinton (served 1993–2001) and Republican George W. Bush (served 2001–2009)—have been able to affect the party identification of young voters.

POLITICAL PREFERENCES AND VOTING BEHAVIOR

Various socioeconomic and demographic factors appear to influence political preferences. These factors include education, income and **socioeconomic status**, religion, race, gender, geographic region, and similar traits. People who share the same religion, occupation, or any other demographic trait are likely to influence one another and may also have common political concerns that follow from the common characteristic. Other factors, such as party identification, perception of the candidates, and issue preferences, are closely connected to the electoral process. Table 6–1 illustrates the impact of some of these variables on voting behavior.

Socioeconomic Status
The value assigned to a person due to occupation or income. An upper-class person, for example, has high socioeconomic status.

DEMOGRAPHIC INFLUENCES

Demographic influences reflect the individual's personal background and place in society. Some factors have to do with the family into which a person was born: race and (for most people) religion. Others may be the result of choices made throughout an individual's life: place of residence, educational achievement, and profession.

It is also clear that many of these factors are interrelated. People who have more education are likely to have higher incomes and to hold professional jobs. Similarly, children born into wealthier families are far more likely to complete college than children from poor families. Many other interrelationships are not so immediately obvious; for example, many people might not guess that 88 percent of African Americans report that religion is very important in their lives, compared with only 57 percent of whites.[6]

Education. In the past, having a college education tended to be associated with voting for Republicans. In recent years, however, this correlation has become weaker. In particular, individuals with a postgraduate education (professors, doctors, lawyers, other managers) have become increasingly Democratic. Also, a higher percentage of voters with only a high school education, who were likely to be blue-collar workers, voted Republican in 2000 and 2004, compared with the pattern in many previous elections, in which that group of voters tended to favor Democrats.

The Influence of Economic Status. Family income is a strong predictor of economic liberalism or conservatism. Those with low incomes tend to favor government action to benefit the poor or to promote economic equality. As indicated in Table 6–2, voters in union households have tended to vote for the Democratic candidate. Those with high incomes tend to oppose government intervention in the economy or to support it only when it benefits business. On economic issues, therefore, the traditional economic spectrum described in Chapter 1 is a useful tool. The rich tend toward the right; the poor tend toward the left.

[6]The Gallup Poll, "A Look at Americans and Religion Today," March 23, 2004.

TABLE 6–1 Votes by Groups in Presidential Elections, 1992–2008 (in Percentages)

	1992			1996		2000		2004		2008	
	CLINTON (DEM.)	BUSH (REP.)	PEROT (REF.)	CLINTON (DEM.)	DOLE (REP.)	GORE (DEM.)	BUSH (REP.)	KERRY (DEM.)	BUSH (REP.)	OBAMA (DEM.)	MCCAIN (REP.)
Total vote	43	38	19	49	41	48	48	48	51	53	46
Gender											
Men	41	38	21	43	44	42	53	44	55	49	48
Women	46	37	17	54	38	54	43	51	48	56	43
Race											
White	39	41	20	43	46	42	54	41	58	43	55
Black	82	11	7	84	12	90	8	88	11	95	3
Hispanic	62	25	14	72	21	67	31	54	44	67	31
Educational Attainment											
Not a high school graduate	55	28	17	59	28	59	39	50	50	63	35
High school graduate	43	36	20	51	35	48	49	47	52	52	46
College graduate	40	41	19	44	46	45	51	46	52	50	48
Postgraduate education	49	36	15	52	40	52	44	54	45	58	40
Religion											
White Protestant	33	46	21	36	53	34	63	32	68	45	54
Catholic	44	36	20	53	37	49	47	47	52	53	45
Jewish	78	12	10	78	16	79	19	75	24	77	22
White fundamentalist	23	61	15	NA	NA	NA	NA	21	79	24	74
Union Status											
Union household	55	24	21	59	30	59	37	59	40	58	40
Family Income											
Under $15,000	59	23	18	59	28	57	37	63	37	73	25
$15,000–29,000	45	35	20	53	36	54	41	57	41	60	37
$30,000–49,000	41	38	21	48	40	49	48	50	49	55	43
Over $50,000	40	42	18	44	48	45	52	43	56	49	49
Size of Place											
Population over 500,000	58	28	13	68	25	71	26	60	40	71	28
Population 50,000 to 500,000	50	33	16	50	39	57	40	50	50	59	40
Population 10,000 to 50,000	39	42	20	48	41	38	59	48	51	45	63
Rural	39	40	20	44	46	37	59	39	60	45	53

NA = not asked

Sources: *The New York Times*; Voter News Service; CBS News; CNN; *Wall Street Journal*.

TABLE 6–2 Percentage of Union Households Voting Republican

Although union members are more likely to identify themselves as Democrats than Republicans and labor organizations are far more likely to support Democratic candidates, the data below show that in eight of the last 14 presidential elections, Republicans have captured at least 40 percent of the votes from union households.

YEAR	UNION HOUSEHOLDS VOTING REPUBLICAN FOR PRESIDENTIAL CANDIDATES	PERCENTAGE
1952	Eisenhower vs. Stevenson	44
1956	Eisenhower vs. Stevenson	57
1960	Kennedy vs. Nixon	36
1964	Johnson vs. Goldwater	17
1968	Nixon vs. Humphrey	44
1972	Nixon vs. McGovern	57
1976	Carter vs. Ford	36
1980	Reagan vs. Carter	45
1984	Reagan vs. Mondale	43
1988	Bush vs. Dukakis	42
1992	Clinton vs. Bush	24
1996	Clinton vs. Dole	30
2000	Bush vs. Gore	37
2004	Bush vs. Kerry	40
2008	Obama vs. McCain	40

Sources: *CQ Researcher*, June 28, 1996, p. 560; *The New York Times*, November 10, 1996, p. 16; and authors' updates.

There are no hard-and-fast rules, however. Some very poor individuals are devoted Republicans, just as some extremely wealthy people support the Democratic Party. Indeed, recent research indicates that a realignment is occurring among those of higher economic status: as just mentioned, professionals now tend to vote Democratic, while small-business owners, managers, and corporate executives tend to vote Republican.[7]

Religious Influence: Denomination. Traditionally, scholars have examined the impact of religion on political attitudes by dividing the population into such categories as Protestant, Catholic, and Jewish. In recent decades, however, such a breakdown has become less valuable as a means of predicting someone's political preferences. It is true that in the past, Jewish voters were notably more liberal than members of other groups on both economic and cultural issues, and they continue to be more liberal today. Persons reporting no religion are very liberal on social issues but have mixed economic views. Northern Protestants and Catholics, however, do not differ that greatly from each other, and neither do Southern Protestants and Catholics. This represents something of a change—in the late 1800s and early 1900s, Northern Protestants were distinctly more likely to vote Republican, and Northern Catholics were more likely to vote Democratic.[8]

Religious Influence: Religiosity and Evangelicals. Nevertheless, two factors do turn out to be major predictors of political attitudes among members of the various Christian denominations. One is the degree of *religiosity*, or practice of beliefs, and the other is whether the

[7]Thomas B. Edsall, "Voters Thinking Less with Their Wallets," *International Herald Tribune*, March 27, 2001, p. 3.
[8]John C. Green, *The Faith Factor: How Religion Influences American Elections* (New York: Praeger, 2007).

RELIGIOUS AFFILIATION and practice impacts political opinions. Individuals who attend religious services frequently tend to be somewhat more conservative than other Americans. (Beth Perkins/ Getty Images)

person holds fundamentalist or evangelical views. A high degree of religiosity is usually manifested by very frequent attendance at church services, at least once or twice a week.

Voters who are more devout, regardless of their church affiliation, tend to vote Republican, whereas voters who are less devout are more often Democrats. In 2000, for example, Protestants who regularly attended church gave 84 percent of their votes to Republican candidate George W. Bush, compared with 55 percent of those who attended church less often. Among Catholics, there was a similar pattern: a majority of Catholics who attended church regularly voted Republican, while a majority of Catholics who were not regular churchgoers voted for Democratic candidate Al Gore.[9] There is an exception to this trend: African Americans of all religious backgrounds have been strongly supportive of Democrats.

Another distinctive group of voters who are also likely to be very religious are those Americans who can be identified as holding fundamentalist beliefs or consider themselves part of an evangelical group. They are usually members of a Protestant church, which may be part of a mainstream denomination or may be an independent congregation. In election studies, these individuals are usually identified by a pattern of beliefs: they may describe themselves as "born again" and believe in the literal word of the Bible, among other characteristics. As voters, these Christians tend to be cultural conservatives but not necessarily economic conservatives.

The Influence of Race and Ethnicity. Although African Americans are, on average, somewhat conservative on certain cultural issues such as same-sex marriage and abortion, they tend to be more liberal than whites on social-welfare matters, civil liberties, and even foreign policy. African Americans voted principally for Republicans until Democrat Franklin Roosevelt's New Deal in the 1930s. Since then, they have largely identified with the Democratic Party. Indeed, Democratic presidential candidates have received, on average, more than 80 percent of the African American vote since 1956. As you

[9]Ronald Brownstein, "Attendance, Not Affiliation, Key to Religious Voters," *The Los Angeles Times*, July 16, 2001, p. A10.

Gender Gap
The difference between the percentage of women who vote for a particular candidate and the percentage of men who vote for the candidate.

learned in Chapter 1, Hispanics also favor the Democrats. Hispanics of Cuban ancestry, however, are predominantly Republican. Most Asian American groups lean toward the Democrats, although often by narrow margins. Muslim American immigrants and their descendants are an interesting category.[10] In 2000, a majority of Muslim Americans of Middle Eastern ancestry voted for Republican George W. Bush because they shared his cultural conservatism and believed that he would do a better job of defending their civil liberties than Democrat Al Gore. In the 2004 election campaign, however, the civil liberties issue propelled many of these voters toward the Democrats.[11]

The Gender Gap. Until the 1980s, there was little evidence that men's and women's political attitudes were very different. Following the election of Ronald Reagan in 1980, however, scholars began to detect a **gender gap**. A May 1983 Gallup poll revealed that men were more likely than women to approve of Reagan's job performance. The gender gap has reappeared in subsequent presidential elections, with women being more likely than men to support the Democratic candidate (see Figure 6–4). In the 2000 elections, 54 percent of women voted for Democrat Al Gore, compared with 42 percent of men.

Women also appear to hold different attitudes from their male counterparts on a range of issues other than presidential preferences. They are much more likely than men to oppose capital punishment and the use of force abroad. Studies also have shown that women are more concerned about risks to the environment, more supportive of social welfare, and more in agreement with extending civil rights to gays and lesbians than are men. In contrast, women are also more concerned than men about the security issues raised by the events of 9/11. This last fact may have pushed women in a more conservative direction, at least for a time. In the 2004 presidential elections, the gender gap narrowed somewhat: 48 percent of women voted for George Bush, the highest percentage voting Republican since 1988. It is also important to note that the gender gap does not appear on other issues facing the American people, including the right to an abortion and economic issues.

[10]At least one-third of U.S. Muslims are actually African Americans whose ancestors have been in this country for a long time. In terms of political preferences, African American Muslims are more likely to resemble other African Americans than Muslim immigrants from the Middle East.
[11]For up-to-date information on Muslim American issues, see the Web site of the Council on American-Islamic Relations at www.cair.com.

FIGURE 6–4 Gender Gap in Presidential Elections, 1980–2008

A gender gap in voting is apparent in the percentage of women and the percentage of men voting in the last several presidential elections. Even when women and men favor the same candidate, they do so by different margins, resulting in a gender gap.

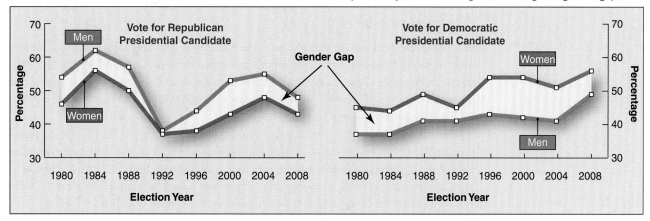

Note: Data in the chart includes votes for Republican and Democratic candidates only. The effect of third party candidates on the gender gap is nominal except in 1992, when H. Ross Perot received 17 percent of the vote among women and 21 percent among men. Perot's impact, if factored into the data, would widen the gap pictured in the chart for 1992, and to a lesser extent in 1996, when his candidacy drew fewer votes.
Sources: Center for American Women and Politics (CAWP); Eagleton Institute of Politics; and Rutgers University.

Reasons for the Gender Gap. What is the cause of the gender gap? A number of explanations have been offered, including the increase in the number of working women, feminism, and women's concerns over abortion rights and other social issues. Researchers Lena Edlund and Rohini Pande of Columbia University, however, found that the major factor leading to the gender gap has been the disparate economic impact on men and women of not being married. In the last three decades, men and women have tended to marry later in life or stay single even after having children. The divorce rate has also risen dramatically. Edlund and Pande argue that this decline in marriage has tended to make men richer and women relatively poorer. Consequently, support for Democrats is high among single women, particularly single mothers.[12]

AN ASIAN AMERICAN FAMILY standing outside their new home. The median family income of Asian Americans is about $10,000 more than the median income for all households. As a result, Asian Americans, especially those from China, India, and Japan, are sometimes seen as succeeding through education and hard work. (Nonetheless, some Asian Americans continue to live in poverty or experience discrimination.) (Ariel Skelley/Corbis)

[12]For an online video presentation of Edlund and Pande's research, go to www.Columbia.edu/cu/news/media/02 /edlund_pande/index.html.

Researchers have also found that the gender gap grows wider as men and women become better educated. This result seems to contradict Edlund and Pande's theory, at least in part—it does not seem likely that well-educated women would be suffering economically, and some evidence suggest that the gender gap persists even among well-educated married women.[13]

Geographic Region. Finally, where you live can influence your political attitudes. In one way, regional differences are less important today than just a few decades ago. The former solid (Democratic) South has crumbled in national elections. Only 43 percent of the votes from the Southern states went to Democrat Al Gore in 2000, while 55 percent went to Republican George W. Bush.

There is a tendency today, at least in national elections, for the South, the Great Plains, and the Rocky Mountain states to favor the Republicans, and for the West Coast and the Northeast to favor the Democrats. Perhaps more important than region is residence—urban, suburban, or rural. People in large cities tend to be liberal and Democratic. Those who live in smaller communities tend to be conservative and Republican.

ELECTION: THE MOST IMPORTANT INFLUENCES

Factors such as party identification, perception of the candidates, and issue preferences all have an effect on how people vote in particular elections. Although strong party identifiers remain loyal in most elections, independent voters change their preferences frequently, and the impact of candidate personality and the issues change with every election.

Party Identification. With the possible exception of race, party identification has been the most important determinant of voting behavior in national elections. Party affiliation is influenced by family and peer groups, by generational effects, by the media, and by the voter's assessment of candidates and issues.

In the middle to late 1960s, party attachment began to weaken. Whereas independent voters were only a little more than 20 percent of the eligible electorate during the 1950s, they constituted more than 30 percent of all voters by the mid-1990s, and their numbers have remained constant since that time. New voters are likely to identify themselves as independent voters, although they may be more ready to identify with one of the major parties by their mid-30s. There is considerable debate among political scientists over whether those who call themselves independents are truly so: when asked, most say that they are "leaning" toward one party or the other. (For further discussion of party affiliation, see Chapter 8).

Perception of the Candidates. The image of the candidate also seems to be important in a voter's choice, especially of a president. To some extent, voter attitudes toward candidates are based on emotions (such as trust or attraction rather than on any judgment about experience or policy). In some years, voters have been attracted to a candidate who appeared to share their concerns and worries. (President Bill Clinton was one example.) In other years, voters have sought a candidate who appeared to have high integrity and honesty. Voters have been especially attracted to these candidates in elections that follow a major scandal, such as Richard Nixon's Watergate scandal (1972–1974) or Clinton's sex scandal (1998–1999). In 2008, Barack Obama was presented as a candidate who represented change and who would bring change to Washington. He ran an "outsider" campaign focusing on the failings of the government under President George W. Bush.

DID YOU KNOW?

That Britain had a major gender gap for much of the 20th century—because women were much more likely than men to support the Conservative Party rather than the more left-wing Labour Party?

---

[13]Susan Page, "'Til Politics Do Us Part: Gender Gap Widens," *USA Today*, December 18, 2003, pp. 1A–2A.

His ability to deliver a charismatic speech along with his youth increased his attractiveness as a candidate. Senator John McCain tried to project the image of a reformer who could also change Washington. His age and long experience in the capital worked against that portrayal.

Issue Preferences. Issues make a difference in presidential and congressional elections. Although personality or image factors may be very persuasive, most voters have some notion of how the candidates differ on basic issues or at least know which candidates want a change in the direction of government policy.

Historically, economic concerns have been among the most powerful influences on public opinion. When the economy is doing well, it is very difficult for a challenger, especially at the presidential level, to defeat the incumbent. In contrast, inflation, unemployment, or high interest rates are likely to work to the disadvantage of the incumbent. Some studies seem to show that people vote on the basis of their personal economic well-being, while other research suggests that people vote on the basis of the nation's overall economic health.[14]

MEASURING PUBLIC OPINION

In a democracy, people express their opinions in a variety of ways, as mentioned in this chapter's introduction. One of the most common means of gathering and measuring public opinion on specific issues is, of course, through the use of **opinion polls**.

THE HISTORY OF OPINION POLLS

During the 1800s, certain American newspapers and magazines spiced up their political coverage by doing face-to-face straw polls (unofficial polls indicating the trend of political opinion) or mail surveys of their readers' opinions. In the early 20th century, the magazine *Literary Digest* further developed the technique of opinion polling by mailing large numbers of questionnaires to individuals, many of whom were its own subscribers, to determine their political opinions. From 1916 to 1936, more than 70 percent of the magazine's election predictions were accurate.

Literary Digest's polling activities suffered a setback in 1936, however, when the magazine predicted, based on more than 2 million returned questionnaires, that Republican candidate Alfred Landon would win over Democratic candidate Franklin D. Roosevelt. Landon won in only two states. A major problem with the *Digest*'s polling technique was its use of nonrepresentative respondents. In 1936, at possibly the worst point of the Great Depression, the magazine's subscribers were, for one thing, considerably more affluent than the average American. In other words, they did not accurately represent all of the voters in the U.S. population.

Several newcomers to the public opinion poll industry accurately predicted Roosevelt's landslide victory. These newcomers are still active in the poll-taking industry today: the Gallup poll founded by George Gallup and the Roper poll founded by Elmo Roper. Gallup and Roper, along with Archibald Crossley, developed the modern polling techniques of market research. Using personal interviews with small samples of selected voters (fewer than 2,000), they showed that they could predict with accuracy the behavior of the total voting population.

Opinion Poll
A method of systematically questioning a small, selected sample of respondents who are deemed representative of the total population.

DID YOU KNOW?

That 30 percent of people asked to participate in an opinion poll refuse?

---

[14]Warren E. Miller and J. Merrill Shanks, *The New American Voter* (Cambridge, MA: Harvard University Press, 1996). See page 270 for voting on the basis of personal income and page 196 for voting on the basis of the state of the economy.

By the 1950s, improved methods of sampling and a whole new science of survey research had been developed. Survey research centers sprang up throughout the United States, particularly at universities. Some of these survey groups are the American Institute of Public Opinion at Princeton, in New Jersey; the National Opinion Research Center at the University of Chicago; and the Survey Research Center at the University of Michigan.

SAMPLING TECHNIQUES

DID YOU KNOW?

That public opinion pollsters typically measure national sentiment among the roughly 200 million adult Americans by interviewing only about 1,500 people?

How can interviewing fewer than 2,000 voters tell us what tens of millions of voters will do? Clearly, it is necessary that the sample of individuals be representative of all voters in the population. Consider an analogy: Let's say we have a large jar containing 10,000 pennies of various dates, and we want to know how many pennies were minted within certain decades (1960–1969, 1970–1979, and so on).

Representative Sampling. One way to estimate the distribution of the dates on the pennies—without examining all 10,000—is to take a representative sample. This sample would be obtained by mixing the pennies up well and then removing a handful of them—perhaps 100 pennies. The distribution of dates might be as follows:

1960–1969: 5 percent
1970–1979: 5 percent
1980–1989: 20 percent
1990–1999: 30 percent
2000–present: 40 percent

If the pennies are very well mixed within the jar, and if you take a large enough sample, the resulting distribution will probably approach the actual distribution of the dates of all 10,000 coins.

The Principle of Randomness. The most important principle in sampling, or poll taking, is randomness. Every penny or every person should have a known chance, and especially an *equal chance*, of being sampled. If this happens, then a small sample should be representative of the whole group, both in demographic characteristics (age, religion, race, region, and the like) and in opinions. The ideal way to sample the voting population of the United States would be to put all voter names into a jar—or a computer—and randomly sample, say, 2,000 of them. Because this is too costly and inefficient, pollsters have developed other ways to obtain good samples. One technique is simply to choose a random selection of telephone numbers and interview the respective households. This technique produces a relatively accurate sample at a low cost.

To ensure that the random samples include respondents from relevant segments of the population—rural, urban, Northeastern, Southern, and so on—most survey organizations randomly choose, say, urban areas that they will consider as representative of all urban areas. Then they randomly select their respondents within those areas. A generally less accurate technique is known as *quota sampling*. Here, survey researchers decide how many persons of certain

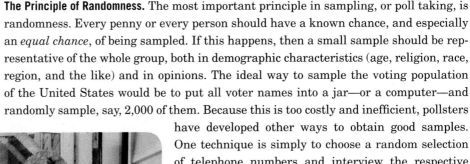

AN INTERVIEWER for a public opinion polling firm speaks with a woman in Jenkintown, Pennsylvania, in a survey of households. (Joseph Kaczmarek/AP/Wide World Photos)

types they need in the survey—such as minorities, women, or farmers—and then send out interviewers to find the necessary number of these types. Not only is this method often less accurate, but it also may be biased if, say, the interviewer refuses to go into certain neighborhoods or will not interview after dark.

Generally, the national survey organizations take great care to select their samples randomly, because their reputations rest on the accuracy of their results. The Gallup and Roper polls usually interview about 1,500 individuals, and their results have a very high probability of being correct—within a margin of three percentage points. The accuracy with which the Gallup poll has predicted presidential election results is shown in Table 6–3.

PROBLEMS WITH POLLS

Public opinion polls are snapshots of the opinions and preferences of the people at a specific moment in time and as expressed in response to a specific question. Given that definition, it is fairly easy to understand situations in which the polls are wrong. For example, opinion polls leading up to the 1980 presidential election showed President Jimmy Carter defeating challenger Ronald Reagan. Only a few analysts noted the large number of undecided respondents a week before the election. Those voters shifted massively to Reagan at the last minute, and Reagan won the election.

The famous photo of Harry Truman showing the front page of the newspaper that declared his defeat in the 1948 presidential elections is another tribute to the weakness of polling. Again, the poll that predicted his defeat was taken more than a week before election day.

Sampling Error
The difference between a sample's results and the true result if the entire population had been interviewed.

Sampling Errors. Polls may also report erroneous results because the pool of respondents was not chosen in a scientific manner; that is, the form of sampling and the number of people sampled may be too small to overcome **sampling error**, which is the difference between the sample result and the true result if the entire population had been interviewed. The sample would be biased, for example, if the poll interviewed people by telephone and did not correct for the fact that more women than men answer the telephone and that some populations (college students and very poor individuals, for example) cannot be found so easily by telephone. Unscientific mail-in polls, telephone call-in polls, Internet polls, and polls completed by the workers in a campaign office are not scientific and do not give an accurate picture of the public's views. Because of these and other problems with polls, some have suggested that polling be regulated by the government.

As polltakers get close to election day, they become even more concerned about

TABLE 6–3 Gallup Poll Accuracy Record

YEAR	GALLUP FINAL SURVEY, PERCENTAGE		ELECTION RESULTS, PERCENTAGE		DEVIATION
2008	55.0	Obama	52.6	Obama	+2.4
2004	49.3	Bush	50.7	Bush	–1.7
2000	50.0	Bush	48.0	Bush	+2.0
1996	52.0	Clinton	49.0	Clinton	+3.0
1992	49.0	Clinton	43.2	Clinton	+5.8
1988	56.0	Bush	53.9	Bush	+2.1
1984	59.0	Reagan	59.1	Reagan	–0.1
1980	47.0	Reagan	50.8	Reagan	–3.8
1976	48.0	Carter	50.0	Carter	–2.0
1972	62.0	Nixon	61.8	Nixon	+0.2
1968	43.0	Nixon	43.5	Nixon	–0.5
1964	64.0	Johnson	61.3	Johnson	+2.7
1960	51.0	Kennedy	50.1	Kennedy	+0.9
1956	59.5	Eisenhower	57.8	Eisenhower	+1.7
1952	51.0	Eisenhower	55.4	Eisenhower	–4.4
1948	44.5	Truman	49.9	Truman	–5.4
1944	51.5	Roosevelt	53.3	Roosevelt	–1.8
1940	52.0	Roosevelt	55.0	Roosevelt	–3.0
1936	55. 7	Roosevelt	62.5	Roosevelt	–6.8

Sources: *The Gallup Poll Monthly*, November 1992; *Time*, November 21, 1994; *The Wall Street Journal*, November 6, 1996; and authors' updates.

MODERN POLLING depends heavily on computerized telephone polling. The respondents are chosen by a random selection of telephone numbers. The interviewer inputs their responses directly into a computer for analysis. (Sven Martson/Image Works)

their sample of respondents. Some pollsters continue to interview eligible voters, meaning those over age 18 and registered to vote. Many others use a series of questions in the poll and other weighting methods to try to identify "likely voters" so that they can be more accurate in their election-eve predictions. When a poll changes its method from reporting the views of eligible voters to reporting those of likely voters, the results tend to change dramatically.

Poll Questions. It makes sense to expect that the results of a poll will depend on the questions that are asked. One of the problems with many polls is the yes/no answer format. For example, suppose the poll question asks, "Do you favor or oppose the war in Iraq?" Respondents might wish to answer that they favored the war at the beginning but not as it is currently being waged or that they favor fighting terrorism but not a military occupation. They have no way of indicating their true position with a yes or no answer. Respondents also are sometimes swayed by the inclusion of certain words in a question: more respondents will answer in the affirmative if the question asks, "Do you favor or oppose the war in Iraq as a means of fighting terrorism?" Furthermore, respondents' answers are also influenced by the order in which questions are asked, by the possible answers from which they are allowed to choose, and, in some cases, by their interaction with the interviewer. To a certain extent, people try to please the interviewer. They answer questions about which they have no information and avoid some answers to try to measure up to the interviewer's expectations.

Push Polls. Some campaigns have begun using "push polls," in which the respondents are given misleading information in the questions asked to persuade them to vote against a candidate. For example, the interviewer might ask, "Do you approve or disapprove of Congressman Smith, who voted to raise your taxes 22 times?" Obviously, the answers given are likely to be influenced by such techniques. Push polls have been condemned by the polling industry and are considered to be unethical. However, other than complaining to the media about such efforts, candidates cannot assure that push polls will not be used.

Because of these problems with polls, you need to be especially careful when evaluating poll results. For some suggestions on how to be a critical consumer of public opinion polls, see the *You Can Make a Difference* feature at the end of this chapter.

THE ACCURACY OF THE 2008 POLLS

The 2008 election year did not begin well for the polls. Virtually all polling organizations predicted that Barack Obama would win the New Hampshire primary by a wide margin. Senator Hillary Clinton campaigned hard in the final days of that primary and won the state. Throughout the year, polling organizations tried to find solutions to a number of issues including whether respondents would tell the truth about voting or not voting for an African American candidate, whether respondents were actually registered to vote, and near the end of the campaign, whether respondents were truly likely to vote. Near election day, there were hundreds of polls reported and fairly great discrepancies between them. Most of the polls actually overestimated Barack Obama's

WHAT IF...

PUBLIC OPINION POLLS WERE REGULATED BY THE GOVERNMENT?

Many public opinion polls are conducted by nonprofit organizations such as the Pew Center or by university research organizations. Hundreds of polls are actually conducted by or for the U.S. government. These include monthly census polls and polls about the financial state of individual Americans. These polls are intended to answer legitimate scientific questions. However, hundreds of polls are conducted by the media, by private polling firms for market research purposes, and by political polling houses. And, as you have read, thousands of media outlets, Internet entrepreneurs, and ordinary individuals post polls on their Web sites or offer call-in polls to their viewers. These are not scientific polls, and their results are certainly doubtful in accuracy.

What if the government placed the regulation of polling under an organization such as the Government Accountability Office for the purpose of setting standards and regulating the methods used by pollsters? Then, if a poll was conducted and publicized that was unscientific, the sponsors could be fined or otherwise punished. Market researchers would argue that such regulation is totally unnecessary. If they want to measure the taste of peanut butter or beer with a certain group, that's a business decision. Television stations admit that their polls are unscientific. Regulation would violate their freedom of expression.

Another aspect of polling that could be regulated is the use of polls that actually present false information, like the "push polls" used in political campaigns. But what government agency could actually decide whether a poll question used false information or conveyed a false impression? Magazines, newspapers, books, and movies are not regulated in that fashion. One of the perils of living in a free democracy is that some information we receive may not be true.

Finally, many commentators and politicians have sought to have polls regulated on election day. As you will read more about in Chapter 10, "Campaigning for Office," election-day polls are used to predict the winners in national elections. If the winners are predicted before all polls close, there is a chance that the prediction will keep some voters in Western states away from the polls. The winner and loser have already been predicted, although the votes have not been counted. In response to public pressure, the television networks have agreed among themselves not to predict the winner in any state until all polls are closed, but they don't address the issue of the overall winner. In any case, pollsters and polling houses clearly believe that any regulation of their on-air predictions would be a violation of the First Amendment and freedom of the press.

Given these considerations, it is unlikely that polls will be regulated, although a serious misuse of polls in an election cycle could bring pressure for polls to be subjected to more scrutiny.

FOR CRITICAL ANALYSIS

1. Should pollsters be required to inform the public about their polling methods?
2. Should all polls conducted by political campaigns be monitored to prevent spreading malicious information about the opposing candidate?
3. Do public opinion polls actually provide new information for voters and citizens?

margin of victory nationally but underestimated it in the battleground states. This was due, in part, to the large number of new voters whose choice was harder to predict.

TECHNOLOGY AND OPINION POLLS

Public opinion polling is based on scientific principles, particularly with respect to randomness. Today, technological advances allow polls to be taken over the Internet, but serious questions have been raised about the ability of pollsters to obtain truly

PRESIDENT HARRY TRUMAN holds up the front page of the *Chicago Daily Tribune* issue that predicted his defeat on the basis of a Gallup poll. The poll had indicated that Truman would lose the 1948 contest for his reelection by a margin of 55.5 to 44.5 percent. The Gallup poll was completed more than a week before the election, so it missed a shift by undecided voters to Truman. (AP Photo/Byron Rollins)

DID YOU KNOW?

That when Americans were asked if they thought race relations were good or bad in the United States, 68 percent said that they were "bad," but when asked about race relations in their own communities, 75 percent said that they were "good"?

random samples using this medium. The same was said not long ago when another technological breakthrough changed public opinion polling—the telephone.

THE ADVENT OF TELEPHONE POLLING

During the 1970s, telephone polling began to predominate over in-person polling. By calling randomly generated telephone numbers within the targeted areas, polls could generate a random sample. Telephone polling quickly proved to be much less expensive than sending interviewers to poll respondents in their homes. Additionally, telephone interviewers do not have to worry about safety problems, particularly in high-crime areas. Finally, telephone interviews can be conducted relatively quickly. They allow politicians or the media to poll one evening and report the results the next day.

Telephone Polling Problems. Somewhat ironically, the success of telephone polling has created major problems for the technique. The telemarketing industry in general has become so pervasive that people increasingly refuse to respond to telephone polls. More than 40 percent of households now use either caller ID or some other form of call screening. This has greatly reduced the number of households that polling organizations can reach. Calls may be automatically rejected, or the respondent may not pick up the call. A potentially greater problem for telephone polling is the popularity of cell phones. Cellular telephone numbers are not yet included in random-digit dialing programs or listed in telephone directories. Furthermore, individuals with cell phones may be located anywhere in the United States or the world, thus confounding attempts to reach people in a particular area. As more people, and especially younger Americans, choose to use only a cell phone and do not have a landline at all, polling accuracy is further reduced because these individuals cannot be included in any sample for a poll.[15]

Nonresponse Rates Have Skyrocketed. Nonresponses in telephone polling include unreachable numbers, refusals, answering machines, and call-screening devices. The nonresponse rate has increased to as high as 80 percent for most telephone polls. Such a high nonresponse rate undercuts confidence in the survey results. In most cases, polling only 20 percent of those on the list cannot lead to a random sample. Even more important for politicians is the fact that polling organizations are not required to report their response rates.

[15]J. Michael Brick et al., "Cell Phone Survey Feasibility in the U.S.: Sampling and Calling Cell Numbers Versus Landline Numbers," *Public Opinion Quarterly*, Vol. 71, Spring 2007, p. 23–39.

ENTER INTERNET POLLING

Obviously, Internet polling is not done on a one-on-one basis, because there is no voice communication. Despite the potential problems, the Harris Poll, a widely respected national polling organization, conducted online polls during the 1998 elections. Its election predictions were accurate in many states. Nonetheless, it made a serious error in one Southern gubernatorial election. The Harris group subsequently refined its techniques and continues to conduct online polls. This organization believes that proper weighting of the results will achieve the equivalent of a random-sampled poll.

Public opinion experts argue that the Harris Poll procedure violates the mathematical basis of random sampling. Nonetheless, the Internet population is looking more like the rest of America: almost as many women (71 percent) go online as men (74 percent), 61 percent of African American adults have Internet access, and so do 72 percent of Hispanics (compared with 73 percent of non-Hispanic whites).[16]

"Nonpolls" on the Internet. Even if organizations such as the Harris Poll succeed in obtaining the equivalent of a random sample when polling on the Internet, another problem will remain: the proliferation of "nonpolls" on the Internet. Every media outlet that maintains a Web site allows anyone to submit her or his opinion. Numerous organizations and for-profit companies send polls to individuals via e-mail. Mister Poll (**www.misterpoll.com**) bills itself as the Internet's largest poll database. Mister Poll allows you to create your own polls just for fun or to include them on your home page. In general, Mister Poll, like many other polling sites, asks a number of questions on various issues and seeks answers from those who log on to its site. Although the Mister Poll Web site states "None of these polls is scientific," sites such as this one undercut the efforts of legitimate pollsters to use the Internet scientifically.

Will Internet Polling Contribute to the Devaluation of Polling Results? Although nonpolls certainly existed before the Internet, the ease with which they can be conducted and disseminated is accelerating another trend: the indiscriminate use of polling by all concerned. Though Americans may not want to be bothered by telemarketers or unwanted telephone polls, they seem to continue to want reports of polling results during presidential elections and news stories about the president's approval ratings and similar topics. When asked, a majority of Americans say that polling results are interesting to them. Yet the proliferation of polls, often on the Internet, with little effort to ensure the accuracy of the results presents perhaps the greatest threat to the science of polling.

As we have noted, totally nonscientific polls sometimes get as much hype from the media as more scientifically conducted surveys. Poll results are broadcast on the Internet with no authentication at all, and the news media regularly encourages viewers to call in to their own unscientific polls. This indiscriminate use of polling may encourage Americans to see all polls as equally truthful or equally fraudulent and to refuse to respond to any poll. Public antipathy toward polling will, in the long run, make it even more difficult for the finest polling organizations to serve their clients.

DID YOU KNOW?

That a straw poll conducted by patrons of Harry's New York Bar in Paris has an almost unbroken record of predicting the outcomes of U.S. presidential contests?

---

[16]Pew Internet and American Life Project, *May–June 2006 Tracking Survey*. The Pew Internet surveys are online at www.pewinternet.org.

PUBLIC OPINION AND THE POLITICAL PROCESS

Public opinion affects the political process in many ways. Politicians, whether in office or in the midst of a campaign, see public opinion as important to their careers. The president, members of Congress, governors, and other elected officials realize that strong support by the public as expressed in opinion polls is a source of power in dealing with other politicians. It is far more difficult for a senator to say no to the president if the president is immensely popular and if polls show approval of the president's policies. Public opinion also helps political candidates identify the most important concerns among the people and may help them shape their campaigns successfully.

During the presidential primary contests, polling becomes extremely important to candidates, contributors, and voters. Individuals who would like to make a campaign contribution to their favorite candidate may decide not to if the polls show that the candidate is not likely to win. Voters do not want to waste their votes on the primary candidates who are doing poorly in the polls. In 2008, the two leading Democratic candidates, Senators Barack Obama and Hillary Clinton, used poll results to try to influence convention delegates of their respective strengths as the party nominee.

Nevertheless, surveys of public opinion are not equivalent to elections in the United States. Although opinion polls may influence political candidates or government officials, elections are the major vehicle through which Americans can bring about changes in their government.

POLITICAL CULTURE AND PUBLIC OPINION

Americans are divided into a multitude of ethnic, religious, regional, and political subgroups. Given the diversity of American society and the wide range of opinions contained within it, how is it that the political process continues to function without being stalemated by conflict and dissension? One explanation is rooted in the concept of the American political culture, which can be described as a set of attitudes and ideas about the nation and the government. As discussed in Chapter 1, our political culture

THE PENTAGON HONOR GUARD renders honors during a memorial ceremony commemorating the fifth anniversary of the September 11, 2001, terrorist attacks on the United States. When Americans express high levels of confidence in the military, which events or which people are they likely to be thinking about? (Mass Communication Specialist 1st Class Chad J. McNeeley/U.S. Navy)

is widely shared by Americans of many different backgrounds. To some extent, it consists of symbols, such as the American flag, the Liberty Bell, and the Statue of Liberty. The elements of our political culture also include certain shared beliefs about the most important values in the American political system, including (1) liberty, equality, and property; (2) support for religion; and (3) community service and personal achievement. The structure of the government—particularly federalism, the political parties, the powers of Congress, and popular rule—is also an important value.

Political Culture and Support for Our Political System. The political culture provides a general environment of support for the political system. If the people share certain beliefs about the system and a reservoir of good feeling exists toward the institutions of government, the nation will be better able to weather periods of crisis. Such was the case after the 2000 presidential elections when, for several weeks, it was not certain who the next president would be and how that determination would be made. At the time, some contended that the nation was facing a true constitutional crisis. Certainly, in many nations of today's world, this would be the case. In fact, however, the broad majority of Americans did not believe that the uncertain outcome of the elections had created a constitutional crisis. Polls taken during this time found that, on the contrary, most Americans were confident in our political system's ability to decide the issue peaceably and in a lawful manner.[17]

Political Trust. The political culture also helps Americans evaluate their government's performance. At times in our history, **political trust** in government has reached relatively high levels. As you can see in Table 6–4, a poll taken two weeks after the September 11 attacks found that trust in government was higher than it had been for more than three decades. At other times, political trust in government has fallen to low levels. For example, in the 1960s and 1970s during the Vietnam War and the Watergate scandals, surveys showed that the overall level of political trust in government had declined steeply. A considerable proportion of Americans seemed to feel that they could not trust government officials and that they could not count on officials to care about the ordinary person. This index of political trust reached an all-time low in the early 1990s but then climbed steadily until 2001.

At times it can be instructive to look at the level of trust that the rest of the world has in the U.S. government. For many years, the United States was a trusted leader

Political Trust
The degree to which individuals express trust in the government and political institutions, usually measured through a specific series of survey questions.

TABLE 6–4 Trends in Political Trust

QUESTION: How much of the time do you think you can trust the government in Washington to do what is right—just about always, most of the time, or only some of the time?

	1972	1976	1978	1980	1982	1984	1986	1988	1990	1992	1994	1996	1998	2000	2002	2006
Percentage saying:																
Always/ Most of the time	53	33	29	25	32	46	42	44	27	23	20	25	34	40	46	32
Some of the time	45	63	67	73	64	51	55	54	73	75	79	71	66	59	52	64

Sources: *New York Times*/CBS News Surveys; University of Michigan Survey Research Center, National Election Studies; Pew Research Center for the People and the Press; Council for Excellence in Government; *Washington Post* poll, September 25–27, 2001; and Gallup polls, Fall 2002, 2004, 2006, and 2008.

[17]As reported in *Public Perspective*, March/April 2002, p. 11, summarizing the results of Gallup/CNN/*USA Today* polls conducted between November 11 and December 10, 2000.

BEYOND OUR B RDERS

WORLD OPINION OF THE UNITED STATES

In the immediate aftermath of the September 11, 2001, terrorist attacks, most of the world expressed a great deal of sympathy toward the United States. Few nations objected to the subsequent American invasion of Afghanistan in 2001 to oust the Taliban government or to the Bush administration's vow to hunt down the terrorists responsible for the 9/11 attacks. When the United States announced plans to invade Iraq in 2003, however, world opinion was not supportive. By 2006, world opinion had become decidedly anti-American, as the United States' ongoing "war on terrorism" continued to offend other nations.

NEGATIVE VIEWS OF AMERICAN UNILATERALISM

The invasion of Iraq in 2003 marked a key turning point in world public opinion toward the United States. Most nations opposed the United States' plan to attack Iraq. They were supportive of continuing inspections by the United Nations and did not agree that Iraq was a sponsor of terrorism. The willingness of American leaders to ignore world opinion with regard to the Iraq situation led to charges of arrogance on the part of the U.S. administration.

Between 2003 and 2007, the Pew Global Attitudes Project conducted surveys of public opinion in more than 40 nations. By 2007, attitudes toward the United States had declined in many regions of the world. For example, the percentage of Canadians who had a favorable view of the United States fell from 71 percent in 2000 to 55 percent in 2007. Declines in favorable views were also found in Western Europe and in some South American countries. While the publics in many former Soviet states had been very supportive of the United States, their favorable views also declined during this period, although not as severely as in Western Europe.

ARAB AND MUSLIM OPINION TOWARD AMERICA AND ITS IDEALS

Among the majority of Middle Eastern states, approval of the United States is especially low among Muslims. This is true in such states as Egypt, Jordan, Pakistan, and Malaysia. There are, however, divisions even among Muslims based on religious views. Sunni Muslims in Lebanon are much more favorably inclined toward the United States than are their Shia countrymen. Many Muslim nations and their peoples are opposed to the United States' action in Iraq and continued aggressive stance toward Iran. While those nations may not support the current regimes, they are more worried that the United States has destabilized the region, and they continue to see the United States as too supportive of the state of Israel. It is worth noting, however, that most Muslim states in Africa have favorable opinions of the United States.*

Many Arabs and Muslims resent the United States' interventionism and presence in the Middle East. This does not mean that they reject all aspects of the United States or its ideals, however. The majority of Muslims do not support religious extremism or terrorism in their own nations. Nor are Arabs and Muslims dismissive of democracy. Recent polls have shown declining support for terrorist groups among Arabs and Muslims, with only 13 percent of Moroccans and 25 percent of Pakistani Muslims expressing positive views toward terrorism. There has also been broad support for democracy in the Middle East. Many individuals believe that democracy is a real possibility in their own country. Indeed, 83 percent of Lebanese and 80 percent of Jordanians believe that democracy could work in their respective nations. However, many are still suspicious of American motives in the region.

FOR CRITICAL ANALYSIS

1. How might the United States reverse its negative image in the world?
2. Some polls have shown that younger Muslims and Arabs have a more positive opinion toward the United States. Why might that be the case?

*The Pew Global Attitudes Project, 2007 Survey, www.pewglobal .org.

in world affairs with many allies. In recent years, however, world opinion toward the United States has soured, as discussed in this chapter's *Beyond Our Borders* feature.

PUBLIC OPINION ABOUT GOVERNMENT

A vital component of public opinion in the United States is the considerable ambivalence with which the public regards many major national institutions. Table 6–5 shows trends from 1983 to 2006 in opinion polls asking respondents, at regularly spaced intervals, how much confidence they had in the institutions listed. Over the years, military and religious organizations have ranked highest. Note, however, the decline in confidence in churches in 2002 following a substantial number of sex-abuse allegations against Catholic priests. Note also the somewhat heightened regard for the military after the first Gulf War in 1991. Since that time, the public has consistently had more confidence in the military than in any of the other institutions shown in Table 6–5. In 2002 and 2003, confidence in the military soared even higher, most likely because Americans recognized the central role being played by the military in the war on terrorism.

The United States Supreme Court and the banking industry have scored well over time. Less confidence is expressed in newspapers, television, big business, and organized labor. In 1991, following a scandal involving congressional banking practices, confidence in Congress fell to a record low of 18 percent. Confidence in Congress has yet to return to the levels reported in the 1970s and 1980s.

At times, popular confidence in all institutions may rise or fall, reflecting optimism or pessimism about the general state of the nation. For example, between 1979 and 1981, there was a collapse of confidence affecting most institutions. This reflected public dissatisfaction with the handling of the hostage crisis in Iran and with some of the

TABLE 6–5 Confidence in Institutions Trend

QUESTION: I am going to read a list of institutions in American society. Would you please tell me how much confidence you, yourself, have in each one—a great deal, quite a lot, some, or very little?

	PERCENTAGE SAYING "A GREAT DEAL" OR "QUITE A LOT"													
	1983	1985	1987	1989	1991	1993	1995	1997	1999	2001	2003	2005	2007	2008
Military	53	61	61	63	69	67	64	60	68	66	82	74	69	71
Church or organized religion	62	66	61	52	56	53	57	56	58	60	50	53	46	48
Banks	51	51	51	42	30	38	43	41	43	44	50	49	41	32
U.S. Supreme Court	42	56	52	46	39	43	44	50	49	50	47	41	34	32
Public schools	39	48	50	43	35	39	40	40	36	38	40	37	33	33
Television news	25	29	28	NA	24	21	33	34	34	34	35	28	23	24
Newspapers	38	35	31	NA	32	31	30	35	33	36	33	28	22	24
Congress	28	39	NA	32	18	19	21	22	26	26	29	22	14	12
Organized labor	26	28	26	NA	22	26	26	23	28	26	28	24	19	20
Big business	28	31	NA	NA	22	23	21	28	30	28	22	22	18	20

NA = Not asked.
Source: Gallup poll, May 21–23, 2004, June 11–14, 2007, June 9–12, 2008.

highest levels of inflation in U.S. history. Some of this confidence was restored by 1985, however, when conditions had improved.

Although people may not have much confidence in government institutions, they nonetheless turn to government to solve what they perceive to be the major problems facing the country. Table 6–6, which is based on Gallup polls conducted from the years 1977 to 2008, shows that the leading problems have changed over time. The public tends to emphasize problems that are immediate and that have been the subject of many stories in the media. When coverage of a particular problem increases suddenly, the public is more likely to see that as the most important problem. Thus, the fluctuations in the "most important problem" cited in Table 6–6 may, in part, be attributed to media agenda-setting. In recent years, the economy and jobs, gas and the heating oil crisis, and the war in Iraq have reached the top of the list.

PUBLIC OPINION AND POLICY MAKING

If public opinion is important for democracy, are policy makers really responsive to public opinion? A study by political scientists Benjamin I. Page and Robert Y. Shapiro suggests that in fact the national government is very responsive to the public's demands for action.[18] In looking at changes in public opinion poll results over time, Page and Shapiro show that when the public supports a policy change, the following occurs: policy changes in a direction consistent with the change in public opinion 43 percent of the time; policy changes in a direction opposite to the change in opinion 22 percent of the time; and policy does not change at all 33 percent of the time. Page and Shapiro also

TABLE 6–6 Most Important Problem Trend, 1977 to Present

1977	High cost of living, unemployment	1993	Health care, budget deficit
1978	High cost of living, energy problems	1994	Crime, violence, health care
1979	High cost of living, energy problems	1995	Crime, violence
1980	High cost of living, unemployment	1996	Budget deficit
1981	High cost of living, unemployment	1997	Crime, violence
1982	Unemployment, high cost of living	1998	Crime, violence
1983	Unemployment, high cost of living	1999	Crime, violence
1984	Unemployment, fear of war	2000	Morals, family decline
1985	Fear of war, unemployment	2001	Economy, education
1986	Unemployment, budget deficit	2002	Terrorism, economy
1987	Unemployment, economy	2003	Terrorism, economy
1988	Economy, budget deficit	2004	War in Iraq, economy
1989	War on drugs	2005	War in Iraq
1990	War in Middle East	2006	War in Iraq, gas prices
1991	Economy	2007	Iraq, economy
1992	Unemployment, budget deficit	2008	Economy, jobs

Sources: *New York Times*/CBS News poll, July 2008; and Gallup polls, 2000 through 2008.

....

[18]See the extensive work of Page and Shapiro in Benjamin I. Page and Robert Y. Shapiro, *The Rational Public: Fifty Years of Trends in Americans' Policy Preferences* (Chicago: University of Chicago Press, 1992).

show, as should be no surprise, that when public opinion changes dramatically—say, by 20 percentage points rather than by just six or seven percentage points—government policy is much more likely to follow changing public attitudes.

Setting Limits on Government Action. Although opinion polls cannot give exact guidance on what the government should do in a specific instance, the opinions measured in polls do set an informal limit on government action. For example, consider the highly controversial issue of abortion. Most Americans are moderates on this issue; they do not approve of abortion as a means of birth control, but they do feel that it should be available under certain circumstances. Yet sizable groups of people express very intense feelings both for and against legalized abortion. Given this distribution of opinion, most elected officials would rather not try to change policy to favor either of the extreme positions. To do so would clearly violate the opinion of the majority of Americans. In this case, as in many others, *public opinion does not make public policy; rather, it restrains officials from taking truly unpopular actions.* If officials do act in the face of public opposition, the consequences will be determined at the ballot box.

To what degree should public opinion influence policy making? It would appear that members of the public view this issue differently than do policy leaders. The results of a recent poll about polls showed that whereas 68 percent of the public feel that public opinion should have a great deal of influence on policy, only 43 percent of policy leaders hold this opinion.[19] Why would a majority of policy leaders *not* want to be strongly influenced by public opinion? One answer to this question is that public opinion polls can provide only a limited amount of guidance to policy makers.

The Limits of Polling. Policy makers cannot always be guided by opinion polls. In the end, politicians must make their own choices. When they do so, their choices necessarily involve trade-offs. If politicians vote for increased spending to improve education, for example, by necessity there must be fewer resources available for other worthy projects.

Individuals who are polled do not have to make such trade-offs when they respond to questions. Indeed, survey respondents usually are not even given a choice of trade-offs in their policy opinions. Pollsters typically ask respondents whether they want more or less spending in a particular area, such as education. Rarely, though, is a dollar amount assigned. Additionally, broad poll questions often provide little guidance for policy makers. What does it mean if a majority of those polled want "free" medical treatment for everyone in need? Obviously, medical care is never free. Certain individuals may receive medical care free of charge, but society as a whole has to pay for it. In short, polling questions usually do not reflect the cost of any particular policy choice. Moreover, to make an informed policy choice requires an understanding not only of the policy area but also of the consequences of any given choice. Virtually no public opinion polls make sure that those polled have such information.

Finally, government decisions cannot be made simply by adding up individual desires. Politicians engage in a type of "horse trading." All politicians know that they cannot satisfy every desire of every constituent. Therefore, each politician attempts to maximize the net benefits to his or her constituents, while keeping within whatever the politician believes the government can afford.

---

[19]Mollyann Brodie et al., "Polling and Democracy: The Will of the People," *Public Perspective*, July/August 2001, pp. 10–14.

You can make a difference

BEING A CRITICAL CONSUMER OF OPINION POLLS

Americans are inundated with the results of public opinion polls. The polls purport to tell us a variety of things: whether the president's popularity is up or down, whether gun control is more in favor now than previously, or who is leading the pack for the next presidential nomination. What must be kept in mind with this blizzard of information is that all poll results are not equally good or equally believable.

WHY SHOULD YOU CARE?

As a critical consumer, you need to be aware of what makes one set of public opinion poll results valid and other results useless or even dangerously misleading. Knowing what makes a poll accurate is especially important if you plan to participate actively in politics. Successful participation depends on accurate information, and that includes knowing what your fellow citizens are thinking. If large numbers of other people really agree with you that a particular policy needs to be changed, there may be a good chance that the policy can actually be altered. If almost no one agrees with you on a particular issue, there may be no point in trying to change policy immediately; the best you can do is to try to sway the opinions of others, in the hope that someday enough people will agree with you to make policy changes possible.

WHAT CAN YOU DO?

Pay attention only to opinion polls that are based on scientific, or random, samples. In these so-called *probability samples*, a known probability is used to select each person interviewed. Do not give credence to the results of opinion polls that consist of shopping-mall interviews or the like. The main problem with this kind of opinion taking is that not everyone has an equal chance of being in the mall when the interview takes place. Also, it is almost certain that the people in the mall are not a reasonable cross section of a community's entire population.

Sometimes, even the most experienced pollsters have unreliable results. The "science" counted on for the 2008 presidential primary polling produced results that were wrong by wide margins. The evening before Super Tuesday 2008, the Reuters/C-SPAN/Zogby poll had Democrat Barack Obama with a 13-point lead over Hillary Clinton in the California primary. This same poll had Republican Mitt Romney with a seven-point lead over John McCain. The final voting results in the California primary showed Clinton ahead of Obama by nine points; McCain held off Romney by almost eight. What happened?

Experts felt there were many reasons that caused such faulty results. The science of political polling tries to create a microcosm of the electorate; 833 Republicans and 895 Democrats were contacted and identified as "likely to vote." Apparently, the sample included too few Latinos and too many younger voters. Also, the "refusal rate" of people unwilling to talk to pollsters is rising. Pollsters have no way of knowing if these refusing voters represent the views of the majority. The 24/7 news cycle also influences the process. Results in the New Hampshire primary demonstrated that up to 15 percent of the voters decided over the weekend before the actual election. Pollsters missed most of those deciders. Many pollsters felt that voters were deciding, especially in the California Democratic primary, in the last 24 hours, making polls conducted days before irrelevant.*

Pay attention as well to how people were contacted for the poll—by mail, by telephone, in person in their homes, or in some other way (such as via the Internet). Because of its lower cost, polling firms have turned more and more to telephone interviewing. This method can produce highly accurate results. Its disadvantage is that telephone interviews typically need to be short and to deal with questions that are fairly easy to answer. Interviews in person are better for getting useful information about why a particular response was given. They take much longer to complete, however. Results from mailed questionnaires should be taken with a grain of salt. Usually, only a small percentage of people send them back.

When viewers or listeners of television or radio shows are encouraged to call in their opinions to an 800 telephone number, the polling results are meaningless. Users of the Internet also have an easy way to make their views known. Only people who own computers and are interested in the topic will take the trouble to respond, however, and that group is not representative of the general public.

*John Diaz, "Why the Polls Are So Wrong," *San Francisco Chronicle*, February 24, 2008, p. G4.

KEY TERMS

agenda setting 223	media 223	political trust 239
consensus 220	nonopinion 220	public opinion 219
divisive opinion 220	opinion leader 223	sampling error 233
gender gap 228	opinion poll 231	socioeconomic status 224
generational effect 223	peer group 222	Watergate break-in 224
lifestyle effect 223	political socialization 220	

CHAPTER SUMMARY

1. Public opinion is the aggregate of individual attitudes or beliefs shared by some portion of the adult population. A consensus exists when a large proportion of the public appears to express the same view on an issue. Divisive opinion exists when the public holds widely different attitudes on an issue. Sometimes, a poll shows a distribution of opinion indicating that most people either have no information about an issue or are not interested enough in the issue to form a position on it.

2. People's opinions are formed through the political socialization process. Important factors in this process are the family, educational experiences, peer groups, opinion leaders, the media, and political events. The influence of the media as a socialization factor may be growing relative to the family. Voting behavior is influenced by demographic factors such as education, economic status, religion, race and ethnicity, gender, and region. It is also influenced by election-specific factors such as party identification, perception of the candidates, and issue preferences.

3. Most descriptions of public opinion are based on the results of opinion polls. The accuracy of polls depends on sampling techniques that include a representative sample of the population being polled and that ensure randomness in the selection of respondents.

4. Problems with polls include sampling errors (which may occur when the pool of respondents is not chosen in a scientific manner), the difficulty of knowing the degree to which responses are influenced by the type and order of questions asked, the use of a yes/no format for answers to the questions, and the interviewer's techniques. Many are concerned about the use of "push polls" (in which the questions "push" the respondent toward a particular candidate).

5. Advances in technology have changed polling techniques over the years. During the 1970s, telephone polling came to be widely used. Today, largely because of extensive telemarketing, people often refuse to answer calls, and nonresponse rates in telephone polling have skyrocketed. Due to the difficulty of obtaining a random sample in the online environment, Internet polls are often "nonpolls." Whether Internet polls can overcome this problem remains to be seen.

6. Public opinion affects the political process in many ways. The political culture provides a general environment of support for the political system, allowing the nation to weather periods of crisis. The political culture also helps Americans to evaluate their government's performance. At times, the level of trust in government has been relatively high; at other times, the level of trust has declined steeply. Similarly, Americans' confidence in government institutions varies over time, depending on a number of circumstances. Generally, though, Americans turn to government to solve what they perceive to be the major problems facing the country. In 2008, Americans ranked the economy and jobs, the war in Iraq, and gas and the heating oil crisis as the three most significant problems facing the nation.

7. Public opinion also plays an important role in policy making. Although polling data show that a majority of Americans would like policy leaders to be influenced to a great extent by public opinion, politicians cannot always be guided by opinion polls. This is because the respondents often do not understand the costs and consequences of policy decisions or the trade-offs involved in making such decisions. An important function of public opinion is to set limits on government action through public pressure.

SELECTED PRINT AND MEDIA RESOURCES

SUGGESTED READINGS

Asher, Herbert. *Polling and the Public: What Every Citizen Should Know.* Washington, DC: CQ Press, 2004. This clearly written and often entertaining book explains what polls are, how they are conducted and interpreted, and how the wording and ordering of survey questions, as well as the interviewer's techniques, can significantly affect the respondents' answers.

Bardes, Barbara A., and Robert W. Oldendick. *Public Opinion: Measuring the American Mind,* 3rd ed. Belmont, CA: Wadsworth, 2006. This examination of public opinion polling looks at the uses of public opinion data and recent technological issues in polling in addition to providing excellent coverage of public opinion on important issues over a period of decades.

Berinsky, Adam J. *Silent Voices: Public Opinion and Political Participation in America.* Princeton, NJ: Princeton University Press, 2004. Berinsky argues that people who do not respond to survey questions may differ significantly from those who do.

Bishop, George F. *The Illusion of Public Opinion: Fact and Artifact in American Public Opinion Polling.* Lanham, MD: Rowman and Littlefield, 2005. This book presents a serious critique of the construction of polls and the use of polling data. Bishop investigates the effects of question wording and other factors on the reliability of results.

Green, John C. *The Faith Factor: How Religion Influences American Elections.* New York: Praeger, 2007. Written by one of the leading researchers in the area of politics and religion, Green shows how the impact of religious belief and practice on elections has changed in the last decades.

Lynch, Marc. *Voices of the New Arab Public: Iraq, al-Jazeera, and Middle East Politics Today.* New York: Columbia University Press, 2006. The author takes an in-depth look at how al-Jazeera and other Arab satellite television stations have transformed Middle Eastern politics over the past decade. Lynch also discusses how this new era of political socialization has affected relations with the United States.

Newport, Frank. *Polling Matters: Why Leaders Must Listen to the Wisdom of the People.* New York: Warner Books, 2004. Newport, the editor-in-chief of the Gallup Poll, offers a spirited defense of the polling process. Newport believes that polls reflect the country's collective wisdom, and he disputes the argument that citizens are too uninformed to offer useful opinions.

MEDIA RESOURCES

Faith and Politics: The Christian Right—This 1995 documentary was hosted by Dan Rather and produced by CBS News. It focuses on the efforts of the Christian conservative movement to affect educational curriculums and public policy. Members of the Christian right who are interviewed include Ralph Reed and Gary Bauer. Critics of the Christian right who are interviewed include Senator Arlen Specter.

Vox Populi: Democracy in Crisis—A PBS special focusing on why public confidence in government, which has plummeted during recent decades, still has not recovered.

Wag the Dog—A 1997 film that provides a very cynical look at the importance of public opinion. The film, which features Dustin Hoffman and Robert De Niro, follows the efforts of a presidential political consultant, who stages a foreign policy crisis to divert public opinion from a sex scandal in the White House.

ONLINE POLLING AND POLL DATA

News organizations, interest groups, not-for-profit groups, and online e-zines are now using online polling to gather the opinions of their readers and viewers. All the user has to do is log on to the Web site and click on the box indicating the preferred response. People can respond to online polls more easily than to call-in polls, and in most cases, they are free to the user. Realize, though, that online polls are totally nonscientific, because the respondents are all self-selected. Essentially, Internet polls are pseudo-polls because only those who choose to do so respond, making the polls much more likely to be biased and based on an unrepresentative sample.

At the same time, the Internet is an excellent source for finding reliable polling reports and data. All of the major polling organizations have Web sites that include news releases about polls they have conducted. Some sites make the polling data available for free to users; others require that a user pay a subscription fee before accessing the polling archives on the site.

LOGGING ON

- Yale University Library, one of the world's great research institutions, offers access to social science libraries and information services. If you want to browse through library sources of public opinion data, this is an interesting site to visit. Go to:
  www.library.yale.edu/socsci/opinion
- According to its home page, the mission of American Election Studies (ANES) "is to produce high-quality data on voting, public opinion, and political participation that serves the research needs of social scientists, teachers, students, and policy makers concerned with understanding the theoretical and empirical founda-

tions of mass politics in a democratic society." This is a good place to obtain information on public opinion. Find it at:
  www.electionstudies.org
- The Polling Report Web site offers polls and their results organized by topic. It is up to date and easy to use:
  www.pollingreport.com
- The Gallup organization's Web site offers not only polling data (although a user must pay a subscription fee to obtain access to many polling reports) but also information on how polls are constructed, conducted, and interpreted. Go to:
  www.gallup.com
- For the most up-to-date poll results and political commentary on any elections as well as an archive of past political polls, go to:
  www.realclearpolitics.com

ONLINE REVIEW

At **www.cengage.com/politicalscience/schmidt/agandpt14e**, you will find a Tutorial Quiz for this chapter providing questions on the chapter contents, including the features. The questions are organized to match the major sections of the chapter. You'll have access to other helpful study tools, including the book's glossary and flashcards, crossword puzzles, and Web links, as well as "Which Side Are You On?" and "Politics and . . ." features written by the authors of the book.

CHAPTER (7)

Congressman Bennie Thompson, a Democrat from Mississippi, is the target of lobbyists Jake James (representing the AFL-CIO) and Samuel L. Maury (of the Business Round-table). James is opposing opening trade with China while Maury is supporting it. (Scott J. Ferrell/Newscom)

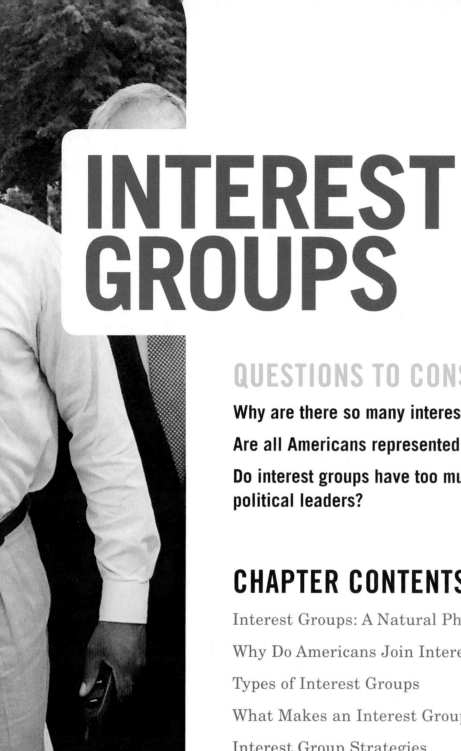

INTEREST GROUPS

Making a DIFFERENCE

LOBBY U

When you hear the word *lobbyist*, do you think of a representative of your college or university? Though you likely do not associate lobbying with your school, almost every institution of higher education (especially public institutions) has an office on campus, and sometimes in Washington, D.C., that actively lobbies government. Usually named government affairs or government relations, these offices are responsible for making sure that the interests of the school are best advocated to those in elective office.

These efforts can take many forms. Often, these offices serve as communication hubs between the university community and the politicians. For example, through Web sites, newsletters, and e-mail updates, politicians alert faculty, staff, students, and alumni when the state legislature or Congress is working on legislation that affects the school. This legislation might be budgetary or regulatory policy or issues pertaining to financial aid or student athletes. If university officials are traveling to Washington, D.C., government relations officers help prepare them and often accompany them on their trips, introducing them to influential members of Congress.

Governmental affairs offices also help keep their schools on the minds of lawmakers. For example, the Massachusetts Institute of Technology (MIT) informs members of Congress when someone from their district has been admitted to MIT.[a] This helps publicize the school to members of Congress. Sometimes government affairs

---

Interest Group
An organized group of individuals sharing common objectives who actively attempt to influence policy makers.

Lobbyist
An organization or individual who attempts to influence legislation and the administrative decisions of government.

BUSINESSES, ENVIRONMENTALISTS, oil drillers, older Americans, African American organizations, doctors, dentists, Native American tribes, colleges and universities, and foreign governments all try to influence the political leaders and policy-making processes of the United States. The structure of American government invites the participation of **interest groups** at various stages of the policy-making process. One reason why so many different types of interest groups and other organized institutions attempt to influence our government is the many opportunities for them to do so. Interest groups can hire **lobbyists** to try to influence members of the House of Representatives, the Senate or any of its committees, or the president or any of his officials. They can file briefs at the Supreme Court or challenge regulations issued by federal agencies. As noted in the *Making a Difference* feature, even colleges and universities and students lobby the government to gain favorable legislation or appropriations. This ease of access to the government is sometimes known as the "multiple cracks" view of our political system. Interests and groups can penetrate the political system through many, many entry points, and, as we will note, their right to do so is protected by the Constitution.

INTEREST GROUPS: A NATURAL PHENOMENON

Alexis de Tocqueville observed in 1834 that "in no country of the world has the principle of association been more successfully used or applied to a greater multitude of objec-

offices work in conjunction with (or are housed with) the public affairs arm of the school. This allows regular, targeted use of press releases to members of Congress to inform them of how the college or university is using tax dollars.

Some government relations offices even organize trips to the nation's capital for their alumni. The University of Missouri hosts a Legislative Day. In addition to providing a schedule of events and contact information for members of Congress, they guide the participants in the following ins and outs of meeting a member of Congress:

- When entering the congressional office, identify yourself as an alumnus of the school.
- Ask to speak with the member of Congress or the legislative aid.
- Keep the discussion focused around the talking points, which are a list of issues of concern to the alumnus. This might be funding for research, or scholarships, or increased access to financial aid.
- Be patient, courteous, and appreciative. Send a follow-up thank-you note.
- There is even a school rally in the Capitol Rotunda![b]

Apart from the efforts of individual colleges and universities, there are student lobbying organizations. The United States Students Association, a student-led advocacy organization, has been in existence since 1947. With its roots in union organizing, this organization has over time been associated with anti-McCarthyism, various student activism efforts in the 1960s, and now characterizes itself as a broad-based progressive advocacy group.[c] Its efforts include lobbying conferences and Lobby Days in Washington, D.C., in which its members learn advocacy and lobbying techniques; attempts to increase voting among young people; and various diversity projects aimed at making higher education accessible to all groups.[d]

[a]http://web.mit.edu/annualreports/pres05/01.03.pdf
[b]www.umsystem.edu/ums/departments/gr/events/index.shtml
[c]www.usstudents.org/who-we-are/history
[d]www.usstudents.org/our-work

---

tives than in America."[1] The French traveler was amazed at the degree to which Americans formed groups to solve civic problems, establish social relationships, and speak for their economic or political interests. James Madison, when he wrote *Federalist Paper No. 10* (see Appendix B), foresaw the importance of having multiple organizations in the political system. He supported the creation of a large republic with many states to encourage the formation of multiple interests. The multitude of interests, in Madison's view, would protect minority views against the formation of an oppressive majority interest. Madison's belief in the power of groups to protect a democracy was echoed centuries later by the work of Robert A. Dahl,[2] a contributor to the pluralist theory of politics, as discussed in Chapter 1. Pluralism sees the political struggle pitting different groups against each other to reach a compromise in the public interest.

Surely, neither Madison nor de Tocqueville foresaw the formation of more than 100,000 associations in the United States. Poll data show that more than two-thirds of all Americans belong to at least one group or association. Although the majority of these affiliations could not be classified as interest groups in the political sense, Americans do understand the principles of working in groups.

Today, interest groups range from elementary school parent-teacher associations and the local "Stop the Sewer Plant Association" to statewide associations of insurance agents. They include small groups such as local environmental organizations

ALEXIS DE TOCQUEVILLE (1805–1859), a French social historian and traveler, commented on Americans' predilection for joining groups. (Réunion des Musées Nationaux/Art Resource, NY)

[1]Alexis de Tocqueville, *Democracy in America*, Vol. 1, edited by Phillips Bradley (New York: Knopf, 1980), p. 191.
[2]Robert A. Dahl, *Who Governs? Democracy and Power in an American City* (New Haven, CT: Yale University Press, 1961).

STAFFERS, LOBBYISTS, and reporters wait in a Capitol hallway outside a Senate Finance Committee hearing. (Scott J. Ferrell/Newscom)

and national groups such as the Boy Scouts of America, the American Civil Liberties Union, the National Education Association, and the American League of Lobbyists. The continuing increase in the number of groups that lobby governments and the multiple ways in which they are involved in the political process has been seen by some scholars as a detriment to an effective government. Sometimes called *hyperpluralism*, the ability of interest groups to mandate policy or to defeat policies needed by the nation may work against the public good.[3]

INTEREST GROUPS AND SOCIAL MOVEMENTS

Social Movement
A movement that represents the demands of a large segment of the public for political, economic, or social change.

Interest groups are often spawned by mass **social movements**. Such movements represent demands by a large segment of the population for change in the political, economic, or social system. Social movements are often the first expression of latent discontent with the existing system. They may be the authentic voice of weaker or oppressed groups in society that do not have the means or standing to organize as interest groups. For example, most mainstream political and social leaders disapproved of the women's movement of the 1800s. Because women were unable to vote or take an active part in the political system, it was difficult for women who desired greater freedoms to organize formal groups. After the Civil War, when more women became active in professional life, the first real women's rights group, the National Woman Suffrage Association, came into being.

African Americans found themselves in an even more disadvantaged situation after the end of the Reconstruction period. They were unable to exercise their political rights in many Southern and border states, and their participation in any form of organization could lead to economic ruin, physical harassment, or even death. The civil rights movement of the 1950s and 1960s was clearly a social movement. Although the movement received support from several formal organizations—including the Southern Christian

[3]Theodore Lowi, *The End of Liberalism* (New York: W. W. Norton, 1979).

Leadership Conference, the National Association for the Advancement of Colored People, and the Urban League—only a social movement could generate the kinds of civil disobedience that took place in hundreds of towns and cities across the country.

Social movements are often precursors of interest groups. They may generate interest groups with specific goals that successfully recruit members through the incentives the group offers. In the case of the women's movement of the 1960s, the National Organization for Women was formed in part out of a demand to end gender-segregated job advertising in newspapers.

WHY SO MANY?

Whether based in a social movement or created to meet an immediate crisis, interest groups continue to form and act in American society. One reason for the multitude of interest groups is that the right to join a group is protected by the First Amendment to the U.S. Constitution (see Chapter 4). Not only are all people guaranteed the right "peaceably to assemble," but they are also guaranteed the right "to petition the Government for a redress of grievances." This constitutional provision encourages Americans to form groups and to express their opinions to the government or to their elected representatives as members of a group. Group membership makes the individual's opinions appear more powerful and strongly conveys the group's ability to vote for or against a representative.

In addition, our federal system of government provides thousands of "pressure points" for interest group activity. Americans can form groups in their neighborhoods or cities and lobby the city council and their state government. They can join statewide groups or national groups and try to influence government policy through Congress or through one of the executive agencies or cabinet departments. Representatives of giant corporations may seek to influence the president personally at social events or fundraisers. When

That at least half of all lobbyists in Washington, D.C., are women?

attempts to influence government through the executive and legislative branches fail, interest groups turn to the courts, filing suit in state or federal courts to achieve their political objectives. Pluralist theorists, as discussed in Chapter 1, point to the openness of the American political structure as a major factor in the power of groups in American politics.

WHY DO AMERICANS JOIN INTEREST GROUPS?

One puzzle that has fascinated political scientists is why some people join interest groups, whereas many others do not. Everyone has some interest that could benefit from government action. For many individuals, however, those concerns remain unorganized interests, or **latent interests**.

According to political theorist Mancur Olson,[4] it simply may not be rational for individuals to join most groups. In his classic work on this topic, Olson introduced the idea of the "collective good." This concept refers to any public benefit that, if available to any member of the community, cannot be denied to any other member, whether or not he or she participated in the effort to gain the good.

Although collective benefits are usually thought of as coming from such public goods as clean air or national defense, benefits are also bestowed by the government on subsets of the public. Price subsidies to dairy farmers and loans to college students are examples. Olson used economic theory to propose that it is not rational for interested individuals to join groups that work for group benefits. In fact, it is often more rational for the individual to wait for others to procure the benefits and then share them. How many college students, for example, join the United States Student Association, an organization that lobbies the government for increased financial aid to students? The difficulty interest groups face in recruiting members when the benefits can be obtained without joining is referred to as the **free rider problem**.

If so little incentive exists for individuals to join together, why are there thousands of interest groups lobbying in Washington? According to the logic of collective action, if the contribution of an individual *will* make a difference to the effort, then it is worth it to the individual to join. Thus, smaller groups, which seek benefits for only a small proportion of the population, are more likely to enroll members who will give time and funds to the cause. Larger groups, which represent general public interests (the women's movement or the American Civil Liberties Union, for example), will find it relatively more difficult to get individuals to join. People need an incentive—material or otherwise—to participate.

SOLIDARY INCENTIVES

Interest groups offer **solidary incentives** for their members. Solidary incentives include companionship, a sense of belonging, and the pleasure of associating with others. Although the National Audubon Society was originally founded to save the snowy egret from extinction, today most members join to learn more about birds and to meet and share their pleasure with other individuals who enjoy bird-watching as a hobby. Even though the incentive might be solidary for many members, this organization nonetheless also pursues an active political agenda, working to preserve the environment and to protect endangered species. Most members may not play any part in working toward larger, national goals

Latent Interests
Public-policy interests that are not recognized or addressed by a group at a particular time.

Free Rider Problem
The difficulty interest groups face in recruiting members when the benefits they achieve can be gained without joining the group.

DID YOU KNOW?

That the activities of interest groups at the state level have been growing much faster than in the nation's capital, with more than 44,000 registered state lobbyists in 2006 and with a growth rate of 50 percent in California, Florida, and Texas in the last 10 years?

Solidary Incentive
A reason or motive having to do with the desire to associate with others and to share with others a particular interest or hobby.

---

[4]Mancur Olson, *The Logic of Collective Action* (Cambridge, MA: Harvard University Press, 1965).

unless the organization can convince them to take political action or unless some local environmental issue arises.

MATERIAL INCENTIVES

For other individuals, interest groups offer direct **material incentives**. A case in point is AARP (formerly the American Association of Retired Persons), which provides discounts, automobile insurance, and organized travel opportunities for its members. After Congress created the prescription drug benefit program that was supported by AARP, it became one of the larger insurers under that program. Because of its exceptionally low dues ($12.50 annually) and the benefits gained through membership, AARP has become the largest—and a very powerful—interest group in the United States. AARP can claim to represent the interests of millions of senior citizens and can show that they actually have joined the group. For most seniors, the material incentives outweigh the membership costs.

Many other interest groups offer indirect material incentives for their members. Such groups as the American Dairy Association and the National Association of Automobile Dealers do not give discounts or freebies to their members, but they do offer indirect benefits and rewards by, for example, protecting the material interests of their members from government policy making that is injurious to their industry or business.

Material Incentive
A reason or motive having to do with economic benefits or opportunities.

PURPOSIVE INCENTIVES

Interest groups also offer the opportunity for individuals to pursue political, economic, or social goals through joint action. **Purposive incentives** offer individuals the satisfaction of taking action when the goals of a group correspond to their beliefs or principles. The individuals who belong to a group focusing on the abortion issue, gun control, or environmental causes, for example, do so because they feel strongly enough about the issues to support the group's work with money and time. They are also the most likely members to have come out of a social movement and see that joining the group will strengthen their influence on an issue of great personal importance.

Some scholars have argued that many people join interest groups simply for the discounts, magazine subscriptions, and other tangible benefits and are not really interested in the political positions taken by the groups. According to William P. Browne, however, research shows that people really do care about the policy stance of an interest group. Members of a group seek people who share the group's views and then ask them to join. As one group leader put it, "Getting members is about scaring the hell out of people."[5] People join the group and then feel that they are doing something about a cause that is important to them.

Purposive Incentive
A reason for supporting or participating in the activities of a group that is based on agreement with the goals of the group. For example, someone with a strong interest in human rights might have a purposive incentive to join Amnesty International.

TYPES OF INTEREST GROUPS

Thousands of groups exist to influence government. Among the major types of interest groups are those that represent the main sectors of the economy. In addition, many public-interest organizations have been formed to represent the needs of the general citizenry, including some single-issue groups. The interests of foreign governments and foreign businesses are also represented in the American political arena. The names and Web addresses of some major interest groups are shown in Tables 7–1 and 7–2.

---

[5]William P. Browne, *Groups, Interests, and U.S. Public Policy* (Washington, DC: Georgetown University Press, 1998), p. 23.

TABLE 7–1 Fortune's "Power 25"—The 25 Most Effective Interest Groups

1.	National Rifle Association of America (the NRA—opposed to gun control): www.nra.org
2.	AARP (formerly the American Association of Retired Persons): www.aarp.org
3.	National Federation of Independent Business: www.nfibonline.com
4.	American Israel Public Affairs Committee (AIPAC—a pro-Israel group): www.aipac.org
5.	American Association for Justice: www.justice.org
6.	American Federation of Labor–Congress of Industrial Organizations (the AFL-CIO—a federation of most U.S. labor unions): www.aflcio.org
7.	Chamber of Commerce of the United States of America (an association of businesses): www.uschamber.com
8.	National Beer Wholesalers Association: www.nbwa.org
9.	National Association of Realtors: www.realtor.com
10.	National Association of Manufacturers (NAM): www.nam.org
11.	National Association of Home Builders of the United States: www.nahb.org
12.	American Medical Association (the AMA—representing physicians): www.ama-assn.org
13.	American Hospital Association: www.aha.org
14.	National Education Association of the United States (the NEA—representing teachers): www.nea.org
15.	American Farm Bureau Federation (representing farmers): www.fb.org
16.	Motion Picture Association of America (representing movie studios): www.mpaa.org
17.	National Association of Broadcasters: www.nab.org
18.	National Right to Life Committee (opposed to legalized abortion): www.nrlc.org
19.	America's Health Insurance Plans: www.ahip.org
20.	National Restaurant Association: www.restaurant.org
21.	National Governors' Association: www.nga.org
22.	Recording Industry Association of America: www.riaa.com
23.	American Bankers Association: www.aba.com
24.	Pharmaceutical Research and Manufacturers of America: www.phrma.org
25.	International Brotherhood of Teamsters (a labor union): www.teamster.org

Source: *Fortune*, May 2005.

ECONOMIC INTEREST GROUPS

More interest groups are formed to represent economic interests than any other set of interests. The variety of economic interest groups mirrors the complexity of the American economy. The major sectors that seek influence in Washington, D.C., include business, agriculture, labor unions and their members, government workers, and professionals.

Business Interest Groups. Thousands of business groups and trade associations work to influence government policies that affect their respective industries. Umbrella groups represent certain types of businesses or companies that deal in a particular type of product. The U.S. Chamber of Commerce, for example, is an umbrella group that represents businesses, and the National Association of Manufacturers is an umbrella group that represents only manufacturing concerns. The American Pet Products Manufacturers Association works for the good of manufacturers of pet food, pet toys, and other pet products, as well as for pet shops. This group strongly opposes increased regulation of stores that sell animals and restrictions on importing pets. Other major organizations that represent business interests, such as the Better Business Bureaus, take positions

TABLE 7–2 Some Other Important Interest Groups (Not on Fortune's "Power 25" List)

American Civil Liberties Union (the ACLU): www.aclu.org
American Legion (a veterans' group): www.legion.org
American Library Association: www.ala.org
The American Society for the Prevention of Cruelty to Animals (the ASPCA): www.aspca.org
Amnesty International USA (promotes human rights): www.amnesty.org
Handgun Control, Inc. (favors gun control): www.bradycampaign.org
League of United Latin American Citizens (LULAC): www.lulac.org
Mothers Against Drunk Driving (MADD): www.madd.org
NARAL Pro-Choice America (formerly the National Abortion and Reproductive Rights Action League—favors legalized abortion): www.naral.org
National Association for the Advancement of Colored People (the NAACP—represents African Americans): www.naacp.org
National Audubon Society (an environmentalist group): www.audubon.org
National Gay and Lesbian Task Force: www.ngltf.org
National Organization for Women (NOW—a feminist group): www.now.org
National Urban League (a civil rights organization): www.nul.org
National Wildlife Federation: www.nwf.org
The Nature Conservancy: www.nature.org
Sierra Club (an environmentalist group): www.sierraclub.org
Veterans of Foreign Wars of the United States: www.vfw.org
World Wildlife Fund: www.wwf.org

on policies but do not actually lobby in Washington, D.C.[6]

Some business groups are decidedly more powerful than others. The U.S. Chamber of Commerce, which has more than 200,000 member companies, can bring constituent influence to bear on every member of Congress. Another powerful lobbying organization is the National Association of Manufacturers. With a staff of more than 60 people in Washington, D.C., the organization can mobilize dozens of well-educated, articulate lobbyists to work the corridors of Congress on issues of concern to its members.

Although business interest groups are likely to agree on anything that reduces government regulation or taxation, they often do not concur on the specifics of policy, and the sector has been troubled by disagreement and fragmentation within its ranks. Large corporations have been far more concerned with federal regulation of their corporate boards and insider financial arrangements, whereas small businesses lobby for tax breaks for new equipment or new employees. One of the key issues on which businesses do not agree is immigration reform. It seems obvious that businesses that employ foreign workers should be responsible for reporting illegal

VICE PRESIDENT Dick Cheney speaks about President Bush's Job and Growth Package at the U.S. Chamber of Commerce in January 2003. Do business interests have undue influence on our government's economic policies? (White House photo by David Bohrer)

[6]Charles S. Mack, *Business, Politics, and the Practice of Government Relations* (Westport, CT: Quorum Books, 1997), p. 14.

FARMERS ARE ONE of the most powerful interests in the country in part because they comprise so many constituencies and in part because most Americans want to protect our own food supply. (Gary Benson/Getty Images)

Labor Movement
Generally, the economic and political expression of working-class interests; politically, the organization of working-class interests.

immigrants, but smaller businesses, particularly in agriculture and construction, argue that checking everyone's immigration status and reporting to the government would be a heavy and expensive burden to bear. Large corporations that are normally under much greater governmental scrutiny and have very professional employment practices comply with immigration rules for their own good.

Business groups and trade associations used to lobby at cross-purposes because they had no way to coordinate their messages. Faced with increasing efforts by organized labor to support Democratic candidates for Congress, business interests agreed in 1996 to form "the Coalition," an informal organization that raises funds specifically to help Republican candidates for Congress.[7]

Agricultural Interest Groups. American farmers and their employees represent less than 2 percent of the U.S. population. Nevertheless, farmers' influence on legislation beneficial to their interests has been significant. Farmers have succeeded in their aims because they have very strong interest groups. They are geographically dispersed and therefore have many representatives and senators to speak for them.

The American Farm Bureau Federation, established in 1919, has several million members (many of whom are not actually farmers) and is usually seen as conservative. It was instrumental in getting government guarantees of "fair" prices during the Great Depression in the 1930s.[8] Another important agricultural interest organization is the National Farmers' Union (NFU), which is considered more liberal. As farms have become larger and agribusiness has become a way of life, single-issue farm groups have emerged. The American Dairy Association, the Peanut Growers Group, and the National Soybean Association, for example, work to support their respective farmers and associated businesses. In recent years, agricultural interest groups have become active on many new issues. Among other things, they have opposed immigration restrictions and are very involved in international trade matters as they seek new markets. One of the newest agricultural groups is the American Farmland Trust, which supports policies to conserve farmland and protect natural resources.

As proof of how powerful the agricultural lobby still is in the United States, in May 2002 President George W. Bush signed the Farm Security and Rural Investment Act, which authorized the largest agricultural subsidy in U.S. history.

Labor Interest Groups. Interest groups representing the **labor movement** date back to at least 1886, when the American Federation of Labor (AFL) was formed. In 1955, the AFL joined forces with the Congress of Industrial Organizations (CIO). Today, the combined AFL-CIO is a large union with a membership of nearly 9 million workers and an active political arm called the Committee on Political Education. In a sense, the AFL-CIO is a union of unions.

_____

[7]H. R. Mahood, _Interest Groups in American National Politics: An Overview_ (New York: Prentice Hall, 2000), p. 34.
[8]The Agricultural Adjustment Act of 1933 (declared unconstitutional) was replaced by the 1938 Agricultural Adjustment Act and later changed and amended several times.

The AFL-CIO experienced severe discord within its ranks during 2005, however, when four key unions left the federation and formed the Change to Win Coalition. The new Change to Win Coalition represents about one-third of the 13 million workers who formerly belonged to the AFL-CIO. Many labor advocates fear that the split will further weaken organized labor's waning political influence. The role of unions in American society has declined in recent decades, as witnessed by the decrease in union membership (see Figure 7–1). In the age of automation and with the rise of the **service sector**, blue-collar workers in basic industries (autos, steel, and the like) represent an increasingly smaller percentage of the total working population. However, in 2007, the number of workers who were members of a union increased by 311,000, which kept the percentage of workers in the United States who are represented by a union steady at 12 percent.

Because of this decline in the industrial sector of the economy, national unions are looking to nontraditional areas for their membership, including migrant farm workers, service workers, and, most recently, public employees—such as police officers, fire-fighting personnel, and teachers, including college professors and graduate assistants. Public-sector unions are the fastest-growing labor organizations.

Although the proportion of the workforce that belongs to a union has declined over the years, American labor unions have not given up their efforts to support sympathetic candidates for Congress or for state office. Currently, the AFL-CIO, under the leadership of John J. Sweeney, has a large political budget, which it uses to help Democratic candidates nationwide. Although interest groups that favor Republicans continue to assist their candidates, the efforts of labor are more sustained and more targeted. Labor offers a candidate (such as Democratic presidential candidate Barack Obama) a corps of volunteers in addition to campaign contributions. A massive turnout by labor union members in critical elections can significantly increase the final vote totals for Democratic candidates.

Service Sector
The sector of the economy that provides services—such as health care, banking, and education—in contrast to the sector that produces goods.

FIGURE 7–1 Decline in Union Membership, 1948 to Present

As shown in this figure, the percentage of the total workforce that is represented by labor unions has declined precipitously over the last 40 years. Note, however, that in contrast to the decline in union representation in the private sector, the percentage of government workers who are unionized has increased significantly since about 1960.

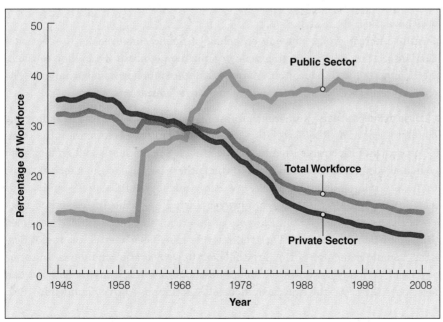

Source: Bureau of Labor Statistics, 2008.

MEMBERS OF THE OPERATING Engineers, Laborers, and Carpenters unions protest the policies of a construction company, claiming that this company's actions are undermining union wages and benefits. Labor unions have wielded considerable political power since the early 1900s. Why has that power declined somewhat in recent years? (AP Photo/The Capital Times/David Sandell)

Public Employee Unions. The degree of unionization in the private sector has declined since 1965, but this has been partially offset by growth in the unionization of public employees. Figure 7–1 displays the growth in public-sector unionization. With a total membership of more than 7.1 million, public-sector unions are likely to continue expanding.

Both the American Federation of State, County, and Municipal Employees and the American Federation of Teachers are members of the AFL-CIO's Public Employee Department. Over the years, public-employee unions have become quite militant and are often involved in strikes. Most of these strikes are illegal, because almost no public employees have the right to strike.

A powerful interest group lobbying on behalf of public employees is the National Education Association (NEA), a nationwide organization of about 2.8 million teachers and others connected with education. Many NEA locals function as labor unions. The NEA lobbies intensively for increased public funding of education.

Interest Groups of Professionals. Numerous professional organizations exist, including the American Bar Association, the Association of General Contractors of America, the Institute of Electrical and Electronic Engineers, and others. Some professional groups, such as lawyers and doctors, are more influential than others because of their social status. Lawyers have a unique advantage, because many members of Congress share their profession. Interest groups that represent lawyers include both the American Bar Association and the Association of Trial Lawyers of America, which has recently renamed itself the Association for Justice.[9] The trial lawyers have been very active in political campaigns, usually being one of the larger donors to Democratic candidates. In terms of money spent on lobbying, however, one professional organization stands head and shoulders above the rest—the American Medical Association (AMA). Founded in 1847,

[9]www.opensecrets.org

THE PRESIDENT of the organization Unidad Honduruena, or Honduran Unity, counsels a young immigrant about taking the proper step to keep his temporary protected status. In this case, an interest group formed to protect nonvoters. How can such an interest group leverage its power when it does not represent voters? (AP Photo/Wilfredo Lee)

it is now affiliated with more than 2,000 local and state medical societies and has a total membership of about 300,000.

The Unorganized Poor. Some have argued that the system of interest group politics leaves out poor Americans or U.S. residents who are not citizens and cannot vote. Americans who are disadvantaged economically cannot afford to join interest groups; if they are members of the working poor, they may hold two or more jobs just to survive, leaving them no time to participate in interest groups. Other groups in the population—including non-English-speaking groups, resident aliens, single parents, disabled Americans, and younger voters—probably do not have the time or expertise even to find out what group might represent them. Consequently, some scholars suggest that interest groups and lobbyists are the privilege of upper-middle-class Americans and those who belong to unions or other special groups.

R. Allen Hays examines the plight of poor Americans in his book *Who Speaks for the Poor?*[10] Hays studied groups and individuals who have lobbied for public housing and other issues related to the poor and concluded that the poor depend largely on indirect representation. Most efforts on behalf of the poor come from a policy network of groups—including public housing officials, welfare workers and officials, religious groups, public-interest groups, and some liberal general-interest groups—that speak loudly and persistently for the poor. Poor Americans remain outside the interest group network and have little direct voice of their own.

ENVIRONMENTAL GROUPS

Environmental interest groups are not new. We have already mentioned the National Audubon Society, which was founded in 1905 to protect the snowy egret from the commercial demand for hat decorations. The patron of the Sierra Club, John Muir, worked for the creation of national parks more than a century ago. But the blossoming of national environmental groups with mass memberships did not occur until the 1970s. Since the first Earth Day, organized in 1970, many interest groups have sprung up to

[10]R. Allen Hays, *Who Speaks for the Poor?* (New York: Routledge, 2001).

protect the environment in general or unique ecological niches. The groups range from the National Wildlife Federation, with a membership of more than 5 million and an emphasis on education, to the more elite Environmental Defense Fund, with a membership of 300,000 and a focus on influencing federal policy. Other groups include the Nature Conservancy, which uses members' contributions to buy up threatened natural areas and either give them to state or local governments or manage them itself, and the more radical Greenpeace Society and Earth First.

PUBLIC-INTEREST GROUPS

Public Interest
The best interests of the overall community; the national good, rather than the narrow interests of a particular group.

Public interest is a difficult term to define because, as we noted in Chapter 6, there are many publics in our nation of about 300 million. It is almost impossible for one particular public policy to benefit everybody, which makes it practically impossible to define the public interest. Nonetheless, over the past few decades, a variety of lobbying organizations have been formed "in the public interest."

Nader Organizations. The best-known and perhaps the most effective public-interest groups are those organized under the leadership of consumer activist Ralph Nader. Nader's rise to the top began in 1965 with the publication of his book *Unsafe at Any Speed*, a lambasting critique of the purported attempt by General Motors (GM) to keep from the public detrimental information about its rear-engine Corvair. Partly as a result of Nader's book, Congress began to consider an automobile safety bill. GM made a clumsy attempt to discredit Nader's background. Nader sued the company, the media exploited the story, and when GM settled out of court for $425,000, Nader became a recognized champion of consumer interests. Since then, Nader has turned over much of his income to the more than 60 public-interest groups that he has formed or sponsored. Nader ran for president in 2000 on the Green Party ticket and again in 2004 and 2008 as an independent.

Other Public-Interest Groups. Partly in response to the Nader organizations, numerous conservative public-interest law firms have sprung up that are often pitted against the consumer groups in court. Some of these are the Mountain States Legal Defense Foundation, the Pacific Legal Foundation, the National Right-to-Work Legal Defense Foundation, the Washington Legal Foundation, the Institute for Justice, and the Mid-Atlantic Legal Foundation.

One of the first groups seeking political reform was Common Cause, founded in 1970. Its goal continues to be moving national priorities toward "the public" and to make governmental institutions more responsive to the needs of the public. Anyone willing to pay dues of $20 per year can become a member. Members are polled regularly to obtain information about local and national issues requiring reassessment. Some of the activities of Common Cause have been (1) helping to ensure the passage of the Twenty-sixth Amendment (giving 18-year-olds the right to vote), (2) achieving greater voter registration in all states, (3) supporting the complete withdrawal of all U.S. forces from South Vietnam in the 1970s, and (4) succeeding in passing campaign finance reform legislation.

While Common Cause has about 300,000 members and is still working for political reforms at the national and state level, it is not as well known today as MoveOn.org. Founded in 1998 by two entrepreneurs from California, the original purpose was to get millions of people to demand that President Clinton be censured instead of impeached and that the country should "move on" to deal with more important problems. What was strikingly different about this organization is that it is—and continues to be—an online interest group. MoveOn (**www.moveon.org**) has more than 3 million members

and is now a family of organizations that are politically active in national campaigns and in pressuring government on specific issues.

Other public-interest groups include the League of Women Voters, founded in 1920. Although nominally nonpartisan, it has lobbied for the Equal Rights Amendment and for government reform. The Consumer Federation of America is an alliance of about 200 local and national organizations interested in consumer protection. The American Civil Liberties Union dates back to World War I (1914–1918), when, under a different name, it defended draft resisters. It generally enters into legal disputes related to Bill of Rights issues.

OTHER INTEREST GROUPS

Single-interest groups, being narrowly focused, may be able to call attention to their causes because they have simple, straightforward goals and because their members tend to care intensely about the issues. Thus, such groups can easily motivate their members to contact legislators or to organize demonstrations in support of their policy goals.

A number of interest groups focus on just one issue. The abortion debate has created various groups opposed to abortion (such as the Right to Life organization) and groups in favor of abortion rights (such as NARAL Pro-Choice America). Other single-issue groups are the National Rifle Association, the Right to Work Committee (an antiunion group), and the American Israel Public Affairs Committee (a pro-Israel group). Still other groups represent Americans who share a common characteristic, such as age or ethnicity. Such interest groups may lobby for legislation that benefits their members in terms of rights or just represent a viewpoint.

AARP, as mentioned earlier, is one of the most powerful interest groups in Washington, D.C., and, according to some, the strongest lobbying group in the United States. It is certainly the nation's largest interest group, with a membership of about 36 million. AARP has accomplished much for its members over the years. It played a significant role in the creation of Medicare and Medicaid, as well as in obtaining cost-of-living increases in Social Security payments. In 2003, AARP supported the Republican bill to

add prescription drug coverage to Medicare. (The plan also made other changes to the system.) Some observers believe that AARP's support tipped the balance and allowed Congress to pass the measure on a closely divided vote.

FOREIGN GOVERNMENTS

Homegrown interests are not the only players in the game. Washington, D.C., is also the center for lobbying by foreign governments as well as private foreign interests. The governments of the largest U.S. trading partners, such as Canada, European Union (EU) countries, Japan, and South Korea, maintain substantial research and lobbying staffs. Even smaller nations, such as those in the Caribbean, engage lobbyists when vital legislation affecting their trade interests is considered. Frequently, these foreign interests hire former representatives or former senators to promote their positions on Capitol Hill. To learn more about how foreign interests lobby the U.S. government, see this chapter's *Beyond Our Borders* feature.

WHAT MAKES AN INTEREST GROUP POWERFUL?

At any time, thousands of interest groups are attempting to influence state legislatures, governors, Congress, and members of the executive branch of the U.S. government. What characteristics make some of those groups more powerful than others and more likely to have influence over government policy? Generally, interest groups attain a reputation for being powerful through their membership size, financial resources, leadership, and cohesiveness.

SIZE AND RESOURCES

No legislator can deny the power of an interest group that includes thousands of his or her own constituents among its members. Labor unions and organizations such as AARP and the American Automobile Association (AAA) are able to claim voters in every Congressional district. Having a large membership—nearly 9 million in the case of the AFL-CIO—carries a great deal of weight with government officials. AARP now has about 36 million members and a budget of $435 million for its operations. In addition, AARP claims to represent all older Americans, who constitute close to 20 percent of the population, whether they join the organization or not.

Having a large number of members, even if the individual membership dues are relatively small, provides an organization with a strong financial base. Those funds pay for lobbyists, television advertisements, mailings to members, a Web site, and many other resources that help an interest group make its point to politicians. The business organization with the largest membership is probably the U.S. Chamber of Commerce, which has more than 200,000 members. The Chamber uses its members' dues to pay for staff and lobbyists, as well as a sophisticated communications network so that it can contact members in a timely way. All of the members can receive e-mail and check the Web site to get updates on the latest legislative proposals.

Other organizations may have fewer members but nonetheless can muster significant financial resources. The pharmaceutical lobby, which represents many of the major drug manufacturers, is one of the most powerful interest groups in Washington due to its financial resources. This lobby has more than 600 registered lobbyists and spent close to $200 million in the 2004 presidential election cycle for lobbying and campaign expenditures.

LEADERSHIP

Money is not the only resource that interest groups need to have. Strong leaders who can develop effective strategies are also important. For example, the American Israel Public Affairs Committee (AIPAC) has long benefited from strong leadership. AIPAC lobbies Congress and the executive branch on issues related to U.S.-Israeli relations, as well as general foreign policy in the Middle East. AIPAC has been successful in facilitating the close relationship that the two nations have enjoyed, which includes between $6 billion and $8 billion in foreign aid that the United States annually bestows on Israel. Despite its modest membership size, AIPAC has won bipartisan support for its agenda and is consistently ranked among the most influential interest groups in America.

Other interest groups, including some with few financial resources, succeed in part because they are led by individuals with charisma and access to power, such as Jesse Jackson of the Rainbow Coalition. Sometimes, choosing a leader with a particular image can be an effective strategy for an organization. The National Rifle Association (NRA) had more than organizational skills in mind when it elected actor Charlton Heston as its president. The strategy of using an actor who is identified with powerful roles as the spokesperson for the organization worked to improve its national image.

COHESIVENESS

Regardless of an interest group's size or the amount of funds in its coffers, the motivation of an interest group's members is a key factor in determining how powerful it is. If

BEYOND OUR BORDERS

LOBBYING AND FOREIGN INTERESTS

Domestic groups are not alone in lobbying the federal government. Many foreign entities hire lobbyists to influence policy and spending decisions in the United States. American lobbying firms are often utilized by foreign groups seeking to advance their agendas. The use of American lobbyists assures greater access and increases the possibility of success. In 2005, for example, more than 700 foreign companies were represented by lobbying firms here. With the United States holding such a dominant position in the global economy and world affairs, it is hardly surprising that foreign entities regularly attempt to influence the U.S. government.

FOREIGN CORPORATIONS AND THE GLOBAL ECONOMY

Economic globalization has had an incalculable impact on public policy worldwide. Given the United States' prominence in the global economy, international and multinational corporations have taken a keen interest in influencing the U.S. government. Foreign corporations spend millions of dollars each year on lobbying in an effort to create favorable business and trade conditions.

As an example of foreign corporations lobbying the United States, consider the pharmaceutical industry. Many of the world's largest manufacturers of prescription drugs are not American corporations. However, firms such as GlaxoSmithKline, based in England, spend extensively on lobbying in the United States to influence Medicare legislation. The coalition of pharmaceutical interests, known as PhRMA, spent $65 million on lobbying between 1998 and 2004.*

Foreign corporations frequently hire former members of Congress to lobby on their behalf. Many overseas companies enlist the most influential lobbyists in Washington. In recent years, however, a few of these companies have found themselves involved in scandals. Some overseas companies had hired lobbyist Jack Abramoff, who pleaded guilty in January 2006 to three felony charges involving fraud in his lobbying activities.

INFLUENCE FROM OTHER NATIONS

Foreign nations also lobby the U.S. government. After it became clear that several Saudi Arabian citizens participated in the September 11, 2001, terrorist attacks, Saudi Arabia became very concerned about its image in the United States. The Saudi government hired Qorvis Communications, LLC, a public and government affairs consulting firm, to spread the message that Saudi Arabia backed the U.S.-led war on terrorism and was dedicated to peace in the Middle East. In 2002 alone, Saudi Arabia spent $14.6 million on lobbying and public relations services provided by Qorvis.

Foreign governments lobby for more specific agendas as well. Numerous developing nations have lobbied Congress to cut back on domestic farm subsidies. If the subsidies were reduced or eliminated, nations with cheaper labor costs could sell their agricultural products in the United States at a lower cost than those produced on American farms. In addition, smaller nations press for free-trade agreements, such as that signed with Canada and Mexico (NAFTA), so they can increase their exports to the United States. In 2008, a leading campaign executive for Hillary Rodham Clinton resigned his position in the campaign after it was disclosed that he was working as a lobbyist for Colombia on the pending free-trade bill. Senator Clinton opposed that legislation.

FOR CRITICAL ANALYSIS

1. Should foreign governments and foreign corporations be permitted to lobby the members of Congress in the same way as American interest groups?
2. Why do these governments prefer to hire former members of Congress?

*Julia DiLaura, "Foreign Companies Pay to Influence U.S. Policy," accessed May 20, 2005, at www.publicintegrity.org.

the members of a group hold their beliefs strongly enough to send letters to their representatives, join a march on Washington, or work together to defeat a candidate, that group is considered powerful. As described earlier, the American labor movement's success in electing Democratic candidates made the labor movement a more powerful lobby.

In contrast, although groups that oppose abortion rights have had little success in influencing policy, they are considered powerful because their members are vocal and highly motivated. Other measures of cohesion include the ability of a group to get its members to contact Washington quickly or to give extra money when needed. The U.S. Chamber of Commerce excels at both of these strategies. In comparison, AARP cannot claim that it can get its 36 million members to contact their Congressional representatives, but it does seem to influence the opinions of older Americans and their views of political candidates.

U2 LEAD SINGER BONO has lobbied world leaders to increase economic aid to Africa. In this 2008 news conference in Paris, he calls on the Group of Eight (the G8) to double assistance by 2010. Why should world leaders or the mass public pay attention to celebrities who take on political causes? (Jacques Brinon/AP/Wide World Photos)

INTEREST GROUP STRATEGIES

Interest groups employ a wide range of techniques and strategies to promote their policy goals. Although few groups are successful at persuading Congress and the president to completely endorse their programs, many are able to block—or at least weaken—legislation that is injurious to their members. The key to success for interest groups is access to government officials. To gain such access, interest groups and their representatives try to cultivate long-term relationships with legislators and government officials. The best of these relationships are based on mutual respect and cooperation. The interest group provides the official with excellent sources of information and assistance, and the official in turn gives the group opportunities to express its views.

The techniques used by interest groups can be divided into direct and indirect techniques. With **direct techniques**, the interest group and its lobbyists approach the officials personally to present their case. With **indirect techniques**, in contrast, the interest group uses the general public or individual constituents to influence the government on behalf of the interest group.

Direct Technique
An interest group activity that involves interaction with government officials to further the group's goals.

Indirect Technique
A strategy employed by interest groups that uses third parties to influence government officials.

DIRECT TECHNIQUES

Lobbying, publicizing ratings of legislative behavior, building coalitions, and providing campaign assistance are the four main direct techniques used by interest groups.

Lobbying Techniques. As might be guessed, the term *lobbying* comes from the activities of private citizens regularly congregating in the lobbies of legislative chambers before a session to petition legislators. In the latter part of the 1800s, railroad and industrial groups openly bribed state legislators to pass legislation beneficial to their interests, giving lobbying a well-deserved bad name. Most lobbyists today are professionals. They are either consultants to a company or interest group or members of one of the Washington, D.C., law firms that specialize in providing such services. As described in the *What If . . .* feature, such firms employ hundreds of former members of Congress and former government officials (e.g., former presidential candidates Bob Dole and Walter Mondale). Lobbyists are valued for their network of contacts in Washington. As Ed Rollins, a former White House aide, put it, "I've got many friends who are all through the agencies and equally important, I don't have many enemies. . . . I tell my clients I can get your case moved to the top of the pile."[11] Lobbyists of all types are becoming more numerous. The number of lobbyists in Washington, D.C., has more than doubled since 2000.

Lobbyists engage in an array of activities to influence legislation and government policy. These include the following:

1. Engaging in private meetings with public officials, including the president's advisors, to make known the interests of the lobbyists' clients. Although acting on behalf of their clients, lobbyists often furnish needed information to senators and representatives (and government agency appointees) that these officials could not easily obtain on their own. It is to the lobbyists' advantage to provide accurate information so that policy makers will rely on this source in the future.
2. Testifying before Congressional committees for or against proposed legislation.
3. Testifying before executive rule-making agencies—such as the Federal Trade Commission or the Consumer Product Safety Commission—for or against proposed rules.
4. Assisting legislators or bureaucrats in drafting legislation or prospective regulations. Often, lobbyists furnish advice on the specific details of legislation.
5. Inviting legislators to social occasions, such as cocktail parties, boating expeditions, and other events, including conferences at exotic locations. Most lobbyists believe that meeting legislators in a relaxed social setting is effective.
6. Providing political information to legislators and other government officials. Often, the lobbyists have better information than the party leadership about how other legislators are going to vote. In this case, the political information they furnish may be a key to legislative success.
7. Supplying nominations for federal appointments to the executive branch.

The Ratings Game. Many interest groups attempt to influence the overall behavior of legislators through their rating systems. Each year, the interest group selects legislation that it believes is most important to the organization's goals and then monitors how legislators vote on it. Each legislator is given a score based on the percentage of times that he or she voted in favor of the group's position. The usual scheme ranges from 0 to 100 percent. In the ratings scheme of the liberal Americans for Democratic Action, for example, a rating of 100 means that a member of Congress voted with the group on every issue and is, by that measure, very liberal.

Ratings are a shorthand way of describing members' voting records for interested citizens. They can also be used to embarrass members. For example, an environmental group identifies the twelve representatives who the group believes have the worst voting records on environmental issues and labels them "the Dirty Dozen," and a watchdog group describes those representatives who took home the most "pork" for their districts or states as the biggest "pigs."

------

[11]As quoted in Mahood, *Interest Groups in American National Politics*, p. 51.

WHAT IF...

RETIRED GOVERMENT EMPLOYEES COULD NOT WORK FOR INTEREST GROUPS?

Interest groups place a high value on lobbyists who "know their way around Washington." Former government employees and elected officials qualify in this regard. Often, retired government employees or congresspersons retain personal friendships with their former colleagues. There are rules in place to prevent former government employees from lobbying their former colleagues for a limited period of time after retirement. Congresspersons and their staff members also face such limits. Still, retirees can immediately engage in activities that do not technically qualify as lobbying, and they can begin full-scale lobbying as soon as the time limits expire. What if retired government employees and members of Congress were banned from lobbying for life? Would this reduce the influence of interest groups on legislation, or would it keep valuable advice out of the public sphere?

A large number of interest groups represent particular industries. Typically, such groups are concerned with legislation and administrative rules that are specific to their industry and are of little interest to the general public. Therefore, the press pays little attention to these laws and regulations. Industry lobbying can pass unnoticed. A retired government employee with expert knowledge of the specific subject matter and of the processes and people involved in making administrative rules can be a formidable lobbyist.

Likewise, a former member of Congress can offer invaluable assistance when an interest group seeks to affect lawmaking. If these knowledgeable retirees were not available to interest groups, those groups would have less influence on administrative rule making and on legislation. It is possible, however, that the insights of a former senator might improve the final legislation due to his or her past experience with such laws.

Industry-specific legislation can include tariffs on imports, tax breaks, and direct subsidies. The cost of this legislation adds up. The Cato Institute, a libertarian research group, estimates that what it calls "corporate welfare" costs nearly $100 billion per year. Barring former government employees from working for interest groups might reduce these kinds of corporate subsidies. Of course, if corporations and other interest groups could not hire members of Congress, they would hire other lobbyists to represent their interests.

Some government employees—and many congresspersons—look forward to lobbying as a final stage of their careers. A government career may be more attractive if it ends with a few years of highly paid, comfortable employment. Banning such employment might make government service less appealing to some. The long-term result might be that fewer well-qualified individuals would choose to enter government and politics as a lifelong career.

FOR CRITICAL ANALYSIS

1. Why would interest groups argue that a ban on hiring retired government employees would be an unfair (or even an unconstitutional) restriction on their activities?
2. In what ways might a ban on hiring retired government employees be unfair to the former employees?

Building Alliances. Another direct technique used by interest groups is to form a coalition with other groups that are concerned about the same legislation. Often, these groups will set up a paper organization with an innocuous name to represent their joint concerns. In the early 1990s, for example, environmental, labor, and consumer groups formed an alliance called the Citizens Trade Campaign to oppose the passage of NAFTA.

Members of such a coalition share expenses and multiply the influence of their individual groups by combining their efforts. Other advantages of forming a coalition are

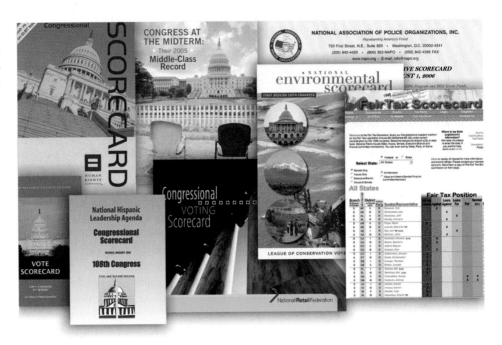

DID YOU KNOW?

That lobbying expenditures in the United States exceed the gross national product of 57 countries?

that it blurs the specific interests of the individual groups involved and makes it appear that larger public interests are at stake. These alliances also are efficient devices for keeping like-minded groups from duplicating one another's lobbying efforts.

Another example of an alliance developed when the Republicans launched the K Street Project. The project, named for the street in Washington, D.C., where the largest lobbying firms have their headquarters, was designed to alter the lobbying community's pro-Democratic tilt. Republicans sought to pressure lobbying firms to hire Republicans in top positions, offering loyal lobbyists greater access to lawmakers in return.

Campaign Assistance. Interest groups have additional strategies to use in their attempts to influence government policies. Groups recognize that the greatest concern of legislators is to be reelected, so they focus on the legislators' campaign needs. Associations with large memberships, such as labor unions, are able to provide workers for political campaigns, including precinct workers to get out the vote, volunteers to put up posters and pass out literature, and people to staff telephone banks for campaign headquarters.

In many states where certain interest groups have large memberships, candidates vie for the groups' endorsements in the campaign. Gaining those endorsements may be automatic, or it may require that the candidates participate in debates or interviews with the interest groups. Endorsements are important, because an interest group usually publicizes its choices in its membership publication and because the candidate can use the endorsement in her or his campaign literature. Traditionally, labor unions have endorsed Democratic Party candidates. Republican candidates, however, often try to persuade union locals at least to refrain from any endorsement. Making no endorsement can then be perceived as disapproval of the Democratic Party candidate.

Despite the passage of the Bipartisan Campaign Finance Act in 2002, the 2008 election boasted record campaign spending. The usual array of interest groups—labor unions, professional groups, and business associations—gathered contributions to their political action committees and distributed them to the candidates. Most labor contributions went to Democratic candidates, while a majority of business contributions went to Republicans. Some groups, such as real estate agents, gave evenly to both parties. At the same time, the newer campaign groups, the so-called 527 organizations—tax-exempt associations focused on influencing political elections—raised more than $425 million in unregulated contributions and used them for campaign activities and advertising. After seeing the success of these groups in raising and spending funds, hundreds of interest groups, private and nonprofit, have founded their 527 organizations to spend funds for advertising and other political activities. The flood of unregulated funds supported massive advertising campaigns in the last months of the campaign.

INDIRECT TECHNIQUES

Interest groups can also try to influence government policy by working through others, who may be constituents or the general public. Indirect techniques mask the interest group's own activities and make the effort appear to be spontaneous. Furthermore, legislators and government officials are often more impressed by contacts from constituents than from an interest group's lobbyist.

Generating Public Pressure. In some instances, interest groups try to produce a groundswell of public pressure to influence the government. Such efforts may include advertisements in national magazines and newspapers, mass mailings, television publicity, and demonstrations. The Internet and satellite links make communication efforts even more effective. Interest groups may commission polls to find out what the public's sentiments are and then publicize the results. The intent of this activity is to convince policy makers that public opinion overwhelmingly supports the group's position.

Some corporations and interest groups also engage in a practice that might be called **climate control**. With this strategy, public relations efforts are aimed at improving the public image of the industry or group and are not necessarily related to any specific political issue. Contributions by corporations and groups in support of public television programs, sponsorship of special events, and commercials extolling the virtues of corporate research are some ways of achieving climate control. For example, to improve its image in the wake of litigation against tobacco companies, Philip Morris began advertising its assistance to community agencies, including halfway houses for teen offenders and shelters for battered women. By building a reservoir of favorable public opinion, groups believe that their legislative goals will be less likely to encounter opposition by the public.

Using Constituents as Lobbyists. Interest groups also use constituents to lobby for the group's goals. In the "shotgun" approach, the interest group tries to mobilize large numbers of constituents to write, phone, or send e-mails to their legislators or the president. Often, the group provides postcards or form letters for constituents to fill out and mail. These efforts are effective on Capitol Hill only with a very large number of responses, however, because legislators know that the voters did not initiate the communications on their own. Artificially manufactured grassroots activity has been aptly labeled *Astroturf lobbying*.

A more powerful variation of this technique uses only important constituents. With this approach, known as the "rifle" technique or the "Utah plant manager theory," the interest group might, for example, ask the manager of a local plant in Utah to contact the senator from Utah.[12] Because the constituent is seen as responsible for many jobs or other resources, the legislator is more likely to listen carefully to the constituent's concerns about legislation than to a paid lobbyist.

Climate Control
The use of public relations techniques to create favorable public opinion toward an interest group, industry, or corporation.

---

[12]Kay Lehman Schlozman and John T. Tierney, *Organized Interests and American Democracy* (New York: Harper & Row, 1986), p. 293.

A GROUP OF PROTESTORS who are against the Bush administration's policies on pollution demonstrate along a highway to gain public and media attention for their cause. Members of the Sierra Club, Common Cause, and Public Citizen are pictured. How might pooling resources help interest groups with overlapping agendas? (Adele Starr/AP Photo)

Boycott
A form of pressure or protest—an organized refusal to purchase a particular product or deal with a particular business.

Unconventional Forms of Pressure. Sometimes, interest groups may employ forms of pressure that are outside the ordinary political process. These can include marches, rallies, civil disobedience, or demonstrations. Such assemblies, as long as they are peaceful, are protected by the First Amendment. In Chapter 5, we described the civil disobedience techniques of the African American civil rights movement in the 1950s and 1960s. The 1963 March on Washington in support of civil rights was one of the most effective demonstrations ever organized. The women's suffrage movement of the early 1900s also employed marches and demonstrations to great effect.

Demonstrations, however, are not always peaceable. Violent demonstrations have a long history in America, dating back to the antitax Boston Tea Party described in Chapter 2. The Vietnam War (1964–1975) provoked many demonstrations, some of which were violent. In 1999, at a meeting of the World Trade Organization in Seattle, demonstrations against globalization turned violent. These demonstrations were repeated throughout the 2000s at various sites around the world. Still, violent demonstrations can be counterproductive—instead of putting pressure on the authorities, they may simply alienate the public. For example, historians continue to debate whether the demonstrations against the Vietnam War were effective or counterproductive.

Another unconventional form of pressure is the **boycott**—a refusal to buy a particular product or deal with a particular business. To be effective, boycotts must command widespread support. One example was the African American boycott of buses in Montgomery, Alabama, during 1955, described in Chapter 5. Another was the boycott of California grapes that were picked by nonunion workers, as part of a campaign to organize Mexican American farmworkers. The first grape boycott lasted from 1965 to 1970; a series of later boycotts was less effective.

REGULATING LOBBYISTS

Congress made its first attempt to control lobbyists and lobbying activities through Title III of the Legislative Reorganization Act of 1946, otherwise known as the Federal Regulation of Lobbying Act. The act actually provided for public disclosure more than for regulation, and it neglected to specify which agency would enforce its provisions. The 1946 legislation defined a *lobbyist* as any person or organization that received money to be used principally to influence legislation before Congress. Such persons and individuals were supposed to register their clients and the purposes of their efforts and report quarterly on their activities.

The legislation was tested in a 1954 Supreme Court case, *United States v. Harriss*,[13] and was found to be constitutional. The Court agreed that the lobbying law did not violate due process, freedom of speech or of the press, or the freedom to petition. The Court narrowly construed the Act, how-

DID YOU KNOW?

That lobbyists have their own lobbying organization, the American League of Lobbyists?

---

[13]347 U.S. 612 (1954).

ever, holding that it applied only to lobbyists who were influencing federal legislation *directly*.

THE RESULTS OF THE 1946 ACT

The immediate result of the act was that a minimal number of individuals registered as lobbyists. National interest groups, such as the National Rifle Association and the American Petroleum Institute, could employ hundreds of staff members who were, of course, working on legislation, but only register one or two lobbyists who were engaged *principally* in influencing Congress. There were no reporting requirements for lobbying the executive branch, federal agencies, the courts, or Congressional staff.

Approximately 7,000 individuals and organizations registered annually as lobbyists, although most experts estimated that 10 times that number were actually employed in Washington to exert influence on the government.

While lobbying firms and individuals who represent foreign corporations must register with Congress, lobbyists who represent foreign governments must register with the Department of Justice under the Foreign Agent Registration Act of 1938. The Department of Justice publishes an annual report listing the lobbyists and the nations that have reported their activities. That report is available online at the Department of Justice Web site (**www.usdoj.gov/criminal/fara**).

THE REFORMS OF 1995

The reform-minded Congress of 1995–1996 overhauled the lobbying legislation, fundamentally changing the ground rules for those who seek to influence the federal government. Lobbying legislation passed in 1995 included the following provisions:

DID YOU KNOW?

That Washington's lobbying industry employs more than four times as many people today as it did in the mid-1960s?

1. A *lobbyist* is defined as anyone who spends at least 20 percent of his or her time lobbying members of Congress, their staffs, or executive-branch officials.
2. Lobbyists must register with the clerk of the House and the secretary of the Senate within 45 days of being hired or of making their first contacts. The registration requirement applies to organizations that spend more than $20,000 in one year or to individuals who are paid more than $5,000 annually for lobbying work.
3. Semiannual (now quarterly and electronic) reports must disclose the general nature of the lobbying effort, specific issues and bill numbers, the estimated cost of the campaign, and a list of the branches of government contacted. The names of the individuals contacted need not be reported.
4. Representatives of U.S.-owned subsidiaries of foreign-owned firms and lawyers who represent foreign entities also are required to register.
5. The requirements exempt grassroots lobbying efforts and those of tax-exempt organizations, such as religious groups.

As they debated the 1995 law, both the House and the Senate adopted new rules on gifts and travel expenses: the House adopted a flat ban on gifts, and the Senate limited gifts to $50 in value and to no more than $100 in gifts from a single source in a year. There are exceptions for gifts from family members and for home-state products and souvenirs, such as T-shirts and coffee mugs. Both chambers banned all-expenses-paid trips, golf outings, and other such junkets. An exception applies for "widely attended" events, however, or if the member is a primary speaker at an event. These gift rules stopped the broad practice of taking members of Congress to lunch or dinner, but the various exemptions and exceptions have caused much controversy as the Senate and House Ethics Committees have considered individual cases.

RECENT LOBBYING SCANDALS

The regulation of lobbying activity again surfaced in 2005, when several scandals came to light. At the center of some publicized incidents was a highly influential and corrupt lobbyist, Jack Abramoff. Using his ties with numerous Republican (and a handful of Democratic) lawmakers, Abramoff brokered numerous deals for the special-interest clients that he represented in return for campaign donations, gifts, and various perks.

In January 2006, Abramoff pled guilty to three criminal felony counts related to the defrauding of American Indian tribes and the corruption of public officials. Investigations have not ceased, however, as lawmakers and Bush administration officials connected with Abramoff and his colleagues are under continued scrutiny. Numerous politicians have attempted to distance themselves from the embattled lobbyist by giving Abramoff's campaign donations to charity.

In 2007, both parties claimed that they wanted to reform lobbying legislation and the ethics rules in Congress. The House Democrats tightened the rules in that body early in the year, as did the Senate. The aptly named Honest Leadership and Open Government Act of 2007 was signed by President Bush in September 2007. The law made reporting requirements for lobbyists tighter, extended the time period before ex-members can accept lobbying jobs (two years for Senators and one year for House members), set up rules for lobbying by the spouses of members, and changed some campaign contribution rules for interest groups. The new rules adopted by the respective houses bar all members from receiving gifts or trips paid for by lobbyists unless preapproved by the Ethics Committee. Within three months after the bill took effect, a loophole was discovered that allows lobbyists to make a campaign contribution to a Senator's campaign, for example, and then go to a fancy dinner where the campaign is allowed to pay the bill.[14] Like most other pieces of lobbying legislation, other loopholes will be discovered and utilized by members and interest groups.

INTEREST GROUPS AND REPRESENTATIVE DEMOCRACY

The role played by interest groups in shaping national policy has caused many to question whether we really have a democracy at all. Most interest groups have a middle-class or upper-class bias. Members of interest groups can afford to pay the membership fees, are generally well educated, and normally participate in the political process to a greater extent than the "average" American. Furthermore, the majority of Americans do not actually join a group outside of their religious congregation or a recreational group. They allow others who do join to represent them.

Furthermore, leaders of some interest groups may constitute an "elite within an elite," in the sense that they usually are from a different economic or social class than most of their members. Certainly, association executives are highly paid individuals who live in Washington, D.C., and associate regularly with the political elites of the country. The most powerful interest groups—those with the most resources and political influence—are primarily business, trade, or professional groups. In contrast, public-interest groups or civil rights groups make up only a small percentage of the interest groups lobbying Congress and may struggle to gain enough funds to continue to exist.

[14]Robert Pear, "Ethics Law Isn't Without Its Loopholes," *The New York Times*, accessed April 20, 2008, from www.nytimes.com.

Thinking about the relatively low number of Americans and their status as middle class or better leads one to conclude that interest groups are really an elitist phenomenon rather than, as discussed in Chapter 1, a manifestation of pluralism. Pluralist theory proposes that these many groups will try to influence the government and struggle to reach a compromise that will be advantageous to both sides. However, if most Americans are not represented by a group, say, on the question of farm subsidies or energy imports, is there any evidence that the final legislation improves life for ordinary Americans?

INTEREST GROUP INFLUENCE

The results of lobbying efforts—Congressional legislation—do not always favor the interests of the most powerful groups, however. In part, this is because not all interest groups have an equal influence on government. Each group has a different combination of resources to use in the policy-making process. While some groups are composed of members who have high social status and significant economic resources, such as the National Association of Manufacturers, other groups derive influence from their large memberships. AARP, for example, has more members than any other interest group. Its large membership allows it to wield significant power over legislators. Still other groups, such as environmentalists, have causes that can claim strong public support even from people who have no direct stake in the issue. Groups such as the National Rifle Association are well organized and have highly motivated members. This enables them to channel a stream of mail or electronic messages toward Congress with a few days' effort.

Even the most powerful interest groups do not always succeed in their demands. Whereas the U.S. Chamber of Commerce may be accepted as having a justified interest in the question of business taxes, many legislators might feel that the group should not engage in the debate over the future of Social Security. In other words, groups are seen as having a legitimate concern in the issues closest to their interests but not necessarily in broader issues. This may explain why some of the most successful groups are those that focus on very specific issues—such as tobacco farming, funding of abortions, or handgun control—and do not get involved in larger conflicts.

You can make a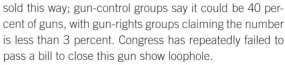

THE GUN CONTROL ISSUE

Some interest groups focus on issues that concern only a limited number of people. Others are involved in causes in which almost everyone has a stake. Gun control is an issue that concerns many people. The question of whether the possession of handguns should be regulated or even banned is at the heart of a long-running heated battle among organized interest groups. The fight is fueled by the 1 million gun incidents occurring in the United States each year—murders, suicides, assaults, accidents, and robberies in which guns are involved.

WHY SHOULD YOU CARE?

Research conducted by the National School Safety Center shows that more than 300 students have died in school shootings in the past 15 years. Student gunmen at Virginia Tech and Northern Illinois University in 2007 and 2008 served as traumatic reminders that campus populations seem increasingly vulnerable to gun violence at the hands of mentally unstable young people. Given the social outcry surrounding these terrible incidents, are interest groups being formed to deal with the crisis?

Many states are now sharing information about certain mentally unstable people with the National Instant Criminal Background Check system, prodded by a measure worked out by Congress and the National Rifle Association, one of the most powerful single-issue groups in the United States. About 32 states have started reporting mental health information to the federal database since the Virginia Tech tragedy, with other states considering laws to improve their reporting. However, people can still buy guns without anyone checking this database. According to current federal law, unlicensed gun dealers at gun shows do not need to conduct a background check before they sell a weapon. It is unclear how many weapons are

sold this way; gun-control groups say it could be 40 percent of guns, with gun-rights groups claiming the number is less than 3 percent. Congress has repeatedly failed to pass a bill to close this gun show loophole.

Gun control advocates would also like to see a reinstatement of the Federal Assault Weapons Ban, which federal lawmakers allowed to expire in 2004. This law would ban the sale of military-style assault weapons and high-capacity ammunition magazines like those used by the Virginia Tech and Northern Illinois University killers.

WHAT CAN YOU DO?

It seems that even with ample warning signs, tragedies can be very difficult to prevent. Both shooters in these university killings were apparently plagued by mental illness. Experts say that we all need to take responsibility for identifying and redirecting the energies of problematic people. We all need social ties and mentoring, especially in large colleges, where counseling staffs are boosting their numbers, offering more walk-in hours, and training faculty and residence hall advisors to become more skilled at identifying students suffering from emotional problems.

Short of installing metal detectors at every building entrance, experts think the majority of these violent events can be handled and prevented by behavioral awareness. College campuses are considering assembling "threat assessment" teams, which would consist of school resource officers and administration personnel, working with lawyers, nurses, and clinical psychologists. These teams would give students and faculty the opportunity to see a warning sign and report it to a group with enough perspective to see a possible threat and the authority to act, if necessary.

Some feel that students and educators should have the right to defend themselves, and that weapons on campus should be part of the plan. A nonprofit organization called Students for Concealed Carry on Campus has 12,000 members nationwide that include college students, faculty, and parents. This group advocates legislation that would allow licensed gun owners to carry concealed weapons on campus, believing that a well-trained citizen could stop a deranged shooter from committing mass murder. Thirteen states are currently considering a form of "concealed carry" legislation for college campuses.

Proponents of The Brady Campaign to Prevent Gun Violence oppose the concealed-carry legislation, believing that it would only heighten the danger on campuses where young people drink heavily and live communally.

To find out more about the National Rifle Association and their positions, contact:

The National Rifle Association
11250 Waples Mill Rd.
Fairfax, VA 22030
703-267-1000
www.nra.org

To learn about the positions of gun-control advocates, contact:

The Coalition to Stop Gun Violence
1023 15th St. N.W., Suite 301
Washington, D.C. 20005
202-408-0061

Brady Center to Prevent Gun Violence
Brady Campaign to Prevent Gun Violence
1225 Eye St. N.W., Suite 1100
Washington, D.C. 20005
Brady Center: 202-289-7319
Brady Campaign: 202-898-0792
www.bradycampaign.org

REFERENCES

Daniel McGinn and Samantha Hening, "Spotting Trouble," *Newsweek*, accessed August 21, 2007, at www.newsweek.com.

Mitch Mitchell, "School-Shooting Expert Answers Tough Questions," *Fort Worth Star Telegram*, accessed February 15, 2008, at www.star-telegram.com/.

Matthew Phillips, "Not Yet Bulletproof," *Newsweek*, accessed October 12, 2007, at www.newsweek.com.

Amanda Ripley, "Ignoring Virginia Tech," *Time*, accessed April 15, 2008, at www.time.com.

Suzanne Smalley, "More Guns on Campus?" *Newsweek*, accessed February 15, 2008, at www.newsweek.com.

KEY TERMS

boycott 272	**interest group** 250	**public interest** 262
climate control 271	**labor movement** 258	**purposive incentive** 255
direct technique 267	**latent interests** 254	**service sector** 259
free rider problem 254	**lobbyist** 250	**social movement** 252
indirect technique 267	**material incentive** 255	**solidary incentive** 254

CHAPTER SUMMARY

1. An interest group is an organization whose members share common objectives and actively attempt to influence government policy. Interest groups proliferate in the United States, because they can influence government at many points in the political structure and because they offer solidary, material, and purposive incentives to their members. Interest groups are often created out of social movements.

2. Major types of interest groups include business, agricultural, labor, public employee, professional, and environmental groups. Other important groups may be considered public-interest groups. In addition, special-interest groups and foreign governments lobby the government.

3. Interest groups use direct and indirect techniques to influence government. Direct techniques include testifying before committees and rule-making agencies, providing information to legislators, rating legislators' voting records, aiding political campaigns, and building alliances. Indirect techniques to influence government include campaigns to rally public sentiment, letter-writing campaigns, efforts to influence the climate of opinion, and the use of constituents to lobby for the group's interests. Unconventional methods of applying pressure include demonstrations and boycotts.

4. The 1946 Legislative Reorganization Act was the first attempt to control lobbyists and their activities through registration requirements. The United States Supreme Court narrowly construed the act as applying only to lobbyists who directly seek to influence federal legislation.

5. In 1995, Congress approved new legislation requiring anyone who spends 20 percent of his or her time influencing legislation to register. Also, any organization spending $20,000 or more and any individual who is paid more than $5,000 annually for his or her work must register. Quarterly reports must include the names of clients, the bills in which they are interested, and the branches of government contacted. The 2007 lobbying reform law tightened the regulations on lobbyists and imposed other rules on members who wish to become lobbyists after leaving office.

SELECTED PRINT AND MEDIA RESOURCES

SUGGESTED READINGS

Berry, Jeffrey M., and Clyde Wilcox. *Interest Group Society*, 4th ed. New York: Longman, 2006. This work examines the expanding influence of interest groups as well as their relationship to the party system.

Goldstein, Kenneth M. *Interest Groups, Lobbying, and Participation in America.* New York: Cambridge University Press, 2003. What kind of people join interest groups, and how do such people seek to influence legislation? The author looks for answers using survey data and interviews with activists.

Patrick, Brian Anse. *The National Rifle Association and the Media: The Motivating Force of Negative Coverage. Vol. 1 of Frontiers in Political Communications.* New York: Peter Lang Publishing, 2004. Patrick argues that the NRA actually benefits from negative media coverage, which has served to mobilize participants in the gun culture.

Sifry, Micah, and Nancy Watzman. *Is That a Politician in Your Pocket? Washington on $2 Million a Day.* New York: John Wiley & Sons, 2004. The authors, who are staff members at Public Campaign, provide a clearly written and detailed exposé of how financial contributions by interest groups drive politics. Chapters cover pharmaceuticals, gun control, agribusiness, oil and chemical corporations, and cable TV.

MEDIA RESOURCES

Bowling for Columbine—Michael Moore's documentary won an Academy Award in 2003. Moore seeks to understand why the United States leads the industrialized world in firearms deaths. While the film is hilarious, it takes a strong position in favor of gun control and is critical of the National Rifl e Association.

Norma Rae—A 1979 Hollywood movie about an attempt by a Northern union organizer to unionize workers in the Southern textile industry; stars Sally Field, who won an Academy Award for her performance.

Organizing America: The History of Trade Unions—A 1994 documentary that incorporates interviews, personal accounts, and archival footage to tell the story of the American labor movement. The film is a Cambridge Educational Production.

The West Wing—A popular television series that was widely regarded as being an accurate portrayal of the issues and political pressures faced by a liberal president and his White House staff.

INTEREST GROUPS AND THE INTERNET

The Internet may have a strong equalizing effect in the world of lobbying and government influence. The first organizations to use electronic means to reach their constituents and drum up support for action were the large economic coalitions, including the Chamber of Commerce and the National Association of Manufacturers. Groups such as these, as well as groups representing a single product such as tobacco, quickly realized that they could set up Web sites and mailing lists to provide information more rapidly to their members. Members could check the Web every day to see how legislation was developing in Congress or anywhere in the world. National associations could send e-mail to all of their members with one keystroke, mobilizing them to contact their representatives in Congress.

LOGGING ON

Almost every interest group or association has its own Web site. To find one, use your favorite search engine (e.g., Lycos, Google, AltaVista, Yahoo!) and search for the association by name. For a sense of the breadth of the kinds of interest groups that have Web sites, take a look at one or two of those listed here.

- Those interested in the gun-control issue may want to visit the National Rifle Association's site at:
  www.nra.org
- You can learn more about the labor movement by visiting the AFL-CIO's site at:
  www.aflcio.org

- AARP (formerly the American Association of Retired Persons) has a site at:
  www.aarp.org
- If you would like to find out the details about how much interest groups spent on elections, go to the site maintained by the Center for Responsive Politics:
  www.opensecrets.org
- Another site that tracks lobbyists and their expenditures is found at:
  www.publicintegrity.org/lobby

ONLINE REVIEW

At **www.cengage.com/politicalscience/schmidt/agandpt14e**, you will find a Tutorial Quiz for this chapter providing questions on the chapter contents, including the features. The questions are organized to match the major sections of the chapter. You'll have access to other helpful study tools, including the book's glossary and flashcards, crossword puzzles, and Web links, as well as "Which Side Are You On?" and "Politics and . . ." features written by the authors of the book.

CHAPTER

(8)

The Democratic precinct chairwoman
explains the rules to the voters at the Iowa
Caucus in January of 2008 before the debate
over the candidates begins. (Dave Weaver/
AP/Wide World Photos)

POLITICAL PARTIES

Making a DIFFERENCE

SHIFTING PARTY COALITIONS

Have you ever heard the expression "politics makes strange bedfellows"? If so, then a coalition of Protestant conservative white voters and Northeastern liberal urban voters from religious and ethnic groups as diverse as Jewish, Irish Catholic, and African American would surely fit the description. This is exactly the New Deal coalition on which Democratic Party victories were based, starting with President Franklin D. Roosevelt's win in 1932. The name, New Deal coalition, refers to those groups who were most helped by President Roosevelt's New Deal programs to address the problems created by the Great Depression. This coalition of disparate groups was a stable electoral force that elected five Democrats to the White House over the next 58 years (Presidents Roosevelt, Truman, Kennedy, Johnson, and Carter).

The electoral landscape for the political parties has changed a great deal from the early to middle 20th century. The Democratic Party, which had supported racial segregation in the South until the 1950s, advocated racial integration and other civil rights policies that drove white, Protestant conservative Southern voters who opposed these initiatives away. First Richard Nixon in 1972 and then Ronald Reagan in 1980 successfully drew these voters to the Republican Party. These voters were also drawn to the Republican Party's social conservatism and rejection of the cultural changes of the 1960s and 1970s. Often self-identifying as working class, these Reagan Democrats were attracted to President Reagan's policies. Motivated by so-called family values, anti-Communism, and strong national defense, by the 1990s they had largely switched their allegiance to the Republican Party.

The 1980 presidential election also saw the first significant gender gap; that is, men and women voting in different patterns, with women voters less likely to support the Republican candidate (see *Making a Difference:*

DURING NATIONAL ELECTION YEARS, whether Congressional years such as 2006 or presidential years like 2004 and 2008, political parties become a much more important feature in the political landscape of the United States. For the first six months of 2008, the political party primary elections focused on choosing a nominee from among their respective candidates. Commentators noted the wide variety of election processes in the Democratic primaries. John McCain, the Republican nominee, earned his party's nod fairly early in the Republican process. For the voters, it became important to know when to vote and what restrictions there might be in voting in the primary: some states allow voters to choose either primary, whereas others restrict voting to declared or registered party "members." In some states, **independent** voters could vote in the primaries, but not in other states.

Notice that in the previous paragraph, party "member" is placed in quotation marks. This is because Americans do not join a party, nor do they really become members. We did this because hardly anyone actually belongs to a political party in the sense of being a card-carrying member. To become a member of a political party, you do not have to pay dues, pass an examination, or swear an oath of allegiance. Furthermore, as discussed in the *Making a Difference* feature, individuals and groups of individuals switch their

Independent
A voter or candidate who does not identify with a political party.

Opinion Gaps and Advocacy in Chapter 6). This trend has held in most presidential elections. Additionally, immigration and differences in birthrates has increased the Latino proportion of the voting age population and decreased the white proportion. Both parties have targeted Latino voters. While George W. Bush was somewhat successful with this group in 2000, with the exception of conservative Cuban Americans, Latinos have largely supported Democratic candidates.

In addition to racial, religious, and ethnic groups, these changing party coalitions can be understood in geographic terms. As the previous discussion indicates, what was once a solidly Democratic region of the country as a vestige of the Civil War,[a] the South, has become a bastion of Republican electoral wins since the late 1980s. The Northeast, which had been moderate and Republican, is now a Democratic stronghold, as is immigrant-rich California. Additionally, the Pacific Northwest began to trend Democratic.[b] This left the Midwest and Central/Mountain West as battleground regions, especially the more populous states like Ohio, Missouri, and Michigan that are crucial to a presidential victory.

Where does this leave the 2008 presidential election? It has broken many records for fundraising and for voter turnout. This is especially true in the Democratic primaries and caucuses, where many voters who were previously turned off by the system found appeal in the historic candidacies of Senator Obama and Senator Clinton (the first viable African American and female presidential candidates, respectively). According to a February 2008 report by the Center for Responsive Politics, the entire group of candidates running for the presidency from both parties raised $582.5 million and spent $481.2 million.[c] Voters have been voting in the Democratic primaries and caucuses in record numbers.

Who are these new Democratic voters? This is a group of younger voters (under 30 years old); some are more affluent (making over $100,000) and more liberal; and they consist of mainly women, African Americans, and Latinos.[d] While this constellation of voters was more likely to support Senator Obama in the Democratic primaries and caucuses, white men, older women, and so-called downscale voters (those in lower earning brackets) were more likely to support Senator Clinton. Indeed, Senator Hillary Clinton won the primary elections in Pennsylvania and Ohio on the strength of these voters. In the general election, almost all of the former Clinton supporters turned out to vote for Barack Obama.

[a]The Republican Party, the party of Lincoln, was associated with the "Yankees" or Union forces long after the close of the Civil War. Local Republican candidates throughout the South were "sacrificial lambs" or candidates with no chance of wining the general election.

[b]Charles S. Bullock, III, Donna R. Hoffman, and Ronald Keith Gaddie, "The Consolidation of the White Southern Vote," *Political Research Quarterly*, vol. 58, no. 2, pp. 231–243, 2005.

[c]www.opensecrets.org/, accessed March 29, 2008.

[d]Ronald Brownstein, "A Party Transformed," *National Journal*, accessed February 29, 2008, at http://nationaljournal.com/about/njweekly/stories/2008/0229nj1.htm.

allegiance from one party to another during critical elections. Therefore, at this point, we can ask an obvious question: If it takes nothing to be a member of a political party, what, then, is a political party?

WHAT IS A POLITICAL PARTY?

A **political party** might be formally defined as a group of political activists who organize to win elections, operate the government, and determine public policy. This definition explains the difference between an interest group and a political party. Interest groups do not want to operate the government, and they do not put forth political candidates—even though they support candidates who will promote their interests if elected or re-elected. Another important distinction is that interest groups tend to sharpen issues, whereas American political parties tend to blur their issue positions to attract voters.

Political parties differ from **factions**, which are smaller groups that are trying to obtain power or benefits.[1] Factions are subgroups within parties that may try to capture a nomination or get a position adopted by the party. A key difference between factions

Political Party
A group of political activists who organize to win elections, operate the government, and determine public policy.

Faction
A group or bloc in a legislature or political party acting in pursuit of some special interest or position.

[1]See James Madison's comments on factions in Chapter 2.

and parties is that factions do not have a permanent organization, whereas political parties do. Factions generally preceded the formation of political parties in American history, and the term is still used to refer to groups within parties that follow a particular leader or share a regional identification or an ideological viewpoint. For example, the Republican Party is sometimes seen as having a Northeastern faction that holds more moderate positions than the dominant conservative majority of the party.

Political parties in the United States engage in a wide variety of activities, many of which are discussed in this chapter. Through these activities, parties perform several functions for the political system. These functions include the following:

1. *Recruiting candidates for public office.* Because it is the goal of parties to gain control of government, they must work to recruit candidates for all elective offices. Often, this means recruiting candidates to run against powerful incumbents. If parties did not search out and encourage political hopefuls, far more offices would be uncontested, and voters would have limited choices.

2. *Organizing and running elections.* Although elections are a government activity, political parties actually organize the voter-registration drives, recruit the volunteers to work at the polls, provide most of the campaign activity to stimulate interest in the election, and work to increase voter participation.

3. *Presenting alternative policies to the electorate.* In contrast to factions, which are often centered on individual politicians, parties are focused on a set of political positions. The Democrats or Republicans in Congress who vote together do so because they represent constituencies that have similar expectations and demands.

4. *Accepting responsibility for operating the government.* When a party elects the president or governor and members of the legislature, it accepts the responsibility for running the government. This includes staffing the executive branch with loyal party supporters and developing linkages among the elected officials to gain support for policies and their implementation.

5. *Acting as the organized opposition to the party in power.* The "out" party, or the one that does not control the government, is expected to articulate its own policies and oppose the winning party when appropriate. By organizing the opposition to the "in" party, the opposition party forces debate on the policy alternatives.

The major functions of American political parties are carried out by a small, relatively loose-knit nucleus of party activists. This arrangement is quite different from the more highly structured, mass-membership party organization typical of many European parties. American parties concentrate on winning elections rather than on signing up large numbers of deeply committed, dues-paying members who believe passionately in the party's program.

A HISTORY OF POLITICAL PARTIES IN THE UNITED STATES

Although it is difficult to imagine a political system in the United States with four, five, six, or seven major political parties, other democratic systems have three-

A DELEGATE LISTENS to Democratic presidential nominee Senator Barack Obama (D.-Ill.) give his acceptance speech at the 2008 Democratic National Convention in Denver, Colorado, August 28, 2008. (Eric Thayer/Reuters/Landov Media)

party, four-party, or even 10-party systems. In some European nations, parties are clearly tied to ideological positions; parties that represent Marxist, socialist, liberal, conservative, and ultraconservative positions appear on the political continuum. Some nations have political parties representing regions of the nation that have separate cultural identities, such as the French-speaking and Flemish-speaking regions of Belgium. Some parties are rooted in religious differences. Parties also exist that represent specific economic interests—agricultural, maritime, or industrial—and some, such as monarchist parties, speak for alternative political systems.

The United States has a **two-party system**, and that system has been around since about 1800. The function and character of the political parties, as well as the emergence of the two-party system, have much to do with the unique historical forces operating from this country's beginning as an independent nation. James Madison (1751–1836) linked the emergence of political parties to the form of government created by the Constitution.

Generally, we can divide the evolution of the nation's political parties into seven periods:

1. The creation of parties, from 1789 to 1816.
2. The era of one-party rule, or personal politics, from 1816 to 1828.
3. The period from Andrew Jackson's presidency to just before the Civil War, from 1828 to 1860.
4. The Civil War and post-Civil War period, from 1860 to 1896.
5. The Republican ascendancy and the progressive period, from 1896 to 1932.
6. The New Deal period, from 1932 to about 1968.
7. The modern period, from approximately 1968 to the present.

Two-Party System
A political system in which only two parties have a reasonable chance of winning.

That the political party with the most seats in the House of Representatives chooses the Speaker of the House, makes any new rules it wants, gets a majority of the seats on each important committee and chooses committee chairs, and hires most of the Congressional staff?

THE FORMATIVE YEARS: FEDERALISTS AND ANTI-FEDERALISTS

The first partisan political division in the United States occurred before the adoption of the Constitution. As you will recall from Chapter 2, the Federalists were those who pushed for adoption of the Constitution, whereas the Anti-Federalists were against ratification.

In September 1796, George Washington, who had served as president for almost two full terms, decided not to run again. In his farewell address, he made a somber assessment of the nation's future. Washington felt that the country might be destroyed by the "baneful [harmful] effects of the spirit of party." He viewed parties as a threat to both national unity and the concept of popular government. Early in his career, Thomas Jefferson did not like political parties either. In 1789, he stated, "If I could not go to heaven but with a party, I would not go there at all."[2]

Nevertheless, in the years after the ratification of the Constitution, Americans realized that something more permanent than a faction would be necessary to identify candidates for office and represent political differences among the people. The result was two political parties. One party was the Federalists, which included John Adams, the second president (served 1797–1801). The Federalists represented commercial interests such as merchants and large planters. They supported a strong national government.

Thomas Jefferson led the other party, which came to be called the Republicans, or Jeffersonian Republicans. (These Republicans should not be confused with the later Republican Party of Abraham Lincoln. To avoid confusion, some scholars refer to

[2]Letter to Francis Hopkinson written from Paris while Jefferson was minister to France. In John P. Foley, ed., *The Jeffersonian Cyclopedia* (New York: Russell & Russell, 1967), p. 677.

THOMAS JEFFERSON, founder of the first Republican Party. His election to the presidency in 1800 was one of the world's first transfers of power through a free election. (Library of Congress, Prints & Photographs Division, Washington, D.C. [LC-USZ62-387])

Era of Good Feelings
The years from 1817 to 1825, when James Monroe was president and there was, in effect, no political opposition.

Democratic Party
One of the two major American political parties evolving out of the Republican Party of Thomas Jefferson.

Whig Party
A major party in the United States during the first half of the 19th century, formally established in 1836. The Whig Party was anti-Jackson and represented a variety of regional interests.

Jefferson's party as the Democratic-Republicans, but this name was never used during the time that the party existed.) Jefferson's Republicans represented artisans and farmers. They strongly supported states' rights. In 1800, when Jefferson defeated Adams in the presidential contest, one of the world's first peaceful transfers of power from one party to another was achieved.

THE ERA OF GOOD FEELINGS

From 1800 to 1820, a majority of U.S. voters regularly elected Republicans to the presidency and to Congress. By 1816, the Federalist Party had virtually collapsed, and two-party competition did not really exist. Although during elections the Republicans opposed the Federalists' call for a stronger, more active central government, they undertook such active government policies as acquiring the Louisiana Territory and Florida and establishing a national bank. Because there was no real political opposition to the Republicans and thus little political debate, the administration of James Monroe (1817–1825) came to be known as the **era of good feelings**. Because political competition now took place among individual Republican aspirants, this period can also be called the *era of personal politics*.

NATIONAL TWO-PARTY RULE: DEMOCRATS AND WHIGS

Organized two-party politics returned in 1824. With the election of John Quincy Adams as president, the Republican Party split into two entities. The followers of Adams called themselves National Republicans. The followers of Andrew Jackson, who defeated Adams in 1828, formed the **Democratic Party**. Later, the National Republicans took the name **Whig Party**, which had been a traditional name for British liberals. The Whigs stood for, among other things, federal spending on "internal improvements" such as roads. The Democrats opposed this policy. The Democrats, who were the stronger of the two parties, favored personal liberty and opportunity for the "common man." It was understood implicitly that the common man was a white man—hostility toward African Americans was an important force holding the disparate Democratic groups together.[3]

The Democrats' success was linked to their superior efforts to involve common citizens in the political process. Mass participation in politics and elections was a new phenomenon in the 1820s, as the political parties began to appeal to popular enthusiasm and themes. The parties adopted the techniques of mass campaigns, including rallies and parades. Lavishing food and drink on voters at polling places also became a common practice. Perhaps of greatest importance, however, was the push to cultivate party identity and loyalty. In large part, the spirit that motivated the new mass politics was democratic pride in participation. By making citizens feel that they were part of the political process, the parties hoped to win lasting party loyalty at the ballot box.

THE CIVIL WAR CRISIS

In the 1850s, hostility between the North and South over the issue of slavery divided both parties. The Whigs were the first party to split apart. The Whigs had been the

[3]Edward Pessen, *Jacksonian America: Society, Personality, and Politics* (Homewood, IL: Dorsey Press, 1969). See especially pages 246–247. The small number of free blacks who could vote were overwhelmingly Whig.

party of an active federal government, but Southerners had come to believe that "a government strong enough to build roads is a government strong enough to free your slaves." The Southern Whigs therefore ceased to exist as an organized party. The Northern Whigs united with antislavery Democrats and members of the radical antislavery Free Soil Party to form the modern **Republican Party**.

THE POST–CIVIL WAR PERIOD

After the Civil War, the Democratic Party was able to heal its divisions. Southern resentment of the Republicans' role in defeating the South and fears that the federal government would intervene on behalf of African Americans ensured that the Democrats would dominate the white South for the next century.

"Rum, Romanism, and Rebellion." Northern Democrats feared a strong government for other reasons. The Republicans thought that the government should promote business and economic growth, but many Republicans also wanted to use the power of government to impose evangelical Protestant moral values on society. Democrats opposed what they saw as culturally coercive measures. Many Republicans wanted to limit or even prohibit the sale of alcohol. They favored the establishment of public schools—with a Protestant curriculum. As a result, Catholics were strongly Democratic. In 1884, Protestant minister Samuel Burchard described the Democrats as the party of "rum, Romanism, and rebellion." This remark was offensive to Catholics, and Republican presidential candidate James Blaine later claimed that it cost him the White House. Offensive as it may have been, Burchard's characterization of the Democrats contained an element of truth.

The Triumph of the Republicans. In this period, the parties were evenly matched in strength. The abolition of the three-fifths rule, described in Chapter 2, meant that African Americans would be counted fully when allocating House seats and electoral votes to the South. The Republicans therefore had to carry almost every Northern state to win, and this was not always possible. In the 1890s, however, the Republicans gained a decisive

ANDREW JACKSON earned the name "Old Hickory" for his exploits during the War of 1812. In 1828, Jackson was elected president as the candidate of the new Democratic Party. He is shown here, shortly before his death in 1845, in a badly scratched daguerreotype produced by the studio of Mathew B. Brady. (Corbis/Bettmann)

Republican Party
One of the two major American political parties. It emerged in the 1850s as an antislavery party and consisted of former Northern Whigs and antislavery Democrats.

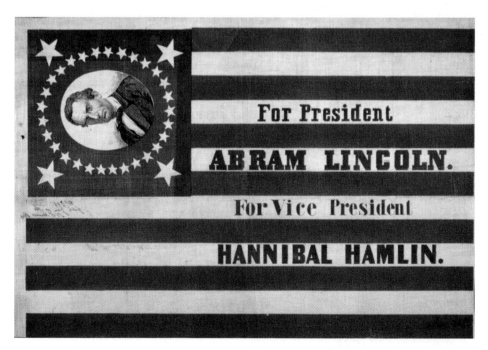

For President
ABRAM LINCOLN.
For Vice President
HANNIBAL HAMLIN.

THIS BANNER was used in the election campaign of 1860 for Republican candidate Abraham Lincoln. Such banners and handbills served the same purpose as today's lawn signs and direct mail advertisements, appealing directly to the voters with the candidate's patriotic image. Why do you think the flag is invoked so often in campaign advertisements? (Library of Congress, Prints & Photographs Division, Washington, D.C. [LC-USZC2-331])

edge. In that decade, the populist movement emerged in the West and South to champion the interests of small farmers, who were often heavily in debt. Populists supported inflation, which benefited debtors by reducing the real value of outstanding debts. In 1896, when William Jennings Bryan became the Democratic candidate for president, the Democrats embraced populism.

As it turned out, the few Western farmers who were drawn to the Democrats by this step were greatly outnumbered by urban working-class voters who believed that inflation would reduce the purchasing power of their paychecks and who therefore became Republicans. William McKinley, the Republican candidate, was elected with a solid majority of the votes. Figure 8–1 shows the states taken by Bryan and McKinley. The pattern of regional support shown in Figure 8–1 persisted for many years. From 1896 until 1932, the Republicans were successfully able to present themselves as the party that knew how to manage the economy.

THE PROGRESSIVE INTERLUDE

In the early 1900s, a spirit of political reform arose in both major parties. Called *progressivism*, this spirit was compounded by a fear of the growing power of great corporations and a belief that honest, impartial government could regulate the economy effectively. In 1912, the Republican Party temporarily split as former Republican president Theodore Roosevelt campaigned for the presidency on a third-party Progressive, or "Bull Moose," ticket. The Republican split permitted the election of Woodrow Wilson, the Democratic candidate, along with a Democratic Congress.

Like Roosevelt, Wilson considered himself a progressive, although he and Roosevelt did not agree on how progressivism ought to be implemented. Wilson's progressivism marked the beginning of a radical change in Democratic policies. Dating back to its foundation, the Democratic Party had been the party of limited government. Under Wilson, the Democrats became for the first time at least as receptive as the Republicans to government action in the economy. (Wilson's progressivism did not extend to race relations—for African Americans, the Wilson administration was something of a disaster.)

THE NEW DEAL ERA

The Republican ascendancy resumed after Wilson left office. It ended with the election of 1932, in the depths of the Great Depression. Republican Herbert Hoover was president when the Depression began in 1929. Although Hoover took some measures to fight the Depression, they fell far short of what the public demanded. Significantly, Hoover

IN 1912, Theodore Roosevelt campaigned for the presidency on a third-party Progressive, or Bull Moose, ticket. Here, you see a charter membership certificate showing Roosevelt and his vice-presidential candidate, Hiram W. Johnson. What was the main result of Roosevelt's formation of this third party? (Bettmann/Corbis)

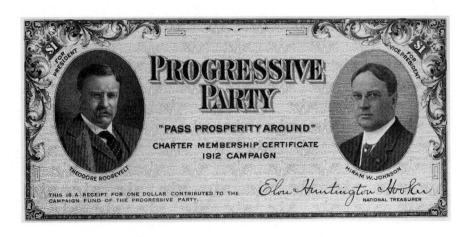

FIGURE 8–1 The 1896 Presidential Election

In 1896, the agrarian, populist appeal of Democrat William Jennings Bryan (blue states) won Western states for the Democrats at the cost of losing more populous Eastern states to Republican William McKinley (red states). This pattern held until the election of Franklin Roosevelt in 1932.

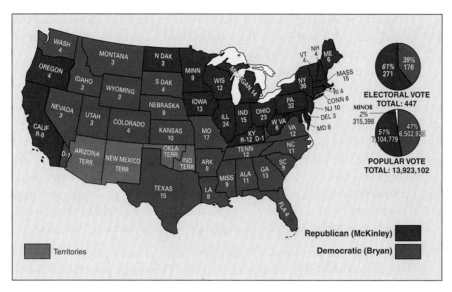

ELECTORAL VOTE TOTAL: 447

POPULAR VOTE TOTAL: 13,923,102

Territories
Republican (McKinley)
Democratic (Bryan)

opposed federal relief for the unemployed and the destitute. In 1932, Democrat Franklin D. Roosevelt was elected president by an overwhelming margin.

The Great Depression shattered the working-class belief in Republican economic competence. Under Roosevelt, the Democrats began to make major interventions in the economy in an attempt to combat the Depression and to relieve the suffering of the unemployed. Roosevelt's New Deal relief programs were open to all citizens, both black and white. As a result, African Americans began to support the Democratic Party in large numbers—a development that would have stunned any American politician of the 1800s.

Roosevelt's political coalition was broad enough to establish the Democrats as the new majority party, in place of the Republicans. In the 1950s, Republican Dwight D. Eisenhower, the leading U.S. general during World War II, won two terms as president. Otherwise, with minor interruptions, the Democratic ascendancy lasted until 1968.

AN ERA OF DIVIDED GOVERNMENT

The New Deal coalition managed the unlikely feat of including both African Americans and whites who were hostile to African American advancement. This balancing act came to an end in the 1960s, a decade that was marked by the civil rights movement, by several years of race riots in major cities, and by increasingly heated protests against the Vietnam War. For many economically liberal, socially conservative voters (especially in the South), social issues had become more important than economic ones, and these voters left the Democrats. These voters outnumbered the new

PRESIDENT FRANKLIN DELANO ROOSEVELT, creator of the modern Democratic Party, speaks to a crowd before his third election victory in 1940. (Fox Photos/Getty Images)

voters who joined the Democrats—newly enfranchised African Americans and former liberal Republicans in New England and the upper Midwest.

The Parties in Balance. The result, since 1968, has been a nation almost evenly divided in politics. In presidential elections, the Republicans have had more success than the Democrats. Until 1994, Congress remained Democratic, but official party labels can be misleading. Some of the Democrats were Southern conservatives who normally voted with the Republicans on issues. As these conservative Democrats retired, they were largely replaced by Republicans.

In the 38 years between the elections of 1968 and 2006, there were only 10 years when one of the two major parties controlled the presidency, the House of Representatives, and the Senate. The Democrats controlled all three institutions during the presidency of Jimmy Carter (1977–1981) and during the first two years of the presidency of Bill Clinton (1993–2001). The Republicans controlled all three institutions during the third through sixth years of George W. Bush's presidency.[4] Before the 1992 elections, the electorate seemed to prefer, in most circumstances, to match a Republican president with a Democratic Congress. Under Bill Clinton, that state of affairs was reversed, with a Democratic president facing a Republican Congress. After the 2006 elections, a Republican president again faced a Democratic Congress.

Red State, Blue State. The pattern of a Republican Congress and a Democratic president would have continued after the election of 2000 if Democratic presidential candidate Al Gore had prevailed. Gore won the popular vote, but lost the electoral college by a narrow margin. Despite the closeness of the result, most states had voted in favor of either Bush or Gore by a fairly wide margin. To many observers, America had become divided between states that were solidly Republican or Democratic in their leanings, with a handful of "swing states." States that had shown strong support for a Republican candidate were deemed "red states" and so-called Democratic states were labeled "blue states."

Despite the presidential victory of Republican George W. Bush and the larger Republican margins of control in the House and Senate, the 2004 elections revealed a nation that continued to be closely divided between the two parties (see Figure 8–2). Bush's 2004 victory may have been the result of cultural politics. In exit polls, more voters chose "moral values" as the most important election issue rather than the war in Iraq or the economy in the exit poll. While this result suggests the importance of cultural issues, the choice of moral issues was never offered to voters in prior elections. The fact that same-sex marriage referenda were on the ballot in many states may have increased the number of conservative voters who turned out and voted Republican.

In 2006, Democratic candidates for Congress seemed to have an edge in national politics. Several Republican members of Congress were forced to resign and face charges on corruption issues, while several others were involved in sex scandals. The Democratic Party mounted a national campaign and won back control of both houses of Congress.

PARTISAN TRENDS IN THE 2008 ELECTIONS

The presidential election year 2008 might be called a "perfect storm" for the Republicans. Although they were able to choose their nominee early, giving him plenty of time

[4]The Republicans also were in control of all three institutions for the first four months after Bush's inauguration. This initial period of control came to an end when Senator James Jeffords of Vermont left the Republican Party, giving the Democrats control of the Senate.

FIGURE 8–3 Republican Issues and Democratic Issues

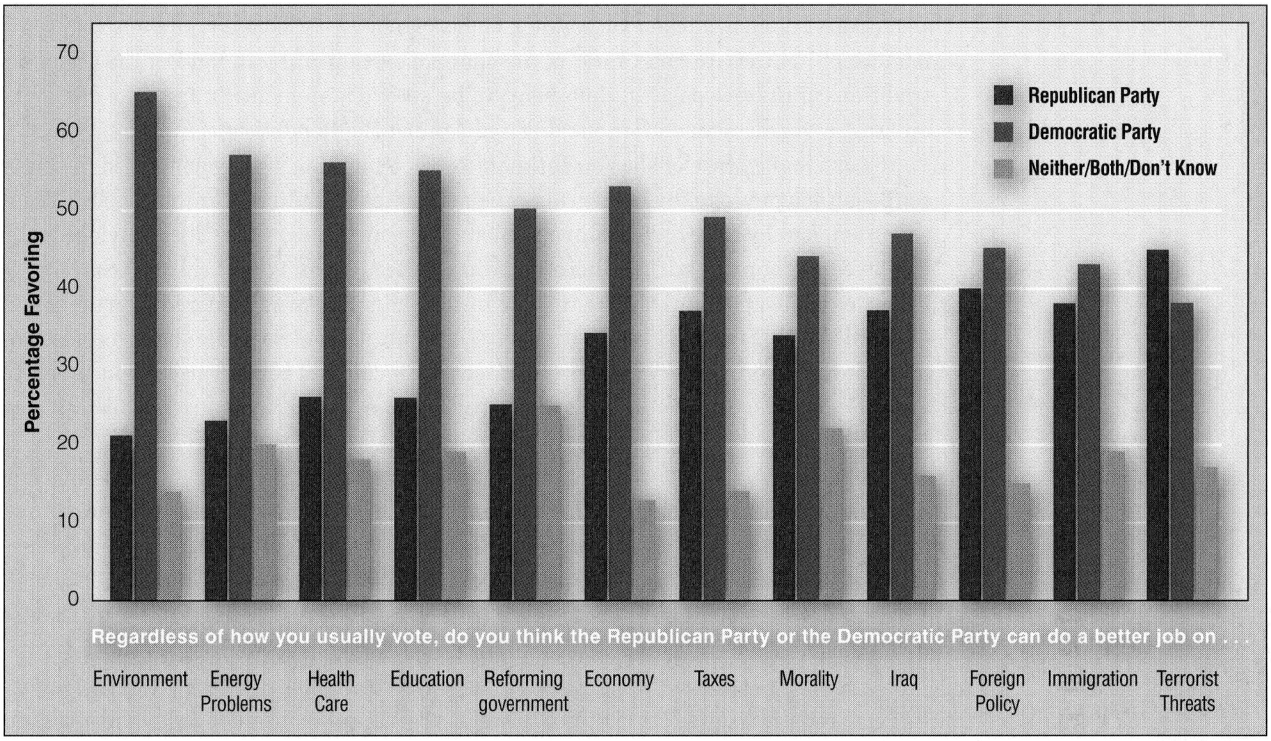

Source: Pew Research Center for the People and the Press. February 28, 2008.

platforms. Republican John McCain adopted a pro-business, less-tax platform, whereas both Democratic contenders for the nomination espoused tax increases for the rich and more tax credits for the poor, as well as taking protectionist positions on trade.

Republican and Democratic Budgets. Other observers have noted a contrast in budgets. Reagan faced a Congress controlled by the Democrats. Clinton in turn faced a Republican Congress for most of his administration. Reagan regularly submitted budgets larger than the ones that the Democratic Congress eventually passed, while Clinton's budgets were typically smaller than those approved by the Republican Congress. During the first three years of George W. Bush's presidency, discretionary federal spending rose by 27 percent, compared with 10 percent under Clinton's two full terms in office. Finally, a Republican majority in Congress passed a new Medicare prescription drug benefit in 2003. In addition, the Bush budgets supporting the war and rebuilding of Iraq added billions to the nation's deficit.

Despite these paradoxes, the perception is that the Democrats still tend to favor the less well off, while the Republicans tend to favor the prosperous. Democrats have argued, for example, that President Bush's tax cuts were weighted heavily toward the upper end of the economic spectrum. In addition, there is another class of issues on which the differences between the parties have become greater than ever—cultural issues.

CULTURAL POLITICS

In recent years, cultural values may have become more important than they previously were in defining the beliefs of the two major parties. For example, in 1987, Democrats were almost as likely to favor stricter abortion laws (40 percent) as Republicans were (48 percent). Today, Republicans are twice as likely to favor stricter abortion laws (50 percent to 25 percent).

Cultural Politics and Socioeconomic Status. Thomas Frank, a writer, noticed the following bumper sticker at a gun show in Kansas City: "A working person voting for the Democrats is like a chicken voting for Colonel Sanders." (Colonel Sanders is the iconic founder of Kentucky Fried Chicken, the chain of restaurants.) In light of the economic traditions of the two parties, this seems to be an odd statement. In fact, the sticker is an exact reversal of an earlier one directed against the Republicans.

You can make sense of such a sentiment by remembering what you learned in Chapter 6—although economic conservatism is associated with higher incomes, social conservatism is relatively more common among lower-income groups. The individual who displayed the bumper sticker, therefore, was in effect claiming that cultural concerns—in this example, presumably the right to own handguns—are far more important than economic ones. Frank argues that despite Republican control of the national government during the George W. Bush administration, cultural conservatives continued to view themselves as embattled "ordinary Americans" under threat from a liberal, cosmopolitan elite.[6]

Also, according to Republican commentator Karl Zinsmeister, many police officers, construction workers, military veterans, and rural residents began moving toward the Republican Party in the 1960s and 1970s. In contrast, many of America's rich and super-rich elite, including financiers, media barons, software millionaires, and entertainers, started slowly, but surely, drifting toward the Democratic Party. Arguably, the major financial backing for Democrats is from the rich and superrich. In contrast, for the Republicans in the last two presidential elections, less than 10 percent of voters in pro-Bush counties earned more than $100,000 per year. All that can be said today is that it is difficult to stereotype what socioeconomic groups support which party.

DID YOU KNOW?

That it took 103 ballots for John W. Davis to be nominated at the Democratic National Convention in 1924?

The Regional Factor in Cultural Politics. Conventionally, some parts of the country are viewed as culturally liberal and others as culturally conservative. On a regional basis, cultural liberalism (as opposed to economic liberalism) may be associated with economic dynamism. The San Francisco Bay Area can serve as an example. The greater Bay Area contains Silicon Valley, the heart of the microcomputer industry; it has the highest per capita personal income of any metropolitan area in America. It also is one of the most liberal regions of the country. San Francisco liberalism is largely cultural—one sign of this liberalism is that the city has a claim to be the "capital" of gay America. There is not much evidence, however, that the region's wealthy citizens are in favor of higher taxes.

IN 2006, Senator John McCain visited Liberty University, a very conservative institution, to shore up his credentials with evangelical Christians in the Republican Party. (The News & Advance, Laura J. Gardner/AP/Wide World Photos)

---

[6]Thomas Frank, *What's the Matter with Kansas?* (New York: Macmillan, 2004).

To further illustrate this point, we can compare the political preferences of relatively wealthy states with relatively poor ones. Of the 10 states with the highest per capita personal incomes in 2004, eight voted for Democrat John Kerry in the presidential election of that year. Of the 25 states with the lowest per capita incomes in 2004, 23 voted for Republican George W. Bush.

Given these data, it seems difficult to believe that upper-income voters really are more Republican than lower-income ones. Within any given state or region, however, upscale voters are more likely to be Republican regardless of whether the area as a whole leans Democratic or Republican. States that vote Democratic are often Northern states that contain large cities. At least part of this **reverse-income effect** may simply be that urban areas are more prosperous, culturally liberal, and Democratic than the countryside, and that the North is more prosperous, culturally liberal, and Democratic than the South.

Reverse-Income Effect
A tendency for wealthier states or regions to favor the Democrats and for less wealthy states or regions to favor the Republicans. The effect appears paradoxical because it reverses traditional patterns of support.

THE 2008 ELECTIONS: ECONOMICS AND NATIONAL SECURITY

Senator Barack Obama and many of the other contenders for the Democratic presidential nomination expressed their opposition to the war in Iraq as well as many other Bush administration foreign policy initiatives long before the primary season began. Indeed, most Democrats doubted that the military surge in Iraq could be effective. National security concerns were still very much on voters' minds in the early period of the primaries as Obama and Senator Hillary Clinton battled for the nomination. After the nomination was clinched in June, national security questions faded in importance. Fewer incidents of violence occurred in Iraq, and the surge seemed to have worked. No terrorist attacks on Americans took place.

Throughout the summer, it seemed clear that the American economy was slowing down, and talk of recession entered the campaigns. As shown in Figure 8–3, voters already believed that Democrats were better able to handle unemployment and the economy than were Republicans. In the general election campaign, the presidential candidates and their respective parties staked out classic positions: Democrats espoused tax cuts for the poor and the middle class and tax increases on the wealthiest Americans. John McCain articulated the Republican view that tax cuts for all levels of income would be a better way to stimulate a sagging economy. As the banking crisis deepened, a majority of voters blamed it on the Republicans and trusted the Democratic Party to bring the country out of recession.

DURING HER PRIMARY battle with Barack Obama, Senator Hillary Clinton campaigned with blue collar Democrats outside an automotive parts plant in Maryland. How do campaign tactics differ in a primary election from the general election? (Jed Kirschbaum/MCT/Landov Media)

THE THREE FACES OF A PARTY

Party-in-the-Electorate
Those members of the general public who identify with a political party or who express a preference for one party over another.

Although American parties are known by a single name and, in the public mind, have a common historical identity, each party really has three major components. The first component is the **party-in-the-electorate**. This phrase refers to all those individuals who claim an attachment to the political party. They need not participate in election campaigns. Rather, the party-in-the-electorate is the large number of Americans who feel some loyalty to the party or who use partisanship as a cue to decide who will earn their vote. Party membership is not really a rational choice; rather, it is an emotional tie somewhat analogous to identifying with a region or a baseball team. Although individuals may hold a deep loyalty to or identification with a political party, there is no need for members of the party-in-the-electorate to speak out publicly, to contribute to campaigns, or to vote all Republican or all Democratic. Needless to say, the party leaders pay close attention to the affiliation of their members in the electorate.

Party Organization
The formal structure and leadership of a political party, including election committees; local, state, and national executives; and paid professional staff.

The second component, the **party organization**, provides the structural framework for the political party by recruiting volunteers to become party leaders; identifying potential candidates; and organizing caucuses, conventions, and election campaigns for its candidates, as will be discussed in more detail shortly. The party organization and its active workers keep the party functioning between elections, as well as make sure that the party puts forth electable candidates and clear positions in the elections. If the party-in-the-electorate declines in numbers and loyalty, the party organization must try to find a strategy to rebuild the grassroots following.

Party-in-Government
All of the elected and appointed officials who identify with a political party.

The **party-in-government** is the third component of American political parties. The party-in-government consists of those elected and appointed officials who identify with a political party. Generally, elected officials do not also hold official party positions within the formal organization, although they often have the informal power to appoint party executives.

PARTY ORGANIZATION

Each of the American political parties is often seen as having a pyramid-shaped organization, with the national chairperson and committee at the top and the local precinct chairperson on the bottom. This structure, however, does not accurately reflect the relative power of the individual components of the party organization. If it did, the national chairperson of the Democratic Party or the Republican Party, along with the national committee, could simply dictate how the organization was to be run, just as if it were the ExxonMobil Corporation or Ford Motor Company. In reality, the political parties have a confederal structure, in which each unit has significant autonomy and is linked only loosely to the other units. The fact that these are not powerful national organizations can be seen in the uneven strength of local and state party organizations. In some states, parties receive significant contributions from individuals and interest groups for their operations, whereas in other states and localities political parties are very weak organizations with very little funding. This is particularly true of the minority party in a state or district where they have little chance to win a seat.

National Convention
The meeting held every four years by each major party to select presidential and vice-presidential candidates, to write a platform, to choose a national committee, and to conduct party business.

THE NATIONAL PARTY ORGANIZATION

Party Platform
A document drawn up at each national convention outlining the policies, positions, and principles of the party.

Each party has a national organization, the most clearly institutional part of which is the **national convention**, held every four years. The convention is used to nominate the presidential and vice-presidential candidates. In addition, the **party platform** is

WHAT IF...

PARTIES WERE SUPPORTED SOLELY BY PUBLIC FUNDING?

Today's major political parties are supported by hundreds of millions of dollars offered by unions, corporations, other groups, and individuals, thereby greatly benefiting the party with the most funding. Not surprisingly, some Americans lament that the winning candidates are merely the "best that money can buy." Over the years, a number of reforms to the system have been proposed to lessen the candidates' dependence on such contributions. One of those reforms would be the public financing of political parties. Such public financing would, of course, come from taxpayers.

What if parties were supported by public funding? Public funding would need to replace the many millions of dollars spent each year to educate the public, register voters, recruit candidates, and support election campaigns. If that amount were significantly reduced, the effectiveness of the political parties would also be reduced. Also, if the public were funding the national parties, there would almost certainly be prohibitions on contributions from corporations, individuals, and interest groups. This would greatly change the current situation, because corporations and interest groups currently give to candidates who they believe will support their interests. For example, labor unions give to Democratic political action committees and chambers of commerce are more likely to give to Republican political action committees.

Currently, candidates for election receive public funds in certain states, such as Arizona, Maine, and Vermont, and a limited amount of public financing is provided for presidential candidates. All such public financing of candidates' campaigns carries with it restrictions on acceptable sources of other funds. If both the major parties and candidates for election were publicly financed, the role of lobbies and lobbyists would be changed. No longer would they be holding fundraising social events for candidates and parties. Instead, they would have to rely on their ability to inform or persuade legislators.

The public financing of the major national parties could either strengthen or weaken their influence over candidates, voters, and campaigns. If only the national parties were funded rather than candidates, contributions would flow to candidates and campaigns. If, however, all public funding was channelled through the parties, candidates would need to be much more attentive to the party platform and its campaign strategies.

MORE POLITICAL PARTIES WOULD BE POSSIBLE

Who is to say that public funding of political parties would be limited to only the two major parties? If we adopted the French system, for example, public funds would be available for numerous political parties. The only requirement would be a minimum number of party members. As you might imagine, the result in France has been the emergence of dozens of small political parties. After all, if public funds are available, someone will figure out a way to obtain them. That means those with strong political ideas would be able to gather like-minded Americans to create a party, spend some effort to obtain like-minded members, and apply for public funds. The major political parties would still be the only serious players in this country, however. In our winner-take-all electoral system, few independent party candidates can win public office.

FOR CRITICAL ANALYSIS

1. If political parties were publicly funded, what would be the appropriate level of funding? More than the parties are spending today, the same, or less?
2. Would it be good to have more than two parties funded by the government?

developed at the national convention. The platform sets forth the party's position on the issues and makes promises to initiate certain policies if the party wins the presidency.

After the convention, the platform frequently is neglected or ignored by party candidates who disagree with it. Because candidates are trying to win votes from a wide spectrum of voters, it is counterproductive to emphasize the fairly narrow and sometimes controversial goals set forth in the platform. Political scientist Gerald M. Pomper discovered decades ago, however, that once elected, the parties do try to carry out platform promises, and that roughly three-fourths of the promises eventually become law.[7] Of course, some general goals, such as economic prosperity, are included in the platforms of both parties.

Convention Delegates. The party convention provides the most striking illustration of the difference between the ordinary members of a party, or party identifiers, and party activists. As a series of studies by the *New York Times* shows, delegates to the national party conventions are quite different from ordinary party identifiers. Delegates to the Democratic National Convention, as shown in Table 8–1, are far more liberal than ordinary Democratic voters. Typically, delegates to the Republican National Convention are far more conservative than ordinary Republicans. Why does this happen? In part, it is because a person, to become a delegate, must gather votes in a primary election from party members who care enough to vote in a primary or be appointed by party leaders. Also, the primaries generally pit presidential candidates against each other on intraparty issues. Competition within each party tends to pull candidates away from the center, and delegates even more so. Often, the most important activity for the convention is making peace among the delegates who support different candidates and persuading them to accept a party platform that will appeal to the general electorate.

FIREWORKS ERUPT at the end of Senator Barack Obama's acceptance speech at the 2008 Democratic National Convention. The first African American presidential nominee gave a stirring speech in Denver's football stadium. (Jim Young/Reuters/Landov Media)

GOVERNOR SARAH PALIN, the vice-presidential nominee for the Republican Party, roused the delegates with her acceptance speech at the Republican National Convention. (Ethan Miller/Getty Images)

[7]Gerald M. Pomper and Susan S. Lederman, *Elections in America: Control and Influence in Democratic Politics*, 2nd ed. (New York: Longman, 1980).

TABLE 8-1 Convention Delegates and Voters: How Did They Compare on the Issues in 2008?

At the time of the national party conventions, the *New York Times* surveys a sample of each convention's delegates, a sample of party voters, and compares their views to those of the average voter. The table below shows that Republican convention delegates tend to be more conservative than their voters and that Democratic delegates are more liberal than their voters.

	PERCENTAGE OF...				
	DEMOCRATIC DELEGATES	DEMOCRATIC VOTERS	ALL VOTERS	REPUBLICAN VOTERS	REPUBLICAN DELEGATES
Rate economy as very or fairly good	2	7	20	40	57
The U.S. did the right thing in taking military action against Iraq.	2	14	37	70	80
Gay couples should be allowed to marry.	55	49	34	11	6
Abortion should be generally available to those who want it.	70	43	33	20	9
Protecting the environment is more a priority for the government than new energy sources.	25	30	21	9	3
It is more important to provide health-care coverage than hold down taxes.	94	90	67	40	7

Source: *The New York Times*, September 1, 2008, p. A14.

The National Committee. At the national convention, each of the parties formally chooses a national standing committee, elected by the individual state parties. This **national committee** directs and coordinates party activities during the following four years. The Democrats include at least two members (a man and a woman) from each state, from the District of Columbia, and from the several territories. Governors, members of Congress, mayors, and other officials may be included as at-large members of the national committee. The Republicans, in addition, include state chairpersons from every state carried by the Republican Party in the preceding presidential, gubernatorial, or Congressional elections. The selections of national committee members are ratified by the delegations to the national convention.

National Committee
A standing committee of a national political party established to direct and coordinate party activities between national party conventions.

One of the jobs of the national committee is to ratify the presidential nominee's choice of a national chairperson, who (in principle) acts as the spokesperson for the party. The national chairperson and the national committee plan the next campaign and the next convention, obtain financial contributions, and publicize the national party.

Picking a National Chairperson. In general, the party's presidential candidate chooses the national chairperson. (If that candidate loses, however, the chairperson is often changed.) The national chairperson performs such jobs as establishing a national party headquarters, raising campaign funds and distributing them to state parties

and to candidates, and appearing in the media as a party spokesperson. The national chairperson, along with the national committee, attempts to maintain some sort of liaison among the different levels of the party organization. In 2008, Democratic National Chairman Howard Dean faced a real challenge as Senators Clinton and Obama battled for the nomination. Many Democrats called for him to convince one of the candidates to drop out of the race for the nomination to build unity among Democrats for the November election. The fact, though, is that the real strength and power of a national party are at the state level.

THE CURRENT CHAIRMAN of the Democratic National Committee is Howard Dean (left). The chairman of the Republican National Committee is Mike Duncan (right). What are some of the jobs carried out by these individuals? (UPI Photo/Kevin Dietsch/Landov and AP Photo/Samira Jafari)

State Central Committee
The principal organized structure of each political party within each state. This committee is responsible for carrying out policy decisions of the party's state convention.

Unit Rule
A rule by which all of a state's electoral votes are cast for the presidential candidate receiving a plurality of the popular vote in that state.

THE STATE PARTY ORGANIZATION

There are 50 states in the Union, plus the District of Columbia and the U.S. territories, and an equal number of party organizations for each major party. Therefore, there are more than 100 state parties (and even more, if we include local parties and minor parties). Because every state party is unique, it is impossible to describe what an "average" state political party is like. Nonetheless, state parties have several organizational features in common.

Each state party has a chairperson, a committee, and local organizations. In theory, the role of the **state central committee**—the principal organized structure of each political party within each state—is similar in the various states. The committee, usually composed of members who represent congressional districts, state legislative districts, or counties, has responsibility for carrying out the policy decisions of the party's state convention. In some states, the state committee can issue directives to the state chairperson.

Also, like the national committee, the state central committee controls the use of party campaign funds during political campaigns. Usually, the state central committee has little, if any, influence on party candidates once they are elected. In fact, state parties are fundamentally loose alliances of local interests and coalitions of often bitterly opposed factions.

State parties are also important in national politics because of the **unit rule**, which awards electoral votes in presidential elections as an indivisible bloc (except in Maine and Nebraska). Presidential candidates concentrate their efforts in states in which voter preferences seem to be evenly divided or in which large numbers of electoral votes are at stake.

LOCAL PARTY MACHINERY: THE GRASSROOTS

The lowest layer of party machinery is the local organization, supported by district leaders, precinct or ward captains, and party workers. Much of the work is coordinated by county committees and their chairpersons.

Patronage and City Machines. In the 1800s, the institution of **patronage**—rewarding the party faithful with government jobs or contracts—held the local organization together. For immigrants and the poor, the political machine often furnished important services and protections. The big-city machine was the archetypal example. Tammany Hall, or the Tammany Society, which dominated New York City government for nearly two centuries, was perhaps the most notorious example of this political form.

The last big-city local political machine to exercise substantial power was run by Chicago's Mayor Richard J. Daley, who was also an important figure in national Democratic politics. Daley, as mayor, ran the Chicago Democratic machine from 1955 until his death in 1976. The current mayor of Chicago, Richard M. Daley, son of the former mayor, does not have the kind of machine that his father had.

City machines are now dead, mostly because their function of providing social services (and reaping the reward of votes) has been taken over by state and national agencies. This trend began in the 1930s, when the social legislation of the New Deal established Social Security and unemployment insurance. The local party machine has little, if anything, to do with deciding who is eligible to receive these benefits.

Local Party Organizations Today. Local political organizations—whether located in cities, in townships, or at the county level—still can contribute a great deal to local election campaigns. These organizations are able to provide the foot soldiers of politics—individuals who pass out literature and get out the vote on election day, which can be crucial in local elections. In many regions, local Democratic and Republican organizations still exercise some patronage, such as awarding courthouse jobs, contracts for street repair, and other lucrative construction contracts. The constitutionality of awarding (or not awarding) contracts on the basis of political affiliation has been subject to challenge, however. The United States Supreme Court has ruled that firing or failing to hire individuals because of their political affiliation is an infringement of the employees' First Amendment rights to free expression.[8] Local party organizations are also the most important

[8]*Rutan v. Republican Party of Illinois*, 497 U.S. 62 (1990).

> **Patronage**
> Rewarding faithful party workers and followers with government employment and contracts.

VOLUNTEERS CHECK their lists as they register voters in South Dade County, Florida. Civil rights organizations trained the volunteers to register voters in hopes of avoiding the chaos of the 2000 elections. (Orjan F. Ellingvag/CORBIS)

vehicles for recruiting young adults into political work, because political involvement at the local level offers activists many opportunities to gain experience.

THE PARTY-IN-GOVERNMENT

After the election is over and the winners are announced, the focus of party activity shifts from getting out the vote to organizing and controlling the government. As you will learn in Chapter 12, party membership plays an important role in the day-to-day operations of Congress, with partisanship determining everything from office space to committee assignments and power on Capitol Hill. For the president, the political party furnishes the pool of qualified applicants for political appointments to run the government. (Although it is uncommon to do so, presidents can and occasionally do appoint executive personnel, such as Cabinet members, from the opposition party.) As we will note in Chapter 13, there are not as many of these appointed positions as presidents might like, and presidential power is limited by the permanent bureaucracy. Judicial appointments also offer a great opportunity to the winning party. For the most part, presidents are likely to appoint federal judges from their own party.

Divided Government. All of these party appointments suggest that the winning political party, whether at the national, state, or local level, has a great deal of control in the American system. Because of the checks and balances and the relative lack of cohesion in American parties, however, such control is an illusion. One reason is that for some time, many Americans have seemed to prefer a **divided government**, with the executive and legislative branches controlled by different parties. The trend toward **ticket splitting**—splitting votes between the president and members of Congress—has increased sharply since 1952. This practice may indicate a lack of trust in government (as discussed in Chapter 6) or the relative weakness of party identification among many voters. Voters have often seemed comfortable with having a president affiliated with one party and a Congress controlled by the other.

The Limits of Party Unity. There are other ways in which the power of the parties is limited. Consider how major laws are passed in Congress. Traditionally, legislation has rarely been passed by a vote strictly along party lines. Although most Democrats may oppose a bill, for example, some Democrats may vote for it. Their votes, combined with the votes of Republicans, may be enough to pass the bill. Similarly, support from some Republicans may enable a bill sponsored by the Democrats to pass. This is not to say that Congress *never* votes along strict party lines. A notable example of such partisan voting occurred in the House of Representatives in 1998. The issue at hand was whether to impeach President Bill Clinton. Almost all votes were strictly along party lines—Democrats against, and Republicans for.

One reason that the political parties find it so hard to rally all of their members in Congress to vote along party lines is that parties have almost no control over who runs for office. In other words, the head of a political party in most instances cannot handpick candidates who share his or her views and who will be loyal to the party's views. In the United States, modern elections are "candidate centered," meaning that candidates choose to run, raise their own funds, build their own organizations, and win elections largely on their own, without significant help from a political party. This means, though, that the parties have very little control over the candidates who run under the party labels. In fact, a candidate could run as a Republican, for example, and advocate beliefs that are repugnant to the national party, such as a socialized health-care system. No one in the Republican Party organization could stop this person from being nominated or

Divided Government
A situation in which one major political party controls the presidency and the other controls the chambers of Congress, or in which one party controls a state governorship and the other controls the state legislature.

Ticket Splitting
Voting for candidates of two or more parties for different offices. For example, a voter splits her ticket if she votes for a Republican presidential candidate and a Democratic Congressional candidate.

even elected, although the likelihood that he or she would attract votes from Republican voters is very slim.

Party Polarization. Despite the forces that act against party-line voting, there have been times when the two parties in Congress have been polarized, and defections from the party line have been rare. One such period was the mid-1990s, after the Republicans gained control of both the House and the Senate. Under House Speaker Newt Gingrich, the Republicans maintained strict discipline in an attempt to use their new majority to sponsor a specific legislative agenda. In 2003, polarization peaked again. "People genuinely hate each other," lamented Louisiana Senator John Breaux, a moderate Democrat.[9]

One cause of polarization is ability of the parties to create House districts that are **safe seats**. The creation of districts will be discussed further in Chapter 12. It is also true that the two parties are each more cohesive today than in many years. That means, for example, that the Republican Party leadership, many of its contributors, and its officeholders share beliefs about government and, to some extent, cultural values. Those beliefs are more conservative than those of the grassroots voter. Democratic leaders and politicians share more liberal views than those of the grassroots voter. This makes it easier for Congresspeople and Senators to vote together and support a common partisan position. With both parties becoming more cohesive, the debate over policies becomes more polarized and divisive.

Safe Seat
A district that returns the legislator with 55 percent of the vote or more.

Writers and advocates in the media, who find that stridency sells, also tend to encourage an atmosphere of polarization. Some commentators, however, do not believe that this spirit of polarization extends very far into the general electorate. They contend that a majority of Americans are strongly committed to tolerance of opposing political views. Supporting this view is Morris Fiorina, who argues that the American people are no more divided over their policy preferences than they have ever been.[10]

WHY HAS THE TWO-PARTY SYSTEM ENDURED?

There are several reasons why two major parties have dominated the political landscape in the United States for almost two centuries. These reasons have to do with (1) the historical foundations of the system, (2) political socialization and practical considerations, (3) the winner-take-all electoral system, and (4) state and federal laws favoring the two-party system.

THE HISTORICAL FOUNDATIONS OF THE TWO-PARTY SYSTEM

As we have seen, at many times in American history, one preeminent issue or dispute has divided the nation politically. In the beginning, Americans were at odds over ratifying the Constitution. After the Constitution went into effect, the power of the federal government became the major national issue. Thereafter, the dispute over slavery divided the nation by section, North versus South. At times—for example, in the North after the Civil War—cultural differences have been important, with advocates

---

[9]Jackie Calmes, "Set This House on Fire," *The Wall Street Journal Europe*, December 1, 2003, p. A7.
[10]Morris Fiorina, *Culture War?: The Myth of a Polarized America* (New York: Longman, 2005).

of government-sponsored morality (such as banning alcoholic beverages) pitted against advocates of personal liberty.

During much of the 1900s, economic differences were preeminent. In the New Deal period, the Democrats became known as the party of the working class, while the Republicans became known as the party of the middle and upper classes and commercial interests. When politics is based on an argument between two opposing points of view, advocates of each viewpoint can mobilize most effectively by forming a single, unified party. Also, when a two-party system has been in existence for almost two centuries, it becomes difficult to imagine an alternative.

POLITICAL SOCIALIZATION AND PRACTICAL CONSIDERATIONS

Given that the majority of Americans identify with one of the two major political parties, it is not surprising that most children learn at a fairly young age to think of themselves as either Democrats or Republicans. This generates a built-in mechanism to perpetuate a two-party system. Also, many politically oriented people who aspire to work for social change consider that the only realistic way to capture political power in this country is to be either a Republican or a Democrat.

THE WINNER-TAKE-ALL ELECTORAL SYSTEM

At virtually every level of government in the United States, the outcome of elections is based on the **plurality**, winner-take-all principle. In a plurality system, the winner is the person who obtains the most votes, even if that person does not receive a majority (more than 50 percent) of the votes. Whoever gets the most votes gets everything. Most legislators in the United States are elected from single-member districts in which only one person represents the constituency, and the candidate who finishes second in such an election receives nothing for the effort.

Presidential Voting. The winner-take-all system also operates in the election of the U.S president. Recall that the voters in each state do not vote for a president directly but

Plurality
A number of votes cast for a candidate that is greater than the number of votes for any other candidate but not necessarily a majority.

THE 2008 REPUBLICAN CONVENTION ended with a traditional balloon drop. In the United States, the major parties expend enormous effort planning their national conventions and attracting a national television audience. What are the parties trying to achieve with these spectacles? (Charles Rex Arbogast/ AP Photo)

vote for **electoral college** delegates who are committed to the various presidential candidates. These delegates are called *electors*.

In all but two states (Maine and Nebraska), if a presidential candidate wins a plurality in the state, then *all* of the state's votes go to that candidate. For example, let us say that the electors pledged to a particular presidential candidate receive a plurality of 40 percent of the votes in a state. That presidential candidate will receive all of the state's votes in the electoral college. Minor parties have a difficult time competing under such a system. Because voters know that minor parties cannot win any electoral votes, they often will not vote for minor-party candidates, even if the candidates are in tune with them ideologically.

Popular Election of the Governors and the President. In most European countries, the chief executive (usually called the prime minister) is elected by the legislature, or parliament. If the parliament contains three or more parties, as is usually the case, two or more of the parties can join together in a coalition to choose the prime minister and the other leaders of the government. In the United States, however, the people elect the president and the governors of all 50 states. There is no opportunity for two or more parties to negotiate a coalition. Here, too, the winner-take-all principle discriminates powerfully against any third party.

Proportional Representation. Many other nations use a system of proportional representation with multimember districts. If, during the national election, party X obtains 12 percent of the vote, party Y gets 43 percent of the vote, and party Z gets the remaining 45 percent of the vote, then party X gets 12 percent of the seats in the legislature, party Y gets 43 percent of the seats, and party Z gets 45 percent of the seats. Because even a minor party may still obtain at least a few seats in the legislature, the smaller parties have a greater incentive to organize under such electoral systems than they do in the United States. To read more about nations that utilize a proportional representation system, see this chapter's *Beyond Our Borders* feature.

The relative effects of proportional representation versus our system of single-member districts are so strong that many scholars have made them one of the few "laws" of political science. Duverger's Law, named after French political scientist Maurice Duverger, states that electoral systems based on single-member districts tend to produce two parties, while systems of proportional representation produce multiple parties.[11] Still, many countries with single-member districts have more than two political parties—Britain and Canada are examples.

STATE AND FEDERAL LAWS FAVORING THE TWO PARTIES

Many state and federal election laws offer a clear advantage to the two major parties. In some states, the established major parties need to gather fewer signatures to place their candidates on the ballot than do minor parties or independent candidates. The criterion for determining how many signatures will be required is often based on the total party vote in the last general election, thus penalizing a new political party that did not compete in that election.

At the national level, minor parties face different obstacles. All of the rules and procedures of both houses of Congress divide committee seats, staff members, and other privileges on the basis of party membership. A legislator who is elected on a minor-party ticket, such as the Conservative Party of New York, must choose to be counted

Electoral College
A group of persons, called electors, who are selected by the voters in each state. This group officially elects the president and the vice president of the United States.

That the Reform Party, established in 1996, used a vote-by-mail process for the first step of its nominating convention and also accepted votes cast by e-mail?

---

[11]As cited in Todd Landman, *Issues and Methods in Comparative Politics* (New York: Routledge, 2003), p. 14.

with one of the major parties to obtain a committee assignment. The Federal Election Commission (FEC) rules for campaign financing also place restrictions on minor-party candidates. Such candidates are not eligible for federal matching funds in either the primary or the general election. In the 1980 election, John Anderson, running for president as an independent, sued the FEC for campaign funds. The commission finally agreed to repay part of his campaign costs after the election in proportion to the votes he received. Giving funds to a candidate when the campaign is over is, of course, much less helpful than providing funds while the campaign is still under way.

THE ROLE OF MINOR PARTIES IN U.S. POLITICS

Third Party
A political party other than the two major political parties (Republican and Democratic).

For the reasons just discussed, minor parties have a difficult (if not impossible) time competing within the American two-party political system. Nonetheless, minor parties have played an important role in our political life. Parties other than the Republicans or Democrats are usually called **third parties**. (Technically, of course, there could be fourth, fifth, or sixth parties as well, but we use the term *third party* because it has endured.) Third parties can come into existence in three ways: (1) they may be founded from scratch by individuals or groups who are committed to a particular interest, issue, or ideology; (2) they can split off from one of the major parties when a group becomes dissatisfied with the major party's policies; and (3) they can be organized around a particular charismatic leader and serve as that person's vehicle for contesting elections.

Third parties have acted as barometers of changes in the political mood. Such barometric indicators have forced the major parties to recognize new issues or trends in the thinking of Americans. Political scientists believe that third parties have acted as safety valves for dissident groups, preventing major confrontations and political unrest. In some instances, third parties have functioned as way stations for voters en route from one of the major parties to the other. Table 8–2 on page 308 lists significant third-party presidential campaigns in American history; Table 8–3 on page 309 provides a brief description of third-party beliefs.

IDEOLOGICAL THIRD PARTIES

The longest-lived third parties have been those with strong ideological foundations that are typically at odds with the majority mind-set. The Socialist Party is an example. The party was founded in 1901 and lasted until 1972, when it was finally dissolved. (A smaller party later took up the name.)

Ideology has at least two functions. First, the members of the minor party regard themselves as outsiders and look to one another for support; ideology provides great psychological cohesiveness. Second, because the rewards of ideological commitment are partly psychological, these minor parties do not think in terms of immediate electoral success. A poor showing at the polls therefore does not dissuade either the leadership or the grassroots participants from continuing their quest for change in American government (and, ultimately, American society).

INDEPENDENT PRESIDENTIAL candidate Ralph Nader (shown here) and former candidate Howard Dean debated the legitimacy of third-party campaigns in July 2004. After Dean's own bid for the presidency failed, the former Vermont governor became the Democratic Party's leading critic of Nader's campaign. Nader ran again in 2008. (REUTERS/Molly Riley/Landov)

BEYOND OUR B RDERS

MULTIPARTY SYSTEMS: THE RULE RATHER THAN THE EXCEPTION

The United States has a two-party system. Occasionally, a third-party candidate enters the race, but really has little chance of winning. Throughout the world, though, many democracies have multiparty systems.

SOME EXAMPLES

In its first legislative elections ever, Afghanistan saw the emergence of six major parties and seven minor parties. In the 2005 Iraqi National Assembly Election, there were a total of 15 parliamentary alliances and parties, plus 20 other parties. In any national election in India, there are six major parties, and in the states, there are a total of 30 parties. (There are also more than 700 registered, but unrecognized, parties in India.)

In the latest elections in Germany, there were major parties and numerous minor ones. In any given presidential election in France, there are even more parties. They include the National Front that represents the extreme right, anti-immigrant part of the electorate. But there was also a party for hunting, fishing, nature, and traditions and one for the Revolutionary Communist League. All in all, there are at least 15 French parties, most of which obtain some public funding.

PROPORTIONAL REPRESENTATION AND COALITIONS

In the German elections of September 2005, the Christian Democrats received about 30 percent of the vote and obtained about 30 percent of the seats in the German Federal Congress, called the *Bundestag*. The Christian Social Union of Bavaria obtained about 8 percent of the votes and almost 8 percent of the seats. Together, these two right-of-center parties obtained 36.8 percent of the seats in Germany's equivalent of our House of Representatives. The opposition on the left, called the Social Demo-

cratic Party of Germany, obtained almost the same—36.2 percent. Not surprisingly, neither the right nor the left in Germany had a high enough percentage of seats in the *Bundestag* to move forward. Consequently, a coalition government was formed, one that had to take account of the more extreme parties represented in the *Bundestag*, including the Free Democratic Party and the so-called Greens (ecologists).

In the latest French elections, the Union for a Presidential Minority, along with assorted other right-of-center parties, obtained a clear majority and therefore did not have to form coalitions with opposition parties on the left.

Coalitions are almost a certainty in a multiparty system. Why? Because usually the leading party does not have a majority of votes in the legislature. The leading party therefore has to make compromises to obtain votes from other parties. These coalitions are subject to change due to the pressures of lawmaking. Often, a minor partner in a coalition finds itself unable to support the laws or policies proposed by its larger partners. Either a compromise will be found, or the coalition will be ended and new partners may be sought to form a government coalition. If we had a multiparty system in the United States, we might have a farmers' party, a Hispanic party, a Western party, a labor party, and others. To gain support for her or his program, a president would have to build a coalition of several parties by persuading each that its members would benefit from the coalition. The major difficulty in a multiparty system is, of course, that the parties will withdraw from the coalition when they fail to benefit from it. Holding a coalition together for more than one issue is sometimes impossible.

FOR CRITICAL ANALYSIS

Are multiparty systems necessarily more representative than the two-party system in the United States? Why or why not?

TABLE 8–2 The Most Successful Third-Party Presidential Campaigns Since 1864

The following list includes all third-party candidates winning more than 5 percent of the popular vote or any electoral votes since 1864. (We ignore isolated "unfaithful electors" in the electoral college who fail to vote for the candidate to which they are pledged.)

YEAR	MAJOR THIRD PARTY	THIRD-PARTY PRESIDENTIAL CANDIDATE	PERCENT OF THE POPULAR VOTE	ELECTORAL VOTES	WINNING PRESIDENTIAL CANDIDATE AND PARTY
1892	Populist	James Weaver	8.5	22	Grover Cleveland (D)
1912	Progressive	Theodore Roosevelt	27.4	88	Woodrow Wilson (D)
	Socialist	Eugene Debs	6.0	—	
1924	Progressive	Robert LaFollette	16.6	13	Calvin Coolidge (R)
1948	States' Rights	Strom Thurmond	2.4	39	Harry Truman (D)
1960	Independent Democrat	Harry Byrd	0.4	15*	John Kennedy (D)
1968	American Independent	George Wallace	13.5	46	Richard Nixon (R)
1980	National Union	John Anderson	6.6	0	Ronald Reagan (R)
1992	Independent	Ross Perot	18.9	0	Bill Clinton (D)
1996	Reform	Ross Perot	8.4	0	Bill Clinton (D)

*Byrd received 15 electoral votes from unpledged electors in Alabama and Mississippi.
Source: *Dave Leip's Atlas of U.S. Presidential Elections*, www.uselectionatlas.org.

Currently active ideological parties include the Libertarian Party and the Green Party. The Libertarian Party supports a *laissez-faire* ("let it be") capitalist economic program, together with a hands-off policy on regulating matters of moral conduct. The Green Party began as a grassroots environmentalist organization with affiliated political parties across North America and Western Europe. It was established in the United States as a national party in 1996 and nominated Ralph Nader to run for president in 2000. Nader campaigned against what he called "corporate greed," advocated universal health insurance, and promoted environmental concerns.[12] He ran again for president as an independent in 2004 and in 2008.

SPLINTER PARTIES

> **Splinter Party**
> A new party formed by a dissident faction within a major political party. Often, splinter parties have emerged when a particular personality was at odds with the major party.

Some of the most successful minor parties have been those that split from major parties. The impetus for these **splinter parties**, or factions, has usually been a situation in which a particular personality was at odds with the major party. The most successful of these splinter parties was the Bull Moose Progressive Party, formed in 1912 to support Theodore Roosevelt for president. The Republican National Convention of that year denied Roosevelt the nomination, although he had won most of the primaries. He therefore left the Republicans and ran against Republican "regular" William Howard Taft in the general election. Although Roosevelt did not win the election, he did split the Republican vote, enabling Democrat Woodrow Wilson to become president.

[12]Ralph Nader offers his own entertaining account of his run for the presidency in 2000 in *Crashing the Party: How to Tell the Truth and Still Run for President* (New York: St. Martin's Press, 2002).

Third parties have also been formed to back individual candidates who were not rebelling against a particular party. Ross Perot, for example, who challenged Republican George H. W. Bush and Democrat Bill Clinton in 1992, had not previously been active in a major party. Perot's supporters, likewise, probably would have split their votes between Bush and Clinton had Perot not been in the race. In theory, Perot ran in 1992 as a nonparty independent; in practice, he had to create a campaign organization. By 1996, Perot's organization was formalized as the Reform Party.

THE IMPACT OF MINOR PARTIES

Third parties have rarely been able to affect American politics by actually winning elections. (One exception is that third-party and independent candidates have occasionally won races for state governorships—for example, Jesse Ventura was elected governor of Minnesota on the Reform Party ticket in 1998.) Instead, the impact of third parties has taken two forms. First, third parties can influence one of the major parties to take up one or more issues. Second, third parties can determine the outcome of a particular election by pulling votes from one of the major-party candidates in what is called the "spoiler effect."

Influencing the Major Parties. One of the most clear-cut examples of a major party adopting the issues of a minor party took place in

THEODORE ROOSEVELT (left) served as president of the United States from 1901 to 1909 as a Republican. Later, after he was unable to secure the Republican nomination for president in 1912, Roosevelt formed a splinter group known as the Bull Moose Progressive Party. Roosevelt was ultimately unsuccessful in his bid to regain the presidency as a minor party candidate. Does a minor party candidate have a realistic chance of winning a presidential election today? (Library of Congress, Prints & Photographs Division, Washington, D.C. [LC-USZC2-6276])

TABLE 8–3 Policies of Selected American Third Parties since 1864

Populist: This pro-farmer party of the 1890s advocated progressive reforms. It also advocated replacing gold with silver as the basis of the currency in hopes of creating a mild inflation in prices. (It was believed by many that inflation would help debtors and stimulate the economy.)

Socialist: This party advocated a "cooperative commonwealth" based on government ownership of industry. It was pro-labor, often antiwar, and in later years, anti-Communist. It was dissolved in 1972 and replaced by nonparty advocacy groups (Democratic Socialists of America and Social Democrats USA).

Communist: This left-wing breakaway from the Socialists was the U.S. branch of the worldwide Communist movement. The party was pro-labor and advocated full equality for African Americans. It was also closely aligned with the Communist-led Soviet Union, which provoked great hostility among most Americans.

Progressive: This name was given to several successive splinter parties built around individual political leaders. Theodore Roosevelt, who ran in 1912, advocated federal regulation of industry to protect consumers, workers, and small businesses. Robert LaFollette, who ran in 1924, held similar viewpoints.

American Independent: Built around George Wallace, this party opposed any further promotion of civil rights and advocated a militant foreign policy. Wallace's supporters were mostly former Democrats who were soon to be Republicans.

Libertarian: This party opposes most government activity.

Reform: The Reform Party was initially built around businessman Ross Perot but later was taken over by others. Under Perot, the party was a middle-of-the-road group opposed to federal budget deficits. Under Patrick Buchanan, it came to represent right-wing nationalism and opposition to free trade.

Green: The Greens are a left-of-center pro-environmental party; they are also generally hostile to globalization.

1896, when the Democratic Party took over the Populist demand for "free silver"—that is, a policy of coining enough new money to create an inflation. As you learned earlier, however, absorbing the Populists cost the Democrats votes overall.

Affecting the Outcome of an Election. The presidential election of 2000 was one instance in which a minor party may have altered the outcome. Green candidate Ralph Nader received almost 100,000 votes in Florida, a majority of which would probably have gone to Democrat Al Gore if Nader had not been in the race. The real question, however, is not whether the Nader vote had an effect—clearly, it did—but whether the effect was important.

The problem is that in an election as close as the presidential election of 2000, *any* factor with an impact on the outcome can be said to have determined the results of the election. Discussing his landslide loss to Democrat Lyndon B. Johnson in 1964, Republican Barry Goldwater wrote, "When you've lost an election by that much, it isn't the case of whether you made the wrong speech or wore the wrong necktie. It was just the wrong time."[13] With the opposite situation, a humorist might speculate that Gore would have won the election had he worn a better tie! Nevertheless, given that Nader garnered almost 3 million votes nationwide, many people believe that the Nader campaign was an important reason for Gore's loss. Should voters ignore third parties to avoid spoiling the chances of a preferred major-party candidate?

MECHANISMS OF POLITICAL CHANGE

What does the 21st century hold for the Democrats and the Republicans? Support for the two major parties is roughly balanced today. In the future, could one of the two parties decisively overtake the other and become the "natural party of government"? The Republicans held this status from 1896 until 1932, and the Democrats enjoyed it for many years after the election of Franklin D. Roosevelt in 1932. Not surprisingly, political advisors in both parties dream of circumstances that could grant them lasting political hegemony, or dominance.

REALIGNMENT

Realignment
A process in which a substantial group of voters switches party allegiance, producing a long-term change in the political landscape.

One mechanism by which a party might gain dominance is called **realignment**. As described in the chapter-opening *Making a Difference* feature, major constituencies shift their allegiance from one party to another, creating a long-term alteration in the political environment. Realignment has often been associated with particular elections, called *realigning elections*. The election of 1896, which established a Republican ascendancy, was clearly a realigning election. So was the election of 1932, which made the Democrats the leading party.

Realignment: The Myth of Dominance. Several myths have grown up around the concept of realignment. One is that in realignment, a newly dominant party must replace the previously dominant party. Actually, realignment could easily strengthen an already dominant party. Alternatively, realignment could result in a tie. This has happened—twice. One example was the realignment of the 1850s, which resulted in Abraham Lincoln's election as president in 1860. After the Civil War, the Republicans and the Democrats were almost evenly matched nationally.

[13]Barry Goldwater, *With No Apologies* (New York: William Morrow, 1979).

The most recent realignment—which also resulted in two closely matched parties—has sometimes been linked to the elections of 1968. Actually, the realignment was a gradual process that took place over many years. It is sometimes referred to as a "rolling realignment." In 1968, Democrat Hubert Humphrey, Republican Richard Nixon, and third-party candidate George Wallace of Alabama all vied for the presidency. Following the Republican victory in that election, Nixon adopted a "Southern strategy" aimed at drawing dissatisfied Southern Democrats into the Republican Party.[14] At the presidential level, the strategy was an immediate success, although years would pass before the Republicans could gain dominance in the South's delegation to Congress or in state legislatures. Nixon's Southern strategy helped create the political environment in which we live today. Another milestone in the progress of the Republicans was Ronald Reagan's sweeping victory in the presidential election of 1980.

Realignment: The Myth of Predictability. A second myth concerning realignments is that they take place, like clockwork, every 36 years. Supposedly, there were realigning elections in 1860, 1896, 1932, and 1968, and therefore 2004 must have been a year for realignment. No such event appears to have taken place. In fact, there is no force that could cause political realignments at precise 36-year intervals. Further, as we observed earlier in this section, realignments are not always tied to particular elections. The most recent realignment, in which conservative Southern Democrats became conservative Southern Republicans, was not closely linked to a particular election. The realignment of the 1850s, following the creation of the modern Republican Party, also took place over a period of years.

Is Realignment Still Possible? The nature of American political parties created the pattern of realignment in American history. The sheer size of the country, combined with the inexorable pressure toward a two-party system, resulted in parties made up of voters with conflicting interests or values. The pre-Civil War party system involved two parties—Whigs and Democrats—with support in both the North and the South. This system could survive only by burying, as deeply as possible, the issue of slavery. We should not be surprised that the structure eventually collapsed. The Republican ascendancy of 1896–1932 united capitalists and industrial workers under the Republican banner, despite serious economic conflicts between the two. The New Deal Democratic coalition after 1932 brought African Americans and ardent segregationists into the same party.

For realignment to occur, a substantial body of citizens must come to believe that their party can no longer represent their interests or values. The problem must be fundamental and not attributable to the behavior of an individual politician. Given the increasing cohesion of each of the parties today, it is unlikely that a realignment is in the offing. The values that unite each party are relatively coherent, and their constituents are reasonably compatible. Therefore, the current party system should be more stable than in the past, and a major realignment is not likely to take place in the foreseeable future.

DEALIGNMENT

Among political scientists, one common argument has been that realignment is no longer likely because voters are not as committed to the two major parties as they were

---

[14]The classic work on Nixon's Southern strategy is Kirkpatrick Sales, *The Emerging Republican Majority* (New Rochelle, NY: Arlington House, 1969).

Dealignment
A decline in party loyalties that reduces long-term party commitment.

Party Identification
Linking oneself to a particular political party.

Straight-Ticket Voting
Voting exclusively for the candidates of one party.

Swing Voters
Voters who frequently swing their support from one party to another.

in the 1800s and early 1900s. In this view, called **dealignment** theory, large numbers of independent voters may result in political volatility, but the absence of strong partisan attachments means that it is no longer easy to "lock in" political preferences for decades.

Independent Voters. Figure 8–4 shows trends in **party identification**, as measured by standard polling techniques from 1937 to the present. The chart displays a rise in the number of independent voters throughout the period, combined with a fall in support for the Democrats from the mid-1960s on. The decline in Democratic identification may be due to the consolidation of Republican support in the South since 1968, a process that by now may be substantially complete. In any event, the traditional Democratic advantage in party identification has vanished.

Not only has the number of independents grown over the last half-century, but voters are also less willing to vote a straight ticket—that is, to vote for all the candidates of one party. In the early 1900s, **straight-ticket voting** was nearly universal. By mid-century, 12 percent of voters engaged in ticket splitting. In recent presidential elections, between 20 and 40 percent of the voters engaged in split-ticket voting. This trend, along with the increase in the number of voters who call themselves independents, suggests that parties have lost much of their hold on the loyalty of the voters.

Not-So-Independent Voters. A problem with dealignment theory is that many "independent" voters are not all that independent. Polling organizations estimate that of the 33 percent of voters who identify themselves as independents, 11 percent vote as if they were Democrats in almost all elections, and 12 percent vote as if they were Republicans. If these "leaners" are deducted from the independent category, only 10 percent of the voters remain. These true independents are **swing voters**—they can swing back and forth between the parties. These voters are important in deciding elections. Some analysts believe, however, that swing voters are far less numerous today than they were two or three decades ago.

FIGURE 8–4 Party Identification from 1937 to the Present

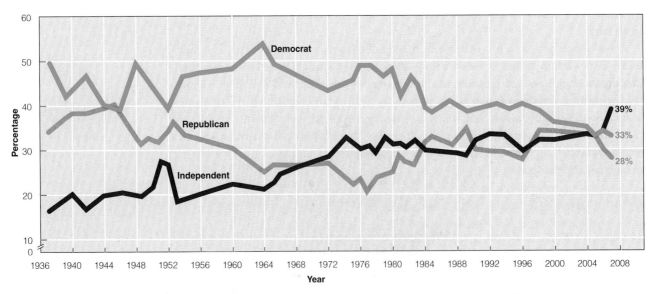

Sources: Gallup Report, August 1995; *New York Times*/CBS poll, June 1996; Gallup Report, February 1998; The Pew Research Center for the People and the Press, November 2003; and authors' updates.

TIPPING

Realignment is not the only mechanism that can alter the political landscape. Political transformation can also result from changes in the composition of the electorate. Even when groups of voters never change their party preferences, if one group becomes more numerous over time, it can become dominant for that reason alone. We call this kind of demographically based change **tipping**. Immigration is one cause of this phenomenon.

Tipping
A phenomenon that occurs when a group that is becoming more numerous over time grows large enough to change the political balance in a district, state, or country.

Tipping in Massachusetts. Consider Massachusetts, where for generations Irish Catholics confronted Protestant Yankees in the political arena. Most of the Yankees were Republican; most of the Irish were Democrats. The Yankees were numerically dominant from the founding of the state until 1928. In that year, for the first time, Democratic Irish voters came to outnumber the Republican Yankees. Massachusetts, which previously had been one of the most solidly Republican states, cast its presidential vote for Democrat Al Smith. Within a few years, Massachusetts became one of the most reliably Democratic states in the nation.

Tipping in California? California may have experienced a tipping effect during the 1990s. From 1952 until 1992, California consistently supported Republican presidential candidates, turning Democratic only in the landslide election of Lyndon Johnson in 1964. In 1992, however, the California electorate gave Democrat Bill Clinton a larger percentage of its votes than he received in the country as a whole. Since then, no Republican presidential candidate has managed to carry California.

The improved performance of the Democrats in California is almost certainly a function of demography. In 1999, California became the third state, after Hawaii and New Mexico, in which non-Hispanic whites do *not* make up a majority of the population. Hispanics and African Americans both give most of their votes to the Democrats. Even before 1999, these groups were numerous enough to tip California into the Democratic column.

ON TO THE FUTURE

Some speculation about the future is reasonable, as long as we remember that unexpected events can make any prediction obsolete. We can anticipate that party advocates will continue to hope that events will propel their party into a dominant position. Either party could lose substantial support if it were identified with a major economic disaster. Noneconomic events could have an impact as well.

Republican strategists will seek to encourage substantial numbers of voters to abandon the Democrats, perhaps on the basis of cultural issues. Some of these strategists believe that the relative conservatism of Hispanic Americans on cultural matters may provide an opening for the Republicans. Others point to the increasing numbers of Americans with investments in the stock market as a possible indicator of growing economic conservatism. Finally, Republicans look at the decline in Democratic Party identification since the 1960s (see Figure 8–4) and project that trend into the future.

Democratic strategists hope that the tolerant spirit of many younger voters (in attitudes toward gay rights, for example) may work to their advantage. Hispanic voters are of interest to the Democrats as well. Demographic changes have turned once-reliably Republican states such as Florida into swing states that can decide national elections. As noted in Chapter 1, some time after 2015, Texas—now among the most Republican states—will no longer have a non-Hispanic white majority. If the Republicans do not succeed in detaching Hispanics from the Democratic Party, Texas could eventually tip into the Democratic column and possibly tip the country as a whole to the Democrats as well.

You can make a difference

ELECTING CONVENTION DELEGATES

The most exciting political party event, staged every four years, is the national convention. State conventions also take place on a regular basis. Surprising as it might seem, there are opportunities for the individual voter to become involved in nominating delegates to a state or national convention or to become a delegate.

WHY SHOULD YOU CARE?

How would you like to exercise a small amount of real political power yourself—power that goes beyond simply voting in an election? You might be able to become a delegate to a county, district, or even state party convention. Many of these conventions nominate candidates for various offices. For example, in Michigan, the state party conventions nominate the candidates for the Board of Regents of the state's three top public universities. The regents set university policies, so these are nominations in which students have an obvious interest. In Michigan, if you are elected as a party precinct delegate, you can attend your party's state convention.

In much of the country, there are more openings for district-level delegates than there are people willing to serve. In such circumstances, almost anyone can become a delegate by collecting a handful of signatures on a nominating petition or by mounting a small-scale write-in campaign. You are then eligible to take part in one of the most educational political experiences available to an ordinary citizen. You will get a firsthand look at how political persuasion takes place, how resolutions are written and passed, and how candidates seek out support among their fellow party members. In some states, party caucuses bring debate even closer to the grassroots level.

WHAT CAN YOU DO?

When the parties choose delegates for the national convention, the process begins at the local level—either the congressional district or the state legislative district. Delegates may be elected in party primary elections or chosen in neighborhood or precinct caucuses. If the delegates are elected in a primary, persons who want to run for these positions must first file petitions with the board of elections. If you are interested in committing yourself to a particular presidential candidate and running for the delegate position, check with the local county committee or with the party's national committee about the rules you must follow.

It is even easier to get involved in the grassroots politics of presidential caucuses. In some states—Iowa being the earliest and most famous example—delegates are first nominated at the local precinct caucus. According to the rules of the Iowa caucuses, anyone can participate in a caucus if he or she is 18 years old, a resident of the precinct, and registered as a party member. These caucuses, in addition to being the focus of national media attention in January or February, select delegates to the county conventions who are pledged to specific presidential candidates. This is the first step toward the national convention.

At both the county caucus and the convention levels, both parties try to find younger members to fill some of the seats. Contact the state or county political party to find out when the caucuses or primaries will be held. Then gather local supporters and friends, and prepare to join in an occasion during which political debate is at its best.

For further information about these opportunities (some states hold caucuses and state conventions in every election year), contact the state party office or your local state legislator for specific dates and regulations. You can also write to the national committee for information on how to become a delegate.

Republican National Committee
Republican National Headquarters
310 First St.
Washington, D.C. 20003
202-863-8500
www.rnc.org

Democratic National Committee
Democratic National Headquarters
430 Capitol St. S.E.
Washington, D.C. 20003
202-863-8000
www.democrats.org

KEY TERMS

CHAPTER SUMMARY

1. A political party is a group of political activists who organize to win elections, operate the government, and determine public policy. Political parties recruit candidates for public office, organize and run elections, present alternative policies to the voters, assume responsibility for operating the government, and act as the opposition to the party in power.

2. The evolution of our nation's political parties can be divided into seven periods: (1) the creation and formation of political parties from 1789 to 1816; (2) the era of one-party rule, or personal politics, from 1816 to 1828; (3) the period from Andrew Jackson's presidency to the Civil War, from 1828 to 1860; (4) the Civil War and post-Civil War period, from 1860 to 1896; (5) the Republican ascendancy and progressive period, from 1896 to 1932; (6) the New Deal period, from 1932 to about 1968; and (7) the modern period, from approximately 1968 to the present.

3. Many of the differences between the two parties date from the time of Franklin D. Roosevelt's New Deal. The Democrats have advocated government action to help labor and minorities, and the Republicans have championed self-reliance and limited government. The constituents of the two parties continue to differ. A close look at policies actually enacted in recent years, however, suggests that despite rhetoric to the contrary, both parties are committed to a large and active government. Today, cultural differences are at least as important as economic issues in determining party allegiance.

4. A political party consists of three components: the party-in-the-electorate, the party organization, and the party-in-government. Each party component maintains linkages to the others to keep the party strong. Each level of the party—local, state, and national—has considerable autonomy. The national party organization is responsible for holding the national convention in presidential election years, writing the party platform, choosing the national committee, and conducting party business.

5. The party-in-government comprises all of the elected and appointed officeholders of a party. The linkage of party members is crucial to building support for programs among the branches and levels of government.

6. Two major parties have dominated the political landscape in the United States for almost two centuries. The reasons for this include (1) the historical foundations of the system, (2) political socialization and practical considerations, (3) the winner-take-all electoral system, and (4) state and federal laws favoring the two-party system. For these reasons, minor parties have found it extremely difficult to win elections.

7. Minor (or third) parties have emerged from time to time, sometimes as dissatisfied splinter groups from within major parties, and have acted as barometers of changes in the political mood. Splinter parties have emerged when a particular personality was at odds with the major party, as when Theodore Roosevelt's differences with the Republican Party resulted in the formation of the Bull Moose Progressive Party. Other minor parties, such as the Socialist Party, have formed around specific issues or ideologies. Third parties can affect the political process (even if they do not win) if major parties adopt their issues or if they determine which major party wins an election.

8. One mechanism of political change is realignment, in which major blocs of voters switch allegiance from one party to another. Realignments were manifested in the elections of 1896 and 1932. Realignment need not leave one party dominant—it can result in two parties of roughly equal strength. Some scholars speak of dealignment—that is, the loss of strong party

attachments. In fact, the share of the voters who describe themselves as independents has grown since the 1930s, and the share of self-identified Democrats has shrunk since the 1960s. Many independents actu-ally vote as if they were Democrats or Republicans, however. Demographic change can also "tip" a district or state from one party to another.

SELECTED PRINT AND MEDIA RESOURCES

SUGGESTED READINGS

Black, Earl, and Merle Black. *The Rise of Southern Republicans.* Cambridge, MA: Belknap Press, 2003. This book analyzes the shift in politics in the Southern states over the last four decades.

Frank, Thomas. *What's the Matter with Kansas?: How Conservatives Won the Heart of America.* New York: Henry Holt & Company, 2005. This book looks at how the Republican Party gained its current dominance in the American heartland. The author examines why so many Americans vote against their own economic interests.

Gould, Lewis. *Grand Old Party: A History of the Republicans.* New York: Random House, 2003. A companion volume to the history of the Democrats by Jules Witcover, listed later. Gould provides a sweeping history of the Republican Party from its origins as an antislavery coalition to the present. A major theme of the work is the evolution of the Republicans from a party of active government to the more conservative party that it is today.

Green, John C., and Paul S. Hernson, eds. *Responsible Partisanship: The Evolution of American Political Parties since 1950.* Lawrence: University Press of Kansas, 2003. This collection of scholarly essays explores the roles and functions of political parties, both as parties-in-the-electorate and as parties-in-government.

McAuliffe, Terry. *What a Party!: My Life among Democrats.* New York: St. Martin's Press, 2007. The former chairperson of the Democratic National Committee discusses his years of experience on the inside of a major political party.

Nader, Ralph. *Crashing the Party: How to Tell the Truth and Still Run for President.* New York: St. Martin's Press, 2002. This is Nader's own entertaining and detailed account of his run for the presidency as a Green in 2000.

Paulson, Arthur. *Electoral Realignment and the Outlook for American Democracy.* University Press of New England, 2006. Paulson seeks to understand recent realignments in the light of political geography and historical divisions.

Sager, Ryan. *The Elephant in the Room: Evangelicals, Libertarians, and the Battle to Control the Republican Party.* New York: Wiley, 2006. The author describes the current coalition of subgroups within the Republican Party and predicts an eventual splintering as the individual groups struggle for greater power within the party.

Witcover, Jules. *Party of the People: A History of the Democrats.* New York: Random House, 2003. A companion volume to the history of the Republicans by Lewis Gould, listed earlier. Witcover describes the transformation of the Democrats from a party of limited government to a party of national authority, but he also finds a common thread that connects modern Democrats to the past—a belief in social and economic justice.

MEDIA RESOURCES

The American President—A 1995 film starring Michael Douglas as a widowed president who must balance partisanship and friendship (Republicans in Congress promise to approve the president's crime bill only if he modifies an environmental plan sponsored by his liberal girlfriend).

The Best Man—A 1964 drama based on Gore Vidal's play of the same name. The film, which deals with political smear campaigns by presidential party nominees, focuses on political party power and ethics.

The Last Hurrah—A classic 1958 political film starring Spencer Tracy as a corrupt politician who seeks his fifth nomination for mayor of a city in New England.

A Third Choice—A film that examines America's experience with third parties and independent candidates throughout the nation's political history.

POLITICAL PARTIES AND THE INTERNET

Today's political parties use the Internet to attract voters, organize campaigns, obtain campaign contributions, and the like. Voters, in turn, can go online to learn more about specific parties and their programs. Those who use the Internet for information on the parties, though, need to exercise some caution. Besides the parties' official sites, there are satirical sites mimicking the parties, sites distributing misleading information about the parties, and sites that are raising money for their own causes rather than for political parties.

LOGGING ON

- The political parties all have Web sites. The Democratic Party is online at:
  www.democrats.org
- The Republican National Committee is at:
  www.rnc.org
- The Libertarian Party has a Web site located at:
  www.lp.org
- The Green Party of the United States can be found at:
  www.gp.org

- Politics1.com offers extensive information on U.S. political parties, including the major parties and 50 minor parties. Go to:
  www.politics1.com/parties.htm
- The Pew Research Center for the People and the Press offers survey data online on how the parties fared during the most recent elections, voter typology, and numerous other issues. To access this site, go to:
  http://people-press.org

ONLINE REVIEW

At **www.cengage.com/politicalscience/schmidt/agandpt14e**, you will find a Tutorial Quiz for this chapter providing questions on the chapter contents, including the features. The questions are organized to match the major sections of the chapter. You'll have access to other helpful study tools, including the book's glossary and flashcards, crossword puzzles, and Web links, as well as "Which Side Are You On?" and "Politics and . . ." features written by the authors of the book.

CHAPTER

(9)

South Carolina voters wait in line to cast their ballots in the 2004 presidential election. (The Charlotte Observer, Diedra Laird/AP Photos)

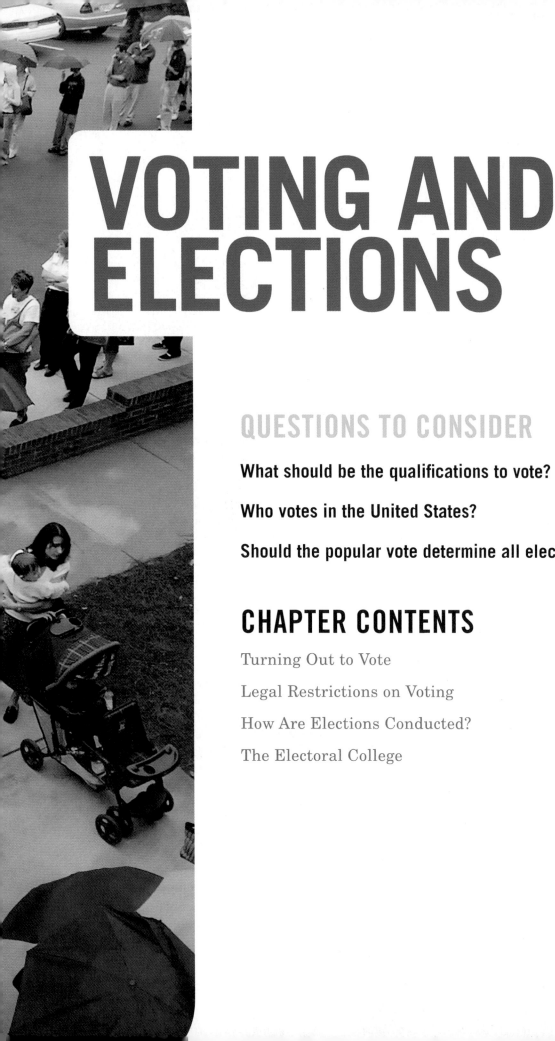

VOTING AND ELECTIONS

Making a DIFFERENCE

LET'S PUT IT TO A VOTE

Have you ever heard someone say, usually in indignation, "There ought to be a law . . . !"? Often this lawmaking happens in state legislatures or in Congress. However, in some states and localities, average citizens (or organized groups of "average citizens") can put an idea to a popular vote.

Why would citizens want to vote on laws themselves? The answer boils down to a debate over what type of democracy a society wants: direct or representative. While representative democracy is much more common, some states explicitly have created a means by which citizens can bypass the legislative process (initiative), revoke the actions of legislatures (referendum), or even remove elected officials from office (recall).

While all states except Delaware require that amendments to the state constitu-

tions go before the voters for final approval,[a] more than half of all states do not have any initiative or referenda. In these 26 states, no mechanism exists for citizens to legislate through initiatives (enact laws by popular vote) or to overrule legislatures through referenda. The 24 states that do give citizens the ability to affect policy changes directly have seen vigorous debates over some of the most divisive and contentious issues of the day.

For example, both gay rights laws (domestic partnership laws, antidiscrimination laws) as well as laws defining marriage as a union between a man and a woman have been put to the direct democracy test. For example, in 2006, an unsuccessful effort was made in Colorado by gay rights advocates to extend domestic partnership rights to same-sex couples through a referendum. In the same year, eight states had ballot issues to amend their constitutions to ban same-sex marriage; the amendment passed in all except one, Arizona.[b] However, in 2007, backers of a planned referendum were unable to place

VOTING IN FREE and fair elections is the basis of any democracy. It is true that people are allowed to vote in China, Cuba, and North Korea, but there are no opposition candidates and no opposition campaign. In other nations, individuals are coerced into staying away from the polls by guerrilla fighters or, in some cases, by the government's own forces. In yet other nations, the incumbent government or candidate may alter the results of elections by fraudulent means. All of those cases fail the test of free and fair elections.

In the United States, it is often said that we have too many elections. As noted in *Making a Difference*, in some states, people can vote directly on laws. In California, there are often dozens of referenda on the ballot at one time. Citizens are often asked to vote three times in one year—in a primary election to choose candidates, in elections for school taxes or other local matters, and in a general election. Americans often elect not only representatives to state and national legislatures and executive officers for the state, but also school superintendents, sheriffs, even the jailer. In addition, many states have elected judges, which can add 50 more offices in a city like Chicago.

on the ballot referenda on two Oregon laws that extended civil rights protections, including domestic partnership, to gays and lesbians.[c] Organizers in Maine are targeting the 2009 election to attempt to add a referendum to the ballot that would repeal that state's law banning discrimination based on sexual orientation.[d]

States choose the process by which a referendum, initiative, or recall effort is allowed on the ballot and the threshold of support necessary for winning. To get on the ballot, signatures are collected on petitions, and the petition is allowed to circulate for a set period of time. States also choose how many signatures are necessary for the effort to get on the ballot. Usually the minimum number is a percentage of either the total number of registered voters or the total turnout in the last general election. Sometimes states specify that the effort has to have support from across the state. Wyoming, for example, mandates that the signatures have to come from at least two-thirds of its counties.[e] Also, the signatures usually have to be from residents of that state who are registered voters. Often opponents of the effort use this stage to mount their attack. For example, in the 2007 Oregon referendum effort, supporters of gay rights were able to thwart the referendum both by challenging the validity of signatures and by effectively mobilizing in a "refuse to sign" campaign.[f]

Once it is on the ballot, the initiative, referendum, or recall must garner a certain percentage of votes. Often held in off-year elections, turnout for these votes may be very small. Some states go to great lengths, however, to ensure that the ballot issue has significant support not just from a majority of people voting in that election but also from the state's voting population. For example, Massachusetts requires that the measure receive a majority of the votes during that election and that those voting on the measure (either for or against) have to constitute in excess of 50 percent of those who voted in the previous general election.[g] Each of these examples illustrates the importance of each vote.

[a]M. Dane Waters, "Initiative and Referendum in the United States," A presentation to the Democracy Symposium, February 16–18, 2002, Williamsburg, VA; accessed at http://ni4d.us/library/waterspaper.pdf.
[b]www.cnn.com/ELECTION/2006/pages/results/ballot.measures; accessed April 11, 2008.
[c]www.basicrights.org/?p=84; accessed April 11, 2008.
[d]www.edgeboston.com/index.php?ch=news&sc=glbt&sc2=news &sc3=&id=72878; accessed April 11, 2008.
[e]Jennifer Drage, "Initiative, Referendum, and Recall: The Process," *Journal of the American Society of Legislative Clerks and Secretaries*, Vol. 5, No. 2, 2000.
[f]www.basicrights.org/?p=84; accessed April 11, 2008.
[g]Jennifer Drage, "Initiative, Referendum, and Recall: The Process," *Journal of the American Society of Legislative Clerks and Secretaries*, Vol. 5, No. 2, 2000.

TURNING OUT TO VOTE

In 2008, the voting-age population was about 231,229,500 million people. Of that number, 127,500,000 million, or 55 percent of the voting-age population, actually went to the polls. When only half of the voting-age population participates in elections, it means, among other things, that the winner of a close presidential election may be voted in by only about one-fourth of the voting-age population (see Table 9–1).

Figure 9–1 shows **voter turnout** for presidential and Congressional elections from 1904 to 2008. According to these statistics, the last good year for voter turnout was 1960, when almost 65 percent of the voting-age population actually voted. Each of the peaks in the figure represents voter turnout in a presidential election. Thus, we can also see that turnout for Congressional elections is influenced greatly by whether there is a presidential election in the same year. Whereas voter turnout during the presidential elections of 2008 was more than 50 percent, it was only 40 percent in the midterm elections of 2006.

Voter Turnout
The percentage of citizens taking part in the election process; the number of eligible voters who actually "turn out" on election day to cast their ballots.

TABLE 9–1 Elected by a Majority?

Most presidents have won a majority of the votes cast in the election. We generally judge the extent of their victory by whether they have won more than 51 percent of the votes. Some presidential elections have been proclaimed *landslides*, meaning that the candidates won by an extraordinary majority of votes cast. As indicated below, however, no modern president has been elected by more than 38 percent of the total voting-age population.

YEAR—WINNER (PARTY)	PERCENTAGE OF TOTAL POPULAR VOTE	PERCENTAGE OF VOTING-AGE POPULATION
1932—Roosevelt (D)	57.4	30.1
1936—Roosevelt (D)	60.8	34.6
1940—Roosevelt (D)	54.7	32.2
1944—Roosevelt (D)	53.4	29.9
1948—Truman (D)	49.6	25.3
1952—Eisenhower (R)	55.1	34.0
1956—Eisenhower (R)	57.4	34.1
1960—Kennedy (D)	49.7	31.2
1964—Johnson (D)	61.1	37.8
1968—Nixon (R)	43.4	26.4
1972—Nixon (R)	60.7	33.5
1976—Carter (D)	50.1	26.8
1980—Reagan (R)	50.7	26.7
1984—Reagan (R)	58.8	31.2
1988—Bush (R)	53.4	26.8
1992—Clinton (D)	43.3	23.1
1996—Clinton (D)	49.2	23.2
2000—Bush (R)	47.8	24.5
2004—Bush (R)	51.0	27.6
2008—Obama (D)	52.6	27.5

Sources: Congressional Quarterly Weekly Report, January 31, 1989, p. 137; *The New York Times*, November 5, 1992; *The New York Times*, November 7, 1996; *The New York Times,* November 12, 2004; *The New York Times*, November 6, 2008; and author's update.

The same is true at the state level. When there is a race for governor, more voters participate both in the general election for governor and in the election for state representatives. Voter participation rates in gubernatorial elections are also greater in presidential election years. The average turnout in state elections is about 14 percentage points higher when a presidential election is held.

Now consider local elections: In races for mayor, city council, county auditor, and the like, it is fairly common for only 25 percent or less of the electorate to vote. Is something amiss here? It would seem that people should be more likely to vote in elections that directly affect them. At the local level, each person's vote counts more (because there are fewer voters). Furthermore, the issues—crime control, school bonds, sewer bonds, and so on— touch the immediate interests of the voters. The facts, however, do not fit the theory. Potential voters are most interested in national elections, when a presidential choice is involved. Otherwise, voter participation in our representative government is very low (and, as we have seen, it is not overwhelmingly great even at the presidential level).

THE EFFECT OF LOW VOTER TURNOUT

There are two schools of thought concerning low voter turnout. Some view low voter participation as a threat to representative democratic government. Too few individuals are deciding who wields political power in society. In addition, low voter participation presumably signals apathy or cynicism about the political system in general. It also may signal that potential voters simply do not want to take the time to learn about the issues or that the issues are too complicated. Others suggest that people do not vote because they do not believe that their vote will make any difference.

Others are less concerned about low voter participation. They believe that low voter participation simply indicates more satisfaction with the status quo. Also, they believe that representative democracy is a reality even if a very small percentage of eligible voters vote. If everyone who does not vote believes that the outcome of the election will accord with his or her own desires, then representative democracy is working. The nonvoters are obtaining the type of government—with the type of people running it—that they want to have anyway.

IS VOTER TURNOUT DECLINING?

During many recent elections, the media have voiced concern that voter turnout is declining. Figure 9–1 appears to show somewhat lower voter turnout in recent years than during the 1960s. Pundits have blamed the low turnout on negative campaigning and broad public cynicism about the political process. But is voter turnout actually as low as it seems?

One problem with widely used measurements of voter turnout—as exemplified by Figure 9–1—is that they compare the number of people who actually vote with the voting-age population, not the population of *eligible voters*. These figures are not the same. The figure for the voting-age population includes felons and ex-felons who have lost the right to vote. Above all, it includes new immigrants who are not yet citizens. Finally, it does not include Americans living abroad, who can cast absentee ballots.

That in August 2000, six people offered to sell their votes for president on eBay, the online auction site? eBay quickly canceled the bidding.

FIGURE 9–1 Voter Turnout for Presidential and Congressional Elections, 1904–2008

The peaks represent turnout in presidential election years; the troughs represent turnout in off-presidential-election years.

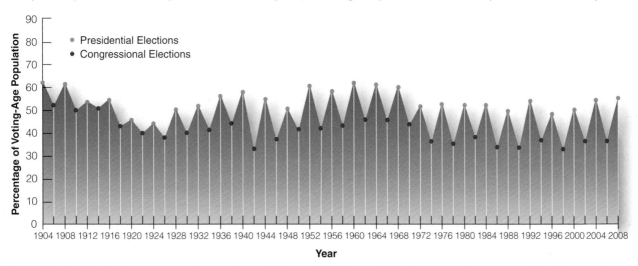

Sources: Historical Data Archive, Inter-university Consortium for Political and Social Research; U.S. Department of Commerce, *Statistical Abstract of the United States: 1980*, 101st ed. (Washington, DC: U.S. Government Printing Office, 1980), p. 515; William H. Flanigan and Nancy H. Zingale, *Political Behavior of the American Electorate*, 5th ed. (Boston: Allyn and Bacon, 1983), p. 20; *Congressional Quarterly*, various issues; and authors' updates.

FIGURE 9–2 Voting in the 2004 Presidential Elections by Age Group

Turnout is given as a percentage of the voting-age citizen population. The data given in this figure is from the Census Bureau. It has been gathered by polling the American public. Generally the Census data is not available for months after the election. The data from the 2008 polls indicates that turnout among older Americans remained high.

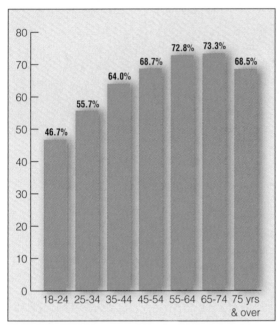

Source: U.S. Bureau of the Census, May 26, 2005

In 2008, the measured voting-age population included 3.2 million ineligible felons and ex-felons and an estimated 17.5 million noncitizens. It did not include 3.3 million Americans abroad. In 2008, the voting-age population was 231.2 million people. The number of eligible voters, however, was only 208.3 million. That means that voter turnout in 2008 was not 55 percent but about 62 percent.

As you learned in Chapter 1, the United States has experienced high rates of immigration in recent decades. Political scientists Michael McDonald and Samuel Popkin argue that the apparent decline in voter turnout since 1972 is entirely a function of the increasing size of the ineligible population, chiefly due to immigration.[1]

FACTORS INFLUENCING WHO VOTES

A clear association exists between voter participation and the following characteristics: age, educational attainment, minority status, income level, and the existence of two-party competition.

1. *Age.* Look at Figure 9–2, which shows the breakdown of voter participation by age group for the 2004 presidential elections. It is very clear that the Americans who have the highest turnout rate are those reaching retirement. The reported turnout increases with each age group. Greater participation with age is very likely because older voters are more settled in their lives, are already registered, and have had more time to experience voting as an expected activity. Older voters may have more leisure time to learn about the campaign and the candidates, and communications, especially those from AARP, target this group.

What is most striking about the turnout figures is that younger voters have the lowest turnout rate. Before 1971, the age of eligibility to vote was 21. Due to the prevailing sentiment that if a man was old enough to be drafted to fight in the Vietnam War, he should be old enough to vote, the U.S. Constitution was amended (Amendment Twenty-six) to lower the voting age to 18. However, young Americans have never exhibited a high turnout rate. In contrast to older Americans, young people are likely to be changing residence frequently, have few ties to the community, and may not see election issues as relevant to them.

Turnout among voters aged 18 to 24 increased significantly between 2000 and 2004, from 36 percent to 47 percent in the presidential election. Evidence suggests that the candidates and political parties devoted much more attention to the younger voters. Candidates appeared on the television shows watched by younger voters, and campaigns began to utilize the Internet and other cybersources to reach younger voters. Younger voters greatly increased their turnout in the 2008 primary elections, with many supporting Barack Obama's campaign for the presidency.

[1]Michael P. McDonald and Samuel L. Popkin, "The Myth of the Vanishing Voter," *American Political Science Review*, Vol. 95, No. 4, December 2001, p. 963.

CALIFORNIA VOTERS vote at the Senior Center in San Jose, California, in 2005. Why do older Americans have such a high turnout rate? (Marcio Jose Sanchez/AP Photos)

2. *Educational attainment.* Education also influences voter turnout. In general, the more education you have, the more likely you are to vote. This pattern is clearly evident in the 2004 election results, as you can see in Figure 9–3. Reported turnout was 30 percentage points higher for those who had some college education than it was for people who had never been to high school.

3. *Minority status.* Race and ethnicity are important, too, in determining the level of voter turnout. Non-Hispanic whites in 2004 voted at a 67.2 percent rate, whereas the non-Hispanic African American turnout rate was 60.0 percent. For Hispanics, the turnout rate was 44.2 percent, and for Asian Americans the rate was slightly lower, at 44.1 percent. These low rates are largely because many Hispanic and Asian American immigrants are not yet citizens.

4. *Income level.* Differences in income also correlate with differences in voter turnout. Wealthier people tend to be overrepresented among voters who turn out on election day. In the 2004 presidential elections, voter turnout for those with the highest annual family incomes was almost three times the turnout for those with the lowest annual family incomes.

5. *Two-party competition.* Another factor in voter turnout is the extent to which elections are competitive within a state. More competitive states generally have higher turnout rates, and turnout increases considerably in states where there is an extremely competitive race in a particular year. In addition, turnout can be increased through targeted get-out-the-vote drives among minority voters.

That computer software now exists that can identify likely voters and likely campaign donors by town, neighborhood, and street?

FIGURE 9–3 Voting in the 2004 Presidential Elections by Education Level

These statistics reinforce one another. White voters are likely to be wealthier than African American voters, who are also less likely to have obtained a college education.

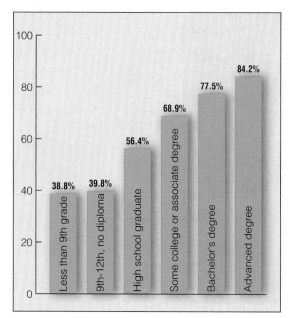

Source: U.S. Bureau of the Census, May 26, 2005

Rational Ignorance Effect
An effect produced when people purposely and rationally decide not to become informed on an issue because they believe that their vote on the issue is not likely to be a deciding one; a lack of incentive to seek the necessary information to cast an intelligent vote.

WHY PEOPLE DO NOT VOTE

For many years, political scientists believed that one reason why voter turnout in the United States was so much lower than in other Western nations was that it was very difficult to register to vote. In most states, registration required a special trip to a public office far in advance of elections. Many experts are now proposing other explanations for low U.S. voter turnout.

Uninformative Media Coverage and Negative Campaigning. Some scholars contend that one of the reasons why some people do not vote has to do with media coverage of campaigns. Many researchers have shown that the news media tend to provide much more news about "the horse race," or which candidates are ahead in the polls, than about the actual policy positions of the candidates. Thus, voters are not given the kind of information that would provide them with an incentive to go to the polls on election day. Additionally, negative campaigning is thought to have an adverse effect on voter turnout. By the time citizens are ready to cast their ballots, most of the information they have heard about the candidates has been so negative that no candidate is appealing.

According to a yearlong study conducted in 2000 by Harvard University's Center on the Press, Politics, and Public Policy, nonvoters and voters alike shared the same criticisms of the way the media cover campaigns: most thought the media treated campaigns like theater or entertainment. Nonvoters, however, were much more cynical about government and politicians than were voters. As the director of the study put it, "All the polls, the spin, the attack ads, the money and the negative news have soured Americans on the way we choose our president."[2]

The Rational Ignorance Effect. Another explanation of low voter turnout suggests that citizens are making a logical choice in not voting. If citizens believe that their votes will not affect the outcome of an election, then they have little incentive to seek the information they need to cast intelligent votes. The lack of incentive to obtain costly (in terms of time, attention, and so on) information about politicians and political issues has been called the **rational ignorance effect**. That term may seem contradictory, but it is not. Rational ignorance is a condition in which people purposely and rationally decide not to obtain information—to remain ignorant.[3]

Why, then, do even one-third to one-half of U.S. citizens bother to show up at the polls? One explanation is that most citizens receive personal satisfaction from the act of voting. It makes them feel that they are good citizens and that they are doing something patriotic, even though they are aware that their one vote will not change the outcome of the election.[4] Even among voters who are registered and who plan to vote, if the cost of voting goes up (in terms of time and inconvenience), the number of registered voters who actually vote will fall. In particular, bad weather on election day means that, on average, a smaller percentage of registered voters will go to the polls.

[2]Thomas E. Patterson, *The Vanishing Voter: Public Involvement in an Age of Uncertainty* (New York: Knopf, 2002). You can continue to track the Vanishing Voter Project at the study's Web site, www.hks.harvard.edu/presspol/vanishvoter.
[3]Anthony Downs, *An Economic Theory of Democracy* (New York: Harper, 1957).
[4]See Ilya Somin, "When Ignorance Isn't Bliss: How Political Ignorance Threatens Democracy," in *Policy Analysis*, September 22, 2004, Washington, DC: The Cato Institute, for a review of the rational ignorance theories.

Plans for Improving Voter Turnout. Mail-in voting, Internet voting, registering to vote when you apply for a driver's license—these are all ideas that have been either suggested or implemented in the hope of improving voter turnout. Nonetheless, voter turnout remains relatively low.

Two other ideas seemed promising. The first was to allow voters to visit the polls up to three weeks before election day. The second was to allow voters to vote by absentee ballot without having to give any particular reason for doing so. The Committee for the Study of the American Electorate discovered, however, that in areas that had implemented these plans, neither plan increased voter turnout. Indeed, voter turnout actually fell in those jurisdictions. In other words, states that did *not* permit early voting or unrestricted absentee voting had better turnout rates than states that did. Apparently, these two innovations appeal mostly to people who already intended to vote.

What is left? One possibility is to declare election day a national holiday. In this way, more eligible voters will find it easier to go to the polls.

LEGAL RESTRICTIONS ON VOTING

Legal restrictions on voter registration have existed since the founding of our nation. Most groups in the United States have been concerned with the suffrage issue at one time or another.

HISTORICAL RESTRICTIONS

In most of the American colonies, only white males who owned property with a certain minimum value were eligible to vote, leaving a greater number of Americans ineligible than eligible to take part in the democratic process.

IN 1944, the Georgia primary was opened to African American voters as the result of a Supreme Court decision. Registrars give instructions on how to cast a ballot. (AP Photo)

Property Requirements. Many government functions concern property rights and the distribution of income and wealth, and some of the founders of our nation believed it was appropriate that only people who had an interest in property should vote on these issues. The idea of extending the vote to all citizens was, according to Charles Pinckney, a South Carolina delegate to the Constitutional Convention, merely "theoretical nonsense."

The logic behind the restriction of voting rights to property owners was questioned seriously by Thomas Paine in his pamphlet *Common Sense*:

> Here is a man who today owns a jackass, and the jackass is worth $60. Today the man is a voter and goes to the polls and deposits his vote. Tomorrow the jackass dies. The next day the man comes to vote without his jackass and cannot vote at all. Now tell me, which was the voter, the man or the jackass?[5]

The writers of the Constitution allowed the states to decide who should vote. Thus, women were allowed to vote in Wyoming in 1870 but not in the entire nation until the Nineteenth Amendment was ratified in 1920. By about 1850, most white adult males in virtually all the states could vote without any property qualification. North Carolina was the last state to eliminate its property test for voting—in 1856.

Further Extensions of the Franchise. Extension of the franchise to black males occurred with the passage of the Fifteenth Amendment in 1870. This enfranchisement was short lived, however, as the "redemption" of the South by white racists had rolled back these gains by the end of the century. As discussed in Chapter 5, African Americans, both male and female, were not able to participate in the electoral process in all states until the 1960s. Women received full national voting rights with the Nineteenth Amendment in 1920. The most recent extension of the franchise occurred when the voting age was reduced to 18 by the Twenty-sixth Amendment in 1971.

Is the Franchise Still Too Restrictive? There continue to be certain classes of people who do not have the right to vote. These include noncitizens and, in most states, convicted felons who have been released from prison. They also include current prison inmates, election law violators, and people who are mentally incompetent. Also, no one under the age of 18 can vote. Some political activists have argued that some of these groups should be allowed to vote. Most other democracies do not prevent persons convicted of a crime from voting after they have completed their sentences. In the 1800s, many states let noncitizen immigrants vote. In Nicaragua, the minimum voting age is 16.

One discussion concerns the voting rights of convicted felons who are no longer in prison or on parole. Some contend that voting should be a privilege, not a right, and we should not want the types of people who commit felonies participating in decision making. Others believe that it is wrong to further penalize those who have paid their debt to society. These people argue that barring felons from the polls injures minority groups because minorities make up a disproportionately large share of former prison inmates.

CURRENT ELIGIBILITY AND REGISTRATION REQUIREMENTS

Voting generally requires **registration**, and to register, a person must satisfy the following voter qualifications, or legal requirements: (1) citizenship, (2) age (18 or older), and (3) residency—the duration varies widely from state to state and with types of elec-

DID YOU KNOW?

That noncitizens were allowed to vote in some states until the early 1920s?

Registration
The entry of a person's name onto the list of registered voters for elections. To register, a person must meet certain legal requirements of age, citizenship, and residency.

[5]Thomas Paine, *Common Sense* (London: H. D. Symonds, 1792), p. 28.

tions. Since 1972, states cannot impose residency requirements of more than 30 days for voting in federal elections.

Each state has different qualifications for voting and registration. In 1993, Congress passed the "motor voter" bill, which requires that states provide voter-registration materials when people receive or renew driver's licenses, that all states allow voters to register by mail, and that voter-registration forms be made available at a wider variety of public places and agencies. In general, a person must register well in advance of an election, although voters in Idaho, Maine, Minnesota, Oregon, Wisconsin, and Wyoming are allowed to register up to, and on, election day. North Dakota has no voter registration at all.

Some argue that registration requirements are responsible for much of the nonparticipation in our political process. Certainly, since their introduction in the late 1800s, registration laws have reduced the voting participation of African Americans and immigrants. There also is a partisan dimension to the debate over registration and nonvoting. Republicans generally fear that an expanded electorate would help to elect more Democrats.

The question arises as to whether registration is really necessary. If it decreases participation in the political process, perhaps it should be dropped altogether. Still, as those in favor of registration requirements argue, such requirements may prevent fraudulent voting practices, such as multiple voting or voting by noncitizens. Several states have passed legislation that requires a would-be voter to show government-issued photo identification before casting a ballot.

VARIOUS MEDIA STARS have often attempted to increase the number of minorities and young voters participating in elections. Here, music and fashion mogul Sean "Diddy" Combs announces the creation of a new voter registration organization called Citizen Change in New York City. (Peter Morgan/Reuters/Corbis)

EXTENSION OF THE VOTING RIGHTS ACT

In the summer of 2006, President Bush signed legislation that extended the Voting Rights Act for 25 more years. As discussed in Chapter 5, the Voting Rights Act was enacted to assure that African Americans had equal access to the polls. Most of the provisions of the 1965 Voting Rights Act became permanent law. The 2006 Act extended certain temporary sections and clarified certain amendments. For example, any new voting practices or procedures in jurisdictions with a history of discrimination in voting have to be approved by the U.S. Department of Justice or the federal district court in Washington, D.C., before being implemented. Section 203 of the 2006 Act ensures that American citizens with limited proficiency in English can obtain the necessary assistance to enable them to understand and cast a ballot. Further, the Act authorizes the U.S. attorney general to appoint federal election observers when there is evidence of attempts to intimidate minority voters at the polls. Those who supported the 2006 Act believe that such provisions will ensure continuing voter participation by minority groups in America.

HOW ARE ELECTIONS CONDUCTED?

The United States uses the **Australian ballot**—a secret ballot that is prepared, distributed, and counted by government officials at public expense. Since 1888, all states have used the Australian ballot. Before that, many states used the alternatives of oral

Australian Ballot
A secret ballot prepared, distributed, and tabulated by government officials at public expense. Since 1888, all states have used the Australian ballot rather than an open, public ballot.

BEYOND OUR B RDERS

WHY DO OTHER NATIONS HAVE HIGHER TURNOUT?

Most nations in the world are now democracies. Some are very new and some are still unstable, but in every democracy the question of voting turnout is important. Some scholars speculated that voting is a matter of historic behavior: those countries, like the democracies of Western Europe, that had the most experience with democratic practice, would naturally have greater voting turnout. Turnout data from the United States would suggest that countries in which citizens are literate and better-off economically would have higher turnout. Australia and Belgium, which both have strictly enforced compulsory voting laws, do have turnout above 80 percent of the voting-age population.

However, the data in Table 9–2 show that high turnout is not restricted to nations with compulsory voting or with highly educated populations. This abbreviated table, which shows a sample of the data from the Institute for Democracy and Electoral Assistance (IDEA), finds Italy at the top of the list of democracies, followed by Iceland, New Zealand, South Africa, Austria, Belgium, Netherlands, Australia, and Denmark. While many of the nations at the head of the list are European, South Africa certainly is not. Most Central and South American countries have higher turnout than the United States, with Venezuela and Belize at 72 percent. The Philippines, Japan, Yugoslavia, and Canada have turnout just under 70 percent. Voting turnout in the United States lags behind 138 nations, at 48.3 percent average turnout for national elections. The only other advanced democracy near the United States is Switzerland at 49.3 percent.

To understand why some nations have such high turnout as compared with others, IDEA looked at voting systems, compulsory voting laws, literacy and other indicators of development, and competitiveness of elections as factors impacting turnout. Their results indicate that literacy and other development factors do increase turnout, but national wealth does not in any systematic way. Proportional voting systems where the results of the election more closely mirror the proportion of votes cast for each party seem to improve turnout, but the factor that seems to be most important across all nations is competitiveness of elections. Voting turnout is considerably greater in nations where the elections are closely fought.* The competitiveness of the 2004 election in the United States following on the contested election of 2000 may well have influenced the increase in turnout here.

IN DECEMBER of 2007, Kenyans turned out to vote in the presidential election. The lines extended more than a mile through this school courtyard in Nairobi. (Roberto Schmidt/AFP/Getty Images)

FOR CRITICAL ANALYSIS

1. Why do you think the United States' turnout is so much lower than many poorer, less-developed nations?
2. Would compulsory voting change election outcomes in the United States?
3. Would uniform voting and election laws across the United States help increase turnout?

*The Institute for Democracy and Electoral Assistance (IDEA), "What Affects Turnout?," www.idea.int/vt.

TABLE 9–2 Turnout in Selected Countries since 1945

COUNTRIES (NO. OF ELECTIONS)	VOTE/VOTING-AGE POPULATION PERCENTAGE
Italy (14)	92.5
Iceland (16)	90.2
New Zealand (18)	86.2
South Africa (1)	85.5
Austria (16)	85.1
Belgium (17)	84.9
Netherlands (15)	84.8
Australia (21)	84.4
Denmark (22)	83.6
Bosnia and Herzegovina (1)	82.8
Germany (13)	80.6
Korea (9)	74.8
Dominican Republic (11)	68.7
Barbados (10)	63.5
India (12)	60.7
Jamaica (12)	58.5
Switzerland (13)	49.3
United States (26)	48.3

Source: IDEA, as cited in *Beyond Our Borders* box.

voting and differently colored ballots prepared by the parties. Obviously, knowing which way a person was voting made it easy to apply pressure on the person to change his or her vote, and vote buying was common.

OFFICE-BLOCK AND PARTY-COLUMN BALLOTS

Two types of Australian ballots are used in the United States in general elections. The first, called an **office-block ballot**, or sometimes a **Massachusetts ballot**, groups all the candidates for a particular elective office under the title of that office. Parties dislike the office-block ballot because it places more emphasis on the office than on the party; it discourages straight-ticket voting and encourages split-ticket voting.

A **party-column ballot** is a form of general election ballot in which all of a party's candidates are arranged in one column under the party's label and symbol. It is also called the **Indiana ballot**. In some states, it allows voters to vote for all of a party's candidates for local, state, and national offices by simply marking a single "X" or by pulling a single lever. Most states use this type of ballot. As it encourages straight-ticket voting, the two major parties favor this form. When a party has an exceptionally strong presidential or gubernatorial candidate to head the ticket, the use of the party-column ballot increases the **coattail effect** (the influence of a popular candidate on the success of other candidates on the same party ticket).

VOTING BY MAIL

Although voting by mail has been accepted for absentee ballots for many decades (for example, for those who are doing business away from home or for members of the armed

Office-Block, or Massachusetts, Ballot
A form of general election ballot in which candidates for elective office are grouped together under the title of each office. It emphasizes voting for the office and the individual candidate, rather than for the party.

Party-Column, or Indiana, Ballot
A form of general-election ballot in which all of a party's candidates for elective office are arranged in one column under the party's label and symbol. It emphasizes voting for the party, rather than for the office or individual.

Coattail Effect
The influence of a popular candidate on the electoral success of other candidates on the same party ticket. The effect is increased by the party-column ballot, which encourages straight-ticket voting.

forces), only recently have several states offered mail ballots to all of their voters. The rationale for using the mail ballot is to make voting easier for the voters. A startling result came in a special election in Oregon in spring 1996: With the mail-only ballot, turnout was 66 percent, and the state saved more than $1 million. In the 2000 presidential elections, in which Oregon voters were allowed to mail in their ballots, voter participation was more than 80 percent. Although voters in several states now have the option of voting by mail, Oregon is the only state to have abandoned precinct polling places completely. A nationwide system of voting by mail would have many pros and cons, which we explore in the *What If...* feature.

VOTE FRAUD

Vote fraud is something regularly suspected but seldom proved. Voting in the 1800s, when secret ballots were rare and people had a cavalier attitude toward the open buying of votes, was probably much more conducive to fraud than are modern elections. Larry J. Sabato and Glenn R. Simpson, however, claim that the potential for vote fraud is high in many states, particularly through the use of phony voter registrations and absentee ballots.[6]

MANY STATES ALLOW paper or electronic ballots to have a "party circle" so the voter can vote for all the candidates of that party for local, state, and national offices with one mark. (Probate Court, Jefferson County, Alabama)

[6]Larry J. Sabato and Glenn R. Simpson, *Dirty Little Secrets: The Persistence of Corruption in American Politics* (New York: Random House, 1996).

OREGON IS THE ONLY STATE that uses only a mail ballot. Special ballot boxes are set up where voters can deposit their ballots. Do you think that mail balloting would work for the entire United States? (Richard Clement/Reuters/Landov Media)

WHAT IF...

VOTING BY MAIL BECAME UNIVERSAL?

As pointed out in the text, so far Oregon is the only state to have eliminated precinct polling places. Washington State has also been a leader in adopting voting by mail. The majority of that state's counties now use a vote-by-mail system.

Typically, with a vote-by-mail system, ballots are mailed to the homes of registered voters, who then fill them out and return them via the postal system. Usually, ballots are sent out about three weeks before the election date. Local voting authorities determine the cut-off date for returning the ballots. In some vote-by-mail jurisdictions, volunteers pick up ballots at voters' homes and take them to drop-off booths or to drive-in quick-drop locations.

What if the Congress passed a law changing all federal elections—Congress and the president—to voting by mail? Many proponents of voting by mail believe that it is the best way to increase voter participation. (Internet voting would be even easier.) Despite some initial concerns that voters would not return their ballots, Oregon has seen the highest percentage of voter participation ever, reaching 87 percent in the 2004 elections.

When questions arise about the accuracy of ballot counts, mail-in votes provide an automatic paper trail. Each vote-by-mail ballot is normally read by optical scanners, and the paper version remains available if a hand recount becomes necessary. Certainly, the elimination of polling places reduces the expense of elections for any jurisdiction. Oregon estimates that it has reduced costs by more than 30 percent since it went to a statewide vote-by-mail system.

Proponents of voting by mail argue that it is preferable to some alternative national standard that would apply new rules to an outdated system of polling places. Voting by mail is low tech, low cost, and convenient.

VOTE BY MAIL: A SUBVERSION OF THE ELECTION PROCESS

Political scientist Norman Ornstein, an early critic of mail-in voting, argues that mail balloting subverts the whole election process. He points out that voters can cast their ballots well before meaningful debates and other exchanges occur between the candidates. As a result, the voter may be casting an uninformed ballot.* The Constitution Project at Georgetown University, as well as a consortium of the Massachusetts Institute of Technology and the California Institute of Technology, came to the same conclusion after an examination of the 2004 elections.

Critics additionally argue that mail-in voting deprives voters of the secrecy guaranteed by voting at a polling place. They also believe that mail-in voting provides more opportunities for fraud. Finally, they contend that it represents the abandonment of an important civic duty of going to the polls on election day.

FOR CRITICAL ANALYSIS

1. Would citizens have more faith in a vote by mail system than they have now?
2. Is there enough new information in the last weeks of a campaign to change votes?
3. Do you believe that the chances of voting fraud are greater or less with a mail-in voting system than with the current polling-place system?

*Norman Ornstein, "Vote-by-Mail: Is It Good for Democracy?" *Campaigns and Elections*, May 1996, p. 47.

The Danger of Fraud. In California, for example, it is very difficult to remove a name from the polling list even if the person has not cast a ballot in the last two years. Thus, many persons are still on the rolls even though they no longer live in California. Enterprising political activists could use these names for absentee ballots. Other states have registration laws that are meant to encourage easy registration and voting. Such laws can be taken advantage of by those who seek to vote more than once.

After the 2000 elections, Larry Sabato again emphasized the problem of voting fraud. "It's a silent scandal," said Sabato, "and the problem is getting worse with increases in

THIS REGISTRAR OF VOTERS in New Orleans reviews absentee ballots sent via fax in April 2006. The fax machines worked day and night prior to that city's first municipal elections after Hurricane Katrina. Are there problems when many voters never step inside a voting booth? If so, what are they? (AP Photo/Cheryl Gerber)

absentee voting, which is the easiest way to commit fraud." He noted that in 2000, one-third of Florida's counties found that more than 1,200 votes were cast illegally by felons, and in one county alone nearly 500 votes were cast by unregistered voters. In two precincts, the number of ballots cast was greater than the number of people who voted.[7]

Mistakes by Voting Officials. Some observers claim, however, that errors leading to fraud are trivial in number, and that a few mistakes are inevitable in a system involving millions of voters. These people argue that an excessive concern with vote fraud makes it harder for minorities and poor people to vote.

For example, in 2000, Katherine Harris, Florida's top election official, oversaw a purge of the voter rolls while simultaneously serving as co-chair of the Florida Bush campaign. According to the *New York Times*, when attempting to remove the names of convicted felons from the list of voters:

> Ms. Harris's office overruled the advice of the private firm that compiled the felon list and called for removing not just names that were an exact match, but ones that were highly inexact. Thousands of Florida voters wound up being wrongly purged. . . . In Missouri, elected officials charged for years that large numbers of St. Louis residents were casting votes from vacant lots. A study conducted by *The* [St. Louis] *Post Dispatch* in 2001 found that in the vast majority of cases, the voters lived in homes that had been wrongly classified by the city.[8]

In both the Florida and Missouri examples, a majority of the affected voters were African American.

As a result of the confusion generated by the 2000 elections, many states are now in the process of improving their voting systems and procedures. Some claim that certain reforms, such as requiring voters to show a voter-registration card or photo identification, may prevent fraud but may also deter first-time voters, new citizens, and people with less educational background. By 2008, 25 states required that voters produce some sort of identification when they go to the polls. In April of that year, the Supreme Court upheld the Indiana law, which was one of the strictest in the nation, by a six-to-three vote.[9] While the court found no direct evidence of the fraud that the Indiana statute is intended to stop, there was also no evidence of any burden being placed on the voter. The ruling makes it likely that other states will pass stricter voter identification laws.

THE IMPORTANCE OF THE VOTING MACHINE

The 2000 presidential election spurred a national debate on the mechanics of how people actually cast their ballots on election day. Up until 2000, states and counties moved from hand-counted paper ballots to mechanical voting machines or electronic touch-

[7]As cited in "Blind to Voter Fraud," *The Wall Street Journal*, March 2, 2001, p. A10.
[8]"How America Doesn't Vote," *The New York Times: The News of the Week in Review*, February 15, 2004, p. 10.
[9]553 U.S.___(2008).

NAPLES, FLORIDA election workers study punch card ballots in the state Supreme Court's ordered recount after the 2000 election. A few minutes after this photograph was taken, the U.S. Supreme Court stopped the recount and announced that it would hear the case. George W. Bush won Florida's electoral votes. (Colin Braley/Reuters/CORBIS)

screen devices as they could afford the move or in response to local election difficulties. The outcome of the 2004 presidential election hinged on winning Florida's electoral votes. The biggest problem lay in Florida's use of punch card ballots. Voters slipped their card into the voting book and then "punched" the number next to the name of the candidate they preferred. Because of the layout of the printed book in 2004, names were spread across two pages, resulting in a "butterfly" ballot. Voters could accidentally punch the wrong number and cast their vote for the wrong candidate.

As the election night came to a close, it was clear that the votes in Florida were "too close to call" between George W. Bush and Al Gore. Ballot problems abounded: some voters invalidated their ballots by voting for both candidates; some punch cards were not punched all the way through, resulting in no vote being counted; some had no vote for president at all. The Democratic Party and its candidates went to court to demand a recount of the votes. The Republican political leaders in Florida tried to stop recounts in fear of losing the election. After a series of dramatic legal battles, the U.S. Supreme Court settled the election by allowing a Florida decision favoring the Republicans to stand. However, the result was a seriously flawed election process that produced tremendous cynicism about the mechanics of voting.

In 2002, Congress passed the Help America Vote Act, which established the U.S. Election Assistance Commission. The charge of the commission is to set standards for voting machines; to distribute funds to help communities acquire new, easier-to-use machines; and to act as a clearinghouse of information for the states. As expected, several companies began to create new machines for use in the voting booth. Most of these depend on digital recording of votes. Given the mistakes that occurred in Florida, many citizens wanted a record of their votes so that a mistake in tallying votes could be checked against a paper record. Election officials are deeply concerned that recording and transmitting vote counts digitally only may be subject to hacking and vote fraud. To date, no system has been devised that is totally immune to some sort of fraud, and voters continue to be concerned about the security of our election system.[10]

[10]The AEI-Brookings Election Reform Project collects data and provides reports on progress in securing the vote at its Web site: www.electionreformproject.org.

THE ELECTORAL COLLEGE

Many people who vote for the president and vice president think that they are voting directly for a candidate. In actuality, they are voting for **electors**, who will cast their ballots in the electoral college. Article II, Section 1, of the Constitution outlines in detail the method of choosing electors for president and vice president. The framers of the Constitution wanted to avoid the selection of president and vice president by the "excitable masses." Rather, they wished the choice to be made by a few supposedly dispassionate, reasonable men (but not women).

Elector
A member of the electoral college, which selects the president and vice president. Each state's electors are chosen in each presidential election year according to state laws.

THE CHOICE OF ELECTORS

Each state's electors are selected during each presidential election year. The selection is governed by state laws. After the national party convention, the electors normally are pledged to the candidates chosen. The total number of electors today is 538, equal to 100 senators, 435 members of the House, and three electors for the District of Columbia (the Twenty-third Amendment, ratified in 1961, added electors for the District of Columbia). Each state's number of electors equals that state's number of senators (two) plus its number of representatives. Figure 9–4 shows how the electoral votes are apportioned by state.

THE ELECTORS' COMMITMENT

When a plurality of voters in a state chooses a slate of electors—except in Maine and Nebraska, where electoral votes are based on Congressional districts—those electors are pledged to cast their ballots on the first Monday after the second Wednesday in December in the state capital for the

DID YOU KNOW?

That 42 states do not indicate on the ballot that the voter is casting a ballot for members of the electoral college rather than for the president and vice president directly?

FIGURE 9–4 Electoral Votes by State Map

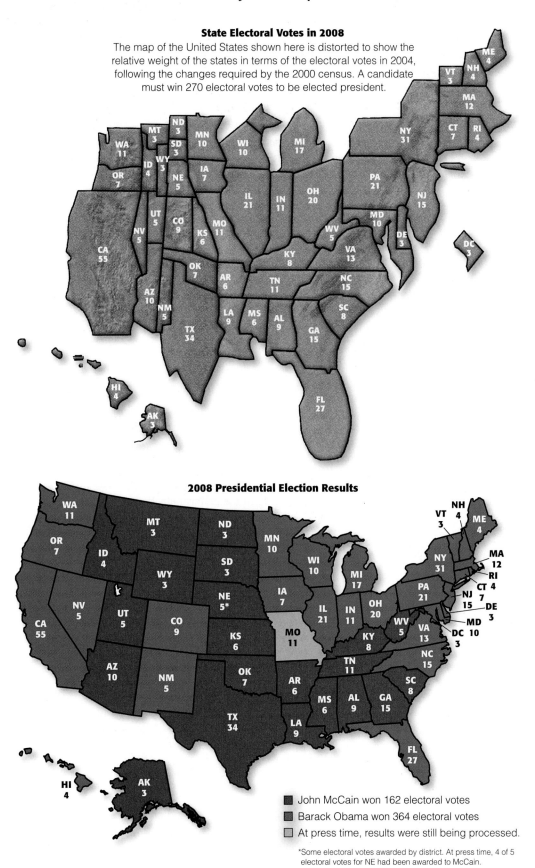

State Electoral Votes in 2008

The map of the United States shown here is distorted to show the relative weight of the states in terms of the electoral votes in 2004, following the changes required by the 2000 census. A candidate must win 270 electoral votes to be elected president.

2008 Presidential Election Results

■ John McCain won 162 electoral votes
■ Barack Obama won 364 electoral votes
☐ At press time, results were still being processed.

*Some electoral votes awarded by district. At press time, 4 of 5 electoral votes for NE had been awarded to McCain.

presidential and vice-presidential candidates of their party. The Constitution does not, however, *require* the electors to cast their ballots for the candidates of their party.

The ballots are counted and certified before a joint session of Congress early in January. The candidates who receive a majority of the electoral votes (270) are certified as president-elect and vice president-elect. According to the Constitution, if no candidate receives a majority of the electoral votes, the election of the president is decided in the House from among the candidates with the three highest numbers of votes, with each state having one vote (decided by a plurality of each state delegation). The selection of the vice president is determined by the Senate in a choice between the two candidates with the most votes, each senator having one vote. Congress was required to choose the president and vice president in 1801 (Thomas Jefferson and Aaron Burr), and the House chose the president in 1825 (John Quincy Adams).[11]

It is possible for a candidate to become president without obtaining a majority of the popular vote. There have been many minority presidents in our history, including Abraham Lincoln, Woodrow Wilson, Harry Truman, John F. Kennedy, Richard Nixon (in 1968), Bill Clinton (1992, 1996), and George W. Bush (in 2000). Such an event becomes more likely when there are important third-party candidates.

Perhaps more distressing is the possibility of a candidate's being elected when an opposing candidate receives a plurality of the popular vote. This has occurred on four occasions—in the elections of John Quincy Adams in 1824, Rutherford B. Hayes in 1876, Benjamin Harrison in 1888, and George W. Bush in 2000, all of whom won elections in which an opponent received a plurality of the popular vote.

CRITICISMS OF THE ELECTORAL COLLEGE

Besides the possibility of a candidate's becoming president even though an opponent obtains more popular votes, there are other complaints about the electoral college. The idea of the Constitution's framers was to have electors use their own discretion to decide who would make the best president. But electors no longer perform the selecting function envisioned by the founders, because they are committed to the candidate who has a plurality of popular votes in their state in the general election.[12]

One can also argue that the current system, which in most states gives all of the electoral votes to the candidate who has a statewide plurality, is unfair to other candidates and their supporters. The current system of voting also means that presiden-

---

[11]For a detailed account of the process, see Michael J. Glennon, *When No Majority Rules: The Electoral College and Presidential Succession* (Washington, DC: Congressional Quarterly Press, 1993), p. 20.
[12]Note, however, that there have been revolts by so-called *faithless electors*—in 1796, 1820, 1948, 1956, 1960, 1968, 1972, 1976, 1988, and 2000.

tial campaigning will be concentrated in those states that have the largest number of electoral votes and in those states in which the outcome is likely to be close. The other states may receive second-class treatment during the presidential campaign. It can also be argued that there is something of a bias favoring states with smaller populations, because including Senate seats in the electoral vote total partly offsets the edge of the more populous states in the House. Wyoming (with two senators and one representative) gets an electoral vote for roughly every 164,594 inhabitants (based on the 2000 census), for example, whereas Iowa gets one vote for every 418,046 inhabitants, and California has one vote for every 615,848 inhabitants. Note that many of the smallest states have Republican majorities.

Many proposals for reform of the electoral college system have been advanced, particularly after the turmoil resulting from the 2000 elections. The most obvious proposal is to eliminate the electoral college system completely and to elect candidates on a popular-vote basis; in other words, a direct election, by the people, of the president and vice president. Because abolishing the electoral college would require a constitutional amendment, however, the chances of electing the president by a direct vote are remote.

The major parties are not in favor of eliminating the electoral college, fearing that this would give minor parties a more influential role. Also, less populous states are not in favor of direct election of the president because they believe they would be overwhelmed by the large-state vote. In recent years, some states have begun to consider yet another way to make the electoral college more responsive to the popular vote. In 2007, the National Popular Vote Movement (NPV) came to public attention. The movement creates a compact between the states that requires that electoral votes from NPV states will be cast for the candidate who wins the national popular vote regardless of the vote in that particular state. So far, two states have approved this law, and several more are considering it. In addition, Massachusetts, South Carolina, Virginia, and Wisconsin are among states considering adopting a district plan like that of Maine.

While the 2000 election caused considerable controversy and cynicism about the national electoral system, it also focused attention on issues that need to be resolved. Efforts to improve registration systems, to make voting easier and more secure, and to make changes to the electoral colleges all will work to make elections in the United States more trustworthy for the voters.

You can make a difference

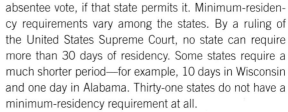

REGISTERING AND VOTING

In nearly every state, before you are allowed to cast a vote in an election, you must first register. Registration laws vary considerably from state to state. Depending in part on how difficult a state's laws make it to register, some states have much lower rates of registration and voting participation than do others.

WHY SHOULD YOU CARE?

To vote, you must register. But why bother to vote? After all, the electorate is large, many elections are not close, and often your vote will not have an important effect on the election outcome. If you do vote, however, you increase the amount of attention that politicians pay to people like you. When Congress, state legislatures, or city councils consider new laws and regulations, these bodies typically give more weight to the interests of groups that are more likely to vote. So even if your single vote does not determine the outcome of an election, it does add, to a small degree, to the voter turnout for your constituency. Your vote therefore increases the chances of legislation that benefits you or that meets with your approval.

WHAT CAN YOU DO?

What do you have to do to register and cast a vote? In general, you must be a citizen of the United States, at least 18 years old on or before election day, and a resident of the state in which you intend to register. Most states require that you meet minimum-residency requirements. In other words, you must have lived in the state in which you plan to be registered for a specified period of time. If you have not lived in the state long enough to register before an upcoming election, you may retain your previous registration in another state and cast an absentee vote, if that state permits it. Minimum-residency requirements vary among the states. By a ruling of the United States Supreme Court, no state can require more than 30 days of residency. Some states require a much shorter period—for example, 10 days in Wisconsin and one day in Alabama. Thirty-one states do not have a minimum-residency requirement at all.

Nearly every state also specifies a closing date by which you must be registered before an election. In other words, even if you have met a residency requirement, you still may not be able to vote if you register too close to the day of the election. The closing date is different in certain states (Connecticut and Delaware) for primary elections than for other elections. The closing date for registration varies from election day itself (Maine, Minnesota, Wisconsin, and Wyoming) to 30 days before the election in 13 states. In North Dakota, no registration is necessary.

In most states, your registration can be revoked if you do not vote within a certain number of years. This process of automatically "purging" the voter-registration lists of nonactive voters happens every two years in about a dozen states, every three years in Georgia, every four years in more than 20 other states, every five years in Maryland and Rhode Island, every eight years in North Carolina, and every 10 years in Michigan. Ten states do not require this purging at all.

Let us look at Iowa as an example. Iowa voters normally register through the local county auditor or when they obtain a driver's license (under the "motor voter" law of 1993). A voter who moves to a new address within the state must change his or her registration by contacting the auditor. Postcard registrations must be postmarked or delivered to the county auditor no later than the 15th day before an election. Voters can declare or change their party affiliation when they register or reregister, or they can change or declare a party when they go to the polls on election day. Postcard registration forms in Iowa are available at many public buildings, from labor unions, at political party headquarters, at the county auditors' offices, or from campus groups. Registrars who will accept registrations at other locations may be located by calling a party headquarters or a county auditor.

For more information on voting registration, contact your county or state officials, party headquarters, labor union, or local chapter of the League of Women Voters.*

*League of Women Voters, www.lwv.org

KEY TERMS

Australian ballot 329
coattail effect 331
elector 336

office-block, or Massachusetts, ballot 331
party-column, or Indiana,
ballot 331

rational ignorance effect 326
registration 328
voter turnout 321

CHAPTER SUMMARY

1. Voter participation in the United States is low compared with that of other countries. Some view low voter turnout as a threat to representative democracy, whereas others believe it simply indicates greater satisfaction with the status quo. There is an association between voting and a person's age, education, minority status, and income level. Another factor affecting voter turnout is the extent to which elections are competitive within a state. It is also true that the number of eligible voters is smaller than the number of people of voting age because of ineligible felons and immigrants who are not yet citizens.

2. In colonial times, only white males with a certain minimum amount of property were eligible to vote. The suffrage issue has concerned, at one time or another, most groups in the United States. Today, to be eligible to vote, a person must satisfy registration, citizenship, and age and residency requirements. Each state has different qualifications. Some claim that these requirements are responsible for much of the nonparticipation in the political process in the United States.

3. The United States uses the Australian ballot, a secret ballot that is prepared, distributed, and counted by government officials. The office-block ballot groups candidates according to office. The party-column ballot groups candidates according to their party labels and symbols.

4. Vote fraud is often charged but not often proven. After the 2000 election, states and local communities are adopting new forms of voting equipment, seeking to provide secure voting systems for elections. The federal government established a commission to test new technologies and provide a clearinghouse for information.

5. The voter technically does not vote directly for president but chooses between slates of presidential electors. In most states, the slate that wins the most popular votes throughout the state gets to cast all the electoral votes for the state. The candidate receiving a majority (270) of the electoral votes wins. Both the mechanics and the politics of the electoral college have been sharply criticized. There have been many proposed reforms, including a proposal that the president be elected on a popular-vote basis in a direct election.

SELECTED PRINT AND MEDIA RESOURCES

SUGGESTED READINGS

Alvarez, R. Michael, and Thad E. Hall. *Electronic Elections: The Perils and Promises of Digital Democracy.* Princeton, NJ: Princeton University Press, 2008. Alvarez and Hall examine all past technologies in voting and look at the new voting machines and processes that are available in the digital age. They suggest standards by which voting systems can be improved.

Fortier, John C. *Absentee and Early Voting: Trends, Promises and Perils.* Washington, DC: AEI, 2006. The author looks at all of the efforts to encourage participation by making early voting and absentee voting easier and then discusses the advantages and disadvantages of these alternatives to going to the polls.

Green, Donald P., and Alan S. Gerber. *Get Out the Vote: How to Increase Voter Turnout.* Washington, DC: Brookings Institution Press, 2004. This volume is a practical guide for activists seeking to mount Get Out The Vote (GOTV) campaigns. It differs from other guides in that it is based on research and experiments in actual electoral settings—Green and Gerber are political science professors at Yale University. The authors discover that many widely used GOTV tactics are less effective than is often believed.

Herrnson, Paul S., Richard G. Niemi, Michael J. Hanmer, Benjamin B. Bederson, Frederick C. Conrad, and Michael W. Traugott. *Voting Technology: The Not-So-Simple Act of Casting a Ballot.* Washington, DC: Brookings Institution, 2008. This book summarizes the data collected by the Brookings Institution on how voting technology impacts voters' behavior.

MEDIA RESOURCES

American Blackout—A 2005 film starring former Congresswoman Cynthia McKinney from Georgia as she investigates the ways in which African American voters can be challenged at the polls and kept from voting.

Election Day—This 2005 film was shot on Election Day 2004 and looks at 14 different individuals who are trying to vote or who are working at the polls themselves.

Mississippi Burning—This 1988 film, starring Gene Hackman and Willem Dafoe, is a fictional version of the investigation of the death of two civil rights workers who came to Mississippi to help register African Americans to vote in 1964.

Trouble in Paradise—Shot in Florida after the contested 2000 presidential election, the film follows Florida residents as they find out what laws have been changed and which aspects of voting are still troubling in their state. The film was released in 2004.

e-mocracy

ELECTIONS AND THE WEB

While the contested election of 2000 certainly spurred interest in American voting systems, the topic has been the subject of research for many decades. Today, the Internet makes it possible for you to learn about voting laws and regulations in your state, at the federal level, and around the world. Investigating different voting systems will help you formulate an opinion about proposals for reform of the voting systems we use here.

LOGGING ON

- To learn more about voting by mail, visit the Oregon secretary of state's Web page dedicated to the topic at **www.sos.state.or.us/elections**. The site includes frequently asked questions and a brief history of voting by mail.
- You can learn about the impact of different voting systems on election strategies and outcomes at the Center for Voting and Democracy, which maintains the following Web site:
  www.fairvote.org
- For a wealth of information about election technologies and the pros and cons of each, see the Web site maintained by the AEI-Brookings Election Reform Project:
  www.electionreformproject.org
- To find out what different states are doing to ensure the vote, go to the Web site of the National Conference of State Legislatures at:
  www.ncsl.org/programs/legismgt/elect/elect.htm
- For information about voting and turnout around the world, go to the Web site of the Institute for Democracy and Electoral Assistance (IDEA):
  www.idea.int

ONLINE REVIEW

At **www.cengage.com/politicalscience/schmidt/agandpt14e**, you will find a Tutorial Quiz for this chapter providing questions on the chapter contents, including the features. The questions are organized to match the major sections of the chapter. You'll have access to other helpful study tools, including the book's glossary and flashcards, crossword puzzles, and Web links, as well as "Which Side Are You On?" and "Politics and . . ." features written by the authors of the book.

CHAPTER (10)

Barack Obama greets supporters as he makes his way into a rally at Bristow, Virginia, on June 5, 2008. He had already clinched the nomination for president. (Mandel Ngan/AFP/Getty Images)

CAMPAIGNING FOR OFFICE

QUESTIONS TO CONSIDER

What are the hallmarks of free and fair elections?

Should all candidates have equal campaign financing?

Should party members or the general public nominate the candidates for president?

CHAPTER CONTENTS

Making a DIFFERENCE

THE EMERGENCE OF 527 GROUPS

Money is the lifeblood of elections. Candidates for office raise and spend hundreds of millions of dollars. For example, the presidential candidates in 2004 spent about $750 million. In the 2008 presidential election, before the national conventions were held, candidates for president, including Senators McCain, Clinton, and Obama, had raised more than $1 billion.[a]

Candidates need these contributions to be successful. However, donors influence the electoral process in other significant ways. As you will learn in this chapter, before the reforms in campaign-finance laws in 2002 (the Bipartisan Campaign Reform Act or BCRA), donors could give unlimited or "soft" money to parties as long as the parties did not explicitly use that money to aid particular candidates. The BCRA outlawed that particular form of soft money, but in its place have risen so-called 527 groups, named for the section of the U.S. Tax Code that provides for these nonprofits to collect donations without having to pay taxes on the money.

The rise of these 527 groups is important for many reasons. By closing the soft money loophole, the BCRA stopped the flow of money from corporations, unions, and wealthy individuals to the political parties. One of the effects of the BCRA was that these donors avoided the provisions of BCRA by redirecting their giving to a relatively new form of organization, the 527. Since the 2002 law, corporations and unions are among the top financial contributors to 527 groups. These groups are not limited in how much money they may accept, nor are they limited in the source of the money. This behavior is related to the way in which they spend their money. The Federal Election Commission (FEC) has ruled that if these groups wish to remain unregulated in fundraising, they may not coordinate with any candidate for a federal election (such as the president or Congress). This means they may not actively campaign for someone running for these offices, nor may they use the "magic words" "vote for" or "vote against" a particular federal candidate in advertisements

FREE ELECTIONS ARE the cornerstone of the American political system. Voters choose one candidate over another to hold political office by casting ballots in local, state, and federal elections. In 2008, the voters chose Barack Obama and Joe Biden to be president and vice president of the United States for the next four years. In addition, voters elected all of the members of the House of Representatives and one-third of the members of the Senate. The campaigns were bitter, long, and extremely expensive, with the Democratic primary contest being the closest and most expensive in history. The total cost for all federal elections in the 2007–2008 cycle was well into the billions of dollars.

Voters and candidates frequently criticize the American electoral process. It is said to favor wealthier candidates, to further the aims of special-interest groups, and to be dominated by older voters and those with better educations and higher incomes. Recent reforms of the campaign-finance laws were tested for the first time in 2004. Although the new laws had some effect on campaign strategy, fundraising outside the system and extensive use of television advertising dominated the election season. New media, especially e-mail, text messaging, and blogging, was used to increase youth participation.

they finance. If they violate these rules, they may become subject to fines. However, they can support issue ads that make clear which issues and, by the way, which candidates they are supporting or opposing.[b]

Despite these limits, these groups are very important players in campaigns. Although the tax status has existed for many years and some groups had limited exposure in 2000,[c] the presidential election of 2004 marked a turning point, making 527 groups a topic of discussion in the mainstream media. One of the more famous, although not the most financially active, groups was the Swift Boat Veterans for Truth. This group was highly critical of the Democratic nominee, Senator John Kerry, attacking his Vietnam War record. By 2008 standards, this group's financial footprint was relatively small; it raised only $158,750 in 2004. Of that sum, Bob J. Perry, a Houston, Texas-based builder, contributed $100,000. In the 2004 cycle, Mr. Perry was the fifth-highest donor to 527 groups (giving $8,085,199), and in 2006, gave the most money ($9,750,000) to 527s. All of this information is publicly accessible either through the FEC or through public-interest groups like the Center for Responsive Politics, which runs a searchable Web site, **www.opensecrets.org**.

These public-interest watchdog groups, such as Democracy 21, the Campaign Legal Center, and the Center for Responsive Politics, are highly critical of the burgeoning influence of 527s. In 2004, they filed a complaint with the FEC against America Coming Together, charging that it has violated the ban on candidate advocacy. This is a Democratic-leaning group whose largest individual contributor, George Soros, donated $7.5 million in 2004.[d] In 2007, the FEC ruled against the 527, levying a fine

of $775,000 against it for making more than $100 million in inappropriate contributions.[e] The public-interest groups protested that the fine was not sufficiently large to deter future 527 actions. As the 2008 primary season progressed, it became obvious that 527s were raising money and running advertisements as they did in 2004. We will not know until well after the 2008 election how much money these groups have raised and spent; however, there is every reason to expect they will remain influential.

[a]As of the end of September 2008, Senator McCain had raised $358 million while Senator Obama had raised more than $639 million. It has been estimated that the total raised for all candidates in this election cycle was almost $2 billion. www .opensecrets.org, accessed November 7, 2008.

[b]www.clcblog.org, accessed April 17, 2008.

[c]In the Republican presidential nominating contest in 2000, Senator John McCain was highly criticized by a 527 group, Republicans for Clean Air. The group was funded in part by individuals who supported then-Governor Bush's candidacy; www.dallasobserver.com/2000-04-06/news/clearing-the-air, accessed April 17, 2008.

[d]www.opensecrets.org/527s/527cmtedetail.asp?cycle=2004& format=&ein=200094706&tname=America%20Coming% 20Together, accessed April 17, 2008.

[e]www.democracy21.org/index.asp?Type=B_PR&SEC=% 7B7248831A-87CA-4C2D-B873-60C64918C920%7D, accessed April 17, 2008.

WHO WANTS TO BE A CANDIDATE?

Democratic political systems require competitive elections, meaning that opposition candidates for each office have a chance to win. If there is no competition for any office—president or local school superintendent—then the public has no ability to make a choice about its leadership or policies to be pursued. Who, then, are the people who seek to run for office?

There are thousands of elective offices in the United States. The political parties strive to provide a slate of candidates for every election. Recruiting candidates is easier for some offices than for others. Political parties may have difficulty finding candidates for the board of the local water control district, but they generally have a sufficient number of candidates for county commissioner or sheriff. The higher the office and the more prestige attached to it, the more candidates are likely to want to run. In many areas of the country, however, one political party may be considerably stronger than the other. In those situations, the minority party may have more difficulty finding nominees for elections in which victory is unlikely.

The presidential campaign provides the most colorful and exciting look at candidates and how they prepare to compete for office—in this instance, the highest office in the land. The men and women who wanted to be candidates in the 2008 presidential campaign faced a long and obstacle-filled path. First, they needed to raise sufficient funds to plan for the early campaigns in Iowa and New Hampshire. Then, they faced an unprecedented number of early **presidential primaries**, which determined if they could win in diverse states. The early primaries were followed by "Super Tuesday" with 22 primaries. Candidates and their campaign organizations needed to have strategies that maximized their strengths across the nation and, at the same time, raised enough donations to keep national campaigns going. They had to keep their organization alive for the primary season, plan to win caucus and primary votes, and, in the case of the Democrats in 2008, convince enough **superdelegates** to win the nomination before the convention. John McCain won his party's primaries early enough to begin raising funds for the general election, while Barack Obama and Hillary Clinton battled throughout the primary season, with Barack Obama ultimately receiving his party's nomination. Each of these candidates raised and spent record amounts of money in their fight for the nomination.

DAYTONA BEACH, FLORIDA, mayoral candidates Mike Shallow, left, and Yvonne Scarlett-Golden answer questions during a political forum for all candidates at Our Lady of Lourdes Catholic Church. Campaigning is just as important for candidates for local office as it is for candidates for the Senate or the presidency. What do voters look for in a personal speech by a candidate? (Daytona Beach News-Journal/Craig Litten/AP Photos)

Presidential Primary
A statewide primary election of delegates to a political party's national convention, held to determine a party's presidential nominee.

Superdelegate
A party leader or elected official who is given the right to vote at the party's national convention. Superdelegates are not elected at the state level.

WHY THEY RUN

People who choose to run for office can be divided into two groups—the self-starters and those who are recruited. The volunteers, or self-starters, get involved in political activities to further their careers, to carry out specific political programs, or in response to certain issues or events. Ralph Nader's campaigns for the presidency in 2000 and 2004 were rooted in his belief that the two major parties were ignoring vital issues, such as environmental protection and the influence of corporate wealth on American politics. Candidates such as Ron Paul, on the Republican side, and Dennis Kucinich, on the Democratic side, run for president to present their positions, even though they know that they have very little chance of winning.

Issues are important, but self-interest and personal goals—status, career objectives, prestige, and income—are central in motivating some candidates to enter political life. Political office is often seen as the stepping-stone to achieving certain career goals. A lawyer or an insurance agent may run for office only once or twice and then return to private life with enhanced status. Other politicians may aspire to long-term political office—for example, county offices such as commissioner or sheriff sometimes offer attractive opportunities for power, status, and income and are in themselves career goals. Finally, we think of ambition as the desire for ever-more-important offices and higher status. Politicians who run for lower offices and then set their sights on Congress or a governorship may be said to have "progressive" ambitions.[1]

_____

[1]See the discussion of this topic in Linda Fowler, _Candidates, Congress, and the American Democracy_ (Ann Arbor: University of Michigan Press, 1993), pp. 56–59.

THE NOMINATION PROCESS

Individuals become official candidates through the process of nomination. Generally, nominating processes for all offices are controlled by state laws and usually favor the two major political parties. For most minor offices, individuals become candidates by submitting petitions to the local election board. Political parties often help individuals obtain the petitions, pay whatever filing fee is required, and gather signatures. In most states, a candidate from one of the two major parties faces far fewer requirements to get on the ballot than a candidate who is an independent or who represents a minor or new party.

For higher-level offices, candidates may need to petition and then be nominated by a party convention at the state level. In other jurisdictions, party caucuses are empowered to nominate candidates. And, as will be discussed later, many contenders for office are nominated through a primary election in which two or more individuals contend for the party's nomination.

The American system of nominations and primary elections is one of the most complex in the world. In most European nations, the political party's choice of candidates is final, and no primary elections are ever held.

DID YOU KNOW?

That five women received votes for vice president at the Democratic convention in 1924, the first held after women received the right to vote in 1920?

WHO IS ELIGIBLE?

There are few constitutional restrictions on who can become a candidate in the United States. As set out in the Constitution, the formal requirements for national office are as follows:

1. *President.* Must be a natural-born citizen, have attained the age of 35 years, and be a resident of the country for 14 years by the time of inauguration.
2. *Vice president.* Must be a natural-born citizen, have attained the age of 35 years, and not be a resident of the same state as the candidate for president.[2]
3. *Senator.* Must be a citizen for at least nine years, have attained the age of 30 by the time of taking office, and be a resident of the state from which elected.
4. *Representative.* Must be a citizen for at least seven years, have attained the age of 25 by the time of taking office, and be a resident of the state from which elected.

The qualifications for state legislators are set by the state constitutions and likewise include age, place of residence, and citizenship. (Usually, the requirements for the upper chamber of a legislature are somewhat more stringent than those for the lower chamber.) The legal qualifications for running for governor or other state office are similar.

WHO RUNS?

Despite these minimal legal qualifications for office at both the national and state levels, a quick look at the slate of candidates in any election—or at the current members of the U.S. House of Representatives—will reveal that not all segments of the population take advantage of these opportunities. Holders of political office in the United States are overwhelmingly white and male. Until the 20th century, presidential candidates were of northern European origin and of Protestant heritage.[3] Laws that effectively denied voting rights made it impossible to elect African American public officials in many areas in which African Americans constituted a significant portion of the population. As a result of the passage of major civil rights legislation in the 1960s, however, the number of African American public officials has increased throughout the United States. By 2007, the number of African American elected officials was estimated at more than 9,500,[4] and 84 percent of Americans said they would be completely comfortable voting for an African American for president.[5]

[2]Technically, a presidential and vice-presidential candidate can be from the same state, but if they are, one of the two must forfeit the electoral votes of their home state.
[3]A number of early presidents were Unitarian. The Unitarian Church is not Protestant, but it is historically rooted in the Protestant tradition.
[4]Ralph Everett, "Number of Black Elected Officials Increases, But Not by Much," *Joint Center Journal*, 2007.
[5]Gallup Poll, February/March 2007.

Women as Candidates. Until recently, women generally were considered to be appropriate candidates only for lower-level offices, such as state legislator or school board member. It was thought that women would be more acceptable to the voting public if they were either running for an office that allowed them to continue their family duties, or were running for an office that focused on local affairs, such as city or school issues. The last 20 years have seen a tremendous increase in the number of women who run for office, not only at the state level but for the U.S. Congress as well. Figure 10–1 shows the increase in female candidates. In 2008, 140 women ran for Congress, and 78 were elected. Of course, one notable female politician is the Speaker of the House of Representatives, Nancy Pelosi, and another is Hillary Rodham Clinton, who has been elected to the U.S. Senate.

In the past, women were not recruited because they had not worked their way up through the male-dominated party organization or because they were thought to have no chance of winning. Women also had a more difficult time raising campaign funds. Since the 1970s, there has been a focused effort to increase the number of women candidates. EMILY's List, a group that raises money to recruit and support liberal women candidates, has had a strong impact on the situation for women candidates. Other organizations with more conservative agendas also raise money for women. Today, it is clear that women can raise the necessary funds to run a campaign, run it effectively, and attract enough voters to win almost any office. According to the Gallup Poll, a vast majority of Americans (86 percent) would vote for a qualified woman for president.[6]

Lawyers as Candidates. Candidates are likely to be professionals, particularly lawyers. Political campaigning and officeholding are simply easier for some occupational groups

FIGURE 10–1 Women Running for Congress (and Winning)

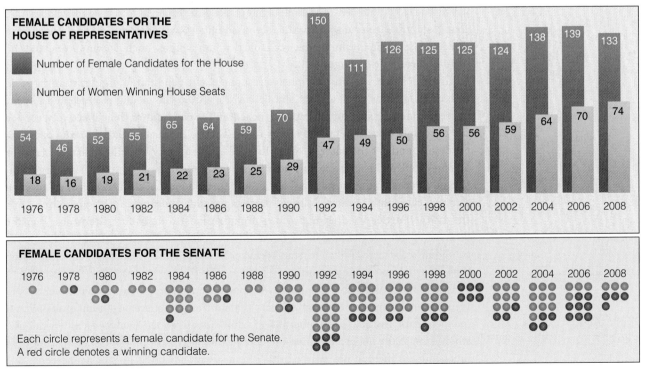

[6]Gallup Poll, September 8–11, 2005.

than for others, and political involvement can make a valuable contribution to certain careers. Lawyers, for example, have more flexible schedules than do many other professionals, can take time off for campaigning, and can leave their jobs to hold public office full-time. Furthermore, holding political office is good publicity for their professional practice, and they usually have partners or associates to keep the firm going while they are in office. Perhaps most important, many jobs that lawyers aspire to—federal or state judgeships, state attorney offices, or work in a federal agency—can be attained by political appointment. Such appointments often go to loyal partisans who have served their party by running for and holding office. For certain groups, then, participation in the political arena may further personal ambitions, whereas it could be a sacrifice for others whose careers demand full-time attention for many years.

THE 21ST CENTURY CAMPAIGN

After the candidates have been nominated, the most exhausting and expensive part of the election process begins—the general election campaign. The contemporary political campaign is becoming more complex and more sophisticated with every election. Even with the most appealing of candidates, today's campaigns require a strong organization; expertise in political polling and marketing; professional assistance in fundraising, accounting, and financial management; and technological capabilities in every aspect of the campaign.

THE CHANGING CAMPAIGN

The goal is the same for all campaigns—to convince voters to choose a candidate or a slate of candidates for office. Part of the reason for the increased intensity of campaigns in the last decade is that they are now centered on the candidate, not on the party. The candidate-centered campaign emerged in response to several developments: changes in the electoral system, the increased importance of television and other forms of electronic media in campaigns, technological innovations such as computers, and the increased cost of campaigning.

To run a successful and persuasive campaign, the candidate's organization must be able to raise funds for the effort, obtain coverage from the media, produce and pay for political commercials and advertising, schedule the candidate's time effectively, convey the candidate's position on the issues to the voters, conduct research on the opposing candidate, and get the voters to go to the polls. When party identification was stronger among voters and before the advent of television campaigning, a strong party organization at the local, state, or national level could furnish most of the services and expertise that the candidate needed. Political parties provided the funds for campaigning until the 1970s. Parties used their precinct organizations to distribute literature, register voters, and get out the vote on election day. Less effort was spent on advertising each candidate's positions and character, because the party label presumably communicated that information to many voters.

One of the reasons that campaigns no longer depend on parties is that fewer people identify with them (see Chapter 8), as is evident from the increased number of political independents. In 1952, about one-fifth of adults identified themselves as independents, whereas in 2008, about one-third considered themselves to be independents. Political independents include not only adults who are well-educated and issue-oriented, but also many individuals who are not very interested in politics or well-informed about candidates or issues.

THE PROFESSIONAL CAMPAIGN

Whether the candidate is running for the state legislature, for the governor's office, for the U.S. Congress, or for the presidency, every campaign has some fundamental tasks to accomplish. Today, in national elections, the lion's share of these tasks is handled by paid professionals, rather than volunteers or amateur politicians. Volunteers and amateurs are primarily used for the last-minute registration or voter turnout activities.

The most sought-after and possibly the most criticized campaign expert is the **political consultant**, who, for a large fee, devises a campaign strategy, creates a campaign theme, oversees the advertising, and possibly chooses the campaign colors and the candidate's official portrait. Political consultants began to displace volunteer campaign managers in the 1960s, about the same time that television became a force in campaigns. The paid consultant monitors the campaign's progress, plans all media appearances, and coaches the candidate for debates. The consultants and the firms they represent are not politically neutral; most will work only for candidates from one party.

Under constant pressure to raise more campaign funds and to comply with the campaign-finance laws, virtually all campaigns need a **finance chairperson**, who plans the fundraising strategy and finds the legal and accounting expertise needed for the organization. Of course, campaigns will either hire an in-house **pollster** or contract with a major polling firm for the tracking polls and focus groups discussed in Chapter 6.

Candidates need to have a clear strategy to gain public attention and to respond to attacks by their opponents. The campaign's **communications director** plans appearances, the themes to be communicated by the candidate at specific points in the campaign, and the responses to any attacks. The campaign's **press secretary** is responsible for dealing directly with the press. Perhaps the most famous example of a successful communication strategy was that of Bill Clinton in his 1992 victory. The campaign organized a "War Room" to instantly respond to any attack by his opponents. At the end of the campaign is the actual election. Campaigns need to find a way to recruit and organize volunteers for the **Get Out the Vote (GOTV)** drive to persuade voters to come to the polls on election day.

Political Consultant
A paid professional hired to devise a campaign strategy and manage a campaign.

Finance Chairperson
The campaign professional who directs fundraising, campaign spending, and compliance with campaign-finance laws and reporting requirements.

Pollster
The person or firm who conducts public opinion polls for the campaign.

Communications Director
A professional specialist who plans the communications strategy and advertising campaign for the candidate.

Press Secretary
The individual who interacts directly with the journalists covering the campaign.

Get Out the Vote (GOTV)
This phrase describes the multiple efforts expended by campaigns to get voters out to the polls on election day.

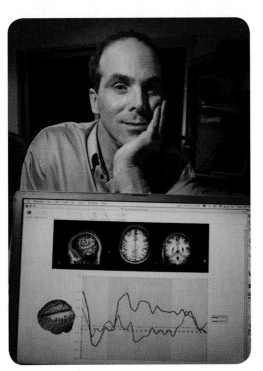

DR. JOSHUA FREEDMAN, a researcher at UCLA, believes that magnetic resonance imaging (MRI) can be used to judge the effectiveness of political ads on television. The graph he shows in this photo is the average of responses of Republicans (red line) and Democrats (blue line) as they watched a pro-George W. Bush video. Clearly, the Republican viewers demonstrated a more positive response than did the Democrats. Why might political consultants be interested in such research? (AP Photo/Reed Saxon)

THE STRATEGY OF WINNING

In the United States, unlike some European countries, there are no rewards for a candidate who comes in second; the winner takes all. A winner-take-all system is also known as a *plurality voting system*. In most situations, the winning candidate does not have to have a majority of the votes. If there are three candidates, the one who gets the most votes wins—that is, "takes it all"—and the other two candidates get nothing. Given this system, the campaign organization must plan a strategy that maximizes the candidate's chances of winning. In American politics, candidates seek to capture all of the votes of their party's supporters, to convince a majority of the independent voters to vote for them, and to gain a few votes from supporters of the other party. To accomplish these goals, candidates must consider their visibility, their message, and their campaign strategy.

CANDIDATE VISIBILITY AND APPEAL

One of the most important concerns is how well known the candidate is. If she or he is a highly visible incumbent, there may be little need for campaigning except to remind the voters of the officeholder's good deeds. If, however, the candidate is an unknown challenger or a largely unfamiliar character attacking a well-known public figure, the campaign must devise a strategy to get the candidate before the public.

In the case of the independent candidate or the candidate representing a minor party, the problem of name recognition is serious. Such candidates must present an overwhelming case for the voter to reject the major-party candidates. Both Democratic and Republican candidates use the strategic ploy of labeling third-party candidates as "not serious"—and therefore not worth the voter's time.

THE USE OF OPINION POLLS

Opinion polls are a major source of information for both the media and the candidates. Poll taking is widespread during the primaries. Presidential hopefuls have private polls taken to make sure that there is at least some chance they could be nominated and, if nominated, elected. During the presidential campaign, polling is even more frequent. Polls are taken not only by the regular pollsters—Roper, Harris, Gallup, and others—but also privately by private use of the candidate and his or her campaign organization. As the election approaches, many candidates and commercial houses use **tracking polls**, which are polls taken almost every day, to find out how well they are competing for votes. Tracking polls enable consultants to fine-tune the advertising and the candidate's speeches in the last days of the campaign.

Tracking Poll
A poll taken for the candidate on a nearly daily basis as election day approaches.

FOCUS GROUPS

Another tactic is to use a **focus group** to gain insights into public perceptions of the candidate. Professional consultants organize a discussion of the candidate or of certain political issues among ten to fifteen ordinary citizens. The citizens are selected from specific target groups in the population—for example, working women, blue-collar men, senior citizens, or young voters. Recent campaigns have tried to reach groups such as "soccer moms," "Wal-Mart shoppers," or "NASCAR dads."[7] The group discusses personality traits of the candidate, political advertising, and other candidate-related

Focus Group
A small group of individuals who are led in discussion by a professional consultant in order to gather opinions on and responses to candidates and issues.

[7]NASCAR stands for the National Association of Stock Car Auto Racing.

issues. The conversation is digitally video recorded (and often observed from behind a mirrored wall). Focus groups are expected to reveal more emotional responses to candidates or the deeper anxieties of voters—feelings that consultants believe often are not tapped into by more impersonal telephone surveys. The campaign then can shape its messages to respond to these feelings and perceptions.

FINANCING THE CAMPAIGN

DID YOU KNOW?

That a candidate can buy lists of all the voters in a precinct, county, or state for only about two cents per name from a commercial firm?

In a book published in 1932 entitled *Money in Elections*, Louise Overacker had the following to say about campaign financing:

> The financing of elections in a democracy is a problem which is arousing increasing concern. Many are beginning to wonder if present-day methods of raising and spending campaign funds do not clog the wheels of our elaborately constructed mechanism of popular control, and if democracies do not inevitably become [governments ruled by small groups].[8]

Although writing more than 70 years ago, Overacker touched on a sensitive issue in American political campaigns—the connection between money and elections. More than $3.5 billion was spent at all levels of campaigning during the 2003–2004 election cycle. Total spending by the presidential candidates in 2004 amounted to about $750 million. For the midterm senatorial election in 2006 in New York State alone, the two candidates together amassed $50 million in contributions for their campaigns. Arizona, Michigan, Minnesota, Missouri, Nebraska, Pennsylvania, and Washington all saw senatorial campaigns costing between $15 million and $30 million. As might be expected, candidates spend much less to retain or obtain a seat in the House of Representatives, because representatives must run for election every two years as opposed to six years for senators. (There are other reasons, too.) Except for the presidential campaigns, all of these funds had to be provided by the candidates and their families, borrowed, or raised by contributions from individuals, political parties, or *political action committees*, described later in this chapter. For the presidential campaigns, some of the funds may come from the federal government.

REGULATING CAMPAIGN FINANCING

The way campaigns are financed has changed dramatically in the last 25 years. Today, candidates and political parties must operate within the constraints imposed by complicated laws regulating campaign financing.

A variety of federal **corrupt practices acts** have been designed to regulate campaign financing. The first, passed in 1925, limited primary and general election expenses for congressional candidates. In addition, it required disclosure of election expenses and, in principle, put controls on contributions by corporations. There were many loopholes in the restrictions, and the acts proved to be ineffective.

The **Hatch Act** (Political Activities Act) of 1939 is best known for restricting the political activities of civil servants. The act also, however, made it unlawful for a political group to spend more than $3 million in any campaign and limited individual contributions to a political group to $5,000. Of course, such restrictions were easily circumvented by creating additional political groups.

Corrupt Practices Acts
A series of acts passed by Congress in an attempt to limit and regulate the size and sources of contributions and expenditures in political campaigns.

Hatch Act
An act passed in 1939 that restricted the political activities of government employees. It also prohibited a political group from spending more than $3 million in any campaign and limited individual contributions to a campaign committee to $5,000.

---

[8]Louise Overacker, *Money in Elections* (New York: Macmillan, 1932), p. vii.

In the 1970s, Congress passed additional legislation to reshape the nature of campaign financing. In 1971, it passed the Federal Election Campaign Act to reform the process. Then in 1974, in the wake of the Watergate scandal (see Chapter 6), Congress enacted further reforms.

THE FEDERAL ELECTION CAMPAIGN ACT

The Federal Election Campaign Act (FECA) of 1971, which became effective in 1972, essentially replaced all past laws. The act placed no limit on overall spending but restricted the amount that could be spent on mass-media advertising, including television. It limited the amount that candidates could contribute to their own campaigns (a limit later ruled unconstitutional) and required disclosure of all contributions and expenditures over $100. In principle, the FECA limited the role of labor unions and corporations in political campaigns. It also provided for a voluntary $1 (now $3) check-off on federal income tax returns for general campaign funds to be used by major-party presidential candidates.

Further Reforms in 1974. For many, the 1971 Act did not go far enough. Amendments to the FECA passed in 1974 did the following:

1. *Created the Federal Election Commission.* This commission consists of six nonpartisan administrators whose duties are to enforce compliance with the requirements of the Act.
2. *Provided public financing for presidential primaries and general elections.* Any candidate running for president who is able to obtain sufficient contributions in at least 20 states can obtain a subsidy from the U.S. Treasury to help pay for primary campaigns. In 2004, however, neither George W. Bush nor John Kerry accepted public financing for the primaries. This allowed both of them to spend much more on advertising and other expenses than they could have if they had accepted public funding. Each of them did accept $74.62 million for the general election campaign.
3. *Limited presidential campaign spending.* Any candidate accepting federal support must agree to limit campaign expenditures to the amount prescribed by federal law.
4. *Limited contributions.* Under the 1974 amendments, citizens could contribute up to $1,000 to each candidate in each federal election or primary; the total limit on all contributions from an individual to all candidates was $25,000 per year. Groups could contribute a maximum of $5,000 to a candidate in any election. (As you will read shortly, some of these limits were changed by the 2002 campaign-reform legislation.)
5. *Required disclosure.* Each candidate must file periodic reports with the FEC, listing who contributed, how much was spent, and for what the funds were spent.

The 1971 and 1974 laws regulating campaign contributions and spending set in place the principles that have guided campaign finance ever since. The laws and those that have enacted subsequently are guided by three principles: (1) set limits on what individuals and groups can give to individual candidates and within one election cycle; (2) provide some public funding for the presidential primaries, conventions, and the general election campaign; and (3) make all contributions and reports public. All contributions that are made to candidates under these laws and principles are usually called **hard money**. As will be detailed later, however, individuals and groups that wish to circumvent these principles have been successful in finding ways to do so.

Hard Money
This refers to political contributions and campaign spending that is recorded under the regulations set forth in law and by the Federal Election Commission.

Buckley v. Valeo. The 1971 Act had limited the amount that each individual could spend on his or her own behalf. The Supreme Court declared the provision unconstitutional in 1976, in *Buckley v. Valeo*,[9] stating that it was unconstitutional to restrict in any way the amount congressional candidates could spend on their own behalf: "The candidate, no less than any other person, has a First Amendment right to engage in the discussion of public issues and vigorously and tirelessly to advocate his own election."

The *Buckley v. Valeo* decision, which has often been criticized, was directly countered by a 1997 Vermont law. The law, known as Act 64, imposed spending limits ranging from $2,000 to $300,000 (depending on the office sought) by candidates for state offices in Vermont. A number of groups, including the American Civil Liberties Union and the Republican Party, challenged the Act, claiming that it violated the First Amendment's guarantee of free speech. In a landmark decision in August 2002, a federal appellate court disagreed and upheld the law. The court stated that Vermont had shown that, without spending limits, "the fund-raising practices in Vermont will continue to impair the accessibility which is essential to any democratic political system. The race for campaign funds has compelled public officials to give preferred access to contributors, selling their time in order to raise campaign funds."[10] In 2006, the U.S. Supreme Court declared that Vermont's campaign spending and donation limits were unconstitutional, thereby in a sense reaffirming the *Buckley v. Valeo* decision.

ATTORNEY JAMES BOPP is shown leaving the Supreme Court building in Washington, D.C., where he argued against the Vermont law that put limits on campaign spending and donations. He won the case, for the Supreme Court, in 2006 in *Randell v. Sorrell*, which ruled that Vermont's law was unconstitutional. Can another state, nonetheless, pass a similar law? Why or why not? (AP Photo/J. Scott Applewhite)

INTEREST GROUPS AND CAMPAIGN FINANCE: REACTION TO NEW RULES

In the last two decades, interest groups and individual companies have found new, very direct ways to support elected officials through campaign donations. Elected officials, in turn, have become dependent on these donations to run increasingly expensive campaigns. Interest groups and corporations funnel money to political candidates through several devices: **political action committees (PACs)**, **soft money** contributions, and **issue advocacy advertising**. These devices developed as a means of circumventing the campaign-financing reforms of the early 1970s, which limited contributions by individuals and unions to set amounts.

PACs AND POLITICAL CAMPAIGNS

The 1974 and 1976 amendments to the Federal Election Campaign Act of 1971 allow corporations, labor unions, and other interest groups to set up PACs to raise funds for candidates. For a federal PAC to be legitimate, the funds must be raised from at least 50 volunteer donors and must be given to at least five candidates in the federal election. PACs can contribute up to $5,000 to each candidate in each election. Each corporation or each union is limited to one PAC. As you might imagine, corporate PACs obtain funds from executives and managers in their firms, and unions obtain PAC funds from their members.

Political Action Committee (PAC)
A committee set up by and representing a corporation, labor union, or special-interest group. PACs raise and give campaign donations.

Soft Money
Campaign contributions unregulated by federal or state law, usually given to parties and party committees to help fund general party activities.

Issue Advocacy Advertising
Advertising paid for by interest groups that support or oppose a candidate or a candidate's position on an issue without mentioning voting or elections.

[9]424 U.S. 1 (1976).
[10]*Randell v. Vermont Public Interest Research Group*, 300 F.3d 129 (2d Cir. 2002).

The number of PACs has grown significantly since 1976, as has the amount they spend on elections. There were about 1,000 PACs in 1976; today, there are more than 4,500. Total spending by PACs grew from $19 million in 1973 to more than $1 billion in 2005–2006. About 43 percent of all campaign funds raised by House candidates in 2006 came from PACs.[11]

Interest groups funnel PAC funds to the candidates they think can do the most good for them. Frequently, they make the maximum contribution of $5,000 per election to candidates who face little or no opposition. The summary of PAC contributions given in Figure 10–2 shows that the great bulk of campaign contributions goes to incumbent candidates rather than to challengers. Table 10–1 shows the amounts contributed by the top 20 PACs during the 2005–2006 election cycle.

As Table 10–1 also shows, many PACs give most of their contributions to candidates of one party. Other PACs, particularly corporate PACs, tend to give funds to Democrats in Congress as well as to Republicans, because, with both chambers of Congress so closely divided, predicting which party will be in control after an election is almost impossible. Why, you might ask, would business leaders give to Democrats who may be more liberal than themselves? Interest groups see PAC contributions as a way to ensure *access* to powerful legislators, even though the groups may disagree with the legislators some of the time. PAC contributions are, in a way, an investment in a relationship.

Campaign-financing regulations clearly limit the amount that a PAC can give to any one candidate, but there is no limit on the amount that a PAC can spend on issue advocacy, either on behalf of a candidate or party or in opposition to one.

FIGURE 10–2 PAC Contributions to Congressional Candidates, 1991–2006

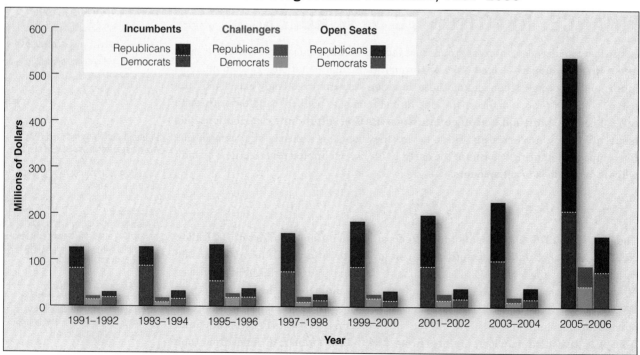

Source: Federal Election Commission, "PAC Activity Continues to Climb," press release, October 5, 2007.

- -

[11]Center for Responsive Politics, at www.opensecrets.org.

TABLE 10–1 The Top 20 Contributors to Federal Candidates, 2005–2006 Election Cycle*

PAC NAME	TOTAL AMOUNT	DEM. %	REP. %
National Association of Realtors	$1,953,005	48%	52%
Association of Trial Lawyers of America	1,806,000	95	4
International Brotherhood of Electrical Workers	1,793,650	96	3
National Beer Wholesalers Association	1,762,500	27	73
Operating Engineers Union	1,697,135	77	22
AT&T, Inc.	1,691,433	33	67
Credit Union National Association	1,631,599	43	57
United Parcel Service	1,565,709	30	70
American Bankers Association	1,555,174	33	67
National Auto Dealers Association	1,541,100	31	69
National Association of Home Builders	1,421,250	25	75
Teamsters Union	1,383,275	90	10
United Auto Workers	1,381,850	98	1
Laborers Union	1,375,150	82	18
Carpenters and Joiners Union	1,349,640	66	33
American Federation of State, County, and Municipal Employees	1,306,671	97	2
International Association of Fire Fighters	1,163,705	71	28
American Federation of Teachers	1,137,000	99	1
Air Line Pilots Association	1,096,500	81	18
Machinists/Aerospace Workers Union	1,069,000	99	0

*Includes subsidiaries and affiliated PACs, if any.
Source: Center for Responsive Politics, 2006.

CAMPAIGN FINANCING BEYOND THE LIMITS

Within a few years after the establishment of the tight limits on contributions, new ways to finance campaigns were developed that skirted the reforms and made it possible for huge sums to be raised, especially by the major political parties.

TABLE 10–2 Soft Money Raised by Political Parties, 1993–2002

	1993–1994	1995–1996	1997–1998	1999–2000	2001–2002
Democratic Party	$45.6 million	$122.3 million	$ 92.8 million	$243.0 million	$199.6 million
Republican Party	$59.5 million	$141.2 million	$131.6 million	$244.4 million	$221.7 million
Total	$105.1 million	$263.5 million	$224.4 million	$487.4 million	$421.3 million

Source: www.opensecrets.org, 2006.

Contributions to Political Parties. Candidates, PACs, and political parties found ways to generate *soft money*—that is, campaign contributions to political parties that escaped the limits of federal election law. Although the FECA limited contributions that would be spent on elections, there were no limits on contributions to political parties for activities such as voter education and voter-registration drives. This loophole enabled the parties to raise millions of dollars from corporations and individuals. It was not unusual for some corporations to give more than $1 million to the Democratic National Committee or to the Republican Party.[12] As shown in Table 10–2, nearly twice as much soft money was raised in the 1999–2000 presidential election cycle as in the previous (1995–1996) presidential election cycle. The parties spent these funds for their conventions, for registering voters, and for advertising to promote the general party position. The parties also sent a great deal to state and local party organizations, which used the soft money to support their own tickets. Although soft money contributions to the national parties were outlawed after election day 2002 (as you will read shortly), political parties saw no contradiction in raising and spending as much soft money as possible during the 2001–2002 election cycle.

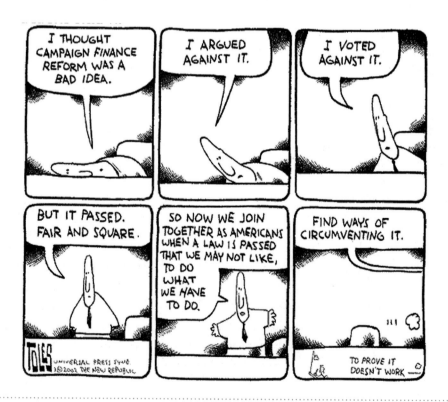

(TOLES © 2004 *The Washington Post.* Reprinted with permission of Universal Press Syndicate)

[12]Paul Allen Beck, *Party Politics in America*, 8th ed. (New York: Longman, 1997), pp. 293–294.

Independent Expenditures. Business corporations, labor unions, and other interest groups discovered that it was legal to make **independent expenditures** in an election campaign, so long as the expenditures were not coordinated with those of the candidate or political party. Hundreds of unique committees and organizations blossomed to take advantage of this campaign tactic. Although a 1990 United States Supreme Court decision, *Austin v. Michigan State Chamber of Commerce*,[13] upheld the right of the states and the federal government to limit independent, direct corporate expenditures (such as for advertisements) on behalf of *candidates*, the decision did not stop businesses and other types of groups from making independent expenditures on *issues*.

Independent Expenditures
Nonregulated contributions from PACs, organizations, and individuals. The funds may be spent on advertising or other campaign activities, so long as those expenditures are not coordinated with those of a candidate.

Issue Advocacy. Indeed, issue advocacy—spending unregulated funds on advertising that promotes positions on issues rather than candidates—has become a common tactic in recent years. Interest groups routinely wage their own issue campaigns. For example, the Christian Coalition, which is incorporated, annually raises millions of dollars to produce and distribute voter guidelines and other direct-mail literature to describe candidates' positions on various issues and to promote its agenda. In 2004, the interest group MoveOn.org began running issue ads attacking the Bush record shortly after Senator John Kerry had clinched the Democratic nomination. The Bush campaign responded by beginning its own advertising campaign.

Although promoting issue positions is very close to promoting candidates who support those positions, the courts repeatedly have held, in accordance with the *Buckley v. Valeo* decision mentioned earlier, that interest groups have a First Amendment right to advocate their positions. In a 1996 decision,[14] the Supreme Court clarified this point, stating that political parties may also make independent expenditures on behalf of candidates—as long as the parties do so *independently* of the candidates. In other words, the parties must not coordinate such expenditures with the candidates' campaigns.

THE BIPARTISAN CAMPAIGN REFORM ACT OF 2002

While both Democrats and Republicans argued for campaign reform legislation during the 1990s, the bill co-sponsored by Senators John McCain, a Republican, and Russ Feingold, a Democrat, finally became the Bipartisan Campaign Reform Act (BCRA) in 2002. This act, which amended the 1971 FECA, took effect on the day after the Congressional elections were held on November 5, 2002.

Key Elements of the New Law. The 2002 law bans the large, unlimited contributions to national political parties that are known as soft money. It places curbs on, but does not entirely eliminate, the use of campaign ads by outside special-interest groups advocating the election or defeat of specific candidates. Such ads are allowed up to 60 days before a general election and up to 30 days before a primary election.

In 1974, contributions by individuals to federal candidates were limited to $1,000 per individual. The 2002 Act increased this limit to $2,000 with annual increases. In addition, the maximum amount that an individual can give to all federal candidates was raised from $25,000 per year to $95,000 over a two-year election cycle. The Act did not ban soft money contributions to state and local parties. These parties can accept such contributions, as long as they are limited to $10,000 per year per individual.

Challenges to the 2002 Act. Almost immediately, the 2002 Act faced a set of constitutional challenges brought by groups negatively affected. In December 2003, however, the Supreme Court upheld almost all of the clauses of the Act.[15]

---

[13]494 U.S. 652 (1990).
[14]*Colorado Republican Federal Campaign Committee v. Federal Election Commission*, 518 U.S. 604 (1996).
[15]*McConnell v. Federal Election Commission*, 540 U.S. 93 (2003).

Soon thereafter, a coalition of conservative and liberal groups called Wisconsin Right to Life brought a lawsuit claiming that the 2002 Act infringed on legitimate grassroots lobbying. Wisconsin Right to Life argued that part of the act violated its right to free speech. In 2006, the Supreme Court unanimously ruled that the Wisconsin group could go back to court to challenge a specific part of the 2002 Act—the federal ban on issue-oriented ads that mention a particular candidate just before an election.[16]

Once the Supreme Court upheld the bulk of the 2002 law, it was left to the FEC to interpret the statute. Slowly but surely, the FEC opened loopholes that allowed campaign finance to return to "business as usual." In 2004, a U.S. district court struck down more than a dozen such commission regulations. When the FEC asked for these rulings to be reversed, a federal appeals court in Washington did not agree.

The Rise of the 527s. Interest groups that previously gave soft money to the parties responded to the 2002 BCRA by setting up new organizations outside the parties, called 527 organizations after the section of the tax code that provides for them. These tax-exempt organizations, which rely on soft money contributions for their funding and generally must report their contributions and expenditures to the Internal Revenue Service, first made a major impact in the 2003–2004 election cycle. While the groups claim to focus on encouraging voter registration and supporting particular issues, they often create advertisements that are meant to impact election outcomes.

Among the most successful 527 groups during the 2004 presidential elections were America Coming Together (ACT), the Media Fund, and the MoveOn.org Voter Fund, which together spent $33 million on television ads attacking Bush's record. The three groups spent another $85 million to register new voters and to run ads explaining the liberal position on issues ranging from health care to international trade. Billionaire George Soros contributed more than $15 million to the three groups. Overall, 527 groups spent more than $600 million in the 2003–2004 election cycle. They continued to be active during the 2005–2006 election cycle, as you can see in Table 10–3.

MOVEON.ORG has become one of the most powerful liberal political groups in the United States with more than 3 million members. By using the Internet, MoveOn.org has continued to increase its membership and raise millions of dollars for campaigning on the issues. (Keyur Khamar/Bloomberg News/Landov Media)

---

[16]*Wisconsin Right to Life, Inc. v. Federal Election Commission*, 126 S. Ct. 1016 (2006).

TABLE 10–3 Committee Activity in 2005–2006 by Type of Group or Interest

TYPE OF GROUP OR INTEREST	TOTAL RECEIPTS	TOTAL EXPENDITURES
Republican/conservative	$17,179,412	$34,150,184
Democratic/liberal	15,045,233	18,001,892
Miscellaneous unions	14,354,031	17,512,894
Public-sector unions	8,957,147	11,335,565
Building trade unions	7,079,956	4,322,358
Women's issues	5,120,785	4,211,303
Environment	2,549,357	1,019,757
Industrial unions	2,496,305	2,773,894
Human rights	1,710,332	2,143,076

Source: Internal Revenue Service.

In contrast to the 527s, charities and true not-for-profit organizations are not allowed to participate directly in any type of political activity. If they do so, they risk fines and the loss of their charitable tax-exempt status. In 2005, the IRS reviewed more than 80 churches, charities, and other tax-exempt organizations. The IRS looked for such banned activities as the distribution of printed materials encouraging members to vote for a specific candidate, contributions of cash to candidates' campaigns, and ministers' use of their pulpits to oppose or endorse specific candidates.

The IRS found that churches played a particularly important role in the 2004 elections. For example, well-known fundamentalist Baptist minister Jerry Falwell used his Web site to endorse President Bush and to urge visitors to the site to donate $5,000 to the Campaign for Working Families. At the All Saints Church in Pasadena, California, a pastor gave a sermon in which he imagined a debate among Senator John Kerry,

RAISING CAMPAIGN FUNDS is an important task for any candidate. Barack Obama speaks to supporters at a fundraiser in Harlem's Apollo Theater in November of 2007, long before he won the nomination for president. How would presidential election campaigns change if they were publicly financed? (Monika Graff/The Image Works)

President George Bush, and Jesus Christ. Although Jesus won, the press reported that the hypothetical debate came out in favor of John Kerry.

Of the 82 churches, charities, and other tax-exempt organizations that the IRS examined, more than 75 percent engaged in prohibited political activity during the 2003–2004 election cycle. The IRS proposed to revoke the tax-exempt status of at least three of these organizations.

CAMPAIGN FINANCING AND THE 2008 ELECTIONS

In 2008, the current campaign financing laws were put to the test and may have failed. Senator John McCain, who authored the most recent revision of the laws, chose not to accept private donations during the general election campaign. As a result, the total amount he raised during 2008 was about $350 million. He did, however, accept about $1 million in PAC contributions. He ran his fall campaign on the $84 million of federal campaign funds granted to him under law. In addition, the Republican National Committee was able to raise and spend funds toward his election.

Taking a completely opposite approach, Senator Barack Obama chose not to accept public funds for the general election campaign. During the 2008 campaign, he raised more than $630 million but accepted no PAC donations. The Obama campaign pioneered new ways for individuals to make contributions over the Internet, and millions of individuals chose to give in that manner. One result of the disparity in funds available was the ability of the Obama campaign to mount an exceptional Get Out the Vote campaign and to purchase four times more advertising time than did McCain. At the end of the campaign came many calls for a reexamination of campaign finance laws to fit these new realities.

RUNNING FOR PRESIDENT: THE LONGEST CAMPAIGN

The American presidential election is the culmination of two different campaigns linked by the parties' national conventions. The presidential primary campaign lasts from January until June of the election year. Traditionally, the final campaign heats up around Labor Day, although if the nominees are known, it will begin even before the conventions.

Primary elections were first mandated in 1903 in Wisconsin. The purpose of the primary was to open the nomination process to ordinary party members and to weaken the influence of party bosses in the nomination procedure. Until 1968, however, there were fewer than twenty primary elections for the presidency. They were often **"beauty contests"** in which the candidates competed for popular votes, but the results had little or no impact on the selection of delegates to the national convention. National conventions were meetings of the party elite—legislators, mayors, county chairpersons, and loyal party workers—who were mostly appointed to their delegations. National conventions saw numerous trades and bargains among competing candidates, and the leaders of large blocs of delegates could direct their delegates to support a favorite candidate.

"Beauty Contest"
A presidential primary in which contending candidates compete for popular votes but the results do not control the selection of delegates to the national convention.

REFORMING THE PRIMARIES

In recent decades, the character of the primary process and the makeup of the national convention have changed dramatically. The public, rather than party elites, now generally controls the nomination process. In 1968, after President Lyndon B. Johnson declined to run for another term, the Democratic Party nomination race was dominated by candidates who opposed the war in Vietnam. After Robert F. Kennedy was assassinated in June 1968, antiwar Democrats faced a convention that would nominate LBJ's choice regardless of popular votes. After the extraordinary disruptive riots outside the

WHAT IF...

SPENDING LIMITS WERE PLACED ON CAMPAIGNS?

After the 2008 presidential primary campaigns ended, more than $7.5 million was distributed by the Federal Election Commission (FEC) to candidates including Joe Biden, Christopher Dodd, John Edwards, Dennis Kucinich, and Ralph Nader. However, the major primary contenders in both parties (including Barack Obama, Hillary Clinton, John McCain, Mitt Romney, and Mike Huckabee) refused the public funding, raising more than $500 million themselves. The political parties each received a little more than $16 million from the FEC for their conventions. In addition, Congress appropriated $50 million to each convention city for help with security and police issues. Both Denver and St. Paul had to raise another $50 to $60 million from private funds to hold the conventions. For the general election, Republican nominee John McCain accepted $85 million for his campaign, but Democratic nominee Barack Obama refused public funding, preferring to raise campaign funds without the restrictions that come with public funds.

One of the most fundamental questions about campaign financing in the United States is the fairness of one candidate who raises more money to finance a strong organization and buy more media advertisements than others. Do voters have an equal chance to hear the positions and promises of all the candidates if some have greater financial resources? Should one candidate be able to buy five times more television time than another? The Supreme Court has said that an individual can spend his or her own funds for their campaign as a practice of free speech. The same principle holds for interest groups that wish to express their views on the issues. So, the tension over regulating campaign finance lies between advocates of free speech and advocates of fairness.

WHAT IF SPENDING LIMITS WERE PLACED ON CAMPAIGNS?

If some sort of limit on campaign spending were found to be constitutional, one consequence would be a decline in the number of candidates with "deep pockets." In other words, fewer of the very rich would attempt to run for office, because they would not be able to use their personal wealth in the effort to win.

A limit on campaign spending would also mean a limit on campaign contributions. Consequently, special-interest groups and lobbying organizations would necessarily diminish in numbers. The lobbying industry would shrink, because one of the best ways to influence legislation is to make sure that the candidate of choice is elected or re-elected. Contributions are certainly helpful in winning elections.

THE IMPACT ON TELEVISION

The television industry would also be affected. Just as the bulk of the public's entertainment time is spent on television, so too is the bulk of campaign spending. Consider that in just the month before the Iowa caucuses in 2008, $9 million was spent on television ads in Des Moines, Iowa, alone. Voters in Iowa's capital saw 22,000 ads for the candidates. In the last week of the presidential campaigns in 2004, the two candidates spent more than $40 million on TV ads. A limit on total campaign spending would, by necessity, dramatically reduce spending on television advertising. Media companies, which count on increased profits in election years, would see a decline in their revenue, and overall advertising prices would decline.

WE HAVE ALREADY ATTEMPTED TO REFORM CAMPAIGNS

Complaints about excessive campaign spending are not new. Even sitting politicians have attempted to clean up elections. The BCRA of 2002 was one such attempt. The law became effective in January 2003. This law prohibited, among other things, so-called soft money contributions and expenditures that were clearly being used to influence federal elections. It also banned supposedly nonpartisan issue ads that were funded by corporations and labor unions. Such ads cannot appear 30 days prior to a primary election or 60 days before a general election. As we saw earlier, however, campaign spending overall has increased dramatically since the act became effective.

FOR CRITICAL ANALYSIS

1. Why would it be extremely difficult to *effectively* limit campaign spending?
2. If campaign spending limits were effective, who would be hurt more—those politicians already in office or those attempting to win an election for the first time? Explain your answer.

SENATOR ROBERT F. KENNEDY tells a press conference on April 1, 1968, that he will pursue the Democratic nomination for president. He was assassinated after winning the California primary election. Then-Vice President Hubert Humphrey won the nomination for president that year but lost the election to Richard Nixon. (Bettmann/CORBIS)

doors of the 1968 Democratic Convention in Chicago, many party leaders pushed for serious reforms of the convention process. They saw the general dissatisfaction with the convention, and the riots in particular, as being caused by the inability of the average party member to influence the nomination system.

The Democratic National Committee appointed a special commission to study the problems of the primary system. Called the McGovern-Fraser Commission, the group formulated new rules for delegate selection over the next several years that had to be followed by state Democratic parties.

The reforms instituted by the Democratic Party, which were imitated in part by the Republicans, revolutionized the nomination process for the presidency. The most important changes require that a majority of the Democratic convention delegates not be nominated by party elites; they must be elected by the voters in primary elections, in caucuses held by local parties (discussed later), or at state conventions. No delegates can be awarded on a "winner-take-all" basis; all must be proportional to the votes for the contenders. Delegates are normally pledged to a particular candidate, although the pledge is not always formally binding at the convention.

The delegation from each state must also include a proportion of women, younger party members, and representatives of the minority groups within the party. At first, virtually no special privileges were given to elected party officials, such as senators and governors. After the conventions chose candidates who were not as strong as the party hoped for, the Democratic Party invented superdelegates, who are primarily elected Democratic officeholders and state leaders. Superdelegates comprise less than 20 percent of the delegate votes.

TYPES OF PRIMARIES

Caucus
A meeting of party members designed to select candidates and propose policies.

Before discussing the types of primaries, we must first examine how some states use a party **caucus**. A caucus is typically a small, local meeting of party regulars who agree on a nominee. Sometimes the results of caucuses are voted on by a broader set of party members in a primary election. (If the party's chosen candidates have no opponents, however, a primary election may not be necessary.)

Alternatively, there may be a local or state party convention at which a slate of nominees of loyal party members is chosen. In any event, the resulting primary elections differ from state to state. The most common types are discussed here.

Closed Primary. In a **closed primary**, only avowed or declared members of a party can vote in that party's primary. In other words, voters must declare their party affiliation, either when they register to vote or at the primary election. A closed-primary system tries to make sure that registered voters cannot cross over into the other party's primary in order to nominate the weakest candidate of the opposing party or to affect the ideological direction of that party.

Open Primary. In an **open primary**, voters can vote in either party primary without disclosing their party affiliation. Basically, the voter makes the choice in the privacy of the voting booth. The voter must, however, choose one party's list from which to select candidates. Open primaries place no restrictions on independent voters.

Blanket Primary. In a *blanket primary*, the voter can vote for candidates of more than one party. Alaska, Louisiana, and Washington have blanket primaries. Blanket-primary campaigns may be much more costly because each candidate for every office is trying to influence all of the voters, not just those in his or her party.

In 2000, the United States Supreme Court issued a decision that altered significantly the use of the blanket primary. The case arose when political parties in California challenged the constitutionality of a 1996 ballot initiative authorizing the use of the blanket primary in that state. The parties contended that the blanket primary violated their First Amendment right of association. Because the nominees represent the party, they argued, party members—not the general electorate—should have the right to choose the party's nominee. The Supreme Court ruled in favor of the parties, holding that the blanket primary violated parties' First Amendment associational rights.[17]

The Court's ruling called into question the constitutional validity of blanket primaries in other states as well. The question before these states is how to devise a primary election system that will comply with the Supreme Court's ruling, yet offer independent voters a chance to participate in the primary elections.

DURING THE 1968 Democratic convention, thousands of protesters gathered in front of the convention headquarters, the Hilton hotel in Chicago. National Guard troops and the Chicago police used military tactics to move the protesters away from the site. (Photograph by Jo Freeman, www.jofreeman.com)

Closed Primary
A type of primary in which the voter is limited to choosing candidates of the party of which he or she is a member.

Open Primary
A primary in which any registered voter can vote (but must vote for candidates of only one party).

---

[17]*California Democratic Party v. Jones*, 530 U.S. 567 (2000).

Front-Runner
The presidential candidate who appears to be ahead at a given time in the primary season.

Front-Loading
The practice of moving presidential primary elections to the early part of the campaign to maximize the impact of these primaries on the nomination.

Runoff Primary. Some states have a two-primary system. If no candidate receives a majority of the votes in the first primary, the top two candidates must compete in another primary, called a *runoff primary*.

FRONT-LOADING THE PRIMARIES

As soon as politicians and potential presidential candidates realized that winning as many primary elections as possible guaranteed them the party's nomination for president, their tactics changed dramatically. For example, candidates running in the 2008 primaries, such as Senator Hillary Clinton, concentrated on building organizations in states that held early, important primary elections. Candidates realized that winning early contests, such as the Iowa caucuses or the New Hampshire primary election (both in January), meant that the media instantly would label the winner as the **front-runner**, thus increasing the candidate's media exposure and escalating the pace of contributions to his or her campaign fund.

The Rush to Be First. The states and state political parties began to see that early primaries had a much greater effect on the outcome of the presidential election and, accordingly, began to hold their primaries earlier in the season to secure that advantage. While New Hampshire held on to its claim to be the first primary, other states moved theirs to the following week. A group of mostly Southern states decided to hold their primaries on the same date, known as Super Tuesday, in the hope of nominating a moderate Southerner at the Democratic convention. When California, which had held the last primary (in June), moved its primary to March, the primary season was curtailed drastically. Due to this process of **front-loading** the primaries, in 2000 the presidential nominating process was over in March, with both George W. Bush and Al Gore having enough convention delegate votes to win their nominations. This meant that the campaign was essentially without news until the conventions in August, a gap that did not appeal to the politicians or the media. Both parties discussed whether more changes in the primary process were necessary.

In 2006, the Democratic Party announced that the Nevada caucus and the South Carolina primary would be held in the same time frame traditionally dominated by New Hampshire and Iowa. The Democrats reasoned that they wanted to add diversity to an early-primary calendar that has been dominated by the predominantly white, rural voices of New Hampshire and Iowa. Nevada boasts a quickly growing Hispanic population, and South Carolina has a long-standing African American community.

Consequences of Early Primaries. Despite the apparent problems with the front-loaded primary season in 2000, the Democratic Party decided to hold some of its primaries even earlier in the 2007–2008 presidential election cycle. For example, the Democratic Iowa caucus was advanced to January 3, to be followed five days later by the New Hampshire primary. The Democrats' goal in moving up their primaries was obvious: settle on a candidate early so that she or he would have a long time during which to raise funds to win the presidency.

In 2005, a private commission headed by former President Jimmy Carter and former Secretary of State James A. Baker III proposed a number of steps to avoid the consequences of early primaries. The Commission on Federal Election Reform was organized by American University. The commission argued in favor of keeping the Iowa caucuses and New Hampshire's early primary because "they test the candidates by genuine

retail, door-to-door campaigning." After that, though, the commission had a radical suggestion—eliminate the state primaries and hold four regional presidential primaries. These regional primaries would be held at monthly intervals in March, April, May, and June, with the order rotated every four years.

The 2008 Primary Contest. The contest for the Democratic nomination drew a large and diverse field of candidates in 2008. Senator Hillary Rodham Clinton, former First Lady, started out as the strongest candidate due to her early fundraising and organizational strengths. In addition, many former staffers from President Bill Clinton's campaigns joined her organization. Many observers saw former vice-presidential candidate John Edwards of North Carolina as the real challenger to Clinton. Other candidates included Senators Joe Biden of Delaware and Chris Dodd of Connecticut, as well as first-term Senator Barack Obama of Illinois. Representative Dennis Kucinich renewed his perennial campaign. Governors Bill Richardson of New Mexico, Tom Vilsack of Iowa, and former Senator Mike Gravel of Alaska also entered the race.

The Iowa caucuses were front-loaded to January 3, 2008. After Iowans trudged through the snow for their local meetings, it became clear that Barack Obama, a senator of mixed race from Illinois, was the true victor and potentially new front-runner. Senator Clinton claimed New Hampshire in a victory not predicted by pollsters, but Obama claimed the most delegates in Nevada and won South Carolina decisively. Michigan and Florida held primaries that were judged illegitimate by the Democratic National Committee, so their votes for Clinton were not counted. Super Tuesday occurred on February 5, with 23 states and territories holding primary elections on that date. After the votes were counted, Clinton and Obama were the clear

U.S. SENATOR Barack Obama (left) spars with U.S. Representative Dennis Kucinich (right) as Senator Hillary Rodham Clinton (center) looks on during the South Carolina Democratic Party Presidential Primary Debate on April 26, 2007, at South Carolina State University in Orangeburg, South Carolina. This was the Democrats' first debate for the 2008 presidential election. (AFP Photo/Stan Honda/Getty Images)

contenders for the nomination. Almost all of the other candidates dropped out and either endorsed one of the remaining candidates or kept silent. Obama had the momentum for a month, but Clinton's victory on "mini-Super Tuesday" in early March showed her strength among blue-collar workers. The two senators battled on through April and May with Senator Clinton showing real strength in the Midwestern "rust belt" states. Both campaigns pressured superdelegates to declare their preferences so that either Clinton or Obama would achieve the majority of the delegates. The Democratic party leadership in Michigan and Florida continued to press the national party to allow their delegate votes to count, even though they had violated party rules in scheduling their respective primaries. Because of the rules for delegate selection, Senator Obama continued to gain delegates even in states where Senator Clinton won by a strong margin. By June it was clear that Senator Obama had the delegate votes to win the nomination, and Senator Clinton stepped aside.

In contrast to the Democratic race, the Republican nominating contest ended fairly early in the season. With winner-take-all rules for delegate counts, the candidate who won a state gained all the delegates at stake. The Republican contest began with a diverse field as well: Former Massachusetts Governor Mitt Romney was a conservative favorite, along with Governor Mike Huckabee of Arkansas. Representative Ron Paul spoke for a libertarian perspective, while Representative Duncan Hunter was concerned about security. Senator John McCain had been working on his campaign for more than a year, but, at the beginning of the primary season, barely had enough funds to keep his organization together. The most moderate Republican candidate was former New York Mayor Rudy Giuliani, who was expected to do well in urban states.

Strategy made all the difference in the Republican race. While Huckabee and Romney sought out conservative Republican votes in Iowa, New Hampshire, and South Carolina, McCain concentrated on larger states. He was greatly advantaged by the new primary schedule, in that Independents and moderate Republican voters in states like Florida could support him early in the campaign. Romney dropped out of the race after Super Tuesday, and Huckabee after the mini-Super Tuesday in March, leaving McCain to build up his campaign war chest and public support for the rest of the spring and summer.

ON TO THE NATIONAL CONVENTION

Presidential candidates have been nominated by the convention method in every election since 1832. The delegates are sent from each state and are apportioned on the basis of state representation. Extra delegates are allowed to attend from states that had voting majorities for the party in the preceding elections. Parties also accept delegates from the District of Columbia, the territories, and certain overseas groups.

Credentials Committee
A committee used by political parties at their national conventions to determine which delegates may participate. The committee inspects the claim of each prospective delegate to be seated as a legitimate representative of his or her state.

Seating the Delegates. At the convention, each political party uses a **credentials committee** to determine which delegates may participate. The credentials committee usually prepares a roll of all delegates entitled to be seated. Controversy may arise when rival groups claim to be the official party organization for a county, district, or state. The Mississippi Democratic Party split along racial lines in 1964 at the height of the civil rights movement in the Deep South. Separate all-white and mixed white/African American sets of delegates were selected, and both factions showed up at the national convention. After much debate on party rules, the committee decided to seat the pro-civil rights delegates and exclude those who represented the traditional "white" party. The 2008 election saw a similar intra-party conflict arise over the delegates from Florida and Michigan. The Clinton and Obama camps eventually agreed to a compromise that seated the delegates but only gave each state half of the votes they were normally

entitled to. The issue was no longer important once Senator Obama had enough pledged delegates to win.

Convention Activities. The typical convention lasts only a few days. The first day consists of speech making, usually against the opposing party. During the second day, there are committee reports, and during the third day, there is presidential balloting. Because delegates generally arrive at the convention committed to presidential candidates, no convention since 1952 has required more than one ballot to choose a nominee, and since 1972, candidates have usually come into the convention with enough committed delegates to win. On the fourth day, a vice-presidential candidate is usually nominated, and the presidential nominee gives the acceptance speech.

In 2008, the Democratic and Republican conventions were scheduled within one week of one another—one right before Labor Day and one immediately after. The Democratic National Convention was held in Denver, Colorado, and was meticulously planned to generate media coverage. Former candidate Senator Hillary Rodham Clinton gave a stirring speech on the second night of the convention, and on the third night, former President Bill Clinton spoke in support of the Obama–Biden ticket. The climax of the convention was Senator Obama's acceptance speech, which was delivered in a stadium to a crowd of more than 80,000 people. Those who wanted to attend lined up for seats hours before the event was to begin for the chance to witness the nomination of the first African American nominee for president.

The Republican convention was ready to kick off in St. Paul, Minnesota, when Hurricane Gustav took aim at Louisiana. The Republicans quickly canceled the first night of speeches to allow the news media to focus on the weather approaching New Orleans and the evacuations there. After it became clear that the hurricane would not be as serious as predicted, the Republican convention returned to normal with speeches by all the former presidential candidates. The high point of the convention, however, was vice-presidential nominee Sarah Palin's acceptance speech. Because she was virtually unknown in the political world, commentators and politicians wondered how well she would do in her first speech. She exceeded all expectations and greatly increased the enthusiasm of all the delegates for their 2008 ticket.

ON TO THE GENERAL ELECTION

Even though the voters may think the presidential election process has gone on for years, the general election campaign actually begins after the two party conventions, when the nominees are officially proclaimed. The general election campaign strategies for each candidate are similar to those used during the primaries, except that each candidate now tries to articulate his or her differences from the opposition in terms of party issues. As noted in Chapter 6, voters respond to the campaigns on the basis of partisanship, the candidates' personalities, and the issues of the day.

Candidates plan their campaigns to use media advertising, debates, and Get Out the Vote (GOTV) campaigns. In addition, campaign strategists must constantly plan to win enough electoral votes to receive the majority. Campaign managers quickly identify those states where their candidate will almost certainly win the popular vote. As illustrated in the endpapers of this book, certain states will quickly line up in the Republican or Democratic column. Those states see relatively light campaign activity and advertising. However, those states that are likely to be close in the popular vote have been tagged **battleground states** and will see intense campaigning up to the very day of the election.

Battleground State
A state that is likely to be so closely fought that the campaigns devote exceptional effort to winning the popular and electoral vote.

In 2000 and 2004, Florida was such a state. States such as Ohio and Wisconsin, which have closely divided electorates, are often in the battleground column. However, it is important to note that the states that will be closely fought change with every presidential election, because the issues and appeals of the two candidates determine race dynamics. In any case, the votes will be counted, the exit polls will be tallied, and the commentators will be heard on election night. In 2008, many of the supposed battleground states were quickly declared Obama victories as a result of how his supporters turned out. Some of these battleground states were won by Obama with large margins. Other states were too close to call for several days after the election. Both candidates had battled hard for the battleground states, even continuing to campaign into election day itself. Toward the end of the campaign, many commentators and political consultants warned of faulty voting machines and the inevitability of voting fraud and discrimination. In the end, election day saw few reports of irregularities but very long voting lines.

You can make a *difference*

STUDENTS ON THE CAMPAIGN TRAIL

The U.S. Congress has 535 members; other elected officials across the nation include more than 7,000 state legislators; 53 governors, attorneys general, treasurers, and secretaries of state; and thousands of mayors and city council members. None of these leaders could run political campaigns without the volunteer efforts of students. What do you believe in? Some students view campaign work as a civic duty. Causes and candidates across the nation would benefit from a volunteer's time and talent.

WHY SHOULD YOU CARE?

The 2008 presidential race sparked interest in many young voters, with 70 percent of 18- to-24 year olds following the campaign closely, according to a Harvard University survey. With the promise of change coming from all candidates in this presidential race, young voters seemed to be inspired to get involved. According to the U.S. Census Bureau, youth voter turnout jumped from 40 percent in the 2000 election to 49 percent in 2004, by far the largest increase of any age group.

Knocking on doors and manning phone banks may not be glamorous work, but these experiences can provide a glimpse into a community that you might not get even by living in the neighborhood. You can talk to people face to face about issues that are important to them. Many students feel that college is the perfect time to work for a candidate or issue, when flexible school schedules and summers lend themselves to the time necessary to devote to a campaign.

You hear much discussion in the media concerning the youth vote but rarely find the opportunity for young people to speak for themselves concerning issues of the day. When you are volunteering for a campaign, opportunities to meet candidates, attend rallies, and engage in debate allow you to voice your opinion firsthand in the context of our political system. Opinions can be diverse even among volunteers within the same campaign affiliation, with some motivated by economic policy and fiscal issues and others by social issues.

WHAT CAN YOU DO?

Most people envision presidential races when first considering campaign volunteer work, but local elections or national hot-button issues such as gun control and local ballot initiatives in your own community feature some form of a campaign. How do you decide which campaign is right

for you? Take into consideration how much time you can devote to the work, how close to home you want to stay, and how much responsibility you are willing to take on.

Campaign work can take many forms for first-time volunteers. You might help with fundraising, weekend canvassing door to door, or getting people out to vote as election day approaches. You might work for one of the party organizations like the Democratic National Committee or the Republican National Committee, or join a campus branch of College Democrats or College Republicans. These clubs host candidates to address students, hold voter registration drives, volunteer at local political events, and work phone banks for candidates and issues. You might also volunteer for an independent political entity, like an issue-oriented nonprofit group or a 527 organization, advocating for candidates and voter mobilization.

Political campaigns offer many opportunities to develop a wide range of skills in a very fast-paced and exciting environment. You get a front-row seat to the electoral process; the work can be grueling but rarely boring. Satisfaction comes from working for a candidate or cause that you respect and support and knowing that your individual efforts can make a difference.

For further information on volunteering for political campaigns, please contact one of the following organizations:

The Democratic National Committee
430 S. Capitol St. SE
Washington, D.C. 20003
202-863-8000
www.democrats.org

College Democrats of America
430 S. Capitol St. SE
Washington, D.C. 20003
202-863-8000
www.collegedems.com

The Republican National Committee
310 First St.
Washington, D.C. 20003
202-863-8500
www.gop.com

College Republican National Committee
600 Pennsylvania Ave. SE, Suite 215
Washington, D.C. 20003
888-765-3564
www.crnc.org

REFERENCES

Sharon Kelly, Justin Levitt, and Amanda Tammen Peterson, "One State, Two State, Red State, Blue State: A Quick Guide to Working on Political Campaigns," Bernard Koteen Office of Public Interest Advising, Harvard Law School, 2007.

Mike Maciag, "BU Students Spread the Word for Candidates," *Peoria Journal Star*, May 4, 2008.

Emily Schultheis, "Students Plan to Hit the Campaign Trail," *Politico*, May 1, 2008.

Mercedes Suarez, "American College Students Embracing U.S. Political Process," America.gov, October 26, 2007.

KEY TERMS

battleground state 372	**front-runner** 368	**political action committee (PAC)** 357
"beauty contest" 364	**Get Out the Vote (GOTV)** 353	**political consultant** 353
caucus 366	**hard money** 356	**pollster** 353
closed primary 367	**Hatch Act** 355	**presidential primary** 348
communications director 353	**independent expenditures** 361	**press secretary** 353
corrupt practices acts 355	**issue advocacy advertising** 357	**soft money** 357
credentials committee 370	**open primary** 367	**superdelegate** 348
finance chairperson 353		**tracking poll** 354
focus group 354		
front-loading 368		

CHAPTER SUMMARY

1. People may choose to run for political office to further their careers, to carry out specific political programs, or in response to certain issues or events. The legal qualifications for holding political office are minimal at both the state and local levels, but holders of political office still are predominantly white and male and are likely to be from the professional class.

2. American political campaigns are lengthy and extremely expensive. In the last decade, they have become more candidate-centered rather than party-centered in response to technological innovations and decreasing party identification. Candidates have begun to rely less on the party and more on paid professional consultants to perform the various tasks necessary to wage a political campaign. The crucial task of professional political consultants is image building. The campaign organization devises a campaign strategy to maximize the candidate's chances of winning. Candidates use public opinion polls and focus groups to gauge their popularity and to test the mood of the country.

3. The amount of money spent in financing campaigns is increasing steadily. A variety of corrupt practices acts have been passed to regulate campaign finance. The Federal Election Campaign Act of 1971 and its amendments in 1974 and 1976 instituted major reforms by limiting spending and contributions; the acts allowed corporations, labor unions, and interest groups to set

up political action committees (PACs) to raise money for candidates. New techniques, including "soft money" contributions to the parties and independent expenditures, were later developed. The Bipartisan Campaign Reform Act (BCRA) of 2002 banned soft money contributions to the national parties, limited advertising by interest groups, and increased the limits on individual contributions.

4. After the Democratic Convention of 1968, the McGovern-Fraser Commission formulated new rules for primaries, which were adopted by all Democrats and by Republicans in many states. These reforms opened up the nomination process for the presidency to all voters.

5. A presidential primary is a statewide election to help a political party determine its presidential nominee at the national convention. Some states use the caucus method of choosing convention delegates. The primary campaign recently has been shortened to the first few months of the election year.

6. The party conventions are held to finalize the nomination of a candidate for president. Normally, the convention is used to unite the party and to introduce the winning candidate to the public. It marks the beginning of the general election campaign. Contested conventions have been rare in the last 50 years.

7. The general election campaign begins after Labor Day in September. Presidential candidates and their campaign organizations use advertising, appearances, speeches, and debates to win support from voters. In recent years, attention is lavished on battleground states where presidential contests are closely fought.

SELECTED PRINT AND MEDIA RESOURCES

SUGGESTED READINGS

Jamieson, Kathleen Hall, ed. *Electing the President 2004: The Insider's View*. Philadelphia: The University of Pennsylvania Press, 2005. This collection of essays explores the inner workings of campaigns, including decisions about themes, advertising, and Get Out the Vote strategies.

Jamieson, Kathleen Hall, et al., eds. *Capturing Campaign Dynamics, 2000 and 2004: The National Annenberg Election Survey*. Philadelphia: University of Pennsylvania Press, 2006. During the contentious 2000 and 2004 presidential elections, the Annenberg Public Policy Center conducted one of the largest studies ever of the American electorate. The data show the dynamic effects of political events as they unfolded during these two important presidential elections.

Lau, Richard R., et al., eds. *How Voters Decide: Information Processing in Election Campaigns*. Cambridge: Cambridge University Press, 2006. The researchers who wrote this book attempted to get "inside the heads" of citizens who confront huge amounts of information during modern presidential campaigns. The researchers argued that we should care not just about which candidates receive the most votes, but also about how many citizens voted "correctly"—that is, in accordance with their own interests.

Magleby, David, Anthony Corrado, and Kelly D. Patterson, eds. *Financing the 2004 Election*. Washington, DC: The Brookings Institution, 2006. This team of authors explores the campaign contributions of parties, candidates, interest groups, and 527 groups and how they influenced the election in 2004.

MoveOn. *MoveOn's 50 Ways to Love Your Country: How to Find Your Political Voice and Become a Catalyst for Change*. Makawao, Maui, Hawaii: Inner Ocean Publishing, 2004. This book contains 50 short chapters in which individuals describe how they sought to make a difference by getting involved in the political process. MoveOn has been called a "shadow party" to the Democrats. Nevertheless, the techniques described here could be used just as easily by Republicans. The volume is also available on audiotape.

Thurber, James A., and Candice J. Nelson, eds. *Campaigns and Elections American Style: Transforming American Politics*. New York: Westview Press, 2004. The articles in this book consider the basics of American campaigns and discuss practical campaign politics. They examine the evolution of campaigns over time, including town meetings, talk radio, infomercials, and focus groups. In this book, you will discover how campaign themes and strategies are determined.

Wayne, Stephen J. *The Road to the White House, 2008: The Politics of Presidential Elections*. Belmont, CA: Wadsworth Publishing, 2008. Stephen Wayne examines the changes in the election process since 1996 and provides an excellent analysis of the presidential selection process.

MEDIA RESOURCES

Bulworth—A 1998 satirical film starring Warren Beatty and Halle Berry. Jay Bulworth, a senator who is fed up with politics and life in general, hires a hit man to carry out his own assassination. He then throws political caution to the wind in campaign appearances by telling the truth and behaving the way he really wants to behave.

The Candidate—A 1972 film, starring a young Robert Redford, that effectively investigates and satirizes the decisions that a candidate for the U.S. Senate must make. It's a political classic.

If You Can't Say Anything Nice—Negative campaigning seems to have become the norm in recent years. This 1999 program looks at the resulting decline in popularity of politics among the electorate and suggests approaches to restoring faith in the process. It is part of the series *Politics As Usual,* available from the Films Media Group.

Money Talks: The Influence of Money on American Politics—Bill Moyers reports on the influence of money on our political system. Produced in 1994.

Primary Colors—A 1998 film starring John Travolta as a Southern governor who is plagued by a sex scandal during his run for the presidency.

e-mocracy

POLITICAL CAMPAIGNS AND THE WEB

Today's voters have a significant advantage over those in past decades. It is now possible to obtain extensive information about candidates and issues simply by going online. Some sites present point-counterpoint articles about the candidates or issues in an upcoming election. Other sites support some candidates and positions and oppose others. The candidates all have Web sites that you can visit if you want to learn more about them and their positions. You can also obtain information online about election results by going to sites such as those listed in the *Logging On* section. While the Internet has proved to be a valuable vehicle for communicating information about elections, it is not clear whether it will be used for actual voting in national elections at some future time. Although Internet voting seems like a great idea, it also raises many concerns, particularly about security.

LOGGING ON

- For detailed information about current campaign-financing laws and for the latest filings of finance reports, see the site maintained by the Federal Election Commission at:
  www.fec.gov

- To find excellent reports on where campaign money comes from and how it is spent, be sure to view the site maintained by the Center for Responsive Politics at:
  www.opensecrets.org
- Another Web site for investigating voting records and campaign-financing information is that of Project Vote Smart. Go to:
  www.vote-smart.org

ONLINE REVIEW

At **www.cengage.com/politicalscience/schmidt/agandpt14e**, you will find a Tutorial Quiz for this chapter providing questions on the chapter contents, including the features. The questions are organized to match the major sections of the chapter. You'll have access to other helpful study tools, including the book's glossary and flashcards, crossword puzzles, and Web links, as well as "Which Side Are You On?" and "Politics and . . ." features written by the authors of the book.

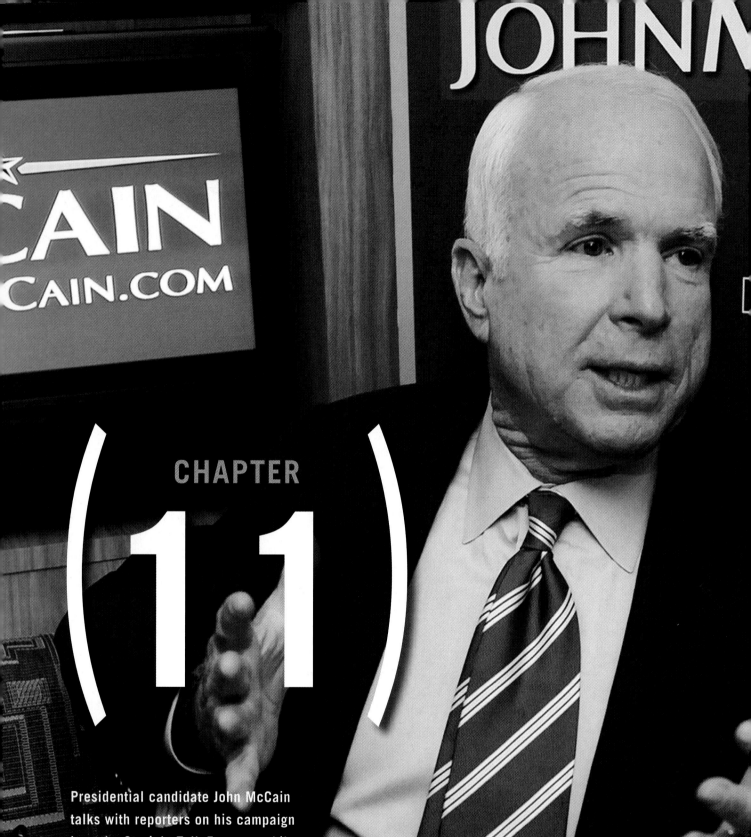

CHAPTER

(11)

Presidential candidate John McCain
talks with reporters on his campaign
bus, the Straight Talk Express, while
traveling in Pennsylvania in July, 2008.
(Clark Van Orden/The Times Leader/AP
Photos)

THE MEDIA AND CYBERPOLITICS

Making a DIFFERENCE

HAVE YOUTUBE AND JON STEWART CHANGED HOW POLITICIANS CAMPAIGN?

"Have you seen *that* video? You know that crazy one that's all over the Net? My friend just texted me the link." If this sounds familiar, you're in good company. "Viral videos" (video clips that spread from person-to-person via e-mail), share sites (like YouTube), and social networking sites (like Facebook and MySpace) have become ubiquitous. The question for politics and politicians is whether these clips are a menace or yet another way to get out their message.

One of the most used share sites, YouTube, has been around since 2006. In the Congressional elections of 2006, it took center stage as embarrassing and/or politically damaging videos surfaced. For example, at a campaign event, Senator George Allen (R.-Va.) called an Indian American staffer of his Democratic opponent (who was present at the event for opposition research) a "macaca," a racial slur.

Not only was the moment captured on a cell phone video camera, but it was also uploaded onto YouTube. In addition to the hundreds of thousands of viewers who saw the video on that site, the "macaca moment" was widely covered by the mainstream media.[a] During the primary campaign in 2008, a remark that Barack Obama made about rural, white gun owners at a private fundraising dinner also made it to the Internet within hours. Hillary Clinton used that quote to bolster a win in the Pennsylvania primary.

In fact, the George Allen event has spawned its own nomenclature; the National Republican Senatorial Campaign Committee has issued guidelines for its 2008 candidates to avoid their own "macaca moments," including respect for the importance of politically influential blogs; remember that you are always "live on film"; and "don't be antisocial," because social network sites like MySpace can work for you.[b]

By the 2008 electoral cycle, candidates had become YouTube savvy and aware of the power of alternative

---

THE STUDY OF PEOPLE and politics—of how people gain the information they need to be able to choose among political candidates, to organize for their own interests, and to formulate opinions on the policies and decisions of the government—must take into account the role played by the media. Historically, the print media played the most important role in informing public debate. The print media developed, for the most part, our understanding of how news is to be reported. Traditional media separated "facts" and "opinion" by having opinion writing confined to editorial pages. Facts were to be laid out in a specific fashion in news columns. Today, however, more than 90 percent of Americans use television news as their primary source of information. In addition, the Internet has become a major source for political communication and fundraising. As Internet use grows, the system of gathering and sharing news and information is changing from one in which the media have a primary role to one in which the individual citizen may play a greater part. As noted in the *Making a Difference* feature, today's citizens use many sources of information, including social networking sites and YouTube videos, to gather information to make political decisions. In this chapter, we will look at the ways in which these contemporary outlets are similar and different from traditional sources of news.

That Alaska residents have the highest percentage of computers at home and residents of Mississippi the lowest?

news sources like Jon Stewart's satirical *The Daily Show* and Stephen Colbert's *The Colbert Report.* Senator John McCain, the Republican nominee for president, made more than nine appearances on Stewart's show. Senator Hillary Clinton, vying for the Democratic nomination, appeared on the show via satellite from Austin, Texas, the night before the nomination contests in that state. In advance of the Pennsylvania primary, Senator Barack Obama made his third appearance on the show.[c]

These candidates were wise to reach out to voters in this fashion. The Pew Research Center regularly conducts surveys on media consumption and news and information sources. Their 2004 survey found that 21 percent of those under age 30 reported getting campaign news from *The Daily Show.*[d] In a study two years later, in addition to being younger than the average TV viewer, *Daily Show* aficionados reported being more likely to self-identify as Democrats, be male, more liberal, and more knowledgeable about politics (though not as knowledgeable as Rush Limbaugh listeners).[e]

The Center also finds evidence for the emerging integration of YouTube into the public consciousness. Their January 2008 report shows that 48 percent of Internet users report going to YouTube. Forty-two percent of younger people report getting campaign news from the Internet, and 2 percent of those cite YouTube as a primary source. Three percent also say they go to MySpace and the Drudge Report for election news.[f]

Candidates and mainstream media outlets have responded. The 2008 presidential election saw jointly sponsored debates by CNN and YouTube, with questions from YouTube video clips. Senator Clinton asked her supporters on YouTube to help her choose a theme song (Celine Dion's "You and I" won). Senator Obama has woven together many tightly knit groups across the country using social networking sites like MySpace and Facebook. So, in the words of "You Choose" (YouTube's citizentube, which is a political blog), have YouTube and Jon Stewart changed campaigning?

[a]www.nytimes.com/2006/08/20/weekinreview/20lizza.html?partner=rssnyt&emc=rss, accessed April 18, 2008.

[b]www.politico.com/news/stories/0607/4483.html, accessed April 18, 2008.

[c]www.thedailyshow.com, accessed April 18, 2008.

[d]Their 2008 report saw a precipitous drop in this figure, down to 12 percent. However, the survey was conducted during a writers' strike that had a serious effect on TV viewership, and the authors of the study attribute the drop to the strike. www.pewinternet.org/pdfs/Pew_MediaSources_jan08.pdf, accessed April 18, 2008.

[e]http://people-press.org/reports/display.php3?ReportID=282, accessed April 18, 2008.

[f]www.pewinternet.org/pdfs/Pew_MediaSources_jan08.pdf, accessed April 18, 2008.

THE MEDIA'S FUNCTIONS

The mass media perform several different functions in any country. In the United States, we can list at least six. Almost all of them can have political implications, and some are essential to the democratic process. These functions are as follows: (1) entertainment, (2) reporting the news, (3) identifying public problems, (4) socializing new generations, (5) providing a political forum, and (6) making profits.

ENTERTAINMENT

By far, the greatest number of radio and television hours are dedicated to entertaining the public. The battle for prime-time and cable ratings indicates how important successful entertainment is to the survival of networks and individual stations. In recent years, the creation of reality shows such as *Survivor* and amateur talent shows including *American Idol* underscores the importance of pure entertainment to the television industry.

Although there is no direct link between entertainment and politics, network dramas often introduce material that may be politically controversial and that may stimulate public discussion. Examples include the TV series *The West Wing* and *Commander in*

Chief, which people believe promoted liberal political values. Made-for-TV movies have focused on many controversial topics, including AIDS, incest, and spousal abuse. The growing number of documentary channels on cable—Discovery, History, National Geographic, and others—often tackle topics such as global warming or other environmental issues that are on the political agenda.

REPORTING THE NEWS

A primary function of the mass media in all their forms—newspapers and magazines, radio, television, cable, and online news services—is the reporting of news. The media provide words and pictures, sound and video about events, facts, personalities, and ideas. The protections of the First Amendment are intended to keep the flow of news as free as possible, because it is an essential part of the democratic process. If citizens cannot obtain unbiased information about the state of their communities and their leaders' actions, how can they make voting decisions? One of the most incisive comments about the importance of the media was made by James Madison, who said, "A people who mean to be their own governors must arm themselves with the power knowledge gives. A popular government without popular information or the means of acquiring it is but a prologue to a farce or a tragedy or perhaps both."[1]

IDENTIFYING PUBLIC PROBLEMS

Public Agenda
Issues that are perceived by the political community as meriting public attention and governmental action.

The power of the media is important not only in revealing what the government is doing but also in determining what the government ought to do—in other words, in setting the **public agenda**. The mass media identify public issues, such as convicted sex offenders living in residential neighborhoods on their release from prison. The media then influence the passage of legislation, such as "Megan's Law," which requires police to notify neighbors about the release and/or resettlement of certain offenders. American journalists also work in a long tradition of uncovering public wrongdoing, corruption, and bribery and of bringing such wrongdoing to the public's attention. Closely related to this investigative function is that of presenting policy alternatives. Public policy is often complex and difficult to make entertaining, but programs devoted to public policy increasingly are being scheduled for prime-time television. Most networks produce shows with a "news magazine" format that sometimes include segments on foreign policy and other issues.

SOCIALIZING NEW GENERATIONS

As mentioned in Chapter 6, the media (particularly television) strongly influence the beliefs and opinions of Americans. Because of this influence, the media play a significant role in the political socialization of the younger generation, as well as immigrants to this country. Through the transmission of historical information (sometimes fictionalized), the presentation of American culture, and the portrayal of the diverse regions and groups in the United States, the media teach young people and immigrants about what it means to be an American. TV talk shows, such as *The Oprah Winfrey Show*, sometimes focus on controversial issues (such as abortion or assisted suicide) that relate to basic American values (such as liberty). Many children's shows are designed not only to entertain young viewers but also to instruct them in the traditional moral values of American society. In recent years, the public has become increasingly concerned about the level of violence depicted on children's programs and on other shows during prime time.

[1]James Madison, "Letter to W. T. Barry" (August 4, 1822), in Gaillard P. Hunt, ed., *The Writings of James Madison* 103 (1910).

THE REAL Hillary Clinton meets her stage double, Amy Poehler, during the March 1, 2008, edition of *Saturday Night Live*. What do candidates gain from appearing on a late night comedy show? (Dana Edelson/NBCU Photobank/AP Photos)

As more young Americans turn to the Internet for entertainment, they are also finding an increasing amount of social and political information there. America's youth today are the Internet generation. Young people do not use the Internet just for chat and e-mail. They also download movies and music, find information for writing assignments, gather news, visit social networking sites, and increasingly get involved in political campaigns and interact online with those campaigns.

PROVIDING A POLITICAL FORUM

As part of their news function, the media also provide a political forum for leaders and the public. Candidates for office use news reporting to sustain interest in their campaigns, while officeholders use the media to gain support for their policies or to present an image of leadership. Presidential trips abroad are an outstanding way for the chief executive to get colorful, positive, and exciting news coverage that makes the president look "presidential." The media also offer ways for citizens to participate in public debate, through letters to the editor, televised editorials, or electronic mail. As noted in the *Making a Difference* feature, 2008 saw the first YouTube live debate during the primaries, and candidates often posted video messages for their followers on their Web sites. The question of whether more public access should be provided will be discussed later in this chapter.

MAKING PROFITS

Most of the news media (including the Internet search engines) in the United States are private, for-profit corporate enterprises. One of their goals is to make profits for expansion and for dividends to the stockholders who own the companies. In general, profits are made as a result of charging for advertising. Advertising revenues usually are related directly to circulation or to listener/viewer ratings.

For the most part, the media depend on advertisers to obtain revenues to make profits. Media outlets that do not succeed in generating sufficient revenues from advertising either go bankrupt or are sold. Consequently, reporters may feel pressure from media owners and from advertisers. Media owners may take their cues from what advertisers want. If an important advertiser does not like the political bent of a particular reporter, the reporter could be asked to alter his or her "style" of writing. The Project for Excellence in Journalism discovered that 53 percent of local news directors said that advertisers try to tell them what to air and what not to air.[2]

Advertisers have been known to pull ads from newspapers and TV stations whenever they read or view negative publicity about their own companies or products. For example, CBS ran a *60 Minutes* show about Dillard's and other department stores that claimed store security guards used excessive force and racial profiling. In response, Dillard's pulled its ads from CBS. This example can be multiplied many times over.

Several well-known media outlets, in contrast, are publicly owned—public television stations in many communities and National Public Radio. These operate without extensive commercials, are locally supported, and are often subsidized by the government and corporations. A complex relationship exists among the for-profit and nonprofit media, the government, and the public. Throughout the rest of this chapter, we examine some of the many facets of this relationship.

DID YOU KNOW?

That the first "wire" story transmitted by telegraph was sent in 1846?

A HISTORY OF THE MEDIA IN THE UNITED STATES

Many years ago, Thomas Jefferson wrote, "Were it left to me to decide whether we should have a government without newspapers, or newspapers without a government, I should not hesitate a moment to prefer the latter."[3] Although the media have played a significant role in politics since the founding of this nation, they were not as overwhelmingly important in the past as they are today. For one thing, politics was controlled by a small elite who communicated personally. For another, during the early 1800s and before, news traveled slowly. If an important political event occurred in New York, it was not known until five days later in Philadelphia; 10 days later in the capital cities of Connecticut, Maryland, and Virginia; and 15 days later in Boston.

Roughly 3,000 newspapers were being published by 1860. Some of these, such as the *New York Tribune*, were mainly sensation mongers that concentrated on crimes, scandals, and the like. The *New York Herald* specialized in self-improvement and what today would be called practical news. Although sensational and biased reporting often created political divisiveness (this was particularly true during the Civil War), many historians believe that the growth of the print media also played an important role in unifying the country.

THE RISE OF THE POLITICAL PRESS

Americans may cherish the idea of an unbiased press, but in the early years of the nation's history, the number of politically sponsored newspapers was significant. The sole reason for the existence of such periodicals was to further the interests of the

[2]Project for Excellence in Journalism, "Gambling with the Future," *Columbia Journalism Review*, November/December 2001.
[3]Thomas Jefferson, "Letter to Edward Carrington" (1787), in Andrew A. Lipscomb and Albert E. Bergh, eds., *The Writings of Thomas Jefferson*, Memorial Edition (Washington, DC, 1903–04), p. 57.

politicians who paid for their publication. As chief executive of our government during this period, George Washington has been called a "firm believer" in **managed news**. Although acknowledging that the public had a right to be informed, he believed that some matters should be kept secret and that news that might damage the image of the United States should be censored (not published). Washington, however, made no attempt to control the press.

THE DEVELOPMENT OF MASS-READERSHIP NEWSPAPERS

Two inventions in the nineteenth century led to the development of mass-readership newspapers. The first was the high-speed rotary press; the second was the telegraph. Faster presses meant lower per-unit costs and lower subscription prices. In addition, by 1848, the Associated Press had developed the telegraph into a nationwide apparatus for the dissemination of all types of information on a systematic basis.

Along with these technological changes came a growing population and increasing urbanization. A larger, more urban population could support daily newspapers, even if the price per paper was only a penny. Finally, the burgeoning, diversified economy encouraged the growth of advertising, which meant that newspapers could obtain additional revenues from merchants who seized the opportunity to promote their wares to a larger public.

THE POPULAR PRESS AND YELLOW JOURNALISM

Students of the history of journalism have ascertained a change in the last half of the 1800s, not in the level of biased news reporting but in its origin. Whereas politically sponsored newspapers had expounded a particular political party's point of view, the post-Civil War mass-based newspapers expounded whatever political philosophy the owner of the newspaper happened to have.

Even if newspaper owners did not have a particular political axe to grind, they often allowed their editors to engage in sensationalism and what is known as **yellow journalism**. The questionable or simply personal activities of a prominent businessperson, politician, or socialite were front-page material. Newspapers, then as now, made their economic way by maximizing readership. As the *National Enquirer* demonstrates with its current circulation of almost 2 million, sensationalism is still rewarded by high levels of readership.

THE AGE OF THE ELECTROMAGNETIC SIGNAL

The first scheduled radio program in the United States featured politicians. On the night of November 2, 1920, KDKA-Pittsburgh transmitted the returns of the presidential election race between Warren G. Harding and James M. Cox. The listeners were a few thousand people tuning in on primitive, homemade sets.

By 1924, there were nearly 1,400 radio stations. But it was not until 8 P.M. on November 15, 1926, that the electronic media came into their own in the United States. On that night, the National Broadcasting Company (NBC) made its debut with a four-hour program broadcast by 25 stations in 21 cities. Network broadcasting had become a reality.

Even with the advent of national radio in the 1920s and television in the late 1940s, many politicians were slow to understand the significance of the **electronic media**. The 1952 presidential campaign was the first to involve a real role for television. Television coverage of the Republican convention helped Dwight Eisenhower win over

Managed News
Information generated and distributed by the government in such a way as to give government interests priority over candor.

DID YOU KNOW?

That the first successful daily newspaper in the United States was the *Pennsylvania Packet & General Advertiser*, which was initially published on September 21, 1784?

Yellow Journalism
A term for sensationalistic, irresponsible journalism. Reputedly, the term is an allusion to the cartoon "The Yellow Kid" in the old *New York World*, a newspaper especially noted for its sensationalism.

Electronic Media
Communication channels that involve electronic transmissions, such as radio, television, and, to an increasing extent, the Internet.

" INTERESTING.....IT'S LIKE A PORTABLE 500K FILE and YOU DON'T HAVE TO WAIT FOR IT TO DOWNLOAD... AND YOU SAY IT'S CALLED A NEWSPAPER ? "

delegates and secure the nomination. His vice-presidential running mate, Richard Nixon, put TV to good use. Accused of hiding a secret slush fund, Nixon replied to his critics with his famous "Checkers" speech. He denied the attacks, cried real tears, and said that the only thing he ever received from a contributor for his personal use was his dog, Checkers, and a "Republican cloth coat" for his wife, Pat. It was a highly effective performance.

Today, television dominates the campaign strategy of every would-be national politician, as well as that of every elected official. Politicians think of ways to continue to be newsworthy, thereby gaining free access to the electronic media. Attacking the president's programs is one way of becoming newsworthy; other ways include holding highly visible hearings on controversial subjects, going on "fact-finding" trips, and employing gimmicks (such as taking a walking tour of a state). In fact, the ideal way to get television coverage is to air a campaign advertisement that is so controversial or "talked about" that the news runs the ad over and over again for free.

THE REVOLUTION IN THE ELECTRONIC MEDIA

Just as technological change was responsible for the end of politically sponsored periodicals, technology is increasing the number of alternative news sources today. The advent of pay TV, cable TV, subscription TV, satellite TV, and the Internet has completely changed the electronic media landscape. With hundreds, if not thousands, of potential outlets for specialized programs, the electronic media are becoming more like the print media in catering to specialized tastes. This is sometimes referred to as **narrowcasting**. Cable and satellite television and the Internet offer the public unparalleled access to specialized information on everything from gardening and home repair to sports and religion. Most viewers are able to choose among several sources for their favorite type of programming.

Narrowcasting
Broadcasting that is targeted to one small sector of the population.

In recent years, narrowcasting has become increasingly prevalent. The broadcast networks' audiences are declining. Between 1982 and 2008, their share of the audience fell from 72 percent to 29 percent. At the same time, the percentage of households having access to the Internet grew from zero to more than 70 percent.

TALK-SHOW POLITICS AND SATELLITE RADIO

Multiple news outlets have given rise to literally thousands of talk shows on television, radio, and the Internet. By 2007, there were more than two dozen national television talk shows; their hosts ranged from Jerry Springer, who is regarded as a sensationalist, to Larry King, whose show has become a political necessity for candidates. In 2003, Arnold Schwarzenegger actually announced his candidacy for governor of California on Jay Leno's *Tonight Show*. Higher-level talk shows like that of Charlie Rose on public television are seen as an important way for politicians to reach upper-income, well-educated audiences.

The real blossoming of "talk" has occurred on the radio. The number of radio stations that program only talk shows has increased from about 300 in 1989 to more than 1,200 today. The topics of talk shows range from business and investment to psychology and politics. There has been considerable criticism of the political talk shows, especially those hosted by Rush Limbaugh, G. Gordon Liddy, and other conservatives, on the grounds that these shows focus on negative politics rather than policy issues. Critics contend that such shows increase the level of intolerance and irrationality in American politics. However, data from the Pew Center show that the audience for most of these talk shows is not very different from the general population.[4]

Responding to conservative dominance of "talk radio," liberal groups began considering the possibilities of left-of-center talk shows. In 2004, liberal comedian Al Franken went live on Air America Radio with his highly partisan take on the news. Franken was willing to match rhetoric with conservative talk-show hosts such as Rush Limbaugh, but the network went bankrupt in 2006. Air America programs were back on the air in 2007 with a new owner.

Satellite radio has also become an important player in talk-show politics. Howard Stern, who was considered an outspoken force in both traditional radio and TV, moved

RADIO TALK SHOW HOST and conservative commentator Rush Limbaugh gives a speech in 2007. Limbaugh considers himself the most influential of the talk radio hosts. Why do you think there are more conservative radio talk shows than liberal ones? (Bill Pugliano/ Stringer/Getty Images)

[4]"News Audiences Increasingly Politicized," The Pew Research Center for the People and the Press, June 8, 2004, accessed at http://people-press.org/reports.

to Sirius satellite radio in 2006. Though Stern spends much of his time on nonpolitical topics, he does interview political guests (whom he usually harasses). The satellite radio system XM, which has merged with Sirius, has its own political commentators, including Bob Edwards, who conducts interviews on XM Public Radio. XM also carries America Right, a channel that features *The G. Gordon Liddy Show* and another show hosted by Michael Reagan, son of the late president Ronald Reagan.

THE INTERNET, BLOGGING, AND PODCASTING

For at least 10 years, every politician has felt the necessity of having a Web site. On the national level, political Web sites were created for the two major-party candidates for president for the first time in 1996. Since then, even the lowliest local politician feels obligated to have a Web site that is updated at least on occasion. Political candidates have used the Internet to raise tens of millions of dollars. Howard Dean and John McCain were early adopters of the Internet to raise money, but Barack Obama became the leader in this practice in 2008. His Web site encouraged millions of supporters to donate small amounts to his primary campaign. His organization even allows individuals to sign up for automatic monthly donations with their credit cards.[5] The inexpensive nature of raising money through the Internet is a great advantage, particularly as compared to a traditional mailing.

Within the last few years, politicians have also felt obligated to post regular blogs on their Web sites. The word *blog* comes from "Web log," a regular updating of one's ideas at a specific Web site. Of course, many people besides politicians are also posting blogs. Not all of the millions of blogs posted daily are political in nature, but many are, and they can have a dramatic influence on events, giving rise to the term *blogosphere politics*. During the 2004 presidential campaign, CBS's Dan Rather reported on television that documents showed that President George W. Bush had failed to fulfill his obligations to the National Guard during the 1970s. Within four hours, a blogger on Freerepublic.com pointed out that the documents shown on CBS appeared to have been created in Microsoft Word, even though personal computers and Microsoft Word did not even exist in the 1970s. Another blogger, Charles Johnson (**Littlegreenfootballs.com**), showed that by using Word default settings he could create documents that matched those from CBS. Eleven days later, CBS admitted that an error had been made, and Dan Rather ultimately lost his job as a news anchor.

----

[5]Joshua Green, "The Amazing Money Machine," *The Atlantic Monthly*, June 2008, accessed at www.theatlantic.com/doc/200806.

By 2004, politicians began to produce their own blogs. Howard Dean actually wrote his own blog, as did his staffers. They chronicled important campaign decisions as well as more mundane activities of the campaign. George Bush and John Kerry also posted blogs, but they were much more than campaign vehicles with galleries of pictures and audio clips. Analysis of these blogs indicated that although they encouraged citizen interaction, they tended to promote one-way communication, sending information from the candidate to the potential voter.[6]

Blogs are clearly threatening the mainstream media. They can be highly specialized, highly political, and highly entertaining—and they are cheap. *The Washington Post* requires thousands of employees, many reams of paper, and tons of ink to generate its offline product and incurs delivery costs to get its papers to readers. A blogging organization such as RealClearPolitics can generate its political commentary with fewer than 10 employees.

Once blogs—written words—became well established, it was only a matter of time before they would end up as spoken words. Enter **podcasting**, so-called because the first Internet-communicated spoken blogs were downloaded onto Apple's iPods. Podcasts, though, can be heard on one's computer or downloaded onto any portable listening device. Podcasting can also include videos. Hundreds of thousands of podcasts are now being generated every day. Basically, anyone who has an idea can easily create a podcast and make it available for downloading. Like blogs, podcasting threatens traditional media sources. Even video podcasting costs virtually nothing with today's inexpensive technology.

Podcasting
A method of distributing multimedia files, such as audio or video files, for downloading onto mobile devices or personal computers.

Although politicians were somewhat slow to adopt this form of communication, many now are using podcasts to keep in touch with their constituents. By the time you read this, there will be thousands, if not tens of thousands, of political podcasts. Certainly, the use of podcasts, blogs, and YouTube became a major part of campaigning during the 2007–2008 election cycle.

THE PRIMACY OF TELEVISION

That the number of people watching the television networks during prime time has declined by almost 25 percent in the last 10 years?

Television is the most influential medium. It is also big business. National news TV personalities such as Katie Couric and Brian Williams earn millions of dollars per year from their TV contracts alone. They are paid so much because they command large audiences, and large audiences command high prices for advertising on national news shows. Indeed, news *per se* has become a major factor in the profitability of TV stations.

THE INCREASE IN NEWS-TYPE PROGRAMMING

In 1963, the major networks—ABC, CBS, and NBC—devoted only 11 minutes daily to national news. A 24/7 news cable channel—CNN—started operating in 1980. With the addition of CNN-Headline News, CNBC, MSNBC, FOX News, and other news-format cable channels since the 1980s, the amount of news-type programming has continued to increase. By 2008, the amount of time the networks devoted to news-type programming each day had increased to about three hours. In recent years, all of the major networks have also added Internet sites to try to capture that market, but they face hundreds of competitors on the Web.

[6]Kaye D. Trammell, "The Blogging of the President," in Andrew Williams and John Tedesco, eds., *The Internet Election: Perspectives on the Web in Campaign 2004* (Lanham, MD: Rowman and Littlefield, 2006).

TELEVISION'S INFLUENCE ON THE POLITICAL PROCESS

Television's influence on the political process today is recognized by all who engage in the process. Television news is often criticized for being superficial, particularly compared with the detailed coverage available in the print media, such as the *New York Times*. In fact, television news is constrained by its technical characteristics, the most important being the limitations of time—stories must be reported in only a few minutes.

The most interesting aspect of television is the fact that it relies on pictures rather than words to attract the viewer's attention. Therefore, the digital videos or slides that are chosen for a particular political story have exaggerated importance. Viewers do not know what other photos may have been taken or what other events may have been digitally recorded—they see only those appearing on their screens. Television news can also be exploited for its drama by well-constructed stories. Some critics suggest that there is pressure to produce television news that has a "story line," like a novel or movie. The story should be short, with exciting pictures and a clear plot. In the extreme case, the news media are satisfied with a **sound bite**, a several-second comment selected or crafted for its immediate impact on the viewer.

Sound Bite
A brief, memorable comment that can easily be fit into news broadcasts.

It has been suggested that these formatting characteristics—or necessities—of television increase its influence on political events. (Newspapers and news magazines are also limited by their formats, but to a lesser extent.) As you are aware, real life is usually not dramatic, nor do all events have a neat or an easily understood plot. Political campaigns are continuing events, lasting perhaps as long as two years. The significance

SENATOR JOHN MCCAIN, right, and Jon Stewart talk during a break in taping *The Daily Show with Jon Stewart* in New York, Tuesday evening, April 24, 2007. McCain announced his candidacy the next day. (Stephan Savoia/AP Photos)

of their daily turns and twists is only apparent later. The "drama" of Congress, with its 535 players and dozens of important committees and meetings, is also difficult for the media to present. Television requires dozens of daily three-minute stories.

Some commentators, including M. B. Zuckerman, editor-in-chief of *U.S. News and World Report*, claim that "policymaking is held hostage to imagery." Zuckerman argues that television networks "distort the meaning of events by failing to provide the context that would help us make sense of these images."[7] The TV newsroom cliché has been—and probably always will be— "if it bleeds, it leads." It is not news to show one hundred rebuilt schools in Iraq, but it is news to show a car bombing that injures or kills civilians.

THE MEDIA AND POLITICAL CAMPAIGNS

All forms of the media—television, newspapers, radio, magazines, blogs, and podcasts—have a significant political impact on American society. Media influence is most obvious during political campaigns. News coverage of a single event, such as the results of the Iowa caucuses or the New Hampshire primary, may be the most important factor in having a candidate be referred to in the media as the front-runner in a presidential campaign. It is not too much of an exaggeration to say that almost all national political figures, starting with the president, plan every public appearance and statement to attract media coverage.

Because television is still the primary news source for the majority of Americans, candidates and their consultants spend much of their time devising strategies that use television to their benefit. Three types of TV coverage are generally employed in campaigns for the presidency and other offices: advertising, management of news coverage, and campaign debates.

ADVERTISING

Perhaps one of the most effective political ads of all time was a 30-second spot created by President Lyndon B. Johnson's media adviser in 1964. In this ad, a little girl stood in a field of daisies. As she held a daisy, she pulled the petals off and quietly counted to herself. Suddenly, when she reached number ten, a deep bass voice cut in and began a countdown: "10, 9, 8, 7, 6 . . ." When the voice intoned "zero," the unmistakable mushroom cloud of an atomic bomb began to fill the screen. Then President Johnson's voice was heard: "These are the stakes. To make a world in which all of God's children can live, or to go into the dark. We must either love each other or we must die." At the end of the commercial, the message read, "Vote for President Johnson on November 3."

To understand how effective this "daisy girl" commercial was, you must know that Johnson's opponent was Barry Goldwater, a Republican conservative candidate known for his expansive views on the role of the U.S. military. The ad's implication was that Goldwater would lead the United States into nuclear war. Although the ad was withdrawn within a few days, it has a place in political campaign history as the classic negative campaign advertisement. The ad's producer, Tony Schwartz, describes the effect in this way: "It was comparable to a person going to a psychiatrist and seeing dirty pictures in a Rorschach pattern. The daisy commercial evoked Goldwater's pro-bomb statements. They were like dirty pictures in the audience's mind."[8]

[7]Mortimer B. Zuckerman, "Why TV Holds Us Hostage," *U.S. News and World Report*, February 20, 2005.
[8]As quoted in Kathleen Hall Jamieson, *Packaging the Presidency: A History and Criticism of Presidential Campaign Advertising*, 3rd ed. (New York: Oxford University Press, 1996), p. 200.

DID YOU KNOW?

That the average length of a quote, or sound bite, for a candidate decreased from 49 seconds in 1968 to less than nine seconds today?

PRESIDENT LYNDON JOHNSON'S "daisy girl" ad contrasted the innocence of childhood with the horror of an atomic attack. Johnson's opponent in the 1964 election was Senator Barry Goldwater, who was more likely to take a strong stance against the Soviet Union. (Democratic National Committee)

Since the daisy girl advertisement, negative advertising has come into its own. Candidates vie with one another to produce "attack" ads and then to counterattack when the opponent responds. The public claims not to like negative advertising, but as one consultant put it, "Negative advertising works." The most important effect of negative advertisements may not be to transfer votes from the candidate who is under attack to the candidate running the ads. Rather, the negative ads can demoralize the supporters of the candidate who is under attack. Some supporters, as a result, may not bother to vote. The widespread use of negative ads, therefore, can lead to reduced political participation and a general cynicism about politics.

Political advertising has become increasingly important for the profitability of television station owners. Hearst-Argyle Television, for example, obtains well over 10 percent of its revenues from political ads during an election year. Political advertising is not restricted to television, however. In addition to typical print ads, online political advertising has been on the rise. The Interactive Advertising Bureau estimates that during the 2008 presidential campaign, as much as $10 billion could be spent on Internet advertising.

MANAGEMENT OF NEWS COVERAGE

Using political advertising to get a message across to the public is a very expensive tactic. Coverage by the news media, however, is free; it simply demands that the campaign

VOTE FOR PRESIDENT JOHNSON ON NOVEMBER 3.

ensure that coverage takes place. In recent years, campaign managers have shown increasing sophistication in creating newsworthy events for journalists to cover. As Doris Graber points out, "To keep a favorable image of their candidates in front of the public, campaign managers arrange newsworthy events to familiarize potential voters with their candidates' best aspects."[9]

The campaign staff uses several methods to try to influence the quantity and type of coverage the campaign receives. First, the campaign staff understands the technical aspects of media coverage—camera angles, necessary equipment, timing, and deadlines—and plans political events to accommodate the press. Second, the campaign organization is aware that political reporters and their sponsors—networks or newspapers—are in competition for the best stories and can be manipulated through the granting of favors, such as a personal interview with the candidate. Third, the scheduler in the campaign has the important task of planning events that will be photogenic and interesting enough for the evening news. A related goal, although one that is more difficult to attain, is to convince reporters that a particular interpretation of an event is correct.

Today, the art of putting the appropriate **spin** on a story or event is highly developed. Each candidate's or elected official's press advisers, often referred to as **spin doctors**, try to convince the journalists that their interpretations of the political events are correct. Each political campaign, and the president's own Office of Communication, send e-mails and faxes to all the major media, setting out their own version of an event virtually in real time. During the 2008 primary campaign, both the Obama campaign and the Clinton campaign spent endless hours "explaining" or "spinning" the results in a specific state or suggesting how the other candidate's "bowling score" or "gun handling" was pandering to voters. More recently, journalists have begun to report on the different spins used by candidates and elected officials to try to manipulate news coverage.

Spin
An interpretation of campaign events or election results that is favorable to the candidate's campaign strategy.

Spin Doctor
A political campaign advisor who tries to convince journalists of the truth of a particular interpretation of events.

GOING FOR THE KNOCKOUT PUNCH—PRESIDENTIAL DEBATES

In presidential elections, perhaps just as important as political advertisements is the performance of the candidates in televised presidential debates. After the first such debate in 1960, in which John F. Kennedy, the young senator from Massachusetts, took on the vice president of the United States, Richard Nixon, candidates became aware of the great potential of television for changing the momentum of a campaign. In general, challengers have much more to gain from debating than do incumbents. Challengers hope that the incumbent will make a mistake in the debate and undermine his "presidential" image. Incumbent presidents are loath to debate their challengers because it puts their opponents on an equal footing with them, but the debates have become so widely anticipated that it is difficult for an incumbent to refuse.

Debates can affect the outcome of a race. Some people believe that Democrat Al Gore hurt himself during the 2000 debates by appearing arrogant. In 2008, the McCain and Obama campaigns agreed on three presidential debates and one vice presidential debate. With the addition of Sarah Palin to the Republican ticket and her stirring convention speech, almost as many Americans tuned in to her debate with Senator Joe Biden as they did to the presidential debates. Each of the presidential debates saw Senator Obama remain calm and composed and Senator McCain try to demonstrate his role as a reformer and cost-cutter. McCain was generally seen as being too assertive and lacking any humor, while Obama won over viewers with his presidential demeanor. Neither candidate made

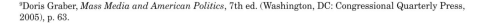

[9]Doris Graber, *Mass Media and American Politics*, 7th ed. (Washington, DC: Congressional Quarterly Press, 2005), p. 63.

any mistakes, nor did either score a knockout punch. Post-debate commentary focused as much on the skill of the moderator as the performance of the candidates.

Although debates are justified publicly as an opportunity for the voters to find out how candidates differ on the issues, the candidates want to capitalize on the power of television to project an image. They view the debate as a strategic opportunity to improve their own images or to point out their opponents' failures. Candidates also know that the morning-after interpretation of the debate by the news media may play a crucial role in what the public thinks. Regardless of the risks of debating, the potential for gaining votes is so great that candidates undoubtedly will continue to seek televised debates. Of course, in today's Internet world, candidates also know that their performances will be "broadcast" on the Internet and that the bloggers will add their own interpretations to those of the mainstream media.

POLITICAL CAMPAIGNS AND THE INTERNET

Without a doubt, the Internet has become an important vehicle for campaign advertising and news coverage, as well as for soliciting campaign contributions. This was made clear during the 2004 presidential elections, when 7 percent of all Internet users participated in online campaign activities. (Internet users included about two-thirds of all American adults.) As pointed out previously, Democratic presidential hopeful Howard Dean (now head of the Democratic Party) used his Internet site and e-mailings to generate millions of dollars in campaign contributions, most of which were very small, such as $50 or $100. Barack Obama was able to raise millions of dollars each month during the primary season, with at least half being small contributions.

During the 2008 election campaigns, the Internet was used not only to advertise the candidates' positions, to solicit donations, and to podcast speeches and debates, but it also was used to target messages. Candidates sought e-mail lists sorted by age, gender, and other demographic variables. Then they e-mailed messages to targeted groups. Members of union households receive, for example, messages about lowering the number of jobs going overseas. Candidates used the Internet to recruit volunteers for Get Out the Vote campaigns. They also used e-mail and blogs to instruct citizens on how to participate in the political caucuses and how to persuade others to support their candidate of choice.

Today, the campaign staff of every candidate running for a significant political office includes an Internet campaign strategist—a professional hired to create and maintain the campaign Web site, blogs, and podcasts. The work of this strategist includes designing a user-friendly and attractive Web site for the candidate, managing the candidate's e-mail communications, and tracking campaign contributions made through the site. Additionally, virtually all major interest groups in the United States now use the Internet to promote their causes. Prior to elections, various groups engage in issue advocacy from their Web sites. At little or no cost, they can promote positions taken by favored candidates and solicit contributions.

Is campaigning on the Internet the most important advance in politics? There are both advantages and disadvantages to a Web campaign. As noted by Robert J. Klotz, using the Internet for campaigning may be a two-edged sword for a candidate. Only individuals who want to look at a Web site will do so, which means few, if any, accidental viewers. This makes it easy to supply lots of information to those who are already interested but difficult to reach undecided voters. In addition, while the Internet may

REPUBLICAN PRESIDENTIAL NOMINEE Senator John McCain, R.-Ariz., left, makes a point during the first U.S. presidential debate with Democratic presidential nominee Senator Barack Obama, D.-Ill., right, at the University of Mississippi in Oxford, Mississippi, September 26, 2008. (Jim Bourg/AP Photo)

encourage blog posting and e-mail to the campaign, it raises expectations that cannot be met. No candidate can spend his or her time answering millions of e-mails. However, a great advantage to Internet campaigning for the candidate is that one minute of exposure costs the same as hours. Followers can view and interact with the Web for hours at a time for no additional cost to the campaign. Compare that strategy with spending millions on television prime-time advertising to a declining audience.[10]

THE MEDIA'S IMPACT ON THE VOTERS

The question of how much influence the media have on voting behavior is difficult to answer. Generally, individuals watch television, read newspapers, or log on to a Web site with certain preconceived ideas about political issues and candidates. These attitudes and opinions act as a kind of perceptual screen that filters out information that makes people feel uncomfortable or that does not fit with their own ideas.

Voters watch campaign commercials and news about political campaigns with "selective attentiveness"—that is, they tend to watch those commercials that support the candidates they favor and tend to pay attention to news stories about their own candidates. This selectivity also affects their perceptions of the content of a news story or commercial and whether it is remembered. Apparently, the media have the most influence on those persons who have not formed an opinion about political candidates or issues. Studies have shown that the flurry of television commercials and debates immediately before election day has the greatest impact on those voters who are truly undecided. Few voters who have already formed their opinions change their minds under the influence of the media.

THE ROLE OF THE MEDIA IN THE 2008 ELECTIONS

As in many past elections, broadcast television dominated media spending during the campaign. In the last midterm elections, $912 million was spent on TV ads. In the 2008 elections, more than $2 billion was spent. The Obama and McCain campaigns produced numerous ads attacking the other's positions and, in some cases, his character. McCain's ads stressed Obama's lack of experience at high levels of office, while the Obama camp painted McCain as a strong supporter of President Bush. While the major media reported on the campaign, commentators and bloggers wrote about how the media treated the two candidates. Rarely have the media been so scrutinized in a presidential campaign. The major networks were frequently charged with being more positive toward Obama and more negative toward McCain in their news stories. Academic studies were published that seemed to back up such a claim. In their defense, the media responded that Obama's historic run for the presidency was more newsworthy then McCain's campaign and that they chose stories solely on news value. Both candidates sought to get beyond the prime-time news by appearing on late-night comedy shows. *Saturday Night Live* recorded some its highest ratings ever with its 2008 political coverage.

THE MEDIA AND THE GOVERNMENT

The mass media not only wield considerable power when it comes to political campaigns, but they also, in one way or another, can wield power over the affairs of government and over government officials. For example, in April 2004, President George W. Bush tried to keep Condoleezza Rice, then the National Security Advisor, from testifying before the bipartisan September 11 investigation commission by citing the doctrine of executive

---

[10]Robert J. Klotz, *The Politics of Internet Communication* (Lanham, MD: Rowman and Littlefield, 2004).

FORMER NATO Supreme Allied Commander (Europe) General Wesley Clark (Ret.) (left) speaks, as former Commander-in-Chief of U.S. Special Operations Command General Wayne Downing (Ret.) (right) listens during an interview on NBC's *Meet the Press* in 2005. In 2007, it became known that such retired military commentators are often briefed by the Pentagon on current military conditions. (Alex Wong/Getty Images for Meet the Press/Getty Images)

privilege. After several weeks, during which this decision was widely criticized in the print and electronic media, Bush reversed himself and allowed Rice to testify.

PREPACKAGED NEWS

In recent years, the public learned that the Bush administration had spent millions of dollars on public relations, including "news" programs that were often created specifically to be rebroadcast on television. In 2005, for example, the Bush administration had to acknowledge that it paid several conservative commentators to write in support of administration-backed programs. Specifically, conservative commentator Armstrong Williams received $240,000 to write favorably about the No Child Left Behind Act and the Department of Education. Additionally, the Bush administration created a video about the new education law that was designed to look like a legitimate news program. The administration used the same technique to promote the law providing a new prescription drug benefit for Medicare recipients.

Is the use of taxpayer dollars to create prepackaged news legal? Some argue that it is because the government is not forcing anyone to broadcast this "covert" propaganda. Others, however, question the ethical underpinnings of government advocacy at the expense of both unbiased journalism and taxpayers' dollars.

In 2008, another more subtle way of influencing the news was exposed. While almost every network has a retired military officer under contract to provide background information on the war in Iraq and other military issues, the networks seemed to be unaware that the Department of Defense included these retired officers in briefings about the current military operations. When this relationship was discovered, the Pentagon announced that it would no longer provide this inside information to the retired commentators.

THE MEDIA AND THE PRESIDENCY

The relationship between the media and the president usually is reciprocal: each needs the other to thrive. Because of this codependency, both the media and the president work hard to exploit one another. The media need news to report, and the president needs coverage.

White House Press Corps
The reporters assigned full-time to cover the presidency.

Press Secretary
The presidential staff member responsible for handling White House media relations and communications.

DID YOU KNOW?

That Franklin D. Roosevelt held approximately 1,000 press conferences during his terms as president?

In the United States, the prominence of the president is accentuated by a **White House press corps** that is assigned full-time to cover the presidency. These reporters even have a lounge in the White House where they spend their days, waiting for a story to break. Most of the time, they simply wait for the daily or twice-daily briefing by the president's **press secretary**. Because of the press corps' physical proximity to the president, the chief executive cannot even take a brief stroll around the Rose Garden without it becoming news. Perhaps no other nation allows the press such access to its highest government official. Consequently, no other democratic nation has its airwaves and print media so filled with absolute trivia regarding the personal lives of the chief executive and his or her family.

One of the first presidents to make truly effective use of the media was President Franklin D. Roosevelt (served 1933–1945), who brought new spirit to a demoralized country and led it through the Great Depression with his radio broadcasts. His "fireside chats" brought hope to millions. Through his speeches, Roosevelt was able to forge a common emotional bond among his listeners.

His decisive announcement in 1933 on the reorganization of the banks, for example, calmed a jittery nation and prevented the collapse of the banking industry. (Nervous depositors were withdrawing their assets, which threatened to create a "run" on the banks.) His famous Pearl Harbor speech, following the Japanese attack on the U.S. Pacific fleet on December 7, 1941 ("a day that will live in infamy"), mobilized the nation for World War II.

SETTING THE PUBLIC AGENDA

According to several studies, the media play an important part in setting the public agenda. Evidence is strong that whatever public problems receive the greatest media treatment will be cited by the public in contemporary surveys as the most important problems. Although the media do not make policy decisions, they do influence to a significant extent the policy issues that will be decided—and this is an important part of the political process. Because those who control the media are not elected representatives of the people, the agenda-setting role of the media necessarily is a controversial

ANNETTE MCLEOD (center), wife of a wounded U.S. Army soldier, wipes away a tear next to wounded U.S. Army Sergeant John Daniel Shannon (left) and wounded U.S. Army Specialist Jeremy Duncan (right) while testifying before a U.S. House subcommittee about the poor conditions at Walter Reed Army Medical Center. Such testimony sets the agenda for future political action. (Chuck Kennedy/MCT/Landov Media)

one. The relationship of the media to agenda setting remains complex, though, because politicians are able to manipulate media coverage to control some of its effects, as well as to exploit the media to further their agendas with the public.

INVESTIGATIVE REPORTING

Most major newspapers and many television networks devote some of their resources to investigative reporting. By finding a problem with a public policy or uncovering official wrongdoing, the media are alerting the public to important political information. Furthermore, the results of investigative reporting can have a very important impact on officeholders and, in the best case, bring about real change for the better. Richard Nixon, for example, barely avoided impeachment and resigned from office due to the investigative reporting of two *Washington Post* reporters. Recently, the *Post* won a Pulitzer Prize for the investigative reporting that found very poor housing conditions at Walter Reed Army Medical Center for wounded veterans.

GOVERNMENT REGULATION OF THE MEDIA

The United States has one of the freest presses in the world. Nonetheless, regulation of the media does exist, particularly of the electronic media. Many aspects of this regulation were discussed in Chapter 4, when we examined First Amendment rights and the press.

The First Amendment does not mention electronic media, which did not exist when the Bill of Rights was written. For many reasons, the government has much greater control over the electronic media than it does over printed media. Through the Federal Communications Commission (FCC), which regulates communications by radio, television, wire, and cable, the number of radio stations has been controlled for many years, even though technologically we could have many more radio stations than now exist. Also, the FCC created a situation in which the three major TV networks dominated the airwaves.

DANA PERINO, press secretary for President George W. Bush in 2007 and 2008, takes questions from the White House Press Corps on her first day in office. What is the relationship between the press corps and the press secretary? (Chip Somodevilla/Getty Images)

WHAT IF...

THE MEDIA HAD TO REVEAL ALL THEIR SOURCES?

Reporters, whether they work for newspapers, newswire services, television stations, magazines, or Internet blogs, typically attempt to "protect their sources." Many of these sources are willing to talk to reporters only on the condition that they remain anonymous. Consequently, untold news stories include phrases such as "informed sources said . . ." or "an anonymous source revealed . . ." Typically, these sources are confident that their names will not be disclosed because so-called shield laws protect reporters from being forced to disclose their sources in court or in other judicial proceedings. In 1972, the U.S. Supreme Court stated that "news gathering is not without First Amendment protections."* The majority on the Court, though, did not see those protections as absolute and held, among other things, that the First Amendment did not protect reporters from federal grand jury subpoenas seeking their confidential sources. In response, state legislatures and courts created their own shield laws.

Assume that at both the federal and state levels, shield laws were abolished. In other words, imagine a world in which reporters could continue to cite anonymous sources but would be subject to subpoenas that legally would require them to reveal their sources. Clearly, news gatherers who could not guarantee confidentiality for many of their sources would find those sources refusing to provide information. In these circumstances, investigative reporting in general could "take a hit." Investigative reporters would discover that fewer individuals would be willing to talk to them, except about minor matters that were not controversial.

Many jurists have predicted the same outcome. One judge stated that compelling a reporter to disclose confidential sources "unquestionably threatens a journalist's ability to secure information that is made available to him only on a confidential basis." The judge continued by saying that the "negative effect of such disclosure on future undercover investigative reporting would be serious and threatens freedom of the press and the public's need to be informed."**

If news gatherers' sources were fair game without any shield-law protection, there would probably be a big increase in litigation. Imagine a person who is unhappy about a story written about him or her. If that person were sufficiently motivated, he or she could go to court to demand the names of the anonymous sources who had provided the information on which the reporter based the detrimental story. The sources might then face a lawsuit. Today, most people tend to rely on trusted news sources and dismiss what might be considered gossip. If trusted news sources engaged in less investigative reporting, though, anonymous bloggers who might or might not be accurate could become increasingly important.

FOR CRITICAL ANALYSIS

1. Is it fair that reporters can shield their sources today? If your answer is yes, under what circumstances might shielding sources be considered unfair?
2. Why do anonymous sources wish to keep their identities secret?

*Branzburg v. Hayes, 408 U.S. 665 (1972).
**Baker v. F & F Investment, 470 F.2d 778 (1972).

CONTROLLING OWNERSHIP OF THE MEDIA

Many FCC rules have dealt with ownership of news media, such as how many stations a network can own. In the past, the FCC auctioned off hundreds of radio frequencies, allowing the expansion of cellular telephone applications.

In 1996, Congress passed legislation that had far-reaching implications for the communications industry—the Telecommunications Act. The Act ended the rule that kept telephone companies from entering the cable business and other communications markets. What this means is that a single corporation—whether Time Warner or Disney—can offer long-distance and local telephone services, cable television, satellite television, Internet services, and, of course, libraries of films and entertainment. The Act opened the door to competition and led to more options for consumers, who now can choose among multiple competitors for all of these services delivered to the home. At the same time, it launched a race among competing companies to control media ownership.

Media Conglomerates. Many media outlets are now owned by corporate conglomerates. A single entity may own a television network, the studios that produce shows, news, and movies, and the means to deliver that content to the home via cable, satellite, or the Internet. The question to be faced in the future is how to ensure competition in the delivery of news so that citizens have access to multiple points of view from the media.

All of the prime-time television networks are owned by major American corporations, including such corporate conglomerates as General Electric (owner of NBC) and Disney (owner of ABC). The Turner Broadcasting/CNN network was also purchased by a major corporation, Time Warner. Later, Time Warner was acquired by America Online (AOL), a merger that combined the world's then-largest media company with the world's then-largest online company. FOX Television has always been a part of Rupert Murdoch's publishing and media empire. In addition to taking part in mergers and acquisitions, many of these companies have formed partnerships with computer software makers, such as Microsoft, for joint electronic publishing ventures.

Increased Media Concentration. The FCC promulgates rules on what media conglomerates can own. One measure of a conglomerate's impact is "audience reach," or the percentage of the national viewing public that has access to the conglomerate's outlets. The FCC

MILEY CYRUS (as Hannah Montana) performs during the ABC *Good Morning America* Summer Concert Series, held in New York's Bryant Park in 2007. The Hannah Montana character is a Disney creation and ABC is owned by the Disney company. (Jennifer Graylock/AP Photos)

places an upper limit on audience reach, known as the "audience-reach cap." A few years ago, the FCC raised the national audience-reach cap from 35 percent to 45 percent and also allowed a corporation to own a newspaper and a television station in the same market. Congress rebelled against this new rule, however, and pushed the national audience-reach cap back below 40 percent. Nevertheless, a corporation can still own up to three TV stations in its largest market. The reality today is that there are only a few independent news operations left in the entire country.

This media concentration has led to the disappearance of localism in the news. Obviously, costly locally produced news cannot be shown anywhere except in that local market. In contrast, the costs of producing a similar show for national broadcast can be amortized over millions and millions of viewers and paid for by higher revenues from national advertisers. Another concern, according to former media mogul Ted Turner, is that the rise of media conglomerates may lead to a decline in democratic debate. The emergence of independent news Web sites, blogs, and podcasts provides an offset to this trend, however. Consequently, the increased concentration of traditional media news organizations may not matter as much as in the past.

GOVERNMENT CONTROL OF CONTENT

On the face of it, the First Amendment would seem to apply to all media. In fact, the United States Supreme Court has often been slow to extend free speech and free press guarantees to new media. For example, in 1915, the Court held that "as a matter of common sense," free-speech protections did not apply to cinema. Only in 1952 did the Court find that motion pictures were covered by the First Amendment.[11] In contrast, the Court extended full protection to the Internet almost immediately by striking down provisions of the 1996 Telecommunications Act.[12] Cable TV also received broad protection in 2000.[13] (To learn about nations that exercise far more control over media content, see this chapter's *Beyond Our Borders* feature.)

Control of Broadcasting. While the Court has held that the First Amendment is relevant to radio and television, it has never extended full protection to these media. The Court has used several arguments to justify this stand—initially, the scarcity of broadcast frequencies. The Court later held that the government could restrict "indecent" programming based on the "pervasive" presence of broadcasting in the home.[14] On this basis, the FCC has the authority to fine broadcasters for indecency or profanity.

Indecency in broadcasting became a major issue in 2004. In the first three months of that year, the FCC levied fines that exceeded those imposed in the previous nine years combined. Including older fines, radio personality Howard Stern cost his employers almost $2 million. Another triggering episode was singer Janet Jackson's "wardrobe malfunction" during a 2004 Super Bowl halftime performance. Legislation was introduced in Congress to increase the maximum fine that the FCC can impose to $500,000 per incident.

Government Control of the Media during the Second Gulf War. During the First Gulf War in 1991, the U.S. government was strongly criticized for not providing accurate information to the media. Stung by this criticism, the Bush administration tried a two-pronged strategy during the Second Gulf War in 2003. Every day, reporters at the central com-

[11]*Joseph Burstyn, Inc. v. Wilson*, 343 U.S. 495 (1952).
[12]*Reno v. American Civil Liberties Union*, 521 U.S. 844 (1997).
[13]*United States v. Playboy Entertainment Group*, 529 U.S. 803 (2000).
[14]*FCC v. Pacifica Foundation*, 438 U.S. 230 (1978). In this case, the Court banned seven swear words (famously used by comedian George Carlin) during hours when children could hear them.

mand post in Qatar were able to hear briefings from top commanders. (Reporters complained, however, that they did not hear enough about the true progress of the war.) The administration also allowed more than five hundred journalists to travel with the combat forces as "embedded" journalists. Reports from the field were very favorable to the military. This was understandable, given that the journalists quickly identified with the troops and their difficulties. The Bush administration, however, was unable to control reports from foreign and Arab media.

The Government's Attempt to Control the Media during the Current War on Terrorism. Certainly, since September 11, 2001, government secrecy has increased, sometimes (apparently) with the public's acceptance. Senator Patrick Leahy (D.-Vt.) argues that the First Amendment would have trouble winning ratification today if it were proposed as a constitutional amendment. He based this assertion on a Knight Foundation survey that found that almost 40 percent of 110,000 students believed that newspapers should have to get "government approval" of news articles before they are published.

In any event, the charter for the Department of Homeland Security, created soon after the September 11 terrorist attacks, includes a provision that allows certain groups to stamp "critical infrastructure information" on the top of documents when they submit information to Homeland Security. This information might include the maps of waterlines or the plans of nuclear power plants. The public has no right to see this information. Additionally, more and more government documents have been labeled "secret" so that they do not have to be revealed to the public.

Despite such measures, since the war on terror and the second war in Iraq started, there have been numerous intelligence leaks to the press. The public did find out about the government's monitoring of telephone calls to suspected terrorists abroad. The tension between needed intelligence secrecy and the public's "right to know" continues to create both legal and military problems.

THE PUBLIC'S RIGHT TO MEDIA ACCESS

Does the public have a right to **media access**? Both the FCC and the courts have gradually taken the stance that citizens do have a right of access to the media, particularly

Media Access
The public's right of access to the media. The Federal Communications Commission and the courts have gradually taken the stance that citizens do have a right to media access.

BEYOND OUR
B🌍RDERS

GOVERNMENT-CONTROLLED MEDIA ABROAD

The First Amendment to the Constitution guarantees freedom of expression in the United States. While there are certainly some restrictions on what Americans say on the radio and television, or even publish, those restrictions are few. This is not so in many other countries today, even though their constitutions may also guarantee freedom of expression.

IRAN'S CONTROL OF THE MEDIA

Broadcasting is run by the state in Iran. The state-run media reflect the views of President Mahmoud Ahmadinejad and those of his allies in the conservative clerical establishment. In Iran, there are no independent newspapers that can present views contrary to the government's conservative clerical views. Every newspaper has to be licensed. Virtually all reformist newspapers have been closed down. In a less-than-totally successful attempt to skirt such censorship, reformist journalists have gone to the Internet.

Because the Internet has become increasingly important as a source of news, Iran has one of the most sophisticated Internet censorship systems in the world, probably as good as or even better than the one used in China (see Chapter 4). Although Internet filtering is ostensibly used to prevent pornographic or immoral materials, the government in reality uses such blocking to censor political content.

THE RUSSIANS HAVE LOST MANY PRESS FREEDOMS, TOO

After the end of communism in Russia, a thriving independent press arose. On television, radio, and in newspapers, Russians could read all sorts of political views. Since Vladimir Putin took over the presidency (he is now prime minister), though, virtually all opposition journalists have been silenced, in one way or another. During his tenure, Putin eliminated most privately owned television stations. In addition, private newspapers are frequently closed if they are too critical of the regime. More frightening to journalists has been the frequent murder of news reporters, especially those who were investigating government issues. By 2006, 13 well-known reporters had been murdered. Of course, the government claimed no involvement in these crimes. Russians are now fed a steady diet of Putin's pronouncements on TV. There is virtually no criticism of Putin's regime that the average Russian can view on TV or hear on the radio. Russians have to seek the foreign press to find out about the corruption that surrounds Putin's administration. Of course, the Internet and blogs still present a problem to the Rus-

FORMER PRESIDENT AND CURRENT PRIME MINISTER
Vladimir Putin makes one of his many speeches, which are duly broadcast and rebroadcast on all available television channels throughout the country. There is virtually no independent television programming in Russia today. (Photo courtesy of Russian Presidential Press and Information Office/Sergeja Velichkina)

sian political hierarchy, but Putin's government attempts to filter the Internet, although less successfully than in Iran or China.

THERE ARE WORSE EXAMPLES, OF COURSE

Currently, if you want to find the worst case of lack of freedom of expression, you have to examine North Korea. The country's dictator, Kim Jong II, makes sure that North Korea's inhabitants have almost no knowledge of the outside world. To a much lesser degree, there are various

restrictions on freedom of the press in Cuba, Egypt, Lebanon, Myanmar (formerly Burma), Saudi Arabia, Syria, Venezuela, and Yemen. In short, the government controls the media in countries in which democracy is either unknown or weak.

FOR CRITICAL ANALYSIS

1. How has technology helped reduce various governments' control of the media?
2. How does the lack of a free press impact the views of the citizens?

the electronic media. The argument is that because the airwaves are public, the government has the right to dictate how they are used. Congress could, for example, pass a law requiring the broadcast networks to provide free airtime to candidates, as is the case in some European nations. Republican presidential nominee Senator John McCain of Arizona, a major proponent of campaign-finance reform, proposed legislation that would provide such free airtime. Broadcast networks that make bigger profits in election years quietly oppose such a law.

Technology is giving more citizens access to the electronic media and, in particular, to television. As more cable operators have more airtime to sell, some of it will remain unused and will be available for public access. At the same time, the Internet makes media access by the public very easy, although not everyone has the resources to take advantage of it.

That the average age of CNN viewers is 44 and that most people who watch the evening network news programs are over age 50?

BIAS IN THE MEDIA

Many studies have been undertaken to try to identify the sources and direction of **bias** in the media, and these studies have reached different conclusions. Some claim that the press has a liberal bias. Others conclude that the press shows a conservative bias. Still others do not see any notable partisan bias.

Bias
An inclination or a preference that interferes with impartial judgment.

DO THE MEDIA HAVE A PARTISAN BIAS?

In a classic study conducted in the 1980s, researchers found that media producers, editors, and reporters (the "media elite") exhibited a notably liberal and "left-leaning" bias in their news coverage.[15] Since then, the contention that the media have a liberal bias has been repeated time and again. Joining the ranks of those who assert that the media has a liberal bias is Bernard Goldberg, a veteran CBS broadcaster. Goldberg argues that liberal bias is responsible for the declining number of viewers who watch network news. He claims that this liberal bias, which "comes naturally to most reporters," has given viewers less reason to trust the big news networks.[16] Conservative journalist

[15]S. Robert Lichter, Stanley Rothman, and Linda S. Lichter, *The Media Elite* (New York: Adler and Adler, 1986).
[16]Bernard Goldberg, *Bias: A CBS Insider Exposes How the Media Distort the News* (Washington, DC: Regnery Publishing, 2001).

William McGowan also claims that the press exhibits a liberal bias. He maintains that most news reporters have liberal views on the issues they cover (he cites a survey of journalists in which more than 80 percent of the respondents said that they were in favor of abortion rights) and that this bias prevents them from investigating and reporting on opposing viewpoints.[17]

In 2005, the University of Connecticut's Department of Public Policy surveyed 300 journalists nationwide. These journalists were asked whom they voted for in the 2004 presidential election. The Democratic challenger, John Kerry, received 52 percent of their votes, while Bush received only 19 percent (27 percent of those queried either refused to disclose their vote or did not vote).[18]

In that same year, there was heated debate about the liberal bias of the government-funded Public Broadcasting Service (PBS). President Bush had already named a Republican, Kenneth Y. Tomlinson, to chair the underlying Corporation for Public Broadcasting. Tomlinson contracted with an outside consultant to track PBS's political leanings on the program *Now with Bill Moyers*. Apparently, Tomlinson wanted proof that PBS had a liberal bias. To counter this supposed liberal bias, Tomlinson encouraged PBS officials to broadcast *The Journal Editorial Report*, a program hosted by Paul Gigot, editor of the conservative editorial page of the *Wall Street Journal*. In his defense, Tomlinson stated that "my goal here is to see programming that satisfies a broad constituency."[19]

A RACIAL BIAS?

Racial profiling is the act of routinely making negative assumptions about individuals based on race. The term was first used to describe the behavior of certain police officers who habitually stopped African American motorists more frequently than white ones, often on minor pretexts. African Americans have described these incidents as stops for "driving while black." Some observers have charged that the media—television in particular—engage in racial profiling in their reporting on minority group members.

Those who believe that the media engage in racial profiling point to common stereotypes that journalists often use when illustrating news stories. For example, a study found that while African Americans constituted 29 percent of the nation's poor, they made up 65 percent of the images of the poor shown on leading network news programs. In addition to being disproportionately portrayed as black, the poor were also largely represented by the persons least likely to command sympathy—unemployed adults. The elderly and the working poor were underrepresented.[20] Critics of racial profiling also argue that African Americans are regularly used to illustrate drug abusers or dealers, even though a majority of users are white, and that images of criminals in general are disproportionately black.

---

[17]William McGowan, *Coloring the News: How Political Correctness Has Corrupted American Journalism* (San Francisco: Encounter Books, 2003).
[18]University of Connecticut, "National Polls of Journalists and the American Public," May 16, 2005.
[19]"Republican Chairman Exerts Pressure on PBS, Alleging Biases," *Washington Times*, May 2, 2005, p. 7.
[20]Martin Gilens, "Race and Poverty in America: Public Misperceptions and the American News Media," *Public Opinion Quarterly*, Vol. 6 (1996).

Americans of Middle Eastern ancestry have also complained about profiling. In this instance, the stereotype is of the Arab terrorist. Of course, such people exist, but like African American criminals, they make up a small part of the group's population.

Today's newsrooms are increasingly diverse. One survey revealed that minority group members made up 18 percent of the employees in television journalism, and African Americans made up 10 percent. Such a substantial minority presence may help prevent egregious examples of racial profiling. Some even argue that racial and ethnic diversity in the workforce leads television journalists to "pull their punches" when reporting on minority group members.

A COMMERCIAL BIAS?

According to Andrew Kohut, director of the Pew Research Center in Washington, D.C., however, the majority of those responding to Pew Research Center polls see no ideological or partisan pattern in media bias. Rather, what people mean when they say the press is biased in its political reporting is that it is biased toward its own self-interest—the need to gain higher ratings and thus more advertising revenues.

Interestingly, even though Bernard Goldberg, as just mentioned, argues that there is a liberal bias in the media, some of the examples he provides in his book would indicate that the bias in the press is more toward commercialism and elitism. For example, he states that during "sweeps" months (when ratings are important), the networks deliberately avoid featuring blacks, Hispanics, and poor or unattractive people on their prime-time news magazine shows. This, asserts Goldberg, is because such coverage might "turn off" the white, middle-class viewers that the networks want to attract so that they can build the ratings that advertisers want.

During the 2008 election, charges and countercharges flew when Hillary Clinton asserted that Barack Obama was receiving more favorable treatment from the media. As an example, Clinton complained that she was always asked the first question in debates, thus allowing Obama to think about the question and respond in a more thoughtful way. Investigation proved the facts of her allegation. A study by the Center for the Media and Public Policy at George Mason University found that the major networks gave much more positive coverage of Obama than of Clinton. Only the FOX network gave balanced coverage of all the candidates. Interestingly, this study was not reported by the other networks. The coverage of Obama most likely resulted from the fact that the success of his campaign was more newsworthy and that, as the first African American candidate to have a chance at the nomination, he was also more newsworthy as a personality.

You can make a difference

BEING A CRITICAL CONSUMER OF THE NEWS

Television and newspapers provide a wide range of choices for Americans who want to stay informed. Still, critics of the media argue that a substantial amount of programming and print is colored either by the subjectivity of editors and producers or by the demands of profit making. Few Americans take the time to become critical consumers of the news.

WHY SHOULD YOU CARE?

Even if you do not plan to engage in political activism, you have a stake in ensuring that your beliefs are truly your own and that they represent your values and interests. To guarantee this result, you need to obtain accurate information from the media and avoid being swayed by subliminal appeals, loaded terms, or outright bias. If you do not take care, you could find yourself voting for a candidate who is opposed to what you believe in or voting against measures that are in your interest.

Many media outlets are attempting to bridge this serious breach in the public's trust of their coverage with public editors or news ombudsmen. These journalists attempt to address their organization's coverage of hot-button issues that generate complaint from the public and examine ethics implementation, critical errors or omissions, and provide more accessibility to their audience. Dozens of newspapers across the country run regular columns from their public editors that deal with specific grievances or issues of broad public interest regarding coverage in their papers. Public editors may also coordinate public forums or reader advisory boards in an effort to reach out to readers.

WHAT CAN YOU DO?

Some media pundits would argue that you are already advocating for yourselves as media consumers, given the amount of information and access that is readily available on the Internet. In many cases, media blogs, or Web diaries updated daily, provide virtual warehouses of information that pull together stories from different media sources all over the world and allow instant comment from readers to be posted and shared. For example, Romenesko, **www .poynter.org**, is a media blog sponsored by the Poynter Institute (school for journalists) that provides journalists and the public at large with brief commentary about, and links to, the big stories of the day, providing a worldwide platform for critical media consumption and comment. However, you must remember that blogs are primarily focused on finding and linking stories, not verifying the original material, so critically evaluating the stories is even more important. Controversial news reports can be spun by the readers through blogs, not just writers or editorial boards.

Watching the evening news can be far more rewarding if you look at how much the news depends on video effects. You will note that stories on the evening news tend to be no more than three minutes long, that stories with excellent videotape get more attention, and that considerable time is taken up with "happy talk" or human interest stories.

Another way to critically evaluate news coverage is to compare how the news is covered in different media. For example, you might compare the evening news with the daily paper. You will see that the paper is perhaps half a day behind television in reporting the news, but that the printed story contains far more information.

If you wish to obtain more information on the media, you can contact one of the following organizations:

National Association of Broadcasters
1771 N St. N.W.
Washington, DC 20036
202-429-5300
www.nab.org

National Newspaper Association
129 Neff Annex
Columbia, MO 65211
1-800-829-4NNA
www.nna.org

Accuracy in Media (a conservative group)
4455 Connecticut Ave. N.W.
Suite 330
Washington, DC 20008
202-364-4401
www.aim.org

People for the American Way (a liberal group)
2000 M St. N.W., Suite 400
Washington, DC 20036
202-467-4999
www.pfaw.org

REFERENCES

"What is ONO?" *Organization of News Ombudsmen*, www .newsombudsmen.org/what.htm.

Simon Dumenco, "Is the Newspaper Ombudsman More or Less Obsolete?" *Advertising Age*, March 24, 2008.

KEY TERMS

bias 405

electronic media 385

managed news 385

media access 403

narrowcasting 386

podcasting 389

press secretary 398

public agenda 382

sound bite 390

spin 393

spin doctor 393

White House press corps 398

yellow journalism 385

CHAPTER SUMMARY

1. The media are enormously important in American politics today. They perform six main functions, including (1) entertainment, (2) news reporting, (3) identifying public problems, (4) socializing new generations, (5) providing a political forum, and (6) making profits.

2. The media have always played a significant role in American politics. In the 1800s and earlier, however, news traveled slowly, and politics was controlled by small groups whose members communicated personally. The high-speed rotary press and the telegraph led to self-supported newspapers and mass readership.

3. Broadcast media (television and radio) have been important means of communication since the early 20th century. New technologies, such as cable television and the Internet, are giving broadcasters the opportunity to air a greater number of specialized programs.

4. The media wield great power during political campaigns and over the affairs of government and government officials by focusing attention on their actions. Today's political campaigns use political advertising and expert management of news coverage. For presidential candidates, how they appear in presidential debates is of major importance.

5. Today's campaigns rely much more heavily on the Internet to reach potential voters and donors. Candidates and their organizations use e-mail, podcasting, Web sites, blogs, and downloadable video and audio to involve people in campaigns. The use of these techniques does rely heavily on self-selection by the user, but the techniques are cheap and effective.

6. The relationship between the media and the president is close; each uses the other—sometimes positively, sometimes negatively. The media play an important role in investigating the government, in getting government officials to understand better the needs and desires of American society, and in setting the public agenda.

7. The electronic media are subject to government regulation. Many Federal Communications Commission rules have dealt with ownership of TV and radio stations. Legislation has removed many rules about co-ownership of several forms of media, although the most recent steps taken by Congress have been to halt any further deregulation.

8. Studies of bias in the media have reached different conclusions. Some claim that the press has a liberal bias; others contend that the press shows a conservative bias. Still others conclude that the press is biased toward its own self-interest—the need to gain higher ratings and thus more advertising revenues. Other studies have found other types of biases, such as a bias in favor of the status quo or a bias against losers.

SELECTED PRINT AND MEDIA RESOURCES

SUGGESTED READINGS

Alterman, Eric. *What Liberal Media? The Truth about Bias and the News.* New York: Basic Books, 2003. Based on extensive research, Alterman's book argues that the media have a conservative bias overall, especially on economic issues.

Gillmor, Dan. *We the Media: Grassroots Journalism by the People, for the People.* Sebastopol, CA: O'Reilly, 2004. Blogs have become an increasingly important part of the media. In 2004, for the first time, bloggers were awarded press credentials to cover the national political conventions. Newspaper journalist Dan Gillmor, also a blogger, covers the new movement.

Goldberg, Bernard. *Arrogance: Rescuing America from the Media Elite.* New York: Warner, 2003. This is Goldberg's second book in which he argues that the media have a liberal bias and is a follow-up to *Bias: A CBS Insider Exposes How the Media Distort the News.* Goldberg argues that the media elite constitute an inbred, insular group.

Howard, Philip N. *New Media Campaigns and the Managed Citizen.* New York: Cambridge University Press, 2006. In this volume, the author investigated the use of the Internet in campaigns and discussed how targeting voters and controlling the news results in undue influence on voters.

Kuypers, Jim. *Bush's War: Media Bias and Justification for War in a Terrorist Age.* Lanham, MD: Rowman & Littlefield, 2006. This researcher examines how the public understood President George W. Bush's justification of military actions since September 11, 2001, as that information was filtered through the news media. The author contends that the public perception of what the president says is shaped by media bias.

Mark, David. *Going Dirty: The Art of Negative Campaigning.* Lanham, MD: Rowman and Littlefield, 2006. Mark, editor-in-chief of *Campaigns and Elections* magazine, discusses the tactics and successes of negative campaigning.

Tremayne, Mark, ed. *Blogging, Citizenship, and the Future of Media.* Oxford: Routledge, 2006. This collection of essays examines the population's growing dependence on blogs for political information. Some of the essays also look at how blog readers differ from the rest of the population. Finally, the book explores the future of traditional media in light of the blogging phenomenon.

MEDIA RESOURCES

All the President's Men—A film, produced by Warner Brothers in 1976, starring Dustin Hoffman and Robert Redford as the two *Washington Post* reporters (Bob Woodward and Carl Bernstein) who broke the story on the Watergate scandal. The film is an excellent portrayal of the *Washington Post* newsroom and the decisions that editors make in such situations.

Citizen Kane—A 1941 film, based on the life of William Randolph Hearst and directed by Orson Welles, that has been acclaimed as one of the best movies ever made. Welles stars as the newspaper tycoon. The film also stars Joseph Cotten and Alan Ladd.

Leveraging Technology for Your Legislative Campaigns: Effectively Using E-Newsletters, E-Mail Alerts, Podcasts, and Your Web Site—This is a series of audio compact discs and MP3 files created by Robert McLean and TheCapitol.net for Capitol Learning that gives you the ins and outs of how modern campaign managers use blogging and podcasts.

e-mocracy

THE MEDIA AND THE INTERNET

Today, the Internet offers a great opportunity to those who want to access the news. All of the major news organizations, including radio and television stations and newspapers, are online. Most local newspapers include at least some of their news coverage and features on their Web sites, and all national newspapers are online. Even foreign newspapers can now be accessed online within a few seconds. Also available are purely Web-based news publications, including e-zines (online news magazines), such as *Slate, Salon*, and *Hotwired*. Because it is relatively simple for anyone or any organization to put up a home page or Web site, a wide variety of sites have appeared that critique the news media or give alternative interpretations of the news and the way it is presented.

LOGGING ON

- The Web site of the *American Journalism Review* includes features from the magazine and original content created specifically for online reading. Go to:
www.ajr.org
- The *Drudge Report* home page, posted by Matt Drudge, provides a handy guide to the Web's best spots for news and opinions. Its mission is one-click access to breaking news and recent columns. It provides links to specific columnists and opinion pages for magazines and major daily newspapers. Go to:
www.drudgereport.com
- The American Review Web page critiques the media, promotes media activism, and calls for media reform. Its URL is:
www.americanreview.us

- To view *Slate*, the e-zine of politics and culture published by Microsoft, go to:
www.slate.com
- Blogs have become a major feature of the Internet. Many blogs deal with political topics. For a listing of several hundred political blogs, go to the Blog Search Engine at:
www.blogsearchengine.com
- For an Internet site that provides links to news media around the world, including alternative media, go to:
www.mediachannel.org
- To read up-to-date research on the public and its use of the media, go to the Web site of the Pew Center for the People and the Press:
www.people-press.org

If you would like to see any of the famous campaign ads from past presidential campaigns, the easiest way is to go to YouTube or Google and use keywords such as "Daisy ad 1964."

ONLINE REVIEW

At **www.cengage.com/politicalscience/schmidt/agandpt14e**, you will find a Tutorial Quiz for this chapter providing questions on the chapter contents, including the features. The questions are organized to match the major sections of the chapter. You'll have access to other helpful study tools, including the book's glossary and flashcards, crossword puzzles, and Web links, as well as "Which Side Are You On?" and "Politics and . . ." features written by the authors of the book.

Speaker of the U.S. House of
Representatives Nancy Pelosi (D.-Cal.),
the first woman to hold that position,
gavels a joint session of Congress into
session for the State of the Union
Address of President George W. Bush
on Capitol Hill in Washington, D.C.
(Jason Reed/Reuters/Corbis)

THE CONGRESS

Making a DIFFERENCE

KEEPING TABS ON CONGRESS

What if we were to tell you that for every dollar you earned, we were going to take 28 cents and would decide how to spend it?[a] And that we could limit what you see on the Internet? And that our actions would influence how much it cost you to fill up your gas tank? You would probably think that if you gave us all this power, you should pay attention to see if we are making good choices, especially since you have a say in whether we keep our jobs.

Congress has these kinds of powers. Along with the president, Congress sets tax law—including gas taxes—and regulates interstate commerce (the Internet), among many other activities. In fact, in any given week early in the legislative session, at least a hundred bills and resolutions are introduced in the U.S. Senate. How is the average citizen supposed to keep track of all of these pieces of potential legislation, any one of which may have an impact on his or her life? And, as you consider voting for your representative or the challenger, how can you know if your member voted in your best interest?

There are a variety of ways to assess substantive representation, the extent to which an elected official's actions match the interests of his or her constituency. The Congressional Record[b] is the official source of information on everything that has happened in Congress. The Library of Congress provides access to the Congressional Record and provides links to other data, such as congressional committees, government reports, and presidential nominations (**http://thomas.loc.gov**).

A quick perusal of these sites illustrates that in addition to the sheer volume of all the bills introduced, the legislative process is extremely complex. There are 22

MOST AMERICANS VIEW Congress in a less than flattering light. In recent years, Congress has appeared to be deeply split, highly partisan in its conduct, and not very responsive to public needs. Polls show that public approval of the Congress rarely reaches more than 40 percent; many times, approval of the Congress is much less than that of the president. Yet individual members of Congress often receive much higher approval ratings from the voters in their districts. This is one of the paradoxes of the relationship between the people and Congress. Members of the public hold the institution in relatively low regard compared with the satisfaction they express with their individual representatives.

Part of the explanation for these seemingly contradictory appraisals is that members of Congress spend considerable time and effort serving their **constituents**. If the federal bureaucracy makes a mistake, the senator's or representative's office tries to resolve the issue. The members of the Congress spend considerable time and effort developing what is sometimes called a **"homestyle"** to gain the trust and appreciation of their constituents through service, local appearances, and the creation of local offices.

Congress, however, was created to work not just for local constituents but also for the nation as a whole. The representatives and senators in their Washington work are creating what might be called a **"hillstyle,"** which refers to their work on legislation and in party leadership to create laws and policies for our nation.[1] In this chapter, we

Constituent
One of the persons represented by a legislator or other elected or appointed official.

Homestyle
The actions and behaviors of a member of Congress aimed at the constituents and intended to win the support and trust of the voters at home.

Hillstyle
The actions and behaviors of a member of Congress in Washington, D.C., intended to promote policies and the member's own career aspirations.

[1]Richard Fenno, *Home Style: House Members in Their Districts* (Boston: Little, Brown, 1978).

House committees, 20 Senate committees, and four joint committees (where membership is shared between the chambers). These bodies all have subcommittees, where the real work of writing laws and holding hearings occurs.

So how can you keep track of legislation that is important to you? You can become familiar with organizations that are vital to the democratic process by making sense of and tracking legislation. For example, certain nonprofit organizations gather information from advocacy groups, such as those discussed in Chapter 7. These nonprofits examine the groups' preferences on legislation pending before Congress and then compare that with how the members of Congress vote. One nonprofit organization, Voter Information Services, hosts a Web site that allows users to create report cards on members of Congress by choosing from a list of advocacy groups.[c]

A closer examination of these report cards illustrates the differences in how particular groups assess the actions of members of Congress. Take, for example, the votes on which NARAL ProChoice America and the National Right to Life Committee (NRLC) "scores" or records whether the member votes as the group wants. In 2006, Congress debated S. 403, the Child Custody Protection Act. NARAL described it as a bill making it a crime for anyone other than a parent "including a grandparent, adult sibling or religious counselor" to take a "young woman across state lines for abortion care." The NRLC described the

same portion of the bill in very different terms, arguing that "abortion clinics' out-of-state advertising in non-notification states . . . frequently highlights the avoidance of parental notification as a selling point. In other cases, young girls are subjected to tremendous pressure from much older males and others who do not have their best interests at heart."[d] Organizations like Voter Information Services allow you to examine these groups' assessments of members of Congress side-by-side. You can decide which groups' positions best match yours and whose assessments of members of Congress you most trust.

Whether you visit advocacy groups online or use the Congressional Record, journalistic sources such as *Congressional Quarterly* or *The National Journal*, or specialized tracking agencies like GalleryWatch.com or CongressNow.com, the information on what our Congress does is readily available. Our role as citizens is to pay attention.

[a]www.irs.gov/pub/irs-pdf/n1036.pdf
[b]http://thomas.loc.gov/home/r110query.html
[c]www.vis.org/crc/groupsincrc.aspx
[d]www.nrlc.org/Federal/CCPA/CCPASenateLetter092806.html

---

describe the functions of Congress, including constituent service, representation, law-making, and oversight of the government. We review how the members of Congress are elected and how Congress organizes itself when it meets. We also examine how bills pass through the legislative process.

WHY WAS CONGRESS CREATED?

The founders of the American republic believed that the bulk of the power that would be exercised by a national government should be in the hands of the legislature. The leading role envisioned for Congress in the new government is apparent from its primacy in the Constitution. Article I deals with the structure, the powers, and the operation of Congress, beginning in Section 1 with an application of the basic principle of separation of powers: "All legislative Powers herein granted shall be vested in a Congress of the United States, which shall consist of a Senate and House of Representatives." These legislative powers are spelled out in detail in Article I and elsewhere.

The **bicameralism** of Congress—its division into two legislative houses—was in part the result of the Connecticut Compromise, which tried to balance the large-state population advantage, reflected in the House, and the small-state demand for equality in policy making, which was satisfied in the Senate. Beyond that, the two chambers of Congress also reflected the social-class biases of the founders. They wished to balance the interests and the numerical superiority of the common citizens with the property

Bicameralism
The division of a legislature into two separate assemblies.

A **VIEW** of the portico and Capitol dome, Washington, D.C. (Donovan Reese/Photodisc/Getty Images)

interests of the less numerous landowners, bankers, and merchants. They achieved this goal by providing in Sections 2 and 3 of Article I that members of the House of Representatives should be elected directly by "the People," whereas members of the Senate were to be chosen by the elected representatives sitting in state legislatures, who were more likely to be members of the elite. (The latter provision was changed in 1913 by the passage of the Seventeenth Amendment, which provides that senators also are to be elected directly by the people.)

The logic of separate constituencies and separate interests underlying the bicameral Congress was reinforced by differences in length of tenure. Members of the House are required to face the electorate every two years, whereas senators can serve for a much more secure term of six years—even longer than the four-year term provided for the president. Furthermore, the senators' terms are staggered so that only one-third of the senators face the electorate every two years, along with all of the House members.

THE FUNCTIONS OF CONGRESS

The bicameral structure of Congress was designed to enable the legislative body and its members to perform certain functions for the political system. These functions include the following: lawmaking, representation, service to constituents, oversight, public education, and conflict resolution. Of these, the two most important and the ones that are most often in conflict are lawmaking and representation.

THE LAWMAKING FUNCTION

Lawmaking
The process of establishing the legal rules that govern society.

The principal and most obvious function of any legislature is **lawmaking**. Congress is the highest elected body in the country charged with making binding rules for all Americans. Lawmaking requires decisions about the size of the federal budget, about health-care reform and gun control, and about the long-term prospects for war or peace. This does not mean, however, that Congress initiates most of the ideas for legislation that it eventually considers. A majority of the bills that Congress acts on originate in the executive branch, and many other bills are traceable to interest groups and political party organizations. Through the processes of compromise and **logrolling** (offering to support a fellow member's bill in exchange for that member's promise to support your bill in the future), as well as debate and discussion, backers of legislation attempt to fashion a winning majority coalition to create policies for the nation.

Logrolling
An arrangement in which two or more members of Congress agree in advance to support each other's bills.

THE REPRESENTATION FUNCTION

Representation
The function of members of Congress as elected officials representing the views of their constituents.

Representation includes both representing the desires and demands of the constituents in the member's home district or state and representing larger national interests

STATE REPRESENTATIVE Aaron Schock (R.-Ill.), left, greets a voter at a diner in Peoria, Illinois, after winning the Republican primary race for the Congressional nomination. Schock, who was only 26 at the time, became the youngest member of Congress when he won his seat in the November 2008 election. (Seth Perlman/AP Photos)

such as farmers or the environment. Because the interests of constituents in a specific district may be in conflict with the demands of national policy, the representation function is often at variance with the lawmaking function for individual lawmakers and sometimes for Congress as a whole. For example, although it may be in the interest of the nation to reduce defense spending by closing military bases, such closures are not in the interest of the states and districts that will lose jobs and local spending. Every legislator faces votes that set representational issues against lawmaking realities.

How should the legislators fulfill the representation function? There are several views on how this should be accomplished.

DID YOU KNOW?

That fewer than three in 10 people can name the House member from their district, and fewer than half can name even one of the two senators from their state?

The Trustee View of Representation. The first approach to the question of how representation should be achieved is that legislators should act as **trustees** of the broad interests of the entire society. They should vote against the narrow interests of their constituents if their conscience and their perception of national needs so dictate. For example, several Republican legislators have supported strong laws regulating the tobacco industry despite the views of some of their constituents.

Trustee
A legislator who acts according to her or his conscience and the broad interests of the entire society.

The Instructed-Delegate View of Representation. Directly opposed to the trustee view of representation is the notion that the members of Congress should behave as **instructed delegates**; that is, they should mirror the views of the majority of the constituents who elected them to power in the first place. On the surface, this approach is plausible and rewarding. For it to work, however, we must assume that constituents actually have well-formed views on the issues that are decided in Congress and, further, that they have clear-cut preferences about these issues. Neither condition is likely to be satisfied very often.

Instructed Delegate
A legislator who is an agent of the voters who elected him or her and who votes according to the views of constituents regardless of personal beliefs.

Generally, most legislators hold neither a pure trustee view nor a pure instructed-delegate view. Typically, they combine both perspectives in a pragmatic mix that is often called the "politico" style.

SERVICE TO CONSTITUENTS

Individual members of Congress are expected by their constituents to act as brokers between private citizens and the imposing, often faceless federal government. This function of providing service to constituents usually takes the form of **casework**. As noted previously, legislators make choices about their "hillstyle," deciding how much time they and their staff will spend on casework activities, such as tracking down a missing Social Security check, explaining the meaning of particular bills to people who may be affected by them, promoting a local business interest, or interceding with a regulatory agency on behalf of constituents who disagree with proposed agency regulations.

Legislators and many analysts of congressional behavior regard this **ombudsperson** role as an activity that strongly benefits the members of Congress. A government characterized by a large, confusing bureaucracy and complex public programs offers innumerable opportunities for legislators to assist (usually) grateful constituents. Morris P. Fiorina once suggested, somewhat mischievously, that senators and representatives prefer to maintain bureaucratic confusion to maximize their opportunities for performing good deeds on behalf of their constituents:

> Some poor, aggrieved constituent becomes enmeshed in the tentacles of an evil bureaucracy and calls upon Congressman St. George to do battle with the dragon. . . . In dealing with the bureaucracy, the congressman is not merely one vote of 435. Rather, he is a nonpartisan power, someone whose phone call snaps an office to attention. He is not kept on hold. The constituent who receives aid believes that his congressman and his congressman alone got results.[2]

Casework
Personal work for constituents by members of Congress.

Ombudsperson
A person who hears and investigates complaints by private individuals against public officials or agencies.

CONGRESSMAN TIM BISHOP,
Democrat, meets with constituents to discuss measures to help drivers afford gasoline. Bishop was elected to represent New York's First Congressional District in 2002 in one of the closest contests in the nation. In 2004, he was re-elected with 56 percent of the vote. Bishop claimed that he had brought more than $65 million in federal funding to his district in his first term. Does "bringing home the bacon," as this activity is often called, constitute part of a representative's function? (Photo courtesy of Tim Bishop)

[2]Morris P. Fiorina, *Congress: Keystone of the Washington Establishment*, 2nd ed. (New Haven, CT: Yale University Press, 1989), pp. 44, 47.

FORMER GOVERNOR Kathleen Babineaux Blanco, D.-La., and Colonel Jeff Smith, deputy director of the Louisiana Office of Homeland Security and Emergency Preparedness, testify before the House Select Katrina Response Investigation Committee hearing on Louisiana's preparedness and response before, during, and after Hurricane Katrina. How do such investigative hearings impact policies for the future? (Scott J. Ferrell/Congressional Quarterly/Getty Images)

Some members of Congress will go to great lengths to please their constituents. In 2006, for example, when gasoline prices increased to more than $3 per gallon, Senate Republicans argued in favor of sending $100 rebate checks to millions of taxpayers, while Senate Democrats campaigned for a 60-day gasoline tax holiday. The latter plan would have cut the price of gasoline by about 20 cents a gallon. Did members of Congress actually believe that a $100 rebate or a 60-day tax holiday would do anything to reduce high gasoline prices in the long run? Certainly not. In private, members of Congress who supported these schemes admitted that they would have been little more than a gesture. Nevertheless, all members of Congress wanted to show their constituents that they were doing something about the problem.

THE OVERSIGHT FUNCTION

Oversight of the bureaucracy is essential if the decisions made by Congress are to have any force. **Oversight** is the process by which Congress follows up on the laws it has enacted to ensure that they are being enforced and administered in the way Congress intended. This is done by holding committee hearings and investigations, changing the size of an agency's budget, and cross-examining high-level presidential nominees to head major agencies. Sometimes Congress establishes a special commission to investigate a problem. For example, after Hurricane Katrina devastated New Orleans and parts of surrounding states in 2005, Congress created a commission to determine how and why the federal government, particularly the Federal Emergency Management Agency (FEMA), had mishandled government aid both during and after that natural disaster. Sometimes a commission may take several years to complete its work. This was the case with the so-called 9/11 Commission, which investigated why the United States was so unprepared for the terrorist attacks in 2001.

Senators and representatives increasingly see their oversight function as a critically important part of their legislative activities. In part, oversight is related to the concept of constituency service, particularly when Congress investigates alleged arbitrariness or wrongdoing by bureaucratic agencies.

Oversight
The process by which Congress follows up on laws it has enacted to ensure that they are being enforced and administered in the way Congress intended.

THE PUBLIC-EDUCATION FUNCTION

Educating the public is a function that is performed whenever Congress holds public hearings, exercises oversight over the bureaucracy, or engages in committee and floor debate on such major issues and topics as political assassinations, aging, illegal drugs, and the concerns of small businesses. In so doing, Congress presents a range of viewpoints on pressing national questions. In recent years, members of Congress and the committees of Congress have greatly improved access to information through their use of the Internet and Web sites. Congress also decides what issues will come up for discussion and decision; this agenda setting is a major facet of its public-education function.

THE CONFLICT-RESOLUTION FUNCTION

Congress is commonly seen as an institution for resolving conflicts within American society. Organized interest groups and representatives of different racial, religious, economic, and ideological interests look on Congress as an access point for airing their grievances and seeking help. This puts Congress in the position of trying to resolve the differences among competing points of view by passing laws to accommodate as many interested parties as possible. To the extent that Congress meets pluralist expectations in accommodating competing interests, it tends to build support for the entire political process.

THE POWERS OF CONGRESS

The Constitution is both highly specific and extremely vague about the powers that Congress may exercise. The first seventeen clauses of Article I, Section 8, specify most of the **enumerated powers** of Congress—that is, powers expressly given to that body.

Enumerated Power
A power specifically granted to the national government by the Constitution. The first 17 clauses of Article I, Section 8, specify most of the enumerated powers of Congress.

ENUMERATED POWERS

The enumerated, or expressed, powers of Congress include the right to impose taxes and import tariffs; borrow funds; regulate interstate commerce and international trade; establish procedures for naturalizing citizens; make laws regulating bankruptcies; coin (and print) money and regulate its value; establish standards of weights and measures; punish counterfeiters; establish post offices and postal routes; regulate copyrights and patents; establish the federal court system; punish illegal acts on the high seas; declare war; raise and regulate an army and a navy; call up and regulate the state militias to enforce laws, to suppress insurrections, and to repel invasions; and govern the District of Columbia.

The most important of the domestic powers of Congress, listed in Article I, Section 8, are the rights to collect taxes, to spend, and to regulate commerce. The most important foreign policy power is the power to declare war. Other sections of the Constitution allow Congress to establish rules for its own members, to regulate the electoral college, and to override a presidential veto. Congress may also regulate the extent of the Supreme Court's authority to review cases decided by the lower courts, regulate relations among states, and propose amendments to the Constitution.

Powers of the Senate. Some functions are restricted to one chamber. The Senate must advise on, and consent to, the ratification of treaties and must accept or reject presidential nominations of ambassadors, Supreme Court justices, and "all other Officers of the United States." But the Senate may delegate to the president or lesser officials the power to make lower-level appointments. In 2005, President George W. Bush faced two vacancies on the Supreme Court. After Justice Sandra Day O'Connor announced her retirement, President Bush nominated John Roberts to the Court, and the Senate appeared likely to approve the appointment. Then, when the death of Chief Justice William Rehnquist created a second vacancy, President Bush immediately changed Roberts' nomination to that of chief justice, and the Senate approved. When President Bush nominated a relatively inexperienced lawyer, Harriet Miers, however, it quickly became clear that the Senate would not approve her nomination. Therefore, President Bush named an experienced federal appeals court judge, Samuel Alito, who was confirmed.

Constitutional Amendments. Amendments to the Constitution provide for other Congressional powers. Congress must certify the election of a president and a vice president or choose these officers if no candidate has a majority of the electoral vote (Twelfth Amendment). It may levy an income tax (Sixteenth Amendment) and determine who will be acting president in case of the death or incapacity of the president or vice president (Twentieth Amendment and Twenty-fifth Amendment). In addition, Congress explicitly is given the power to enforce, by appropriate legislation, the provisions of several other amendments.

SUPREME COURT nominee Samuel Alito answers questions on the third day of his Senate Judiciary Committee confirmation hearings on Capitol Hill in 2006. Why are some nominees for the Supreme Court rejected by the Senate? (Dennis Cook/AP Photos)

THE NECESSARY AND PROPER CLAUSE

Beyond these numerous specific powers, Congress enjoys the right under Article I, Section 8 (the "elastic" or "necessary and proper" clause), "[t]o make all Laws which shall be necessary and proper for carrying into Execution the foregoing Powers [of Article I], and all other Powers vested by this Constitution in the Government of the United States, or in any Department or Officer thereof." As discussed in Chapter 3, this vague statement of Congressional responsibilities provided, over time, the basis for a greatly expanded national government. It also constituted, at least in theory, a check on the expansion of presidential powers.

CHECKS ON THE CONGRESS

When you consider all of the powers of Congress and its ability to override a presidential veto, there can be no doubt that it is the most powerful branch of government. However, because of the diversity of the United States and the corresponding diverse interests of members of the Congress, rarely is there enough unanimity to override presidential vetoes. So, one check on the Congress is the veto of the president. Another constitutional check is the power of the Supreme Court to hold a law passed by the Congress as unconstitutional. Additionally, the members of the House face election every two years. If the Congress were to exercise too much power in the eyes of the public, it is likely that many members would be voted out of office. And on the other side of Capitol Hill sits the Senate, which often curbs the House by not agreeing with proposals from the "other house."

HOUSE–SENATE DIFFERENCES

Congress is composed of two markedly different—but coequal—chambers. Although the Senate and the House of Representatives exist within the same legislative institution, each has developed certain distinctive features that clearly distinguish one from the other. A summary of these differences is given in Table 12–1.

SIZE AND RULES

The central difference between the House and the Senate is simply that the House is much larger than the Senate. The House has 435 representatives, plus delegates from the District of Columbia, Puerto Rico, Guam, American Samoa, and the Virgin Islands, compared with just 100 senators. This size difference means that a greater number of formal rules are needed to govern activity in the House, whereas correspondingly looser procedures can be followed in the less crowded Senate.

The effect of the difference in size is most obvious in the rules governing debate on the floors of the two chambers. The House operates with an elaborate system to control the agenda and allot time fairly in such a large assembly. For each major bill, the **Rules Committee** normally proposes a **Rule** for debate that includes time limitations for the debate, divides the time between the majority and the minority, and specifies whether amendments can be proposed. The House debates and approves the Rule, which will govern the debate on that specific legislation. As a consequence of its stricter time limits on debate, the House, despite its greater size, often is able to act on legislation more quickly than the Senate.

Rules Committee
A standing committee of the House of Representatives that provides special rules under which specific bills can be debated, amended, and considered by the House.

Rule
The proposal by the Rules Committee of the House that states the conditions for debate for one piece of legislation.

TABLE 12–1 Differences between the House and the Senate

HOUSE*	SENATE*
Constitutional Differences	
Members chosen from local districts	Members chosen from an entire state
Two-year term	Six-year term
Originally elected by voters	Originally (until 1913) elected by state legislatures
May impeach (indict) federal officials	May convict federal officials of impeachable offenses
Process and Culture	
Larger (435 voting members)	Smaller (100 members)
More formal rules	Fewer rules and restrictions
Debate limited	Debate extended
Less prestige and less individual notice	More prestige and more media attention
More partisan	More individualistic
Specific Powers	
Originates bills for raising revenues	Has power to advise the president on, and to consent to, presidential appointments and treaties

*Some of these differences, such as the term of office, are provided for in the Constitution. Others, such as debate rules, are not.

DEBATE AND FILIBUSTERING

In the Senate, the rules governing debate are much less limiting. In fact, for legislation to reach the floor of the Senate, the body must have approved the rules of debate by a **Unanimous Consent Agreement**, which means that the entire body agrees to the rules of debate. The Senate tradition of the **filibuster**, or the use of unlimited debate as a blocking tactic, dates back to 1790. In that year, a proposal to move the U.S. capital from New York to Philadelphia was stalled by such time-wasting maneuvers. This unlimited-debate tradition—which also existed in the House until 1811—is not absolute, however.

In 2005, use of the filibuster became the subject of national debate. Senate Democrats had been using the filibuster for some time to block confirmation votes on many of President Bush's most controversial nominees to the federal courts of appeals. Frustrated by this tactic, Republican senators threatened to utilize what some called the "nuclear option," under which Senate rules would be revised to disallow filibusters against judicial nominees. In the end, though, a bipartisan group engineered a temporary compromise to preserve the filibuster.

Under Senate Rule 22, debate may be ended by invoking *cloture*. Cloture shuts off discussion on a bill. Amended in 1975 and 1979, Rule 22 states that debate may be closed off on a bill if 16 senators sign a petition requesting it and if, after two days have elapsed, three-fifths of the entire membership (60 votes, assuming no vacancies) vote for cloture. After cloture is invoked, each senator may speak on a bill for a maximum of one hour before a vote is taken.

In 1979, the Senate refined Rule 22 to ensure that a final vote must take place within 100 hours of debate after cloture has been imposed. It further limited the use of multiple amendments to stall postcloture final action on a bill.

Unanimous Consent Agreement
An agreement on the rules of debate for proposed legislation in the Senate that is approved by all the members.

Filibuster
The use of the Senate's tradition of unlimited debate as a delaying tactic to block a bill.

ORRIN HATCH, R.-Utah, speaks in the Senate chamber. Hatch chairs the Senate Judiciary Committee. Hatch spoke during the 39th hour of a marathon session organized by Republicans to protest Democratic filibusters. The Democrats were blocking Bush nominees for federal court judgeships. Why might senators seek to block a president's judicial candidates? (AP Photo/APTN)

PRESTIGE

As a consequence of the greater size of the House, representatives generally cannot achieve as much individual recognition and public prestige as can members of the Senate. Senators are better able to gain media exposure and to establish careers as spokespersons for large national constituencies. To obtain recognition for his or her activities, a member of the House generally must do one of two things. He or she might survive in office long enough to join the ranks of the leadership on committees or within the party. Alternatively, the representative could become an expert on some specialized aspect of legislative policy, such as tax laws, the environment, or education.

CONGRESSPERSONS AND THE CITIZENRY: A COMPARISON

Members of the U.S. Senate and the U.S. House of Representatives are not typical American citizens. Members of Congress are older than most Americans, partly because of constitutional age requirements and partly because a good deal of political experience normally is an advantage in running for national office. Members of Congress are also disproportionately white, male, and trained in high-status occupations. Lawyers are by far the largest occupational group among congresspersons, although the proportion of lawyers in the House is lower now than it was in the past. Compared with the average American citizen, members of Congress are well paid. In 2008, annual congressional salaries were $169,300. Increasingly, members of Congress are also much wealthier than the average citizen. Whereas less than 1 percent of Americans have assets exceeding $1 million, about one-third of the members of Congress are millionaires. Table 12–2 summarizes selected characteristics of the members of Congress.

Compared with the composition of Congress over the past 200 years, however, the House and Senate today are significantly more diverse in gender and ethnicity than ever before. There are 74 women in the House of Representatives (17 percent) and 17 women in the U.S. Senate (17 percent). Minority group members fill over 15 percent of the seats in the House. The 111th Congress has significant numbers of members born in 1946 or later, the so-called Baby Boomers. A majority of House members and an even larger minority of the Senate belong to this postwar generation. This shift in the character of Congress may prompt consideration of the issues that will affect the Boomers, such as Social Security and Medicare.

CONGRESSIONAL ELECTIONS

The process of electing members of Congress is decentralized. Congressional elections are conducted by the individual state governments. The states, however, must conform to the rules established by the U.S. Constitution and by national statutes. The Constitution states that representatives are to be elected every second year by popular ballot, and the number of seats awarded to each state is to be determined every 10 years by the results of the census. It is important to note that the decennial census is viewed as crucial by members of Congress and by the states. If the census is not accurate, perhaps recording an undercount of individuals living in a state, then that

TABLE 12–2 Characteristics of the 110th Congress, 2007–2008

CHARACTERISTIC	U.S. POPULATION (2000)*	HOUSE	SENATE
Age (median)	35.3	56.0	61.9
Percentage minority	24.9	15.9	5
Religion			
Percentage church members	61.0	90.6	99
Percentage Roman Catholic	39.0	29.4	24
Percentage Protestant	56.0	55.6	56
Percentage Jewish	4.0	6.7	13
Percentage female	50.9	16.1	16
Percentage with advanced degrees	5.0	66.7	78
Occupation			
Percentage lawyers	0.4	38.4	58
Percentage blue-collar workers	20.1	1.6	3
Income			
Percentage of families earning more than $50,000 annually	22.0	100.0	100
Percentage with assets over $1 million**	0.7	16.0	33

Source: Congressional Quarterly.
*Estimates based on 2000 census.
**108th Congress.

state might lose a representative in Congress. Each state has at least one representative, with most congressional districts having about half a million residents. Senators are elected by popular vote (since the passage of the Seventeenth Amendment) every six years; approximately one-third of the seats are chosen every two years. Each state has two senators. Under Article I, Section 4, of the Constitution, state legislatures are given control over "[t]he Times, Places and Manner of holding Elections for Senators and Representatives"; however, "the Congress may at any time by Law make or alter such Regulations."

Only states can elect members of Congress. Therefore, territories such as Puerto Rico and Guam are not represented, though they do elect nonvoting delegates who sit in the House. The District of Columbia is also represented only by a nonvoting delegate. The District is not represented in the Senate at all. There have been several proposals to give D.C. voting representation in Congress. In 1978, Congress approved a constitutional amendment to give the District the representation it would have if it were a state, including two senators. The amendment was not ratified, however. More recently, District citizens have campaigned to make D.C. a state. New states can be admitted to the union without amending the Constitution. Another proposal is to allow District citizens to vote either with Maryland or Virginia, as they did in the 18th century. However, this solution would not give the citizens of the District the attention they believe is necessary to meet their interests. Democrats in Congress have generally supported more representation for the District because the majority of its citizens are African American and vote overwhelmingly Democratic. Republicans are generally not supportive of giving voting powers to D.C.'s representative.

CANDIDATES FOR CONGRESSIONAL ELECTIONS

Candidates for House and Senate seats may be self-selected. The qualifications for the two houses do differ: Members of the House must be at least 25 years old, a citizen for seven years, and live in the state they will represent, whereas senators must be 30 years old, a citizen for nine years, and a resident of the state they represent. In Congressional districts where one party is very strong, however, there may be a shortage of candidates willing to represent the weaker party. In such circumstances, leaders of the weaker party must often actively recruit candidates. Candidates may resemble the voters of the district in ethnicity or religion, but they are also likely to be very successful individuals who have been active in politics before. House candidates are especially likely to have local ties to their districts. Candidates usually choose to run because they believe they would enjoy the job and its accompanying status. They also may be thinking of a House seat as a stepping-stone to future political office as a senator, governor, or president. Individuals who seek Senate seats may also have plans to run for governor in their home state or be considering a run for the presidency.

Direct Primary
An intraparty election in which the voters select the candidates who will run on a party's ticket in the subsequent general election.

Party Identifier
A person who identifies with a political party.

Congressional Campaigns and Elections. Congressional campaigns have changed considerably in the past two decades. Like all other campaigns, they are much more expensive, with the average cost of a winning Senate campaign now $7.1 million and a winning House campaign averaging more than $1.1 million. Campaign funds include direct contributions by individuals, contributions by political action committees (PACs), and "soft money" funneled through state party committees. As you read in Chapter 10, all of these contributions are regulated by laws, including the Federal Election Campaign Act of 1971, as amended, and most recently the Bipartisan Campaign Reform Act of 2002. Once in office, legislators spend time almost every day raising funds for their next campaign.

Most candidates for Congress must win the nomination through a **direct primary**, in which **party identifiers** vote for the candidate who will be on the party ticket in the general election. To win the primary, candidates may take more liberal or more conservative positions to get the votes of party identifiers. In the general election, they may moderate their views to attract the votes of independents and voters from the other party.

DRESSED AS GEORGE WASHINGTON, a demonstrator protests the District of Columbia's lack of Congressional representation at a rally for the D.C. delegates to the Democratic National Convention. The delegates are gathered at Union Station in Washington before a train trip to Boston. Why do you think the two major parties grant the District representation at their national conventions? (AP Photo/Lauren Burke)

Presidential Effects. Congressional candidates are always hopeful that a strong presidential candidate on the ticket will have "coattails" that will sweep in senators and representatives of the same party. In fact, coattail effects have been quite limited, and in recent presidential elections have not materialized at all. One way to measure the coattail effect is to look at the subsequent midterm elections, held in the even-numbered years following the presidential contests. In these years, voter turnout falls sharply. In the past, the party controlling the White House normally lost seats in Congress in the midterm elections, in part because the coattail effect ceased to apply. Members

of Congress who were from contested districts or who were in their first term were more likely not to be reelected.

Table 12–3 shows the pattern for midterm elections since 1942. The president's party lost seats in every election from 1942 to 1998. In that year, with President Bill Clinton under the threat of impeachment, voters showed their displeasure with the Republicans by voting in five more Democrats. In 2002, Republicans bucked the normal slump by winning five more Republican seats in the House. Most commentators believed that these midterm victories were based on public support for the president after the September 11 attacks. In 2006, the Republicans suffered a fairly normal midterm defeat, comparable to the midterm defeat in 1958, the sixth year of the Eisenhower presidency.

THE POWER OF INCUMBENCY

The power of incumbency in the outcome of Congressional elections cannot be overemphasized. Once members are elected and survive the second election, they build up considerable loyalty among their constituents, and they are frequently reelected as long as they wish to serve. Table 12–4 shows that more than 90 percent of representatives and a slightly smaller proportion of senators who decide to run for re-election are successful. This conclusion holds for both presidential-year and midterm elections. Several scholars contend that the pursuit of re-election is the strongest motivation behind the activities of members of Congress. The re-election goal is pursued in several ways. Incumbents develop their homestyle, using the mass media, making personal appearances with constituents, and sending newsletters—all to produce a favorable image and to make the incumbent's name a household word. Members of Congress generally try to present themselves as informed, experienced, and responsive to people's needs. Legislators also can point to things that they have done to benefit their constituents—by fulfilling the congressional casework function or by bringing money for mass transit to the district, for example. Finally, incumbents can demonstrate the positions that they have taken on key issues by referring to their voting records in Congress.

PARTY CONTROL OF CONGRESS AFTER THE 2008 ELECTIONS

The Democratic Party gained control of both the House and the Senate in 2006. In the 2008 elections, Democrats gained six seats in the Senate and close to 30 seats in the House of Representatives. With a margin of 58 Democrats to 40 Republicans and two Independents, the Democratic majority in the Senate approached the magic number of 60 votes, which would cut off filibusters. This means that on crucial votes, the majority has enough votes to overcome any obstructionist tactics used by the minority party. However, some Democratic senators are fairly moderate and do not necessarily vote with the majority all of the time. In the House of Representatives, the Democratic majority already had fairly tight control of the institution. With their new margin of about 255 Democrats to 173 Republicans, the majority will rarely need any Republican

TABLE 12–3 Midterm Gains and Losses by the Party of the President, 1942 to 2006

SEATS GAINED OR LOST BY THE PARTY OF THE PRESIDENT IN THE HOUSE OF REPRESENTATIVES	
1942	–45 (D.)
1946	–55 (D.)
1950	–29 (D.)
1954	–18 (R.)
1958	–47 (R.)
1962	–4 (D.)
1966	–47 (D.)
1970	–12 (R.)
1974	–48 (R.)
1978	–15 (D.)
1982	–26 (R.)
1986	–5 (R.)
1990	–8 (R.)
1994	–52 (D.)
1998	+5 (D.)
2002	+5 (R.)
2006	–30 (R.)

DID YOU KNOW?

That 2004 was the first time since 1866 that Republicans increased their majority in the House of Representatives in two consecutive elections?

TABLE 12–4 The Power of Incumbency

	ELECTION YEAR														
	1980	1982	1984	1986	1988	1990	1992	1994	1996	1998	2000	2002	2004	2006	2008*
HOUSE															
Number of incumbent candidates	398	393	411	394	409	406	368	387	384	402	403	393	404	405	389
Re-elected	361	354	392	385	402	390	325	349	361	395	394	383	397	382	372
Percentage of total	90.7	90.1	95.4	97.7	98.3	96.0	88.3	90.2	94.0	98.3	97.8	97.5	98.3	94.3	95.6
Defeated	37	39	19	9	7	16	43	38	23	7	9	10	7	23	17
In primary	6	10	3	3	1	1	19	4	2	1	3	3	1	2	3
In general election	31	29	16	6	6	15	24	34	21	6	6	7	6	21	17
SENATE															
Number of incumbent candidates	29	30	29	28	27	32	28	26	21	29	29	28	26	29	32
Re-elected	16	28	26	21	23	31	23	24	19	26	23	24	25	23	23
Percentage of total	55.2	93.3	89.6	75.0	85.2	96.9	82.1	92.3	90.5	89.7	79.3	85.7	96.2	79.3	81.3
Defeated	13	2	3	7	4	1	5	2	2	3	6	4	1	6	3
In primary	4	0	0	0	0	0	1	0	1	0	0	1	0	1*	0
In general election	9	2	3	7	4	1	4	2	1	3	6	3	1	6	3

*Joe Lieberman of Connecticut lost the Democratic primary but won the general election as an independent. He chose to organize with the Senate Democrats.
Sources: Norman Ornstein, Thomas E. Mann, and Michael J. Malbin, *Vital Statistics on Congress, 2001–2002* (Washington, DC: The AEI Press, 2002); and authors' update.

seats to pass legislation. In addition, the ratio of Democrats to Republicans on all of the standing committees will greatly enhance the influence of the Democratic majority in formulating legislation.

CONGRESSIONAL APPORTIONMENT

Reapportionment
The allocation of seats in the House of Representatives to each state after each census.

Redistricting
The redrawing of the boundaries of the congressional districts within each state.

Justiciable Question
A question that may be raised and reviewed in court.

Two of the most complicated aspects of congressional elections are apportionment issues—**reapportionment** (the allocation of seats in the House to each state after each census) and **redistricting** (the redrawing of the boundaries of the districts within each state). In a landmark six-to-two vote in 1962, the United States Supreme Court made the apportionment of state legislative districts a **justiciable** (that is, a reviewable) **question**.[3] The Court did so by invoking the Fourteenth Amendment principle that no state can deny to any person "the equal protection of the laws." In 1964, the Court held that *both* chambers of a state legislature must be apportioned so that all districts are equal in population.[4] Later that year, the Court applied this "one person,

[3]*Baker v. Carr*, 369 U.S. 186 (1962). The term *justiciable* is pronounced "juhs-tish-a-buhl."
[4]*Reynolds v. Sims*, 377 U.S. 533 (1964).

one vote" principle to U.S. Congressional districts on the basis of Article I, Section 2, of the Constitution, which requires that members of the House be chosen "by the People of the several States."[5]

Severe malapportionment of Congressional districts before 1964 resulted in some districts containing two or three times the populations of other districts in the same state, thereby diluting the effect of a vote cast in the more populous districts. This system generally benefited the conservative populations of rural areas and small towns and harmed the interests of the more heavily populated and liberal cities. In fact, suburban areas have benefited the most from the Court's rulings, as suburbs account for an increasingly larger proportion of the nation's population, while cities include a correspondingly smaller segment of the population.

GERRYMANDERING

Although the general issue of apportionment has been dealt with fairly successfully by the one person, one vote principle, the **gerrymandering** issue has not yet been resolved. This term refers to the legislative boundary-drawing tactics that were used under Elbridge Gerry, the governor of Massachusetts, in the 1812 elections (see Figure 12–1). A district is said to have been gerrymandered when its shape is altered substantially by the dominant party in a state legislature to maximize its electoral strength at the expense of the minority party.

Gerrymandering
The drawing of legislative district boundary lines to obtain partisan or factional advantage. A district is said to be gerrymandered when its shape is manipulated by the dominant party in the state legislature to maximize electoral strength at the expense of the minority party.

FIGURE 12–1 The Original Gerrymander

The practice of "gerrymandering"—the excessive manipulation of the shape of a legislative district to benefit a certain incumbent or party—is probably as old as the Republic, but the name originated in 1812. In that year, the Massachusetts legislature carved out of Essex County a district that historian John Fiske said has a "dragonlike contour." When the painter Gilbert Stuart saw the misshapen district, he penciled in a head, wings, and claws and exclaimed, "That will do for a salamander!" Editor Benjamin Russell replied, "Better say a Gerrymander" (after Elbridge Gerry, then-governor of Massachusetts).

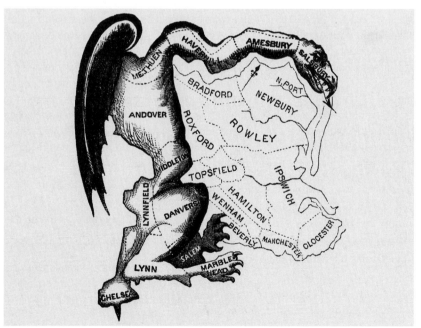

Source: *Congressional Quarterly's Guide to Congress*, 3rd ed. (Washington, DC: Congressional Quarterly Press, 1982), p. 695.

[5]*Wesberry v. Sanders*, 376 U.S. 1 (1964).

WHAT IF...

NONPARTISAN PANELS DREW CONGRESSIONAL DISTRICTS?

In almost all states, district lines are drawn by a small group of party leaders in the state legislature. Whichever party controls the process in a specific state attempts to arrange Congressional districts so that most districts are "safe seats," where an incumbent has an almost a 100 percent chance of being re-elected. Consider that in the 2004 elections, only 23 of the 435 Congressional districts were decided by 10 percentage points or fewer.

Such lack of competition is not surprising, given that in most states during 2001, sophisticated computer modeling was used to create new districts that would be "safe seats." In response to such blatant partisan redistricting, California governor Arnold Schwarzenegger and others have proposed that the responsibility for redrawing Congressional district lines be taken away from politicians and given to a panel of nonpartisan retired judges.

WHAT IF REDRAWING DISTRICTS WAS TRULY NONPARTISAN?

If nonpartisan panels or state commissions were used to draw Congressional districts every 10 years, an immediate question would be, who should be the members? As mentioned previously, some politicians have suggested retired judges. Other possible participants might be current or retired law professors, political scientists teaching at major universities, or some combination of these.

Above all, the members of the panels or commissions would have to be nonpartisan. In other words, panel participants could receive no benefit from the outcome of the redistricting. Perhaps prospective panel members would have to declare that they favored neither Republicans nor Democrats. Alternatively, a panel could consist of an equal number of declared Democrats and Republicans who are dedicated to drawing nonpartisan districts.

NONPARTISAN PANELS ALREADY EXIST

Nonpartisan boards for redistricting already exist in Britain and Canada, where they apparently have been highly successful. The boundaries are universally respected, and the legislative seats are often more competitive than in the United States. Some states, such as Arizona, Iowa, and Minnesota, already use nonpartisan redistricting, employing a panel of retired judges to draw district lines. Many who live in those states claim that the districts are more competitive than those in other states. If you look at the map of Iowa districts, for example, in Figure 12–2, you will see that the districts lack the strange wiggles and odd shapes of gerrymandered districts in other states.

IMPLICATIONS OF MORE COMPETITIVE CONGRESSIONAL ELECTIONS

Assuming that nonpartisan panels were able to redistrict in an unbiased way, the result would be more competitive Congressional races. One consequence might be increased spending by challengers because the probability of a challenger winning would be greater. The makeup of Congress would also change. Fewer members would remain in the House of Representatives for decades. Hence, there would be more turnover in the powerful committee chairs. In other words, there would be fewer old-timers holding the reins of power in Congress and the House of Representatives. On the one hand, having many newcomers in power could bring new ideas, but on the other hand, more turnover could result in the loss of many experienced members.

FOR CRITICAL ANALYSIS

1. What types of people do you think would be the most unbiased participants in a redistricting panel or commission? Why?
2. Some argue that less politically homogeneous districts might result in divisive elections. Do you believe this might be a problem? Why or why not?

FIGURE 12–2 Congressional Districts of Iowa

Iowa's five Congressional districts are drawn by a nonpartisan commission. As you can see, the districts are compact, easily understood by the voters, and relate to the geography of the state.

Congressional Districts
1 2 3 4 5

Congressional District Map of Iowa

MILES
0 10 20 30 40 50 60
Albers equal area projection

In 1986, the Supreme Court heard a case that challenged gerrymandered congressional districts in Indiana. The Court ruled for the first time that redistricting for the political benefit of one group could be challenged on constitutional grounds. In this specific case, *Davis v. Bandemer*,[6] however, the Court did not agree that the districts were drawn unfairly, because it could not be proved that a group of voters would consistently be deprived of influence at the polls as a result of the new districts.

[6]478 U.S. 109 (1986).

REDISTRICTING AFTER THE 2000 CENSUS

In the meantime, political gerrymandering continues. For example, New York Democratic Representative Maurice Hinchey's district resembles a soup ladle. Why? That shape guarantees that he will always be able to pick up enough votes in Ithaca and Binghamton to win re-election. Right next to that district is Republican Representative Sherwood Boehlert's district, which has been said to resemble a "napping Bugs Bunny."

Redistricting decisions are often made by a small group of political leaders within a state legislature. Typically, their goal is to shape voting districts in such a way as to maximize their party's chances of winning state legislative seats as well as seats in Congress. Two of the techniques they use are called "packing" and "cracking." With the use of powerful computers and software, they *pack* voters supporting the opposing party into as few districts as possible or *crack* the opposing party's supporters into different districts. Consider that in Michigan, the Republicans who dominated redistricting efforts succeeded in packing six Democratic incumbents into only three congressional seats.

Clearly, partisan redistricting aids incumbents. The party that dominates a state's legislature will be making redistricting decisions. Through gerrymandering tactics such as packing and cracking, districts can be redrawn in such a way as to ensure that party's continued strength in the state legislature or Congress. As pointed out before, some have estimated that only between 30 and 50 of the 435 seats in the House of Representatives were open for any real competition in the most recent elections.

In 2004, the United States Supreme Court reviewed an obviously political redistricting scheme in Pennsylvania. The Court concluded, however, that the federal judiciary would not address purely political gerrymandering claims.[7] Two years later, the Supreme Court reached a similar conclusion with respect to most of the new Congressional districts created by the Republicans in the Texas legislature in 2003. Again, except for one district in Texas, the Court refused to intervene in what was clearly a political gerrymandering plan.[8]

"MINORITY-MAJORITY" DISTRICTS

In the early 1990s, the federal government encouraged a type of gerrymandering that made possible the election of a minority representative from a "minority-majority" area. Under the mandate of the Voting Rights Act of 1965, the Justice Department issued directives to states after the 1990 census instructing them to create Congressional districts that would maximize the voting power of minority groups—that is, create districts in which minority voters were the majority. The result was several creatively drawn Congressional districts—see, for example, the depiction of Illinois's Fourth Congressional District in Figure 12–3, which is commonly described as "a pair of earmuffs."

CONSTITUTIONAL CHALLENGES

Many of these "minority-majority" districts were challenged in court by citizens who claimed that creating districts based on race or ethnicity alone violates the equal protection clause of the Constitution. In 1995, the Supreme Court agreed with this argument when it declared that Georgia's new Eleventh District was unconstitutional. The district stretched from Atlanta to the Atlantic, splitting eight counties and five munici-

[7]*Vieth v. Jubelirer*, 541 U.S. 267 (2004).
[8]*League of United Latin American Citizens v. Perry*, 399 F.Supp. 2d 756 (2006).

FIGURE 12–3 The Fourth Congressional District of Illinois

This district, which is mostly within Chicago's city limits, was drawn to connect two Hispanic neighborhoods separated by an African American majority district.

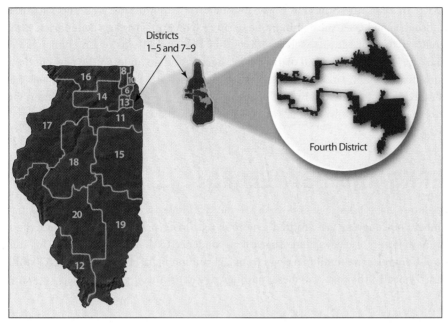

Source: *The New York Times*, July 15, 2001, p. 16.

palities along the way. The Court referred to the district as a "monstrosity" linking "widely spaced urban centers that have absolutely nothing to do with each other." The Court went on to say that when a state assigns voters on the basis of race, "it engages in the offensive and demeaning assumption that voters of a particular race, because of their race, think alike, share the same political interests, and will prefer the same candidates at the polls." The Court also chastised the Justice Department for concluding that race-based districting was mandated under the Voting Rights Act of 1965: "When the Justice Department's interpretation of the Act compels race-based districting, it by definition raises a serious constitutional question."[9] In subsequent rulings, the Court affirmed its position that when race is the dominant factor in the drawing of Congressional district lines, the districts are unconstitutional.

CHANGING DIRECTIONS

In the early 2000s, the Supreme Court seemed to take a new direction on racial redistricting challenges. In a 2000 case, the Court limited the federal government's authority to invalidate changes in state and local elections on the basis that the changes were discriminatory. The case involved a proposed school redistricting plan in Louisiana. The Court held that federal approval for the plan could not be withheld simply because the plan was discriminatory. Rather, the test was whether the plan left racial and ethnic minorities worse off than they were before.[10]

DID YOU KNOW?

That before the Republicans reorganized House services in 1995, all members had buckets of ice delivered to their offices each day, at an annual cost of $500,000?

[9]*Miller v. Johnson*, 515 U.S. 900 (1995).
[10]*Reno v. Bossier Parish School Board*, 528 U.S. 320 (2000).

In 2001, the Supreme Court reviewed, for a second time, a case involving North Carolina's Twelfth District. The district was 165 miles long, following Interstate 85 for the most part. According to a local joke, the district was so narrow that a car traveling down the interstate highway with both doors open would kill most of the voters in the district. In 1996, the Supreme Court had held that the district was unconstitutional because race had been the dominant factor in drawing the district's boundaries. Shortly thereafter, the boundaries were redrawn, but the district was again challenged as a racial gerrymander. A federal district court agreed and invalidated the new boundaries as unconstitutional. In 2001, however, the Supreme Court held that there was insufficient evidence for the lower court's conclusion that race had been the dominant factor when the boundaries were redrawn.[11] The Twelfth District's boundaries remained as drawn.

PERKS AND PRIVILEGES

Legislators have many benefits that are not available to most workers. For example, members of Congress are granted generous **franking** privileges that permit them to mail newsletters, surveys, and other correspondence to their constituents. The annual cost of Congressional mail has risen from $11 million in 1971 to more than $70 million today. Typically, the costs for these mailings rise substantially during election years.

PERMANENT PROFESSIONAL STAFFS

More than 30,000 people are employed in the Capitol Hill bureaucracy. About half of them are personal and committee staff members. The personal staff includes office clerks and secretaries; professionals who deal with media relations, draft legislation, and satisfy constituency requests for service; and staffers who maintain local offices in the member's home district or state.

The average Senate office on Capitol Hill employs about 30 staff members, and twice that number work on the personal staffs of senators from the most populous states. House office staffs typically are about half as large as those of the Senate. The number of staff members has increased dramatically since 1960. With the bulk of those increases coming in assistants to individual members, some scholars question whether staff members are really advising on legislation or are primarily aiding constituents and gaining votes in the next election.

Congress also benefits from the expertise of the professional staffs of agencies that were created to produce information for members of the House and Senate. For example, the Congressional Research Service, the Government Accountability Office, and the Congressional Budget Office all provide reports, audits, and policy recommendations for review by members of Congress.

PRIVILEGES AND IMMUNITIES UNDER THE LAW

Members of Congress also benefit from some special constitutional protections. Under Article I, Section 6, of the Constitution, they "shall in all Cases, except Treason, Felony and Breach of the Peace, be privileged from Arrest during their Attendance at the Session of their respective Houses, and in going to and returning from the same; and for any Speech or Debate in either House, they shall not be questioned in any other Place." The arrest immunity clause is not really an important provision today. The "speech or debate" clause, however, means that a member may make any allegations or other

---

[11]*Easley v. Cromartie*, 532 U.S. 234 (2001).

statements he or she wishes in connection with official duties and normally not be sued for libel or slander or otherwise be subject to legal action.

CONGRESSIONAL CAUCUSES: ANOTHER SOURCE OF SUPPORT

All members of Congress are members of one or more caucuses. The most important caucuses are those established by the parties in each chamber. These Democratic and Republican meetings provide information to the members and devise legislative strategy for the party. Other caucuses have been founded, such as the Democratic Study Group and the Congressional Black Caucus, to support subgroups of members. In 1995, concerned with the growth of caucuses supported by public funds, the Republican majority in the House passed a rule that prohibited using free space for caucuses or using public funds to finance them.

The number of caucuses has not declined, however. Instead, the number has increased. There are now more than two hundred caucuses, including small ones (the Albanian Issues Caucus, the Potato Caucus) and large ones (the Sportsmen's Caucus). These organizations, which are now funded by businesses and special interests, provide staff assistance and information for members of Congress, and help them build support among specific groups of voters.

RETIRED NORTH CAROLINA Supreme Court Chief Justice Henry Frye (left) swears in members of the Congressional Black Caucus of the 109th Congress on January 4, 2005. The Congressional Black Caucus has been an effective influence within Congress for several decades. (Alex Wong/Getty Images)

THE COMMITTEE STRUCTURE

Most of the actual work of legislating is performed by the committees and subcommittees within Congress. Thousands of bills are introduced in every session of Congress,

and no single member can possibly be adequately informed on all the issues that arise. The committee system is a way to provide for specialization, or a division of the legislative labor. Members of a committee can concentrate on just one area or topic—such as taxation or energy—and develop sufficient expertise to draft appropriate legislation when needed. The flow of legislation through both the House and the Senate is determined largely by the speed with which the members of these committees act on bills and resolutions.

THE POWER OF COMMITTEES

Sometimes called "little legislatures," committees usually have the final say on pieces of legislation.[12] Committee actions may be overturned on the floor by the House or Senate, but this rarely happens. Legislators normally defer to the expertise of the chairperson and other members of the committee who speak on the floor in defense of a committee decision. Chairpersons of committees exercise control over the scheduling of hearings and formal action on a bill. They also decide which subcommittee will act on legislation falling within their committee's jurisdiction.

Committees only very rarely are deprived of control over a bill—although this kind of action is provided for in the rules of each chamber. In the House, if a bill has been considered by a standing committee for 30 days, the signatures of a majority (218) of the House membership on a **discharge petition** can pry a bill out of an uncooperative committee's hands. From 1909 to 2007, however, although more than 900 such petitions were initiated, only slightly more than two dozen resulted in successful discharge efforts. Of those, 20 resulted in bills that passed the House.[13]

Discharge Petition
A procedure by which a bill in the House of Representatives may be forced (discharged) out of a committee that has refused to report it for consideration by the House. The petition must be signed by an absolute majority (218) of representatives and is used only on rare occasions.

TYPES OF CONGRESSIONAL COMMITTEES

Over the past two centuries, Congress has created several different types of committees, each of which serves particular needs of the institution.

Standing Committees. By far the most important committees in Congress are the **standing committees**—permanent bodies that are established by the rules of each chamber of Congress and that continue from session to session. A list of the standing committees of the 111th Congress is presented in Table 12–5. In addition, most of the standing committees have created subcommittees to carry out their work. For example, in the 110th Congress, there were 68 subcommittees in the Senate and 88 in the House.[14] Each standing committee is given a specific area of legislative policy jurisdiction, and almost all legislative measures are considered by the appropriate standing committees.

Standing Committee
A permanent committee in the House or Senate that considers bills within a certain subject area.

Because of the importance of their work and the traditional influence of their members in Congress, certain committees are considered to be more prestigious than others. Seats on standing committees that handle spending issues are especially sought after because members can use these positions to benefit their constituents. Committees that control spending include the Appropriations Committee in either chamber and the Ways and Means Committee in the House. Members also normally seek seats on committees that handle matters of special interest to their constituents. A member of the House from an agricultural district, for example, will have an interest in joining the House Agriculture Committee.

DID YOU KNOW?

That Samuel Morse demonstrated his telegraph to Congress in 1843 by stretching wire between two committee rooms?

---

[12]The term *little legislatures* is from Woodrow Wilson, *Congressional Government* (New York: Meridian Books, 1956 [first published in 1885]).

[13]Congressional Quarterly, Inc., *Guide to Congress,* 5th ed. (Washington, DC: CQ Press, 2000); and authors' update.

[14]*Congressional Directory* (Washington, DC: U.S. Government Printing Office, various editions).

TABLE 12–5
Standing Committees of the 111th Congress, 2009–2011

HOUSE COMMITTEES	SENATE COMMITTEES
Agriculture	Agriculture, Nutrition, and Forestry
Appropriations	Appropriations
Armed Services	Armed Services
Budget	Banking, Housing, and Urban Affairs
Education and the Workforce	Budget
Energy and Commerce	Commerce, Science, and Transportation
Financial Services	Energy and Natural Resources
Government Reform	Environment and Public Works
Homeland Security	Finance
House Administration	Foreign Relations
International Relations	Governmental Affairs
Judiciary	Health, Education, Labor, and Pensions
Resources	Judiciary
Rules	Rules and Administration
Science	Small Business and Entrepreneurship
Small Business	Veterans Affairs
Standards of Official Conduct	
Transportation and Infrastructure	
Veterans Affairs	
Ways and Means	

Select Committees. In principle, a **select committee** is created for a limited time and for a specific legislative purpose. For example, a select committee may be formed to investigate a public problem, such as child nutrition or aging. In practice, a select committee, such as the Select Committee on Intelligence in each chamber, may continue indefinitely. Select committees rarely create original legislation.

Select Committee
A temporary legislative committee established for a limited time period and for a special purpose.

Joint Committees. A **joint committee** is formed by the concurrent action of both chambers of Congress and consists of members from each chamber. Joint committees, which may be permanent or temporary, have dealt with the economy, taxation, and the Library of Congress.

Joint Committee
A legislative committee composed of members from both chambers of Congress.

Conference Committees. Special joint committees—**conference committees**—are formed to achieve agreement between the House and the Senate on the exact wording of legislative acts when the two chambers pass legislative proposals in different forms. The bill is reported out of the conference committee if it is approved by the majority of members from both houses who sit on the committee. It is then returned to the House and Senate for final votes. No bill can be sent to the White House to be signed into law unless it first passes both chambers in identical form. Sometimes called the "third house" of Congress, conference committees are in a position to make significant alterations to legislation and frequently become the focal point of policy debates.

Conference Committee
A special joint committee appointed to reconcile differences when bills pass the two chambers of Congress in different forms.

The House Rules Committee. Because of its special "gatekeeping" power over the terms on which legislation will reach the floor of the House of Representatives, the House Rules

U.S. ASSISTANT SECRETARY OF STATE for Intelligence and Research Randall Fort, Federal Bureau of Investigation Director Robert Mueller, Director of National Intelligence Mike McConnell, Central Intelligence Agency Director Michael Hayden, and Defense Intelligence Agency Director Lieutenant General Michael Maples attend a hearing before the Senate (Select) Intelligence Committee on February 5, 2008. The Committee held the hearing to assess threats and challenges the nation is facing. No matter how important the federal official, they are often called to Capitol Hill. (Alex Wong/Getty Images)

Committee holds a uniquely powerful position. A special committee rule sets the time limit on debate and determines whether and how a bill may be amended. This practice dates back to 1883. The Rules Committee has the unusual power to meet while the House is in session, to have its resolutions considered immediately on the floor, and to initiate legislation on its own.

THE SELECTION OF COMMITTEE MEMBERS

In both chambers, members are appointed to standing committees by the Steering Committee of their party. The majority-party member with the longest term of continuous service on a standing committee can be given preference when the leadership nominates chairpersons. Newt Gingrich, during his time as Speaker in the House, restricted chairpersons' terms to six years. Additionally, he bypassed seniority to appoint chairpersons loyal to his own platform.

Seniority System
A custom followed in both chambers of Congress specifying that the member of the majority party with the longest term of continuous service will be given preference when a committee chairperson (or a holder of some other significant post) is selected.

Respecting seniority is an informal, traditional process, and it applies to other significant posts in Congress as well. The **seniority system**, although it deliberately treats members unequally, provides a predictable means of assigning positions of power within Congress. The most senior member of the minority party is called the *ranking committee member* for that party.

The general pattern until the 1970s was that members of the House or Senate who represented **safe seats** would be reelected continually and eventually would accumulate enough years of continuous committee service to enable them to become the chairpersons of their committees. In the 1970s, a number of reforms in the chairperson selection process somewhat modified the seniority system. The reforms introduced the use of a secret ballot in electing House committee chairpersons and allowed for the possibility of choosing a chairperson on a basis other than seniority. The Democrats immediately replaced three senior chairpersons who were out of step with the rest of their party. The Republican leadership in the House has also taken more control over the selection of committee chairpersons.

Safe Seat
A district that returns a legislator with 55 percent of the vote or more.

THE FORMAL LEADERSHIP

The limited amount of centralized power that exists in Congress is exercised through party-based mechanisms. Congress is organized by party. When the Democratic Party, for example, wins a majority of seats in either the House or the Senate, Democrats control the official positions of power in that chamber, and every important committee has a Democratic chairperson and a majority of Democratic members. The same process holds when Republicans are in the majority.

Generally speaking, the leadership organizations in the House and the Senate look alike on paper. However, leaders in the House of Representatives have more control over the agenda of the body and, often, over their own party's members. Senate leaders, due to the power of individual members, must work closely with the other party's leaders to achieve success. Although the party leaders in both the House and the Senate are considered to be the most powerful members of the Congress, their powers pale compared to those given to the leaders in true "party government" legislatures. The differences between those legislatures and the U.S. Congress are detailed in the *Beyond Our Borders* feature.

Speaker of the House
The presiding officer in the House of Representatives. The Speaker is always a member of the majority party and is the most powerful and influential member of the House.

LEADERSHIP IN THE HOUSE

The House leadership is made up of the Speaker, the majority and minority leaders, and the party whips.

The Speaker. The foremost power holder in the House of Representatives is the **Speaker of the House**. The Speaker's position is technically a nonpartisan one, but in fact, for the better part of two centuries, the Speaker has been the official leader of the majority party in the House. When a new Congress convenes in January of odd-numbered years, each party nominates a candidate for Speaker. All Democratic members of the House are expected to vote for their party's nominee, and all Republicans are expected to support their candidate. The vote to organize the House is the one vote in which representatives must vote with their party. In a sense, this vote defines a member's partisan status.

The influence of modern-day Speakers is based primarily on their personal prestige, persuasive ability, and knowledge of the legislative process—plus the acquiescence or active support of other representatives. In recent years, both the Republican and Democratic parties in the House have given their leaders more power in making appointments and controlling the agenda. The major formal powers of the Speaker include the following:

1. Presiding over meetings of the House.
2. Appointing members of joint committees and conference committees.

WHEN THE DEMOCRATS took control of the House of Representatives after the 2006 midterm elections, John Boehner (R.-Ohio) was named House Minority Leader by the Republicans. What benefits could a state receive when one of its representatives wins such a leadership post? (Photo courtesy of the U.S. Congress)

BEYOND OUR BORDERS

SHOULD PARTIES CONTROL LEGISLATURES (AND GOVERNMENTS)?

The Congress of the United States is, as you know, a bicameral legislature. The American-style legislature differs from most of the legislatures in the world in several significant ways. Because the U.S. government is composed of three branches, separate structures sharing powers, we frequently have "divided" government, meaning that the party that controls one or both houses of Congress does not control the presidency. Does this mean that the government is hopelessly deadlocked? Not usually. Members of Congress, especially in the House, frequently support their party leaders, but on many other votes, they "cross the aisle" to vote with members of the other side, thinking it best for their constituency or for re-election.

Most Americans think that our legislature is modeled on the British parliament. However, the parliament of Great Britain, as well as that of many other Western

nations, is based on the idea of "party government." No separation of powers exists between the legislature and the executive branch. What does this mean? When a political party wins a majority of seats in the House of Parliament (the lower and only powerful house), that party then selects the prime minister, who is also the party leader. The prime minister and his cabinet members actually sit in parliament during debates, where they play an active role. The party, which may have promised "lemonade in every drinking fountain" or a better welfare system, votes the new law into effect, and the prime minister implements the new policy.*

Similar systems with two major parties and some minor parties are in effect in Canada and other nations as well. Another variation on this type of party government occurs when a nation such as Germany, Italy, or Israel has a multiparty system. In that case, no party wins a majority of seats. The party with the plurality of the seats chooses the leader and then negotiates with other parties to form a coalition in order to constitute a government and pass new legislation. Governing as part of a coalition is much more difficult, however, because if one of the partners does not agree with the proposed policy, the coalition may fall apart, and new elections may be necessary.

Consider the important relationship between the executive (prime minister or president) and the legislature. In the U.S. system, even if the Congress and the president are of the same party, this does not guarantee that the president's agenda will be fully carried out. Think about the Bush administration from 2000 to 2008. While the Republicans were able to pass a great deal of the president's bills, absolutely no movement occurred with health care, Medicare reform, or Social Security reform. In fact, both the Democrats and the Republicans in the House were so cohesive throughout much of those years that some scholars believed it was a form of "conditional party government."*** In a true party government system, everything on the Republicans' agenda would be law, and the president would be selected by the Congress.

Although Americans complain bitterly about ineffective Congresses, they generally prefer divided government due to fear that one party will have too much power.

FOR CRITICAL ANALYSIS

1. Would the United States ever give the kind of power to the president to achieve his agenda that is given to the prime minister of Great Britain?
2. What is more important—controlling government power or having a more effective legislature?
3. How would the United States Congress be different if three or four parties were represented there?

*For information on the world's legislatures, go to the Web site of the Inter-Parliamentary Union at www.ipu.org.
**The "conditional party government" thesis has been developed by David Rohde, *Parties and Leaders in the PostReform House* (Chicago: University of Chicago Press, 1991).

3. Scheduling legislation for floor action.
4. Deciding points of order and interpreting the rules with the advice of the House parliamentarian.
5. Referring bills and resolutions to the appropriate standing committees of the House.

A Speaker may take part in floor debate and vote, as can any other member of Congress, but recent Speakers usually have voted only to break a tie. Since 1975, the Speaker, when a Democrat, has also had the power to appoint the Democratic Steering Committee, which determines new committee assignments for House party members.

In general, the powers of the Speaker are related to his or her control over information and communications channels in the House and the degree of support received from members. This is a significant power in a large, decentralized institution in which information is a very important resource. With this control, the Speaker attempts to ensure the smooth operation of the chamber and to promote the party's agenda.

The Majority Leader. The **majority leader of the House** is elected by a caucus of the majority party to foster cohesion among party members and to act as a spokesperson for the party. The majority leader influences the scheduling of debate and acts as the chief supporter of the Speaker. The majority leader cooperates with the Speaker and other party leaders, both inside and outside Congress, to formulate the party's legislative program and to guide that program through the legislative process in the House. The Democrats often recruit future Speakers from those who hold that position.

The Minority Leader. The **minority leader of the House** is the candidate nominated for Speaker by a caucus of the minority party. Like the majority leader, the leader of the minority party has as her or his primary responsibility the maintaining of cohesion within the party's ranks. The minority leader works for cohesion among the party's members and speaks on behalf of the president if the minority party controls the White House. In relations with the majority party, the minority leader consults with both the Speaker and the majority leader on recognizing members who wish to speak on the floor, on House rules and procedures, and on the scheduling of legislation. Minority leaders have no actual power in these areas, however.

Majority Leader of the House
A legislative position held by an important party member in the House of Representatives. The majority leader is selected by the majority party in caucus or conference to foster cohesion among party members and to act as spokesperson for the majority party in the House.

Minority Leader of the House
The party leader elected by the minority party in the House.

That the Constitution does not require that the Speaker of the House of Representatives be an elected member of the House?

Whip
A member of Congress who aids the majority or minority leader of the House or the Senate.

Whips. The leadership of each party includes assistants to the majority and minority leaders, known as whips. The **whips** are members of Congress who assist the party leaders by passing information down from the leadership to party members and by ensuring that members show up for floor debate and cast their votes on important issues. Whips conduct polls among party members about the members' views on legislation, inform the leaders about whose vote is doubtful and whose is certain, and may exert pressure on members to support the leaders' positions. In the House, serving as a whip is the first step toward positions of higher leadership.

LEADERSHIP IN THE SENATE

The Senate is less than one-fourth the size of the House. This fact alone probably explains why a formal, complex, and centralized leadership structure is not as necessary in the Senate as it is in the House.

President Pro Tempore
The temporary presiding officer of the Senate in the absence of the vice president.

The two highest-ranking formal leadership positions in the Senate are essentially ceremonial in nature. Under the Constitution, the vice president of the United States is the president (that is, the presiding officer) of the Senate and may vote to break a tie. The vice president, however, is only rarely present for a meeting of the Senate. The Senate elects instead a **president pro tempore** ("pro tem") to preside over the Senate in the vice president's absence. Ordinarily, the president pro tem is the member of the majority party with the longest continuous term of service in the Senate. The president pro tem is mostly a ceremonial position. Junior senators take turns actually presiding over the sessions of the Senate.

Senate Majority Leader
The chief spokesperson of the majority party in the Senate, who directs the legislative program and party strategy.

Senate Minority Leader
The party officer in the Senate who commands the minority party's opposition to the policies of the majority party and directs the legislative program and strategy of his or her party.

The real leadership power in the Senate rests in the hands of the **Senate majority leader**, the **Senate minority leader**, and their respective whips. The Senate majority and minority leaders have the right to be recognized first in debate on the floor and generally exercise the same powers available to the House majority and minority leaders. They control the scheduling of debate on the floor in conjunction with the majority party's Policy Committee, influence the allocation of committee assignments for new members or for senators attempting to transfer to a new committee, influence the selection of other party officials, and participate in selecting members of conference committees. The leaders are expected to mobilize support for partisan legislative initiatives or

AFTER THE DEMOCRATS took control of the U.S. Senate in the 2006 elections, Republican Senator Mitch McConnell of Kentucky (left) was elected Senate minority leader for the 110th Congress. Democratic Senator Harry Reid of Nevada (right), who had been elected Senate minority leader at the beginning of the 109th Congress, became the Senate majority leader. It is very rare for a Congressional leader to become president. How might a leadership position interfere with presidential aspirations? (Photos courtesy of Senator McConnell and Senator Reid)

for the proposals of a president who belongs to their party. The leaders act as liaisons with the White House when the president is of their party, try to obtain the cooperation of committee chairpersons, and seek to facilitate the smooth functioning of the Senate through the senators' unanimous consent. The majority and minority leaders are elected by their respective party caucuses.

Senate party whips, like their House counterparts, maintain communication within the party on platform positions and try to ensure that party colleagues are present for floor debate and important votes. The Senate whip system is far less elaborate than its counterpart in the House, simply because there are fewer members to track.

A list of the formal party leaders of the 110th Congress is presented in Table 12–6. Party leaders are a major source of influence over the decisions about public issues that senators and representatives must make every day.

That in 2004, on the urging of representative Don Young (R.-Alaska), the House approved a new bridge to connect a town of 7,845 people with an island of 50 residents—a $200 million structure with a longer span than the George Washington Bridge in New York?

HOW MEMBERS OF CONGRESS DECIDE

Each member of Congress casts hundreds of votes in each session. Each member compiles a record of votes during the years that he or she spends in the national legislature. There are usually several different reasons why any particular vote is cast. Research shows that the best predictor of a member's vote is party affiliation. Obviously, party members do have common opinions on some, if not all, issues facing the nation. In

TABLE 12–6 Party Leaders in the 111th Congress, 2009–2011

POSITION	INCUMBENT	PARTY/STATE	LEADER SINCE
House			
Speaker	Nancy Pelosi	D.-Calif.	Jan. 2007
Majority leader	Steny Hoyer	D.-Md.	Jan. 2007
Majority whip	James Clyburn	D.-S.C.	Jan. 2007
Chair of the Democratic Caucus	Rahm Emanuel	D.-Ill.	Jan. 2007
Minority leader	John Boehner	R.-Ohio	Jan. 2007
Minority whip	Roy Blunt	R.-Mo.	Jan. 2007
Chair of the Republican Conference	Adam Putnam	R.-Fla.	Jan. 2007
Senate			
President pro tempore	Robert Byrd	D.-W.Va.	Jan. 2007
Majority leader	Harry Reid	D.-Nev.	Jan. 2007
Majority whip	Dick Durbin	D.-Ill.	Jan. 2007
Vice Chair of the Democratic Conference	Charles E. Schumer	D.-N.Y.	Jan. 2007
Minority leader	Mitch McConnell	R.-Ky.	Jan. 2007
Minority whip	Trent Lott	R.-Miss.	Jan. 2007
Chair of the Republican Conference	Jon Kyl	R.-Ariz.	Jan. 2007

addition, the party leadership in each house works hard to build cohesion and agreement among the members through the activities of the party caucuses and conferences. In recent years, the increase in partisanship in both the House and the Senate has meant that most Republicans are voting in opposition to most Democrats.

THE CONSERVATIVE COALITION

Political parties are not always unified. In the 1950s and 1960s, the Democrats in Congress were often split between Northern liberals and Southern conservatives. This division gave rise to the **conservative coalition**, a voting bloc made up of conservative Democrats and conservative (which is to say, most) Republicans. This coalition was able to win many votes over the years. Today, however, most Southern conservatives are Republicans, so the coalition has almost disappeared. There are, however, some Democrats in Congress who represent more moderate states or districts. The votes of these members, who are known as **Blue Dog Democrats**, are frequently sought after by Republican leaders.

"CROSSING OVER"

On some votes, individual representatives and senators will vote against their party, "crossing over to the other side," because the interests of their states or districts differ from the interests that prevail within the rest of their party. In some cases, members vote a certain way because of the influence of regional or national interests. Other voting decisions are based on the members' religious or ideological beliefs. Votes on issues such as abortion or gay rights may be motivated by a member's religious views.

There are, however, far too many voting decisions for every member to be fully informed on each issue. Research suggests that many voting decisions are based on cues provided by trusted colleagues or the party leadership. A member who sits on the committee that wrote a law may become a reliable source of information about that law. Alternatively, a member may turn to a colleague who represents a district in the same state or one who represents a similar district for cues on voting. Cues may also come from fellow committee members, leaders, and the administration.

LOGROLLING, EARMARKS, AND "PORK"

Sometimes, leaders on either side of the aisle will offer incentives to get needed votes for the passage of legislation. Even the president has been known to offer opportunities for the member to better serve his or her district through "bringing home the bacon." When a member "trades" his or her vote on a particular bill with another member in exchange for their votes on other legislation, the practice known as logrolling described earlier in the chapter. Often members request that special appropriations for projects back home are attached to a bill to gain their votes. If the actual project is named, this is referred to as an **earmark**. The term comes from the V-shaped mark that is cut in a pig's ear to identify the animal. The special projects that are so identified are often referred to as **pork**, as in bringing home the bacon or pork. Although the practice of special appropriations has a long history, the amounts now being earmarked equal more than $30 billion in most years. Efforts have been made to force lawmakers to reveal all of their special projects, but new methods have been found to hide these special appropriations from the public eye.

Politicians and reformers often rail against the practice of earmarks, and some projects seem absolutely silly to everyone except the people or state that will benefit. In

Conservative Coalition
An alliance of Republicans and Southern Democrats that can form in the House or the Senate to oppose liberal legislation and support conservative legislation.

Blue Dog Democrats
Members of Congress from more moderate states or districts who sometimes "cross over" to vote with Republicans on legislation.

That the term "Blue Dog Democrat" was coined by a Texas Democratic congressman who said that the extreme liberals were choking some Democrats blue?

Earmarks
Funding appropriations that are specifically designated for a named project in a member's state or district.

Pork
Special projects or appropriations that are intended to benefit a member's district or state; slang term for earmarks.

some cases, earmarks truly are needed; in others, they are seen as the key to keeping a member of Congress in office. As Senator Robert Byrd of West Virginia has been known to remark, "One man's pork is another man's job."[15]

HOW A BILL BECOMES LAW

Each year, Congress and the president propose and approve many laws. Some are budget and appropriations laws that require extensive bargaining but must be passed for the government to continue to function. Other laws are relatively free of controversy and are passed with little dissension. Still other proposed legislation is extremely controversial and reaches to the roots of differences between Democrats and Republicans and between the executive and legislative branches.

As detailed in Figure 12–4, each law begins as a bill, which must be introduced in either the House or the Senate. Often, similar bills are introduced in both chambers. A "money bill," however, must start in the House. In each chamber, the bill follows similar steps. It is referred to a committee and its subcommittees for study, discussion, hearings, and rewriting ("markup"). When the bill is reported out to the full chamber, it must be scheduled for debate (by the Rules Committee in the House and by the leadership in the Senate). After the bill has been passed in each chamber, if it contains different provisions, a conference committee is formed to write a compromise bill, which must be approved by both chambers before it is sent to the president to sign or veto.

Another form of congressional action, the *joint resolution*, differs little from a bill in how it is proposed or debated. Once it is approved by both chambers and signed by the president, it has the force of law.[16] A joint resolution to amend the Constitution, however, after it is approved by two-thirds of both chambers, is sent not to the president but to the states for ratification.

That retiring members of Congress can start collecting a pension at age 50 after 20 years of work or at age 60 after 10 years of service?

HOW MUCH WILL THE GOVERNMENT SPEND?

The Constitution is very clear about where the power of the purse lies in the national government: all taxing or spending bills must originate in the House of Representatives. Today, much of the business of Congress is concerned with approving government expenditures through the budget process and with raising the revenues to pay for government programs.

From 1922, when Congress required the president to prepare and present to the legislature an **executive budget**, until 1974, the Congressional budget process was so disjointed that it was difficult to visualize the total picture of government finances. The president presented the executive budget to Congress in January. It was broken down into 13 or more appropriations bills. Some time later, after all of the bills had been debated, amended, and passed, it was more or less possible to estimate total government spending for the next year.

Frustrated by the president's ability to impound, or withhold, funds and dissatisfied with the entire budget process, Congress passed the Budget and Impoundment Control Act of 1974 to regain some control over the nation's spending. The Act required the

Executive Budget
The budget prepared and submitted by the president to Congress.

---

[15]"Just Say No to Earmarks," *The Wall Street Journal*, Editorial, October 4, 2006.
[16]In contrast, *simple resolutions* and *concurrent resolutions* do not carry the force of law, but rather are used by one or both chambers of Congress, respectively, to express facts, principles, or opinions. For example, a concurrent resolution is used to set the time when Congress will adjourn.

FIGURE 12–4 How a Bill Becomes Law

This illustration shows the most typical way in which proposed legislation is enacted into law. Most legislation begins as similar bills introduced into the House and the Senate. The process is illustrated here with two hypothetical bills, House bill No. 100 (HR 100) and Senate bill No. 200 (S 200). The path of HR 100 is shown on the left, and that of S 200, on the right.

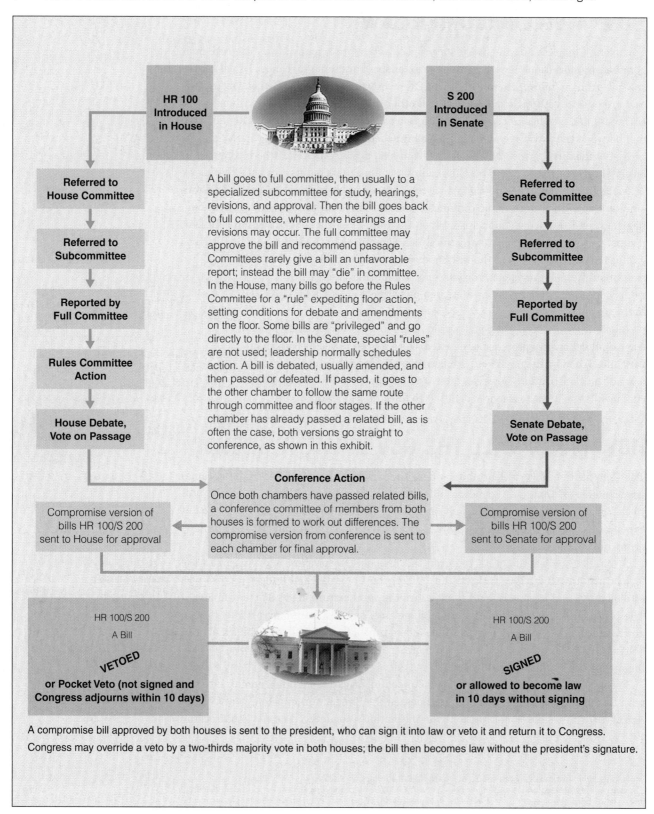

HR 100 Introduced in House

S 200 Introduced in Senate

Referred to House Committee

Referred to Senate Committee

Referred to Subcommittee

Referred to Subcommittee

Reported by Full Committee

Reported by Full Committee

Rules Committee Action

House Debate, Vote on Passage

Senate Debate, Vote on Passage

A bill goes to full committee, then usually to a specialized subcommittee for study, hearings, revisions, and approval. Then the bill goes back to full committee, where more hearings and revisions may occur. The full committee may approve the bill and recommend passage. Committees rarely give a bill an unfavorable report; instead the bill may "die" in committee. In the House, many bills go before the Rules Committee for a "rule" expediting floor action, setting conditions for debate and amendments on the floor. Some bills are "privileged" and go directly to the floor. In the Senate, special "rules" are not used; leadership normally schedules action. A bill is debated, usually amended, and then passed or defeated. If passed, it goes to the other chamber to follow the same route through committee and floor stages. If the other chamber has already passed a related bill, as is often the case, both versions go straight to conference, as shown in this exhibit.

Conference Action

Once both chambers have passed related bills, a conference committee of members from both houses is formed to work out differences. The compromise version from conference is sent to each chamber for final approval.

Compromise version of bills HR 100/S 200 sent to House for approval

Compromise version of bills HR 100/S 200 sent to Senate for approval

HR 100/S 200

A Bill

HR 100/S 200

A Bill

VETOED

SIGNED

or Pocket Veto (not signed and Congress adjourns within 10 days)

or allowed to become law in 10 days without signing

A compromise bill approved by both houses is sent to the president, who can sign it into law or veto it and return it to Congress.

Congress may override a veto by a two-thirds majority vote in both houses; the bill then becomes law without the president's signature.

president to spend the funds that Congress had appropriated, ending the president's ability to kill programs by withholding funds. The other major accomplishment of the act was to force Congress to examine total national taxing and spending at least twice in each budget cycle.

The budget cycle of the federal government is described in the rest of this section. (See Figure 12–5 for a graphic illustration of the budget cycle.)

PREPARING THE BUDGET

The federal government operates on a **fiscal year (FY)** cycle. The fiscal year runs from October through September, so that fiscal 2009, or FY09, runs from October 1, 2008, through September 30, 2009. Eighteen months before a fiscal year starts, the executive branch begins preparing the budget. The Office of Management and Budget (OMB) receives advice from the Council of Economic Advisers and the Treasury Department. The OMB outlines the budget and then sends it to the various departments and agencies. Bargaining follows, in which—to use only two of many examples—the Department of Health and Human Services argues for more welfare spending, and the armed forces argue for more defense spending.

Even though the OMB has only 600 employees, it is one of the most powerful agencies in Washington. It assembles the budget documents and monitors federal agencies throughout each year. Every year, it begins the budget process with a **spring review**, in which it requires all of the agencies to review their programs, activities, and goals. At the beginning of each summer, the OMB sends out a letter instructing agencies to submit their requests for funding for the next fiscal year. By the end of the summer, each agency must submit a formal request to the OMB.

In actuality, the "budget season" begins with the **fall review**. At this time, the OMB looks at budget requests and, in almost all cases, routinely cuts them back. Although the OMB works within guidelines established by the president, specific decisions often are left to the OMB director and the director's associates. By the beginning of November, the director's review begins. The director meets with Cabinet secretaries and budget officers. Time becomes crucial. The budget must be completed by January so that it can be included in the *Economic Report of the President*.

Fiscal Year (FY)
A 12-month period that is used for book-keeping, or accounting purposes. Usually, the fiscal year does not coincide with the calendar year. For example, the federal government's fiscal year runs from October 1 through September 30.

Spring Review
The annual process in which the Office of Management and Budget requires federal agencies to review their programs, activities, and goals and submit their requests for funding for the next fiscal year.

Fall Review
The annual process in which the Office of Management and Budget, after receiving formal federal agency requests for funding for the next fiscal year, reviews the requests, makes changes, and submits its recommendations to the president.

FIGURE 12–5 The Budget Cycle

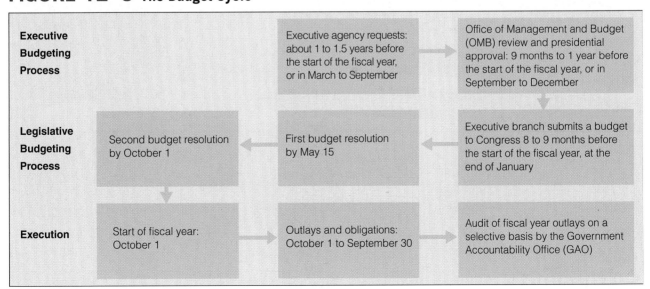

CONGRESS FACES THE BUDGET

In January, nine months before the fiscal year starts, the president takes the OMB's proposed budget, approves it, and submits it to Congress. Then the Congressional budgeting process takes over. The budgeting process involves two steps. First, Congress must authorize funds to be spent. The **authorization** is a formal declaration by the appropriate Congressional committee that a certain amount of funding may be available to an agency. Congressional committees and subcommittees look at the proposals from the executive branch and the Congressional Budget Office in making the decision to authorize funds. After the funds are authorized, they must be appropriated by Congress. The appropriations committees of both the House and the Senate forward spending bills to their respective bodies. The **appropriation** of funds occurs when the final bill is passed.

The budget process involves large sums. For example, President George W. Bush's proposed budget for fiscal year 2007 called for expenditures of $2.77 trillion, or $2,770,000,000,000. When forming the budget for a given year, Congress and the president must take into account revenues, primarily in the form of taxes, as well as expenditures to balance the budget. If spending exceeds the amount brought in by taxes, the government runs a budget deficit (and increases the public debt). For example, although President Bush's proposed budget for fiscal year 2007 called for expenditures of approximately $2.77 trillion, projected revenues from taxes amounted to only about $2.416 trillion—leaving a deficit of $354 billion.

Authorization
A formal declaration by a legislative committee that a certain amount of funding may be available to an agency. Some authorizations terminate in a year; others are renewable automatically, without further Congressional action.

Appropriation
The passage, by Congress, of a spending bill specifying the amount of authorized funds that actually will be allocated for an agency's use.

SPEAKER OF THE HOUSE Nancy Pelosi (D.-Ca.) (left) and Senate Majority Leader Harry Reid (D.-Nev.) hold a news conference in 2007 to declare that the Democratic majority would pass a budget to cut taxes and balance the budget by 2012. (Chip Somodevilla/Getty Images)

With these large sums in play, representatives and senators who chair key committees find it relatively easy to slip spending proposals into a variety of bills. These proposals may have nothing to do with the ostensible purpose of the bill. Are such earmarked appropriations good policy?

BUDGET RESOLUTIONS

The **first budget resolution** by Congress is scheduled to be passed in May of each year. It sets overall revenue goals and spending targets. During the summer, bargaining among all the concerned parties takes place. Spending and tax laws that are drawn up during this period are supposed to be guided by the May Congressional budget resolution.

By September, Congress is scheduled to pass its **second budget resolution**, one that will set "binding" limits on taxes and spending for the fiscal year beginning October 1. Bills passed before that date that do not fit within the limits of the budget resolution are supposed to be changed.

In actuality, between 1978 and 1996 Congress did not pass a complete budget by October 1. In other words, generally, Congress does not follow its own rules. Budget resolutions are passed late, and when they are passed, they are not treated as binding. In each fiscal year that starts without a budget, every agency operates on the basis of a **continuing resolution**, which enables the agency to keep on doing whatever it was doing the previous year with the same amount of funding. Even continuing resolutions have not always been passed on time.

First Budget Resolution
A resolution passed by Congress in May that sets overall revenue and spending goals for the following fiscal year.

Second Budget Resolution
A resolution passed by Congress in September that sets "binding" limits on taxes and spending for the following fiscal year.

Continuing Resolution
A temporary funding law that Congress passes when an appropriations bill has not been decided by the beginning of the new fiscal year on October 1.

You can make a difference

LEARNING ABOUT YOUR REPRESENTATIVES

Do you know the names of your senators and your representative in Congress? A surprising number of Americans do not. Even if you know the names and parties of your elected delegates, there is still much more you could learn about them that would be useful.

WHY SHOULD YOU CARE?

The legislation that Congress passes can directly affect your life. Consider, for example, the Medicare prescription drug benefit passed in November 2003. Some might think that such a benefit, which only helps persons over the age of 65, would be of no interest to college students. Actually, legislation such as this could affect you long before you reach retirement age. Funding the new benefit may mean that you will have to pay higher taxes when you join the workforce. Also, some students may be affected even sooner than that. Most students are part of a family,

and family finances are often important in determining whether a family will help pay for the student's tuition. There are families in which the cost of medicine for the oldest members is a substantial burden.

You can make a difference in our democracy simply by going to the polls on election day and voting for the candidates you would like to represent you in Congress. It goes without saying, though, that to cast an informed vote, you need to know how your Congressional representatives stand on the issues and, if they are incumbents, how they have voted on bills that are important to you.

WHAT CAN YOU DO?

To contact a member of Congress, start by going to the Web sites of the U.S. House of Representatives (**www .house.gov**) and the U.S. Senate (**www.senate.gov**).

Not all Congressional Web sites are equally informative. Often, these Web sites post pictures of lawmakers, state flags, and pictures from their districts. Many sites contain Congressional biographies, constituent services, sponsored legislation, and contact information. Some Congressional Web sites have interactive polls and regularly updated blogs. In 2007, the Sunlight Foundation conducted the Congressional Web Site Investigation Project. This group wanted to examine how well members of Congress spend taxpayer money to maintain official Web sites. They used everyday citizens to evaluate their own Congressional representatives' Web sites for transparency and accountability. Do these Web sites allow responsible citizens to exercise oversight over their representatives and hold them accountable for their performance? Go to **www.sunlightlabs.com** to find the project's results.

You can also contact your representatives using one of the following addresses or phone numbers:

United States House of Representatives
Washington, DC 20515
202-224-3121

United States Senate
Washington, DC 20510
202-224-3121

Interest groups also track the voting records of members of Congress and rate the members on the issues. Project Vote Smart is supported by thousands of volunteers, conservative and liberal, who research the backgrounds and records of thousands of political candidates and elected officials to provide citizens with their voting records, campaign contributions, public statements, biographical data, and evaluations from more than 150 competing special-interest groups. You can contact Project Vote Smart at:

Project Vote Smart
One Common Ground
Philipsburg, MT 59858
1-888-VOTE-SMART (1-888-868-3762)
www.votesmart.org

Nonpartisan, independent, and nonprofit, the Center for Responsive Politics (CRP) educates voters through research that tracks campaign contributions and lobbying data. They "count cash to make change" in government and strive to inform voters about how money in politics affects their lives. You can contact the CRP at:

The Center for Responsive Politics
1101 14th St. NW, Suite 1030
Washington, DC 20005-5635
202-857-0044
www.opensecrets.org

REFERENCES

Kelly McCormack, "Congressional Websites: The Bright, Bland and Bizarre," The Hill.com, accessed June 20, 2007.

Conor Kenny, "Participatory Democracy: Rate Your Senator's and Representative's Web Pages," PRWatch.org, accessed February 21, 2007.

"About Project Vote Smart," www.votesmart.org/program_about_pvs.php?q=print.

"Our Mission," www.opensecrets.org/about/index.php.

KEY TERMS

appropriation 448
authorization 448
bicameralism 415
Blue Dog Democrats 444
casework 418
conference committee 437
conservative coalition 444
constituent 414
continuing resolution 449
direct primary 426
discharge petition 436
earmarks 444
enumerated power 420
executive budget 445
fall review 447
filibuster 423
first budget resolution 449
fiscal year (FY) 447

franking 434
gerrymandering 429
hillstyle 414
homestyle 414
instructed delegate 417
joint committee 437
justiciable question 428
lawmaking 416
logrolling 416
majority leader of the
    House 441
minority leader of the
    House 441
ombudsperson 418
oversight 419
party identifier 426
pork 444
president pro tempore 442

reapportionment 428
redistricting 428
representation 416
Rule 422
Rules Committee 422
safe seat 439
second budget resolution 449
select committee 437
Senate majority leader 442
Senate minority leader 442
seniority system 438
Speaker of the House 439
spring review 447
standing committee 436
trustee 417
**Unanimous Consent
    Agreement** 423
whip 442

CHAPTER SUMMARY

1. The authors of the Constitution believed that the bulk of national power should be in the legislature. The Constitution states that Congress will consist of two chambers. A result of the Connecticut Compromise, this bicameral structure established a balanced legislature, with the membership in the House of Representatives based on population and the membership in the Senate based on the equality of states.

2. The functions of Congress include (1) lawmaking, (2) representation, (3) service to constituents, (4) oversight, (5) public education, and (6) conflict resolution.

3. The first 17 clauses of Article I, Section 8, of the Constitution specify most of the enumerated, or expressed, powers of Congress, including the right to impose taxes, to borrow money, to regulate commerce, and to declare war. Besides its enumerated powers, Congress enjoys the right to "make all Laws which shall be necessary and proper for carrying into Execution the foregoing Powers, and all other Powers vested by this Constitution in the Government of the United States, or in any Department or Officer thereof." This is called the elastic, or necessary and proper, clause.

4. There are 435 members in the House of Representatives and 100 members in the Senate. Owing to its larger size, the House has more formal rules. The Senate tradition of unlimited debate (filibustering) dates back to 1790 and has been used over the years

to frustrate the passage of bills. Under Senate Rule 22, cloture can be used to shut off debate on a bill.

5. Members of Congress are not typical American citizens. They are older and wealthier than most Americans, disproportionately white and male, and more likely to be trained in professional occupations.

6. Congressional elections are operated by the individual state governments, which must abide by rules established by the Constitution and national statutes. Most candidates for Congress must win nomination through a direct primary. The overwhelming majority of incumbent representatives and a smaller proportion of senators who run for re-election are successful. A complicated aspect of congressional elections is apportionment—the allocation of legislative seats to constituencies. The Supreme Court's "one person, one vote" rule has been applied to equalize the populations of congressional and state legislative districts.

7. Members of Congress are well paid and enjoy benefits such as franking privileges. Members of Congress have personal and committee staff members available to them and also receive many legal privileges and immunities.

8. Most of the actual work of legislating is performed by committees and subcommittees within Congress. Legislation introduced into the House or Senate is assigned to the appropriate standing committees for review. Select committees are created for a limited

time for a specific purpose. Joint committees are formed by the concurrent action of both chambers and consist of members from each chamber. Conference committees are special joint committees set up to achieve agreement between the House and the Senate on the exact wording of legislative acts passed by both chambers in different forms. The seniority rule, which is usually followed, specifies that the longest-serving member of the majority party will be the chairperson of a committee.

9. The foremost power holder in the House of Representatives is the Speaker of the House. Other leaders are the House majority leader, the House minority leader, and the majority and minority whips. Formally, the vice president is the presiding officer of the

Senate, with the most senior member of the majority party serving as the president pro tempore to preside when the vice president is absent. Actual leadership in the Senate rests with the majority leader, the minority leader, and their whips.

10. A bill becomes law by progressing through both chambers of Congress and their appropriate standing and joint committees to the president.

11. The budget process for a fiscal year begins with the preparation of an executive budget by the president. This is reviewed by the Office of Management and Budget and then sent to Congress, which is supposed to pass a final budget by the end of September. Since 1978, Congress generally has not followed its own time rules.

SELECTED PRINT AND MEDIA RESOURCES

SUGGESTED READINGS

Barone, Michael, and Grant Ujifusa. *The Almanac of American Politics, 2008*. Washington, DC: National Journal, 2006. This book, which is published biannually, is a comprehensive summary of current political information on each member of Congress, his or her state or Congressional district, recent Congressional election results, key votes, ratings by various organizations, sources of campaign contributions, and records of campaign expenditures.

Davidson, Roger H., and Walter J. Oleszek. *Congress and Its Members*, 11th ed. Washington, DC: CQ Press, 2008. This classic looks carefully at the "two Congresses," the one in Washington and the role played by congresspersons at home.

Just, Ward S. *The Congressman Who Loved Flaubert*. New York: Carrol and Graf Publishers, 1990. This fictional account of a career politician was first published in 1973 and is still a favorite with students of political science. Ward Just is renowned for his political fiction, and particularly for his examination of character and motivation.

Mann, Thomas B., and Norman J. Ornstein. *The Broken Branch: How Congress Is Failing America and How to Get It Back on Track*. New York: Oxford University Press, 2006. These two political scientists believe that Congress is more dysfunctional now than ever before. They argue that there is too much partisan bickering and internal rancor. These two scholars of government and politics present a blueprint for reform.

Rangel, Charles B., and Leon Wynter. . . . *And I Haven't Had a Bad Day Since: The Memoir of Charles B. Rangel's Journey from the Streets of Harlem to the Halls of Congress*. New York: Scribner, 2007. This biographical account of one of Congress's most flamboyant members tells his story from (obviously) the streets of Harlem to the halls of Congress. Rangel, a high school dropout, became a lawyer and then a member of Congress. He helped create the earned-income tax credit for working families.

MEDIA RESOURCES

The Congress—In one of his earliest efforts (1988), filmmaker Ken Burns profiles the history of Congress. Narration is by David McCullough, and those interviewed include David Broker, Alistair Cooke, and Cokie Roberts. PBS Home Video re-released this film on DVD in 2003.

Congress: A Day in the Life of a Representative—From political meetings to social functions to campaigning, this 1995 program examines what politicians really do. Featured representatives are Tim Roemer (a Democrat from Indiana) and Sue Myrick (a Republican from North Carolina).

Mr. Smith Goes to Washington—A 1939 film in which Jimmy Stewart plays the naïve congressman who is quickly educated in Washington. A true American political classic.

The Seduction of Joe Tynan—A 1979 film in which Alan Alda plays a young senator who must face serious decisions about his political role and his private life.

THE CONGRESS AND THE WEB

Almost all senators and representatives now have Web sites that you can find simply by keying their names into a search engine. As you read in this chapter's *You Can Make a Difference* feature, you can easily learn the names of your Congressional representatives by going to the Web site of the House or Senate (see the following *Logging On* section for the URLs for these sites). Once you know the names of your representatives, you can go to their Web sites to learn more about them and their positions on specific issues. You can also check the Web sites of the groups listed in the *You Can Make a Difference* feature to track your representatives' voting records and discover the names of their campaign contributors.

Note that some members of Congress also provide important services to their constituents via their Web sites. Some sites, for example, allow constituents to apply for internships in Washington, D.C., apply for appointments to military academies, order flags, order tours of the Capitol, and register complaints electronically. Other sites may provide forms from certain government agencies, such as the Social Security Administration, that constituents can use to request assistance from those agencies or register complaints.

LOGGING ON

- To find out about the schedule of activities taking place in Congress, use the following Web sites:
  www.senate.gov
  www.house.gov

- The Congressional Budget Office is online at:
  www.cbo.gov
- The URL for the Government Printing Office is:
  www.gpoaccess.gov
- For the real inside facts on what's going on in Washington, D.C., you can look at the following resources: *RollCall*, the newspaper of the Capitol:
  www.rollcall.com
- *Congressional Quarterly*, a publication that reports on Congress:
  www.cq.com
- *The Hill*, which investigates various activities of Congress:
  www.hillnews.com

ONLINE REVIEW

At **www.cengage.com/politicalscience/schmidt/agandpt14e**, you will find a Tutorial Quiz for this chapter providing questions on the chapter contents, including the features. The questions are organized to match the major sections of the chapter. You'll have access to other helpful study tools, including the book's glossary and flashcards, crossword puzzles, and Web links, as well as "Which Side Are You On?" and "Politics and . . ." features written by the authors of the book.

CHAPTER

(13)

THE PRESIDENT

QUESTIONS TO CONSIDER

Why has the presidency become more powerful than was intended?

How is presidential success judged?

How important are the personal qualities of the president to success in office?

CHAPTER CONTENTS

Making a DIFFERENCE

"FOR THE RECORD" VERSUS "THAT'S PRIVILEGED INFORMATION"

Do we have a right to know everything our government does? What circumstances might justify the president keeping his activities or those of his administration secret? These questions raise complex issues, and common sense says the answers lie somewhere in between the two extremes. How this balance is struck has been the subject of intense political debate.

After the Watergate scandal (see the "Abuses of Executive Power and Impeachment" section for an explanation of these events), Congress passed the Presidential Records Act of 1978 (PRA) to address control of the historical record of a presidential administration.[a] Immediately upon the inauguration of the successor, the

National Archives physically takes control of all presidential and vice-presidential records. For a period of 12 years, the National Archives is responsible for processing these papers and reviewing and examining each document for national security issues or other reasons that would preclude it from being made public. Under the PRA, after the 12-year period and as the archivists finish their work, the records are released to the presidential libraries. Each library—staffed by archivists employed by the federal government—houses all of the papers of that administration.[b] However, current or former presidents can request that certain documents not be released, claiming executive privilege (discussed in the "Special Uses of Presidential Power" section).[c]

President Reagan's records were the first to be processed under the PRA. In February 2001, President Bush was notified that one of the first batches of Reagan

---

THE WRITERS OF the Constitution created the presidency of the United States without any models to follow. Nowhere else in the world was there a democratically selected chief executive. What the founders did not want was a king. In fact, given their previous experience with royal governors in the colonies, many of the delegates to the Constitutional Convention wanted to create a very weak executive who could not veto legislation. Other delegates, especially those who had witnessed the need for a strong leader in the Revolutionary Army, believed a strong executive would be necessary for the new republic.

Overall, however, the delegates did not spend much time discussing the actual powers to be granted to the president, leaving those questions to the Committee on Detail. The delegates, in the end, created a chief executive who had enough powers granted in the Constitution to balance those of Congress.[1]

The power exercised by each president who has held the office has been scrutinized and judged by historians, political scientists, the media, and the public. The personalities and foibles of each president have also been investigated and judged by many. Indeed, it would seem that Americans are fascinated by presidential power and by the persons who hold the office. In this chapter, after looking at who can become president and at the

DID YOU KNOW?

That George Washington's salary of $25,000 in 1789 was the equivalent of about $600,000 in today's dollars?

---

[1]Forrest McDonald, *The American Presidency: An Intellectual History* (Lawrence: University Press of Kansas, 1994), p. 179.

documents was scheduled for release, as the 12-year period was set to expire. The President's subsequent Executive Order (E.O. 13233) in November 2001 significantly altered the PRA. Under E.O. 13233, instead of the process described previously, the National Archives now cannot release documents until the current and former presidents have approved their release. Researchers who may want access to these records bear the burden of arguing before a federal court that there is no reason for the president to withhold the records. The burden of proof has shifted away from the current or former presidents who formerly had to demonstrate a compelling reason to keep the public away from the records. Now the burden is on the public to substantiate their need to know.

A coalition of scholars, researchers, journalists, and public-interest lobby groups joined in a suit to stop the implementation of President Bush's executive order. Among the groups joining the 2002 suit filed by a public-interest group called Public Citizen were the Association of American University Presses (AAUP), the Association of American Publishers, the Society of American Historians, and the Society of Professional Journalists. The group won a partial victory in October 2007 when a federal court struck down the portion of E.O. 13233 allowing current and former presidents to screen the release of documents.[d]

In 2007, Congressional partisan control reverted to the Democrats, and Representative Henry Waxman (D.-Ca.)

became chair of the House Government and Oversight Committee. In addition to numerous investigations that his committee has launched into the Republican White House, Congressman Waxman co-authored HR 1255: The Presidential Records Act Amendments of 2007, which would repeal E.O. 13233. Having passed the House in March of 2007, the bill remains stuck in the Senate, as several Republican senators have blocked the legislation's progress. When the bill passed the House, President Bush issued a Statement of Administration Policy threatening to veto it should it pass the Senate on the grounds that "Executive privilege is not subject to Congressional regulation, but rather arises directly from the Constitution itself."[e] As you will learn in this chapter, these Constitutional and political arguments are inextricably intertwined.

[a]www.archives.gov/presidential-libraries/laws/1978-act.html

[b]For a complete list of the presidential libraries, see www.archives.gov/presidential-libraries.

[c]If someone wants access to an unreleased document, the person can file a Freedom of Information Act (FOIA) request. Archivists trained with an understanding of the PRA, FOIA, and any other governing statutes determine whether to release the documents. This process remains in place today.

[d]http://aaupnet.org/news/press/PRAamicus.pdf

[e]www.whitehouse.gov/omb/legislative/sap/110-1/hr1255sap-h.pdf

---

process involved, we will examine closely the nature and extent of the constitutional powers held by the president, including whether the president can decide which papers will be private and which will be public, as discussed in the *Making a Difference* feature.

DID YOU KNOW?

That the salary of the president did not increase from 1969 until 2001, when it was raised to $400,000?

WHO CAN BECOME PRESIDENT?

The requirements for becoming president, as outlined in Article II, Section 1, of the Constitution, are not overwhelmingly stringent:

> No person except a natural born Citizen, or a Citizen of the United States, at the time of the Adoption of this Constitution, shall be eligible to the Office of President; neither shall any Person be eligible to that Office who shall not have attained to the Age of thirty-five Years, and been fourteen Years a Resident within the United States.

The only question that arises about these qualifications relates to the term *natural-born citizen*. Does that mean only citizens born in the United States and its territories? What about a child born to a U.S. citizen (or to a couple who are U.S. citizens) visiting or living in another country? Although the Supreme Court has never directly addressed the question, it is reasonable to expect that someone would be eligible if her or his

parents were Americans. The first presidents, after all, were not even American citizens at birth, and others were born in areas that did not become part of the United States until later. These questions were debated when George Romney, who was born in Chihuahua, Mexico, made a serious bid for the Republican presidential nomination in the 1960s.[2] Similar questions were raised about the 2008 Republican candidate, John McCain, who was born in Panama on an American military base. Those questions were quickly dismissed because it is clear that children born abroad to American citizens are considered natural-born Americans.

When Arnold Schwarzenegger became governor of California, many of his supporters suggested that he might be a potential presidential candidate. But Schwarzenegger, who was born in Austria, is a naturalized U.S. citizen and therefore is ineligible to become president under the Constitution. Early in his administration, a movement began to amend the Constitution to allow *naturalized* citizens to become president; however, as time passed, the idea lost support.

The American dream is symbolized by the statement that "anybody can become president of this country." It is true that in modern times, presidents have included a haberdasher (Harry Truman—for a short period of time), a peanut farmer (Jimmy Carter), and an actor (Ronald Reagan). But if you examine the list of presidents on the inside back cover of your textbook, you will see that the most common previous occupation of presidents in this country has been the law. Out of 43 presidents, 26 have been lawyers, and many have been wealthy. (There have been fewer lawyers in the last century, in part because senators, who are likely to be lawyers, have had a difficult time being elected president. Senators have often faced the problem of defending their voting records.)

Although the Constitution states that the minimum-age requirement for the presidency is 35 years, most presidents have been much older than that when they assumed office. John F. Kennedy, at the age of 43, was the youngest elected president, and the old-

[2]George Romney was governor of Michigan from 1963 to 1969. Romney was not nominated for the presidency, and the issue remains unresolved.

est was Ronald Reagan, at age 69. The average age at inauguration has been 54. There has clearly been a demographic bias in the selection of presidents. All have been male, white, and from the Protestant tradition, except for John F. Kennedy, who was a Roman Catholic. Presidents have been men of great stature (such as George Washington) and men in whom leadership qualities were not so pronounced (such as Warren Harding; served 1921–1923). A presidential candidate usually has experience as a vice president, senator, or state governor. Former governors have been especially successful at winning the presidency, because they can make the legitimate claim to have executive experience as well as being electable.

THE PROCESS OF BECOMING PRESIDENT

Major and minor political parties nominate candidates for president and vice president at national conventions every four years. As discussed in Chapter 9, the nation's voters do not elect a president and vice president directly, but rather cast ballots for presidential electors, who then vote for president and vice president in the electoral college.

Because winning the election requires winning the majority of electoral votes, it is conceivable that someone could be elected to the office of the presidency without having a majority of the popular vote cast. In four cases, candidates won elections even though their major opponents received more popular votes. One of those cases occurred in 2000, when George W. Bush won the electoral college vote and became president even though his opponent, Al Gore, won the popular vote. In elections when more than two candidates were running for office, many presidential candidates have won with less than 50 percent of the total popular votes cast for all candidates—including Abraham Lincoln, Woodrow Wilson, Harry Truman, John F. Kennedy, Richard Nixon, and, in 1992, Bill Clinton. Independent candidate Ross Perot garnered a surprising 19 percent of the vote in 1992. Remember from Chapter 9 that no president has won a majority of votes from the entire voting-age population.

Twice, the electoral college has failed to give any candidate a majority. At this point, the election is thrown into the House of Representatives. The president is then chosen from among the three candidates having the most electoral college votes, as noted in Chapter 9. Thomas Jefferson and Aaron Burr tied in the electoral college in 1800. This happened because the Constitution had not been explicit in indicating which of the two electoral votes were for president and which were for vice president. In 1804, the **Twelfth Amendment** clarified the matter by requiring that the president and vice president be chosen separately. In 1824, the House again had to make a choice, this time among William H. Crawford, Andrew Jackson, and John Quincy Adams. It chose Adams, even though Jackson had more electoral and popular votes.

Twelfth Amendment
An amendment to the Constitution, adopted in 1804, that specifies the separate election of the president and vice president by the electoral college.

THE MANY ROLES OF THE PRESIDENT

The Constitution speaks briefly about the duties and obligations of the president. Based on this brief list of powers and on the precedents of history, the presidency has grown into a very complicated job that requires balancing at least five constitutional roles: (1) head of state, (2) chief executive, (3) commander in chief of the armed forces, (4) chief diplomat, and (5) chief legislator of the United States. Here we examine each of these significant presidential functions, or roles. It is worth noting that one person plays all these roles simultaneously and that the needs of these roles may at times come into conflict.

HEAD OF STATE

Head of State
The role of the president as ceremonial head of the government.

Every nation has at least one person who is the ceremonial head of state. In most democratic governments, the role of **head of state** is given to someone other than the chief executive, who leads the executive branch of government. In Britain, for example, the head of state is the queen. In much of Europe, the prime minister is the chief executive, and the head of state is the president. But in the United States, the president is both chief executive and head of state. According to William Howard Taft, as head of state the president symbolizes the "dignity and majesty" of the American people.

As head of state, the president engages in many activities that are largely symbolic or ceremonial, such as the following:

- Decorating war heroes.
- Throwing out the first pitch to open the baseball season.

PRESIDENT GEORGE W. BUSH
escorts Britain's Queen Elizabeth II to a state dinner in her honor. Both are heads of state, although the Queen has no political power. (Brooks Kraft/CORBIS)

- Dedicating parks and post offices.
- Receiving visiting heads of state at the White House.
- Going on official state visits to other countries.
- Making personal telephone calls to astronauts.
- Representing the nation at times of national mourning, such as after the terrorist attacks of September 11, 2001, after the loss of the space shuttle Columbia in 2003, and after the destruction from Hurricane Katrina in 2005.

That 21 presidents have served only one term in office?

Some students of the American political system believe that having the president serve as both the chief executive and the head of state drastically limits the time available to do "real" work. Not all presidents have agreed with this conclusion, however—particularly those presidents who have skillfully blended these two roles with their role as politician. Being head of state gives the president tremendous public exposure, which can be an important asset in a campaign for re-election. When that exposure is positive, it helps the president deal with Congress over proposed legislation and increases the chances of being re-elected—or getting the candidates of the president's party elected.

CHIEF EXECUTIVE

According to the Constitution, "The executive Power shall be vested in a President of the United States of America. . . . [H]e may require the Opinion, in writing, of the principal Officer in each of the executive Departments, upon any Subject relating to the Duties of their respective Offices . . . and he shall nominate, and by and with the Advice and Consent of the Senate, shall appoint . . . Officers of the United States. . . . [H]e shall take Care that the Laws be faithfully executed."

As **chief executive**, the president is constitutionally bound to enforce the acts of Congress, the judgments of federal courts, and treaties signed by the United States. The duty to "faithfully execute" the laws has been a source of constitutional power for presidents. Is the president allowed to reject certain parts of legislation if he or she believes that they are unconstitutional? This question relates to so-called **signing statements**, which are written declarations made by presidents that accompany legislation.

Chief Executive
The role of the president as head of the executive branch of the government.

Signing Statement
A written declaration that a president may make when signing a bill into law. Usually, such statements point out sections of the law that the president deems unconstitutional.

DURING 2006, President George W. Bush came under fire because of his extensive use of signing statements. Here, Deputy Assistant Attorney General Michelle Boardman appeared before the Senate Judiciary Committee to defend Bush's actions. Do you think future presidents would abide by a signing statement? (AP Photo/Dennis Cook)

For at least 175 years, presidents have used signing statements to make substantive constitutional pronouncements on the bill being signed. In 1830, President Andrew Jackson created a controversy when he signed a bill and at the same time sent to Congress a message that restricted the reach of the statute. In 1842, President John Tyler expressed misgivings in a signing statement about the constitutionality and policy of an entire act. Presidents Abraham Lincoln, Andrew Johnson, Theodore Roosevelt, Woodrow Wilson, and Franklin Roosevelt all used signing statements.

As for the legality of the practice, the Department of Justice has advised the last four administrations that the Constitution provides the president with the authority to decline to enforce a clearly unconstitutional law. Four justices of the Supreme Court joined in an opinion that the president may resist laws that encroach upon presidential powers by "disregarding them when they're unconstitutional."[3]

After George W. Bush took office, he issued signing statements on more than 800 statutes, more than all of the previous presidents combined. He also tended to use the statements for a different purpose. When earlier presidents issued signing statements, they were normally used to instruct agencies on how to execute the laws or for similar purposes. In contrast, many (if not most) of Bush's signing statements served notice that he believed parts of bills that he signed were unconstitutional or might violate national security.

Some members of Congress are not so concerned about Bush's signing statements. Senator John Cornyn (R.-Tex.) says that Bush's signing statements are only "expressions of presidential opinion" and carry no legal weight. According to Cornyn, federal courts would be unlikely to consider the statements when interpreting the laws with which they were issued.[4]

The Powers of Appointment and Removal. To assist in the various tasks of the chief executive, the president has a federal bureaucracy (see Chapter 14), which consists of more than 2.7 million federal civilian employees. You might think that the president, as head of the largest bureaucracy in the United States, wields enormous power. The president, however, only nominally runs the executive bureaucracy. Most government positions are filled by **civil service** employees, who generally gain government employment through a merit system rather than presidential appointment.[5] Therefore, even though the president has important **appointment power**, it is limited to Cabinet and subcabinet jobs, federal judgeships, agency heads, and about 2,000 lesser jobs. This means that most of the 2.7 million federal employees owe no political allegiance to the president. They are more likely to owe loyalty to Congressional committees or to interest groups representing the sector of the society that they serve. Table 13–1 shows what percentage of the total employment in each executive department is available for political appointment by the president.

The president's power to remove from office those officials who are not doing a good job or who do not agree with the president is not explicitly granted by the Constitution and has been limited with regard to certain agencies. In 1926, however, a Supreme Court decision prevented Congress from interfering with the president's ability to fire those executive-branch officials whom the president had appointed with Senate approval.[6] There are 10 agencies whose directors the president can remove at any time, including the Arms Control and Disarmament Agency, the Commission on Civil Rights,

DID YOU KNOW?

That Thomas Jefferson was the first president to be inaugurated in Washington, D.C., where he walked to the Capitol from a boardinghouse, took the oath, made a brief speech in the Senate chamber, and then walked back home?

Civil Service
A collective term for the body of employees working for the government. Generally, civil service is understood to apply to all those who gain government employment through a merit system.

Appointment Power
The authority vested in the president to fill a government office or position. Positions filled by presidential appointment include those in the executive branch and the federal judiciary, commissioned officers in the armed forces, and members of the independent regulatory commissions.

[3]*Freytag v. C.I.R.*, 501 U.S. 868 (1991).
[4]T. J. Halstead, "Presidential Signing Statements: Constitutional and Institutional Implications" (Washington, DC: Congressional Research Service September 17, 2007).
[5]See Chapter 14 for a discussion of the Civil Service Reform Act.
[6]*Meyers v. United States*, 272 U.S. 52 (1926).

TABLE 13–1 Total Civilian Employment in Cabinet Departments Available for Political Appointment by the President

EXECUTIVE DEPARTMENT	TOTAL NUMBER OF EMPLOYEES	POLITICAL APPOINTMENTS AVAILABLE	PERCENTAGE
Agriculture	100,084	384	0.43
Commerce	39,151	324	1.13
Defense	670,568	655	0.06
Education	4,581	260	4.06
Energy	15,689	469	2.75
Health and Human Services	63,323	418	0.61
Homeland Security	165,085	453	0.27
Housing and Urban Development	10,154	152	1.53
Interior	72,982	283	0.32
Justice	126,711	569	0.39
Labor	16,016	219	1.17
State	28,054	1,287	3.79
Transportation	64,131	271	0.42
Treasury	159,274	175	0.14
Veterans Affairs	223,137	361	0.14
TOTAL	1,593,855	6,280	0.39

Source: *Policy and Supporting Positions* (Washington, DC: Government Printing Office, 2004). This text, known as the "Plum Book" (see Chapter 14), is published after each presidential election. The numbers of employees cited in this table are from 2004, the year in which the last edition of this book was published.

the Environmental Protection Agency, the General Services Administration, and the Small Business Administration. In addition, the president can remove all heads of Cabinet departments, all individuals in the Executive Office of the President, and all of the 6,280 political appointees listed in Table 13–1.

Harry Truman spoke candidly of the difficulties a president faces in trying to control the executive bureaucracy. On leaving office, he referred to the problems that Dwight Eisenhower, as a former general of the army, was going to have: "He'll sit here and he'll say do this! do that! and nothing will happen. Poor Ike—it won't be a bit like the Army. He'll find it very frustrating."[7]

The Power to Grant Reprieves and Pardons. Section 2 of Article II of the Constitution gives the president the power to grant **reprieves** and **pardons** for offenses against the United States except in cases of impeachment. All pardons are administered by the Office of the Pardon Attorney in the Department of Justice. In principle, a pardon is granted to remedy a mistake made in a conviction.

The United States Supreme Court upheld the president's power to grant reprieves and pardons in a 1925 case concerning a pardon granted by the president to an individual

Reprieve
A formal postponement of the execution of a sentence imposed by a court of law.

Pardon
A release from the punishment for or legal consequences of a crime; a pardon can be granted by the president before or after a conviction.

[7]Quoted in Richard E. Neustadt, *Presidential Power: The Politics of Leadership* (New York: Wiley, 1960), p. 9. Truman may not have considered the amount of politics involved in decision making in the upper echelon of the army.

convicted of contempt of court. The judiciary had contended that only judges had the authority to convict individuals for contempt of court when court orders were violated and that the courts should be free from interference by the executive branch. The Court simply stated that the president could grant reprieves or pardons for all offenses "either before trial, during trial, or after trial, by individuals, or by classes, conditionally or absolutely, and this without modification or regulation by Congress."[8]

The power to pardon can also be used to apply to large groups of individuals who may be subject to indictment and trial. In 1977, President Jimmy Carter extended amnesty to all of the Vietnam War resisters who avoided the military draft by fleeing to Canada. More than 50,000 individuals were allowed to come back to the United States, free from the possibility of prosecution. The power to reprieve individuals allows the president to extend clemency to federal prisoners, usually on humanitarian grounds. However, in 1999, President Bill Clinton extended a conditional offer of clemency to a group of Puerto Rican nationalists who had been tried for planning terrorist attacks in the United States. The condition was for them to renounce the use of terrorist tactics and to not associate with other nationalists who advocate violence. Twelve accepted the offer, while two refused to accept the conditions.

In a controversial decision, President Gerald Ford pardoned former president Richard Nixon for his role in the Watergate affair before any charges were brought in court. Just before George W. Bush's inauguration in 2001, President Clinton announced pardons for almost 200 persons. Some of these pardons were controversial and appeared to be political favors.

COMMANDER IN CHIEF

The president, according to the Constitution, "shall be Commander in Chief of the Army and Navy of the United States, and of the Militia of the several States, when called into the actual Service of the United States." In other words, the armed forces are under civilian, rather than military, control.

Wartime Powers. Certainly, those who wrote the Constitution had George Washington in mind when they made the president the **commander in chief**. The founders did not, however, expect presidents to lead the country into war without Congressional authorization. Remember from Chapters 2 and 12 that Congress is given the power to declare war. As the United States grew in military power and global reach, presidents became much more likely to send troops into armed combat either in crisis situations or with an authorizing resolution short of a declaration of war. The last war to be fought under a Congressional declaration was World War II.

Although we do not expect our president to lead the troops into battle, presidents as commanders in chief have wielded dramatic power. Harry Truman made the difficult decision to drop atomic bombs on Hiroshima and Nagasaki in 1945 to force Japan to surrender and thus bring World War II to an end. Lyndon B. Johnson ordered bombing missions against North Vietnam in the 1960s, and he personally selected some of the targets. Richard Nixon decided to invade Cambodia in 1970, which was widely condemned as going beyond his power as commander in chief.

The president is the ultimate decision maker in military matters and, as such, has the final authority to launch a nuclear strike using missiles or bombs. Everywhere the president goes, so too goes the "football"—a briefcase filled with all the codes necessary to order a nuclear attack. Only the president has the power to order the use of nuclear force.

Commander in Chief
The role of the president as supreme commander of the military forces of the United States and of the state National Guard units when they are called into federal service.

---

[8]*Ex parte Grossman*, 267 U.S. 87 (1925).

IN OCTOBER, 1983, United States medical students to be evacuated from the island of Grenada stand with an armed United States soldier looking up while waiting for their military transport plane. The students were being evacuated from the island due to the United States invasion in progress. (Bettmann/CORBIS)

The use of military force by presidents has raised some very thorny issues for the balance between Congress and the presidency. Harry Truman sent U.S. troops to Korea under a United Nations resolution, and Lyndon Johnson escalated the U.S. involvement in Vietnam under the quickly passed Gulf of Tonkin Resolution. George W. Bush invaded Iraq with Congressional authorization. In none of these cases did Congress and the public expect extended wars with many casualties.

Presidents have also used military force without any Congressional authorization, particularly in emergency situations. Ronald Reagan sent troops to Grenada to stop a supposedly Communist coup, and Lyndon Johnson invaded the Dominican Republic. George H. W. Bush sent troops to Panama, and numerous presidents have ordered quick air strikes on perceived enemies.

The War Powers Resolution. In an attempt to gain more control over such military activities, in 1973 Congress passed the **War Powers Resolution**—over President Nixon's veto—requiring that the president consult with Congress when sending American forces into action. Once they are sent, the president must report to Congress within 48 hours. Unless Congress approves the use of troops within 60 days or extends the 60-day time limit, the forces must be withdrawn. The War Powers Resolution was tested in the fall of 1983, when Reagan requested that troops be left in Lebanon. The resulting compromise was a Congressional resolution allowing troops to remain there for 18 months. Shortly after the resolution was passed, however, more than 240 sailors and Marines were killed in a suicide bombing of a U.S. military housing compound in Beirut. That event provoked a furious congressional debate over the role that American troops were playing in the Middle East, and all troops were withdrawn shortly thereafter.

War Powers Resolution
A law passed in 1973 spelling out the conditions under which the president can commit troops without Congressional approval.

Despite the War Powers Resolution, the powers of the president as commander in chief have continued to expand. The attacks of September 11, 2001, were the first on U.S. soil since Pearl Harbor. The imminent sense of threat supported passage of legislation that gave the president and the executive branch powers that had not been seen since World War II. President Bush's use of surveillance powers and other powers granted by the PATRIOT Act have caused considerable controversy. However, as long as international terrorist groups threaten the United States, presidents are likely to have these enhanced powers.

CHIEF DIPLOMAT

Advice and Consent
Terms in the Constitution describing the U.S. Senate's power to review and approve treaties and presidential appointments.

Chief Diplomat
The role of the president in recognizing foreign governments, making treaties, and effecting executive agreements.

Diplomatic Recognition
The formal acknowledgment of a foreign government as legitimate.

The Constitution gives the president the power to recognize foreign governments; to make treaties, with the **advice and consent** of the Senate; and to make special agreements with other heads of state that do not require Congressional approval. In addition, the president nominates ambassadors. As **chief diplomat**, the president dominates American foreign policy, a role that has been supported many times by the Supreme Court.

Diplomatic Recognition. An important power of the president as chief diplomat is that of **diplomatic recognition**, or the power to recognize—or refuse to recognize—foreign governments. In the role of ceremonial head of state, the president has always received foreign diplomats. In modern times, the simple act of receiving a foreign diplomat has been equivalent to accrediting the diplomat and officially recognizing his or her government. Such recognition of the legitimacy of another country's government is a prerequisite to diplomatic relations or treaties between that country and the United States.

Deciding when to recognize a foreign power is not always simple. The United States, for example, did not recognize the Soviet Union until 1933—16 years after the Russian Revolution of 1917. It was only after all attempts to reverse the effects of that revolution—including military invasion of Russia and diplomatic isolation—had proved futile that Franklin Roosevelt extended recognition to the Soviet government. U.S. presidents faced a similar problem with the Chinese Communist revolution. In December 1978, long after the Communist victory in China in 1949, Jimmy Carter granted official recognition to the People's Republic of China.[9]

A diplomatic recognition issue that faced the Clinton administration involved recognizing a former enemy—the Republic of Vietnam. Many Americans, particularly those who believed that Vietnam had not been forthcoming in the efforts to find the remains of missing American soldiers or to find out about former prisoners of war, opposed any

PRESIDENT RICHARD NIXON and First Lady Pat Nixon lead the way as they take a tour of China's famed Great Wall, near Beijing, February 21, 1972. Why was Nixon's visit to China so historic? (AP/Wide World Photos)

[9]The Nixon administration first encouraged new relations with the People's Republic of China by allowing a cultural exchange of ping-pong teams.

formal relationship with that nation. After the U.S. government had negotiated with the Vietnamese government for many years over the missing-in-action issue and engaged in limited diplomatic contacts for several years, President Clinton announced on July 11, 1995, that the United States would recognize the government of Vietnam and move to establish normal diplomatic relations.

Proposal and Ratification of Treaties. The president has the sole power to negotiate treaties with other nations. These treaties must be presented to the Senate, where they may be modified and must be approved by a two-thirds vote. After ratification, the president can approve the senatorial version of the treaty. Approval poses a problem when the Senate has tacked on substantive amendments or reservations to a treaty, particularly when such changes may require reopening negotiations with the other signatory governments. Sometimes a president may decide to withdraw a treaty if the senatorial changes are too extensive, as Woodrow Wilson did with the Versailles Treaty in 1919. Wilson believed that the senatorial reservations would weaken the treaty so much that it would be ineffective. His refusal to accept the senatorial version of the treaty led to the eventual refusal of the United States to join the League of Nations.

President Carter was successful in lobbying for the treaties that provided for the return of the Panama Canal to Panama by the year 2000 and neutralizing the canal. President Bill Clinton won a major political and legislative victory in 1993 by persuading Congress to ratify the North American Free Trade Agreement (NAFTA). In so doing, he had to overcome opposition from Democrats and most of organized labor. In 1998, he worked closely with Senate Republicans to ensure Senate approval of a treaty governing the use of chemical weapons. In 2000, President Clinton won another major legislative victory when Congress voted to normalize trade relations with China permanently.

Before September 11, 2001, President George W. Bush indicated his intention to steer the United States in a unilateral direction on foreign policy. He rejected the Kyoto Agreement on global warming and proposed ending the 1972 Anti-Ballistic Missile (ABM) Treaty that was part of the first Strategic Arms Limitation Treaty (SALT I). After the terrorist attacks of September 11, 2001, however, President Bush sought cooperation from U.S. allies in the war on terrorism. Bush's return to multilateralism was exemplified in the signing of a nuclear weapons reduction treaty with Russia in 2002. Nonetheless, his attempts to gain international support for a war against Iraq to overthrow that country's government were not as successful as he had hoped. During the continuing occupation of Iraq, the Bush administration saw even more erosion in other countries' support of his actions.

Executive Agreements. Presidential power in foreign affairs is enhanced greatly by the use of **executive agreements** made between the president and other heads of state. Such agreements do not require Senate approval, although the House and Senate may refuse to appropriate the funds necessary to implement them. Whereas treaties are binding on all succeeding administrations, executive agreements require each new president's consent to remain in effect.

Among the advantages of executive agreements are speed and secrecy. The former is essential during a crisis; the latter is important when the administration fears that open senatorial debate may be detrimental to the best interests of the United States or to the interests of the president.[10] There have been far more executive agreements

Executive Agreement
An international agreement made by the president, without senatorial ratification, with the head of a foreign state.

---

[10]The Case Act of 1972 requires that all executive agreements be transmitted to Congress within 60 days after the agreement takes effect. Secret agreements are transmitted to the foreign relations committees as classified information.

(about 13,000) than treaties (about 1,300). Many executive agreements contain secret provisions calling for American military assistance or other support. For example, Franklin Roosevelt (served 1933–1945) used executive agreements to bypass Congressional isolationists when he traded American destroyers for British Caribbean naval bases and when he arranged diplomatic and military affairs with Canada and Latin American nations.

CHIEF LEGISLATOR

Constitutionally, presidents must recommend to Congress legislation that they judge necessary and expedient. Not all presidents have wielded their powers as **chief legislator** in the same manner. Some presidents have been almost completely unsuccessful in getting their legislative programs implemented by Congress. Presidents Franklin Roosevelt and Lyndon Johnson, however, saw much of their proposed legislation put into effect. Each year, the *Congressional Quarterly Weekly Review* publishes an analysis of presidential success in terms of legislation passed that the president has publicly supported. As illustrated by the graph in Figure 13–1, presidents tend to have a high success rate at the beginning of their administration, with a steep decline toward the end of their term. George W. Bush had more than a 70 percent success rate during the years he had a Republican controlled Congress, but it fell to 34 percent after the Democrats won control of Congress in the 2006 elections.

In modern times, the president has played a dominant role in creating the Congressional agenda. In the president's annual **State of the Union message**, which is required by the Constitution (Article II, Section 3) and is usually given in late January shortly after Congress reconvenes, the president, as chief legislator, presents a program. The message gives a broad, comprehensive view of what the president wishes the legislature to accomplish during its session. Originally, presidents simply sent a written memo to the Congress, which clearly satisfies the constitutional requirement. In modern times, however, presidents see the State of the Union address as a tool to advance their policy agenda. The president is able to command the media stage and set out his or her goals. President Ronald Reagan began the practice of referring to ordinary citizens and bringing the subjects of those stories to sit in the balcony during the speech. Today, the president, the opposition party, and the commentators all recognize the impact of the State of the Union message on public opinion.

Getting Legislation Passed. The president can propose legislation. Congress, however, is not required to pass—or even introduce—any of the administration's bills. How, then, does the president get those proposals made into law? One way is by exercising the power of persuasion. The president writes to, telephones, and meets with various Congressional leaders;

Chief Legislator
The role of the president in influencing the making of laws.

State of the Union Message
An annual message to Congress in which the president proposes a legislative program. The message is addressed not only to Congress but also to the American people and to the world.

FIGURE 13–1 Presidential Success Rate by Year of Presidency

The graph illustrates the president's success rate on bills on which he had taken a position. Note that presidents do very well at the beginning of their terms, especially when they have control of Congress. When the other party controls Congress, the presidential success rate falls.

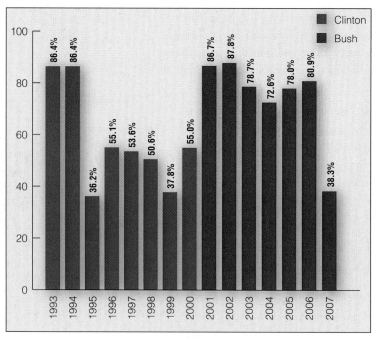

makes public announcements to influence public opinion; and, as head of the party, exercises legislative leadership through the congresspersons of that party. Most presidents also have an Office of Congressional Liaison within the White House Office. Such an office is staffed by individuals with extensive Washington experience, including former members of the Congress, who lobby the Congress on behalf of the president and monitor the progress of legislation on Capitol Hill. Presidents may also decide to use social events to lobby the Congress, inviting the members and their spouses to parties at the White House. A more negative strategy is for the president to threaten to veto legislation if it does not correspond to his position.

Saying No to Legislation. The president has the power to say no to legislation through use of the veto, by which the White House returns a bill unsigned to Congress with a **veto message** attached.[11] Because the Constitution requires that every bill passed by the House and the Senate be sent to the president before it becomes law, the president must act on each bill.

That one member of the Cabinet must not attend the State of the Union speech so that someone in the line of succession to the presidency would survive in case of an attack on the Capitol?

Veto Message
The president's formal explanation of a veto when legislation is returned to Congress.

. . . .

[11]*Veto* in Latin means "I forbid."

PRESIDENT GEORGE W. BUSH gets a standing ovation from both sides of the aisle when he discusses military benefits during his final State of the Union address to Congress on Capitol Hill in Washington on January 28, 2008. The Republicans are on the left and the Democrats are to the right. (UPI Photo/Pat Benic/Landov Media)

BEYOND OUR BORDERS

DO WE NEED A PRESIDENT *AND* A KING?

In the United States, the president is the head of state and the head of government. In many democratic societies, the government has a head of government, who actually guides government policy and is the political leader, and a head of state, who is the symbolic head of government. As noted in Chapter 12, in parliamentary systems the head of government is actually elected by his or her peers in the majority party in the legislature. In Great Britain, after the election, the leader of the majority party is asked by the Queen of England (in her role as head of state) if he or she will serve as the prime minister. The Queen has no political power whatsoever. She cannot refuse to name the leader of the majority party. When she opens the parliamentary session, she reads a speech written for her by the prime minister. Similar political systems with royal families and parliamentary leadership are found in Denmark, Sweden, Spain, and a few smaller European nations. The advantage of this system is that the head of state, the monarch, symbolically represents the nation. Public fascination with the royal family and the queen generally means that the prime minister can do his or her job without all the gossip and journalistic coverage that surrounds the president of the United States.

In other democracies, including Italy, France, and Germany, there are no royal families. The president of the nation is separately elected for a longer term but has little political power. He or she is the head of state and may counsel the head of the government, but political and executive power rests with the prime minister or premier. In some democratic states, the president and the premier are elected, although with different terms.

Until 2008, Vladimir Putin was the president of Russia, but his two terms were limited by the 1993 Constitution. In the most recent election, his chosen successor, Dmitry Medvedev, won the election for president, and his party won 80 percent of the seats in the legislature. Some Russians who opposed Putin suggested that elections were not fair and that opposition leaders and journalists have been suppressed. Soon after the election, Medvedev named Putin as his premier. It seemed clear that Putin would still be running the government of Russia, even though his position had changed from head of government to head of state. So, in the case of Russia and some other states, the head of state is the president (who is elected) and who then can name the premier and the cabinet ministers. The intent of this system is for the president to be popularly elected and to exercise political leadership, while the premier runs the everyday operations of government and leads the legislative power. But, such a system can degenerate into a rivalry between the president and the premier. How can citizens know which one really has the power of the leader?

FOR CRITICAL ANALYSIS

1. Why is it important to separate the roles of head of state and head of government?
2. Can the existence of a symbolic head of state, such as a monarch, make the elected leader more effective?
3. Is there too much burden put on the president who is both head of state and head of government?

1. If the bill is signed, it becomes law.
2. If the bill is not sent back to Congress after 10 congressional working days, it becomes law without the president's signature.
3. The president can reject the bill and send it back to Congress with a veto message setting forth objections. Congress then can change the bill, hoping to secure presi-

dential approval and pass it again. Or, Congress can simply reject the president's objections by overriding the veto with a two-thirds roll-call vote of the members present in both the House and the Senate.

4. If the president refuses to sign the bill and Congress adjourns within 10 working days after the bill has been submitted to the president, the bill is killed for that session of Congress. This is called a **pocket veto**. If Congress wishes the bill to be reconsidered, the bill must be reintroduced during the following session.

Presidents employed the veto power infrequently until after the Civil War, but it has been used with increasing vigor since then (see Table 13–2). The total number of vetoes from George Washington through the middle of George W. Bush's second term in office was 2,552, with about two-thirds of those vetoes being exercised by Grover Cleveland, Franklin Roosevelt, Harry Truman, and Dwight Eisenhower.

Not since Martin Van Buren (served 1837–1841) has a president served a full term in office without exercising the veto power. George W. Bush, who had the benefit of a Republican Congress that passed legislation he was willing to sign, did not veto any legislation during his first term. Only in the summer of 2006 did Bush finally issue a veto, saying "no" to stem-cell research legislation passed by Congress. He occasionally threatened to use the veto and certainly used it when he was governor of Texas. After the Democrats took control of Congress in 2006, Bush used the veto more frequently, even on bills with bipartisan majorities.

The Line-Item Veto. Ronald Reagan lobbied strenuously for Congress to give to the president another tool, the **line-item veto**, which would allow the president to veto

Pocket Veto
A special veto exercised by the chief executive after a legislative body has adjourned. Bills not signed by the chief executive die after a specified period of time. If Congress wishes to reconsider such a bill, it must be reintroduced in the following session of Congress.

Line-Item Veto
The power of an executive to veto individual lines or items within a piece of legislation without vetoing the entire bill.

PRESIDENT GEORGE W. BUSH, after vetoing the Iraq War Funding Bill in a private ceremony, makes a statement to the news media on May 1, 2007. (Shawn Thew/CORBIS)

TABLE 13–2 Presidential Vetoes, 1789 to Present

YEARS	PRESIDENT	REGULAR VETOES	VETOES OVERRIDDEN	POCKET VETOES	TOTAL VETOES
1789–1797	Washington	2	0	0	2
1797–1801	J. Adams	0	0	0	0
1801–1809	Jefferson	0	0	0	0
1809–1817	Madison	5	0	2	7
1817–1825	Monroe	1	0	0	1
1825–1829	J. Q. Adams	0	0	0	0
1829–1837	Jackson	5	0	7	12
1837–1841	Van Buren	0	0	1	1
1841–1841	W. Harrison	0	0	0	0
1841–1845	Tyler	6	1	4	10
1845–1849	Polk	2	0	1	3
1849–1850	Taylor	0	0	0	0
1850–1853	Fillmore	0	0	0	0
1853–1857	Pierce	9	5	0	9
1857–1861	Buchanan	4	0	3	7
1861–1865	Lincoln	2	0	5	7
1865–1869	A. Johnson	21	15	8	29
1869–1877	Grant	45	4	48	93
1877–1881	Hayes	12	1	1	13
1881–1881	Garfield	0	0	0	0
1881–1885	Arthur	4	1	8	12
1885–1889	Cleveland	304	2	110	414
1889–1893	B. Harrison	19	1	25	44
1893–1897	Cleveland	42	5	128	170
1897–1901	McKinley	6	0	36	42
1901–1909	T. Roosevelt	42	1	40	82
1909–1913	Taft	30	1	9	39
1913–1921	Wilson	33	6	11	44
1921–1923	Harding	5	0	1	6
1923–1929	Coolidge	20	4	30	50
1929–1933	Hoover	21	3	16	37
1933–1945	F. Roosevelt	372	9	263	635
1945–1953	Truman	180	12	70	250
1953–1961	Eisenhower	73	2	108	181
1961–1963	Kennedy	12	0	9	21
1963–1969	L. Johnson	16	0	14	30
1969–1974	Nixon	26*	7	17	43
1974–1977	Ford	48	12	18	66
1977–1981	Carter	13	2	18	31
1981–1989	Reagan	39	9	39	78
1989–1993	G. H. W. Bush	29	1	15	44
1993–2001	Clinton	37**	2	1	38
2001–2008	G. W. Bush	11	4	1	12
TOTAL		**1,495**	**110**	**1,067**	**2,563**

*Two pocket vetoes by President Nixon, overruled in the courts, are counted here as regular vetoes.
**President Clinton's line-item vetoes are not included.
Source: Office of the Clerk.

specific spending provisions of legislation that was passed by Congress. In 1996, Congress passed the Line Item Veto Act, which provided for the line-item veto. Signed by President Clinton, the law granted the president the power to rescind any item in an appropriations bill unless Congress passed a resolution of disapproval. Of course, the Congressional resolution could be, in turn, vetoed by the president. The law did not take effect until after the 1996 election.

The Act was soon challenged in court as an unconstitutional delegation of legislative powers to the executive branch. In 1998, by a six-to-three vote, the United States Supreme Court agreed and overturned the Act. The Court stated that "there is no provision in the Constitution that authorizes the president to enact, to amend or to repeal statutes."[12]

Congress's Power to Override Presidential Vetoes. A veto is a clear-cut indication of the president's dissatisfaction with Congressional legislation. Congress, however, can override a presidential veto, although it rarely exercises this power. Consider that two-thirds of the members of each chamber who are present must vote to override the president's veto in a roll-call vote. This means that if only one-third plus one of the members voting in one of the chambers of Congress do not agree to override the veto, the veto holds. Congress first overrode a presidential veto during the administration of John Tyler (served 1841–1845). In the first 65 years of American federal government history, out of 33 regular vetoes, Congress overrode only one, or about 3 percent. Overall, only about 7 percent of all regular vetoes have been overridden.

OTHER PRESIDENTIAL POWERS

The powers of the president just discussed are called **constitutional powers**, because their basis lies in the Constitution. In addition, Congress has established by law, or statute, numerous other presidential powers, such as the ability to declare national emergencies. These are called **statutory powers**. Both constitutional and statutory powers have been labeled the **expressed powers** of the president, because they are expressly written into the Constitution or into law.

Presidents also have what have come to be known as **inherent powers**. These depend on the statements in the Constitution that "the executive Power shall be vested in a President" and that the president should "take Care that the Laws be faithfully executed." The most common example of inherent powers are those emergency powers invoked by the president during wartime. Franklin Roosevelt, for example, used his inherent powers to move the Japanese and Japanese Americans living in the United States into internment camps for the duration of World War II.

Clearly, modern U.S. presidents have many powers at their disposal. According to some critics, among the powers exercised by modern presidents are certain powers that rightfully belong to Congress but that Congress has yielded to the executive branch.

THE PRESIDENT AS PARTY CHIEF AND SUPERPOLITICIAN

Presidents are by no means above political partisanship, and one of their many roles is that of chief of party. Although the Constitution says nothing about the function of the president within a political party (the mere concept of political parties was abhorrent

DID YOU KNOW?

That President William Henry Harrison gave the longest inaugural address (8,445 words) of any American president, lasting two hours (the weather was chilly and stormy, and Harrison caught a cold, got pneumonia and pleurisy, and died a month later)?

Constitutional Power
A power vested in the president by Article II of the Constitution.

Statutory Power
A power created for the president through laws enacted by Congress.

Expressed Power
A power of the president that is expressly written into the Constitution or into statutory law.

Inherent Power
A power of the president derived from the statements in the Constitution that "the executive Power shall be vested in a President" and that the president should "take Care that the Laws be faithfully executed"; defined through practice rather than through law.

---

[12]*Clinton v. City of New York*, 524 U.S. 417 (1998).

to most of the authors of the Constitution), today presidents are the actual leaders of their parties.

THE PRESIDENT AS CHIEF OF PARTY

Patronage
The practice of rewarding faithful party workers and followers with government employment and contracts.

As party leader, the president chooses the national committee chairperson and can try to discipline party members who fail to support presidential policies. One way of exerting political power within the party is through **patronage**—appointing political supporters to government or public jobs. This power was more extensive in the past, before the establishment of the civil service in 1883 (see Chapter 14), but the president retains important patronage power. As noted earlier, the president can appoint several thousand individuals to jobs in the Cabinet, the White House, and the federal regulatory agencies.

Perhaps the most important partisan role that the president played in the late 1900s and early 2000s was that of fundraiser. The president is able to raise large amounts for the party through appearances at dinners, speaking engagements, and other social occasions. President Clinton may have raised more than half a billion dollars for the Democratic Party during his two terms. President George W. Bush was even more successful than Clinton.

Presidents have other ways of exerting influence as party chief. The president may make it known that a particular congressperson's choice for federal judge will not be appointed unless that member of Congress is more supportive of the president's legislative program.[13] The president may agree to campaign for a particular program or for a particular candidate. Presidents also reward loyal members of Congress with support for the funding of local projects, tax breaks for regional industries, and other forms of "pork."

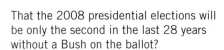

That the 2008 presidential elections will be only the second in the last 28 years without a Bush on the ballot?

THE PRESIDENT'S POWER TO PERSUADE

According to political scientist Richard E. Neustadt, without the power to persuade, no president can lead very well. After all, even though the president is in the news virtually every day, the Constitution gives Congress most of the authority in the U.S. political system. The Constitution does not give the executive branch enough constitutional power to keep the president constantly in a strong leadership position. Therefore, the president must convince Congress, the bureaucracy, and the public to support what the president wants. As Neustadt argues, "presidential power is the power to persuade."[14]

CONSTITUENCIES AND PUBLIC APPROVAL

All politicians worry about their constituencies, and presidents are no exception. Presidents with high approval ratings are able to leverage those ratings with the members of Congress who would prefer not to vote against the opinions of their own constituents.

Presidential Constituencies. According to Neustadt, presidents have not just one constituency, but many. In principle, they are beholden to the entire electorate—the public of the United States—even those who did not vote. They are certainly beholden to their party

[13]"Senatorial courtesy" (see Chapter 15) often puts the judicial appointment in the hands of the Senate, however.
[14]Richard E. Neustadt, *Presidential Power and the Modern Presidents: The Politics of Leadership from Roosevelt to Reagan*, rev. ed. (New York: Free Press, 1991).

because its members helped to put them in office. The president's constituencies also include members of the opposing party whose cooperation the president needs. Finally, the president must take into consideration a constituency that has come to be called the **Washington community**. This community consists of individuals who—whether in or out of political office—are intimately familiar with the workings of government, thrive on gossip, and measure on a daily basis the political power of the president.

Washington Community
Individuals regularly involved with politics in Washington, D.C.

Public Approval. All of these constituencies are impressed by presidents who maintain a high level of public approval, partly because this is very difficult to accomplish. Presidential popularity, as measured by national polls, gives the president an extra political resource to use in persuading legislators or bureaucrats to pass legislation. As you will note from Figure 13–2, there are common patterns for almost all presidents. Presidential approval ratings tend to be very high when a new president takes office (the honeymoon period), and certainly decline to a low in the last two years of the second term. Spikes in public approval apart from that cycle tend to occur when the United States sends troops in harm's way. This is called the "rally 'round the flag" effect. Take a look at George H. W. Bush's ratings. Popular approval of the president reached a new high at the beginning of the Persian Gulf War, but that approval had no staying power, and his ratings declined precipitously in the year following the victory. Bill Clinton defied all tradition by having high ratings even while he was fighting the impeachment.

George W. Bush and the Public Opinion Polls. The impact of popular approval on a president's prospects was placed in sharp relief by the experiences of President Bush. Immediately after September 11, 2001, Bush had the highest approval ratings ever recorded. His popularity then entered a steep decline that was interrupted only briefly by high ratings during the early phases of the Second Gulf War. Such a decline appeared to threaten his re-election. In the end, however, Bush's popularity stabilized at just more

FIGURE 13–2 Public Popularity of Modern Presidents

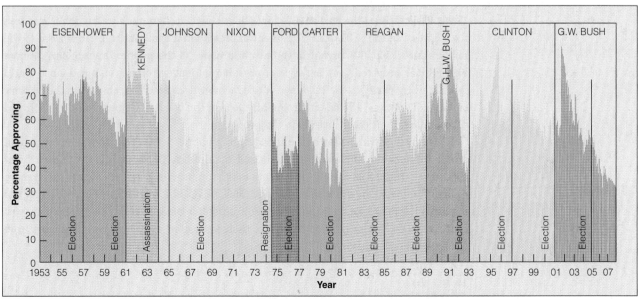

Sources: The Roper Center for Public Opinion Research; Gallup and *USA Today*/CNN Polls, March 1992 through September 2008.

PRESIDENT BUSH points to a reporter during his news conference in the Brady Press Briefing Room of the White House in Washington, Tuesday, December 4, 2007. What do presidents try to achieve in such appearances? (Pablo Martinez Monsivais/AP/Wide World Photos)

than 50 percent, reflecting the continued support of his political base. Bush's support may have come from a narrow majority of the voters, but their support was firm. During his second term, Bush's approval ratings reached new lows, falling to 31 percent during May 2006. During the summer of that year, more than 56 percent of citizens polled disapproved of the job he was doing as president.

"Going Public." Since the early 1900s, presidents have spoken more to the public and less to Congress. In the 1800s, only 7 percent of presidential speeches were addressed to the public; since 1900, 50 percent have been addressed to the public. One scholar, Samuel Kernell, has proposed that the style of presidential leadership has changed since World War II, owing partly to the influence of television, with a resulting change in the balance of national politics.[15] Presidents frequently go over the heads of Congress and the political elites, taking their cases directly to the people.

This strategy, which Kernell dubbed "going public," gives the president additional power through the ability to persuade and manipulate public opinion. By identifying their own positions so clearly, presidents make compromises with Congress much more difficult and weaken the legislators' positions. Given the increasing importance of the media as the major source of political information for citizens and elites, presidents will continue to use public opinion as part of their arsenal of weapons to gain support from Congress and to achieve their policy goals.

[15]Samuel Kernell, *Going Public: New Strategies of Presidential Leadership*, 3rd ed. (Washington, DC: Congressional Quarterly Press, 1997).

SPECIAL USES OF PRESIDENTIAL POWER

Presidents have at their disposal a variety of special powers and privileges not available in the other branches of the U.S. government: (1) emergency powers, (2) executive orders, and (3) executive privilege.

EMERGENCY POWERS

If you read the Constitution, you will find no mention of the additional powers that the executive office may exercise during national emergencies. The Supreme Court has indicated that an "emergency does not create power."[16] But it is clear that presidents have used their inherent powers during times of emergency, particularly in the realm of foreign affairs. The **emergency powers** of the president were first enunciated in the Supreme Court's decision in *United States v. Curtiss-Wright Export Corp.*[17] In that case, President Franklin Roosevelt, without authorization by Congress, ordered an embargo on the shipment of weapons to two warring South American countries. The Court recognized that the president may exercise inherent powers in foreign affairs and that the national government has primacy in these affairs.

Examples of emergency powers are abundant, coinciding with crises in domestic and foreign affairs. Abraham Lincoln suspended civil liberties at the beginning of the Civil War (1861–1865) and called the state militias into national service. These actions and his subsequent governance of conquered areas and even of areas of Northern states were justified by claims that they were essential to preserve the Union. Franklin Roosevelt declared an "unlimited national emergency" following the fall of France in World War II (1939–1945) and mobilized the federal budget and the economy for war.

President Harry Truman authorized the federal seizure of steel plants and their operation by the national government in 1952 during the Korean War. Truman claimed that he was using his inherent emergency power as chief executive and commander in chief to safeguard the nation's security, as an ongoing strike by steelworkers threatened the supply of weapons to the armed forces. The Supreme Court did not agree, holding that the president had no authority under the Constitution to seize private property or to legislate such action.[18] According to legal scholars, this was the first time a limit was placed on the exercise of the president's emergency powers.

After September 11, the Bush administration pushed several laws through the Congress that granted more power to the Department of Justice and other agencies to investigate possible terrorists. Many of these provisions of the PATRIOT Act and other laws have been reaffirmed by Congress in subsequent years, while others have been revised. In 2006, it became clear that President Bush had also authorized federal agencies to eavesdrop on international telephone calls without a court order when the party overseas was suspected of having information about terrorism or who might be a suspect in a terrorist plot. This eavesdropping had not been authorized under the legislation. Many

"I don't think you can distance yourself from the White House on this one. After all, you are the President." (© 2002 The New Yorker Collection from cartoonbank.com. All rights reserved.)

Emergency Power
An inherent power exercised by the president during a period of national crisis.

That the shortest inaugural address was George Washington's second one at 135 words?

---

[16]*Home Building and Loan Association v. Blaisdell*, 290 U.S. 398 (1934).
[17]299 U.S. 304 (1936).
[18]*Youngstown Sheet and Tube Co. v. Sawyer*, 343 U.S. 579 (1952).

scholars claimed that this exercise of presidential power was far beyond what could be claimed an emergency power.[19] The Bush administration claimed that it was entirely within the president's power to make such an authorization, although they did not claim it to be within the Supreme Court's definition of "emergency power." Following these disclosures, the administration pursued an expanded law to allow such wiretapping, but provisions of that new bill proved too controversial to pass in 2008.

EXECUTIVE ORDERS

Executive Order
A rule or regulation issued by the president that has the effect of law. Executive orders can implement and give administrative effect to provisions in the Constitution, to treaties, and to statutes.

Congress allows the president (as well as administrative agencies) to issue **executive orders** that have the force of law. These executive orders can do the following: (1) enforce legislative statutes, (2) enforce the Constitution or treaties with foreign nations, and (3) establish or modify rules and practices of executive administrative agencies.

An executive order, then, represents the president's legislative power. The only requirement is that under the Administrative Procedure Act of 1946, all executive orders must be published in the *Federal Register*, a daily publication of the U.S. government. Executive orders have been used to establish procedures to appoint noncareer administrators, to implement national affirmative action regulations, to restructure the White House bureaucracy, to ration consumer goods and to administer wage and price controls under emergency conditions, to classify government information as secret, to regulate the export of restricted items, and to establish military tribunals for suspected terrorists.

Federal Register
A publication of the U.S. government that prints executive orders, rules, and regulations.

It is important to note that executive orders can be revoked by succeeding presidents. George H. W. Bush issued an order to ban foreign aid to countries that included abortion in their family planning strategies, because that provision (known as the Hyde Amendment) could not make it through Congress as legislation. President Clinton revoked the order. The George W. Bush administration revoked many of the thousands of executive orders and regulations issued in the last months of the Clinton administration.

EXECUTIVE PRIVILEGE

Another inherent executive power that has been claimed by presidents concerns the ability of the president and the president's executive officials to withhold information from or refuse to appear before Congress or the courts. This is called **executive privilege**, and it relies on the constitutional separation of powers for its basis.

Executive Privilege
The right of executive officials to withhold information from or to refuse to appear before a legislative committee.

Presidents have frequently invoked executive privilege to avoid having to disclose information to Congress on actions of the executive branch. For example, President George W. Bush claimed executive privilege to keep the head of the newly established Office of Homeland Security, Tom Ridge, from testifying before Congress. The Bush administration also resisted attempts by the congressional Government Accountability Office to obtain information about meetings and documents related to Vice President Dick Cheney's actions as chair of the administration's energy policy task force. Bush, like presidents before him, claimed that a certain degree of secrecy is essential to national security. Critics of executive privilege believe that it can be used to shield from public scrutiny actions of the executive branch that should be open to Congress and to the American citizenry.

Limiting Executive Privilege. Limits to executive privilege went untested until the Watergate affair in the early 1970s. Five men had broken into the headquarters of the Democratic National Committee and were caught searching for documents that would

[19]Elizabeth Drew, "Power Grab," *New York Review of Books*, Vol. 53, No. 11, June 22, 2006.

damage the candidacy of the Democratic nominee, George McGovern. Later investigation showed that the break-in was planned by members of Richard Nixon's campaign committee and that Nixon and his closest advisors had devised a strategy for impeding the investigation of the crime. After it became known that all of the conversations held in the Oval Office had been tape-recorded on a secret system, Nixon was ordered to turn over the tapes to the special prosecutor.

Nixon refused to do so, claiming executive privilege. He argued that "no president could function if the private papers of his office, prepared by his personal staff, were open to public scrutiny." In 1974, in one of the Supreme Court's most famous cases, *United States v. Nixon*,[20] the justices unanimously ruled that Nixon had to hand over the tapes. The Court held that executive privilege could not be used to prevent evidence from being heard in criminal proceedings.

Clinton's Attempted Use of Executive Privilege. The claim of executive privilege was also raised by the Clinton administration as a defense against the aggressive investigation of Clinton's relationship with White House intern Monica Lewinsky by Independent Counsel Kenneth Starr. The Clinton administration claimed executive privilege for several presidential aides who might have discussed the situation with the president. In addition, President Clinton asserted that his White House counsel did not have to testify before the Starr grand jury due to attorney-client privilege. Finally, the Department of Justice claimed that members of the Secret Service who guard the president could not testify about his activities due to a "protective function privilege" inherent in their duties. The federal judge overseeing the case denied the claims of privilege, however, and the decision was upheld on appeal.

ABUSES OF EXECUTIVE POWER AND IMPEACHMENT

Presidents normally leave office either because their first term has expired and they have not sought (or won) re-election or because, having served two full terms, they are not allowed to be elected for a third term (owing to the Twenty-second Amendment, passed in 1951). Eight presidents have died in office. But there is still another way for a president to leave office—by **impeachment** and conviction. Articles I and II of the Constitution authorize the House and Senate to remove the president, the vice president, or other civil officers of the United States for committing "Treason, Bribery, or other high Crimes and Misdemeanors." According to the Constitution, the impeachment process begins in the House, which impeaches (accuses) the federal officer involved. If the House votes to impeach the officer, it draws up articles of impeachment and submits them to the Senate, which conducts the actual trial.

In the history of the United States, no president has ever actually been impeached and also convicted—and thus removed from office—by means of this process.

Impeachment
An action by the House of Representatives to accuse the president, vice president, or other civil officers of the United States of committing "Treason, Bribery, or other high Crimes and Misdemeanors."

RICHARD NIXON says goodbye outside the White House after his resignation on August 9, 1974, as he prepares to board a helicopter for a flight to nearby Andrews Air Force Base. Nixon addressed members of his staff in the East Room prior to his departure. Was Nixon impeached? (AP Photo/Bob Daughtery)

[20]318 U.S. 683 (1974).

WHAT IF...

THERE WERE NO EXECUTIVE PRIVILEGE?

If there were no executive privilege, a president would have to be aware that all of his or her words, documents, and actions could be made public. We know from 20th-century history that when a president does not have full executive privilege to protect information, the results can be devastating. President Richard Nixon (served 1969–1974) had tape-recorded hundreds of hours of conversations in the Oval Office. During a scandal involving a cover-up (the Watergate scandal), Congress requested those tapes. Nixon invoked executive privilege and refused to turn them over. Ultimately, the Supreme Court ordered him to do so, however, and the tapes provided damning information about Nixon's role in the purported cover-up of illegal activities. Rather than face impeachment, Nixon resigned the presidency.

Clearly, if executive privilege were eliminated, it is unlikely that conversations between the president and other members of the executive branch would be recorded or otherwise documented. As a result, we would have fewer records of an administration's activities than we do today.

Following the terrorist attacks on September 11, 2001, Attorney General John Ashcroft advised federal agencies "to lean toward withholding information whenever possible." In some instances, the Bush administration attempted to withhold information from Congress and the courts, not just the public. In one troubling example, a top civil servant was threatened with being fired if he told Congress the true projected cost of the administration's Medicare prescription drug bill. Yet among the documents that were withdrawn from public access were the plans for federal buildings, blueprints for the Navy's ships, and the maps of nuclear power plants. Public documents make it too easy for enemies to get information needed for terrorism.

If executive privilege were eliminated, the White House would have a difficult time regulating the flow of past presidential records into the public forum. Future presidents, of course, would know that virtually every word and act could be released to the public. The behavior of presidents and their administrations would certainly change. They might simply insist that there be no record of sensitive conversations. If so, future Americans would lose much of the historical background for America's domestic and international actions.

FOR CRITICAL ANALYSIS

1. The history of executive privilege dates back to 1796, when President George Washington refused a request by the House for certain documents. Given the changes that have taken place since that time, should executive privilege be eliminated? Or should it be retained as even more necessary today than it was at that time?
2. What would be the costs to the nation if executive privilege were eliminated?

President Andrew Johnson (served 1865–1869), who succeeded to the office after the assassination of Abraham Lincoln, was impeached by the House but acquitted by the Senate. More than a century later, the House Judiciary Committee approved articles of impeachment against President Richard Nixon for his involvement in the cover-up of the Watergate break-in of 1972. Informed by members of his own party that he had no hope of surviving the trial in the Senate, Nixon resigned on August 9, 1974, before the full House voted on the articles. Nixon is the only president to have resigned from office.

ON DECEMBER 19, 1998, the House of Representatives voted to impeach President Bill Clinton for perjury and obstruction of justice. That same day, Clinton addressed lawmakers and staff outside the Oval Office, surrounded by supporters. President Clinton was later acquitted by the Senate, but the events raised important issues about presidential privacy and ethics. To what extent should the president's personal life be the subject of public scrutiny while he or she is in office? (AP Photo/Doug Mills)

The second president to be impeached by the House but not convicted by the Senate was President Bill Clinton. In September 1998, Independent Counsel Kenneth Starr sent to Congress the findings of his investigation of the president on the charges of perjury and obstruction of justice. The House approved two charges against Clinton: lying to the grand jury about his affair with Monica Lewinsky and obstruction of justice. The articles of impeachment were then sent to the Senate, which acquitted Clinton.

THE EXECUTIVE ORGANIZATION

Gone are the days when presidents answered their own mail, as George Washington did. It was not until 1857 that Congress authorized a private secretary for the president, to be paid by the federal government. Woodrow Wilson typed most of his correspondence, even though he did have several secretaries. At the beginning of Franklin Roosevelt's long tenure in the White House, the entire staff consisted of 37 employees. With the New Deal and World War II, however, the presidential staff became a sizable organization.

Today, the executive organization includes a White House office staff of about 600, including some workers who are part-time employees and others who are borrowed from their departments by the White House. The more than 360 employees who work in the White House Office are closest to the president. The employees who work for the numerous councils and advisory groups are supposed to advise the president on policy and coordinate the work of departments. The group of appointees who perhaps are most helpful to the president is the Cabinet, each member of which is the principal officer of a government department.

THE CABINET

Although the Constitution does not include the word *cabinet*, it does state that the president "may require the Opinion, in writing, of the principal Officer in each of the executive Departments." Since the time of George Washington, there has been an advisory group, or **Cabinet**, to which the president turns for counsel.

Cabinet
An advisory group selected by the president to aid in making decisions. The Cabinet includes the heads of 15 executive departments and others named by the president.

Members of the Cabinet. Originally, the Cabinet consisted of only four officials—the secretaries of state, treasury, and war, and the attorney general. Today, the Cabinet numbers 14 department secretaries and the attorney general. (See Table 13–1 for the names of the Cabinet departments and Chapter 14 for a detailed discussion of these units.) The Cabinet may include others as well. The president can, at his or her discretion, ascribe Cabinet rank to the vice president, the head of the Office of Management and Budget, the national security advisor, the ambassador to the United Nations, or others.

Kitchen Cabinet
The informal advisors to the president.

Often, a president will use a **kitchen cabinet** to replace the formal Cabinet as a major source of advice. The term *kitchen cabinet* originated during the presidency of Andrew Jackson, who relied on the counsel of close friends who often met with him in the kitchen of the White House. A kitchen cabinet is a very informal group of advisors; usually, they are friends with whom the president worked before being elected.

Presidential Use of Cabinets. Because neither the Constitution nor statutory law requires the president to consult with the Cabinet, its use is purely discretionary. Some presidents have relied on the counsel of their Cabinets more than others. Dwight Eisenhower was used to the team approach to solving problems from his experience as supreme allied commander during World War II, and therefore he frequently turned to his Cabinet for advice on a wide range of issues. More often, presidents have solicited the opinions of their Cabinets and then did what they wanted to do anyway. Lincoln supposedly said—after a Cabinet meeting in which a vote was seven nays against his one aye—"Seven nays and one aye, the ayes have it." In general, few presidents have relied heavily on the advice of their Cabinet members.

It is not surprising that presidents tend not to rely on their Cabinet members' advice. Often, the departmental heads are more responsive to the wishes of their own staffs or to their own political ambitions than they are to the president. They may be more concerned with obtaining resources for their departments than with achieving the goals of the president. So there is often a strong conflict of interest between presidents and their Cabinet members.

THE EXECUTIVE OFFICE OF THE PRESIDENT

When President Franklin Roosevelt appointed a special committee on administrative management, he knew that the committee would conclude that the president needed help. The committee proposed a major reorganization of the executive branch. Congress did not approve the entire reorganization, but it did create the **Executive Office of the President (EOP)** to provide staff assistance for the chief executive and to help coordinate the executive bureaucracy. Since that time, many agencies have been created within the EOP to supply the president with advice and staff help. These agencies include the following:

Executive Office of the President (EOP)
An organization established by President Franklin D. Roosevelt to assist the president in carrying out major duties.

- White House Office
- White House Military Office
- Office of the Vice President
- Council of Economic Advisers
- President's Critical Infrastructure Protection Board
- Office of Management and Budget

- Office of National Drug Control Policy
- Office of Science and Technology Policy
- Office of the United States Trade Representative
- Council on Environmental Quality
- National Security Council
- President's Foreign Intelligence Advisory Board
- Office of National AIDS Policy

Several of the offices within the EOP are especially important, including the White House Office, the Office of Management and Budget, and the National Security Council.

The White House Office. The **White House Office** includes most of the key personal and political advisors to the president. Among the jobs held by these aides are those of legal counsel to the president, secretary, press secretary, and appointments secretary. Often, the individuals who hold these positions are recruited from the president's campaign staff. Their duties—mainly protecting the president's political interests—are similar to campaign functions. In fact, most observers of the presidency agree that contemporary presidents continue their campaigning after inauguration. The **permanent campaign** is a long-term strategy planned by the White House Office of Communications with the press secretary to keep the president's approval ratings high and to improve his support in Congress. The campaign includes staged events, symbolic actions, and controlled media appearances. In all recent administrations, one member of the White House Office has been named **chief of staff**. This person, who is responsible for coordinating the office, is also one of the president's chief advisors.

The president may establish special advisory units within the White House to address topics the president finds especially important. Under George W. Bush, these units also include the Office of Faith-Based and Community Initiatives and the USA Freedom Corps. The White House Office also includes the staff members who support the first lady.

In addition to civilian advisors, the president is supported by a large number of military personnel, who are organized under the White House Military Office. These members of the military provide communications, transportation, medical care, and food services to the president and the White House staff.

Employees of the White House Office have been both envied and criticized. The White House Office, according to most former staffers, grants its employees access and power. They are able to use the resources of the White House to contact virtually anyone in the world by telephone, cable, fax, or electronic mail, as well as to use the influence of the White House to persuade legislators and citizens. Because of this influence, staffers are often criticized for overstepping the bounds of the office. The appointments secretary is able to grant or deny senators, representatives, and Cabinet secretaries access to the president. The press secretary grants the press and television journalists access to any information about the president.

White House staff members are closest to the president and may have considerable influence over the administration's decisions. When presidents are under fire for their decisions, the staff is often accused of keeping the chief executive too isolated from criticism or help. Presidents insist that they will not allow the staff to become too powerful, but, given the difficulty of the office, each president eventually turns to staff members for loyal assistance and protection.

The Office of Management and Budget. The **Office of Management and Budget (OMB)** was originally the Bureau of the Budget, which was created in 1921 within the Department of the Treasury. Recognizing the importance of this agency, Franklin Roosevelt moved it into the White House Office in 1939. Richard Nixon reorganized the Bureau of the Budget in 1970 and changed its name to reflect its new managerial function. It is headed by a director, who must make up the annual federal budget that the president presents to Congress each January for approval. In principle, the director of the OMB has broad fiscal powers in planning and estimating various parts of the federal budget, because all agencies must submit their proposed budget to the OMB for approval. In

White House Office
The personal office of the president, which tends to presidential political needs and manages the media.

Permanent Campaign
A coordinated and planned strategy carried out by the White House to increase the president's popularity and support.

Chief of Staff
The person who is named to direct the White House Office and advise the president.

That the 2008 presidential elections will be the first since 1952 without an incumbent president or vice president running?

Office of Management and Budget (OMB)
A division of the Executive Office of the President. The OMB assists the president in preparing the annual budget, clearing and coordinating departmental agency budgets, and supervising the administration of the federal budget.

reality, it is not so clear that the OMB truly can affect the greater scope of the federal budget. Rather, the OMB may be more important as a clearinghouse for legislative proposals initiated in the executive agencies.

The National Security Council. The **National Security Council (NSC)** is a link between the president's key foreign and military advisors and the president. Its members consist of the president, the vice president, and the secretaries of state and defense, plus other informal members. Included in the NSC is the president's special assistant for national security affairs. In 2001, Condoleezza Rice became the first woman to serve as a president's national security advisor.

> **National Security Council (NSC)**
> An agency in the Executive Office of the President that advises the president on national security.

THE VICE PRESIDENCY

The Constitution does not give much power to the vice president. The only formal duty is to preside over the Senate, which is rarely necessary. This obligation is fulfilled when the Senate organizes and adopts its rules and when the vice president is needed to decide a tie vote. In all other cases, the president pro tem manages parliamentary procedures in the Senate. The vice president is expected to participate only informally in senatorial deliberations, if at all.

THE VICE PRESIDENT'S JOB

Vice presidents have traditionally been chosen by presidential nominees to balance the ticket to attract groups of voters or appease party factions. If a presidential nominee is from the North, it is not a bad idea to have a vice-presidential nominee who is from the South. If the presidential nominee is from a rural state, perhaps someone with an urban background would be most suitable as a running mate. Presidential nominees who are strongly conservative or strongly liberal would do well to have vice-presidential nominees who are more in the middle of the political road.

Strengthening the Ticket. In recent presidential elections, vice presidents have often been selected for other reasons. Bill Clinton picked Al Gore to be his running mate in 1992, even though both were Southern and moderates. The ticket appealed to Southerners and moderates, both of whom were crucial to the election. In 2000, both vice-presidential selections were intended to shore up the respective presidential candidates' perceived weaknesses. Republican George W. Bush, who was subject to criticism for his lack of federal government experience and his "lightweight" personality, chose Dick Cheney, a former member of Congress who had also served as secretary of defense. Democrat Al Gore chose Senator Joe Lieberman of Connecticut, whose reputation for moral integrity (as an Orthodox Jew) could help counteract the effects of Bill Clinton's sex scandals. In 2004, Democratic presidential candidate John Kerry made a more traditional choice in Senator John Edwards of North

VICE PRESIDENT DICK CHENEY addresses an audience assembled at the Pentagon in 2006 to commemorate the 186 persons killed during the September 11, 2001, attack on that building. To what extent does a vice president actually represent the president? (R. D. Ward/Department of Defense)

Carolina. Edwards provided regional balance and also a degree of socioeconomic balance because, unlike Kerry, he had been born into relatively humble circumstances. Both presidential candidates in 2008 sought to balance their perceived weaknesses with their vice presidential choices. Barack Obama chose Senator Joseph Biden to add experience and foreign policy knowledge to his ticket, and John McCain chose Sarah Palin to add youth and an appeal to the Christian right to his ticket.

Supporting the President. The job of vice president is not extremely demanding, even when the president gives some specific task to the vice president. Typically, vice presidents spend their time supporting the president's activities. During the Clinton administration (1993–2001), however, Vice President Al Gore did much to strengthen the position of vice president by his aggressive support for environmental protection policies on a global basis. He also took a special interest in areas of emerging technology and lobbied Congress to provide subsidies to public schools for Internet use.

Vice President Dick Cheney, as one of President George W. Bush's key advisors, clearly has been an influential figure in the Bush administration. Although many of the Washington elite were happy to see Dick Cheney as vice president because of his intelligence and wide range of experience, he quickly became a controversial figure. President Bush, especially after the September 11 attacks, seemed to turn frequently to Cheney for advice. He was known to be a supporter of a tough foreign and military policy and to have encouraged Bush to attack Iraq. Cheney was far more influential as vice president than most of his predecessors. However, the duties and influence of the next vice president will be completely dependent on the president's desires. Of course, the vice presidency takes on more significance if the president becomes disabled or dies in office and the vice president becomes president.

Vice presidents sometimes have become elected presidents in their own right. John Adams and Thomas Jefferson were the first two vice presidents to do so. Richard Nixon was elected president in 1968 after he had served as Dwight D. Eisenhower's vice president from 1953 to 1961. In 1988, George H. W. Bush was elected to the presidency after eight years as Ronald Reagan's vice president.

SENATOR JOE BIDEN, the vice-presidential nominee for the Democratic Party, greets young voters in Detroit. (Manuel Dunand/AFP/Getty Images)

PRESIDENTIAL SUCCESSION

Eight vice presidents have become president because of the death of the president. John Tyler, the first to do so, took over William Henry Harrison's position after only one month. No one knew whether Tyler should simply be a caretaker until a new president could be elected three and a half years later or whether he actually should be president. Tyler assumed that he was supposed to be the chief executive and he acted as such, although he was commonly referred to as "His Accidency." Since then, vice presidents taking over the position of the presidency because of the incumbent's death have assumed the presidential powers.

But what should a vice president do if a president becomes incapable of carrying out necessary duties while in office? When James Garfield was shot

DID YOU KNOW?

That President Richard Nixon served 56 days without a vice president, and that President Gerald Ford served 132 days without a vice president?

in 1881, he remained alive for two and a half months. What was Vice President Chester Arthur's role? This question was not addressed in the original Constitution. Article II, Section 1, says only that "[i]n Case of the Removal of the President from Office, or of his Death, Resignation, or Inability to discharge the Powers and Duties of the said Office, the same shall devolve on [the same powers shall be exercised by] the Vice President." There have been many instances of presidential disability. When Dwight Eisenhower became ill a second time in 1958, he entered into a pact with Richard Nixon specifying that the vice president could determine whether the president was incapable of carrying out his duties if the president could not communicate. John F. Kennedy and Lyndon Johnson entered into similar agreements with their vice presidents. Finally, in 1967, the **Twenty-fifth Amendment** was passed, establishing procedures in case of presidential incapacity.

Twenty-fifth Amendment
A 1967 amendment to the Constitution that establishes procedures for filling presidential and vice-presidential vacancies and makes provisions for presidential disability.

THE TWENTY-FIFTH AMENDMENT

According to the Twenty-fifth Amendment, when a president believes that he or she is incapable of performing the duties of office, the president must inform Congress in writing. Then the vice president serves as acting president until the president can resume normal duties. When the president is unable to communicate, a majority of the Cabinet, including the vice president, can declare that fact to Congress. Then the vice president serves as acting president until the president resumes normal duties. If a dispute arises over the return of the president's ability, a two-thirds vote of Congress is required to decide whether the vice president shall remain acting president or whether the president shall resume normal duties.

In 2002, President George W. Bush formally invoked the Twenty-fifth Amendment for the first time by officially transferring presidential power to Vice President Dick Cheney while the president underwent a colonoscopy, a 20-minute procedure. He commented that he undertook this transfer of power "because we're at war," referring to the war on terrorism. The only other time the provisions of the Twenty-fifth Amendment have been used was during President Reagan's colon surgery in 1985, although Reagan did not formally invoke the Amendment.

AN ATTEMPTED ASSASSINATION of Ronald Reagan occurred on March 31, 1981. In the foreground, two men bend over Press Secretary James Brady, who lies seriously wounded. In the background, President Reagan is watched over by a U.S. Secret Service agent with an automatic weapon. A Washington D.C. police officer, Thomas Delahanty, lies to the left after also being shot. (AP Photo/Ron Edmonds)

WHEN THE VICE PRESIDENCY BECOMES VACANT

The Twenty-fifth Amendment also addresses the issue of how the president should fill a vacant vice presidency. Section 2 of the amendment simply states, "Whenever there is a vacancy in the office of the Vice President, the President shall nominate a Vice President who shall take office upon confirmation by a majority vote of both Houses of Congress." This is exactly what occurred when Richard Nixon's vice president, Spiro Agnew, resigned in 1973 because of his alleged receipt of construction contract kickbacks during his tenure as governor of Maryland. Nixon turned to Gerald Ford as his choice for vice president. After extensive hearings, both chambers of Congress confirmed the appointment. Then, when Nixon resigned on August 9, 1974, Ford automatically became president and nominated Nelson Rockefeller as his vice president. Congress confirmed Ford's choice. For the first time in the history of the country, neither the president nor the vice president had been elected to their positions.

The question of who shall be president if both the president and vice president die is answered by the Succession Act of 1947. If the president and vice president die, resign, or are disabled, the Speaker of the House will become president, after resigning from Congress. Next in line is the president pro tem of the Senate, followed by the Cabinet officers in the order of the creation of their departments (see Table 13–3).

TABLE 13–3 Line of Succession to the Presidency of the United States

1.	Vice President
2.	Speaker of the House of Representatives
3.	Senate President Pro Tempore
4.	Secretary of State
5.	Secretary of the Treasury
6.	Secretary of Defense
7.	Attorney General (head of the Justice Department)
8.	Secretary of the Interior
9.	Secretary of Agriculture
10.	Secretary of Commerce
11.	Secretary of Labor
12.	Secretary of Health and Human Services
13.	Secretary of Housing and Urban Development
14.	Secretary of Transportation
15.	Secretary of Energy
16.	Secretary of Education
17.	Secretary of Veterans Affairs
18.	Secretary of Homeland Security

You can make a difference

WATCHING THE WHITE HOUSE

As our head of state, chief executive, commander in chief, and chief legislator, the president of the United States wields massive power over matters at home and abroad. However, the times we live in also present major challenges to this individual, and it is up to us as citizens to monitor our president's performance and balance our country's place in the world.

WHY SHOULD YOU CARE?

A recent panel convened at the Center for Public Leadership at Harvard's John F. Kennedy School of Government to discuss the challenges facing the president-elect in the 2008 election. Foreign-policy issues topped concerns cited, with the continued U.S. presence in Iraq debated, and the nuclear potential of Iran and North Korea studied. Our new president will inherit the largest ongoing deployments of U.S. military forces in combat since the Vietnam War, while trying to overcome the unprecedented unpopularity of America in the world.

Domestically, five challenges were listed as needing resolution: (1) reforming America's financial institutions, (2) lessening inequality between society's richest 1 percent and the bottom 80 percent on the income scale, (3) improving the health-care system, (4) creating a more open global economy, and (5) providing energy security while reducing climate change. This is a daunting to-do list for any president and, to make things even more complex, what needs to be done in each of these areas is not completely clear.

A high degree of public trust in our elected leaders forms one of the basic premises of representative government, but Americans today express less trust in the president than at any point in the past decade. Gallup's annual 2007 Governance Survey found trust in the executive branch of government at 43 percent, only slightly better than the 40 percent support for Richard Nixon about four months before he resigned as president amid the Watergate scandal.

WHAT CAN YOU DO?

Perhaps this public distrust of the president will encourage you to watch the White House through the many checks and balances built into our system. In his 1980 acceptance speech at the Republican National Convention, Ronald Reagan commented on the "trust me" form of government, where there is no need for oversight or limits on presidential power: "Trust me government is government that asks that we concentrate our hopes and dreams on one man; that we trust him to do what's best for us. My view of government places trust not in one person or one party, but in those that transcend persons and parties. The trust is where it belongs—in the people."

You can begin to monitor the president at the home page of the White House, **www.whitehouse.gov**. This Web site has current news; links to the Web pages of the president, vice president, and first lady; categories for public policy; pages for the president's Cabinet; and interactive links where you can register your comments. The Web site also allows you to subscribe to free White House e-mail updates that focus on certain issues, such as homeland security, the economy, education, health care, and the war on terrorism. On a 24-hour comment line, 202-456-1111, an operator will record your message and forward it to the president's office. Letters to the president should be addressed to:

The President of the United States
The White House
1600 Pennsylvania Avenue N.W.
Washington, DC 20500

Countless Web sites provide daily updates to focus on the president and the White House. White House Watch, **www.washingtonpost.com/whitehousewatch**, is published every weekday and includes White House-related items from newspapers, magazines, broadcast Web sites, and blogs. The White House Watch Links on the site include the latest White House salary list, a map of the West Wing, presidential approval polls, and a list of correspondents covering the White House for major news outlets. Politicalticker, a blog for CNNPolitics.com, features the latest political news and has a special category devoted to the President. BeltwayConfidential, **http://blogs.chron .com/beltwayconfidential**, is a blog run by the *Houston Chronicle* that features "The President of America," with daily updates from media sources around the country and opportunities to post your comments.

Finally, if you would like to check the factual accuracy of statements made by the president or about him or her in the media, you can go to **www.factcheck.org**, a project of the Annenberg Public Policy Center (APPC) of the University of Pennsylvania. The APPC was established in 1994 to create a community of scholars to address public policy issues at the local, state, and federal levels.

REFERENCES

Glenn Greenwald, "Trust Us Government," Salon.com, accessed January 29, 2008, at www.salon.com.

Jeffrey Jones, "Low Trust in Federal Government Rivals Watergate Era Levels," Gallup News Service, accessed September 26, 2007, at www.gallup.com.

http://blogs.chron.com/beltwayconfidential/the_president_of_america

http://politicalticker.blogs.cnn.com

www.factcheck.org

www.washingtonpost.com/whitehousewatch

www.whitehouse.gov

KEY TERMS

advice and consent 466
appointment power 462
Cabinet 481
chief diplomat 466
chief executive 461
chief legislator 468
chief of staff 483
civil service 462
commander in chief 464
constitutional power 473
diplomatic recognition 466
emergency power 477
executive agreement 467
**Executive Office of the
   President (EOP)** 482

executive order 478
executive privilege 478
expressed power 473
Federal Register 478
head of state 460
impeachment 479
inherent power 473
kitchen cabinet 482
line-item veto 471
**National Security Council
   (NSC)** 484
**Office of Management and
   Budget (OMB)** 483
pardon 463
patronage 474

permanent campaign 483
pocket veto 471
reprieve 463
signing statement 461
**State of the Union
   message** 468
statutory power 473
Twelfth Amendment 459
Twenty-fifth Amendment 486
veto message 469
War Powers Resolution 465
Washington community 475
White House Office 483

CHAPTER SUMMARY

1. The office of the presidency in the United States, combining as it does the functions of head of state and chief executive, was unique when it was created. The framers of the Constitution were divided over whether the president should be a weak or a strong executive.

2. The requirements for the office of the presidency are outlined in Article II, Section 1, of the Constitution. The president's roles include both formal and informal duties. The roles of the president include head of state, chief executive, commander in chief, chief diplomat, chief legislator, and party chief.

3. As head of state, the president is ceremonial leader of the government. As chief executive, the president is bound to enforce the acts of Congress, the judgments of the federal courts, and treaties. The chief executive has the power of appointment and the power to grant reprieves and pardons.

4. As commander in chief, the president is the ultimate decision maker in military matters. As chief diplomat, the president recognizes foreign governments, negotiates treaties, signs agreements, and nominates and receives ambassadors.

5. The role of chief legislator includes recommending legislation to Congress, lobbying for the legislation, approving laws, and exercising the veto power. In addition to

constitutional and inherent powers, the president has statutory powers written into law by Congress. Presidents are also leaders of their political parties. Presidents use their power to persuade and their access to the media to fulfill this function.

6. Presidents have a variety of special powers that are not available to other branches of the government. These include emergency power and the power to issue executive orders and invoke executive privilege.

7. Abuses of executive power are dealt with by Articles I and II of the Constitution, which authorize the House and Senate to impeach and remove the president, vice president, or other officers of the federal government for committing "Treason, Bribery, or other high Crimes and Misdemeanors."

8. The president receives assistance from the Cabinet and from the Executive Office of the President (including the White House Office).

9. The vice president is the constitutional officer assigned to preside over the Senate and to assume the presidency in the event of the death, resignation, removal, or disability of the president. The Twenty-fifth Amendment, passed in 1967, established procedures to be followed in case of presidential incapacity and when filling a vacant vice presidency.

SELECTED PRINT AND MEDIA RESOURCES

SUGGESTED READINGS

Clinton, Bill. *My Life.* New York: Knopf, 2004. President Clinton's autobiography devotes ample space to illuminating stories from his childhood. In contrast, some may find the account of his presidential years excessively detailed. Still, the book is essential source material on one of the most important and controversial political figures of our time.

Crenson, Matthew, and Benjamin Ginsberg. *Presidential Power: Unchecked and Unbalanced.* New York: W. W. Norton, 2007. The authors return to the idea that the president has become too powerful and show how presidents over the last 30 years have expanded the power of the office.

Genovese, Michael A., and Lori Cox Han, eds. *The Presidency and the Challenge of Democracy.* Boston: Palgrave Macmillan, 2006. This collection of essays by leading scholars probes the current trend of expanding presidential powers.

Mann, James. *Rise of the Vulcans: The History of Bush's War Cabinet.* New York: Viking Books, 2004. This is a collective biography of the foreign-policy team (not all of whom were actually in the Cabinet) during George W. Bush's first term. The self-described Vulcans included Donald Rumsfeld, secretary of defense; Vice President Dick Cheney; Colin Powell, secretary of state; Paul Wolfowitz, deputy secretary of defense; Richard Armitage, deputy secretary of state; and Condoleezza Rice, national security advisor. While these individuals were never in perfect agreement, they shared basic values.

Skowronek, Stephen. *Presidential Leadership in Political Time: Reprise and Reappraisal.* Lawrence: University Press of Kansas, 2008. In this updating of a well-known book, the author expands on his thesis that presidents' successes are, in part, constrained by the political events of the day. He includes both Bill Clinton and George W. Bush in his analysis.

MEDIA RESOURCES

Fahrenheit 9/11—Michael Moore's scathing 2004 critique of the Bush administration has been called "one long political attack ad." It is also the highest-grossing documentary ever made. While the film may be biased, it is—like all of Moore's productions—entertaining.

The Guns of October—This film explores the Cuban Missile Crisis of 1962. It portrays the Kennedy decision-making process in deciding not to attack Cuba.

LBJ: A Biography—An acclaimed biography of Lyndon Johnson that covers his rise to power, his presidency, and the events of the Vietnam War, which ended his presidency; produced in 1991 as part of PBS's *The American Experience* series.

Nixon—An excellent 1995 film exposing the events of Richard Nixon's troubled presidency. Anthony Hopkins plays the embattled but brilliant chief executive.

Sunrise at Campobello—An excellent portrait of one of the greatest presidents, Franklin Delano Roosevelt; produced in 1960 and starring Ralph Bellamy.

e-mocracy

THE PRESIDENCY AND THE INTERNET

Today, the Internet has become such a normal part of most Americans' lives that it is difficult to imagine what life was like without it. Certainly, accessing the latest press releases from the White House was much more difficult 10 years ago than it is today. It was not until the Clinton administration (1993–2001) that access to the White House via the Internet became possible. President Bill Clinton supported making many White House documents available on the White House Web site.

Correspondence with the president and the first lady quickly moved from ordinary handwritten letters to e-mail. During the Clinton presidency, most agencies of the government, as well as Congressional offices, also began to provide access and information on the Internet. Today, you can access the White House Web site (see the following *Logging On* section) to find White House press releases, presidential State of the Union messages and other speeches, historical data on the presidency, and much more.

LOGGING ON

- This site offers extensive information on the White House and the presidency:
  www.whitehouse.gov
- Inaugural addresses of American presidents from George Washington to George W. Bush can be found at:
  www.bartleby.com/124

- You can find an excellent collection of data and maps describing all U.S. presidential elections at Dave Leip's Atlas of U.S. Presidential Elections. Go to:
  www.uselectionatlas.org
- There is a wonderful collection of presidential photographs, documents, audio, and video archived at the Presidency Project at the University of California at Santa Barbara. Check the Web site at:
  www.presidency.ucsb.edu

ONLINE REVIEW

At **www.cengage.com/politicalscience/schmidt/agandpt14e**, you will find a Tutorial Quiz for this chapter providing questions on the chapter contents, including the features. The questions are organized to match the major sections of the chapter. You'll have access to other helpful study tools, including the book's glossary and flashcards, crossword puzzles, and Web links, as well as "Which Side Are You On?" and "Politics and . . ." features written by the authors of the book.

An aerial view of multiple federal buildings, including the IRS building and the Old Post Office Building. (Hisham Ibrahim/Photov.com/Alamy Limited)

(CHAPTER

(14)

THE BUREAUCRACY

CHAPTER CONTENTS

Making a DIFFERENCE

HOLDING GOVERNMENT ACCOUNTABLE

If $17 million were stolen from the federal government, the thieves should be held to account.[a] If our nation's airport security system were not keeping pace with emerging terrorist threats, policy makers in a position to act should be informed.[b] If sensitive U.S. military equipment like F-14 antennae, nuclear biological chemical gear, and pieces of body armor plates could be bought freely on Internet auction sites, an investigation should be launched to shut this practice down.[c] Keeping all aspects of government accountable and investigating possible fraud, waste, and abuse are among the key responsibilities of the Government Accountability Office (GAO).

Created by Congress in 1921, the GAO (originally named the General Accounting Office) was designed to audit and review executive branch agencies.[d] Sometimes called Congress's watchdog, GAO is part of the executive branch and is headed by the Comptroller General, who is appointed by the president and confirmed by the Senate for a 12-year nonrenewable term. The size, responsibilities, and reach of GAO have changed over time, hitting their zenith in the early 1990s. In 2004, its name was changed to the Government Accountability Office to reflect the way the agency had expanded from its original mission. The examples cited earlier are just a few of the many investigations it launches each year. With a staff of more than 3,000 people and a budget of more than $488 million, GAO conducts reviews, writes reports, and investigates (often undercover) alleged wrongdoing on the part of individuals within the federal government.[e]

FACELESS BUREAUCRATS—this image provokes a negative reaction from many, if not most, Americans. Polls consistently report that the majority of Americans support "less government." The same polls, however, report that the majority of Americans support almost every specific program that the government undertakes. The conflict between the desire for small government and the benefits that only a large government can provide has been a constant feature of American politics. For example, the goal of preserving endangered species has widespread support. At the same time, many people believe that restrictions imposed under the Endangered Species Act violate the rights of landowners. Helping the elderly pay their medical bills is a popular objective, but hardly anyone enjoys paying the Medicare tax that supports this effort.

In addition, everyone complains about the inefficiency and wastefulness of government, in general and at federal, state, and local levels. The media regularly uncovers examples of failures in governmental programs. However, investigations and reports of the Governmental Accountability Office, as described in the *Making a Difference* feature, are rarely the subject of news coverage. In this chapter, we describe the size, organization, and staffing of the federal bureaucracy. We review modern attempts at bureaucratic reform and the process by which Congress exerts ultimate control over the bureaucracy. We also discuss the bureaucracy's role in making rules and setting policy.

THE NATURE OF BUREAUCRACY

Every modern president, at one time or another, has proclaimed that his administration was going to "fix the government." All modern presidents also have put forth plans

One of the ways GAO keeps tabs on government is to list areas within the federal government that are at high risk for "fraud, waste, abuse, and mismanagement."[f] Some agencies like the Medicare Program and the Department of Defense Supply Chain Management have remained on the list since 1990. An example of an agency recently removed from the list is the U.S. Postal Service. The Postal Service was originally added to the list because of concerns about its fiscal health. The GAO determined that significant changes, including retiring its debt and implementing $5 billion in cost savings, were made to justify removing it from the list.

The information GAO provides is critical in a democracy, where citizens need to be informed about the actions of government. The GAO issues many reports each year on topics like understanding how the government spends taxpayers' dollars, the safety of our food supply, and successful strategies for monitoring convicted sex offenders. Many reports are available online, through your college or university library, or ordered directly from GAO (**www.gao .gov/cgi-bin/ordtab.pl**).

If this sort of investigative and analysis work sounds interesting, you might consider employment with GAO or another similar agency among the many you will discover in this chapter. Students can intern with these organizations to gain valuable work experience.[g] Those close to graduating should visit **www.usajobs.opm.gov**, which is a gateway to government employment opportunities. Whether you plan to be a chemist, or are studying animal husbandry or criminal justice, the federal bureaucracy needs your talents.

[a]www.gao.gov/new.items/d07724t.pdf

[b]http://oversight.house.gov/documents/20071114175647.pdf

[c]www.gao.gov/new.items/d08644t.pdf

[d]Frederick M. Kaiser, CRS Report for Congress (GAO: Government Accountability Office and General Accounting Office, 2007), updated June 22, 2007, Order Code RL30349, www.fas.org/sgp/crs/misc/RL30349.pdf, accessed May 15, 2007.

[e]www.gao.gov/about/gglance.html

[f]www.gao.gov/new.items/d07310.pdf

[g]www.studentjobs.gov/searchvol.asp

to end government waste and inefficiency. For instance, Bill Clinton's plan was called Reinventing Government, followed by Performance-Based Budgeting under George W. Bush. The success of plans such as these has been, in a word, underwhelming. Presidents generally have been powerless to affect the structure and operation of the federal bureaucracy significantly.

A **bureaucracy** is the name given to a large organization that is structured hierarchically to carry out specific functions. Generally, most bureaucracies are characterized by an organization chart. The units of the organization are divided according to the specialization and expertise of the employees.

Bureaucracy
A large organization that is structured hierarchically to carry out specific functions.

PUBLIC AND PRIVATE BUREAUCRACIES

We should not think of bureaucracy as unique to government. Any large corporation or university can be considered a bureaucratic organization. The fact is that the handling of complex problems requires a division of labor. Individuals must concentrate their skills on specific, well-defined aspects of a problem and depend on others to solve the rest of it.

Public or government bureaucracies differ from private organizations in some important ways, however. A private corporation, such as Microsoft, has a single set of leaders—its board of directors. Public bureaucracies, in contrast, do not have a single set of leaders. Although the president is the chief administrator of the federal system, all bureaucratic agencies are subject to Congress for their funding, staffing, and their continued existence. Furthermore, public bureaucracies supposedly serve the citizenry.

A HUGE FEMA TRAILER PARK houses displaced families from New Orleans exactly one year after Hurricane Katrina flooded the city. Why do you think Hurricane Katrina was such as diasaster? (Mario Tama/Getty Images)

One other important difference between private corporations and government bureaucracies is that government bureaucracies are not organized to make a profit. Rather, they are supposed to perform their functions as efficiently as possible to conserve the taxpayers' dollars. Perhaps this ideal makes citizens hostile toward government bureaucracy when they experience inefficiency and red tape.

MODELS OF BUREAUCRACY

Several theories have been offered to help us better understand the ways in which bureaucracies function. Each of these theories focuses on specific features of bureaucracies.

Weberian Model. The classic model, or **Weberian model**, of the modern bureaucracy was proposed by the German sociologist Max Weber.[1] He argued that the increasingly complex nature of modern life, coupled with the steadily growing demands placed on governments by their citizens, made the formation of bureaucracies inevitable. According to Weber, most bureaucracies—whether in the public or private sector—are organized hierarchically and governed by formal procedures. The power in a bureaucracy flows from the top downward. Decision-making processes in bureaucracies are shaped by detailed technical rules that promote similar decisions in similar situations. Bureaucrats are specialists who attempt to resolve problems through logical reasoning and data analysis instead of instinct and guesswork. Individual advancement in bureaucracies is supposed to be based on merit rather than political connections. The modern bureaucracy, according to Weber, should be an apolitical organization.

Acquisitive Model. Other theorists do not view bureaucracies in terms as benign as Weber's. Some believe that bureaucracies are acquisitive in nature. Proponents of the **acquisitive model** argue that top-level bureaucrats will always try to expand, or at least to avoid any reductions in, the size of their budgets. Although government bureau-

Weberian Model
A model of bureaucracy developed by the German sociologist Max Weber, who viewed bureaucracies as rational, hierarchical organizations in which decisions are based on logical reasoning.

Acquisitive Model
A model of bureaucracy that views top-level bureaucrats as seeking to expand the size of their budgets and staffs to gain greater power.

[1]Max Weber, *Theory of Social and Economic Organization*, edited by Talcott Parsons (New York: Oxford University Press, 1974).

cracies are not-for-profit enterprises, bureaucrats want to maximize the size of their budgets and staffs, because these things are the most visible trappings of power in the public sector. These efforts are also prompted by the desire of bureaucrats to "sell" their products—national defense, public housing, agricultural subsidies, and so on—to both Congress and the public.

Monopolistic Model. Because government bureaucracies seldom have competitors, some theorists have suggested that these bureaucratic organizations may be explained best by a **monopolistic model**. The analysis is similar to that used by economists to examine the behavior of monopolistic firms. Monopolistic bureaucracies—like monopolistic firms—essentially have no competitors and act accordingly. Because monopolistic bureaucracies usually are not penalized for chronic inefficiency, they have little reason to adopt cost-saving measures or to use their resources more productively. Some economists have argued that such problems can be cured only by privatizing certain bureaucratic functions.

Monopolistic Model
A model of bureaucracy that compares bureaucracies to monopolistic business firms. Lack of competition in either circumstance leads to inefficient and costly operations.

BUREAUCRACIES COMPARED

The federal bureaucracy in the United States enjoys a greater degree of autonomy than do federal or national bureaucracies in many other nations. Much of the insularity that is commonly supposed to characterize the bureaucracy in this country may stem from the sheer size of the government organizations needed to implement an annual budget that is about $3 trillion. Because the lines of authority often are not well defined, some bureaucracies may be able to operate with a significant degree of autonomy.

The federal nature of the American government also means that national bureaucracies regularly provide financial assistance to their state counterparts. Both the Department of Education and the Department of Housing and Urban Development, for example, distribute funds to their counterparts at the state level. In contrast, most bureaucracies in European countries have a top-down command structure so that national programs may be implemented directly at the lower level. This is due not only

COMMISSIONER NANCY NORD of the U.S. Consumer Product Safety Commission announces the recall of about 9 million Mattel toys made in China during a press conference in Bethesda, Maryland. Mattel, the world's largest toy company, announced its second major recall in a month of Chinese-made toys contaminated with lead paint. How could such an oversight occur in the importation of products? (Shawn Thew/epa/CORBIS)

to the smaller size of most European countries but also to the fact that public ownership of such businesses as telephone companies, airlines, railroads, and utilities is far more common in Europe than in the United States.

The fact that the U.S. government owns relatively few enterprises does not mean, however, that its bureaucracies are comparatively powerless. Many **administrative agencies** in the federal bureaucracy—such as the Environmental Protection Agency, the Nuclear Regulatory Commission, and the Securities and Exchange Commission—regulate private companies.

> **Administrative Agency**
> A federal, state, or local government unit established to perform a specific function. Administrative agencies are created and authorized by legislative bodies to administer and enforce specific laws.

THE SIZE OF THE BUREAUCRACY

In 1789, the new government's bureaucracy was minuscule. There were three departments—State (with nine employees), War (with two employees), and Treasury (with 39 employees)—and the Office of the Attorney General (which later became the Department of Justice). The bureaucracy was still small in 1798. At that time, the secretary of state had seven clerks and spent a total of $500 (about $8,545 in 2008 dollars) on stationery and printing. In that same year, the Appropriations Act allocated $1.4 million to the War Department (or $23.9 million in 2008 dollars).[2]

That the federal government spends more than $1 billion every five hours, every day of the year?

Times have changed, as we can see in Figure 14–1, which lists the various federal agencies and the number of civilian employees in each. Excluding

FIGURE 14–1 Federal Agencies and Their Respective Numbers of Civilian Employees

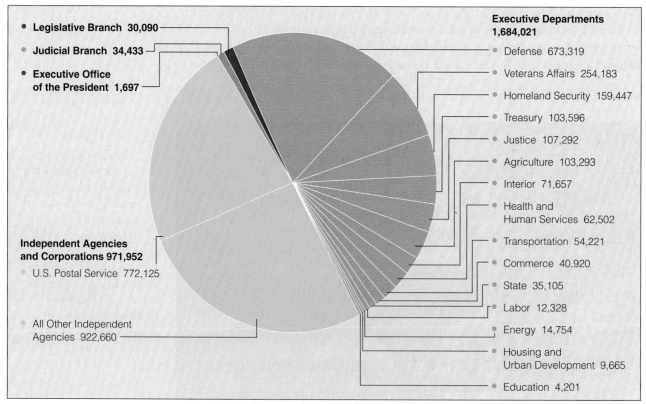

Source: The U.S. Office of Personnel Management, *Factbook*, September 2007.

[2]Leonard D. White, *The Federalists: A Study in Administrative History, 1789–1801* (New York: Free Press, 1948).

the military, the federal bureaucracy includes approximately 2.7 million government employees. That number has remained relatively stable for the last several decades. It is somewhat deceiving, however, because many other individuals work directly or indirectly for the federal government as subcontractors or consultants and in other capacities. In fact, according to some studies, the federal workforce vastly exceeds the number of official federal workers.[3]

The figures for federal government employment are only part of the story. Figure 14–2 shows the growth in government employment at the federal, state, and local levels. Since 1970, this growth has been mainly at the state and local levels. If all government employees are included, more than 16 percent of all civilian employment is accounted for by government. The costs of the bureaucracy are commensurately high. The share of the gross domestic product accounted for by all government spending was only 8.5 percent in 1929. Today, it exceeds 30 percent. Could we reduce the cost of government by eliminating unnecessary spending? We look at one example of questionable spending in the discussion of AMTRAK in the "Government Corporations" section.

THE ORGANIZATION OF THE FEDERAL BUREAUCRACY

Within the federal bureaucracy are several different types of government agencies and organizations. Figure 14–3 outlines the several bodies within the executive branch, as well as the separate organizations that provide services to Congress, to the courts, and directly to the president. In Chapter 13, we discussed those agencies that are considered to be part of the Executive Office of the President.

The executive branch, which employs most of the government's staff, has four major types of structures: (1) Cabinet departments, (2) independent executive agencies, (3) independent regulatory agencies, and (4) government corporations. Each has a distinctive relationship to the president, and some have unusual internal structures, overall goals, and grants of power.

CABINET DEPARTMENTS

The 15 **Cabinet departments** are the major service organizations of the federal government. They can also be described in management terms as **line organizations**. This means that they are directly accountable to the president and are responsible for performing government functions, such as printing money and training troops. These departments were created by Congress when the need for each department arose. The first department to be created was State, and the most recent one was Homeland Security, established in 2003. The difficulties faced in creating that new department are discussed in the "Reorganizing to Stop Terrorism" section. A president might ask that a new department be created or an old one abolished, but the president has no power to do so without legislative approval from Congress.

Each department is headed by a secretary (except for the Justice Department, which is headed by the attorney general). Each also has several levels of undersecretaries, assistant secretaries, and so on.

Presidents theoretically have considerable control over the Cabinet departments, because presidents are able to appoint or fire all of the top officials. As discussed in

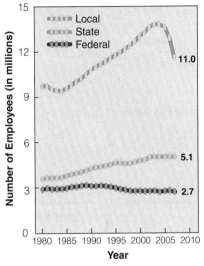

FIGURE 14–2
Government Employment at the Federal, State, and Local Levels
There are more local government employees than federal or state employees combined.

Source: Bureau of Labor Statistics, 2006.

Cabinet Department
One of the 15 departments of the executive branch (State, Treasury, Defense, Justice, Interior, Agriculture, Commerce, Labor, Health and Human Services, Homeland Security, Housing and Urban Development, Education, Energy, Transportation, and Veterans Affairs).

Line Organization
In the federal government, an administrative unit that is directly accountable to the president.

[3]See, for example, Paul C. Light, *The True Size of Government* (Washington, DC: Brookings Institution Press, 1999).

FIGURE 14–3 Organization Chart of the Federal Government

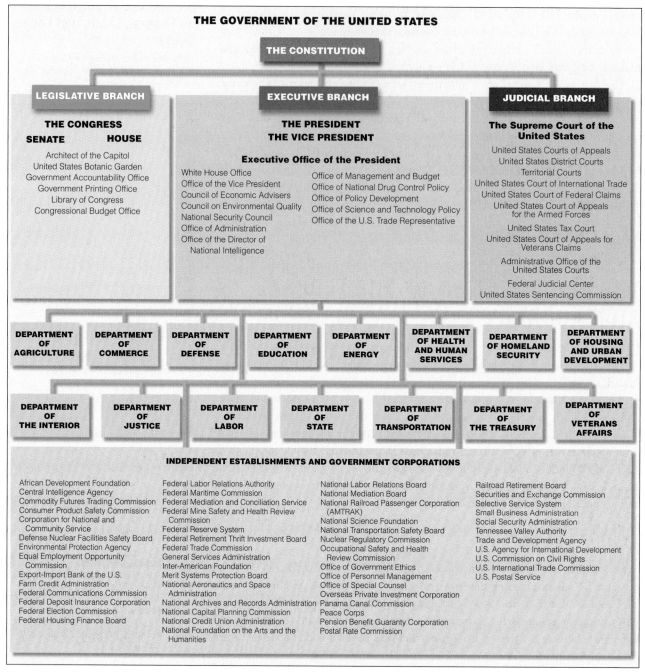

Source: *United States Government Manual, 2007–2008* (Washington, DC: U.S. Government Printing Office, 2007).

Chapter 13, these positions are listed in the Plum Book. Even Cabinet departments do not always respond to the president's wishes, though. One reason that presidents are frequently unhappy with their departments is that the entire bureaucratic structure below the top political levels is staffed by permanent employees, many of whom are committed to established programs or procedures and who resist change. Table 14–1 on page 502 shows that each Cabinet department employs thousands of individuals, only a handful of whom are under the control of the president. The table also describes some of the functions of each of the departments.

INDEPENDENT EXECUTIVE AGENCIES

Independent executive agencies are bureaucratic organizations that are not located within a department but report directly to the president, who appoints their chief officials. When a new federal agency is created—the Environmental Protection Agency, for example—Congress decides where it will be located in the bureaucracy. In recent decades, presidents often have asked that a new organization be kept separate or independent rather than added to an existing department, particularly if a department may be hostile to the agency's creation. The Smithsonian Institution, which runs the government's museums and the National Zoo, was formed in 1846 and is an example of an independent executive agency. Another example is the Central Intelligence Agency (CIA). Formed in 1947, the CIA gathers and analyzes political and military information about foreign countries and conducts covert operations outside the United States. You can read more about the CIA in Chapter 18.

TREASURY SECRETARY HENRY PAULSON, left, accompanied by Federal Reserve Chairman Ben Bernanke, right, testifies on Capitol Hill in Washington in July, 2008. By late September, Bernanke and Paulson returned to Congress urgently seeking a bailout of troubled Wall Street banking institutions. (Manuel Balce Ceneta/AP/Wide World Photos)

INDEPENDENT REGULATORY AGENCIES

The **independent regulatory agencies** are typically responsible for a specific type of public policy. Their function is to make and implement rules and regulations in a particular sphere of action to protect the public interest. The earliest such agency was the Interstate Commerce Commission (ICC), which was established in 1887 when Americans began to seek some form of government control over the rapidly growing business and industrial sector. This new form of organization, the independent regulatory agency, was supposed to make technical, nonpolitical decisions about rates, profits, and rules that would benefit all and that did not require congressional legislation. In the years that followed the creation of the ICC, other agencies were formed to regulate communication (the Federal Communications Commission), nuclear power (the Nuclear Regulatory Commission), and so on. (The ICC was abolished on December 30, 1995.)

The Purpose and Nature of Regulatory Agencies. In practice, the regulatory agencies are administered independently of all three branches of government. They were set up because Congress felt it was unable to handle the complexities and technicalities required to carry out specific laws in the public interest. The regulatory commissions in fact combine some functions of all three branches of government—executive, legislative, and judicial. They are legislative in that they make rules that have the force of law. They are executive in that they enforce those rules. They are judicial in that they decide disputes involving the rules they have made.

Members of regulatory agency boards or commissions are appointed by the president with the consent of the Senate, although they do not report to the president. By law, the members of regulatory agencies cannot all be from the same political party. Members may be removed by the president only for causes specified in the law creating the agency. Presidents can influence regulatory agency behavior by appointing people of their own parties or individuals who share their political views when vacancies occur, in particular when the chair is vacant. For example, President George W. Bush placed people on the Federal Communications Commission (FCC) who shared his belief in

Independent Executive Agency
A federal agency that is not part of a Cabinet department but reports directly to the president.

Independent Regulatory Agency
An agency outside the major executive departments charged with making and implementing rules and regulations.

TABLE 14–1 Executive Departments

DEPARTMENT AND YEAR ESTABLISHED	PRINCIPAL FUNCTIONS
State (1789) (33,945 employees)	Negotiates treaties; develops foreign policy; protects citizens abroad
Treasury (1789) (109,077 employees)	Pays all federal bills; borrows money; collects federal taxes; mints coins and prints paper currency; supervises national banks
Interior (1849) (67,138 employees)	Supervises federally owned lands and parks; supervises Native American affairs
Justice (1870)* (105,873 employees)	Furnishes legal advice to the president; enforces federal criminal laws; supervises federal prisons
Agriculture (1889) (95,289 employees)	Assists farmers and ranchers; conducts agricultural research; works to protect forests
Commerce (1913)* (39,184 employees)	Grants patents and trademarks; conducts national census; monitors weather; protects interests of businesses
Labor (1913)* (15,279 employees)	Administers federal labor laws; promotes interests of workers
Defense (1947)** (675,111 employees)	Manages the armed forces; operates military bases; civil defense
Housing and Urban Development (1965) (9,685 employees)	Deals with nation's housing needs; develops and rehabilitates urban communities; oversees resale of mortgages
Transportation (1967) (53,337 employees)	Finances improvements in mass transit; develops and administers programs for highways, railroads, and aviation
Energy (1977) (14,759 employees)	Promotes energy conservation; analyzes energy data; conducts research and development
Health and Human Services (1979)*** (60,375 employees)	Promotes public health; enforces pure food and drug laws; conducts and sponsors health-related research
Education (1979)*** (4,230 employees)	Coordinates federal education programs and policies; administers aid to education; promotes educational research
Veterans Affairs (1988) (235,654 employees)	Promotes welfare of U.S. veterans
Homeland Security (2003) (165,085 employees)	Attempts to prevent terrorist attacks within the U.S.; controls U.S. borders; minimizes damage from natural disasters

*Formed from the Office of the Attorney General (created in 1789).
**Formed from the Department of Commerce and Labor (created in 1903).
***Formed from the Department of War (created in 1789) and the Department of the Navy (created in 1798).
****Formed from the Department of Health, Education, and Welfare (created in 1953).
Employment figures as of September 2006.

the need to curb obscene language in the media. Not surprisingly, the FCC soon thereafter started to "crack down" on obscenities on the air. One victim of this regulatory effort was Howard Stern, a nationally syndicated radio and television personality. His response was to switch from commercial radio and TV to unregulated satellite radio, where he can be heard every day on Sirius.

Agency Capture. Over the last several decades, some observers have concluded that these agencies, although nominally independent, may in fact not always be so. They contend that many independent regulatory agencies have been **captured** by the very industries and firms they were supposed to regulate. The results have been less competition rather than more competition, higher prices rather than lower prices, and less choice rather than more choice for consumers.

Capture
The act by which an industry being regulated by a government agency gains direct or indirect control over agency personnel and decision makers.

Deregulation and Re-regulation. During the presidency of Ronald Reagan (served 1981–1989), some significant deregulation (the removal of regulatory restraints—the opposite of regulation) occurred, much of which had started under President Jimmy Carter (served 1977–1981). For example, President Carter appointed a chairperson of the Civil Aeronautics Board (CAB), who gradually eliminated regulation of airline fares and routes. Then, under Reagan, the CAB was eliminated on January 1, 1985.

During the administration of George H. W. Bush (served 1989–1993), calls for re-regulation of many businesses increased. During that administration, the Americans with Disabilities Act of 1990, the Civil Rights Act of 1991, and the Clean Air Act Amendments of 1991, all of which increased or changed the regulation of many businesses, were passed. Additionally, the Cable Re-regulation Act of 1992 was passed.

Under President Bill Clinton (served 1993–2001), the Interstate Commerce Commission was eliminated, and the banking and telecommunications industries, along with many other sectors of the economy, were deregulated. At the same time, extensive regulation protected the environment. In the wake of the mortgage crisis of 2007 and failure of several large investment houses in 2008, the administration and most members of Congress called for a bailout of the troubled firms and a return to more regulation.

That the Commerce Department's U.S. Travel and Tourism Administration gave away $440,000 in disaster relief to Western ski resort operators because there hadn't been enough snow?

GOVERNMENT CORPORATIONS

Another form of bureaucratic organization in the United States is the **government corporation**. Although the concept is borrowed from the world of business, distinct differences exist between public and private corporations.

A private corporation has shareholders (stockholders) who elect a board of directors, who in turn choose the corporate officers, such as president and vice president. When a private corporation makes a profit, it must pay taxes (unless it avoids them through various legal loopholes). It either distributes part or all of the after-tax profits to shareholders as dividends or plows the profits back into the corporation to make new investments.

A government corporation has a board of directors and managers, but it does not have any stockholders. We cannot buy shares of stock in a government corporation. If the government corporation makes a profit, it does not distribute the profit as dividends. Also, if it makes a profit, it does not have to pay taxes; the profits remain in the corporation.

Two of the best-known government corporations are the U.S. Postal Service, which is approaching solvency, and AMTRAK, the domestic passenger railroad corporation. Thirty-five years ago, after several private rail companies went bankrupt, Congress created a public railway system called AMTRAK. Today, AMTRAK links 500 American towns and cities in 46 states with more than 22,000 miles of rail. AMTRAK runs 41 long-distance routes, such as the "Sunset Limited" between Orlando, Florida, and Los Angeles, California, but its most popular routes are along the Northeast corridor. While AMTRAK appears impressive, it has many critics both inside and outside of Congress.

During AMTRAK's existence, American taxpayers have subsidized it to the tune of more than $25 billion. Current subsidies typically exceed $1 billion per year—$1.8 billion was requested in 2006, and $2 billion was requested for 2007. As Republican Representative Harold Rogers of Kentucky has pointed out, "Every time a passenger boards a train, Uncle Sam

Government Corporation
An agency of government that administers a quasi-business enterprise. These corporations are used when activities are primarily commercial.

That the Pentagon and the Central Intelligence Agency spent more than $11 million on psychics who were supposed to provide special insights regarding various foreign threats?

writes a check for $138.71, on average." Those in favor of the AMTRAK subsidies argue that AMTRAK provides essential transportation for the poor. However, the majority of daily passengers are middle-class commuters on the Eastern corridor routes.

For many years, critics of this government corporation have said that the benefits of AMTRAK, including reducing congestion on the highways, are less than the costs. Some have suggested that the passenger service be privatized—that is, sold to a private corporation. However, as the price of gasoline rose in 2008 and the issue of the future supply of oil became critical, AMTRAK became more popular with travelers. Faced with skyrocketing gas prices, rail transportation may see expansion rather than contraction in the next decade.

CHALLENGES TO THE BUREAUCRACY

With Cabinet departments, independent executive agencies, independent regulatory agencies, and government corporations, the federal bureaucracy is both complex and very specialized. Each agency, corporation, or line department has its own mission, its own goals, and, in many cases, its own constituents either at home or, in the case of the State Department, abroad. However, some problems and crises require the attention of multiple agencies. In these cases, overlapping jurisdictions can cause confusion, or there may be problems that no agency has the authority to solve.

There is a famous story about the Carter administration that makes this point: President Jimmy Carter believed he smelled something dead behind his Oval Office wall—probably a mouse. His staff called the General Services Administration, which has responsibility for the White House, but those bureaucrats claimed it was not their problem. They had fumigated recently, so the mouse must have come in from outside. The Department of the Interior, which has responsibility for the gardens and grounds, refused to help since the mouse was now inside. Eventually, an interagency task force was created to remove the mouse. If solving this small problem was complicated for the federal bureaucracy, consider larger issues such as terrorism and natural disasters.

REORGANIZING TO STOP TERRORISM

After September 11, 2001, the nation saw that no single agency was responsible for coordinating antiterrorism efforts. Nor was one person able to muster a nationwide response to a terrorist attack. Fighting terrorism involves so many different aspects— screening baggage at airports, inspecting freight shipments, and protecting the border, to name just a few—that coordinating them would be impossible unless all of these functions were combined into one agency.

The creation of the Department of Homeland Security (DHS) in 2003 was the largest reorganization of the U.S. government since 1947. Twenty-two agencies with responsibilities for preventing terrorism were merged into a single department. The Congress and the president agreed that combining the Federal Emergency Management Agency (FEMA), Customs and Border Protection, the Coast Guard, the Secret Service, and many other organizations into a single agency would promote efficiency and improve coordination. This sprawling agency now has more than 165,000 employees and an estimated budget of $43 billion (as of 2007).

One of the main challenges facing the new department was integrating agencies whose missions were very different. Some commentators suggested that the bureaucratic cultures of those agencies that were focused on law enforcement, such as the Secret Service and the Border Patrol, would have difficulty working with the agencies that focus on the problems faced by citizens in a time of natural disasters, such as the

THE U.S. COAST GUARD patrols the waters of Boston Harbor in preparation for the 2004 Democratic convention. Since September 11, 2001, such precautions have become normal in the United States. (William B. Plowman/Reuters/CORBIS)

Federal Emergency Management Agency (FEMA). Indeed, when FEMA became part of the DHS, not only was its funding reduced, but more importantly, it received less attention because the focus of the DHS has been on fighting terrorism, not on responding to natural disasters.

Perhaps even more importantly, the DHS did not actually unify all U.S. antiterrorism efforts. The most important antiterrorist agencies are the Federal Bureau of Investigation (FBI) and the Central Intelligence Agency (CIA), but neither is part of the DHS. Many believe that the number-one problem in addressing terrorism is the failure of the FBI and CIA to exchange information with each other. To try to address this problem, President Bush created a Terrorist Threat Integration Center in *addition* to the DHS, the FBI, and the CIA. In 2004, Congress established the new Office of the Director of National Intelligence to coordinate the nation's intelligence efforts, and in 2005, President Bush appointed John Negroponte to be the Director of National Intelligence to try once again to coordinate the nation's intelligence agencies.

DEALING WITH NATURAL DISASTERS

As George H. W. Bush faced a tough re-election campaign in 1992, Hurricane Andrew struck southern Florida, one of only three Category Five storms to hit the United States in the 20th century. Hurricane Andrew destroyed many communities south of Miami,

A FAMILY waits for help on the roof of their house after Hurricane Katrina flooded the city of New Orleans in August, 2005. (Vincent Laforet/Pool/Reuters/CORBIS)

Florida, leaving hundreds of thousands of people without power and without homes. Although the total death toll was only 65, the cost of the storm was more than $25 billion in damage and losses. The Bush administration was widely criticized for not getting aid to the victims quickly enough, and the president was chided for not putting in a personal appearance.

Supposedly, FEMA was strengthened and improved after Hurricane Andrew. FEMA did deal with hundreds of natural disasters in the years that followed, including tornados, floods, and blizzards. However, in 2005, a year in which five major hurricanes made landfall in the United States, FEMA again proved unable to meet the challenges of a massive natural disaster. When Hurricane Katrina headed toward New Orleans, all authorities warned of a possible flooding situation. No one dreamed of flooding that would trap thousands of residents in their homes for a week or more and destroy whole neighborhoods in New Orleans. No one had planned to evacuate thousands of people with no transportation of their own or to house them for years after the storm.

A natural disaster such as Hurricane Katrina can only be met by coordinated action from local, state, and federal authorities. Clearly, miscommunication occurred among all those levels of government in the case of Katrina. Responding to Hurricane Katrina involved the Army Corps of Engineers (responsible for the New Orleans levees), FEMA, the National Guard, the Departments of Energy (oil rigs and refineries), Health and Human Services (hospitals, health services, vaccines), Housing and Urban Development (housing and rebuilding), and the Department of Education (schools destroyed throughout Louisiana). While FEMA is charged with emergency management, it does not have any direct control over these other federal agencies. Again, the sitting president was criticized for the lack of federal response and, in this case, George W. Bush was chastised for flying over New Orleans rather than walking around the city. The Bush administration responded to the criticism by noting that having a president on the ground diverts many police and rescue officials from their primary duty to aid the victims.

What Hurricane Katrina illustrates is the huge challenge faced by bureaucracies when dealing with natural disasters. So many agencies and levels of government must be coordinated that sometimes responses are delayed and aid does not get to the victims

SECRETARY OF STATE Condoleezza Rice shakes hands with State Department employees on January 27, 2005, the day she took over as the 66th person to hold that office. (Evan Vucci/AP/Wide World Photos)

in a timely way. Media coverage of these tragedies focuses on the struggles of citizens, while the struggles of the bureaucrats take place in back rooms. The Department of Homeland Security now includes many of the agencies needed to meet another hurricane disaster, but it remains to be seen whether the response will be more effective.

STAFFING THE BUREAUCRACY

There are two categories of bureaucrats: political appointees and civil servants. As noted earlier, the president is able to make political appointments to most of the top jobs in the federal bureaucracy. The president can also appoint ambassadors to foreign posts. As noted in Chapter 13, these jobs are listed in the Plum Book. The rest of the national government's employees belong to the civil service and obtain their jobs through a much more formal process.

POLITICAL APPOINTEES

To fill the positions listed in the Plum Book, the president and the president's advisors solicit suggestions from politicians, businesspersons, and other prominent individuals. Appointments to these positions offer the president a way to pay off outstanding political debts. But the president must also consider such things as the candidate's work experience, intelligence, political affiliations, and personal characteristics. Presidents have differed in the importance they attach to appointing women and minorities to plum positions. Presidents often use ambassadorships, however, to reward individuals for their campaign contributions.

We should note here that even though the president has the power to appoint a government official, that does not mean an appointment will pass muster. Before making any nominations, the administration requires potential appointees to undergo a detailed screening process and answer questions such as the following: What are your accomplishments? Did you ever *not* pay taxes for your nannies or housekeepers? What kinds of investments have you made? What have your past partisan affiliations been?

Such a process takes months, and after completing it, the appointees must be confirmed by the Senate. Even with such a screening process, the Bush administration has made some serious errors. For example, as mentioned previously, the president's appointment of Michael Brown to head FEMA turned out to be a big mistake, because Brown had no experience in emergency planning and relief efforts. As another example, the president's appointee to the National Aeronautics and Space Administration (NASA) had to resign when officials at Texas A&M University confirmed that he had *not* graduated from that university, contrary to what he indicated on his résumé.

The Aristocracy of the Federal Government. Political appointees are in some sense the aristocracy of the federal government. But their powers, although appearing formidable on paper, are often exaggerated. Like the president, a political appointee will occupy her or his position for a comparatively brief time. Political appointees often leave office before the president's term actually ends. In fact, the average term of service for political appointees is less than two years. As a result, most appointees have little background for their positions and may be mere figureheads. Often, they only respond to the paperwork that flows up from below. Additionally, the professional civil servants who make up the permanent civil service may not feel compelled to carry out their current boss's directives quickly, because they know that he or she will not be around for very long.

The Difficulty in Firing Civil Servants. This inertia is compounded by the fact that it is very difficult to discharge civil servants. In recent years, less than one-tenth of 1 percent of federal employees have been fired for incompetence. Because discharged employees may appeal their dismissals, many months or even years can pass before the issue is resolved conclusively. This occupational rigidity helps ensure that most political appointees, no matter how competent or driven, will not be able to exert much meaningful influence over their subordinates, let alone implement dramatic changes in the bureaucracy itself.

HISTORY OF THE FEDERAL CIVIL SERVICE

When the federal government was formed in 1789, it had no career public servants but rather consisted of amateurs who were almost all Federalists. When Thomas Jefferson took over as president, few people in his party were holding federal administrative jobs, so he fired more than 100 officials and replaced them with his own supporters. Then, for the next 25 years, a growing body of federal administrators gained experience and expertise, becoming in the process professional public servants. These administrators stayed in office regardless of who was elected president. The bureaucracy had become a self-maintaining, long-term element within government.

To the Victor Belong the Spoils. When Andrew Jackson took over the White House in 1828, he could not believe how many appointed officials (appointed before he became president, that is) were overtly hostile toward him and his Democratic Party. Because the bureaucracy was reluctant to carry out his programs, Jackson did the obvious: he fired federal officials—more than had all his predecessors combined. The **spoils system**—an application of the principle that to the victor belong the spoils—became the standard method of filling federal positions. Whenever a new president was elected from a party different from the party of the previous president, there would be an almost complete turnover in the staffing of the federal government.

The Civil Service Reform Act of 1883. Jackson's spoils system survived for several years, but it became increasingly corrupt. Also, as the size of the bureaucracy increased by 300

Spoils System
The awarding of government jobs to political supporters and friends.

ON SEPTEMBER 19, 1881, President James A. Garfield was assassinated by a disappointed office seeker, Charles J. Guiteau. The long-term effect of this event was to replace the spoils system with a permanent career civil service. This process began with the passage of the Pendleton Act in 1883, which established the Civil Service Commission. (Library of Congress, Prints & Photographs Division, Washington, D.C. [LC-USZ62-7622])

percent between 1851 and 1881, the cry for civil service reform became louder. Reformers began to look to the example of several European countries, Germany in particular, which had established a professional civil service that operated under a **merit system**, in which job appointments were based on competitive examinations.

In 1883, the **Pendleton Act**—or **Civil Service Reform Act**—was passed, placing the first limits on the spoils system. The Act established the principle of employment on the basis of open, competitive examinations and created the **Civil Service Commission** to administer the personnel service. Initially, only 10 percent of federal employees were covered by the merit system. Later laws, amendments, and executive orders, however, increased the coverage to more than 90 percent of federal employees. The effects of these reforms were felt at all levels of government.

The Supreme Court strengthened the civil service system in *Elrod v. Burns*[4] in 1976 and *Branti v. Finkel*[5] in 1980. In those two cases, the Court used the First Amendment to forbid government officials from discharging or threatening to discharge public employees solely for *not* being supporters of the political party in power unless party affiliation is an appropriate requirement for the position. Additional enhancements to the civil service system were added in *Rutan v. Republican Party of Illinois*[6] in 1990. The Court's ruling effectively prevented the use of partisan political considerations as the basis for hiring, promoting, or transferring most public employees. An exception was permitted, however, for senior policy-making positions, which usually go to officials who will support the programs of the elected leaders.

The Civil Service Reform Act of 1978. In 1978, the Civil Service Reform Act abolished the Civil Service Commission and created two new federal agencies to perform its duties. To administer the civil service laws, rules, and regulations, the Act created the Office of Personnel Management (OPM), which is empowered to recruit, interview, and test potential government workers and determine who should be hired. The OPM makes recommendations to the individual agencies as to which persons meet the standards

Merit System
The selection, retention, and promotion of government employees on the basis of competitive examinations.

Pendleton Act (Civil Service Reform Act)
An act that established the principle of employment on the basis of merit and created the Civil Service Commission to administer the personnel service.

Civil Service Commission
The initial central personnel agency of the national government, created in 1883.

[4]427 U.S. 347 (1976).
[5]445 U.S. 507 (1980).
[6]497 U.S. 62 (1990).

(typically, the top three applicants for a position), and the agencies then decide whom to hire. To oversee promotions, employees' rights, and other employment matters, the Act created the Merit Systems Protection Board (MSPB), which evaluates charges of wrongdoing, hears employee appeals from agency decisions, and can order corrective action against agencies and employees.

Federal Employees and Political Campaigns. In 1933, when President Franklin D. Roosevelt set up his New Deal, a virtual army of civil servants was hired to staff the numerous new agencies that were created. Because the individuals who worked in these agencies owed their jobs to the Democratic Party, it seemed natural for them to campaign for Democratic candidates. The Democrats controlling Congress in the mid-1930s did not object. But in 1938, a coalition of conservative Democrats and Republicans took control of Congress and forced through the Hatch Act—or Political Activities Act—of 1939. The Act prohibited federal employees from actively participating in the political management of campaigns. It also forbade the use of federal authority to influence nominations and elections and outlawed the use of bureaucratic rank to pressure federal employees to make political contributions.

The Hatch Act created a controversy that lasted for decades. Many contended that the Act deprived federal employees of their First Amendment freedoms of speech and association. In 1972, a federal district court declared the Act unconstitutional. The United States Supreme Court, however, reaffirmed the challenged portion of the Act in 1973, stating that the government's interest in preserving a nonpartisan civil service was so great that the prohibitions should remain.[7] Twenty years later, Congress addressed the criticisms of the Hatch Act by passing the Federal Employees Political Activities Act of 1993. This Act, which amended the Hatch Act, lessened the harshness of the 1939 Act in several ways. Among other things, the 1993 Act allowed federal employees to run for office in nonpartisan elections, participate in voter-registration drives, make campaign contributions to political organizations, and campaign for candidates in partisan elections.

That federal officials spent $333,000 building a deluxe, earthquake-proof outhouse for hikers in Pennsylvania's remote Delaware Water Gap recreation area?

MODERN ATTEMPTS AT BUREAUCRATIC REFORM

As long as the federal bureaucracy exists, there will continue to be attempts to make it more open, efficient, and responsive to the needs of U.S. citizens. The most important actual and proposed reforms in the last several decades include sunshine and sunset laws, privatization, incentives for efficiency, and more protection for so-called whistleblowers.

SUNSHINE LAWS BEFORE AND AFTER SEPTEMBER 11

Government in the Sunshine Act
A law that requires all committee-directed federal agencies to conduct their business regularly in public session.

In 1976, Congress enacted the **Government in the Sunshine Act**. It required for the first time that all multiheaded federal agencies—agencies headed by a committee instead of an individual—hold their meetings regularly in public session. The bill defined *meetings* as almost any gathering, formal or informal, of agency members, including a conference telephone call. The only exceptions to this rule of openness are discussions of matters such as court proceedings or personnel problems, and these exceptions are specifically listed in the bill. Sunshine laws now exist at all levels of government.

7*United States Civil Service Commission v. National Association of Letter Carriers*, 413 U.S. 548 (1973).

Information Disclosure. Sunshine laws are consistent with the policy of information disclosure that has been supported by the government for decades. For example, beginning in the 1960s, several consumer protection laws have required that certain information be disclosed to consumers when purchasing homes, borrowing funds, and so on. In 1966, the federal government passed the Freedom of Information Act, which required federal government agencies, with certain exceptions, to disclose to individuals, on their request, any information about them contained in government files.

Curbs on Information Disclosure. Since September 11, 2001, the trend toward government in the sunshine and information disclosure has been reversed at both the federal and state levels. Within weeks after September 11, 2001, numerous federal agencies removed hundreds, if not thousands, of documents from Internet sites, public libraries, and reading rooms found in various federal government departments. Information contained in some of the documents included diagrams of power plants and pipelines, structural details on dams, and safety plans for chemical plants. The military also immediately started restricting information about its current and planned activities, as did the FBI. These agencies were concerned that terrorists could use this information to plan attacks. The federal government has also gone back into the archives to remove an increasing quantity of not only sensitive information but also sometimes seemingly unimportant information.

In making some public documents inaccessible to the public, the federal government was ahead of state and local governments, but they quickly followed suit. State and local governments control and supervise police forces, dams, electricity sources, and water supplies. Consequently, it is not surprising that many state and local governments followed in the footsteps of the federal government in curbing access to certain public records and information. Most local agencies, however, do include the public in their planning for emergencies.

SUNSET LAWS

Potentially, the size and scope of the federal bureaucracy can be controlled through **sunset legislation**, which places government programs on a definite schedule for Congressional consideration. Unless Congress specifically reauthorizes a particular federally operated program at the end of a designated period, it would be terminated automatically; that is, its sun would set.

Sunset Legislation
Laws requiring that existing programs be reviewed regularly for their effectiveness and be terminated unless specifically extended as a result of these reviews.

AN ARMED NUCLEAR SECURITY OFFICER patrols the coastal area of the Diablo Canyon nuclear power plant on May 5, 2004, in Avila Beach, California. Since September 11, all American utilities have increased the security at their facilities. Do you think that the increased awareness of a possible terrorist attack has actually prevented such an event? (Michael A. Mariant/AP/Wide World Photos)

The idea of sunset legislation was initially suggested by Franklin D. Roosevelt when he created the plethora of New Deal agencies in the 1930s. His assistant, William O. Douglas, recommended that each agency's charter should include a provision allowing for its termination in 10 years. Only an act of Congress could revitalize it. The proposal was never adopted. It was not until 1976 that a state legislature—Colorado's—adopted sunset legislation for state regulatory commissions, giving them a life of six years before their suns set. Today, most states have some type of sunset law.

PRIVATIZATION

Privatization
The replacement of government services with services provided by private firms.

Another approach to bureaucratic reform is **privatization**, which occurs when government services are replaced by services from the private sector. For example, the government might contract with private firms to operate prisons. Supporters of privatization argue that some services could be provided more efficiently by the private sector. Another scheme is to furnish vouchers to "clients" in lieu of services. For example, instead of supplying housing, the government could offer vouchers that recipients could use to "pay" for housing in privately owned buildings.

The privatization, or contracting out, strategy has been most successful at the local level. Municipalities, for example, can form contracts with private companies for such things as trash collection. This approach is not a cure-all, however, as many functions, particularly on the national level, cannot be contracted out in any meaningful way. For example, the federal government could not contract out most of the Defense Department's functions to private firms. Nonetheless, the U.S. military has contracted out many services in Iraq and elsewhere, as you'll learn in this chapter's *Beyond Our Borders* feature.

INCENTIVES FOR EFFICIENCY AND PRODUCTIVITY

An increasing number of state governments are beginning to experiment with a variety of schemes to run their operations more efficiently and capably. They focus on maximizing the efficiency and productivity of government workers by providing incentives for

BEYOND OUR B RDERS

PRIVATIZING THE U.S. MILITARY ABROAD

Privatization has been a hot topic for several decades now, at least domestically. All levels of government—federal, state, and local—have privatized at least some activities. Less well known, however, is that for more than a decade, the U.S. military has been employing private companies abroad to perform several functions that were previously done by military personnel. After the American military was downsized following the fall of the Berlin Wall in 1989, the military responded by outsourcing many functions to the private sector. Before the First Gulf War, the Pentagon was already spending about 8 percent of its overall budget on private companies.

PRIVATE CONTRACTORS GALORE

Today, private contractors are everywhere in Iraq. By 2006, there were more than 100,000 private contractors/workers on the ground in Iraq employed in some capacity by the U.S. government. By 2008, the number reached almost 150,000, about as many as there are U.S. military personnel. What do all these private contractors actually do? They provide food and water for the troops, transport supplies for the coalition troops and for civilians stationed in Iraq, repair equipment, and are employed as guards for prisoners. In addition, most major construction on American bases and air fields is done by contractors.

THE NUMBERS TELL IT ALL

One of the reasons that the U.S. military has felt obligated to hire private contractors in Iraq and elsewhere is that the army in particular has been downsized. During the First Gulf War, active-duty troops in the army numbered 711,000. Today, that number has been reduced by almost one-third, to only about 485,000. As a result, the Pentagon says that it has to fill ancillary jobs and programs by contracting with private companies that either send their workers abroad or hire workers there. The Army Corps of Engineers and the Navy Seabees did a great deal of the construction in World War II, but today, neither of these forces has the manpower to do similar work in Iraq.

Hiring private contractors to work in a combat zone has some real complications. First, private contractors are often subject to combat conditions resulting in the risk of capture, injury, or death. Several contractors, both American and European, have been captured and held as hostages. A few of these have been murdered. More than 1,100 civilian contractors have been killed in their line of work. In addition, private contractors can commit acts that are crimes against Iraqi civilians or against other contractors. In accordance with a recently approved amendment to the Uniform Code of Military Justice, contractors who are accused of crimes are tried in military court-martials.

Who is hiring these contractors, and where are they being hired? Large international firms, some of which are based in the United States, are the major employers. Kellogg, Brown and Root, a firm based in Houston, Texas, is the largest employer with more than 54,000 contractors in Iraq. Another firm, MPRI, has employees providing management services and technical training to Iraqis, while the 6,500 employees of Titan are linguists. You might wonder where Titan found 6,500 Americans who could be used as translators in Iraq. In fact, most of the civilian contractors are not Americans; only 27,000 of the 150,000 workers are Americans.* Many are Iraqis who are using their talents working for these firms and incurring the risks involved.

FOR CRITICAL ANALYSIS

Is there any national security argument against using private contractors to do U.S. military work?

*David Ivanovich, "Contractor Deaths Up 17 Percent across Iraq in 2007," *Houston Chronicle,* February 9, 2008.

improved performance.[8] For example, many governors, mayors, and city administrators are considering ways in which government can be made more entrepreneurial. Some of the most promising measures have included such tactics as permitting agencies that do not spend their entire budgets to keep some of the difference and rewarding employees with performance-based bonuses.

Government Performance and Results Act. At the federal level, the Government Performance and Results Act of 1997 was designed to improve efficiency in the federal workforce. The Act required that all government agencies (except the CIA) describe their new goals and establish methods for determining whether those goals are met. Goals may be broadly crafted (e.g., reducing the time it takes to test a new drug before allowing it to be marketed) or narrowly crafted (e.g., reducing the number of times a telephone rings before it is answered).

The performance-based budgeting implemented by President George W. Bush took this results-oriented approach a step further. Performance-based budgeting links agency funding to actual agency performance. Agencies are given specific performance criteria to meet, and the Office of Management and Budget rates each agency to determine how well it has performed. In theory, the amount of funds that each agency receives in the next annual budget should be determined by the extent to which it has met the performance criteria.

Bureaucracy Changed Little, Though. Efforts to improve bureaucratic efficiency are supported by the assertion that although society and industry have changed enormously in the past century, the form of government used in Washington, D.C., and in most states has remained the same. Some observers believe that the nation's diverse economic base cannot be administered competently by traditional bureaucratic organizations. Consequently, the government must become more responsive to cope with the increasing number of demands placed on it. Political scientists Joel Aberbach and Bert Rockman take issue with this contention. They argue that the bureaucracy has changed significantly over time in response to changes desired by various presidential administrations. In their opinion, many of the problems attributed to the bureaucracy are, in fact, a result of the political decision-making process. Therefore, attempts to reinvent government by reforming the bureaucracy are misguided.[9] Public assessment of bureaucratic services would provide another way to get more feedback from the public.

Other analysts have suggested that the problem lies not so much with traditional bureaucratic organizations as with the people who run them. According to policy specialist Taegan Goddard and journalist Christopher Riback, what needs to be reinvented is not the machinery of government, but public officials. After each election, new appointees to bureaucratic positions may find themselves managing complex, multimillion-dollar enterprises, yet they often are untrained for their jobs. According to these authors, if we want to reform the bureaucracy, we should focus on preparing newcomers for the task of "doing" government.[10]

Saving Costs through E-Government. Many contend that the communications revolution brought about by the Internet has not only improved the efficiency with which government agencies deliver services to the public but also helped reduce the cost of government. Agencies can now communicate with members of the public, as well as other

[8]See, for example, David Osborne and Ted Gaebler, *Reinventing Government: How the Entrepreneurial Spirit Is Transforming the Public Sector* (Reading, MA: Addison-Wesley, 1992); and David Osborne and Peter Plastrik, *Banishing Bureaucracy: The Five Strategies for Reinventing Government* (Reading, MA: Addison-Wesley, 1997).
[9]Joel D. Aberbach and Bert A. Rockman, *In the Web of Politics: Three Decades of the U.S. Federal Executive* (Washington, DC: Brookings Institution Press, 2000).
[10]Taegan D. Goddard and Christopher Riback, *You Won—Now What? How Americans Can Make Democracy Work from City Hall to the White House* (New York: Scribner, 1998).

WHAT IF...

THE PUBLIC GRADED FEDERAL BUREAUCRACIES?

Congress has repeatedly reformed the civil service since 1883. In addition, each modern administration has claimed that it would make bureaucrats more accountable. Despite all efforts, however, bureaucrats are far from accountable to their bosses in the executive branch, to Congress, and, least of all, to the public—the taxpayers who fund their salaries. Would bureaucrats be more accountable if report cards graded their efforts?

WHAT IF THE PUBLIC CREATED THE REPORT CARD?

Upon taking office, President George W. Bush implemented a plan known as "performance-based budgeting" to increase bureaucratic accountability. As part of this plan, the Office of Management and Budget (OMB) was to examine how well each agency met specific performance criteria and create a report card for each agency.

The government could also prepare report cards that summarize public input. Many commercial businesses actively solicit feedback from their customers on whether staff members were polite, whether problems were resolved quickly, and whether the customer was satisfied with the transaction overall. Similarly, the government could print evaluation forms to be distributed to citizens every time they interacted with the government. Taxpayers could even insert their evaluations of the Internal Revenue Service into the same envelope as their tax returns.

THE PUBLIC'S IMPLICIT GRADING AFTER HURRICANE KATRINA

In one recent example, public opinion polls provided an actual evaluation of a federal agency's performance. In the immediate aftermath of Hurricane Katrina, residents of New Orleans were extremely critical of the assistance provided by FEMA. Criticism of FEMA's management led to a change in leadership at the agency. Interestingly, though, a Gallup poll taken in October 2005, a month after the hurricane, found that half of the city's residents believed that FEMA had been very helpful to them.

USING THE EVALUATIONS

Under the Bush administration's plan for performance-based budgeting, budgetary payouts were to be linked to specific performance criteria for each program. Unfortunately, it is not always possible to cut the funding of a program that is performing poorly. The program may be so essential that it cannot be cut. It may be performing poorly because it is underfunded—and cutting back will only make matters worse.

Bad publicity might be a better tool for making bureaucrats more responsive. Already, numerous private groups are ridiculing the federal government by publicizing laughable programs and actions by federal bureaucrats that virtually no one could justify. If agencies were compared with other agencies and had to fear criticism if their performance fell below average, they might have an incentive to improve the quality of their work.

A BASIS FOR DISCIPLINE

Many observers believe that the greatest obstacle to making the federal bureaucracy responsive is that it is very difficult to fire federal bureaucrats. If bureaucrats in private businesses do not perform, their bosses simply fire them. The federal bureaucracy, in contrast, is so extensively governed by rules and regulations about firing that virtually no one is ever dismissed. Congress could make it easier for bureaucrats to be fired. If it did so, perhaps poor performance on a public report card could lead to discipline and, in due course, discharge.

FOR CRITICAL ANALYSIS

1. What specific items ought to be listed on a report card that is used to evaluate a federal bureaucracy?
2. Which agencies or departments do you think would get the worst grades?

Whistleblower
Someone who brings to public attention gross governmental inefficiency or an illegal action.

agencies, via e-mail. Additionally, every federal agency now has a Web site to which citizens can go to find information about agency services instead of calling or appearing in person at a regional agency office. Since 2003, federal agencies have also been required by the Government Paperwork Elimination Act of 1998 to use e-commerce whenever it is practical to do so and will save on costs.

HELPING OUT THE WHISTLEBLOWERS

The term **whistleblower** as applied to the federal bureaucracy has a special meaning: it is someone who blows the whistle on a gross governmental inefficiency or illegal action. Whistleblowers may be clerical workers, managers, or even specialists, such as scientists.

Laws Protecting Whistleblowers. The 1978 Civil Service Reform Act prohibits reprisals against whistleblowers by their superiors, and it set up the Merit Systems Protection Board as part of this protection. Many federal agencies also have toll-free hotlines that employees can use anonymously to report bureaucratic waste and inappropriate behavior. About 35 percent of all calls result in agency action or follow-up.

Further protection for whistleblowers was provided in 1989, when Congress passed the Whistle-Blower Protection Act. That Act established an independent agency, the Office of Special Counsel (OSC), to investigate complaints brought by government employees who have been demoted, fired, or otherwise sanctioned for reporting government fraud or waste. Congress is currently considering legislation that would extend whistleblower protections to civil servants at national security agencies, employees of government contractors, and federal workers who expose the distortion of scientific data for political reasons.

Some state and federal laws encourage employees to blow the whistle on their employers' wrongful actions by providing monetary incentives to the whistleblowers. At the federal level, the False Claims Act of 1986 allows a whistleblower who has disclosed information about a fraud against the U.S. government to receive a monetary award. If the government chooses to prosecute the case and wins, the whistleblower receives between 15 and 25 percent of the proceeds. If the government declines to intervene, the whistleblower can bring suit on behalf of the government, and if the suit is successful, will receive between 25 and 30 percent of the proceeds.

The Problem Continues. Despite these endeavors to help whistleblowers, there is little evidence that potential whistleblowers truly have received more protection. More than 40 percent of the employees who turned to the OSC for assistance in a recent three-year period stated that they were no longer employees of the government agencies on which they blew the whistle.

Additionally, in a significant 2006 decision, the U.S. Supreme Court placed restrictions on lawsuits brought by public workers. The case, *Garcetti v. Ceballos*,[11] involved an assistant district attorney, Richard Ceballos, who wrote a memo asking if a county sheriff's deputy had lied in a search warrant affidavit. Ceballos claimed that he was subsequently demoted and denied a promotion for trying to expose the lie. The outcome of the case turned on an interpretation of an employee's right to freedom of speech—whether it included the right to criticize an employment-related action. In a close (five-to-four) and controversial decision, the Supreme Court held that when public employees make statements relating to their official duties, they are not speaking as citizens for First Amendment purposes. The Court deemed that when he wrote his memo, Ceballos was

---

[11]126 S. Ct. 1951 (2006).

speaking as an employee, not a citizen, and was thus subject to his employer's disciplinary actions. The ruling will affect millions of governmental employees.

BUREAUCRATS AS POLITICIANS AND POLICY MAKERS

Because Congress is unable to oversee the day-to-day administration of its programs, it must delegate certain powers to administrative agencies. Congress delegates the power to implement legislation to agencies through what is called **enabling legislation**. For example, the Federal Trade Commission was created by the Federal Trade Commission Act of 1914, the Equal Employment Opportunity Commission was created by the Civil Rights Act of 1964, and the Occupational Safety and Health Administration was created by the Occupational Safety and Health Act of 1970. The enabling legislation generally specifies the name, purpose, composition, functions, and powers of the agency.

Enabling Legislation
A statute enacted by Congress that authorizes the creation of an administrative agency and specifies the name, purpose, composition, functions, and powers of the agency being created.

In theory, the agencies should put into effect laws passed by Congress. Laws are often drafted in such vague and general terms, however, that they provide relatively little guidance to agency administrators as to how the laws should be implemented. This means that the agencies must decide how best to carry out the wishes of Congress.

The discretion given to administrative agencies is not accidental. Congress has long realized that it lacks the technical expertise and the resources to monitor the implementation of its laws. Hence, the administrative agency is created to fill the gaps. This gap-filling role requires the agency to formulate administrative rules (regulations) to put flesh on the bones of the law. But it also forces the agency to become an unelected policy maker.

THE RULE-MAKING ENVIRONMENT

Rule making does not occur in a vacuum. Suppose that Congress passes a new air-pollution law. The Environmental Protection Agency (EPA) might decide to implement the new law through a technical regulation on factory emissions. This proposed regulation would be published in the *Federal Register*, a daily government publication, so that interested parties would have an opportunity to comment on it. Individuals and companies that opposed the rule (or parts of it) might then try to convince the EPA to revise or redraft the regulation. Some parties might try to persuade the agency to withdraw the proposed regulation altogether. In any event, the EPA would consider these comments in drafting the final version of the regulation following the expiration of the comment period.

Waiting Periods and Court Challenges. Once the final regulation has been published in the *Federal Register*, there is a 60-day waiting period before the rule can be enforced. During that period, businesses, individuals, and state and local governments can ask Congress to overturn the regulation. After that 60-day period has lapsed, the regulation can still be challenged in court by a party having a direct interest in the rule, such as a company that expects to incur significant costs in complying with it. The company could argue that the rule misinterprets the applicable law or goes beyond the agency's statutory purview. An allegation by the company that the EPA made a mistake in judgment

THE FARMERS FROM KLAMATH LAKE, California, confronted the Bureau of Reclamation guards at the headgate of Canal A. The water was shut off to protect endangered sucker fish that live in Upper Klamath Lake and Coho salmon that live in the Klamath River downstream. (Peter Essick/Getty Images)

probably would not be enough to convince the court to throw out the rule. The company instead would have to demonstrate that the rule was "arbitrary and capricious." To meet this standard, the company would have to show that the rule reflected a serious flaw in the EPA's judgment.

Controversies. How agencies implement, administer, and enforce legislation has resulted in controversy. Decisions made by agencies charged with administering the Endangered Species Act have led to protests from farmers, ranchers, and others whose economic interests have been harmed. For example, the government decided to cut off the flow of irrigation water from Klamath Lake in Oregon in the summer of 2001. That action, which affected irrigation water for more than one thousand farmers in southern Oregon and northern California, was undertaken to save endangered suckerfish and salmon. It was believed that the lake's water level was so low that further use of the water for irrigation would harm these fish. The results of this decision were devastating for many farmers.

Another controversy has involved the George W. Bush administration for several years. The Congress of the United States created the Environmental Protection Agency in 1970 and has passed laws requiring the reduction of air pollution from multiple sources. During the Bush administration, the EPA issued decisions that seemed to weaken the enforcement of air-pollution laws. In 1999, several environmental groups petitioned the EPA to set new standards for automobiles to reduce greenhouse gas emissions. In 2003, the EPA refused to do so, claiming that it did not have the legal authority to do this. Massachusetts and other states that passed laws regulating automobiles in their own states sued the EPA. In 2007, the Supreme Court ruled, by a five-to-four majority, that the EPA cannot refuse to assess environmental hazards and issue appropriate regulations. As Justice John Paul Stevens wrote, "This is the Congressional design. EPA has refused to comply with this clear statutory command."[12] This was an

[12]*Commonwealth of Massachusetts v. EPA*, 127 S. Ct. 1438 (2007).

unusual situation in that the states actually challenged a regulatory agency to issue stronger regulations. Often, challenges to regulatory agencies are intended to weaken new regulations.

NEGOTIATED RULE MAKING

Since the end of World War II (1939–1945), companies, environmentalists, and other special-interest groups have challenged government regulations in court. In the 1980s, however, the sheer wastefulness of attempting to regulate through litigation became more and more apparent. Today, a growing number of federal agencies encourage businesses and public-interest groups to become directly involved in drafting regulations. Agencies hope that such participation may help prevent later courtroom battles over the meaning, applicability, and legal effect of the regulations.

Congress formally approved such a process, which is called *negotiated rule making*, in the Negotiated Rule-making Act of 1990. The Act authorizes agencies to allow those who will be affected by a new rule to participate in the rule-drafting process. If an agency chooses to engage in negotiated rule making, it must publish in the *Federal Register* the subject and scope of the rule to be developed, the parties affected significantly by the rule, and other information. Representatives of the affected groups and other interested parties then may apply to be members of the negotiating committee. The agency is represented on the committee, but a neutral third party (not the agency) presides over the proceedings. Once the committee members have reached agreement on the terms of the proposed rule, a notice is published in the *Federal Register*, followed by a period for comments by any person or organization interested in the proposed rule. Negotiated rule making often is conducted under the condition that the participants promise not to challenge in court the outcome of any agreement to which they were a party.

BUREAUCRATS ARE POLICY MAKERS

Theories of public administration once assumed that bureaucrats do not make policy decisions but only implement the laws and policies promulgated by the president and legislative bodies. Many people continue to make this assumption. A more realistic view, which is now held by most bureaucrats and elected officials, is that the agencies and departments of government play important roles in policy making. As we have seen, many government rules, regulations, and programs are in fact initiated by bureaucrats, based on their expertise and scientific studies. How a law passed by Congress eventually is translated into concrete action—from the forms to be filled out to decisions about who gets the benefits—usually is determined within each agency or department. Even the evaluation of whether a policy has achieved its purpose usually is based on studies that are commissioned and interpreted by the agency administering the program.

The bureaucracy's policy-making role has often been depicted by what traditionally has been called the "iron triangle." Recently, the concept of an "issue network" has been viewed as a more accurate description of the policy-making process.

Iron Triangles. In the past, scholars often described the bureaucracy's role in the policy-making process by using the concept of an **iron triangle**—a three-way alliance among legislators in Congress, bureaucrats, and interest groups. Consider as an example the development of agricultural policy. Congress, as one component of the triangle (as illustrated in Figure 14–4), includes two major committees concerned with agricultural policy, the House Committee on Agriculture and the Senate Committee on Agriculture, Nutrition, and Forestry. The Department of Agriculture, the second component

Iron Triangle
The three-way alliance among legislators, bureaucrats, and interest groups to make or preserve policies that benefit their respective interests.

FIGURE 14–4 Iron Triangle

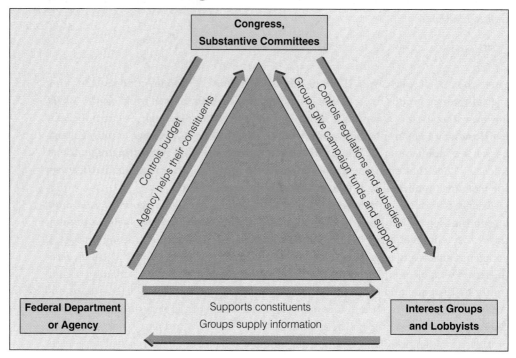

of the triangle, has more than 95,000 employees, plus thousands of contractors and consultants. Agricultural interest groups, the third component of the iron triangle in agricultural policy making, include many large and powerful associations, such as the American Farm Bureau Federation, the National Cattleman's Association, and the Corn Growers Association. These three components of the iron triangle work together, formally or informally, to create policy.

For example, the various agricultural interest groups lobby Congress to develop policies that benefit their groups' interests. Members of Congress cannot afford to ignore the wishes of interest groups, because those groups are potential sources of voter support and campaign contributions. The legislators in Congress also work closely with the Department of Agriculture, which, in implementing a policy, can develop rules that benefit—or at least do not hurt—certain industries or groups. The Department of Agriculture, in turn, supports policies that enhance the department's budget and powers. In this way, according to theory, agricultural policy is created that benefits all three components of the iron triangle.

Issue Networks. To be sure, the preceding discussion presents a simplified picture of how the iron triangle works. With the growth in the complexity of government, policy making also has become more complicated. The bureaucracy is larger, Congress has more committees and subcommittees, and interest groups are more powerful than ever. Although iron triangles still exist, often they are inadequate as descriptions of how policy is actually made. Frequently, different interest groups concerned about a certain area of policy have conflicting demands, making agency decisions difficult. Additionally, divided government in some years has meant that departments are sometimes pressured by the president to take one approach and by Congress to take another.

Many scholars now use the term *issue network* to describe the policy-making process. An **issue network** consists of individuals or organizations that support a particular policy position on the environment, taxation, consumer safety, or some other issue. Typically, an issue network includes legislators and/or their staff members, interest

Issue Network
A group of individuals or organizations—which may consist of legislators and legislative staff members, interest group leaders, bureaucrats, the media, scholars, and other experts—that supports a particular policy position on a given issue.

groups, bureaucrats, scholars and other experts, and representatives from the media. Members of a particular issue network work together to influence the president, members of Congress, administrative agencies, and the courts to affect public policy on a specific issue. Each policy issue may involve conflicting positions taken by two or more issue networks.

CONGRESSIONAL CONTROL OF THE BUREAUCRACY

Many political pundits doubt whether Congress can meaningfully control the federal bureaucracy. Nevertheless, Congress does have some means of exerting control.

WAYS CONGRESS DOES CONTROL THE BUREAUCRACY

These commentators forget that Congress specifies in an agency's "enabling legislation" the powers of the agency and the parameters within which it can operate. Additionally, Congress has the power of the purse and theoretically could refuse to authorize or appropriate funds for a particular agency (see the discussion of the budgeting process in Chapter 12). Whether Congress would actually take such a drastic measure would depend on the circumstances. It is clear, however, that Congress does have the legal authority to decide whether to fund or not to fund administrative agencies. Congress can also exercise oversight over agencies through investigations and hearings.

Congressional committees conduct investigations and hold hearings to oversee an agency's actions, reviewing them to ensure compliance with congressional intentions. The agency's officers and employees can be ordered to testify before a committee about the details of an action. Through these oversight activities, especially in the questions and comments of members of the House or Senate during the hearings, Congress indicates its positions on specific programs and issues.

Congress can ask the Government Accountability Office (GAO) to investigate particular agency actions as well. The Congressional Budget Office (CBO) also conducts oversight studies. The results of a GAO or CBO study may encourage Congress to hold further hearings or make changes in the law. Even if a law is not changed explicitly by Congress, however, the views expressed in any investigations and hearings are taken seriously by agency officials, who often act on those views.

In 1996, Congress passed the Congressional Review Act. The Act created special procedures that can be employed to express Congressional disapproval of particular agency actions. These procedures have rarely been used, however. Since the Act's passage, the executive branch has issued more than 15,000 regulations. Yet only eight resolutions of disapproval have been introduced, and none of these was passed by either chamber.

REASONS WHY CONGRESS CANNOT EASILY OVERSEE THE BUREAUCRACY

Despite the powers just described, one theory of Congressional control over the bureaucracy suggests that Congress cannot possibly oversee all of the bureaucracy. Consider two possible approaches to Congressional control—(1) the "police patrol" and (2) the "fire alarm" approach. Certain Congressional activities, such as annual budget hearings, fall under the police patrol approach. This regular review occasionally catches *some* deficiencies in a bureaucracy's job performance, but it usually fails to detect most problems.

In contrast, the fire alarm approach is more likely to discover gross inadequacies in a bureaucracy's job performance. In this approach, Congress and its committees react to scandal, citizen disappointment, and massive negative publicity by launching a full-scale investigation into whatever agency is suspected of wrongdoing. Clearly, this is what happened when Congress investigated the inadequacies of the CIA after the terrorist attacks of September 11, 2001. Congress was also responding to an alarm when it investigated the failures of FEMA after Hurricane Katrina. Fire alarm investigations will not catch all problems, but they will alert bureaucracies that they need to clean up their procedures before a problem arises in their own agencies.[13]

[13]Matthew D. McCubbins and Thomas Schwartz, "Congressional Oversight Overlooked: Police Patrols versus Fire Alarms," *American Journal of Political Science*, February 28, 1984, p. 165–179.

You can make a difference

WHAT THE GOVERNMENT KNOWS ABOUT YOU

The federal government collects billions of pieces of information on tens of millions of Americans each year. These data are stored in files and sometimes are exchanged among agencies. You are probably the subject of several federal records (e.g., in the Social Security Administration, the Internal Revenue Service, and, if you are a male, the Selective Service).

WHY SHOULD YOU CARE?

Verifying the information that the government has on you can be important. On several occasions, the records of two people with similar names have become confused. Sometimes innocent persons have had the criminal records of other persons erroneously inserted into their files. Such disasters are not always caused by bureaucratic error. One of the most common crimes in today's world is identity theft, in which one person uses another person's personal identifiers (such as a Social Security number) to commit fraud. In some instances, identity thieves have been arrested or even jailed under someone else's name.

WHAT CAN YOU DO?

The 1966 Freedom of Information Act (FOIA) requires that the federal government release, at your request, any identifiable information it has about you or about any other subject. Ten categories of material are exempted, however (classified material, confidential material on trade secrets, internal personnel rules, personal medical files, and the like). To request material, write directly to the FOIA officer at the agency in question (say, the Department of Education). You must have a relatively specific idea about the document or information you want to obtain.

A second law, the Privacy Act of 1974, gives you access specifically to information the government may have collected about you. This law allows you to review records on file with federal agencies and to check those records for possible inaccuracies. If you want to look at any records or find out if an agency has a record on you, write to the agency head or Privacy Act officer, and address your letter to the specific agency. State that "under the provisions of the Privacy Act of 1974, 5 U.S.C. 522a, I hereby request a copy of (or access to) _____." Then describe the record that you wish to investigate.

The American Civil Liberties Union (ACLU) has published a manual, called *Your Right to Government Information*, that guides you through the steps of obtaining information from the federal government. You can order it online at **www.aclu.org**. Alternatively, you can order the manual from the ACLU at the following address:

ACLU Publications
P.O. Box 4713
Trenton, NJ 08650-4713
1-800-775-ACLU

KEY TERMS

acquisitive model 496
administrative agency 498
bureaucracy 495
Cabinet department 499
capture 502
Civil Service Commission 509
enabling legislation 517
government corporation 503
Government in the Sunshine
Act 510

independent executive
agency 501
independent regulatory
agency 501
iron triangle 519
issue network 520
line organization 499
merit system 509

monopolistic model 497
Pendleton Act (Civil Service
Reform Act) 509
privatization 512
spoils system 508
sunset legislation 511
Weberian model 496
whistleblower 516

CHAPTER SUMMARY

1. Bureaucracies are hierarchical organizations characterized by a division of labor and extensive procedural rules. Bureaucracy is the primary form of organization of most major corporations and universities as well as governments.

2. Several theories have been offered to explain bureaucracies. The Weberian model posits that bureaucracies are rational, hierarchical organizations in which decisions are based on logical reasoning. The acquisitive model views top-level bureaucrats as pressing for ever-larger budgets and staffs to augment their own sense of power and security. The monopolistic model focuses on the environment in which most government bureaucracies operate, stating that bureaucracies are inefficient and excessively costly to operate because they have no competitors.

3. Since the founding of the United States, the federal bureaucracy has grown from 50 to about 2.7 million employees (excluding the military). Federal, state, and local employees together make up more than 16 percent of the nation's civilian labor force. The federal bureaucracy consists of 15 Cabinet departments, as well as a large number of independent executive agencies, independent regulatory agencies, and government corporations. These entities enjoy varying degrees of autonomy, visibility, and political support.

4. A federal bureaucracy of career civil servants was formed during Thomas Jefferson's presidency. Andrew Jackson implemented a spoils system through which he appointed his own political supporters. A civil service based on professionalism and merit was the goal of the Civil Service Reform Act of 1883. Concerns that

the civil service be freed from the pressures of politics prompted the passage of the Hatch Act in 1939. Significant changes in the administration of the civil service were made by the Civil Service Reform Act of 1978.

5. There have been many attempts to make the federal bureaucracy more open, efficient, and responsive to the needs of U.S. citizens. The most important reforms have included sunshine and sunset laws, privatization, strategies to provide incentives for increased productivity and efficiency, and protection for whistleblowers.

6. Congress delegates much of its authority to federal agencies when it creates new laws. The bureaucrats who run these agencies may become important policy makers, because Congress has neither the time nor the technical expertise to oversee the administration of its laws. In the agency rule-making process, a proposed regulation is published. A comment period follows, during which interested parties may offer suggestions for changes. Because companies and other organizations have challenged many regulations in court, federal agencies now are authorized to allow parties that will be affected by new regulations to participate in the rule-drafting process.

7. Congress exerts ultimate control over all federal agencies because it controls the federal government's purse strings. It also establishes the general guidelines by which regulatory agencies must abide. The appropriations process may provide a way to send messages of approval or disapproval to particular agencies, as do congressional hearings and investigations of agency actions.

SELECTED PRINT AND MEDIA RESOURCES

SUGGESTED READINGS

Goodsell, Charles T. *The Case for Bureaucracy: A Public Administration Polemic*, 4th ed. Washington, DC: CQ Press, 2003. Goodsell argues for the excellence of the federal bureaucracy, introducing all types of performance measures and examining numerous public opinion polls that demonstrate satisfaction with government agencies.

Gronlund, Ake, ed. *Electronic Government: Design, Applications, and Management*. Hershey, PA: Idea Group Publishing, 2002. This collection of essays focuses on how electronic government might improve government services as well as increase citizen participation in democratic processes.

Hilts, Philip J. *Protecting America's Health: The FDA, Business, and One Hundred Years of Regulation*. New York: Knopf, 2003. This history of the Food and Drug Administration (FDA) explains the origin and nature of the drug-approval process and the importance of clinical trials. The book provides a thorough examination of an important regulatory agency. Hilts is sympathetic to the agency and relatively critical of the pharmaceutical industry.

Meier, Kenneth J., and Lawrence J. O'Toole, Jr. *Bureaucracy in a Democratic State: A Governance Perspective*. Baltimore, MD: Johns Hopkins University Press, 2006. This study employs a governance approach to the bureaucracy. The authors examine the details of bureaucracy and demonstrate that bureaucracy can actually promote democracy.

Osborne, David, and Peter Plastrik. *Banishing Bureaucracy: The Five Strategies for Reinventing Government*. San Francisco: David Osborne Publishing, 2006. In 1992, David Osborne (with Ted Gaebler) wrote a best seller entitled *Reinventing Government*. *Vanishing Bureaucracy* is his sequel, which goes one step further—it outlines specific strategies that can help transform public systems and organizations into engines of efficiency. The book focuses on clarifying a bureaucracy's purpose, creating incentives, improving accountability, redistributing power, and nurturing the correct culture.

Weiner, Tim. *Legacy of Ashes: The History of the CIA*. New York: Doubleday, 2007. The author has written a very readable account of the CIA with the general view that many of its directors and major players have been less than competent. The book provides real insight into the CIA's role in recent American history.

MEDIA RESOURCES

The Bureaucracy of Government: John Lukacs—In a 1988 Bill Moyers special, historian John Lukacs discusses the common political lament over the giant but invisible mechanism called bureaucracy.

Yes, Minister—A new member of the British cabinet bumps up against the machinations of a top civil servant in a comedy of manners. This popular 1980 BBC comedy is now available on DVD.

E-GOVERNMENT

All federal government agencies (and virtually all state agencies) now have Web pages. Citizens can access these Web sites to find information and forms that, in the past, could normally be obtained only by going to a regional or local branch of the agency. For example, if you or a member of your family wants to learn about Social Security benefits available to you upon retirement, you can simply access the Social Security Administration's Web site to find that information. Several federal government agencies have also been active in discovering and prosecuting fraud perpetrated on citizens via the Internet.

LOGGING ON

- Numerous links to federal agencies and information on the federal government can be found at the U.S. government's official Web site. Go to:
  www.firstgov.gov
- You may want to examine two publications available from the federal government to learn more about the federal bureaucracy. The first is the *Federal Register*, which is the official publication for executive-branch documents. You can find it at:
  www.gpoaccess.gov/fr/browse.html
- The second is the *United States Government Manual*, which describes the origins, purposes, and administrators of every federal department and agency. It is available at:
  www.gpoaccess.gov/gmanual/index.html

- The Plum Book, which lists the bureaucratic positions that can be filled by presidential appointment, is online at:
  www.gpoaccess.gov/plumbook/index.html
- To find telephone numbers for government agencies and personnel, you can go to:
  www.firstgov.gov/Agencies.shtml

ONLINE REVIEW

At **www.cengage.com/politicalscience/schmidt/agandpt14e**, you will find a Tutorial Quiz for this chapter providing questions on the chapter contents, including the features. The questions are organized to match the major sections of the chapter. You'll have access to other helpful study tools, including the book's glossary and flashcards, crossword puzzles, and Web links, as well as "Which Side Are You On?" and "Politics and . . ." features written by the authors of the book.

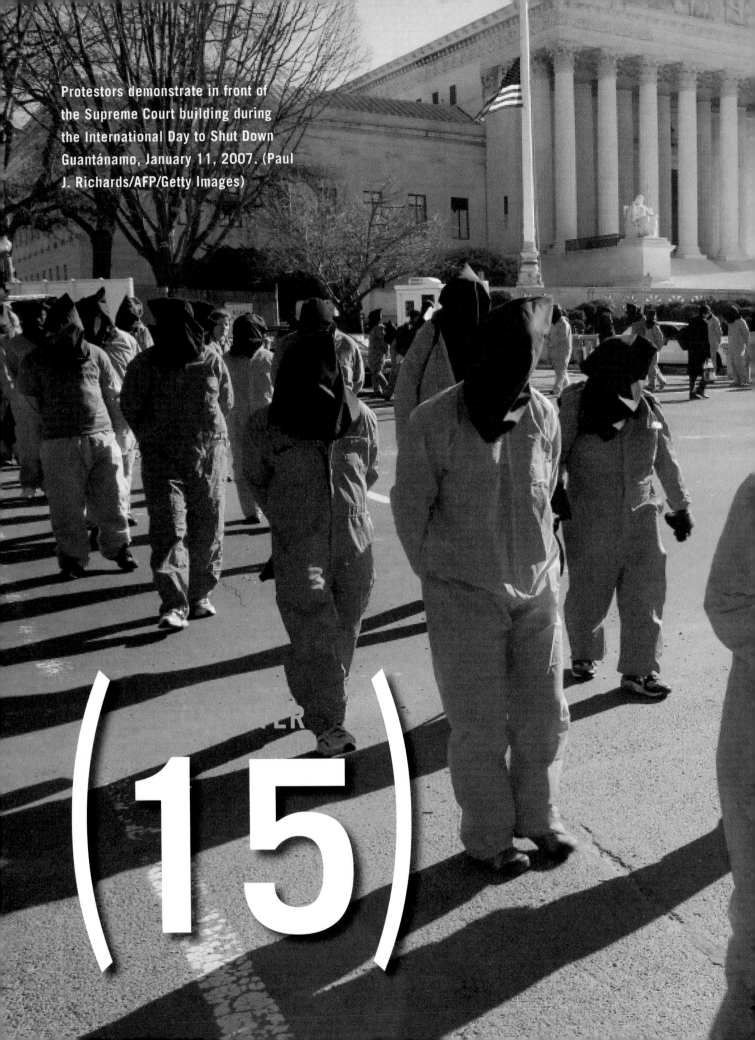

Protestors demonstrate in front of the Supreme Court building during the International Day to Shut Down Guantánamo, January 11, 2007. (Paul J. Richards/AFP/Getty Images)

(15)

THE COURTS

QUESTIONS TO CONSIDER

Why are appointed judges so powerful in a democracy?

Should the Supreme Court make law?

Why are judicial appointments so controversial?

CHAPTER CONTENTS

Making a DIFFERENCE

POLITICAL STRUGGLES FOUGHT IN THE COURT

Complaints about activist judges, a hotly contested election with partisan opponents hurling nasty insults, and debates about big government. One might argue that this is a description of politics in the 21st century. However, it also describes the presidential election of 1800, the aftermath of which led to *Marbury v. Madison*, one of the most important Supreme Court cases whose influence is felt today.

Marbury v. Madison established the doctrine of judicial review, or the ability of the Court to rule an act of government to be unconstitutional. It was precipitated by the presidential election of 1800, in which the incumbent president, John Adams, was defeated by his vice president, Thomas Jefferson. Not only did this event mark the first

election where issues divided the emerging political parties, but the election was also intensely and personally fought. President Adams was a member of the Federalist Party, which had emerged victorious in the fights over ratification of the Constitution. Jefferson was an Anti-Federalist and the leader of the ascendant Jeffersonian Republicans. These two groups disagreed on the power of the federal government. In addition, the two men bitterly disagreed with each other's politics.

While Thomas Jefferson would eventually win the election, he would not take office until March 1801.[a] In the interim between the election and inauguration, the Federalist-controlled Congress passed a series of laws creating additional judicial positions that would be staffed with Federalist appointments. One of these positions was District of Columbia Justice of the Peace, a relatively low-level judicial appointment whose term would expire in five years. William Marbury was confirmed as one of these

THE JUSTICES OF the Supreme Court are not elected, but rather are appointed by the president and confirmed by the Senate. The same is true for all other federal court judges. This fact does not mean that the federal judiciary is apolitical, however. American courts play a larger role in making public policy than courts in most other countries in the world today. Much of that power to make public policy stems from the practice of **judicial review**, which originated in the *Marbury v. Madison* case discussed in the *Making a Difference* feature.

> **Judicial Review**
> The process for deciding whether a law is contrary to the mandates of the Constitution.

As Alexis de Tocqueville, a French commentator on American society in the 1800s, noted, "scarcely any political question arises in the United States that is not resolved, sooner or later, into a judicial question."[1] Our judiciary forms part of our political process. The instant that judges interpret the law, they become actors in the political arena—policy makers working within a political institution. The most important political force within our judiciary is the United States Supreme Court.

How do courts make policy? Why do the federal courts play such an important role in American government? The answers to these questions lie, in part, in our colonial heritage. Most of American law is based on the English system, particularly the English *common-law tradition*. In that tradition, the decisions made by judges constitute an important source of law. We open this chapter with an

DID YOU KNOW?

That the Supreme Court was not provided with a building of its own until 1935, in the 146th year of its existence?

[1] Alexis de Tocqueville, *Democracy in America* (New York: Harper & Row, 1966), p. 248.

appointments. The day before inauguration, the appointment papers were signed and sealed, but not delivered. John Marshall was to deliver the appointment, but he had his own appointment to become Chief Justice of the Supreme Court. Upon taking office, President Jefferson ordered his secretary of state, James Madison, not to deliver the commissions. Marbury and two others brought suit to the Supreme Court, asking that the Court force Jefferson to deliver the commissions.

Some accounts argue that Marbury took this action, not because he wanted the appointment, but because he wanted to provoke a fight with Jefferson. Marbury was a committed Federalist who believed that the Jeffersonian argument to reduce federal government control and give power back to state governments was deeply flawed. These Federalists were very unhappy with the outcome of the election and were seeking mechanisms to remain influential.[b]

By then, the Chief Justice of the Supreme Court was John Marshall, a Federalist appointed by the former President Adams. Marshall had a real dilemma to resolve in this case. He knew that if he ordered Jefferson to honor the commission, the President would likely ignore the order, resulting in an unacceptably dangerous constitutional crisis for the young country, and the Supreme Court would be weakened. Marshall, writing for the Court, issued a decision that found Marbury's rights had been denied but that the law passed by Congress that would have granted the Court the power of redress was unconstitutional. In other words,

Marshall said that the Supreme Court was not where Marbury should have sought a solution, arguing for the first time that the Court had the power to "say what the law is."[c]

There are many interpretations of John Marshall's role and of the legal arguments he used in deciding the case.[d] Without dispute, however, this case marked the formal articulation of judicial review, a power that in the 20th century would touch Americans' most basic liberties and rights. Even more significantly, the case illustrates that the intense battles waged by groups to make a difference in contemporary politics (e.g., *Roe v. Wade* and *Bush v. Gore*) are as old as the Republic.

[a]This election was also noteworthy for illustrating the flaw in the electoral college that resulted in a tie between Jefferson and his running mate, Aaron Burr. Breaking the tie in the House of Representatives took six days and 36 ballots. www.historynow.org/09_2004/historian4b.html, accessed May 16, 2008.

[b] www.claremont.org/publications/crb/id.1183/article_detail.asp#, accessed May 17, 2008.

[c]*Marbury v. Madison*, 5 U.S. 137 (1803).

[d]See, for example, Alexander M. Bickel, *The Least Dangerous Branch: The Supreme Court at the Bar of Politics* (New Haven, CT: Yale University Press, 1986); and William E. Nelson, *Marbury v. Madison: The Origins and Legacy of Judicial Review* (Lawrence: University Press of Kansas, 2000).

examination of this tradition and of the various sources of American law. We then look at the federal court system—its organization, how its judges are selected, how these judges affect policy, and how they are restrained by our system of checks and balances.

THE COMMON-LAW TRADITION

In 1066, the Normans conquered England, and William the Conqueror and his successors began the process of unifying the country under their rule. One of the ways they did this was to establish king's courts. Before the conquest, disputes had been settled according to local custom. The king's courts sought to establish a common or uniform set of rules for the whole country. As the number of courts and cases increased, portions of the most important decisions of each year were compiled in *Year Books*. Judges settling disputes similar to ones that had been decided before used the *Year Books* as the basis for their decisions. If a case was unique, judges had to create new laws, but they based their decisions on the general principles suggested by earlier cases. The body of judge-made law that developed under this system is still used today and is known as the **common law**.

The practice of deciding new cases with reference to former decisions—that is, according to **precedent**—became a cornerstone of the English and American judicial systems and is embodied in the doctrine of ***stare decisis*** (pronounced *ster*-ay dih-*si*-ses),

Common Law
Judge-made law that originated in England from decisions shaped according to prevailing custom. Decisions were applied to similar situations and gradually became common to the nation.

Precedent
A court rule bearing on subsequent legal decisions in similar cases. Judges rely on precedents in deciding cases.

Stare Decisis
To stand on decided cases; the judicial policy of following precedents established by past decisions.

GEORGIA SUPREME COURT Chief Justice Leah War Sears questions attorneys during oral arguments concerning Georgia's constitutional amendment to ban same-sex marriages. In 2006, the Georgia Supreme Court restored the state's constitutional ban on gay marriage, reversing a lower court judge's ruling. (AP Photo/Ric Feld)

a Latin phrase that means "to stand on decided cases." The doctrine of *stare decisis* obligates judges to follow the precedents set previously by their own courts or by higher courts that have authority over them.

For example, a lower state court in California would be obligated to follow a precedent set by the California Supreme Court. That lower court, however, would not be obligated to follow a precedent set by the supreme court of another state, because each state court system is independent. Of course, when the United States Supreme Court decides an issue, all of the nation's other courts are obligated to abide by the Court's decision, because the Supreme Court is the highest court in the land.

The doctrine of *stare decisis* provides a basis for judicial decision making in all countries that have common-law systems. Today, the United States, Britain, and several dozen other countries have common-law systems. Generally, those countries that were once British colonies, such as Australia, Canada, and India, have retained their English common-law heritage. An alternative legal system based on Muslim *sharia* is discussed in this chapter's *Beyond Our Borders* feature.

SOURCES OF AMERICAN LAW

The body of American law includes the federal and state constitutions, statutes passed by legislative bodies, administrative law, and case law—the legal principles expressed in court decisions. The power of case law rests in the principle of judicial review.

CONSTITUTIONS

The constitutions of the federal government and the states set forth the general organization, powers, and limits of government. The U.S. Constitution is the supreme law of the land. A law in violation of the Constitution, no matter what its source, may be declared unconstitutional and thereafter cannot be enforced. Similarly, the state constitutions are supreme within their respective borders (unless they conflict with the U.S. Constitution or federal laws and treaties made in accordance with it). The Constitution thus defines the political playing field on which state and federal powers are reconciled. The idea that the Constitution should be supreme in certain matters stemmed from widespread dissatisfaction with the weak federal government that had existed previously under the Articles of Confederation adopted in 1781.

STATUTES AND ADMINISTRATIVE REGULATIONS

Although the English common law provides the basis for both our civil and criminal legal systems, statutes (laws enacted by legislatures) increasingly have become important in defining the rights and obligations of individuals. Federal statutes may relate to any subject that is a concern of the federal government and may apply to areas ranging from hazardous waste to federal taxation. State statutes include criminal codes, commercial laws, and laws covering a variety of other matters. Cities, counties, and other

BEYOND OUR BORDERS

THE LEGAL SYSTEM BASED ON *SHARIA*

Hundreds of millions of Muslims throughout the world are governed by a system of law called *sharia*. In this system, religious laws and precepts are combined with practical laws relating to common actions, such as entering into contracts and borrowing funds.

THE AUTHORITY OF *SHARIA*

It is said that *sharia*, or Islamic law, is drawn from two major sources and one lesser source. The first major source is the Qur'an (Koran) and the specific guidelines laid down in it. The second major source, called *sunnah*, is based on the way the Prophet Muhammad lived his life. The lesser source is called *ijma*; it represents the consensus of opinion in the community of Muslims. *Sharia* law is comprehensive in nature. All possible actions of Muslims are divided into five categories: obligatory, meritorious, permissible, reprehensible, and forbidden.

THE SCOPE OF *SHARIA* LAW

Sharia law covers many aspects of daily life, including the following:

Dietary rules
Relations between married men and women
The role of women
Holidays
Dress codes, particularly for women
Speech with respect to the Prophet Muhammad
Crimes, including adultery, murder, and theft
Business dealings, including the borrowing and lending
    of funds

WHERE *SHARIA* LAW IS APPLIED

The degree to which *sharia* is used varies throughout Muslim societies today. Several of the countries with the largest Muslim populations (e.g., Bangladesh, India, and Indonesia) do not have Islamic law. Other Muslim countries have dual systems of *sharia* courts and secular courts. In 2008, many British citizens were surprised by the remarks of the Archbishop of Canterbury, the religious leader of all Episcopalians, that there was a need for accommodation of *sharia* law in Great Britain.* He was referring to a system of *sharia* courts that have been functioning in Muslim neighborhoods for the last 20 years. The comments followed news that a *sharia* court had released some Somali youth who had stabbed another young man after ordering the assailants to compensate the victim and apologize. This incident led to national debate over whether the *sharia* court was performing functions that should be reserved for criminal and civil courts. In other parts of England, *sharia* courts deal mainly with Islamic laws regarding divorce and the rights of women, much in the same way the Catholic Church decides the status of its own members.**

Canada, which has a *sharia* arbitration court in Ontario, is the first North American country to establish a *sharia* court. Some countries, including Iran and Saudi Arabia, maintain religious courts for all aspects of jurisprudence, including civil and criminal law. Recently, Nigeria has reintroduced *sharia* courts.

FOR CRITICAL ANALYSIS

1. Do you think that a nation can have two different systems of law at the same time?
2. How should decisions about religious law be regarded by civil legal systems?

*"Sharia Law Courts Are Already Dealing with Crime on the Streets of London, It Has Emerged," *Evening Standard*, London, February 8, 2008.
**"The View from Inside a Sharia Court," BBC News, February 11, 2008.

local political bodies also pass statutes, which are called ordinances. These ordinances may deal with such issues as zoning proposals and public safety. Rules and regulations issued by administrative agencies are another source of law. Today, much of the work of the courts consists of interpreting these laws and regulations and applying them to circumstances in cases before the courts.

CASE LAW

Case Law
Judicial interpretations of common-law principles and doctrines, as well as interpretations of constitutional law, statutory law, and administrative law.

Because we have a common-law tradition, in which the doctrine of *stare decisis* (described under "The Common-Law Tradition" section) plays an important role, the decisions rendered by the courts also form an important body of law, collectively referred to as **case law**. Case law includes judicial interpretations of common-law principles and doctrines, as well as interpretations of the types of law just mentioned—constitutional provisions, statutes, and administrative agency regulations. As you learned in previous chapters, it is up to the courts—and particularly the Supreme Court—to decide what a constitutional provision or a statutory phrase means. In doing so, the courts, in effect, establish law.

JUDICIAL REVIEW

The process for deciding whether a law is contrary to the mandates of the Constitution is known as judicial review. This power is nowhere mentioned in the U.S. Constitution. Rather, this judicial power was first established in the famous case of *Marbury v. Madison* (as discussed at the beginning of the chapter in the *Making a Difference* feature). In that case, Chief Justice Marshall insisted that the Supreme Court had the power to decide that a law passed by Congress violated the Constitution:

> It is emphatically the province and duty of the Judicial Department to say what the law is. Those who apply the rule to a particular case must, of necessity, expound and interpret that rule. If two laws conflict with each other, the courts must decide on the operation of each.[2]

The Supreme Court has ruled parts or all of acts of Congress to be unconstitutional less than 200 times in its history. State laws, however, have been declared unconstitutional by the court much more often—more than a 1,000 times. The court has been more active in declaring federal or state laws unconstitutional since the beginning of the 20th century.

The Supreme Court, through its power of judicial review, can effectively define the separation of powers between the branches. In 1983, for example, the Court outlawed the practice of the legislative veto by which one or both chambers of Congress could overturn decisions made by the president or by executive agencies. This single decision overturned dozens of separate statutes and reinforced the Court's position as the arbiter of institutional power.

THE FEDERAL COURT SYSTEM

The United States has a dual court system. There are state courts and federal courts. Each of the 50 states, as well as the District of Columbia, has its own independent system of courts. This means that there are 52 court systems in total. The federal court

......

[2]5 U.S. (1 Cranch) 137 (1803).

FIGURE 15–1 Dual Structure of the American Court System

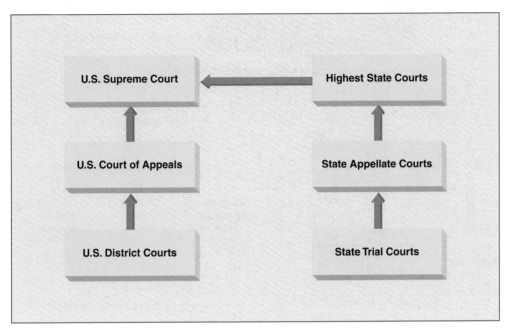

derives its power from the U.S. Constitution, Article III, Section 1, and is organized according to Congressional legislation. State courts draw their authority from state constitutions and laws. Court cases that originate in state court systems reach the Supreme Court only after they have been appealed to the highest possible state court. Figure 15–1 shows the basic components of the state and federal court systems.

BASIC JUDICIAL REQUIREMENTS

In any court system, state or federal, before a case can be brought before a court, certain requirements must be met. Two important requirements are jurisdiction and standing to sue.

Jurisdiction. A state court can exercise **jurisdiction** (the authority of the court to hear and decide a case) over the residents of a particular geographic area, such as a county or district. A state's highest court, or supreme court, has jurisdictional authority over all residents within the state. Because the Constitution established a federal government with limited powers, federal jurisdiction is also limited.

Article III, Section 1, of the U.S. Constitution limits the jurisdiction of the federal courts to cases that involve either a federal question or diversity of citizenship. A **federal question** arises when a case is based, at least in part, on the U.S. Constitution, a treaty, or a federal law. A person who claims that her or his rights under the Constitution, such as the right to free speech, have been violated could bring a case in a federal court. **Diversity of citizenship** exists when the parties to a lawsuit are from different states, or (more rarely) when the suit involves a U.S. citizen and a government or citizen of a foreign country. The amount in controversy must be at least $75,000 before a federal court can take jurisdiction in a diversity case, however.

Standing to Sue. Another basic judicial requirement is standing to sue, or a sufficient "stake" in a matter to justify bringing suit. The party bringing a lawsuit must have suffered a harm, or have been threatened by a harm, as a result of the action that led

Jurisdiction
The authority of a court to decide certain cases. Not all courts have the authority to decide all cases. Two jurisdictional issues are where a case arises as well as its subject matter.

Federal Question
A question that has to do with the U.S. Constitution, acts of Congress, or treaties. A federal question provides a basis for federal jurisdiction.

Diversity of Citizenship
The condition that exists when the parties to a lawsuit are citizens of different states, or when the parties are citizens of a U.S. state and citizens or the government of a foreign country. Diversity of citizenship can provide a basis for federal jurisdiction.

FIGURE 15–2 The Federal Court System

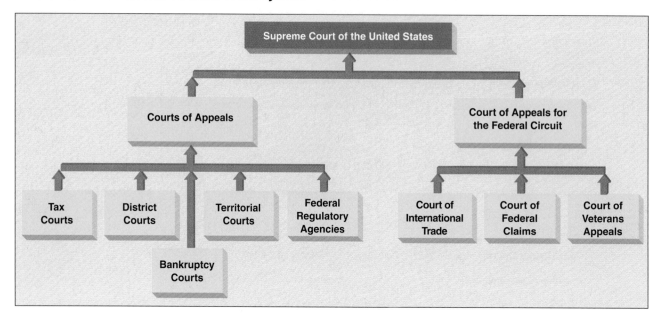

to the dispute in question. Standing to sue also requires that the controversy at issue be a justiciable controversy. A *justiciable controversy* is a controversy that is real and substantial, as opposed to hypothetical or academic. In other words, a court will not give advisory opinions on hypothetical questions.

TYPES OF FEDERAL COURTS

As you can see in Figure 15–2, the federal court system is basically a three-tiered model consisting of (1) U.S. district courts and various specialized courts of limited jurisdiction (not all of the latter are shown in the figure); (2) intermediate U.S. courts of appeals; and (3) the United States Supreme Court. Other specialized courts in the federal system are discussed in a later section. In addition, the U.S. military has its own system of courts, which are established under the Uniform Code of Military Justice. Cases from these other federal courts may also reach the Supreme Court.

U.S. District Courts. The U.S. district courts are trial courts. A **trial court** is what the name implies—a court in which trials are held and testimony is taken. The U.S. district courts are courts of **general jurisdiction**, meaning that they can hear cases involving a broad array of issues. Federal cases involving most matters typically are heard in district courts. The other courts on the lower tier of the model shown in Figure 15–2 are courts of **limited jurisdiction**, meaning that they can try cases involving only certain types of claims, such as tax claims or bankruptcy petitions.

There is at least one federal district court in every state. The number of judicial districts can vary over time as a result of population changes and corresponding caseloads. Currently, there are 94 federal judicial districts. A party who is dissatisfied with the decision of a district court can appeal the case to the appropriate U.S. court of appeals, or federal **appellate court**. Figure 15–3 shows the jurisdictional boundaries of the district courts (which are state boundaries, unless otherwise indicated by dotted lines within a state) and of the U.S. courts of appeals.

U.S. Courts of Appeals. There are 13 U.S. courts of appeals—also referred to as U.S. circuit courts of appeals. Twelve of these courts, including the U.S. Court of Appeals for

Trial Court
The court in which most cases begin.

General Jurisdiction
Exists when a court's authority to hear cases is not significantly restricted. A court of general jurisdiction normally can hear a broad range of cases.

Limited Jurisdiction
Exists when a court's authority to hear cases is restricted to certain types of claims, such as tax claims or bankruptcy petitions.

Appellate Court
A court having jurisdiction to review cases and issues that were originally tried in lower courts.

FIGURE 15–3 Geographic Boundaries of Federal District Courts and Circuit Courts of Appeals

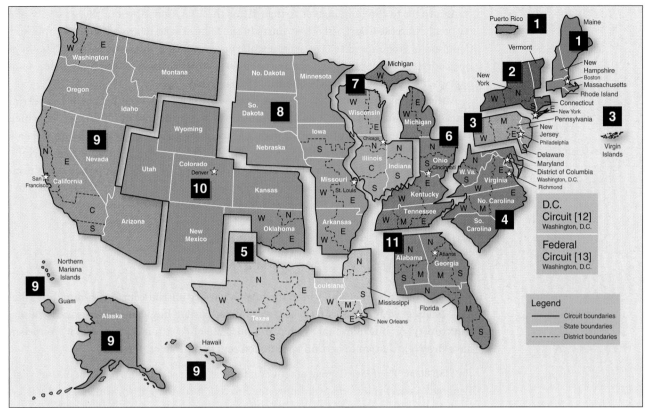

Source: Administrative Office of the United States Courts.

the District of Columbia, hear appeals from the federal district courts located within their respective judicial circuits (geographic areas over which they exercise jurisdiction). The Court of Appeals for the Thirteenth Circuit, called the Federal Circuit, has national appellate jurisdiction over certain types of cases, such as cases involving patent law and those in which the U.S. government is a defendant.

Note that when an appellate court reviews a case that was decided in a district court, the appellate court does not conduct another trial. Rather, a panel of three or more judges reviews the record of the case on appeal, which includes a transcript of the trial proceedings, and determines whether the trial court committed an error. Usually, appellate courts do not look at questions of *fact* (such as whether a party did, in fact, commit a certain action, such as burning a flag) but at questions of *law* (such as whether the act of burning a flag is a form of speech protected by the First Amendment to the Constitution). An appellate court will challenge a trial court's finding of fact only when the finding is clearly contrary to the evidence presented at trial or when no evidence supports the finding.

A party can petition the United States Supreme Court to review an appellate court's decision. The likelihood that the Supreme Court will grant the petition is slim, however, because the Court reviews very few of the cases decided by the appellate courts. This means that decisions made by appellate judges are usually final.

The United States Supreme Court. The highest level of the three-tiered model of the federal court system is the United States Supreme Court. When the Supreme Court came into existence in 1789, it had five justices. Congress passes laws that determine the number of justices and other aspects of the court. In the following years, more justices were added. Since 1869, there have been nine justices on the Court at any given time.

According to the language of Article III of the U.S. Constitution, there is only one national Supreme Court. All other courts in the federal system are considered "inferior." Congress is empowered to create other inferior courts as it deems necessary. The inferior courts that Congress has created include the district courts, the federal courts of appeals, and the federal courts of limited jurisdiction.

Although the Supreme Court can exercise original jurisdiction (that is, act as a trial court) in certain cases, such as those affecting foreign diplomats and those in which a state is a party, most of its work is as an appellate court. The Court hears appeals not only from the federal appellate courts but also from the highest state courts. Note, though, that the United States Supreme Court can review a state supreme court decision only if a federal question is involved. Because of its importance in the federal court system, we will look more closely at the Supreme Court in a later section.

SPECIALIZED FEDERAL COURTS AND THE WAR ON TERRORISM

As noted, the federal court system includes a variety of trial courts of limited jurisdiction, dealing with matters such as tax claims, patent law, Native American claims, bankruptcy, or international trade. The government's attempts to combat terrorism have drawn attention to certain specialized courts that meet in secret.

The FISA Court. The federal government created the first secret court in 1978. In that year, Congress passed the Foreign Intelligence Surveillance Act (FISA), which established a court to hear requests for warrants for the surveillance of suspected spies. Officials can request warrants without having to reveal to the suspect or the public the information used to justify the warrant. The FISA court has approved almost all of the thousands of requests for warrants that the U.S. attorney general's office and other officials have submitted. The seven judges on the FISA court (who are also federal district judges from across the nation) meet in secret, with no published opinions or orders. There is also no public access to the court's proceedings or records. Hence, when the court authorizes surveillance, most suspects do not even know that they are under scrutiny. Additionally, during the Clinton administration, the court was given the authority to approve physical as well as electronic searches, which means that officials may search a suspect's property without obtaining a warrant in open court and without notifying the subject.

In the aftermath of the terrorist attacks on September 11, 2001, the Bush administration expanded the powers of the FISA court. Previously, the FISA allowed secret domestic surveillance only if the target was spying by an agent of another nation. Post-September 11 amendments allow warrants if a "significant purpose" of the surveillance is to gather foreign intelligence and allow surveillance of groups who are not agents of a foreign government.

Alien "Removal Courts." The FISA court is not the only court in which suspects' rights have been reduced. In response to the Oklahoma City bombing in 1995, Congress passed the Anti-Terrorism and Effective Death Penalty Act of 1996. The Act included a provision creating an alien "removal court" to hear evidence against suspected "alien terrorists." The judges rule on whether there is probable cause for deportation. If so, a public deportation proceeding is held in a U.S. district court. The prosecution does not need to follow procedures that normally apply in criminal cases. In addition, the defendant cannot see the evidence that the prosecution used to secure the hearing.

In some cases, the United States Supreme Court ruled against the George W. Bush administration's efforts to use secret legal proceedings in dealing with suspected terrorists. In 2004, the Supreme Court ruled that enemy combatants who are U.S. citizens and who have been taken prisoner by the United States cannot be denied due process rights. Justice Sandra Day O'Connor wrote that "due process demands that a citizen held in the United States as an enemy combatant be given a meaningful opportunity to contest the factual basis of that detention before a neutral decision maker. . . . A state of war is not a blank check for the president when it comes to the rights of the nation's citizens."[3] The Court also found that noncitizen detainees held at Guantánamo Bay in Cuba were entitled to challenge the grounds for their confinement.[4]

THE PRISON AT GUANTÁNAMO BAY, Cuba, where the detainees from Afghanistan and Iraq are held until their military trials. While the number of prisoners has declined a great deal, many of the remaining detainees are from Yemen. To date, there has been no agreement between the United States and Yemen on how some of these men can be returned to that nation. Why did the United States create the prison at Guantánamo Bay? (Brennan Linsley/AP/Wide World Photos)

In response to the court rulings, the Bush administration asked Congress to enact a law establishing military tribunals to hear the prisoners' cases at Guantánamo. In 2006, the Court held that these tribunals did not meet due-process requirements for a fair hearing. The central issue in the case was whether the entire situation at the prison camp violated the prisoners' right of *habeas corpus*—the right of a detained person to challenge the legality of his or her detention before a judge or other neutral party. Congress then passed the Military Commissions Act of 2006, which eliminated federal court jurisdiction over *habeas corpus* challenges by enemy combatants. This law was also tested in court, but the Supreme Court refused to hear the case, so the law, as upheld by an appellate court, stands.[5]

Finally, in 2008, the Supreme Court, by a five-to-four majority, held that enemy combatants have the right to challenge their detention in front of a federal court if they have not been charged with a crime. This ruling essentially grants the detainees at Guantánamo Bay the right of *habeas corpus*, a right that the majority said Congress cannot restrict.[6]

PARTIES TO LAWSUITS

In most lawsuits, the parties are the plaintiff (the person or organization that initiates the lawsuit) and the defendant (the person or organization against whom the lawsuit is brought). There may be numerous plaintiffs and defendants in a single lawsuit. In the last several decades, many lawsuits have been brought by interest groups (see Chapter 7). Interest groups play an important role in our judicial system, because

---

[3]*Hamdi v. Rumsfeld*, 542 U.S. 507 (2004).
[4]Hamdi was eventually released following a settlement with the government under which he agreed to renounce his U.S. citizenship and return to Saudi Arabia.
[5]*Boumediene v. Bush*, 476 F.3d 981 (D.C. Cir. 2007).
[6]*Boumediene v. Bush*, 553 U.S. ____ (2008).

Litigate
To engage in a legal proceeding or seek relief in a court of law; to carry on a lawsuit.

Class-Action Suit
A lawsuit filed by an individual seeking damages for "all persons similarly situated."

they **litigate**—bring to trial—or assist in litigating most cases of racial or gender-based discrimination, virtually all civil liberties cases, and more than one-third of the cases involving business matters. Interest groups also file *amicus curiae* (pronounced ah-*mee*-kous *kur*-ee-eye) briefs, or "friend of the court" briefs, in more than 50 percent of these kinds of cases.

Sometimes interest groups or other plaintiffs will bring a **class-action suit**, in which whatever the court decides will affect all members of a class similarly situated (such as users of a particular product manufactured by the defendant in the lawsuit). The strategy of class-action lawsuits was pioneered by such groups as the National Association for the Advancement of Colored People (NAACP), the Legal Defense Fund, and the Sierra Club, whose leaders believed that the courts would offer a more sympathetic forum for their views than would Congress.

PROCEDURAL RULES

Both the federal and the state courts have established procedural rules that shape the litigation process. These rules are designed to protect the rights and interests of the parties, to ensure that the litigation proceeds in a fair and orderly manner, and to identify the issues that must be decided by the court, thus saving court time and costs. Court decisions may also apply to trial procedures. For example, the Supreme Court has held that the parties' attorneys cannot discriminate against prospective jurors on the basis of race or gender. Some lower courts have also held that people cannot be excluded from juries because of their sexual orientation or religion.

The parties must comply with procedural rules and with any orders given by the judge during the course of the litigation. When a party does not follow a court's order, the court can cite him or her for contempt. A party who commits *civil* contempt (failing to comply with a court's order for the benefit of another party to the proceeding) can be taken into custody, fined, or both, until the party complies with the court's order. A party who commits *criminal* contempt (obstructing the administration of justice or bringing the court into disrespect) also can be taken into custody and fined but cannot avoid punishment by complying with a previous order.

A COURTROOM ARTIST'S rendering of the sentencing trial for Zacarias Moussaoui at the Federal Courthouse. The confessed September 11 conspirator testified he knew about the terrorist plot when he was arrested a month before the attacks and lied to FBI agents because he wanted the mission to go forward. (Art Lein/epa/CORBIS)

Throughout this book, you have read about how technology is affecting all areas of government. The judiciary is no exception. Today's courts continue to place opinions and other information online. Increasingly, lawyers are expected to file court documents electronically. There is little doubt that in the future we will see more court proceedings being conducted through use of the Internet.

THE SUPREME COURT AT WORK

The Supreme Court begins its regular annual term on the first Monday in October and usually adjourns in late June or early July of the next year. Special sessions may be held after the regular term ends, but only a few cases are decided in this way. More commonly, cases are carried over until the next regular session.

Of the total number of cases that are decided each year, those reviewed by the Supreme Court represent less than one-half of 1 percent. Included in these, however, are decisions that profoundly affect our lives. In recent years, the United States Supreme Court has decided issues involving capital punishment, affirmative action programs, religious freedom, assisted suicide, abortion, property rights, busing, term limits for congresspersons, sexual harassment, pornography, states' rights, limits on federal jurisdiction, and many other matters with significant consequences for the nation. Because the Supreme Court exercises a great deal of discretion over the types of cases it hears, it can influence the nation's policies by issuing decisions in some types of cases and refusing to hear appeals in others, thereby allowing lower court decisions to stand.

JUSTICE RUTH BADER GINSBURG being interviewed in 2008. She noted the presence of two Jewish justices on the court and that their religion plays no role in their decisions. (Kevin Wolf/AP/Wide World Photos)

WHICH CASES REACH THE SUPREME COURT?

Many people are surprised to learn that in a typical case, there is no absolute right of appeal to the United States Supreme Court. The Court's appellate jurisdiction is almost entirely discretionary; the Court can choose which cases it will decide. The justices never explain their reasons for hearing certain cases and not others, so it is difficult to predict which case or type of case the Court might select. Former Chief Justice William Rehnquist, in his description of the selection process in *The Supreme Court: How It Was, How It Is*,[7] said that the decision of whether to accept a case "strikes me as a rather subjective decision, made up in part of intuition and in part of legal judgment."

Factors That Bear on the Decision. Factors that bear on the decision include whether a legal question has been decided differently by various lower courts and needs resolution by the highest court, whether a lower court's decision conflicts with an existing Supreme Court ruling, and whether the issue could have significance beyond the parties to the dispute.

Another factor is whether the solicitor general is pressuring the Court to take a case. The solicitor general, a high-ranking presidential appointee within the Justice Department, represents the national government before the Supreme Court and promotes presidential policies in the federal courts. He or she decides what cases the government

[7]William H. Rehnquist, *The Supreme Court: How It Was, How It Is* (New York: Morrow, 1987).

should ask the Supreme Court to review and what position the government should take in cases before the Court.

Writ of *Certiorari*
An order issued by a higher court to a lower court to send up the record of a case for review.

Granting Petitions for Review. If the Court decides to grant a petition for review, it will issue a **writ of *certiorari*** (pronounced sur-shee-uh-*rah*-ree). The writ orders a lower court to send the Supreme Court a record of the case for review. More than 90 percent of the petitions for review are denied. A denial is not a decision on the merits of a case, nor does it indicate agreement with the lower court's opinion. (The judgment of the lower court remains in force, however.) Therefore, denial of the writ has no value as a precedent. The Court will not issue a writ unless at least four justices approve of it. This is called the **rule of four**.[8]

Rule of Four
A United States Supreme Court procedure by which four justices must vote to grant a petition for review if a case is to come before the full court.

DECIDING CASES

Once the Supreme Court grants *certiorari* in a particular case, the justices do extensive research on the legal issues and facts involved in the case. (Of course, some preliminary research is necessary before deciding to grant the petition for review.) Each justice is entitled to four law clerks, who undertake much of the research and preliminary drafting necessary for the justice to form an opinion.[9]

Oral Arguments
The verbal arguments presented in person by attorneys to an appellate court. Each attorney presents reasons to the court why the court should rule in her or his client's favor.

The Court normally does not hear any evidence, as is true with all appeals courts. The Court's consideration of a case is based on the abstracts, the record, and the briefs. The attorneys are permitted to present **oral arguments**. All statements and the justices' questions are tape-recorded during these sessions. Unlike the practice in most courts, lawyers addressing the Supreme Court can be (and often are) questioned by the justices at any time during oral argument.

The justices meet to discuss and vote on cases in conferences held throughout the term. In these conferences, in addition to deciding cases currently before the Court, the justices determine which new petitions for *certiorari* to grant. These conferences take place in the oak-paneled chamber and are strictly private—no stenographers, tape recorders, or video cameras are allowed. Two pages used to be in attendance to wait on the justices while they were in conference, but fear of information leaks caused the Court to stop this practice.[10]

DECISIONS AND OPINIONS

Opinion
The statement by a judge or a court of the decision reached in a case. The opinion sets forth the applicable law and details the reasoning on which the ruling was based.

Affirm
To declare that a court ruling is valid and must stand.

Reverse
To annul or make void a court ruling on account of some error or irregularity.

Remand
To send a case back to the court that originally heard it.

When the Court has reached a decision, its opinion is written. The **opinion** contains the Court's ruling on the issue or issues presented, the reasons for its decision, the rules of law that apply, and other information. In many cases, the decision of the lower court is **affirmed**, resulting in the enforcement of that court's judgment or decree. If the Supreme Court believes that a reversible error was committed during the trial or that the jury was instructed improperly, however, the decision will be **reversed**. Sometimes the case will be **remanded** (sent back to the court that originally heard the case) for a new trial or other proceeding. For example, a lower court might have held that a party was not entitled to bring a lawsuit under a particular law. If the Supreme Court holds to the contrary, it will remand (send back) the case to the trial court with instructions that the trial proceed.

[8]The "rule of four" is modified when seven or fewer justices participate, which occurs from time to time. When that happens, as few as three justices can grant *certiorari*.
[9]For a former Supreme Court law clerk's account of the role these clerks play in the high court's decision-making process, see Edward Lazarus, *Closed Chambers: The First Eyewitness Account of the Epic Struggles inside the Supreme Court* (New York: Times Books, 1998).
[10]It turned out that one supposed information leak came from lawyers making educated guesses.

The Court's written opinion sometimes is unsigned; this is called an opinion *per curiam* ("by the court"). Typically, the Court's opinion is signed by all the justices who agree with it. When in the majority, the Chief Justice assigns the opinion and often writes it personally. When the Chief Justice is in the minority, the senior justice on the majority side decides who writes the opinion.

When all justices unanimously agree on an opinion, the opinion is written for the entire Court (all the justices) and can be deemed a **unanimous opinion**. When there is not a unanimous opinion, a **majority opinion** is written, outlining the views of the majority of the justices involved in the case. Often, one or more justices who feel strongly about making or emphasizing a particular point that is not made or emphasized in the unanimous or majority written opinion will write a **concurring opinion**. That means the justice writing the concurring opinion agrees (concurs) with the conclusion given in the majority written opinion, but for different reasons. Finally, in other than unanimous opinions, one or more **dissenting opinions** are usually written by those justices who do not agree with the majority. The dissenting opinion is important because it often forms the basis of the arguments used years later if the Court reverses the previous decision and establishes a new precedent.

Shortly after the opinion is written, the Supreme Court announces its decision from the bench. At that time, the opinion is made available to the public at the office of the clerk of the Court. The clerk also releases the opinion for online publication. Ultimately, the opinion is published in the *United States Reports*, which is the official printed record of the Court's decisions.

Some have complained that the Court reviews too few cases each term, thus giving the lower courts less guidance on important issues. The number of signed opinions issued by the Court has dwindled notably since the 1980s. For example, in its 1982–1983 term, the Court issued signed opinions in 151 cases. By the early 2000s, this number dropped to between 70 and 80 per term. In the term ending in June 2006, the number dropped to 69, the lowest number of signed opinions by the Court in one term since 1953.

Some scholars suggest that one of the reasons why the Court hears fewer cases today than in the past is the growing conservatism of the judges sitting on lower courts. More than half of these judges have now been appointed by Republican presidents. As a result, the government loses fewer cases in the lower courts, which lessens the need for the government to appeal the rulings through the solicitor general's office. Some support for this conclusion is given by the fact that the number of petitions filed by that office has declined by more than 50 percent since George W. Bush became president.

Unanimous Opinion
A court opinion or determination on which all judges agree.

Majority Opinion
A court opinion reflecting the views of the majority of the judges.

Concurring Opinion
A separate opinion prepared by a judge who supports the decision of the majority of the court but who wants to make or clarify a particular point or to voice disapproval of the grounds on which the decision was made.

Dissenting Opinion
A separate opinion in which a judge dissents from (disagrees with) the conclusion reached by the majority on the court and expounds his or her own views about the case.

THE SELECTION OF FEDERAL JUDGES

All federal judges are appointed. The Constitution, in Article II, Section 2, states that the president appoints the justices of the Supreme Court with the advice and consent of the Senate. Congress has provided the same procedure for staffing other federal courts. This means that the Senate and the president jointly decide who shall fill every vacant judicial position, no matter what the level.

There are more than 850 federal judgeships in the United States. Once appointed to such a judgeship, a person holds that job for life. Judges serve until they resign, retire voluntarily, or die. Federal judges who engage in blatantly illegal conduct may be removed through impeachment, although such action is rare.

JUDICIAL APPOINTMENTS

Judicial candidates for federal judgeships are suggested to the president by the Department of Justice, senators, other judges, the candidates, and lawyers' associations and other interest groups. In selecting a candidate to nominate for a judgeship, the president considers not only the person's competence but also other factors, including the person's political philosophy (as will be discussed shortly), ethnicity, and gender.

The nomination process—no matter how the nominees are obtained—always works the same way. The president makes the actual nomination, transmitting the name to the Senate. The Senate then either confirms or rejects the nomination. To reach a conclusion, the Senate Judiciary Committee (operating through subcommittees) invites testimony, both written and oral, at its various hearings. A practice used in the Senate, called **senatorial courtesy**, is a constraint on the president's freedom to appoint federal district judges. Senatorial courtesy allows a senator of the president's political party to veto a judicial appointment in her or his state. During much of American history, senators from the "opposition" party (the party to which the president did not belong) also have enjoyed the right of senatorial courtesy, although their veto power has varied over time.

Senatorial Courtesy
In federal district court judgeship nominations, a tradition allowing a senator to veto a judicial appointment in his or her state.

Federal District Court Judgeship Nominations. Although the president officially nominates federal judges, in the past the nomination of federal district court judges actually originated with a senator or senators of the president's party from the state in which there was a vacancy. In effect, judicial appointments were a form of political patronage. President Jimmy Carter (served 1977–1981) ended this tradition by establishing independent commissions to oversee the initial nomination process. President Ronald Reagan (served 1981–1989) abolished Carter's nominating commissions and established complete presidential control of nominations.

SENATOR EDWARD M. KENNEDY, D.-Mass., right, confers with Senate Judiciary Committee Chairman Arlen Specter, R.-Pa., before the start of the panel for final deliberations on Samuel Alito's Supreme Court nomination, on Tuesday, January 24, 2006. (J. Scott Applewhite/AP/Wide World Photos)

In 2000, Orrin Hatch, Republican chair of the Senate Judiciary Committee, announced that the opposition party (at that point, the Democrats) would no longer be allowed to invoke senatorial courtesy. The implementation of the new policy was delayed when Republican Senator James Jeffords of Vermont left the Republican Party. Jeffords' departure turned control of the Senate over to the Democrats. After the 2002 elections, however, when the Republicans regained control of the Senate, they put the new policy into effect.[11]

Federal Courts of Appeals Appointments. Appointments to the federal courts of appeals are far less numerous than federal district court appointments, but they are more important. This is because federal appellate judges handle more important matters, at least from the point of view of the president, and therefore presidents take a keener interest in the nomination process for such judgeships. Also, the U.S. courts of appeals have become stepping stones to the Supreme Court.

Supreme Court Appointments. As we have described, the president nominates Supreme Court justices.[12] As you can see in Table 15–1, which summarizes the background of all Supreme Court justices to 2008, the most common occupational background of the justices at the time of their appointment has been private legal practice or state or federal judgeship. Those nine justices who were in federal executive posts at the time of their appointment held the high offices of secretary of state, comptroller of the treasury, secretary of the navy, postmaster general, secretary of the interior, chairman of the Securities and Exchange Commission, and secretary of labor. In the "Other" category under "Occupational Position before Appointment" in Table 15–1 are two justices who were professors of law (including William H. Taft, a former president) and one justice who was a North Carolina state employee with responsibility for organizing and revising the state's statutes.

The Special Role of the Chief Justice. Although ideology is always important in judicial appointments, as described next, when a Chief Justice is selected for the Supreme Court, other considerations must also be taken into account. The Chief Justice is not only the head of a group of nine justices who interpret the law. He or she is also in essence the chief executive officer (CEO) of a large bureaucracy that includes

---

[11]John Anthony Maltese, "Anatomy of a Confirmation Mess: Recent Trends in the Federal Judicial Selection Process," April 15, 2004. This article is available as part of a *Jurist* online symposium. Go to jurist.law.pitt.edu/forum/symposium-jc/index.php.

[12]For a discussion of the factors that may come into play during the process of nominating Supreme Court justices, see David A. Yalof, *Pursuit of Justices: Presidential Politics and the Selection of Supreme Court Nominees* (Chicago: University of Chicago Press, 1999).

TABLE 15–1 Background of U.S. Supreme Court Justices to 2008

Number of Justices (110 = Total)

OCCUPATIONAL POSITION BEFORE APPOINTMENT	
Private legal practice	25
State judgeship	21
Federal judgeship	30
U.S. Attorney General	7
Deputy or Assistant U.S. Attorney General	2
U.S. Solicitor General	2
U.S. senator	6
U.S. representative	2
State governor	3
Federal executive post	9
Other	3
RELIGIOUS BACKGROUND	
Protestant	83
Roman Catholic	13
Jewish	6
Unitarian	7
No religious affiliation	1
AGE ON APPOINTMENT	
Under 40	5
41–50	32
51–60	59
61–70	14
POLITICAL PARTY AFFILIATION	
Federalist (to 1835)	13
Jeffersonian Republican (to 1828)	7
Whig (to 1861)	1
Democrat	44
Republican	44
Independent	1
EDUCATIONAL BACKGROUND	
College graduate	94
Not a college graduate	16
GENDER	
Male	108
Female	2
RACE	
White	108
African American	2

Sources: Congressional Quarterly, *Congressional Quarterly's Guide to the U.S. Supreme Court* (Washington, DC: Congressional Quarterly Press, 1996); and authors' updates.

all of the following: 1,200 judges with lifetime tenure, more than 850 magistrates and bankruptcy judges, and more than 30,000 staff members.

The Chief Justice is also the chair of the Judicial Conference of the United States, a policy-making body that sets priorities for the federal judiciary. That means that the Chief Justice also indirectly oversees the $5.5 billion budget of this group.

Finally, the Chief Justice appoints the director of the Administrative Office of the United States Courts. The Chief Justice and this director select judges who sit on judicial committees that examine international judicial relations, technology, and a variety of other topics.

PARTISANSHIP AND JUDICIAL APPOINTMENTS

Ideology plays an important role in the president's choices for judicial appointments. In most circumstances, the president appoints judges or justices who belong to the president's own political party. Presidents see their federal judiciary appointments as the one sure way to institutionalize their political views long after they have left office. By 1993, for example, Presidents Ronald Reagan and George H. W. Bush together had appointed nearly three-quarters of all federal court judges. This preponderance of Republican-appointed federal judges strengthened the legal moorings of the conservative social agenda on a variety of issues, ranging from abortion to civil rights. Nevertheless, President Bill Clinton had the opportunity to appoint about 200 federal judges, thereby shifting the ideological makeup of the federal judiciary.

During the first two years of his second term, President George W. Bush was able to nominate two relatively conservative justices to the Supreme Court—John Roberts, who became Chief Justice, and Samuel Alito. Both are Catholics and have relatively, but not consistently, conservative views. In fact, during his first term as Chief Justice, Roberts voted most of the time with the Court's most conservative justices, Antonin Scalia and Clarence Thomas. Nonetheless, Roberts and Alito may not cause the Supreme Court to "tilt to the right" as much as some people anticipated. The reason is that the two newest Supreme Court members replaced justices who were moderate to conservative. Thus, the makeup of the Court did not necessarily change.

Interestingly, some previous conservative justices have shown a tendency to migrate to a more liberal view of the law. Sandra Day O'Connor, the first female justice and a conservative, gradually shifted to the left on several issues, including abortion. In 1981, during her confirmation hearing before the Senate Judiciary Committee, she said, "I am opposed to it [abortion], as a matter of birth control or otherwise." By 1992, she was part of a five-to-four majority that agreed that the Constitution protects a woman's right to an abortion.

JOHN ROBERTS raises his right hand as he takes the oath of office to be sworn in as the 17th Chief Justice of the United States during a ceremony in the East Room of the White House in Washington, September 29, 2005. Chief Justice Roberts clerked for the court after law school and practiced before the court in later years. Do you think these experiences made his confirmation easier? (Jim Bourg/Reuters/Landov/Landov Media)

THE SENATE'S ROLE

Ideology also plays a large role in the Senate's confirmation hearings, and presidential nominees to the Supreme Court have not always been confirmed. In fact, almost 20 percent of presidential nominations to the Supreme Court have been either rejected or not acted on by the Senate. There have been many acrimonious battles over Supreme Court appointments when the Senate and the president have not seen eye to eye about political matters.

The U.S. Senate had a long record of refusing to confirm the president's judicial nominations from the beginning of Andrew Jackson's presidency in 1829 to the end of Ulysses Grant's presidency in 1877. From 1894 until 1968, however, only three nominees were not confirmed. Then, from 1968 through 1987, four presidential nominees to the highest court were rejected. One of the most controversial Supreme Court nominations was that of Clarence Thomas, who underwent an extremely volatile confirmation hearing in 1991, replete with charges against him of sexual harassment. He was ultimately confirmed by the Senate, however, and has been a stalwart voice for conservatism ever since.

President Bill Clinton had little trouble gaining approval for both of his nominees to the Supreme Court: Ruth Bader Ginsburg and Stephen Breyer. President George W. Bush's nominees faced hostile grilling in their confirmation hearings, and various interest groups mounted intense media advertising blitzes against them. Bush had to forgo one of his nominees, Harriet Miers, when he realized that she could not be confirmed by the Senate. Both Clinton and Bush had trouble securing Senate approval for their judicial nominations to the lower courts. In fact, during the late 1990s and early 2000s, the duel between the Senate and the president aroused considerable concern about the consequences of the increasingly partisan and ideological tension over federal judicial appointments. On several occasions, presidents have appointed federal judges using a temporary "recess appointment." This procedure is always used for the same reason—to avoid the continuation of an acrimonious and perhaps futile Senate confirmation process.

Although the confirmation hearings on Supreme Court nominees get all of the media attention, the hearings on nominees for the lower federal courts are equally bitter, leading some to ask whether the politicization of the confirmation process has gone too far. According to Fifth Circuit Court Judge Edith Jones, judicial nominations have turned into battlegrounds because so many federal judges now view the courts as agents of social change. Jones argues that when judge-made law (as opposed to legislature-made law) enters into sensitive topics, it provokes a political reaction. Thus, the ideology and political views of the potential justices should be a matter of public concern and political debate.

Politics has played a role in selecting judges since the administration of George Washington. The classic case cited earlier, *Marbury v. Madison*, was rooted in partisan politics. Nonetheless, most nominees are confirmed without dispute. As of 2006, the vacancy rate on the federal bench was at its lowest point in 15 years. Those nominees who run into trouble are usually the most conservative Republican nominees or the most liberal Democratic ones. It is legitimate to evaluate a candidate's judicial ideology when that ideology is strongly held and likely to influence the judge's rulings.

POLICY MAKING AND THE COURTS

The partisan battles over judicial appointments reflect an important reality in today's American government: the importance of the judiciary in national politics. Because appointments to the federal bench are for life, the ideology of judicial appointees can affect national policy for years to come. Although the primary function of judges in our system of government is to interpret and apply the laws, inevitably judges make policy when carrying out this task. One of the major policy-making tools of the federal courts is their power of judicial review.

"Do you ever have one of those days when everything seems un-Constitutional?" (© 2002 The New Yorker Collection from cartoonbank .com. All rights reserved.)

JUDICIAL REVIEW

If a federal court declares that a federal or state law or policy is unconstitutional, the court's decision affects the application of the law or policy only within that court's jurisdiction. For this reason, the higher the level of the court, the greater the impact of the decision on society. Because of the Supreme Court's national jurisdiction, its decisions have the greatest impact. For example, when the Supreme Court held that an Arkansas state constitutional amendment limiting the terms of congresspersons was unconstitutional, laws establishing term limits in 23 other states were also invalidated.[13]

Some claim that the power of judicial review gives unelected judges and justices on federal court benches too much influence over national policy. Others argue that the powers exercised by the federal courts, particularly the power of judicial review, are necessary to protect our constitutional rights and liberties. Built into our federal form of government is a system of checks and balances. If the federal courts did not have the power of judicial review, there would be no governmental body to check Congress's lawmaking authority.

JUDICIAL ACTIVISM AND JUDICIAL RESTRAINT

> **Judicial Activism**
> A doctrine holding that the Supreme Court should take an active role by using its powers to check the activities of governmental bodies when those bodies exceed their authority.

Judicial scholars like to characterize different judges and justices as being either "activist" or "restraintist." The doctrine of **judicial activism** rests on the conviction that the federal judiciary should take an active role by using its powers to check the activities of Congress, state legislatures, and administrative agencies when those governmental bodies exceed their authority. One of the Supreme Court's most activist eras was the period from 1953 to 1969, when the Court was headed by Chief Justice Earl Warren. The Warren Court propelled the civil rights movement forward by holding, among other things, that laws permitting racial segregation violated the equal protection clause.

> **Judicial Restraint**
> A doctrine holding that the Supreme Court should defer to the decisions made by the elected representatives of the people in the legislative and executive branches.

In contrast, the doctrine of **judicial restraint** rests on the assumption that the courts should defer to the decisions made by the legislative and executive branches, because members of Congress and the president are elected by the people, whereas members of the federal judiciary are not. Because administrative agency personnel normally have more expertise than the courts do in the areas regulated by the agencies, the courts likewise should defer to agency rules and decisions. In other words, under the doctrine of judicial restraint, the courts should not thwart the implementation of legislative acts and agency rules unless they are clearly unconstitutional.

Judicial activism sometimes is linked with liberalism, and judicial restraint with conservatism. In fact, though, a conservative judge can be activist, just as a liberal judge can be restraintist. In the 1950s and 1960s, the Supreme Court was activist and liberal. Some observers believe that the Rehnquist Court, with its conservative majority, became increasingly activist during the early 2000s. Some go even further and claim that the federal courts, including the Supreme Court, wield too much power in our democracy.

STRICT VERSUS BROAD CONSTRUCTION

> **Strict Construction**
> A judicial philosophy that looks to the "letter of the law" when interpreting the Constitution or a particular statute.

Other terms that are often used to describe a justice's philosophy are *strict construction* and *broad construction*. Justices who believe in **strict construction** look to the "letter

---

[13]*U.S. Term Limits v. Thornton*, 514 U.S. 779 (1995).

of the law" when they attempt to interpret the Constitution or a particular statute. Those who favor **broad construction** try to determine the context and purpose of the law.

As with the doctrines of judicial restraint and judicial activism, strict construction is often associated with conservative political views, whereas broad construction is often linked with liberalism. These traditional political associations sometimes appear to be reversed, however. Consider the Eleventh Amendment to the Constitution, which rules out lawsuits in federal courts "against one of the United States by Citizens of another State, or by Citizens or Subjects of any Foreign State." Nothing is said about citizens suing their *own* states, and strict construction would therefore find such suits to be constitutional. Conservative justices, however, have construed this amendment broadly to deny citizens the constitutional right to sue their own states in most circumstances. John T. Noonan, Jr., a federal appellate court judge who was appointed by a Republican president, has described these rulings as "adventurous."[14]

Broad construction is often associated with the concept of a "living constitution." Supreme Court Justice Antonin Scalia has said that "the Constitution is not a living organism, it is a legal document. It says something and doesn't say other things." Scalia believes that jurists should stick to the plain text of the Constitution "as it was originally written and intended."

> **Broad Construction**
> A judicial philosophy that looks to the context and purpose of a law when making an interpretation.

IDEOLOGY AND THE REHNQUIST COURT

William H. Rehnquist became the 16th Chief Justice of the Supreme Court in 1986, after 15 years as an associate justice. He was known as a strong anchor of the Court's conservative wing until his death in 2005. With Rehnquist's appointment as Chief Justice, it seemed to observers that the Court would necessarily become more conservative.

Indeed, that is what happened. The Court began to take a rightward shift shortly after Rehnquist became Chief Justice, and the Court's rightward movement continued as other conservative appointments to the bench were made during the Reagan and George H. W. Bush administrations. During the late 1990s and early 2000s, three of the justices (William Rehnquist, Antonin Scalia, and Clarence Thomas) were notably conservative in their views. Four of the justices (John Paul Stevens, David Souter, Ruth Bader Ginsburg, and Stephen Breyer) held liberal-to-moderate views. The middle of the Court was occupied by two moderate-to-conservative justices, Sandra Day O'Connor and Anthony Kennedy. O'Connor and Kennedy usually provided the swing votes on the Court in controversial cases.

Although the Court seemed to become more conservative under Rehnquist's leadership, its decisions were not always predictable. Many cases were decided by very close votes, and results seemed to vary depending on the issue. For example, the Court ruled in 1995 that Congress had overreached its powers under the commerce clause when it attempted to regulate the possession of guns in schoolyards. According to the Court, the possession of guns in school zones had nothing to do with the commerce clause.[15] Yet in 2005, the Court upheld Congress's power under the commerce clause to ban marijuana use even when a state's law permitted such use.[16] In other areas such as civil rights, the Court generally issued conservative opinions.

THE ROBERTS COURT

In 2006, a new Chief Justice was appointed to the court. John Roberts had a distinguished career as an attorney in Washington, D.C. He had served as a clerk to the

---

[14]John T. Noonan, Jr., *Narrowing the Nation's Power: The Supreme Court Sides with the States* (Berkeley: University of California Press, 2002).
[15]*United States v. Lopez*, 514 U.S. 549 (1995).
[16]*Gonzales v. Raich*, 545 U.S. 1 (2005).

Supreme Court while in law school and was well-liked by the justices. The confirmation process had been quite smooth, and many hoped that he would be a moderate leader of the Court.

During John Roberts's first term (2005–2006) as Chief Justice, the Court ruled on several important issues, but no clear pattern was discernible in the decisions. Under Roberts, the Court ruled in 2006 that the due-process clause of the Constitution does not prohibit Arizona's use of an insanity test stated solely in terms of the accused's capacity to tell whether an act charged as a crime was right or wrong. In the same year, the Court held that federal courts can assess the procedures used in military tribunals when the accused is not a member of the military. With respect to capital punishment, the Roberts Court ruled that the capital sentencing statute in Kansas was constitutional.

In the years following his appointment, Roberts was more likely to vote with the conservative justices—Scalia, Thomas, and Alito—than with the moderate-to-liberal bloc. Thus, several important decisions were handed down with close votes. In an important case for environmentalist groups, the Court held that the Environmental Protection Agency (EPA) did have the power under the Clean Air Act to regulate greenhouse gasses. The vote was five to four, with the Chief Justice on the minority side.[17] Similarly, when the Court upheld the 2003 federal law banning partial-birth abortions, Roberts was on the conservative side in a five-to-four vote.[18]

Later in 2007, the Supreme Court issued a very important opinion on school integration. By another five-to-four vote, the Court ruled that school district policies that included race as a determining factor in admission to certain schools were unconstitutional on the ground that they violated the equal protection clause of the Constitution.[19] These decisions of the Roberts Court suggest that there may often be a conservative

[17]*Massachusetts v. EPA*, 127 St. Ct. 1438 (2007).
[18]*Gonzales v. Carhart*, 127 St. Ct. 1610 (2007).
[19]*Parents Involved in Community Schools v. Seattle School District*, N. 1, 127 St. Ct. 2162 (2007).

majority on the Supreme Court, but the majority is razor thin, and swing votes can change the outcome in many cases.

WHAT CHECKS OUR COURTS?

Our judicial system is one of the most independent in the world, but the courts do not have absolute independence, for they are part of the political process. Political checks limit the extent to which courts can exercise judicial review and engage in an activist policy. These checks are exercised by the executive branch, the legislature, the public, and, finally, the judiciary.

EXECUTIVE CHECKS

President Andrew Jackson was once supposed to have said, after Chief Justice John Marshall made an unpopular decision, "John Marshall has made his decision; now let him enforce it."[20] This purported remark goes to the heart of **judicial implementation**—the enforcement of judicial decisions in such a way that those decisions are translated into policy. The Supreme Court simply does not have any enforcement powers, and whether a decision will be implemented depends on the cooperation of the other two branches of government. Rarely, though, will a president refuse to enforce a Supreme Court decision, as President Jackson did. To take such an action could mean a significant loss of public support because of the Supreme Court's stature in the eyes of the nation.

FEDERAL TROOPS were sent by President Eisenhower to guard Little Rock High School and to ensure the safety of the African American students who were going to attend that school. (A. Y. Owen/Getty Images)

Judicial Implementation
The way in which court decisions are translated into action.

More commonly, presidents exercise influence over the judiciary by appointing new judges and justices as federal judicial seats become vacant. Additionally, as mentioned earlier, the U.S. Solicitor General plays a significant role in the federal court system, and the person holding this office is a presidential appointee.

Executives at the state level may also refuse to implement court decisions with which they disagree. A notable example of such a refusal occurred in Arkansas after the Supreme Court ordered schools to desegregate "with all deliberate speed" in 1955.[21] Arkansas Governor Orval Faubus refused to cooperate with the decision and used the state's National Guard to block the integration of Central High School in Little Rock. Ultimately, President Dwight Eisenhower had to federalize the Arkansas National Guard and send federal troops to Little Rock to quell the violence that had erupted.

---

[20]The decision referred to was *Cherokee Nation v. Georgia*, 30 U.S. 1 (1831).
[21]*Brown v. Board of Education*, 349 U.S. 294 (1955)—the second *Brown* decision.

LEGISLATIVE CHECKS

Courts may make rulings, but often the legislatures at local, state, and federal levels are required to appropriate funds to carry out the courts' rulings. A court, for example, may decide that prison conditions must be improved, but the legislature authorizes the funds necessary to carry out the ruling. When such funds are not appropriated, the court that made the ruling, in effect, has been checked.

Constitutional Amendments. Courts' rulings can be overturned by constitutional amendments at both the federal and state levels. Many of the amendments to the U.S. Constitution (such as the Fourteenth, Fifteenth, and Twenty-sixth Amendments) check the state courts' ability to allow discrimination, for example. Proposed constitutional amendments that were created in an effort to reverse courts' decisions on school prayer and abortion have failed.

Rewriting Laws. Finally, Congress or a state legislature can rewrite (amend) old laws or enact new ones to overturn a court's rulings if the legislature concludes that the court is interpreting laws or legislative intentions erroneously. For example, Congress passed the Civil Rights Act of 1991 in part to overturn a series of conservative rulings in employment-discrimination cases. In 1993, Congress enacted the Religious Freedom Restoration Act (RFRA), which broadened religious liberties, after Congress concluded that a 1990 Supreme Court ruling restricted religious freedom to an unacceptable extent.[22]

According to political scientist Walter Murphy, "A permanent feature of our constitutional landscape is the ongoing tug and pull between elected government and the courts."[23] Certainly, over the last few decades, the Supreme Court has been in conflict with the other two branches of government. Congress at various times has passed laws that, among other things, made it illegal to burn the American flag and attempted to curb pornography on the Internet. In each instance, the Supreme Court ruled that those laws were unconstitutional. The Court also invalidated the RFRA.

Whenever Congress does not like what the judiciary does, it threatens to censure the judiciary for its activism. One member of the Senate Judiciary Committee, John Cornyn (R.-Tex.), claimed that judges are making "political decisions yet are unaccountable to the public." He went on to say that violence against judges in the courtroom can be explained by the public's distress at such activism.

The states can also negate or alter the effects of Supreme Court rulings, when such decisions allow it. A good case in point is *Kelo v. City of New London*.[24] In that case, the Supreme Court allowed a city to take private property for redevelopment by private businesses. Since that case was decided, a majority of states have passed legislation limiting or prohibiting such takings.

PUBLIC OPINION

Public opinion plays a significant role in shaping government policy, and certainly the judiciary is not exempt from this rule. For one thing, persons affected by a Supreme Court decision that is noticeably at odds with their views may simply ignore it. Officially sponsored prayers were banned in public schools in 1962, yet it was widely known that the ban was (and still is) ignored in many Southern districts. What can the courts do in this situation? Unless someone complains about the prayers and initiates a lawsuit, the courts can do nothing. The public can also pressure state and local government officials

---

[22]*Employment Division, Department of Human Resources of Oregon v. Smith*, 494 U.S. 872 (1990).
[23]As quoted in Neal Devins, "The Last Word Debate: How Social and Political Forces Shape Constitutional Values," *American Bar Association Journal*, October 1997, p. 48.
[24]545 U.S. 469 (2005).

WHAT IF...

SUPREME COURT JUSTICES HAD TERM LIMITS?

The nine justices who sit on the Supreme Court are not elected officials. Rather, they are appointed by the president (and confirmed by the Senate). Barring gross misconduct, they also hold their offices for life. Given the long life span of Americans, it is not unusual for justices to be actively serving on the court after they turn 80 years old. Would the justices be more in tune with the ideas of Americans and less likely to use their power to make policy if they did not hold permanent seats? One way to make the justices even more responsive to public opinion might be to limit their tenure in office.

If Supreme Court justices had term limits, what should be the length of the term? Perhaps an appropriate one would be the average time on the bench from the founding of our nation until 1970—15 years. In other words, after confirmation by the Senate, a person could serve only 15 years on the bench and then would have to retire. Perhaps the most important result of term limits would be a reduction in the rancor surrounding confirmation hearings. Today, the confirmation of a Supreme Court nominee—one chosen by the president to fit his or her views—is a major political event because that person may be on the Court for the next three decades.

Consider the current Chief Justice, John Roberts. When he took the Supreme Court bench at age 50, Americans could potentially anticipate that his conservative ideology would influence Supreme Court decisions for as long as 30 years. Knowing this, those who did not share his views or philosophy fought bitterly to prevent him from being confirmed. If term limits were in existence, in contrast, less would have been at stake—probably about half as many years of his influence.

TERM LIMITS WOULD PUT THE UNITED STATES IN LINE WITH OTHER DEMOCRACIES

In having no term limits for federal judges, the United States is somewhat out of step. Not only does just one state—Rhode Island—appoint state supreme court justices for life, but virtually every other major democratic nation has age or term limits for judges. Thus, term limits in the United States for federal judges would not be an anomaly. Even with term limits, Supreme Court justices would still be independent, which is what the framers of the Constitution desired.

MORE INFUSION OF NEW BLOOD

With term limits of, say, 15 years, vacancies would be created on a more or less regular basis. Consequently, Supreme Court justices would have less temptation to time their retirements for political purposes. Thus, liberal-leaning justices would not necessarily delay their retirements until a Democratic president was in office, and conservative-leaning justices would not necessarily wait for a Republican. In other words, fewer justices would follow the example of Justice Thurgood Marshall, who often said that he was determined to hang on to his judicial power until a Democratic president was in office to appoint his successor. After many years on the bench, he joked, "I have instructed my clerks that if I should die, they should have me stuffed—and continue to cast my votes."

In short, virtually every president, whether he or she was Republican or Democrat, would get a chance to fill a Supreme Court vacancy every few years. As a result, "new blood" would be infused into the Supreme Court more often. We would no longer face the risk of having Supreme Court justices who become less than enthusiastic about their work and less willing to examine new intellectual arguments. Term limits would also avoid the decrepitude that has occurred with several very old Supreme Court justices. In the last 30 years, some truly have stayed until the last possible minute. The public might prefer at least to have a mandatory retirement age.

FOR CRITICAL ANALYSIS

1. What are the benefits of having lifetime appointments to the Supreme Court?
2. Just because a president can appoint whomever he or she wishes to the Supreme Court, does that necessarily mean that the successful nominee will always reflect the president's political philosophy? Explain your answer.

to refuse to enforce a certain decision. As already mentioned, judicial implementation requires the cooperation of government officials at all levels, and public opinion in various regions of the country will influence whether such cooperation is forthcoming.

Additionally, the courts necessarily are influenced by public opinion to some extent. After all, judges are not isolated in our society; their attitudes are influenced by social trends, just as the attitudes and beliefs of all persons are. Courts generally tend to avoid issuing decisions that they know will be noticeably at odds with public opinion.[25] In part, this is because the judiciary, as a branch of the government, prefers to avoid creating divisiveness among the public. Also, a court—particularly the Supreme Court—may lose stature if it decides a case in a way that markedly diverges from public opinion. For example, in 2002, the Supreme Court ruled that the execution of mentally retarded criminals violates the Eighth Amendment's ban on cruel and unusual punishment. In its ruling, the Court indicated that the standards of what constitutes cruel and unusual punishment are influenced by public opinion and that there is "powerful evidence that today our society views mentally retarded offenders as categorically less culpable than the average criminal."[26]

JUDICIAL TRADITIONS AND DOCTRINES

Supreme Court justices (and other federal judges) typically exercise self-restraint in fashioning their decisions. In part, this restraint stems from their knowledge that the other two branches of government and the public can exercise checks on the judiciary, as previously discussed. To a large extent, however, this restraint is mandated by various judicially established traditions and doctrines. For example, in exercising its discretion to hear appeals, the Supreme Court will not hear a meritless appeal just so it can rule on the issue. Also, when reviewing a case, the Supreme Court typically narrows its focus to just one issue or one aspect of an issue involved in the case. The Court rarely makes broad, sweeping decisions on issues. Furthermore, the doctrine of *stare decisis* acts as a restraint because it obligates the courts, including the Supreme Court, to follow established precedents when deciding cases. Only rarely will courts overrule a precedent.

Hypothetical and Political Questions. Other judicial doctrines and practices also act as restraints. As already mentioned, the courts will hear only what are called justiciable disputes, which arise out of actual cases. In other words, a court will not hear a case that involves a merely hypothetical issue. Additionally, if a political question is involved, the Supreme Court often will exercise judicial restraint and refuse to rule on the matter. A **political question** is one that the Supreme Court declares should be decided by the elected branches of government—the executive branch, the legislative branch, or those two branches acting together. For example, the Supreme Court has refused to rule on the controversy regarding the rights of gays and lesbians in the military, preferring instead to defer to the executive branch's decisions on the matter. Generally, fewer questions are deemed political questions by the Supreme Court today than in the past.

The Impact of the Lower Courts. Higher courts can reverse the decisions of lower courts. Lower courts can act as a check on higher courts, too. Lower courts can ignore—and have ignored—Supreme Court decisions. Usually, this is done indirectly. A lower court might conclude, for example, that the precedent set by the Supreme Court does not apply to the exact circumstances in the case before the court; or the lower court may decide that the Supreme Court's decision was ambiguous with respect to the issue before the lower court. The fact that the Supreme Court rarely makes broad and clear-cut statements on any issue makes it easier for the lower courts to interpret the Supreme Court's decisions in a different way.

Political Question
An issue that a court believes should be decided by the executive or legislative branch.

. . . .

[25]One striking counterexample is the *Kelo v. City of New London* decision mentioned earlier.
[26]*Atkins v. Virginia*, 536 U.S. 304 (2002).

You can make a difference

THE INNOCENCE PROJECT

News stories of people sent to jail after being convicted of crimes they did not commit seem to appear regularly in the media these days. Have you ever wondered how often the courts send innocent people to jail? Just how vulnerable is our criminal justice system to wrongful convictions? DNA testing and a group called The Innocence Project are changing such injustices.

WHY SHOULD YOU CARE?

About 2 million people are in American jails and prisons. Since its inception in 1992, the Innocence Project, a non-profit legal clinic located at the Cardozo School of Law at Yeshiva University in New York, is dedicated to exonerating wrongfully convicted people through DNA testing. Law students handle casework while supervised by practicing attorneys. Affiliated offices can be found in nearly every major city and state across the country, as well as in Australia, Canada, New Zealand, and the United Kingdom. The organization has helped to exonerate more than 200 people, including 16 who were sentenced to death. Those released spent an average of 12 years in prison.

People have been wrongly imprisoned for many reasons, including eyewitness misidentification, negligence, misconduct, poor training in forensic labs, false confessions, the use of jailhouse informants, incompetent or inadequate defense lawyers, and police mistakes or misconduct. Clients come from all walks of life, with some being veterans or college students. A disproportionate number are Latinos or African Americans who, due to their imprisonment, had become indigent. To date, 16 people had received death sentences before DNA proved their innocence. About 70 percent of those people exonerated by DNA testing are members of a minority group. A study conducted in 2004 by the University of Michigan suggested that the leading causes of wrongful convictions for murder were false confessions among those most vulnerable to suggestion and intimidation, such as the mentally retarded, the mentally ill, and juveniles. When innocent people are incarcerated, criminals still on the streets commit crimes and make a more dangerous society for us all.

WHAT CAN YOU DO?

DNA testing leading to the subsequent exoneration of innocent people suggests flaws in our criminal justice system. Freeing people who have been wrongly convicted provides proof of those flaws and reveals the need for action and reform. The Innocence Project is dedicated to enacting those reforms and boosting confidence in our justice system. Volunteers from across the nation are working on eyewitness identification reform, the problem of false confessions, access to post-conviction DNA testing, evidence preservation, crime lab oversight, criminal justice reform commissions, and compensation for innocent people sent to jail.

The Innocence Project Web site, **www.innocenceproject.org**, provides state-by-state comparisons dealing with exonerations, causes of wrongful convictions, reforms enacted, and a link to affiliated organizations around the United States and the world. Some individual state groups also accept cases outside their state or the country. You can find further information regarding successful outcomes and pending cases awaiting their day in court. Like many nonprofit organizations, The Innocence Project and affiliated groups cannot function without volunteer support. In most cases, volunteers are required to live in close proximity to the offices because of the nature of the work involved. If you would like more information regarding volunteer opportunities, e-mail The Innocence Project at info@innocenceproject.org, or contact them at:

Innocence Project
100 Fifth Avenue, 3rd Floor
New York, NY 10011
212-364-5340

REFERENCES

Adam Liptak, "Study Suspects Thousands of False Convictions," *The New York Times*, April 19, 2004, accessed at www.truthinjustice.org/exoneration-study.htm.
http://innocenceproject.org
www.truthinjustice.org

KEY TERMS

CHAPTER SUMMARY

1. American law is rooted in the common-law tradition, which is part of our heritage from England. The common-law doctrine of *stare decisis* (which means "to stand on decided cases") obligates judges to follow precedents established previously by their own courts or by higher courts that have authority over them. Precedents established by the United States Supreme Court, the highest court in the land, are binding on all lower courts. Fundamental sources of American law include the U.S. Constitution and state constitutions, statutes enacted by legislative bodies, regulations issued by administrative agencies, and case law.

2. Article III, Section 1, of the U.S. Constitution limits the jurisdiction of the federal courts to cases involving (1) a federal question, which is a question based, at least in part, on the U.S. Constitution, a treaty, or a federal law; or (2) diversity of citizenship, which arises when parties to a lawsuit are from different states or when the lawsuit involves a foreign citizen or government. The federal court system is a three-tiered model consisting of (1) U.S. district (trial) courts and various lower courts of limited jurisdiction; (2) U.S. courts of appeals; and (3) the United States Supreme Court. Cases may be appealed from the district courts to the appellate courts. In most cases, the decisions of the federal appellate courts are final because the Supreme Court hears relatively few cases.

3. The Supreme Court's decision to review a case is influenced by many factors, including the significance of the issues involved and whether the solicitor general is pressing the Court to take the case. After a case is accepted, the justices undertake research (with the help of their law clerks) on the issues involved in the case, hear oral arguments from the parties, meet in confer-

ence to discuss and vote on the issue, and announce the opinion, which is then released for publication.

4. Federal judges are nominated by the president and confirmed by the Senate. Once appointed, they hold office for life, barring gross misconduct. The nomination and confirmation process, particularly for Supreme Court justices, is often extremely politicized. Democrats and Republicans alike realize that justices may occupy seats on the Court for decades and naturally want to have persons appointed who share their basic views. Nearly 20 percent of all Supreme Court appointments have been either rejected or not acted on by the Senate.

5. In interpreting and applying the law, judges inevitably become policy makers. The most important policy-making tool of the federal courts is the power of judicial review. This power was not mentioned specifically in the Constitution, but John Marshall claimed the power for the Court in his 1803 decision in *Marbury v. Madison*.

6. Judges who take an active role in checking the activities of the other branches of government sometimes are characterized as "activist" judges, and judges who defer to the other branches' decisions sometimes are regarded as "restraintist" judges. The Warren Court of the 1950s and 1960s was activist in a liberal direction, whereas the Rehnquist Court became increasingly activist in a conservative direction. Several politicians and scholars argue that judicial activism has gotten out of hand. It is too early to know what direction the Roberts Court will take.

7. Checks on the powers of the federal courts include executive checks, legislative checks, public opinion, and judicial traditions and doctrines.

SELECTED PRINT AND MEDIA RESOURCES

SUGGESTED READINGS

Baird, Vanessa. *Answering the Call of the Court: How Justices and Litigants Set the Supreme Court Agenda.* Charlottesville: University of Virginia Press, 2006. The author attempts to relate the justices' political and philosophical priorities to the way the Court's agenda has expanded in recent years. This is one of the first studies of the Court's agenda-setting process.

Foskett, Ken. *Judging Thomas: The Life and Times of Clarence Thomas.* New York: William Morrow, 2004. Foskett, an Atlanta journalist, delves into the intellectual development of Justice Thomas, one of the nation's most prominent African American conservatives.

Greenburg, Jan Crawford. *Supreme Conflict: The Inside Story of the Struggle for the Control of the United States Supreme Court.* New York: Penguin Books, 2008. A newspaper and PBS reporter, Greenburg developed close relationships with justices and staff at the Supreme Court. She tells the inside story of which justices were really powerful and which were the followers.

Klarman, Michael J. *From Jim Crow to Civil Rights: The Supreme Court and the Struggle for Racial Equality.* New York: Oxford University Press, 2004. Klarman, a professor of constitutional law, provides a detailed history of the Supreme Court's changing attitudes toward equality. Klarman argues that the civil rights movement would have revolutionized the status of African Americans even if the Court had not outlawed segregation.

O'Connor, Sandra Day. *The Majesty of the Law: Reflections of a Supreme Court Justice.* New York: Random House, 2003. As the Supreme Court's most prominent swing vote during her years on the bench, Justice O'Connor may have been the most powerful member of that body. O'Connor gives a basic introduction to the Court, reflects on past discrimination against women in the law, tells amusing stories about fellow justices, and calls for improving the treatment of jury members.

Zimmerman, Joseph F. *Interstate Disputes: The Supreme Court's Original Jurisdiction.* Buffalo: State University of New York, 2006. This well-researched study examines the role of the Court in settling disputes between the states. The author concludes that states should enter into more interstate compacts rather than taking their disputes to the Supreme Court.

MEDIA RESOURCES

Amistad—A 1997 movie, starring Anthony Hopkins, about a slave ship mutiny in 1839. Much of the story revolves around the prosecution, ending at the Supreme Court, of the slave who led the revolt.

truTV—This TV channel covers high-profile trials, including those of O. J. Simpson, the Unabomber, British nanny Louise Woodward, and Timothy McVeigh. (You can learn how to access truTV from your area at its Web site—see the *Logging On* section in this chapter's *e-mocracy* feature for its URL.)

Gideon's Trumpet—A 1980 film, starring Henry Fonda as the small-time criminal James Earl Gideon, which makes clear the path a case takes to the Supreme Court and the importance of cases decided there.

Justice Sandra Day O'Connor—In a 1994 program, Bill Moyers conducts Justice O'Connor's first television interview. Topics include women's rights, O'Connor's role as the Supreme Court's first female justice, and her difficulties breaking into the male-dominated legal profession. O'Connor defends her positions on affirmative action and abortion.

The Magnificent Yankee—A 1950 movie, starring Louis Calhern and Ann Harding, that traces the life and philosophy of Oliver Wendell Holmes, Jr., one of the Supreme Court's most brilliant justices.

Marbury v. Madison—A 1987 video on the famous 1803 case that established the principle of judicial review. This is the first in a four-part series, *Equal Justice Under Law: Landmark Cases in Supreme Court History*, produced by Judicial Conference of the United States.

COURTS ON THE WEB

Most courts in the United States now have Web sites, which vary in what information they include. Some courts simply display contact information for court personnel. Others include recent judicial decisions along with court rules and forms. Many federal courts permit attorneys to file documents electronically. The information available on these sites continues to grow as courts try to avoid being left behind in the information age. One day, courts may decide to implement *virtual courtrooms*, in which judicial proceedings take place totally via the Internet. The Internet may ultimately provide at least a partial solution to the twin problems of overloaded dockets and the high time and money costs of litigation.

LOGGING ON

- The home page of the federal courts is a good starting point for learning about the federal court system in general. At this site, you can even follow the path of a case as it moves through the federal court system. Go to:
 www.uscourts.gov
- To access the Supreme Court's official Web site, on which Supreme Court decisions are made available within hours of their release, go to:
 supremecourtus.gov
- Several Web sites offer searchable databases of Supreme Court decisions. You can access Supreme Court cases since 1970 at FindLaw's site:
 www.findlaw.com

- The following Web site also offers an easily searchable index to Supreme Court opinions, including some important historic decisions:
 www.law.cornell.edu/supct/index.html
- You can find information on the justices of the Supreme Court, as well as their decisions, at:
 www.oyez.org/oyez/frontpage
- The Web site of truTV (formerly Court TV) offers information like its program schedule—featuring six hours of daily trial coverage—and a Crime Library, which includes case histories as well as selected documents filed with the court and court transcripts. At the site, you can click on CNN Crime for trial news. You can access this site at:
 www.trutv.com

ONLINE REVIEW

At **www.cengage.com/politicalscience/schmidt/agandpt14e**, you will find a Tutorial Quiz for this chapter providing questions on the chapter contents, including the features. The questions are organized to match the major sections of the chapter. You'll have access to other helpful study tools, including the book's glossary and flashcards, crossword puzzles, and Web links, as well as "Which Side Are You On?" and "Politics and . . ." features written by the authors of the book.

California traffic running heavy between Hercules and the Bay Bridge near Berkeley, California. Interstate highways are constructed and maintained by states with federal funds. (Mark Constantini/CORBIS)

CHAPTER

(16)

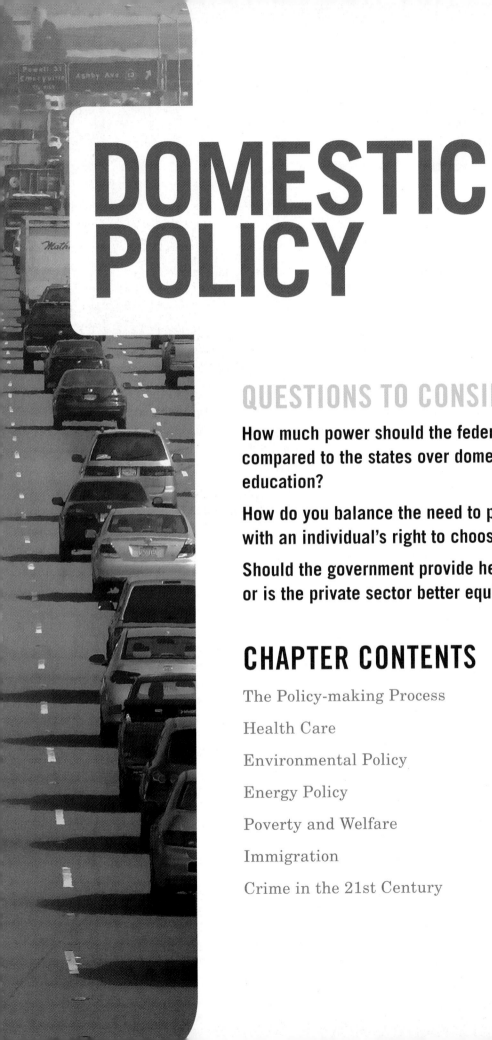

DOMESTIC POLICY

QUESTIONS TO CONSIDER

How much power should the federal government have compared to the states over domestic issues such as education?

How do you balance the need to protect the environment with an individual's right to choose how to live?

Should the government provide health care to all Americans, or is the private sector better equipped to do so?

CHAPTER CONTENTS

Making a DIFFERENCE

DEFINING PROBLEMS AND FINDING SOLUTIONS IN EDUCATION

What's in a name? Policy makers often choose names for legislation as a way of directing attention to a particular policy problem. For example, President George W. Bush's No Child Left Behind (NCLB) landmark education bill[a] was designed to focus on specific problems the President had identified: inadequate accountability of schools to the public; tax dollars not having their intended effect on education; and disturbing trends showing disparate rates of success in school among children of different socioeconomic groups.

As governor of Texas, President Bush had been a proponent of the reforms that had grown in popularity during the late 1980s and early 1990s. Accountability advocates favored standardized testing throughout a child's educational career to measure concretely the progress schools were making toward specific educational goals. The results of these tests would factor significantly into teacher raises and funding for particular schools and school districts across the state.[b]

The President also identified what he called the "soft bigotry of low expectations," referring to the lower test scores of specific groups of children.[c] In an effort to close these gaps, NCLB mandates that test scores must be reported separately for specific racial and ethnic groups, for low-income children, for children for whom English is a second language, and for children with disabilities. States are charged with setting educational goals, assessing how close to the goals schools were at the time of passage of the law, and using the differential to determine "adequate yearly progress" (AYP) benchmarks the schools must hit each year. If any one of the subgroups listed does not make AYP, the entire school is listed as "needs improvement"; NCLB allows children in these schools to transfer to better-performing schools.

WHEN PEOPLE ARE ASKED what the national government is supposed to do for them, generally they will answer that the government should defend our nation and solve our national problems. Americans expect the federal government to pay attention to the issues that impact the lives of American citizens. The legislation and regulation that are passed to address these problems is usually called domestic policy. **Domestic policy** can be defined as all of the laws, government planning, and government actions that affect each individual's daily life in the United States. Consequently, the span of such policies is enormous. Domestic policies range from relatively simple issues, such as what the speed limit should be on interstate highways, to more complex ones, such as how best to address the impact of global warming on our nation and reduce our contribution to climate change or how to improve the performance of schools across the nation.

> **Domestic Policy**
> Public plans or courses of action that concern internal issues of national importance, such as poverty, crime, and the environment.

As noted in the *Making a Difference* feature, improving the educational achievement of all children involves the federal government, state governments, local governments, parents, and teachers. This is typical of domestic policies that are formulated and implemented by the federal government, but many others are the result of the combined efforts of federal, state, and local governments.

In this chapter, we look at domestic policy issues involving health care, the environment and energy, poverty and welfare, immigration, and crime. Before we start our analysis, though, we must look at how public policies are made.

NCLB passed Congress with bipartisan support and without major opposition from teachers' groups and unions. Interestingly, these groups had been an active part of the dialogue on school reform for several decades. For example, in 1983, the Department of Education issued a report entitled "A Nation at Risk," in which it asserted: "the educational foundations of our society are presently being eroded by a rising tide of mediocrity that threatens our very future as a Nation and a people."[d] One group, the American Federation of Teachers (AFT), was more supportive of the call for reform than another, the National Education Association (NEA). The AFT's immediate response to NCLB was similar to their response in the 1980s—to embrace goals to close the gaps between groups of children. The NEA, on the other hand, has been vocal in its opposition to NCLB, even threatening to sue to overturn the law.[e] In recent years, both groups have been critical of the testing, arguing that its high-stakes nature drives curriculum, creating a "teaching to the test" mentality.

These teacher groups have been joined by others in opposition to the implementation of the law. Disability and immigration advocates argue that NCLB does not meet the special needs of children with disabilities and immigrant children.[f] Some conservative groups are frustrated by what they see as an inappropriate growth of federal government power.[g] All of these criticisms have been voiced in the debate over the bill's reauthorization in the 2007–2008 Congressional session. For example, a coalition of conservative legislators favors Academic Part-

nerships Lead Us to Success (A-PLUS),[h] an alternative to NCLB that would give states the ability to opt out of the national mandates. The issue at hand may now be shifting away from reforming education to reforming the reform.

[a]Signed by the President on January 8, 2002, PL 107-110.
[b]E. DeBray, K. McDermott, and P. Wohlstetter, "Introduction to the Special Issue on Federalism Reconsidered: The Case of the No Child Left Behind Act," *Peabody Journal of Education*, Vol. 80, 2005, pp. 1–18.
[c]The President used this phrase many times in the lead-up to the legislation and during its implementation. An example of the latter is in a speech made to the National Association for the Advancement of Colored People (NAACP) in June 2006, available at www.whitehouse.gov/news/releases/2006/07/20060720.html.
[d]www.ed.gov/pubs/NatAtRisk/risk.html
[e]J. Koppich, "A Tale of Two Approaches—The AFT, the NEA, and NCLB," *Peabody Journal of Education*, Vol. 80, 2005, pp. 137–155.
[f]www.ncd.gov/newsroom/news/2003/r03-419.htm; www.urban.org/publications/411469.html
[g]www.heritage.org/Press/Commentary/ed031707a.cfm
[h]An alternative to NCLB proposed by a coalition of Republican lawmakers. www.heritage.org/Press/Commentary/ed031707a.cfm, accessed May 25, 2008.

THE POLICY-MAKING PROCESS

How does any issue get resolved? First, the issue must be identified as a problem. Often, policy makers simply have to open their local newspapers—or letters from their constituents—to discover that a problem is brewing. On rare occasions, a crisis, such as that brought about by the terrorist attacks of September 11, 2001, creates the need to formulate policy. Like most Americans, however, policy makers receive much of their information from the national media. Finally, various lobbying groups provide information to members of Congress.

As an example of policy making, consider the Medicare reform bill. Medicare is a program that pays health-care expenses for Americans older than age 65. As initially created in the 1960s, Medicare did not cover the cost of prescription drugs. The new bill provided a direct drug benefit beginning in 2006. (Certain discounts were available immediately.)

No matter how simple or how complex the problem, those who make policy follow several steps. We can divide the process of policy making into at least five steps: agenda building, policy formulation, policy adoption, policy implementation, and policy evaluation (see Figure 16–1).

AGENDA BUILDING

First, the issue must get on the agenda. In other words, Congress must become aware that an issue requires Congressional action. Agenda building may occur as the result of

FIGURE 16–1

The Policy-making Process: The Medicare Reform Bill

Four of the five steps of the policy-making process, as exemplified by the Medicare reform bill of 2003. The fifth step—evaluation—could not begin until 2006, when all provisions of the new act went into effect.

AARP protest (Gail Oskin/AP Photo)

Lobbyist (AP Photo/Susan Walsh)

Bush with card (Paul Morse/White House photo)

Roundtable (Eric Draper/White House Photo)

Nancy Pelosi (AP Photo/Dennis Cook)

Bipartisan (Paul Morse/White House Photo)

Members (Courtesy of the House Committee on Ways and Means)

Bill Frist *et al.* (AP Photo/Terry Ashe)

AARP executives (AP Photo/Susan Walsh)

Bush signs bill (White House photo by Paul Morse)

Q&As on cards (AP Photo/Stephen J. Carrera)

Bush at pharmacy (AP Photo/Susan Walsh)

AGENDA BUILDING

June 3, 1997
AARP members rally to show their strong support for Medicare benefits.

July 3, 1997
John Rother, chief lobbyist of AARP, with mail from retirees. "We got Congress to pay attention," he said.

July 12, 2001
President Bush with a copy of a proposed discount card for lower prices on prescription drugs for seniors.

POLICY FORMULATION

June 12, 2003
President Bush speaks to seniors during a round-table discussion about Medicare at a Connecticut hospital.

June 17, 2003
House Minority Leader Nancy Pelosi criticizes a Republican version of the Medicare drug bill in committee hearings.

June 18, 2003
Bush in a bipartisan meeting with senators on Medicare reform in the White House.

POLICY ADOPTION

July 15, 2003
Members of the House-Senate Conference Committee on Medicare legislation begin their meeting at the Capitol.

November 24, 2003
Senate Majority Leader Bill Frist with Republican leaders after the Senate voted to end debate on the Medicare drug bill.

November 25, 2003
AARP executives speak about AARP's support of the Medicare bill during a news conference.

POLICY IMPLEMENTATION

December 8, 2003
President Bush signs the Medicare Prescription Drug, Improvement, and Modernization Act of 2003 at Constitution Hall in Washington, D.C.

May 3, 2004
On the first day senior citizens can sign up for the Medicare prescription drug discount cards, seniors meet with House Speaker Dennis Hastert to raise questions and express confusion about the new program.

June 14, 2004
President Bush meets the employees at a Hy-Vee Pharmacy in Liberty, Missouri and participates in a discussion about health care, including Medicare and the new prescription drug card.

a crisis, technological change, or mass media campaigns, as well as through the efforts of strong political personalities and effective lobbying groups.

Advocates for the elderly, including AARP (formerly the American Association of Retired Persons), had demanded a Medicare drug benefit for years. Traditionally, liberals have advocated such benefits. Yet the benefit was created under President George W. Bush—a conservative Republican. Bush's advocacy of Medicare reform was essential to its success and shored up his support among more moderate voters.

POLICY FORMULATION

During the next step in the policy-making process, various policy proposals are discussed among government officials and the public. Such discussions may take place in the printed media, on television, and in the halls of Congress. Congress holds hearings, the president voices the administration's views, and the topic may even become a campaign issue.

Many Republicans in Congress were opposed to any major new social-spending program, partly because they did not want to see more government control over the economy and partly because it would be very costly. Conservative members of Congress believed that insurance programs should be run by private businesses. To win their support, the Republican leadership advocated a degree of privatization. Under this plan, private companies would administer the drug benefit. In a six-city demonstration project, plans administered by private companies would compete with traditional Medicare. The Democratic leadership opposed privatization, claiming that it threatened the existence of Medicare, although the drug prescription plan was a new program entirely.

The Republicans also proposed measures that would benefit the insurance and pharmaceutical industries. For example, the government would not use its immense bargaining power to obtain lower prices for Medicare drugs and would discourage the importation of lower-cost drugs from Canada. Finally, the Republicans proposed that to keep the cost of the bill down, not all drug expenses would be covered. To reduce costs, the Republican plan had a "doughnut hole" in which out-of-pocket drug expenses greater than $2,250 but less than $3,600 were not covered. Republicans argued that these limits would provide good, basic prescription coverage for most senior citizens but would require those with a certain level of income to pay a portion of their prescription costs. Poorer seniors were covered entirely.

POLICY ADOPTION

The third step in the policy-making process involves choosing a specific policy from among the proposals that have been discussed. In the end, the Republican proposals were adopted, and the bill passed by the narrowest of margins. The progress of the bill through Congress revealed some of the intense partisan behavior that has become common in recent years. For example, the Republicans refused to allow any Democrats from the House to participate in the conference committee that reconciled the House and Senate versions of the bill—a startling departure from tradition.

Almost at the last minute, AARP endorsed the bill, which may have guaranteed its success. A significant minority of the Democratic members of Congress broke with their party to support the bill, and that was enough to balance out the Republicans who refused to vote for it.

DID YOU KNOW?

That in the mid-1930s, during the Great Depression, Senator Huey P. Long of Louisiana proposed that the government confiscate all personal fortunes of more than $5 million and all incomes of more than $1 million and use the funds to give every American family a house, a car, and an annual income of $2,000 or more (about $25,000 in today's dollars)?

POLICY IMPLEMENTATION

The fourth step in the policy-making process involves the implementation of the policy alternative chosen by Congress. Government action must be implemented by bureaucrats, the courts, police, and individual citizens. In the example of the Medicare reform bill, the main portion of the legislation was not to come into effect until 2006. For the most part, therefore, implementation did not begin immediately. Some sections of the bill did become effective in 2004, however. These included a series of drug discount cards, sponsored by the government in cooperation with various insurance companies, which would provide some savings on prescription drugs right away. Because the Bush administration hoped to elicit a positive political response to the Medicare reform, it organized a major advertising campaign for the new cards, paid for by taxpayers through the Department of Health and Human Services. In May 2004, however, the federal Government Accountability Office ruled that the advertisements were illegal.

POLICY EVALUATION

After a policy has been implemented, it is evaluated. Groups inside and outside the government conduct studies to determine what actually happens after a policy has been in place for a given period of time. Based on this feedback and the perceived success or failure of the policy, a new round of policy-making initiatives will be undertaken to improve on the effort. Given that the new prescription drug benefit was the most significant expansion of Medicare since its creation 40 years ago, there was certain to be mixed feedback. In this instance, much of the initial feedback was negative because of the multiplicity of plans and confusion over which drugs would be covered. As the program was fully implemented, both Congress and the Bush administration began to propose changes, including increasing premiums for higher-income beneficiaries to help pay for the program.

After the Democrats gained control of Congress in 2006, legislation was passed in the House that would require the Secretary of Health and Human Services to negotiate drug prices with the pharmaceutical companies, although the bill was killed in the Senate. The program, overall, is very popular with senior citizens, with more than 1 million prescriptions filled every day. It will likely be revised many times in years to come.

HEALTH CARE

Undoubtedly, one of the most important problems facing the nation is how to guarantee affordable health care for all Americans at a cost the nation can bear. Spending for health care is estimated to account for about 15 percent of the total U.S. economy. In 1965, about 6 percent of our income was spent on health care, and that percentage has been increasing ever since, exceeding 15 percent by 2005 and projected to reach 16 percent by 2010. Per capita spending on health care is greater in the United States than almost anywhere else in the world. Measured by the percentage of the *gross domestic product* (GDP) devoted to health care, America spends almost twice as much as Australia or Canada (see Figure 16–2). (The GDP is the dollar value of all final goods and services produced in a one-year period.)

THE RISING COST OF HEALTH CARE

Numerous explanations exist for why health-care costs have risen so much. At least one has to do with changing demographics—the U.S. population is getting older. Life expectancy has gone up, as shown in Figure 16–3. The top 5 percent of those using health care incur more than 50 percent of all health-care costs. The bottom 70 percent of health-care users account for only 10 percent of health-care expenditures. Not sur-

FIGURE 16–2 Cost of Health Care in Economically Advanced Nations

Cost is given as a percentage of total gross domestic product (GDP).

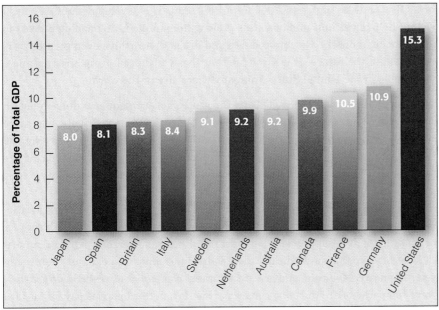

Source: Organization for Economic Cooperation and Development, *OECD Health Data*, 2006.

FIGURE 16–3 Life Expectancy in the United States

Along with health-care spending, life expectancy has gone up. Therefore, we are presumably getting some return for our spending.

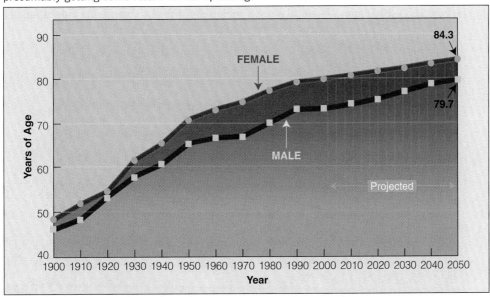

Source: Social Security Administration, Office of the Chief Actuary.

prisingly, the elderly make up most of the top users of health-care services, including nursing home care and long-term care for those suffering from debilitating diseases.

Advanced Technology. Another reason why health-care costs have risen so dramatically is advancing technology. A computerized tomography (CT) scanner costs around $1 million. A magnetic resonance imaging (MRI) scanner can cost more than $2 million. A positron emission tomography (PET) scanner costs approximately $4 million. All of these machines have become increasingly available in recent decades and are in demand around the country. Typical fees for procedures using these scanners range from $300 to $500 for a CT scan to as high as $2,000 for a PET scan. The development of new technologies that help physicians and hospitals prolong human life is an ongoing process in an ever-advancing industry. New procedures and drugs that involve even greater costs can be expected in the future. It is also true that these advanced procedures are more readily available in the United States than anywhere else in the world.

The Government's Role in Financing Health Care. Currently, government spending on health care constitutes about 45 percent of total health-care spending. Private insurance accounts for about 35 percent of payments for health care. The remainder—less than 20 percent—is paid directly by individuals or by philanthropy. Medicare and Medicaid are the main sources of hospital and other medical benefits for 35 million U.S. residents, most of whom are older than age 65.

    Medicare is specifically designed to support the elderly, regardless of income. **Medicaid**, a joint state–federal program, is in principle a program to subsidize health care for the poor. In practice, it often provides long-term health care to persons living in nursing homes. (To become eligible for Medicaid, these individuals must first exhaust their financial assets.) Medicare, Medicaid, and private insurance companies are called *third parties*. Caregivers and patients are the two primary parties. When third parties pay for medical care, the demand for such services increases; health-care recipients have no incentive to restrain their use of health care. One result is some degree of wasted resources.

MEDICARE

The Medicare program, which was created in 1965 under President Lyndon B. Johnson (served 1963–1969), pays hospital and physicians' bills for U.S. residents older than age

Medicare
A federal health-insurance program that covers U.S. residents older than age 65. The costs are met by a tax on wages and salaries.

Medicaid
A joint state–federal program that provides medical care to the poor (including indigent elderly persons in nursing homes). The program is funded out of general government revenues.

A PHYSICIAN examines a patient. Managed-care programs, which have become popular with employers in recent years, often reimburse only a limited number of health-care providers. How might we allow patients to visit physicians of their own choosing and simultaneously control health care costs? (Corbis)

65. As already mentioned, beginning in 2006, Medicare also pays for at least part of the prescription drug expenses of the elderly. In return for paying a tax on their earnings (currently set at 2.9 percent of wages and salaries) while in the workforce, retirees are ensured that the majority of their hospital and physicians' bills will be paid for with public funds.

Over the past 40 years, Medicare has become the second-largest domestic spending program, after Social Security. Government expenditures on Medicare have routinely turned out to be far in excess of the expenditures forecast at the time the program was put into place or expanded. In Chapter 17, you will learn about Medicare's impact on the current federal budget and the impact it is likely to have in the future. For now, consider only that the total outlays on Medicare are high enough to create substantial demands curtail its costs.

One response by the federal government to soaring Medicare costs has been to impose arbitrary reimbursement caps on specific procedures. To avoid going over Medicare's reimbursement caps, however, hospitals have an incentive to discharge patients quickly. The government has also cut rates of reimbursement to individual physicians and physician groups, such as health maintenance organizations (HMOs). One consequence has been a nearly 15 percent reduction in the amount the government pays for Medicare services provided by physicians. As a result, physicians and HMOs have become reluctant to accept Medicare patients. Several of the nation's largest HMOs have withdrawn from certain Medicare programs. A growing number of physicians now refuse to treat Medicare patients.

MEDICAID

In a few short years, the joint federal–state taxpayer-funded Medicaid program for the "working poor" has generated one of the biggest expansions of government entitlements in the last 50 years. In 1997, Medicaid spending was around $150 billion. Ten years later, it exceeded $300 billion. At the end of the last decade, 34 million people were enrolled in the program. Today, there are more than 50 million. When you add Medicaid coverage to Medicare and the military and federal employee health plans, the government has clearly become the nation's primary health insurer. More than 100 million people—one in three—in the United States have government coverage.

Why Has Medicaid Spending Exploded? One of the reasons Medicaid has become such an important health-insurance program is that the income ceiling for eligibility has increased to more than $40,000 per year in most states. In other words, a family of four can earn around $40,000 and still obtain health insurance through Medicaid for its children. Indeed, many low-income workers choose Medicaid over health insurance offered by employers. Why? The reason is that Medicaid is less costly and sometimes covers more medical expenses. For most recipients, Medicaid is either free or almost free.

Medicaid and the States. On average, the federal government pays almost 60 percent of Medicaid's cost; the states pay the rest. Certain states, particularly in the South, receive even higher reimbursements. In general, such states are not complaining about the expansion of Medicaid. Other states, however, such as New York, have been overwhelmed by the rate of increase in Medicaid spending. Even with the federal government's partial reimbursement, the portion paid by the states has increased so rapidly that the states are becoming financially strapped. Florida, for example, had to

drastically revise its Medicaid eligibility rules to reduce the number of families using Medicaid. Otherwise, the state projected a budget deficit that it would not be able to handle.

THE UNINSURED

More than 45 million Americans—15 percent of the population—do not have health insurance. The proportion of the population that is uninsured varies from one part of the country to another. In Hawaii and Minnesota, only 7 percent of working adults lack coverage. In Texas, however, the figure is 27 percent. According to the Congressional Black Caucus Foundation, African Americans, Hispanics, and Asian/Pacific Islanders make up more than half of the year-round uninsured, even though they constitute only 29 percent of the total U.S. population. Hispanic Americans are the most likely to be uninsured, with only 35 percent of working Hispanic adults having coverage.

According to surveys, being uninsured has negative health consequences. People without coverage are less likely to get basic preventive care, such as mammograms; less likely to have a personal physician; and more likely to rate their own health as only poor or fair.

The Uninsured Employed. The uninsured population is relatively young, in part due to Medicare, which covers almost everyone older than age 65. Also, younger workers are more likely to be employed in entry-level jobs that do not come with health-insurance benefits so, to maximize their income, they choose not to buy health insurance. The current system of health care in the United States assumes that employers will provide health insurance. Many small businesses, however, simply cannot afford to offer their workers health insurance. Insurance costs are now approaching an average of $9,000 per year for each employee.

Shifting Costs to the Uninsured. A further problem faced by the uninsured is that when they do seek medical care, they must usually pay much higher fees than would be paid on their behalf if they had insurance coverage. Large third-party insurers, private or public, normally strike hard bargains with hospitals and physicians over how much

WHAT IF...

WE HAD UNIVERSAL HEALTH CARE?

We must first distinguish between universal health insurance and universal health care. Here we are discussing the latter—providing access to health care for those who are uninsured. We are not talking about setting up a universal, government-administered health-insurance system. With universal health care, those in need of basic medical care who lack insurance would have access to physicians, clinics, hospitals, and the like.

THE SAN FRANCISCO EXPERIMENT

To understand how universal health care might work, we can go to San Francisco, California, where a universal health-care plan was approved in the summer of 2006. The San Francisco Health Access Plan, as it is called, is financed by local government, mandatory contributions from employers, and income-adjusted premiums from users.

Enrollment fees range from $3 to $201, and most participants will pay $35 per month. Uninsured San Franciscans can then seek comprehensive primary care in the city's public and private clinics and hospitals. San Francisco Mayor Gavin Newsom described the city's historic undertaking as a "moral obligation."

Not everybody in the city is happy about the new plan, however. To offset the estimated annual price tag of more than $200 million, firms with 20 or more workers have to contribute about one dollar per hour worked by any employee. Those with more than a hundred workers have to pay $1.60 per hour, up to a monthly maximum of $180 per worker.

Many small-business owners in San Francisco predict that new businesses will no longer locate there. They also argue that goods and services within the city will become more expensive as employers pass on the added health-care costs to customers.

THE RELATIONSHIP BETWEEN UNIVERSAL HEALTH-CARE ACCESS AND THE NUMBER OF UNINSURED

Economic analysis yields a simple relationship between price and quantity demanded—the lower the price, the higher the quantity demanded. Medical care is a service like any other. If medical care is provided at a lower price to those who desire it, more medical care will be demanded.

We can predict that if a universal health-care plan is implemented, the number of people without health insurance will increase. To understand this, consider how people will behave if universal health-care access becomes a reality. Over time, some individuals and families will choose not to renew their health insurance, because they will know that they can rely on universal health-care access. Consequently, the existence of universal health care will actually increase the number of those who do not have health insurance in the United States. As this happens, the burden on hospitals and clinics will increase, as will the costs to the government.

In essence, universal health-care coverage is the equivalent of having a zero deductible for primary care. Note that this does not mean that people will become sicker if they have access to universal health care, but it does mean that they will make greater use of health-care facilities.

FOR CRITICAL ANALYSIS

1. Administratively, what is the difference between setting up universal health care and providing universal health insurance?
2. If universal health-care access becomes a reality, what will happen to hospital emergency rooms?

they will pay for procedures and services. The uninsured have less bargaining power. As a result, hospitals attempt to recover from the uninsured the revenues they lost in paying third-party insurers.

In any given year, most people do not require expensive health care. Young, healthy people in particular can be tempted to do without insurance. One benefit of insurance coverage, however, is that it protects the insured against catastrophic costs resulting from unusual events. Medical care for life-threatening accidents or diseases can run into thousands or even hundreds of thousands of dollars. An uninsured person who requires this kind of medical care may be forced into bankruptcy.

ONE ALTERNATIVE: NATIONAL HEALTH INSURANCE

National Health Insurance
A plan to provide universal health insurance under which the government provides basic health-care coverage to all citizens. In most such plans, the program is funded by taxes on wages or salaries.

Single-Payer Plan
A plan under which one entity has a monopoly on issuing a particular type of insurance. Typically, the entity is the government, and the insurance is basic health coverage.

The United States is the only advanced industrial country with a large pool of citizens who lack health insurance. Western Europe, Japan, Canada, and Australia all provide systems of universal coverage. Such coverage is provided through **national health insurance**. In effect, the government takes over the economic function of providing basic health-care coverage. Private insurers are excluded from this market. The government collects premiums from employers and employees on the basis of their ability to pay and then pays physicians and hospitals for basic services to the entire population.

Because the government provides all basic insurance coverage, national health-insurance systems are often called **single-payer plans**. Such plans can significantly reduce administrative overhead, because physicians need only deal with a single set of forms and requirements. The number of employees required to process claims is also lowered. In France, for example, which has national health insurance, administrative overhead is 5 percent of total costs, compared to 14 percent in the United States.[1] The French experience suggests that containing unnecessary procedures may be more difficult with a single-payer plan, however. National health-insurance systems are also sometimes called *socialized medicine*. It should be noted, though, that only health insurance is socialized. The government does not employ most physicians, and in many countries the hospitals are largely private as well.[2] Americans seeking an example of national health insurance often look to the Canadian system, which we examine in this chapter's *Beyond Our Borders* feature.

ANOTHER ALTERNATIVE: A HEALTH SAVINGS ACCOUNT

Republicans in Congress have enacted a health savings account (HSA) program as an alternative to completely changing the U.S. health-care industry. Most taxpayers can set up a tax-free HSA, which must be combined with a high-deductible health-insurance policy. Eligible individuals or families can make an annual tax-deductible contribution to an HSA up to a maximum of $2,900 for an individual and $5,800 for a family. Funds in the HSA accumulate tax free, and distributions of HSA funds for medical expenses are also exempt. Any funds remaining in an HSA after an individual reaches age 65 can be withdrawn tax free. The benefits can be impressive: a single person depositing around $1,500 each year with no withdrawals will have hundreds of thousands of dollars in the account after 40 years.

For those using an HSA, the physician–patient relationship remains intact, because third-party payers do not intervene in paying or monitoring medical expenses. The patients, rather than third parties, have an incentive to discourage their physicians

[1]Paul V. Dutton, "Health Care in France and the United States: Learning from Each Other," Washington, DC: The Brookings Institution, 2002. This article is online at www.brookings.edu/fp/cusf/analysis/dutton.htm.
[2]Britain is an exception. Under the British "National Health," most (but not all) physicians are employed by the government.

BEYOND OUR BORDERS

THE CANADIAN HEALTH-CARE SYSTEM

Canada's national health-insurance system is often viewed as a potential model for solving some of the health-care woes affecting many Americans. Canada's program, however, is atypical in many respects. Until very recently, Canada was the only country that in effect outlawed private parallel health-care services.

THE HIDDEN COSTS OF THE CANADIAN HEALTH-CARE SYSTEM

Canadians have found that their "free" health care entails some unexpected costs. Because physicians are unwilling to provide as many services as people wish to purchase at the below-market fees dictated by the Canadian government, long waiting lists are a fixture of the Canadian system. The average waiting time to see a specialist after referral by a general practitioner is more than four months.* Individuals experiencing debilitating back pain often must wait at least a year for neurosurgery. Even people diagnosed with life-threatening cancers typically have to wait six weeks before they have an initial examination by a cancer specialist. It is not surprising that a Gallup poll in 2005 found that only 9 percent of Canadians rated their health-care system as "excellent."

CANADIANS LOOK FOR PRIVATE TREATMENT

The long waits for officially approved health care in Canada have led to the establishment of private health-care clinics on Native American reservations, where physicians can legally accept private payments. This health-

care system is very costly to that nation's residents. In 2005, the Canadian Supreme Court ruled that the long waits for treatment in Quebec actually violated patients "life and personal security, inviolability and freedom," and that prohibition of private health insurance was unconstitutional.** After that decision, Canadians living in the province of Quebec can use their public health insurance cards for some surgeries at private clinics. Private insurance is also available for some procedures, such as cataract surgery and orthopaedic surgeries. Other nations, such as Germany, also allow for a two-tier system: higher-earning citizens can opt out of the public insurance system and buy private insurance. But this means that fewer citizens are paying for the public system.

FOR CRITICAL ANALYSIS

1. Why are some services not available in a timely way to Canadians?
2. Would Americans be willing to wait several months for heart surgery, for example?

*June E. O'Neill and Dave M. O'Neill, "Health Status, Health Care and Inequality: Canada vs. the U.S.," Working Paper No. 13429, National Bureau of Economic Research, September 2007, www.nber.org/papers/w13429.

**Chaoulli vs. Quebec, 1 S.C.R. 791, 2005 S.C.C. 35. For more information, see Colleen M. Flood, Kent Roach, and Lorne Sossin, editors, Access to Care, Access to Justice: The Legal Debate over Private Health Insurance in Canada (Toronto: University of Toronto Press, 2005).

from ordering expensive tests for every minor ache and pain, because they are allowed to keep any funds saved in the HSA. Some critics argue that HSA participants may also forgo necessary medical attention and develop more serious medical problems as a consequence. Also, HSAs do not address the issue of universal access to health care. After all, even if HSAs become common, not everyone will be willing or able to participate.

ENVIRONMENTAL POLICY

Americans have paid increasing attention to environmental issues in the last three decades. A major source of concern for the general public has been the emission of pollutants into the air and water. Each year, the world atmosphere receives 20 million metric tons of sulfur dioxide, 18 million metric tons of ozone pollutants, and 60 million metric tons of carbon monoxide.

ENVIRONMENTALISM

Environmental issues are not limited to concerns about pollution. A second major concern is the protection of the natural environment. The protection of endangered species is an example of this type of issue. The movement to protect the environment has

THESE THREE PHOTOS illustrate some of the environmental problems that persuaded Congress to pass the National Environmental Policy Act of 1969.

Top: The Cuyahoga River in 1969—firefighters extinguish a fire that started on the river and spread to a wooden trestle bridge. (Photo courtesy of the Environmental Protection Agency)

Lower left: Workers clean a beach after a 1969 oil spill in Santa Barbara, California. (Photo courtesy of the California Environmental Protection Agency)

Lower right: In 1945, municipal workers spray the pesticide DDT at Jones Beach, New York, while children frolic. (Library of Congress)

been based on two major strands of thought since its beginnings in the early 1900s. One point of view calls for *conservation*—that is, a policy under which natural resources should be used, but not abused. A second view advocates *preservation*. Under this policy, natural preserves are established that are isolated from the effects of human activity.

The Environmentalist Movement. In the 1960s, an environmentalist movement arose that was much more focused on pollution issues than the previous conservation movement. A series of high-profile events awoke environmental interest. In 1962, Rachel Carson of the U.S. Fish and Wildlife Service published the book *Silent Spring*,[3] in which she detailed the injurious effects of pesticides on a variety of wild species. In 1969, an oil spill off the coast of Santa Barbara, California, drew national attention. That same year, the Cuyahoga River in Cleveland actually caught fire due to flammable chemicals floating on top of the water.

In 1970, the environmental movement organized the first Earth Day (April 22), which proved to be very successful in drawing attention to environmentalism and its concerns. Pollution control was a popular goal, and during the 1960s and 1970s, Congress passed numerous bills aimed at cleaning up the nation's air and water. We will describe some of these efforts in greater detail shortly.

Ecology. In the 1970s, many environmental activists began to advocate policies that were more controversial than pollution control. These policies represented a radical elaboration of the older preservationist philosophy and a rejection of the conservationist principle of wise use. Not only did the new line of thought reject the conservation of natural resources for use by people, but some activists also argued that the human race itself was the problem. Along with the new thinking came a new label—the ecology movement. *Ecology* refers to the total pattern of relationships between organisms and their environment.

CLEANING UP THE AIR AND WATER

The government has been responding to pollution problems since before the American Revolution, when the Massachusetts Bay Colony issued regulations to try to stop the pollution of Boston Harbor. In the 1800s, states passed laws controlling water pollution after scientists and medical researchers convinced most policy makers that dumping sewage into drinking and bathing water caused disease. At the national level, the Federal Water Pollution Control Act of 1948 provided research and assistance to the states for pollution-control efforts, but little was done.

The National Environmental Policy Act. The year 1969 marked the start of the most concerted national government involvement in solving pollution problems. As mentioned, in that year, the conflict between oil-exploration interests and environmental interests literally erupted when an oil well six miles off the coast of Santa Barbara, California, exploded, releasing 235,000 gallons of crude oil. The result was an oil slick that covered an area of 800 square miles and washed up on the city's beaches and killed plant life, birds, and fish. Hearings in Congress revealed that the Interior Department had no guidance in the energy–environment trade-off. Congress soon passed the National Environmental Policy Act of 1969. This landmark legislation established, among other things, the Council on Environmental Quality. It also mandated that an **environmental impact statement (EIS)** be prepared for all major federal actions that could significantly affect the quality

That some economists estimate that the Environmental Protection Agency's new ozone standards, when fully implemented, will cost nearly $100 billion per year?

Environmental Impact Statement (EIS)
A report that must show the costs and benefits of major federal actions that could significantly affect the quality of the environment.

[3]Boston: Houghton Mifflin, 1962; repr., Boston: Mariner Books, 2002.

of the environment. The Act gave citizens and public-interest groups who were concerned with the environment a weapon against the unnecessary and inappropriate use of natural resources by the government.

Curbing Air Pollution. Beginning in 1975, the government began regulating tailpipe emissions from cars and light trucks in an attempt to curb air pollution. In 1990, after years of lobbying by environmentalists, Congress passed the Clean Air Act of 1990. The Act established tighter standards for emissions of nitrogen dioxide (NO_2) and other pollutants by newly built cars and light trucks. California was allowed to establish its own, stricter standards. By 1994, the maximum allowable NO_2 emissions (averaged over each manufacturer's "fleet" of vehicles) were about one-fifth of the 1975 standard. The "Tier 2" system, phased in between 2004 and 2007, reduced maximum fleet emissions by cars and light trucks to just over 2 percent of the 1975 standard. In 2008–2009, the standards will be extended to trucks weighing between 6,000 and 8,500 pounds.

Stationary sources of air pollution were also subjected to more regulation under the 1990 Act. The Act required 110 of the oldest coal-burning power plants in the United States to cut their emissions by 40 percent by 2001. Controls were placed on other factories and businesses in an attempt to reduce ground-level ozone pollution in 96 cities to healthful levels by 2005 (except in Los Angeles, which has until 2010 to meet the standards). The Act also required that the production of chlorofluorocarbons (CFCs) be stopped completely by 2002. CFCs are thought to deplete the ozone layer in the upper atmosphere and increase the levels of harmful radiation reaching the earth's surface. CFCs were formerly used in air-conditioning and other refrigeration units.

In 1997, in light of evidence that very small particles (2.5 microns, or millionths of a meter) of soot might be dangerous to our health, the Environmental Protection Agency (EPA) issued new particulate standards for motor vehicle exhaust systems and other sources of pollution. The EPA also established a more rigorous standard for ground-level ozone, which is formed when sunlight combines with pollutants from cars and other sources. Ozone is a major component of smog.

Water Pollution. One of the most important acts regulating water pollution is the Clean Water Act of 1972, which amended the Federal Water Pollution Control Act of 1948. The Clean Water Act established the following goals: (1) make waters safe for swimming; (2) protect fish and wildlife; and (3) eliminate the discharge of pollutants into the water. The Act set specific time schedules, which were subsequently extended by further legislation. Under these schedules, the EPA establishes limits on discharges of types of pollutants based on the technology available for controlling them. The 1972 Act also required municipal and industrial polluters to apply for permits before discharging wastes into navigable waters.

The Clean Water Act also prohibits the filling or dredging of wetlands unless a permit is obtained from the Army Corps of Engineers. The EPA defines *wetlands* as "those areas that are inundated or saturated by surface or ground water at a frequency and duration sufficient to support, and that under normal circumstances do support, a prevalence of vegetation typically adapted for life in saturated soil conditions." In recent years, the broad interpretation of what constitutes a wetland that is subject to the regulatory authority of the federal government has generated substantial controversy.

Perhaps one of the most controversial regulations concerning wetlands was the "migratory-bird rule" issued by the Army Corps of Engineers. Under this rule, any bodies of water that could affect interstate commerce, including seasonal ponds or waters "used or suitable for use by migratory birds" that fly over state borders,

were "navigable waters" subject to federal regulation under the Clean Water Act as wetlands. In 2001, after years of controversy, the United States Supreme Court struck down the rule. The Court stated that it was not prepared to hold that isolated and seasonal ponds, puddles, and "prairie potholes" become "navigable waters of the United States" simply because they serve as a habitat for migratory birds.[4]

COST-EFFECTIVE SOLUTIONS

Before the mid-1980s, environmental politics seemed to be couched in terms of "them against us." "Them" was everyone involved in businesses that cut down rain forests, poisoned rivers, and created oil spills. "Us" was the government, and it was the government's job to stop "them." Today, particularly in the United States, more people are aware that the battle lines are blurred.

According to the EPA, the U.S. is spending about $210 billion annually to comply with federal environmental rules. There is a bright side, however. A report issued by the Office of Management and Budget in 2003 concluded that the health and social benefits of enforcing tough new clean-air regulations are five to seven times greater than the costs of compliance. The government has become interested in how to solve the nation's environmental problems at the lowest cost. Moreover, U.S. corporations are becoming increasingly engaged in producing recyclable and biodegradable products, as well as helping to solve some environmental problems.

The Costs of Clean Air. Cost concerns clearly were on the minds of the drafters of the Clean Air Act of 1990 when they tackled the problem of sulfur emissions from electric power plants. Rather than tightening the existing standards, the law simply limited total sulfur emissions. Companies had a choice of either rebuilding old plants or buying rights to pollute. The result was that polluters had an incentive to not even attempt to deal with exceptionally dirty plants. When closing down such plants, they could sell their pollution rights to those who valued them more. The law is straightforward: An electric utility power plant is allowed to emit up to one ton of sulfur dioxide into the air in a given year. If the plant emits one ton of sulfur dioxide, the allowance disappears. If a plant switches to a fuel low in sulfur dioxide, for example, or installs "scrubbing equipment" that reduces sulfur dioxide, it may end up emitting less than one ton. In this circumstance, it can sell or otherwise trade its unused pollution allowance, or it can bank it for later use.

These rights to pollution allowances are being traded in the marketplace. Indeed, a well-established market in "smog futures" is offered on the Chicago Board of Trade and the New York Mercantile Exchange.

There Have Been Improvements. The United States is making fairly substantial strides in the war on toxic emissions. According to the EPA, in the last 30 years U.S. air pollution has been cut in half. Airborne lead is 3 percent of what it was in 1975, and the lead content of the average American's blood is one-fifth of what it was in that year. Airborne sulfur dioxide concentrations are one-fifth of the levels found in the 1960s. Carbon monoxide concentrations are one-quarter of what they were in 1970. Water pollution is also down. Levels of six persistent pollutants in U.S. freshwater fish are about one-fifth of their 1970 levels. One reason for these successes is the increased awareness of the American public of the need for environmental protection. To a large extent, this increased awareness has been brought about through the efforts of various environmental interest groups, which have also exerted pressure on Congress to take action.

----

[4]*Solid Waste Agency of Northern Cook County v. U.S. Army Corps of Engineers*, 531 U.S. 159 (2001).

IN 1978, construction on the multimillion-dollar Tellico Dam was stopped dead in its tracks when a group of environmentalists argued that it endangered the snail darter fish, shown on the right. Several years later, the snail darter was found to be thriving in other locations, and shortly thereafter, it was removed from the government's endangered species list. How does a society balance environmental issues with economics ones? (Courtesy of the Tennessee Valley Authority and the U.S. Fish and Wildlife Service)

THE ENDANGERED SPECIES ACT

Inspired by the plight of disappearing species, Congress passed the Endangered Species Preservation Act in 1966. In 1973, Congress passed a completely new Endangered Species Act (ESA), which made it illegal to kill, harm, or otherwise "take" a species listed as endangered or threatened. The government could purchase habitat critical to the survival of a species or prevent landowners from engaging in development that would harm a listed species.

The ESA proved to be a powerful legal tool for the ecology movement. In a famous example, environmental groups sued to stop the Tennessee Valley Authority from completing the Tellico Dam on the ground that it threatened habitat critical to the survival of the snail darter, a tiny fish. In 1978, the United States Supreme Court ruled in favor of the endangered fish.[5] Further controversy erupted in 1990, when the Fish and Wildlife Service listed the spotted owl as a threatened species. The logging industry blamed the ESA for a precipitous decline in national forest timber sales in subsequent years.

The ESA continues to be a major subject of debate. There are signs, however, that the government and environmentalists may be seeking common ground. Both sides are shifting toward incentives for landowners who participate in protection programs. "Regulatory incentives really do result in landowners doing good things for their land," said William Irvin of the World Wildlife Fund.[6] Still, environmental groups accused the Bush administration of underfunding the Act and undermining the species-listing process by shifting control from the Fish and Wildlife Service to the secretary of the interior.

GLOBAL WARMING

In the 1990s, scientists working on climate change began to conclude that average world temperatures will rise significantly in the 21st century. Gases released by human activity,

[5]*Tennessee Valley Authority v. Hill*, 437 U.S. 153 (1978). In 1979, Congress exempted the snail darter from the ESA. In 1980, snail darters were discovered elsewhere, and the species turned out not to be in danger.
[6]"Endangered Species Act Turns 30 as Environmental Strategy Shifts," *The Charleston Post and Courier*, Charleston, SC, January 2, 2004.

principally carbon dioxide, may produce a "greenhouse effect," trapping the sun's heat and slowing its release into outer space. In fact, many studies have shown that global warming has already begun, although the effects of the change are still modest. Christine Todd Whitman, who headed the EPA from 2001 to 2003, called global warming "one of the greatest environmental challenges we face, if not the greatest."

The Kyoto Protocol. In 1997, delegates from around the world gathered in Kyoto, Japan, for a global climate conference sponsored by the United Nations. The conference issued a proposed treaty aimed at reducing emissions of greenhouse gases to 5.2 percent below 1990 levels by 2012. Only 38 developed nations were mandated to reduce their emissions, however—developing nations including China and India faced only voluntary limits. The U.S. Senate voted unanimously in 1997 that it would not accept a treaty that exempted developing countries, and in 2001 President Bush announced that he would not submit the Kyoto protocol to the Senate for ratification. By 2007, 124 nations had ratified the protocol. Its rejection by the United States, however, raised the question of whether it could ever be effective.

Even in those European countries that most enthusiastically supported the Kyoto protocol and signed it, the results have not been overly positive. Thirteen of the 15 original European Union signatories will miss their 2010 emission targets. For example, Spain will miss its target by 33 percentage points. Denmark had agreed to reduce its levels of greenhouse gas emissions by 21 percent, but so far its emissions have *increased* by more than 6 percent since 1990. Greece has seen its greenhouse gas emissions increase by 23 percent since 1990. Closer to home, Prime Minister Paul Martin of Canada lambasted the United States for its lack of a "global conscience." But since 1990, Canada's emissions have risen by 24 percent, much faster than the U.S. rate.

The Global Warming Debate. While the majority of scientists who perform research on the world's climate believe that global warming will be significant, there is considerable disagreement as to how much warming will actually occur. It is generally accepted that world temperatures have already increased by at least 0.6 degrees Celsius over the last century. Scenarios by the United Nations Intergovernmental Panel on Climate Change predict increases ranging from 2.0 to 4.5 degrees Celsius by the year 2100. More conservative estimates, such as those by climate experts James Hansen and Patrick Michaels, average around 0.75 degrees Celsius.[7]

Global warming has become a major political football to be kicked back and forth by conservatives and liberals. Some conservatives have seized on the work of scientists who believe that global warming does not exist at all. (Some of these researchers work for oil companies.) If this were true, there would be no reason to limit emissions of carbon dioxide and other greenhouse gases. A more sophisticated argument by conservatives is that major steps to limit emissions in the near future would not be cost effective. Bjørn Lomborg, a critic of the environmental movement, believes that it would be more practical to take action against global warming later in the century, when the technology to do so is better and when renewable energy sources have become more competitive in price.[8]

BJØRN LOMBORG, the director of the Copenhagen Consensus Center at the Copenhagen Business School, wrote a book called *Cool It: The Skeptical Environmentalist's Guide to Global Warming*. In his book, Lomborg argues that limiting emissions of carbon dioxide and other greenhouse gases is not a cost-effective policy today. He also argues that global warming, while a significant issue, is not as serious as other problems facing the world. (Suzanne Plunkett Bloomberg News/Landov)

[7]J. E. Hansen, "Can We Defuse the Global Warming Time Bomb," *Scientific American*, March 2004, pp. 69–77. This article is also online at www.sciam.com/media/pdf/hansen.pdf.
[8]Bjørn Lomborg, *The Skeptical Environmentalist* (Cambridge, England: Cambridge University Press, 2001), pp. 258–324.

ENERGY POLICY

The United States has always had enormous energy resources, whether from coal, oil, natural gas, or alternative sources such as wind or solar power. However, the American economy depends almost totally on fossil fuel, namely oil, coal, and natural gas. **Energy policy**—that is, laws that are concerned with how much energy is needed and used—and the regulation of energy producers tends to become important only during a crisis. In 1973, the Organization of Petroleum Exporting Countries (OPEC), the cartel of oil-producing nations, instituted an embargo on shipments of petroleum to the United States because of our support of Israel in the Arab–Israeli conflict of that year. President Nixon declared that the United States would achieve energy independence through reducing speed limits and meeting Corporate Average Fuel Economy (CAFE) standards by a certain time.

In 1977, President Carter also found himself facing shortages of oil and natural gas. The Department of Energy was created, and numerous programs were instituted to assist citizens in buying more energy-efficient appliances and improving the energy profile of their homes. In addition, legislation created the National Petroleum Reserve, and incentives for researching alternative forms of energy were instituted. However,

FIGURE 16–4 Oil Consumption by the Top 15 Oil Producers, 2007

The United States is by far the largest consumer of petroleum products and the third largest producer. The only other producer in this list that consumes more than it produces is China.

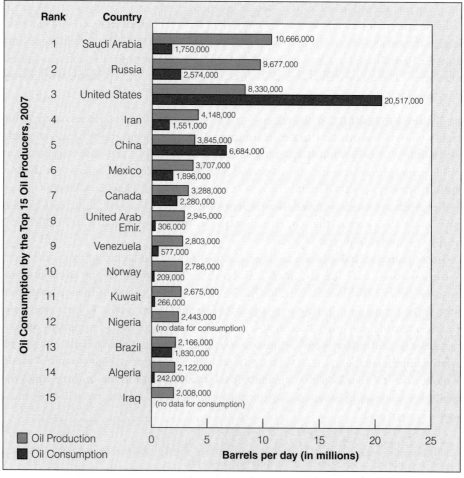

Source: Department of Energy, Energy Information Administration, 2008.

over time, Americans sought to replace their smaller, more efficient cars with sport utility vehicles (SUVs) and light trucks. Airline traffic grew. Suburbs were built farther from cities and jobs. America's dependence on foreign oil has grown, as has the nation's overall appetite for energy.

In 2007, the United States consumed about 20 million barrels of petroleum per day, with half of this used as gasoline for transportation. Of those 20 million barrels per day, more than 65 percent is imported. As shown in Figure 16–4, the United States is the third largest producer of oil but the largest consumer among the major producers. As shown in Figure 16–5, the price of gasoline closely tracks the price per barrel for crude oil. When the price for crude began to rise after 2003, the gasoline price rose quickly as well. The figure also shows the earlier eras of oil shortages in 1981 and 1990. The rapid increase in the price of crude since 2003 appears to be caused by the loss of Iraqi oil fields during the war, the growing demand for oil (especially by India and China), and speculation on future prices.

ENERGY AND THE ENVIRONMENT

Because of the effects of producing energy and burning fuels, energy policy is deeply entangled with environmental policy.[9] Using gasoline to power a car is the normal practice. However, burning gasoline produces serious emissions that contribute to the buildup of smog in the atmosphere. As noted previously, through a series of laws passed over the last 20 years, the EPA has forced cities to implement procedures to reduce smog

FIGURE 16–5 U.S. Crude Oil and Retail Gasoline Prices, 1976–2008

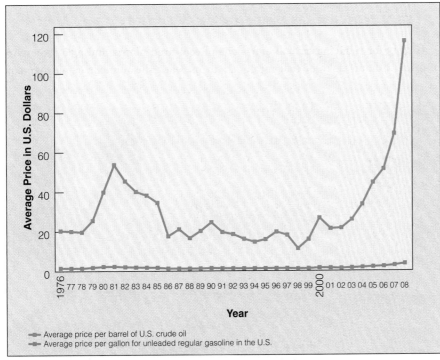

Source: Department of Energy, Energy Information Administration, 2008;
http://www.fueleconomy.gov/feg/gasprices/

[9]For a comprehensive look at all energy resources in the United States, go to the Web site of the Department of Energy: www.energy.gov/energysources.

and to require cleaner-burning gasoline. In addition, Congress has mandated that 10 percent of fuels sold in the years to come include ethanol as an ingredient. In response, the production of corn, which is used to make ethanol, has shot up, but still not enough is being grown to overcome the rising market for corn and the accompanying rise in price.

The United States continues to pump oil from existing wells and offshore platforms. However, more areas exist where oil could be found and extracted, but in most cases, environmental risks would be incurred. Following an oil spill in Santa Barbara, California, from an offshore drilling rig, most Americans welcomed laws that forbade drilling in new areas off Florida, Louisiana, Texas, and California. In addition, large areas of the Arctic National Wilderness Reserve (ANWR) have also been protected from oil exploration. Drilling in the ANWR is an extremely controversial issue because of the pristine nature of the land and the potential danger to native wildlife in that area of Alaska. As the cost of gasoline rose in 2008, however, with no likely possibility of prices declining, the debate reopened over drilling in the ANWR and offshore.

Another dilemma facing the United States involves domestic power production and the need for cleaner air. The majority of electric power generated in the United States comes from coal-fired plants in the Midwest and Central regions of the nation. For many years, these plants spewed carbon emissions into the air. As scientists became aware of the impact of these emissions on the environment, new laws required the plants to reduce their emissions by installing scrubbers or, after reaching the legal "cap" on their carbon emissions, buying or trading for the right to produce more. The EPA, under the Bush administration, issued regulations for coal-burning plants that reduced their burden to meet the standards. States that felt they received the most damage from some of these emissions sued to make the EPA issue standards that meet the letter of the Clean Air Act. The Supreme Court agreed with these states, and the EPA began to prepare stricter standards.

NUCLEAR POWER—AN UNPOPULAR SOLUTION

One strategy for reducing carbon emissions of coal-fired plants and also the environmental and human risks of coal mining is to increase the number of nuclear power

THE SUN SETS behind the Three Mile Island nuclear power plant after the accident in 1979. The crippled reactor, the round building on the left of the cooling towers, was in the process of cooling down. What was the impact of Three Mile Island on American energy policy? (Bettmann/CORBIS)

plants in the United States. Nuclear power plants are very efficient and emit very low levels of greenhouse gases.[10] However, the accident at the Three Mile Island plant in Pennsylvania in 1979 and the disaster at Chernobyl in the Soviet Union in 1986 have almost destroyed any support for nuclear power in the United States. Not only do people fear the possibility of an accident at such a plant, but nuclear plants also provide a superb target for terrorist attacks.

Finally, nuclear plants produce spent fuel, which must be stored until it is safe. No state wants to be the repository for nuclear waste, and few citizens want the waste trucked through their neighborhoods. The United States, though, is alone among industrialized nations in its fear of nuclear power. While Europe depends on oil, gas, coal, and nuclear power for electricity, hundreds of nuclear plants in Europe and the former states of the Soviet Union have operated safely for decades, and hundreds more are planned throughout the world. As the United States has become more concerned about carbon emissions, attention has begun to turn to nuclear power again, and permits have been issued to plan a few new plants.

ALTERNATIVE APPROACHES TO AN ENERGY CRISIS

Several alternative sources of energy can be used to reduce the nation's dependence on fossil fuels. Huge wind farms in California generate energy for cities there. Research continues on harnessing the power

of the ocean waves to produce electricity and the most efficient ways to use geothermal energy from below the surface of the earth.[11] However, the technology does not yet exist to use any of these sources to produce the quantity of energy needed to replace our coal plants or other current energy sources. And, in some areas, citizens consider wind farms as extremely disturbing to the environment and area wildlife.

The rising price of gasoline in 2008 spurred a much greater demand for hybrid automobiles and for smaller, more fuel-efficient cars. In addition, people began to ride motor scooters for city commutes and increased their use of mass transit. Homes closer to the city center became somewhat more attractive, although it will be many years before the trend of living in the suburbs will be reversed. Both political parties seemed supportive of new legislation encouraging energy efficiency in home building, using energy-efficient light bulbs, and giving incentives to buy hybrid vehicles. In many ways, these initiatives repeat the measures of the 1970s, but as the worldwide demand for energy is predicted to grow quickly, it may be time for energy policy to play a more important role in the lives of Americans.

MANY ENVIRONMENTALISTS and commentators suggest that a much greater use of wind power could reduce the nation's dependence on fossil fuels. This California windmill farm produces energy for Palm Springs. However, windmill farms cannot be successful everywhere in the United States. (Jim Corwin)

[10]Larry Parker and Mark Holt, "Nuclear Power: Outlook for New U.S. Reactors" (Washington, DC: Congressional Research Service, March 9, 2007).
[11]For a discussion of these new technologies, see Jay Inslee and Bracken Henricks, *Apollo's Fire* (Island Press, 2007).

POVERTY AND WELFARE

Throughout the world, poverty has historically been accepted as inevitable. The United States and other industrialized nations, however, have sustained enough economic growth in the past several hundred years to eliminate mass poverty. In fact, considering the wealth and high standard of living in the United States, the persistence of poverty here appears bizarre and anomalous. How can so much poverty exist in a nation of so much abundance? And what can be done about it?

A traditional solution has been **income transfers**. These are methods of transferring income from relatively well-to-do to relatively poor groups in society, and as a nation, we have been using such transfers for a long time. Before we examine these efforts, let us look at the concept of poverty in more detail and at the characteristics of the poor.

Income Transfer
A transfer of income from some individuals in the economy to other individuals. This is generally done by government action.

THE LOW-INCOME POPULATION

We can see in Figure 16–6 that the number of people classified as poor fell steadily from 1961 to 1968—that is, during the presidencies of John Kennedy and Lyndon Johnson. The number remained level until the recession of 1981–1982, during Ronald Reagan's presidency, when it increased substantially. The number fell during the Internet boom of 1994–2000, but then it started to rise again. Over the last 50 years, the number of Americans who are classified as poor has ranged from a high of 40 million in 1959 to a low of 25 million. The percentage has remained fairly low. In 2007, about 36.5 million Americans, or about 12.3 percent, were classified as poor.

The threshold income level that is used to determine who falls into the poverty category was originally based on the cost of a nutritionally adequate food plan designed by the U.S. Department of Agriculture in 1963. The threshold was determined by multiplying the food-plan cost times three, on the assumption that food expenses constitute approximately one-third of a poor family's expenditures. Until 1969, annual revisions of the threshold level were based only on changes in food prices. After 1969, the adjustments were made on the basis of changes in the consumer price index (CPI). The CPI is based on the average prices of a specified set of goods and services bought by wage earners in urban areas.

The low-income poverty threshold thus represents the income needed to maintain a specified standard of living as of 1963, with the purchasing-power value increased year by year to reflect the general increase in prices. For 2006, for example, the official poverty level for a family of four was about $20,000.

The official poverty level is based on pretax income, including cash but not **in-kind subsidies**—food stamps, housing vouchers, and the like. If we correct poverty levels for such benefits, the percentage of the population that is below the poverty line drops dramatically. To put the official U.S. poverty level in perspective, consider that this income level for the United States is twice as high as the world's average per capita income level. According to the World Bank, only 26 countries have per capita incomes higher than the poverty income threshold defined by the U.S. government.

In-Kind Subsidy
A good or service—such as food stamps, housing, or medical care—provided by the government to low-income groups.

THE ANTIPOVERTY BUDGET

It is not always easy to determine how much the government spends to combat poverty. In part, this is because it can be difficult to decide whether a particular program is an antipoverty program. Are grants to foster parents an antipoverty measure? What about job-training programs? Are college scholarships for low-income students an antipoverty

FIGURE 16–6 The Official Number of Poor in the United States

The number of individuals classified as poor fell steadily from 1961 through 1968. It then increased during the 1981–1982 recession. After 1994, the number fell steadily until 2000, when it started to rise again.

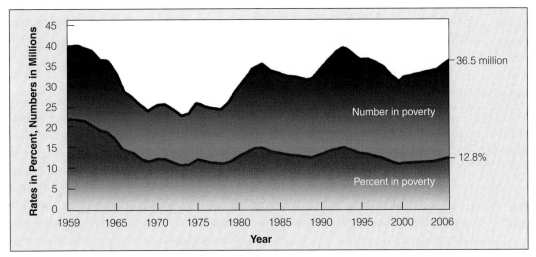

Note: The data points represent the midpoints of the respective years.
Source: U.S. Census Bureau, Current Population Reports, *Income, Poverty, and Health Insurance Coverage in the United States: 2007*, Washington, D.C.: Government Printing Office (2007).

measure? President George W. Bush's federal budget for 2009 allocated $18 billion for such scholarships.

Bush's 2009 budget allocated about $700 billion, or about one-fourth of all federal expenditures, to federal programs that support persons of limited income (scholarships included).[12] Of this amount, $206 billion was for Medicaid, which funds medical services for the poor, as discussed earlier. The states were expected to contribute an additional $150 billion to Medicaid. Medical care is by far the largest portion of the antipoverty budget. One reason why medical spending is high is the widespread belief that everyone should receive medical care that at least approximates the care received by an average person. No such belief supports spending for other purposes, such as shelter or transportation. Elderly people receive 70 percent of Medicaid spending.

BASIC WELFARE

The program that most people think of when they hear the word *welfare* is now called **Temporary Assistance to Needy Families (TANF)**. With the passage in 1996 of the Personal Responsibility and Work Opportunity Reconciliation Act, popularly known as the Welfare Reform Act, the government created TANF to replace an earlier program known as Aid to Families with Dependent Children (AFDC). The AFDC program provided "cash support for low-income families with dependent children who have been deprived of parental support due to death, disability, continued absence of a parent, or unemployment."

Under the TANF program, the U.S. government turned over to the states, in the form of block grants, funds targeted for welfare assistance. The states, not the national government, now bear the burden of any increased welfare spending. For example, if a state wishes to increase the amount of TANF payments over what the national government supports, the state has to pay the additional costs.

Temporary Assistance to Needy Families (TANF)
A state-administered program in which grants from the national government are used to provide welfare benefits. The TANF program replaced the Aid to Families with Dependent Children (AFDC) program.

[12]This sum does not include the earned-income tax credit, which is not part of the federal budget.

One of the aims of the Welfare Reform Act was to reduce welfare spending. To do this, the Act made two significant changes in the basic welfare program. One change was to limit most welfare recipients to only two years of assistance at a time. The second change was to impose a lifetime limit on welfare assistance of five years. The Welfare Reform Act has largely met its objectives. During the first five years after the Act was passed, the number of families receiving welfare payments was cut in half. The 2009 federal budget allocated $17 billion to the TANF block grants.

WELFARE CONTROVERSIES

Whether known as AFDC or TANF, the basic welfare program has always been controversial. Conservative and libertarian voters often object to welfare spending as a matter of principle, believing that it reduces the incentive to find paid employment. Because AFDC and TANF have largely supported single-parent households, some also believe that such programs are anti-marriage. Finally, certain people object to welfare spending out of a belief that welfare recipients are "not like us." In fact, non-Hispanic whites made up only 30 percent of TANF recipients in the mid-2000s. As a result of all these factors, basic welfare payments in the United States are relatively low when compared with similar payments in other industrialized nations. In 2006, the average monthly TANF payment nationwide was about $700 for a family of four.

OTHER FORMS OF GOVERNMENT ASSISTANCE

Supplemental Security Income (SSI)
A federal program established to provide assistance to elderly persons and persons with disabilities.

Food Stamps
Benefits issued by the federal government to low-income individuals to be used for the purchase of food; originally provided as coupons, but now typically provided electronically through a card similar to a debit card.

Earned-Income Tax Credit (EITC) Program
A government program that helps low-income workers by giving back part or all of their Social Security taxes.

The **Supplemental Security Income (SSI)** program was established in 1974 to provide a nationwide minimum income for elderly persons and persons with disabilities who do not qualify for Social Security benefits. The 2009 budget allocated $41 billion to this program.

The government also issues **food stamps**, benefits that can be used to purchase food; they are usually provided electronically through a card similar to a debit card. Food stamps are available to low-income individuals and families. Recipients must prove that they qualify by showing that they have a low income (or no income at all). Food stamps go to a much larger group of people than do TANF payments. President Bush's 2009 budget allocated $40 billion to the food stamp program. The food stamp program has become a major part of the welfare system in the United States, although it was started in 1964 mainly to benefit farmers by distributing surplus food through retail channels.

The **earned-income tax credit (EITC) program** was created in 1975 to help low-income workers by giving back part or all of their Social Security taxes. Currently, about 15 percent of all taxpayers claim an EITC, and an estimated $39 billion per year is rebated to taxpayers through the program.

HOMELESSNESS—STILL A PROBLEM

The plight of the homeless remains a problem. Some observers argue that the Welfare Reform Act of 1996 has increased the number of homeless persons. No hard statistics on the homeless are available, but estimates of the number of people without a home on any given night in the United States range from a low of 230,000 to as many as 750,000 people.

It is difficult to estimate how many people are homeless because the number depends on how the homeless are defined. There are *street people*—those who sleep in bus stations, parks, and other areas. Many of these people are youthful runaways. There are also the so-called *sheltered homeless*—those who sleep in government-supported or privately funded shelters. Many of these individuals used to live with their families or friends. Whereas street people are almost always single, the sheltered homeless include many families with children. Homeless families are the fastest-growing subgroup of the homeless population. The homeless problem pits liberals against conservatives. Conservatives argue that there are not really that many homeless people and that most of them are alcoholics, drug users, or the mentally ill. Conservatives contend that these individuals should be dealt with by either the mental-health system or the criminal justice system. In contrast, many liberals argue that homelessness is caused by a reduction in welfare benefits and by excessively priced housing.

Some cities have "criminalized" homelessness. Many municipalities have outlawed sleeping on park benches and sidewalks, as well as panhandling and leaving personal property on public property. In some cities, police sweeps remove the homeless, who then become part of the criminal justice system. In general, Northern cities have assumed a responsibility to shelter the homeless in bad weather. Cities in warmer climates are most concerned with a year-round homeless problem. No new national policies on the homeless have been initiated, in part because of disagreement about the causes and solutions for the problem.

Since 1993, the U.S. Department of Housing and Urban Development has spent billions of dollars on programs designed to combat homelessness. Yet because of the intense disagreement about the number of homeless persons, the reasons for homelessness, and the possible cures for the problem, no consistent government policy has resulted. Whatever policies have been adopted usually have been attacked by one group or another.

IMMIGRATION

Time and again, this nation has been challenged and changed—and culturally enriched—by immigrant groups. All of these immigrants have faced the problems involved in living in a new and different political and cultural environment. Most of them have had to overcome language barriers, and many have had to deal with discrimination in one form or another because of their skin color, their inability to speak English fluently, or their customs. The civil rights legislation passed during and since the 1960s has done much to counter the effects of prejudice against immigrant groups by ensuring that they obtain equal rights under the law.

One of the questions facing Americans and their political leaders today is the effect of immigration on American politics and government. Another issue is whether immigration is having a positive or negative impact on the United States and the form immigration reform should take.

THE CONTINUED INFLUX OF IMMIGRANTS

Today, immigration rates are among the highest they have been since their peak in the early 20th century. Every year, more than 1 million people immigrate to this country, and people who were born on foreign soil now constitute more than 10 percent of the U.S. population—twice the percentage of 30 years ago.

Minority Groups' Importance on the Rise. Since 1977, four out of five immigrants have come from Latin America or Asia. Hispanics have overtaken African Americans as the nation's largest minority. If current immigration rates continue, by the year 2060, minority groups collectively will constitute the "majority" of Americans. If Hispanics, African Americans,

A MOTHER FROM SOMALIA and her three children wait at a shelter in Columbus, Ohio, for housing assistance. They represent the hundreds of thousands of legal immigrants to the United States who come from many different nations. (Terry Gilliam/AP/Wide World Photos)

and perhaps Asians were to form coalitions, they could increase their political power dramatically and would have the numerical strength to make significant changes. According to Ben Wattenberg of the American Enterprise Institute, in the future the "old guard" white majority will no longer dominate American politics.

The Advantages of High Rates of Immigration. Some regard the high rate of immigration as a plus for America, because it offsets the low birthrate and aging population. Immigrants expand the workforce and help support, through their taxes, government programs that benefit older Americans, such as Medicare and Social Security. If it were not for immigration, contend these observers, the United States would be facing even more serious problems than it already does with funding these programs (see Chapter 17). In contrast, nations that do not have high immigration rates, such as Japan, are experiencing serious fiscal challenges due to their aging populations.

ATTEMPTS AT IMMIGRATION REFORM

A significant number of U.S. citizens, however, believe that immigration—both legal and illegal—negatively affects America. They argue, among other things, that the large number of immigrants seeking work results in lower wages for Americans, especially those with few skills. They also worry about the cost of providing immigrants with services such as schools and medical care.

Not surprisingly, before the 2006 elections, members of Congress were in favor of enacting a sweeping immigration reform bill, but the two houses could not agree on what it should do. Some versions of the bill in the House would have made every illegal immigrant in the United States a felon. The Senate, in contrast, came up with a much softer immigration reform system, one that was similar to a proposal made by President Bush. The Senate bill in its various forms in 2006 would have allowed illegal immigrants to gradually become citizens. None of these immigration reform bills came

to fruition. Later in the year, however, Congress did pass legislation authorizing the construction of a 700-mile-long fence between the United States and Mexico. The fence is to be a real fence in some areas and a "virtual fence" using cameras and surveillance technologies in other areas. In 2007, some members of Congress indicated that Congress, now under Democratic leadership, may review that legislation when working on a comprehensive immigration reform bill.

Conservative talk radio show hosts took up the cause of defeating the Senate's comprehensive immigration bill because it was seen to offer "amnesty" for illegal immigrants. Members of Congress were content to let the bill die rather than face constituents in an election year. By 2008, the debate seemed to have changed, with virtually all of the candidates for president, except the most conservative, supporting legislation that would tighten the borders, force employers to check the papers of their workers, and eventually build a path to citizenship. In the meantime, many illegal workers were "swept up" by law enforcement and deported, while others quietly left the country to avoid arrest. Some states and cities enacted laws making it illegal for undocumented residents to access public services or to get drivers' licenses.

CRIME IN THE 21st CENTURY

In 2006, overall crime rates in the United States dropped below those in many other countries, such as Britain. Nonetheless, virtually all polls taken in the United States in the last 10 years have shown that crime remains one of the public's major concerns. A related issue that has been on the domestic policy agenda for decades is controlling the use and sale of illegal drugs—activities that are often associated with crimes of violence. Additionally, finding ways to deal with terrorism has become a priority for the nation's policy makers.

CRIME IN AMERICAN HISTORY

In every period in the history of this nation, people have voiced apprehension about crime. Some criminologists argue that crime was probably as frequent around the time of the American Revolution as it is today. During the Civil War, mob violence and riots erupted in several cities. After the Civil War, people in San Francisco were told that "no decent man is in safety to walk the streets after dark; while at all hours, both night and day, his property is jeopardized by incendiarism [arson] and burglary."[13] In 1886, *Leslie's Weekly* reported, "Each day we see ghastly records of crime . . . murder seems to have run riot and each citizen asks . . . 'who is safe?'" From 1860 to 1890, the crime rate rose twice as fast as the population.[14] In 1910, one author stated that "crime, especially in its more violent forms and among the young, is increasing steadily and is threatening to bankrupt the Nation."[15]

From 1900 to the 1930s, social violence and crime increased dramatically. Labor union battles and race riots were common. Only during the three-decade period from the mid-1930s to the early 1960s did the United States experience, for the first time in its history, stable or slightly declining overall crime rates.

What most Americans are worried about is violent crime. From the mid-1980s to 1994, its rate rose relentlessly. The murder rate per 100,000 people in 1964 was 4.9, whereas in 1994 it was estimated at 9.3, an increase of almost 100 percent. Between 1995 and 2004, violent crime rates declined. Some argue that this decline was a result of the growing economy the United States has generally enjoyed since about 1993. Others claim that the $3 billion of additional funds the federal government has spent to curb crime in the last few years has led to less crime. Still others claim that an increase in the number of persons who are jailed or imprisoned is responsible for the reduction in crime. Some have even argued that legalized abortion has reduced the population that is likely to commit crimes. You can see changes in the rate of violent crimes in Figure 16–7.

Many people have heard that the United States has the highest crime rates in the world. This is not actually true. Total crime rates are higher in some other countries, including Britain, Denmark, and Sweden, than in the United States. You are much more likely to be robbed in London than in New York City. What the United States has is not a high total crime rate, but a *murder* rate that is unusually high for an advanced industrialized nation. Explanations for this fact vary from easy access to firearms to a cultural predisposition for settling disputes with violence. It is worth noting, however, that many countries in Asia, Africa, and Latin America have much higher homicide rates than the United States.

CRIMES COMMITTED BY JUVENILES

A disturbing aspect of crime is the number of serious crimes committed by juveniles, although the number of such crimes is also dropping. The political response to this rise in serious juvenile crimes has been varied. Some cities have established juvenile curfews. Several states have begun to try more juveniles as adults, particularly juveniles who have been charged with homicides. Still other states are operating "boot camps" to try to "shape up" less violent juvenile criminals. Additionally, victims of juvenile crime and victims' relatives are attempting to pry open the traditionally secret juvenile court system.[16]

DID YOU KNOW?

That a University of Southern California evaluation of a gang prevention program discovered that when the program lost funding, the gang broke up and the gang's crime rate declined?

---

[13]President's Commission on Law Enforcement and Administration of Justice, *Challenge of Crime in a Free Society* (Washington, DC: Government Printing Office, 1967), p. 19.
[14]Richard Shenkman, *Legends, Lies, and Cherished Myths of American History* (New York: HarperCollins, 1988), p. 158.
[15]President's Commission, *Challenge of Crime*, p. 19.
[16]See Chapter 5 for details on the rights of juveniles in our legal system.

FIGURE 16-7 Violent Crime Rates

Violent crime rates have declined since 1994, reaching the lowest level ever recorded in 2002. The crimes included in this chart are rape, robbery, aggravated and simple assault, and homicide.

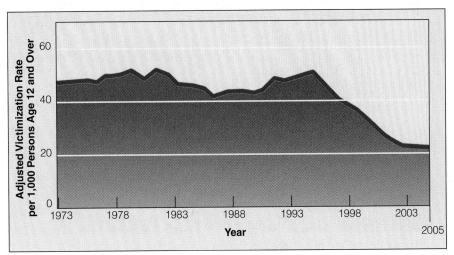

Sources: U.S. Department of Justice; rape, robbery, and assault data are from the *National Crime Victimization Survey*; the homicide data are from the Federal Bureau of Investigation's *Uniform Crime Reports*.

Some worry that the decline in serious juvenile crimes is only temporary. The number of youths between the ages of 15 and 17 will rise from about 9 million today to almost 13 million in the year 2010. As a result, the grave concern about preventing an even worse juvenile crime problem in the years to come is understandable.

SCHOOL SHOOTINGS

School shootings are a form of violent crime that, for most people, is particularly shocking and difficult to understand. Perhaps the most widely publicized of all school shootings in the United States occurred in 1999 in Littleton, Colorado. In what has become known as the Columbine High School massacre, two teenaged students went on a shooting rampage, killing 12 students and a teacher, and wounding 24 others, before committing suicide.

School shootings occur not only in secondary schools but also in elementary schools and on college campuses. Even a one-room school in Lancaster County, Pennsylvania, was not immune from such violence: in October 2006, a milk-truck driver held 10 Amish girls hostage before shooting five of them and then himself at the small schoolhouse. The deadliest school shooting to date, however, occurred on a college campus. On April 16, 2007, the nation was stunned to learn that a South Korean student at Virginia Polytechnic Institute and State University (Virginia Tech) in Blacksburg, Virginia, had killed 32 students and wounded some 29 others before killing himself.

The perception of school shootings as a growing form of violence is reinforced, to some extent, by the extraordinary media attention that such killings receive. Even while homicide rates in the schools were declining from 1993 to 2002, media attention increased in 2007 due to the many victims at the Virginia Tech campus. Overall, it remains true that students continue to face less risk of being victims of serious violent crimes while at school than while out of school. According to the National School Safety

Center, the annual probability of a school experiencing a student-perpetuated homicide
is about 1 in 11,520.[17]

THE COST OF CRIME TO AMERICAN SOCIETY

For the perpetrator, crime may pay in certain circumstances—a successful robbery or
embezzlement, for example—but crime certainly costs the American public. One study
suggests that when everything is added up, including the expenses of the legal system,
the costs of private deterrence, losses by victims, and the value of time wasted by criminals and victims, the annual burden of crime in the United States exceeds a trillion
dollars each year.[18]

The Office for Victims of Crime, a unit of the U.S. Department of Justice, has estimated that the direct tangible costs to crime victims, including the costs of medical
expenses, lost earnings, and victim assistance, are $105 billion annually. Pain, suf-
fering, and reduced quality of life increase the cost to $450 billion annually. Check
fraud costs an estimated $10 billion each year. Fraud involving stocks, bonds, and com-
modities costs about $40 billion per year. Telemarketing fraud costs another $40 billion
(though the recently established "do not call" list may have curbed this expense somewhat). Insurance fraud costs about $80 billion per year.[19]

THE PRISON POPULATION BOMB

Many Americans believe that the best solution to the nation's crime problem is to impose
stiff prison sentences on offenders. Such sentences, in fact, have become national policy.
By 2008, U.S. prisons and jails held 2.3 million people. About two-thirds of the incarcerated population was in state or federal prisons, with the remainder held in local jails.

----

[17]National School Safety Center, *Indicators of School Crime and Safety, 2006* (Washington, DC: Bureau of
Justice Statistics, 2006).
[18]David A. Anderson, "The Aggregate Burden of Crime," *Journal of Law and Economics*, Vol. 42, No. 2, October
1999.
[19]These estimates are online at www.ojp.usdoj.gov/ovc/ncvrw/2006/welcome.html.

About 60 percent of the persons held in local jails were awaiting court action. The other 40 percent were serving sentences.

The number of incarcerated persons has grown rapidly in recent years. In 1990, for example, the total number of persons held in U.S. jails or prisons was still only 1.1 million. From 1995 to 2002, the incarcerated population grew at an average of 3.8 percent annually. The rate of growth has slowed since 2002, however. You might ask why the prison population has grown so much when the crime rate was declining in the last decade. As noted previously, many states and localities have increased the list of crimes for which a criminal may receive a mandatory sentence. In addition, many individuals who are in prison were convicted of drug offenses. Many states operate under a "three strikes" law, which means that on the third drug conviction, even if it involves possession of a small amount of drugs, the individual is automatically sentenced to prison for a specified length of time.

The Incarceration Rate. Some groups of people are much more likely to find themselves behind bars than others. Men are more than 10 times more likely to be incarcerated than women. Prisoners are also disproportionately African American. To measure how frequently members of particular groups are imprisoned, the standard statistic is the **incarceration rate**. This rate is the number of people incarcerated for every 100,000 persons in a particular population group. To put it another way, an incarceration rate of 1,000 means that 1 percent of a particular group is in custody. Using this statistic, we can say that U.S. men have an incarceration rate of 1,309, compared to a rate of 113 for U.S. women. Table 16–1 on the next page shows selected incarceration rates by gender, race, and age. Note the very high incarceration rate for African Americans between the ages of 25 and 29—at any given time, almost 12 percent of this group is in jail or prison.

Incarceration Rate
The number of persons held in jail or prison for every 100,000 persons in a particular population group.

International Comparisons. The United States has more people in jail or prison than any other country in the world. That fact is not necessarily surprising, because the United States also has one of the world's largest total populations. More to the point, the United States has the highest reported incarceration rate of any country on earth.[20] Figure 16–8 compares U.S. incarceration rates, measured by the number of prisoners per 100,000 residents, with incarceration rates in other major countries.

Prison Construction. To house a growing number of inmates, prison construction and management have become sizable industries in the United States. Ten years ago, prison overcrowding was a major issue. In 1994, for example, state prisons had a rated capacity of about 500,000 inmates but actually held 900,000 people.

FIGURE 16–8 Incarceration Rates Around the World, 2007

Incarceration rates of major nations measured by the number of prisoners per 100,000 residents. Some authorities believe that the estimate for China is too low.

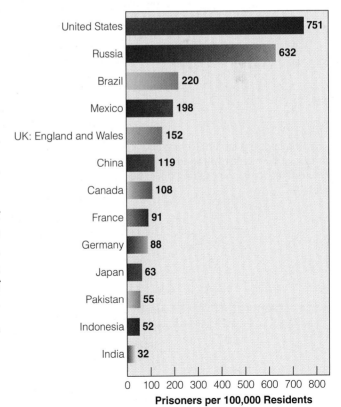

Source: Kings College, London, International Centre for Prison Studies, 2007.

[20]North Korea probably has a higher incarceration rate than the United States, but that nation does not report its incarceration statistics. The incarceration rate for political prisoners alone is estimated to be between 650 and 900 per 100,000 inhabitants. North Korea also holds an unknown number of prisoners as common criminals. See Pierre Rigoulot, "Comparative Analysis of Concentration Camps in Nazi Germany, the Former Soviet Union, and North Korea," 2002. This article is online at the Web site of Human Rights without Frontiers. Go to www .hrwf.net/north_korea/cf_north_korea_political_pri.html.

TABLE 16–1 Incarceration Rates per 100,000 Persons for Selected U.S. Population Groups

	MEN	WOMEN
Non-Hispanic white, total	736	94
Non-Hispanic white, aged 25–29	1,685	226
Non-Hispanic black, total	4,789	358
Non-Hispanic black, aged 25–29	11,695	716
Hispanic, total	1,862	152
Hispanic, aged 25–29	3,912	305
All groups	1,384	129

Source: U.S. Department of Justice, "Prison and Jail Inmates at Midyear 2006," *Bureau of Justice Statistics Bulletin,* 2007.

The prisons were therefore operating at 80 percent above capacity. Today, after a major prison construction program, state prisons are operating between 1 and 16 percent above capacity, although the federal prison system is still 31 percent above capacity. Since 1980, Texas has built 120 new prisons, Florida has built 84, and California has built 83. In 1923, there were only 61 prisons in the entire United States.

Effects of Incarceration. When imprisonment keeps truly violent felons behind bars longer, it prevents them from committing additional crimes. The average predatory street criminal commits 15 or more crimes each year when not behind bars. But most prisoners are in for a relatively short time and are released on parole early, often because of prison overcrowding. Then many ex-convicts find themselves back in prison because they have violated parole, typically by using illegal drugs. Of the more than 1.5 million people who are arrested each year, the majority are arrested for drug offenses. Given that from 20 to 40 million Americans violate one or more drug laws each year, the potential supply of prisoners seems virtually limitless. Consequently, it may not matter how many prisons are built; overcrowding will remain as along as we maintain the same legislation on illegal drugs.

That the odds are one in 20 that an American born today will wind up in jail or prison at some point during his or her lifetime?

FEDERAL DRUG POLICY

Illegal drugs are a major cause of crime in America. A rising percentage of arrests are for illegal drug trafficking. The latest major illegal drug has contributed to an increase in the number of drug arrests. That drug is methamphetamine, sometimes known as meth or speed. Methamphetamine is often made in small home laboratories using toxic household chemicals. Raids on meth labs around the country have become common news stories. The violence that often accompanies the illegal drug trade occurs for several reasons. One is that drug dealers engage in "turf wars" over the territories in which drugs can be sold. Another is that when drug deals go bad, drug dealers cannot turn to the legal system for help, so they resort to violence. Finally, drug addicts who do not have the income to finance their habits often engage in crime—assault, robbery, and sometimes murder.

The war on drugs and the increased spending on drug interdiction over the years have had virtually no effect on overall illegal drug consumption in the United States. Mandatory sentences, which have been imposed by the federal government since the late 1980s for all federal offenses, including the sale or possession of illegal drugs, are also not an ideal solution. Mandatory sentences lead to a further problem—overcrowded prisons. Furthermore, almost half of the 1.5 million people arrested each year in the United States on drug charges are arrested for marijuana offenses—and of these, almost 90 percent are charged with possession only.

While the federal government has done little to modify its drug policy, state and local governments have been experimenting with new approaches to the problem. Many states now have special drug courts for those arrested for illegal drug use. In these courts, offenders typically are sentenced to a rehabilitation program.

CONFRONTING TERRORISM

Of all of the different types of crimes, terrorism can be the most devastating. The victims of terrorist attacks can number in the hundreds—or even in the thousands, as was the case when hijacked airplanes crashed into the Pentagon and the World Trade Center on September 11, 2001. Additionally, locating the perpetrators is often extremely difficult. In a suicide bombing, the perpetrators have themselves been killed, so the search is not for the perpetrators, but for others who might have conspired with them in planning the attack.

Terrorism is certainly not a new phenomenon in the world, but it is a relatively new occurrence on U.S. soil. And certainly, the September 11 attacks made many Americans aware for the first time of the hatred of America harbored by some foreigners—in this case, a network of religious fundamentalists in foreign countries. As you have read elsewhere in this text, the U.S. government took many actions immediately after September 11, including launching a war in Afghanistan as part of a war on terrorism. Congress quickly passed new legislation to fund these efforts, as well as many other acts, such as the Aviation Security Act.

Some of the actions taken in the wake of September 11, such as the war in Afghanistan, were widely supported by the public. Others, such as the enactment of the USA PATRIOT Act and President Bush's executive order establishing military tribunals, have been criticized for infringing too much on Americans' civil liberties. Worldwide, terrorists' acts have continued since September 11. Among others, they include bomb attacks on the subway system and a bus in London, which killed more than 50 people, and bomb attacks on the public transportation system in Madrid, which killed more than 200 people. In the summer of 2006, the British government foiled what could have been one of the worst terrorist attacks yet. Ten or more individuals had prepared to take clear liquids into planes departing for the United States. These liquids were in fact bomb materials, and they were going to be detonated with electronic devices, such as MP3 players (or what appeared to be these devices). Certainly, at this point no end is in sight to the war on terrorism. As with all policies, the nation's policy with respect to terrorism will be evaluated—and perhaps modified—over time.

You can make a *difference*

DOING YOUR PART: GLOBAL WARMING

While debate continues over the causes of global warming, consensus exists among most scientists and climate researchers that global warming is here and will make an enormous impact on our planet. Sea levels, rainfall patterns, and snow and ice cover are all changing as a result of increasing greenhouse gas levels in the atmosphere. Human beings probably are tipping the ecological balance in the atmosphere with increased population, deforestation, cars, factories, and power plants.

WHY SHOULD YOU CARE?

Global warming is changing the Earth's climate, and is already affecting people, animals, and plants in different ways. The seas are rising, the glaciers are shrinking, trees are blooming earlier, and ice on lakes and rivers is freezing later and breaking up earlier. In the United States, scientists believe that most areas will continue to warm, with increased precipitation and evaporation. Drier soil is predicted for middle parts of the country. Northern regions, including Alaska, are forecast to experience the most drastic warming. Extreme periods of heat, cold, and storms can affect human health; climate-related diseases will increase, and smog episodes will rise. Doctors at the Harvard Medical School have linked recent U.S. outbreaks of dengue fever, malaria, and hantavirus to our changing climate. The eight warmest years on record (official records date to 1850) have all happened since 1998.

Some of the world's most respected climate scientists believe that we have a single decade, when today's college students will be in their 30s, to slow the growth of carbon emissions. Your generation will have to live with the consequences, and global warming is a defining issue on college campuses today.

WHAT CAN YOU DO?

Thinking about global problems can be overwhelming, but acting locally lets everyone participate and contribute to a solution. Action that starts at home can set the stage for national policy change. Tell your representatives in Congress and the Senate that you want to see a national plan to address global warming. Find out about all political candidates' positions on energy and global warming before voting.

Here are 10 actions we can all take to reduce our own carbon imprint on the planet:

1. Save energy at home by switching to Energy Star fluorescent lightbulbs. If every household in the United States replaced five conventional bulbs in the most frequently used fixtures, we would prevent greenhouse gas emissions equivalent to nearly 10 million cars.
2. Every gallon of gas burned emits 20 pounds of carbon dioxide; that's several times your car's weight every year. Try walking, taking public transportation, or riding a bike.
3. Recycle as much as possible; any reduction in trash going to the landfill makes a difference.
4. Buy recycled products; in some cases, products made from recycled materials require less energy to produce. Also look for goods with less packaging that will have less waste going to the landfill.
5. Many utilities are offering the choice to buy green electricity, generated by wind or solar power. Support this or any renewable energy development.
6. Make informed choices about the products and services you buy. Use businesses that make an effort to protect the climate, and let them know why you chose their services. Buy local produce whenever possible, because this food does not have to be shipped great distances, burning more fossil fuel to get to your table (and often tastes better, too!).
7. Educate yourself about global warming and climate change; many sources of information confuse the issues, and the ability to think critically is important when reading the paper or watching the news.
8. Let your elected representatives know you care about global warming; urge them to support actions to reduce pollution and save energy.

9. Create a climate-friendly environment on your college campus by working with school administrators to increase energy efficiency, develop an inventory of the school's greenhouse gas emissions, and create a campus climate action plan.
10. Seek out and support nonprofit groups that support green legislation and offer positions on environmental issues.

The EPA's Web site, **www.epa.gov**, provides details on actions by states and local agencies to address global warming. Find out what your region/state's climate action plan is all about.

Clean Air–Cool Planet has partnered with several universities in the Northeastern United States to develop a Campus Climate Action Plan Toolkit, available to anyone who is interested in making colleges more climate-friendly. For more information, please go to **www.cleanair-coolplanet .org**.

Focus the Nation is a national effort to focus attention on global warming issues at American college campuses. A national teach-in in 2008 provided a climate change seminar with more than 10,000 volunteers on more than 1,300 campuses. About 1 million people participated across the nation; another teach-in is planned for 2009. Their Web site offers opportunities to blog with other students and educators, events to get your campus involved, contests promoting creative solutions, and dozens of ways to participate politically. For more information, contact:

Focus the Nation Headquarters
4160 SW Haven St.
Lake Oswego, OR 97035
503-200-2313
www.focusthenation.org

REFERENCES

Daniel Horgan, "College Students Seeing Green as the Way to Go," *USA Today*, accessed March 12, 2008, at www.usatoday .com.

Bryan Walsh, "Changing the Climate on Campus," *Time*, accessed February 8, 2008, at www.time.com.

www.clearnair-coolplanet.org
www.epa.gov/climatechange
www.focusthenation.org
www.stopglobalwarming.org

KEY TERMS

CHAPTER SUMMARY

1. Domestic policy consists of all of the laws, government planning, and government actions that affect the lives of American citizens. Policies are created in response to public problems or public demand for government action. Major policy problems discussed in this chapter include health care, poverty and welfare, immigration, crime, and the environment.

2. The policy-making process is initiated when policy makers become aware—through the media or from their constituents—of a problem that needs to be addressed by the legislature and the president. The process of policy making includes five steps: agenda building, policy formulation, policy adoption, policy implementation, and policy evaluation. All policy actions necessarily result in both costs and benefits for society.

3. Health-care spending is about 15 percent of the U.S. economy and is growing. Reasons for this growth include the increasing number of elderly persons, advancing technology, and higher demand because costs are picked up by third-party insurers. A major third party is Medicare, the federal program that pays health-care expenses of U.S. residents older than age 65. The federal government has tried to restrain the growth in Medicare spending, but it has also expanded the program to cover prescription drugs.

4. About 15 percent of the population does not have health insurance—a major political issue. Most uninsured adults work for employers that cannot afford to offer health benefits. Hospitals tend to charge the uninsured higher rates than they charge insurance companies or the government. One proposal for addressing this problem is a national health-insurance system under which the government provides basic coverage to all citizens. Another alternative is the use of health savings accounts (HSAs) that allow people to save for their medical expenses tax free.

5. Pollution problems continue to plague the United States and the world. Since the 1800s, several significant federal acts have been passed in an attempt to curb the pollution of our environment. The National Environmental Policy Act of 1969 established the Council on Environmental Quality. That Act also mandated that environmental impact statements be prepared for all legislation or major federal actions that might significantly affect the quality of the environment. The Clean Water Act of 1972 and the Clean Air Act amendments of 1990 constituted the most significant government attempts at cleaning up our environment. Recent environmental controversies have centered on the Endangered Species Act and global warming.

6. Energy policy in the United States has generally sought to stabilize the supply of cheap energy to meet the demands of Americans. When energy sources are threatened, new policies have been adopted, increasing efficiency standards for automobiles, funding research on new technologies, and supporting the use of alternative energy. All energy policies are deeply interconnected with environmental issues, because the use of fossil fuels contributes to air pollution and climate change. Reducing the use of energy and using new technologies for cleaner energy makes all energy more expensive for Americans. However, reduced future supplies are likely to mean more reforms in the future.

7. Despite the wealth of the United States as a whole, a significant number of Americans live in poverty or are homeless. The low-income poverty threshold represents the income needed to maintain a specified standard of living as of 1963, with the purchasing-power value increased year by year based on the general increase in prices. The official poverty level is based on pretax income, including cash, and does not take into consideration in-kind subsidies (food stamps, housing vouchers, and so on).

8. The 1996 Welfare Reform Act transferred more control over welfare programs to the states, limited the number of years people can receive welfare assistance, and imposed work requirements on welfare recipients. The Reform Act succeeded in reducing the number of welfare recipients in the United States by at least 50 percent.

9. America has always been a land of immigrants and continues to be so. Today, more than 1 million immigrants from other nations enter the United States each year, and more than 10 percent of the U.S. population consists of foreign-born persons. The civil rights legislation of the 1960s and later has helped immigrants to overcome some of the effects of prejudice and discrimination against them.

10. There is widespread concern in this country about violent crime, particularly the large number of crimes that are committed by juveniles. However, the overall rate of violent crime, including crimes committed by juveniles, declined between 1995 and 2004. In response to crime concerns, the United States has incarcerated an unusually large number of persons. Crimes associated with illegal drug sales and use have also challenged policy makers. A pressing issue facing Americans and their government today is terrorism—one of the most devastating forms of crime. Government attempts to curb terrorism will no doubt continue for some time to come.

SELECTED PRINT AND MEDIA RESOURCES

SUGGESTED READINGS

Blundell, Katherine, and Fraser Armstrong. *Energy . . . Beyond Oil.* Cambridge: Oxford University Press, 2007. Written by two British scientists, the book reviews all of the major new technologies for energy generation and discusses whether or when the technologies can make a contribution to world energy needs.

Davis, Devra Lee. *When Smoke Ran Like Water: Tales of Environmental Deception and the Battle against Pollution.* New York: Basic Books, 2004. Davis, an epidemiologist, describes the health consequences of polluted air. She provides historical examples, such as the Donora Fog of 1948 that sickened a small town in Pennsylvania.

Ehrenreich, Barbara. *Nickel and Dimed: On (Not) Getting By in America.* New York: Owl Books, 2002. Released on audio CD in 2004. What is life like for the working poor? Commentator and humorist Barbara Ehrenreich sought to live for a few months working at minimum-wage jobs. Here, she describes her experiences.

Hage, Dave. *Reforming Welfare by Rewarding Work: One State's Successful Experiment.* Minneapolis: University of Minnesota Press, 2004. Hage describes the Minnesota Family Investment Program, a pilot program in welfare reform. He illustrates the story with firsthand accounts of three families.

Miller, Roger LeRoy, et al. *The Economics of Public Issues,* 15th ed. Reading, MA: Addison-Wesley, 2005. Chapters 4, 8, 11, 13, 19, 20, 22, 24, and 27 are especially useful. The authors use short essays of three to seven pages to explain the purely economic aspects of numerous social problems, including health care, the environment, and poverty.

Schellenberger, Michael, and Ted Nordhaus. *Break Through: From the Death of Environmentalism to the Politics of Possibility.* New York: Houghton-Mifflin, 2007. The authors argue that the environmentalist movement is no longer useful nor effective. A new approach to policy embracing research and societal needs will succeed in their view.

Sered, Susan Starr, and Rushika Fernandopulle. *Uninsured in America: Life and Death in the Land of Opportunity.* Berkeley: University of California Press, 2006. Based on interviews with 120 uninsured individuals and numerous policy makers and medical providers, this book looks at the growing ranks of Americans lacking health insurance and the problems with the nation's current health-care policies.

Zuberi, Dan. *Differences that Matter: Social Policy and the Working Poor in the United States and Canada.* Ithaca, NY: Cornell University Press, 2006. The author takes a comparative approach to the lives of the working poor in the United States and Canada, looking at vital issues ranging from health care to labor policies.

MEDIA RESOURCES

A Day's Work, A Day's Pay—This 2002 documentary by Jonathan Skurnik and Kathy Leichter follows three welfare recipients in New York City from 1997 to 2000. When forced to work at city jobs for well below the prevailing wage and not allowed to go to school, the three fight for programs that will help them get better jobs.

The Age of Terror: A Survey of Modern Terrorism—A four-part series, released in 2002, that contains unprecedented interviews with bombers, gunmen, hijackers, and kidnappers. The interviews are combined with photos from police and news archives. The four tapes are *In the Name of Liberation, In the Name of Revolution, In the Name of God,* and *In the Name of the State.*

America's Promise: Who's Entitled to What?—A four-part series that examines the current state of welfare reform and its impact on immigrant and other populations.

Drugs and Punishment: Are America's Drug Policies Fair?—In this 1996 BBC production, British journalist Charles Wheeler examines America's drug use and the hail of new drug laws instituted under the Reagan administration. Former drug czar William Bennett defends the government's position.

Traffic—A 2001 film, starring Michael Douglas and Benicio Del Toro, that offers compelling insights into the consequences of failed drug policies. (Authors' note: Be aware that this film contains material of a violent and sexual nature that may be offensive.)

Young Criminals, Adult Punishment—An ABC program that examines the issue of whether the harsh sentences given out to adult criminals, including capital punishment, should also be applied to young violent offenders.

e-mocracy

THE INTERNET AND DOMESTIC POLICY

Today, the Web offers opportunities for you to easily access information about any domestic policy issue. The *Logging On* section that follows lists a variety of Web sites where you can learn more about domestic policy issues and how they affect you. Many other sites are available as well. For example, would you like to learn more about prisons and imprisonment rates in different countries? The Web site of the International Centre for Prison Studies (ICPS), **www.kcl.ac.uk/depsta/rel/icps/worldbrief/world_ brief.html**, can help. Would you like to take a turn at proposing a federal budget and allocating spending among different programs, domestic or otherwise? You can find a budget-simulation game at **www.kowaldesign.com/ budget**. Of course, most news media outlets have their own Web sites, which are useful for keeping up to date on the latest domestic policy developments.

LOGGING ON

- To find more information on poverty in the United States and the latest research on this topic, go to the Web site of the Institute for Research on Poverty at:
  www.ssc.wisc.edu/irp
- For current statistics on poverty in the United States, go to:
  www.census.gov/hhes/www/poverty.html
- The National Governors Association offers information on the current status of welfare reform and other topics at:
  www.nga.org

- The Federal Bureau of Investigation offers information about crime rates at its Web site:
  www.fbi.gov/ucr/ucr.htm
- You can also find statistics and other information on crime in the United States at the Web site of the Bureau of Justice Statistics. Go to:
  www.ojp.usdoj.gov/bjs

ONLINE REVIEW

At **www.cengage.com/politicalscience/schmidt/agandpt14e**, you will find a Tutorial Quiz for this chapter providing questions on the chapter contents, including the features. The questions are organized to match the major sections of the chapter. You'll have access to other helpful study tools, including the book's glossary and flashcards, crossword puzzles, and Web links, as well as "Which Side Are You On?" and "Politics and . . ." features written by the authors of the book.

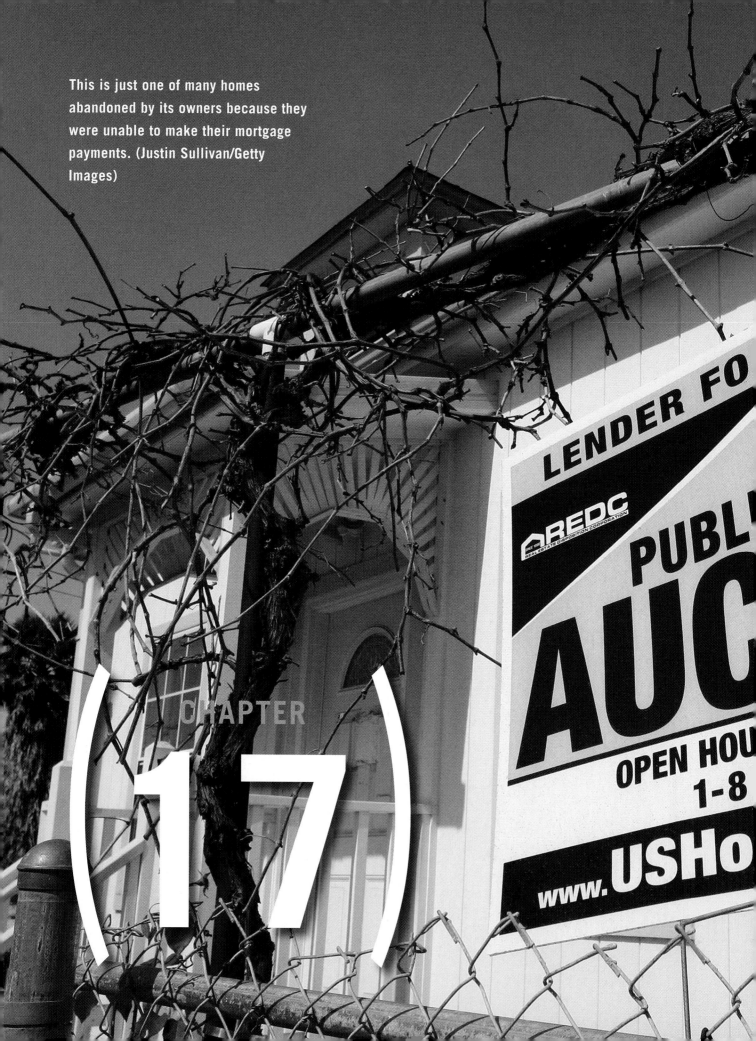

This is just one of many homes abandoned by its owners because they were unable to make their mortgage payments. (Justin Sullivan/Getty Images)

CHAPTER

(17)

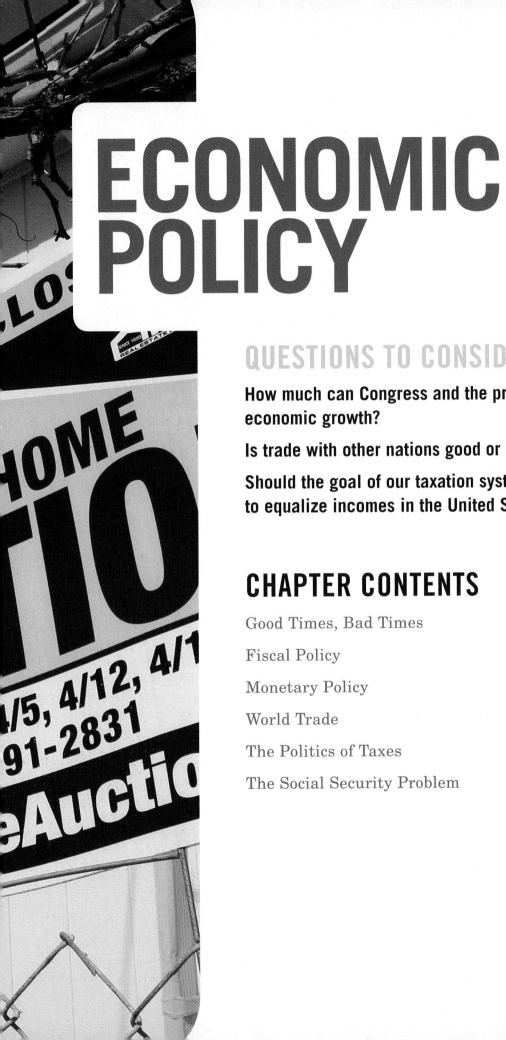

ECONOMIC POLICY

QUESTIONS TO CONSIDER

How much can Congress and the president do to encourage economic growth?

Is trade with other nations good or bad for the United States?

Should the goal of our taxation system be to raise money or to equalize incomes in the United States?

CHAPTER CONTENTS

Making a DIFFERENCE

MANAGING YOUR MONEY

Have you ever worried that your paycheck will not cover your monthly expenses, about how you are going to pay your bills, or about repaying your college loans? Most of us experience these concerns at one time or another and are forced to find solutions. Maybe we become more fiscally disciplined and stick to a budget. Maybe we find a way to increase revenue. Maybe one of your motivations for going to college is economic security.

The federal government faces similar dilemmas, only on a much larger and more complicated scale. As you will learn in this chapter, the federal government has, at various times, engaged in deficit spending—that is, spending more on services and programs than it has in generated in tax revenue. Prolonged periods of deficit spending cumulate to the federal debt.

Many organizations track deficit spending and the national debt carefully out of concern for the health and stability of the national economy. The Concord Coalition (**www.concordcoalition.org**) is a bipartisan organization advocating a "generationally responsible fiscal policy." As an advocacy group (see Chapter 7), its mission involves creating public awareness and lobbying government for reduced spending, fiscal discipline, and balanced budgets.

The Concord Coalition encourages public awareness of government spending.[a] Imagine if you had 100 pennies. Think about how you would divide those pennies among the various categories of spending: defense, education, interest on the debt, foreign aid, Social Security, welfare, health, the environment, and other programs like homeland security and agriculture. Each penny represents 1 percent of all federal spending. Interest on the federal debt alone is almost 10 percent.

NOWHERE ARE THE principles of public policy making more obvious than in the economic decisions made by the federal government. The president and Congress (and to a growing extent, the judiciary) are constantly faced with questions of economic policy. A major economic policy issue is how to maintain stable economic growth without falling into either excessive unemployment or **inflation** (rising prices). Inflation is defined as a sustained upward movement in the average level of prices.

Inflation
A sustained rise in the general price level of goods and services.

Another policy issue that is always under discussion is the state of the federal budget, because it is rarely balanced. You read about the debate over whether the government should continually engage in deficit financing in the *Making a Difference* feature. Other issues discussed in this chapter include fiscal and monetary policy, world trade, taxes, and the impact that Social Security will have on the federal budget in future years.

GOOD TIMES, BAD TIMES

Other than the fundamental tasks of maintaining law, order, and national security, no governmental objective is more important than the maintenance of economic stability. Like any economy that is fundamentally capitalist, the U.S. economy experiences ups and downs. Good times—booms—are followed by lean years. If a slowdown is so severe

So is it a problem that the government often spends more money than it takes in? Conflicting opinions exist. The Concord Coalition clearly advocates against deficit spending. At a 2004 forum, then-Federal Reserve Board Governor Edward M. Gramlich argued, "When the government runs deficits, it siphons off private savings . . . leaving less available for capital investment."[b]

By contrast, some argue that keeping tax rates low will have the most positive impact on the economy, regardless of the effect on the government. Some are openly hostile to the deficit hawks, calling them representative of the "Chicken Little deficit reduction myopia that was once the rage in the Republican Party."[c] These "supply siders" argue that taxes need to be held to a minimum in order for businesses to keep a maximum amount of their profits to reinvest in the economy. Some among them who also advocate for a smaller government that engages in fewer programs would also argue that lower taxes are a way to "starve" the federal government into being leaner and more efficient.[d] These conservatives argue that a "budget with Federal spending at 15 percent of GDP [gross domestic product], and a deficit of 3 percent of GDP, is far preferable to a balanced budget with Federal spending at 35 percent of GDP."[e] In other words, they prioritize low government spending over a balanced budget. Similarly, they point to rising costs of entitlement programs as a major threat to economic growth.

As a candidate, Senator Obama's platform included fiscal reform, citing the debt and deficit spending as barriers to "responsible fiscal policies." As president, he will need to work with Congress to translate these campaign promises into policy initiatives.[f]

[a]www.concordcoalition.org/learn/educators/penny-game, accessed October 10, 2008.

[b]www.concordcoalition.org/issues/primers/fiscal-responsibility .html, accessed May 28, 2008.

[c]www.nationalreview.com/moore/moore121102.asp, accessed May 28, 2008.

[d]www.businessweek.com/print/magazine/content/04_52/ b3914021_mz007.htm?chan=gl, accessed May 28, 2008.

[e]www.spectator.org/dsp_article.asp?art_id=13277, accessed May 28, 2008.

[f]www.barackobama.com/issues/fiscal, accessed June 2, 2008.

that the economy actually shrinks for six or more months, it is called a **recession**. Recessions—in part because they bring increased unemployment—are political poison for a sitting president, even though a president's power to control the economy is actually not that great. The government tries to moderate the effects of such downturns. In contrast, booms are historically associated with another economic problem that the government must address: rising prices, or inflation. We will turn to the topic of inflation shortly. First, we consider the problem of excessive unemployment.

Recession
Two or more successive quarters in which the economy shrinks instead of grows.

UNEMPLOYMENT

One political goal of any administration is to keep the rate of unemployment down. **Unemployment** is the inability of those who are in the workforce to find jobs. Individuals may become unemployed for several reasons. Some people enter the labor force for the first time and have to look for a job. Some people are fired or laid off and have to look for a job. Others just want to change occupations. **Full employment** is defined as a level of unemployment that makes allowances for normal movement between jobs. Full employment is widely considered to be a desirable state of affairs, but the nation does not always have it. During recessions, unemployment rises well above the full-employment level. For example, during the last serious business slowdown in 2001–2002, the rate of unemployment increased from 4.0 to 6.5 percent. By late 2005, the unemployment

Unemployment
The inability of those who are in the labor force to find a job; defined as the total number of those in the labor force actively looking for a job but unable to find one.

Full Employment
An arbitrary level of unemployment that corresponds to "normal" friction in the labor market. In 1986, a 6.5 percent rate of unemployment was considered full employment. Today, it is assumed to be around 5 percent.

rate fell to less than 5 percent and stayed there until spring 2008, when it reached 5.5 percent. The economy had slowed partly because of the increase in oil prices and the weakening of the housing market.

Unemployment Becomes an Issue. For much of American history, unemployment was not a problem that the federal government was expected to address. In the early years of the Republic, most people would have thought that the national government could not do much about unemployment. By the late 1800s, many people had come to believe that as a matter of principle, the government should not fight unemployment. This belief followed from an economic philosophy that was dominant in those years—*laissez-faire economics*. (You learned about the concept of *laissez-faire*—French for "let it be"—in Chapter 1.) Advocates of this philosophy believed then (and believe now) that government intervention in the economy is almost always misguided and likely to lead to negative results. A second barrier to any federal government action against unemployment was the doctrine of *dual federalism*, which was described in Chapter 3. Under this theory, *only* state governments had the right to address a problem such as unemployment. For the most part, however, ups and downs in the economy were a matter of the capitalist system and not a matter for government.

The Great Depression of the 1930s ended popular support for dual federalism and *laissez-faire* economics. As the Depression took hold, unemployment initially exceeded 25 percent. Relatively high rates of unemployment—more than 15 percent—persisted for more than 10 years. One of the methods that the Roosevelt administration adopted to combat the effects of the Depression was direct government employment of those without jobs through such programs as the Civilian Conservation Corps and the Works Progress Administration.

Since the passage of the Social Security Act of 1935, the federal government has also offered a program of unemployment insurance. The program is the government's single most important source of assistance to the jobless. Not all unemployed workers are eligible, however. In fact, only about one-third of the unemployed receive benefits. Benefits are not available to employees who quit their jobs voluntarily or are fired for cause (for example, constantly showing up late for work). They are also not paid to workers who are entering the labor force for the first time but cannot find a job. Unemployment insurance is a joint state–federal program and is paid for by a tax on employers.

Measuring Unemployment. Estimates of the number of unemployed are prepared by the U.S. Department of Labor. The Bureau of the Census also generates estimates using survey research data. Figure 17–1 shows how unemployment has fluctuated over the course of American history.

Critics of the published unemployment rate calculated by the federal government believe that it fails to reflect the true numbers of discouraged workers and "hidden unemployed." Although no exact definition of discouraged workers or a way to measure them exists, the Department of Labor defines them as people who have dropped out of the labor force and are no longer looking for a job because they believe that the job market has little to offer them.

INFLATION

Rising prices, or inflation, can also be a serious political problem for any sitting administration, especially if prices are rising fast. As previously stated, inflation is a sustained upward movement in the average level of prices. Inflation can also be defined as a decline in the purchasing power of money over time. The government measures inflation using the **consumer price index (CPI)**. The Bureau of Labor Statistics (BLS) identifies a market basket of goods and services purchased by the typical consumer and regularly

Consumer Price Index (CPI)
A measure of the change in price over time of a specific group of goods and services used by the average household.

checks the price of that basket. Over a period of many years, inflation can add up. For example, today's dollar is worth (very roughly) one-twentieth of what a dollar was worth a century ago. Figure 17–2 shows the changing rates of inflation in the United States since 1860. While interest rates have not increased very much in the mid-2000s, the increase in the price of oil and, thus, all transportation costs, has begun to drive up all prices of consumer goods. Inflation is once again a concern for the nation. Predicted inflation rates are still in excess of 3 to 4 percent per year. That might not seem very high, but an inflation rate of 4 percent per year leads to a *doubling* of the price index in 18 years.

FIGURE 17–1 More than a Century of Unemployment

Unemployment reached lows during World Wars I and II of less than 2 percent and a high during the Great Depression of more than 25 percent.

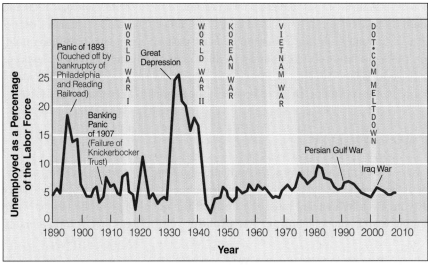

Source: U.S. Department of Labor, Bureau of Labor Statistics.

FIGURE 17–2 Changing Rates of Inflation, 1860 to the Present

From the Civil War until World War II, the United States experienced alternating inflation and deflation. (*Deflation* is a sustained decrease in the average price level.) Since World War II, deflation has not been a problem. The vertical yellow bars represent wartime.

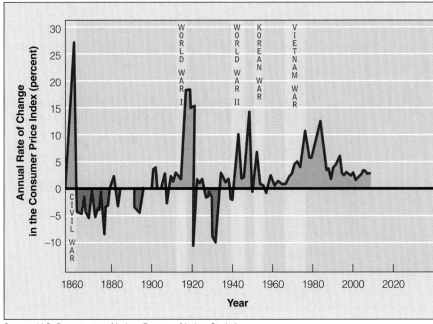

Source: U.S. Department of Labor, Bureau of Labor Statistics.

THE BUSINESS CYCLE

As noted earlier in the chapter, the economy passes through boom times and recessions. Economists refer to the regular succession of economic expansions and contractions as the *business cycle*. This term may be less appropriate than it used to be, because *cycle* implies regular recurrence, and in the years since World War II (1939–1945), contractions and expansions have varied greatly in length. Figure 17–3 shows business cycles since 1880. Note that the long-term upward trend line is shown as horizontal, so all changes in business activity focus around that trend line.

An extremely severe recession is called a *depression*, as in the example of the Great Depression. By 1933, actual output was 35 percent below the nation's productive capacity. By 1932, the net income of farm operators was barely 20 percent of its 1929 level, even though total farm output had risen by 3 percent in the interim. Between 1929 and 1932, more than 5,000 banks (one out of every five) failed, and their customers' deposits vanished. Compared to that catastrophe, most modern recessions have been mild. However, the bank failures of 2008 and the stock market plunge may lead to another worldwide depression. The United States government as well as the governments of every major power try to prevent such economic disasters by every means available.

FISCAL POLICY

> **Fiscal Policy**
> The federal government's use of taxation and spending policies to affect overall business activity.

To smooth out the ups and downs of the national economy, the government has several policy options. One is to change the level of taxes or government spending. The other possibility involves influencing interest rates and the money side of the economy. We will examine taxing and spending, or **fiscal policy**, first. Fiscal policy is the domain

FIGURE 17–3 National Business Activity, 1880 to the Present
Variations around the trend of U.S. business activity have been frequent since 1880.

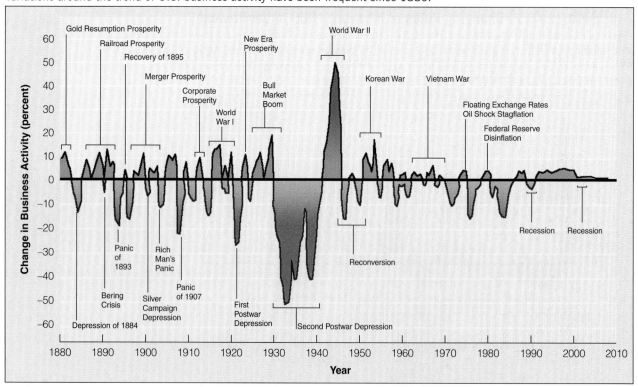

Sources: *American Business Activity from 1790 to Today*, 67th ed. (AmeriTrust Co., January 1996); and authors' updates.

of Congress and the president. Generally, the incumbent president and his party are blamed by the public for an economic downturn. However, any real changes in fiscal policy are likely to be initiated by the president and then passed by the Congress. A fiscal policy approach to stabilizing the economy is often associated with a 20th-century economist named John Maynard Keynes.

Keynesian Economics. The British economist John Maynard Keynes (1883–1946) originated the school of thought called **Keynesian economics**, which supports the use of government spending and taxing to help stabilize the economy. (*Keynesian* is pronounced *kayn*-zee-un.) Keynes believed that a need for government intervention in the economy existed, in part because after falling into a recession or depression, a modern economy may become trapped in an ongoing state of less than full employment.

Keynesian Economics
A school of economic thought that tends to favor active federal government policy making to stabilize economy-wide fluctuations, usually by implementing discretionary fiscal policy.

Government Spending. Keynes developed his fiscal policy theories during the Great Depression. He believed that the forces of supply and demand operated too slowly on their own in such a serious recession. Unemployment meant people had less to spend, and because they could not buy things, more businesses failed, creating additional unemployment. It was a vicious cycle. Keynes's idea was simple: in such circumstances, the government should step in and undertake the spending that is needed to return the economy to a more normal state.[1]

Government Borrowing. Government spending can be financed in several ways, including increasing taxes and borrowing. For government spending to have the effect Keynes wanted, however, it was essential that the spending be financed by borrowing, and not by taxes. In other words, the government should run a **budget deficit**, which was discussed in the chapter-opening *Making a Difference* feature—it should spend more than it receives. If the government financed its spending during a recession by taxation, the government would be spending funds that would, for the most part, otherwise have been spent by taxpayers.

Budget Deficit
Government expenditures that exceed receipts.

Normally, businesses constantly borrow funds to expand future production. Consumers also borrow to finance items that cannot be paid for out of current income, such as a house or a car. In a recession, however, borrowing slows down. Businesses may not believe that they can sell the new goods or services that would allow them to repay the funds they might borrow. Consumers may be fearful of incurring long-term obligations at a time when their jobs might be threatened.

When the government borrows during a recession, this borrowing replaces the borrowing that businesses and consumers would normally undertake. By running a budget deficit, therefore, the government makes up not only for reduced spending by businesses and consumers, but for reduced private borrowing as well.

Discretionary Fiscal Policy. Keynes originally developed his fiscal theories as a way of lifting an economy out of a major disaster such as the Great Depression. Beginning with the presidency of John F. Kennedy (served 1961–1963), however, policy makers have attempted to use Keynesian methods to fine-tune the economy. This is discretionary fiscal policy—*discretionary* meaning left to the judgment or discretion of a policy maker. For example, President George W. Bush pushed his tax cuts of 2001 and 2003 as a method of stimulating the economy to halt the economic slowdown of those years. During 2006, Bush repeatedly pointed out that since his tax cuts were put into effect, the economy grew so much that federal tax revenues increased more than anticipated, thereby reducing the federal budget deficit below the level that had been predicted. As Bush

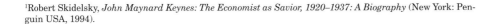

[1]Robert Skidelsky, *John Maynard Keynes: The Economist as Savior, 1920–1937: A Biography* (New York: Penguin USA, 1994).

approached the end of his second term, he noted that the 2008 budget submitted to Congress would reduce the budget deficit and, if his proposals were followed, the budget would produce a surplus by 2012.

Kennedy was the first American president to explicitly adopt Keynesian economics. In 1963, during a mild business slowdown, Kennedy proposed a tax cut. Congress did not actually pass the necessary legislation until early 1964, after Kennedy had been assassinated. The economy picked up—and the tax cut was a success.

An aide to President George W. Bush gave this succinct description of federal priorities: "It helps to think of the government as an insurance company with an army"?

Discretionary Fiscal Policy Failures. Subsequent presidents did not have the same success as Kennedy with their fiscal policies. Lyndon B. Johnson, Kennedy's successor, presided over a boom that was partially fueled by spending on the Vietnam War (1964–1975). In principle, Johnson should have asked for a tax increase to pay for the war. He was afraid of the political consequences, however; the Vietnam War was unpopular enough already. Instead of raising taxes, Congress borrowed and ran a budget deficit. This is the exact opposite of what Keynes would have recommended. One of the results seemed to be inflation.

Ending an inflationary spiral can be politically dangerous. It may result in a recession. Johnson's successors, Presidents Richard Nixon, Gerald Ford, and Jimmy Carter, were reluctant to take that risk and, in any event, may have lacked the political support needed for serious anti-inflationary measures. Nixon, in particular, chose to fight inflation not with fiscal or monetary policies but by instituting a comprehensive system of **wage and price controls**. Eventually, Nixon had to lift the controls, and when he did, measured inflation came roaring back stronger than ever. In the end, inflation was halted through the use of monetary policy, which you will read about shortly.

Wage and Price Controls
Government-imposed controls on the maximum prices that may be charged for specific goods and services, plus controls on permissible wage increases.

THE THORNY PROBLEM OF TIMING

Attempts to fine-tune the economy face a timing problem. Have you ever taken a shower, turned on the hot water, and had the water come out cold? Then, in frustration, you gave the hot water faucet another turn and were scalded? What happened was a lag between the time you turned on the faucet and the time the hot water actually reached the showerhead. Policy makers concerned with short-run stabilization face similar difficulties.

It takes a while to collect and assimilate economic data. Time may go by before an economic problem can be identified. After an economic problem is recognized, a solution must be formulated. There will be an action time lag between the recognition of a problem and the implementation of policy to solve it. Getting Congress to act can easily take a year or two. Finally, after fiscal policy is enacted, it takes time for the policy to act on the economy. Because fiscal policy time lags are long and variable, a policy designed to combat a recession may not produce results until the economy is already out of the recession.

AUTOMATIC STABILIZERS

Automatic, or Built-in, Stabilizers
Certain federal programs that cause changes in national income during economic fluctuations without the action of Congress and the president. Examples are the federal income tax system and unemployment compensation.

Not all changes in taxes or in government spending require new legislation by Congress. Certain automatic fiscal policies—called **automatic**, or **built-in, stabilizers**—include the tax system and government transfer payments such as unemployment insurance.

You know that if you work less, you are paid less, and therefore you pay lower taxes. The amount of taxes that our government collects falls automatically during a recession. Some economists consider this an automatic tax cut. Like other tax cuts, it may help reduce the extent of a recession.

Similar to the tax system, unemployment compensation payments may boost total economy-wide demand. When business activity drops, many laid-off workers automati-

cally become eligible for unemployment compensation from their state governments. They continue to receive income, although certainly it is less than they earned when they were employed.

DEFICIT SPENDING AND THE PUBLIC DEBT

The federal government typically borrows by selling **U.S. Treasury bonds**. The sale of these federal government bonds to corporations, private individuals, pension plans, foreign governments, foreign businesses, and foreign individuals adds to this nation's *public debt*. In the last few years, foreigners have come to own about 50 percent of the U.S. public debt. Thirty years ago, the share of the U.S. public debt held by foreigners was only 15 percent.

U.S. Treasury Bond
Debt issued by the federal government.

The Public Debt in Perspective. Did you know that the federal government has accumulated trillions of dollars in debt? Does that scare you? It certainly would if you thought that we had to pay it back tomorrow, but we do not.

There are two types of public debt—gross and net. The **gross public debt** includes all federal government interagency borrowings, which really do not matter. This is similar to your taking an IOU ("I owe you") out of your left pocket and putting it into your right pocket. Currently, federal interagency borrowings account for close to $3 trillion of the gross public debt. What is important is the **net public debt**—the public debt that does not include interagency borrowing. Table 17–1 shows the net public debt of the federal government since 1940.

Gross Public Debt
The net public debt plus interagency borrowings within the government.

Net Public Debt
The accumulation of all past federal government deficits; the total amount owed by the federal government to individuals, businesses, and foreigners.

This table does not consider two very important variables: inflation and increases in population. A better way to examine the relative importance of the public debt is to compare it to the **gross domestic product (GDP)**, as is done in Figure 17–4. (The *gross domestic product* is the dollar value of all final goods and services produced in a one-year period.) There you see that the public debt reached its peak during World War II and fell thereafter. Since about 1960, the net public debt as a percentage of GDP has ranged between 30 and 50 percent.

Gross Domestic Product (GDP)
The dollar value of all final goods and services produced in a one-year period.

TABLE 17–1 Net Public Debt of the Federal Government

YEAR	TOTAL (BILLIONS OF CURRENT DOLLARS)	YEAR	TOTAL (BILLIONS OF CURRENT DOLLARS)
1940	$42.7	1998	3,870.0
1945	235.2	1999	3,632.9
1950	219.0	2000	3,448.6
1960	237.2	2001	3,200.3
1970	284.9	2002	3,528.7
1980	709.3	2003	3,878.4
1990	2,410.1	2004	4,295.0
1992	2,998.6	2005	4,592.0
1993	3,247.5	2006	4,895.0
1994	3,432.1	2007	5,035.0
1995	3,603.4	2008	5,232.0*
1996	3,747.1	2009	5,443.0*
1997	3,900.0		

*Estimate.
Source: Congressional Budget Office.

FIGURE 17–4 Net Public Debt as a Percentage of the Gross Domestic Product

During World War II, the net public debt as a percentage of GDP grew dramatically. It fell thereafter but rose again from 1975 to 1995. The percentage fell after 1995, began to rise again after the events of September 11, 2001, and then fell again, starting in 2004.

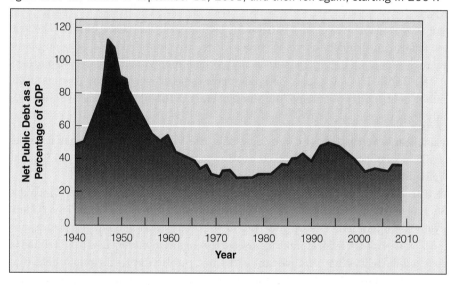

Are We Always in Debt? From 1960 until the last few years of the 20th century, the federal government spent more than it received in all but two years. Some observers consider these ongoing budget deficits to be the negative result of Keynesian policies. Others argue that the deficits actually result from the abuse of Keynesianism. Politicians have been more than happy to run budget deficits in recessions, but they have often refused to implement the other side of Keynes's recommendations—to run a budget surplus during boom times.

In 1993, however, President Bill Clinton (served 1993–2001) obtained a tax increase as the nation emerged from a mild recession. For the first time, the federal government implemented the more painful side of Keynesianism. In any event, between the tax

WHAT IF...

THE FEDERAL GOVERNMENT WERE REQUIRED TO BALANCE ITS BUDGET?

To understand the ramifications of a balanced federal budget, you first have to consider how it would be balanced. Let's assume that an amendment requiring a balanced budget is added to the U.S. Constitution. Initially, the two possible ways to balance the federal budget would be to raise taxes and increase user fees or to reduce the amount of federal government spending. Alternatively, a combination of these two actions could be undertaken.

INCREASED TAXES

On the revenue side of the equation, one way to balance the budget is to increase taxes on individuals and corporations. If the government did this by increasing taxes on individuals, then the tax rates paid by the middle class would have to rise significantly. Why? The reason is simply that the middle class is the source of most tax revenues for the federal government. The rich and the super-rich pay a more-than-proportionate share in taxes, but not enough households in that group exist to increase the revenues enough to balance the budget. Thus, middle-class Americans would see their taxes go up rather dramatically.

Taxes on corporations might increase significantly, too. Corporations, though, exist only as legal entities. Therefore, increased corporate taxes would mean reduced income for owners of corporate stock, lower salaries for employees of corporations, and higher prices for consumers.

It would also be possible to increase user fees for all federal government services, perhaps to keep them more in line with the actual costs of the federal government. The fees to visit national parks would likely be raised, as one example.

REDUCED FEDERAL GOVERNMENT SPENDING

On the spending side of the equation, a reduction in federal government spending could mean dramatic changes for many Americans. Fewer pork-barrel spending projects would be available for members of Congress to get for their states and districts, but these projects actually make up a very small proportion of the federal budget.

Much more spending would have to be reduced to balance the budget (unless taxes were raised at the same time). So there might be across-the-board cuts of, say, 6 percent in every department. Each department would then have to decide how much to cut from its own programs. Obviously, the public would be outraged as popular programs were either cut back substantially or eliminated altogether.

FOREIGN OWNERSHIP OF U.S. TREASURY BONDS

Another effect of a balanced federal budget would be a reduction in the amount of U.S. Treasury bonds held by foreign residents and governments. When the federal government runs a deficit, it creates debt obligations, usually in the form of U.S. Treasury bonds. Currently, foreigners buy a significant portion of those bonds, up to 50 percent. If the government had to balance its budget, foreigners would no longer be able to buy U.S. debt. Many Americans are uncomfortable knowing that foreigners own so much of our accumulated federal deficits, and would therefore view this change as beneficial.

FOR CRITICAL ANALYSIS

1. Of the two methods of reducing the deficit to zero—raising taxes or decreasing government spending—which method do you believe would be perceived by most people to be less painful? Why?
2. How can the federal government spend more than it receives every year, whereas a family would have a hard time doing the same thing year in and year out?

increase and the dot-com boom, the United States had a budget surplus each year from 1998 to 2002. Some commentators predicted that we would be running federal government surpluses for years to come. All of those projections went by the wayside because of several events.

One event was the dot-com bust followed by the 2001–2002 recession, which was caused by the terrorist attacks on September 11, 2001. These events lowered the rate of growth of not only the economy but also the federal government's tax receipts. Another event was a series of large tax cuts passed by Congress in 2001 and 2003 at the urging of President George W. Bush. Finally, the government had to pay for the war in Iraq in 2003 and the occupation of that country thereafter, which turned out to be far more costly than ever imagined. The federal budget deficit for 2007 was close to $270 billion. Few people now think that government budget surpluses will occur in the near future, although President Bush claimed they will happen by 2012. Citizens often wonder why the United States, as rich a nation as it is, continues to run its government in deficit. Wouldn't it be possible for the government to be "in the black?"

MONETARY POLICY

Federal Reserve System (the Fed)
The agency created by Congress in 1913 to serve as the nation's central banking organization.

Controlling the rate of growth of the money supply is called *monetary policy*. This policy is the domain of the **Federal Reserve System**, also known simply as **the Fed**. The Fed is the most important regulatory agency in the U.S. monetary system.

The Fed performs several important functions. Perhaps the Fed's most important ability is that it is able to regulate the amount of money in circulation, which can be defined loosely as checkable account balances and currency. The Fed also provides a system for transferring checks from one bank to another. In addition, it holds reserves deposited by most of the nation's banks, savings and loan associations, savings banks, and credit unions.

ORGANIZATION OF THE FEDERAL RESERVE SYSTEM

Federal Open Market Committee
The most important body within the Federal Reserve System. The Federal Open Market Committee decides how monetary policy should be carried out.

A board of governors manages the Fed. This board consists of seven full-time members appointed by the president with the approval of the Senate. The 12 Federal Reserve district banks have 25 branches. The most important unit within the Fed is the **Federal Open Market Committee**. This is the body that actually determines the future growth of the money supply and other important economy-wide financial variables. This committee is composed of the members of the Board of Governors, the president of the New York Federal Reserve Bank, and presidents of four other Federal Reserve banks, rotated periodically.

The Board of Governors of the Federal Reserve System is independent. The president can attempt to influence the board, and Congress can threaten to merge the Fed into the Treasury Department, but as long as the Fed retains its independence, its chairperson and governors can do what they please. Hence, any talk about "the president's monetary policy" or "Congress's monetary policy" is inaccurate. To be sure, the Fed has, on occasion, yielded to presidential pressure, and for a while the Fed's chairperson had to observe a Congressional resolution requiring him to report monetary targets over each six-month period. But now, more than ever before, the Fed remains one of the truly independent sources of economic power in the government.[2]

[2]Axel Krause, "The American Federal Reserve System: Functioning and Accountability" (Paris, France: Groupement d'études et de recherches, Notre Europe, Research and Policy Paper No. 7, 1999). This paper is available online at www.notre-europe.eu/en/axes.

LOOSE AND TIGHT MONETARY POLICIES

The Federal Reserve System seeks to stabilize nationwide economic activity by controlling the amount of money in circulation. Changing the amount of money in circulation is a major aspect of **monetary policy**. You may have read a news report in which a business executive complained that money is "too tight." This means that the Federal Reserve has increased the interest rate that it charges banks, making it more expensive to borrow money. You may have run across a story about an economist who has warned that money is "too loose." In this instance, the Fed has lowered the interest rate in hopes of stimulating borrowing by businesses and individuals. The businesses will then use that money to invest in new equipment and create new jobs. When the interest rate is lowered, it is easier, theoretically, for businesses and individuals to borrow money, thus stimulating the economy.

How do the actions of the Federal Reserve affect the life of the ordinary citizen? The answer to that question depends on what kinds of loans an individual might have. If you have a 30-year fixed-rate mortgage on your home, for example, nothing the Fed does will change the interest rate of your loan. However, if you have a low adjustable-rate mortgage, the rate will increase as the Fed increases the prime rate. This happened to millions of homeowners and investors in 2005 to 2007, with payments increasing so much that many homes were foreclosed on by the banks. Generally, interest on credit cards remains high no matter what the Fed does. It is important to remember that the Fed is more interested in stimulating business activity than it is in stimulating individuals to buy more homes.[3]

If the Fed implements a **loose monetary policy** (often called an "expansionary" policy), the supply of credit increases and its cost falls. If the Fed implements a **tight monetary policy** (often called a "contractionary" policy), the supply of credit falls and its cost increases. A loose money policy is often implemented as an attempt to encourage economic growth. You may be wondering why any nation would want a tight money policy. The answer is to control inflation. If money becomes too plentiful too quickly, prices (and ultimately the price level) increase, and the purchasing power of the dollar decreases.

Monetary Policy
The utilization of changes in the amount of money in circulation to alter credit markets, employment, and the rate of inflation.

Loose Monetary Policy
Monetary policy that makes credit inexpensive and abundant, possibly leading to inflation.

Tight Monetary Policy
Monetary policy that makes credit expensive in an effort to slow the economy.

TIME LAGS FOR MONETARY POLICY

You learned earlier that policy makers who implement fiscal policy—the manipulation of budget deficits and the tax system—experience problems with time lags. The Fed faces similar problems when it implements monetary policy. Sometimes accurate information about the economy is not available for months. Once the state of the economy is known, time may elapse before any policy can be put into effect. Still, the time lag when implementing monetary policy is usually much shorter than the lag involved in fiscal policy. The Federal Open Market Committee meets eight times per year and can put a policy into effect relatively quickly. Nevertheless, a change in the money supply may not have an effect for several months.

Time lags were a major reason why the Fed's implementation of monetary policy had dismal results for much of the 20th century. Researchers point out that until the last two decades or so, the Fed's policies turned out to be procyclical rather than anticyclical—that is, by the time the Fed started pumping money into the economy, it was usually time to do the opposite. By the time the Fed started reducing the rate of growth of the money supply, it was usually time to start increasing it.

[3]For data on Federal Reserve prime rates and mortgage rates, see the Historical Data series from the Federal Reserve Board of Governors at www.federalreserve.gov.

The Fed's greatest blunder occurred during the Great Depression. The Fed's policy actions at that time resulted in an almost one-third decrease in the amount of money in circulation. Some economists believe that the Fed was responsible for turning a severe recession into a full-blown depression.

In the early years of the 21st century, the United States experienced a housing boom and a rapid increase in the values of homes and condominiums. Credit was easily available, and the Fed, seeking to keep the economy growing, kept rates low. Then rates began to increase to stop inflation, and many millions of Americans found themselves with mortgages that were becoming more expensive. The housing market declined, values of homes declined, and people ended up owning homes that were not worth the mortgage value. Some people lost their homes, whereas others simply let the bank take over their investments. As the crisis continued, Congress struggled to create legislation to help homeowners who found themselves in this situation. Some analysts criticized the Fed for lowering interest rates too far and stimulating borrowing, whereas other commentators blamed the lending institutions and financial houses that borrowed funds against overvalued mortgages. The mortgage crisis was not limited to the United States: European banks shared the banking crisis.[4]

THE WAY FEDERAL RESERVE POLICY IS ANNOUNCED

Whatever the Fed's intentions, it signifies its current monetary policy by announcing an interest rate target. Nevertheless, when the chair of the Fed states that the Fed is lowering the interest rate from, say, 4.75 percent to 4.50 percent, something else is really meant. The interest rate referred to is the *federal funds rate*, or the rate at which banks can borrow excess reserves from other banks. The direct impact of this interest rate on the economy is modest. To have a significant effect on interest rates throughout the economy, the Fed must increase or restrain the growth in the money supply.

MONETARY POLICY VERSUS FISCAL POLICY

A tight monetary policy is effective as a way of taming inflation. (Some would argue that, ultimately, a tight monetary policy is the only way that inflation can be fought.) If interest rates go high enough, people *will* stop borrowing. How effective, though, is a loose monetary policy at ending a recession?

Under normal conditions, a loose monetary policy will spur an expansion in economic activity. At any given time, many businesses are considering whether to borrow. If interest rates are low, the businesses are more likely to do so. Low interest rates also reduce the cost of new houses or cars and encourage consumers to spend.

Recall from earlier in the chapter, however, that in a serious recession, businesses may not want to borrow no matter how low the interest rate falls. Likewise, consumers may be reluctant to make major purchases even if the interest rate is zero. In these circumstances, monetary policy is ineffective. Using monetary policy in this situation has been described as "pushing on a string," because the government has no power to *make* people borrow. Here is where fiscal policy becomes important. The borrowing *can* take place—if the government does it itself.

WORLD TRADE

Most of the consumer electronic goods you purchase—flat-screen television sets, portable media players, cell phones, and digital cameras—are made in other countries.

4"CSI: Credit Crunch," *The Economist*, October 18, 2007, www.economist.com/specialreports.

Many of the raw materials used in manufacturing in this country are also purchased abroad. For example, more than 90 percent of bauxite, from which aluminum is made, is brought in from other nations.

World trade, however, is a controversial topic. Since 1999, meetings of major trade bodies such as the World Trade Organization have been marked by large and sometimes violent demonstrations against "globalization." Opponents of globalization often refer to "slave" wages in developing countries as a reason to restrict imports from those nations. Others argue that we should restrict imports from countries that do not follow the same environmental standards as the United States.

Although economists of all political persuasions are strong believers in the value of international trade, this is not true of the general public. In 2008, when the *Los Angeles Times*/Bloomberg Poll asked a sampling of Americans whether they believe increased trade between the United States and other countries helped or hurt the economy, 50 percent said that it hurt the economy, as compared to 28 percent who said it helped.[5]

IMPORTS AND EXPORTS

Imports are those goods (and services) that we purchase from outside the United States. Today, imports make up about 15 percent of the goods and services that we buy. This is a significant share of the U.S. economy, but actually it is quite small in comparison with many other countries.

Imports
Goods and services produced outside a country but sold within its borders.

We not only import goods and services from abroad, but we also sell goods and services abroad, called **exports**. Each year we export more than $900 billion worth of goods. In addition, we export about $300 billion worth of services. The United States exports about 13 percent of the GDP. Like our imports, our exports are a relatively small part of our economy compared with those of many other countries.

Exports
Goods and services produced domestically for sale abroad.

[5]*Los Angeles Times*/Bloomberg Poll, May 1–8, 2008.

A SYMBOL OF GLOBAL TRADE, a ship full of containers, transits the Panama Canal. Such ships are built to meet the maximum size of the canal. (Robert Harding Picture Library/Alamy Limited)

Back in the 1950s, imports and exports comprised only about 4 percent of the U.S. GDP. In other words, international trade has become more important for the United States. This is also true for the world as a whole. Since the 1950s, world trade has increased by more than 22 times, although the output of all nations has only increased by eight times.

THE IMPACT OF IMPORT RESTRICTIONS ON EXPORTS

What we gain as a country from international trade is the ability to import the things we want. We must export other things to pay for those imports. A fundamental proposition for understanding international trade is the following: *In the long run, imports are paid for by exports.*

In the short run, imports can also be paid for by the sale (or export) of U.S. assets, such as title to land, stocks, and bonds, or through an extension of credit from other countries. Other nations, however, will not continue to give us credit forever for the goods and services that we import from them.

Economists point out that if we restrict the ability of the rest of the world to sell goods and services to us, then the rest of the world will not be able to purchase all of the goods and services that we want to sell to them. This argument runs contrary to the beliefs of people who want to restrict foreign competition to protect domestic jobs. Although it is certainly possible to preserve jobs in certain sectors of the economy by restricting foreign competition, there is evidence that import restrictions actually reduce the total number of jobs in the economy. Why? The reason is that ultimately such restrictions lead to a reduction in employment in export industries.

Protecting American Jobs. When imports are restricted to save jobs, one effect is to reduce the supply of a particular good or service, and thus to raise its price to consumers. Economists calculate that restrictions on imports of clothing have cost U.S. consumers $45,000 *per year* for each job saved. In the steel industry, the cost of preserving a job has been estimated at approximately $750,000 per year.

One of the best examples of how import restrictions raise prices to consumers has been in the automobile industry, where "voluntary" restrictions on Japanese car imports were in place for more than a decade. Due in part to the enhanced quality of imported cars, sales of domestically produced automobiles fell from 9 million units per year in the late 1970s to an average of 6 million units annually between 1980 and 1982. The U.S. automakers and the United Automobile Workers demanded protection from import competition.

The United States and Japan entered into a "voluntary agreement" to reduce imports of Japanese cars from 1981 into the late 1990s. The result was more demand for Japanese cars than supply, and their prices went up. Domestic car-makers then increased their prices to match those of the imported cars. The estimated cost in one year to consumers was $6.5 billion, or $250,000 for each of the 26,000 American jobs saved. The price was paid by American consumers.

Quotas and Tariffs. The U.S. government uses two key tools to restrict foreign trade: import quotas and tariffs. An **import quota** is a restriction imposed on the value or the number of units of a particular good that can be brought into the United States. **Tariffs** are taxes specifically on imports. Tariffs can be set as a particular dollar amount per unit—say, 10 cents per pound—or as a percentage of the value of the imported commodity.

Tariffs have been a part of the import landscape for two centuries. One of the most famous examples of the use of tariffs was the Smoot-Hawley Tariff Act of 1930.

Import Quota
A restriction imposed on the value or number of units of a particular good that can be brought into a country. Foreign suppliers are unable to sell more than the amount specified in the import quota.

Tariffs
Taxes on imports.

It included tariff schedules for more than 20,000 products, raising taxes on affected imports by an average of 52 percent. The Smoot-Hawley Tariff Act encouraged similar import-restricting policies by the rest of the world. Britain, France, the Netherlands, and Switzerland soon adopted high tariffs, too. The result was a massive reduction in international trade. According to many economists, this worsened the ongoing Great Depression.

Free-Trade Areas and Common Markets. To lower or even eliminate restrictions on free trade among nations, some nations and groups of nations have created free-trade areas, sometimes called common markets. The oldest and best-known common market is today called the European Union (EU). As of 2008, the EU consisted of 27 member nations. These countries have eliminated almost all restrictions on trade in both goods and services among themselves.

On our side of the Atlantic, the best-known free-trade zone consists of Canada, the United States, and Mexico. This free-trade zone was created by the North American Free Trade Agreement (NAFTA), approved by Congress in 1993. A more recent trade agreement is the Central American–Dominican Republic Free Trade Agreement (CAFTA-DR), which was signed into law by President George W. Bush in 2005. This agreement was formed by Costa Rica, the Dominican Republic, El Salvador, Guatemala, Honduras, Nicaragua, and the United States. Once the parties agree on an effective date, CAFTA-DR will reduce trade tariffs and improve market access among all of the signatory nations, including the United States.

THE WORLD TRADE ORGANIZATION

Since 1997, the principal institution overseeing tariffs throughout the world has been the World Trade Organization (WTO). The goal of the nations that created the WTO was to lessen trade barriers throughout the world, so that all nations can benefit from freer international trade.

What the WTO Does. The WTO's many tasks include administering trade agreements, acting as a forum for trade negotiations, settling trade disputes, and reviewing national trade policies. Today, the WTO has more than 140 member nations, accounting for more than 97 percent of world trade. Another 30 countries are negotiating to obtain membership. Since the WTO came into being, it has settled many trade disputes between countries, sometimes involving the United States.

For example, a few years ago, the United States, backed by five Latin American banana-exporting nations, argued before the WTO that the banana import rules of the European Union (EU) favored former European colonies in Africa and the Caribbean at the expense of Latin American growers and U.S. marketing companies. Specifically, Chiquita Banana claimed that its earnings had fallen because its competitors' bananas received preferential treatment from the EU. Because the EU would not back down, the United States imposed a 100 percent tariff on almost $200 million worth of EU items in nine categories. The right of the United States to impose the tariffs was backed by the WTO. Finally, the WTO brokered a deal between the United States and the EU. The EU agreed to dismantle its banana import policy that favored European multinationals and former European colonies. The United States agreed to drop the 100 percent tariff.

The WTO and Globalization. Opponents of globalization have settled on the WTO as the embodiment of their fears. As noted in Chapter 7, WTO meetings in recent years have been the occasion for widespread and sometimes violent demonstrations. The WTO raises serious political questions for many Americans. Although the WTO has arbitration boards to settle trade disputes, no country has veto power. Some people claim that a vetoless America will be repeatedly outvoted by the countries of Western Europe and East Asia. Some citizens' groups have warned that the unelected WTO bureaucrats based in Geneva, Switzerland, might be able to weaken environmental, health, and consumer safety laws, if such laws affect international trade flows.

The work of the WTO has met opposition in many regions of the world. During the 2003 meetings in Cancun, Mexico, African nations walked out of the "Doha Round" of negotiations because they disagreed with the more-developed nations over new rules for investments and cross-border transfers. One of the areas of the greatest disagreement in the WTO is the treatment of agriculture. Most developed nations subsidize their own farmers and want to protect them from competition from other countries. The United States and Europe are currently at odds over the reduction of agricultural subsidies, and further talks are stalled.[6]

THE BALANCE OF TRADE AND THE CURRENT ACCOUNT BALANCE

Balance of Trade
The difference between the value of a nation's exports of goods and the value of its imports of goods.

Current Account Balance
The current account balance includes the balance of trade in services, unilateral transfers, and other items. This is a wider concept than the balance of trade.

You may have heard on the news that the U.S. **balance of trade** is "negative" by some large figure. What does this announcement mean? To begin with, a negative balance of trade exists when the value of goods imported into a country is greater than the value of its exports. This situation is called a *trade deficit*. The United States has consistently had a large trade deficit since the late 1970s.

The Current Account Balance. The balance of trade is limited to trade in goods. A broader concept is the **current account balance**, which includes trade in services and sev-

---

[6]Jonathan Lynn, "Doha Round Negotiators Bear Down in Hopes of Deal This Year," *International Herald Tribune*, March 9, 2008.

eral other items. The United States has enjoyed a positive balance of trade in *services* for a long time. (Does the recent practice of outsourcing service jobs abroad change this fact? We examine this question in this chapter's *Beyond Our Borders* feature.) Like the balance of trade, however, the current account balance is negative and has been growing more negative for years. Figure 17–5 shows the growth in the current account deficit.

Are We Borrowing Too Much from Other Countries? If we run a current account deficit, as we have in recent years, we can finance it only by increasing our obligations to other countries. The increasing current account deficit shown in Figure 17–5 can also be viewed as an increase in the claims that foreigners have on our economy. These obligations to other countries can take a variety of forms. Foreigners can buy stocks on Wall Street. They can buy American businesses or real estate. Above all, they can buy U.S. Treasury bonds issued by the government to fund the federal budget deficit.

Have our obligations abroad, which by 2007 were increasing by more than $700 billion per year, become too large? It is true that during the last 20 years, the United

FIGURE 17–5 The Current Account Deficit

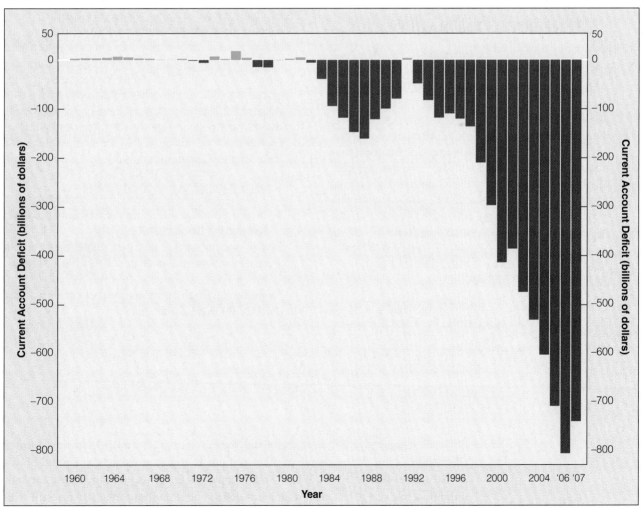

Source: U.S. Department of Commerce, Bureau of Economic Analysis, U.S. International Transactions Accounts Data, Table 1, June 18, 2006.

BEYOND OUR
B⊕RDERS

SENDING WORK OVERSEAS

For hundreds of years, nations have bought goods and services from abroad. Nonetheless, Americans have always perceived the purchase of services from other countries as a way of allowing those countries to "steal" American jobs. Today, such activity is called either *off-shoring* or *outsourcing*. During the 2008 presidential election campaigns, outsourcing continued to be a hot topic, particularly as factories continue to close in the United States.

OUTSOURCING PROBABLY EXAGGERATED

The latest data about outsourcing from the McKinsey Global Institute show that about 300,000 jobs per year are lost to overseas outsourcing firms. This may sound like a lot, but we must put that number in perspective: the U.S. labor market has close to 140 million workers! In any one month, more than 4 million U.S. residents start new jobs with new employers. Also, consider that from 1999 to 2003, according to the Institute for International Economics, the United States lost 125,000 programming jobs to foreign outsourcing, but it added 425,000 jobs for higher-skilled software analysts and engineers.

OUTSOURCING CHANGES TO MEET THE TIMES

Outsourcing is here to stay, but the countries to which jobs are outsourced may change. India and China were the leading "villains" in the outsourcing debate a few years ago, but other countries may soon take their place. Why? Wages for outsourcing services are rising rapidly in both of those countries. This means that other low-wage countries, such as the Philippines and Indonesia, may become larger providers of services.

Outsourcing service providers in India and China have seen the handwriting on the wall. In response, they are attempting to move into higher-tech activities. In India, for example, calls for customer service are increasingly being handled by automated systems, thereby reducing the demand for low-cost Indian workers in this low-tech field. A recent report suggested that Indian business sees legal processing as a profitable target for outsourcing. Legal processing would employ white-collar, highly trained individuals to do legal investigations, prepare contracts, write patents, and perform legal research for clients in other English-speaking, common law countries such as the United States, Canada, and Australia.*

FOR CRITICAL ANALYSIS

1. Do you think that outsourcing of jobs is an economic threat to the United States?
2. Will legal documents prepared abroad be an advantage in an American court or not?

*www.washingtonpost.com/wp-dyn/content/article/2008/05/10/AR2008051002355.html

States has enjoyed a larger share of the world's economic growth than any country other than China. Many people in other nations therefore consider the United States an attractive place to invest. While foreign appetites for investment in America are not unlimited, the rise in the current account deficit suggests that foreigners are still willing to invest in the United States.

THE POLITICS OF TAXES

Taxes are enacted by members of Congress. Today, the Internal Revenue Code encompasses thousands of pages, thousands of sections, and thousands of subsections—our tax system is very complex.

Americans pay a variety of different taxes. At the federal level, the income tax is levied on most sources of income. Social Security and Medicare taxes are assessed on wages and salaries. There is an income tax for corporations, which has an indirect effect on many individuals. The estate tax is collected from property left behind by those who have died. State and local governments also assess taxes on income, sales, and land. Altogether, the value of all taxes collected by the federal government and by state and local governments is about 30 percent of GDP. This is a substantial sum, but it is less than what many other countries collect, as you can see in Figure 17–6.

FEDERAL INCOME TAX RATES

Individuals and businesses pay taxes based on tax rates. Not all of your income is taxed at the same rate. The first few dollars you make are not taxed at all. The highest rate is imposed on the "last" dollar you make. This highest rate is the *marginal* tax rate. Table 17–2 shows the 2008 marginal tax rates for individuals and married couples. The higher the tax rate—the action on the part of the government—the greater the public's reaction to that tax rate. If the highest tax rate you pay on the income you make is 15 percent, then any method you can use to reduce your taxable income by one dollar saves you 15 cents in tax liabilities that you owe the federal government. Individuals paying a 15 percent rate have a relatively small incentive to avoid paying taxes, but consider the individuals who faced a marginal tax rate of 94 percent in the 1940s. They had a tremendous incentive to find legal ways to reduce their taxable incomes. For every dollar of income that was somehow deemed nontaxable, these taxpayers would reduce tax liabilities by 94 cents.

FIGURE 17–6 Total Amount of Taxes Collected as a Percentage of Gross Domestic Product (GDP) in Major Industrialized Nations

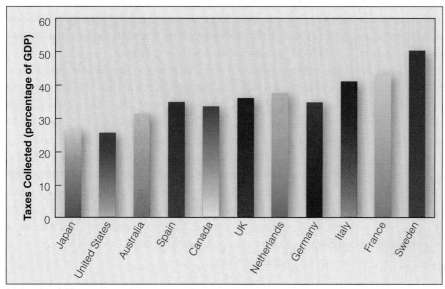

Source: The OECD Observer, *OECD in Figures—Volume 2006*, Supplement 1 (Organization for Economic Cooperation and Development, 2005).

TABLE 17–2 Marginal Tax Rates for Single Persons and Married Couples (2008)

SINGLE PERSONS		MARRIED FILING JOINTLY	
MARGINAL TAX BRACKET	MARGINAL TAX RATE	MARGINAL TAX BRACKET	MARGINAL TAX RATE
$0–$7,825	10%	$0–$15,650	10%
$7,825–$31,850	15%	$15,650–$63,700	15%
$31,850–$77,100	25%	$63,700–$128,500	25%
$77,100–$160,850	28%	$128,500–$195,850	28%
$160,850–$349,700	33%	$195,850–$349,700	33%
$349,700 and higher	35%	$349,700 and higher	35%

LOOPHOLES AND LOWERED TAXES

Loophole
A legal method by which individuals and businesses are allowed to reduce the tax liabilities owed to the government.

Individuals and corporations facing high tax rates will adjust their earning and spending behavior to reduce their taxes. They will also make concerted attempts to get Congress to add **loopholes** to the tax law that allow them to reduce their taxable incomes. When Congress imposed very high tax rates on high incomes, it also provided for more loopholes than it does today. For example, special provisions enabled investors in oil and gas wells to reduce their taxable incomes.

In 2001, President George W. Bush fulfilled a campaign pledge by persuading Congress to enact new legislation lowering tax rates for a period of several years. In 2003, rates were lowered again, retroactive to January 2003; these rates are reflected in Table 17–2. As a result of other changes contained in the new tax laws, the U.S. tax code became even more complicated than it was before. President Bush tried several times to renew his tax rate cuts on a permanent basis, but after Democrats took over Congress in 2006, the possibility of the cuts becoming permanent was gone.

Progressive Tax
A tax that rises in percentage terms as incomes rise.

Regressive Tax
A tax that falls in percentage terms as incomes rise.

Progressive and Regressive Taxation. As Table 17–2 shows, the greater your income, the higher the marginal tax rate. Persons with large incomes pay a larger share of their income in income tax. A tax system in which rates go up with income is called a **progressive tax** system. The federal income tax is clearly progressive.

The income tax is not the only tax you must pay. For example, the federal Social Security tax is levied on wage and salary income at a flat rate of 6.2 percent. (Employers pay another 6.2 percent, making the total effective rate 12.4 percent.) In 2008, however, there was no Social Security tax on wages and salaries in excess of $102,000. (This threshold changes from year to year.) Persons with very high salaries therefore pay no Social Security tax on much of their wages. In addition, the tax is not levied on investment income (including capital gains, rents, royalties, interest, dividends, or profits from a business). The wealthy receive a much greater share of their income from these sources than do the poor. As a result, the wealthy pay a much smaller portion of their income in Social Security taxes than do the working poor. The Social Security tax is therefore a **regressive tax**.

Who Pays? The question of whether the tax system should be progressive—and if so, to what degree—is subject to vigorous political

debate. Democrats in general and liberals in particular favor a tax system that is significantly progressive. Republicans and conservatives are more likely to prefer a tax system that is proportional or even regressive. For example, President Bush's tax cuts made the federal system somewhat less progressive, largely because they significantly reduced taxes on nonsalary income. If you look at Figure 17–7, you will see that almost half of all American households pay no federal income taxes at all, while the top 25 percent of all households pay more than 85 percent of all income taxes. Thus, the federal income tax is progressive, but the tax burden overall is much more complicated.

Overall, what kind of tax system do we have? The various taxes Americans pay pull in different directions. The Medicare tax, as applied to wages and salaries, is entirely flat—that is, neither progressive nor regressive. Because it is not levied on investment income, however, it is regressive overall. Sales taxes are regressive because the wealthy spend a relatively smaller portion of their income on items subject to the sales tax. Table 17–3 lists the characteristics of major taxes. Add everything up, and the tax system as a whole is probably slightly progressive.[7]

FIGURE 17–7 Federal Tax Burden by Income Group, 2005

Percentage of federal taxes paid as compared to percentage of gross national income earned by tiers, 2005.

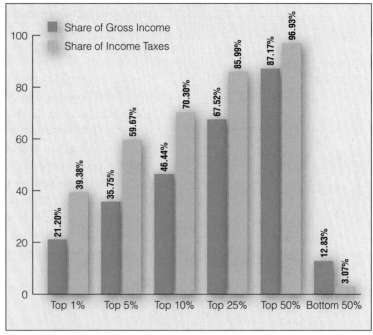

Source: The Tax Foundation, 2007. http://www.taxfoundation.org.

THE SOCIAL SECURITY PROBLEM

Closely related to the question of taxes in the United States is the viability of the Social Security system. Social Security taxes came into existence when the Federal Insurance Contribution Act (FICA) was passed in 1935. Social Security was established as a means of guaranteeing a minimum level of pension benefits to all persons. Today, many people regard Social Security as a kind of "social compact"—a national promise to successive generations that they will receive support in their old age.

TABLE 17–3 Progressive versus Regressive Taxes

PROGRESSIVE TAXES	REGRESSIVE TAXES
Federal Income Tax	Social Security Tax
State Income Taxes	Medicare Tax
Federal Corporate Income Tax	State Sales Taxes
Estate Tax	Local Real Estate Taxes

[7]Brian Roach, "GDAE Working Paper No. 03–10: Progressive and Regressive Taxation in the United States: Who's Really Paying (and Not Paying) Their Fair Share?" (Medford, MA: Global Development and Environment Institute, Tufts University, 2003). This paper is online at www.ase.tufts.edu/gdae/Pubs/wp/03-10-Tax_ Incidence.pdf.

FIGURE 17–8 Workers Per Social Security Retiree

The average number of workers per Social Security retiree has declined dramatically since the program began.

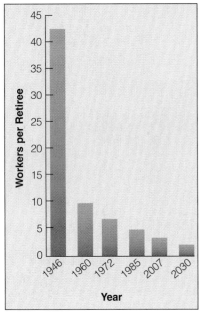

Sources: Social Security Administration; and authors' estimates.

To pay for Social Security, as of 2008, a 6.2 percent rate is imposed on each employee's wages up to a maximum of $102,000. Employers must pay in ("contribute") an equal percentage. In addition, a combined employer/employee 2.9 percent tax rate is assessed for Medicare on all wage income, with no upper limit. (Medicare is a federal program, begun in 1965, that pays hospital and physicians' bills for persons over the age of 65. See Chapters 7 and 16.)

SOCIAL SECURITY IS NOT A PENSION FUND

One of the problems with the Social Security system is that people who pay into Social Security think that they are actually paying into a fund, perhaps with their name on it. This is what you do when you pay into a private pension plan. It is not the case, however, with the federal Social Security system, which is basically a pay-as-you-go transfer system in which those who are working are paying benefits to those who are retired.

Currently, the number of people who are working relative to the number of people who are retiring is declining. Therefore, those who continue to work will have to pay more in Social Security taxes to fund the benefits of those who retire. In 2025, when the retirement of the Baby Boomer generation is almost complete, benefits are projected to cost almost 25 percent of taxable payroll income in the economy, compared with the current rate of 16 percent. In today's dollars, that amounts to more than $1 trillion of additional taxes annually.

WORKERS PER RETIREE

One way to think about the future bill that today's college students (and their successors) could face in the absence of fundamental changes in Social Security is to consider the number of workers available to support each retiree. As you can see in Figure 17–8, roughly three workers now provide for each retiree's Social Security, plus his or her Medicare benefits. Unless the current system is changed, by 2030 only two workers will be available to pay the Social Security and Medicare benefits due each recipient.

The growing number of people claiming the Social Security retirement benefit may pose less of a problem than the ballooning cost of Medicare. In the first place, an older population will require greater expenditures on medical care. In addition, however, medical expenditures *per person* are also increasing rapidly. Given continuing advances in medical science, Americans may logically wish to devote an ever-greater share of the national income to medical care. This choice puts serious pressure on federal and state budgets, however, because a large part of the nation's medical bill is funded by the government. The projected future increases in Medicaid (health insurance for the poor), Social Security, and Medicare are shown in Figure 17–9. As you can see, while Social Security expenditures will grow from 4.2 percent of the GDP to 6.1 percent, Medicare expenditures are expected to quadruple, going from 2.7 percent of the GDP in 2005 to 8.9 percent in 2050. To put this another way, by 2050, almost 20 percent of the gross domestic product of the United States will be devoted to entitlement spending, mostly on older Americans.

WHAT WILL IT TAKE TO SALVAGE SOCIAL SECURITY?

The facts just discussed illustrate why efforts to reform Social Security and Medicare have begun to dominate the nation's public agenda. What remains to be seen is how the government ultimately will resolve the problem. What, if anything, might be done?

Raise Taxes. One option is to raise the combined Social Security and Medicare payroll tax rate. A 2.2 percentage point hike in the payroll tax rate, to an overall rate of 17.5 percent, would yield an $80 billion annual increase in contributions. Such a tax increase would keep current taxes above current benefits until 2020, after which the system would again technically be in "deficit." Another option is to eliminate the current cap on the level of wages to which the Social Security payroll tax is applied; this measure would also generate about $80 billion per year in additional tax revenues. Nevertheless, even a combined policy of eliminating the wage cap and implementing a 2.2 percentage point tax increase would not keep tax collections above benefit payments over the long run.

Other Options. Proposals are also on the table to increase the age of full benefit eligibility, perhaps to as high as 70. In addition, many experts believe that increases in immigration offer the best hope of dealing with the tax burdens and workforce shrinkage of the future. Unless Congress changes the existing immigration system to permit the admission of a much larger number of working-age immigrants with useful skills, however, immigration is unlikely to relieve fully the pressure building due to our aging population.

FIGURE 17–9 Medicare, Medicaid, and Social Security Spending as a Percentage of GDP, 2005–2050

Projections of the increase in spending on these three programs as a proportion of the gross domestic product.

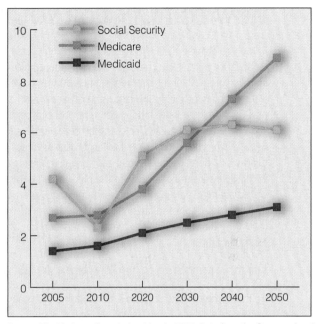

Source: The Heritage Foundation, March, 2008. Data from the Congressional Budget Office Long-term Budget Outlook, December, 2007.

Privatizing Social Security. Still another proposal calls for partially privatizing the Social Security system in the hope of increasing the rate of return on individuals' retirement contributions. Privatization would allow workers to invest a specified portion of their Social Security payroll taxes in the stock market and possibly in other investment options, such as bonds or real estate. Although such a solution would have been unthinkable in past decades, today there is some support for the idea. If the economy is good and the stock market grows, then the increased value of these investments would provide more benefits to individuals when they retire. Indeed, President George W. Bush's proposal that Social Security be partially privatized in this way drew significant support from younger Americans but total opposition from most members of Congress and the AARP.

Several groups oppose the concept of partial privatization. These groups fear that the diversion of Social Security funds into individual investment portfolios could jeopardize the welfare of future retirees, who could be at the mercy of the volatile stock market. Opponents of partial privatization point out that such a plan might mean that workers would have to pay for two systems for many years—the benefits for today's retirees cannot simply be abolished.

Obviously, solving the problem of increasing Social Security and Medicare obligations is a task for future presidents and Congresses. While it will be a controversial issue, most Americans are aware that it must be solved.

You can make a difference

HOW TO PLAN FOR YOUR FUTURE

If you are between 20 and 40 today, you may likely live to be 100 years old. That might sound incredible, but how do you plan for a retirement that could last 40 years? Retirement is probably the last thing on your mind right now, with college loans and credit card debt to be paid. Today's college graduates kick off their careers more than $20,000 in debt, on average. College costs have soared; tuition has increased 28 percent for private colleges and 38 percent for public colleges in the past 10 years. Meanwhile, average earnings have not kept pace; men with a bachelor's degree today earn only 5.45 percent more than they did a decade ago, with women earning about 10.4 percent more.

WHY SHOULD YOU CARE?

As the common saying goes, a comfortable retirement is based on a "three-legged stool" of Social Security, pensions, and savings. Several trends are working against today's college graduates. Unless reforms are enacted to shore up the system, Social Security benefits for future retirees, who are now in their 20s, could be cut by more than 20 percent and be reduced every year thereafter. The traditional pension is disappearing from the workplace, with more employers favoring 401(k) plans that allow you to save with pre-tax contributions. Today's young employees are expected to invest in these employer-sponsored retirement plans, which allow them to choose from a mix of investment options and may have employers matching contributions. You may also choose to save through individual retirement accounts (IRAs), stocks, bonds, mutual funds, and cash accounts such as bank savings accounts, certificates of deposit (CDs), and money market funds.

The point of this is that when it comes to retirement, young workers are on their own and need a plan for future financial security.

WHAT CAN YOU DO?

Money compounds over time, so the earlier you invest, the greater your yield will be. Compound interest means that you earn interest on the original amount you've saved, and you continue to earn interest on the interest. The longer your money is invested, the more compounding can work for you. The earlier you start, the less you have to save to reach your goal. The longer you wait, the harder it is to make up for lost interest earnings. For example, if you have a goal to save $100,000 and have 20 years to do so, at a conservative 4 percent rate of return, you would need to invest $3,272 per year; compounding will do the rest of the work for you. If you needed to save the same $100,000 and only had 10 years to do so, you would have to save more and take more risk. Even with an 8 percent rate of return, you would need to save $6,559 each year.

When you make saving money a part of your lifestyle at a young age, it will become a habit, not an option. As you begin your career, make sure you take advantage of all savings options at your disposal. Here are a few key questions you should ask any potential or current employer:

Is there a traditional benefit pension plan?
Is there a 401(k) or other contribution plan and, if so, are your contributions matched?
How soon can you join the plan?
What are the plan's vesting rules, and what happens to your money if you leave the company?

Your employer may have plans to help you save for your future, but the responsibility really lies with you. Financial experts agree on a few simple rules to keep you on track to your goals: avoid credit card debt, track expenses and spend within a monthly budget, maintain three to six months of savings equivalent to living expenses in a short-term account, contribute the maximum allowed to your 401(k), take advantage of any "free money" company matches, and maintain savings beyond employer-sponsored plans, like individual retirement accounts (IRAs).

Choose to Save, a program of the nonprofit Employee Benefit Research Institute and the American Savings Education Council, was created in 1996 to promote individual savings. Their Web site, **www.choosetosave.org**, provides free savings tools and information to help plan for financial security. Retirement planning worksheets, interactive financial calculators, DVDs, and other materials are available. You can also contact them at:

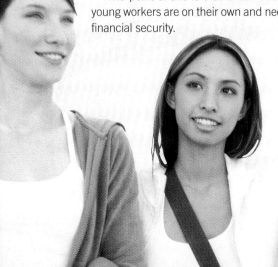

Choose to Save
1100 13th St. NW, Suite 878
Washington, DC 20005
202-659-0670

To monitor reforms in Social Security, you can contact them at:

Social Security Administration
Office of Public Inquiries
Windsor Park Bldg.
6401 Security Blvd.
Baltimore, MD 21235
800-772-1213
www.ssa.gov

REFERENCES

Aleksandra Todorova, "What Will Retirement Be Like for Gens X and Y?" *Smart Money*, May 15, 2007. www.smartmoney .com.
www.choosetosave.org
www.ssa.gov

KEY TERMS

automatic, or built-in, stabilizers 608
balance of trade 618
budget deficit 607
consumer price index (CPI) 604
current account balance 618
exports 615
Federal Open Market Committee 612
Federal Reserve System (the Fed) 612

fiscal policy 606
full employment 603
gross domestic product (GDP) 609
gross public debt 609
import quota 616
imports 615
inflation 602
Keynesian economics 607
loophole 622
loose monetary policy 613

monetary policy 613
net public debt 609
progressive tax 622
recession 603
regressive tax 622
tariffs 616
tight monetary policy 613
unemployment 603
U.S. Treasury bond 609
wage and price controls 608

CHAPTER SUMMARY

1. One of the most important policy goals of the federal government is to maintain economic growth without falling into either excessive unemployment or inflation (rising prices). Inflation is commonly measured using the Consumer Price Index (CPI) published by the U.S. Bureau of Labor Statistics. The regular fluctuations in the economy are called business cycles. If the economy fails to grow for six months or more, the nation is experiencing a recession.

2. Fiscal policy is the use of taxes and spending to affect the overall economy. Economist John Maynard Keynes is credited with developing a theory under which the government should run budget deficits during recessions to stimulate the economy. Keynes also advocated budget surpluses in boom times, but political leaders have been reluctant to implement this side of the policy. Time lags in implementing fiscal policy can create serious difficulties.

3. The federal government has run a deficit in most years since the 1930s. The deficit is met by U.S. Treasury borrowing. This adds to the public debt of the U.S. government. Although the budget was temporarily in surplus from 1998 to 2002, deficits now seem likely for many years to come.

4. Monetary policy is controlled by the Federal Reserve System, or the Fed. Monetary policy involves changing the rate of growth of the money supply in an attempt to either stimulate or cool the economy. A loose monetary policy, in which more money is created, encourages economic growth. A tight monetary policy, in which less money is created, may be the only effective way of ending an inflationary spiral. Monetary policy may, however, be ineffectual in pulling the economy out of a severe recession—fiscal policy may be required.

5. World trade has grown rapidly since 1950. The United States imports and exports goods as well as services.

While economists of all persuasions strongly support world trade, the public is less enthusiastic. Restrictions on imports to protect jobs are often popular. Ultimately, however, imports are paid for by exports. Restricting imports restricts exports as well, with resulting loss of employment in export industries. Trade restrictions also increase the cost of the affected goods to consumers.

6. Groups of nations have established free-trade blocs to encourage trade among themselves. Examples include the European Union and the North American Free Trade Association (NAFTA). The World Trade Organization (WTO) is an international organization that oversees trade disputes and provides a forum for negotiations to reduce trade restrictions. The WTO has been a source of controversy in American politics.

7. The current account balance includes the balance of trade, which is limited to goods, and also the balance in the trade of services and other items. A possible problem for the future is the growing size of the U.S. current account deficit, which is funded by foreign investments in the United States.

8. U.S. taxes amount to about 30 percent of the gross domestic product, which is not particularly high by international standards. Individuals and corporations that pay taxes at the highest rates will try to pressure Congress into creating exemptions and tax loopholes, which allow high-income earners to reduce their taxable incomes. The federal income tax is progressive; that is, tax rates increase as income increases. Some other taxes, such as the Social Security tax and state sales taxes, are regressive—they take a larger share of the income of poorer people. As a whole, the tax system is slightly progressive.

9. Closely related to the question of taxes is the viability of the Social Security and Medicare systems. As the number of people who are retired increases relative to the number of people who are working, those who are working may have to pay more for the benefits of those who retire. Proposed solutions to the problem include raising taxes, reducing benefits, allowing more immigration, and partially privatizing the Social Security system in hopes of obtaining higher rates of return on contributions.

SELECTED PRINT AND MEDIA RESOURCES

SUGGESTED READINGS

Friedman, Milton, and Walter Heller. *Monetary versus Fiscal Policy.* New York: Norton, 1969. This is a classic presentation of the pros and cons of monetary and fiscal policy given by a noninterventionist (Friedman) and an advocate of federal government intervention in the economy (Heller).

Hira, Ron, and Anil Hira. *Outsourcing America: The True Cost of Shipping Jobs Overseas and What Can be Done About It.* New York: AMACON, 2008. The authors look closely at the effects of outsourcing on the American economy and make suggestions to political leaders on how to bring jobs back to the United States.

Hundt, Reed. *In China's Shadow: The Crisis of American Entrepreneurship.* New Haven, CT: Yale University Press, 2006. The author explores the foreseeable challenges that the American economy faces from China.

Kotlikoff, Laurence J., and Scott Burns. *The Coming Generational Storm: What You Need to Know about America's Economic Future.* Cambridge, MA: MIT Press, 2004. The authors explain how an aging population will create a crisis in Social Security and Medicare funding. One possible flaw in the authors' argument is their unquestioning use of very long-term demographic projections, which are inherently uncertain.

Phillips, Kevin. *Bad Money, Reckless Finance, Failed Politics, and the Global Crisis of American Capitalism.* New York: Viking, 2008. This best-selling author and former reporter for *The New York Times* investigates the deterioration of U.S. influence in the world and the causes of the prime mortgage crisis.

MEDIA RESOURCES

Alan Greenspan—This rather laudatory biography of the former chair of the Federal Reserve was released in 1999. Using Greenspan as an example, the film looks at factors that influence the world and national economies.

e-mocracy

SHOW ME THE E-MONEY

The age of e-commerce has brought with it several challenges for economic policy makers. One economic policy issue has to do with electronic money, or *e-money*. In one type of e-money, a balance of funds is recorded on a magnetic stripe on a card; each time the card is used, a computer terminal debits funds from the balance. Another type uses a microprocessor chip embedded in a so-called *smart card*. E-money is sometimes referred to as *e-cash*, because it can be used like cash, meaning that no personally identifiable records are created. The problem for policy makers is that e-cash moves outside the network of banks, checks, and paper currency. With the growth of e-cash, the traditional definition of money will no longer hold, giving the Federal Reserve less ability to control the money supply.

LOGGING ON

- You can keep up with actions taken by the Federal Reserve by checking the home page of the Federal Reserve Bank of San Francisco at:
  www.frbsf.org
- For further information on Social Security, access the Social Security Administration's home page at:
  www.ssa.gov

- For information on the 2009 budget of the U.S. government, go to:
  www.whitehouse.gov/omb/budget/fy2007
- If you are interested in federal tax policy and would like to read several studies on its impact, go to the Web site of the Tax Foundation, a private think tank, at:
  www.taxfoundation.org
- For more information about world trade and the World Trade Organization, go to:
  www.wto.org

ONLINE REVIEW

At **www.cengage.com/politicalscience/schmidt/agandpt14e**, you will find a Tutorial Quiz for this chapter providing questions on the chapter contents, including the features. The questions are organized to match the major sections of the chapter. You'll have access to other helpful study tools, including the book's glossary and flashcards, crossword puzzles, and Web links, as well as "Which Side Are You On?" and "Politics and . . ." features written by the authors of the book.

A Somali boy helps push a donkey cart filled with food aid given to refugee families by the United Nations World Food Program. The aid was sent from the United States to feed refugees displaced by violence in that country. (Roberto Schmidt/Getty Images)

CHAPTER

(18)

FOREIGN POLICY AND NATIONAL SECURITY

QUESTIONS TO CONSIDER

What should be the goals of American foreign policy?

Should the United States play the role of global police officer?

Who should formulate foreign policy: the president or Congress?

CHAPTER CONTENTS

Making a DIFFERENCE

THINK TANKS

Why is the price of gasoline so high? What is the effect of the demand for oil from emerging markets like China? Should the United States empty out its Strategic Petroleum Reserves to combat the low production from oil-producing nations?[a] Would that have a detrimental effect on our ability to respond should we need to send troops and ships into a military situation? Can the United States meet the oil-price crisis alone, or would a coalition of nations have more influence on oil producers?

Policy makers need experts to help them answer these questions, and they often turn to think tanks for this expertise. Former State Department advisor Richard Haas called the influence of these "idea factories" "among the most important and least appreciated."[b] Emerging at the beginning of the 20th century, think tanks were named for the small rooms in which research scientists and military strategists plotted the conduct of World War II. They have proliferated; more than 2,000 of these organizations are based in the United States alone. Most are nonprofit and nonpartisan, although many advocate particular ideological perspectives. Some are so-called legacy organizations, like the Carter Center, the Hoover Institute, or the Nixon Center for Peace and Freedom. Some are attached to universities, like the Harvard Kennedy School, and some are independent, like the RAND Corporation.[c] Throughout the 1960s and 1970s, advocacy think tanks emerged, such as the conservative Heritage Foundation (1973) and the libertarian Cato Institute (1977), named for the libertarian pamphlets written during the American Revolution.[d]

In addition to seeking ideas from think tanks, there is a revolving door between think tanks and government.[e] Many U.S. government officials have worked for think tanks, often serving as officials in previous presidential administrations. For example, Zbigniew Brzezinski, who was President Carter's national security advisor, is a counselor for the Center for Strategic and International Studies. Lee Feinstein has been a Senior Fellow for U.S. Foreign Policy and International Law at the Council on Foreign

ON SEPTEMBER 11, 2001, Americans were forced to change their view of national security and of our relations with the rest of the world—literally overnight. No longer could citizens of the United States believe that national security issues involved only threats overseas or that the American homeland could not be attacked. No longer could Americans believe that regional conflicts in other parts of the world had no direct impact on the United States.

Within a few days, it became known that the attacks on the World Trade Center and on the Pentagon had been planned and carried out by a terrorist network named al Qaeda that was funded and directed by the radical Islamist leader Osama bin Laden. The network was closely linked to the Taliban government of Afghanistan, which had ruled that nation since 1996.

Americans were shocked by the complexity and the success of the attacks. They wondered how our airport security systems could have failed so drastically. How could the Pentagon, the heart of the nation's defense, have been successfully attacked? Shouldn't our intelligence community have known about and defended against this network? And, finally, how could our foreign policy have been so blind to the anger voiced by Islamist groups throughout the world?

Relations and was a senior official in President Clinton's Department of State. James Baker was the Secretary of State under George H. W. Bush and now is the honorary head of the James A. Baker III Institute for Public Policy at Rice University.[f] Aside from providing personnel for executive branch policy positions, think tanks also try to influence opinion through publications, press releases, opinion editorials (op-eds), and media appearances.

Returning to the questions posed earlier about rising oil prices, in a 2006 op-ed in the *Washington Times*, an analyst for RAND argued that the United States has little control over oil prices and that the government should encourage alternative fuels like ethanol and increase supply by opening up drilling in the protected Arctic National Wildlife Reserve (ANWR),[g] a move opposed by some environmental groups. Similarly, in 2008, representatives from the Cato Institute recommended drilling in ANWR as well as opening up federally protected land in the Mountain West to oil shale development. Cato also advocates draining the Strategic Petroleum Reserves, arguing that threats to our national security from worldwide oil embargoes against us are exaggerated.[h] While the American Enterprise Institute places the "blame" for high oil prices on increased demand from emerging markets,[i] George Soros (whose foundation has funded several advocacy groups and think tanks) has argued the cause involves the complex relationship among competing and complicated factors.[j] As we watch the foreign policy of the new presidential administration take shape, we will surely see its connections to these powerful think tanks.

[a]The Strategic Petroleum Reserves is a large stockpile of emergency petroleum, controlled by the U.S. Department of Energy, created after the 1973–74 oil embargo. www.fossil.energy.gov/programs/reserves/#Strategic%20Petroleum%20Reserve, accessed June 4, 2008.

[b]Richard Haass, "Think Tanks and U.S. Foreign Policy: A Policy-Maker's Perspective," *U.S. Foreign Policy Agenda, An Electronic Journal of the U.S. Department of State*, Vol. 7, 2000, pp. 5–8, accessed June 1, 2008, at http://usinfo.state.gov/journals/itps/1102/ijpe/ijpe1102.pdf.

[c]Donald E. Abelson, "Think Tanks and U.S. Foreign Policy: An Historical View," *U.S. Foreign Policy Agenda, An Electronic Journal of the U.S. Department of State*, Vol. 7, 2000, pp. 9–12.

[d]www.cato.org/about.php, accessed June 5, 2008.

[e]*U.S. Foreign Policy Agenda, An Electronic Journal of the U.S. Department of State*, Vol. 7, 2000, pp. 39–40, accessed June 1, 2008, at http://usinfo.state.gov/journals/itps/1102/ijpe/ijpe1102.pdf.

[f]*Ibid.*

[g]www.rand.org/commentary/051906WT.html

[h]www.cato.org/pub_display.php?pub_id=9438

[i]www.aei.org/publications/pubID.27426,filter.all/pub_detail.asp

[j]He argues that subsidies foreign countries place on their production of oil, the profit margins on oil exploration and development, and speculative buying on world commodities markets have all driven the price of oil upward. www.salon.com/tech/htww/2008/06/03/soros_oil_bubble_2/, accessed June 3, 2008.

In this chapter, we examine the tools of foreign policy and national security policy in light of the many challenges facing the United States today. As indicated in the *Making a Difference* feature, many schools of thought about how to meet these challenges exist, and many of the experts from think tanks will become members of the new president's administration.

FACING THE WORLD: FOREIGN AND DEFENSE POLICY

The United States is only one nation in a world with more than 200 independent countries, each of which has its own national goals and interests. What tools does our nation have to deal with the many challenges to its peace and prosperity? One tool is **foreign policy**. By this term, we mean both the goals the government wants to achieve in the world and the techniques and strategies used to achieve them. For example, if one national goal is to achieve stability in the Middle East and to encourage the formation of pro-American governments there, U.S. foreign policy in that area may be carried out through **diplomacy, economic aid, technical assistance**, or military intervention.

Foreign Policy
A nation's external goals and the techniques and strategies used to achieve them.

Diplomacy
The process by which states carry on political relations with each other; settling conflicts among nations by peaceful means.

Economic Aid
Assistance to other nations in the form of grants, loans, or credits to buy the assisting nation's products.

Technical Assistance
The practice of sending experts in such areas as agriculture, engineering, or business to aid other nations.

Sometimes foreign policies are restricted to statements of goals or ideas, such as helping to end world poverty, whereas at other times foreign policies are comprehensive efforts to achieve particular objectives, such as changing the regime in Iraq.

As you will read later in this chapter, in the United States, the **foreign policy process** usually originates with the president and those agencies that provide advice on foreign policy matters. Congressional action and national public debate often affect foreign policy formulation.

Foreign Policy Process
The steps by which foreign policy goals are decided and acted on.

NATIONAL SECURITY POLICY

As one aspect of overall foreign policy, **national security policy** is designed primarily to protect the independence and the political integrity of the United States. It concerns itself with the defense of the United States against actual or potential (real or imagined) enemies, domestic or foreign.

U.S. national security policy is based on determinations made by the Department of Defense, the Department of State, and many other federal agencies, including the National Security Council (NSC). The NSC acts as an advisory body to the president, but it has increasingly become a rival to the State Department in influencing the foreign policy process.

Defense policy is a subset of national security policy. Generally, defense policy refers to the set of policies that direct the scale and size of the U.S. armed forces. Among the questions defense policy makers must consider is the number of major wars the United States should be prepared to fight simultaneously. Defense policy also considers the types of armed forces units we need to have, such as Rapid Defense Forces or Marine Expeditionary Forces, and the types of weaponry that should be developed and maintained for the nation's security. Defense policies are proposed by the leaders of the nation's military forces and the Secretary of Defense and are greatly influenced by Congressional decision makers.

National Security Policy
Foreign and domestic policy designed to protect the nation's independence and political and economic integrity; policy that is concerned with the safety and defense of the nation.

Defense Policy
A subset of national security policies having to do with the U.S. armed forces.

DIPLOMACY

Diplomacy is another aspect of foreign policy. Diplomacy includes all of a nation's external relationships, from routine diplomatic communications to summit meetings among heads of state. More specifically, diplomacy refers to the settling of disputes and conflicts among nations by peaceful methods. Diplomacy is the set of negotiating techniques by which a nation attempts to carry out its foreign policy.

Diplomacy can be carried out by individual nations, by groups of nations, or by international organizations. The United Nations often spearheads diplomatic actions in the interests of maintaining peace in certain areas. For example, in 2006, several incidents set off an ever-escalating war between Israel and Hezbollah, a militant Shiite Islamist group that attempts to control Lebanon. While Israeli aircraft bombed Hezbollah's positions and Hezbollah fighters shelled Israeli cities, diplomatic efforts persisted at the United Nations, eventually reaching a peace settlement.

Over the past 50 years, American presidents have often exercised diplomacy to encourage peace in the Middle East. The most successful example was President Jimmy Carter's efforts in 1978 to get Israel and Egypt to agree to a path to peaceful relations. The Camp David Accords were negotiated in the United States by the leaders of Egypt and Israel, with the direct mediation of President Carter. The two countries agreed to work toward peace between them, including mutual recognition.[1]

[1]To read the text of the Camp David Accords, go to: www.jimmycarterlibrary.org/documents/campdavid/accords/phtml.

Diplomacy can be successful only if the parties are willing to negotiate. Diplomacy clearly failed before the First Gulf War and perhaps before the second (some observers believe that the United States did not give diplomacy a long enough time to work to avoid the Second Gulf War). The United States continues to work with European allies to pressure Iran to reject the development of nuclear weapons and—through talks including Russia, China, Japan, South Korea, and North Korea—to persuade North Korea to end its weapons development. In the summer of 2008, North Korea agreed to hand over its long-awaited nuclear program declaration to Chinese officials, and it blew up a cooling tower at one of its nuclear facilities to demonstrate its desire to move forward in ending its weapons program.

MORALITY VERSUS REALITY IN FOREIGN POLICY

From the earliest years of the republic, Americans have felt that their nation had a special destiny. The American experiment in democratic government and capitalism, it was thought, would provide the best possible life for men and women and be a model for other nations. As the United States assumed greater status as a power in world politics, Americans came to believe that the nation's actions on the world stage should be guided by American political and moral principles. As Harry Truman stated, "The United States should take the lead in running the world in the way that it ought to be run."

MORAL IDEALISM

This view of America's mission has led to the adoption of many foreign policy initiatives that are rooted in **moral idealism**. This philosophy sees the world as fundamentally benign and assumes that most nations can be persuaded to take moral considerations into account when setting their policies.[2] In this perspective, nations should come

Moral Idealism
A philosophy that sees nations as normally willing to cooperate and to agree on moral standards for conduct.

AN AMERICAN PEACE CORPS volunteer works with students in a Kenyan school. (Courtesy of the Peace Corps Press Office)

[2]Eugene R. Wittkopf, Charles W. Kegley, and James M. Scott, *American Foreign Policy*, 6th ed. (Belmont, CA: Wadsworth Publishing, 2002).

together and agree to keep the peace, as President Woodrow Wilson (served 1913–1921) proposed for the League of Nations. Many of the foreign policy initiatives taken by the United States have been based on this idealistic view of the world. The Peace Corps, which was created by President John Kennedy in 1961, is one example of an effort to spread American goodwill and technology that has achieved some of its goals. In fact, Kennedy once said that the United States would "pay any price" and "bear any burden" to further liberty in the world.

POLITICAL REALISM

Political Realism
A philosophy that sees each nation acting principally in its own interest.

In opposition to the moral perspective is **political realism**, often called *realpolitik* (a German word meaning "realistic politics"). Realists see the world as a dangerous place in which each nation strives for its own survival and interests regardless of moral considerations. The United States must also base its foreign policy decisions on cold calculations without regard for morality. Realists believe that the United States must be prepared to defend itself militarily, because all other nations are, by definition, out to improve their own situations. A strong defense will show the world that the United States is willing to protect its interests. The practice of political realism in foreign policy allows the United States to sell weapons to military dictators who will support its policies, to support American business around the globe, and to repel terrorism through the use of force.

AMERICAN FOREIGN POLICY—A MIXTURE OF BOTH

It is important to note that the United States has never been guided by only one of these principles. Instead, both moral idealism and political realism affect foreign policy making. President George W. Bush drew on the tradition of morality in foreign policy when he declared that the al Qaeda network of Osama bin Laden was "evil" and that fighting terrorism was fighting evil. To actually wage war on the Taliban in Afghanistan, however, U.S. forces needed the right to use the airspace of India and Pakistan, neighbors of Afghanistan. The United States had previously criticized both of these South Asian nations because they had developed and tested nuclear weapons. In addition, the United States had taken the moral stand that it would not deliver certain fighter aircraft to Pakistan as long as it continued its weapons program. When it became absolutely necessary to work with India and Pakistan, the United States switched to a realist policy, promising aid and support to both regimes in return for their assistance in the war on terrorism.

The Second Gulf War that began in 2003 also revealed a mixture of idealism and realism. While the primary motive for invading Iraq was realistic (the interests of U.S. security), another goal of the war reflected idealism—the liberation of the Iraqi people from an oppressive regime and the establishment of a democratic model in the Middle East. The reference to the war effort as Operation Iraqi Freedom emphasized this idealistic goal.

In 2008, Secretary of State Condoleezza Rice wrote about the future of American foreign policy, noting that "The old dichotomy between realism and idealism has never really applied to the United States, because we do not really accept that our national interest and our universal ideals are at odds. . . . Even when our interests and our ideals come into tension in the short run, we believe that in the long run they are indivisible."[3]

_____

[3]Condoleezza Rice, "Rethinking the National Interest: American Realism for a New World," *Foreign Affairs*, July/August 2008.

THE MAJOR FOREIGN POLICY THEMES

Although some observers might suggest that U.S. foreign policy is inconsistent and changes with each occupant of the White House, the long view of American diplomatic ventures reveals some major themes underlying foreign policy. In the early years of the nation, presidents and the people generally agreed that the United States should avoid foreign entanglements and concentrate instead on its own development. From the beginning of the 20th century until today, however, a major theme has been increasing global involvement. The theme of the post-World War II years was the containment of communism. The theme for at least the first part of the 21st century may be the containment of terrorism.

THE FORMATIVE YEARS: AVOIDING ENTANGLEMENTS

Foreign policy was largely nonexistent during the formative years of the United States. Remember that the new nation was operating under the Articles of Confederation. The national government had no right to levy or collect taxes, no control over commerce, no right to make commercial treaties, and no power to raise an army (the Revolutionary army was disbanded in 1783). The government's lack of international power was made clear when Barbary pirates seized American hostages in the Mediterranean. The United States was unable to rescue the hostages and ignominiously had to purchase them in a treaty with Morocco.

The founders of this nation had a basic mistrust of European governments. George Washington said it was the U.S. policy "to steer clear of permanent alliances," and Thomas Jefferson echoed this sentiment when he said America wanted peace with all nations but "entangling alliances with none." This was also a logical position at a time when the United States was so weak militarily that it could not influence European development directly. Moreover, being protected by oceans that took weeks to traverse certainly allowed the nation to avoid entangling alliances. During the 1800s, therefore, the United States generally stayed out of European conflicts and politics. In this hemisphere, however, the United States pursued an actively expansionist policy. The nation purchased Louisiana in 1803, annexed Texas in 1845, gained substantial territory from Mexico in 1848, purchased Alaska in 1867, and annexed Hawaii in 1898.

The Monroe Doctrine. President James Monroe, in his message to Congress on December 2, 1823, stated that the United States would not accept foreign intervention in the Western Hemisphere. In return, the United States would not meddle in European affairs. The **Monroe Doctrine** was the underpinning of the U.S. **isolationist foreign policy** toward Europe, which continued throughout the 1800s.

The Spanish-American War and World War I. The end of the isolationist policy started with the Spanish-American War in 1898. Winning the war gave the United States possession of Guam, Puerto Rico, and the Philippines (which gained independence in 1946). On the

AN ELDERLY IRAQI WOMAN casts her vote in a ballot box at the Al-Zahraa hospital in Al-Sadr city, east of Baghdad, Iraq. (Karim Kadim/AP Photo)

Monroe Doctrine
A policy statement made by President James Monroe in 1823, which set out three principles: (1) European nations should not establish new colonies in the Western Hemisphere; (2) European nations should not intervene in the affairs of independent nations of the Western Hemisphere; and (3) the United States would not interfere in the affairs of European nations.

Isolationist Foreign Policy
A policy of abstaining from an active role in international affairs or alliances, which characterized U.S. foreign policy toward Europe during most of the 1800s.

heels of that war came World War I (1914–1918). In his re-election campaign of 1916, President Woodrow Wilson ran on the slogan "He kept us out of war." Nonetheless, the United States declared war on Germany on April 6, 1917, because that country refused to give up its campaign of sinking all ships headed for Britain, including passenger ships. (Large passenger ships of that time commonly held more than a thousand people, so the sinking of such a ship was a disaster comparable to the attack on the World Trade Center.)

In the 1920s, the United States went "back to normalcy," as President Warren G. Harding urged it to do. U.S. military forces were largely disbanded, defense spending dropped to about 1 percent of total annual national income, and the nation returned to a period of isolationism.

THE ERA OF INTERNATIONALISM

Isolationism was permanently shattered by the bombing of the U.S. naval base at Pearl Harbor, Hawaii, on December 7, 1941. The surprise attack by the Japanese caused the deaths of 2,403 American servicemen and wounded 1,143 others. Eighteen warships were sunk or seriously damaged, and 188 planes were destroyed at the airfields. The American public was outraged. President Franklin Roosevelt asked Congress to declare war on Japan immediately, and the United States entered World War II. This unequivocal response was certainly due to the nature of the provocation. American soil had not been attacked by a foreign power since the occupation of Washington, D.C., by the British in 1814.

The United States was the only major participating country to emerge from World War II with its economy intact, and even strengthened. Britain, France, Germany, Italy, Japan, the Soviet Union, and several minor participants in the war were economically devastated. The United States was also the only country to have control over opera-

A PORTRAIT OF President James Monroe by Gilbert Stuart. The Monroe Doctrine essentially made the Western Hemisphere the concern of the United States. (Library of Congress Prints & Photographs Division, Washington, D.C. [LC-USZ62-117118])

BRITISH PRIME MINISTER Winston Churchill, U.S. President Franklin Roosevelt, and Soviet leader Joseph Stalin met at Yalta from February 4 to 11, 1945, to resolve their differences over the shape that the international community would take after World War II. (Library of Congress Prints & Photographs Division, Washington, D.C. [LC-USZ62-7449])

tional nuclear weapons. President Harry Truman had made the decision to use two atomic bombs, on August 6 and August 9, 1945, to end the war with Japan. (Historians still argue over the necessity of this action, which ultimately killed more than 100,000 Japanese and left an equal number permanently injured.) The United States truly had become the world's superpower.

The Cold War. The United States had become an uncomfortable ally of the Soviet Union after Adolf Hitler's invasion of that country. Soon after World War II ended, relations between the Soviet Union and the West deteriorated. The Soviet Union wanted a weakened Germany, and to achieve this, it insisted that Germany be divided in two, with East Germany becoming a buffer against the West. Little by little, the Soviet Union helped install communist governments in Eastern European countries, which began to be referred to collectively as the **Soviet bloc**. In response, the United States encouraged the rearming of Western Europe. The **Cold War** had begun.[4]

In Fulton, Missouri, on March 5, 1946, Winston Churchill, in a striking metaphor, declared that from the Baltic to the Adriatic Sea "an iron curtain has descended across the [European] continent." The term **iron curtain** became even more appropriate when Soviet-dominated East Germany built a wall separating East Berlin from West Berlin in August 1961.

Containment Policy. In 1947, a remarkable article was published in *Foreign Affairs*. The article was signed by "X." The actual author was George F. Kennan, chief of the policy-planning staff for the State Department. The doctrine of **containment** set forth in the article became—according to many—the bible of Western foreign policy. The author "X" argued that whenever and wherever the Soviet Union could successfully challenge the West, it would do so. He recommended that our policy toward the Soviet Union be "firm and vigilant containment of Russian expansive tendencies."[5]

The containment theory was expressed clearly in the **Truman Doctrine**, which was enunciated by President Harry Truman in his historic address to Congress on March 12, 1947. In that address, he announced that the United States must help countries in which a communist takeover seemed likely. Later that year, he backed the Marshall Plan, an economic assistance plan for Europe that was intended to prevent the expansion of communist influence there. By 1950, the United States had entered into a military alliance with the European nations commonly called the North Atlantic Treaty Organization (NATO). The combined military power of the United States and the European nations worked to contain Soviet influence to Eastern Europe and to maintain a credible response to any Soviet military attack on Western Europe. Figure 18–1 shows the face-off between the U.S.-led NATO alliance and the Soviet-led Warsaw Pact.

Soviet Bloc
The Soviet Union and the Eastern European countries that installed communist regimes after World War II and were dominated by the Soviet Union.

Cold War
The ideological, political, and economic confrontation between the United States and the Soviet Union following World War II.

Iron Curtain
The term used to describe the division of Europe between the Soviet bloc and the West; coined by Winston Churchill.

Containment
A U.S. diplomatic policy adopted by the Truman administration to contain communist power within its existing boundaries.

Truman Doctrine
The policy adopted by President Harry Truman in 1947 to halt communist expansion in Southeastern Europe.

SUPERPOWER RELATIONS

During the Cold War, there was never any direct military conflict between the United States and the Soviet Union. Rather, confrontations among "client" nations were used to carry out the policies of the superpowers. Only on occasion did the United States directly enter a conflict in a significant way. Two such occasions were in Korea and in Vietnam.

After the end of World War II, northern Korea was occupied by the Soviet Union, and southern Korea was occupied by the United States. The result was two rival Korean governments. In 1950, North Korea invaded South Korea. Under United Nations authority,

---

[4]See John Lewis Gaddis, *The United Nations and the Origins of the Cold War* (New York: Columbia University Press, 1972).
[5]X, "The Sources of Soviet Conduct," *Foreign Affairs*, July 1947, p. 575.

the United States entered the war, which prevented an almost certain South Korean defeat. When U.S. forces were on the brink of conquering North Korea, however, China joined the war on the side of the North, resulting in a stalemate. An armistice signed in 1953 led to the two Koreas that exist today. U.S. forces have remained in South Korea ever since.

The Vietnam War (1964–1975) also involved the United States in a civil war between a communist North Vietnam and pro-Western South Vietnam. When the French army in Indochina was defeated by the communist forces of Ho Chi Minh and the two Vietnams were created in 1954, the United States assumed the role of supporting the South Vietnamese government against North Vietnam. President John Kennedy sent 16,000 "advisors" to help South Vietnam, and after Kennedy's death in 1963, President Lyndon B. Johnson greatly increased the scope of that support. More than 500,000 American troops were in Vietnam at the height of the U.S. involvement. More than 58,000 Americans were killed and 300,000 were wounded in the conflict. A peace agreement in 1973 allowed U.S. troops to leave the country, and in 1975 North Vietnam easily occupied Saigon (the South Vietnamese capital) and unified the nation. The debate over U.S. involvement in Vietnam became extremely heated and, as mentioned previously, spurred Congressional efforts to limit the ability of the president to commit forces to armed combat. The military draft was also a major source of contention during the Vietnam War.

The Cuban Missile Crisis. Perhaps the closest the two superpowers came to a nuclear confrontation was the Cuban missile crisis in 1962. The Soviets installed missiles in Cuba, 90 miles off the U.S. coast, in response to Cuban fears of an American invasion and to try to balance an American nuclear advantage. President Kennedy and his advisors rejected the option of invading Cuba and set up a naval blockade around the island instead. When Soviet vessels appeared near Cuban waters, the tension reached

FIGURE 18–1 Europe During the Cold War

This map shows the face-off between NATO (led by the United States) and the Soviet bloc (the Warsaw Pact). Note that France was out of NATO from 1966 to 1996, and Spain did not join until 1982.

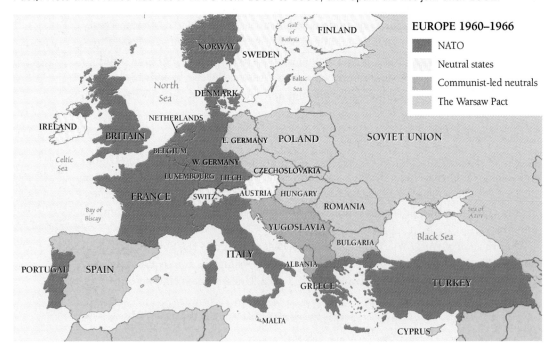

MISSILE EQUIPMENT
MARIEL PORT FACILITY
4 NOVEMBER 1962

4 MISSILE TRANSPORTERS

OXIDIZER TRAILERS

OXIDIZER TRAILERS

FUEL TRAILERS

RUSSIAN MISSILE TRANSPORTERS
and fuel trucks in Mariel, Cuba, in 1962, as captured in a photo from an American spy plane. This picture brought the United States and the Soviet Union to the brink of war in the Cuban Missile Crisis. (Bettmann/CORBIS)

its height. After intense negotiations between Washington and Moscow, the Soviet ships turned around on October 25, and on October 28, the Soviet Union announced the withdrawal of its missile operations from Cuba. In exchange, the United States agreed not to invade Cuba in the future and to remove some of its own missiles that were located near the Soviet border in Turkey.

A Period of *Détente*. The French word *détente* means a relaxation of tensions. By the end of the 1960s, it was clear that some efforts had to be made to reduce the threat of nuclear war between the United States and the Soviet Union. The Soviet Union gradually had begun to catch up in the building of strategic nuclear delivery vehicles in the form of bombers and missiles, thus balancing the nuclear scales between the two countries. Each nation acquired the military capacity to destroy the other with nuclear weapons.

As the result of lengthy negotiations under Secretary of State Henry Kissinger and President Nixon, the United States and the Soviet Union signed the **Strategic Arms Limitation Treaty (SALT I)** in May 1972. That treaty "permanently" limited the development and deployment of antiballistic missiles (ABMs) and limited the number of offensive missiles each country could deploy. To further reduce tensions, new scientific and cultural exchanges were arranged with the Soviets, as well as new opportunities for Jewish emigration out of the Soviet Union.

The policy of *détente* was not limited to the U.S. relationship with the Soviet Union. Seeing an opportunity to capitalize on increasing friction between the Soviet Union and the People's Republic of China, Kissinger secretly began negotiations to establish a new relationship with that nation. President Nixon eventually visited China in 1972. The visit set the stage for the formal diplomatic recognition of that country, which occurred during the Carter administration (1977–1981).

Détente
A French word meaning a relaxation of tensions. The term characterized U.S.–Soviet relations as they developed under President Richard Nixon and Secretary of State Henry Kissinger.

Strategic Arms Limitation Treaty (SALT I)
A treaty between the United States and the Soviet Union to stabilize the nuclear arms competition between the two countries. SALT I talks began in 1969, and agreements were signed on May 26, 1972.

The Reagan–Bush Years. President Ronald Reagan took a hard line against the Soviet Union during his first term, proposing the strategic defense initiative (SDI), or "Star Wars," in 1983. The SDI was designed to serve as a space-based defense against enemy missiles. Reagan and others in his administration argued that the program would deter nuclear war by shifting the emphasis of defense strategy from offensive to defensive weapons systems.

In November 1985, however, President Reagan and Mikhail Gorbachev, the Soviet leader, began to work on an arms reduction compact. The negotiations resulted in a historic agreement signed by Reagan and Gorbachev in Washington, D.C., on December 8, 1987. The terms of the Intermediate-Range Nuclear Force (INF) Treaty, which was ratified by the Senate, required the superpowers to dismantle a total of 4,000 intermediate-range missiles within the first three years of the agreement.

Beginning in 1989, President George H. W. Bush continued the negotiations with the Soviet Union to reduce the number of nuclear weapons and the number of armed troops in Europe. Subsequent events, including developments in Eastern Europe, the unification of Germany, and the dissolution of the Soviet Union (in December 1991), changed the world order. American and other Western leaders now worked to find and control the weapons that had formerly been in the inventory of the Soviet Union. Agreements were signed with Russia and with other former Soviet republics to reduce the weapons threat.

That Russia suffered more battle deaths in putting down the rebellion in Chechnya than the Soviet Union experienced in its decades-long attempt to subdue Afghanistan?

The Dissolution of the Soviet Union. After the fall of the Berlin Wall in 1989, it was clear that the Soviet Union had relinquished much of its political and military control over the states of Eastern Europe that formerly had been part of the Soviet bloc. Figure 18–2 shows the current alliances in Europe. No one expected the Soviet Union to dissolve into separate states as quickly as it did, however. Though Gorbachev tried to adjust the Soviet constitution and political system to allow greater autonomy for the republics within the union, demands for political, ethnic, and religious autonomy grew. Since 1991, Russia has struggled to develop a democratic system of government. Boris Yeltsin, president of Russia from 1991 to 1999, attempted to lead needed reforms on the government and electoral system. In 2000, Yeltsin, whose health was failing, named Vladimir Putin as acting president. After completing his terms as an elected president, Putin became the premier of Russia in 2008.

Although Putin has claimed that Russia's most important task is to "develop as a free and democratic state," his actions belie his words. Throughout his time in office, he has slowly but surely limited freedom of the press and freedom of speech. Most strangely, quite a few opposition journalists have been murdered in Russia with no arrests for their assassins. In addition, he has reduced the number of political offices that are filled by free elections. Some argue that without the huge revenues that the Russian government is obtaining as a result of the high price of oil, Putin would face popular discontent and would be unable to carry out his antidemocratic actions.[6]

CHALLENGES IN WORLD POLITICS

The foreign policy of the United States, whether moralistic, realistic, or both, must be formulated to deal with world conditions. Early in its history, the United States was a weak, new nation facing older nations well equipped for world domination. In the 21st century, the United States faces different challenges. Now it must devise foreign and

---

[6]Martha Brill Olcott, "Vladimir Putin and Russia's Oil Policy," Carnegie Moscow Center, Issue 1, 2005.

FIGURE 18–2 Europe After the Fall of the Soviet Union

This map shows the growth in European unity as marked by the participation in transnational organizations. The United States continues to lead NATO (and would be orange if it were on this map). Note the reunification of Germany and the creation of new states from former Yugoslavia and the former Soviet Union.

defense policies that will enhance its security in a world in which it is the global superpower and has no equal. Among the challenges that must be faced are the growth of new economic and military powers, the threat of terrorism, war in Iraq and Afghanistan, the proliferation of nuclear weapons, and numerous regional conflicts, including the ongoing violence in the Middle East.

THE EMERGING WORLD ORDER

From 1945 until 1989, the world watched as two superpowers, the United States and the Soviet Union, dueled for power in the world. Both nations had their allies and fought wars through their surrogates. Both nations built up huge arsenals of nuclear weapons and were militarily prepared to destroy each other and the world itself. After the Berlin Wall fell in 1989, the entire Soviet bloc disintegrated with surprising speed. East Germany, one of the strongest allies of the Soviet Union, merged with West Germany to become one nation, democratic and capitalistic. The United States was quick to establish strong relationships with Estonia, Latvia, and Lithuania, the three Baltic states that were occupied by the Soviet Union after World War II. All of the other Eastern bloc nations became truly independent states, and the Soviet Union was divided into Russia and several other states that are part of the Russian Federation.

The U.S. military and U.S. nuclear scientists worked closely with their Russian counterparts to account for the nuclear arsenal of the Soviet Union and to try to control these weapons. For a time, as Russia held democratic elections, U.S. political consultants were hired to help Russian candidates market their campaigns just as in the United States. Moscow quickly developed into a major capital with luxury shops and condominiums. Russia supported the U.S. war against terrorism, even as it fought terrorists within Chechnya.

After the Persian Gulf War in 1991, it was clear that the American military was the finest in the world and that U.S. advances in technology and weaponry were far superior to those of any other nation. What this meant was that the United States was the sole military global superpower. Under the Clinton administration, the Pentagon tried to plan for a post-Cold War world. What should be the objectives of the nation in terms of national security? How should the military be structured? How many wars should the United States be equipped to handle at one time? What kinds of intelligence gathering would now be important if the Soviets were no longer a threat? All of these questions and more needed to be answered in terms of American foreign and national security policy.

The Clinton administration, with the approval of Congress, began to change the size and scope of the American military. By 2001, the active-duty military was one-third less than it had been in 1990, dropping from 2.1 million in 1989 to 1.4 million in 1999.[7] Fewer appropriations were made to build new ships and acquire new equipment. The Central Intelligence Agency was ordered to focus more on economic intelligence and less on military intelligence. However, the United States continued to lead NATO and maintain this military alliance of European nations. Russia objected on the grounds that this alliance was no longer needed. Instead, many of the former Soviet bloc nations, beginning with Poland, expressed interest in joining NATO and, by 2008, the alliance included the 27 members who joined at the beginning of or before the fall of the Soviet Union, as well as the Czech Republic, Hungary, Poland, Bulgaria, Estonia, Latvia, Lithuania, Romania, Slovakia, and Slovenia, all former allies of Russia.

At the same time, other developments in the world challenged American policy. The European Union became a single economic unit, competing with American exports around the world. China began to become an economic force in the world and, a few years later, India followed suit. By 2008, China was a major trading partner of the United States and, with its newly generated cash, a major holder of the securities of the U.S. government. China became a major military power as well, with nuclear weapons and missile capabilities. Other nations such as Brazil and Australia became important economic players in the world.

By 2001, when terrorists attacked the World Trade Center in New York, the United States was focused more on economic growth and economic competition in the world. The United States military was prepared for crisis situations and technologically sophisticated warfare, but not for a long engagement on the ground. The wars in Afghanistan and, later, Iraq, exhausted the uniformed military in terms of resources. Many began to ask whether the United States should institute the military draft again to ensure a ready supply of troops in this new world.

THE THREAT OF TERRORISM

Dissident groups, rebels, and other revolutionaries have long engaged in terrorism to gain attention and to force their enemies to the bargaining table. Over the last two decades, however, terrorism has increasingly threatened world peace and the lives of ordinary citizens.

Terrorism and Regional Strife. Terrorism can be a weapon of choice in regional or domestic strife. The conflict in the Middle East between Israel and the Arab states is an example. Until recently, the conflict had been lessened by a series of painfully negotiated agree-

[7]Edward F. Bruner, "Military Forces: What is the Appropriate Size for the United States?" Congressional Research Service Report for Congress, updated February 10, 2005.

WHAT IF...

THE UNITED STATES BROUGHT BACK THE DRAFT?

By law, male residents of the United States are required to register for the military draft after their 18th birthdays. From 1948 through 1973, all American men were subject to the draft, and draftees filled the ranks of the armed forces during war and peace. Since 1973, however, the armed forces have been composed entirely of volunteers.

Beginning in 2004, coalition troops in Iraq faced major uprisings. U.S. forces were stretched thin. The Department of Defense was compelled to extend the tours of duty for units that were about to be brought home. In particular, this meant extending the service of National Guard units. Most members of the National Guard had never anticipated that they would serve in a war zone. To meet the shortfall of trained military personnel, the country could bring back the draft.

BRINGING BACK THE DRAFT WOULD PROMOTE FAIRNESS

Those who advocate bringing back the draft believe that universal service would be fairer than the current system. Now, almost no children of wealthy families enter the military. Only four members of the 107th Congress had children in one of the services. Draft advocates say that the military should not be limited to the lower classes; everyone should give something back to society. Alternative civilian service could be provided for those who do not wish to join the armed forces, but complete exemption should be unavailable.

A draft would prevent the kinds of troop shortages that the military is currently experiencing. In particular, it could eliminate the unfairness involved in stationing National Guard troops abroad for long periods of time. Finally, if there were a universal draft, Congress might be more cautious about endorsing wars.

THE DRAFT IS UNFAIR AND UNNECESSARY

Others fundamentally oppose forcing young people to give up one or more years of their lives to the government. The draft, they say, is a "tax" that falls most strongly on those who value their independence. If the government wants more soldiers, let it offer higher pay and better benefits. A draft would worsen already existing divisions in the country, as it did during the Vietnam War. Furthermore, the military really needs highly trained members who will reenlist, not large numbers of "warm bodies" who will leave as soon as they can.

GOING ONLINE

Draft registration is administered by the Selective Service System, which maintains a Web site at **www.sss.gov**. At this site, you can actually register online. An antidraft site that advocates civil disobedience is at **www.draftresistance.org**.

FOR CRITICAL ANALYSIS

1. Why do you think the draft has not been reinstituted since the Vietnam War?
2. Do you think all Americans should be required to serve their country in some capacity?

ments between Israel and some of the Arab states. Those opposed to the peace process, however, have continued to disrupt the negotiations through assassinations, mass murders, and bomb blasts in the streets of major cities within Israel. Other regions have also experienced terrorism. In September 2004, terrorists acting on behalf of Chechnya, a breakaway republic of Russia, seized a school at Beslan in the nearby Russian republic of North Ossetia. In the end, at least 330 people—most of them children—were dead.

In Colombia, the Farc terrorist group, supported in some part by the Venezuelan president, Hugo Chavez, continues to capture civilians, both Colombians and foreigners, and hold them as hostages. By the spring of 2008, more than 700 hostages were being held in the jungle, including a former candidate for president, Ingrid Betancourt, and at least three Americans. President Chavez of Venezuela assisted in getting two hostages released in January 2008 and four former legislators released one month later. Betancourt, the Americans, and several other hostages were freed on July 13, 2008, in a daring raid conducted by the Colombian army. Hundreds of hostages are still being held, some for ransom and others to exchange for Farc guerrillas who have been arrested and imprisoned.8

Terrorist Attacks against Foreign Civilians. In other cases, terrorist acts are planned against civilians of foreign nations traveling abroad to make an international statement. One of the most striking attacks was that launched by Palestinian terrorists against Israeli athletes at the Munich Olympics in 1972, during which 11 athletes were murdered. Other attacks have included ship and airplane hijackings, as well as bombings of embassies. For example, in 1998, terrorist bombings of two American embassies in Africa killed 257 people, including 12 Americans, and injured more than 5,500 others.

September 11. In 2001, terrorism came home to the United States in ways that few Americans could have imagined. In a well-coordinated attack, 19 terrorists hijacked four airplanes and crashed three of them into buildings—two into the World Trade Center towers in New York City and one into the Pentagon in Washington, D.C. The fourth airplane crashed in a field in Pennsylvania, after the passengers fought the hijackers. Why did the al Qaeda network plan and launch attacks on the United States? Apparently, the leaders of the network, including Osama bin Laden, were angered by the presence of U.S. troops on the soil of Saudi Arabia, which they regard as sacred. They also saw the United States as the primary defender of Israel against the Palestinians and as the defender of the royal family that governs Saudi Arabia. The attacks were intended to so frighten and demoralize the American people that they would convince their leaders to withdraw American troops from the Middle East.

London Bombings. On July 7, 2005, terrorists carried out synchronized bombings of the London Underground (subway) and bus network. Four suicide bombers, believed to have been of Middle Eastern descent, claimed the lives of 52 people and wounded hundreds more in the attacks. On July 21, a second group of bombers attempted to carry out a similar plot, but no one was killed. Following the attacks, security was heightened in Britain and elsewhere (including New York City).

In August 2006, British authorities foiled a plot to bring down 10 planes scheduled to leave London's Heathrow Airport for the United States. If successful, it would have been the largest terrorist attack since September 11. The alleged bombers planned to blow up the airplanes with liquid chemicals that could be combined to make a bomb. The chemicals were to be carried onboard in containers for bottled water and other ordinary liquids, mixed together on the plane, and then ignited using triggers installed in what appeared to be MP3 players and other small electronic devices. After the suspects were arrested, the London airport was shut down, flights to the United States were canceled, and travel by air was extremely difficult in England for a few days. Travel in the United States was severely disrupted, too, as carry-on luggage was given extra screening.

8"Colombian Hostages Freed by Farc," BBC News, February 28, 2008, www.bbbc.co.uk.

TERRORIST BOMBINGS have become increasingly destructive.

LEFT: The wreckage of a bus with its seats open to the elements and its roof blown off after an explosion in London in 2005. Nearby, simultaneous explosions rocked the London subway and a double-decker bus during the morning rush hour, causing 52 deaths and sending bloodied victims fleeing from debris-strewn blast sites. (AP Photo/Sergio Dionisio)

CENTER: Rescue workers cover bodies following train explosions in Madrid, Spain, just three days before Spain's general elections in 2004. The bombs killed more than 170 and wounded more than 500. (AP Photo/Paul White)

UPPER RIGHT: The bombing of a nightclub on the island of Bali in Indonesia in 2002 killed more than 180 tourists, most of them Australian. Al Qaeda was blamed for the bombing. (Achmad Ibrahim/AP Photo)

BOTTOM RIGHT: Palestinians carry sacks of food through the remains of a market in Bethlehem, destroyed after a stand-off between Israeli troops and Palestinians in 2002. (David Guttenfelder/AP Photo)

THE WAR ON TERRORISM

After September 11, President George W. Bush implemented stronger security measures to protect homeland security and U.S. facilities and personnel abroad. The president sought and received Congressional support for heightened airport security, new laws allowing greater domestic surveillance of potential terrorists, and new funding for the military. The Bush administration has also conducted two military efforts as part of the war on terrorism.

Military Responses. The first military effort was directed against al Qaeda camps in Afghanistan and the Taliban regime, which had ruled that country since 1996. In late 2001, after building a coalition of international allies and anti-Taliban rebels within Afghanistan, the United States defeated the Taliban and fostered the creation of an interim government that did not support terrorism. However, by 2008, it was clear that the Taliban were still active in the mountainous regions of the nation, and attacks on coalition forces were escalating.

Then, during 2002 and early 2003, the U.S. government turned its attention to the threat posed by Saddam Hussein's government in Iraq. (The war in Iraq and the subsequent occupation of that country will be discussed in detail later in this chapter under "The Iraq Wars.")

A New Kind of War. Terrorism has posed a unique challenge for U.S. foreign policy makers. The Bush administration's response was unique. In September 2002, President

Bush enunciated what has since become known as the "Bush doctrine" or the doctrine of preemption:

> We will . . . [defend] the United States, the American people, and our interests at home and abroad by identifying and destroying the threat before it reaches our borders. While the United States will constantly strive to enlist the support of the international community, we will not hesitate to act alone, if necessary, to exercise our right of self-defense by acting preemptively against such terrorists, to prevent them from doing harm against our people and our country.[9]

The concept of "preemptive war" as a defense strategy is a new element in U.S. foreign policy. The concept is based on the assumption that in the war on terrorism, self-defense must be *anticipatory*. As President Bush stated on March 17, 2003, just before launching the invasion of Iraq, "Responding to such enemies only after they have struck first is not self-defense, it is suicide."

The Bush doctrine has not been without its critics. Some point out that preemptive wars against other nations have traditionally been waged by dictators and rogue states—not democratic nations. By employing such tactics, the United States would seem to be contradicting its basic values. Others claim that launching preemptive wars will make it difficult for the United States to further world peace in the future. By endorsing such a policy itself, the United States could hardly argue against the decisions of other nations to do likewise when they feel threatened.

THE IRAQ WARS

On August 2, 1990, the Persian Gulf became the setting for a major challenge to the international system set up after World War II (1939–1945). President Saddam Hussein of Iraq sent troops into the neighboring oil sheikdom of Kuwait, occupying that country. This was the most clear-cut case of aggression against an independent nation in half a century.

The Persian Gulf—The First Gulf War. At the formal request of the king of Saudi Arabia, American troops were dispatched to set up a defensive line at the Kuwaiti border. After the United Nations (UN) approved a resolution authorizing the use of force if Saddam Hussein did not respond to sanctions, the U.S. Congress reluctantly also approved such an authorization. On January 17, 1991, two days after a deadline for Hussein to withdraw, U.S.-led coalition forces launched a massive air attack on Iraq. After several weeks, the ground offensive began. Iraqi troops retreated from Kuwait a few days later, and the First Gulf War ended, although many Americans criticized President George H. W. Bush for not sending troops to Baghdad to depose Saddam Hussein.

As part of the cease-fire that ended the Gulf War, Iraq agreed to abide by all UN resolutions and to allow UN weapons inspectors to search for and oversee the destruction of its medium-range missiles and all weapons of mass destruction, including any chemical and nuclear weapons, and related research facilities. Economic sanctions were to be imposed on Iraq until the weapons inspectors finished their work. In 1999, however, Iraq placed so many obstacles in the path of the UN inspectors that they withdrew from the country.

The Iraq War. After the terrorist attacks on the United States on September 11, 2001, President George W. Bush called Iraq and Saddam Hussein part of an "axis of evil" that

---

[9]George W. Bush, September 17, 2002. The full text of the document from which this statement is taken can be accessed at www.whitehouse.gov/nsc/nssall.html.

threatened world peace. In 2002 and early 2003, Bush called for a "regime change" in Iraq and began assembling an international coalition that might support further military action in Iraq.

Having tried and failed to convince the UN Security Council that the UN should take action to enforce its resolutions, Bush decided to create a coalition of 35 other nations, including Britain, to join the United States to invade Iraq. Within three weeks, the coalition forces had toppled Hussein's decades-old dictatorship and were in control of Baghdad and most of the other major Iraqi cities.

The process of establishing order and creating a new government in Iraq turned out to be extraordinarily difficult, however. In the course of the fighting, the Iraqi army, rather than surrendering, disbanded itself. Soldiers simply took off their uniforms and made their way home. As a result, the task of maintaining law and order fell on the shoulders of a remarkably small coalition expeditionary force. Coalition troops were unable to put an immediate halt to the wave of looting and disorder that spread across Iraq in the wake of the invasion. Saddam Hussein was found and later tried and executed by an Iraqi court for crimes against the Kurdish people, but that did not stop the insurgent resistance movement against the coalition forces.

Occupied Iraq. The people of Iraq are divided into three principal groups by ethnicity and religion. The Kurdish-speaking people of the North, who had in practice been functioning as an American-sponsored independent state since the First Gulf War, were overjoyed by the invasion. The Arabs adhering to the Shiite branch of Islam live principally in the South and constitute a majority of the population. The Shiites were glad that Saddam Hussein, who had murdered many thousands of Shiites, was gone. They were deeply skeptical of U.S. intentions, however. The Arabs belonging to the Sunni branch of Islam live in the center of the country, west of Baghdad. Although the Sunnis constituted only a minority of the population, they had controlled the government under Hussein. Many of them considered the occupation to be a disaster. Figure 18–3 shows the distribution of major ethnic and religious groups in Iraq.

The Situation Worsens. In April 2004, four non-Iraqi civilian security personnel were murdered in the Sunni city of Fallujah, and their bodies were publicly defiled. U.S. Marines entered the city to locate and arrest the perpetrators. Almost at the same time, authorities in Baghdad closed a newspaper run by followers of the Shiite cleric Muqtada al-Sadr. Al-Sadr, a radical, was the son of a famous Shiite martyr. The paper was closed on the ground that it had been fomenting violence. The result was simultaneous uprisings in the "Sunni triangle" west of Baghdad and in neighborhoods dominated by al-Sadr's militia in Baghdad and southern cities.

After several weeks, fighting was confined to Fallujah and the Shiite city of Najaf, where al-Sadr had established his headquarters. Public opinion polls in Iraq revealed that hostility toward the occupation forces had grown dramatically. To make matters worse, in May 2004, graphic photographs were published showing that U.S. guards at Abu Ghraib prison in Baghdad had subjected prisoners to physical and sexual abuse.

While coalition forces were able to maintain control of the country, they were now suffering monthly casualties comparable to those experienced during the initial invasion. Casualties continued to increase in the years that followed, and the unpopularity of the war among the American people dragged President Bush's approval rating to historic lows.

FIGURE 18–3 Ethnic/Religious Groups in Iraq

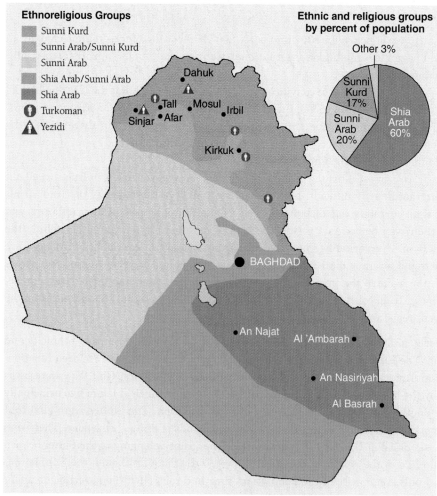

Source: The Central Intelligence Agency, as adapted by www.globalsecurity.org.

The Continuing Insurgency. Certainly, establishing a stable Iraqi government has proved difficult, particularly because of the problems with Sunni participation. As mentioned earlier, the Sunnis dominated the political landscape when Saddam Hussein was in power, even though they were a minority. Now, with Hussein gone, the Shiites, who are a majority of the population, are the dominant political force. The Sunnis clearly are participating in the insurgency to prevent the Shiites from controlling the political scene.

Additionally, the insurgency may be fed by Iran, which is a Shiite country. Much information shows that Iran is pressing Shiite militia to step up attacks against American-led forces. In August 2006, while the war between Hezbollah and Israel was being waged in Lebanon, tens of thousands of followers of a major Shiite cleric held a rally in Baghdad in support of Hezbollah. Now there is concern that the rise of the majority Shiites in Iraq will lead to the creation of a "Shiite crescent" across the Middle East, with groups in Iran, Iraq, and Lebanon working together against such common enemies as Sunni Arabs, Israel, and the United States.

By 2007, it was clear that al Qaeda terrorist cells were also participating in the insurgency. This turn of events is certainly ironic, in that one of the justifications for invading Iraq was a supposed link between al Qaeda and Saddam Hussein. It is clear that such a link did not exist then, but al Qaeda is involved in Iraq currently. In spring 2007, President Bush and his commanders in the field requested additional troops for a surge of military activity to defeat the insurgency. Although many in Congress and the public did not believe that the surge would be successful, by late 2007, violence in many parts of Iraq had decreased, and the Iraqi military forces were taking the lead in operations against the insurgents.

While the Bush administration stood firm in its commitment to defeating the insurgents in 2008 and made few promises of bringing the troops home, the question of how to exit Iraq was a major issue in the primary campaigns. By the time of the general election in November, 2008, both John McCain and Barack Obama held fairly similar views on the conditions under which American troops would come home, although they differed on whether an American presence in Iraq was necessary in the long term. It was clear by then that the situation in Afghanistan was worsening. The Taliban gained strength, and the new president would need to send more troops into that country while reducing troop strength in Iraq.

NUCLEAR WEAPONS

In 1945, the United States was the only nation to possess nuclear weapons. Several nations quickly joined the "nuclear club," however, including the Soviet Union in 1949, Great Britain in 1952, France in 1960, and China in 1964. Few nations have made public their nuclear weapons programs since China's successful test of nuclear weapons in 1964. India and Pakistan, however, detonated nuclear devices within a few weeks of each other in 1998, and North Korea conducted an underground nuclear explosive test in October 2006. Several other nations are suspected of possessing nuclear weapons or the capability to produce them in a short time.

The United States and the Soviet Union. More than 32,000 nuclear warheads are known to be stocked worldwide, although the exact number is uncertain, because some countries do not reveal the extent of their nuclear stockpiles. Although the United States and Russia have dismantled some of their nuclear weapons systems since the end of the Cold War and the dissolution of the Soviet Union in 1991, both still retain sizable nuclear arsenals. Even more troublesome is nuclear proliferation—that is, the development of nuclear weapons by additional nations.

Nuclear Proliferation. The United States has attempted to influence late arrivals to the nuclear club through a combination of rewards and punishments. In some cases, the United States has promised aid to a nation to gain cooperation. In other cases, such as those of India and Pakistan, it has imposed economic sanctions as a punishment for carrying out nuclear tests. In the end, Pakistan demonstrated its ability to explode nuclear bombs in 1998. Despite the United States' disagreement with these countries, President Bush signed a new nuclear pact with India in March 2006.

In 1999, President Bill Clinton presented the Comprehensive Nuclear Test Ban Treaty to the Senate for ratification. The treaty, formed in 1996, prohibits all nuclear test explosions worldwide and established a global network of monitoring stations. Ninety-three nations have ratified the treaty. Among those that have not are China, Israel, India, and Pakistan. In a defeat for the Clinton administration, the U.S. Senate rejected the treaty in 1999.

President George W. Bush described both North Korea and Iran as members of an "axis of evil," and the fear exists that one of them could supply nuclear materials to terrorists. In addition, Israel is known to possess more than one hundred nuclear warheads. South Africa developed six nuclear warheads in the 1980s but dismantled them in 1990. In 2003, Libya announced that it was abandoning a secret nuclear weapons program. Also, since the dissolution of the Soviet Union in 1991, the security of its nuclear arsenal has declined. There have been reported thefts, smugglings, and illicit sales of nuclear material from the former Soviet Union in the past 15 years.

For years, the United States, the European Union, and the UN have tried to prevent Iran from becoming a nuclear power. Today, though, many observers believe that Iran has already developed nuclear capability or is close to doing so. Continued diplomatic attempts to at least slow down Iran's quest for a nuclear bomb have proved ineffectual at best.

With nuclear weapons, materials, and technology available worldwide, it is conceivable that terrorists could develop a nuclear device and use it in a terrorist act. In fact, a U.S. federal indictment filed in 1998, after the attack on the American embassies in Kenya and Tanzania, charged Osama bin Laden and his associates with trying to buy components for a nuclear bomb "at various times" since 1992.

REGIONAL CONFLICTS

The United States has played a role—sometimes alone, sometimes with other powers—in many regional conflicts during the 1990s and 2000s.

Cuba. Tensions between the United States and Cuba have been frequent since Fidel Castro took power in Cuba in 1959. Relations with Cuba continue to be politically important in the United States, because the Cuban American population can influence election outcomes in Florida, a state that all presidential candidates try to win. When Fidel Castro became seriously ill and underwent surgery in the summer of 2006, his brother, Raul, temporarily assumed power. In 2008, Fidel named his brother as his official successor. Although no major changes have occurred in relationships with the United States, Raul Castro immediately legalized cell phones for Cuban citizens. Other reforms in Cuban society seem likely, although no one knows when relations with the United States might be normalized.

Israel and the Palestinians. As a longtime supporter of Israel, the United States has undertaken to persuade the Israelis to negotiate with the Palestinian Arabs who live in the

---

DID YOU KNOW?

That including the Civil War, more than 1 million American soldiers have been killed in the nation's wars?

THIS CIA PHOTOGRAPH shows Yongbyon in North Korea. The area marked in red contains a nuclear research center and associated reprocessing facilities. What, if anything, can the United States legitimately offer to North Korea if that country abandons its nuclear weapons program? (Globalsecurity .org)

Normal Trade Relations (NTR) Status
A status granted through an international treaty by which each member nation must treat other members at least as well as it treats the country that receives its most favorable treatment. This status was formerly known as most-favored-nation status.

BEYOND OUR BORDERS

CHINA: A SUPERPOWER UNDER THE SPOTLIGHT

China has experienced rapid economic growth for the last 30 years, and today is one of the world's great economic powers. Adjusted for purchasing power, China's gross domestic product (GDP) is now second only to that of the United States and is almost double that of Japan. This fact does not mean that all Chinese are rich. Per capita income in China is well below that of the United States and Europe.

Between 2001 and 2007, China's industrial output increased by almost 50 percent. China now produces more steel than America and Japan combined. Such rapid growth requires massive amounts of raw materials. China consumes 40 percent of the world's output of cement, for example. China's growing demand for raw materials has contributed to dramatic increases in the world prices of many commodities, including oil. Although economists around the world have been predicting that China's growth will slow down, it had yet to do so by the beginning of 2007.

CHINA'S ECONOMIC PROSPECTS

Goldman Sachs, a U.S. investment firm, has projected that China's GDP will surpass that of the United States by 2039, making China's economy the largest in the world. In fact, this projection may underestimate China's prospects, because it uses growth rates that are substantially lower than the actual rates China has posted during the last 30 years.

CHINESE–AMERICAN RELATIONS

Since Richard Nixon's visit to China in 1972, American policy has been to gradually engage the Chinese in diplomatic and economic relationships in the hope of turning the nation in a more pro-Western direction. In 1989, however, when Chinese students engaged in extraordinary demonstrations against the government, the Chinese government crushed the demonstrations, killing several students and protesters and imprisoning others. The result was a distinct chill in Chinese–American relations.

After initially criticizing the administration of George H. W. Bush (served 1989–1993) for not being hard enough on China, President Bill Clinton came around to a policy of diplomatic outreach to the Chinese. An important reason for this change was the large and growing trade ties between the two countries. China was granted *most-favored-nation status* for tariffs and trade policy on a year-to-year basis. In 2001, Congress granted China permanent **Normal Trade Relations (NTR) Status**, thus endorsing China's admission to the World Trade Organization (WTO). For a country that is officially communist, China already permits a striking degree of free enterprise, and the rules China must follow as a WTO member will further increase the role of the private sector in China's economy.

In recent years, China did support the American efforts against terrorists but did not support the war in Iraq. Although the two nations have had diplomatic differences, China has joined the six-party talks, working with the United States, Japan, Russia, South Korea, and North Korea to negotiate with North Korea to end its pursuit of nuclear weapons.

CHINA IN THE SPOTLIGHT

In 2008, China became the center for world attention. First, an enormous earthquake struck the area near Chengdu, causing thousands of deaths and billions of dollars of destruction. For the first time since World War II, the Chinese government chose to be open to the media and to allow foreign journalists to report the tragedy. The Chinese government used every resource possible to help the people in the region and to encourage truthful reporting. The openness shown by China in this situation may well have been related to China's pride in hosting the 2008 Olympics in Beijing. Although already an economic and military superpower, the Chinese government and the Chinese people placed a great deal of importance on enhancing the nation's standing in the world by producing the most successful Olympic games ever seen.

FOR CRITICAL ANALYSIS

1. Can China truly be recognized as a superpower if it does not become more democratic?
2. What are some of the issues involving trade that have tarnished China's image in recent years?

territories occupied by the state of Israel. The conflict, which began in 1948, has been extremely difficult to resolve. The internationally recognized solution is for Israel to yield the West Bank and the Gaza Strip to the Palestinians in return for effective security commitments and abandonment by the Palestinians of any right of return to Israel proper. Unfortunately, the Palestinians have been unwilling to stop terrorist attacks on Israel, and Israel has been unwilling to dismantle all of its settlements in the occupied territories. Furthermore, the two parties have been unable to come to an agreement on how much of the West Bank should go to the Palestinians and on what compensation (if any) the Palestinians should receive for abandoning all claims to settlement in Israel proper.

In December 1988, the United States began talking directly to the Palestine Liberation Organization (PLO), and in 1991, under great pressure from the United States, the Israelis opened talks with representatives of the Palestinians and other Arab states. In 1993, both parties agreed to set up Palestinian self-government in the West Bank and the Gaza Strip. The historic agreement, signed in Cairo on May 4, 1994, put in place a process by which the Palestinians would assume self-rule in the Gaza Strip and in the town of Jericho. In the months that followed, Israeli troops withdrew from much of the occupied territory, the new Palestinian Authority assumed police duties, and many Palestinian prisoners were freed by the Israelis.

The Collapse of the Israeli–Palestinian Peace Process. Although negotiations between the Israelis and the Palestinians resulted in more agreements in Oslo, Norway, in 2000, the agreements were rejected by Palestinian radicals, who began a campaign of suicide bombings in Israeli cities. In 2002, the Israeli government responded by moving tanks and troops into Palestinian towns to kill or capture the terrorists. One result of the Israeli reoccupation was an almost complete collapse of the Palestinian authority. Groups such as Hamas (the Islamic Resistance Movement), which did not accept the concept of peace with Israel even in principle, moved into the power vacuum.

In 2003, President Bush attempted to renew Israeli–Palestinian negotiations by sponsoring a "road map" for peace. First, the road map called for an end to terrorism by

TO PROTECT ISRAELI civilians from terrorism, Israel has built a wall to separate Palestinian settlements from Jewish neighborhoods. (Andrija Ilic for Dallas Morning News/CORBIS)

the Palestinians. Later, it held out hopes for a Palestinian state alongside Israel. In its weakened condition, however, the Palestinian authority was unable to make any commitments, and the road map process ground to a halt. In February 2004, Israeli Prime Minister Ariel Sharon announced a plan under which Israel would withdraw from the Gaza Strip regardless of whether a deal could be reached with the Palestinians. Sharon's plan met with strong opposition within his own political party, but ultimately the withdrawal took place.

After the death of Palestinian leader Yasir Arafat in 2004, a moderate prime minister was elected. In January 2006, however, the militant group Hamas won a majority of the seats in the Palestinian legislature. American and European politicians hoped that after it became part of the legitimate government, Hamas would agree to rescind its avowed desire to destroy Israel, but so far, it has not done so.

Wars and AIDS in Africa. The continent of Africa presents many extremely serious challenges to the United States and the rest of the world. Many African nations are still underdeveloped, with enormous health problems and unstable regimes. Tribal rivalries lead to civil wars and, in the worst cases, genocide. The United States has worked with the United Nations to try to end conflicts and improve the situation on the continent.

During the early 2000s, the disease AIDS (acquired immune deficiency syndrome) spread throughout southern Africa. This disease infects one-fourth of the populations of Botswana and Zimbabwe and is endemic in most other nations in the southernmost part of the continent. Millions of adults are dying from AIDS, leaving orphaned children. The epidemic is taking a huge economic toll on the affected countries because of the cost of caring for patients and the loss of skilled workers. The disease may be the greatest single threat to world stability emanating from Africa. The Bush administration put in place a special aid package directed at this problem amounting to $15 billion over five years.

The year 1994 brought disaster to the African nation of Rwanda. Following the death of that country's president, members of the Hutu tribe launched a campaign of genocide against the Tutsi tribe. More than half a million people were killed in a matter of weeks. The genocide campaign ended abruptly as a Tutsi guerrilla force, sponsored by neighboring Uganda, overthrew the Rwandan government. A large number of Hutus then fled from Rwanda. The United States played almost no part in this crisis until small military and civilian contingents were sent to assist the Hutu refugees.

That the United States invaded and occupied part of Russia in 1919?

In Angola, wars dating back as far as 1961 ended in 2002 with the death of rebel leader Jonas Savimbi, who had received U.S. support for several years in the 1970s. In 1996, civil war broke out in Zaire (now named the Democratic Republic of the Congo; also known as Congo-Kinshasa). Rebels were aided by Rwandan and Ugandan forces, while Angolan and Zimbabwean forces entered the country to support the government. The civil war officially ended in 2002, and a coalition government was established in 2003. Several million deaths, primarily due to disease and malnutrition, have been attributed to the war. At the present time, more than 17,000 United Nations peacekeepers are trying to keep the coalition government stabilized.

In 2004, the world woke up to a growing disaster in Darfur, a western province of Sudan. In the spring of 2004, Sudan had reached a tenuous agreement with rebels in the southern part of the country, but the agreement did not cover a separate rebellion in Darfur. Government-sponsored militias drove more than a million inhabitants of Darfur from their homes and into refugee camps, where they faced starvation. Despite a cease-fire, fighting renewed during the summer of 2006 and continued to plague the region.

DISPLACED CHILDREN in Kalma camp near Nyala in South Darfur wait in the shade while their mother works in nearby fields for income. This work is very dangerous, as relief workers report that women who venture from the camps are often targets of Jingaweit attacks, including rape and murder. Why have the continued killings in Darfur not created more outrage throughout the world? (Photo courtesy of USAID)

WHO MAKES FOREIGN POLICY?

Given the vast array of challenges in the world, developing a comprehensive U.S. foreign policy is a demanding task. Does this responsibility fall to the president, to Congress, or to both acting jointly? There is no easy answer to this question, because, as constitutional authority Edwin S. Corwin once observed, the U.S. Constitution created an "invitation to struggle" between the president and Congress for control over the foreign policy process. Let us look first at the powers given to the president by the Constitution.

CONSTITUTIONAL POWERS OF THE PRESIDENT

The Constitution confers on the president broad powers that are either explicit or implied in key constitutional provisions. Article II vests the executive power of the government in the president. The presidential oath of office given in Article II, Section 1, requires that the president "solemnly swear" to "preserve, protect and defend the Constitution of the United States."

War Powers. In addition, and perhaps more importantly, Article II, Section 2, designates the president as "Commander in Chief of the Army and Navy of the United States." Starting with Abraham Lincoln, all presidents have interpreted this authority dynamically and broadly. Since George Washington's administration, the United States has been involved in at least 125 undeclared wars that were conducted under presidential authority. For example, in 1950, Harry Truman ordered U.S. armed forces in the Pacific to counter North Korea's invasion of South Korea. Dwight Eisenhower threatened China and North Korea with nuclear weapons if the Korean peace talks were not successfully concluded. Bill Clinton sent troops to Haiti and Bosnia. In 2001, George W. Bush authorized an attack against the al Qaeda terrorist network and the Taliban government in Afghanistan. As described earlier, in 2003, after receiving authorization to use force from Congress, Bush sent military forces to Iraq to destroy Saddam Hussein's government.

Treaties and Executive Agreements. Article II, Section 2, of the Constitution also gives the president the power to make treaties, provided that two-thirds of the senators present concur. Presidents usually have been successful in getting treaties through the Senate. In addition to this formal treaty-making power, the president uses executive agreements (discussed in Chapter 13). Since World War II (1939–1945), executive agreements have accounted for almost 95 percent of the understandings reached between the United States and other nations.

Executive agreements have a long and important history. During World War II, Franklin Roosevelt reached several agreements with the Soviet Union and other countries. One agreement with long-term results was concluded at Yalta in the Soviet Crimea. In other important agreements, Presidents Eisenhower, Kennedy, and Johnson all promised support to the government of South Vietnam. In all, since 1946, more than 8,000 executive agreements with foreign countries have been made. There is no way to obtain an accurate count, because perhaps as many as several hundred of these agreements have been secret.

Other Constitutional Powers. An additional power conferred on the president in Article II, Section 2, is the right to appoint ambassadors, other public ministers, and consuls. In Section 3 of that article, the president is given the power to recognize foreign governments by receiving their ambassadors.

INFORMAL TECHNIQUES OF PRESIDENTIAL LEADERSHIP

Other broad sources of presidential power in the U.S. foreign policy process are tradition, precedent, and the president's personality. The president can employ a host of informal techniques that give the White House overwhelming superiority within the government in foreign policy leadership.

First, the president has access to information. The Central Intelligence Agency (CIA), the State Department, and the Defense Department make more information available to the president than to any other governmental official. This information carries with it the ability to make quick decisions—and the president uses that ability often. Second, the president is a legislative leader who can influence the funds that are allocated for different programs. Third, the president can influence public opinion. President Theodore Roosevelt once made the following statement:

> People used to say to me that I was an astonishingly good politician and divined what the people are going to think.... I did not "divine" how the people were going to think; I simply made up my mind what they ought to think and then did my best to get them to think it.[10]

Presidents are without equal with respect to influencing public opinion, partly because of their ability to command the media. Depending on their skill in appealing to patriotic sentiment (and sometimes fear), they can make people believe that their course in foreign affairs is right and necessary. Public opinion often seems to be impressed by the president's decision to make a national commitment abroad. President George W. Bush's speech to Congress shortly after the September 11 attacks rallied the nation and brought new respect for his leadership. It is worth noting that presidents normally, although certainly not always, receive the immediate support of the American people in a foreign policy crisis.

Finally, the president can commit the nation morally to a course of action in foreign affairs. Because the president is the head of state and the leader of one of the most powerful nations on earth, once the president has made a commitment for the United States, it is difficult for Congress or anyone else to back down on that commitment.

OTHER SOURCES OF FOREIGN POLICY MAKING

In addition to the president, there are at least four foreign policy-making sources within the executive branch: (1) the Department of State, (2) the National Security Council, (3) the intelligence community, and (4) the Department of Defense.

The Department of State. In principle, the State Department is the executive agency that has primary authority over foreign affairs. It supervises U.S. relations with the more than 200 independent nations around the world and with the United Nations and other multinational groups, such as the Organization of American States. It staffs embassies and consulates throughout the world. It has about 32,000 employees. This number may sound impressive, but it is small compared with, say, the 67,000 employees of the Department of Health and Human Services. Also, the State Department had an annual budget of only $9.1 billion in fiscal year 2009, one of the smallest budgets of the Cabinet departments.

Newly elected presidents usually tell the American public that the new secretary of state is the nation's chief foreign policy advisor. Nonetheless, the State Department's preeminence in foreign policy has declined since World War II. The State Department's image within the White House Executive Office and Congress (and even with foreign governments) is quite poor—a slow, plodding, bureaucratic maze of inefficient, indecisive individuals. Reportedly, Premier Nikita Khrushchev of the Soviet Union urged President John F. Kennedy to formulate his own views rather than rely on State Department officials who, according to Khrushchev, "specialized in why something had not worked forty years ago."[11] In any event, since the days of Franklin Roosevelt, the State Department has often been bypassed or ignored when crucial decisions are made.

That it is estimated that the Central Intelligence Agency has more than 16,000 employees, with about 5,000 in the clandestine services?

---

[10]Sidney Warren, *The President as World Leader* (New York: McGraw-Hill, 1964), p. 23.
[11]Theodore C. Sorensen, *Kennedy* (New York: Harper & Row, 1965), pp. 554–555.

It is not surprising that the State Department has been overshadowed in foreign policy. It has no natural domestic constituency as does, for example, the Department of Defense, which can call on defense contractors for support. Instead, the State Department has what might be called **negative constituents**—U.S. citizens who openly oppose the government's policies. One of the State Department's major functions, administering foreign aid, often elicits criticisms. There is a widespread belief that the United States spends much more on foreign aid than it actually does. For 2007, President Bush's budget request allocated $25 billion to foreign economic aid, or about 88 cents for every 100 dollars of federal spending.

The National Security Council. The job of the National Security Council (NSC), created by the National Security Act of 1947, is to advise the president on the integration of "domestic, foreign, and military policies relating to the national security." Its larger purpose is to provide policy continuity from one administration to the next. As it has turned out, the NSC—consisting of the president, the vice president, the secretaries of state and defense, the director of emergency planning, and often the chairperson of the joint chiefs of staff and the director of the CIA—is used in just about any way the president wants to use it.

The role of national security advisor to the president seems to adjust to fit the player. Some advisors have come into conflict with heads of the State Department. Henry A. Kissinger, Nixon's flamboyant and aggressive national security advisor, rapidly gained ascendancy over William Rogers, the secretary of state. More recently, Condoleezza Rice played an important role as national security advisor during George W. Bush's first term. Rice eventually became secretary of state.

The Intelligence Community. No discussion of foreign policy would be complete without some mention of the **intelligence community**. This consists of the 40 or more government agencies or bureaus that are involved in intelligence activities. They are as follows:

1. Central Intelligence Agency (CIA)
2. National Security Agency (NSA)
3. Defense Intelligence Agency (DIA)
4. Offices within the Department of Defense
5. Bureau of Intelligence and Research in the Department of State
6. Federal Bureau of Investigation (FBI)
7. Army intelligence
8. Air Force intelligence
9. Drug Enforcement Administration (DEA)
10. Department of Energy
11. Directorate of Information Analysis and Infrastructure Protection in the Department of Homeland Security
12. Office of the Director of National Intelligence

The CIA, created as part of the National Security Act of 1947, is the lead organization of the intelligence community.

U.S. AMBASSADOR ANNE PATTERSON takes part in a groundbreaking ceremony in Pakistan. She is emblematic of the diversity of today's career diplomats who represent the United States in every country. (Shakil Adil/AP Photo)

Negative Constituents
Citizens who openly oppose the government's policies.

Intelligence Community
The government agencies that gather information about the capabilities and intentions of foreign governments or that engage in covert actions.

Covert Actions. Intelligence activities consist mostly of overt information gathering, but covert actions also are undertaken. Covert actions, as the name implies, are carried out in secret, and the American public rarely finds out about them. The CIA covertly aided in the overthrow of the Mossadegh regime of Iran in 1953 and the Arbenz government of Guatemala in 1954. The agency was instrumental in destabilizing the Allende government in Chile from 1970 to 1973.

During the mid-1970s, the "dark side" of the CIA was partly uncovered when the Senate undertook an investigation of its activities. One of the major findings of the Senate Select Committee on Intelligence was that the CIA had routinely spied on American citizens domestically—supposedly a prohibited activity. Consequently, the CIA was scrutinized by oversight committees within Congress, which restricted the scope of its operations. By 1980, however, the CIA had regained much of its lost power to engage in covert activities.

Criticisms of the Intelligence Community. By 2001, the CIA had come under fire for several lapses, including the discovery that one of its agents was spying on behalf of a foreign power, the failure to detect the nuclear arsenals of India and Pakistan, and, above all, the failure to obtain advance knowledge about the September 11 terrorist attacks. With the rise of terrorism as a threat, the intelligence agencies have received more funding and enhanced surveillance powers, but these moves have also provoked fears of civil liberties violations. In 2004, the bipartisan September 11 Commission called for a new intelligence czar to oversee the entire intelligence community, with full control of all agency budgets. After initially balking at this recommendation, President Bush eventually called for a partial implementation of the commission's report. Legislation enacted in 2004 established the Office of the Director of National Intelligence to oversee the intelligence community. In 2005, Bush appointed John Negroponte to be the first director. The current director is Admiral Mike McConnell, who formerly held the position of Director of the National Security Agency.

AN AERIAL VIEW of the Pentagon, the headquarters of the U.S. Department of Defense (DoD), located between the Potomac River and Arlington National Cemetery. The Pentagon employs approximately 23,000 military and civilian personnel and is one of the world's largest office buildings, with three times the floor space of the Empire State Building in New York City. In the background, the obelisk of the Washington Monument is visible. When the media refer to The Pentagon, what do they mean? (Johnny Bivera, U.S. Navy)

The Department of Defense. The Department of Defense (DoD) was created in 1947 to bring all of the various activities of the American military establishment under the jurisdiction of a single department headed by a civilian secretary of defense. At the same time, the joint chiefs of staff, consisting of the commanders of the various military branches and a chairperson, was created to formulate a unified military strategy.

Although the Department of Defense is larger than any other federal department, it declined in size after the fall of the Soviet Union in 1991. In the subsequent 10 years, the total number of civilian employees was reduced by about 400,000, to about 665,000. Military personnel were also reduced in number. The defense budget remained relatively flat for several years, but with the advent of the war on terrorism and the use of military forces in Afghanistan and Iraq, funding has again been increased.

CONGRESS BALANCES THE PRESIDENCY

A new interest in the balance of power between Congress and the president on foreign policy questions developed during the Vietnam War (1964–1975). Sensitive to public frustration over the long and costly war and angry at Richard Nixon for some of his other actions as president, Congress attempted to establish limits on the power of the president in setting foreign and defense policy. In 1973, Congress passed the War Powers Resolution over President Nixon's veto. The act limited the president's use of troops in military action without Congressional approval (see Chapter 13). Most presidents, however, have not interpreted the "consultation" provisions of the act as meaning that Congress should be consulted before military action is taken. Instead, Presidents Ford, Carter, Reagan, George H. W. Bush, and Clinton ordered troop movements and then informed Congressional leaders. Critics note that it is quite possible for a president to commit troops to a situation from which the nation could not withdraw without incurring heavy losses, whether or not Congress is consulted.

Congress has also exerted its authority by limiting or denying presidential requests for military assistance to various groups (such as Angolan rebels and the government of El Salvador) and requests for new weapons (such as the B-1 bomber). In general, Congress has been far more cautious in supporting the president in situations in which military involvement of American troops is possible. Since 2001, however, Congress has shown a willingness to support the administration of George W. Bush in the use of military force to fight the war on terrorism.

That in the name of national security, the United States spends at least $5.6 billion annually to keep information classified?

Congress has its limits, of course, and often these are based on political considerations about election campaigns. Prior to the 2006 elections, Democrats found that antiwar platforms could be very effective during their campaigns. Certainly, the Iraq War and the future foreign policy direction of the United States were very important issues in the presidential and Congressional elections of 2008.

DOMESTIC SOURCES OF FOREIGN POLICY

The making of foreign policy is often viewed as a presidential prerogative because of the president's constitutional power in that area and the resources of the executive branch that the president controls. Foreign policy making is also influenced by various other sources, however, including elite and mass opinion and the *military-industrial complex*, described in a following section.

ELITE AND MASS OPINION

Public opinion influences the making of U.S. foreign policy through several channels. Elites in American business, education, communications, labor, and religion try to influence presidential decision making through several strategies. A number of elite organizations, such as the Council on Foreign Relations and the Trilateral Commission, work to increase international cooperation and to influence foreign policy through conferences, publications, and research. The members of the American elite establishment also exert influence on foreign policy through the general public by encouraging debate about foreign policy positions, publicizing the issues, and using the media.

Generally, the efforts of the president and the elites are most successful with the segment of the population called the **attentive public**. This sector of the mass public, which probably constitutes 10 to 20 percent of all citizens, is more interested in foreign affairs than are most other Americans, and members of the attentive public are likely to transmit their opinions to the less interested members of the public through conversation and local leadership.

Attentive Public
That portion of the general public that pays attention to policy issues.

THE MILITARY-INDUSTRIAL COMPLEX

Civilian fear of the relationship between the defense establishment and arms manufacturers (the **military-industrial complex**) dates back many years. During President Eisenhower's eight years in office, the former five-star general of the army experienced firsthand the kind of pressure that could be brought against him and other policy makers by arms manufacturers. Eisenhower decided to give the country a solemn and—as he saw it—necessary warning of the consequences of this influence. On January 17, 1961, in his last official speech, he said:

Military-Industrial Complex
The mutually beneficial relationship between the armed forces and defense contractors.

> In the councils of government, we must guard against the acquisition of unwarranted influence, whether sought or unsought, by the military-industrial complex. The potential for the disastrous rise of misplaced power exists and will persist. . . . Only an alert and knowledgeable citizenry can compel the proper meshing of the huge industrial and military machinery of defense with our peaceful methods and goals, so that security and liberty may prosper together.[12]

The Pentagon has supported a large sector of our economy through defense contracts. It has also supplied retired army officers as key executives to large defense-contracting firms. Perhaps the Pentagon's strongest allies have been members of Congress whose districts or states benefit economically from military bases or contracts. After the Cold War ended in the late 1980s, the defense industry looked abroad for new customers. Sales of some military equipment to China raised serious issues for the Clinton administration. The war on terrorism provoked a new debate about what types of weaponry would be needed to safeguard the nation in the future. When President George W. Bush proposed legislation in 2002 to increase the Defense Department's budget substantially, weapons manufacturers looked forward to increased sales and profits.

That the Pentagon's stockpile of strategic materials includes 1.5 million pounds of quartz crystals used in pre-Great Depression radios and 150,000 tons of tannin used in tanning cavalry saddles?

---

[12]*Congressional Almanac* (Washington, DC: Congressional Quarterly Press, 1961), pp. 938–939.

You can make a *difference*

WORKING FOR HUMAN RIGHTS

In many countries throughout the world, human rights are not protected. In some nations, people are imprisoned, tortured, or killed because they oppose the current regime. In other nations, certain ethnic or racial groups are oppressed by the majority population. Monks in Myanmar, lawyers in Pakistan, food rioters in Bangladesh, Egypt, and Haiti, and women activists in Iran have all landed on the front pages of our newspapers in the past year, fighting for the basic human rights of millions of people in the world. More than 200,000 people in Darfur alone have died since 2003, as a direct result of the Sudanese government's actions to displace an entire population.

WHY SHOULD YOU CARE?

The strongest reason for involving yourself with human rights issues in other countries is simple moral altruism—unselfish regard for the welfare of others. The defense of human rights is unlikely to put a single dollar in your pocket. A broader consideration, however, is that human rights abuses are often associated with the kind of dictatorial regimes that are likely to provoke wars. To the extent that the people of the world can create a climate in which human rights abuses are unacceptable, they may also create an atmosphere in which national leaders believe that they must display peaceful conduct generally. This, in turn, might reduce the frequency of wars, some of which could involve the United States. Less war would mean preserving peace and human life, not to mention reducing the financial burden.

WHAT CAN YOU DO?

What can you do to work for the improvement of human rights in other nations? One way is to join an organization that attempts to keep watch over human rights violations. (Two such organizations are listed at the end of this feature.) By publicizing human rights violations, such organizations try to pressure nations into changing their practices. Sometimes, these organizations are able to apply enough pressure and cause enough embarrassment that victims may be freed from prison or allowed to emigrate.

Another way to work for human rights is to keep informed about the state of affairs in other nations and to write personally to governments that violate human rights or to their embassies, asking them to cease these violations.

If you want to receive general information about the position of the United States on human rights violations, you can contact the State Department:

U.S. Department of State
Bureau of Democracy, Human Rights, and Labor
2201 C St. N.W.
Washington, DC 20520
202-647-4000
www.state.gov/g/drl/hr

The following organizations are well known for their watchdog efforts in countries that violate human rights for political reasons:

Amnesty International U.S.A.
5 Penn Plaza
New York, NY 10001
212-807-8400
www.amnestyusa.org

American Friends Service Committee
1501 Cherry St.
Philadelphia, PA 19102
215-241-7000
www.afsc.org
www.amnestyusa.org
www.eyesondarfur.org

KEY TERMS

attentive public 662

Cold War 639

containment 639

defense policy 634

détente 641

diplomacy 633

economic aid 633

foreign policy 633

foreign policy process 634

intelligence community 659

iron curtain 639

isolationist foreign policy 637

military-industrial
    complex 662

Monroe Doctrine 637

moral idealism 635

national security policy 634

negative constituents 659

Normal Trade Relations (NTR)
    Status 652

political realism 636

Soviet bloc 639

Strategic Arms Limitation
    Treaty (SALT I) 641

technical assistance 633

Truman Doctrine 639

CHAPTER SUMMARY

1. Foreign policy includes national goals and the techniques used to achieve them. National security policy, which is one aspect of foreign policy, is designed to protect the independence and the political and economic integrity of the United States. Diplomacy involves the nation's external relationships and is an attempt to resolve conflict without resort to arms. U.S. foreign policy is sometimes based on moral idealism and sometimes on political realism.

2. Three major themes have guided U.S. foreign policy. In the early years of the nation, isolationism was the primary strategy. With the start of the 20th century, isolationism gave way to global involvement. From the end of World War II through the 1980s, the major goal was to contain communism and the influence of the Soviet Union.

3. During the 1800s, the United States had little international power and generally stayed out of European conflicts and politics, and so these years have been called the period of isolationism. The Monroe Doctrine of 1823 stated that the United States would not accept foreign intervention in the Western Hemisphere and would not meddle in European affairs. The United States pursued an actively expansionist policy in the Americas and the Pacific area, however.

4. The end of the policy of isolationism toward Europe started with the Spanish-American War of 1898. U.S. involvement in European politics became more extensive when the United States entered World War I on April 6, 1917. World War II marked a lasting change in American foreign policy. The United States was the only major country to emerge from the war with its economy intact and the only country with operating nuclear weapons.

5. Soon after the close of World War II, the uncomfortable alliance between the United States and the Soviet Union ended, and the Cold War began. A policy of containment, which assumed an expansionist Soviet Union, was enunciated in the Truman Doctrine. Following the frustrations of the Vietnam War and the apparent arms equality of the United States and the Soviet Union, the United States adopted a policy of *détente*. Although President Reagan took a tough stance toward the Soviet Union during his first term, his second term saw serious negotiations toward arms reduction, culminating in the signing of the Intermediate-Range Nuclear Force Treaty in 1987. After the fall of the Soviet Union, Russia emerged as a less threatening state and signed the Strategic Arms Reduction Treaty with the United States in 1992. The United States and Russia have agreed on some issues in recent years, such as the fight against terrorism, but have disagreed on other matters, such as the war against Iraq in 2003.

6. After the dissolution of the Soviet Union, the United States assumed the position of global superpower without a military competitor. However, the United States has maintained the NATO alliance with its European allies and has added several former Soviet bloc states to the alliance. Russia has remained a powerful nation, one that is becoming increasingly a one-party state. The European Union continues to increase its influence as an economic superpower and competitor to the United States, while the rapidly developing economies of India and China continue to push those nations into the global power structure.

7. Terrorism has become a major challenge facing the United States and other nations. The United States waged war on terrorism after the September 11

attacks. U.S. armed forces occupied Afghanistan in 2001 and Iraq in 2003.

8. Nuclear proliferation continues to be an issue as a result of the breakup of the Soviet Union and loss of control over its nuclear arsenal, along with the continued efforts of other nations to gain nuclear warheads. More than 32,000 nuclear warheads are known to exist worldwide.

9. Ethnic tensions and political instability in many regions of the world provide challenges to the United States. In the Caribbean, Cuba requires American attention because of its proximity. Civil wars have torn apart Rwanda and other countries. The Middle East continues to be a hotbed of conflict despite efforts to continue the peace process. In 1991 and again in 2003, the United States sent combat troops to Iraq. The Second Gulf War in 2003 succeeded in toppling the decades-long dictatorship in Iraq.

10. The formal power of the president to make foreign policy derives from the U.S. Constitution, which designates the president as commander in chief of the army and navy. Presidents have interpreted this authority broadly. They also have the power to make treaties and executive agreements. In principle, the State Department is the executive agency with primary authority over foreign affairs. The National Security Council also plays a major role. The intelligence community consists of government agencies engaged in activities varying from information gathering to covert operations. In response to presidential actions in the Vietnam War, Congress attempted to establish some limits on the power of the president to intervene abroad by passing the War Powers Resolution in 1973.

SELECTED PRINT AND MEDIA RESOURCES

SUGGESTED READINGS

Chomsky, Noam, and Gilbert Achcar. *Perilous Power: The Middle East and U.S. Foreign Policy Dialogues on Terror, Democracy, War, and Justice.* Boulder, CO: Paradigm, 2006. Chomsky is one of the most vocal critics of U.S. foreign policy, and he shows it in the essays in this book. Achcar is a specialist in Middle Eastern affairs who has lived in the region. These authors examine key questions relating to terrorism, conspiracies, democracy, anti-Semitism, and anti-Arab racism. This book can serve as an introduction to understanding the Middle East today.

Hoffmann, Stanley. *Chaos and Violence: What Globalization, Failed States, and Terrorism Mean for U.S. Foreign Policy.* Lanham, MD: Rowman & Littlefield, 2006. What is the proper place of the United States in a world that has been defined by the terrorist acts of September 11, 2001? What are the ethics of intervention, and what is the morality of human rights? These are questions the author answers. He also attempts to show how our broken relationship with Europe can be repaired. He believes that America has engaged in too much unilateralism.

Kang, David. *China Rising: Peace, Power, and Order in East Asia.* New York: Columbia University Press, 2007. Kang examines the history of China and suggests that the ascendance of China to great power status is not

a destabilizing force in the world, but that the Chinese rise to power will be peaceful and an asset to other Asian nations.

Meredith, Martin. *The Fate of Africa: From the Hopes of Freedom to the Heart of Despair.* New York: Public Affairs Press, 2005. A journalist and historian, Meredith gives an overview of the continent of Africa, examines the postcolonial regimes that have succeeded, and investigates the failed nations and civil wars in the region.

O'Hanlon, Michael, and Mike M. Mochizuki. *Crisis in the Korean Peninsula: How to Deal with a Nuclear North Korea.* New York: McGraw-Hill, 2003. The authors provide a comprehensive introduction to the dangers posed by North Korea, which could become a greater threat to world peace than the current terrorist movements. They also offer a possible "grand bargain" to defuse the crisis.

Woodward, Bob. *State of Denial.* New York: Simon and Schuster, 2006. This is the third of Woodward's masterful inside accounts of policy making in George W. Bush's administration. *Bush at War* (2002) dealt with September 11 and the war in Afghanistan. *Plan of Attack* (2004) covered the Second Gulf War in Iraq and its aftermath. *State of Denial* provides the fullest, and most critical, account of the development and implementation of the Bush administration's Iraq policy.

MEDIA RESOURCES

The Aftermath: A Visit to Postwar Iraq—A 2003 program that features interviews with Iraqi clerics, business-persons, scholars, and street protesters, and also with U.S. soldiers and their commanders.

Black Hawk Down—This 2002 film recounts the events in Mogadishu, Somalia, in October 1993, during which two U.S. Black Hawk helicopters were shot down. The film, which is based on reporter Mark Bowden's best-selling book by the same name, contains graphic scenes of terrifying urban warfare.

The Fall of Milosevic—A highly acclaimed 2003 documentary by Norma Percy and Brian Lapping, this film covers the final years of the crisis in former Yugoslavia, including the war in Kosovo and the fall of Slobodan Milosevic, the Serb nationalist leader and alleged war criminal. Except for Milosevic, almost all top Serb and Albanian leaders are interviewed, as are President Bill Clinton and British Prime Minister Tony Blair.

The 50 Years War—Israel and the Arabs—This is a two-volume PBS Home Video released in 2000. More balanced than some accounts, this film includes interviews with many leaders involved in the struggle, including (from Israel) Yitzhak Rabin, Shimon Peres, Benjamin Netanyahu, and Ariel Sharon, (from the Arab world) Egypt's Anwar al-Sadat, Jordan's King Hussein, and Yasir Arafat, and (from the United States) Presidents Jimmy Carter, George H. W. Bush, and Bill Clinton.

Osama bin Laden: In the Name of Allah—A 2001 biography of the leader responsible for the terrorist attacks of September 11, 2001.

e-mocracy

ATTACKING GOVERNMENT COMPUTER SYSTEMS

Attacks on the government's computer systems occur often and are sometimes successful. In 1996, hackers caused mischief at the computers of the CIA and the Justice Department and destroyed the Air Force's home page. In early 1998, computer hackers accessed a series of unclassified sites, caused major university and NASA computers to crash, and defaced military base home pages. It is clear from these episodes that the electronic network used by U.S. military and intelligence organizations is susceptible to access by amateurs, criminals, and spies.

Perhaps even more damage could be caused by interruptions to the global economic and banking systems. During 1997, a survey of banks, universities, and companies showed that more than 60 percent had been accessed "illegitimately" during that year alone. In 2000, a series of computer viruses crippled businesses around the world. One of the most destructive viruses was eventually traced to a graduate student in the Philippines whose thesis had been rejected.

The potential consequences of successful attacks on government or business computer systems are great. Among the networks that, if impaired or destroyed, could interfere with the nation's activities are those that connect the military services; guide satellites for communications and defense; guide submarines; and control all air traffic, credit card transactions, interbank transactions, and utility grids throughout the nation. The collapse of the World Trade Center towers in 2001 damaged telecommunications and Internet communications for all of lower Manhattan.

LOGGING ON

- Our government and the governments of other nations maintain hundreds of Web sites on foreign and defense policy. If you are interested in information about visas, passports, and individual countries, you can access the site maintained by the Department of State at:
  www.state.gov
- For information about human rights, national security, and other issues from a European point of view, check a Web site maintained by the Swiss government, the International Relations and Security Network, at:
  www.css.ethz.ch
- The Brookings Institution, a Washington, D.C., think tank, provides access to its research reports at the following Web site:
  www.brook.edu
- The Global Affairs Agenda, an interest group that promotes a progressive or liberal foreign policy, provides information about many topics at:
  www.fpif.org/gaa/index.html
- For information about the intelligence community and about foreign countries, go to the Web site of the Central Intelligence Agency at:
  www.cia.gov
- Freedom House, an organization that promotes its vision of democracy around the world, rates all nations on their democratic practices at:
  www.freedomhouse.org

ONLINE REVIEW

At **www.cengage.com/politicalscience/schmidt/agandpt14e**, you will find a Tutorial Quiz for this chapter providing questions on the chapter contents, including the features. The questions are organized to match the major sections of the chapter. You'll have access to other helpful study tools, including the book's glossary and flashcards, crossword puzzles, and Web links, as well as "Which Side Are You On?" and "Politics and . . ." features written by the authors of the book.

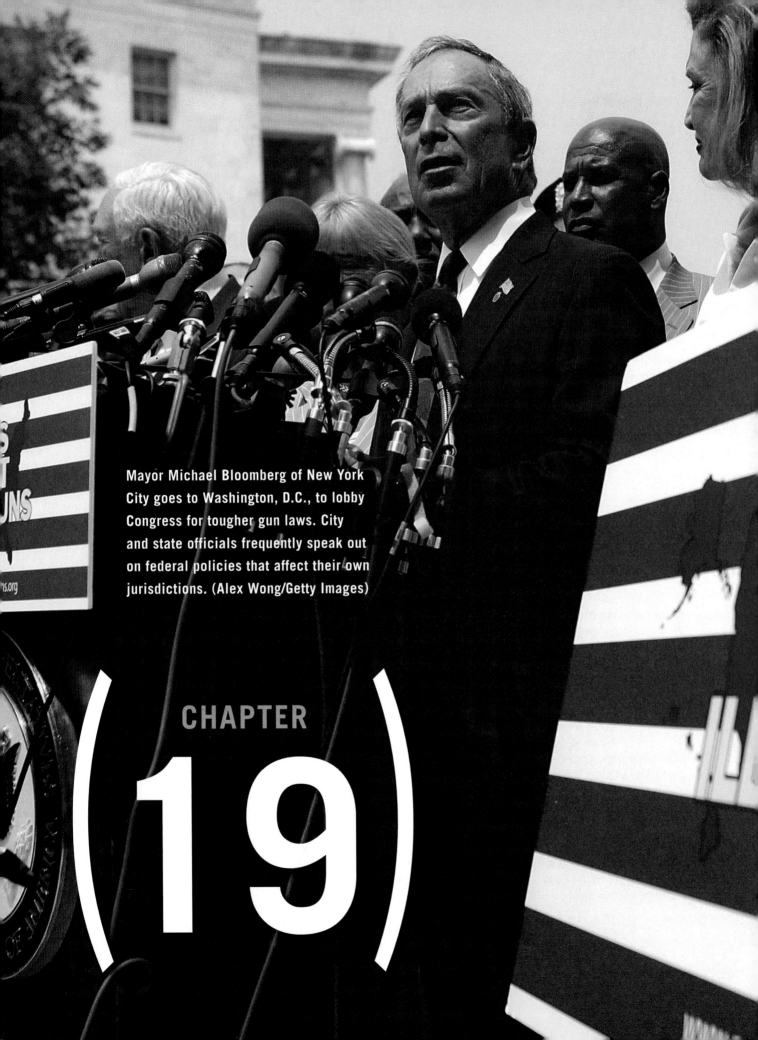

Mayor Michael Bloomberg of New York City goes to Washington, D.C., to lobby Congress for tougher gun laws. City and state officials frequently speak out on federal policies that affect their own jurisdictions. (Alex Wong/Getty Images)

CHAPTER

(19)

STATE AND LOCAL GOVERNMENT

QUESTIONS TO CONSIDER

What are the most important functions of state governments?

What is the value of keeping independent state governments?

What level of government is most responsive to citizens?

CHAPTER CONTENTS

Making a DIFFERENCE

WHO SHOULD RUN THE CITY, "PROFESSIONALS" OR POLITICIANS?

Who is the mayor of your city or town? Does she or he have executive branch powers like making appointments, proposing a city budget, and managing day-to-day business? If your mayor is well known and has this kind of authority, your town likely has a strong mayor system. In this type of system, the mayor is elected independently of the town or city council, as opposed to being chosen from the council. Large cities tend to have a strong mayor system, so-called for the executive-type powers the office controls.

Contrast this with a system where the city council is the most powerful elected municipal body. The council members might vie for the mayor's spot, which is usually ceremonial. In this council-manager system, the council will appoint a professional city manager, who will take on the daily management of the municipality.

Cities and towns must make choices about municipal government while considering how best to provide essential services (e.g., water, police, waste management) with limited resources. Advocates for the city manager system say it is more economical. They argue that trained professionals are able to hire and fire staff unencumbered by political patronage and have the educational and vocational background to eliminate waste and inefficiency.[a]

Many city manager systems were created during the Progressive Era, which fostered a meritocracy over patronage. These Progressive reformers at the turn of the 20th century valued expertise and skill and formed the modern bureaucracy we see at all levels of government:

FOR MOST AMERICANS, state and local governments have the most day-to-day impact on their lives. To get a driver's license, you must meet directly with a representative of the state government and complete state-required forms and tests to be certified to drive a car. You attended elementary and secondary schools that are provided by local governmental units, typically called school boards. Local governments determine the cost of a traffic ticket and the day that your street is cleaned. Because they shape the environments in which all Americans live, the more than 89,000 local governmental units in the United States play a vital role in our federal system.

From a practical point of view, it is impossible to understand American politics and government today without knowledge of how state and local governments operate—the topic of this chapter. We begin by examining the constitutional powers of the states as set forth by the founders in the U.S. Constitution. As you will see, local governments were not mentioned in the Constitution. The founders left their existence in the hands of state government. The *Making a Difference* feature highlights some different views on how local governments can be efficient and responsive to people's needs.

THE U.S. CONSTITUTION AND THE STATE GOVERNMENTS

We live in a federal system in which there are 50 separate state governments and one national government. The U.S. Constitution reserves a broad range of powers for state

city, state, and national. A professionalized city management assumed that "scientific management" was superior to political control, which would lead to "cronyism . . . and inferior standards."[b]

On the other side are proponents of the strong mayor system, where the mayor is elected and has the power to run the day-to-day operations of the municipality, including budget creation, management of personnel, and responsibility for delivery of essential goods and services. While almost half of all cities with more than 2,500 people use a council-manager system,[c] moderate to large-sized cities with city manager systems sometimes flirt with this strong mayor system. Though the larger the city, the greater likelihood of adopting this system, the reasons for success or failure of strong mayor initiatives seem to be specific to the particular city. For example, Miami-Dade, Florida, passed a strong mayor initiative in 2007, moving away from the council-manager system with a weak mayor, despite the strong opposition from some labor groups and city council members.[d] The popularity of the then mayor and general public support paved the way for the change.[e]

By contrast, the efforts of the pro-strong mayor groups in Dallas, Texas, were stymied by a coalition of community activists, African American and Latino civic leaders, and some leaders in the business community. A long history of political wrangling among these groups, as well as between the groups and the mayor, resulted in tensions that served as a contentious backdrop, making the strong mayor proposal even less likely to pass.

So, what has happened to cities that have switched to a strong mayor form of government away from a weak mayor/council-manager system? Little systematic evidence exists. Our federal system allows local governments to decide what structure of leadership they want at the helm of their municipality, and these decisions are examined on a case-by-case basis.

[a]www.council-manager.org/index.php, accessed June 5, 2008.
[b]www.hogriver.org/issues/v02n04/politics.htm, accessed June 5, 2008.
[c]www.council-manager.org/index.php, accessed June 5, 2008.
[d]"Strong Mayor Isn't a Cure-all," *St. Petersburg Times* (Florida), February 1, 2007, p. 16A.
[e]http://metropolitan.fiu.edu/downloads/HeraldStrongMayor.pdf, accessed June 5, 2008.

governments. It also prohibits state governments from engaging in certain activities. The U.S. Constitution does not say explicitly what the states actually may do. Rather, state powers are simply reserved, or residual: states may do anything that is not prohibited by the Constitution or anything that is not expressly within the realm of the national government.

The major reserved powers of the states are the powers to tax, spend, and regulate intrastate commerce (commerce within a given state). The states also have general police power, meaning that they can impose their will on their citizens in the areas of safety (through, say, traffic laws), health (immunizations), welfare (child-abuse laws), and morals (regulation of pornographic materials).

Restrictions on state and local governmental activity are implied by the Constitution in Article VI, Clause 2:

> This Constitution, and the Laws of the United States which shall be made in Pursuance thereof; and all Treaties made, or which shall be made, under the Authority of the United States, shall be the supreme Law of the Land; and the Judges in every State shall be bound thereby, any Thing in the Constitution or Laws of any State to the Contrary notwithstanding.

In other words, the U.S. Constitution is the supreme law of the land. No state or local law can be in conflict with the Constitution, with laws made by the national Congress, or with treaties entered into by the national government. State and local governments, however, will create policies that are at odds with federal policies or adopt policies

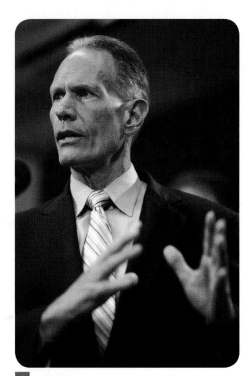

MIAMI-DADE MAYOR Carlos Alvarez speaks during a press conference about the federal government seizing control of the Miami-Dade Housing Agency in August 2007 in Miami, Florida. The government accused the county of grossly mismanaging housing programs for some of its neediest families. (Joe Raedle/Getty Images)

The Texas constitution declares that banks may use automated teller machines, and that the New York constitution specifies the width of ski trails?

that the federal government has not yet adopted. In recent years, states, especially those along the Mexican border, have passed their own policies to deal with illegal immigrants, in part because the Congress has not yet agreed on a new immigration policy. In Arizona, for example, a referendum passed in 2004 denies all social services to illegal immigrants, and laws passed by the Arizona legislature have toughened penalties on employers of illegal immigrants.[1] If, in the future, the U.S. Congress passes legislation that conflicts with the Arizona law, the United States Supreme Court would be the final arbiter of any conflict between the Arizona laws and the federal law.

STATE CONSTITUTIONS

The U.S. Constitution is a model of brevity, although at the cost of specificity. State constitutions, however, typically are excessively long and detailed. The U.S. Constitution has endured for 200 years and has been amended only 27 times. State constitutions are another matter. Louisiana has had 11 constitutions; Georgia, 10; South Carolina, seven; and Alabama, Florida, and Virginia, six. The number of amendments that have been submitted to voters borders on the absurd. For example, the citizens of Alabama have adopted 771 amendments to their state constitution.

WHY ARE STATE CONSTITUTIONS SO LONG?

According to historians, the length and mass of detail of many state constitutions reflect the loss of popular confidence in state legislatures between the end of the Civil War and the early 1900s. During that period, 42 states adopted or revised their constitutions. Those constitutions adopted before or after that period are shorter and contain fewer restrictions on the powers of state legislatures. Another equally important reason for the length and detail of state constitutions is that state constitution makers apparently have had a difficult time distinguishing between constitutional and statutory law. Does the Louisiana constitution need an amendment to declare Huey Long's birthday a legal holiday? Is it necessary for the constitution of South Dakota to authorize a cordage and twine plant at the state penitentiary? Does the California constitution need to discuss the tax-exempt status of the Huntington Library and Art Gallery? The U.S. Constitution contains no such details. It leaves to the legislature the nuts-and-bolts activity of making specific statutory laws.

In all fairness to the states, their courts do not interpret their constitutions as freely as the United States Supreme Court interprets the U.S. Constitution. Therefore, the states feel compelled to be more specific in their own constitutions. Additionally, the framers of state constitutions may feel obliged to fill in the gaps left by the very brief federal constitution.

THE CONSTITUTIONAL CONVENTION AND THE CONSTITUTIONAL INITIATIVE

Two of the several ways to effect constitutional changes are the state constitutional convention and the constitutional initiative. As of 2007, more than 230 state constitutional

[1]Mark K. Matthews, "Arizona Lashes out at Illegal Immigration," August 31, 2005, www.stateline.org.

conventions had been used to write an entirely new constitution or to attempt to amend an existing one. In 18 states, the constitution can be amended by **constitutional initiative**.[2] An initiative allows citizens to place a proposed amendment on the ballot without calling a constitutional convention. The number of signatures required to get a constitutional initiative on the ballot varies from state to state; it is usually between 5 and 10 percent of the total number of votes cast for governor in the last election. The initiative process has been used most frequently in California and Oregon. Relatively few initiative amendments are approved by the electorate.

THE STATE EXECUTIVE BRANCH

All state governments in the United States have executive, legislative, and judicial branches. Here the similarity with the federal government ends. State governments do not always have strong executive branches.

A WEAK EXECUTIVE

During the colonial period, governors were appointed by the Crown and had the power to call the colonial assembly (the colonial legislative body) into session, recommend legislation, exercise veto power, and dissolve the assembly. The colonial governor acted as commander in chief of the colony's military forces and was also the head of the judiciary.

---

[2]These states are Arizona, Arkansas, California, Colorado, Florida, Illinois, Massachusetts, Michigan, Mississippi, Missouri, Montana, Nebraska, Nevada, North Dakota, Ohio, Oklahoma, Oregon, and South Dakota.

DID YOU KNOW?

That the first woman to become governor of a state was Nellie Taylor Ross, who became governor of Wyoming in 1925?

Constitutional Initiative
An electoral device whereby citizens can propose a constitutional amendment through petitions signed by the required number of registered voters.

KANSAS GOVERNOR KATHLEEN SEBELIUS AND TOM VILSACK, former governor of Iowa, both Democrats, chat at the National Governors Convention. Governors are often seen as potential presidential or vice-presidential candidates because of their administrative and campaign experience. (Tom Mihalek/AP Photo)

Not surprisingly, the colonies' revolt against British rule centered on the all-powerful colonial governors. When the first states were formed after the Declaration of Independence, hostility toward the governor's office ensured a weak executive branch and an extremely strong legislative branch. By the 1830s, however, the state executive office had become more important. Since Andrew Jackson's presidency, all governors (except in South Carolina) have been elected directly by the people. Simultaneously, there was an effort to democratize state government by popularly electing other state government officials as well.

Under the tenets of Jacksonian democracy, the more public officials who are elected (and not appointed), the more democratic (and better) the system will be. Even today, some states have many state offices with independently elected officials. The direct election of so many executive officials makes it likely that no one will have much power, because each official is working to secure his or her own political support. Only if the elected officials happen to be able to work together cohesively can they get much done.

A slight majority of the states require that the candidates for governor and lieutenant governor run for election as a team. In some states where this is not required, however, the voters have at times chosen a governor from one political party and a lieutenant governor from another. In a few states, this has actually created a situation in which the governor is unwilling to leave the state in order to prevent the lieutenant governor from exerting power during the governor's absence.

DID YOU KNOW?

That the Louisiana legislature passed a law requiring students from kindergarten through fifth grade to address teachers as "sir" and "ma'am"?

REFORMING THE SYSTEM

Most states follow the practice of electing numerous executive officials. Nonetheless, governors have exercised the authority of their office with increasing frequency in recent years. Governors, for example, have become a significant force in legislative policy making. In theory, the governor enjoys the same advantage that the president has over Congress in his or her ability to make policy decisions and to embody these in a program on which the state legislative body can act. How the governor exercises this ability often depends on her or his powers of persuasion. A strong personality can make for a strong executive office. Personal skill, the strength of political parties and special-interest groups, and the governor's use of the media can affect how much actual power she or he has.

Reorganization of the state executive branch to achieve greater efficiency has been attempted many times and in many states. There are some obstacles to reorganizing state executive branches, however. Voters do not want to lose their ability to influence politics directly. Both the voters and the legislators fear that reorganization will concentrate too much authority in the hands of the governor. Finally, many believe that numerous governmental functions, such as control of the highway program, should remain administrative rather than political.

Despite the fragmentation of executive power and doubts about the concentration of power in an executive's hands, the trend toward modernization has increased the powers of many of the states' highest executives. Based on a governor's ability to make major appointments, formulate a state budget, veto legislation, and exercise other powers, the National Governors Association ranks the governors of at least 25 states as powerful or very powerful executives. Only 11 states are assessed as giving their executives little or very little power.

Moreover, state governors—as well as legislators—are playing increasingly important roles as the states assume more authority over programs, such as welfare, that for decades were controlled by the national government. The trend toward states' rights during the 1990s and 2000s has allowed governors to become models of leadership on several issues affecting national politics, including crime, welfare, and education. A state governorship may also be a stepping-stone to the U.S. presidency. Seventeen of the nation's 43 presidents (39 percent), including several recent presidents (Jimmy Carter, Ronald Reagan, Bill Clinton, and George W. Bush), served as state governors before assuming the presidential office. For these reasons, elections to state governorships tend to receive more national attention than in the past.

THE GOVERNOR'S VETO POWER

The veto power gives the president of the United States immense leverage. Simply the threat of a presidential veto often means that legislation will not be passed by Congress. In some states, governors have strong veto power, but in other states, governors have no veto power at all. Some states give the governor veto power but allow only five days in which to exercise it. Thirteen states give the governor pocket veto power.

In 43 states, the governor has some form of **item veto** power on appropriations, which gives the governor an opportunity to decrease legislative spending. If the governor in such a state does not like one item, or line, in an appropriations bill, he or she can veto that item. In 12 states, the governor can reduce the amount of the appropriation but cannot eliminate it altogether. Nineteen states give governors the ability to use the item veto on more than just appropriations.

Item Veto
The power exercised by the governors of most states to veto particular sections or items of an appropriations bill, while signing the remainder of the bill into law.

THE STATE LEGISLATURE

Although there has been a move in recent years to increase the power of governors, state legislatures are still an important force in state politics and state governmental decision making. The task of these assemblies is to legislate on such matters as taxes and the regulation of business and commerce, highways, school systems and the funding of education, and welfare payments. Allocation of funds and program priorities are vital issues to local residents and communities, and conflicts between regions within the state or between the cities and the rural areas are common.

State legislatures have been criticized for being unprofessional and less than effective. It is true that state legislatures sometimes spend their time considering trivial legislation (such as the official state pie in Florida), and lobbyists often have too much influence in state capitals. At the same time, state legislators are often given few resources with which to work. In many states, legislatures are limited to meeting only part of the year, and in some the pay is a disincentive to real service. In several states, state legislators are paid less than $15,000 per year. The National Council of State Legislatures actually categorizes state legislatures as fully professional, hybrid, or volunteer/part-time, according to the characteristics discussed here. A complete list of state legislators' salaries, as well as other characteristics of state legislatures, is given in Table 19–1.

We have seen earlier (Chapter 12) how a bill becomes a law in the U.S. Congress. A similar process occurs at the state level. Figure 19–1 on page 678 traces how an idea becomes a law in the Florida legislature. Similar steps are followed in other states (note that Nebraska has a unicameral legislature, however, so there is no second chamber process).

LEGISLATIVE APPORTIONMENT

Drawing up legislative districts—state as well as federal—has long been subject to gerrymandering (creative cartography designed to guarantee that

DID YOU KNOW?

That Missouri state legislators approved a five-pound, 1,012-page bill aimed at reducing state paperwork?

TABLE 19–1 Characteristics of State Legislatures

	SEATS IN SENATE	LENGTH OF TERM	SEATS IN HOUSE	LENGTH OF TERM	YEARS SESSIONS ARE HELD	SALARY*
Alabama	35	4	105	4	Annual	$10(d)†
Alaska	20	4	40	2	Annual	24,012†
Arizona	30	2	60	2	Annual	24,000†
Arkansas	35	4	100	2	Odd	14,765†
California	40	4	80	2	Even**	113,098†
Colorado	35	4	65	2	Annual	30,000†
Connecticut	36	2	151	2	Annual	28,000
Delaware	21	4	41	2	Annual	42,000
Florida	40	4	120	2	Annual	30,996†
Georgia	56	2	180	2	Annual	17,342†
Hawaii	25	4	51	2	Annual	35,900†
Idaho	35	2	70	2	Annual	16,116†
Illinois	59	‡	118	2	Annual	57,619†
Indiana	50	4	100	2	Annual	11,600†
Iowa	50	4	100	2	Annual	25,000†
Kansas	40	4	125	2	Annual	84.8(d)†
Kentucky	38	4	100	2	Annual	180.54(d)†
Louisiana	39	4	105	4	Annual	16,800†
Maine	35	2	151	2	Even	12,713§†
Maryland	47	4	141	4	Annual	43,500†
Massachusetts	40	2	160	2	Biennial**	58,237.15†
Michigan	38	4	110	2	Annual	79,650†
Minnesota	67	4	134	2	Biennial	31,141†
Mississippi	52	4	122	4	Annual	10,000†
Missouri	34	4	163	2	Annual	31,351†
Montana	50	4	100	2	Odd	82.67(d)†
Nebraska	49	4	—	—	Annual	12,000"
Nevada	21	4	42	2	Odd	137.9(d)†

one political party maintains control of a particular voting district). Malapportionment is the skewed distribution of voters in a state's legislative districts. The United States Supreme Court ruled in 1962 that malapportioned state legislatures violate the equal protection clause of the Fourteenth Amendment.[3] In a series of cases that followed, the Court held that legislative districts must be as nearly equal as possible in terms of population, and the grossest examples of state legislative malapportionment were eliminated.[4] The Supreme Court, however, allowed "benevolent, bipartisan gerrymandering" in certain states.

[3]*Baker v. Carr*, 369 U.S. 186 (1962).
[4]*Reynolds v. Sims*, 377 U.S. 533 (1964); and other cases.

Characteristics of State Legislatures—continued

	SEATS IN SENATE	LENGTH OF TERM	SEATS IN HOUSE	LENGTH OF TERM	YEARS SESSIONS ARE HELD	SALARY*
New Hampshire	24	2	400	2	Annual	200(b)
New Jersey	40	4	80	2	Biennial	49,000
New Mexico	42	4	70	2	Annual	—†
New York	62	2	150	2	Annual	79,500†
North Carolina	50	2	120	2	Odd††	13,951†
North Dakota	47	4	94	4	Odd	125(d)†
Ohio	33	4	99	2	Biennial	58,934
Oklahoma	48	4	101	2	Annual	38,400†
Oregon	30	4	60	2	Odd	18,408†
Pennsylvania	50	4	203	2	Odd**	73,613†
Rhode Island	38	2	75	2	Annual	13,089
South Carolina	46	4	124	2	Biennial	10,400†
South Dakota	35	2	70	2	Annual	12,000†
Tennessee	33	4	99	2	Biennial	18,123†
Texas	31	4	150	2	Odd	7,200†
Utah	29	4	75	2	Annual	130(d)†
Vermont	30	2	150	2	Annual	600.78(w)†
Virginia	40	4	100	2	Annual	18,000‡‡
Washington	49	4	98	2	Annual	36,311†
West Virginia	34	4	100	2	Annual	15,000†
Wisconsin	33	4	99	2	Biennial	47,413†
Wyoming	30	4	60	2	Biennial	150(d)†

*Salaries annual unless otherwise noted as (d)—per day, (b)—biennium, or (w)—per week.
†Plus *per diem* living expenses.
‡Terms vary from two to four years.
§For odd year; $8,655 for even year.
‖Unicameral legislature.
**Two-year session (that is, it meets every year).
††Annual at option of legislature.
‡‡Senate; House is $17,640.
Source: Council of State Governments, *Book of the States*, Vol. 38, (2006 Edition).

Minority Representation. In 1977, the Supreme Court held that a state had an obligation under the 1965 Voting Rights Act to draw district boundaries to maximize minority legislative representation.[5] Thus, each decade, state and federal legislative districts must be redrawn to ensure that every person's vote is roughly equal and that minorities are represented adequately.

By the mid-1990s, the Supreme Court had reversed its position on what has been called "racial gerrymandering." In a series of cases, the Court held that voting districts that are redrawn solely with the goal of maximizing the electoral strength and representation

[5]*United Jewish Organizations of Williamsburg v. Cary*, 430 U.S. 144 (1977).

FIGURE 19–1 How an Idea Becomes a Law

A simplified chart showing the route a bill takes through the Florida legislature. Bills may originate in either house. This bill originated in the House of Representatives.

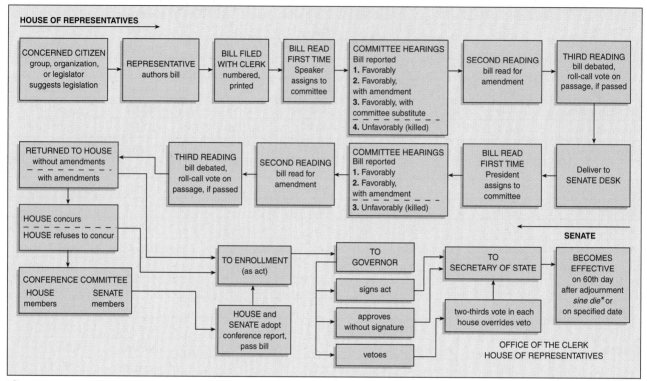

Sine die means "without assigning a day for a further meeting."
Source: Allen Morris and Joan Perry Morris, compilers, *The Florida Handbook, 2005–2006*, 30th ed. (Tallahassee, FL: Peninsular Books, 2005).

of minority groups violate the equal protection clause.[6] (See Chapter 12 for a more detailed discussion of this issue.)

Political Gerrymandering. In recent years, political gerrymandering that benefits both of the major political parties has become a significant issue. Using sophisticated computer programs, legislators can draw district lines that virtually guarantee the re-election of incumbents. In many states, Republican and Democratic legislators conspire to ensure the safety of incumbents, regardless of party. In 2004, for example, not a single seat in the California state legislature changed hands. Some have said that instead of the voters choosing their legislators, the legislators now choose their voters. The Supreme Court has not blocked this practice. In 1986, the Court did hold that it was at least conceivable that an instance of political gerrymandering might be unconstitutional.[7] In 2004 and 2006, however, the Court in effect withdrew the possibility that it might ever issue such a ruling.[8]

Citizens in states ranging from Massachusetts to California have organized campaigns to win new laws that curb political gerrymandering. Iowa and Arizona already use nonpartisan commissions to draw district lines instead of leaving the job to the legislature and the governor. In California, Governor Arnold Schwarzenegger has called for such a system, so far without success. Some experts believe that regional political loyalties have become so entrenched that nonpartisan plans can create only a handful of competitive districts.[9]

[6]*Miller v. Johnson*, 515 U.S. 900 (1995); *Shaw v. Hunt*, 517 U.S. 899 (1996); and *Bush v. Vera*, 517 U.S. 952 (1996).
[7]*Davis v. Bandemer*, 478 U.S. 109 (1986).
[8]*Vieth v. Jubelirer*, 541 U.S. 267 (2004); and *League of Latin American Citizens v. Perry*, 126 S.Ct. 2594 (2006).
[9]Steven Hill, "Schwarzenegger vs. Gerrymander," *The New York Times*, February 19, 2005, p. A29.

TERM LIMITS FOR STATE LEGISLATORS

For more than a decade, many states have agreed that a legislator's tenure should be limited. Although the restrictions vary, 15 states have laws restricting the number of terms for which a legislator can serve. In four other states—Massachusetts, Oregon, Washington, and Wyoming—term-limit laws were thrown out by the respective state supreme courts, while Idaho and Utah's legislatures repealed their own term-limit laws. Advocates of term limits argue that lawmakers who have not spent years in public office will best represent the interests of voters. Special-interest groups will have less chance to influence a politician who does not have a future campaign to finance. Opponents of term limits argue that the same newly elected lawmakers who are less likely to be swayed by special interests are also more likely to lack the experience that is required to understand state policy. Ironically, such opponents include current politicians who once voted for term limits but are now subject to their consequences.

Making service in the legislature a part-time job rather than a full-time one is another way states try to keep legislators in tune with their fellow citizens. In some states, especially large states such as California and New York, state legislators receive a salary that is large enough to live on. In these states, service in the legislature is considered a full-time job, and the members of the state house and senate are referred to as professional legislators. In a majority of the states, however, legislative service is considered part-time work, and salaries reflect this expectation. Such states are said to have citizen legislators. New Hampshire is an extreme example of this system. The four hundred members of its house are paid only $200 per session, with no allowance for expenses. New Hampshire has only about 1.3 million people, so it is relatively easy for a political activist to become part of the legislature.

Advocates of a professional legislature recognize that this system would be a hard sell in a state with a small population, such as Montana. Still, these advocates believe that a part-time legislature creates significant problems and that larger states such as Texas should not rely on such a system. Paid only $7,200 per year, Texas legislators have a powerful incentive to represent and take payments from corrupt special interests. Paying legislators a living wage would actually make it easier for ordinary citizens to run for office. Service should not be limited to the retired, the wealthy, and lawyers who represent the powerful. Those who support a citizen legislature do not believe that states with professional legislators have better laws. They contend that much of the extra time spent by professional legislators is likely to be wasted and that making legislators full-time professionals encourages careerism and a lack of responsiveness to the voters.

ETHICS AND CAMPAIGN FINANCE REFORM IN THE STATES

Regulations for campaign contributions and the disclosure of contributors for all federal offices, including representatives, senators, and the president, are the result of legislation passed by the Congress and rules put forward by the Federal Elections Commission. However, regulations that affect candidates for office at the state level are the responsibility of state legislatures and the governor. States differ a great deal on the degree to which they regulate campaign contributions and the disclosure of donors. For example, while most states require that all contributions be disclosed to the public through some sort of quarterly reporting system, the amount of information that is disclosed about the donors varies widely, as does the public's access to the information. Some states require that the donor's name, occupation, address, and employer be disclosed, whereas 12 states do not require either the donor's occupation or employer be disclosed, thus hiding contributions from those industries that might benefit from legislation. Almost all states require that candidates report expenditures, but several do not require the amount or purpose of the expenditure to be revealed. Report requirements have greatly increased in recent years, but 17 states still do not audit these reports in any way.[10]

Similarly, states have struggled to enact and enforce ethics legislation. If a legislature is composed of volunteer legislators meeting, perhaps, for four or five months per year, and being paid less than $15,000, it seems unlikely that the legislators depend on their elected position for their livelihood. Most part-time legislators have real careers and earn their living through those positions. However, there are always questions of conflicts of interest, lobbying gifts and parties, and opportunities for a legislator or the staff to benefit from a particular piece of legislation. There are numerous examples of legislators and governors who have suffered legal action from lapses in ethical decision making. Generally, states have tried to adopt ethics codes that would prohibit legislators and other officeholders from accepting gifts or free dinners from lobbyists or to disclose gifts over a minimum amount. In Tennessee, legislators must disclose any contribution over $250. In addition, states are passing ethics laws that prohibit former legislators from becoming lobbyists at the state capitol for a certain period of time. Six states have a two-year period before a legislator can become a lobbyist, whereas 20 states require sitting out for only one year.[11] Sometimes, it appears that ethics rules can go too far. Recently, a Colorado amendment to the constitution passed by voters in 2006 prevented any state official's child from receiving a college scholarship or any Colorado college professor from accepting the Nobel Prize.[12]

DIRECT DEMOCRACY: THE INITIATIVE, REFERENDUM, AND RECALL

There is a major difference between the legislative process as outlined in the U.S. Constitution and the legislative process as outlined in the various state constitutions. Many states exercise a type of direct democracy through the initiative, the referendum, and the recall—procedures that allow voters to control the government directly.

The Initiative. One technique lets citizens bypass legislatures by proposing new statutes or changes in government for citizen approval. Most states that permit the citizen legislative require that the initiative's backers circulate a petition to place the issue on the ballot and that a certain percentage of the registered voters in the last gubernatorial election sign the petition. Twenty-four states use the legislative initiative, typically those states in which political parties are relatively weak and nonpartisan groups are strong. Legislative initiatives have involved a range of issues, including crime victims' rights, campaign contributions, corporate spending on ballot questions, affirmative action, physician-assisted suicide, and the medical use of marijuana. In some instances, voters have passed state initiatives that are contrary to federal policy. For example, several states passed initiatives legalizing the use of marijuana for medical purposes, a policy that conflicts with federal law.

[10]"Grading Campaign Disclosure 2007," The Campaign Disclosure Project, www.campaigndisclosure.org.
[11]"Ethics Reform," Center for Policy Alternatives, National Council of State Legislatures, www.cfpa.org.
[12]Karl Kurtz, "Colorado Ethics Initiative Blocked by Court," The Thicket at State Legislatures, July 1, 2007, http://ncsl.typepad.com/the_thicket.

The Referendum. The referendum is similar to the initiative, except that the issue (or constitutional change) is proposed first by the legislature and then directed to the voters for their approval. The referendum is most often used for approval of local school bond issues and for amendments to state constitutions. In several states that provide for the referendum, a bill passed by the legislature may be suspended by obtaining the required number of voters' signatures on petitions. A statewide referendum election is then held. If a majority of the voters disapprove of the bill, it is no longer valid.

The referendum was not initially intended for regular use, and it was employed infrequently in the past. Its opponents argue that it is an unnecessary check on representative government and that it weakens legislative responsibility. In recent years, the referendum has become increasingly popular as citizens have attempted to control their state and local governments. Interest groups have been active in sponsoring the petition drives necessary to force a referendum. More than two-thirds of the states provide for the referendum.

The Recall. The right of citizens to recall (or remove) elected officials is not exercised frequently. Recall is a provision written into the constitutions of 15 states. It allows voters to remove elected state officials, including the governor, before the expiration of their terms of office. In the case of judges, the recall can terminate a lifetime appointment.

Citizens begin the recall process by circulating petitions demanding a statewide vote to remove the offending officeholder. The number of signatures required to bring about the election ranges from 10 to 40 percent of the last vote for the office in question. If the required number of signatures is obtained, the matter of whether to remove the incumbent is decided in a general election.

The recall and the initiative are examples of "pure democracy," in which the people as a whole vote directly on important issues. Such measures are distinct in theory and in practice from the norms of "representative democracy," in which the people govern only indirectly through their elected representatives.

THE STATE JUDICIARY

In addition to the federal courts, each of the 50 states, as well as the District of Columbia, has its own separate court system. Figure 19–2 shows a sample state court system. Like the federal court system, it has several tiers, including trial courts, intermediate courts of appeals, and a supreme court.

TRIAL COURTS

All states have major trial courts, commonly called circuit courts, district courts, or superior courts. The number of judges and their terms in office vary widely. As in the federal court system, the trial courts are of two types: those having limited jurisdiction and those having general jurisdiction.[13] Cases heard before these courts can be appealed to the state intermediate appellate court and ultimately to the state supreme court.

APPELLATE COURTS

About three-fourths of the states have intermediate appellate courts between the trial courts of original jurisdiction and the highest state appellate court, or the supreme

DID YOU KNOW?

That the most expensive ballot initiative in history was California's Proposition 5 (the opposing sides of the 1998 proposition, which permitted video slot machines and card games on Indian reservations, spent a total of approximately $100 million)?

[13]See Chapter 15 for a definition of these terms.

FIGURE 19–2 A Sample State Court System

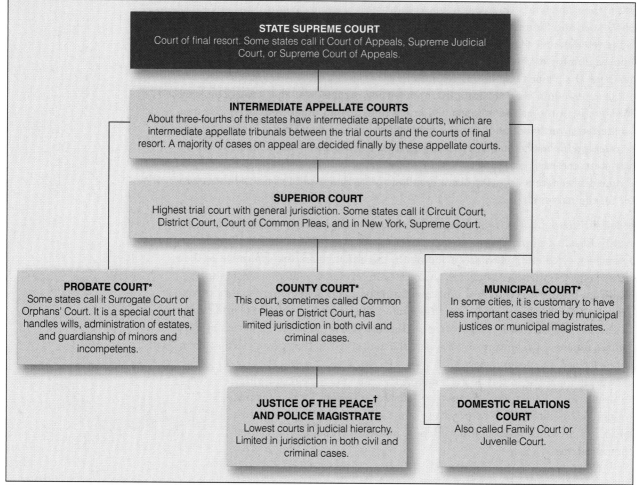

STATE SUPREME COURT
Court of final resort. Some states call it Court of Appeals, Supreme Judicial Court, or Supreme Court of Appeals.

INTERMEDIATE APPELLATE COURTS
About three-fourths of the states have intermediate appellate courts, which are intermediate appellate tribunals between the trial courts and the courts of final resort. A majority of cases on appeal are decided finally by these appellate courts.

SUPERIOR COURT
Highest trial court with general jurisdiction. Some states call it Circuit Court, District Court, Court of Common Pleas, and in New York, Supreme Court.

PROBATE COURT*
Some states call it Surrogate Court or Orphans' Court. It is a special court that handles wills, administration of estates, and guardianship of minors and incompetents.

COUNTY COURT*
This court, sometimes called Common Pleas or District Court, has limited jurisdiction in both civil and criminal cases.

MUNICIPAL COURT*
In some cities, it is customary to have less important cases tried by municipal justices or municipal magistrates.

JUSTICE OF THE PEACE†
AND POLICE MAGISTRATE
Lowest courts in judicial hierarchy. Limited in jurisdiction in both civil and criminal cases.

DOMESTIC RELATIONS COURT
Also called Family Court or Juvenile Court.

*Courts of special jurisdiction, such as probate, family, or juvenile courts, and the so-called inferior courts, such as common pleas or municipal courts, may be separate courts or may be part of the trial court of general jurisdiction.
†Justices of the peace do not exist in all states. Their jurisdiction varies greatly from state to state when they do exist.
Source: William P. Statsky, *Essentials of Paralegalism: Perspectives, Problems, and Skills,* 4th ed. (Clifton Park, NY: Thomson Delmar Learning, 2006).

DID YOU KNOW?

That until 1975, the United States Supreme Court allowed the states to exclude women from jury duty?

court. These are usually called courts of appeals. Salaries of state judges vary widely, but higher pay is given to appellate and supreme court members.

The highest state appellate courts are usually called simply supreme courts, although they are also labeled the supreme judicial court (Maine and Massachusetts), the court of appeals (Maryland and New York), the court of criminal appeals (Oklahoma and Texas, which also have separate supreme courts for appeals in noncriminal cases), or the supreme court of appeals (West Virginia). The decisions of each state's highest court on all questions of state law are final. Only when issues of federal law are involved can a decision made by a state's highest court be overruled by the United States Supreme Court.

JUDICIAL ELECTIONS AND APPOINTMENTS

State court judges are either elected or appointed, depending on the state and (often) on the level of court involved—the procedures vary widely from state to state. In some states, including Delaware, the procedure is similar to the way federal judges are appointed: the judges are appointed by the governor and confirmed by the upper chamber of the legislature. In other states, all state court judges are elected, either on a partisan ballot (as in Alabama) or on a nonpartisan ballot (as in Kentucky). In several states, judges in some of the lower courts are elected, while those in the appellate courts are appointed. Additionally, depending on the state, judges who are appointed may have to run for re-election if they wish to serve a second term.

In the 38 states that elect judges, many of these elections are turning into hard-fought political battles. This is happening even in states with nonpartisan elections. A little-noted Supreme Court decision has changed the old rules for judicial campaigning. In 2002, the Court overturned a state law that barred judicial candidates from commenting on controversies they might have to resolve.[14] Now groups with strong opinions on abortion or same-sex marriage can grill candidates on these issues. In some states, judicial races have turned into fights between trial lawyers who sue businesses and the businesses that they sue. Some judges now advocate replacing judicial elections with an appointive system. The American Bar Association has called for public financing of judicial campaigns so that candidates will not have to seek private contributions.

HOW LOCAL GOVERNMENT OPERATES

Local governments are difficult to describe because of their great dissimilarities and because, if we include municipalities, counties, towns, townships, and special districts, there are so many of them. We limit the discussion here to the most important types and features of local governments.

THE LEGAL EXISTENCE OF LOCAL GOVERNMENT

As mentioned earlier, the U.S. Constitution makes no mention of local governments. Article IV, Section 4, merely states that "[t]he United States shall guarantee to every State in this Union a Republican Form of Government." Actually, then, the states do not even need to have local governments. Consequently, every local government is a creature of the state. The state can create a local government, and the state can terminate the right of a local government to exist. States often have abolished entire counties, school districts, cities, and special districts. Since World War II (1939–1945), almost 20,000 school districts have gone out of existence as they were consolidated with other school districts.

Because the local government is the legal creation of the state, does that mean the state can dictate everything the local government does? For many years, that seemed to be the case. The narrowest possible view of the legal status of local governments follows **Dillon's rule**, outlined by Judge John F. Dillon in his *Commentaries on the Law of Municipal Corporations* in 1872. He stated that municipal corporations may possess only powers "granted in express words . . . [that are] necessarily or fairly implied in or incident to the powers expressly granted."[15] Cities governed under Dillon's rule have sometimes been dominated by the state legislatures, depending on the extent of the authority granted to the cities by the legislatures. Those communities wishing to obtain the status of a municipal corporation have petitioned the state legislature for a **charter**.

In a revolt against state legislative power over municipalities, the home rule movement began. It was based on **Cooley's rule**, derived from an 1871 decision by Michigan judge Thomas Cooley stating that cities should be able to govern themselves.[16] Since 1900, about four-fifths of the states have allowed **municipal home rule**, but only with

Dillon's Rule
The narrowest possible interpretation of the legal status of local governments, outlined by Judge John E. Dillon, who in 1872 stated that a municipal corporation can exercise only those powers expressly granted by state law.

Charter
A document issued by a government that grants to a person, a group of persons, or a corporation the right to carry on one or more specific activities. A state government can grant a charter to a municipality.

Cooley's Rule
The view that cities should be able to govern themselves, presented in an 1871 Michigan decision by Judge Thomas Cooley.

Municipal Home Rule
The power vested in a local unit of government to draft or change its own charter and to manage its own affairs.

[14]*Republican Party of Minnesota v. White*, 536 U.S. 765 (2002).
[15]John F. Dillon, *Commentaries on the Law of Municipal Corporations*, 5th ed. (Boston: Little, Brown, 1911), Vol. 1, Sec. 237.
[16]*People v. Hurlbut*, 24 Mich. 44 (1871).

respect to local concerns for which no statewide interests are involved. A municipality must choose to become a **home rule city**; otherwise, it operates as a **general law city**. In the latter case, the state makes certain general laws relating to cities of different sizes, which are designated as first-class cities, second-class cities, or towns. Once a city, by virtue of its population, receives such a ranking, it follows the general law established by the state. Only if it chooses to be a home rule city can it avoid such state government restrictions. In many states, only cities with populations of 2,500 or more can choose home rule.

LOCAL GOVERNMENTAL UNITS

There are four major types of local governmental units: municipalities, counties, towns and townships, and special districts.

Municipalities. A municipality is a political entity created by the people of a city or town to govern themselves locally. Currently, there are more than 19,000 municipalities within the 50 states. Almost all municipalities are fairly small cities. Only about 200 cities have populations more than 100,000, and only nine cities (Chicago, Dallas, Houston, Los Angeles, New York, Philadelphia, Phoenix, San Antonio, and San Diego) have populations more than 1 million. City expenditures are primarily for water supply and other utilities, police and fire protection, and education. About three-fourths of municipal tax revenues come from property taxes. Municipalities often rely heavily on financial assistance from both the federal and state governments.

Counties. The difference between a **county** and a municipality is that a county is usually not created at the behest of its inhabitants. The state sets up counties on its own initiative to serve as political extensions of the state government. Counties apply state law and administer state business at the local level.

There are more than 3,000 counties within the United States; they vary greatly in both size and population. San Bernardino County in California is the largest geographically, with 20,102 square miles. New York County in New York is possibly the smallest, with less than 22 square miles. County populations within California alone range from millions of residents, as in Los Angeles County, to barely a thousand, as in Alpine County.

County governments' responsibilities include zoning, building regulations, health, hospitals, parks, recreation, highways, public safety, justice, and recordkeeping. Typically, when a municipality is established within a county, the county withdraws most of its services from the municipality; for example, the municipal police force takes over from the county police force. County governments are extremely complex entities, a product of the era of Jacksonian democracy and its effort to bring government closer to the people. There is no easy way to describe their operation in summary form. The county has been called by one scholar "the dark continent of American politics."[17]

Towns and Townships. A unique governmental creation in the New England states is the **New England town**—not to be confused with the word *town* (meaning a small city). In Connecticut, Maine, Massachusetts, New Hampshire, and Vermont, the unit called the town combines the roles of city and county in one governing unit. A New England

Home Rule City
A city permitted by the state to let local voters frame, adopt, and amend their own charter.

General Law City
A city operating under general state laws that apply to all local governmental units of a similar type.

DID YOU KNOW?

That there are more than 100,000 elementary and secondary schools in the United States?

County
The chief governmental unit set up by the state to administer state law and business at the local level. Counties are drawn up by area, rather than by rural or urban criteria.

New England Town
A governmental unit in the New England states that combines the roles of city and county in one unit.

---

[17]Henry S. Gilbertson, *The County, the "Dark Continent of American Politics"* (New York: National Short Ballot Association, 1917).

town typically consists of one or more urban settlements and the surrounding rural areas. Consequently, counties have little importance in New England. In Connecticut, for example, they are simply geographic units.

From the New England town is derived the tradition of the **town meeting**, an annual meeting at which direct democracy was—and continues to be—practiced. Each resident of a town is summoned to the annual meeting at the town hall. Those who attend levy taxes, pass laws, elect town officers, and appropriate money for different activities.

Normally, few residents show up for town meetings today unless an item of high interest is on the agenda or unless family members want to be elected to office. The town meeting takes a day or more, and few citizens are able to set aside such a large amount of time. Because of the declining interest in town meetings, many New England towns have adopted a **town manager system**: the voters simply elect three **select-persons**, who then appoint a professional town manager. The town manager in turn appoints other officials.

Townships operate somewhat like counties, though on a lower level. Where they exist, there may be several dozen within a county. They perform some of the functions that the county would otherwise perform. Most Midwestern states have townships, and they are also found in New Jersey, New York, and Pennsylvania. A township is not the same thing as a New England town, because it is meant to be a rural government rather than a city government. Moreover, it is never the principal unit of local government, as are New England towns. The boundaries of most townships are based on federal land surveys that began in the 1780s, mapping the land into six-square-mile blocks called townships. They were then subdivided into 36 blocks of one square mile each, called sections. Typically, a road was built along the boundaries of each section.

Although townships have few functions in many parts of the nation, they are still politically important in others. In some metropolitan areas, townships are the political unit that provides most public services to residents who live in suburban **unincorporated areas**.

Special Districts and School Districts. The most numerous local government units are special districts. Currently, there are more than 35,000 special districts (see Table 19–2). Special districts are one-function governments that usually are created by the state legislature and governed by a board of directors. Special districts may be called authorities, boards, corporations, or simply districts.

One important feature of special districts is that they cut across geographic and governmental boundaries. Sometimes special districts even cut across state lines. For example, the Port Authority of New York and New Jersey was established by an interstate compact between the two states in 1921 to develop and operate the harbor

Town Meeting
The governing authority of a New England town. Qualified voters may participate in the election of officers and the passage of legislation.

Town Manager System
A form of town government in which voters elect three selectpersons, who then appoint a professional town manager, who in turn appoints other officials.

Selectperson
A member of the governing group of a town.

Township
A rural unit of government based on federal land surveys of the American frontier in the 1780s. Townships have declined significantly in importance.

Unincorporated Area
An area not located within the boundary of a municipality.

TABLE 19–2 Local Governments in the United States

Counties	3,033
Municipalities (mainly cities and towns)	19,492
Townships (less extensive powers)	16,519
Special districts (water supply, fire protection, hospitals, libraries, parks and recreation, highways, sewers, and the like)	37,381
School districts	13,051
Total	**89,476**

Source: U.S. Census Bureau, Preliminary Report, 2007 Census of Governments.

facilities in the area. A mosquito control district may cut across both municipal and county lines. A metropolitan transit district may provide bus service to dozens of municipalities and to several counties.

School districts, although listed separately in Table 19–2, are essentially a type of special district. Except for school districts, the typical citizen is not very aware of most special districts. Most citizens do not know who furnishes their weed control, mosquito abatement, water, or sewage service. Part of the reason for the low profile of special districts is that most special district administrators are appointed, not elected, and therefore receive little public attention.

CONSOLIDATION OF GOVERNMENTS

> **Consolidation**
> The union of two or more governmental units to form a single unit.

With more than 80,000 separate and often overlapping governmental units within the United States, the trend toward consolidation in recent years is understandable. **Consolidation** is the union of two or more governmental units to form a single unit. Typically, a state constitution or a state statute will designate consolidation procedures.

Consolidation is often recommended for metropolitan-area problems, but to date there have been few consolidations within metropolitan areas. The most successful consolidations have been **functional consolidations**, particularly of city and county police, health, and welfare departments. In some situations, functional consolidation is a satisfactory alternative to the complete consolidation of governmental units. One of the most successful examples of functional consolidation was started in 1957 in Dade County, Florida. The county government, now called Miami-Dade, is a union of 26 municipalities. Each municipality has its own governmental entity, but the county government has the authority to furnish water, planning, mass transit, and police services and to set minimum standards of performance. The governing body of Miami-Dade is an elected board of county commissioners, which appoints an executive mayor.

> **Functional Consolidation**
> Cooperation by two or more units of local government in providing services to their inhabitants. This is generally done by unifying a set of departments (e.g., the police departments) into a single agency.

A special type of consolidation is the **council of governments (COG)**, a voluntary organization of counties and municipalities that attempts to deal with area-wide problems. More than two hundred COGs have been established, mainly since 1966. The impetus for their establishment was, and continues to be, federal government grants. COGs are an alternative means of treating major regional problems that various communities are unwilling to tackle on a consolidated basis, either by true consolidation of governmental units or by functional consolidation.

> **Council of Governments (COG)**
> A voluntary organization of counties and municipalities concerned with area-wide problems.

The power of COGs is advisory only. Each member unit simply selects its council representatives, who report back to the unit after COG meetings. Nonetheless, today several COGs have gained considerable influence on regional policy. These include the Metropolitan Washington Council of Governments in Washington, D.C., the Supervisors' Inter-County Commission in Detroit, and the Association of Bay Area Governments in the San Francisco Bay area.

HOW MUNICIPALITIES ARE GOVERNED

We can divide municipal representative governments into four general types of plans: (1) the commission plan, (2) the council-manager plan, (3) the mayor-administrator plan, and (4) the mayor-council plan.

The Commission Plan. The commission form of municipal government consists of a commission of three to nine members who have both legislative and executive powers. The salient aspects of the commission plan are as follows:

1. Executive and legislative powers are concentrated in a small group of individuals, who are elected at large on a (normally) nonpartisan ballot.
2. Each commissioner is individually responsible for heading a particular municipal department, such as the department of public safety.
3. The commission is collectively responsible for passing ordinances and controlling spending.
4. The mayor (an office that is only ceremonial) is selected from the members of the commission.

The commission plan, originating in Galveston, Texas, in 1901, had its greatest popularity during the first 20 years of the 20th century. It appealed to municipal government reformers. They looked on it as a type of business organization that would eliminate the problems they believed to be inherent in the long ballot and in partisan municipal politics. Unfortunately, vesting both legislative and executive power in the hands of a small group of individuals means that there are no checks and balances on administration and spending. Also, because the mayoral office is ceremonial, there is no provision for strong leadership. Not surprisingly, only about one hundred cities today use the commission plan—Atlantic City, Mobile, Salt Lake City, Topeka, and Tulsa are a few of them.

The Council-Manager Plan. In the council-manager form of municipal government, a city council appoints a professional manager, who acts as the chief executive. He or she typically is called the city manager. In principle, the manager is there simply to see that the general directions of the city council are carried out. The important features of the council-manager plan are as follows:

1. A professional, trained manager can hire and fire subordinates and is responsible to the council.
2. The council or commission consists of five to seven members, elected at large on a nonpartisan ballot.
3. The mayor may be chosen from within the council or from outside, but he or she has no executive function. As with the commission plan, the mayor's job may be largely ceremonial, or it may be limited to chairing council meetings. The city manager works for the council, not the mayor (unless, of course, the mayor is part of the council).

Today, about two thousand cities use the council-manager plan. About one-third of the cities with populations of more than 5,000 and about one-half of the cities with populations of more than 25,000 operate with this type of plan. Only four large cities—Cincinnati, Dallas, San Antonio, and San Diego—have adopted this plan.

The major defect of the council-manager scheme, as with the commission plan, is that there is no single, strong political executive leader. It is therefore not surprising that large cities rarely use such a plan.

The Mayor-Administrator Plan. The mayor-administrator plan is often used in large cities where there is a strong mayor. It is similar to the council-manager plan except that the political leadership is vested in the mayor. The mayor is an elected chief executive. She or he appoints an administrative officer, whose function is to free the mayor from routine administrative tasks, such as personnel direction and budget supervision.

The Mayor-Council Plan. The mayor-council form of municipal government is the oldest and most widely used. The mayor is an elected chief executive, and the council is the legislative body. Virtually all councils are unicameral. The council typically has five to nine members, except in very large cities. For example, in Chicago, the council has 50

DID YOU KNOW?

That the first African American mayors of big cities were Richard G. Hatcher of Gary, Indiana, and Carl B. Stokes of Cleveland, Ohio, both elected in 1967?

members. Council members are popularly elected for terms as long as six, but normally four, years.

The mayor-council plan can either be a strong-mayor type or a weak-mayor type. In the *strong mayor-council plan*, the mayor is the chief executive and has virtually complete control over hiring and firing employees, as well as preparing the budget. The mayor exercises strong and positive leadership in the formation of city policies. The *weak mayor-council plan* separates executive and legislative functions completely. The mayor is elected as chief executive officer; the council is elected as the legislative body. This traditional division of powers allows for checks and balances on spending and administration.

About 50 percent of American cities use some form of the mayor-council plan. Most recently, the mayor-council plan has lost ground to the council-manager plan in small and middle-sized cities.

MACHINE VERSUS REFORM IN CITY POLITICS

For much of the late 19th and early 20th centuries, many major cities were run by "the machine." The machine was an integrated political organization. Each city block within the municipality had an organizer, each neighborhood had a political club, each district had a leader, and all of these parts of the machine had a boss—such as William Tweed in New York, Richard Daley in Chicago, Edward Crump in Memphis, or Tom Pendergast in Kansas City. The machine became a popular form of city political organization in the 1840s, when the first waves of European immigrants came to the United States to work in urban factories. Those individuals, often lacking the ability to communicate in English, needed help—and the machine was created to help them.[18] The urban machine drew on the support of the dominant ethnic groups to forge a strong political institution that was able to keep the boss (usually the mayor) in office year after year. The machine was oiled by patronage—rewarding faithful party workers and followers with government employment and contracts. The party in power was often referred to as the patronage party.[19]

[18]See Harvey W. Zorbaugh, *The Gold Coast and the Slum: A Sociological Study of Chicago's Near North Side* (Chicago: University of Chicago Press, 1929).
[19]See, for example, Harold F. Gosnell, *Machine Politics: Chicago Model* (Chicago: University of Chicago Press, 1937).

According to sociologist Robert Merton, the machine offered personalized assistance to the needy, helped establish local businesses, opened avenues of upward social mobility for the underprivileged, and afforded a locus of strong political authority and responsibility.[20] Others, however, viewed party machines and the behind-the-scenes government that they often involved as contrary to our principles of government. In their classic work on city politics, Edward Banfield and James Q. Wilson also gave a critical appraisal of machine politics:

> [M]achine government is, essentially, a system of organized bribery. The destruction of machines . . . permit[s] government on the basis of appropriate motives, that is, public-regarding ones. In fact it has other highly desirable consequences—especially greater honesty, impartiality, and (in routine matters) efficiency.[21]

When the last of the big-city bosses, Mayor Richard Daley of Chicago, died in December 1976, an era died with him. The big-city machine began to be in serious trouble in the 1960s, when community activists organized to work for a more professional and efficient municipal government. Soon, governments of administrators rather than politicians began to appear. Fewer offices were elective; more were appointive.

Switching from a political to an administrative form of urban government was a way to break up the centralized urban political machine. In some cities, the results have been beneficial to most citizens. In others, decentralization has gone so far that no strong leader exists to pull together discordant factions to create and follow a coherent policy. Consequently, in cities with a highly decentralized government typified by numerous independent commissions and boards, much that should be done does not get done, particularly when an area-wide concern is involved. This is an especially severe problem for less economically privileged people, who used to be able to rely on machine-sponsored activities and on the machine's political clout to help them compete against wealthier citizens for a share of the city's services. Reform is in some ways a middle-class preoccupation, whereas the less advantaged may believe they are better served by machine politics.

THE "BRAINS"

THAT ACHIEVED THE TAMMANY VICTORY AT THE ROCHESTER DEMOCRATIC CONVENTION.

A THOMAS NAST CARTOON shows Boss Tweed represented as having a money-bag face. The caption reads, "The 'Brains' that achieved the Tammany Victory at the Rochester Democratic Convention." Another identifying feature is a famous $15,500 diamond stickpin. Why are there no true big-city "machine" bosses anymore in the United States? (Library of Congress Prints & Photographs Division, Washington, D.C. [LC-USZ6-787])

GOVERNING METROPOLITAN AREAS

Large cities are often faced with problems that develop in part from a shrinking employment base. When employers move out of a city, there is a smaller tax base, and more people are out of work. Less tax revenue means fewer funds to pay for schools and to meet other municipal obligations, including fighting crime and assisting those who are unemployed. These developments feed on themselves, leading to more crime, more poverty, an even smaller job base, and other problems.

But crime, as well as problems such as traffic congestion and pollution, is not contained within municipal political boundaries. For this reason, solutions are sometimes sought for a metropolitan area as a whole. Annexation by a city of the surrounding suburbs is one solution; consolidation of city and county governments into a single-government

---

[20]Robert Merton, *Social Theory and Social Structure* (Glencoe, IL: Free Press, 1957), pp. 71–81.
[21]Edward C. Banfield and James Q. Wilson, *City Politics* (New York: Vintage Books, 1963), p. 12.

MEMBERS OF PHILADELPHIA'S
Community Preservation Network
protest the City of Philadelphia's
use of eminent domain to take
property. After the Supreme Court
decision in 2005 to allow cities to
use the right of eminent domain for
economic development, citizens
created protest groups across the
United States, and some states
then banned the practice.(Matt
Rourke/AP Photo)

is another. People who live in the suburbs often oppose such measures, however, particularly when they and the residents of a city are of different races or social classes, or have different political agendas.

A third possible solution to problems that spread beyond limited political boundaries is to set up a system of metropolitan government. With this method, a single entity, such as a county, concerns itself with the problems of an entire metropolitan area, and smaller entities, such as individual city governments, concern themselves with local matters. People who live in the suburbs often oppose this solution, however, for the same reasons that they oppose other measures: they want to preserve their communities and lifestyles as they are.

A fourth solution is the creation of special districts, each of which is concerned with a specific service—an area's water supply or public transportation system, for example. Special districts are more popular than the other solutions, in part because they can deal with a single matter relatively more efficiently without concern for social issues or class conflict.

PAYING FOR STATE AND LOCAL GOVERNMENT

Examining the spending habits of a household often gives relevant information about the personalities and priorities of the household members. Examination of the expenditure patterns of state and local governments likewise can be illuminating.

STATE AND LOCAL GOVERNMENT EXPENDITURES

Table 19–3 shows state expenditures, by function, in percentages. Table 19–4 shows these data for local governments. Education and highways are major expenses at both the state and local level. (Most state spending on education is for colleges and universities; most local spending is for elementary and secondary schools.) Because of the growth of Medicaid—the health-care program for the poor—welfare is now the leading expense at the state level. Local governments, in contrast, spend heavily on utilities such as water, electricity, gas, sewers, and garbage collection.

Compare state and local spending on education with spending by the federal government, which allocates only about 4 percent of its budget to education. Despite high expenditures, state and local governments are finding that their educational programs are not always producing well-educated students. Many states have begun issuing vouchers for children to attend nonpublic schools. What would happen if all states offered school vouchers?

STATE AND LOCAL GOVERNMENT REVENUES

State and local expenditures have to be paid for somehow. Until the 20th century, almost all state and local expenditures were paid for by state and local revenues raised within

TABLE 19–3 State Expenditures (in percentages)

EXPENDITURE	PERCENTAGE
Welfare, including Medicaid	28.7
Education	17.8
Employee retirement	11.0
Highways	7.4
Unemployment compensation	4.7
Governmental administration	4.3
Hospitals	3.9
Jails and prisons	3.6
Interest on general debt	3.2
Health	2.9
Utilities	2.6
Parks and natural resources	2.1
Workers' compensation	1.2
Police	0.9
Other	5.5

Source: U.S. Census Bureau, July 2006.

TABLE 19–4 Local Expenditures (in percentages)

EXPENDITURE	PERCENTAGE
Education	38.8
Water, gas, and electricity	7.9
Police and jails	6.4
Highways and airports	5.0
Governmental administration	4.6
Hospitals	4.5
Sewers and solid waste	4.1
Interest on general debt	3.9
Welfare	3.5
Transit	2.9
Health	2.7
Housing and community development	2.6
Parks and natural resources	2.6
Fire protection	2.3
Other	8.1

Source: U.S. Census Bureau, July 2006.

state borders. Starting in the 20th century, however, federal grants to state and local governmental units began to pay some of these costs.

Figure 19–3 shows the percentages of revenues in various categories received by state and local governments. The most important tax at the state level is the **general sales tax**. Whereas the federal government obtains about 45 percent of its total revenues from the personal income tax, states obtain only about 9 percent in this way. By 2007, seven states still did not have a personal income tax. Other taxes assessed by

General Sales Tax
A tax levied as a proportion of the retail price of a commodity at the point of sale.

FIGURE 19–3 State and Local Government Revenues

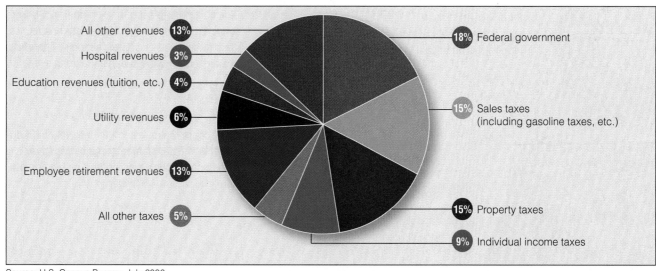

Source: U.S. Census Bureau, July 2006.

WHAT IF...

ALL STATES OFFERED SCHOOL VOUCHERS?

Many observers argue that the low achievement of American students requires drastic changes. They propose that the easiest way to improve the system is to make schools compete with each other. Currently, parents normally are required to send their children to a public school in the particular district where the family's home is located. Generally, only families that are willing to spend from $3,000 to $10,000 per year for tuition at private schools (in addition to the property taxes they pay to support their local public school districts) have a choice as to which school their children will attend.

WHAT IF STATES GAVE PARENTS MONEY TO CHANGE SCHOOLS?

School choice can involve open districts, meaning that parents can choose to send their children to public schools outside of their districts. The type of school choice that generates controversy, however, usually involves giving families vouchers, representing state funds that can be used at any school, public or private. In other words, a voucher is worth some specified amount of money, such as $5,000, but only if it is redeemed by a bona fide public or private school. Any such plan has to be set up by state or local government, because that is where the responsibility for education currently lies.

Under such a system, parents determine where their children go to school. The children may attend the same local public school, a public school in another district, or a private school anywhere. Private schools can accept the vouchers as full payment for tuition fees or require that additional fees be paid.

COMPETITION WOULD BECOME EVIDENT

Certainly, with a voucher system, competition for students would develop. Public schools would have to compete not only among themselves (as they currently do in areas that have open districts) but also with private schools. Private schools would have to compete with all schools.

Some critics of school choice, particularly public school teachers and administrators, are uncomfortable with treating public education like a business. Because of the competitive environment that would be created by school choice, some public schools might not be able to keep and attract enough students to survive. These schools, unless further subsidized by state and local governments, would go bankrupt and disappear. Still, in Milwaukee, Wisconsin, where the first voucher program was established in 1990, the program has raised test scores at both private and public schools. School board members and some liberals who formerly opposed the plan now accept it.

THE CONSTITUTIONAL ISSUE

Other critics of school vouchers claim that such programs violate the federal Constitution or state constitutions because they allow state funds to be used for education at religious schools. For example, in Cleveland, Ohio, children from low-income families received state funds, in the form of vouchers, to attend the schools of their choice. Most of the 4,000 children in the program left public schools to attend Catholic educational institutions.

According to opponents, the use of tax dollars to support religious education violated the establishment clause of the First Amendment to the Constitution, which requires the separation of church and state (see Chapter 4). In 2002, however, the Supreme Court held that the voucher program was constitutional because families theoretically could use the vouchers to send their children not only to religious schools but also to secular private academies, suburban public schools, or charter schools. Therefore, the program did not unconstitutionally entangle church and state.

FOR CRITICAL ANALYSIS

1. Why are teachers' unions, such as the National Education Association, so adamantly against vouchers?
2. Do you see school choice as hurting or helping students from low-income families?

states include corporate income taxes and fees, permits, and licenses at both the state and local governmental levels, as well as inheritance and gift taxes at the state level. At the local level, the most important tax is the **property tax**. More than 95 percent of property tax revenues are raised by local governments. Generally, the types of taxes that states levy vary widely from state to state.

There is considerable variation in the amounts of state and local taxes collected per capita. According to the most recently available statistics, state and local governments in Delaware, New York, and Wyoming collect $7,000 or more per capita, while governments in Georgia, Kansas, and Texas collect only about $4,000. There is also substantial variation in the degree to which taxes are collected at the state level, as opposed to locally. The state governments of Arkansas, Delaware, and Hawaii collect more than four-fifths of the state and local taxes, while the state governments of Colorado, New York, and Texas collect less than half of the state and local total.

Nontax revenue includes federal grants to state and local governments. Today, federal grants to state and local governments provide about 18 percent of state government income. The grants are not always without "strings," however. Federal programs in such areas as education, highway construction, health care, and law enforcement may dispense cash subject to certain conditions (see Chapter 3).

Revenues from publicly operated services and businesses are additional sources of income for state and local governments. Publicly operated services include universities and hospitals, as well as municipal utilities such as water, electric power, and bus systems. More than one-third of the states sell liquor at a profit through state-operated stores. Other state-run businesses include Washington's ferries and North Dakota's commercial banks. Further nontax revenue sources include court fines and interest on loans and investments. In the 1980s, state lotteries became an increasingly popular way to raise revenues.

Most revenue from publicly operated services and businesses is earmarked for the services that earned it. Tuition goes only to colleges, and state hospitals keep the revenue they generate. A special and rather sizable source of earmarked revenue is the income from state employee retirement plans. In principle, these sums should be used only to pay the pensions of retired state employees.

THE STRUGGLE TO BALANCE STATE BUDGETS

During the 1990s, most states expanded their spending on health care, education, and criminal justice. During the dot-com boom of that decade, tax revenues were more than sufficient to fund the increases in most states. Some states even cut their tax rates. The dot-com bust of 2001, however, hit state governments hard. In 2002, as a result of the dot-com collapse, state tax revenue dropped by 7.8 percent. Tax revenue dropped another 3.5 percent in 2003. Both the sales tax and the income tax are sensitive to changes in the economic environment, and many states depend on revenue from these two taxes. Furthermore, most states are formally required to balance their budgets and cannot automatically fund a deficit by issuing bonds as the federal government does when it faces a deficit.

By 2003, Texas faced a budget deficit of $10 billion, and California's shortfall had reached $38 billion. The 2003 revenue shortfalls were 23 percent of the budget in Alaska and Arizona and 24 percent in New York. Only Wyoming and New Mexico managed to avoid running a deficit. The National Governors Association announced that the states faced "the most dire fiscal situation since World War II." Governors and state legislators found themselves caught between two highly vocal groups—those who opposed cutting spending on education, health care, and other services, and those who opposed higher taxes.

That as of fiscal 2007, South Dakota was the only state with less than $1 billion in revenues, while California's revenues were about $100 billion?

Getting into Trouble: Borrowing Too Much. Although every state constitution except that of Vermont requires the state to balance its budget, states have shown great ingenuity in evading this requirement. Even if states cannot automatically borrow to meet a budget deficit, their legislatures can still find ways to borrow. Such practices only postpone the problem, though; eventually, the debt must be repaid.

New York is an example of a state that has engaged in what many consider excessive borrowing despite constitutional restrictions. New York's constitution ostensibly requires that voters approve state borrowing. Nevertheless, by 2004, New York's debt had reached $46.9 billion, or $2,420 for every inhabitant of the state. In 2000, the state had adopted a new law designed to curb borrowing, but despite the law, borrowing actually accelerated. According to many observers, New York was falling into a pattern of borrowing to fund day-to-day expenses rather than long-term capital improvements such as roads or bridges.

Getting into Trouble: Poor Productivity. An additional problem for the states is that the tasks they perform are somewhat resistant to productivity improvements. Over the years, America's farms and factories have posted dramatic improvements in the volume of goods produced by the labor of each individual farmer or worker—in other words, these industries have improved their productivity. It is more difficult to attain such improvements in service industries. Some services, notably education and law enforcement, require face-to-face interaction with the public. It is difficult to cut the amount of such interaction without reducing the quality of the service. Still, from 1993 to 2000, productivity in a typical private-sector service industry rose by about 20 percent. The productivity of government services rose by much less.

Getting into Trouble: Health-Care Costs. Increased health-care costs were a major part of the states' budget problems in the early 2000s, and they continue to be a major threat to the solvency of state governments. One problem is the rising cost of health-insurance premiums for state and local government employees. Nationwide, the cost of health-insurance premiums rose by 50 percent from 2000 to 2007, and such costs for state employees grew as well. A much greater problem is Medicaid, the program that provides health-care services to the poor. State Medicaid spending rose by 9 percent per year on average between 2000 and 2007.

Recovery from the Crisis. In 2004, fiscal pressures on state governments began to ease. Tax revenues increased by 3.2 percent in 2004 and 4.9 percent in 2005, and estimates indicate that they grew at an even greater rate in 2006. For the most part, the economic recovery was responsible for the higher revenues, although some states raised tax rates as well.

An easing in the rate of growth of spending on Medicaid also contributed to the states' fiscal recovery. By fiscal year 2006, 16 states were actually projecting lower Medicaid expenditures than they incurred in fiscal 2005. From fiscal 2002 to 2003, California's expenditures on Medicaid grew by 11.9 percent. From fiscal 2006 to 2007, however, California projected an increase of only 1.8 percent.

The slowdown in Medicaid spending growth reflected major cost-containment efforts by the states. Changes in federal policy also gave state governments more flexibility to experiment with less expensive methods of providing health care. The business slowdown of 2001–2003 had a serious effect on many state budgets. By 2002, the states were forced to address Medicaid costs. Between fiscal years 2002 and 2006, every state reduced payment rates to health-care providers such as hospitals, physicians, and nursing homes. Eligibility standards were tightened in 43 states, and 39 states reduced benefits.

How did the states get into this situation? Certainly, health-care costs have been rising across the board for many years. Some people argue, however, that there is a special reason that Medicaid spending rose so much. They believe that the rise was due, in part, to the federal subsidy. A typical state receives $3 in federal funds for every $2 it spends on Medicaid. This is an attractive proposition even for conservative lawmakers. Conservative state legislators may advocate low tax rates, but they rarely object when federal funds come into their state. Consider again a typical state: A reduction of $1 in the state's Medicaid spending leads to a $1.50 reduction in federal receipts.

The states are responsible for controlling costs, while the federal government pays most of the bill. According to some observers, the result is what the insurance industry calls a *moral hazard*. This term refers to the danger that people will take greater risks with a home or car when it is insured, because if something happens to it, they will not lose financially. Similarly, during the boom years of the 1990s, the states may not have controlled the growth in Medicaid costs as much as they would have if they had been paying the entire bill.

Entrepreneurial Federalism. Another factor that influences state finances is the business environment provided by the state. The 50 states have 50 different systems of laws and regulations that help or hinder commerce. Further, states often compete with each other to attract business by offering tax incentives to favored enterprises. Such competition has been called *entrepreneurial federalism*. Tax incentives to individual businesses certainly reduce state revenues in the short run, but advocates of these benefits argue that in the long run they promote the state's economic growth and increase its tax base.

States as Policy Pioneers. State budgets are also influenced by the mix of public policies adopted by the state to serve the citizens. Over the past two centuries, states have often pioneered innovative policies that were later adopted by the federal government. For example, several states have experimented with requiring all residents to have health insurance either through their employer, their school, or through state-run insurance plans. Massachusetts was the most recent state to adopt such a plan, and many other states are watching the implementation of the plan to see if it is successful.

States are also in the forefront of environmental policies, in part because of their unique geographic and demographic situations. California, with its immense population growth and propensity to develop smog in the coastal areas, has been much stricter about emission controls for automobiles than the federal government for more than 30 years. Recently, the California Air Resources Board released a draft plan for reducing greenhouse gas emissions to 1990 levels by creating a carbon credit trading system, using landfills to produce methane, reducing urban sprawl, and changing the law for automobile emissions. The comprehensive plan would impact virtually every industry in California. While the draft plan needs much more analysis and would need implementation from the legislature, it illustrates the degree to which states can create innovative new policies and experiment with new ways to address public issues.

You can make a difference

LEARNING ABOUT LOCAL POLITICS AND GOVERNMENT IN YOUR COMMUNITY

Your local government bodies are usually close by. If you would like to learn how government operates, local government is a logical place to start.

WHY SHOULD YOU CARE?

What government does or fails to do in the areas of education, health, employment, and crime affects you, your family, and your friends. Your sense of adventure, concern, curiosity, or injustice may urge you to take an active part in the government of a society with which you might not be particularly content. Yet getting involved on the national level may seem complicated, and national issues may not be of immediate concern. You may not even know exactly where you stand on many of those issues.

Every week, however, decisions are being made in your community that directly affect your local environment, transportation, education, health, employment, rent, schools, utility rates, freedom from crime, and overall quality of life. The local level is a good place to begin discovering who you are politically.

WHAT CAN YOU DO?

Many neighborhoods have formed neighborhood associations to protect their interests. One way to learn about issues that directly affect you (such as whether a street in your neighborhood should be widened or a park created) is to attend a local neighborhood association meeting. Another way to familiarize yourself with local political issues is to attend a city council meeting. Think about the

issues being discussed. How do these issues and their outcomes concern you as an individual? What is your position on each issue?

If you are interested in education and educational reform, you can attend a school board meeting. Typically, the board will devote a substantial amount of time to budgetary decisions. Pay close attention to how the board believes school funds should be allocated. What are the board's primary concerns and priorities? Do you agree with the board's views? Find out if the school district is considering proposals to implement innovative educational programs.

Getting involved in a campaign for a local or state office is another way to learn about political issues that affect your community or your state. You can also participate at the local level in campaigns by candidates seeking national office, such as candidates running for Congress. Working at the grassroots level for a political candidate gives you firsthand knowledge of how the politics of democracy actually works.

Finally, to observe the judicial branch of government at work, you can watch the proceedings in your local courts. An important court at the local level is the small claims court. Small claims courts hear disputes involving claims under a certain amount, such as $2,500 or $5,000 (the amount varies from state to state). Lawyers are not required, and many small claims courts do not permit lawyers. Other local courts are described in Figure 19–2. For information on your local courts and on when you can attend court proceedings, call the courthouse clerk.

KEY TERMS

charter 683

consolidation 686

constitutional initiative 673

Cooley's rule 683

council of governments
   (COG) 686

county 684

Dillon's rule 683

functional consolidation 686

general law city 684

general sales tax 691

home rule city 684

item veto 675

municipal home rule 683

New England town 684

property tax 693

selectperson 685

town manager system 685

town meeting 685

township 685

unincorporated area 685

CHAPTER SUMMARY

1. The United States has more than 89,000 separate governmental units. State and local governments perform a wide variety of highly visible functions, such as education and police and fire protection.

2. Under the U.S. Constitution, powers not delegated expressly to the federal government are reserved to the states. The states may exercise taxing, spending, and general police powers. State constitutions are often very long. One reason for their length is that a loss of popular confidence in state legislatures in the late 1800s caused the framers of the constitutions to include many provisions that would normally be considered statutory law. Other reasons include state courts' reluctance to interpret state constitutions as freely as the United States Supreme Court interprets the U.S. Constitution.

3. In colonial America, the governors of the colonies were vested with extensive powers. Following the Revolutionary War, most states established forms of government in which the governor received very limited powers. After Andrew Jackson's presidency, however, all governors (except in South Carolina) were elected directly by the people. Most governors have the right to exercise some sort of veto power; many enjoy item veto power.

4. State legislatures deal with matters such as taxes, schools, highways, and welfare. They must also redraw state and federal legislative districts each decade to ensure that every person's vote is roughly equal to that of others and that minorities are adequately represented in both the state legislature and Congress. Voters may exercise some direct control over state government through the use of the initiative, referendum, and recall. Every state has its own court system. Most such systems have several levels of courts, including trial courts, intermediate courts of appeals, and a supreme court.

5. There are more than 19,000 municipalities in the United States, most of which are small cities. The more than 3,000 counties in this country are merely extensions of state authority and apply state laws at the local level. In New England, many of the functions of municipalities and counties are combined in towns. Municipalities may be governed by a commission consisting of members with executive and legislative powers, or they may be administered according to a council-manager, mayor-administrator, or mayor-council plan. Most major cities used to be run by political machines, which freely dispensed favors to supporters. In recent decades, however, political machines have become almost completely extinct.

6. State spending is funded by sales and personal income taxes and is concentrated on welfare (including Medicaid), higher education, and highways. Local spending, which is mainly funded by property taxes, goes largely to the public schools and to utility services such as water, electricity, gas, sewers, and garbage collection.

SELECTED PRINT AND MEDIA RESOURCES

SUGGESTED READINGS

Cannon, Lou. *Governor Reagan: His Rise to Power.* New York: Public Affairs, 2003. With two books on Reagan under his belt, Lou Cannon is the recognized expert on the late former president. Here, he assesses Reagan's years as governor of California. Despite Reagan's fame as a conservative standard-bearer, his policies for the state were pragmatic, and his term in office was a political success.

Deckman, Melissa M. *School Board Battles: The Christian Right in Local Politics.* Washington, DC: Georgetown University Press, 2004. Deckman, a college professor, provides a judicious look at a controversial topic. Deckman contends that members of the Christian Right and their opponents tend to demonize each other in local races and that the Christian Right is more complicated than it is usually portrayed.

Gray, Virginia, and Russell Hanson, eds. *Politics in the American States*, 8th ed. Washington, DC: CQ Press, 2007. Twenty authors compare policies and processes as well as the political climate across the states.

Grunwald, Michael. *The Swamp: The Everglades, Florida, and the Politics of Paradise.* New York: Simon & Schuster, 2006. Grunwald, a *Washington Post* reporter, tells the story of how local Florida interests first sought to drain the Everglades and then to restore it. The book contains entertaining vignettes on the environmental activists who sought to turn back the "march of progress" beginning in the 1960s.

Karch, Andrew. *Democratic Laboratories: Policy Diffusion among the American States.* Ann Arbor: University of Michigan Press, 2007. In this scholarly book, the author examines the process by which policy ideas from one state are translated to another and how some federal policies may be resisted by states.

Siegel, Fred. *The Prince of the City: Giuliani, New York and the Genius of American Life.* New York: Encounter Books, 2005. This work is as much a history of late-20th-century New York City as a biography of Rudolph Giuliani, the city's mayor during the September 11 terrorist attacks. Crime rates went down under Giuliani, and he was also unusually successful in curbing spending. But his leadership during September 11 made him the national figure he is today.

MEDIA RESOURCES

Can the States Do It Better?—This is a program examining devolution—shifting federal powers back to the states—and what this means for the states with respect to, among other things, school reform.

City Hall—A 1996 drama about corruption at City Hall in New York and a mayor, played by Al Pacino, who is willing to break the law to fulfill his presidential aspirations.

The Last Hurrah—A film based, in part, on the career of James Curley (1874–1958) of Massachusetts, who played a leading role in creating and running Boston's political machine in the first half of the 20th century. When Curley was convicted of mail fraud and sent to prison in 1947, he refused to resign as mayor and maintained his office while in jail.

Our Town—A 1980 film based on Thornton Wilder's play about day-to-day life and politics in a small, picturesque community—Peterborough ("Grover's Corners" in the play) in New Hampshire.

e-mocracy

PUBLIC ACCESS TO INFORMATION ON THE INTERNET IS GROWING

Individuals conduct only a tiny fraction—less than 1 percent—of their fund transactions with federal, state, and local governments over the Internet each year. This percentage should increase sharply over the next decade as activities such as voting, paying fines, and registering automobiles become more accessible on the Internet.

The type of information one can access on the Internet is also growing and is certainly not limited to government resources. Now the places where that information can be accessed are growing as well. Children are becoming more exposed to cyberspace as public schools add computers to their classroom tools. Community centers, public libraries, and other local organizations or entities often have computers that can be used by patrons who otherwise would not have the means to obtain such access or information. Shoppers at a mall in Medford, Oregon, can use computers in an office space run by the Oregon Department of Employment to look for available job opportunities. As a result of these innovations, standing in long lines at the post office to file taxes or at the employment office to apply for a job might one day become a thing of the past.

LOGGING ON

- If you are interested in state law codes (statutes) and state court cases, go to:
  www.findlaw.com/casecode/state.html
- Information on state governments, including their constitutional powers, education, and finances, can be accessed by going to:
  www.vote-smart.org/resource_govt101_09.php

- Another excellent source for information on state governments is the Web site of the Council of State Governments at:
  www.csg.org.
- The National Governors Association offers a wide variety of information on issues and data relating to state governments at:
  www.nga.org
- The National Conference of State Legislatures is a good source for state information as well:
  www.ncsl.org
- You can find a wealth of data on state and local governments at the "Map Stats" site of the U.S. Census Bureau by simply clicking on states and counties on the maps. Go to:
  quickfacts.census.gov/qfd/index.html
- HelloMetro offers a Web site with numerous links to state and local government resources. You can access this site at:
  www.statelocalgov.net

ONLINE REVIEW

At **www.cengage.com/politicalscience/schmidt/agandpt14e**, you will find a Tutorial Quiz for this chapter providing questions on the chapter contents, including the features. The questions are organized to match the major sections of the chapter. You'll have access to other helpful study tools, including the book's glossary and flashcards, crossword puzzles, and Web links, as well as "Which Side Are You On?" and "Politics and . . ." features written by the authors of the book.

APPENDIX A

the *Declaration* OF INDEPENDENCE

IN CONGRESS, JULY 4, 1776

A Declaration by the Representatives of the United States of America, in General Congress assembled. When in the Course of human Events, it becomes necessary for one People to dissolve the Political Bands which have connected them with another, and to assume among the Powers of the Earth, the separate and equal Station to which the Laws of Nature and of Nature's God entitle them, a decent Respect to the Opinions of Mankind requires that they should declare the causes which impel them to the Separation.

We hold these Truths to be self-evident, that all Men are created equal, that they are endowed by their Creator with certain unalienable Rights, that among these are Life, Liberty, and the Pursuit of Happiness—That to secure these Rights, Governments are instituted among Men, deriving their just Powers from the Consent of the Governed, that whenever any Form of Government becomes destructive of these Ends, it is the Right of the People to alter or to abolish it, and to institute new Government, laying its Foundation on such Principles, and organizing its Powers in such Forms, as to them shall seem most likely to effect their Safety and Happiness. Prudence, indeed, will dictate that Governments long established should not be changed for light and transient Causes; and accordingly all Experience hath shewn, that Mankind are more disposed to suffer, while Evils are sufferable, than to right themselves by abolishing the Forms to which they are accustomed. But when a long Train of Abuses and Usurpations, pursuing invariably the same Object, evinces a Design to reduce them under absolute Despotism, it is their Right, it is their Duty, to throw off such Government, and to provide new Guards for their future Security. Such has been the patient Sufferance of these Colonies; and such is now the Necessity which constrains them to alter their former Systems of Government. The History of the present King of Great-Britain is a History of repeated Injuries and Usurpations, all having in direct Object the Establishment of an absolute Tyranny over these States. To prove this, let Facts be submitted to a candid World.

He has refused his Assent to Laws, the most wholesome and necessary for the public Good.

He has forbidden his Governors to pass Laws of immediate and pressing Importance, unless suspended in their Operation till his Assent should be obtained; and when so suspended, he has utterly neglected to attend to them.

He has refused to pass other Laws for the Accommodation of large Districts of People, unless those People would relinquish the Right of Representation in the Legislature, a Right inestimable to them, and formidable to Tyrants only.

He has called together Legislative Bodies at Places unusual, uncomfortable, and distant from the Depository of their Public Records, for the sole Purpose of fatiguing them into Compliance with his Measures.

He has dissolved Representative Houses repeatedly, for opposing with manly Firmness his Invasions on the Rights of the People.

He has refused for a long Time, after such Dissolutions, to cause others to be elected; whereby the Legislative Powers, incapable of Annihilation, have returned to the People at large for their exercise; the State remaining in the mean time exposed to all the Dangers of Invasion from without, and Convulsions within.

He has endeavoured to prevent the Population of these States; for that Purpose obstructing the Laws for Naturalization of Foreigners; refusing to pass others to encourage their Migrations hither, and raising the Conditions of new Appropriations of Lands.

He has obstructed the Administration of Justice, by refusing his Assent to Laws for establishing Judiciary Powers.

He has made Judges dependent on his Will alone, for the Tenure of their offices, and the Amount and payment of their Salaries.

He has erected a Multitude of new Offices, and sent hither Swarms of Officers to harass our People, and eat out their Substance.

He has kept among us, in Times of Peace, Standing Armies, without the consent of our Legislatures.

He has affected to render the Military independent of, and superior to the Civil Power.

He has combined with others to subject us to a Jurisdiction foreign to our Constitution, and unacknowledged by our Laws; giving his Assent to their Acts of pretended Legislation:

For quartering large Bodies of Armed Troops among us:

For protecting them, by a mock Trial, from Punishment for any Murders which they should commit on the Inhabitants of these States:

For cutting off our Trade with all Parts of the World:

For imposing Taxes on us without our Consent:

For depriving us, in many cases, of the Benefits of Trial by Jury:

For transporting us beyond Seas to be tried for pretended Offences:

For abolishing the free System of English Laws in a neighbouring Province, establishing therein an arbitrary Government, and enlarging its Boundaries, so as to render it at once an Example and fit Instrument for introducing the same absolute Rule into these Colonies:

For taking away our Charters, abolishing our most valuable Laws, and altering fundamentally the Forms of our Governments:

For suspending our own Legislatures, and declaring themselves invested with Power to legislate for us in all Cases whatsoever.

He has abdicated Government here, by declaring us out of his Protection and waging War against us.

He has plundered our Seas, ravaged our Coasts, burnt our towns, and destroyed the Lives of our People.

He is, at this Time, transporting large Armies of foreign Mercenaries to compleat the works of Death, Desolation, and Tyranny, already begun with circumstances of Cruelty and Perfidy, scarcely paralleled in the most barbarous Ages, and totally unworthy the Head of a civilized Nation.

He has constrained our fellow Citizens taken Captive on the high Seas to bear Arms against their Country, to become the Executioners of their Friends and Brethren, or to fall themselves by their Hands.

He has excited domestic Insurrections amongst us, and has endeavoured to bring on the Inhabitants of our Frontiers, the merciless Indian Savages, whose known Rule of Warfare, is an undistinguished Destruction, of all Ages, Sexes and Conditions.

In every state of these Oppressions we have Petitioned for Redress in the most humble Terms: Our repeated Petitions have been answered only by repeated Injury. A Prince, whose Character is thus marked by every act which may define a Tyrant, is unfit to be the Ruler of a free People.

Nor have we been wanting in Attentions to our British Brethren. We have warned them from Time to Time of Attempts by their Legislature to extend an unwarrantable Jurisdiction over us. We have reminded them of the Circumstances of our Emigration and Settlement here. We have appealed to their native Justice and Magnanimity, and we have conjured them by the Ties of our common Kindred to disavow these Usurpations, which, would inevitably interrupt our Connections and Correspondence. They too have been deaf to the Voice of Justice and of Consanguinity. We must, therefore, acquiesce in the Necessity, which denounces our Separation, and hold them, as we hold the rest of Mankind, Enemies in War, in Peace, Friends.

We, therefore, the Representatives of the UNITED STATES OF AMERICA, in General Congress Assembled, appealing to the Supreme Judge of the World for the Rectitude of our Intentions, do, in the Name, and by the Authority of the good People of these Colonies, solemnly Publish and Declare, That these United Colonies are, and of Right ought to be, Free and Independent States; that they are absolved from all Allegiance to the British Crown, and that all political Connection between them and the State of Great-Britain, is and ought to be totally dissolved; and that as Free and Independent States, they have full Power to levy War, conclude Peace, contract Alliances, establish Commerce, and to do all other Acts and Things which Independent States may of right do. And for the support of this declaration, with a firm Reliance on the Protection of divine Providence, we mutually pledge to each other our lives, our Fortunes, and our sacred Honor.

APPENDIX B

*the*Federalist Papers

Nos. 10 and 51

In 1787, after the newly drafted U.S. Constitution was submitted to the 13 states for ratification, a major political debate ensued between the Federalists (who favored ratification) and the Anti-Federalists (who opposed ratification). Anti-Federalists in New York were particularly critical of the Constitution, and in response to their objections, Federalists Alexander Hamilton, James Madison, and John Jay wrote a series of 85 essays in defense of the Constitution. The essays were published in New York newspapers and reprinted in other newspapers throughout the country.

For students of American government, the essays, collectively known as the Federalist Papers, *are particularly important because they provide a glimpse of the founders' political philosophy and intentions in designing the Constitution—and, consequently, in shaping the American philosophy of government.*

We have included in this appendix two of these essays: Federalist Papers *No. 10 and No. 51. Each essay has been annotated by the authors to indicate its importance in American political thought and to clarify the meaning of particular passages.*

FEDERALIST PAPER NO. 10

Federalist Paper No. 10, penned by James Madison, has often been singled out as a key document in American political thought. In this essay, Madison attacks the Anti-Federalists' fear that a republican form of government will inevitably give rise to "factions"—small political parties or groups united by a common interest—that will control the government. Factions will be harmful to the country because they will implement policies beneficial to their own interests but adverse to other people's rights and to the public good. In this essay, Madison attempts to lay to rest this fear by explaining how, in a large republic such as the United States, there will be so many different factions, held together by regional or local interests, that no single one of them will dominate national politics.

Madison opens his essay with a paragraph discussing how important it is to devise a plan of government that can control the "instability, injustice, and confusion" brought about by factions.

Among the numerous advantages promised by a well-constructed Union, none deserves to be more accurately developed than its tendency to break and control the vio-lence of faction. The friend of popular governments never finds himself so much alarmed for their character and fate as when he contemplates their propensity to this dangerous vice. He will not fail, therefore, to set a due value on any plan which, without violating the principles to which he is attached, provides a proper cure for it. The instability, injustice, and confusion introduced into the public councils have, in truth, been the mortal diseases under which popular governments have everywhere perished, as they continue to be the favorite and fruitful topics from which the adversaries to liberty derive their most specious declamations. The valuable improvements made by the American constitutions on the popular models, both ancient and modern, cannot certainly be too much admired; but it would be an unwarrantable partiality to contend that they have as effectually obviated the danger on this side, as was wished and expected. Complaints are everywhere heard from our most considerate and virtuous citizens, equally the friends of public and private faith and of public and personal liberty, that our governments are too unstable, that the public good is disregarded in the conflicts of rival parties, and that measures are too often decided, not according to the rules of justice and the rights of the minor party, but by the superior force of an interested and overbearing majority. However anxiously we may wish that these complaints had no foundation, the evidence of known facts will not permit us to deny that they are in some degree true. It will be found, indeed, on a candid review of our situation, that some of the distresses under which we labor have been erroneously charged on the operation of our governments; but it will be found, at the same time, that other causes will not alone account for many of our heaviest misfortunes; and, particularly, for that prevailing and increasing distrust of public engagements and alarm for private rights which are echoed from one end of the continent to the other. These must be chiefly, if not wholly, effects of the unsteadiness and injustice with which a factious spirit has tainted our public administration.

Madison now defines what he means by the term faction.

By a faction I understand a number of citizens, whether amounting to a majority or minority of the whole, who are united and actuated by some common impulse of passion, or of interest, adverse to the rights of other citizens, or the permanent and aggregate interests of the community.

Madison next contends that there are two methods by which the "mischiefs of faction" can be cured: by removing the causes of faction or by controlling their effects. In the following paragraphs, Madison explains how liberty itself nourishes factions. Therefore, to abolish factions would involve abolishing liberty—a cure "worse than the disease."

There are two methods of curing the mischiefs of faction: the one, by removing its causes; the other, by controlling its effects.

There are again two methods of removing the causes of faction: the one, by destroying the liberty which is essential to its existence; the other, by giving to every citizen the same opinions, the same passions, and the same interests.

It could never be more truly said than of the first remedy that it was worse than the disease. Liberty is to faction what air is to fire, an aliment without which it instantly expires. But it could not be a less folly to abolish liberty, which is essential to political life, because it nourishes faction than it would be to wish the annihilation of air, which is essential to animal life, because it imparts to fire its destructive agency.

The second expedient is as impracticable as the first would be unwise. As long as the reason of man continues fallible, and he is at liberty to exercise it, different opinions will be formed. As long as the connection subsists between his reason and his self-love, his opinions and his passions will have a reciprocal influence on each other; and the former will be objects to which the latter will attach themselves. The diversity in the faculties of men, from which the rights of property originate, is not less an insuperable obstacle to a uniformity of interests. The protection of these faculties is the first object of government. From the protection of different and unequal faculties of acquiring property, the possession of different degrees and kinds of property immediately results; and from the influence of these on the sentiments and views of the respective proprietors ensues a division of the society into different interests and parties.

The latent causes of faction are thus sown in the nature of man; and we see them everywhere brought into different degrees of activity, according to the different circumstances of civil society. A zeal for different opinions concerning religion, concerning government, and many other points, as well of speculation as of practice; an attachment to different leaders ambitiously contending for pre-eminence and power; or to persons of other descriptions whose fortunes have been interesting to the human passions, have, in turn, divided mankind into parties, inflamed them with mutual animosity, and rendered them much more disposed to vex and oppress each other than to co-operate for their common good. So strong is this propensity of mankind to fall into mutual animosities that where no substantial occasion presents itself the most frivolous and fanciful distinctions have been sufficient to kindle their unfriendly passions and excite their most violent conflicts. But the most common and durable source of factions has been the various and unequal distribution of property. Those who hold and those who are without property have ever formed distinct interests in society. Those who are creditors, and those who are debtors, fall under a like discrimination. A landed interest, a manufacturing interest, a mercantile interest, a moneyed interest, with many lesser interests, grow up of necessity in civilized nations, and divide them into different classes, actuated by different sentiments and views. The regulation of these various and interfering interests forms the principal task of modern legislation and involves the spirit of party and faction in the necessary and ordinary operations of government.

No man is allowed to be a judge in his own cause, because his interest would certainly bias his judgment, and, not improbably, corrupt his integrity. With equal, nay with greater reason, a body of men are unfit to be both judges and parties at the same time; yet what are many of the most important acts of legislation but so many judicial determinations, not indeed concerning the rights of single persons, but concerning the rights of large bodies of citizens? And what are the different classes of legislators but advocates and parties to the causes which they determine? Is a law proposed concerning private debts? It is a question to which the creditors are parties on one side and the debtors on the other. Justice ought to hold the balance between them. Yet the parties are, and must be, themselves the judges; and the most numerous party, or in other words, the most powerful faction must be expected to prevail. Shall domestic manufacturers be encouraged, and in what degree, by restrictions on foreign manufacturers? [These] are questions which would be differently decided by the landed and the manufacturing classes, and probably by neither with a sole regard to justice and the public good. The apportionment of taxes on the various descriptions of property is an act which seems to require the most exact impartiality; yet there is, perhaps, no legislative act in which greater opportunity and temptation are given to a predominant party to trample on the rules of justice. Every shilling with which they overburden the inferior number is a shilling saved to their own pockets.

It is in vain to say that enlightened statesmen will be able to adjust these clashing interests and render them all subservient to the public good. Enlightened statesmen will not always be at the helm. Nor, in many cases, can such an adjustment be made at all without taking into view indirect and remote considerations, which will rarely prevail over the immediate interest which one party may find in disregarding the rights of another or the good of the whole.

The inference to which we are brought is that the *causes* of faction cannot be removed and that relief is only to be sought in the means of controlling its *effects*.

Having concluded that "the causes of faction cannot be removed," Madison now looks in some detail at the other method by which factions can be cured—by controlling their effects. This is the heart of his essay. He begins by positing a significant question: How can you have self-government without risking the possibility that a ruling faction, particularly a majority faction, might tyrannize over the rights of others?

If a faction consists of less than a majority, relief is supplied by the republican principle, which enables the majority to defeat its sinister views by regular vote. It may clog the administration, it may convulse the society; but it will be unable to execute and mask its violence under the forms of the Constitution. When a majority is included in a faction, the form of popular government, on the other hand, enables it to sacrifice to its ruling passion or interest both the public good and the rights of other citizens. To secure the public good and private rights against the danger of such a faction, and at the same time to preserve the spirit and the form of popular government, is then the great object to which our inquiries are directed. Let me add that it is the great desideratum by which alone this form of government can be rescued from the opprobrium under which it has so long labored and be recommended to the esteem and adoption of mankind.

Madison now sets forth the idea that one way to control the effects of factions is to ensure that the majority is rendered incapable of acting in concert in order to "carry into effect schemes of oppression." He goes on to state that in a democracy, in which all citizens participate personally in government decision making, there is no way to prevent the majority from communicating with each other and, as a result, acting in concert.

By what means is this object attainable? Evidently by one of two only. Either the existence of the same passion or interest in a majority at the same time must be prevented, or the majority, having such coexistent passion or interest, must be rendered, by their number and local situation, unable to concert and carry into effect schemes of oppression. If the impulse and the opportunity be suffered to coincide, we well know that neither moral nor religious motives can be relied on as an adequate control. They are not found to be such on the injustice and violence of individuals, and lose their efficacy in proportion to the number combined together, that is, in proportion as their efficacy becomes needful.

From this view of the subject it may be concluded that a pure democracy, by which I mean a society consisting of a small number of citizens, who assemble and administer the government in person, can admit of no cure for the mischiefs of faction. A common passion or interest will, in almost every case, be felt by a majority of the whole; a communication and concert results from the form of government itself; and there is nothing to check the inducements to sacrifice the weaker party or an obnoxious individual.

Hence it is that such democracies have ever been spectacles of turbulence and contention; have ever been found incompatible with personal security or the rights of property; and have in general been as short in their lives as they have been violent in their deaths. Theoretic politicians, who have patronized this species of government, have erroneously supposed that by reducing mankind to a perfect equality in their political rights, they would at the same time be perfectly equalized and assimilated in their possessions, their opinions, and their passions.

Madison now moves on to discuss the benefits of a republic with respect to controlling the effects of factions. He begins by defining a republic and then pointing out the "two great points of difference" between a republic and a democracy: a republic is governed by a small body of elected representatives, not by the people directly; and a republic can extend over a much larger territory and embrace more citizens than a democracy can.

A republic, by which I mean a government in which the scheme of representation takes place, opens a different prospect and promises the cure for which we are seeking. Let us examine the points in which it varies from pure democracy, and we shall comprehend both the nature of the cure and the efficacy which it must derive from the Union.

The two great points of difference between a democracy and a republic are: first, the delegation of the government, in the latter, to a small number of citizens elected by the rest; secondly, the greater number of citizens and greater sphere of country over which the latter may be extended.

In the following four paragraphs, Madison explains how in a republic, particularly a large republic, the delegation of authority to elected representatives will increase the likelihood that those who govern will be "fit" for their positions and that a proper balance will be achieved between local (factional) interests and national interests. Note how he stresses that the new federal Constitution, by dividing powers between state governments and the national government, provides a "happy combination in this respect."

The effect of the first difference is, on the one hand, to refine and enlarge the public views by passing them through the medium of a chosen body of citizens, whose wisdom may best discern the true interest of their country and whose patriotism and love of justice will be least likely to sacrifice it to temporary or partial considerations. Under such a regulation it may well happen that the public voice, pronounced by the representatives of the people, will be more consonant to the public good than if pronounced by the people themselves, convened for the purpose. On the other hand, the effect may be inverted. Men of factious tempers, of local prejudices, or of sinister designs, may, by intrigue, by corruption, or by other means, first obtain the suffrages, and then betray the interests of the people. The question resulting is, whether small or extensive republics are most favorable to the election of proper guardians of the public weal; and it is clearly decided in favor of the latter by two obvious considerations.

In the first place, it is to be remarked that however small the republic may be the representatives must be raised to a certain number in order to guard against the cabals of a few; and that however large it may be, they must be limited to a certain number in order to guard against the confusion of a multitude. Hence, the number of representatives in the two cases not being in proportion to that of the constituents, and being proportionally greater in the small republic, it follows that if the proportion of fit characters be not less in the large than in the small republic, the former will present a greater option, and consequently a greater probability of a fit choice.

In the next place, as each representative will be chosen by a greater number of citizens in the large than in the small republic, it will be more difficult for unworthy candidates to practice with success the vicious arts by which elections are too often carried; and the suffrages of the people being more free, will be more likely to center on men who possess the most attractive merit and the most diffusive and established characters.

It must be confessed that in this, as in most other cases, there is a mean, on both sides of which inconveniencies will be found to lie. By enlarging too much the number of electors, you render the representative too little acquainted with all their local circumstances and lesser interests; as by reducing it too much, you render him unduly attached to these, and too little fit to comprehend and pursue great and national objects. The federal Constitution forms a happy combination in this respect; the great and aggregate interests being referred to the national, the local and particular to the State legislatures.

Madison now looks more closely at the other difference between a republic and a democracy—namely, that a republic can encompass a larger territory and more citizens than a democracy can. In the remaining paragraphs of his essay, Madison concludes that in a large republic, it will be difficult for factions to act in concert. Although a factious group—religious, political, economic, or otherwise—may control a local or regional government, it will have little chance of gathering a national following. This is because in a large republic, there will be numerous factions whose work will offset the work of any one particular faction ("sect"). As Madison phrases it, these numerous factions will "secure the national councils against any danger from that source."

The other point of difference is the greater number of citizens and extent of territory which may be brought within the compass of republican than of democratic government; and it is this circumstance principally which renders factious combinations less to be dreaded in the former than in the latter. The smaller the society, the fewer probably will be the distinct parties and interests composing it; the fewer the distinct parties and interests, the more frequently will a majority be found of the same party; and the smaller the number of individuals composing a majority, and the smaller the compass within which they are placed, the more easily will they concert and execute their plans of oppression. Extend the sphere and you take in a greater variety of parties and interests; you make it less probable that a majority of the whole will have a common motive to invade the rights of other citizens; or if such a common motive exists, it will be more difficult for all who feel it to discover their own strength and to act in unison with each other. Besides other impediments, it may be remarked that, where there is a consciousness of unjust or dishonorable purposes, communication is always checked by distrust in proportion to the number whose concurrence is necessary.

Hence, it clearly appears that the same advantage which a republic has over a democracy in controlling the effects of faction is enjoyed by a large over a small republic—is enjoyed by the Union over the States composing it. Does this advantage consist in the substitution of representatives whose enlightened views and virtuous sentiments render them superior to local prejudices and to schemes of injustice? It will not be denied that the representation of the Union will be most likely to possess these requisite endowments. Does it consist in the greater security afforded by a greater variety of parties, against the event of any one party being able to outnumber and oppress the rest? In an equal degree does the increased variety of parties comprised within the Union increase this security. Does it, in fine, consist in the greater obstacles opposed to the concert and accomplishment of the secret wishes of an unjust and interested majority? Here again the extent of the Union gives it the most palpable advantage.

The influence of factious leaders may kindle a flame within their particular States but will be unable to spread a general conflagration through the other States. A religious sect may degenerate into a political faction in a part of the Confederacy; but the variety of sects dispersed over the entire face of it must secure the national councils against any danger from that source. A rage for paper money, for an abolition of debts, for an equal division of property, or for any other improper or wicked project, will be less apt to pervade the whole body of the Union than a particular member of it, in the same proportion as such a malady is more likely to taint a particular county or district than an entire State.

In the extent and proper structure of the Union, therefore, we behold a republican remedy for the diseases most incident to republican government. And according to the degree of pleasure and pride we feel in being republicans ought to be our zeal in cherishing the spirit and supporting the character of federalists.

Publius
(James Madison)

FEDERALIST PAPER NO. 51

Federalist Paper No. 51, also authored by James Madison, is another classic in American political theory. Although the Federalists wanted a strong national government, they had not abandoned the traditional American view, particularly notable during the revolutionary era, that those holding powerful government positions could not be trusted to put national interests and the common good above their own personal interests. In this essay, Madison explains why the separation of the national government's powers into three branches—executive, legislative, and judicial—and a federal structure of government offer the best protection against tyranny.

To what expedient, then, shall we finally resort, for maintaining in practice the necessary partition of power among the several departments as laid down in the Constitution? The only answer that can be given is that as all these exterior provisions are found to be inadequate the defect must be supplied, by so contriving the interior structure of the government as that its several constituent parts may, by their mutual relations, be the means of keeping each other in their proper places. Without presuming to undertake a full development of this important idea I will hazard a few general observations which may perhaps place it in a clearer light, and enable us to form a more correct judgment of the principles and structure of the government planned by the convention.

In the next two paragraphs, Madison stresses that for the powers of the different branches (departments) of government to be truly separated, the personnel in one branch should not be dependent on another branch for their appointment or for the "emoluments" (compensation) attached to their offices.

In order to lay a due foundation for that separate and distinct exercise of the different powers of government, which to a certain extent is admitted on all hands to be essential to the preservation of liberty, it is evident that each department should have a will of its own; and consequently should be so constituted that the members of each should have as little agency as possible in the appointment of the members of the others. Were this principle rigorously adhered to, it would require that all the appointments for the supreme executive, legislative, and judiciary magistracies should be drawn from the same fountain of authority, the people, through channels having no communication whatever with one another. Perhaps such a plan of constructing the several departments would be less difficult in practice than it may in contemplation appear. Some difficulties, however, and some additional expense would attend the execution of it. Some deviations, therefore, from the principle must be admitted. In the constitution of the judiciary department in particular, it might be inexpedient to insist rigorously on the principle: first, because peculiar qualifications being essential in the members, the primary consideration ought to be to select that mode of choice which best secures these qualifications; second, because

the permanent tenure by which the appointments are held in that department must soon destroy all sense of dependence on the authority conferring them.

It is equally evident that the members of each department should be as little dependent as possible on those of the others for the emoluments annexed to their offices. Were the executive magistrate, or the judges, not independent of the legislature in this particular, their independence in every other would be merely nominal.

In the following passages, which are among the most widely quoted of Madison's writings, he explains how the separation of the powers of government into three branches helps to counter the effects of personal ambition on government. The separation of powers allows personal motives to be linked to the constitutional rights of a branch of government. In effect, competing personal interests in each branch will help to keep the powers of the three government branches separate and, in so doing, will help to guard the public interest.

But the great security against a gradual concentration of the several powers in the same department consists in giving to those who administer each department the necessary constitutional means and personal motives to resist encroachments of the others. The provision for defense must in this, as in all other cases, be made commensurate to the danger of attack. Ambition must be made to counteract ambition. The interest of the man must be connected with the constitutional rights of the place. It may be a reflection on human nature that such devices should be necessary to control the abuses of government. But what is government itself but the greatest of all reflections on human nature? If men were angels, no government would be necessary. If angels were to govern men, neither external nor internal controls on government would be necessary. In framing a government which is to be administered by men over men, the great difficulty lies in this: you must first enable the government to control the governed; and in the next place oblige it to control itself. A dependence on the people is, no doubt, the primary control on the government; but experience has taught mankind the necessity of auxiliary precautions.

This policy of supplying, by opposite and rival interests, the defect of better motives, might be traced through the whole system of human affairs, private as well as public. We see it particularly displayed in all the subordinate distributions of power, where the constant aim is to divide and arrange the several offices in such a manner as that each may be a check on the other—that the private interest of every individual may be a sentinel over the public rights. These inventions of prudence cannot be less requisite in the distribution of the supreme powers of the State.

Madison now addresses the issue of equality between the branches of government. The legislature will necessarily predominate, but if the executive is given an "absolute negative" (absolute veto power) over legisla-

tive actions, this also could lead to an abuse of power. Madison concludes that the division of the legislature into two "branches" (parts, or chambers) will act as a check on the legislature's powers.

But it is not possible to give to each department an equal power of self-defense. In republican government, the legislative authority necessarily predominates. The remedy for this inconveniency is to divide the legislature into different branches; and to render them, by different modes of election and different principles of action, as little connected with each other as the nature of their common functions and their common dependence on the society will admit. It may even be necessary to guard against dangerous encroachments by still further precautions. As the weight of the legislative authority requires that it should be thus divided, the weakness of the executive may require, on the other hand, that it should be fortified. An absolute negative on the legislature appears, at first view, to be the natural defense with which the executive magistrate should be armed. But perhaps it would be neither altogether safe nor alone sufficient. On ordinary occasions it might not be exerted with the requisite firmness, and on extraordinary occasions it might be perfidiously abused. May not this defect of an absolute negative be supplied by some qualified connection between this weaker department and the weaker branch of the stronger department, by which the latter may be led to support the constitutional rights of the former, without being too much detached from the rights of its own department?

If the principles on which these observations are founded be just, as I persuade myself they are, and they be applied as a criterion to the several State constitutions, and to the federal Constitution, it will be found that if the latter does not perfectly correspond with them, the former are infinitely less able to bear such a test.

In the remainder of the essay, Madison discusses how a federal system of government, in which powers are divided between the states and the national government, offers "double security" against tyranny.

There are, moreover, two considerations particularly applicable to the federal system of America, which place that system in a very interesting point of view.

First. In a single republic, all the power surrendered by the people is submitted to the administration of a single government; and the usurpations are guarded against by a division of the government into distinct and separate departments. In the compound republic of America, the power surrendered by the people is first divided between two distinct governments, and then the portion allotted to each subdivided among distinct and separate departments. Hence a double security arises to the rights of the people. The different governments will control each other, at the same time that each will be controlled by itself.

Second. It is of great importance in a republic not only to guard the society against the oppression of its rulers, but to guard one part of the society against the injustice of the other part. Different interests necessarily exist in different classes of citizens. If a majority be united by a common interest, the rights of the minority will be insecure. There are but two methods of providing against this evil: the one by creating a will in the community independent of the majority—that is, of the society itself; the other, by comprehending in the society so many separate descriptions of citizens as will render an unjust combination of a majority of the whole very improbable, if not impracticable. The first method prevails in all governments possessing an hereditary or self-appointed authority. This, at best, is but a precarious security; because a power independent of the society may as well espouse the unjust views of the major as the rightful interests of the minor party, and may possibly be turned against both parties. The second method will be exemplified in the federal republic of the United States. Whilst all authority in it will be derived from and dependent on the society, the society itself will be broken into so many parts, interests and classes of citizens, that the rights of individuals, or of the minority, will be in little danger from interested combinations of the majority.

In a free government the security for civil rights must be the same as that for religious rights. It consists in the one case in the multiplicity of interests, and in the other in the multiplicity of sects. The degree of security in both cases will depend on the number of interests and sects; and this may be presumed to depend on the extent of country and number of people comprehended under the same government. This view of the subject must particularly recommend a proper federal system to all the sincere and considerate friends of republican government, since it shows that in exact proportion as the territory of the Union may be formed into more circumscribed Confederacies, or States, oppressive combinations of a majority will be facilitated; the best security, under the republican forms, for the rights of every class of citizen, will be diminished; and consequently the stability and independence of some member of the government, the only other security, must be proportionally increased. Justice is the end of government. It is the end of civil society. It ever has been and ever will be pursued until it be obtained, or until liberty be lost in the pursuit. In a society under the forms of which the stronger faction can readily unite and oppress the weaker, anarchy may as truly be said to reign as in a state of nature, where the weaker individual is not secured against the violence of the stronger; and as, in the latter state, even the stronger individuals are prompted, by the uncertainty of their condition, to submit to a government which may protect the weak as well as themselves; so, in the former state, will the more powerful factions or parties be gradually induced, by a like motive, to wish for a government which will protect all parties, the weaker as well as the more powerful.

It can be little doubted that if the State of Rhode Island was separated from the Confederacy and left to itself, the insecurity of rights under the popular form of government within such narrow limits would be displayed by such reiterated oppressions of factious majorities that some power altogether independent of the people would soon be called for by the voice of the very factions whose misrule had proved the necessity of it. In the extended republic of the United States, and among the great variety of interests, parties, and sects which it embraces, a coalition of a majority of the whole society could seldom take place on any other principles than those of justice and the general good; whilst there being thus less danger to a minor from the will of a major party, there must be less pretext, also, to provide for the security of the former, by introducing into the government a will not dependent on the latter, or, in other words, a will independent of the society itself. It is no less certain than it is important, notwithstanding the contrary opinions which have been entertained, that the larger the society, provided it lie within a practicable sphere, the more duly capable it will be of self-government. And happily for the republican cause, the practicable sphere may be carried to a very great extent by a judicious modification and mixture of the *federal principle*.

Publius
(James Madison)

GLOSSARY

A

Acquisitive Model A model of bureaucracy that views top-level bureaucrats as seeking to expand the size of their budgets and staffs to gain greater power.

Actual Malice Either knowledge of a defamatory statement's falsity or a reckless disregard for the truth.

Administrative Agency A federal, state, or local government unit established to perform a specific function. Administrative agencies are created and authorized by legislative bodies to administer and enforce specific laws.

Advice and Consent Terms in the Constitution describing the U.S. Senate's power to review and approve treaties and presidential appointments.

Affirm To declare that a court ruling is valid and must stand.

Affirmative Action A policy in educational admissions or job hiring that gives special attention or compensatory treatment to traditionally disadvantaged groups in an effort to overcome present effects of past discrimination.

Agenda Setting Determining which public-policy questions will be debated or considered.

Amicus Curiae **Brief** A legal document filed by an organization that is not a party to a lawsuit to provide additional information and attempt to influence the outcome of the case.

Anarchy The absence of any form of government or political authority.

Anti-Federalist An individual who opposed the ratification of the new Constitution in 1787. The Anti-Federalists were opposed to a strong central government.

Appellate Court A court having jurisdiction to review cases and issues that were originally tried in lower courts.

Appointment Power The authority vested in the president to fill a government office or position. Positions filled by presidential appointment include those in the executive branch and the federal judiciary, commissioned officers in the armed forces, and members of the independent regulatory commissions.

Appropriation The passage, by Congress, of a spending bill specifying the amount of authorized funds that actually will be allocated for an agency's use.

Aristocracy Rule by the "best"; in reality, rule by an upper class.

Arraignment The first act in a criminal proceeding, in which the defendant is brought before a court to hear the charges against him or her and enter a plea of guilty or not guilty.

Attentive Public That portion of the general public that pays attention to policy issues.

Australian Ballot A secret ballot prepared, distributed, and tabulated by government officials at public expense. Since 1888, all states have used the Australian ballot rather than an open, public ballot.

Authoritarianism A type of regime in which only the government is fully controlled by the ruler. Social and economic institutions exist that are not under the government's control.

Authority The right and power of a government or other entity to enforce its decisions and compel obedience.

Authorization A formal declaration by a legislative committee that a certain amount of funding may be available to an agency. Some authorizations terminate in a year; others are renewable automatically, without further Congressional action.

Automatic, or Built-in, Stabilizers Certain federal programs that cause changes in national income during economic fluctuations without the action of Congress and the president. Examples are the federal income tax system and unemployment compensation.

B

Balance of Trade The difference between the value of a nation's exports of goods and the value of its imports of goods.

Battleground State A state that is likely to be so closely fought that the campaigns devote exceptional effort to winning the popular and electoral vote.

"Beauty Contest" A presidential primary in which contending candidates compete for popular votes but the results do not control the selection of delegates to the national convention.

Bias An inclination or a preference that interferes with impartial judgment.

Bicameralism The division of a legislature into two separate assemblies.

Bicameral Legislature A legislature made up of two parts, called chambers. The U.S. Congress, composed of the House of Representatives and the Senate, is a bicameral legislature.

Block Grants Federal programs that provide funds to state and local governments for general functional areas, such as criminal justice or mental-health programs.

Blue Dog Democrats Members of Congress from more moderate states or districts who sometimes "cross over" to vote with Republicans on legislation.

Boycott A form of pressure or protest—an organized refusal to purchase a particular product or deal with a particular business.

Broad Construction A judicial philosophy that looks to the context and purpose of a law when making an interpretation.

Budget Deficit Government expenditures that exceed receipts.

Bureaucracy A large organization that is structured hierarchically to carry out specific functions.

Busing In the context of civil rights, the transportation of public school students from areas where they live to schools in other areas to eliminate school segregation based on residential patterns.

C

Cabinet An advisory group selected by the president to aid in making decisions. The Cabinet includes the heads of 15 executive departments and others named by the president.

Cabinet Department One of the 15 departments of the executive branch (State, Treasury, Defense, Justice, Interior, Agriculture, Commerce, Labor, Health and Human Services, Homeland Security, Housing and Urban Development, Education, Energy, Transportation, and Veterans Affairs).

Capitalism An economic system characterized by the private ownership of wealth-creating assets, free markets, and freedom of contract.

Capture The act by which an industry being regulated by a government agency gains direct or indirect control over agency personnel and decision makers.

Case Law Judicial interpretations of common-law principles and doctrines, as well as interpretations of constitutional law, statutory law, and administrative law.

Casework Personal work for constituents by members of Congress.

Categorical Grants Federal grants to states or local governments that are for specific programs or projects.

Caucus A meeting of party members designed to select candidates and propose policies.

Charter A document issued by a government that grants to a person, a group of persons, or a corporation the right to carry on one or more specific activities. A state government can grant a charter to a municipality.

Checks and Balances A major principle of the American system of government whereby each branch of the government can check the actions of the others.

Chief Diplomat The role of the president in recognizing foreign governments, making treaties, and effecting executive agreements.

Chief Executive The role of the president as head of the executive branch of the government.

Chief Legislator The role of the president in influencing the making of laws.

Chief of Staff The person who is named to direct the White House Office and advise the president.

Civil Disobedience A nonviolent, public refusal to obey allegedly unjust laws.

Civil Law The law regulating conduct between private persons over noncriminal matters. Under civil law, the government provides the forum for the settlement of disputes between private parties in such matters as contracts, domestic relations, and business interactions.

Civil Liberties Those personal freedoms that are protected for all individuals. Civil liberties typically involve restraining the government's actions against individuals.

Civil Rights Generally, all rights rooted in the Fourteenth Amendment's guarantee of equal protection under the law.

Civil Service A collective term for the body of employees working for the government. Generally, civil service is understood to apply to all those who gain government employment through a merit system.

Civil Service Commission The initial central personnel agency of the national government, created in 1883.

Class-Action Suit A lawsuit filed by an individual seeking damages for "all persons similarly situated."

Clear and Present Danger Test The test proposed by Justice Oliver Wendell Holmes for determining when government may restrict free speech. Restrictions are permissible, he argued, only when speech creates a *clear and present danger* to the public order.

Climate Control The use of public relations techniques to create favorable public opinion toward an interest group, industry, or corporation.

Closed Primary A type of primary in which the voter is limited to choosing candidates of the party of which he or she is a member.

Coattail Effect The influence of a popular candidate on the electoral success of other candidates on the same party ticket. The effect is increased by the party-column ballot, which encourages straight-ticket voting.

Cold War The ideological, political, and economic confrontation between the United States and the Soviet Union following World War II.

Commander in Chief The role of the president as supreme commander of the military forces of the United States and of the state National Guard units when they are called into federal service.

Commerce Clause The section of the Constitution in which Congress is given the power to regulate trade among the states and with foreign countries.

Commercial Speech Advertising statements, which increasingly have been given First Amendment protection.

Common Law Judge-made law that originated in England from decisions shaped according to prevailing custom. Decisions were applied to similar situations and gradually became common to the nation.

Communications Director A professional specialist who plans the communications strategy and advertising campaign for the candidate.

Communism A revolutionary variant of socialism that favors a partisan (and often totalitarian) dictatorship, government control of all enterprises, and the replacement of free markets by central planning.

Concurrent Powers Powers held jointly by the national and state governments.

Concurring Opinion A separate opinion prepared by a judge who supports the decision of the majority of the court but who wants to make or clarify a particular point or to voice disapproval of the grounds on which the decision was made.

Confederal System A system consisting of a league of independent states, each having essentially sovereign powers. The central government created by such a league has only limited powers over the states.

Confederation A political system in which states or regional governments retain ultimate authority except for those powers they expressly delegate to a central government. A voluntary association of independent states, in which the member states agree to limited restraints on their freedom of action.

Conference Committee A special joint committee appointed to reconcile differences when bills pass the two chambers of Congress in different forms.

Consensus General agreement among the citizenry on an issue.

Consent of the People The idea that governments and laws derive their legitimacy from the consent of the governed.

Conservatism A set of beliefs that includes a limited role for the national government in helping individuals, support for traditional values and lifestyles, and a cautious response to change.

Conservative Coalition An alliance of Republicans and Southern Democrats that can form in the House or the Senate to oppose liberal legislation and support conservative legislation.

Consolidation The union of two or more governmental units to form a single unit.

Constituent One of the persons represented by a legislator or other elected or appointed official.

Constitutional Initiative An electoral device whereby citizens can propose a constitutional amendment through petitions signed by the required number of registered voters.

Constitutional Power A power vested in the president by Article II of the Constitution.

Consumer Price Index (CPI) A measure of the change in price over time of a specific group of goods and services used by the average household.

Containment A U.S. diplomatic policy adopted by the Truman administration to contain communist power within its existing boundaries.

Continuing Resolution A temporary funding law that Congress passes when an appropriations bill has not been decided by the beginning of the new fiscal year on October 1.

Cooley's Rule The view that cities should be able to govern themselves, presented in an 1871 Michigan decision by Judge Thomas Cooley.

Cooperative Federalism The theory that the states and the national government should cooperate in solving problems.

Corrupt Practices Acts A series of acts passed by Congress in an attempt to limit and regulate the size and sources of contributions and expenditures in political campaigns.

Council of Governments (COG) A voluntary organization of counties and municipalities concerned with area-wide problems.

County The chief governmental unit set up by the state to administer state law and business at the local level. Counties are drawn up by area, rather than by rural or urban criteria.

Credentials Committee A committee used by political parties at their national conventions to determine which delegates may participate. The committee inspects the claim of each prospective delegate to be seated as a legitimate representative of his or her state.

Criminal Law The law that defines crimes and provides punishment for violations. In criminal cases, the government is the prosecutor because crimes are violations of the public order.

Current Account Balance The current account balance includes the balance of trade in services, unilateral transfers, and other items. This is a wider concept than the balance of trade.

D

Dealignment A decline in party loyalties that reduces long-term party commitment.

De Facto Segregation Racial segregation that occurs because of past social and economic conditions and residential racial patterns.

Defamation of Character Wrongfully hurting a person's good reputation. The law imposes a general duty on all persons to refrain from making false, defamatory statements about others.

Defense Policy A subset of national security policies having to do with the U.S. armed forces.

***De Jure* Segregation** Racial segregation that occurs because of laws or administrative decisions by public agencies.

Democracy A system of government in which political authority is vested in the people. Derived from the Greek words *demos* ("the people") and *kratos* ("authority").

Democratic Party One of the two major American political parties evolving out of the Republican Party of Thomas Jefferson.

Democratic Republic A republic in which representatives elected by the people make and enforce laws and policies.

Détente A French word meaning a relaxation of tensions. The term characterized U.S.–Soviet relations as they developed under President Richard Nixon and Secretary of State Henry Kissinger.

Devolution The transfer of powers from a national or central government to a state or local government.

Dillon's rule The narrowest possible interpretation of the legal status of local governments, outlined by Judge John E. Dillon, who in 1872 stated that a municipal corporation can exercise only those powers expressly granted by state law.

Diplomacy The process by which states carry on political relations with each other; settling conflicts among nations by peaceful means.

Diplomatic Recognition The formal acknowledgment of a foreign government as legitimate.

Direct Democracy A system of government in which political decisions are made by the people directly, rather than by their elected representatives; probably attained most easily in small political communities.

Direct Primary An intraparty election in which the voters select the candidates who will run on a party's ticket in the subsequent general election.

Direct Technique An interest group activity that involves interaction with government officials to further the group's goals.

Discharge Petition A procedure by which a bill in the House of Representatives may be forced (discharged) out of a committee that has refused to report it for consideration by the House. The petition must be signed by an absolute majority (218) of representatives and is used only on rare occasions.

Dissenting Opinion A separate opinion in which a judge dissents from (disagrees with) the conclusion reached by the majority on the court and expounds his or her own views about the case.

Diversity of Citizenship The condition that exists when the parties to a lawsuit are citizens of different states, or when the parties are citizens of a U.S. state and citizens or the government of a foreign country. Diversity of citizenship can provide a basis for federal jurisdiction.

Divided Government A situation in which one major political party controls the presidency and the other controls the chambers of Congress, or in which one party controls a state governorship and the other controls the state legislature.

Divisive Opinion Public opinion that is polarized between two quite different positions.

Domestic Policy Public plans or courses of action that concern internal issues of national importance, such as poverty, crime, and the environment.

Dominant Culture The values, customs, and language established by the group or groups that traditionally have controlled politics and government in a society.

Dual Federalism A system in which the states and the national government each remain supreme within their own spheres. The doctrine looks on nation and state as co-equal sovereign powers. Neither the state government nor the national government should interfere in the other's sphere.

E

Earmarks Funding appropriations that are specifically designated for a named project in a member's state or district.

Earned-Income Tax Credit (EITC) Program A government program that helps low-income workers by giving back part or all of their Social Security taxes.

Economic Aid Assistance to other nations in the form of grants, loans, or credits to buy the assisting nation's products.

Elastic Clause, or Necessary and Proper Clause The clause in Article I, Section 8, that grants Congress the power to do whatever is necessary to execute its specifically delegated powers.

Elector A member of the electoral college, which selects the president and vice president. Each state's electors are chosen in each presidential election year according to state laws.

Electoral College A group of persons, called electors, who are selected by the voters in each state. This group officially elects the president and the vice president of the United States.

Electronic Media Communication channels that involve electronic transmissions, such as radio, television, and, to an increasing extent, the Internet.

Elite Theory A perspective holding that society is ruled by a small number of people who exercise power to further their self-interest.

Emergency Power An inherent power exercised by the president during a period of national crisis.

Eminent Domain A power set forth in the Fifth Amendment to the U.S. Constitution that allows government to take private property for public use under the condition that just compensation is offered to the landowner.

Enabling Legislation A statute enacted by Congress that authorizes the creation of an administrative agency and specifies the name, purpose, composition, functions, and powers of the agency being created.

Energy Policy Laws concerned with how much energy is needed and used.

Enumerated Powers Powers specifically granted to the national government by the Constitution. The first 17 clauses of Article I, Section 8, specify most of the enumerated powers of the national government.

Environmental Impact Statement (EIS) A report that must show the costs and benefits of major federal actions that could significantly affect the quality of the environment.

Equality As a political value, the idea that all people are of equal worth.

Era of Good Feelings The years from 1817 to 1825, when James Monroe was president and there was, in effect, no political opposition.

Establishment Clause The part of the First Amendment prohibiting the establishment of a church officially supported by the national government. It is applied to questions of state and local government aid to religious organizations and schools, the legality of allowing or requiring school prayers, and the teaching of evolution versus intelligent design.

Exclusionary Rule A policy forbidding the admission at trial of illegally seized evidence.

Executive Agreement An international agreement made by the president, without senatorial ratification, with the head of a foreign state.

Executive Budget The budget prepared and submitted by the president to Congress.

Executive Office of the President (EOP) An organization established by President Franklin D. Roosevelt to assist the president in carrying out major duties.

Executive Order A rule or regulation issued by the president that has the effect of law. Executive orders can implement and give administrative effect to provisions in the Constitution, to treaties, and to statutes.

Executive Privilege The right of executive officials to withhold information from or to refuse to appear before a legislative committee.

Exports Goods and services produced domestically for sale abroad.

Expressed Power A power of the president that is expressly written into the Constitution or into statutory law.

Extradite To surrender an accused or convicted criminal to the authorities of the state from which he or she has fled; to return a fugitive criminal to the jurisdiction of the accusing state.

F

Faction A group or bloc in a legislature or political party acting in pursuit of some special interest or position.

Fall Review The annual process in which the Office of Management and Budget, after receiving formal federal agency requests for funding for the next fiscal year, reviews the requests, makes changes, and submits its recommendations to the president.

Fascism A 20th-century ideology—often totalitarian—that exalts the national collective united behind an absolute ruler. Fascism rejects liberal individualism, values action over rational deliberation, and glorifies war.

Federalism A system of government in which power is divided by a written constitution between a central government and regional or subdivisional governments. Each level must have some domain in which its policies are dominant and some genuine constitutional guarantee of its authority.

Federalist The name given to one who was in favor of the adoption of the U.S. Constitution and the creation of a federal union with a strong central government.

Federal Mandate A requirement in federal legislation that forces states and municipalities to comply with certain rules.

Federal Open Market Committee The most important body within the Federal Reserve System. The Federal Open Market Committee decides how monetary policy should be carried out.

Federal Question A question that has to do with the U.S. Constitution, acts of Congress, or treaties. A federal question provides a basis for federal jurisdiction.

Federal Register A publication of the U.S. government that prints executive orders, rules, and regulations.

Federal Reserve System (the Fed) The agency created by Congress in 1913 to serve as the nation's central banking organization.

Federal System A system of government in which power is divided between a central government and regional, or subdivisional, governments. Each level must have some domain in which its policies are dominant and some genuine political or constitutional guarantee of its authority.

Feminism The movement that supports political, economic, and social equality for women.

Filibuster The use of the Senate's tradition of unlimited debate as a delaying tactic to block a bill.

Finance Chairperson The campaign professional who directs fundraising, campaign spending, and compliance with campaign-finance laws and reporting requirements.

First Budget Resolution A resolution passed by Congress in May that sets overall revenue and spending goals for the following fiscal year.

Fiscal Policy The federal government's use of taxation and spending policies to affect overall business activity.

Fiscal Year (FY) A 12-month period that is used for bookkeeping, or accounting purposes. Usually, the fiscal year does not coincide with the calendar year. For example, the federal government's fiscal year runs from October 1 through September 30.

Focus Group A small group of individuals who are led in discussion by a professional consultant in order to gather opinions on and responses to candidates and issues.

Food Stamps Benefits issued by the federal government to low-income individuals to be used for the purchase of food; originally provided as coupons, but now typically provided electronically through a card similar to a debit card.

Foreign Policy A nation's external goals and the techniques and strategies used to achieve them.

Foreign Policy Process The steps by which foreign policy goals are decided and acted on.

Franking A policy that enables members of Congress to send material through the mail by substituting their facsimile signature (frank) for postage.

Free Exercise Clause The provision of the First Amendment guaranteeing the free exercise of religion.

Free Rider Problem The difficulty interest groups face in recruiting members when the benefits they achieve can be gained without joining the group.

Front-Loading The practice of moving presidential primary elections to the early part of the campaign to maximize the impact of these primaries on the nomination.

Front-Runner The presidential candidate who appears to be ahead at a given time in the primary season.

Full Employment An arbitrary level of unemployment that corresponds to "normal" friction in the labor market. In 1986, a 6.5 percent rate of unemployment was considered full employment. Today, it is assumed to be around 5 percent.

Full Faith and Credit Clause This section of the Constitution requires states to recognize one another's laws and court decisions. It ensures that rights established under deeds, wills, contracts, and other civil matters in one state will be honored by other states.

Functional Consolidation Cooperation by two or more units of local government in providing services to their inhabitants. This is generally done by unifying a set of departments (e.g., the police departments) into a single agency.

G

Gag Order An order issued by a judge restricting the publication of news about a trial or a pretrial hearing to protect the accused's right to a fair trial.

Gender Discrimination Any practice, policy, or procedure that denies equality of treatment to an individual or to a group because of gender.

Gender Gap The difference between the percentage of women who vote for a particular candidate and the percentage of men who vote for the candidate.

General Jurisdiction Exists when a court's authority to hear cases is not significantly restricted. A court of general jurisdiction normally can hear a broad range of cases.

General Law City A city operating under general state laws that apply to all local governmental units of a similar type.

General Sales Tax A tax levied as a proportion of the retail price of a commodity at the point of sale.

Generational Effect A long-lasting effect of the events of a particular time on the political opinions of those who came of political age at that time.

Gerrymandering The drawing of legislative district boundary lines to obtain partisan or factional advantage. A district is said to be gerrymandered when its shape is manipulated by the dominant party in the state legislature to maximize electoral strength at the expense of the minority party.

Get Out the Vote (GOTV) This phrase describes the multiple efforts expended by campaigns to get voters out to the polls on election day.

Government The institution in which decisions are made that resolve conflicts or allocate benefits and privileges. It is unique because it has the ultimate authority within society.

Government Corporation An agency of government that administers a quasi-business enterprise. These corporations are used when activities are primarily commercial.

Government in the Sunshine Act A law that requires all committee-directed federal agencies to conduct their business regularly in public session.

Grandfather Clause A device used by Southern states to disenfranchise African Americans. It restricted voting to those whose grandfathers had voted before 1867.

Great Compromise The compromise between the New Jersey and Virginia plans that created one chamber of the Congress based on population and one chamber representing each state equally; also called the Connecticut Compromise.

Gross Domestic Product (GDP) The dollar value of all final goods and services produced in a one-year period.

Gross Public Debt The net public debt plus interagency borrowings within the government.

H

Hard Money This refers to political contributions and campaign spending that is recorded under the regulations set forth in law and by the Federal Election Commission.

Hatch Act An act passed in 1939 that restricted the political activities of government employees. It also prohibited a political group from spending more than $3 million in any campaign and limited individual contributions to a campaign committee to $5,000.

Head of State The role of the president as ceremonial head of the government.

Hillstyle The actions and behaviors of a member of Congress in Washington, D.C., intended to promote policies and the member's own career aspirations.

Hispanic Someone who can claim a heritage from a Spanish-speaking country (other than Spain). The term is used only in the United States or other countries that receive immigrants—Spanish-speaking persons living in Spanish-speaking countries do not normally apply the term to themselves.

Home Rule City A city permitted by the state to let local voters frame, adopt, and amend their own charter.

Homestyle The actions and behaviors of a member of Congress aimed at the constituents and intended to win the support and trust of the voters at home.

I

Ideology A comprehensive set of beliefs about the nature of people and about the role of an institution or government.

Impeachment An action by the House of Representatives to accuse the president, vice president, or other civil officers of the United States of committing "Treason, Bribery, or other high Crimes and Misdemeanors."

Import Quota A restriction imposed on the value or number of units of a particular good that can be brought into a country. Foreign suppliers are unable to sell more than the amount specified in the import quota.

Imports Goods and services produced outside a country but sold within its borders.

Incarceration Rate The number of persons held in jail or prison for every 100,000 persons in a particular population group.

Income Transfer A transfer of income from some individuals in the economy to other individuals. This is generally done by government action.

Incorporation Theory The view that most of the protections of the Bill of Rights apply to state governments through the Fourteenth Amendment's due process clause.

Independent A voter or candidate who does not identify with a political party.

Independent Executive Agency A federal agency that is not part of a Cabinet department but reports directly to the president.

Independent Expenditures Nonregulated contributions from PACs, organizations, and individuals. The funds may be spent on advertising or other campaign activities, so long as those expenditures are not coordinated with those of a candidate.

Independent Regulatory Agency An agency outside the major executive departments charged with making and implementing rules and regulations.

Indirect Technique A strategy employed by interest groups that uses third parties to influence government officials.

Inflation A sustained rise in the general price level of goods and services.

Inherent Power A power of the president derived from the statements in the Constitution that "the executive Power shall be vested in a President" and that the president should "take Care that the Laws be faithfully executed"; defined through practice rather than through law.

Initiative A procedure by which voters can propose a law or a constitutional amendment.

In-Kind Subsidy A good or service—such as food stamps, housing, or medical care—provided by the government to low-income groups.

Institution An ongoing organization that performs certain functions for society.

Instructed Delegate A legislator who is an agent of the voters who elected him or her and who votes according to the views of constituents regardless of personal beliefs.

Intelligence Community The government agencies that gather information about the capabilities and intentions of foreign governments or that engage in covert actions.

Interest Group An organized group of individuals sharing common objectives who actively attempt to influence policy makers.

Interstate Compact An agreement between two or more states. Agreements on minor matters are made without Congressional consent, but any compact that tends to increase the power of the contracting states relative to other states or relative to the national government generally requires the consent of Congress. Such compacts serve as a means by which states can solve regional problems.

Iron Curtain The term used to describe the division of Europe between the Soviet bloc and the West; coined by Winston Churchill.

Iron Triangle The three-way alliance among legislators, bureaucrats, and interest groups to make or preserve policies that benefit their respective interests.

Isolationist Foreign Policy A policy of abstaining from an active role in international affairs or alliances, which characterized U.S. foreign policy toward Europe during most of the 1800s.

Issue Advocacy Advertising Advertising paid for by interest groups that support or oppose a candidate or a candidate's position on an issue without mentioning voting or elections.

Issue Network A group of individuals or organizations—which may consist of legislators and legislative staff members, interest group leaders, bureaucrats, the media, scholars, and other experts—that supports a particular policy position on a given issue.

Item Veto The power exercised by the governors of most states to veto particular sections or items of an appropriations bill, while signing the remainder of the bill into law.

J

Joint Committee A legislative committee composed of members from both chambers of Congress.

Judicial Activism A doctrine holding that the Supreme Court should take an active role by using its powers to check the activities of governmental bodies when those bodies exceed their authority.

Judicial Implementation The way in which court decisions are translated into action.

Judicial Restraint A doctrine holding that the Supreme Court should defer to the decisions made by the elected representatives of the people in the legislative and executive branches.

Judicial Review The process for deciding whether a law is contrary to the mandates of the Constitution.

Jurisdiction The authority of a court to decide certain cases. Not all courts have the authority to decide all cases. Two jurisdictional issues are where a case arises as well as its subject matter.

Justiciable Question A question that may be raised and reviewed in court.

K

Keynesian Economics A school of economic thought that tends to favor active federal government policy making to stabilize economy-wide fluctuations, usually by implementing discretionary fiscal policy.

Kitchen Cabinet The informal advisors to the president.

L

Labor Movement Generally, the economic and political expression of working-class interests; politically, the organization of working-class interests.

Latent Interests Public-policy interests that are not recognized or addressed by a group at a particular time.

Lawmaking The process of establishing the legal rules that govern society.

Legislature A governmental body primarily responsible for the making of laws.

Legitimacy Popular acceptance of the right and power of a government or other entity to exercise authority.

Libel A written defamation of a person's character, reputation, business, or property rights.

Liberalism A set of beliefs that includes the advocacy of positive government action to improve the welfare of individuals, support for civil rights, and tolerance for political and social change.

Libertarianism A political ideology based on skepticism or opposition toward almost all government activities.

Liberty The greatest freedom of individuals that is consistent with the freedom of other individuals in the society.

Lifestyle Effect The phenomenon of certain attitudes occurring at certain chronological ages.

Limited Government The principle that the powers of government should be limited, usually by institutional checks.

Limited Jurisdiction Exists when a court's authority to hear cases is restricted to certain types of claims, such as tax claims or bankruptcy petitions.

Line-Item Veto The power of an executive to veto individual lines or items within a piece of legislation without vetoing the entire bill.

Line Organization In the federal government, an administrative unit that is directly accountable to the president.

Literacy Test A test administered as a precondition for voting, often used to prevent African Americans from exercising their right to vote.

Litigate To engage in a legal proceeding or seek relief in a court of law; to carry on a lawsuit.

Lobbyist An organization or individual who attempts to influence legislation and the administrative decisions of government.

Logrolling An arrangement in which two or more members of Congress agree in advance to support each other's bills.

Loophole A legal method by which individuals and businesses are allowed to reduce the tax liabilities owed to the government.

Loose Monetary Policy Monetary policy that makes credit inexpensive and abundant, possibly leading to inflation.

M

Madisonian Model A structure of government proposed by James Madison in which the powers of the government are separated into three branches: executive, legislative, and judicial.

Majoritarianism A political theory holding that in a democracy, the government ought to do what the majority of the people want.

Majority Full age; the age at which a person is entitled by law to the right to manage her or his own affairs and to the full enjoyment of civil rights.

Majority Leader of the House A legislative position held by an important party member in the House of Representatives. The majority leader is selected by the majority party in caucus or conference to foster cohesion among party members and to act as spokesperson for the majority party in the House.

Majority Opinion A court opinion reflecting the views of the majority of the judges.

Majority Rule A basic principle of democracy asserting that the greatest number of citizens in any political unit should select officials and determine policies.

Managed News Information generated and distributed by the government in such a way as to give government interests priority over candor.

Mandatory Retirement Forced retirement when a person reaches a certain age.

Material Incentive A reason or motive having to do with economic benefits or opportunities.

Media Channels of mass communication.

Media Access The public's right of access to the media. The Federal Communications

Commission and the courts have gradually taken the stance that citizens do have a right to media access.

Medicaid A joint state–federal program that provides medical care to the poor (including indigent elderly persons in nursing homes). The program is funded out of general government revenues.

Medicare A federal health-insurance program that covers U.S. residents older than age 65. The costs are met by a tax on wages and salaries.

Merit System The selection, retention, and promotion of government employees on the basis of competitive examinations.

Military-Industrial Complex The mutually beneficial relationship between the armed forces and defense contractors.

Minority Leader of the House The party leader elected by the minority party in the House.

Monetary Policy The utilization of changes in the amount of money in circulation to alter credit markets, employment, and the rate of inflation.

Monopolistic Model A model of bureaucracy that compares bureaucracies to monopolistic business firms. Lack of competition in either circumstance leads to inefficient and costly operations.

Monroe Doctrine A policy statement made by President James Monroe in 1823, which set out three principles: (1) European nations should not establish new colonies in the Western Hemisphere; (2) European nations should not intervene in the affairs of independent nations of the Western Hemisphere; and (3) the United States would not interfere in the affairs of European nations.

Moral Idealism A philosophy that sees nations as normally willing to cooperate and to agree on moral standards for conduct.

Municipal Home Rule The power vested in a local unit of government to draft or change its own charter and to manage its own affairs.

N

Narrowcasting Broadcasting that is targeted to one small sector of the population.

National Committee A standing committee of a national political party established to direct and coordinate party activities between national party conventions.

National Convention The meeting held every four years by each major party to select presidential and vice-presidential candidates, to write a platform, to choose a national committee, and to conduct party business.

National Health Insurance A plan to provide universal health insurance under which the government provides basic health-care coverage to all citizens. In most such plans, the program is funded by taxes on wages or salaries.

National Security Council (NSC) An agency in the Executive Office of the President that advises the president on national security.

National Security Policy Foreign and domestic policy designed to protect the nation's independence and political and economic integrity; policy that is concerned with the safety and defense of the nation.

Natural Rights Rights held to be inherent in natural law, not dependent on governments. John Locke stated that natural law, being superior to human law, specifies certain rights of "life, liberty, and property." These rights, altered to become "life, liberty, and the pursuit of happiness," are asserted in the Declaration of Independence.

Necessaries In contract law, necessaries include whatever is reasonably necessary for suitable subsistence as measured by age, state, condition in life, and so on.

Negative Constituents Citizens who openly oppose the government's policies.

Net Public Debt The accumulation of all past federal government deficits; the total amount owed by the federal government to individuals, businesses, and foreigners.

New England Town A governmental unit in the New England states that combines the roles of city and county in one unit.

Nonopinion The lack of an opinion on an issue or policy among the majority.

Normal Trade Relations (NTR) Status A status granted through an international treaty by which each member nation must treat other members at least as well as it treats the country that receives its most favorable treatment. This status was formerly known as most-favored-nation status.

O

Office-Block, or Massachusetts, Ballot A form of general election ballot in which candidates for elective office are grouped together under the title of each office. It emphasizes voting for the office and the individual candidate, rather than for the party.

Office of Management and Budget (OMB) A division of the Executive Office of the President. The OMB assists the president in preparing the annual budget, clearing and coordinating departmental agency budgets, and supervising the administration of the federal budget.

Oligarchy Rule by the few in their own interests.

Ombudsperson A person who hears and investigates complaints by private individuals against public officials or agencies.

Open Primary A primary in which any registered voter can vote (but must vote for candidates of only one party).

Opinion The statement by a judge or a court of the decision reached in a case. The opinion sets forth the applicable law and details the reasoning on which the ruling was based.

Opinion Leader One who is able to influence the opinions of others because of position, expertise, or personality.

Opinion Poll A method of systematically questioning a small, selected sample of respondents who are deemed representative of the total population.

Oral Arguments The verbal arguments presented in person by attorneys to an appellate court. Each attorney presents reasons to the court why the court should rule in her or his client's favor.

Order A state of peace and security. Maintaining order by protecting members of society from violence and criminal activity is the oldest purpose of government.

Oversight The process by which Congress follows up on laws it has enacted to ensure that they are being enforced and administered in the way Congress intended.

P

Pardon A release from the punishment for or legal consequences of a crime; a pardon can be granted by the president before or after a conviction.

Party-Column, or Indiana, Ballot A form of general-election ballot in which all of a party's candidates for elective office are arranged in one column under the party's label and symbol. It emphasizes voting for the party, rather than for the office or individual.

Party Identification Linking oneself to a particular political party.

Party-in-Government All of the elected and appointed officials who identify with a political party.

Party-in-the-Electorate Those members of the general public who identify with a political party or who express a preference for one party over another.

Party Identifier A person who identifies with a political party.

Party Organization The formal structure and leadership of a political party, including election committees; local, state, and national executives; and paid professional staff.

Party Platform A document drawn up at each national convention outlining the policies, positions, and principles of the party.

Patronage The practice of rewarding faithful party workers and followers with government employment and contracts.

Peer Group A group consisting of members sharing common social characteristics. These groups play an important part in the socialization process, helping to shape attitudes and beliefs.

Pendleton Act (Civil Service Reform Act) An act that established the principle of employment on the basis of merit and created the Civil Service Commission to administer the personnel service.

Permanent Campaign A coordinated and planned strategy carried out by the White House to increase the president's popularity and support.

Picket-Fence Federalism A model of federalism in which specific programs and policies (depicted as vertical pickets in a picket fence) involve all levels of government—national, state, and local (depicted by the horizontal boards in a picket fence).

Pluralism A theory that views politics as a conflict among interest groups. Political decision making is characterized by bargaining and compromise.

Plurality A number of votes cast for a candidate that is greater than the number of votes for any other candidate but not necessarily a majority.

Pocket Veto A special veto exercised by the chief executive after a legislative body has adjourned. Bills not signed by the chief executive die after a specified period of time. If Congress wishes to reconsider such a bill, it must be reintroduced in the following session of Congress.

Podcasting A method of distributing multimedia files, such as audio or video files, for downloading onto mobile devices or personal computers.

Police Power The authority to legislate for the protection of the health, morals, safety, and welfare of the people. In the United States, most police power is reserved to the states.

Political Action Committee (PAC) A committee set up by and representing a corporation, labor union, or special-interest group. PACs raise and give campaign donations.

Political Consultant A paid professional hired to devise a campaign strategy and manage a campaign.

Political Culture The collection of beliefs and attitudes toward government and the political process held by a community or nation.

Political Party A group of political activists who organize to win elections, operate the government, and determine public policy.

Political Question An issue that a court believes should be decided by the executive or legislative branch.

Political Realism A philosophy that sees each nation acting principally in its own interest.

Political Socialization The process through which individuals learn a set of political attitudes and form opinions about social issues. Families and the educational system are two of the most important forces in the political socialization process.

Political Trust The degree to which individuals express trust in the government and political institutions, usually measured through a specific series of survey questions.

Politics The struggle over power or influence within organizations or informal groups that can grant or withhold benefits or privileges.

Pollster The person or firm who conducts public opinion polls for the campaign.

Poll Tax A special tax that must be paid as a qualification for voting. The Twenty-fourth Amendment to the Constitution outlawed the poll tax in national elections, and in 1966, the Supreme Court declared it unconstitutional in all elections.

Popular Sovereignty The concept that ultimate political authority is based on the will of the people.

Pork Special projects or appropriations that are intended to benefit a member's district or state; slang term for earmarks.

Precedent A court rule bearing on subsequent legal decisions in similar cases. Judges rely on precedents in deciding cases.

Presidential Primary A statewide primary election of delegates to a political party's national convention, held to determine a party's presidential nominee.

President Pro Tempore The temporary presiding officer of the Senate in the absence of the vice president.

Press Secretary The presidential staff member responsible for handling White House media relations and communications, or the individual who interacts directly with the journalists covering a campaign.

Prior Restraint Restraining an action before the activity has actually occurred. When expression is involved, this means censorship.

Privatization The replacement of government services with services provided by private firms.

Privileges and Immunities Special rights and exceptions provided by law. States may not discriminate against one another's citizens.

Progressive Tax A tax that rises in percentage terms as incomes rise.

Property Anything that is or may be subject to ownership. As conceived by the political philosopher John Locke, the right to property is a natural right superior to human law (laws made by government).

Property Tax A tax on the value of real estate. This tax is a particularly important source of revenue for local governments.

Public Agenda Issues that are perceived by the political community as meriting public attention and governmental action.

Public Figure A public official, movie star, or other person known to the public because of his or her position or activities.

Public Interest The best interests of the overall community; the national good, rather than the narrow interests of a particular group.

Public Opinion The aggregate of individual attitudes or beliefs shared by some portion of the adult population.

Purposive Incentive A reason for supporting or participating in the activities of a group that is based on agreement with the goals of the group. For example, someone with a strong interest in human rights might have a purposive incentive to join Amnesty International.

R

Ratification Formal approval.

Rational Ignorance Effect An effect produced when people purposely and rationally decide not to become informed on an issue because they believe that their vote on the issue is not likely to be a deciding one; a lack of incentive to seek the necessary information to cast an intelligent vote.

Realignment A process in which a substantial group of voters switches party allegiance, producing a long-term change in the political landscape.

Reapportionment The allocation of seats in the House of Representatives to each state after each census.

Recall A procedure allowing the people to vote to dismiss an elected official from state office before his or her term has expired.

Recession Two or more successive quarters in which the economy shrinks instead of grows.

Redistricting The redrawing of the boundaries of the Congressional districts within each state.

Referendum An electoral device whereby legislative or constitutional measures are referred by the legislature to the voters for approval or disapproval.

Registration The entry of a person's name onto the list of registered voters for elections. To register, a person must meet certain legal requirements of age, citizenship, and residency.

Regressive Tax A tax that falls in percentage terms as incomes rise.

Remand To send a case back to the court that originally heard it.

Representation The function of members of Congress as elected officials representing the views of their constituents.

Representative Assembly A legislature composed of individuals who represent the population.

Representative Democracy A form of government in which representatives elected by the people make and enforce laws and policies; may retain the monarchy in a ceremonial role.

Reprieve A formal postponement of the execution of a sentence imposed by a court of law.

Republic A form of government in which sovereignty rests with the people, as opposed to a king or monarch.

Republican Party One of the two major American political parties. It emerged in the 1850s as an antislavery party and consisted of former Northern Whigs and antislavery Democrats.

Reverse To annul or make void a court ruling on account of some error or irregularity.

Reverse Discrimination The charge that an affirmative action program discriminates against those who do not have minority status.

Reverse-Income Effect A tendency for wealthier states or regions to favor the Democrats and for less wealthy states or regions to favor the Republicans. The effect appears paradoxical because it reverses traditional patterns of support.

Rule The proposal by the Rules Committee of the House that states the conditions for debate for one piece of legislation.

Rule of Four A United States Supreme Court procedure by which four justices must vote to grant a petition for review if a case is to come before the full court.

Rules Committee A standing committee of the House of Representatives that provides special rules under which specific bills can be debated, amended, and considered by the House.

S

Safe Seat A district that returns the legislator with 55 percent of the vote or more.

Sampling Error The difference between a sample's results and the true result if the entire population had been interviewed.

Second Budget Resolution A resolution passed by Congress in September that sets "binding" limits on taxes and spending for the following fiscal year.

Select Committee A temporary legislative committee established for a limited time period and for a special purpose.

Selectperson A member of the governing group of a town.

Senate Majority Leader The chief spokesperson of the majority party in the Senate, who directs the legislative program and party strategy.

Senate Minority Leader The party officer in the Senate who commands the minority party's opposition to the policies of the majority party and directs the legislative program and strategy of his or her party.

Senatorial Courtesy In federal district court judgeship nominations, a tradition allowing a senator to veto a judicial appointment in his or her state.

Seniority System A custom followed in both chambers of Congress specifying that the member of the majority party with the longest term of continuous service will be given preference when a committee chairperson (or a holder of some other significant post) is selected.

Separate-but-Equal Doctrine The doctrine holding that separate-but-equal facilities do not violate the equal protection clause.

Separation of Powers The principle of dividing governmental powers among different branches of government.

Service Sector The sector of the economy that provides services—such as health care, banking, and education—in contrast to the sector that produces goods.

Sexual Harassment Unwanted physical or verbal conduct or abuse of a sexual nature that interferes with a recipient's job performance, creates a hostile work environment, or carries with it an implicit or explicit threat of adverse employment consequences.

Signing Statement A written declaration that a president may make when signing a bill into law. Usually, such statements point out sections of the law that the president deems unconstitutional.

Single-Payer Plan A plan under which one entity has a monopoly on issuing a particular type of insurance. Typically, the entity is the government, and the insurance is basic health coverage.

Slander The public uttering of a false statement that harms the good reputation of another. The statement must be made to, or within the hearing of, persons other than the defamed party.

Social Contract A voluntary agreement among individuals to secure their rights and welfare by creating a government and abiding by its rules.

Socialism A political ideology based on strong support for economic and social equality. Socialists traditionally envisioned a society in which major businesses were taken over by the government or by employee cooperatives.

Social Movement A movement that represents the demands of a large segment of the public for political, economic, or social change.

Socioeconomic Status The value assigned to a person due to occupation or income. An upper-class person, for example, has high socioeconomic status.

Soft Money Campaign contributions unregulated by federal or state law, usually given to parties and party committees to help fund general party activities.

Solidary Incentive A reason or motive having to do with the desire to associate with others and to share with others a particular interest or hobby.

Sound Bite A brief, memorable comment that can easily be fit into news broadcasts.

Soviet Bloc The Soviet Union and the Eastern European countries that installed communist regimes after World War II and were dominated by the Soviet Union.

Speaker of the House The presiding officer in the House of Representatives. The Speaker is always a member of the majority party and is the most powerful and influential member of the House.

Spin An interpretation of campaign events or election results that is favorable to the candidate's campaign strategy.

Spin Doctor A political campaign advisor who tries to convince journalists of the truth of a particular interpretation of events.

Splinter Party A new party formed by a dissident faction within a major political party. Often, splinter parties have emerged when a particular personality was at odds with the major party.

Spoils System The awarding of government jobs to political supporters and friends.

Spring Review The annual process in which the Office of Management and Budget requires federal agencies to review their programs, activities, and goals and submit their requests for funding for the next fiscal year.

Standing Committee A permanent committee in the House or Senate that considers bills within a certain subject area.

Stare Decisis To stand on decided cases; the judicial policy of following precedents established by past decisions.

State A group of people occupying a specific area and organized under one government; may be either a nation or a subunit of a nation.

State Central Committee The principal organized structure of each political party within each state. This committee is responsible for carrying out policy decisions of the party's state convention.

State of the Union Message An annual message to Congress in which the president proposes a legislative program. The message is addressed not only to Congress but also to the American people and to the world.

Statutory Power A power created for the president through laws enacted by Congress.

Straight-Ticket Voting Voting exclusively for the candidates of one party.

Strategic Arms Limitation Treaty (SALT I) A treaty between the United States and the Soviet Union to stabilize the nuclear arms competition between the two countries. SALT I talks began in 1969, and agreements were signed on May 26, 1972.

Strict Construction A judicial philosophy that looks to the "letter of the law" when interpreting the Constitution or a particular statute.

Subpoena A legal writ requiring a person's appearance in court to give testimony.

Suffrage The right to vote; the franchise.

Sunset Legislation Laws requiring that existing programs be reviewed regularly for their effectiveness and be terminated unless specifically extended as a result of these reviews.

Superdelegate A party leader or elected official who is given the right to vote at the party's national convention. Superdelegates are not elected at the state level.

Supplemental Security Income (SSI) A federal program established to provide assistance to elderly persons and persons with disabilities.

Supremacy Clause The constitutional provision that makes the Constitution and federal laws superior to all conflicting state and local laws.

Supremacy Doctrine A doctrine that asserts the priority of national law over state laws. This principle is rooted in Article VI of the Constitution, which provides that the Constitution, the laws passed by the national government under its constitutional powers, and all treaties constitute the supreme law of the land.

Swing Voters Voters who frequently swing their support from one party to another.

Symbolic Speech Nonverbal expression of beliefs, which is given substantial protection by the courts.

T

Tariffs Taxes on imports.

Technical Assistance The practice of sending experts in such areas as agriculture, engineering, or business to aid other nations.

Temporary Assistance to Needy Families (TANF) A state-administered program in which grants from the national government are used to provide welfare benefits. The TANF program replaced the Aid to Families with Dependent Children (AFDC) program.

Third Party A political party other than the two major political parties (Republican and Democratic).

Ticket Splitting Voting for candidates of two or more parties for different offices. For example, a voter splits her ticket if she votes for a Republican presidential candidate and a Democratic Congressional candidate.

Tight Monetary Policy Monetary policy that makes credit expensive in an effort to slow the economy.

Tipping A phenomenon that occurs when a group that is becoming more numerous over time grows large enough to change the political balance in a district, state, or country.

Totalitarian Regime A form of government that controls all aspects of the political and social life of a nation.

Town Manager System A form of town government in which voters elect three selectpersons, who then appoint a professional town manager, who in turn appoints other officials.

Town Meeting The governing authority of a New England town. Qualified voters may participate in the election of officers and the passage of legislation.

Township A rural unit of government based on federal land surveys of the American frontier in the 1780s. Townships have declined significantly in importance.

Tracking Poll A poll taken for the candidate on a nearly daily basis as election day approaches.

Trial Court The court in which most cases begin.

Truman Doctrine The policy adopted by President Harry Truman in 1947 to halt communist expansion in Southeastern Europe.

Trustee A legislator who acts according to her or his conscience and the broad interests of the entire society.

Twelfth Amendment An amendment to the Constitution, adopted in 1804, that specifies the separate election of the president and vice president by the electoral college.

Twenty-fifth Amendment A 1967 amendment to the Constitution that establishes procedures for filling presidential and vice-presidential vacancies and makes provisions for presidential disability.

Two-Party System A political system in which only two parties have a reasonable chance of winning.

U

Unanimous Consent Agreement An agreement on the rules of debate for proposed legislation in the Senate that is approved by all the members.

Unanimous Opinion A court opinion or determination on which all judges agree.

Unemployment The inability of those who are in the labor force to find a job; defined as the total number of those in the labor force actively looking for a job but unable to find one.

Unicameral Legislature A legislature with only one legislative chamber, as opposed to a bicameral (two-chamber) legislature, such as the U.S. Congress. Today, Nebraska is the only state in the Union with a unicameral legislature.

Unincorporated Area An area not located within the boundary of a municipality.

Unitary System A centralized governmental system in which local or subdivisional governments exercise only those powers given to them by the central government.

Unit Rule A rule by which all of a state's electoral votes are cast for the presidential candidate receiving a plurality of the popular vote in that state.

Universal Suffrage The right of all adults to vote for their representatives.

U.S. Treasury Bond Debt issued by the federal government.

V

Veto Message The president's formal explanation of a veto when legislation is returned to Congress.

Voter Turnout The percentage of citizens taking part in the election process; the number of eligible voters who actually "turn out" on election day to cast their ballots.

W

Wage and Price Controls Government-imposed controls on the maximum prices that may be charged for specific goods and services, plus controls on permissible wage increases.

War Powers Resolution A law passed in 1973 spelling out the conditions under which the president can commit troops without Congressional approval.

Washington Community Individuals regularly involved with politics in Washington, D.C.

Watergate Break-In The 1972 illegal entry into the Democratic National Committee offices by participants in President Richard Nixon's re-election campaign.

Weberian Model A model of bureaucracy developed by the German sociologist Max Weber, who viewed bureaucracies as rational, hierarchical organizations in which decisions are based on logical reasoning.

Whig Party A major party in the United States during the first half of the 19th century, formally established in 1836. The Whig Party was anti-Jackson and represented a variety of regional interests.

Whip A member of Congress who aids the majority or minority leader of the House or the Senate.

Whistleblower Someone who brings to public attention gross governmental inefficiency or an illegal action.

White House Office The personal office of the president, which tends to presidential political needs and manages the media.

White House Press Corps The reporters assigned full-time to cover the presidency.

White Primary A state primary election that restricts voting to whites only; outlawed by the Supreme Court in 1944.

Writ of *Certiorari* An order issued by a higher court to a lower court to send up the record of a case for review.

Writ of *habeas corpus* *Habeas corpus* means, literally, "you have the body." A writ of *habeas corpus* is an order that requires jailers to bring a prisoner before a court or judge and explain why the person is being held.

Y

Yellow Journalism A term for sensationalistic, irresponsible journalism. Reputedly, the term is an allusion to the cartoon "The Yellow Kid" in the old *New York World*, a newspaper especially noted for its sensationalism.

CREDITS

INDEX

Presidents of the United States

	Term of Service	Age at Inauguration	Political Party	College or University	Occupation or Profession
1. George Washington	1789–1797	57	None		Planter
2. John Adams	1797–1801	61	Federalist	Harvard	Lawyer
3. Thomas Jefferson	1801–1809	57	Jeffersonian Republican	William and Mary	Planter, Lawyer
4. James Madison	1809–1817	57	Jeffersonian Republican	Princeton	Lawyer
5. James Monroe	1817–1825	58	Jeffersonian Republican	William and Mary	Lawyer
6. John Quincy Adams	1825–1829	57	Jeffersonian Republican	Harvard	Lawyer
7. Andrew Jackson	1829–1837	61	Democrat		Lawyer
8. Martin Van Buren	1837–1841	54	Democrat		Lawyer
9. William H. Harrison	1841	68	Whig	Hampden-Sydney	Soldier
10. John Tyler	1841–1845	51	Whig	William and Mary	Lawyer
11. James K. Polk	1845–1849	49	Democrat	U. of N. Carolina	Lawyer
12. Zachary Taylor	1849–1850	64	Whig		Soldier
13. Millard Fillmore	1850–1853	50	Whig		Lawyer
14. Franklin Pierce	1853–1857	48	Democrat	Bowdoin	Lawyer
15. James Buchanan	1857–1861	65	Democrat	Dickinson	Lawyer
16. Abraham Lincoln	1861–1865	52	Republican		Lawyer
17. Andrew Johnson	1865–1869	56	National. Union†		Tailor
18. Ulysses S. Grant	1869–1877	46	Republican	U.S. Mil. Academy	Soldier
19. Rutherford B. Hayes	1877–1881	54	Republican	Kenyon	Lawyer
20. James A. Garfield	1881	49	Republican	Williams	Lawyer
21. Chester A. Arthur	1881–1885	51	Republican	Union	Lawyer
22. Grover Cleveland	1885–1889	47	Democrat		Lawyer
23. Benjamin Harrison	1889–1893	55	Republican	Miami	Lawyer
24. Grover Cleveland	1893–1897	55	Democrat		Lawyer
25. William McKinley	1897–1901	54	Republican	Allegheny College	Lawyer
26. Theodore Roosevelt	1901–1909	42	Republican	Harvard	Author
27. William H. Taft	1909–1913	51	Republican	Yale	Lawyer
28. Woodrow Wilson	1913–1921	56	Democrat	Princeton	Educator
29. Warren G. Harding	1921–1923	55	Republican		Editor
30. Calvin Coolidge	1923–1929	51	Republican	Amherst	Lawyer
31. Herbert C. Hoover	1929–1933	54	Republican	Stanford	Engineer
32. Franklin D. Roosevelt	1933–1945	51	Democrat	Harvard	Lawyer
33. Harry S. Truman	1945–1953	60	Democrat		Businessman
34. Dwight D. Eisenhower	1953–1961	62	Republican	U.S. Mil. Academy	Soldier
35. John F. Kennedy	1961–1963	43	Democrat	Harvard	Author
36. Lyndon B. Johnson	1963–1969	55	Democrat	Southwest Texas State	Teacher
37. Richard M. Nixon	1969–1974	56	Republican	Whittier	Lawyer
38. Gerald R. Ford‡	1974–1977	61	Republican	Michigan	Lawyer
39. James E. Carter, Jr.	1977–1981	52	Democrat	U.S. Naval Academy	Businessman
40. Ronald W. Reagan	1981–1989	69	Republican	Eureka College	Actor
41. George H. W. Bush	1989–1993	64	Republican	Yale	Businessman
42. Bill Clinton	1993–2001	46	Democrat	Georgetown	Lawyer
43. George W. Bush	2001–2009	54	Republican	Yale	Businessman
44. Barack Obama	2009–	47	Democrat	Columbia	Lawyer

*Church preference; never joined any church.
†The National Union Party consisted of Republicans and War Democrats. Johnson was a Democrat.

**Inaugurated Dec. 6, 1973, to replace Agnew, who resigned Oct. 10, 1973.
‡Inaugurated Aug. 9, 1974, to replace Nixon, who resigned that same day.
§Inaugurated Dec. 19, 1974, to replace Ford, who became president Aug. 9, 1974.